THE OXFORD HISTORY OF THE CHRISTIAN CHURCH

Edited by
Henry and Owen Chadwick

Reformation in Britain and Ireland

FELICITY HEAL

OXFORD
UNIVERSITY PRESS

OXFORD

UNIVERSITY PRESS

Great Clarendon Street, Oxford OX2 6DP

Oxford University Press is a department of the University of Oxford.
It furthers the University's objective of excellence in research, scholarship,
and education by publishing worldwide in

Oxford New York

Auckland Bangkok Buenos Aires Cape Town Chennai
Dar es Salaam Delhi Hong Kong Istanbul Karachi Kolkata
Kuala Lumpur Madrid Melbourne Mexico City Mumbai Nairobi
São Paulo Shanghai Taipei Tokyo Toronto

Oxford is a registered trade mark of Oxford University Press
in the UK and in certain other countries

Published in the United States
by Oxford University Press Inc., New York

British Library Cataloguing in Publication Data
Data available

Library of Congress Cataloging in Publication Data
Heal, Felicity.
Reformation in Britain and Ireland / Felicity Heal.
p. cm. – (The Oxford history of the Christian church)
Includes bibliographical references.
1. Reformation–Great Britain. 2. Great Britain–Church history–16th century.
3. Reformation–Ireland. 4. Ireland–Church history–16th century. I. Title. II. Series.
BR375 .H43 2003
274.1'06–dc21   2002038186
ISBN 0-19-826924-2

3 5 7 9 10 8 6 4 2

Typeset by Kolam Information Services, Pvt Ltd, India
Printed in Great Britain on acid-free paper by
Biddles Ltd. King's Lynn, Norfolk

To my Mother, for all her support

PREFACE

It was almost a decade ago that the General Editor wrote to ask if I would be interested in contributing to the Oxford History of the Christian Church. The volume he suggested would address the early English Reformation, with a concluding date in the first years of Elizabeth's reign. Or so I read Owen Chadwick's letter. A more careful rereading added a distinctive dimension to the task: what was needed was a study of the British churches, or rather those of Britain and Ireland, to match volumes being prepared on the Continental Reformations. It was that additional information that seduced me from the paths of social history and persuaded me to sign. In the first half of the 1990s there were at last exciting developments in the integrated and comparative study of the British Isles, following the ideas first proposed by John Pocock a decade and a half earlier. Collections of essays on the British dimension of early modern history began to proliferate. The time had come to try to stretch the understanding of a 'mere English' historian and to think about the ways in which the three kingdoms, and four nations of the British archipelago, responded to the most traumatic experience of the sixteenth century, the coming of the Reformation.

I added only one caveat to the Editor's proposal. It was no longer possible to halt the story of religious change at 1560, or even 1570. It is at present fashionable to argue that the Reformation has to be understood as a long process, finishing, according to taste, in 1640, in the 1680s, or even in the eighteenth century. This seems unnecessarily extended, though there is an obvious logic in continuing the narrative of changes in religious politics up to the war of the three kingdoms in 1642, a point made by Professor Chadwick. Instead Reformation historians would now most usually argue that it is important to proceed a generation or two beyond 1560: to understand the impact of religious crisis both on those who lived through the great transitions in public policy and those who followed them. The latter, as credal Protestants or conscious recusants, had a very different relationship to religious change from their mothers and fathers, and needed to be studied to understand how post-Reformation culture emerged. So, the Editor and I agreed to compromise: both the ecclesiastical narrative and the study of post-Reformation beliefs would have a terminal date around the turn of the sixteenth century. The latter possessed an intellectual logic; the former the recognition that James VI and I's arrival in England provides a temporary caesura for each of his three kingdoms.

At about the time that *Reformation in Britain and Ireland* became more than a contract with a rather distant submission date, Diarmaid MacCulloch proposed to Judith Maltby, Susan Brigden, and myself, that we establish an Oxford seminar on Religion in the British Isles 1400–1700. This has now been a regular feature of the Trinity Term calendar for some years, with Christopher Haigh joining to replace Susan four years ago. It has proved a most stimulating seminar, and my gratitude goes to my fellow organizers who have kept my faith in the intellectual project going in what have sometimes proved difficult circumstances. We often disagree about the nature of the Reformation, and about the significance of its 'British' dimensions, but for all of us the Thursday evenings of Trinity Term have proved a high point in the academic calendar.

A number of the speakers and participants at the seminar have been generous in offering me advice and comments. Jane Dawkins, Linda Dunbar, Donald Meek, and Margo Todd have helped to guide my faltering footsteps on the Scottish Reformation. I am particularly grateful to Margo Todd for allowing me to read a chapter of her book on Scottish Protestantism in draft. Jenny Wormald has also been a great source of information and stimulating discussion on Scotland, as well as a constant friend. Alan Ford and Raymond Gillespie provided important discussion and references on the Irish Reformation. Glanmor Williams, the doyen of Welsh Reformation studies, gave inspiration through his seminar, but above all through his written works. Bill Sheils, Alec Ryrie, Craig d'Alton, Peter Sherlock, Alison Wall, and Peter Marshall all offered illumination on England. Cliff Davies reminded me that the Channel Islands had to be taken into account. Beyond the seminar I have benefited from valuable help from Michael Lynch on Scotland and Steven Ellis on Ireland. Tony Shaw has been stimulating on the dissolution of the monasteries. Roger Bowers and Brett Usher were both kind enough to show me unpublished work on the Elizabethan Settlement and the first Elizabethan bench of bishops respectively, and to discuss their findings with me. My graduates have been an important source of inspiration and friendship: in particular Kevin Dillow, Christine Peters, Helen Parish, Greg Duke, and Mark Bell have all contributed directly or indirectly to my thinking on this project.

Diarmaid MacCulloch read the material in Chapter 8, and saved me from a number of theological errors. Owen Chadwick has been a most patient and supportive general editor, and has read the whole text systematically. Hilary O'Shea at the Oxford University Press has also waited uncomplainingly as administrative burdens delayed the completion of the book for longer than was reasonable. That it is completed at all must be attributed partly to the administrative support of two colleagues and friends: Diane Price, who sustained me as senior tutor of my college, and Sue Bennett, who has been a tower of strength in the History Faculty.

I owe particular personal debts to my uncle, Revd Donald Johnson, for sustained interest in the project, and intermittent reminders that it was time it was finished, and to my colleague John Walsh, who (rightly) wondered from time to time if it was wise to commit to a large project of this kind, but who has always been enthusiastic about discussing it. As always my greatest debt has been to my husband, Clive Holmes. Though we have parted intellectual ways since writing together on the gentry, he remains my greatest academic support and critic, always ready to read drafts, debate ideas, encourage, and drive me forward.

F. H.

Jesus College, Oxford
Easter 2002

CONTENTS

ILLUSTRATIONS

ABBREVIATIONS

AHR	*American Historical Review*
APC	*Acts of the Privy Council of England*, ed. J. R. Dasent, 32 vols. (1890–1907)
APS	*Acts of the Parliaments of Scotland*, ed. T. Thomson (1814–75)
ARG	*Archiv für Reformationsgeschichte*
BIHR	*Bulletin of the Institute of Historical Research* (see also *HR*)
BL	British Library
Bodl	Bodleian Library, Oxford
BUK	*The Booke of the Universall Kirk: Acts and Proceedings of the General Assemblies of the Kirk of Scotland*, ed. T. Thomson, 3 vols. (Bannatyne Club, 1839–45)
C16J	*Sixteenth-Century Journal*
Calderwood	*History of the Church of Scotland by Mr David Calderwood*, ed T. Thomson, 8 vols. (Wodrow Society, Edinburgh, 1842–9)
CPR	*Calendar of Patent Rolls*
CPR Irl	*Calendar of Patent and Close Rolls of Ireland*
CS	Camden Society
CSPD	*Calendar of State Papers Domestic*
CSP For	*Calendar of State Papers Foreign*
CSP Irl	*Calendar of State Papers Ireland*
CSP Sc	*Calendar of State Papers Scotland*
CSP Sp	*Calendar of State Papers Spanish*
CSP Ven	*Calendar of State Papers Venetian*
CWTM	*Complete Works of St Thomas More*, 10 vols. (New Haven, Conn., 1963–90)
DNB	*Dictionary of National Biography*
EETS	Early English Text Society
EHR	*English Historical Review*
Foxe	J. Foxe, *Acts and Monuments*, ed. G. Townshend and S. R. Cattley, 8 vols. (1837–41)
HJ	*Historical Journal*
HMC	Historical Manuscripts Commission

HR	*Historical Research*
IHS	*Irish Historical Studies*
JBS	*Journal of British Studies*
JEH	*Journal of Ecclesiastical History*
JRH	*Journal of Religious History*
Knox	J. Knox, *Works*, ed. D. Laing, 6 vols. (Wodrow Society, Edinburgh, 1846)
LP	*Letters and Papers, Foreign and Domestic, of the Reign of Henry VIII*, ed. J. S. Brewer *et al.*, 23 vols. (1862–1932)
LPL	Lambeth Palace Library
LRS	Lincoln Record Society
OL	*Original Letters Relative to the English Reformation*, ed. H. Robinson, 2 vols. (PS, Cambridge, 1846–7)
PP	*Past and Present*
PRO	Public Record Office, London
PS	Parker Society
RSCHS	*Records of the Scottish Church History Society*
RSTC	*Revised Short Title Catalogue of Books Printed in England, Scotland and Ireland . . . before 1640*, ed. W.A. Jackson and F.S. Ferguson, 3 vols. (1976–91)
SCH	Studies in Church History: Ecclesiastical History Society
SHR	*Scottish Historical Review*
SHS	Scottish Historical Society
SP HVIII	*State Papers of King Henry VIII*, 11 vols. (1830–52)
SRS	Scottish Record Society
STS	Scottish Text Society
TRHS	*Transactions of the Royal Historical Society*
TRP	*Tudor Royal Proclamations*, ed. P.L. Hughes and J.F. Larkin, 2 vols. (New Haven, Conn., 1964, 1969)
VAI	*Visitation Articles and Injunctions of the Period of the Reformation*, 3 vols., ed. W.H. Frere and W.M. Kennedy (Alcuin Club, 14–16, 1910)
Wilkins, *Concilia*	*Concilia Magnae Britanniae et Hibernicae*, ed. D. Wilkins, 4 vols. (1737)
YAJ	*Yorkshire Archaeological Journal*
ZL	*Zurich Letters, 1558–1579*, ed. H. Robinson, 2 vols. (PS, Cambridge, 1842)

NOTE ON CONVENTIONS AND MONEY

All spellings have been modernized, except in the case of verse where original spelling is pertinent to pronunciation. Dates are given in Old Style, but with the year beginning on 1 January, not 25 March. The place of publication is London unless otherwise specified.

Figures for ecclesiastical income are given in the national currencies, that is pounds English, Irish, and Scots. Until 1460 Irish pounds were equivalent to English. Thereafter they diverged: in the early sixteenth century a pound English was worth 30 shillings Irish. Scottish and English pounds diverged after the mid-fourteenth century. The relationship between the value of the two varied markedly over our period. Between 1475 and 1565 the shift was from a ratio of 4:1 to 5:1. Thereafter the value of the Scottish pound collapsed: by 1603 the ratio was 12:1.

INTRODUCTION

Early one morning in mid-August 1553 John Bale, Protestant polemicist, dramatist, and bishop of Ossory in the Irish marches, fled from his episcopal see to Dublin. Thence he made his escape by sea, intending to go to Scotland, but, after a series of picaresque adventures with pirates, eventually arriving in the Low Countries. There, in the wearisome years of Mary I's reign, he published his *Vocacyon*, one of the first pieces of writing in English that can claim the status of autobiography.[1] It is, however, autobiography of a narrowly circumscribed kind. Bale describes his calling to the see of Ossory by Edward VI in 1552, his experiences in Dublin and Kilkenny in the months before his flight, and the complex sea journeying that led him to Flanders. The context of the work is scriptural and providential: Bale had experienced calling, persecution, and deliverance, and in this he resembled the saints of the true Church in all ages. The bishop's particular models were Jeremiah, John the Baptist, and St Paul: all were 'called from their mother's womb to that heavenly office of preaching', each suffered under tyrants, and each was finally 'delivered in this life from parlous dangers and in death from sin, hell and damnation'.[2] Though Bale had not been called upon to suffer direct physical martyrdom, the cross that he bore was heavy, involving the fear of death, the killing of several of his servants in Ireland, exile, and the tragic loss of his collection of books.[3]

Bale's precipitate flight was one small incident in a summer of profound crisis for the Protestant cause. His stay in Ireland was so brief that he scarcely had time to disturb the surface of Irish religious politics and neither his coming nor his going can be said to have changed much in the Tudor crown's second realm. However, the bishop's account of his

---

[1] The critical edition with facsimile reproduction of the text is P. Happé and J.N. King (eds.), *The vocacyon of Johan Bale*, Medieval and Renaissance Texts and Studies 70 (Binghamton, N.Y., 1990).

[2] Ibid., 32.

[3] Ibid., introduction. See also A. Hadfield, 'Translating the Reformation: John Bale's Irish *Vocacyon*', in B. Bradshaw, A. Hadfield, and W. Maley (eds.), *Representing Ireland: Literature and the Origins of the Conflict, 1534–1660* (Cambridge, 1993), 43–59; S. Ellis, 'John Bale, bishop of Ossory, 1552–3', *Journal of the Butler Society* 2 (1984), 283–93.

experiences is remarkably revealing, both about the nature of evangelical Protestantism, and about religious change in sixteenth-century Britain and Ireland. Bale was one of the most vigorous protagonists of the 'hot gospelling' generation: men whose objective, in Margaret Aston's vivid phrase, was not 'to re-educate, but to re-convert the world'.[4] Steeped in the scriptures—Henry VIII was King David, Edward VI a wise Solomon, the popish clergy of Ireland the spawn of Antichrist—Bale was wholly uncompromising in his determination to preach the gospel. He initiated a crucial sermon cycle from the pulpit of Kilkenny cathedral, preaching repentance, Christ's saving merits and sole capacity to save, while lambasting the clergy for their maintenance of 'white gods of their making', which were 'no gods but idols'.[5] When challenged by his cathedral establishment after Mary's proclamation as Queen he first 'took Christ's testament in my hand' and then, after preaching at the market cross, organized the young men of the town to perform 'a Tragedy of Gods promises in the old law' followed by 'a Comedy of Saint John Baptists preaching'. Both plays were probably by Bale, whose reforming interludes were famous long before he left for Ireland.[6] It may be the sheer vigour and passion of the bishop's approach that won him friends and supporters in the hostile environment of Kilkenny. His own assessment was that he had numbers of ordinary lay adherents, who helped among other things to protect him from murder in 1553, while his enemies were the clergy and a coterie of influential gentry and magistrates. When his servants were killed in the countryside 300 local men carried him back to Kilkenny 'the young men singing psalms and godly songs all the way'.[7]

But John Bale's gospelling, as he narrated it, was of a distinctive sort, regulated by the Royal Supremacy, and insistent on obedience to an established Tudor order. His 'vocation' was not generated by some internal divine calling, but by the summons of Edward VI to take up episcopal office, articulated in a conciliar letter that he proudly prints in full in his text. It was, he claimed, the doctrine of obedience that led him to insist that he and his colleague Hugh Goodacre be consecrated in Dublin according to the new ordinal of 1550. George Browne, the archbishop of Dublin, wanted to use the old text on the grounds that the new had not been sanctioned by the act of an Irish parliament. But Bale argued that 'if England and Ireland be under one king, they are both bound to the obedience of one law under him'. And his view prevailed because it had

[4] M. Aston, *England's Iconoclasts: Laws Against Images* (Oxford, 1988), 9.
[5] Happé and King, *Vocacyon*, 54.
[6] On Bale's career as dramatist see L.P. Fairfield, *John Bale: Mythmaker for the English Reformation* (Purdue, Ind., 1976).
[7] Happé and King, *Vocacyon*, 64.

the support of Sir Thomas Cusack, the Irish chancellor.[8] Once Edward's death was known the bishop tried every shift legally to avoid restoring the old religion, including arguing that there was no Irish lord deputy in residence to whom he could appeal. Law and conscience finally came directly into conflict when Mary's proclamation allowing the Mass was made public and 'the priests...suddenly set up the altars and images in the cathedral church'. At this point Bale could no longer retain any conviction in his appeal to authority and fled shaking the dust of the wicked off his feet 'according to Christ's commandment'.[9]

Bale's Irish adventures can usefully introduce many of the issues that are of central importance to this study of the Reformation in Britain and Ireland. The first is that the Tudor Reformation was incontrovertibly political. Historians are currently more attracted to the investigation of 'popular' religion and of forms of religious identity than to the ecclesiastical proceedings of Henry VIII and Elizabeth I.[10] But an understanding of the nature of the Reformation demands above all careful analysis of exactly this type of religious politics. The principle of *cuius regio, eius religio* was well understood by the subjects of the Tudors long before it became one of the assumptions of the Peace of Augsburg (1555). This doctrine of obedience to the conscience of the prince could take extreme forms. John Foxe cites a remarkable speech by the chronicler Edward Hall to the 1539 parliament, in which he asserts the duty of subjects to obey their prince in matters of religion, following what he, with the advice of the clergy, 'shall at any time please to set forth to be observed or believed'.[11] Bale's Protestantism was not erastian in this way: the conscience of the individual maintained a sovereignty that could not be displaced by prince or parliament. However, obedience to the spiritual will of the monarch, and to the political choices that resulted, was an essential aspect of his behaviour and that of most other leaders of the English church and state.[12] The

---

[8] Ibid., 52–3.   [9] Ibid., 67.

[10] Among the important recent studies of religion in early modern England that adopt this approach are E. Duffy, *The Stripping of the Altars: Traditional Religion in England 1400–1580* (New Haven, Conn., 1992); C. Marsh, *Popular Religion in Sixteenth Century England* (Basingstoke, 1998); M. Spufford (ed.), *The World of Rural Dissenters, 1520–1725* (Cambridge, 1995); T. Watt, *Cheap Print and Popular Piety, 1550–1640* (Cambridge, 1992); and A. Walsham, *Providence in Early Modern England* (Oxford, 2000). For Ireland there is R. Gillespie, *Devoted People: Belief and Religion in Early Modern Ireland* (Manchester, 1997). Studies which balance the investigation of high politics and ecclesiology with that of lay beliefs include C. Haigh, *English Reformations: Religion, Politics and Society under the Tudors* (Oxford, 1993); D. MacCulloch, *The Later Reformation in England, 1547–1603*, 2nd edn. (Basingstoke, 2001) and *Tudor Church Militant: Edward VI and the Protestant Reformation* (1999); and for Wales, G. Williams, *Wales and the Reformation* (Cardiff, 1997).

[11] Foxe, vi. 505.

[12] R. Rex, 'The crisis of obedience: God's Word and Henry's Reformation', *HJ* 39 (1996), 863–94.

export of religious change to Ireland was also a matter of political choice and will. Bale's remarks on the importance of Cusack's support in Dublin acknowledge that reformation could only be achieved with the help of the magistrate. A prime explanation for the final failure of reform in the Irish Pale was that the principle of *cuius regio, eius religio* was simply not accepted by enough of those who had to implement the crown's will.[13]

The Scottish Reformation seems, at first glance, less obviously politicized than its English, Welsh, and Irish counterpart. The monarchy did not make the Scottish Reformation. However, the Lords of the Congregation did, and without their political support, and that of Elizabeth's regime, the ministerial revolution of John Knox and his colleagues would probably have been stillborn. Power to enforce change rested in the hands of the lay elite, though since authority in the Scottish realm was far more decentralized and local than south of the border, the ministers were offered opportunities for political intervention that would have amazed Bale, and that appalled later English bishops.[14] In the late years of the century, under a mature monarch, conflicts at the centre of Scottish politics became ever more closely associated with issues about the governance of the Kirk.[15] So dramatic, and sometimes violent, were these conflicts, that they have tended to mesmerize historians of Scottish reform, who have been slower than their English or Irish counterparts to turn aside from ecclesiastical politics to the study of religious behaviour.[16]

The Reformation, Henry Kamen has observed, became institutionalized in northern Europe through the support of state, of lay elites, and of

---

[13] There is a vast historiography seeking to explain the failure of Reformation in Ireland. The best introduction is the debate conducted in article form over the past twenty-five years: B. Bradshaw, 'Sword, word and strategy in the Reformation in Ireland', *HJ* 21 (1978), 475–502; N. Canny, 'Why the Reformation failed in Ireland: une question mal posée', *JEH* 30 (1979), 423–50; K.S. Bottigheimer, 'The failure of the Reformation in Ireland: une question bien posée', *JEH* 36 (1985), 196–207; K.S. Bottigheimer and U. Lotz-Heumann, 'The Irish Reformation in European perspective', *ARG* 89 (1998), 268–309; K. Bottigheimer and B. Bradshaw, 'Revisionism and the Irish Reformation: a debate', *JEH* 51 (2000), 581–92; H.A. Jefferies, 'The early Tudor Reformation in the Irish Pale', *JEH* 52 (2001), 34–62.

[14] The best brief introduction to the relationship between politics and religion in Scotland is in J. Wormald, *Court, Kirk and Community: Scotland 1470–1625* (1981). The formal narrative is provided by G. Donaldson, *The Scottish Reformation* (Cambridge, 1960). On power relations between nobility and Kirk see J. Wormald, '"Princes" and the regions in the Scottish Reformation', in N. MacDougall (ed.), *Church, Politics and Society* (Edinburgh, 1983), 65–84.

[15] For a thorough survey see A.R. MacDonald, *The Jacobean Kirk, 1567–1625* (Aldershot, 1998).

[16] An honourable exception is I.B. Cowan, *The Scottish Reformation: Church and Society in Sixteenth-Century Scotland* (1982). The study by Margo Todd on the post-Reformation Scottish Kirk is the first that seeks systematically to study belief and behaviour in the congregation: M. Todd, *The Culture of Protestantism in Early Modern Scotland* (New Haven, Conn., 2002). This important volume was published too late to be reflected fully in the present study.

towns.[17] For John Bale this secular formulation would have omitted the one estate below the crown that was of fundamental importance: the clergy. His Irish venture was structured around monarchical and lay support for reform but the opposition of the conservative clergy was sufficient constantly to destabilize his mission. And Bale perceived that he and his opponents were not just locked in conflict about ceremonial or behaviour: he moved unhesitatingly into preaching on the key doctrinal themes of justification, grace, and salvation through Christ's merits. The minister was far more than an agent of an official reformation. Just as the Catholic priest claimed the key intermediary role between God and man through the operation of the sacraments, so the Protestant became the medium for the edification of the congregation through the lively preaching of the Word.[18] The clergy might be beleaguered by the greed and ignorance of lay society: they still had to bear witness to the truth of the gospel and recognize the popish priests as their greatest enemies. Of course, sources like Bale's, or like Knox's far more influential *History of the Reformation*, have a tendency to distort the historical record with their belief in the heroic witness of the godly ministers and their sharp binary division of the world into the forces of light and darkness.[19] The British clergy might, by the early seventeenth century, have deserved Joseph Hall's epithet '*Stupor mundi clericus Britannicus*' (The clergy of Britain is the wonder of the world).[20] It had, however, arrived at that point through a series of crises and disasters, compromises and processes of accommodation that appeared far from wonderful. Only perhaps in its contributions to learning, translation, and doctrinal debate, can the British clergy lay claim to Hall's observation from the very beginning of the Protestant Reformation.

[17] H. Kamen, 'Spain', in R. Scribner, R. Porter, and M. Teich (eds.), *The Reformation in National Context* (Cambridge, 1994), 211. See also G. Parker, 'Success and failure during the first century of the Reformation', *PP* 136 (1992), 43–82.

[18] Key studies of the role of the clergy in England are, for the pre-Reformation period, P. Marshall, *The Catholic Priesthood and the English Reformation* (Oxford, 1994) and P. Heath, *The English Parish Clergy on the Eve of the Reformation* (1969); for the early Reformation, D. MacCulloch, *Thomas Cranmer* (New Haven, Conn., 1996); and for the Elizabethan period, P. Collinson, *The Religion of Protestants* (Oxford, 1982) and R. O'Day, *The English Clergy: The Emergence and Consolidation of a Profession* (Leicester, 1979). On Scotland see J. Kirk, *Patterns of Reform: Continuity and Change in the Reformation Kirk* (Edinburgh, 1989) and, for the end of the century, D.G. Mullan, *Scottish Puritanism 1590–1638* (Oxford, 2000). On Ireland see H.A. Jefferies, *Priests and Prelates in Armagh, 1518–1558* (Dublin, 1997) and A. Ford, *The Protestant Reformation in Ireland 1590–1641* (Dublin, 1997).

[19] J. Kirk, 'John Knox and the historians', in R.A. Mason (ed.), *John Knox and the British Reformations* (Aldershot, 1998), 14–15, though Kirk points out that it is the ministers as a group whom Knox trumpets, not his own role.

[20] P. Wynter (ed.), *The Works of Joseph Hall*, 10 vols. (Oxford, 1843), x. 29. Quoted by Collinson, *Religion of Protestants*, 92. Hall chooses to single out the intellectual luminaries of the English church from Jewel and Humphrey to Willett and White.

Bale's Catholic clergy and conservative magistrates endeavoured to impede the true work of reformation: the conversion of the people. Bale had, he argued, been sent 'to seek the peoples health', which must be achieved by the preaching of pure doctrine combined with good discipline. 'For doctrine without discipline and restraint of vices maketh dissolute hearers. And on the other side discipline without doctrine maketh either hypocrites or else desperate doers.'[21] The reformation of parish, congregation, and individual was the objective of all zealous ministers. The ambition was for nothing less than a regeneration of society: an aim that often existed in tension with the Calvinist conviction that only a minority would be saved. In Bale's narrative we can see hints that he sought to reconcile himself to the failures of general conversion by singling out groups which showed evidence of regeneration, particularly the psalm-singing, thespian youths of Kilkenny. Sermon-gadding laymen in Elizabethan England, or committed congregations like that of the kirk of St Andrews in Scotland, offered the same promising material to their clerical mentors.[22] But the process of conversion was hard, and in practice the ambitions of the clergy for many of the laity extended little further than the conformity that was a requirement of the churches. The very language of conversion indicated a sharp rupture between past and present behaviour that was unlikely to be achieved in most ordinary parochial environments. The establishment of full discipline of the kind contemplated by Bale and largely enacted by the Scottish reformers assisted in redirecting the laity. However, the principal process by which ordinary Catholics became Protestant was one of accommodation and adjustment. The displacement of the old—the loss of the Catholic liturgy, of saints, of prayer for the dead—was followed by slow reconstruction, as conformity was built into acceptance of new liturgy, preaching, and Bible reading.[23]

Studies of religious change and reformation in lands that became Protestant have routinely had a national character.[24] The practical complexity of researching and explaining something as fundamental as a transformation

---

[21] Happé and King, *Vocacyon*, 54–5.

[22] P. Collinson, 'Elizabethan and Jacobean Puritanism as forms of popular culture', in C. Durston and J. Eales (eds.), *The Culture of English Puritanism 1560–1700* (Basingstoke, 1996), 20–3. J. Dawson, '"The face of the perfyt reformed Kyrk": St Andrews and the early Scottish Reformation', SCH Subsidia 8 (Oxford, 1991), 413–35.

[23] This is broadly the revisionist position now accepted by most historians of the English Reformation, who accept the substance of Haigh's argument for a 'slow Reformation' only gradually achieved over the late sixteenth century. Haigh, *English Reformations*, 12–21, 285–95. In recent years there has been more interest in the nature of post-Reformation popular belief than in the speed of religious change. See, in particular, Walsham, *Providence*; J. Maltby, *Prayer Book and People in Elizabethan and Early Stuart England* (Cambridge, 1998).

[24] Scribner, Porter, and Teich, *The Reformation in National Context*.

in official ideology and popular religious behaviour has contributed to this pattern. So too has the difficulty of identifying a logical structure of analysis of a supranational kind. Historians of doctrine and ideas have found it easiest to transcend fixed boundaries, for the reformers themselves formed a 'republic of letters', albeit one often divided on critical issues of interpretation. Like their humanist predecessors, Bucer, Bullinger, and Calvin consciously promoted the pursuit of pan-European religious harmony through correspondence, formal debate, and mission.[25] But when the reception of these ideas and their assimilation into the political mainstream is at issue, national historians have a tendency to revert to claims of local exceptionalism. Protestantism itself, of course, legitimated these national impulses, with its acceptance that the true Church could have many particular manifestations, unified only by the possession of the proper 'marks' of faithful preaching and proper ministration of the sacraments.[26] In Germany after Augsburg the way was opened for a full-blooded acceptance that reforming churches could proceed autonomously under their own prince. National autonomy is enshrined in the very fabric of the Reformation.

English and Scottish historians have been among the most committed proponents of a view of reform founded upon the nation. The Scots acquired a rigorous form of Calvinism and forged it into a powerful system of religious identity that also became a major source of political unity. The preachers were already praising its distinctive Reformation at the end of the sixteenth century, and understanding the Scots and their faith has been a major preoccupation of historians ever since.[27] English claims to uniqueness have been less concerned with purity of faith, but have constructed the Reformation as part of the manifest destiny of the English people. While historians no longer subscribe to such teleological theories, they remain intrigued by the contribution made by the Reformation to the emergence of a sense of national identity.[28] They may also be seduced by the distinctiveness of the structure of the Church of England, which has traditionally led to claims of separateness. To privilege the study of religious change in England is at best to acknowledge that distinctiveness, which can be analysed through rich and abundant sources. At worst it can contribute to the 'fog in the Channel, Continent isolated' view of English history.

Irish historians have their own claims to uniqueness, based not of course on the acceptance of Reformation, but on its triumphal rejection.

---

[25] P.D.L. Avis, *The Church in the Theology of the Reformers* (1981).

[26] D.F. Wright (ed.), *Martin Bucer: Reforming Church and Community* (Cambridge, 1994).

[27] For reflections on this theme see M. Lynch, 'A nation born again? Scottish identity in the sixteenth and seventeenth centuries', in D. Brown, R.J. Finlay, and M. Lynch (eds.), *Image and Identity: The Making and Re-making of Scotland through the Ages* (Edinburgh, 1998), 82–104.

[28] See particularly P. Collinson, *The Birthpangs of Protestant England* (Basingstoke, 1988).

In a northern European world in which rulers claimed to control the consciences of their subjects, goes the argument, the Irish alone resisted. It was, to quote Brendan Bradshaw, 'a kingdom in which the vast majority of the subjects persisted in refusing to conform to the religion of the monarch "as by law established"'.[29] Irish historians, like their English and Scottish counterparts, have retreated from claims that the success of Catholicism was inevitable, but their readings of religious experience remain coloured by a conviction of the uniqueness of the island's experience.

The development of 'new British history' since the 1970s has provided one form of riposte to national essentialists in the various parts of the archipelago. As articulated by John Pocock the new approach was designed to counter Anglocentric narrative in which the 'matter of Britain' if it was considered at all was constantly identified with 'the matter of England'.[30] Instead, the new British history should endeavour to understand the 'cultural pluralism and partial domination' that was the story of the three kingdoms or four nations. The results have been mixed for the early modern period and for the study of the Reformation. There has been valuable comparative work on the impact of religious change in Ireland and Wales, and on the relationship between religion and politics in these two territories.[31] Gaelic scholars have reminded Anglophone historians of the internationalism of the Gaelic world, and of some of its responses to religious and political upheaval.[32] Religious change in the sixteenth century has been considered, briefly, as the context for the more visibly British crises of religion in the Stuart period.[33] A first attempt has

[29] B. Bradshaw, 'The Tudor Reformation and revolution in Wales and Ireland: the origins of the British problem', in B. Bradshaw and J. Morrill (eds.), *The British Problem c.1534–1707: State Formation in the Atlantic Archipelago* (Basingstoke, 1996), 39–40.

[30] The 'Ur' text is J.G.A. Pocock, 'British history: a plea for a new subject', *Journal of Modern History* 47 (1975), 601–28. The quotations are from Geoffrey of Monmouth, used as the focus of R.R. Davies's Oxford inaugural lecture: *The Matter of Britain and the Matter of England* (Oxford, 1996).

[31] Bradshaw, 'The Tudor Reformation' and idem, 'The English Reformation and identity formation in Ireland and Wales', in B. Bradshaw and P. Roberts (eds.), *British Consciousness and Identity: The Making of Britain 1533–1707* (Cambridge, 1998), 43–111. S. Ellis, 'Economic problems of the Church: why the Reformation failed in Ireland', *JEH* 41 (1990), 239–65. C. Brady, 'Comparable histories? Tudor reform in Wales and Ireland', in S.G. Ellis and S. Barber (eds.), *Conquest and Union: Fashioning a British State 1485–1725* (Harlow, 1995), 64–86. This comparative project has been driven by Irish historians, and Karl Bottigheimer and Ute Lotz-Heumann have warned of its narrowness and its tendency to confirm a nationalist view of Irish exceptionalism: Bottigheimer and Lotz-Heumann, 'Irish Reformation', 274–5.

[32] M. MacCraith, 'The Gaelic reaction to the Reformation', in Ellis and Barber, *Conquest and Union*, 139–61.

[33] J. Morrill, 'A British patriarchy? Ecclesiastical imperialism under the early Stuarts', in A. Fletcher and P. Roberts (eds.), *Religion, Culture and Society in Early Modern Britain* (Cambridge, 1994), 209–37.

been made to reflect comparatively on popular religious practice.[34] The most stimulating work, since it studies interconnection between reformers and provides a genuine challenge to national exceptionalism, is that of Jane Dawson on Anglo-Scottish relations.[35]

The disinclination of historians of the English Reformation to participate thus far in this wider analysis of religion in the British Isles is striking. It could be read as an implicit affirmation of older claims of English distinctiveness: there are more important things to be said about England alone than about English religion in relation to the whole of Britain and Ireland. But a more telling assumption is that, in so far as the Reformation was international, it was its European dimensions that most affected English belief and behaviour. Diarmaid MacCulloch's work on Cranmer, for example, emphasizes the influence of Continental reformers on the archbishop's plans for the English church.[36] Thirdly, the exclusion of the other British realms may be understood as a response to surviving evidence. One of Pocock's 'bons mots' in his plea for a new British history was that 'a highly governed society is a highly literate society'.[37] There can be no doubt that the English church and state accumulated documents and preserved them in a systematic manner; and that lay and clerical elites were also generous in their use of paper and printed text. Scotland, Ireland, and initially even Wales, were less administratively centralized, less disposed to elaborate methods of preservation, less routinely able to resort to the printing press. It is easier, though never of course easy, for historians to hear the voices of Englishmen than those of the Irish, the Welsh, or the Scots.[38]

Each of these challenges to a Reformation history of the British Isles carries some weight. The evidential issue is the most significant for the working historian. While the study of political process can be conducted on an equal footing across much of Britain and Ireland the same is not true of ecclesiastical organization or of the study of lay belief and behaviour. Two acute contrasts may stand as exemplary: over 200 sets of churchwardens' accounts survive for England during the Tudor period;

---

[34] R. Gillespie, 'Differing devotions: patterns of religious practice in the British Isles, 1500–1700', in S.J. Connolly (ed.), *Kingdoms United? Great Britain and Ireland since 1500* (Dublin, 1999), 67–77.

[35] J. Dawson, 'Anglo-Scottish Protestant culture and the integration of sixteenth-century Britain', in Ellis and Barber, *Conquest and Union*, 87–114. See also S. Alford, *The Early Elizabethan Polity* (Cambridge, 1999) and the collection of essays on John Knox, R.A. Mason (ed.), *John Knox and the British Reformations* (Aldershot, 1998).

[36] MacCulloch, *Cranmer, passim.*

[37] Pocock, 'British history', 611.

[38] Note the title of Eamon Duffy's local study of a Devon parish: *Voices of Morebath: Reformation and Rebellion in an English Village* (New Haven, Conn., 2001).

Scotland and Ireland have none.[39] Episcopal visitation records are patchy throughout the British Isles, but they are available in some quantity in England while they seem rarely to have been kept by the Irish prelates.[40] Only when the kirk sessions become available in Scotland after the Reformation is there a comparable source to English church court records.[41] Moreover, differences in the way local records have been used by historians can compound the problem: in Scotland, for example, the kirk session records are only now being used to gain access to the attitudes of the laity.[42] Evidence about lay religious behaviour in the Gaelic territories is almost non-existent before 1600, and indeed it proves impossible to write a convincing history of lay religion in Ireland before that date.[43]

Other doubts about the study of reformation in the British Isles are more readily answered. To consider the relationship between the component parts of the isles does not preclude an awareness of the Continental contacts of reforming divines, or the broad influence of international politics on British behaviour. There are circumstances, for example, that of the Geneva exile in the late 1550s, where an understanding of British identities enhances the significance of the European perspective.[44] The earlier diaspora of Scottish Protestants during the reign of James V also exposes fascinating networks of contact across the Protestant world, placing England in its broader context.[45] As for a lingering enthusiasm for English exceptionalism: the comparative study of other Reformations often in practice serves as a reminder that the uniqueness of Tudor experience can easily be exag-

---

[39] R. Hutton, 'The local impact of the Tudor Reformations', in C. Haigh (ed.), *The English Reformation Revised* (Cambridge, 1987), 114–15.

[40] Not only are visitation records very rare for Ireland, Dr Jefferies believes that the most basic records of episcopal administration, the registers, were not kept in most Irish sees *inter hibernicos*: Jefferies, 'Early Tudor Reformation', 37. In the case of Scotland Gordon Donaldson also doubted if registers were routinely kept: G. Donaldson, 'Church records', *The Scottish Genealogist* 2/3 (1955), 14. However, it is likely that much was destroyed at the Reformation: D. MacRoberts, 'Material destruction caused by the Scottish Reformation', *Innes Review* 10 (1959), 169.

[41] M.J. Graham, *The Uses of Reform: 'Godly Discipline' and Popular Behaviour in Scotland and Beyond, 1560–1610* (Leiden, 1996).

[42] See particularly the work of Margo Todd on post-Reformation Scotland.

[43] Gillespie, *Devoted People*, draws some examples from the sixteenth century, but is essentially a study in seventeenth- and eighteenth-century devotion, comprehending Catholics and Protestants.

[44] C. Kellar, ' "To enrich with gospel truth the neighbour kingdom": Religion and Reform in England and Scotland 1534–1561', University of Oxford D.Phil. (2000), 161–91, is the first detailed study of these links, though see J.E.A. Dawson, 'Trumpeting resistance: Christopher Goodman and John Knox', in Mason, *John Knox*, 131–53.

[45] J. Kirk, 'The religion of early Scottish Protestants', in J. Kirk (ed.), *Humanism and Reform: The Church in Europe, England and Scotland 1400–1643*, SCH Subsidia 8 (Oxford, 1991), 371–84. J. Durkan, 'Scottish "Evangelicals" in the patronage of Thomas Cromwell', *RSCHS* 21 (1982), 127–56.

gerated. This is most obviously the case in the years before Henry VIII's break with Rome: each part of the British Isles existed within a universal Church that had a theology, pattern of worship, and institutional organization that was essentially the same. Differences were probably less significant than similarities, and a fault line, if it existed, divided a Gaelic from an anglophone environment rather than realms from one another.[46] Difference assumes a far greater significance after 1534 but, among the reformers, doctrinal affinity and a division of the world between the true and the false Church discouraged too precise an obsession with national boundaries. Only once in his narrative does Bishop Bale remember that he is among the 'wild Irish' as a separate racial group.[47]

This study of religious change and reformation consciously follows Pocock's prescription that we should study both cultural pluralism and partial domination in the history of the British Isles. It pursues national histories of reform, but places them in the context of supranational relationships. It recognizes that the constant interweaving of the narrative of religious change in the four nations is largely a consequence of English claims to hegemony. Not only was this true in politics. When John Foxe chose in his martyrology to describe persecutions 'in this realm of England and also of Scotland', his Scottish colleagues might legitimately have suspected an implicit assumption of English leadership of the true Church.[48] Those political and ideological ambitions provide the foundation for the British dimensions of this study. The fact that the English Reformation was not confined to the borders of the old kingdom is surely one of its most crucial features. And the response of the Scots and the Irish to English pressures for religious change in the sixteenth century constructed a subsequent history of political breakdown and civil war. The study of cultural pluralism, on the other hand, provides the opportunity to move aside from this English focus into comparative histories of individual territories and into the study of the broader divisions of the British Isles, especially those that separated Celtic and Anglo-Norman societies. Reformation demanded popular evangelism, the use of new methods of communication, the manipulation of language and text: in all of these areas the cultural diversity of Britain and Ireland provides an important stimulus for the ensuing analysis.[49]

---

[46] J.A. Watt, *The Church in Medieval Ireland* (Dublin, 1972).

[47] Happé and King, *Vocacyon*, 58, this was in the period of violence against the English that followed the death of Edward VI.

[48] Foxe, i. 1.

[49] The story of the Counter-Reformation is not the objective of this present study, but would be susceptible to similar treatment. A start has been made on this approach by T. McCoog, *The Society of Jesus in Ireland, Scotland and England, 1541–88* (Leiden, 1996).

In the narrative of the coming of reform it is as difficult for historians to delineate a time as a place. The English Reformation was once thought to have begun in the late 1520s and to have been concluded in its essentials once the Elizabethan Settlement was completed.[50] Now academic fashion has moved, and there are exponents of the 'Long Reformation' not concluded until the seventeenth, or even the eighteenth, century.[51] Meanwhile Irish historians, as part of their escape from teleology, have extended the possible dates for the failure of reform in Ireland into the early seventeenth century.[52] And even in Scotland, where the emphasis on the Reformation as transformative moment remains strongest, some historians now emphasize the slow and partial acceptance of religious change.[53] There is certainly nothing of a very specific kind that marks out 1500 as the beginning of a process or 1600 as its end. The former date simply offers the benefit of studying the Church, its relations with the states, and the nature of popular belief, for a whole generation before the bright eyes of Anne Boleyn turned the English world upside-down. The latter takes us forty years beyond the Scottish and English 'settlements', into a period when both Reformations had gained a certain political and ideological maturity and, conversely, when commentators were beginning to acknowledge that the Reformation in Ireland had failed. The narrower logic of 1600 is, of course, that it pre-dates the Union of the Crowns and hence the beginning of a new cycle of ecclesiastical politics. By then James VI, in *Basilikon Doron*, was already looking forward from a Scottish Reformation that was wrought 'by popular tumult and rebellion', albeit 'extraordinarily wrought by God', to the happiness of a Church 'proceeding from the Princes order'.[54] Reformation history was already being reconstructed in the interests of what the king hoped would be a truly British state.

---

[50] The classic modern exponent of this view is usually taken to be A.G. Dickens, *The English Reformation*, 2nd edn. (1989), though in fact Dickens is more cautious on the nature of popular commitment to the Settlement than some of his critics allow.

[51] See especially N. Tyacke (ed.), *England's Long Reformation 1500–1800* (1998).

[52] See above at n. 13.

[53] This is a view particularly favoured by Graham, *The Uses of Reform*, and M. Lynch, *Edinburgh and the Reformation* (Edinburgh, 1981), and 'Preaching to the converted? Perspectives on the Scottish Reformation', in A.A. MacDonald, M. Lynch, and I.B. Cowan (eds.), *The Renaissance in Scotland* (Leiden, 1994), 301–43.

[54] J. Craigie (ed.), *The basilikon doron of King James VI*, 2 vols., STS 11, 18 (1944–50), i. 74.

PART I

THE TRADITIONAL ORDER

I

AUTHORITY AND CONTROL

Papacy

On an October day in 1521 John Clerk, Henry VIII's orator at Rome, stood before Leo X and presented him with a luxurious copy of his master's defence of Catholic orthodoxy against the attacks of Luther, the *Assertio Septem Sacramentorum*. In his accompanying speech Clerk expatiated on the theme of devotion to the papacy; a devotion displayed both in the sentiments and actions of his monarch, and in the attitudes of his countrymen. 'Let others speak of other Nations, certainly my Britainy (called England by our Modern Cosmographers) Situated in the furthermost end of the World, and separated from the Continent by the Ocean: As it has never been behind in the Worship of God, and True Christian Faith, and due Obedience to the Roman Church, either to Spain, France, Germany or Italy: Nay to Rome itself; so likewise, there is no Nation which more Impugns this Monster [Luther], and the Heresies broached by him...'.[1] The occasion demanded florid sentiments and Leo is not likely to have judged England's commitment to the papacy by such words. An Italian observer had felt otherwise two decades earlier: 'the kingdom of England is not quite independent, I do not mean of the Empire, but of the Apostolic See'. The last view clearly proved more prophetic: the identity of the monarch and his people to the cause of Rome, and indeed to the universalism of the Church that it expressed, was to endure only another decade.[2]

The peoples of the British Isles should have had few illusions about their position in late medieval Western Catholicism. They remained physically peripheral, and often politically marginal, in the great game of papal politics. Du Boulay, considering fifteenth-century Anglo-Papal relations, suggested that a glance at Creighton or Pastor indicates how little England figured in the vision of Rome.[3] Scotland received even more scant

---

[1] Henry VIII, *An Assertion of the Seven Sacraments against Martin Luther*, trans T.W. (1687), sig. Ai
[2] C.A. Sneyd (ed.), *A Relation of the Island of England about the Year 1500*, CS os 37 (1847), 53.
[3] F. Du Boulay, 'England and the papacy in the fifteenth century', in C.H. Lawrence (ed.), *The English Church and the Papacy in the Middle Ages* (1965), 217.

attention, and Ireland merits only two references in Pastor's study of the period to the end of the pontificate of Alexander VI.[4] There is, of course, far more than this to be said about papal relations with the British Isles in the fifteenth century, yet even a recent commentator like Margaret Harvey would acknowledge that by the end of the Hundred Years' War the papacy only looked intermittently to these northern lands.[5] It was in part this very absence from the stormy heart of papal politics that made possible the ostentatious displays of loyalty and affinity proffered in 1521. The jurisdictional relationship between England and the papacy was already clear in all its essentials. The English monarch was proximate to his clergy and, usually, powerful: the papacy was distant and, for much of the fifteenth century, politically vulnerable. Under the statutes against provisions the crown had secured to itself the general right to control clerical taxation, and had gradually inhibited all but a small group of payments, including annates and Peter's Pence, from being transmitted to the papal treasury. Lunt's calculations put the transmitted figure for regular taxes in the fifteenth century at only *c.* £250 per annum. On the eve of the Reformation Scarisbrick's figure for all dues including episcopal payments for common services is much higher, something under £5,000, but even so not a dramatic flow of wealth from this loyal corner of Western Christendom. The right of provision to benefices other than bishoprics was effectively cut off after 1407. Episcopal patronage remained formally with Rome, but with the full acknowledgement that the crown nominated to all senior posts. By the early sixteenth century no pope could expect to exercise his claim to provisions without royal assent.[6]

The Scottish monarchy had established these controls somewhat later than England. Gradual *de facto* incursions upon papal nominations had been occurring throughout the fifteenth century. The attempt to reassert papal control by finally establishing St Andrews as the metropolitical see in 1472 backfired, since James III was quickly able to establish one of his own men, William Scheves, in control. Finally in 1487 Innocent III formally granted James III the right to have eight months' delay in the case of livings worth more than 200 gold florins before papal nomination occurred, thereby securing both the king's influence over appointments and his interim profit from temporalities. When the Scottish crown was relatively stable this agreement held, but in times of weakness, such as the

---

[4] L. Pastor, *The History of the Popes from the Close of the Middle Ages*, 40 vols. (1890–1953), vols. i–vi. Ireland only features among lists of countries asked to participate in various papal crusades. J.A.F. Thomson, *Popes and Princes, 1417–1517* (1980), 213–14.

[5] M. Harvey, *England, Rome and the Papacy, 1417–64* (Manchester, 1993), 130–213.

[6] W. Lunt, *Financial Relations of the Papacy with England, 1327–1534* (Cambridge, Mass., 1962), 436–46. J.J. Scarisbrick, 'Clerical taxation in England, 1485–1547', *JEH* 11 (1960), 41–54.

years after Flodden, the papacy sometimes exercised its remaining rights vigorously, as in the appointment of Innocenzo Cibo, nephew to Leo X, to the see of St Andrews. This, however, was unusual, and the Scottish crown, like its English neighbour, seems to have established an effective *modus vivendi* with the papacy on nominations.[7]

By the eve of the Reformation the major area of difficulty in monarchical control over appointments remained Gaelic and marcher Ireland. Since Henry VII and Henry VIII (until 1541) were merely lords over a section of Ireland, the majority of Irish sees were in theory, and often in practice, beyond their control. Here the papal right to provide to benefices commanded significantly greater influence than in England, Wales, or Scotland. Unfortunately, curial knowledge of the native church was so uncertain, and local political patterns so fluid, that provisions were often made to sees not actually vacant, and double nominations occasionally occurred. In 1492, for example, Richard O'Guanach was preferred to Elphin in Tuam province, only to be challenged by Nicholas O'Flanagan, whom the papacy had presumed dead in 1487.[8] A more difficult conflict concerned the see of Cork and Cloyne, an area on the margins of English influence, for which Henry VII supported a candidate of the Geraldine interest, eventually prevailing despite deep uncertainty at Rome about who had been properly provided to the bishopric in the previous generation. It was often easier for the papacy to listen to the cardinal protector of the English, who would promote his master's case for reliable candidates, rather than confront the mass of competing interests that surrounded Irish candidates.[9]

The insularity of the northern lands should not, however, be exaggerated. The revitalized Tudor monarchy, and the vigour of the 'auld alliance' between Scotland and France, did something to persuade the ambitious popes of the Italian Wars period to reconsider their English and Scottish subjects.[10] The enlarged political chessboard of these years demanded that the papacy calculated more fully than before distant events such as conflict on the Anglo-Scottish border. In 1514, for example, Leo X had an ambassador, Balthasar Stuart, resident in Scotland for a whole year, endeavouring to broker peace with England after the debacle of Flodden.[11] Leo might be irritated by the tortuous diplomacy of Henry VIII and Wolsey, and by their reluctance to yield any revenues for his planned

[7] L. MacFarlane, 'The primacy of the Scottish Church, 1472–1521', *Innes Review* 20 (1969), 125–8. Cibo was never resident as archbishop, holding the see with numerous others.

[8] S. Ellis, *Tudor Ireland: 1470–1603* (1985), 184–6.

[9] W.E. Wilkie, *The Cardinal Protectors of England: Rome and the Tudors before the Reformation* (Cambridge, 1974), 63–73. K. Walsh, 'The beginnings of a national protectorate', *Archivium Hibernicum* 32 (1974), 72–80.

[10] Du Boulay, 'England and the papacy', 235–6.

[11] J.A.F. Thomson, 'Innocent VIII and the Scottish church', *Innes Review* 19 (1968), 26.

crusade, but he could not afford to reject the papalist enthusiasm that the young king developed as a consequence of their exchanges.[12]

Conversely the importance of the papacy both for control of the Church and for international diplomacy encouraged the English and Scottish kings to adopt cardinal protectors in the curia: men who could mediate between their own agents and the papal court and speak the language of curial politics with confidence. Hostility from the revived fifteenth-century papacy to such 'national' protectors gave way to official acceptance under Innocent VIII and Alexander VI. Giovanni and Silvester de Gigli, successively bishops of Worcester, and the most important Roman agents of Henry VII and his successor, were never cardinals, but they 'managed' key connections with Cardinals Piccolomini, Medici, and Campeggio, around whom English influence was built.[13] Meanwhile Scottish interests were directed by two generations of the Accolti family, uncle and nephew. The oddest figure in this group is that of Christopher Bainbridge, archbishop of York, cardinal in 1511 and resident at the papal court until 1514. In the fourteenth century there had been an expectation that cardinals would reside with the papacy: by the early sixteenth century it was a feature of the growing national identity of the Western churches that men such as John Morton and Thomas Wolsey expected to stay at home to serve their princes. Bainbridge identified himself as strongly with the interests of Julius II as with those of England and, until the rise of Wolsey, he conceived his political and perhaps his spiritual role as bridging the gap between his native land and the curia. The ultimate thanks that he received, characteristic of Renaissance power politics at their worst, was gradual exclusion by Wolsey and his local agent Gigli, and an abrupt death, which led to persistent rumours of poisoning.[14]

These spokesmen for the English and Scottish crown had a threefold pattern of responsibilities that indicate the needs of their home regimes. They had to represent the political interests of their monarchs, to facilitate the transaction of routine ecclesiastical business, and to secure royal nominations to key office. The importance of the last task, interconnected with the first, is shown most intriguingly in the intermittent attempts of the Tudor crown to extend its hegemony over the churches of the British Isles through its Roman agents. The Irish church has already been mentioned: by the beginning of Henry VIII's reign the cardinal protectors were managing royal nominations for Ireland in exactly the same way as England, and much of the earlier confusion about provisions had been resolved. Even earlier there was an abortive plan by Alexander VI to

[12] MacFarlane, 'Primacy', 111–20. J.J. Scarisbrick, *Henry VIII* (1968), 97–134.
[13] Wilkie, *Cardinal Protectors, passim.*
[14] D.S. Chambers, *Cardinal Bainbridge in the Court of Rome* (Oxford, 1965).

allow English bishops to reform the Irish church. The extension of English influence over Scotland was also a possibility at moments of Scottish weakness with the assistance of men at the curia. It was probable that Henry VIII's assertion of 1513 that all Scottish bishoprics should be subordinate to York as they had been originally was intended as no more than a gesture. But there were attempts to influence Scottish provisions, both in that year and again in the mid-1520s. In the latter period the French interest was virtually excluded, and Henry's agents in Rome consistently promoted the candidates presented in the name of the young James V by his mother, Henry's sister. But the cardinal protectors usually bent to the power in the ascendant in their individual realms: Accolti had no difficulty in accepting James's countermanding of the previous nomination of an Anglophile bishop of Moray when he came to majority.[15]

It is not easy to estimate how powerful an identity with the papacy lay behind these political and institutional encounters. The language used by Clerk to Leo X deploys a rhetoric much favoured in official circles in England and Scotland in the post-conciliar period. These northern isles were not to be outdone in their expressions of loyalty to the Holy See; were apparently enthusiastic adherents of such papal initiatives as crusades; and in general wished to assert their centrality within the community of Catholic Christendom.[16] In 1512, for example, Henry used his loyalty to Rome and to the Catholic Church as a justification for declaring war on the schismatic French, who had just participated in the Council of Pisa. His boundless enthusiasm for the attack on Luther in 1521 can be explained as a diplomatic propaganda exercise, which showed identity with the Emperor and Rome in a period when conflict with France was becoming likely again. England had had its great representative of vigorous ideological anti-papalism in Wyclif, whose reputation as a scourge of the papacy owed much to a particularly low moment in relations between European powers and Rome. Yet even the indigenous heretical tradition of Lollardy showed less specific interest in challenging the pope after the early years of the fifteenth century, focusing much of its anti-clerical energies instead on those nearer home.[17] It is perhaps easiest to argue the

---

[15] Wilkie, *Cardinal Protectors*, 161–8, 172–5. Walsh, 'National protectorate', 78.

[16] On the diplomatic significance of the *Assertio*, and its connection to attacks on heresy, see C.W. D'Alton, 'The Suppression of Heresy in Early Henrician England', University of Melbourne Ph.D. (1999), 125–7.

[17] In the Norwich heresy trials of 1428–31 there were fourteen examples of attacks on the papacy, as against ten challenges to other orders within the Church: N. Tanner (ed.), *Norwich Heresy Trials, 1428–31*, CS 4th ser. 20 (1977), 11. In later Lollard trials there was also only limited evidence of interest in the papacy, though a scattering of references to the pope as antichrist: Foxe, iv. 208. A. Hudson, *The Premature Reformation: Wycliffite Texts and Lollard History* (Oxford, 1988), 469.

essential acceptance of papal authority by negation. In England there was little political enthusiasm for the most obvious alternative to papal authority: conciliarism. After the critical period of Constance the English church took only limited part in the conciliar movement. There were English delegates at Basel in 1433–4, but their major objectives were to assail the Bohemian heretics and to use the medium of the Council to negotiate about the Anglo-French wars.[18] The English were represented at the Fifth Lateran Council of 1512–17 in a basic show of unity with papal aims, as well as a means of distancing themselves from the competing Council of Pisa. Even the Scots, whose ideological commitment to conciliarism was an abiding feature of the late medieval period, did not always feel the need to be loyal to the practice: James V stressed to Leo X that the Scots had not supported Pisa, despite the obvious temptation to further the 'auld alliance' by pleasing the French in this matter.[19]

The doctrine of papal supremacy met with no direct challenge from British theologians in the early sixteenth century. Zealous support of full claims of papal plenitude of power, however, was quite another matter in the period before positions hardened in the 1520s. The Observant Franciscans seem to have offered the proudest defence of papal authority; their basic commitment to the pope as their only superior being strongly reinforced by Leo X's decision finally to separate them from the Conventuals as an independent order.[20] Among English theologians Bishop Fisher stands out in arguing, as early as 1519, in his *De Unica Magdalena*, that papal pronouncements should have priority in discussion of doctrine. Henry VIII's defence of papal supremacy in *Assertio*, on the other hand, was less than doctrinally exhaustive: 'I will not wrong the Bishop of Rome so much', he wrote, 'as troublesomely or carefully to dispute His Right, as if it were a matter doubtful.' He proceeded to assert the universal consent of nations, the precedents of the past, and the habits of the American Indians, who 'do submit themselves to the See of Rome'.[21] Thomas More's hand in the *Assertio* may go some way to explaining this less-than-wholehearted papalism: Henry's comments on the papal primacy seemed to him too enthusiastic and he advised his monarch to 'leave out that point, or else touch it more slenderly'.[22] More began to move to-

---

[18] A.N.E.D. Schofield, 'The first English delegation to the Council of Basel', *JEH* 12 (1961), 167–96.

[19] On the Fifth Lateran Council see W. Ullmann, 'Julius II and the schismatic cardinals', in D. Baker (ed.), *Schism, Heresy and Religious Protest*, SCH 9 (1972), 177–94.

[20] On the Observants see K.D. Brown, 'The Franciscan Observants in England, 1482–1559', University of Oxford D.Phil. (1986).

[21] R. Rex, *The Theology of John Fisher* (Cambridge, 1991), 102–3. Henry VIII, *Assertio*, 5–6.

[22] E.F. Rogers (ed.), *The Correspondence of Sir Thomas More* (Princeton, N.J., 1947), 199.

wards a full articulation of papal supremacy in his defence of the universal Church in *Responsio ad Lutherum*, but even then he showed a reluctance to dilate on his new-found commitment: 'I am moved', he wrote, 'to obedient submission to this see by all those arguments which learned and holy men have assembled in support of this point' and by fear of the disorder that would ensue without the power of one head.[23] Only Fisher, the papalist, in his *Assertionis Lutheranae Confutatio*, provided a full testimony in favour of the authority of Rome, based largely on scriptural argument for the precedence of Peter, backed by a wide-ranging appeal to the support of the Fathers.[24]

Conciliarist sentiment might be of limited practical significance for the British churches, but like claims to papal sovereignty it could be revived. There was an acceptance that the universal Church was on occasions best represented by a general council in conjunction with the papacy. On the relationship between popes and councils the position articulated by John Fisher probably commanded most English assent. He assumed that consensus would normally operate between pope and council, that to be a proper body the latter would be convened by the former, and that a council could only admonish and reprove a pope who had fallen from the path of righteousness.[25] His colleague Thomas More may well have begun with the same assumptions, but circumstances led him by a wavering path to an acceptance of conciliarism. More in his later years, despite his growing support for papal monarchism, asserted that a true council could depose a pope.[26] By the 1520s circumstances began to force a reconsideration of the nature of authority on traditional theologians. For example, it has recently been shown that Fisher's writings against Luther produced in the young Thomas Cranmer a surprisingly vigorous defence of the papalist position. This was, however, already tempered by conciliarist views. Cranmer's marginal annotations on his copy of Fisher's *Confutatio* denounce above all the 'impious' German heretic for his argument that a general council, as well as the papacy, can err.[27]

Scottish theologians and canonists were better equipped than their English counterparts for a reopening of the debate on authority. Many had had some of their training in the schools of Paris, where the strongest intellectual commitment to conciliarism survived into the sixteenth century.[28] Thus John Major, the greatest among them, published in 1518 a

---

[23] *CWTM* v. 607–9.   [24] Rex, *Theology of Fisher*, 79–81.   [25] Ibid., 102, 107–9.

[26] *CWTM* v. 768, 771–2. There is much debate on More's commitment to conciliarism: see F. Oakley, 'Headley, Marius and the matter of Thomas More's conciliarism', *Moreana* 64 (1980), 82–8.

[27] D. MacCulloch, *Thomas Cranmer* (1996), 28–30.

[28] J. Burns, 'The conciliarist tradition in Scotland', *SHR* 42 (1963), 89–104.

tract entitled *Disputatio de auctoritate concilii supra pontificem maximum*. This rehearsed a number of the old arguments of the fifteenth century: in particular the right of a council to depose a heretical pope was reaffirmed. Major in his turn taught many of the generation of Scottish clerics who were to be engaged in the Reformation conflicts: his views are, for example, generally believed to have had influence on the thinking of the young George Buchanan.[29] On the other hand we should be cautious about attributing radical influence to the conciliarism of Major and his contemporaries. There was no intention to offer any intellectual denial of normal papal authority, and the interest of the Scots in the issue seems to have been constitutional rather than reformist. There was little discussion of the possible role a council might have in promoting active reform 'of head and members'.[30]

One further group within the Church had a particularly strong interest in the defence of papal interest: the canonists. They looked to the authority of Rome to uphold the structures and principles of the universal law by which the Church was governed.[31] This was less an issue of the ability to appeal directly to the supreme pontiff than of a conceptual and institutional preoccupation with the origins of legitimacy. In the distinctive case of English Ireland it has been argued that this canonist belief in the authority of the papacy provided much of the apparatus for maintaining the peculiar claims of the Church to a civilizing and hegemonic role within the island. The original papal bull *Laudabiliter*, which had sanctioned English overlordship, became the justification for the spiritual way of life established in the Pale. This was explicitly designed to conform to the best standards of the universal Church, and was vigorously defended by canon lawyers and senior clerics who feared the contaminating 'degeneracy' of the Gaelic peoples. In these peculiar circumstances Rome acquired totemic status as the guarantor of a way of life through its more general status as the guarantor of the Church's system of law.[32]

It would be unwise, therefore, to place too much emphasis on the homogeneity of views about authority in the late medieval Church. Ac-

---

[29] F. Oakley, 'Almain and Major: conciliar theory on the eve of the Reformation', *AHR* 70 (1965), 671–90.

[30] The general interest in conciliarism among Scottish theologians is indicated as much by surviving texts, such as those of Gerson and d'Ailly, in Scottish libraries, as in actual writings by Scots: J. Durkan and A. Ross, 'Early Scottish libraries', *Innes Review* 9 (1958), 5–172.

[31] R.A. Helmholz, *Roman Canon Law in Reformation England* (Cambridge, 1990), 4–20, though Helmholz notes that the lawyers managed well enough without the appellate jurisdiction of Rome.

[32] J. Murray, 'The Tudor Diocese of Dublin: Episcopal Government, Ecclesiastical Politics and the Enforcement of the Reformation, c.1534–1590', University of Dublin (TCD) Ph.D. (1997), 68 ff.

ceptance of the broad supremacy of the papacy, and integration of that belief with some notion that general councils also played a role in the rulership of the Church, left niches for other views as well. In particular a number of English theologians pointed to views that can only be described as proto-Gallican. Richard Ullerstone and Thomas Gascoigne, influenced by the work of Grosseteste, stressed the merits of local episcopal autonomy in matters of discipline and reform. 'The Lord', Gascoigne critically noted, 'gives great power to his vicar the pope of the church that he may reform great ills and give great edification of good acts.'[33] Instead the papacy intruded into the provinces of the Church with demands for money and the issue of inappropriate licences. The best agent for change, in the opinion of several of these writers, was the reforming bishop in his diocese, resident and preaching in person after the manner of the early Church.[34]

Beyond the ranks of the theologians and politicians there is little to suggest that the position of the papacy stirred passions in England or Scotland before the late 1520s. The arch of customary authority was upheld: a man who scorned the papal bull excommunicating rebels against Henry VII was popularly believed to have been punished for his sacrilege by instant death.[35] On the other hand particular popes, like individual clergy, could be the focus of popular contempt. Edward Hall (scarcely an unbiased witness) claimed that in 1527, with the Sack of Rome, 'the commonalty little mourned for it, and said the Pope was a ruffian, and not meet for the room: wherefore they said that he began the mischief, and so he was well served'.[36] Humphrey Bonner preached an anti-curial sermon in 1516, but he was incited to do so by particular conflicts with the apostolic auditor. Bonner felt the latter was discriminating against his superior, the abbot of St Werburgh's, Chester, in a poisonous dispute with the bishop of Coventry and Lichfield.[37] Most negative English comment on the papacy was the product of such particular circumstances, especially during the Wolsey era, when the legatine authority was readily labelled as abusive by interested parties.[38] Conversely, it is difficult to read earlier beliefs from the evidence of resistance in the 1530s. Questioning of the

[33] Harvey, *England, Rome and the Papacy*, 230.

[34] Ibid., 229–42. Harvey is at pains to stress that there is no shared theological enterprise here, more a tendency, one among several of the interests of fifteenth-century authors.

[35] C. Harper-Bill, *The Pre-Reformation Church in England, 1400–1523* (1989), 23.

[36] E. Hall, *Henry VIII*, ed. C. Whibley (1904), ii. 95.

[37] *LP* ii. i, no. 2692. On the St Werburgh dispute see R.V.H. Burne, 'The dissolution of St Werburgh's Abbey', *Journal of Chester and North Wales Archaeological and Historical Society* NS 37 (1948), 16–17.

[38] Gwyn argues for limited opposition to Wolsey's legatine powers: P. Gwyn, *The King's Cardinal: The Rise and Fall of Thomas Wolsey* (1990), 284–9.

royal supremacy there certainly was, and a number of examples have accumulated of failure to expunge the name of the pope from liturgical material when required to do so by the crown. Some groups of the clergy offered principled resistance as long as they dared: those of the Irish Pale being conspicuous among them.[39] But while the cause of Rome was clearly defended by more than the handful of martyrs of the 1530s, the old notion that it was difficult to lead a counter-revolution on behalf of a distant and indifferent Rome has much to commend it. Even the Gaelic Irish took some time to refocus their loyalties on the papacy: in the early 1540s the English regime had much success in persuading the Gaelic bishops and chiefs to a basic acknowledgement of the supremacy. The early papal missions associated with Archbishop Wauchope of Armagh were conspicuous failures.[40]

This is also surely connected with what men saw, and were taught, daily in the parishes. The bishop of Rome appeared in the liturgical texts, but not on the walls of the church, except in the occasional Last Judgement, where the mighty could be found among the damned as well as the saved. The preaching of the friars, and not just the Observants, no doubt appealed to the authority of Rome from time to time, but surviving preaching manuals make little mention of the theme. It is no accident that Eamon Duffy's massive analysis of the traditional religion of the English people, their liturgy, their forms of devotion, the methods by which they were instructed in the faith, includes scarcely a mention of the importance of the papacy.[41] When Thomas Cromwell's agents and informants began to report on discontent within the realm in the 1530s, it looks as though a lack of enthusiasm for the curious and novel idea of a secular head of the Church was more prominent among men's anxieties than a passionate support for the bishop of Rome.[42]

The most significant modification to this general view of the papacy is the evidence that has been accumulating in recent years of the regularity of individual lay and clerical access to Rome on the eve of the Reformation. A steady flow of litigants and petitioners moved between the north

---

[39] Murray, 'Diocese of Dublin', 110–16: it is interesting that one of the English clerical defenders of the papacy, John Travers, moved to Dublin in 1533, apparently because he believed his views would be more sympathetically received there.

[40] Ellis, *Tudor Ireland*, 192. J. Durkan, 'Robert Wauchope, Archbishop of Armagh', *Innes Review* 1 (1950), 51–62.

[41] E. Duffy, *The Stripping of the Altars: Traditional Religion in England, 1400–1580* (1992).

[42] See, for example, Christopher Haigh's view that 'the papacy had become, for the English, not much more than a symbol of the unity of Christendom', *English Reformations: Religion, Politics and Society under the Tudors* (Oxford, 1993), 8. Among recent 'revisionist' views of the early Reformation, only that of Richard Rex argues strongly for the spiritual relevance of the papacy, citing the hostility to the supremacy revealed by Cromwell's archive: R. Rex, *Henry VIII and the English Reformation* (1993), 32–5.

and the papal capital, and proctors made a living from the business of those who did not wish to make the tedious journey. *The Calendar of Entries in Papal Registers*, now available to 1513, shows the wide range of contacts that existed, and this records only a part of the business that took English and Irish men to Rome.[43] A combination of litigation and pilgrimage kept the English hospice at Rome active throughout the early Tudor years: there were 205 visitors in 1506 and 1507, and by 1518 Wolsey received a complaint that increasing numbers were adding to the costs of the hospital.[44] The Scottish hospice is less well documented, but was certainly active from the Jubilee of 1450 onwards.[45] More men invested in papal services at a distance. While clerical petitioners were clearly prominent there is consistent evidence of lay involvement as well. Dispensations were regularly given for marriage where there was the impediment of consanguinity: in 1445 William Suthirland and his wife Dalmagyn Marley, for example, alleged that their marriage within the third degree of consanguinity had been contracted in order to end murders and scandals among their kinsmen. They therefore sought and obtained dispensation from incest and the legitimization of their offspring.[46] It has been suggested that the major problem of the Renaissance papacy, when it faced the need for reform, was the pressure created by the demands for litigation, dispensations, indulgences, licences, and the like, all of which stimulated the grossly enlarged bureaucracy of the curia.[47] The records of the papal penitentiary, only recently and partially opened to historians, reveal the great diversity of problems referred to Rome. An aged parish priest from Meltham, Yorkshire, sought permission to employ a housekeeper; Patrick Cantwell from Dublin diocese, son of a bishop, asked for ordination in spite of his parent; Thomas Caylart wanted exoneration from a potentially simoniacal promotion; a layman from St David's sought relief from the penalties of excommunication, imposed on him by his bishop whose horses he had stolen. Most ordinary laymen who needed the administrative or legal assistance of the Church seem to have had no difficulty in accepting the Roman curia as 'a well of grace sufficient for their suits'.[48]

---

[43] *Calendar of Entries in the Papal Registers relating to Great Britain and Ireland*, 19 vols. (1893–1988). For Scotland see *Calendar of Scottish Supplications to Rome*, 4 vols. covering 1418–47.

[44] Harvey, *England, Rome and the Papacy*, 52–67, has an extensive analysis of Rome's hospices in the fifteenth century.

[45] D. McRoberts, 'The Scottish national churches in Rome', *Innes Review* 1/2 (1950), 110–19.

[46] A.I. Dunlop and D. MacLauchlan (eds.), *Scottish Supplications to Rome, 1433–1447*, SHS 4th ser. 7 (1982), 301–2.

[47] Harvey, *England, Rome and the Papacy*, 101–14.

[48] J.A.F. Thomson, '"The Well of Grace": Englishmen and Rome in the fifteenth century', in *The Church, Politics and Patronage in the Fifteenth Century*, ed. R.B. Dobson (Gloucester, 1984), 99–114.

Most of the English litigants stopped short of full appeal to the Roman courts. Litigation was an expensive business, and the limited number of English cases recorded in the *Rota*, the principal Roman court of appeal, may in part indicate this.[49] However, the effective control exercised over the Church by the English ecclesiastical courts provides a more convincing explanation. Long legal battles seem to have been the prerogative of a few wealthy clergy like Archbishop Morton, who twice defended his authority in the courts.[50] There is here a striking contrast with the Scots: approximately 370 Scottish cases were heard by the *Rota* between 1464 and 1560, compared to twenty English cases up to 1534.[51] The difference lies above all in the Scottish resolution of benefice disputes before the papal court. It was a source of some anxiety to the Scottish crown: in 1493 the Scottish parliament passed an act ordering home all litigants before the Holy See: to little apparent effect.[52] The Gaelic church also made prolific use of appeal to Rome: indeed it has been suggested that one of the numerous explanations for a measure of continuing loyalty to Rome on the part of the Irish church was that 'Rome running' was a congenial means of dispute resolution far beyond the centralist reach of the English authorities.[53]

There is some paradoxical sense in which the more efficient and accessible the local agents of the universal Church, the less the papacy could or did play a crucial part in the religious life of individual realms. The later medieval papacy had itself contributed to this process by the devolution of powers to legates, nuncios, and judge-delegates. While there is no systematic pattern in such forms of devolved authority, there was a tendency for them to become normative in the years before the Reformation. In the case of judge-delegates, appointed usually for short periods to engage in a particular commissioned mission, or hear a specific cause, Rome was only weakened by a reduction of direct contact with its petitioners.[54] The higher clergy, both secular and regular, routinely acted as judge-delegates in cases not heard in Rome considering election disputes, conflicts between monks and their bishops, tithe misappropriation, and matrimonial

---

[49] R.N. Swanson, *Church and Society in Late Medieval England* (Oxford, 1989), 11–16. J.A.F. Thomson, *The Early Tudor Church and Society: 1485–1529* (1993), 29–31.

[50] Harper-Bill, *Pre-Reformation Church*, 12, 19–20.

[51] J. Robertson, 'Scottish legal research in the Vatican Archives: a preliminary report', *Renaissance Studies* 2 (1988), 339–46.

[52] McRoberts, 'Scottish National Churches', 114.

[53] Ellis, *Tudor Ireland*, 191. D.B. Quinn and K.W. Nicholls, 'Ireland in 1534', in T.W. Moody, F.X. Martin, and F.J. Bryne (eds.), *A New History of Ireland,* vol. iii: *Early Modern Ireland* (Oxford, 1976), 29–31.

[54] R.A. Schmutz, 'Medieval papal representatives: legates, nuncios and judges-delegate', *Studia Gratiana,* 15 (1972), 443–63.

causes. Most of these issues were clerical in nature, but laymen still util-
ized the delegated power of Rome, as in 1518 when the London Court of
Aldermen sought clarification of their tithe obligations.[55] In England,
within a strongly regulated church, the system of judge-delegates seems to
have functioned effectively. When such local control was lacking, however, it could expose the papal system to abuse, as in Gaelic Ireland,
where petitioners would often be able to nominate delegates in cases such
as contested collation to benefices.[56] When Maurice Flellian, canon of
Limerick cathedral, was delegated to hear a convoluted case of dispute
between the chancellor of the diocese and the bishop, in which the
former needed absolution from a multitude of offences including abetting
his temporal lord in violent crimes and appearing at Mass while excommunicate, it is unlikely that he could have achieved any judicial impartial-
ity in the conflicts.[57]

The nuncios, more difficult to characterize simply, often combined the
office of papal collector with that of agent. Giovanni Gigli is the best-
known English example: he also occupied the see of Worcester and was
followed in all three offices by his nephew. As Italians closely connected
to the papal court their loyalties were divided, but both men came to play
important roles in English government, thereby weakening the hold of
the papacy upon them.[58] More conventional ambassadorial nuncios, dispatched from Rome to promote crusade, reconcile warring monarchs, or
promote papal interests against schismatics, should not be overlooked. A
series of papal interventions in Scotland, the last as late as 1547, came
when Petrus Lippomanus was dispatched to be 'near that realm [England],
for the purpose of taking advantage of any opportunity that might arise'.[59]
Three years later Julius III pursued the same line of thought for Ireland,
when Robert Wauchope, the papally nominated archbishop of Armagh,
was made apostolic nuncio to the whole island on the eve of his journey
to his see.[60]

The legateship was, however, the most significant and contentious
delegated office at the disposal of the papacy, possessing proctorial powers.
The primates of Canterbury and York had, of course, long been *legati nati*,
but this usual arrangement could be enhanced as it was, for example, by

[55] S. Brigden, 'Tithe controversy in Reformation London', *JEH* 32 (1981), 293.

[56] Thomson, *Early Tudor Church*, 32–3. Swanson, *Church and Society*, 14–15. J. Watt, *The Church in Medieval Ireland* (Dublin, 1972), 189–92.

[57] A. Gwynn, *Anglo-Irish Church Life in the Fourteenth and Fifteenth Centuries* (Dublin, 1968), 73. A.P. Fuller (ed.), *Calendar of Entries in the Papal Registers, 1492–1503* (1994), no. 485.

[58] Wilkie, *Cardinal Protectors*, 9–10.

[59] C.G. Buschbell (ed.), *Concilium Tridentinum . . . Epistularum*, ii. i (Freiburg im Breisgau, 1923), 821.

[60] Durkan, 'Wauchope', 63.

Henry VII and Archbishop Morton who persuaded the papacy that visitation rights over exempt monasteries should be exercised by the archbishop of Canterbury.[61] The final creation of the archiepiscopacy and then primateship of St Andrews, plus the slightly later erection of the archiepiscopacy of Glasgow, gave the same indigenous authority to the Scottish church. But it was the greater prize of the legateship *a latere* that drew ambitious prelates and their political masters. Full legatine powers gave much of the authority and jurisdictional control of the papacy into the hands of its nominees, for the legate more explicitly personated the monarchical authority of the pope than did a nuncio. In the crisis following Flodden, Andrew Forman, nominated to St Andrews, was temporarily given the powers of legate *a latere*, although the fury of the English at the promotion of an enemy quickly robbed him of the status.[62] Wolsey achieved his steadier and more famous ascent to legatine glory first by being given matching authority to that of the papal legate, Campeggio, sent to negotiate for crusade in 1518. His powers were steadily extended until they became a life grant in 1524, by which time, as we have seen, he was handling much of the petitioning that would previously have been addressed to Rome. His unusual powers once again reflected on the vulnerability of the papacy, and especially on its political needs: Leo X could not afford to alienate Henry VIII, whose commitment to the jurisdictional authority of his cardinal was made abundantly clear.[63] The later grants of legateship to Scottish primates, Beaton in 1545 and Hamilton thereafter, reveal much the same pattern, though it is worth noting that Paul III, deeply suspicious of James V's ambition for control of the local kirk, withheld the grant to Beaton until after the king's death.[64]

With the existence of a powerful legateship many of those appeals for dispensations and the like that would routinely have been addressed to the curia could be heard locally instead. Evidence survives for only one year of Wolsey's office, but in that time he granted approximately a hundred dispensations, yielding fees of about £200. The policy also had potential for English control of the Irish church. A letter from a John, possibly John Rawson, prior of Kilmain, to Wolsey, expressed anxiety about the difficulty of persuading Archbishop Inge, the lord chancellor of Ireland, to grant dispensations in the legate's name:

---

[61] C. Harper-Bill, 'Archbishop John Morton and the Province of Canterbury, 1486–1500', *JEH* 29 (1978), 6–11.

[62] Wilkie, *Cardinal Protectors*, 83–5, 142–4, 146–9.

[63] Gwyn, *The King's Cardinal*, 265–337.

[64] M. Mahoney, 'The Scottish hierarchy, 1513–1565', in D. McRoberts (ed.), *Essays on the Scottish Reformation* (Glasgow, 1962), 68–75.

whereof hath ensued the decay of the Church of Ireland, for, when an idle person goeth to the Court of Rome, the compositions be to Irishmen so small for their poverty, that by him many other exorbitant matters be sped. So that, in this land, your Graces dispensations be necessary to be granted with less difficulty than else where, for the avoiding of contempt of holy canons, and the occasion of the inconvenience that followeth of the Rome runners.[65]

But Wolsey's legatine control over Ireland remained uncertain. He sought a bull in 1528 to clarify the position and another drastically to reduce the number of Irish sees to make them more financially viable. All of this came too late to have much effect in the period before the Cardinal's fall.[66]

Finally the legateships raise the question of how far the papacy endeavoured to transcend its jurisdictional, fiscal, and political relationship with the British churches. Was reform ever a significant part of its wider agenda in the decades before Trent? It is possible to argue that at least it was expected that, in return for the grant of unusual regional powers, popes required gestures of renewal and renovation. Andrew Forman, during his brief period of delegated power, promulgated the decrees of the Fifth Lateran Council in Scotland. A generation later, admittedly now in the period overshadowed by the growth of Protestant dissent, Archbishop Hamilton held major provincial councils in 1549 and 1552 and made serious efforts to revitalize Scottish Catholicism.[67] And Wolsey exercised his legatine powers in a variety of reforming gestures including the calling of a council that issued new constitutions in 1518.[68] On the effect of this last, historians have been as divided as the cardinal's colleagues: Bishop Fox enthused that it opened the way for reform, while Bishop Fisher's biographer may have reflected the jaundiced view of his subject when he wrote that the synod was held 'rather to notify to the world his great authority...than for any great good he meant to do'.[69] It may suffice here to note that even if these provincial attempts at reform achieved something, they scarcely did anything to reinforce the positive influence of the papacy in the two realms. When Fox wrote to Wolsey on the merits of the synod his focus was most explicitly upon the English people and their religious destiny:

in reading your grace's letter I see before me a more entire and whole reformation of the ecclesiastical hierarchy of the English people than I could have

---

[65] PRO SP 1/2/103–4 [*LP* iv. 5625].

[66] Gwyn, *The King's Cardinal*, 252–3.

[67] T. Winning, 'Church councils in sixteenth-century Scotland', in McRoberts, *Scottish Reformation*, 332–58.

[68] Gwyn, *The King's Cardinal*, 267–70.

[69] R. Bayne (ed.), *The Life of Bishop Fisher*, EETS extra ser. 27 (1921), 34.

expected, or ever hoped to see completed, or even so much attempted in this age.[70]

Crown and Church

The term *ecclesia Anglicana* may not have readily translated into Church *of* England before the Reformation, but many of the institutional attributes of independence were already in place. Moreover, as Fox's letter suggests, there was a perception of the Church as integral with the realm. The first two Tudor monarchs, while ever willing to parade their devotion to the universal Church, more frequently acted as though they were lords of their own religious destiny. Royal behaviour was often at its most paradoxical in the endeavour to combine devotion and autonomy. The early Tudors had an outstanding prototype in their Lancastrian predecessor Henry V, whose deep and ostentatious piety is not in doubt, but who identified devotion with his regalian authority.[71] Henry VII, Anthony Goodman has suggested, was much influenced by the model of religiosity espoused at the court of the dukes of Brittany with whom he lived in exile.[72] This involved the lavish invocation of papal support for the legitimacy of the monarchy: in Henry's case papal confirmation of title, and of Henry's marriage to Elizabeth of York, backed by the full sanction of excommunication for those who challenged it. Yet the enhanced religious authority with which Henry sought to invest his kingship consisted in the main of the gestures of a 'royal religion': support for the reform of the monastic orders, for the canonization of Henry VI, and for the foundation of the Savoy. There was an intention to stamp a monarchical vision of piety and authority on the realm. His son, equally ostentatious in his piety, articulated the potentially schizophrenic nature of this royal influence when he told a bemused Thomas More that 'we are so much bounden unto the See of Rome that we cannot do too much honour unto it ... For we received from that See our crown Imperial.'[73] The situation in Scotland was little different in fundamentals, though some allowance must be made for the greater plurality and localism of Scottish power.

---

[70] P.S. and H.M. Allen (eds.), *The Letters of Richard Fox* (1929), 114–15.

[71] J. Catto, 'Religious change under Henry V', in G. Harriss (ed.), *Henry V: The Practice of Kingship* (Oxford, 1985), 110–15. On the rather oppressive quality of Henry's devotion see W.N. Mackay, 'Sheen Charterhouse from its Foundation to its Dissolution', University of Oxford D.Phil. (1992), 74–5.

[72] A. Goodman, 'Henry VII and Christian renewal', in K. Robbins (ed.), *Religion and Humanism*, SCH 17 (Oxford, 1981), 115–25.

[73] E.V. Hitchcock (ed.), *William Roper's Life of Sir Thomas More, Knight* (1935), 68. R. Koebner, 'The imperial crown of this realm', *BIHR* 26 (1953), 29–52. On the erratic evolution of Henry VIII's ideas on imperial authority see Scarisbrick, *Henry VIII*, 245–50.

James IV and James V both valued papal support on occasions and both produced serious gestures of devotion to the universal Church. James IV complicated European politics in the period before Flodden by his enthusiasm for a crusade: his son was an appropriate scourge of heretics in the years before Solway Moss. But like their English counterparts these adult monarchs were committed to determining the essential directions in which their national churches should evolve.[74]

For most practical purposes it was the bishops, keeping a wary eye on their royal masters, who governed the English and Scottish churches, ensuring essential conformity with the wider Catholic community through a shared canon law and correspondence with the papacy. The crown meanwhile routinely permitted itself and its agents to intervene in the affairs of its spiritual servants, not directly denying jurisdictional authority, yet tempering its practical consequences. The two issues of most immediate relevance to the Tudor monarchy, provisions and taxation, had clearly been resolved in its favour long before this period. This is shown most dramatically in the case of taxation raised from the Church, an old right given new vigour by the first two Tudors. Figures vary markedly, and are in any event difficult to calculate from the surviving material, but by the 1520s the clergy were being asked to produce a loan of £60,000 in 1522, a subsidy of £120,000 spread over the five following years, and then the Amicable Grant of a third of income on top.[75] This is dramatic, yet Henry VII had also squeezed large revenues from his clergy: four separate grants of tenths were made between 1487 and 1496, and to these were added demands for benevolences and loans from the most affluent. There was little protest from the Church. Only the Amicable Grant of 1525, which produced such vigorous resentment in lay society, generated complaints. Then Archbishop Warham reported on the clergy's 'untowardness' and their fear that they would have to 'live in continual poverty'.[76] Nothing as ambitious as this could be contemplated in the Scotland of the 1510s, yet by the 1530s James V was able to follow the precedents of his southern neighbour, burdening the Church with a range of exactions reluctantly sanctioned by Clement VII.[77]

[74] J. Wormald, *Court, Kirk and Community: Scotland 1470–1625* (1981), 78–9. J.H. Burns, 'The political background of the Reformation, 1513–1625', in McRoberts, *Scottish Reformation*, 5–9.

[75] Scarisbrick, 'Clerical taxation', 49–50. F. Heal, 'Clerical tax-collection under the Tudors', in R.O'Day and F. Heal (eds.), *Continuity and Change: Personnel and Administration of the Church in England, 1500–1642* (Leicester, 1976), 97–102.

[76] *LP* iv. i. 1267. G. Bernard, *War, Taxation and Rebellion in Early Tudor England* (Brighton, 1986), 101–3.

[77] W.S. Reid, 'Clerical taxation: the Scottish alternative to dissolution of the monasteries, 1530–1560', *Catholic Historical Review* 35 (1948), 129–53.

The great years of jurisdictional conflict between the English crown and its clerical subjects were long past by the late fifteenth century. However, Henry VII's reign revealed a tendency by the crown to support the claims of the common law against those of the church courts when any contest did emerge. In the years of Morton's ascendancy (1486–1500) these tendencies were kept in check: thereafter they emerged in the support given to the issuing of writs of prohibition, evoking disputes from the church courts into those of the king.[78] There had long been a conviction on the part of the common lawyers that papal claims to jurisdiction in areas covered by common law were invalid. In Henry's reign some key areas, especially defamation involving the imputation of crime, were systematically prohibited by the royal courts; by the end of the reign all cases of this kind were under secular control. In this, and in other areas, the secular courts succeeded partly because they offered adequate remedy. The same was true of benefice disputes involving property right: while in Scotland these arguments moved through the system of ecclesiastical jurisdiction and might easily end in Rome, in England they were under the control of the common law, and might end in Common Pleas.[79]

While the common lawyers and in some measure the litigants themselves helped to promote the movement away from ecclesiastical jurisdiction, the crown's sensitivity to any jurisdictional challenge was visible as well. Henry VII began a process of restricting some of the liberties granted by earlier monarchs grateful for ecclesiastical support in difficult times. Two acts of 1489 and 1497 limited benefit of clergy: more dramatically there were ten cases of *praemunire* before King's Bench in the last two law terms of the reign. Bishop Nykke of Norwich, the principal sufferer, complained bitterly to Warham in 1504 that he would 'curse all such promoters and maintainers of *praemunire* as heretics'.[80] Then in 1512 Parliament returned to the attack, prohibiting all clerks in minor orders from claiming benefit of clergy for certain serious crimes.[81] This act eventually produced a vigorous clerical reaction when, in a St Paul's sermon of 1515, Richard Kidderminster, abbot of Winchcombe, preached in defence of the sacrosanctity of all orders major and minor. Henry Standish, warden of the London Grey Friars, became the spokesman of crown interest against the seculars at the subsequent Blackfriars Conference summoned

---

[78] M.J. Kelly, 'Canterbury Jurisdiction and Influence during the Episcopate of William Warham, 1503–32', University of Cambridge Ph.D. (1963), 98–110.

[79] R. Houlbrooke, 'The decline of ecclesiastical jurisdiction under the Tudors', in O'Day and Heal, *Continuity and Change*, 241–2.

[80] 4 HVII c. 13; 12 HVII c. 7. PRO SC 1/44, fo. 83: quoted in Houlbrooke, 'Decline', 241.

[81] Gwyn, *The King's Cardinal*, 43–50. G. Gabel, *Benefit of Clergy in England in the Later Middle Ages* (New York, 1969).

to debate the act. The issues debated were made more complex by one of the few actions of the Fifth Lateran Council that had impact in England: two papal bulls of 1514 specifically invoked the powers of the Church against any lay interference with the clergy. Standish was eventually cited before convocation, which was in its turn threatened with *praemunire* by the royal judges.[82] The final gesture and threat in this crisis was explicitly Henry's, when he declared at a conference at Baynard's Castle in November 1515 that 'by the ordinance and sufferance of God we are King of England, and the kings of England in time past have never had any superior but God alone'.[83]

It is customary to see the events of 1515 as evidence of a crown determination to signal clearly to the clergy the limitations of their jurisdictional autonomy. What is less frequently noted is that the dispute arose out of a willingness by the clergy to assert that autonomy. It has recently been suggested that an aspect of the generally recognized energy and efficiency of the last generations of pre-Reformation prelates was a growing clericalism, a toughness and self-confidence in the assertion of rights and authority that risked confrontation with royal interests.[84]

There are obvious dangers, however, in reading relations between the Church and the monarchy in the light of the English break with Rome and the Scottish Reformation. The key to the weaknesses of the religious establishments is to be found rather in too intimate an association with the lay authorities than in overt conflict, or even subliminal tension. Crown control of senior appointments within the Church could be employed with various degrees of beneficence or otherwise, but it always tended to affirm the identity of prelates and other higher clergy as kings' men. The best test of this proposition is the English bench, which historians generally agree to have been of impressive quality in the pre-Reformation years. Among the forty promotions of Englishmen between 1485 and 1529 there were few disasters, in the sense of administrative or moral failures. If Wolsey is discounted, only James Stanley, the aristocratic bishop of Ely, can be criticized under both heads. While there were a few nonentities, such as Penny and Leyburn, the vast majority of the early Tudor bishops were men of learning, capacity, and great administrative experience. Most were graduates who had been trained in the laws and all but four had held some office under the crown before reaching the bench. It is important for an understanding of later religious change to analyse the

---

[82] A. Fox and J. Guy, *Reassessing the Henrician Age: Humanism, Politics and Reform 1500–1550* (Oxford, 1986), 167. Gwyn, *The King's Cardinal*, 47–50.

[83] A. Ogle, *The Tragedy of the Lollards' Tower* (1949), 151.

[84] For an interesting, if not wholly convincing, argument along these lines see R.N. Swanson, 'Problems of the priesthood in pre-Reformation England', *EHR* 105 (1990), 845–69.

ways in which these admirable prelates were vulnerable. They rarely failed
their dioceses at the level of basic administrative control, left of course on
a daily basis in the hands of their deputies. Many, for example successive
bishops of Lincoln, were energetic in ensuring that the clergy, both regular and secular, were disciplined through visitation, that their church
courts were maintained in full vigour and that intruders upon their jurisdiction were challenged. A number took a positive interest in learning,
displayed most notably through the founding of colleges, but also through
endowments within their cathedrals or the promotion of better standards
among the parish clergy. It has recently been suggested that they collectively adopted an intelligent humanist-reformist view of the early stages of
Lutheran heresy. No doubt many were remote from the ordinary religion
of the parishes, but this was scarcely an unusual feature of any episcopate,
and most juggled their dual role as royal administrators and diocesan
overlords with some skill.[85] The guilt expressed by Bishop Fox that 'to
serve worldly' was 'the damnation of my soul and many other souls
whereof I have the cure' was the reaction of a politician who had temporarily failed to reconcile these roles.[86] The risk of such imbalance was
always present but, given that the daily routines of a diocese rarely needed
the attention of a prelate, most seem to have coped with their broader
directive duties.

The weakness of the late medieval bishops came rather from the very
confidence instilled by their essentially harmonious relationship with the
crown. Their training was most commonly in the two laws, and as canonists they might be expected, in Maitland's memorable phrase, to be
'steeped and soaked . . . in the papal law-books'.[87] Yet that absorption no
longer appeared to demand eternal vigilance about ecclesiastical autonomy
of the kind that had marked church–state relationships since the Investi-
ture Contest. The environment in which these capable men operated was,

[85] There is an extensive literature on the early Tudor prelates, with few voices raised in
criticism of their activities. Much of the best work is contained in two dissertations, J.J. Scarisbrick, 'The Conservative Episcopate in England, 1529–35', University of Cambridge Ph.D.
(1955) and S. Thompson, 'The Pastoral Work of the English and Welsh Bishops, 1500–1558',
University of Oxford D.Phil. (1984). B. Bradshaw and E. Duffy (eds.), *Humanism, Reform and
Reformation: The Career of Bishop John Fisher* (Cambridge, 1989), app. 3. Thompson shows that
many pre-Reformation prelates were resident in their dioceses at least 75 per cent of the time.
There is a useful summary in Thomson, *Early Tudor Church*, 46–60. M. Bowker, *The Secular
Clergy of the Diocese of Lincoln, 1495–1520* (Cambridge, 1968) and *The Henrician Reformation: The
Diocese of Lincoln under John Longland, 1521–1547* (Cambridge, 1981). D'Alton, 'The Suppression
of Heresy', *passim*.
[86] Allen and Allen, *Letters of Fox*, 83. See also his famous protestation of the renunciation of
worldly duties, 30 April 1517: ibid., 93.
[87] F.W. Maitland, *The Roman Canon Law in the Church of England* (1898), 93. R.J. Schoeck,
'Canon law in England on the eve of the Reformation', *Medieval Studies* 25 (1963), 131.

to use the words of a recent historian, slightly 'stuffy'.[88] They were well-attuned to detecting threats to the integrity of the Church from heresy, and threats to the crown from political subversion, less well-armed against inappropriate behaviour by God's anointed. While prelates could often detach themselves from the obligations of secular office in their later years and tend to their benefices and souls, they could not so readily escape from the political and patronage identities of the English state. Bishop Fox expressed these anxieties to Wolsey on several occasions, especially at the time of the attempted legatine reforms of 1518:

As far as I can see this reformation of the clergy and religious will so abate the calumnies of the laity, so advance the honour of the clergy, and so reconcile our sovereign lord the king and his nobility to them... that I intend to devote to its furtherance the few remaining years of my life.[89]

The reactions of the bench to the one great exception to all rules, Thomas Wolsey, are indicative of the difficulties of the Church under a strong monarch. No amount of historical rehabilitation of the cardinal as politician or putative reformer can disguise the contrasts between his behaviour and that of his colleagues. His appropriation of power, and even his flouting of moral norms, had the visible support of the young king. The hostility of some of the episcopate, and especially of Archbishop Warham, to his jurisdictional claims, has been meticulously documented, but so has their failure to make any essential difference to the cardinal's authority. Wolsey was the king's man, and as such the prelates had to accommodate to him, indeed had to regard him as the source of much of their own power and patronage. What we seem to observe here is not just a recognition of the realities of royal power, but an acceptance that that power in some sense legitimated Wolsey's activities: the beginnings perhaps of a displacement of moral authority from church to state? Scarisbrick's comment on the cardinal's secular policies, 'his sins were scarlet, but his writs were read', is a fitting acknowledgement of the ambiguities of power that the leaders of the Henrician bench had to accommodate.[90]

While English bishops have received general approbation from recent historians, the prelates of the Scottish and Irish, and even the Welsh,

---

[88] D. MacCulloch, 'Henry VIII and the reformation of the Church', in D. MacCulloch (ed.), *The Reign of Henry VIII: Politics, Policy and Piety* (Basingstoke, 1998), 161.

[89] Strype, *Ecclesiastical Memorials*, i. app. 18. The original Latin is printed in Allen and Allen, *Letters of Fox*, 116.

[90] Kelly, 'Canterbury Jurisdiction', 176–94. J.J. Scarisbrick, 'Cardinal Wolsey and the common weal', in E.W. Ives, R.J. Knecht, and J.J. Scarisbrick (eds.), *Wealth and Power in Tudor England: Essays Presented to S.T. Bindoff* (1978), 67. Gwyn, *The King's Cardinal*, takes a very different view, arguing that Wolsey simply did not possess the power traditionally attributed to him.

churches are still, like the curate's egg, considered good only in parts. This is often represented as a matter of wealth, dividing the British and Irish churches along economic fault lines. The seventeen English sees (excluding Sodor and Man) had an average income according to the figures of the 1535 *Valor Ecclesiasticus* of £1,594.[91] The four Welsh sees averaged only £233. Figures for Ireland are complicated by the nature of English power there and cannot be given exhaustively for the period on the eve of the Reformation. But among the thirty-two dioceses, those within the Englishry that were assessed in Henry's reign varied in value from Dublin at £535 IR (£357) to six bishoprics worth less than £75 each. Bishoprics within the Irishry were probably even poorer.[92] Scotland's figures have to be drawn from a later date when, in the early years of the Reformation, ecclesiastical rentals were recorded for dividing resources between the crown and the old and new kirks. These show an episcopate divided between comfort and relative poverty, with the fault line largely corresponding to the highland and lowland zones. St Andrews, Glasgow, Moray, and Dunkeld were prosperous, with incomes in money and kind of between £2,500 and £6,000 (Scots): Caithness and Galloway had barely any income in kind and only £1,200–1,300 in money. In Scotland a cleric with powerful connections was likely to aspire to one of the key lowland sees.[93]

Yet the weaknesses of these other churches, the Welsh perhaps excepted, are more usually attributed to the deficiencies of the lay patronage system than to absolute poverty. The Scottish hierarchy, in particular, has commonly been seen as the collective victim of ambitious but poor monarchs, ruthless nobles, and long royal minorities. The crown needed all the patronage advantage it could obtain, so both James IV and James V were guilty of such blatant actions as giving the see of St Andrews to a royal bastard (James IV) and nominating five illegitimate children to hold five of the great Scottish abbeys in commendation (James V). Neither monarch was overly squeamish about the elevation of men of known immorality either: James V's promotion of Patrick Hepburn to Ross being the prime example. Long periods of minority and the bitter rivalries of Scottish politics produced a bench with at least 50 per cent noble blood, and the tastes and interests to accompany affinity to that social

[91] F. Heal, *Of Prelates and Princes: A Study of the Economic and Social Position of the Tudor Episcopate* (Cambridge, 1980), 20–34.

[92] S.G. Ellis, 'Economic problems of the Church: why the Reformation failed in Ireland', *JEH* 41 (1990), 249–51.

[93] J. Kirk (ed.), *The Books of the Assumptions of Thirds: Scottish Ecclesiastical Rentals at the Reformation*, British Academy Records of Social and Economic History NS 21 (1995), pp. xlvi–xlviii.

group. Such men could, of course, on occasions be rather successful in resisting royal pressures, but usually only in the equally secular interests of their own families.[94] Historians are now sometimes disposed to express surprise at the relative success of some Scottish prelates, rather than to dwell upon this gloomy tale. The most distinguished bishop was without question William Elphinstone, bishop of Aberdeen from 1483 to 1514, an important royal servant, but a diocesan bishop who combined administrative skill with a desire to evangelize his flock. He founded the University of Aberdeen and laboured to improve the educational standards of his clergy. Above all he sponsored a specifically Scottish approach to liturgy and the saints through his *Martyrology of Aberdeen* and *Aberdeen Breviary*. Both emphasized national Scottish saints such as Ninian, eliminating a number of English saints from the calendar. Elphinstone also showed some of the spirit in defence of ecclesiastical interest that seemed essential for the preservation of institutional stability. He fought both king and other patrons to establish control over 'his' patronage in Aberdeen diocese. Yet Elphinstone also shows the vulnerability of the late medieval episcopate: he was excluded from Aberdeen for five years after 1483 because his episcopal revenues had been pocketed by the crown and he could not pay his common services to the curia.[95]

Revisionists can certainly list a number of effective Scottish prelates to place beside Elphinstone: the learned Robert Reid of Orkney, or Archbishop Blacadder of Glasgow. The two most famous archbishops of St Andrews, James Beaton and John Hamilton, both exercised themselves in defence of the kirk: Beaton resisted James V's passion for the feuing of church lands, Hamilton summoned reforming councils. It is, however, difficult to escape the impression that the Scottish hierarchy was remarkably ill-equipped to withstand any of the demands of the crown, or to bring much moral suasion to bear upon the nobility bent on the expropriation of ecclesiastical property.[96]

The Gaelic church in Ireland, beyond the regular reach of the English crown, also had its own problems of episcopal authority and lay control. Here the prelacy was deeply integrated into the system of familial control characteristic of the clan culture. Thus the Diocese of Clogher, Fermanagh,

---

[94] Mahoney, 'Scottish hierarchy', 39–84. MacFarlane, 'Primacy', 111–29. L. MacFarlane, 'Was the Scottish church reformable by 1513?' in N. MacDougall (ed.), *Church, Politics and Society. Scotland 1408–1929* (Edinburgh, 1983), 23–43.

[95] L. Macfarlane, *William Elphinstone and the Kingdom of Scotland* (Aberdeen, 1995), 217–89, 192–3. James IV actively supported Elphinstone's liturgical endeavours: he sponsored the printing of the *Breviary*, the first volume to be printed on a Scottish press.

[96] For a reasonably positive assessment of the episcopate see Wormald, *Court, Kirk and Community*, 80–2. The older view, of weakness and worldliness, is presented by G. Donaldson, *The Scottish Reformation* (Cambridge, 1960), 13–26.

was dominated by the clerical dynasty of MacCawells, who shared with the local Maguires the rulership of the see for most of the fifteenth and early sixteenth centuries.[97] The papacy itself compounded this problem by allowing procedures to circumvent the canon law requirement that no son should succeed to a father's benefice. Where local competition for power made the issue less certain, and Roman candidates were inserted into bishoprics, the results were often absenteeism as friars, for example, supplemented their positions in England or elsewhere from Irish benefices. Even on the rare occasions when a man of distinction was promoted within this confused system, it did not necessarily benefit the local establishment. For example, Maurice O'Fihilly, the only distinguished Irish theologian of the early sixteenth century, was promoted to the archbishopric of Tuam in 1506. Yet he spent scarcely any time in Ireland before his death in 1513.[98]

The ecclesiastical hierarchies of the British Isles may in many ways be said to mirror the polities in which they were located. Where authority was strong and centralist, as it was in England, the episcopate was vigorous and effective. It was also rather firmly committed to a perception of the Church as a national body, not detached from the universal Church but whole unto itself. Where political authority was weak, and/or fractured, as it was in Ireland, the episcopate either adhered to the norms of secular society or sought patronage and support outside the island, from the papacy or from England. Where a strong underlying perception of political unity was regularly disrupted by power struggles, as in Scotland, the episcopate followed the fortunes of the politically strong. In all cases lay power profoundly influenced ecclesiastical behaviour: in all, except perhaps Gaelic Ireland, there was until the Reformation sufficient adjustment between God and Caesar to ensure the stable management of the institutional Church.

The Distribution of Power

The jurisdictional and organizational complexity of the late medieval churches need detain us here only in so far as they have relevance for the future and reveal something of the strengths and weaknesses of the traditional order. Medieval Catholicism might be monarchical, with only general councils contesting the high ground of control, but it was a monarchy in which power was constantly devolved and evolved away from the curial centre. Provincial councils and synods legislated on many matters of regional import; bishops exercised high judicial powers and of

---

[97] Gwynn, *Anglo-Irish Church Life*, 72.   [98] Watt, *The Church in Medieval Ireland*, 185–7.

course bowed to the will of their political masters. The devolution continued to the sub-diocesan level of archdeaconry, commissary, and rural deanery. Meanwhile the regulars presented another hierarchy of control: often independent of local episcopal management, and integrated instead with their universal order, sometimes with their own provincial chapters, always governed by their own heads of house.

Such complexity was not automatically a source of either strength or weakness. The long evolution of the medieval church had led to the establishment of reasonably clear patterns of hierarchical order and explicit definitions of obligation and duty that were cumulatively functional and only intermittently confusing. A few distinctive jurisdictional patterns can be itemized for the British Isles. In the case of England and Wales the fixity of the Northern and Southern provinces, and the absence of a separate Welsh province, are the most notable features. The primacy of Canterbury over York had been fully acknowledged by the sixteenth century, but could still generate tensions when due form was not observed. After three centuries of dispute titles had been settled: Canterbury had 'the primacy of all England' while York was known as 'primate of England'.[99] The distinctive quality of the convocations of Canterbury was that they met concurrently with Parliament. For a brief period during Wolsey's legateship the division of provinces ceased to have much meaning and a more genuinely national church emerged in embryonic form.[100] Relations between the seculars and the regulars were characterized by the generally high level of disciplinary control that the former exercised over the latter. But there were major exceptions: the Cluniacs, Premonstratensians, Carthusians, Gilbertines, and Cistercians maintained their exempt status and were not subject to episcopal visitation.[101] Above all the orders of friars preserved their autonomy and their capacity profoundly to annoy the leaders of the secular Church. Finally, though this is by no means exclusive to the English church, the pattern of peculiar or exempt jurisdictions, well demonstrated in Swanson's map of medieval Yorkshire, is revealing of the limitations of authority even in a rather centralized and hierarchical corner of Christendom.

The key organizational and structural features of the Scottish church arise partly from the late establishment of the two archiepiscopal sees of St Andrews and Glasgow. This left an unresolved issue of primacy: first superiority was given to St Andrews but then the elevation of Glasgow, as

[99] Swanson, *Church and Society*, 16–26. J.C. Dickinson, *An Ecclesiastical History of England: The Later Middle Ages from the Norman Conquest to the Eve of the Reformation* (1979), 66–8.

[100] D.B. Weske, *Convocation of the Clergy* (1937).

[101] D. Knowles, *The Monastic Orders in England*, 3 vols. (Cambridge, 1959), iii. 28, 33, 39, 222.

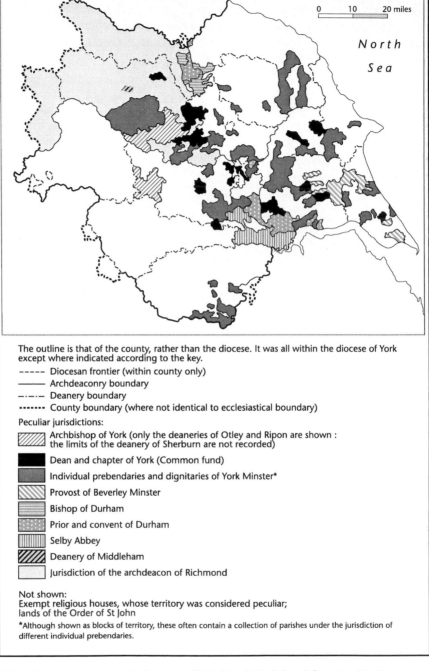

The outline is that of the county, rather than the diocese. It was all within the diocese of York except where indicated according to the key.

----- Diocesan frontier (within county only)

——— Archdeaconry boundary

—·—·— Deanery boundary

······· County boundary (where not identical to ecclesiastical boundary)

Peculiar jurisdictions:

Archbishop of York (only the deaneries of Otley and Ripon are shown : the limits of the deanery of Sherburn are not recorded)

Dean and chapter of York (Common fund)

Individual prebendaries and dignitaries of York Minster*

Provost of Beverley Minster

Bishop of Durham

Prior and convent of Durham

Selby Abbey

Deanery of Middleham

Jurisdiction of the archdeacon of Richmond

Not shown:
Exempt religious houses, whose territory was considered peculiar; lands of the Order of St John

*Although shown as blocks of territory, these often contain a collection of parishes under the jurisdiction of different individual prebendaries.

'Peculiars, or exempt jurisdictions of Medieval Yorkshire' from R. N. Swanson,
Church and Society in Late Medieval England (1989).

a consequence of the skilled political manoeuvring of Archbishop Blacadder, gave the latter control over four of the thirteen Scottish sees. Historical opinion is divided upon whether it was this separation that prevented the calling of provincial councils before 1536, but there was certainly bitter conflict about the symbols of precedence such as the displaying of the cross of St Andrews in Glasgow Cathedral.[102] The abbeys and priories of Scotland were increasingly identified with a highly developed system of commendation: from the 1530s onwards, noble houses established a lay control over many of the great monasteries that was in practice hereditary.[103] It is also worth remarking that while the jurisdictional and institutional densities of the church in the Scottish Lowlands were essentially similar to those of England, the structure of the Highland zone was a complete contrast. There diocesan organization was thin and weak, the parochial structure ineffective, and the monastic orders almost absent—on the eve of the Reformation there were only five small houses in the Highland zone, and the only friary, at Kingussie, had already failed.[104]

The institutional peculiarities of the Irish churches are, in the main, the predictable product of the political division of the island. The separation of dioceses, so that they were of either the Englishry or the Irishry or, in the case of Armagh, into deaneries *inter Hibernicos* and *inter Anglicos*, was of defining importance. Provincial synods were held with some regularity in the early sixteenth century for those of the Englishry, December assemblies, being used for the granting of tax, and July meetings for general legislation for the whole province. Medieval historians, studying the surviving records of the province of Armagh, have been at pains to emphasize that there were sustained attempts to treat the two 'nations' in a similar manner.[105] However, history, politics, and the ideology of the canonists who led the church of the Pale conspired to keep the systems apart.[106] The Rome-running of the Gaelic sees was a response to an ecclesiastical system that had not been able to evolve the administrative complexity of its English counterpart. Moreover, the common routines of appeal to Rome produced some distinctive features at home: the Armagh court of audience, for example, acted as a tutorial court, protecting the property rights of those litigating at the curia.[107] A final feature that is

---

[102] MacFarlane, 'Primacy', 118–25. Donaldson, *Scottish Reformation*, 25–6.

[103] I.B. Cowan, *The Scottish Reformation* (1982), 29–36.

[104] I.B. Cowan and D.E. Easson, *Medieval Religious Houses: Scotland* (1976), 77–8, 83–4, 89, 94, 101–2.

[105] M.A.J. Burrows, 'Fifteenth-century Irish provincial legislation', in W.J. Sheils and D. Wood (eds.), *The Churches, Ireland and the Irish*, SCH 25 (Oxford, 1989), 57–9.

[106] Murray, 'Diocese of Dublin', 54–7.

[107] J.A. Watt, 'The Church and the two nations in late medieval Armagh', in W.J. Sheils and D. Wood (eds.), *The Churches, Ireland and the Irish*, SCH 25 (Oxford, 1989), 37–54.

worth remark is the density of monastic penetration, especially in Gaelic Ireland: there were almost as many houses of regulars as there were in England on the eve of the Reformation and the society had never fully lost its origins as a monastic church.[108]

Jurisdictional and institutional plurality became problematic for the Church when it resulted in litigiousness. Conflicts about primacy and provincial autonomy afflicted all areas of the British Isles, not perhaps very seriously in the case of Canterbury and York, but very visibly in Ireland and Scotland: in the former case the archbishops of Armagh refused to attend Dublin synods when that archbishopric made a bid for the supremacy.[109] Some areas of jurisdiction, notably control over testamentary provisions, were a source of much hostility between the archbishops of Canterbury and their suffragans, and later between Archbishop Warham and Wolsey.[110] Throughout the system there was a general defensiveness about individual jurisdictional claims and an eagerness to assert full or extended rights against others. This was in part because the Church was serviced by an elaborate hierarchy of courts, each under the control of a group of professionals who had a strong vested interest in protecting their own. Compositions were at times necessary to define jurisdictional boundaries more closely. Since, as we have already seen, the higher clergy had to be alert to the need to fend off intrusions from the crown and the laity it is scarcely surprising if they appeared collectively to be more concerned about their own claims to authority than about discipline, preaching, or reform. When we include the zealousness with which individual clergy litigated against one another, at least in Ireland and Scotland, about possession of benefices, it is possible to paint a dismal picture of ecclesiastical introversion and greed.[111]

Yet these conflicts were rarely seen by contemporaries as a sign of terminal decline, or as the opportunity to challenge the authority of the institution in fundamental ways. Reform in 'head and members' was a rhetoric shared by the British churches and their Continental counterparts. The abiding evidence of the thirty years before the English broke with Rome, however, is that few felt that a fundamental jurisdictional revolution was needed and that even fewer anticipated that such a thing might occur.

[108] B. Bradshaw, *The Dissolution of the Religious Orders in Ireland under Henry VIII* (Cambridge, 1974).

[109] H.A. Jefferies, 'Diocesan synods and convocations in Armagh on the eve of the Tudor reformations', *Seanchas ard Mhacha* 16 (1995), 120–32. Watt, 'Church and two nations', 46.

[110] Kelly, 'Canterbury Jurisdiction', *passim*.

[111] Watt, 'Church and two nations', 46.

2

THE STATE OF THE CLERGY

John Colet, preaching his famous sermon before the Convocation of Canterbury in 1512, cited St Bernard with approval. 'The dignity of priests ...is greater than either the king's or the emperor's: it is equal with the dignity of angels.'[1] He was not alone in appealing to such a high clericalist view as the standard against which his contemporaries should be measured. A few years earlier John Alcock had preached in much the same vein to a synod of the Ely clergy; somewhat later William Melton, the long-serving chancellor of York, was equally emphatic on the need for the clergy to measure up to high standards of spiritual renewal.[2] The preachers had, of course, an agenda and an audience that led to a distinctive emphasis on the dignity of the priesthood, as well as on the failures of many of its individual representatives. That agenda may in part be characterized as humanist: the attempt to establish the clergy as models for lay piety, men worthy of the association with the angels because of their learning and wisdom, as well as their probity of life and spiritual leadership. But, though broadly in tune with humanist aspirations, the ambitions of these churchmen were also rather distinct from Erasmian ideals. Erasmus, in a characteristic moment in his *Sileni Alcibiades*, had identified the Church not with the priests, bishops and popes that 'the followers of the world' assume but with 'the whole Christian people'.[3] This conventional sentiment also articulates difference. Those who urged the clergy to follow the example of St Bernard would not have denied the Erasmian premise, yet they sought to centre the Church in the leadership of its priesthood, in those consecrated and ordained to an estate that transcended mundanity.[4]

It scarcely needed the words of an Alcock or Colet to remind the clergy that they were in an exposed social and moral position. Numbers,

[1] Colet's sermon is printed in full in C.H. Williams (ed.), *English Historical Documents* (1971), 652–60. C. Harper-Bill, 'Dean Colet's Convocation sermon and the pre-Reformation Church in England', *History* 73 (1988), 191–210.

[2] J. Alcock, *Gallicantus in Sinodo apud Bernwell* (1498). R.N. Swanson, 'Problems of the priesthood in pre-Reformation England', *EHR* 105 (1990), 862–3.

[3] D. Erasmus, 'The Silene of Alcibiades', in D. Wootton (ed.), *Thomas More: Utopia* (Indianapolis, Ind., 1999), 179.

[4] N. Tanner, *The Church in Late Medieval Norwich* (Toronto, 1984), 1.

wealth, and structural influence constantly reminded the laity that, though the priesthood was only a part of the Church universal, it was one which placed high demands upon the culture in return for the spiritual services that it rendered. Even those elements of the priestly order that can be subject to a crude Gross Domestic Product calculation are revealing: between a quarter and a third of English acreage was still owned by the Church, while in parts of Ireland it was nearer a half.[5] The demesne revenues of the Scottish crown amounted to little more than £8,000 (Scots) at the end of the fifteenth century, while the incomes of the wealthiest monasteries in their last half-century were between £7,500 and £13,000 (Scots).[6] Numbers of clerics were high, both in absolute terms and as a proportion of population: one estimate for Scotland puts the ratio of clergy to laity at 1:32 in the early sixteenth century.[7] If a fairly conservative multiplier of three clergy is applied to each English and Welsh parish and the approximately 6,000 regulars are added, a figure of around 33,000 priests in major orders is produced. A much more precise microcalculation for the city of Norwich gives a figure of 4 to 6 per cent of the male population as in major orders.[8] All these estimates would suggest that there would have been few lay people without some personal or kin connection to the clergy. The clerical order was therefore very visible: collectively, if not individually, it was wealthy and powerful. It was also extremely diverse: for example, although the percentage engaged in secular activities was almost certainly declining by the early sixteenth century, fewer than half of the Scottish clergy were reckoned to be in strictly 'spiritual' employment. Estimates for pluralism in England—approximately a fifth of livings being held in this way at the beginning of the sixteenth century—offer some indication of the number of clerics diversified away from parochial cures or from service as chaplains.[9]

---

[5] W.J. Sheils, *The English Reformation, 1530–1570* (Harlow, 1989), 27. The Irish evidence is very uncertain, but Bradshaw gives one telling example of church power when he compares the revenues of the earl of Kildare's estates with those of the Cistercian order in the Pale, Ormond, and county Wexford: the latter were worth £100 more than the former per annum: B. Bradshaw, *The Dissolution of the Religious Orders in Ireland under Henry VIII* (Cambridge, 1974), 33.

[6] J. Kirk (ed.), *The Books of the Assumption of Thirds*, British Academy Records of Social and Economic History NS 21 (1995), pp. lvi–lvii.

[7] L.B. Macfarlane, *William Elphinstone and the Kingdom of Scotland* (Aberdeen, 1995), 164. J. Cameron, *James V: The Personal Rule, 1528–42* (Edinburgh, 1998), 257. L. Macfarlane, 'Was the Scottish church reformable by 1513?' in N. MacDougall (ed.), *Church, Politics and Society: Scotland 1408–1929* (Edinburgh, 1983), 39.

[8] R.N. Swanson, *Church and Society in Late Medieval England* (Oxford, 1989), 30–6. Tanner, *Norwich*, 19–20.

[9] P. Marshall, *The Catholic Priesthood and the English Reformation* (Oxford, 1994), 109. J.A. Lipkin, 'Pluralism in pre-Reformation England: A Quantitative Analysis of Ecclesiastical Incumbency, c.1490–1539', Catholic University of America Ph.D. (1979), 155–65.

There was a constant pressure in this culture to evaluate the clergy, to question whether they could live up to the high vision offered by humanist reformers. It must have been difficult enough for ordinary clerks even to realize the ideal already expressed in the fifteenth century: the priest should be a preacher, as well as a man of prayer, a generous giver of hospitality, and a peace-maker.[10] These qualities had no doubt always been demanded in general: the distinctive feature of the century preceding the Reformation was that the laity were increasingly likely to articulate their views of the clergy through wills and other instruments of literacy. Similarly the laity had always had opportunities to 'employ' chosen clerics through parochial patronage, domestic chaplaincies, and court favour: all these continued but were notably enhanced by the growth of employment in the singing of Masses for the dead, through either chantries, or guilds and fraternities. So judgement was likely to be pronounced upon the clergy both by their own colleagues and by laymen who had a variety of investments in the Church.[11] To these evaluations the historian must perforce add that of hindsight: the fashion of revisionist historiography has been to insist that the experience of the Church in the early sixteenth century should not be read through the distorting lens of our knowledge of Luther or of Henry VIII's marital problems. Nevertheless, there is an inescapable awareness of the imminence of the break with Rome, and it is important to interrogate the preparedness of the clergy for the coming cataclysm.

The Religious

Colet's sermon was addressed to the whole body of the clergy, yet it said little about the regulars who comprised between a quarter and a third of those in orders. There was a passing remark about the desirability of withdrawal from the world for those who had the appropriate vocation: the rest was silence. This is perhaps to be expected in a humanist who, though not hostile to the religious, had imbibed the Erasmian praise of the active life. There may be a sense in which the historian of the Reformation should follow Colet's example, and simply note the existence and wealth of the regulars before passing on to those who did survive the cataclysm. But monks, nuns, and friars are important not merely because

---

[10] See for example the comments of Bernardino of Siena, and the same view was espoused by Thomas Gascoigne: B. Manning, *The People's Faith in the Time of Wyclif* (Hassocks, 1975), 18; R.N. Swanson, 'Problems of the priesthood in pre-Reformation England', *EHR* 105 (1990), 846.

[11] Marshall, *Catholic Priesthood*, is an important study of this process of lay evaluation, as seen primarily through wills. Swanson, 'Problems', 846.

of their numbers, or because their wealth attracted the most obvious greed of the laity. In some ways the orders offer the most interesting test of the health of the clerical estate: like an archaeological site they can reveal layer by layer the reforming impulses of the Church, and they display the appeal that forms of spirituality articulated at a particular moment in time could have in a later and different context. They also offer some of the most intriguing comparative material across the British Isles since the religious orders experienced remarkably different fortunes in England, Wales, Scotland, and Ireland.

In terms of wealth, power, and numbers it was still the black monks who dominated the English monastic scene. Barbara Harvey's study based on Westminster is a major reminder that the Benedictines were still entrenched at the heart of the life of the capital in the mid-1530s.[12] St Albans, Durham, Canterbury, Bury, Peterborough, and a number of lesser houses all show the general signs of good institutional health on the eve of the dissolutions. Recruitment was strong: the order as a whole experienced a growth of more than 30 per cent between 1400 and 1500, and in many cases numbers continued to rise into the 1530s. Finances had benefited from the general economic recovery being experienced by landlords in the first years of the sixteenth century; scandal was confined to a limited number of glaring cases.[13] Examples of new building are again sufficient to counter any general idea of decline. Abbot Kirton's retrochoir at Peterborough (*c.*1510) and the crossing tower at Gloucester are the finest surviving ecclesiastical structures: the rich range of lodgings at Glastonbury built by Abbot Bere is perhaps more characteristic of the constructions undertaken by the last monastic generation.[14] The Benedictines also remained dominant in the fields of education and scholarship. They played particularly critical roles at Oxford, through their shared foundation, Gloucester College, and in the last generation before the Reformation were a more potent force in the university than the friars.[15] In the previous century the number of schools run by the monks had increased, and in the 1530s the monks of St Albans offered a rare example of enthusiasm for the potential of new technology when they established the only printing press to operate outside London.[16] The black monks also still

---

[12] B. Harvey, *Living and Dying in Medieval England 1100–1540: The Monastic Experience* (Oxford, 1995).

[13] D. Knowles, *The Religious Orders in England*, 3 vols. (Cambridge, 1959), iii. 9–10.

[14] D. Knowles and R.N. Hadcock, *Medieval Religious Houses: England and Wales* (1971), 61–5, 73. J. Leland, *Itineraries*, 5 vols., ed. L. Toulmin-Smith (1906–8), ii. 289.

[15] R.B. Dobson, 'The religious orders, 1370–1540', in J.I. Catto and T.A.R. Evans (eds.), *The History of the University of Oxford: Late Medieval Oxford* (Oxford, 1992), 546–8, 573–9.

[16] J.G. Clark, 'Reformation and reaction at St Alban's Abbey, 1530–1558', *EHR* 115 (2000), 304–14.

featured in the consciousness of the laity: where will benefactions have been analysed they show that giving was by no means confined to the newer orders: in Norwich testators actually gave to the priory in a larger percentage of cases in the pre-dissolution years than in the early fifteenth century. In Salisbury diocese the last century of monasticism saw a steady increase in giving to the newer order of the Carthusians, but almost 50 per cent of benefactions went to Benedictine houses.[17]

It is customary, and no doubt largely appropriate, to see the statement of the 1536 Act dissolving the poorer monastic houses that the great monasteries were places 'wherein...religion is right well kept and observed' as the merest persiflage.[18] But, while the neat division articulated by a cynical regime has no formal justification, there is a sense that the traditional orders of the black monks and canons were vulnerable, not in the great establishments, rather in the large number of small houses that dotted the English landscape. Here the story of vitality, of levels of recruitment, and of general lay support is more varied: examples of energy and revivalism in the last generations, as at Winchcombe under the great Abbot Richard Kidderminster, can be found, but there are counter-examples of atrophy, weakness, or downright decay.[19] Visitation returns must always be regarded with the utmost caution, but the Norwich visitations between 1492 and 1532 show problems of a failure of conventual order most commonly occurring in the houses with few recruits. There was presumably a vicious circle in the case of a house like Walsingham Priory, where disciplinary and economic problems were matched by problems of recruitment.[20] Even well-organized houses with small numbers of monks often had to struggle to maintain the full *opus dei* that was their prime duty.[21] While it is rarely possible to judge the motives of those who entered the regular life through the old orders, it may be inferred that parents, guardians and even the recruits themselves sought a measure of stability and security not always available in these small establishments.

---

[17] Tanner, *Norwich*, 120. A.D. Brown, *Popular Piety in Late Medieval England: The Diocese of Salisbury 1250–1550* (Oxford, 1995), 29.

[18] 27 HVIII, c. 28.

[19] W. Dugdale (ed.), *Monasticon Anglicanum*, 6 vols. (1817–30), ii. 301. W.A. Pantin, 'Abbot Kidderminster and monastic studies', *Downside Review* 47 (1929), 198–211. Knowles, *Religious Orders*, iii. 93–4.

[20] A. Jessop (ed.), *Visitations of Norwich, 1492–1532*, CS 2nd ser. 43 (1888). Bowker shows some correlation between size and good order for Lincoln, though it is not wholly consistent: M. Bowker, *The Henrician Reformation: The Diocese of Lincoln under John Longland 1521–47* (Cambridge, 1981), 17–28.

[21] P. Heath (ed.), *Bishop Geoffrey Blythe's Visitations, ca. 1515–25*, Staffordshire Record Society, 4th ser. 7 (1973), pp. xxxviii–xxxix, liii.

In Wales, Scotland, and Ireland the old orders of the Benedictines and Cluniacs played a very insignificant part in regular life. They were visible only where Norman influence had penetrated in significant ways: and they rarely functioned in the role of cathedral chapter as so commonly in England.[22] On the other hand the Cistercians and Premonstratensians and other 'reformed' Benedictines were spread far more evenly across Britain and Ireland and not exclusively confined to the wilderness. The spiritual colonization of upland Wales owed much to the Cistercians: yet in Scotland, and in lesser measure in Ireland, there seems to have been a willingness to found houses wherever convenience, and the support of patrons, justified it.[23] The Cistercians lack the appearance of stability and internal growth that characterizes the Benedictines, oscillating between internal decline and determined attempts at revival. The former state was often explained by adverse external circumstances. In Ireland it was reported at the end of the fifteenth century that all forty-four houses, with the two exceptions of Dublin and Mellifont, were impoverished by warfare and desolate.[24] The Welsh Cistercian houses had great difficulty in recovering from the crises of the early fifteenth-century Glyndŵr rebellions: indeed only Strata Florida and Tintern were in a reasonably healthy state on the eve of the Reformation.[25] The Scottish Cistercian houses were heavily concentrated in the Borders, and were physically vulnerable even before the sustained crisis of the Anglo-Scottish wars of the 1540s.[26] A part of the decay, however, was more internal to the order: charges of moral and institutional transgression were common in Ireland and Scotland, and not absent from Cistercian visitations even of the great English houses. The struggle to sustain the conventual life in what were often adverse economic conditions created by the choice of environment often defeated the smaller houses: Grace Dieu in Wales, for example, was valued at only £19 at the dissolution, had two monks, and had long been in trouble for failure to pay appropriate dues.[27]

On the other hand, there are signs both of continuing Cistercian strength and of attempts at spiritual renewal. There were houses that recruited well at least until the 1520s: Cleeve Abbey in Somerset offers a

---

[22] There is only one Irish example of a capitular monastery staffed by Benedictines: that at Down. There were only three Benedictine houses in Ireland and seven in Scotland by the dissolution period. A. Gwynn and R.N. Hadcock, *Medieval Religious Houses: Ireland* (1970). I.B. Cowan and D.F. Easson, *Medieval Religious Houses: Scotland*, 2nd edn. (1976).

[23] R. Cooper, *Abbeys and Priories of Wales* (Swansea, 1992), 57–8.

[24] B. Bradshaw, *The Dissolution of the Religious Orders in Ireland under Henry VIII* (Cambridge, 1974), 16–38.

[25] G. Williams, *Wales and the Reformation* (Cardiff, 1997), 72–7.

[26] M. Dilworth, *Scottish Monasteries: Monastic Life in the Sixteenth Century* (Edinburgh, 1994), 26–7.

[27] Knowles and Hadcock, *Religious Houses: England and Wales*, 120.

good example. There was also one vigorous monastic leader in the shape of Marmaduke Huby, abbot of Fountains, great builder, and energetic political leader of his movement. Under his leadership the number of professed monks at Fountains rose from twenty-two to about fifty-two.[28] Since the houses of these orders were exempt from visitation, and were still formally linked to the founding establishments in France via the general chapters of Cîteaux, it was always a possibility that new life would be breathed into the collectivity of houses through externally generated religious renewal. There were attempts at regulation in all three realms in the early sixteenth century. In Ireland there was what Bradshaw describes as a flickering attempt to resuscitate the Cistercians, with two zealous abbots of Mellifont leading the efforts, but little was achieved.[29] Scotland witnessed a rather more sustained renewal: visitations orchestrated by Cîteaux became more regular after 1500, the general chapter was willing to support abbots elected by their own monks against royal nominees, albeit unsuccessfully, and in 1531 there was a famous visitation by Simon Postel, abbot of Chaalis, which issued in general reforming instructions to the order.[30] The English province was more isolated from Cîteaux than its Scottish counterpart, but visitations by provincial commissaries continued, and Huby's vigilant eye ensured that reform was not wholly neglected.[31] These efforts at discipline and improvement did not occur in a political vacuum. In both England and Scotland the monarchy and the legates, for their own purposes, intervened to encourage reform in the orders. In 1497 Henry VII urged support for Cistercian reform and praised the monastic life: half a generation later Wolsey as legate sought to override exempt jurisdictions and undertake his own programme of change.[32] The Scottish monarchy more consistently intervened in the affairs of the Cistercians, most obviously when James V actually requested the abbot of Cîteaux to send a reforming visitor in 1531.[33]

---

[28] R.W. Dunning, 'The last days of Cleeve Abbey', in C.M. Barron and C. Harper-Bill (eds.), *The Church in Pre-Reformation Society* (Woodbridge, 1985), 58–67. Knowles, *Religious Orders*, iii. 29–37, 39–50.

[29] Bradshaw, *Dissolution*, 33, 36–7.

[30] Cowan and Easson, *Religious Houses: Scotland*, 26.

[31] C.H. Talbot (ed.), *Letters from the English Abbots to the Chapter at Cîteaux, 1442–1521*, CS 4th ser. 4 (1967), 83, 97–8, 120, 123. The English Premonstratensians, closely supervised in the early sixteenth century by Bishop Redman, provide a parallel case of the concern for reform from above. At least ten of the twenty-nine houses seem to have been consistently exemplary in behaviour, with few glaring deficiencies elsewhere: Knowles, *Religious Orders*, iii. 39–51.

[32] A. Goodman, 'Henry VII and Christian renewal', in K. Robbins (ed.), *Religion and Humanism*, SCH 17 (Oxford, 1981), 117. P. Gwyn, *The King's Cardinal: The Rise and Fall of Thomas Wolsey* (1990), 273–4.

[33] R.K. Hannay and D. Hay (eds.), *The Letters of James V* (Edinburgh, 1954), 187, 202, 210–11. Dilworth, *Scottish Monasteries*, 35–8.

Some parts of the Cistercian order may have suffered from that very disposition to colonize the wilderness that was central to St Bernard's original vision. Lay support, both political and economic, was more likely to be directed to the orders in their midst, especially the friars and the urban monasteries. Robert Aske's hymn of praise to the monasteries can be read as indicating continuing general enthusiasm for the great houses at the time of the Pilgrimage of Grace, but recent historians have suggested that there is a dearth of supporting evidence for this proposition.[34] A greater danger for all the old monastic orders was creeping laicization of the material assets of a house. As so often, this was revealed at its most extreme in Ireland: to quote Bradshaw, 'dilapidation, rather than con-cubinage, must be considered the most characteristic aberration of late medieval Irish monasticism'.[35] It was routine in areas of Irish, or Anglo-Norman, hegemony for local magnate and local abbot to be kin-related, or at least deeply bound together by the clientage system, and for leases and property therefore to pass readily from the latter to the former.[36] The Scottish system of commendation had some of the same results, though the commendators themselves remained clerics and were not so automat-ically under magnate control. In the Scottish case the shift to the feuing of church lands after the 1520s secured for the laity a control of church wealth that had previously been unthinkable.[37] As always, the closer polit-ical control exercised by the crown in England made it more difficult for a crude secularism to flourish without its assent, yet lay identities with the abbeys were extended through long leases and stewardships. These rela-tionships had some value in providing the monasteries with protectors, and indeed voices for the defence when the final challenge came. It also ensured that there were local men well placed to finish the work of appropriation once the crown had decreed an end to the orders.[38]

The debate about spiritual vitality of British monasticism is as old as the dissolutions themselves. A part of the problem in providing convincing

[34] C. Cross, 'Monasticism and society in the Diocese of York, 1520–1540', *TRHS* 5th ser. 38 (1988), 131–45. R. Hoyle, *The Pilgrimage of Grace and the Politics of the 1530s* (Oxford, 2001), 47–50.

[35] Bradshaw, *Dissolution*, 27.

[36] They could, indeed, be one and the same person, like Rory MacDermot, who died in 1568, and who had been both the lord of Moylung and the abbot of the Premonstratensian house of Lough Key for sixty years. The *Annals of Loch Cé* praise him as chief and plunderer, not as churchman: K.W. Nicholls, *Gaels and Gaelicised Ireland in the Middle Ages* (Dublin, 1972), 109.

[37] Dilworth, *Scottish Monasteries*, 21–4, 39 ff., though Dilworth is properly cautious about a simplified reading of creeping secularism. For an older and more robust condemnation of contemporary practice see G. Donaldson, *The Scottish Reformation* (Cambridge, 1960), 2–4.

[38] J. Youings, *The Dissolution of the Monasteries* (1969), 19–20, provides a useful summary of these issues.

responses lies in the manner of posing the question. There is no absolute standard to which to appeal for a judgement upon proper monastic spirituality, and the best that historians can usually do is to appeal to the zeal of the founding fathers and the dynamic thrust of the young movements of reform from the tenth to the twelfth centuries. Thereafter, runs one side of the argument, there was a steady glissade towards, at best, middle-aged complacency; at worst, downright abandonment of the original ideals. But a functional spirituality, suitable to its social environment, may not require the white heat of the evangelizing zeal of a St Bernard. If the monasteries continued to provide the cycle of canonical prayer and avoided moral depravity or extreme secularism it might be argued that they served with an appropriate spirituality. This is the essence of a famous complaint from the black monks against Wolsey's attempted reforms in the 1520s: few nowadays, they argued, wished to live lives of extreme austerity, and if all monasteries had to follow the example of the Carthusians, Bridgettines, and Observants, they would soon be depopulated.[39] The clear inference was that such austerity was not essential to an effective life as a regular. It is an approach that carries some conviction, given the diverse strengths of the Benedictines. But diversity, and its accompanying ease with the secular world, carried its own risk, particularly that of a loss of the uniqueness of the monastic calling. It is easy to argue that laymen valued the monasteries: English will evidence, for example, places them explicitly within the economy of prayer for the dead.[40] It is less clear that they appreciated the uniqueness of the monasteries, as against the various other agencies—friaries, guilds, confraternities, and chantries—that could provide similar spiritual service. Alternative focuses of devotion were readily available when the attack on monasticism began. Scottish evidence also suggests an acceptance of a continuing role for the monasteries, yet little sense of their centrality in the religious life of the nation. When the Reformation crisis finally came it was the friaries, not the monasteries, which were attacked, the latter were largely left to atrophy in a new and hostile climate of belief.[41]

Among the claustral orders it remains almost obligatory to single out, as did the black monks' petition, the unusual role of the Carthusians and Bridgettines. They arrived late upon the English scene, and did not influence Scotland, Ireland, or Wales at all, with the exception of one Charterhouse at Perth. Even in England the powerful influence of the Carthusians

[39] W.A. Pantin (ed.), *Chapters of the English Black Monks*, 2 vols., CS 3rd ser. 47, 53 (1933, 1937), ii. 123–4.

[40] J.J. Scarisbrick, *The Reformation and the English People* (Oxford, 1984), 1–18.

[41] See for example M.B. Sanderson, *Ayrshire and the Reformation* (E. Linton, E. Lothian, 1997), 12, 126–8. Cowan, *The Scottish Reformation* (1982), 39–43.

was regionalized, with London and Yorkshire as the most important centres, and the Bridgettines remained confined to their one royal foundation at Syon. But it is commonplace to argue that this limited number of houses had an influence out of all proportion to their size, both because of the powerful example of their spirituality and because their royal and elite patronage enabled them to do much to determine the tenor of lay piety at the heart of the political regime. The tragic end of the London Charterhouse, and the heroic resistance to Henry VIII's will by a scattering of men from all the houses, tends to magnify their influence in historical hindsight: it does not gainsay it. Knowles, in a telling comparison, relates the Bridgettine house to Port Royal, the great centre of French Jansenism.[42] The importance of these orders, apart from the sheer vitality of their spiritual life, obviously derives from their proximity to laymen and women, and the strength of their example despite the demands of enclosure. They were in the position to preach, write, and, in the case of the Bridgettines, to act as confessors in ways that helped to determine late medieval spirituality.[43] The process of transmission is beautifully encapsulated in the story of a Passion devotion recorded in a fifteenth-century text. The cycle of devotion emanated from the London Carthusians, whence it was transmitted to Mount Grace in Yorkshire. A monk sent it to a pious parish priest, who in turn shared it with his parishioners. One husbandman in his turn used the meditations, and was so grateful that they revived his ox, that he went and requested a full copy in writing from the monastery.[44] The vulnerability of these godly houses, especially those in London, lay in their close identity with the court. Syon and Sheen, in particular, were treated by monarchs as extensions of their own spirituality, and unlike the husbandman, they were not always humbly and unobtrusively grateful for the activities of their ghostly advisers.[45] While all the evidence suggests that the monks and nuns themselves were extraordinarily adroit at avoiding worldly entanglement, assumptions were made about their loyalty and gratitude, and about their willingness to serve the interests of the crown, which proved in the crisis to be misplaced.

The story of the powerful influence of the Charterhouses and Syon is one of individuals as much as orders, and we might note two elements

---

[42] Knowles, *Religious Orders*, iii. 215.

[43] Knowles, *Religious Orders*, iii. 212–40. M. Beckwith, 'The Bridgettine Monastery of Syon, with Special Reference to its Monastic Usages', University of Oxford D.Phil. (1975).

[44] E. Duffy, *The Stripping of the Altars: Traditional Religion in England 1400–1580* (New Haven, Conn., 1992), 296–7. The story is taken from a fifteenth-century Passion devotion, the 'Revelation of the Hundred Paternosters'.

[45] W.N. Mackay, 'Sheen Charterhouse from its Foundation to its Dissolution', University of Oxford D.Phil. (1992).

that seem to mark them off from the more general monastic movement. The first is that there is reasonably sustained evidence of late vocations among those entering these houses, at least in the last generations and in London. This means that a number of the Carthusians and the advisers of Syon came late to their vows, often with university training, or knowledge of the secular Church, behind them. Late vocations were, of course, not unknown elsewhere, and in particular the taking of the habit as a form of spiritual retirement was widely accepted. But for the Carthusians the commitment of mature men who were equipped intellectually and spiritually to defend the order was a particularly important development.[46] The second is that the nuns of Syon, and in lesser degree some of the Carthusians, were distinguished by high social status. This has long been known, but only recently has the significance of this situation been underlined by careful research on the wider corporation of nuns. Barbara Harris has shown that few aristocratic women entered nunneries in the century before the Reformation: of 958 nuns in the dissolutions lists, only thirty-six can be shown to have come from noble or knightly families, while in the whole century fewer than a hundred seem to have been destined by families for the cloister. This lack of enthusiasm for placing elite daughters in convents underlines the distinctiveness of Syon, where such women were relatively common. It must be assumed that it was through this one house that the ideal of enclosed female spirituality was made visible to the leaders of early Tudor society.[47]

Enclosed orders continued to play a part in late medieval society, and even the oldest and most traditional possessed some residual cultural vitality. Yet only the few houses of the Carthusians seem to have possessed the inner strength to play a major role in the Reformation crisis. Individual monks, forcibly released from the cloister, sometimes became dynamic adherents either of religious change or of Catholic tradition, but their numbers were limited and the majority simply melted into the new environment of parochial livings and marginal chaplaincies. Of more interest for the narrative of religious change is the situation of the friars. The mendicant orders possessed characteristics that made them more visible actors in the story of late medieval religious behaviour and indicated that they would play significant roles in the Reformation drama. Although the first religious fervour of the four main orders had in some measure been dissipated by the late fourteenth century, they continued to be shaken by more vigorous winds of external and internal change than did the en-

[46] Mackay, 'Sheen Charterhouse', 163 ff.

[47] Beckwith, 'Bridgettine Monastery of Syon', 69–70. B. Harris, 'A new look at the Reformation: aristocratic women and nunneries, 1450–1540', *JBS* 32 (1993), 89–113.

closed orders. The friars had embedded themselves firmly in the urban landscape of England, Scotland, and Ireland, and their close integration into local communities meant that they were able to influence and be influenced by patterns of lay pietism.[48] Their preaching role seems to have continued with some vigour until the eve of the dissolutions, as did their capacity to annoy the secular Church with their attacks on possessioners and worldly clerics. The last notable crisis provoked by such preaching in England occurred in the 1460s, when Carmelite preaching in London led to appeals to Rome and the imprisonment of the head of the order, but Archbishop Morton was still fulminating against them in the 1480s.[49] Henry Standish's support for the royal cause against claims of clerical immunity in 1515 is consistent with this tradition. Episcopal preaching licences for the 1530s indicate that friars remained the key to sermon-giving: Archbishop Lee of York, for example, licensed twenty-nine preachers in 1534, twenty-six of them mendicants.[50] Secondly, the urban positioning of the friars and their growing participation in the economy of prayer for the dead seems to have made them the focus of more enduring lay benefaction than the monasteries. This seems to be true whether elite giving or that of ordinary townspeople is studied. Thirty-three per cent of Kentish knights and 27 per cent of esquires left bequests to the friars in their wills in the century after 1422. In Salisbury 40 per cent of fifteenth-century wills gave to the friars; in Norwich it was 44 per cent of wills made between 1370 and 1532, though the percentages declined in the last two decades before the Reformation; in York it was 33 per cent in the last three decades. London is particularly interesting because the proportion giving to mendicants in their wills was actually increasing on the eve of the break with Rome.[51]

The presence of the friars in the universities also maintained their vitality and their access to religious debate. The greatest days of the Franciscans and Dominicans at Oxford had passed by the later fifteenth century, and there were no figures to rival the opponents of FitzRalph or Wyclif.

---

[48] For general overviews see Knowles, *Religious Orders*, iii. 52–9; Bradshaw, *Dissolution*, 8–16; Cowan, *Scottish Reformation*, 44–8; Williams, *Wales and Reformation*, 73.

[49] F.R.H. Du Boulay, 'The quarrel between the Carmelite friars and the secular clergy of London, 1464–1468', *JEH* 6 (1955), 156–74. C. Harper-Bill, 'Archbishop Morton and the Province of Canterbury', *JEH* 29 (1978), 12.

[50] S. Wabuda, 'The Provision of Preaching during the Early Reformation, with special reference to Itineration, c.1530 to 1547', University of Cambridge Ph.D. (1991), 89. The same was true in Worcester diocese, where almost all the thirty-six preachers in these years were friars.

[51] P.W. Fleming, 'Charity, faith and the gentry of Kent, 1422–1529', in A.J. Pollard (ed.), *Property and Politics* (Gloucester, 1984), 48–9. Brown, *Salisbury*, 44–5. Tanner, *Norwich*, 119. D. Palliser, *Tudor York* (Oxford, 1979), 227. S. Brigden, *London and the Reformation* (Oxford, 1989), 73–4.

Yet the *studia* remained large, and investigation of surviving library evidence suggests that the orders remained open to new ideas.[52] In Scotland the young universities drew heavily upon the resources of the friars: at St Andrews, for example, a new Dominican house was built with money left by Bishop Elphinstone in 1516.[53]

The rise of the observant movement was of crucial importance for the Franciscans and influenced the Dominicans and Augustinians to a lesser degree. Observantism was not native to the British Isles: its concerns for close observation of the rule, and adherence to the spirit of mendicancy, was developed mainly in France and Italy in the late fourteenth century.[54] By the third decade of the fifteenth century Franciscan and Dominican observance made a limited appearance in Ireland, and by the end of the century the movement assumed major significance.[55] In Scotland observants from the Low Countries became influential and established new foundations after the 1460s.[56] In England, by contrast, observantism was a deliberate royal introduction in the 1480s, and only led to the foundation, or reallocation from the conventuals, of seven Franciscan houses.[57] It is important first to note that, despite different patterns of foundation, there was a common belief in all three realms in the spiritual merits of the observant movement. Moreover the spiritual vitality of observantism on the eve of the Reformation meant that it routinely presented an obstacle to those who sought to initiate change. Even without major constitutional or doctrinal upheaval, the observants could be an irritant to authority. They adhered in extreme form to the general fraternal identification with the authority of the papacy, so much so that when Wolsey endeavoured to visit the Observants of Greenwich nineteen took the extreme step of fleeing from their monastery in disobedience to their superior rather than accept an intermediary power.[58]

These shared and very significant characteristics of the observant movement have to be compared with differences that were to have considerable long-term import for the religious history of the British Isles. The sharpest contrast is between England and Ireland: in the former observantism was

[52] Dobson, 'Religious orders', 556–65.

[53] Cowan and Easson, *Religious Houses: Scotland*, 119–20.

[54] D. Nimmo, *Reform and Division in the Medieval Franciscan Order* (Rome, 1987), pt. iii.

[55] T.S. Flynn, *The Irish Dominicans, 1536–1641* (Dublin, 1994), 3–8. F.X. Martin, 'The Irish Friars and the observant movement in the fifteenth century', *Proceedings of the Irish Catholic Historical Commission* (1960), 10–16.

[56] J. Durkan, 'The observant Franciscan province in Scotland', *Innes Review* 35 (1984), 51–5.

[57] A.G. Little, 'The introduction of the observant Friars into England', *Proceedings of the British Academy* 10 (1921–3), 455–71.

[58] K.B. Brown, 'Wolsey and ecclesiastical order: the case of the Franciscan Observants', in S.J. Gunn and P.G. Lindley (eds.), *Cardinal Wolsey: Church, State and Art* (Cambridge, 1991), 178–218.

introduced only as a consequence of royal patronage, and was sustained mainly by the desire of Edward IV and Henry VII to mirror the fashionable religiosity of the Burgundian and French courts.[59] It became a formidable spiritual force and a major challenge to Cromwell, but numbers were always relatively low and there was no general movement from other parts of the mendicant orders into its ranks. Various explanations have been advanced by historians: the most convincing perhaps is that the English orders, including the Franciscan conventuals, were in reasonable spiritual health, had high educational standards and had maintained much of the original vision of poverty. Reforming ministers of the conventuals had been defeated in the early fifteenth century, and thereafter the pressure for change was limited. The English province had no difficulty in sustaining the decree of Eugenius IV that conventual houses should not be given to the observants: the three that changed did so by royal fiat.[60]

The situation in Ireland presents a total contrast. There the arrival of observantism seems to defy all the generalizations normally applied to the mendicants. The early houses, and the attempts at reform within existing structures, were all concentrated in Gaelic regions, especially in Ulster and Connacht. This meant that it grew in rural areas and that its patrons were local lords, like Cormac, Lord of Muskerry, who founded Kilcrea in 1465 and was buried in the choir in Franciscan habit, or Margaret O'Brien, wife of Ewghan O'Rourke, who founded Dromahair in 1508. As the movement spread it attracted all three of the main mendicant orders, and led to internal reform within existing houses, in many cases happily defying the papal ban on the transfer from Franciscan conventuals to observants. It reached urban areas and the Pale from the west, presumably as a result of the zeal of existing houses. And the scale of change, although not unique in Europe, was very marked: by the 1530s two-thirds of the sixty Franciscan houses were observant and, while only eight Dominican and eight Augustinian houses had explicitly changed, in these orders there was no clear division into two categories and the influence of observantism was more widely diffused. In addition there was a completely new growth of the Franciscan Third Order Regular, an order that had evolved from St Francis's confraternity of sympathetic laymen to become a regular grouping in its own right. It may have had as many as forty houses at the time of the suppression.[61]

Explanations for this vigorous growth usually revolve around the inherent attraction which monasticism still held for Irish culture and, more specifically, the racial divisions of the island that prevented a close identity with English-

---

[59] Little, 'Observant Friars', 460–1.

[60] K.B. Brown, 'The Franciscan Observants in England: 1482–1559', University of Oxford D.Phil. (1986), 20–3, 25–34.

[61] Gwynn and Hadcock, *Religious Houses: Ireland*, 218–67. Martin, 'Irish Friars', 13–15.

dominated forms of rule. The historian of the Franciscan Observants argues that they tended to appear whenever the influence of the English crown over Irish affairs was in retreat, and that the great attraction of the movement was that it was free of English jurisdictional interference, which dogged the steps of the existing orders. One of the rare moments when the advance of observantism seemed to be halted was when a Gael, William O'Reilly, was elected as the conventual provincial in 1469, and a number of friars who had migrated petitioned to return to their old houses.[62] The Dominicans suffered particularly from this English intrusion: there were conflicts in the late fifteenth century about the election of the first Irish provincial, and only in 1536 was Paul III finally persuaded to rescind a bull of 1397 which had prohibited the establishment of a separate Gaelic province.[63] It is interesting that the Carmelites, who seem to have been least influenced by observantism, had managed with difficulty to hold on to their own provincial and from about 1440 were always governed by an Irishman.[64]

While the impulses governing Irish observant expansion may in part have been political, the consequences were to produce a movement that was still energetically expansionist, and still had powerful popular support in Henry VIII's reign. Its learning, where it can be tested as in the surviving library catalogues for Youghal, was impressive, if essentially traditional, and its one scholar of international repute, Maurice O'Fihilly, was a vigorous defender of the interests of Rome.[65] All of this constructed a powerful form of opposition to the attempts at religious change of the 1530s and to the dissolution itself. One of the great 'what ifs...' of the failed Irish Reformation must be, what if there had been no mendicant revival, or it had been confined largely to those areas within the ambit of the English crown?

This sharp contrast between England and Ireland has left aside Scottish mendicancy. In purely quantitative terms Scotland conforms more closely to the former than the latter. The Franciscan Observant movement arrived rather belatedly and was sustained by crown initiative. The Augustinians barely existed north of the Border: the Dominicans, who were an important group, for a time rested on the laurels of having achieved provincial separation from England in 1481, although under John Adamson, provincial in 1511, they were exposed to more sustained reform and a new friary was established at Dundee. As in England, Franciscan

---

[62] P. Conlan, *Franciscan Ireland* (Dublin, 1988), 22–6, 94.

[63] Flynn, *Irish Dominicans*, 4–8.

[64] P. O'Dwyer, 'The Carmelite Order in pre-Reformation Ireland', *Proceedings of the Irish Catholic Historical Commission* (1969), 57–8.

[65] J. Coleman (ed.), 'A medieval Irish library catalogue', *Bibliographical Society of Ireland* 2 (1921–5), 111–20. Bradshaw, *Dissolution*, 15–16, though it should be noted that O'Fihilly was essentially an international figure, rarely resident in his native land.

Observance owed most to royal effort: the crown established the first four houses and then James IV played some part in the erection of a further five.[66] The movement remained true to the general traditions of mendicancy by working in and through the towns and playing a part in the revival of learning through the universities: no attempt was made to plant houses in the desert and there is little evidence of active support from the Scottish nobility, highland or lowland. Yet these changes are not always given the weight they deserve in general narratives of the period: the limited revival seems to have imparted enough vigour to the friars to make them major actors in the Reformation drama. A quite disproportionate number of those Scots charged with heresy in the 1530s and 1540s were friars, but so also were some of the most energetic defenders of the status quo. On one side one may quickly list John Willock, Alexander Dick, Alexander Seton, and Friar Rough, on the other John Black, the formidable defender of orthodoxy in Edinburgh, or Robert Veitch, head of the Greyfriars in Stirling who was still proselytizing for Catholicism in the 1580s.[67] It is often pointed out that it was the friaries, not the monasteries, which the zealous reformers of the 1540s and 1550s attacked and 'cast down'. This was partly a result, no doubt, of proximity: it also reflects the conviction that such establishments were a particular threat to the progress of reform: they were assailed because they were effective.[68]

The mendicant orders in England were suppressed before there was much likelihood of popular aggression against them and, with the exception of the observants, they vanished with no more than the occasional brave sermon of protest. But they shared with the Scottish houses complex individual responses to reform. The wholehearted adherence of a Richard Ingworth or George Browne to the interests of Cromwell can be compared to the sustained opposition of the Greenwich Observants, and of men like Friar Peto and Friar Elstow who returned to refound their house under Mary.[69] In all of this we should, of course, perceive self-interest at work in very adverse circumstances: we should also note what Dobson calls the radical subjectivism of the friars that made them sit uneasily under the rule of obedience.[70] To return for a moment to the

---

[66] Cowan and Easson, *Religious Houses: Scotland*, 13–14, 114–34. Cowan, *Scottish Reformation*, 44, 47, 92, 101.

[67] M. Lynch, *Edinburgh and the Reformation* (Edinburgh, 1981), 114–15, 175–6. M.J. Yellowlees, 'The ecclesiastical establishment of the Diocese of Dunkeld at the Reformation', *Innes Review* 36 (1985), 81.

[68] D. McRoberts, 'Material destruction caused by the Scottish Reformation', in D. McRoberts (ed.), *Essays on the Scottish Reformation* (Glasgow, 1962), 418–20.

[69] Knowles, *Religious Orders*, iii. 438–40.

[70] B. Dobson, 'Mendicant ideal and practice in late medieval York', in P.V. Addyman and V.E. Black (eds.), *Archaeological Papers from York Presented to M.W. Barley* (York, 1984), 111.

Greenwich Observants who fled from Wolsey's visitation: we have embodied in this both the passionate commitment to the rule that legitimated the deepest possible protest under obedience, and the passion that could transmute that commitment into essentially anarchic action. Clement VII, intervening rather ineffectually in the quarrel, urged 'for gods sake to use mercy with those friars, seeing that they be as desperate beasts past shame, that can lose nothing by clamours'. It was from such devout 'beasts' that some of the most powerful advocacy on both sides of a fractured Christendom was to emerge in subsequent decades.[71]

The Seculars

The circumstances of the secular Church are far less amenable to succinct summary than those of the regulars. The clergy were everywhere, and so intimately a part of the everyday religious life of all sixteenth-century people that to separate them and categorize them under the institutional headings normally employed by historians is to risk misunderstanding of their essential roles. They were those men who particularly represented the divine to the rest of the society: who marked out a Christian society by the discharge of their specialist functions and by the calibre of their lives.[72] Such duties and expectations could be said to be perdurable, but the late medieval priest was also set apart by high claims made for his mediatory powers, which constructed him, according to the *Sermones Discipuli*, as 'higher than kings, more blessed than angels, the maker of his Maker'.[73] The priest as celebrant and the priest as confessor were essential to the laity. Through the sacraments men gained access to spiritual reward, and in the central drama of the Mass experienced Christ in their midst. Through the cycle of confession, contrition, and penance they sought their own spiritual cleansing, and also often the purging of the community in the interests of charity and harmony.[74] These were not simple tasks. They might be practically burdensome when they involved the cure of souls in a parish with a large population or problems of access: at Doncaster the chantry commissioners under Henry VIII reported that there were

[71] Brown, 'Wolsey', 225–9.

[72] On the expectations contemporaries had of the seculars see Marshall, *Catholic Priesthood*; Swanson, 'Problems', P. Heath, *English Parish Clergy on the Eve of the Reformation* (1969), 1–18; M. Bowker, *The Secular Clergy in the Diocese of Lincoln, 1495–1520* (Cambridge, 1968), 110–13.

[73] J. Herolt, *Sermones Discipuli* (Rothomagi, 1511), fo. 111. Herolt's sermons were left in more English clerical wills of this period than the Bible: Marshall, *Catholic Priesthood*, 89.

[74] The role of confessor, in particular, was more doctrinally charged in the period before the Reformation than it had previously been: J. Bossy, 'The social history of confession in the age of the Reformation', *TRHS* 25 (1975), 21–38; L.G. Duggan, 'Fear and confession on the eve of the Reformation', *ARG* 75 (1984), 153–75.

'2000 houseling people' and excessive work for seven priests.[75] They were certainly spiritually burdensome, since they set the priest apart, making him both mediator between the divine and human and the exemplar to his flock. As the *Imitation of Christ* expressed it: 'When a priest sayeth Mass he honoureth God; he maketh angels glad; he edifieth the church; he helpeth the people that be living, and giveth rest to them that be dead, and maketh himself part-taker of all good deeds.'[76]

Sixteenth-century laymen may not have subscribed to the boldest claims of this high clericalism, but they had firm expectations of their rectors, vicars, or curates, chantry priests or guild chaplains. These could be summarized as the fulfilment of First Table duties by the faithful performance of the sacraments, and Second Table duties via a high standard of behaviour in society. The limited English visitation material available for the early sixteenth century seems consistently to show that parishioners complained most vocally about sexual and social misconduct on the one hand, and about failure to provide adequate services on the other. In the well-known returns for Lincoln diocese between 1514 and 1521 there were twenty-five accusations of sexual misconduct, and seventeen cases of complaint that services were not provided, small numbers when over 1,000 parishes were visited, but nevertheless more significant than other issues.[77] The sort of complaint made in 1480 against the priest of Kingston chapel in Bere Regis, Dorset, that he was not administering the sacraments every day, as was customary, is characteristic of lay anxieties.[78] Less common is the sort of positive affirmation of priestly behaviour shown in the case of Sir Robert Rhind, chaplain of Perth, who in 1547 was given the freedom of the city because he was so conscientious in saying the Mass that 'the whole community and neighbours, who rise early to their labours' could hear it.[79]

Laymen were confident in their judgements partly because they routinely hired and fired their local clergy. Parochial curates and guild chaplains were often directly accountable to the laity, especially in urban communities.[80] They were recruited because of their 'good fame' and dismissed for incontinency or incompetence. Ipswich parishioners referred to one of their inadequate chaplains as 'little Sir John' and at Ayr in 1534 the burgh council took the extreme step of firing all their hired chaplains

[75] Marshall, *Catholic Priesthood*, 13.
[76] E.J. Klein (ed.), *The Imitation of Christ from the First Edition of an English Translation Made c.1530 by Richard Whitford* (New York, 1941), 234: section from the Latin text is bk. 4, ch. 5.
[77] A.H. Thompson (ed.), *Visitations in the Diocese of Lincoln, 1517–1531*, LRS 33, 35 (1940–4).
[78] Brown, *Salisbury*, 80.
[79] D. McKay, 'Parish life in Scotland, 1500–1560', in McRoberts, *Scottish Reformation*, 90.
[80] J.J. Scarisbrick, *The Reformation and the English People* (Oxford, 1984), 24–5.

'till their dispositions improved'.[81] It is from wills that the clearest evidence emerges of what such men expected, especially of the 'specialized' priests that they proposed to employ to sing Masses after their death. Peter Marshall's striking finding was that over 80 per cent of his large sample of testators leaving money for Masses between 1500 and 1546 specified in some form the moral qualifications they expected in their employees. Priests were to be 'honest', 'virtuous', and 'of good conversation', indicating attitudes which risk being labelled quasi-Donatist, since they sit uneasily with the Church's *ex opere operato* understanding of the sacraments. Orthodox opinion moreover insisted that the priest did not need to be in a state of grace to render the sacrament efficacious: to argue otherwise would be to accept heretical criticism stretching from the Donatists to the Lollards.[82] More put the point most explicitly in his *Dialogue Concerning Heresies* when he argued that the sin of the priest does not detract from the nature of his liturgical actions, making the sacrifice 'to God as acceptable and to us as available for the thing itself, as though it were offered by a better man'.[83] In practice laymen seem to be untroubled by the doctrinal tension, accepting the automatic efficacy of sacramental grace without surrendering a sense that their priests should be men of virtue.[84]

Priests who had this access to the sacred were also liable to be the focus of lay expectations that migrated between the territories of 'orthodox' belief and 'magic', territories that were not neatly separated in contemporary perception.[85] The Welsh clergy, whose reputation as cursers was solemnly recorded by Tyndale, also had more positive roles as the creators of charms.[86] Salt and water blessed by the priest before the Mass each Sunday offered protection against the supernatural and disease. Holy girdles and other items blessed in this way, unlike the sacraments themselves, derived their power from the consecrator. Sacred things were possessed of objective power and, through the mediation of the priesthood, a world of sacramentals was constructed which provided necessary protection and security.[87] The obligation of the clergy in all of this was to remind laymen

[81] D. MacCulloch and J. Blatchly, 'Pastoral provision in the parishes of Tudor Ipswich', *C16J* 22 (1991), 458–9. J. Durkan, 'Chaplains in late medieval Scotland', *RSCHS* 20 (1979), 96.

[82] Marshall, *Catholic Priesthood*, 47–55.

[83] *CWTM*, vi. 299.

[84] Tanner, *Norwich*, 109. Swanson, 'Problems', 861.

[85] Ideas about the relationship between 'belief' and 'magic' in late medieval Europe have, of course, generated a vast literature. Most pertinent for the idea of separation between 'elite' or 'official' belief and popular practice are J. Delumeau, *Catholicism from Luther to Voltaire* (1977), and K.V. Thomas, *Religion and the Decline of Magic* (1971).

[86] G. Williams, *The Welsh Church from Conquest to Reformation* (Cardiff, 1976), 333–5.

[87] E. Duffy, *The Stripping of the Altars: Traditional Religion in England, 1400–1580* (1992), 281–2. For a good analysis of the significance of sacramentals in a European context see R.W. Scribner, *Popular Culture and Popular Movements in Reformation Germany* (1987), 5–8.

of the nature of sacred power. One Irish cleric in the early sixteenth century approved the use of holy water to cure cattle, provided that it ensured men did not turn to wise men, but that they linked prayer and trust in divine grace to the process of sprinkling.[88] Dependence on these offerings of the Church, as Eamon Duffy has forcefully argued, was not a matter of a popular set of beliefs manifesting themselves primarily in some Celtic 'twilight' zone, but in some measure the possession of all the devout and orthodox.[89] But belief in the automatic efficacy of holy things was always close to a mechanistic belief in the power of priestly actions to guarantee good fortune. And priests at times nurtured this belief, as in the rubric of the prayer recorded in Salisbury Cathedral: 'whosoever sayeth this prayer following in the worship of God and St Rock shall not die of the pestilence by the grace of God'.[90]

The other enduring obligation of the priesthood was that of instruction: a particular duty enjoined upon those who had the cure of souls, but in a more general sense a duty inherent in the office as part of the *imitatio christi*. The classic statement of this obligation in medieval England was Archbishop Pecham's provincial decree of 1281, ordering parish priests with cure of souls to expound the faith four times a year to their flock. They were to explain the fourteen articles of faith, the ten commandments and their gospel gloss, the seven works of mercy, principal virtues and deadly sins, and the seven sacraments.[91] Pecham's decree continued to be seen as a useful tool of parochial instruction until the eve of the Reformation. It was re-issued in England with official support at the York Convocation of 1518, Fox of Winchester and West of Ely were still encouraging its use in the last generation before the Reformation. In 1526 all priests in the Diocese of Armagh *inter anglicos* were instructed to acquire a copy.[92] *Ignorantia Sacerdotum* had earlier been translated into English by Bishop Stafford of Bath and Wells for the benefit of '*simplex sacerdos*'. Pecham's decree also distinguished clearly between the forms priestly instruction should normally take: a four-fold division of preaching, catechizing, confession, and the expounding of

---

[88] R. Gillespie, *Devoted People: Belief and Religion in Early Modern Ireland* (Manchester, 1997), 6, 68.

[89] Duffy, *Stripping of the Altars*, 266 ff. See also J. Bossy, 'Holiness and society', *PP* 75 (1977), 110–37.

[90] W.K. Clay (ed.), *Private Prayers Put forth by Authority during the Reign of Queen Elizabeth* (PS, Cambridge, 1851), 392 n. 1.

[91] Heath, *Parish Clergy*, 86–103. Marshall, *Catholic Priesthood*, 86–107.

[92] R.M. Haines, *Ecclesia Anglicana: Studies of the English Church in the Later Middle Ages* (Toronto, 1989), 134–5, 161. R. Houlbrooke, *Church Courts and People during the English Reformation* (Oxford, 1979), 199–200. F. Heal, 'Parish clergy and the Reformation in the Diocese of Ely', *Cambridge Antiquarian Society* 66 (1977), 149. H.A. Jefferies, 'Diocesan synods and convocations in Armagh on the eve of the Tudor Reformation', *Seanchas ard Mhacha* 16/2 (1995), 122.

sentences of excommunication. Not only was the decree regularly reiterated in subsequent legislation, it became the basis of several of the sermon cycles or homilies produced to support the practice of preaching in late medieval England.[93] There was, most famously, John Mirk's *Festial*, with its dependence upon the stories of the *Golden Legend*, but also the *quatuor sermones* and the *sermones discipuli*. All feature with some regularity in clerical wills—ten copies of the *sermones discipuli* for example in Peter Heath's study of Norwich clerical wills between 1500 and 1550—and evidence for their use can also be found occasionally in sources such as clerical commonplace books.[94]

Lay expectations are more difficult to penetrate here than in the case of the sacramental duties of the priesthood: no complaints of failure by the clergy to preach are found in Warham's 1511 visitation of Canterbury and only a handful in the great Lincoln visitations.[95] Wills, though they reveal a scattering of bequests for sermons, inevitably subordinate instruction to the singing of Masses. They also rather rarely included a desire for preaching even in elaborate arrangements for funerals and commemorations. And when sermons were requested, they seem to have been perceived less as forms of edification than as suffrages; a functional equivalent to Masses for the dead.[96] It would, however, be unwise to move from the proper assumption that instruction by the clergy concerned the laity less than the sacraments, to an argument that preaching and teaching were rejected. Pulpits became a regular feature of late medieval churches: England has over 200 surviving examples, and their ubiquity at the time is suggested by the 1529 Devonshire will of John Lane, who left money to a hundred neighbouring churches 'to pray for me in their pulpits'.[97] Where iconography survives, it indicates that teaching as well as prayer was supposed to be undertaken from these structures. It is clear that some laymen had high expectations of the preaching of some seculars, as well as regulars. While the friars may have been the traditional vehicles for powerful evangelizing sermons, urban elites also congregated to hear star preachers whatever their background.[98] The comment of the great fourteenth-

[93] G.H. Russell, 'Vernacular instruction of the laity in the later Middle Ages in England', *JRH* 2 (1962–3), 98–119.

[94] Heath, *Parish Clergy*, 87–9.

[95] K.L. Wood-Legh (ed.), *Kentish Visitations of Archbishop Warham and his Deputies, 1511–1512*, Kent Records 24 (1984). A.H. Thompson (ed.), *Visitations in the Diocese of Lincoln, 1517–1531*, LRS 33, 35 (1940–4).

[96] Duffy, *Stripping of the Altars*, 57. Wabuda, 'Provision of Preaching', 183–4. One London document of the late fifteenth century rated sermons as less efficacious than Masses but preferable to 'private or vocal prayer'.

[97] R. Whiting, *The Blind Devotion of the People: Popular Religion and the English Reformation* (Cambridge, 1989), 237.

[98] M. Dowling, 'John Fisher and the preaching ministry', *ARG* 82 (1991), 287–309.

century preacher Thomas Brinton, that it was best to preach in London for there men were more discerning and better informed than in the rest of the realm, has many sixteenth-century resonances.[99] In a more modest market centre, King's Lynn, Margery Kempe had recorded in the early fifteenth century 'how fast the people came running to hear the sermon'.[100]

There has been a tendency in recent studies of sixteenth-century religion to privilege the role of the secular clergy as spiritual mentors and agents of the divine at the expense of the evaluation of their institutional experience. While such an approach may have the merit of enabling us better to see how contemporaries wished their clergy to behave, and even on occasions how the latter performed, the institutional experience cannot be neglected. Men were trained, recruited, organized, paid, and disciplined as part of a system which must have appeared almost as divinely ordained as the Mass or the rites of passage. Certainly one of its most questionable features, adherence to hierarchy and hence to acceptance of sharp differences of wealth, privilege, and responsibility, was so integral that none except a few radically heretical voices saw fit to challenge it. A rather larger number of voices questioned the level of the institution's involvement with the lay world: the most effective of these were often found in the ranks of the clergy themselves. However, the realities of power inevitably led to accommodation with the existing order of things.

Training and recruitment of the clergy has recently been judged a moderate success story in Britain and Ireland in the half-century before the reformations. The output of a graduate elite from the universities increased, especially in Scotland, where the new foundations of St Andrews, Glasgow, and Aberdeen began to make their mark on the upper ranks of the clergy.[101] Some of this elite found its way into parochial livings, even in Ireland, where graduates were a very small minority of the secular clergy; the names of those gaining benefices in the poor diocese of Dromore in the 1530s include a number of those styled *magister*.[102] In the great diocese of Lincoln laymen, perhaps the group of patrons least concerned with educational qualifications, were appointing 11.5 per cent graduate clergy by the early sixteenth century.[103] At the apex of the

---

[99] Ibid., 293.

[100] S.B. Meech and H.E. Allen (eds.), *The Book of Margery Kempe*, EETS os 212 (1940), 149.

[101] Cowan, *Scottish Reformation*, 15–20.

[102] H.A. Jefferies, 'The Diocese of Dromore on the eve of the Tudor Reformation', in L. Proudfoot (ed.), *Down: History and Society* (Dublin, 1997), 128.

[103] Bowker, *Secular Clergy*, 42–6. It is important to note that those who are *magistri*, that is who should have covered the full masters' course to graduate, are not necessarily a majority of those who had attended university. Estimates suggest that only a third of matriculands may have proceeded to a BA and only a sixth to an MA.

English system, in London, at least 60 per cent of those holding benefices between 1521 and 1546 were graduates.[104] This last figure was, however, wholly exceptional. For the vast majority, who did not have access to university, little changed in this period, though it may be that some extension in formal educational provision slightly shifted the balance between the numbers attending school and those who had to manage merely with informal local resources. Moran's study of educational provision in late medieval York shows a sharp increase in both reading and grammar schools between 1501 and 1548.[105]

General recruitment levels to the priesthood were high for most areas that can be adequately documented. The average of 187 ordinations per year for seculars in York diocese in the period from the 1470s to the 1530s is unusual, but in Lincoln the average between 1496 and 1520 was 105 elevated to the priesthood, though this includes regulars as well as seculars.[106] At Lichfield the figure for major and minor orders together was always over 100 between the 1470s and 1530. Only in some southern dioceses, notably Chichester, do there seem to have been periods of sluggish recruitment, and even there a vigorous bishop like Robert Sherburne could increase numbers in the last generation before the Reformation.[107] Beyond England it is impossible to calculate recruitment levels from ordination lists, and numerical success has to be inferred from the availability of clergy to fill chantries and collegiate posts, as well as parochial benefices.[108] It would seem that on the eve of the Reformation many English dioceses had a ratio of unbeneficed to beneficed clergy of between one and two to one, and the same may be true in favoured parts of Scotland. In some of the northern English sees there was an even higher ratio in favour of the unbeneficed.[109] Although the percentage of the unbeneficed had fallen in most areas between the figures available from the 1377 poll tax and those for the 1522 subsidy, local examples still sometimes show

[104] S. Brigden, *London and the Reformation* (Oxford, 1989), 58. An average figure for these decades would probably be nearer to 30 per cent.
[105] J.A. Moran, 'Clerical recruitment in the Diocese of York, 1340–1530', *JEH* 34 (1983), 53.
[106] Moran, 'Recruitment', 49–51. Bowker, *Secular Clergy*, 38–9.
[107] Swanson, *Church and Society*, 34–6. S. Lander, 'The Diocese of Chichester: Episcopal Reform under Robert Sherburne and its Aftermath', University of Cambridge Ph.D. (1974), 190–5.
[108] See for example Sanderson, *Ayrshire*, 12–14. J. Durkan, 'Chaplains in late medieval Scotland', *RSCHS* 20 (1979), 91–103.
[109] In Lancashire and parts of Durham, for example, the ratio of the beneficed to parochial curates was nearer to 4:1, because of the nature of the large upland parishes: C. Haigh, *Reformation and Resistance in Tudor Lancashire* (Cambridge, 1975), 32–3. L.M. Stevens-Benham, 'The Durham clergy 1494–1540: a study of continuity and mediocrity among the unbeneficed', in D. Marcombe (ed.), *The Last Principality: Politics, Religion and Society in the Bishopric of Durham, 1494–1660* (Nottingham, 1987), 17.

extraordinary concentrations of clergy, like the case of Holy Trinity, Hull, where there were seventeen chaplains in 1525.[110] In Scotland, with its roughly 1,200 parishes, it has been estimated that there were approximately 3,000 clergy in the mid-sixteenth century. Here also the burghs, each with only one central parish, could display great concentrations of clerics, like the forty or so who served the altars in St Giles, Edinburgh.[111] Among the various complaints about the state of the Church, absence of manpower is one that rarely features in Britain or Ireland. When parochial livings, or even bishoprics in the case of Ireland, were vacant or untended the explanation was usually economic or bound up with complex legal or personal issues, rather than a consequence of shortage of recruits.[112] Indeed the problems of the Church were if anything those created by an excess of specialists: long delays before preferment was available; fragmentation of parochial funding among too many individual priests; insecurity because of the temporary nature of much employment. The energy that the Gaelic clergy of Ireland and of the Scottish Highlands put into 'Rome running' offers another possible indication of an imbalance between supply and demand in the clerical estate.[113] Thomas More, as so often, acknowledged the problem, and then turned it to critical purpose: 'there is more plenty of priests than of good men... Now runneth every rascal and boldly offereth himself for able.' In Utopia there were only thirteen priests in each city.[114]

Those 'bold' men who pursued the priesthood as a means of social mobility were all too liable to be disappointed. The Church adhered to degree and hierarchy almost as firmly as lay society. Degree was affirmed by the separation of orders—minor from major, the diaconate from the priesthood—and by the patterns of office holding—rural dean, archdeacon and bishop, canon and dean. Less formally hierarchy was affirmed by the gap that existed between the beneficed and the unbeneficed, and between the ordinary parochial clergy and those whose qualifications or connections marked them out as likely pluralists, sinecurists and officeholders. There is plenty of evidence that the beneficed and unbeneficed were sharply differentiated by contemporaries, even when the context of

---

[110] A.K. McHardy, 'Careers and disappointments in the late medieval Church: some English evidence', in W. Sheils and D. Woods (eds.), *The Ministry, Clerical and Lay*, SCH 26 (1989), 113–17. 'The East Riding clergy in 1525–6', *YAJ* 24 (1917), 73–4.

[111] Donaldson, *Scottish Reformation*, 16. Lynch, *Edinburgh and the Reformation*, 28–9.

[112] M. Zell, 'Economic problems of the parochial clergy in the sixteenth century', in R. O'Day and F. Heal (eds.), *Princes and Paupers in the English Church, 1500–1800* (Leicester, 1981), 19–44.

[113] J. Bannerman, 'The Lordship of the Isles', in J. Brown (ed.), *Scottish Society in the Fifteenth Century* (1977), 230.

[114] *CWTM*, vi. 1. 301; iv. 227. Brigden, *London*, 46.

office was not particularly significant.[115] The English subsidy commissioners of 1522, for example, always distinguished between the two categories when making their returns.[116] This careful separation seems largely to conform to social and economic reality. Chaplains, stipendiaries, and chantry priests gained benefices rather rarely in England in the early sixteenth century: in the archdeaconry of Leicester, for example, only nine curates found a benefice between 1520 and 1547. In Kent, just over 10 per cent of the clerical proletariat gained benefices between 1538 and 1550.[117] If the chaplain or curate did succeed in crossing this crucial status division, it often took many years to do so. Of the twenty-six curates recorded in Boston, Lincolnshire, in 1500, eight had received livings by 1526, but in several cases the process had taken more than ten years.[118] Degree and differentiation were also visible in the forms of employment offered to the unbeneficed. They might have some security of tenure as perpetual curates or as vicars pensionary, but were more likely to be salaried, paid either by an absentee cleric or by the laity to perform various duties. This could, in some cases, threaten the deference that ecclesiastics believed was due to the clerical estate.[119]

It is more difficult to pattern the difference between the 'ordinary' incumbent, whether rector or vicar with cure of souls, and the rest of the secular clergy. The obligation to reside, to exercise cure, provides one measure of contrast, sinecurists in orders being common enough in all parts of the British Isles, but most routinely found where appropriation of benefices was at its densest: in Scotland, Wales, and parts of Ireland. A second measure of contrast comes from the system of licensing non-residence for those who did have cure of souls. Margaret Bowker's close study of this process in Lincoln diocese from 1514 to 1521 showed that those licensed were usually those able for whatever reason to pursue wider financial advantage. More than a third of the absentees were graduates, a significantly larger group than that of all graduates appointed to benefices, the largest number were 'pure' pluralists, but many were also studying at university, or were in service to crown or private individuals. Among the Lincoln pluralists many cannot now be distinguished by any pattern of connection or career, but there were significant concentrations of men linked to the great families of the diocese, and personnel of cathedrals or collegiate

---

[115] Zell, 'Parochial clergy', 21–30.

[116] J. Cornwall, *Wealth and Society in Early Sixteenth Century England* (1988), 87–94.

[117] J.F. Fuggles, 'The parish clergy in the Archdeaconry of Leicester, 1520–1540', *Transactions of the Leicestershire Archaeological and Historical Society* 46 (1970–1), 26.

[118] Bowker, *Secular Clergy*, 71–2.

[119] Heath, *Parish Clergy*, 24–6. I B. Cowan, 'Vicarages and the cure of souls in medieval Scotland', *RSCHS* 16 (1963), 123.

churches.[120] Pluralism and absenteeism in a Scottish diocese like Dunblane can be linked to much the same pattern of ambition—men serving the crown, or acting as agents of the nobility: graduates absent by virtue of academic status.[121] The Lincoln categories serve to identify the types of commitment undertaken by the secular clergy who were either wholly detached from their benefices or might, in an infelicitous piece of language, be called 'partially parochial'. The last might be absent for specific periods, or at particular points in their careers; they were often compelled into residence by the efforts of their ordinaries. They also included many whose intentions were to continue to evade the mundane business of parochial ministry.[122]

It is impossible to attach any effective statistics to what these absentees were doing with their time. The various categories of diocesan official, and especially the prebends of cathedrals, undoubtedly absorbed many livings. In any one diocese this group might not be unduly weighty. If we take, for example, a medium-sized diocese like Chichester, which had 278 benefices, its senior personnel can be readily identified as the bishop, two archdeacons, the chancellor, registrar, a small number of proctors and apparitors to staff the diocesan courts, a dean, and thirty prebendaries, only between two and six of the last normally being residentiaries.[123] Since the diocese happened to have only two collegiate churches one might reasonably conclude that it was hierarchical without being unduly top-heavy. It has been estimated that there were fifty-five 'internal pluralists' drawing revenues from the Chichester parishes. Of course there were also some absentee rectors and vicars engaged far more widely in affairs of church and state, unconstrained by diocesan boundaries. An extreme example was Thomas Brent, a lawyer and chaplain to Henry VII, who held six rectories or vicarages (not always in conjunction) plus prebends in Warwick and London, the deanery of South Malling and the hospital of St Bartholomew by Rye. What Brent was actually *doing* during a long career was to serve at court, as almoner and executor to Elizabeth Woodville as well as royal chaplain. Chichester seems to have been fortunate in having only a limited number of rich benefices that were attractive to this sort of pluralist, though even a handful of examples, like the livings in the gift of the earl of Arundel, contributed to absenteeism.[124] When large

---

[120] Bowker, *Secular Clergy*, 85–109.

[121] J.R. Todd, 'Pre-Reformation cure of souls in Dunblane diocese', *Innes Review* 26 (1975), 28–34.

[122] Jefferies, 'Dromore', 125.

[123] Thomson, *Early Tudor Church*, 60–72. S. Lander, 'The church courts and the Reformation in the Diocese of Chichester, 1500 to 1558', in R. O'Day and F. Heal (eds.), *Continuity and Change: Personnel and Administration of the Church in England, 1500–1642* (Leicester, 1976), 215–23.

[124] Heath, *Parish Clergy*, 51–2. Lander, 'Chichester', 211–12.

parishes produced significant wealth the scale of absenteeism was greater: in Lancashire in 1500 83 per cent of the graduate incumbents were non-residents.[125]

English dioceses seem to have been able to sustain this third tier of the clergy, partly because of the number of its parishes, over 9,000, and the relative wealth of many of its benefices. There had also been some decline since the fourteenth century in the number of clergy occupied by secular tasks, thereby limiting one reason for absenteeism.[126] In Scotland, where one specialist estimates that more than half the clerical body was still employed upon secular tasks in the early sixteenth century, the situation was far worse. There appropriation of 86 per cent of rectories and at least 56 per cent of perpetual vicarages released men and money from the parishes on a grand scale.[127] A good idea of the pattern at diocesan level can be gained by looking at Dunkeld, where the cathedral staff has been estimated at fifty in a diocese comprising sixty-nine parish churches.[128] The Scots were also proportionately far more susceptible to absenteeism created by the development of collegiate churches than their English counterparts. With thirteen cathedrals and forty collegiate churches to sustain in a system with just over 1,000 parishes, many of them poor, strain was inevitable. The Irish churches in some ways resemble the Scots: appropriation of benefices was the norm and in English Ireland was used largely to sustain a body of cathedral clergy who employed stipendiary curates to serve their cures. St Patrick's, Dublin, was the very model of an English secular cathedral, but its prebendaries had few lands and had to maintain themselves almost entirely from the income of the parishes. Bishop Montgomery's optimistic assertion of 1609 that the benefices were bestowed on those training for priest's orders was far from the truth.[129]

Even though the laicization of parts of the bureaucracy of the late medieval state may have curtailed the employment opportunities of some of the well-connected clergy, there was still the expectation that with proper training and contacts men would prosper in non-parochial jobs.

---

[125] Haigh, *Lancashire*, 29.

[126] R.N. Swanson, 'Learning and livings: university study and clerical careers in late medieval England', *History of Universities* 6 (1986–7), 81–103.

[127] Macfarlane, 'Scottish church', 39. I.B. Cowan, 'Some aspects of the appropriation of parish churches in Scotland', *RSCHS* 13 (1959), 204–5.

[128] Yellowlees, 'Dunkeld', 74–5.

[129] J. Murray, 'The Tudor Diocese of Dublin', University of Dublin, Trinity College Dublin, Ph.D. (1997), 38–42. The Irish situation was complicated by marked differences between Gaelic areas and those of Norman settlement, but also between Ulster and the West; K.W. Nicholls, 'Rectory, vicarage and parish in western Irish dioceses', *Journal of the Royal Society of Antiquities of Ireland* 101 (1971), 53–84. P.K. Egan, 'Diocesan organisation: Clonfert', *Proceedings of the Irish Catholic Historical Commission* (1956), 4–8.

And for the graduates of the century before the Reformation proper training meant study of the laws. In Oxford and Cambridge, in St Andrews,
Aberdeen, and Glasgow, the higher degrees in law flourished in some
cases at the expense of theology, which could be undertaken only after
the long initial training in arts.[130] Arts training in itself was no necessary
guarantee of success within the Church. As a group the lawyers were
highest on the ladder of promotion. Hence a steady pressure, despite the
founders' intentions, to shift colleges like New and Magdalen at Oxford
towards a fellowship dominated by lawyers. The Scottish colleges also
showed a marked preference for canon law studies, though at Glasgow
John Major's efforts to revive theology at the expense of the laws did bear
fruit.[131] The absence of universities in Ireland did not prevent a number
of potential clergy from studying abroad, usually at Oxford in this period,
and they seem almost universally to have studied law if they had moved
beyond a master's degree.[132] This training, and the rewards within and
without the Church that routinely accrued to those well qualified in the
laws, may have been of little relevance to the parishes, but as we have
seen it may well have fostered litigiousness on the part of the higher clergy
that was at odds with ideas of charity and good pastoral service. It also
risked depriving the Church of active preachers and controversialists if
there were a threat to orthodoxy.[133]

It was the financing of the clergy that inevitably produced some of the
closest and most difficult encounters with the laity, since it was the latter's
tithes or teinds that sustained much of the grand edifice of the possessioner
Church. The higher clergy took what most regarded as their share of the
offerings of the faithful through the system of appropriated rectories or
vicarages. The burden of appropriations on parish finance was significant,
and the pressure was increasing in the century before the Reformation.
Between 1291 and 1535 the number of appropriated parishes in England
rose from under 2,000 to about 3,300, most of the late increase coming
from grants to new educational foundations or collegiate churches. Yet this
high figure still left two-thirds of English livings unappropriated, with a
higher percentage in some of the prosperous dioceses in the south and
east.[134] Scottish appropriation followed a similar pattern, though it was the

---

[130] Catto and Evans, *Late Medieval Oxford*, 526–9, 582. There is an extensive debate on the
career prospects for university graduates in the late medieval period: see Swanson, 'Learning
and livings', 85–7.

[131] J. Durkan and J. Kirk, *The University of Glasgow 1451–1577* (Glasgow, 1977), 132–3, 158–62.

[132] A. Lynch, 'Religion in late medieval Ireland', *Archivium Hibernicum* 36 (1981), 4–6, 11–12.

[133] R.W. Hays, 'Welsh students at Oxford and Cambridge Universities in the Middle Ages',
Welsh History Review 4 (1968–9), 325–61. Six per cent of Oxford's recorded alumni were from
Ireland, Scotland, and Wales before 1500.

[134] Swanson, *Church and Society*, 44.

rapid growth in university colleges and the fashion for collegiate foundations that produced massive expropriations. Some Scottish appropriations redirected funds away from the parish on a scale rarely found in England. The vicarage of Dunblane, for example, was worth 320 marks Scots, and formed part of the dean's prebend; its vicar pensionary had an income of £8, £2 less than the basic sum thought necessary by the Scottish church for its clergy before the inflation of the sixteenth century became significant.[135] The experience of the Welsh and Irish churches was not dissimilar. In Wales some 65 per cent of all benefices were appropriated by the 1530s, and once again the late grants were often made to diocesan officials or colleges, to men of the secular Church rather than the regulars. In the 1490s the bishop and chapter of St David's had one of those temporary moments of self-denial that indicated the unease of the possessioners. No more parochial revenues were to be taken since 'the sustenance of the sowers of the Divine Word is taken away and want evidently increases every day among our subjects to the detriment... of our whole diocese of St David's'.[136] Ireland *inter anglicos* experienced similar pressures to those in Wales, with 85 per cent of benefices appropriated in the diocese of Dublin.[137] In the Gaelic lands, tithe had long been divided between those who served the cures and the hereditary 'erenaghs' and 'coarbs', or heads of the tenants occupying church lands within the parish. The erenaghs might simply be laymen, but many of them were priestly families and supplied many of the parishes with their incumbents. Such lineages could hold important livings at the diocesan level as well, an interweaving of layman and priest, parish incumbent and higher clergy, that makes it difficult to make comparisons with other parts of the British Isles.[138]

Those who were left to staff the parishes, usually vicars or curates, had to manage either upon the share of the tithe left to their portion, or on a combination of salary and offerings. Taxation rarely produces the best of sentiments in either payer or payee, and the pre-Reformation Church provides plenty of cases of clerics who, unlike Chaucer's parson, were not slow to 'cursen for their tithe'.[139] Occasionally a confrontation about tithe could

---

[135] Cowan, *Scottish Reformation*, 59–61. J. Kirk (ed.), *The Books of the Assumptions of the Thirds of Benefices*, British Academy Records in Economic and Social History 21 (1995), p. xxxii.

[136] Williams, *Welsh Church*, 168–9.

[137] Murray, 'Tudor Diocese of Dublin', 297. A. Ford, 'The Protestant Reformation in Ireland', in C. Brady and R. Gillespie (eds.), *Natives and Newcomers: The Making of Irish Colonial Society, 1534–1641* (Dublin, 1986), 68, gives the lower figure of 60 per cent for all dioceses *inter Anglicos*.

[138] K. Simms, 'Frontiers in the Irish church—regional and cultural', in T. Barry, R. Frame, and K. Simms (eds.), *Colony and Frontier in Medieval Ireland* (1995), 177–8. Nicholls, 'Rectory', 66.

[139] For figures and interpretations see B.L. Woodcock, *Medieval Ecclesiastical Courts in the Diocese of Canterbury* (1952), 86. Tanner, *Norwich*, 6. R. Houlbrooke, *Church Courts and People during the English Reformation* (Oxford, 1979), 101–40.

assume principled proportions even though no other evidence of heterodoxy was involved. David Straiton of Woodstone in Angus was burned for
heresy although his principal fault was to challenge the right of the prior of
St Andrews to the teinds of fish.[140] The issues more usually at stake in tithe
litigation are not so much the principle of payment, or even resentment
against those parts of the payment that went to absentees, but arguments
about methods of assessment. New crops, such as saffron in eastern England,
were guaranteed to produce dispute and evasion, and problems could be
created by awkward parochial boundary arrangements or shared community rights. As a generalization English evidence seems to suggest that there
was a greater likelihood of tithe disputes in or near urban communities than
in fully rural parishes. The extreme manifestation of this is the problem of
London, where the personal, rather than agricultural (or predial), nature of
tithe offerings made them difficult to collect. Between 1520 and 1546 over a
third of city parishes are known to have had tithe disputes that reached
court, and, while the individual causes of conflict were very diverse, underlying many was the problem of an equitable agreement of dues in a complex
commercial environment.[141] Elsewhere real acrimony was often it seemed
generated by anxieties that were only partially financial: as in the case of the
parson of Swainsthorpe in Norfolk who collected his tithe on horseback,
with his supposed mistress on the pillion.[142] The other aspect of tithe litigation that is worth noting is that cases often did not involve lay–clerical
relations, but were between incumbents and clerical appropriators. A third
of the cases that came before the Norwich consistory court in the early
sixteenth century were of this last type.[143]

The evidence of tithe disputes does not support an argument that the
laity were disposed to any fundamental rejection of clerical rights. The
same may broadly be true of sources of revenue that in aggregate were
common to more of the parochial clergy than tithe: offerings and mortuaries. Mortuaries seem to have been the most unpopular of the various
dues that could be demanded by clerics, and this not merely because of
Hunne's case.[144] There are other examples of solemn protests such as that

---

[140] F. Bardgett, *Scotland Reformed: The Reformation in Angus and the Mearns* (Edinburgh, 1989), 22.
[141] Swanson, *Church and Society*, 212–15. J.A.F. Thomson, 'Tithe disputes in later medieval
London', *EHR* 53 (1963), 15–16. Brigden, *London*, 52.
[142] Heath, *Parish Clergy*, 149.
[143] Houlbrooke, *Church Courts*, 146.
[144] Richard Hunne challenged the London clergy on three separate issues in 1511–12. The
most famous of the three was his refusal to give his dead son's winding sheet as mortuary fee to
the parson of St Mary Matfelon, Whitechapel, for burying the child. The complexity of the
case, and Hunne's mysterious death in the Lollards' Tower, have produced a wide range of
historical interpretations. Good recent discussions are in Brigden, *London*, 98–103 and
W.R. Cooper, 'Richard Hunne', *Reformation*, 1 (1996), 221–51.

made by the inhabitants of Kingston-on-Thames in 1514 that the present incumbent 'hath taken and daily taketh and withholds the old ancient custom with us in taking of mortuaries otherwise than hath been taken and used time out of mind'.[145] Disputes about mortuary were the most common source of litigation before the commissary for Buckinghamshire in the early sixteenth century, and the more limited Scottish evidence indicates similar resentment.[146] Issues included who could claim exemption, at what rate mortuary could be levied, and in what circumstances local custom could be modified. The alacrity with which some parishes opposed mortuaries after the 1529 legislation also hints at earlier resentments.[147] Christopher St German, scarcely a disinterested observer, chose an obvious target when he claimed that 'there were few things within this realm that caused more variance among the people'.[148] Yet the payments of offerings and dues for services rendered seem to have been largely acceptable, and the clergy must often have adjusted their demands to customs that were likely to secure good community relations.

Conflict about tithes and dues could readily be caused by bad judgement or greed on the part of individual clergy or laymen. If any cause has to be generalized, however, the most obvious explanation would surely be that clerical poverty must often have driven the demands of individuals. The gaping financial gulfs between the possessioner Church and many of those who served the parishes are readily documented. Some of the most systematic sources of evidence available to the ecclesiastical historian are the returns of the 1535 survey the *Valor Ecclesiasticus* and its Irish equivalent. These can be supplemented for England with the subsidy figures for 1522. In Scotland there is nothing so early, but prior to the assumption of the thirds of benefices by the crown in 1561 a general survey of church wealth was undertaken.[149] From these sources historians have been able to deduce significant evidence of poverty in all parochial systems. In Scottish parishes, vicars pensionary, the group most easily traced in 1561, were often paid no more than £6 to £8 Scots, although church councils had long since established that 10 marks was inadequate, and by 1559 had set a level of 24 marks as the minimum clerical stipend.[150] In Ireland the complex figures derived from the *Valor* show 64 per cent of benefices in the

---

[145] Heath, *Parish Clergy*, 155.

[146] Bowker, *Secular Clergy*, 149–51. Durkan, 'Chaplains', 99–100.

[147] Whiting, *Blind Devotion*, 132–3 for Devon cases post-1529.

[148] C. St German, 'A treatise concerning the division between the spirituality and temporalty', in *CWTM*, ix. 194.

[149] *Valor Ecclesiasticus*, 6 vols. (Record Comm., 1825–34). *Valor Beneficiorum Ecclesiasticorum in Hibernia* (Dublin, 1741). Cornwall, *Wealth and Society*. Kirk, *Thirds of Benefices*, pp. xxxii–xxxiii.

[150] Kirk, *Thirds of Benefices*, p. xxxii.

documented dioceses with incomes of under £5 sterling, and no less than 85 per cent worth less than £10.[151] £10 is usually taken as the figure necessary to keep an incumbent above the poverty line in England. In Wales 70 per cent of livings fell below the £10 boundary, though only a third of these were in the poorest category.[152] The beneficed in England fared somewhat better, but almost half still apparently fell beneath the crucial boundary. Moreover the proletariat of chaplains, stipendary curates, and the like, were poorly paid: the average paid to North Lanca-shire curates and chaplains in 1524 was £2. 9s. 6d. per annum, while in the East Riding of Yorkshire it was about £4.[153] On the other hand Ken-tish chaplains averaged £5 to £6 and in general chantry chaplains fared better, a norm in the south-east of England being £6. 13s. 4d. The only legislation governing such payments in England was a fifteenth-century statute that set the maximum payment for chaplains at £5. 6s. 8d.[154]

It is more difficult to extract full meaning from these figures. Two issues had an obvious bearing on the situation of the parochial clergy. The first is whether the apparent poverty of stipends and benefices was re-flected in actual deprivation among the priesthood. Here the availability of additional income from dues and services not easily quantified has to be taken into account, as does access to glebe or other forms of exploiting additional resources. Moreover, cost of living calculations should be a necessary part of evaluation. It is evident from the English figures that it was more expensive to employ a chaplain in the south-east than elsewhere and that this must reflect in part a difference in cost of living.[155] At the other extreme, the exiguity of Irish livings appears somewhat less grim when mapped against differentials in cost of living and in the economic expectations of the rest of the society. Nevertheless, such mitigating factors do not serve to disguise the reality of clerical poverty. A surplus of priests, at least in England and Lowland Scotland, helped to constrict pay rises in a time of inflation. Bishop Stokesley of London faced a protest from local curates in 1531 complaining that 'twenty nobles [£6. 13s. 4d.] a year is but a bare living for a priest, for now victual and everything in manner is so dear'.[156] Studies of wills and inventories of the unbeneficed in England show some examples of those who by good fortune or effi-

[151] S.G. Ellis, 'Economic problems of the Church: why the Reformation failed in Ireland', *JEH* 41 (1990), 248–57.
[152] Williams, *Welsh Church*, 273, 285.
[153] Heath, *Parish Clergy*, 173–4.
[154] Zell, 'Economic problems', 26–7.
[155] Zell, 'Economic problems', 27. The absence of any attempt to compare wealth creates problems in the analyses of both Williams and Ellis.
[156] Brigden, *London*, 49.

ciency accumulated some goods, but also plenty of evidence of the sort of poverty that left behind movables worth only a pound or two.[157]

The second, perhaps unanswerable, question, is what influence relative or absolute deprivation had on the quality of spiritual services rendered by the parish clergy. In some instances, where benefices were left empty and parishes not served, the failures of the system were evident. A handful of parishes in Kent at the time of Warham's visitation in 1511 were explicitly stated to be neglected because of the poverty of the living.[158] But, as we have already seen, given available manpower it was unusual to find parishes left without any curate for significant periods. Poverty might also be associated with failure to maintain the material fabric of the church, and so provide parishioners with the proper environment for worship. However, chancels were the responsibility of the most prosperous group of clergy, the rectors, and it was often rich absentees, rather than residents, who were most at fault.[159] In Ireland the parishes of the Pale and marches *inter Anglicos* could only be staffed by appointing Gaelic clergy to fill livings insufficiently attractive to the English. The bishops thereby breached the legal bar against Gaels established in the fourteenth century, and stored trouble for the future when evangelism for the new faith needed English-speaking clerics.[160] Beyond the acknowledgement of these identifiable problems contemporaries usually argued about the consequences of poverty from predisposing values. Thus humanists regularly linked poverty and ignorance as the vices of the parochial system, regarding the latter as tantamount to neglect.[161] Modern historians have, crudely, divided between those who follow humanist analysis and those who argue that it was more important that the clergy had a certain standing in local society, and could perform key sacramental duties efficiently, than that they were well-paid or learned. If we take parochial complaints against the clergy at face value the latter view has much to commend it, though two caveats may be in order. Parishioners seem to have been most inclined to complain about clergy at the two extremes of the hierarchical system. They assailed the affluent possessioners, whether individuals or monastic appropriators, who neglected church fabric and sometimes failed to provide proper deputies, and they also challenged the unbeneficed, whose deficiencies might indeed at times be associated with that combination of poverty and ignorance that so troubled reforming humanists.

---

[157] J. Pound, 'Clerical poverty in the early sixteenth century: some East Anglian evidence', *JEH* 37 (1986), 389–96. Stevens-Benham, 'Durham clergy', 21.
[158] *Visitations of Warham*, 133–4, 223–4.
[159] The best analysis of the problems of maintenance is in Bowker, *Secular Clergy*, 125–36.
[160] M.A. Lyons, *Church and Society in County Kildare, c. 1470–1547* (Dublin, 2000), 74–8.
[161] Marshall, *Catholic Priesthood*, 213–14.

The deficiency of the lesser clergy that apparently most often exercised the laity was sexual misdemeanour. Having a woman within the household produced the largest number of comments in Lincoln visitations between 1514 and 1521, 126 from 1,000 parishes; and even though many of these women were *non suspecte*, only twenty-five being clearly reported as undesirable, there was always an edge of anxiety in the presentation of women associated with priests.[162] Chichester produced 15 per cent of parishes in which there was complaint about clerical incontinency in the first decade of the sixteenth century.[163] Other figures were lower: like the 1499 visitation of Suffolk that produced only five complaints of immorality among 478 parishes.[164] Small numbers of complaints of this last kind have been taken to indicate either that there were few delinquents, or that failures did not trouble the laity. In the case of England, the latter supposition is unconvincing: popular literature was replete with examples of jesting hostility against lewd priests, and Protestant polemic found a rich vein of existing complaint on which to build when it attacked the depravity of the clergy.[165] Laymen who denounced specific priests often did so in unequivocally hostile form. The constable of St Breock, Cornwall, described Sir Matthew Poldon as having 'ordered his life and living contrary to the laws of Almighty God'.[166] The parson of Shawell in Leicestershire was attacked by one of his parishioners as 'a man of evil disposition . . . [an] evil example of all good Christian people'.[167] Even Tyndale thought that the English had assimilated the Hildebrandine reforms more fully than much of Europe and that laymen would take their clergy to law 'to put away their whores'.[168]

It may therefore be that the actual standards of clerical chastity reflected in the visitation records possess some objective reality—anxiety displayed whenever there was a hint of vice; a small, but deeply troublesome number of cases of real scandal. On the distinction between general sexual misdemeanour and concubinage there is ambiguity in the records. Historians can cite plenty of cases in which *de facto* toleration of 'hearthmates' and their bastards seems to have occurred, Bishop Bonner being the most famous offspring of such a union in this period.[169] Yet Peter Marshall is

---

[162] Bowker, *Secular Clergy*, 116–20.

[163] Lander, 'Church courts', 218.

[164] C. Harper-Bill, 'A late medieval visitation: the Diocese of Norwich in 1499', *Proceedings of the Suffolk Institute of Archaeology and History* 34 (1977), 35–48.

[165] Marshall, *Catholic Priesthood*, 143–6. H.L. Parish, *Clerical Marriage and the English Reformation: Precedent, Policy and Practice* (Aldershot, 2000).

[166] Whiting, *Blind Devotion*, 129.

[167] Marshall, *Catholic Priesthood*, 152.

[168] H. Walter (ed.), *Doctrinal Treatises of William Tyndale* (PS, Cambridge, 1848), 41.

[169] Haigh, *Lancashire*, 50.

surely correct to argue that any display of unchastity was thought by many to pollute the sacraments that offered access to salvation.[170] There are still some troubling problems to consider, especially in relation to the apparent chasm between English standards and those of the rest of the archipelago. If the historian possessed merely the surviving evidence from provincial councils and episcopal decrees it might be legitimate to assume that the same standards of sexual discipline were being enforced throughout these islands. Wolsey's provincial constitutions of 1518 reiterated a decree of William Greenfield that threatened women living as priests' concubines with excommunication and possible denial of ecclesiastical burial.[171] Irish provincial and diocesan synods sternly forbade concubinage and individual priests were sometimes admonished before these meetings. The Scots chose to use the decree of the Council of Basel against concubinage as the first of their reforming measures to be enacted by the 1549 Provincial Council.[172]

But differences of cultural assumption were displayed on this issue more fully than in any other within late medieval Catholicism in Britain and Ireland. In Gaelic Ireland, in much of Scotland, and in Celtic Wales concubinage, or rather what is better described as civil marriage, remained a norm for the secular clergy.[173] Its commonplace quality is suggested by the fact that at least three Welsh Tudor bishops, William Glyn, Richard Davies, and Rowland Meyrick, were the product of such unions.[174] This has to be understood, as Irish historians have argued most fully, in terms of the different laws of inheritance, which produced for both laity and clergy an acceptance of concubinage contracts throughout the culture. So, when the reforming friars began in the fifteenth century to write against unchaste clergy in Ireland, one of their key targets was the dowry that gave 'wives' their security and status. The uphill nature of their task is suggested by the comment of the *Annals of Ulster* on Cathal Óg Maguire, canon of Clogher and father of at least twelve children, who died in 1498: '[a] gem of purity... [a] dove for purity of heart and [a] turtle for chastity'.[175] The legal position of clerical companions seems almost as critical in Wales, where both English and Welsh law gave them some of the security that

---

[170] Marshall, *Catholic Priesthood*, 142 ff.

[171] Wilkins, *Concilia*, iii. 670; iv. 47–8.

[172] M.A.J. Burrows, 'Fifteenth-century Irish provincial legislation and pastoral care', in W. Sheils and D. Wood (eds.), *The Churches, Ireland and the Irish*, SCH 25 (Oxford, 1989), 57. T. Winning, 'Church councils in sixteenth-century Scotland', in McRoberts, *Scottish Reformation*, 338.

[173] Simms, 'Frontiers in the Irish church', 194–9. J. Watt, *The Church in Medieval Ireland* (Dublin, 1972), 186. Lyons, *County Kildare*, 78.

[174] Williams, *Welsh Church*, 339–46.

[175] B. MacCarthy (ed.), *Annals of Ulster*, 4 vols. (Dublin, 1895), iii. 429.

made it difficult to displace them. Married clergy and their children were recognized as tenants of the bishop of St David's, and the children of 'civil' unions were acknowledged as legitimate in most legal documents. In Scotland it was also recognized that the relatively easy acceptance of the legal position of priests' children remained an encouragement to concubinage: the councils of 1549 and 1552 endeavoured to restrict the dower and land that might be left to such offspring.[176] One possible measure of the difference between England and its neighbours might be the papal dispensations from the stigma of illegitimacy required by sons of priests if they were to take orders: between 1447 and 1492 there were 578 such dispensations for Ireland and Scotland, and only eight for England. The last figure is quite unconvincing, if only because the papal collectors in England were sometimes given power to dispense from the stigma of bastardy, but it articulates a gap in social behaviour that was real enough.[177]

But explaining the existence of 'civil' relationships with reference to inheritance practices is frankly curious, if neighbouring territories—even in the case of Wales territories that are part of the same ecclesiastical jurisdiction—were filled with devout Christians horrified by the pollution of sacramental processes. At the very least life in the borderlands must have been odd: for example, David ap John of Monmouth, ministering in the Diocese of Hereford, persisted in keeping a concubine and prompted the unusually drastic step by the ecclesiastical authorities of warning parishioners not to attend his Masses.[178] Edmund Earl Grey, marcher lord of Dyffryn Clwyd in the fifteenth century, was so disturbed by concubinage among the clergy that he conducted his own campaign of moral purification.[179] When the difference of custom and habit was known it could be explained away by dismissive assumptions about racial superiority, which is what More seems to be doing with the Welsh example in his *Dialogues*.[180] Priests in English Ireland seem to have been deeply troubled by any idea of clerical marriage, which they associated with Gaelic 'degeneracy'.[181] Similarly the attacks of the friars on Irish and Welsh practice could be used to articulate difference, though in this case of spiritual, rather than

---

[176] D.H. Robertson, *The Reformation in Scotland* (Edinburgh, 1909), 62, 71–7. McKay, 'Parish life in Scotland, 1500–1560', in D. McRoberts (ed.), *Essays on the Scottish Reformation* (Glasgow, 1962), 95.

[177] Lynch, 'Religion in Ireland', 8, notes that the readiness of Rome to grant dispensation undermined the efforts of Irish councils to eliminate concubinage.

[178] Thomson, *Early Tudor Church*, 169.

[179] R.I. Jack, 'Religious life in a Welsh marcher lordship: the lordship of Dyffryn Clwyd in the later Middle Ages', in C. Barron and C. Harper-Bill (eds.), *Church in Pre-Reformation Society* (Woodbridge, 1985), 153–7.

[180] *CWTM*, vi. 1. 309.

[181] Murray, 'Tudor Diocese of Dublin', 144, 209.

racial, standards. But we might also use the evidence of Wales and Ireland to raise questions about how general the anxiety about the pollution of clerical sexuality was even in England. Sobriety, good neighbourliness, and diligence were the qualities men most sought in their priests. These must most often have been allied with assumptions about chastity, but it was surely relationships flaunted before the parish in defiance of good order that were the prime cause of offence. When a priest like Robert Becket of Lincoln diocese had to be presented by his parishioners for offering the wife of William Tailboys a noble to go to bed with him the churchwardens sounded reluctant to prosecute because the man served the cure well and 'doth his duty'.[182] The English laity was undoubtedly acculturated to the Hildebrandine reforms, and, like many human groups, found charges of sexual delinquency an important way of demarcating the pure from the impure. The practice of social relations was more complex, and the processes of accommodation between the lay and clerical more malleable than some of the ideological statements of contemporaries would suggest.

In 1503 the University of Cambridge obtained a bull from Alexander VI allowing the appointment of twelve preachers who would act as itinerant evangelists, preaching throughout England, Scotland, and Ireland (there was no mention of Wales). The next year, in a related move, Bishop Fisher encouraged the foundation of the Lady Margaret preachership, designed to educate youths who would then 'spread the gospel of Christ throughout the land of Britain with superabundant fruit'.[183] The preacher himself was to provide sermons annually in London, Westminster, Hertfordshire, Cambridgeshire and Lincolnshire. Finally, in the statutes of the new foundation of St John's College, Fisher planned that there should be English preaching by the fellowship for the benefit of the laity. Behind these moves lay his own fervent conviction that 'true faith cannot be gotten but by hearing of this Word; this hearing of this Word shall not be had but by means of preaching...'[184] The breadth of the vision, and its unusual geographical inclusiveness are impressive. Here the voice of reformed Catholicism speaks vigorously against the assumption that all was well with the early sixteenth-century clergy. It is unfashionable to accept the judgement of the humanists that ignorance and idleness were the vices of the clergy: instead historians look to institutional weaknesses; the close interdependence of church and state; the involvement of the

---

[182] Bowker, *Secular Clergy*, 120–1.

[183] Dowling, 'John Fisher', 288. C. Cooper, *Annals of Cambridge*, 4 vols. (Cambridge, 1842–52), i. 260.

[184] Dowling, 'John Fisher', 294.

clergy in lay society; the appropriation of parochial resources by the higher clergy. Various parts of the British and Irish churches exhibited one or more of these weaknesses: none seems fundamentally to have challenged the laity's acceptance of the key functions of the priesthood. On the other hand, this was a church that depended more often on the intellectual instruction first promulgated in the thirteenth century than on an acceptance of Fisher's challenge to offer new insight via the scriptures.[185] In circumstances of religious change this was to prove a costly mistake.

---

[185] This was Pecham's decree discussed above, p. 62. In addition to the examples given there it is interesting to note that Fisher's friend, Bishop West, was still promulgating the decrees in Ely diocese in 1528: F. Heal, 'The Bishops of Ely and their Diocese, 1515–*ca.*1600', University of Cambridge Ph.D. (1972), 55.

3

COMMUNITIES AND BELIEFS

Parish and Guild

Laymen in early sixteenth-century Britain and Ireland could belong to a series of intersecting and overlapping communities, whose purposes were wholly or partially religious. The pattern of those communities, and the extent to which they were generally available, tells us much about the nature of religious behaviour on the eve of the Reformation. Christian laymen in this culture were above all corporate souls: members of the body of Christ, with its visible expression in local structures.[1] This in no way precluded personal devotion, but may legitimately be regarded as prior to personal piety. Collective Christianity was not, of course, an unchanging entity, nor were communities necessarily highly functional, bonded groups dedicated to collective spiritual goals. Contrasts and conflicts are as significant in this analysis as harmony and good order.[2] But the structures remain crucial: they offer a frame of reference that was inescapable for contemporaries and is indispensable for historians. Parish and guild, chantry and household provide a grid on which to map the religious life of ordinary Christians.[3]

The parish was the prime expression of this corporate identity for the vast majority of the populations of the British Isles. The process of parochialization had been completed even in Gaelic Scotland and Ireland during the thirteenth century and remained largely fixed up to, and usu-

---

[1] The language of corporate Christians is derived from E. Duffy, *The Stripping of the Altars: Traditional Religion in England 1400–1580* (New Haven, Conn., 1992), ch. 4.

[2] To use the term 'communities' is to enter a historiographical minefield, see C. Carpenter, 'Gentry and community in medieval England', *JBS* 33 (1994), 340–3 and B. Short, *The English Rural Community: Image and Analysis* (Cambridge, 1992), but it still seems possible to apply this language to the parish and its sub-units without undue emphasis on some idealized sense of mutuality. For a very sensible recent discussion see the introduction to A. Shepard and P. Withington (eds.), *Communities in Early Modern England: Networks, Place, Rhetoric* (Manchester, 2000).

[3] B. Kümin, *The Shaping of a Community: The Rise and Reformation of the English Parish, c.1400–1560* (Aldershot, 1996), 1–2.

ally well beyond, the Reformation.[4] It provided every layman with his or her formal association with a mother church, which was almost invariably the focus for the rites of passage, and for the payment of tithe, and usually the environment for access to the Mass and the Church's liturgical cycle. Within the parish church individual Christians experienced the same liturgy wherever they lived and there would have been little overt contrast between attending worship in the Orkneys, Calais, or Galway. Roger Martyn of Long Melford, Suffolk, writing at the end of his long life lived mainly under the new Church, looked back with longing to his Henrician youth. Then the ceremonial year in Long Melford was marked at every stage by the singing of the Mass, bell-ringing, and processions. There was the beating of the bounds at Rogation, bonfires on the eves of the feasts of St James, St Peter, St Paul and St Thomas.[5] In prosperous southern and midland England the parish church was the repository for a rich array of vestments, liturgical vessels, paintings, and images to support this ceremoniousness. Often it would have been wholly or partially reconstructed in the century before the Reformation as a suitable setting for worship. In varying degrees most English parishes seem to have striven to provide a fit setting for the Mass and for the corporate expression of religious devotion.

But not every parish was Long Melford, or even its more modest counterpart, Morebath in Devon, where the accounts of the priest, Sir Christopher Trychay, show strong corporate piety on the eve of the Reformation.[6] There were the obvious contrasts provided by wealth and poverty, and the availability of an adequate supply of conscientious clerics. Parishes also tended to be divided into two categories according to their regional position. The first was characteristic of the Gaelic territories of Scotland and Ireland, and in more limited measure of parts of Wales and lowland Scotland. The second was the normal parish of lowland England, and parts of Scotland and English Ireland, where the area of the parish was normally small, and the community nucleated. Despite the formal parochialization of the first type of area, and the construction of the churches that provided their focus, the parish as community remained relatively weak. The overwhelming importance of kin relationships in defining the

---

[4] On the early history of the parish see for England Kumin, *Shaping of a Community*, 13–17; for Scotland, I.B. Cowan, *The Medieval Church in Scotland* (Edinburgh, 1995), 1–11; for Ireland, K.W. Nicholls, 'Rectory, vicarage and parish in western Irish dioceses', *Journal of the Royal Society of Antiquaries of Ireland* 101 (1971), 53–84; for Wales, G. Williams, *The Welsh Church from Conquest to Reformation* (Cardiff, 1976), 14–17.

[5] W. Parker, *The History of Long Melford* (1873), 70–3. C. Haigh, *English Reformations* (Oxford, 1994), 1–11, and Duffy, *Stripping of the Altars*, 39–41, 137–8.

[6] J.E. Binney (ed.), *The Accounts of the Wardens of the Parish of Morebath, Devon, 1520–1573* (Exeter, 1904). See the important new study by E. Duffy, *The Voices of Morebath: Reformation and Rebellion in an English Parish* (New Haven, Conn., 2001).

social structure meant that everyday religious behaviour was largely focused upon these identities, and indeed parochial boundaries themselves often seem to have been constructed to conform to ancient family groups.[7] The absence of towns, and often of any significant nucleated communities, the scattered nature of population, and the need to have large parochial territories for financial reasons, all contributed to a pattern of religious behaviour very different to that characteristic of the Anglophone British Isles. The report to the papacy in 1517 on the town of Clogher offers an extreme image of this contrast. Clogher was inhabited only in the winter, since its herdsmen practised transhumance, and in the cathedral, the only stone building, Mass was celebrated only on Sundays.[8] This could suggest partly simple neglect, but the point is not so much absence of basic services in the Gaelic lands as their necessary adaptation to different geographical and social patterns. In both Ireland and Scotland these patterns were further complicated by the disposition to build churches on holy sites associated with the Celtic saints rather than in any natural territorial centre, and then to use those churches as focuses mainly for pilgrimage or special festivals.[9] It is therefore unsurprising to find that our fragmentary evidence for the devotional life of the laity is to be found in the household or friary, rather than in the parochial round. John Bossy's view that kinship relations often dominated religious behaviour before the sixteenth-century reformations has not found much support from English historians, but seems far more pertinent in the context of other parts of Britain and Ireland.[10]

The sheer size of parishes in the Celtic lands obviously inhibited the construction of communities centred on the mother church. The Welsh uplands, for example, had many parishes of over 20,000 acres.[11] In Ireland there was a marked contrast between areas of Norman and of Gaelic settlement: Armagh's parishes *inter Anglicos* averaged somewhat over 2,000 acres, while in the Hibernian deaneries they averaged more than 11,000 acres in all cases.[12] Some of the Scottish Gaidhealtachd parishes were

---

[7] K. Simms, 'Frontiers in the Irish church: regional and cultural', in T. Barry, R. Frame, and K. Simms (eds.), *Colony and Frontier in Medieval Ireland* (1995), 178–84. I.B. Cowan, 'The medieval Church in Argyll and the Isles', *RSCHS* 20 (1978), 15–29.

[8] M.J. Haren, 'A description of Clogher Cathedral in the early sixteenth century', *Clogher Record* 12/1 (1985), 52.

[9] For a more generally sympathetic view of parochial units *inter hibernicos* see H.A. Jefferies, *Priests and Prelates of Armagh in the Age of Reformations* (Dublin, 1997), 62–82. J. Dawson, 'Calvinism and the Gaidhealtachd in Scotland', in A. Duke, G. Lewis, and A. Pettegree (eds.), *Calvinism in Europe* (Cambridge, 1994), 243.

[10] J. Bossy, 'The Counter-Reformation and the people of Catholic Europe', *PP* 47 (1970), 51–70.

[11] G. Williams, *Wales and The Reformation* (Cardiff, 1997), 28.

[12] Jefferies, *Priests and Prelates*, 20, 64–5.

twenty miles long, and few had settlements of any size as a heart.[13] The
English uplands often show a similar pattern: the three great parishes of
the central Lake District measured 188,026 acres between them.[14] Lancashire offers the best-known English case: there the large parishes averaged
33 square miles. For comparison we have an average of 4 square miles or
less in the Midland and South-Eastern parishes. Large size was usually
linked to low population density. The dispersed parishes of Carlisle diocese are estimated to have had an average of about 450 inhabitants in
1563.[15]

The best solution to the problem of isolation was the construction of
chapels of ease. The inhabitants of Newchurch in Rossendale, Lancashire,
described how they had founded a chapelry because the parish church was
twelve miles away and in winter 'infants borne to church are in great peril
of their lives . . . and the dead corpses there like to remain unburied at such
times for want of carriage'.[16] Such problems were not confined to the
uplands: the inhabitants of Hindon in Wiltshire petitioned the papacy for a
new chapel because the woods between it and its mother church, two miles
distant, were filled with robbers, and in wintry weather access to Enford for
burials was difficult.[17] This last example is redolent of special pleading: long
after the Reformation Archbishop Bancroft was to comment caustically
that he had known 'great suits in law for the maintenance of a chapel of ease
within half a mile of the parish church'.[18] But often chapelries were a
crucial way of providing for the spiritual life of scattered congregations. In
England, at least, they meant that few had to go far to hear Mass celebrated.
In a vast parish like that of Kendal the antiquary Leland noted that 'there
belongeth about a 30 chapels and hamlets to the head church'.[19] Cornwall
possessed, it has been estimated, 700 chapelries of one kind or another.[20]
Ireland and Scotland are less well documented and studied, but in both
there is evidence of chapels in various forms supplementing parochial

---

[13] Dawson, 'Calvinism and the Gaidhealtachd', 243.

[14] M. Clark, 'Northern light? Parochial life in a "dark corner" of Tudor England', in
K.L. French, G.G. Gibbs, and B.A. Kumin (eds.), *The Parish in English Life, 1400–1600* (Manchester, 1997), 56–7.

[15] C. Haigh, *Reformation and Resistance in Tudor Lancashire* (Cambridge, 1975), 22–3.

[16] T. Whitaker, *A History of the Original Parish of Whalley* (Manchester, 1872), 318.

[17] A.D. Brown, *Popular Piety in Late Medieval England: The Diocese of Salisbury, 1250–1550*
(Oxford, 1995), 76.

[18] C. Kitching, 'Church and chapelry in sixteenth century England', in D. Baker (ed.), *The
Church in Town and Countryside*, SCH 16 (Oxford, 1979), 279–90.

[19] L. Toulmin-Smith (ed.), *The Itinerary of John Leland*, 5 vols. (Carbondale, Ill., 1964), v. 47.
Kumin, *Shaping of a Community*, 167–79.

[20] Adams, 'The medieval chapels of Cornwall', *Journal of the Royal Institution of Cornwall* 3
(1947), 48. For a useful summary of the role of chapels before and after the Reformation see
N.J.G. Pounds, *A History of the English Parish* (Cambridge, 2000), 91–6.

centres. A rare example of being able to count these chapels comes from the deanery of Tullyhogue in Armagh diocese, where twelve chapels can be identified to supplement twenty-three parish churches.[21] When there were no chapels of ease private provision sometimes made good the deficiency: in Scotland John Major claimed that, since as many as thirty villages sometimes had to depend on one kirk, the private chapels of the lairds ensured that 'all may have a chance to hear divine service'.[22]

How rich a mimesis of full parochial life these small chapelries could achieve must be questionable. The aspiration seems to have been the regular service of a priest and hence the celebration of the Mass on Sundays, feast days, and some weekdays, 'and all other sacraments as necessary'.[23] The reality was more mixed. For example, the congregation of Carleton chapel in Yorkshire had celebrations of Mass only on Monday, Wednesday, and Friday in the late fifteenth century since they shared their priest with the parish church of Husthwaite. Some communities had Mass only at the six major festivals of the year, though this seems to have been rare. The limitations were not only those of access to priests: the surrender of full parochial rights, especially those of burial, to a chapelry, were very uncommon, and the financial demands of the mother church were rarely relaxed. Since surviving petitions suggest that being able to have easy access to the rites of passage was one of the two major concerns of scattered congregations tensions not infrequently issued in disputes before the church courts.[24]

Many of the upland chapels of Britain and Ireland were therefore a necessary response to population dispersal, offering a relatively simple focus for the spiritual life of corporate Christians. However, the story of the chapels is complicated by the existence of some that were neither physically isolated nor particularly impoverished. These could build their own church life just as effectively as the full parish. Some chapels, like the one which served the rapidly growing community of Liverpool, or that of Farnworth which has surviving churchwardens' accounts, were parishes in all but name.[25] They were there because three centuries earlier canon law had 'laid its cold hand on the parishes of Europe and froze[n] the pattern'.[26] The relative fixity of parochial boundaries after the thirteenth century meant that there was little opportunity to adapt to social and

---

[21] Jefferies, *Priests and Prelates*, 64.

[22] A.J.G. Mackay (ed.), *History of Greater Britain, Compiled by John Major*, SHS 10 (1892), 30.

[23] Kitching, 'Church and Chapelry', 283–4.

[24] Kumin, *Shaping of a Community*, 167–79.

[25] Kitching, 'Church and Chapelry', 280. G. Tupling, 'The pre-Reformation parishes and chapelries of Lancashire', *Transactions of the Lancashire and Cheshire Antiquarian Society* 67 (1957), 10.

[26] C.N.L. Brooke, 'The missionary at home: the Church and the towns, 1000–1250', in G.J. Cuming (ed.), *The Mission of the Church and the Propagation of the Faith*, SCH 6 (Cambridge, 1970), 72.

economic change. Large parishes had been created in Lancashire because of low population, but when population increased in the early sixteenth century, there was scarcely any commensurate increase in the number of parishes. The consequence was that Lancashire incumbents were responsible for many souls: Haigh suggests an average of 1,700 per parish by 1563.[27] Scotland offers a variant on this pattern in the burgh churches that had been established to cover a whole territory before there was significant urban growth. Dundee, for example, had 4,500 parishioners in 1480. For a comparison one could point to the old city of York, whose approximately 8,000 souls were serviced through forty parish churches.[28]

Although chapelries could provide a full corporate Christian life this did not prevent congregations from seeking to gain full parochial status. A major motive was fiscal, since the mother church rarely surrendered its rights to tithes and dues, and burdens on chapelries could therefore be heavy. For example, when the wardens of Tywardreath in Cornwall reached a compromise about rights with the chapel of Golant, the latter were conceded the right to bury, but had to maintain mortuary payments to the rector.[29] The separate funding of a priest meant double charges for spiritual services. But a desire for parity with the mother church in their religious life was also an implicit objective of the ambitious chapelries. This is suggested both by Bancroft's observation and by the sort of complaint made by the vicar of Barton Stacey, that the inhabitants of Newton expected him to perform exactly the same services in their chapel as in the parish church. There is a splendid example of conflict in Margery Kempe's narrative of the attempt of two King's Lynn chapelries to separate themselves from the parish by establishing baptismal rights. Despite a papal bull, and the sympathy of Bishop Alnwick, the ambitious merchants were doomed to failure when Margery prayed against them, seeking and gaining the Deity's protection for the existing order of things.[30] However, separations sometimes succeeded, as in the three parishes created out of Weston Zoyland, Somerset, in 1515. There it was acknowledged by the incumbent that the two dependent chapelries had the equipment, buildings, and resources for a proper liturgical existence. Even when efforts failed in the face of entrenched interests supported by canon law, the fact that laymen often tried to make themselves into full parishioners is indicative of the value placed on the corporate community.[31]

---

[27] Haigh, *Tudor Lancashire*, 22–3.
[28] M. Lynch, 'The religious life of medieval Scotland', in S. Gilley and W.J. Sheils (eds.), *A History of Religion in Britain* (Oxford, 1994), 120. D. Palliser, *Tudor York* (Oxford, 1979), 226.
[29] Kumin, *Shaping of a Community*, 175–8.
[30] S.B. Meech and H.E. Allen (eds.), *The Book of Margery Kempe*, EETS os 212 (1940), 58–9.
[31] J.A.F. Thomson, *The Early Tudor Church and Society, 1485–1529* (1993), 285–6.

A major benefit of parochial status was the assurance it provided that the resources of the faithful, tithes apart, could be fully directed to the building, repair and embellishment of the local church. And in much of the British Isles parishioners willingly undertook these tasks in the century before the Reformation. They reflected the view that the church, particularly in the lowlands, was the centre of community: providing it with its cultural and social identity as well as its religious focus. Laymen were, in Andrew Brown's words, 'bound to their parishes, pastorally and financially, from cradle to grave'.[32] The ideal essence of the parish was spiritual and social inclusiveness: men and women worshipped together, celebrated the feasts of the liturgical year together, and organized the financial support of the church together under the auspices of the churchwardens. The author of the fifteenth-century tract *Dives and Pauper* argued that the common prayer of the 'community in church' was most pleasing to God.[33] If the parish were part of a wider urban community, as in London and Coventry, its members would process through the city for thanksgivings and other special occasions.[34] Church ales, shooting matches, and the like, which were major forms of fund-raising in most parishes, also served to bind men together, as did the gestures of those who in their wills left funds for a general parochial feast. The first deacon of Holy Trinity, Coventry, for example, had an obligation to serve the parishioners with bread and ale, 'at Mylborne's dirge, and Meynley's, and other dirges that be made of the church's cost'.[35] Sacramentals, such as the holy loaf distributed at the end of Mass, were provided for the whole parish by individuals on a rota system. The prayers of the living for the souls of the dead extended the idea of the parish in time and space. And so finally it is no surprise that the overwhelming majority of parishioners seem to have chosen burial in their local church or adjacent cemetery.[36]

A curious testimony to the power of the parish as a focus of devotion is provided by the attitudes of Lollards. Late Lollardy is, as Patrick Collinson has argued, better seen as a conventicling tendency than as a separated church.[37] The *Lanterne of Light* had argued that 'our church material . . . is

---

[32] Brown, *Popular Piety*, 67.

[33] P.H. Barnum (ed.), *Dives and Pauper*, 2 vols., EETS os 280 (1976–80), i. 196.

[34] S. Brigden, *London and the Reformation* (Oxford, 1989), 23–4. C. Phythian-Adams, *The Desolation of a City: Coventry and the Urban Crisis of the Late Middle Ages* (Cambridge, 1979), 162.

[35] Phythian-Adams, *Coventry*, 169.

[36] R. Dinn, '"Monuments Answerable to Mens Worth": Burial patterns, social status and gender in late medieval Bury St Edmunds', *JEH* 46 (1995), 242–3. V. Harding, 'Burial choice and burial location in late medieval London', in S. Bassett (ed.), *Death in Towns* (Leicester, 1992), 120–1.

[37] P. Collinson, 'The English conventicle', in W.J. Sheils and D. Wood (eds.), *Voluntary Religion*, SCH 23 (Oxford, 1986), 223–59.

ordained for parishioners, when they come together' and ordinary Lollards seem to have assumed that they had a part in this 'church material'.[38] But those suspected of heresy were not all quiet nicodemists, serving out their necessary time in the pews to avoid the denunciation of neighbours. In Buckinghamshire at least they sometimes played active roles in the parish community. The Saunders of Amersham had patronage control over the holy-water clerkship of the town in the 1520s; one of the Bartlet family, a veritable network of Buckinghamshire Lollards, was churchwarden of Upton in 1519; and numerous wills of known or suspected heretics left bequests for the repair of their parish church or sought burial within its walls.[39] There is also the spectacular case of the well-known Essex Lollard, William Sweeting, who was holy-water clerk of Boxted for seven years early in his career and at Colchester even after his first abjuration of heresy. It is, of course, difficult to judge the spirit in which these radicals involved themselves in corporate experience. When Henry Phip of Hitchenden was chosen to be keeper of the roodloft he is alleged to have said that he must go and tend a candle before 'Block Almighty'.[40] London heretics sometimes deliberately avoided parochial involvement and there were ideological objections to the concept of the church as consecrated space since the church of the chosen did not depend on buildings for worship.[41] But it is intriguing that at least some of this most alienated group of early Tudor laymen largely accepted the need for identity with the parish.

The ideal of spiritual inclusiveness should not, however, blind us to the reality that parishes and their churches existed in a social universe that was both stratified and liable to division. Even the most basic definition of what it was to be a parishioner was contentious. Eamon Duffy has made a powerful case for the bede-roll, the list recited annually at the requiem for the benefactors of the church, as the key document of parish identity. To be included on the roll was to be one of the 'good doers and well-willers' who supported the church, or had sustained it in the past. Good doing needed money. The sum that had to be given could be small, like the two-pence donations carefully recorded by the priest of Morebath, but some must have been excluded from the full membership of this giving community.[42] Then there was the further expectation that proper observance

[38] L.M. Swinburn (ed.), *The Lanterne of Light*, EETS os 151 (1917), 41.

[39] D. Plumb, 'Social and economic spread of rural Lollardy: a reappraisal', in W.J. Sheils and D. Wood (eds.), *Voluntary Religion*, SCH 23 (Oxford, 1986), 111–29; 'A gathered church? Lollards and their society', in M. Spufford (ed.), *The World of Rural Dissenters, 1520–1725* (Cambridge, 1995), 132–63.

[40] Foxe, iv. 237–8.

[41] Brigden, *London*, 82–92.

[42] Duffy, *Stripping of the Altars*, 153–4, 332–7.

of hierarchy would mark the church just as it did society as a whole. After the Reformation pews finally became a most powerful mode of status display. This trend had already begun in the fifteenth century, especially for those gentry and noble families who could link chantry chapels or aisles to separated seating.[43] More general in the pre-Reformation period is the patterning of burial as an indicator of status. In late medieval Bury St Edmund's there was a clear correlation between wealth displayed in a will and explicit choice of burial site: the richer parishioners usually chose the church, and defined their preferred site carefully.[44] Ritual behaviour could also articulate status. The most famous example is the kissing of the pax board: clerical moralists denounced what they saw as the tendency of parishioners to subordinate the devoutness of this act to their concerns for status in its passage. The scattering of cases recorded by the church courts suggest that there was some basis for the criticism: for example, blood flowed at Theydon-Garnon in Essex in 1522 when the clerk offered the pax to Francis Hamden before John Browne.[45]

Disputes such as these were deeply regretted, as a threat to the harmony of the *corpus Christiani*, but proper hierarchical display was accepted as a proper expression of the natural order, as logical as the process of gender segregation that was a consistent feature of congregations. Indeed, properly managed, the marks of status could be used to provide a frame for corporate identities. Hence the minute attention that was paid to levels of parochial dues, to the proper ordering of the bede-roll and so forth. The same argument is now often applied to that other way in which early Tudor parishioners expressed their religious identity: guilds and fraternities. The religious guilds and fraternities provided a crucial focus for devotional behaviour in much of Britain and Ireland in the century before the Reformation.[46] It has been estimated that there may have been as many as 30,000 guilds spread through the land, and though the calculation may seem improbably high it can be underpinned by evidence from some

---

[43] N. Alldridge, 'Loyalty and identity in Chester parishes, 1540–1640', in S. Wright (ed.), *Parish, Church and People: Local Studies in Lay Religion, 1350–1750* (1988), 94–7. On the use of ecclesiastical space to express hierarchy, and often to claim power, see C. Pamela Graves, 'Social space in the English medieval parish church', *Economy and Society* 18 (1989), 297–322.

[44] Dinn, 'Monuments answerable', 248–55. The status correlation is less clear in London, Harding, 'Burial choice', 124–7.

[45] Duffy, *Stripping of the Altars*, 126–7.

[46] There is now a vast literature on the parish guilds. A. Westlake, *The Parish Gilds of Medieval England* (1919), remains the starting-point. See particularly G. Rosser, 'Communities of parish and guild in the later Middle Ages', in Wright (ed.) *Parish, Church and People*, 29–55 and 'Parochial conformity and voluntary religion in late medieval England', *TRHS* 6th ser. 1 (1991), 173–89. C.M. Barron, 'The parish fraternities of medieval London', in C.M. Barron and C. Harper-Bill (eds.), *The Church in Pre-Reformation Society: Essays in Honour of F.R.H. Du Boulay* (Woodbridge, 1985), 13–37.

local studies. In Cambridgeshire, for example, 350 guilds are documented in the two centuries before the Reformation. Not all had a continuous existence, but they remained a popular form of religious association throughout this period: 152 were apparently the product of the half-century before the dissolution.[47] For Cornwall the number is only 140, but this is for a handful of parishes, which, if extrapolated for the whole county, might produce a figure of 1,200.[48] Guilds were to be found in most parts of the British Isles: in anglicized Ireland they were established by royal charter in the hundred years before the Reformation, preponderantly in the towns, but also in some rural communities of the Pale counties.[49] In lowland Scotland they were once again a feature of the burghs, though trade guilds, rather than general fraternities, continued to be the key here to local solidarity.[50] In Wales they appear to have been most common in the south and on the eastern borders.[51] Only the Celtic regions, and some upland areas like Cumbria, seem to have been little touched by this form of lay association. Fraternities, one commentator suggests, ran counter to the nature of these societies, which were independent in attitude and able to turn to true kin networks, not their artificial alternative.[52] But it may also be that in Gaelic Ireland, at least, the development of the tertiary orders associated with friaries offered some of the same active spiritual engagement for the laity.

The formal purposes of the guilds are articulated in statutes that survive in quantity for England. They were voluntary associations principally of lay men and women who joined together to promote a particular devotion, typically to Corpus Christi, the Trinity, the Virgin, or a particular saint; to maintain a chapel, or light, or candles at the appropriate feasts; to provide for the burial of members and for prayers for their souls; and to offer other forms of support both to members and often to the parish church. The nature of their devotional engagements will be considered below: here we need to address the difficult question of their relationship with the less voluntary corporate community of the parish. The impulses that led to the founding of fraternities would seem to be both inclusive

---

[47] V.R. Bainbridge, *Gilds in the Medieval Countryside: Social and Religious Change in Cambridgeshire, c.1350–1558* (Woodbridge, 1996).

[48] J. Mattingley, 'The medieval parish gilds of Cornwall', *Journal of the Royal Institute of Cornwall* NS 10 (1989), 290–329.

[49] M.V. Ronan, 'Religious customs of Dublin medieval gilds', *Irish Ecclesiastical Record* 5th ser. 26 (1925), 364–85.

[50] There seems to be little specialist research on religion and the Scottish guilds, though see Lynch, 'Medieval Scotland', 11, and *Edinburgh and the Reformation*, 55–61; A.-B. Fitch, 'The Search for Salvation: Lay Faith in Scotland: 1480–1560', University of Glasgow Ph.D. (1994), 289–90.

[51] Williams, *Welsh Church*, 288–92.

[52] Clark, 'Northern light?' 63–4.

and exclusive.[53] There is plenty of evidence to link the fraternities with broad support for the parish church. The first is that membership was in many cases limited to the community, in practice if not in theory. While great urban guilds had a wider scope, sometimes having almost a national character as in the example of the Holy Trinity Guild in Coventry, rural associations tended to limit themselves to logical local boundaries.[54] If a rural parish spawned only one guild this must have made the boundaries between voluntary and involuntary association very fluid. In Bassingbourn, Cambridgeshire, for example, the priest employed by the Trinity Guild kept the churchwardens' accounts, and left most of his goods for the general improvement of the church.[55] It is the routine concern in guild records to embellish the parish church and maintain its lights properly that also indicates identity: repairs of roofs and walls, as well as of particular altars or saints' images, often fell to the lot of a particular fraternity. When churches needed expansion, guilds might be organized to provide the necessary funding: at Golant, Cornwall, in 1509 the guilds contributed to the new roof and had their names recorded on it.[56]

Yet historians seem currently too anxious to deny difference between the experience of being a parishioner and of guild membership. Guilds were well-organized, highly practical, entities that created a familial solidarity and bonding. This concept was clearly expressed in the use of the language of 'brothers' and 'sisters' to describe membership. Guild popularity is indicative of a desire by the laity to provide a more focused form of collective devotion and more sustained pattern of intercession than that offered by the ordinary parochial round. Rosser is surely right to suggest that the guild Mass and the guild feast both provided a para-liturgical bonding, linking the members in honourable common spiritual and social purposes.[57] It is widely accepted that this often provided the laity with an organizational role, for example in hiring and firing their own chaplains, which they would not otherwise have possessed.[58] Given the diversity of guild membership and the choice of association available at least in urban society, this role was quite widely diffused, and could even in some circumstances embrace

[53] Duffy, in his account of corporate Christians, places overwhelming emphasis on the inclusive elements in guild behaviour: *Stripping of the Altars*, 141–54. For a more questioning view see Rosser, 'Communities of parish and guild', 37–45.

[54] Phythian-Adams, *Coventry*, 22.

[55] W.M. Palmer, 'Village gilds of Cambridgeshire', *Transactions of the Cambridgeshire and Huntingdonshire Archaeological Society* 39 (1938–9), 366–70.

[56] R. Whiting, *The Blind Devotion of the People: Popular Religion and the English Reformation* (Cambridge, 1989), 87.

[57] G. Rosser, 'Going to the fraternity feast: commensality and social relations in late medieval England', *JBS* 33 (1994), 430–6. M. Rubin, *Corpus Christi: The Eucharist in Late Medieval Culture* (Cambridge, 1991), 232–43.

[58] J.J. Scarisbrick, *The Reformation and the English People* (Oxford, 1984), 19–39.

women or the relatively poor. The guilds were also well adapted to give expression to particular voluntarist needs within the broad church. Sometimes they provided very specifically for their own, filling gaps in parochial provision not unlike chapels of ease. In the Isle of Ely, where settlement centres did not necessarily correlate closely with parish boundaries, some of the guilds seem to have existed specifically to provide for small nucleated communities.[59] When a new town was established without proper parochial provision, as at Weymouth, a guild might supply the need.[60] The same might happen where population was too great for the parochial structure: all but one of the large extramural parishes of London had more than one fraternity, which, when one considers the 3,500 souls to be housled in Southwark, was an almost essential way of disaggregating religious activity.[61] All guilds placed considerable emphasis on their separate identity, even when contributing financially or otherwise to the collective well-being of the parish. Brethren might eat together several times a week, not just at the grand fraternity feast, or sit together within the body of the church. None of this was an automatic recipe for conflict with the wider corporate body, but it created separate interest groups of active Christians.

Guilds have been described as the 'poor man's chantry' and the two certainly have identical intercessory functions. Perpetual chantries did not normally structure the experience of living laymen, as did the fraternities. There were circumstances, however, for example in the use of chantry chapels for general worship in isolated areas, when intercession for the dead influenced the community of the living. The importance of chantries used for communal worship north of the border is evident on the very eve of the Reformation. Eleven colleges for votive Masses were established between 1450 and 1500 and a further thirteen were initiated before the Reformation. Most were erected within existing parish churches, though in some cases, most spectacularly the rebuilt St Giles, Edinburgh, collegiate status was linked to new building.[62] In England, such collegiate foundations had declined in the early sixteenth century, though the impulse was not entirely dead. At the dissolution of the monasteries the duke of Norfolk endeavoured to turn Thetford Priory into a collegiate church to protect his familial interest.[63]

There are, however, two more general comparisons that can be made between the social purposes of the guild and the chantry. The first is the evidence that those who funded these sub-parish structures often had in

---

[59] Bainbridge, *Gilds*, 20–2, 27.

[60] Rosser, 'Communities of parish and guild', 34–5.

[61] Barron, 'Parish fraternities', 28.

[62] Lynch, 'Medieval Scotland', 117. I.B. Cowan and D.F. Easson, *Medieval Religious Houses: Scotland*, 2nd edn. (1976), 213–28.

[63] J. Rosenthal, *The Purchase of Paradise: Gift Giving and the Aristocracy, 1307–1485* (1972). *LP* xiv. 2. 815, 816.

mind the desirability of supplementing parochial provision. Bristol testators, who have been studied in some detail, showed an anxiety to have their priests contribute to the 'increase of Divine worship', by saying general services and singing in the choir. This suggests that the well-being of the whole parish could often drive intercessory investment. It was, as Burgess has suggested, evidence of the penitential motive in action.[64] But there is a second dimension to chantry and guild provisions. They concerned themselves with intercession for the individual and his or her immediate family; both were also likely to involve an identity with wider kin, natural or artificial, as community before extending themselves to prayer for all Christian souls. When Geoffrey Spring, a London draper, left money for a perpetual chantry in his native Cambridgeshire he established a priest to sing for his father and mother and 'for the souls of all them that I am most bound to pray for' and finally for all Christian souls.[65] In Scotland there was a particular tendency to offer the benefits of prayer and protection to vassals and tenants as well as family, thereby mimicking this world's power structures in hope of the world to come.[66]

The public face of worship in the late medieval parish was intimately bound up with the physical boundaries of the sacred and the secular. The proper use of the sacred space of the church was one old theme routinely contested between reforming clergy and the laity. There was a concern in England to restrain sociable use of the body of the church. For example, Archbishop Warham's visitation of Kent in 1511 attempted to abolish drinking in church, thereby provoking resentment among parishioners. The wardens of Willesborough reported that there was an unwillingness to offer at obits and churchings because 'they cannot drink in the church'.[67] Guild regulations, however, indicate that such drinking continued, and members of the elite, as well as ordinary parishioners, apparently found this mixed use acceptable. Regulations for baptism for the earl of Northumberland's household required the consumption of wine at several points during the religious ceremony.[68] More generally, quarrelling, unsocial behaviour, and bringing dogs into church were all thought by church authorities to be inappropriate activities in sacred space. The contentious ground was primarily that of the nave, the territory of the laity. The chancel, usually firmly isolated by the rood screen, was in

---

[64] C. Burgess, '"For the Increase of Divine Service": chantries in the parish in late medieval Bristol', *JEH* 36 (1985), 46–65; '"A Fond thing vainly invented": an essay on purgatory and pious motivation in later medieval England', in Wright, *Parish, Church and People*, 56–79.

[65] C. Marsh, *Popular Religion in Sixteenth Century England* (Basingstoke, 1998), 66.

[66] G. Donaldson, *The Faith of the Scots* (1990), 51.

[67] K.L. Wood-Legh (ed.), *Kentish Visitations of Archbishop William Warham and his Deputies, 1511–12*, Kent Records 24 (1984), 156.

[68] Bodl. MS, Eng. Hist. B 208, fos. 15 ff.

theory held sacred from lay intrusion except when by grace men were allowed to come to view the elevation of the host.[69]

The same cannot always be said in Ireland, where a powerful sense of the holy seems to have been compatible with almost casual desecration of both nave and sanctuary. Rapine and even murder were not unknown, and since the churches were often used to deposit valuable goods, provincial councils had to legislate against robbery as well. The annals of the Four Masters report in 1484 that Gilla-Patrick, son of Maguire 'was treacherously slain by his own five brothers' at the altar of the church of Aghalurcher.[70] A recent historian of Irish religion explains this indifference to consecrated space as part of the common coin of Gaelic ideas of conflict.[71] When there was a Dublin riot involving the men of the earls of Ormond and Kildare in 1493, the clergy lamented that St Patrick's Cathedral had been polluted with slaughter, the images defaced, and altars destroyed. Kildare could be brazen about such desecration: when charged before Henry VII with the burning of Cashel church, he is supposed to have responded, 'By Jesus....I would never have done it, had it not been told me that the Archbishop was within.'[72] To explain is hardly to justify, but perhaps the Irish evidence should be considered as simply the extreme example of lay attitudes, which accepted the power of the holy, and saw it as intimately woven into everyday social experience.

The church itself, with its altars and consecrated host, was the most explicitly sanctified territory. But the sacrosanctity of the whole community was expressed through processions, Rogationtide, Corpus Christi, and the circulation of the host that often accompanied these occasions. Ceremony, and with it the sense of the holy, was taken outwards from the church when, especially during the 'ritualistic' half of the year from Christmas to Midsummer, the parish dramatized itself in processions, plays, and holy day celebrations. Of course, it was not only the individual parish that was involved in this construction of the community as holy: in towns and cities, as in the famous case of Coventry, procession and religious drama were directed to articulating the whole society in this way.[73] On St Giles's Day, 1 September, Edinburgh was reconsecrated to its saint as his image was led through the town to the sound of 'tabors and trum-

---

[69] P. Marshall, *The Catholic Priesthood and the English Reformation* (Oxford, 1994), 42–3.

[70] Jefferies, *Priests and Prelates*, 23.

[71] S. Meigs, *The Reformations in Ireland* (Basingstoke, 1997), 42–5.

[72] M.A. Lyons, 'Sidelights on the Kildare ascendancy: a survey of Geraldine involvement in the church, c.1470–c.1520', *Archivium Hibernicum* 48 (1994), 76–8.

[73] C. Phythian-Adams, 'Ceremony and the citizen: the communal year in Coventry, 1450–1550', in P. Clark and P. Slack (eds.), *Crisis and Order in English Towns* (1972), 57–85. M. James, 'Ritual, drama and the social body in the late medieval town', *PP* 98 (1983), 3–29. Rubin, *Corpus Christi*, 243–87.

pets'.[74] Not all ceremony was directed to sacred ends: the division of the year into 'ritualistic' and 'urban' halves in the cities showed clearly that public action could be differentiated in the minds of contemporaries. But the ceremonial life of the parishes indicates above all a belief that the idea of sanctity was extended to the whole community, not confined by the uniqueness of the church as place or the clergy as mediators of the divine.[75]

The Household and Piety

The diffusion of the idea of the holy may have encouraged the growth of individual lay piety. Individual devotions could be private, confined to an isolated closet or oratory. They could also be articulated in separate prayer within corporate worship. The popularity of primers in early sixteenth-century England seems to indicate a desire both to follow the nature of public worship and to have a measure of control over individual prayer. The appearance of separate pews for elites within the parish church, taken by Colin Richmond as a sign that the gentry wished to set themselves apart from parochial worship, could instead be seen as an example of continuing commitment to corporate behaviour. It merely employed new, fashionable forms of status symbol to support it.[76] Yet the capacity of families, groups, and individuals to pursue part of their religious life apart from the community should not be ignored, indeed without an understanding of this we may find responses to the challenge of reformation extremely difficult to fathom.

The pluralistic patterns of devotional behaviour characteristic of the later Middle Ages make it understandable that private oratories and domestic chapels should have been popular. The so-called 'free' chapels for noble households and their tenants had long been a feature of the English religious landscape: in this period they were supplemented by more intimate arrangements for worship. The episcopal licensing of private oratories is common: 187 were granted in the Diocese of Salisbury in the second

---

[74] J. Smith (ed.), *The Hammermen of Edinburgh and their Altar in St Giles* (Edinburgh, 1906), xxxviii–xlvii.

[75] R. Gillespie, 'Differing devotions: patterns of religious practice in the British Isles, 1500–1700', in S.J. Connolly (ed.), *Kingdoms United? Great Britain and Ireland since 1500* (Dublin, 1999), 68–9.

[76] C. Richmond, 'Religion and the fifteenth-century English gentleman', in B. Dobson (ed.), *The Church, Politics and Patronage* (Gloucester, 1984), 193–208; 'The English gentry and religion c.1500', in C. Harper-Bill (ed.), *Religious Belief and Ecclesiastical Careers in Late Medieval England* (Woodbridge, 1991), 121–50. For a strong rebuttal of this argument see C. Carpenter, 'The religion of the gentry in fifteenth-century England', in D. Williams (ed.), *England in the Fifteenth Century* (Woodbridge, 1987), 53–74.

half of the fourteenth century, for example.[77] Regional studies for Yorkshire and Warwickshire tell the same tale.[78] Since the papacy could also be approached directly for separate licence for a portable altar, there must have been a vast number of formal locations of worship outside the parish church and its network of dependent chapelries. In cases where details of such licences survive the diocesan authorities seem to have adhered to the canon law requirement of attendance at the parochial church at least on the major festivals. But the liturgical cycle of the greater gentry and noble households of fifteenth-century England seems to have focused more fully on internal devotions than on the collective worship of the parish. Not only was Mass said regularly by chaplains in most of these houses, thereby obviating the need to attend the parish church, but particular feasts were celebrated in much the same way as the patronal festivals of the churches. The Stonors, for example, had a particularly rich liturgical cycle in which the household venerated the Trinity, St Anne, and St Katherine.[79] And there may have been practical consequences for the church of such elite separation: a study of the gentry of Kent shows those with private chapels giving less to church repairs at death than those who regularly worshipped with the community.[80]

The household, as both Protestant and Catholic reformers were to discover, was a notably difficult territory to regulate. In most instances it seems to have provided a focus for worship that was sensitive to social hierarchy but firmly orthodox: indeed much of the clearest evidence of sophisticated lay piety derives from a household context. Women had a particular advantage in this world, with its private confessors, books of hours, and close association with domestic routine. The devout households of Lady Margaret Beaufort, Cecily, duchess of York, and Margaret, Lady Hungerford, provide well-documented paradigms of orthodox, though sometimes avant garde, devotion.[81] Lady Margaret Beaufort offers an unusual example of the latter trend in her use of her household to promote the new cult of the Name of Jesus, venerated within her walls, with the Office actually developed there, and then preached by her chaplains far beyond.[82] A rather

---

[77] Brown, *Popular Piety*, 204–5.

[78] J. Hughes, *Pastors and Visionaries: Religion and Secular Life in Late Medieval Yorkshire* (Woodbridge, 1988), 10–14. C. Carpenter, *Locality and Polity: A Study of Warwickshire Society, 1401–1499* (Cambridge, 1992), 225.

[79] R.G.K.A. Mertes, 'The household as a religious community', in J. Rosenthal and C. Richmond (eds.), *People, Politics and Community in the Later Middle Ages* (Gloucester, 1987), 123–39.

[80] P.W. Fleming, 'Charity, faith and the gentry of Kent, 1422–1529', in A.F. Pollard (ed.), *Property and Politics: Essays in Late Medieval English History* (Gloucester, 1984), 36–58.

[81] M.A. Hicks, 'The piety of Margaret, Lady Hungerford', *JEH* 38 (1987), 19–38.

[82] M.K. Jones and M.G. Underwood, *The King's Mother: Lady Margaret Beaufort, Countess of Richmond and Derby* (Cambridge, 1992), 174–5.

different approach to household worship is offered by the work of Richard Whytford, whose *Werke for Housholders* (1530) assumed that his household-ers, perhaps first and foremost the urban middling sort, would attend parish Mass rather than hearing it in their own chapels. He saw the household instead as a centre for religious training in which the literate man should 'gather your neighbours about you on the holy day, especially the young sort, and read to them this poor lesson'.[83] The development from the mid-fifteenth century of the cult of St Anne and the Holy Family is one dimen-sion of a religious pluralism that focused on households.[84]

But the household could, and did, also provide the locus for a hetero-dox alternative to established belief. A network of families sustained Eng-lish Lollardy on the eve of the Reformation, normally holding their private conventicles in houses of leading members of the group. The Durdant household, of Iver Court near Staines, provides a particularly well-documented example. There one accused Lollard described how Robert Durdant read from the Epistle of St James to the extended family and their sympathizers seated at dinner, while on other occasions there were all-night reading parties and a wedding, the last an almost unique example of the Lollards providing separate rites of passage.[85] Women could thrive in these unorthodox environments as well: Roger Bennet, from the notorious Lollard centre of Amersham, described how a group of women met together on holidays 'when they go and come from the church' and 'there keep their conventicle'.[86] The household played a similar, though rather more evangelical, role in Scotland in the years preceding the Reformation when the 'privy kirks' of the 1550s evolved out of an earlier conventicling movement often centred in the households of nobles and lairds. Here, as in Amersham or Iver, it was often reading and hearing the scriptures that provided the content of devotion.[87]

The ultimate physical withdrawal from the community of the parish was into the private closet for prayer and contemplation. Elements in the mystical and *devotio moderna* traditions of the late medieval Church obvi-ously encouraged such withdrawal and the process of self-examination that accompanied it. A profound suspicion of the life of contemplation occasionally emerges in the clerical writers of the period, most notably in

[83] R. Whytford, *A Werke for Housholders*, ed. J. Hogg, Salzburg Studies in English Literature 89 (1979), v. 11–12.

[84] J. Bossy, 'Privacy, Christianity and the state, 1400–1650', in J.Ph. Genet and B. Vincent (eds.), *Etat et Eglise dans la Genèse de l'Etat Moderne* (Madrid, 1986), 105–7.

[85] Plumb, 'A gathered church?', 120–2.

[86] A. Hope, 'Lollardy: the stone the builders rejected?' in P. Lake and M. Dowling (eds.), *Protestantism and the National Church in Sixteenth Century England* (Beckenham, 1987), 10–11. Foxe, iv. 224.

[87] J. Kirk, *Patterns of Reform* (Edinburgh, 1989), 1–15.

the eccentric Reginald Pecock, who used a substantial section of his *Reule of Crysten Religoun* for denouncing prayer, and arguing that it was 'but a means' to 'outward works'.[88] The fear was that the contemplative in-volved a denial of the social, that the inward response to sin diminished the anxiety about shame that was integral to public religious performance. The sin of spiritual pride was to be avoided at all cost, and hence the mystics themselves, especially the influential Walter Hilton, urged a com-bination of the withdrawn life of meditation and proper attention to the active life of the corporate religious community.[89] An ideal is represented by the advice given to a devout fifteenth-century layman by his confessor. There should be constant meditation in a private closet and routine reflec-tion upon unworthiness and sinfulness, even during meals. In addition daily Mass should be heard in church with devout attention to the actions of the priest, and household godliness should be inculcated through col-lective prayers and instruction.[90] This is an elite example, but, as the incorporation into some of the primers of Jean Quentin's *The Maner to Lyve Well, Devoutly and Salutarily Every Day for all Persons of Meane Estate* indicates, there was an intention to construct inward Christians as well as corporate ones in late medieval manuals. Duffy's argument that private prayer, in closet or pew, should not be seen as antagonistic to collective devotion, is no doubt correct, but it is naive to suggest that no differenti-ation was to be found in religious behaviour or social attitude. If we return to the earlier emphasis on cultural practice, on the use to which a standard liturgy and ideological system could be put, then such differenti-ation seems an obvious outcome.[91]

The Sacramental Economy

'The liturgy', to quote Eamon Duffy, 'lay at the heart of medieval religion and the Mass lay at the heart of the liturgy.'[92] Lay belief and behaviour were centred upon the Mass, with its constant renewal of Christ's sacrifice for mankind and its re-articulation of the unity of the Church that he founded. This had, of course, been true of the Christian community throughout the Middle Ages, but the centuries preceding the Reforma-

---

[88] Reginald Pecock, *The Reule of Crysten Religoun*, ed. W.C. Greet, EETS os 171 (1927), 391–7.

[89] Hughes, *Pastors and Visionaries*, 357–60. Hughes stresses that no separate devotional sects were founded in England.

[90] W.A. Pantin, 'Instructions for a devout and literate layman', in J.J.G. Alexander and M.T. Gibson (eds.), *Medieval Learning and Literature* (Oxford, 1976), 389–422.

[91] *This Prayer of Salisbury Use etc.*, printed by F. Regnault (Paris, 1531), fos.15–17. Duffy, *Stripping of the Altars*, 132–4.

[92] Duffy, *Stripping of the Altars*, 91.

tion intensified this preoccupation with the sacramental mediation of the Eucharist. The causes are less our concern here than the consequences for ordinary Christians. Hearing daily Mass became the accepted standard of devout behaviour for early Tudor Englishmen, advocated by the instructional manuals of the Church, but also attested in sources such as Archbishop Warham's Kentish Visitations of 1511–12.[93] At the church men and women should, according to Jean Quentin, 'abide... the space of a low Mass', saying their prayers and reading their primers. Their principal duty, however, was to reverence the host at the moment of elevation, 'kneeling and knocking' as a demonstration of faith.[94] This was particularly manageable at the regular Masses celebrated by chantry priests at the side altars of the parish church. Regularity of celebration and physical intimacy enabled parishioners to experience God daily. Cranmer was later bitterly to denounce arrangements which 'made the people to run from their seats to the altar, and from altar to altar, and from sacring to sacring, peeping, tooting and gazing at that thing which the priest held up in his hands'. Their objective was to assure themselves that they had 'seen [their] Maker', without which they could not go quietly about their business.[95]

What for Cranmer was a matter of reproof must have been for most laymen part of the repertoire of learned behaviour that demonstrated their basic understanding of the central message of Christianity. Parishioners were supposed to be given formal instruction upon the sacrament as part of the curriculum initiated by Archbishop Pecham's Provincial Decrees, and many versions of such guidance exist for the late medieval period. A fourteenth-century reworking of Pecham is typical:

The fourth sacrament is Gods body in form of bread that the priest consecrates at Mass. That every Christian man shall believe that it is verylike Gods body that is born of the maid Mary and hanged on the rood.[96]

Commonplace books, as well as the formal manuals, indicate that laymen regularly had access to these basic forms of guidance about the centrality of the Mass. Versions of the appropriate catechetical material appear in the book of the Norfolk yeoman Robert Reynes in the mid-fifteenth century, and in that of the Londoner Richard Hilles early in the sixteenth century.[97] Visual instruction was offered by sources such as the sacrament fonts of Norfolk, which may have been constructed to provide an ortho-

---

[93] Wood-Legh, *Kentish Visitations*, 56, 98.

[94] *This Prayer of Salisbury*, fo.16. Richard Whitford gave the same advice in his *Werke for Housholders*, 34.

[95] T. Cranmer, *Miscellaneous Writings and Letters*, ed. J.E. Cox (PS, Cambridge, 1846), 442.

[96] R. Dyboski (ed.), *Songs, Carols and other Miscellaneous Poems*, EETS ES 101 (1907), no. 71.

[97] C. Louis (ed.), *The Commonplace Book of Robert Reynes of Acle* (New York, 1980), 180–1.

dox rebuttal of Lollard views.[98] The Church also consciously promoted
the veneration of the Host that Cranmer so disapproved through its support of the cult of Corpus Christi, with its processions and regular display
of Christ's consecrated body.[99]

The forms which heretical denial of the Mass took on the eve of the
Reformation reveal much about its prime meanings for contemporaries.
Lollards interrogated by Bishops Smith and Longland in Lincoln diocese,
by Blythe and Audley in Salisbury, and by Tunstal in London, frequently
made the Mass the focus of their hostility. Of course the evidence is
tainted both by the determination of the ecclesiastical authorities to elicit
confessions on precisely this issue and by the standardization of the interrogatories. But the general approach of the late Lollards is not very different from earlier Wycliffite commentaries.[100] Those examined, when they
addressed the Eucharist, were largely in accord in their denial of the
miracle of transubstantiation. Richard Colins of Ginge's views were typical: 'the sacrament of the altar is not very God, but a certain figurative
thing of Christ in bread'. When Lollards were bold enough to make a
public statement about their faith in the church they sometimes did so by
failing to co-operate in the central moments of the Mass. A group of those
denounced in Buckinghamshire in 1521 were said to 'come to church,
and especially at the elevation time, would say no prayers, but did sit
mum like beasts'.[101] This is not to suggest that heretics approved of other
aspects of the sacrament, simply that they (and the church authorities)
believed that they knew where their principal criticism should be
directed.

For the orthodox, on the other hand, the centrality of the miracle of
the Mass did not detract from the plurality of its meanings and uses.
Diversity began with the liturgy itself, in the articulation of new feasts and
forms of Eucharistic celebration, of which Corpus Christi was only the
most famous. From the 1470s onwards the Mass of the Holy Name
became a highly popular devotion, promoted, as we have seen, by Lady
Margaret Beaufort, but sustained at the parochial level by a rapidly growing number of Jesus fraternities.[102] New votive Masses such as that of the
Five Wounds also achieved very wide support, and one of the most
regular forms of requests for Masses in wills on the eve of the Reformation was for the trental of St Gregory. Particular devotion to the Virgin

[98] A.E. Nichols, *Seeable Signs: The Iconography of the Seven Sacraments, 1350–1544* (1994).

[99] Rubin, *Corpus Christi*, 97–108.

[100] J.A.F. Thomson, *The Later Lollards, 1414–1520* (Oxford, 1965), 241–2. A. Hudson, *The Premature Reformation: Wycliffite Texts and Lollard History* (Oxford, 1988), 468–9.

[101] Foxe, iv. 235.

[102] R.W. Pfaff, *New Liturgical Feasts in Late Medieval England* (Oxford, 1970).

or to an aspect of the sacrament could be expressed in the form of benefactions.[103] Sir Edmund Leversedge of Frome, for example, who believed
that he had been saved from a horrendous death and damnation by his
devotion to the Blessed Sacrament, left much of his substance to found a
Corpus Christi fraternity to say Masses in honour of Christ's blood.[104]
Christocentric devotion of this kind is one of the aspects of Scottish pre-
Reformation piety that is well documented: sacrament houses or aumbrys
can be found in at least thirty-five medieval churches, and half of these
date from the period after 1500. The feast of the Holy Name also attracted
Scottish support.[105] New devotions did not necessarily exclude the old, as
the continuing popularity of traditional shrines and images attests, but they
did offer different forms of contemplation, often connected with continental fashions of the Rhineland and Low Countries.

Pluralism and diversity also manifested themselves in the world of para-
liturgy and sacramentals that gave meaning to lay approaches to the holy.
The range of possibilities offered by late medieval ritual is here so great as
to defy easy categorization. On the one hand there were rituals that 'spun
out' of the experience of Christ's sacrifice. Easter sepulchres, with their
symbolic burying and raising of Christ during Easter week, became a
common feature of English churches, and the sepulchre sometimes
became a setting for the display of the host in a piece of merged symbolism.[106] The holy bread dispensed at the end of the parish Mass was another tangible example of a desire to participate actively in the meaning of
the ritual. In a rather different category were the customs and beliefs
associated with lay concern to see the Host regularly. The blessing it
conferred would, it was believed, protect against evil and disaster so that:

> Thy fote that day shall not the fayll;
> Thyn eyen from ther syght shall not blynd.[107]

Conversely medieval literature was full of moralized tales of those who
abused or ignored the Eucharist, and came to horrible ends. Miracle
stories of Lollard priests who made the Blood of Hailes boil or Jews who
violated the host and suffered gruesome fates were, of course, literary
constructs of the clergy, but they probably reflected general belief in the
power and efficacy of the consecrated bread.[108] And this combination of
powerful belief and flexible practice readily ended in the world where

---

[103] R.W. Pfaff, 'The English devotion of St Gregory's Trental', *Speculum* 49 (1974), 75–90.

[104] Brown, *Popular Piety*, 1–2, 24–5.

[105] Lynch, 'Medieval Scotland', 118–19. D. MacRoberts, 'Scottish sacrament houses', *Trans-actions of the Scottish Ecclesiological Society* 15 (1965), 30–56.

[106] Duffy, *Stripping of the Altars*, 125–7.   [107] Ibid., 100.

[108] Rubin, *Corpus Christi*, 294–7.

pieces of the host were stolen to facilitate magic, or divination, and the quest for lost goods depended upon the assurance of the Mass.[109]

Reformers were aware from the fifteenth century onwards that some line had to be drawn around the practice of the Mass and its multiplicity of meanings. The problem was perhaps located less where Keith Thomas identified it a generation ago, in the territory of magic or popular behaviour detached from a full understanding of the sacrament and yet dependent upon it for social meaning.[110] Rather it lay in what Miri Rubin has called the over-determination of the symbol: the vast range of competing meanings and claims attached to a universal act, through lay and sacerdotal claims, art and drama, individual and collective investment.[111] English devotion to the Eucharist, Lollard dissent notwithstanding, does not seem to be in question, and the limited evidence for the rest of the British Isles confirms the same tale. But in the multiplicity of uses and devotions, in the desire to quantify access to the divine through, for example, increased Masses for the dead, is represented the quest to appropriate the holy for sectional and lay benefit. That the symbol nevertheless largely survived may be due more to the power still exercised by the mediating priesthood than to any profoundly centripetal force inherent in the Mass itself.[112]

The sacramental economy of late medieval Britain and Ireland often seems to overvalue the Eucharist. But for the individual Christian the Mass represented only a stage in the cycle of salvation, in that process by which with the assistance of divine grace he or she could through confession, contrition, and absolution ultimately become worthy of redemption. The formal sacrament, the 'houseling' that looms large in the manuals for medieval priests, was normally only an annual affair, conducted in Lent in preparation for the Easter communion.[113] It was, if properly conducted, a burdensome activity, involving the clergy in interrogating parishioners on their basic knowledge of the catechetical programme of the Church as well as on their particular sins. When the Pastons 'advertised' their benefice of Oxnead, asking contacts for names of suitable priests, they stressed its attractions by arguing that there were no more than twenty people to be confessed annually.[114] Contrast this with the difficulties that must have arisen in the great burgh churches of Scotland, where there were often

---

[109] K.V. Thomas, *Religion and the Decline of Magic* (Oxford, 1971), 36–40, 60–1.

[110] Ibid., 36–7.

[111] Rubin, *Corpus Christi*, 348–50. T.F. Ruiz, 'Unsacred monarchy: the kings of Castile in the late Middle Ages', in S. Wilentz (ed.), *Rites of Power: Symbolism, Ritual and Politics since the Middle Ages* (Philadelphia, 1985), 109–44.

[112] J. Bossy, 'The Mass as a social institution, 1200–1700', *PP* 100 (1983), 29–61.

[113] Marshall, *Catholic Priesthood*, 5–13. Duffy, *Stripping of the Altars*, 59–63.

[114] N. Davis (ed.), *Paston Letters and Papers of the Fifteenth Century*, 2 vols. (Oxford, 1971), i. 178.

several thousand parishioners.[115] We have scattered evidence that the Easter reception of the Eucharist was taken very seriously in pre-Reformation England, and that it was preceded by carefully organized confession.[116] The Norfolk sacrament fonts show careful organization of penitents, provision of kneeling desks and priests' chairs, and some attempt at privacy during the rite.[117] In confession, as elsewhere, there was an enlarged form of lay piety that demanded more than this annual cycle. Confessors with responsibilities for particular families were regularly licensed by the bishops from the fourteenth century onwards, and bequests to 'my ghostly father' become a routine feature of late medieval wills.[118]

By far the most explicit evidence of general lay assumptions about the importance of confession comes from the deathbed. The need to 'housle and shrift at my last ending' is recurrent in popular literature, in wills, and in the anxious fears of parishioners that careless or temporarily absent priests might not be available to hear their last repentance.[119] For example, the wardens of Bampton, Oxfordshire, complained that John Taylor had died without 'the sacraments of the church' through the neglect of their curate.[120] Primers assured devout readers that if they used the correct prayers they 'shall not perish with sudden death'. Through the genre of the *ars moriendi* laymen were taught that they must make full confession of their sins, putting their trust in Christ, the Virgin, and the whole company of heaven, and seeking absolution. The good deathbed confession became part of that great weight of 'last things' that late medieval laymen were convinced were necessary to protect the soul from the pains of purgatory.[121] Historians disagree on whether the preoccupation with purgatory disturbed the balance of lay religiosity, making it a 'cult of the living in service of the dead'. Those who underline the obsession are perhaps unduly influenced by the nature of our sources, which is rich with information about chantries, monuments, and wills, and certainly disposes us to a clearer understanding of the wishes of the dying rather

[115] Lynch, 'Medieval Scotland', 120. Doncaster had 2,000 'houseling people' according to the chantry commissioners.

[116] L. Duggan, 'Fear and confession on the eve of the Reformation', *ARG* 75 (1984), 153–75.

[117] A.E. Nicholls, 'The etiquette of pre-Reformation confession in East Anglia', *C16J* 17 (1986), 145–63.

[118] Brigden, *London*, 44–6. Brown, *Popular Piety*, 203–5. Quentin proposed weekly, or at least fortnightly, shriving, *This Prayer of Salisbury*, fo. 16ᵛ. Marshall, *Catholic Priesthood*, 13–15.

[119] Duffy, *Stripping of the Altars*, 310–27.

[120] A. Hamilton-Thompson (ed.), *Visitations in the Diocese of Lincoln, 1517–31*, 3 vols., LRS 33, 35, 37, vol. ii, 50.

[121] A. Galpern, 'The legacy of late medieval religion in sixteenth-century Champagne', in C. Trinkhaus and H. Oberman (eds.), *The Pursuit of Holiness* (1974), 149. P. Aries, *The Hour of Our Death* (1981).

than those of the living.[122] Even these sources do not necessarily indicate total preoccupation with the horrors of the afterlife. Chantries served the function of supporting the living, through the network of Masses, the linkage of kin, natural and artificial, and sometimes teaching or preaching. Monuments, even when they displayed cadavers and worms, might speak of the worth of a good name and above all of the need for charitable deeds. The purpose of their horrors was to stir men to early penitence since: 'penance is health in the man whole, and it is sick and feeble in the man unsteadfast'.[123]

Yet death and in particular the doctrine of purgatory did haunt the living; did require a level of thought, anxiety, and financial investment from ordinary men and women that is distinctive in Christian history. Even those aspects of devotion that seemed least structurally linked to mortality flourished because of the fears of the living. Pilgrimages were often undertaken with an eye to the afterlife.[124] Margery Kempe travelled to shrines largely to gain indulgences, and she was given money by others to pray for them at shrines where such benefits could be found.[125] One of the most famous sites, that of St Patrick's Purgatory, at Lough Derg, provoked visions of the sufferings of the souls being purged, such as that of William of Stranton, a fifteenth-century pilgrim from Durham, which both warned against the horrors to come and offered protection against them.[126] Penitential bequests might help in the general provision of Masses, and might assist parochial regimes: their purpose, however, was unequivocally to protect individuals and families from the full threat of purgatory. This required not just careful general investment in the singing of Masses, the maintenance of lights, and the like. It came to involve precise calculations about how the soul might progress through its torments. Wills, for example, often laid great stress on the importance of a rapid sequence of Masses immediately after death because this was when prayer was most efficacious and made the soul 'strong to suffer...pain with the more patience'.[127] It might even secure a quick release from purgatory. The multiplication of Masses indicates a belief that each one

---

[122] G.R. Keiser, 'The progress of purgatory: visions of the afterlife in late medieval English literature', *Analecta Cartusiana* 107 (1987), 72–100. For a determinedly positive reading see Duffy *Stripping of the Altars* and 338 ff.

[123] *The Arte or Crafte to Lyve Well and to Dye Well* (1505), fos. lxxxxxiv–v [*sic*].

[124] R.C. Finucane, *Miracles and Pilgrimages: Popular Beliefs in Medieval England* (1977), 191–202.

[125] *Book of Margery Kempe*, 79, 106.

[126] R. Easting (ed.), *St Patrick's Purgatory*, EETS os 288 (1998), 79–117.

[127] T. Erbe (ed.), *Mirk's Festial: A Collection of Homilies*, EETS es 96 (1905), 296. Another example of the same direct association between prayer and time off purgatory is the 'Fifteen Oes', which promised the release of fifteen souls from purgatory. E. Hoskins, *Horae Beatae Mariae Virginis* (1901), 124–7.

represented a unit of merit, and the rich do seem to have believed that they were purchasing advantage in the next life having had it in this. No amount of historical enthusiasm for late medieval piety will quite erase the sense that the Church manipulated this spiritual calculus in its use of indulgences. Its objectives were often worthy—the support of a shrine, of hospitals, of bridges, and so on—the explicit claims to a number of days of remission less so.[128]

Images and Pilgrimages

When John Foxe summarized the grounds on which Lollards objected to Catholic doctrine he singled out, in addition to the Eucharist, pilgrimages and the adoration of images. The two themes are clearly interconnected, as they were in the jeering attack of Elizabeth Sampson on the pilgrimage image of Our Lady of Willesden, who 'was a burnt arsed elf and a burnt arsed stock' who would not have allowed 'her tail to have been burnt' if she could have helped her worshippers.[129] Radical Lollards hated pilgrimages as 'the second trap of the fiend', though a number of the comments in the early sixteenth-century interrogations suggest mainly contempt for a worthless and wasteful activity.[130] William Sweeting, burned for heresy in 1511, had an orthodox wife whom he despised for her pursuit of shrines, and Thomas Geoffrey maintained that the only true pilgrimage was going barefoot to visit the poor and sick.[131] Images were more explicitly hated because they led to idolatry and therefore the denial of the Decalogue, and they led the innocent astray by substituting 'sticks and stones' for the living power of the Word.[132] Agnes Hignell of Newbury went further: when devout Christian people 'be offering their candle to the image of St Erasmus I would I had a hatchet in my hand'.[133] On occasions such views led to direct action, as they did at Rickmansworth in 1522, when all the images in the church were deliberately burned by unknown arsonists.[134]

---

[128] On the parochial advantages of chantries see C. Burgess, '"For the Increase of Divine Service": chantries in the parish in late medieval Bristol', *JEH* 36 (1985), 46–65. N. Tanner, *The Church in Late Medieval Norwich* (Toronto, 1984), 105–6.

[129] Foxe, iv. 218.

[130] M. Aston, *Faith and Fire: Popular and Unpopular Religion, 1350–1600* (1993), 24. L.M. Swinburn (ed.), *The Lanterne of Light* EETS os 151 (1917), 84.

[131] Foxe, iv. 215.

[132] Foxe, iv. 221. M. Aston, *England's Iconoclasts*, vol. i: *Laws against Images* (Oxford, 1988), 96–143.

[133] D.P. Wright (ed.), *The Register of Thomas Langton, Bishop of Salisbury, 1485–93*, Canterbury and York Society 74 (1985), 495.

[134] Aston, *Faith and Fire*, 231–60.

At the other end of the reforming spectrum doubts about the merits of cultivating images were shared by humanists concerned to improve devotional standards. Most famous is Erasmus's outspoken criticism of images and pilgrimages, particularly his witty demolition of the paraphernalia of the Walsingham and Becket shrines. In the *Enchiridion* (1503) he had earlier expressed deep reservations about the popular tendency to confuse sign and signifier through images: 'you honour a likeness of Christ's face that has been crudely shaped out of rock or wood...much more to be honoured is that likeness of his mind...portrayed in the words of the gospels'.[135] The localization of the holy in images and sites was criticized within the *devotio moderna* tradition.[136] Thomas More, even in the heady pre-Lutheran days, was less disposed than Erasmus and his colleagues to direct denunciation of holy helpers, but he contributed some of the most memorable criticisms of popular, or rather female, credulity. London wives, he complained, gaped at the Virgin by the Tower until they believed she smiled at them. And the competing devotions to the Virgin were satirized in the narrative of the wives who challenged one another with '"I love best our lady of Walsingham." "And I", saith the other, "our lady of Ipswich".'[137] John Fisher, standing as so often at the most traditional end of the humanist spectrum, does not indulge in this sort of critique, but in his sermons avoids discussion of saints and pilgrimages in favour of strongly Christocentric and biblical piety. Other forms of devotion aroused anxieties, but none seemed to orthodox reformers to be so open to lay abuse.[138]

These fears were generated partly by the sheer scale and diversity of late medieval cults. Duffy has shown that English churches were literally stuffed with images: Faversham in Kent, for example, had approximately thirty-five in the early sixteenth century, each with their own lights and a number with their own altars or chapels.[139] In addition we have the surviving evidence of the rood screens, especially of East Anglia and Devon, on which cycles of saints served as the supporters of the rood itself, with its central image and Mary and John on either side. The screens are particularly valuable evidence of lay attitudes to the saints, since there was no absolutely fixed iconography and in many cases it can

[135] Aston, *England's Iconoclasts*, 195–201. R. Himelick (ed.), *The Enchiridion of Erasmus* (Bloomington, Ind., 1963), 112.

[136] C.M.N. Eire, *War against the Idols: The Reformation of Worship from Erasmus to Calvin* (Cambridge, 1986), 11–22.

[137] *CWTM*, vi. 1. 230–2.

[138] J.E.B. Mayor (ed.), *The English Works of John Fisher*, EETS ES 27 (1876), 289–310, 388–428. S. Wabuda, 'The Provision of Preaching during the English Reformation', University of Cambridge Ph.D. (1991), 65.

[139] Duffy, *Stripping of the Altars*, 155–60.

be shown that they were constructed with lay benefactions. Apostles and prophets were a recurrent feature of the screens as, more interestingly, were the four Latin doctors of the Church, the latter perhaps intended to reinforce the significance of orthodoxy in the face of dissent.[140] Amid the diversity of ordinary saints it is difficult to offer generalities about the most popular groupings of saints, but two sets of wide significance may be noted. This first were the holy helpers, such as St Margaret, St Agatha, St Barbara, St Erasmus and St George, who were protectors of childbirth, marriage, and the home, and guarantors of health and stability. These saints provided, to adapt Duffy's phrase, fire-insurance and medical cover. Then there were the images that can only be explained as part of local cults: St Edmund, St Wulfstan, and even the uncanonized, such as St Etheldreda and Master John Schorne, in the case of Norfolk. Most of the latter group have their focus in shrines accessible for local pilgrimage and therefore offer an identity as old as saint cult itself with a site of spiritual power.

Throughout Britain and Ireland the cult of the saints and the pursuit of pilgrimage continued to have these dual, though interconnected, focuses. The lives of the universal holy helpers were made more routinely accessible through the printed editions of the *Legenda Aurea*, which ran through seven editions between 1483 and 1527. The stock of individual helpers might rise and fall with national or regional fashion—among the male saints, for example, Roche and Sebastian seem to have enjoyed growing prestige.[141] Meanwhile local cult identities also proved remarkably tenacious. This was partly because of determined clerical sponsorship: the old equation of pilgrimage sites with spiritual prestige and wealth endured. But the enthusiasm of the laity cannot be ignored. For example, the cult of St Osmund of Salisbury was strongly sponsored by the cathedral: yet it drew offerings, bequests, and reports of miracles until the eve of the dissolutions.[142] St Urith of Chittlehampton, Devon, was the focus of a strong local cult still vital in the 1530s: offerings to her image had helped to fund the late-Perpendicular tower of the church, and contributed approximately £50 to its coffers per annum.[143]

---

[140] E. Duffy, 'The parish, piety and patronage in late medieval East Anglia: the evidence of rood screens', in French *et al.*, *Parish in English Life*, 133–62. For an important study of the screen of Ashton, Devon, which is directed towards the clergy and the donor family's private pew, see M. Glassoe, 'Late medieval paintings in Ashton church, Devon', *Journal of the British Archaeological Association* 140 (1987), 182–90.

[141] Duffy, *Stripping of the Altars*, 169–83.

[142] Brown, *Popular Piety*, 57–63.

[143] Whiting, *Blind Devotion*, 54–5.

It is impossible to quantify patterns of pilgrimage, but it might be noted that this is an area in which popular devotion in the Celtic lands is particularly visible. The Welsh, Irish, and Scots had the particular advantage of a host of Celtic saints to whom to turn. In Wales St David offered a national cult, while figures of the second rank, such as Teilo, Beuno, and the 20,000 saints of Bardsey Island, provided regional sites to venerate.[144] The Scots focused much of their energy on Saints Ninian and Duthac, and in the century before the Reformation royal patronage played a significant part in affirming their importance.[145] The most famous Irish example was St Patrick's Purgatory on Lough Derg, but saints' sites derived from the Celtic tradition continued to be popular, especially where they were associated with the holy wells that were a general feature of the Western landscapes of Britain and Ireland.[146] St Winifred, for example, was able to preserve the reputation for sanctity of her well in North Wales even though her remains had been translated to Shrewsbury.[147] However, it is important to emphasize that the Irish and the Welsh were not caught up in some Celtic twilight directing all their devotions to local saints whose deeds were unknown to Rome. Most of those appearing on Irish tombs are universal figures, and the fifteen places of pilgrimage visited by the penitent Heneas MacNichaill in 1539 includes Marian shrines and the abbey at Holy Cross as well as sacred rocks, wells, and the Arran Islands. Several of the greatest Welsh shrines were focuses of Marian devotion.[148]

It is even more difficult to read the mind of a parishioner in prayer before an image, or on pilgrimage, than it is to judge response to the Mass or confession. But we might note that, while the belief in the intercessory powers of the saints in the business of this world seems to have been a constant, concern for their role as petitioners for the soul probably grows in importance in conjunction with the preoccupation with purgatory. The point is best shown in relation to the greatest of all the cults, that of the Virgin. Marian devotion has so many aspects in late medieval Britain and Ireland that it is impossible to do it any justice within a few lines. Every aspect of the humanity and sanctity of the Virgin produced its share of poems and prayers, statues and shrines. The Book of Hours that

---

[144] Williams, *Welsh Church*, 485–90.

[145] Lynch, 'Medieval Scotland', 121. D. McKay, 'Parish life in Scotland, 1500–1560', in D. McRoberts (ed.), *Essays on the Scottish Reformation* (Glasgow, 1962), 109–10. See above, p. 37.

[146] C. Lennon, *Sixteenth-Century Ireland: The Incomplete Conquest* (Dublin, 1994), 132.

[147] T. Charles-Edwards, *Saint Winefride and her Well* (1964).

[148] Meigs, *Reformations in Ireland*, 119–21. L.P. Murray, 'A Calendar of the Register of Primate George Dowdall', *Journal of the County Louth Archaeological Society*, 6 (1927), 152.

became the primer of lay devotion was constructed around the Little Office of the Blessed Virgin, and the meditations on her joys and sorrows were central to the pious routines of Englishmen.[149] They seem to have been just as significant to the Irish, but with the local variant that their relationship with the Mother of God was perceived as an extension of earthly kin-bonds. 'May she, my sister and His nurse, help me for God's sake in virtue of her kinship,' wrote one of the fifteenth-century poets.[150] Rosary devotions loomed large in Scottish piety: they are to be found, for example, in the poems recorded in Arundel MS 285, and on the banner of Edinburgh's Holy Blood fraternity.[151] The greatest of late medieval English pilgrimage sites, like those of Wales, were dedicated to the Virgin, with Our Lady of Walsingham as the most outstanding.[152] There are, however, signs that it was intercession for the soul in torment that was seen as the prime function of Mary and her saintly supporters on the eve of the Reformation.[153] In the final section of the lengthy Marian prayer 'Obsecro te' the suppliant lists the benefits of her intercession. They include spiritual and bodily health, correct living, peace, and so on, but are aimed above all at procuring the spiritual benefits needed at the hour of death, when Mary's intercession would be crucial.[154]

Popular Dissent

This rapid survey of religious belief and practice has been deliberately exclusionary. Little has been said of the massive investment in church building that characterized most parts of England in the later fifteenth century, is almost equally evident in Scotland, and can be identified on a more modest scale in Wales and Ireland.[155] Nor have we exhausted the devotional possibilities of late medieval religion or the complexities of sacramental mediation. These additions would not, however, significantly change the image of lay commitment to the structures and patterns of the faith already outlined. The centripetal influence of the liturgy held

---

[149] Hoskins, *Horae*, 66–7.

[150] Meigs, *Reformations in Ireland*, 31.

[151] Fitch, 'Search for Salvation', 471.

[152] Finucane, *Miracles and Pilgrimages*, 195–202. Williams, *Welsh Church*, 490–2.

[153] C. Peters, 'Women and the Reformation: Social Relations and Attitudes in Rural England, *ca.*1470–1570', University of Oxford D.Phil. (1992), 264–80.

[154] Fitch, 'Search for Salvation', 490–7.

[155] For England see C. Platt, *The Parish Churches of Medieval England* (1981), 138–89. For Wales, Williams, *Welsh Church*, 428–9; R.I. Jack, 'Religious life in a Welsh marcher lordship: the lordship of Dyffryn Clwyd in the later Middle Ages', in C. Barron and C. Harper-Bill (eds.), *The Church in Pre-Reformation Society* (Woodbridge, 1985), 155–7. For Ireland, Jefferies, *Priests and Prelates*, 22–5. For Scotland, R. Fawcett, *Scottish Architecture from the Accession of the Stewarts to the Reformation, 1371–1560* (Edinburgh, 1994), 142 ff.

together a diverse and pluralistic set of religious behaviour, most of which could be accommodated within the broad frame of the holy. A tension certainly existed between the assumptions of reforming clergy and the wilder reaches of lay experience: in the cult of the saints, in understanding of the sacred and the secular, and in the use to which the sacraments and sacramentals of the Church might be put. Most of the time the strictures of the reformers neither destabilized the local church nor, it must be said, probably changed lay behaviour significantly.

This raises the obvious question of why any sane layman would have dissented from this comprehensive, but rather permissive, *corpus Christiani*. But dissent a number of them did, especially in Essex, Buckinghamshire, and London, the areas of greatest late Lollard strength.[156] Formal dissent has to be put in perspective, of course. So far as can be judged from the surviving archives there was no challenge to the established Church in Ireland or Wales, very little in Northern England or the West Country and only one 'nest of heretics' in Scotland.[157] The only evidence of heretical activity in Wales is that a Lollard Bible seems to have influenced the first passage of scriptural translation into Welsh.[158] In Scotland there was the shadowy group described by Knox as the Lollards of Kyle, thirty-four of whom were accused in 1494. The most solid evidence that we have of their continuing importance comes from the New Testament in Scots that Murdoch Nisbet translated from the Purvey text in the 1520s, a version that was never published.[159] The limited geographical scope of late dissent, as well as the essentially quietist nature much of it seems to possess, has led in recent years to casual dismissals of its significance. However, where it did exist there is sometimes evidence of quite wide-spread sympathy or interest from lay men and women across the social spectrum. The extreme example is Amersham, where as many as a quarter of the population seem to have Lollard links in the 1520s.[160] Elsewhere it is more difficult to be confident about the presence or absence of dissent: in Salisbury diocese, for example, there were scattered prosecutions for heresy in the early sixteenth century, but little evidence of cells of Lollards being detected by the bishops.[161] Those who were detected appear well

---

[156] On Lollard distribution see R.G. Davies, 'Lollardy and locality', *TRHS* 6th ser. 1 (1991), 200–7.

[157] Sceptical views about numbers can be found in Haigh, *English Reformations*, 54–5, and R.N. Swanson, *Church and Society in Late Medieval England* (Oxford, 1989), 342–5.

[158] Williams, *Wales and Reformation*, 15.

[159] Knox, i. 7–12. M. Sanderson, *Ayrshire and the Reformation* (East Linton, East Lothian, 1997), 40–3. T.G. Law (ed.), *The New Testament in Scots*, 3 vols., STS 46, 49, 52 (1901–5), vol. i, pp. x–xiv.

[160] On Amersham see Plumb, 'A gathered church?', 132–63.

[161] Brown, *Popular Piety*, 215–22.

integrated into local society. Are they therefore merely the vocal end of a more silent sympathy with heterodoxy?

Numbers matter, as does social status, but the most interesting question in the current historiographical climate is why groups found it necessary to oppose the powerful embrace of the Church and the diverse communal expectations that were associated with it. The evidence that family networks often sustained heresy provides a part of the answer: Lollardy was an inherited avocation. Another partial explanation may lie in those sectors of society prone to general restiveness: Lollardy in cloth towns or in London may be a symptom of economic and social alienation. But beliefs must surely be central: denials of aspects of the sacramental system and of the mediatory role of the saints, and the allied conviction that access to the Bible was essential to salvation.[162] Attacks on the existing sacramental scheme might, very tentatively, be divided between those who denied the entire mediatory role of the priesthood, hence the sacrifice of the Mass and transubstantiation, and those whose recorded comments addressed the abuses of popular religion. In the latter category, the most significant issue of saint cult has already been discussed, but a list could be accumulated including pilgrimage, prayers for the dead, and the elaboration of the liturgy. For example, a number of those accused of heresy in Coventry in 1485 were said to have denied purgatory and to have insisted that men 'incontinent after death' go to either heaven or hell.[163] The doctrines of baptism, of confession before a priest, and of the authority of the papacy, were all challenged from time to time, though interestingly the last was rarely found in late Lollardy. There is also evidence that Lollards sought to justify their position by turning their critique of ceremony to positive ends. True fasting was fasting from sin; true pilgrimage the visiting of the sick.[164]

Above all Lollards were a people of the text, insistent that men must understand their faith by reading and exposition. They tended to displace, even if they did not utterly reject, the symbolic articulation of belief. The devout man was one who, like Robert Pope, sat up until midnight reading his text.[165] Concern that there should be access to Scripture linked together the Ayrshire Lollards.[166] The vernacular Bible was the core issue,

---

[162] The time seems ripe for a new analysis of the Lollard beliefs that emerge from trials in the late period. Meanwhile Thomson, *Later Lollards*, offers a good general survey, though it places undue emphasis on the negations in Lollard testimony. See also Hope, 'Lollardy', 12–25. A. Hudson, *The Premature Reformation: Wycliffite Texts and Lollard History* (Oxford, 1988), 468–73.

[163] Foxe, iv. 133–4.

[164] Hudson, *Premature Reformation*, 307–8.

[165] Hope, 'Lollardy', 19–21.

[166] Sanderson, *Ayrshire*, 41.

though in practice few ordinary Lollards could have access to the whole of the banned text, and they were highly dependent on smaller bindings being passed between them, or on the oral transmission offered by visiting preachers. And within Scripture they privileged the tradition of law and works: the Ten Commandments, the Sermon on the Mount, the Epistle of St James. Like humanists, Lollards seem to have accepted that knowledge was the essential prerequisite for proper action, the doing of good works for their own sake, not as part of the calculus of salvation.[167]

Lollards were convinced of a conspiracy by the priesthood to deny knowledge to the laity, a theme vividly articulated by Tyndale in his attack on priestly authority and widely accepted in subsequent historical narrative.[168] More recently Duffy and others have fiercely contested this analysis, pointing to the sustained catechetical literature of the late medieval Church, to the insistence on basic doctrinal knowledge for the taking of communion, to the translation of prayers and the dissemination of homilies. The ploughman was supposed to learn his *pater noster* and the medieval parish church was often replete with mnemonic devices to help him do so.[169] The only denials, on this reading, were of those texts explicitly identified as heterodox, and of the whole Bible in the mother tongue. Even that last prohibition could be alleviated by episcopal licence, permitting the influential to read the scriptures. But a more fundamental denial was involved. Traditional lay religion in pre-Reformation England is flexible and vibrant, able to adapt itself to various spiritual needs, to enter into a dialogue and exchange of power with ecclesiastical authority. Through the rich catechetical and devotional literature of the period it was offered the opportunity for intellectual as well as affective engagement with the faith. What was denied was any legitimate means of checking the claims of the Church against the Word. Such a questioning was no doubt irrelevant for the vast majority of the laity. For a small minority who quickly extended beyond the immediate ranks of the Lollards, it became an issue of vital spiritual significance.

---

[167] Foxe, iv. 222, 224–6. *LP*, iv. 2. 4029. J.F. Davis, *Heresy and Reformation in the South East of England 1520–1559* (1983), 57–8.

[168] W. Tyndale, 'Obedience of a Christian Man', in *Doctrinal Treatises*, ed. H. Walter (PS, Cambridge, 1848), 144–62.

[169] Duffy, *Stripping of the Altars*, 53–87. *How the plowman lerned his pater noster* (Wykyn de Worde, 1505). Graves, 'Social space', 305–6. Nichols, *Seeable Signs*, 147–57. The commonplace book of Robert Reynes is also full of counting devices, presumably intended to aid learning: Louis, *Robert Reynes*, 152, 154, 287.

PART II

THE COMING OF REFORMATION

4

THE POLITICS OF REFORM, 1530–1558

The powr of princys, ys gevyn fro god above
And as saythe Salomon, ther hartes the lord dothe move
God spekyth in ther lyppes, whan they gave jugement
The lawys that they make, are by the lordes appoyntment
Christ wylled not his [disciples] the[ir] princes to correct
But to ther prescepttes, rether to be subjecte.

J. Bale, *King Johan*, ll. 1343–8[1]

The English and Scottish monarchies were regularly exposed to the enthusiastic political advice of their writers and poets in the long-established tradition of the *regnum principum*. It was the duty of the author to counsel princes to reform themselves and their realms: weak kings, misled by their own sensuality and weakness, failed to secure order among their subjects and to produce harmony in the commonweal. Hence the royal characters of the morality plays—Skelton's Magnificence or Lindsay's King Humanitie—are being led to an apprehension of good government through the representation of the seductive power of the vices.[2] Effective monarchs could discipline their own fallen natures and provide proper remedies for the failures of their subjects. In the opening session of the Reformation parliament More spoke of Henry VIII as a 'good shepherd', governing the realm by 'vigilantly foreseeing things to come' and seeking to compensate for the 'frail condition of man' by making good laws to reform abuses.[3]

These topoi were rarely passive commonplaces: instead they should be read as rhetorical strategies, designed to elicit an appropriate dialectical response in their audiences. The latter were both the monarch directly addressed or described and those who might in practice have the power of persuasion—nobles, counsellors, clergy, estates, and parliaments. Imaginative writers sought to persuade of the need for proper distributive justice, of the desirability of strong political control and careful financial manage-

---

[1] J.H. Pafford (ed.), *King Johan by John Bale* (Malone Society, Oxford, 1931).
[2] G. Walker, *Plays of Persuasion: Drama and Politics at the Court of Henry VIII* (Cambridge, 1991), 60–101, 169–221. R. Lyall (ed.), *Sir David Lindsay of the Mount: Ane Satyre of the Thrie Estaitis* (Edinburgh, 1989).
[3] E. Hall, *Chronicle: Life of King Henry VIII*, ed. C. Whibley, 2 vols. (1804), ii. 164.

ment, of the significance of fostering learning, and a host of related
themes. Challenging the behaviour of the clergy was part of these traditional topoi, but suddenly from the late 1520s began to assume a deadly
political earnestness as Henry VIII sought some way out of his unwanted
marriage to Catherine of Aragon. Pleas for reform quickly became comprehensive calls for the reconstruction of church and state. For Bale,
writing at the end of the 1530s, royal power over the Church was represented as the means to effect a full Protestantism in England. For Sir
David Lindsay, writing *The Thrie Estates* in the Scotland of the early
1550s, King Humanitie, supported by his Estates, was to enact laws to:

> fortifie
> The Kirk of Christ and His religioun,
> Without dissimulance or hypocrisie,[4]

and the drama proceeds to list acts that form a thorough reformation.
Even drama that upheld the Catholic faith, such as *Respublica*, which dates
from the beginning of Mary's reign, turned to the crown as the agent of
regeneration and renewal. Mary was represented by the author as Nemesis
sent:

> To reform th'abuses which hitherto have been:
> And that ills which long time have reigned uncorrect
> Shall now, for ever, be redressed with effect.[5]

The appeal to monarchy as agent of renewal and reform helps to explain why cultures that usually identified change with danger and instability assimilated radical shifts in religious organization and belief without
collapsing into profound disorder. By investigating the politics of religious
change before examining ideology or religious behaviour the ensuing
analysis will partially subscribe to these readings. Reformation in England,
Wales, and Ireland was initiated from above as a consequence of political
choices. It was driven by monarchical will and sustained as much by
the identification of sections of the political elite with that will as by the
commitment and hope of the clerical reformers. The crown could not act
alone, but it often appeared that it alone could direct the religious destinies of its dominions. The situation of Scotland was very different both
because of the biological crises experienced by the monarchy and because
the state was inherently less centralized. In each realm, however, it is
essential to begin by understanding the matrix of political circumstances
that made reformation, or its rejection, possible for the rulers.

---

[4] Lyall, *Ane Satyre*, ll. 3827–9.
[5] W.W. Greg (ed.), *Respublica*, EETS os 226 (1952), ll. 50–2.

Divorce and Supremacy

In 1521 Henry VIII's political interests had been served by his trenchant stand against Luther, articulated in the *Assertio* dedicated to Pope Leo. Half a decade later circumstances had changed: Cardinal Wolsey still wove plans for universal peace and accord, hoping to snatch high reputation for his monarch, even from the crisis created by the sack of Rome in 1527. For Henry, however, the behaviour of Charles V's troops was of moment mainly because it resulted in the imprisonment of Clement VII, the total dislocation of pontifical business, and the threat of long-term Habsburg dominance of the papacy. These were critical problems because by the early months of 1527 divorce from Catherine of Aragon had become Henry's central concern and was rapidly coming to determine the whole direction of English politics.[6] Bitter frustration at the absence of an heir and the appearance of the bright eyes of Anne Boleyn, with her failure to accept the mere status of royal mistress, provided Henry with his immediate motives for action. It was, however, one of the defining moments of the king's own attitudes to authority and belief that he turned to the Bible, and to his knowledge of two Levitical texts against a man's marriage to his brother's widow, to justify his repudiation of Catherine. These texts seem to have been Henry's own 'discovery', despite later attempts to identify either Wolsey or the king's confessor, John Longland, as the guiding spirit. Of course, Henry had no intention in 1527 of denying the principle of papal right to act on the divorce: his manoeuvres, for example, included a botched attempt to seek dispensation for what amounted to bigamy. But he rapidly acknowledged that his expedient purposes had to be underpinned by divine sanction and moved with enthusiasm into the jurisdictional and ideological minefield that Wolsey was seeking to control. His favourite argument based on Leviticus remained unshakeable throughout the divorce crisis: no pope could dispense from the law of God, therefore the dispensation granted by Julius II so that Henry could marry his brother's widow was invalid.[7]

The two years which followed Henry's first overt pressure for divorce were occupied by Wolsey's increasingly desperate attempts to have the

---

[6] The best narrative of the divorce proceedings remains J.J. Scarisbrick, *Henry VIII* (1968), 147–240. See also E.W. Ives, *Anne Boleyn* (Oxford, 1986), 77–182.

[7] V. Murphy, 'The literature and propaganda of Henry VIII's first divorce', in D. MacCulloch (ed.), *The Reign of Henry VIII: Politics, Policy and Piety* (Basingstoke, 1995), 135–58, offers an important argument for the early dating of Henry's insistence that the pope could not dispense from divine law. For the particular issues raised in the divorce proceedings see H.A. Kelly, *The Matrimonial Trials of Henry VIII* (Stanford, Calif., 1976). Henry's Leviticus texts were 18: 16 and 20: 21. J. Harpsfield, *The Life and Death of Sir Thomas Moore, Knight*, ed. E.V. Hitchcock and R.S. Chambers, EETS os 186 (1932), 41.

whole matter of the divorce remitted to judgement in England, and by
the growing political influence of Anne Boleyn and her supporters. Clement VII devolved much authority on Wolsey and on Cardinal Campeggio,
who in June 1529 finally began to sit as commissioners on the divorce case
at Blackfriars. Immediately the cardinals were faced by fierce and effective
opposition from Bishop Fisher and the rest of Catherine's defence team.
They also entered a minefield of complex legal arguments. Catherine
herself appealed to Rome in disregard of the delegated commissioners.
Any opportunity that Wolsey and the papacy might jointly have had to
compromise the issue without further breakdown was then foreclosed by
imperial success over the French at the battle of Landriano.[8] On 16 July
1529, Clement formally revoked the divorce case to Rome. In London,
on the arrival of the news, the duke of Suffolk thumped the table in the
legatine court, declaring 'there was never legate nor cardinal that did good
in England'.[9] This was not, of course, the end of the road in the attempts
to extract either the divorce itself, or agreement that it might be judged in
England, from Rome, but henceforth the crown increasingly resorted to
threats to the Church as the means of gaining its dynastic ends.[10]

The early stages of Henry VIII's quest for divorce are replete with
'what if...' questions, with a sense that success was snatched from Wolsey
and his monarch by a series of unfortunate accidents. From the sack of
Rome to the battle of Landriano external events moved against accommodation with the papacy. Within the realm Cardinal Campeggio's constant delays in establishing the legatine court frustrated Henry's objectives:
the discovery in Spain of a second brief of dispensation for the Aragonese
marriage complicated Henry's case: Catherine was resolute in resisting
persuasion from Campeggio as well as the king to take the veil and make
the monarch a spiritual widower.[11] It is difficult to argue that Clement's
final failure to give Henry his wish was based on any profound moral
objections: his vacillating conduct could not, for example, be a sharper
contrast with the resolution of Bishop Fisher as Catherine's prime defend-
ant. Yet Clement knew that Henry's case was weak in law, and deeply
resented the bullying tactics of king and minister, and if the objective of
the divorce had been achieved through pressure on Rome it would, at the
very least, have left a legacy of profound mistrust by the clergy of royal
intentions. The 'what ifs...' on the king's side are even more intriguing.
Had Henry achieved his marital goal would he have abandoned the cri-

---

[8] Scarisbrick, *Henry VIII*, 198–228.
[9] Hall, *Chronicle*, ii. 153.
[10] E. Surtz and V. Murphy (eds.), *The Divorce Tracts of Henry VIII* (Angers, 1988), introduction.
[11] Kelly, *Matrimonial Trials*, 54–131; the second brief is discussed at 62–4.

tique of papal power to dispense from divine law which he and his divorce team had so painfully assembled? Was the challenge to Roman jurisdiction already a crisis waiting to happen before Wolsey had failed?[12]

On 1 November 1528 Wolsey wrote an agonized letter to Casale, one of the king's agents in Rome, denouncing the delays in establishing the legatine court, and the inhuman treatment of Henry, and prognosticating the ruin of the Church in England and the destruction of the pope's power within the realm.[13] This was in part a rhetorical gesture in the campaign of persuasion, but it expressed fears that the cardinal certainly had for his own future and for that of the existing order of the Church. Before the debacle of the legatine court it seems unlikely that Henry had moved far towards formulating any serious alternative to forcing consent out of Rome. Yet during 1529 his mind was moving upon new paths. As early as April he was telling Campeggio that ecclesiastics 'live very wickedly' especially at the Roman court, and was being influenced by what the legate described as 'certain Lutheran books in English'.[14] Access to these ideas, or rather the evidential detail to support these generalizations, was almost certainly provided by Anne Boleyn and her circle, now in dominant positions at court. Anne is supposed to have provided Henry with a copy of Tyndale's *Obedience of a Christian Man*, with its thoroughgoing defence of monarchical powers over the Church.[15] Others ensured that he saw Simon Fish's *A Supplication for the Beggars*, which provided the negative attack upon greedy and worldly clerics. In October the king revealed his changing view of the crisis to the new Imperial ambassador, Eustace Chapuys. He denounced the vaingloriousness of the Roman curia, urged the need for reform in the Church, praised Luther's stand against the corruption of the clergy, and claimed that he proposed to institute reform in his own lands as the Emperor should in his territories.[16] Then on 3 November 1529 the Reformation parliament met for the first time, aware that the king would look favourably on attacks on the Church, and especially on the embodiment of its grandeur, Cardinal Wolsey.[17]

[12] P. Gwyn, *The King's Cardinal: The Rise and Fall of Thomas Wolsey* (1990), 502–4.

[13] *LP* iv. ii. 4897.

[14] *LP* iv. iii. 5416.

[15] The involvement of Anne Boleyn in the presentation to Henry of the work of Tyndale rests on late evidence: see Ives, *Anne Boleyn*, 161–3.

[16] *CSP Sp* iv. i. 349–50.

[17] Lehmberg points out that the parliament was summoned to deal with the vacuum left by Wolsey, not with the aftermath of Clement's revocation of the cause to Rome, since summons for the session were issued on 9 August before news of the revocation had arrived: S. Lehmberg, *The Reformation Parliament, 1529–36* (Cambridge, 1970), 2–4.

The summoning of the Reformation parliament acquires full significance only with historical hindsight. Henry's encouragement of its anticlerical complaints were part of the campaign of pressure upon the pope and of his direct grievances against Wolsey.[18] The attacks on probate, mortuaries, pluralism, and non-residence were probably orchestrated by sectional interests—the London Mercers, some of the common lawyers—and encouraged by the court groupings bent on destroying the cardinal.[19] The anticlerical debates occupied a rather limited part of the first six-week session, which passed twenty-six statutes in all, only four of them specifically addressing ecclesiastical issues. The most dramatic moment of the session, a vigorous challenge by John Fisher to the bills emanating from the Commons, may have been triggered by a petition advocating disendowment of the Church which emanated from the group of nobles who were subverting Wolsey.[20] Yet the nature of Fisher's speech, as reported by his biographer, is clear evidence that the consequences of Henry's 'great matter' were no longer readily contained within the spheres of diplomacy and court faction. The laity, he complained, were merely greedy for the property of the Church, not seeking clerical reform. He raised the spectre of Germany, and announced that 'all these mischiefs among them arise through lack of faith'.[21] This last observation provoked an angry Commons' response and a demand from Henry that Fisher explain himself. This he did by denying that he had claimed Englishmen lacked faith.[22] Precedents had been set, both for the engagement of Parliament in anticlerical legislation and for the intrusion of religious conflict into a public and secular sphere.

The divorce proceedings also began to impinge on broader issues through the pursuit of historical and legal precedents. This occupied Henry's growing team of specialists between 1530 and 1532. In much of this effort the target remained the justification of the Levitical texts. This was the issue on which the theological experts of Europe were consulted in 1530 at the suggestion of that rising star Thomas Cranmer.[23] It also formed the substance of one of the two major collections of documents accumulated by the team: a work translated into English by Cranmer and

---

[18] Lehmberg, *Reformation Parliament*, 76–104.

[19] J.A. Guy, *The Political Career of Sir Thomas More* (Brighton, 1980), 117–24. C. Haigh, *English Reformations* (Oxford, 1993), 97–9, claims that the anticlericalism of the 1529 session was not particularly significant.

[20] On the 1529 petition see R.W. Hoyle, 'The origins of the dissolution of the monasteries', *HJ* 38 (1995), 284–8 and the convincing suggestion there made that Lord Darcy, and possibly the dukes of Norfolk and Suffolk, were associated with the petition.

[21] R. Bayne (ed.), *The Life of Fisher*, EETS ES 27 (1921), 68–70.

[22] Edward Hall also remarks a Fisher denunciation of the laity. However, Hall claims that it was the spectre of Bohemia that was raised: Hall, *Chronicle*, ii. 168.

[23] D. MacCulloch, *Thomas Cranmer* (1996), 46–57.

published in late 1531 under the title *The Determinations of the most famous and most excellent Universities of France and Italy*. However, it was the parallel efforts of another group, almost certainly orchestrated by Edward Foxe, to demonstrate that the divorce case could be heard in England, that proved of most significance for the crown. By the end of 1530 they had accumulated an eclectic document containing over two hundred sides of citation from Scripture, the Fathers and medieval commentators 'proving' that Rome did not necessarily possess jurisdictional superiority in a case like Henry's. The *Collectanea satis copiosa* deployed historical and conciliarist arguments, as well as those of acknowledged ecclesiastical authorities, to show that provincial hierarchies could resist papal authority if appeals made to Rome were frivolous or if judgements rendered by the papacy might contravene divine law.[24] Some of Foxe's collection also articulated the implications for monarchs. Henry, who read and annotated the text, was particularly enthused by the letter (a medieval forgery of John's reign) supposedly written by Pope Eleutherius to the legendary King Lucius of Britain in the second century.[25] In it the king was urged to rule by a law above that of Rome: '*divinam legem et fidem Christi*'. The king was described as *vicarius dei*, a man fully able to rule in his own kingdom without external intervention. Thus Henry was presented with an ideological structure for resolving his matrimonial problems in the fullest possible manner, by claiming for himself the caesaropapist right to imperial power within his realms.

By the time aspects of the *Collectanea* had been incorporated into the first edition of the propaganda text for the divorce, *The Glasse of Truth*, probably late in 1531, the king had assimilated much of its radical message. His first direct assault on the clerical estate in the previous autumn had involved the charge that a group of sixteen churchmen had been guilty of *praemunire*: that is they had permitted the exercise of improper jurisdictional power. The overt complaint was that they had aided and abetted Wolsey in the exercise of his legatine jurisdiction: the sub-texts an attack on Catherine's leading supporters and a desire to extract money.[26] Henry

---

[24] On the *Collectanea* we are still primarily dependent on the unpublished dissertation of G. Nicholson, 'The Nature and Function of Historical Argument in the Henrician Reformation', University of Cambridge Ph.D. (1977), some of the key themes of which are summarized in his 'The Act of Appeals and the English Reformation', in C. Cross, D. Loades, and J.J. Scarisbrick (eds.), *Law and Government under the Tudors* (Cambridge, 1988), 19–30.

[25] On the significance of the King Lucius story see A. Fox and J. Guy, *Reassessing the Henrician Age* (Oxford, 1986), 157–64. Below, pp. 389–90.

[26] J. Guy, 'Henry VIII and the *praemunire* manoeuvres of 1530–31', *EHR* 97 (1982), 481–503. Scarisbrick, *Henry VIII*, 273–7, though this places crucial shifts in Henry's position as early as the summer of 1530, and credits the king with too much planning and foresight about the *praemunire* attack.

achieved the last when the next January the convocation of Canterbury promised £100,000 in order to gain a general pardon. By March, however, the king reacted to the clergy's cautious gestures with a full challenge to the rights of the courts Christian to exercise their authority without royal sanction. He bullied two unhappy convocations into some acceptance of his title of supreme head of the Church, thereby provoking a more vigorous backlash.[27] The convocation of Canterbury insisted on qualifying their agreement with the phrase 'so far as the law of Christ allowed'. Cuthbert Tunstal, presiding as bishop of Durham over the Northern Convocation, had a formal protest against the royal style entered in the register. When Tunstal followed this with a courageous letter to Henry defending the jurisdiction of Rome, he was rebuffed by a claim that each Christian prince was the *supremum caput* of the congregation of the Church in his realm.[28]

After the summer of 1531 few of the English political nation can have doubted Henry's absolute determination to secure his divorce at any cost, and the well-informed must have understood that the Church was likely to pay much of the price. But how these ends were to be achieved remained in some question. At a practical political level there was strong opposition to overcome from the clergy, and the hounding of Convocation that finally resulted in the Submission of the Clergy on 15 May 1532 was one of the least edifying moments in the whole Reformation crisis. By then Thomas Cromwell had emerged as the key figure orchestrating parliamentary actions. He was almost certainly responsible for the drafting of the Supplication against the Ordinaries that provided Henry with his ammunition against the bishops and probably played a part in the earlier bill laid before Parliament, for the halting of annates paid to Rome. There seems no reason to question that Cromwell, in early 1532 as later, saw Parliament as the key to effecting a political revolution.[29] His views were shared by, indeed anticipated by, others, most notably Christopher St German, the common lawyer who in 1531 in a supplement to his tract *Doctor and Student* had already set out a model of parliamentary control of clerical jurisdiction.[30] It was St German who first clearly expressed the idea that the king-in-parliament was 'the high sovereign over the people, which hath not only charge on the bodies, but also on the souls of his subjects'.[31]

---

[27] Nicholson, 'Henrician Reformation', 126–31.

[28] Wilkins, *Concilia*, iii. 745, 762 ff.

[29] For a narrative of these events that remains largely convincing see G.R. Elton, *Reform and Reformation* (1976), 273–95.

[30] Fox and Guy, *Henrician Age*, 99–102, 168–70.

[31] T.F.T. Plucknett and J.L. Barton (eds.), *St German's Doctor and Student*, Selden Society 91 (1974), 327.

Although Henry placed much of the structural responsibility for the divorce process and the growing separation from Rome in the hands of Cromwell, in 1532 it was by no means certain that his parliamentary and common law approach to the crisis would emerge as dominant. The king himself spoke of the prerogatives of the crown, of imperial kingship and of a caesaropapist exercise of authority over the clergy. The first draft of the crucial Act in Restraint of Appeals (1533), which finally secured internal jurisdiction over the divorce case, talked of jurisdiction as 'derived and depended of the imperial crown of this realm'. By the time the legislation reached the statute book these high claims to royal control had been eliminated by Cromwell, though they seem to reflect the king's views with some accuracy.[32] The Henrician Reformation, as it finally emerged, was an amalgam of the personal, divinely sanctioned view of royal authority over the Church and the institutional legalism of St German and Cromwell. In 1532 there was also a 'third way', or rather a significant variant on the personal view of royal authority, that was mooted in various writings of Henry's clerical apologists, including Edward Foxe. This largely acknowledged the king as the source of all authority, with duties to correct sin and suppress heresy. It anticipated, however, that the monarch would function in concert with his clergy. Parliament was either to be excluded from decision-making or used only to provide sanctions for clerical programmes.[33] In the early stages of the propaganda campaign this view was linked to an advocacy of appeal to a general council of the Church. As this solution became less viable Foxe and his colleagues continued to favour a 'synodal' answer to the king's dilemmas, focusing jurisdictional submission, and later positive legislation, on Convocation, rather than Parliament. Foxe's views, which Melanchthon later found too favourable to 'prelatical religion', were apparently displaced in the first stages of the parliamentary revolution.[34] However, they represented a significant strand in Henrician debate and policy-making, and were to return to haunt clerical–lay relations throughout the later Reformation.

There was no easy high road to English autonomy from Rome, even with the skilled parliamentary management of Thomas Cromwell.[35] But by fits and starts the legislation restraining appeals to Rome, denying payments to the papacy, and eventually acknowledging the royal supremacy was enacted. The acknowledgement of Henry's marriage to Anne in May 1533 brought the beginning of the end of the king's great matter. It

[32] G.R. Elton, 'The evolution of a reformation statute', *EHR* 64 (1949), 174–97.
[33] Nicholson, 'Henrician Reformation', 161–3, 244 ff.
[34] E. Foxe, *Of True Dyfferens*, trans. Henry, Lord Stafford (1548), fo. 15^{r-v}.
[35] For the spasmodic quality even of the government's actions in 1533 to early 1534 see Haigh, *English Reformations*, 116–20.

began the process of defending his actions against internal and external threat. Internally the second half of 1533 saw the commencement of sermon propaganda against the papacy and in favour of the Boleyn marriage, which was followed by the 1534 Succession Act, making actions or words against it treasonable and fixing inheritance upon Henry and Anne's heirs. The Treasons Act provided the coercive force to defend what was, by the end of the 1534 parliamentary session, the king's revolution. Concurrently the king's propagandists began to write their formal defences of the new status quo. Thomas Swinnerton produced the memorably named *Little treatise against the muttering of some papists in corners* (1534), deploying the full range of anti-papal rhetoric for the first time. In the following year William Marshall published his tendentiously annotated translation of Marsilius of Padua's *Defensor Pacis* and that reluctant revolutionary Stephen Gardiner wrote *De Vera Obedientia*, the tract that was to haunt the rest of his career.[36] Obedience to the royal view of order became the new credo.[37] And Henry sought, unsuccessfully, to export his revolution by persuading Francis I to join him in repudiating the jurisdiction of Rome.[38]

If Francis was an unlikely candidate to follow Henry's leadership, the king had higher hopes of another monarch: the young James V of Scotland. The latter was emerging as a mature ruler just as England was engaged in the divorce crisis. On 17 May 1532, he had addressed the Scottish Parliament on a range of issues, promising to defend the Kirk as his ancestors had done.[39] Conventional enough language: yet it suggested a high view of royal protectorship not unlike that of his English uncle, and James's actions in the next few years revealed that he did indeed have an imperious understanding of his relationship with churchmen. The puzzling thing for his royal relative was that he persisted in combining this with the most explicit statements of loyalty to Rome. Indeed at the height of the crisis created by the Kildare revolt in Ireland the Scottish king flirted with the idea of an alliance with the pope and Charles V against 'heresy'.[40] It is not surprising that from time to time there should be diplomatic overtures from Henry to James, firm reminders of the perfidy

---

[36] S. Lockwood, 'Marsilius of Padua and the case for the royal ecclesiastical supremacy', *TRHS* 6th ser. 1 (1990), 89–119. S. Gardiner, *Obedience in Church and State*, ed. P. Janelle (Cambridge, 1930). R. Pogson, 'God's law and man's: Stephen Gardiner and the problem of loyalty', in Cross *et al.*, *Law and Government*, 71–4.

[37] R. Rex, 'The crisis of obedience: God's Word and Henry's Reformation', *HJ* 39 (1996), 880–3.

[38] D. Potter, 'Foreign policy', in MacCulloch, *Reign of Henry VIII*, 119.

[39] *APS* ii. 335–6.

[40] M. O'Siochru, 'Foreign involvement in the revolt of Silken Thomas, 1534–5', *Proceedings of the Royal Irish Academy*, sect. C 96 (1996), 59–60.

of the papacy and of the benefits that had accrued to the English king once he had been freed from his jurisdictional blindness.[41]

In 1536 Bishop Barlow, as Henry's ambassador, was briefed to urge James to reject Rome, reform the clergy and restore all church emoluments to the crown, to which they rightly belonged. James responded with dramatic horror at the thought that he should follow his uncle into heresy, and the Deity reinforced his pious revulsion with a providential thunder-clap during the ambassador's presentation.[42] Four years later the English tried again, spurred on by a report of a conversation between Lord Eure and Thomas Bellenden, one of James's advisers. The Scottish king had been stung by a court play performed in 1540 that was critical of the clergy, into threatening that he would 'send six of the proudest of them [the bishops] unto his uncle of England'.[43] Sadler was dispatched to the north, with secret information about Cardinal Beaton's dealings with Rome and dire warnings about clerical power. The objectives of such diplomacy were of course to neutralize the political threat posed by James's alliances, especially the French connection.[44] But Henry also appears to have taken some pleasure in the idea of goading his nephew into action against Rome. Meanwhile, if relations turned sour, there was always the English claim to Scotland to resuscitate. The *Collectanea* had revived Edward I's imperialist claims to Scotland as part of its tireless quest for historical proofs of regal authority.[45] Bishop Foxe thought it worth repeating them in his *De Vera Differentia* (1534), though he can hardly have guessed how important they would prove to be in the subsequent decade.[46]

Jurisdiction and Authority in King Henry's Realms

The 1534 Act of Supremacy acknowledged Henry VIII as Head of the Church in England: in 'the Church called *Anglicana Ecclesia*'.[47] Much of the rest of the decade was to be devoted to articulating the nature of that supremacy and to enforcing it within England. There were major prob-

---

[41] As early as 1534 Cromwell had sought to persuade Adam Otterburn of the merits of the Henrician settlement: *LP* vi. 1571; vii. 4.

[42] C. Patrick Hotle, *Thorns and Thistles: Diplomacy between Henry VIII and James V, 1528–42* (1996), 79–81. *LP* ix. 730; x. 141.

[43] *LP* xv. 136.

[44] See Sadler's advice on his 1540 mission, Hotle, *Thorns and Thistles*, 145–51.

[45] Nicholson, 'Henrician Reformation', 172–8.

[46] Foxe, *True Dyfferens*, fos. 80 ff. Henry had always been disposed to offer other princes unsolicited advice on their religious affairs: as early as 1524 he had urged the three dukes of Saxony to follow his example and uphold orthodoxy: C. D'Alton, 'The Suppression of Heresy in Early Henrician England', University of Melbourne Ph.D. (1999), 128–9.

[47] 26 HVIII, c. 1.

lems of authority within the Church. For example, the first attempt at
procuring oaths from the clergy renouncing the authority of Rome foundered because it was undertaken as part of Cranmer's metropolitical visitation, and the bishops challenged the archbishop's authority, fearing that
they might be exposed to a second charge of *praemunire* in five years. The
possibility of a clericalist solution to the issue of authority, with the king
merely providing the temporal support to a policy enforced by the episcopate, led by a series of stages to the appointment of Cromwell as full
vicegerent in spirituals in 1536.[48] The first notion was that the minister
would simply exercise rights under the royal supremacy during the royal
visitation instituted in January 1535. This in turn, by addressing a wide
variety of issues of religious discipline, confirmed the quasi-sacerdotal role
of the supreme head. The bishops' fears about their jurisdictions led the
king to grant enhanced powers to his vicegerent: and authority was restored to the ordinaries only at his, and the king's, pleasure. Finally in July
1536 the vicegerency was made permanent. The process had been slow,
and not necessarily self-consciously planned, but the outcome was not in
doubt. Cromwell could intervene at will in the affairs of the Church: the
jurisdictional authority of the supreme head was not to be challenged.[49]

Clarifying the structure of authority did not necessarily render the task
of enforcement any easier. Much of the theory of obedience to the supreme headship was supplied by Tyndale's *Obedience of a Christian Man* and
other Lutheran writings. The means for achieving this obedience were
various: for the clergy the most significant were the preaching campaigns
in which they were required to proclaim the abolition of Roman authority
and the nature of King Henry's new-found status.[50] In June 1535 Cromwell ordered that the bishops preach on the royal supremacy each
Sunday.[51] The next year a royal circular commanded bishops to institute
preaching against 'the filthy and corrupt abominations of the bishop of
Rome', associating the preaching of the 'word of God' with the promotion of the supremacy. Cranmer was one of several bishops who initiated
their own preaching campaigns in these years.[52] Prelates like John Longland of Lincoln, and Thomas Goodrich of Ely, organized circulars to all
parishes on the abolition of Roman authority and preaching circuits by

---

[48] S.E. Lehmberg, 'Supremacy and vicegerency: a re-examination', *EHR* 81 (1966), 225–35,
gives an outline narrative, but the discussion of the dating of the commission for the vicegerency has been superseded by F.D. Logan, 'Thomas Cromwell and the vicegerency in spirituals:
a revisitation', *EHR* 103 (1988), 658–67.

[49] M. Bowker, 'The supremacy and the episcopate: the struggle for control, 1534–1540',
HJ 18 (1975), 227–43.

[50] Rex, 'crisis of obedience', 881–94.   [51] *LP* x. 45.

[52] P. Ayris, 'Continuity and change in diocese and province: the role of a Tudor bishop',
HJ 39 (1996), 290.

licensed clergy.[53] At Paul's Cross the pulpit resounded regularly with defence of the supreme head from late 1534 until 1539 and the theme was resuscitated whenever the political situation appeared threatening.[54] When Henry referred in his proclamation of 9 June 1535 to the preaching campaign, he associated the dissemination of 'the very true and sincere word of God' with the denunciation of the 'great and innumerable enormities and abuses' of the bishop of Rome.[55] The clergy were required to engage in an intense effort to win hearts and minds, and to instil the religious fear that would secure obedience. However, the key labour of ensuring that there was no active dissent from the king's policies fell to the secular arm, the local magistrates whose reports to Cromwell formed the basis of Elton's definitive study of the enforcement of the supremacy.[56]

The Act of Supremacy, like all the legislation of the Reformation parliament, was intended to apply with as much force in Henry VIII's scattered dominions as in the heartland of the *Anglicana Ecclesia*. There is no reason to suppose that the parliamentary draftsmen saw any problems in law when they announced that this applied to 'any person, subject or resident within this realm or elsewhere within the King's dominions'. In the cases of Wales, Calais, the Channel Islands, and the Isle of Man the regime could largely make good these claimed rights to obedience, though even in these territories it quickly became clear that the new jurisdictional pattern presented complications.[57] The Channel Islands were governed directly from London by nominated governors, but their ecclesiastical position was anomalous. Until 1496 they remained under the diocese of Coutances, Normandy, and, although Henry VII then obtained papal bulls transferring them first to Salisbury and then to Winchester, in practice Coutances was where appointments to benefices continued to be registered.[58] There was the added embarrassment that they had been granted especial papal protection by Sixtus IV as a safeguard against piracy. Political acceptance of Henry's headship seems to have proved largely uncontentious on Jersey and Guernsey: the royal courts of the islands emphasized their obedience and, so far as can be judged in the absence of good internal records, their ecclesiastical traditions continued much as

---

[53] S. Wabuda, 'The Provision of Preaching during the Early English Reformation, with special reference to Itineration, *c*.1530 to 1547', University of Cambridge Ph.D. (1991), 92–9.

[54] M. MacLure, *The Paul's Cross Sermons, 1534–1642* (Toronto, 1958), 27 ff.

[55] *TRP* i. 230.

[56] G.R. Elton, *Policy and Police: The Enforcement of the Reformation in the Age of Thomas Cromwell* (Cambridge, 1972).

[57] G. Williams, *Wales and the Reformation* (Cardiff, 1997), 105–6.

[58] A.J. Eagleston, *The Channel Islands under Tudor Government, 1485–1642* (Cambridge, 1949), 35, 171. C.S.L. Davies, 'International politics and the establishment of presbyterianism in the Channel Islands: the Coutances connection', *JEH* 50 (1999), 498–522.

before.[59] Only later under Elizabeth did the problems of weak ecclesiastical control become manifest. Calais was far more closely regulated under the watchful eye of Lord Lisle as deputy and of Archbishop Cranmer, since it was part of the peculiar jurisdiction of Canterbury.[60] The problems of Calais were not an absence of control, but an excess of competing jurisdictions: those of the deputy, the merchant Staple and the local corporation on the secular side, and of the archbishop in spiritual matters. The volatile combination of a large English-language garrison, a mixed French and English civilian population, and visitors constantly moving across the Channel, always made Calais difficult to govern. It remained the gateway to France and was central to the interests of a king for whom rivalry with his Valois neighbour was accounted little less than an article of faith. In the 1530s the addition of ideological conflict, and of a deputy who was profoundly opposed to religious change, made the town one of the flash-points of Henrician politics.[61]

The case of Wales is again distinct. There was no question about the crown's claims to enforce religious policy: Welsh sees were simply subsumed within the *Anglicana Ecclesia*. The principality and marches were not jurisdictionally identical to English shires, but the king's writ unquestionably ran in them. Rowland Lee, bishop of Coventry and Lichfield, presided over a rejuvenated Council of the Marches from 1534. This was explicitly designed both to suppress endemic Welsh disorder and to facilitate the enforcement of the supremacy.[62] In the prelude to the full break with Rome Welsh politics had been destabilized by Henry's attack on Rhys ap Gruffudd, his key regional governor in the south-west. Gruffudd was accused of planning to ally himself with James V and raise forces in Ireland, Scotland, and the Isle of Man to depose the king. Although there was little basis to the charges, Gruffudd was executed for treason in 1531, leaving behind him a resentful clientage led by his unstable

---

[59] D.M. Ogier, *Reformation and Society in Guernsey* (Woodbridge, 1996), 22–38. It is remarkable that there is no surviving evidence of attempts to enforce religious change on the islands, beyond the dissolution of the one small monastery still extant on Guernsey, until 1547. This was partly because the bulk of the monastic property had been seized in the reign of Henry V under the legislation against alien priories. I am grateful for information on Jersey to Helen Evans.

[60] MacCulloch, *Cranmer*, 110–12.

[61] P. Ward, 'The politics of religion: Thomas Cromwell and the Reformation in Calais, 1534–40', *JRH* 17 (1992), 155–64. The conflicts are revealed in unusual depth in Lisle's surviving papers: M. St Byrne (ed.), *The Lisle Letters*, 6 vols. (1980). In an indicative letter Cranmer wrote to Cromwell in 1535 that Calais was a place of 'great ignorance and blindness as well as of the heads now resident there, as of the common and vulgar people': *LP* ix. 561.

[62] Williams, *Wales and the Reformation*, 106–9. P. Roberts, 'Tudor Wales, national identity and the British inheritance', in B. Bradshaw and P. Roberts (eds.), *British Consciousness and Identity: The Making of Britain, 1533–1707* (Cambridge, 1998), 8–11.

uncle.[63] Chapuys, the imperial ambassador, remained hopeful that the Welsh would rise in defence of the interests of Catherine of Aragon at the time of the Kildare revolt.[64] Careful management of Wales was therefore a high priority for the Henrician regime.

Lee's appointment was the first of a series of moves that culminated in the first Act of Union of 1536. The regime's motives for the incorporation of Wales are not entirely easy to analyse. There was, no doubt, a strong impulse for increased centralized control: the abolition of the marcher lordships was complemented by the general legislation abolishing lordships and franchises throughout the realm. In a crude dichotomy the legislation might be described as Henrician in that it made the king's claims to imperial power territorial as well as jurisdictional, Cromwellian in that it made jurisdiction uniform and constructed the new identity through statute.[65] But the statute was also probably a conscious appeal to the Welsh elite, persuaded by the removal of all legal disabilities and the promise of enhanced local control through the shiring system, to co-operate fully in the enforcement of Henry's Reformation. Thus was developed one of the most successful of Tudor political collaborations: the Welsh gentry achieved a local control that had not previously been possible; the monarchy gained effective support from a territory whose general religious conservatism might otherwise have posed a significant threat.[66]

It was, of course, in Ireland that the jurisdictional and political limitations of the Henrician settlement were most brutally exposed. Henry's suzereignty as lord of Ireland was vulnerable both in theory and practice and the events of the 1530s forced a fundamental rethinking of his position. Theoretical authority rested in the lordship, which claimed some jurisdiction over the whole island, but notionally from the time of John onwards as a fiefdom of the papacy. The papal bull *Laudabiliter* remained a crucial justification for English rule over the barbarous Gaels.[67] When the

---

[63] G. Williams, *Recovery, Reorientation and Reformation: Wales c.1415–1642* (Oxford, 1987), 255–7. *LP* v. 563, 683, 720 (14). The events leading to Rhys ap Gruffudd's execution are obscure, but it seems that his uncle, James, imprisoned with him, may have accused him as a result of family quarrels: R.A. Griffiths, *Sir Rhys ap Thomas and his Family* (Cardiff, 1993), 291–2.

[64] *CSP Sp* iv. ii. 853.

[65] There is, however, some danger in making the 1536 legislation sound too coherent and final. As Roberts points out elsewhere, the act was ill prepared and its clauses on judicial provision so uncertain that the king was permitted to suspend its provisions under the great seal if need be. P. Roberts, 'Wales and England after the Tudor "union": crown, principality and parliament, 1543–1624', in Cross et al., *Law and Government*, 112–13.

[66] B. Bradshaw, 'The English Reformation and identity formation in Ireland and Wales', in B. Bradshaw and P. Roberts (eds.), *British Consciousness and Identity* (Cambridge, 1998), 72–88.

[67] For good narratives of the political background to the Kildare revolt and its course see S. Ellis, *Tudor Frontiers and Noble Power: The Making of the British State* (Oxford, 1995), 173–232 and C. Lennon, *Sixteenth Century Ireland: The Incomplete Conquest* (Dublin, 1994), 93–112.

earl of Kildare sought foreign support for his revolt his chaplain was sent to Pope Paul III to remind him that the papacy still possessed authority over the whole island.[68] It had, however, been the consistent policy of the English crown to ignore both its own and the papacy's large claims in favour of the everyday attempt to control the Pale and the marches. Henry VII and Henry VIII, like their predecessors, usually employed methods of indirect rule through the great regional magnates. In the early Tudor period this meant overwhelmingly the earls of Kildare, though intermittently Ormond and Desmond were invoked as counterbalance. Mistrust between crown and magnates was common, and the Irish peers had periods of enforced residence in England, or even imprisonment in the Tower, which punctuated their years of control in Ireland.

The crisis which led to the 1534 Kildare revolt appeared at first as little more than one of these breakdowns: the rule of the ninth earl as governor was challenged by a factional grouping eagerly abetted by his predecessor, Lord Skeffington, and the earl was summoned to England in 1533. His son, Lord Thomas, made his deputy in his absence, tried to exert pressure to sustain the political control of the family. In the tense circumstances of the divorce and break with Rome the king now chose to interpret this as outright rebellion, thereby precipitating exactly this outcome.[69] Chapuys hoped that Kildare's uprising would become part of a more general challenge to Henry's heresy, and since Kildare ultimately chose to present himself as leading a Catholic crusade, his speculation was not wholly unfounded.[70] During 1533 English spies had been kept busy investigating contacts between the Irish, the Scots, and the disaffected Welshman, James ap Gruffudd ap Hywel, now seeking revenge for his nephew's death. James was received by James V, the former claiming that he 'with the Lion of Scotland should subdue all England'.[71] During the Kildare rebellion clan networks brought highlanders to the aid of the Irish, and the ubiquitous James ap Gruffudd appeared from the Low Countries, possibly bringing some military assistance. Meanwhile the earl appealed to Rome, to the emperor, and to James V.[72] All three dabbled cautiously in Irish affairs: Charles V, in particular, kept his agents to Ireland busy with verbal interest and support, though his preparations for the Tunisian cru-

[68] O'Siochru, 'Foreign involvement', 49–66. *LP* vi. 907; vii. 957, 1057, 1141.

[69] B. Bradshaw, 'Cromwellian reform and the origins of the Kildare rebellion, 1533–34', *TRHS* 5th ser. 27 (1977), 69–94. S. Ellis, 'The Kildare rebellion and the early Henrician Reformation', *HJ* 19 (1976), 807–30.

[70] For a detailed analysis of the 'British' implications of 1533/4, see C. Kellar, '"To Enrich with Gospell Truth the Neighbour Kingdom": Religion and Reform in England and Scotland, 1534–1561', University of Oxford D.Phil. (1999), 21–6.

[71] PRO SP 1/81, fo. 59ᵛ.

[72] *LP* vii. 1193. O'Siorchu, 'Foreign involvement', 55–60.

sade left him with no capacity to intervene more directly.[73] For the Henrician regime it was, however, the first alarming evidence that religious disaffection might unite the other territories of Britain and Ireland against England.[74]

Even without the Kildare debacle the process of enforcing the royal supremacy in Ireland would have been fraught with difficulty. The king's title was personal, and therefore not dependent upon parliamentary legislation, but obedience to it was enforced by English statute that had application in Ireland, though was fully secure only when certified and ratified by an Irish parliament. It is understandable that in these circumstances Thomas Skeffington, who returned to Ireland as lord deputy to oppose Kildare, should have been instructed merely to attack papal jurisdiction 'according to the statutes thereupon provided, and the like to be enacted there the next parliament'.[75] Plans to summon that parliament were initially delayed by the suppression of the revolt, and then in later 1535 by the death of Skeffington and his replacement by Lord Grey. The Irish Reformation parliament therefore only met finally in May 1536 and completed its business in 1537. In the first session the principal statutes paralleling those of England were passed—for supremacy, succession, first fruits, and restraint of annates, as well as a version of the Treasons Act. There was consistent and tenacious opposition to the legislation from the clergy in both Houses.[76] The 1536 session was followed by the beginning of a campaign for enforcement as the new archbishop of Dublin, George Browne, exacted the Oath of Supremacy from his diocesan clergy, and Lord Grey began to do the same in piecemeal fashion from civic officials. Grey, in particular, brought no very great urgency to the task of ensuring conformity.[77] In 1538, when he was supposed to be supporting Browne's campaign against images, he was alleged to have gone to the pilgrimage site at Trim and 'very devoutly kneeling' before the image of Our Lady, heard three or four Masses. In the same year he licensed a deputation of friars to visit England to petition for the preservation of their order.[78] But more was at stake than a hesitant start to the enforcement of religious discipline. First, the end of the Kildare ascendancy made it necessary to

[73] Earlier, in July 1533 an English spy in Spain reported that it was said that Charles would set the Scots and the Irish against England: *LP* vi. 821.

[74] Williams, *Wales and the Reformation*, 57–8. Ellis, 'Kildare rebellion', 825–30.

[75] R.W.D. Edwards, 'The Irish Reformation parliament of Henry VIII, 1536–7', *Historical Studies* 6 (1968), 60.

[76] Ibid., 59–84. B. Bradshaw, 'The opposition to the ecclesiastical legislation in the Irish Reformation parliament', *IHS* 16 (1968–9), 285–303. The consistent opposition of the clergy to the Henrician legislation provided a critical complication for the Henrician regime.

[77] H.A. Jefferies, 'The early Tudor Reformation in the Irish Pale', *JEH* 52 (2001), 53–6.

[78] PRO sp 60/6/127. Jefferies, 'Early Tudor Reformation', 54.

redefine the nature of political control in the lordship. Secondly, Gaelic chieftains and dissident marcher lords now became more than a general threat to law and order in the Englishry, they became potential agents of the Roman antichrist and his imperial minions.[79]

Cromwell's solution, as elsewhere, was to promote direct government from London, with accompanying reform of the Irish council to make it a more effective agent of control under an English-appointed lord deputy.[80] But strict and straight control would only be viable with resources that London, and especially Henry, was unwilling to commit. Hence on Grey's failure to resolve the problems posed by the Geraldine league of Gaelic princes by military action in 1539 a new approach was adopted. Anthony St Leger arrived as lord deputy in July 1540, committed to the royal supremacy, but otherwise uninterested in disturbing the religious peace. Instead he began the policy of surrender and regrant, persuading the Gaelic chiefs to agree to hold their lands of the king, and accept his title as supreme head, in return for a surrender of his unenforceable feudal rights. At its heart was the idea of acknowledging Henry king of Ireland, a project first mooted by Bishop Staples of Meath in 1537 and enacted by the Irish parliament in June 1541.[81] The initiative was undoubtedly from Ireland: the king had serious reservations about the enlarged responsibilities implied in the change of style, and only roused himself to action when he understood that the Irish parliament had named him as king, rather than merely recognizing the pre-existent justice of his title. This was 'corrected' by further legislation in 1542.[82] But the potential for enlarged political influence was immense and, as St Leger began the painstaking business of negotiating the surrender of individual chieftains, the political Reformation appeared institutionalized throughout Henry's realms.

Henrician Policy

Acceptance of Henry's imperial title and of his jurisdictional authority over the English and Irish church was an end in itself, but it was never likely to be the only consequence of the breach with Rome. Ministers, churchmen, and courtiers all had their own agendas for change after 1534, and the king himself was initially more than willing to probe the extent of his newly acquired power. Making sense of Henrician religious politics is a trying business: living them must often have had a nightmarish quality,

---

[79] Ellis, 'Kildare rebellion', 823–30.
[80] S. Ellis, 'Thomas Cromwell and Ireland, 1532–40', *HJ* 23 (1980), 497–519.
[81] B. Bradshaw, *The Irish Constitutional Revolution of the Sixteenth Century* (Cambridge, 1979), 98–106, 233–8.
[82] *SP HVIII* ii. 480.

as men sought to second-guess the monarch's latest views. It is most commonly argued by historians that the consequence was policies that oscillated sharply, driven by whichever individual or grouping commanded the king's ear, or by Henry's own erratic and eclectic reading of the duties of the supreme head.[83] The latter, it is suggested, were underpinned not by a coherent theology, but by little more than a 'ragbag of emotional preferences'.[84] It has recently been urged, however, that the king was both deeply engaged in the making of policy, and possessed his own consistent assumptions about moderate reform pursued along a middle path.[85] He leant, in Cromwell's words to Parliament in May 1540, 'neither to the right nor the left hand...but set the pure and sincere doctrine of the Christian faith only before his eyes'.[86] The theme was reprised in many different contexts during the later years of the reign. Marillac, the French ambassador, was assured that it explained Henry's dealings with the Lutherans: Sadler, on embassy to Scotland in 1543, was told to justify the king's position as 'neither swerving to the left hand of iniquity neither the right hand with other pretence of holiness than is agreeable to God's truth'.[87] Those who deviated from this path were to be 'duly corrected and punished', as was the unfortunate Cromwell in 1540. In some of these pronouncements the balanced Aristotelian mean was genuinely invoked. But Cromwell's language, directly quoting the Bible on the godly Josiah, should alert us to the fact that the 'middle way' was itself a contested concept.[88] It could be represented as the righteous path from which the monarch was in no circumstances to be deflected.

This dimension of Henry's thinking was reinforced in his later years by his growing identification with Old Testament monarchs, notably David and Josiah. They, like him, had articulated the divine will through law and adherence to the word. Josiah had purged the idols: David had defended his people and served them in righteousness.[89] These representations served

---

[83] For interpretations, each markedly different, that emphasize the influence of others in the making of policy, see Elton, *Reform and Reformation*, 273–95; D. Starkey, *Henry VIII: Personalities and Politics* (1985); and E. Duffy, *The Stripping of the Altars: Traditional Religion in England 1400–1580* (New Haven, Conn., 1992), 379–447.

[84] D. MacCulloch, 'Henry VIII and the reform of the Church', in MacCulloch, *Reign of Henry VIII*, 178.

[85] The revival of the rational and controlling Henry is to be found in G. Bernard's recent work, especially 'The making of religious policy, 1533–1546: Henry VIII and the search for the middle way', *HJ* 41 (1998), 321–49, but see also the important earlier article by G. Redworth, 'Whatever happened to the English Reformation?', *History Today* 37 (1987), 29–35.

[86] *Lords Journals*, i. 128–9.   [87] *LP* xiv. ii. 388; xviii. i. 364. *SP HVIII* viii. no. 901.

[88] 2 Kings 22: 2.

[89] P. Tudor-Craig, 'Henry VIII and King David', in D. Williams (ed.), *Early Tudor England* (Woodbridge, 1989), 183–205. J.N. King, 'Henry VIII as David: the king's image and Reformation politics', in P.C. Herman (ed.), *Rethinking the Henrician Era* (Urbana, Ill., 1994), 78–92.

those committed to reform, and were vigorously promoted by them, as in the use of David on the frontispieces of the Coverdale and Great Bibles. But Henry's internalization of this latter parallel is strongly suggested by his approval of the Psalter presented to him by Jean Mallard, a French courtier, with its miniatures representing him as the Israelite king.[90] Henry annotated this volume heavily, identifying particularly with the suffering monarch assailed by his enemies. Neither the adulterous nor the penitential aspects of King David were emphasized by Mallard, who claimed that the psalms represented a guide to ideal kingship. Henry's annotations also avoid reflection on penitence. But even if Davidic images defined the king's sense of his religious role, the ideological direction of his church policy remained unclear to many of those at the heart of the regime. The result was deep conflict in court, council and the assemblies of the bishops.[91]

Hostility to the papacy, and its obverse, the elevation of the authority and responsibility of the supreme head, was the guiding theme of Henry's rhetoric throughout the later 1530s and 1540s. The content of policy should best be seen as following where the king's current belief in his duty led. This often involved claiming a commitment to reform and renewal in the Church, while simultaneously insisting on unity and on the essential truths of the Catholic faith.[92] Each, or all, of these elements can be found in official pronouncements throughout the later years of the reign. The king and his clergy, began the King's Book of 1543, 'by the help of God and his word have travailed to purge and cleanse our realm' of the enormities of superstition and hypocrisy.[93] Reform involved access to the Word and, after 1536, the purging of idolatrous images. In 1538 Henry took particular pleasure in the destruction of the shrine of Thomas Becket, that martyr to papal interest and clerical autonomy. And in the same year the linkage between usurped papal power and false idolatry was attested dramatically in the burning of Friar Forest. The Observant defender of papal supremacy was burned with the wreckage of the image of St Derfel from Llandderfel, North Wales.[94] As for the king's understand-

---

[90] There is disagreement about the dating of Mallard's gift, but agreement that Henry's annotations post-date the break with Rome.

[91] Some of the more interesting recent readings of Henry's policy do not argue with Bernard for full coherence of policy or dominance by Henry, but accept the significance of the king's configuration of his own authority in terms of Old Testament law and kingship: R. Rex, *Henry VIII and the English Reformation* (Basingstoke, 1993), 173–5; and D. MacCulloch, 'Henry VIII', in MacCulloch, *Reign of Henry VIII*, 179–80.

[92] Bernard, 'Making of religious policy', 321–39.

[93] C. Lloyd (ed.), *Formularies of Faith put forth by authority during the reign of Henry VIII* (Oxford, 1825), 215.

[94] P. Marshall, 'The Rood of Boxley, the Blood of Hailes and the defence of the Henrician church', *JEH* 46 (1995), 695.

ing of the essential truths of Catholicism: the annotations of his private psalter suggest they included belief in the sacrifice of the Mass, confession, and the salvific efficacy of works.[95] Unity was to be achieved by the careful regulation of official confessions, by setting out 'plain and sincere' doctrine, and, as the Act of Six Articles (1539) has it, by legislating for the 'abolishing of diversity in opinions'.[96]

Reform and tradition, however, were always likely to be in conflict: if the middle way was to be one of unity rather than compromise it had to possess a certain clarity and the capacity to command consent. Henry presumably did not have in mind the sort of horse-trading among the bishops that marked the passage of the Bishops' Book (1537), in which each article was fought phrase by phrase and then often compromised.[97] His contempt for this clerical in-fighting resonates through his parliamentary speech of 1545 in which he denounced the priests for lack of charity and intellectual arrogance.[98] Instead, the king's aims suggest the need for a certain olympian detachment and disinterest, which would allow him to act solely in accord with the demands of his conscience, that 'highest and supreme court for judgement and justice' as he once notably called it.[99] But the real king was not a self-fashioning isolate, and his middle way had to be sold in the marketplace of Tudor politics. The pressures of foreign policy, of internal dissent, and of conflicting political advice all militated against his desire to order the trinity of reform, tradition, and unity.

Henry and his ministers saw foreign hostility as the gravest threat to England's new-found imperial status. The abiding fear of the anger of Charles V, and of the danger that he might bury his differences with Francis I and launch a crusade against the heretic English, resonates through the 1530s and was not wholly buried in the 1540s. Jean du Bellay, the French ambassador, observed that the divorce would be a means 'to bring the King of England to his knees'.[100] The more contentious issue for historians is how far internal religious politics were driven or distorted by that fear. The timing of certain stages of the attack on church wealth—in 1534 and again in 1538—certainly seems to have owed something to enhanced anxieties about hostile coalitions in Ireland or on the Continent.

[95] Tudor-Craig, 'Henry VIII and King David', 196.
[96] 31 Henry VIII, c. 8.
[97] The process of negotiation is recalled in Gardiner's letters, though the struggles are registered independently by Latimer: J.A. Muller (ed.), *The Letters of Stephen Gardiner* (Cambridge, 1933), 351. *LP* xii. ii. 295.
[98] Hall, *Chronicle*, ii. 356.
[99] M. St Clare Byrne (ed.), *The Letters of King Henry VIII* (1936), 86.
[100] D. Potter, 'Foreign policy', in MacCulloch, *Reign of Henry VIII*, 119–23.

In the second half of the 1530s Henry was less able than he would have wished to play the 'natural' game of balancing between the two great European powers. His need for friends, especially in the dark days when Franco-Imperial rapprochement threatened possible invasion in 1538/9, drove him to German powers and the Schmalkaldic League.[101] Lutheran encounters were not new. Henry had dabbled with German contacts as early as 1528, when he began to consider gaining their goodwill in relation to his divorce. In 1534–5 Bishop Foxe was assigned the task of negotiating with the League, with a view to achieving a measure of concord between the churches. From these exchanges came a compromise document known as the Wittenberg Articles, which did something to shape the English confession of the Ten Articles of 1536. However, the compromise was never published or officially acknowledged in either England or Germany: its influence lay in the countenance that it gave to Cranmer and his allies as they sought to establish the first formularies of the new church.[102] The contacts of 1538 were altogether different: they had a higher political profile and were cemented a year later by the ill-fated Cleves marriage. Their doctrinal objectives, from the German perspective, were acceptance by the English of the essential principles of the Augsburg Confession. The king willed the proposed alliance, but saw the ideological cost as too high: from his summer progress he demolished the envoys' views on clerical celibacy, communion in one kind, and intercessory Masses. The Lutherans retired in disgust, only to be wooed again from January 1539 when Henry actually offered to join the League, displaying an urgency they had never seen in the previous years. A new delegation was sent to England in the spring, immediately to be confronted with the passage of the Act of Six Articles, and to experience violent debate with Henry over clerical marriage.

Thus expressed it would appear that Henry was not deflected from his internal religious politics by the Lutheran negotiations. But a closer look at 1538 to 1540 indicates that the king did respond to the threats posed by France and the Empire with internal manoeuvring, and that the local volatility of this period owes much to foreign danger. The negotiations with the Germans, in 1538 as earlier, encouraged evangelicals internally, and were one of the elements challenging the balance the king sought. His response, during the autumn and winter of that year, was to signal a return to tradition: a return realized in the passage of the Act of Six

---

[101] The definitive work on Henry VIII and the Lutherans is now R. McEntegart, 'England and the League of Schmalkalden', London School of Economics Ph.D. (1992), but see also N.S. Tjernagel, *Henry VIII and the Lutherans: A Study of Anglo-Lutheran Relations from 1521 to 1547* (St Louis, Mo., 1965).

[102] MacCulloch, *Cranmer*, 355–6.

Articles the following spring.[103] At least one motive, albeit secondary to internal considerations, was the signal of increased orthodoxy that was given to foreign powers. The Treaty of Toledo, engineered by the papacy to facilitate crusade against England, had been signed in January 1539 between France and the Empire, and ambassadors had been recalled, though they had returned in time to be impressed by the parliamentary action. Marillac, the French ambassador, commented that the king had 'taken up again all the old opinions and constitutions, excepting only papal obedience'.[104] Yet within two months the atmosphere had changed again. In June Henry staged a spectacular anti-papal pageant on the Thames: in July he agreed to the Cleves marriage.[105] The former gesture reminded the world of the firmness of his commitment to supremacy, but the latter seems to reflect a disappointment at his fellow monarchs' lack of response to his trumpeted doctrinal orthodoxy. And with the marriage treaty came, once again, the promise of serious negotiations with the Germans and the predictable fillip to reforming hopes as Cromwell once again appeared in the ascendant.

The political seesaw continued in 1540 as the Cleves marriage proved disastrous, the Germans were once again too demanding, and, most crucially, Francis and Charles resumed their quarrels. The Franco-Imperial breakdown does not necessarily explain Cromwell's fall: it does explain why Henry could again reconfigure his internal religious politics. During the ensuing French and Scottish wars Henry seems to have felt less constrained in his domestic choices, but in the last year of the reign some of the violent swings of politics may be connected to the European situation. This was the year that produced a short flurry of diplomacy as Henry seems to have toyed very briefly with abandoning the royal supremacy and, as the Schmalkaldic War in Germany reached a crisis, he seems to have wavered between reform and conservatism with an eye once again on the emperor. John Hooper's caustic judgement from exile was that Henry would turn to the gospel if Charles was defeated: if he was victorious 'he [Henry] will then retain his impious mass'.[106]

Internal opposition to royal policy is a theme for a later chapter. The only moment at which it might be argued to have changed Henry's mind is in the aftermath of the Pilgrimage of Grace. The scale of the uprising, its interlinkage with the Lincolnshire revolt, and the aftershock of the Bigod revolt in January 1537 all destroyed his sense that opposition was confined

---

[103] G. Redworth, 'A study in the formulation of policy: the genesis and evolution of the Act of Six Articles', *JEH* 37 (1986), 42–67. Scarisbrick, *Henry VIII*, 355–83.

[104] *LP* xiv. i. 1260.

[105] MacCulloch, *Cranmer*, 254–7.

[106] *LP* xiv. i. 1137. *OL* i. 41.

to fanatical monks, a few Catholic intellectuals, and alehouse dissent.[107] The regime's immediate reactions were angry justification and repression, followed at some distance by a desire to persuade. Henry's letters to the rebels defended his settlement while expressing fury at their sin against God's anointed, and at the first politically possible moment he demanded ferocious retribution. He also concluded that, for the common people, ignorance was at the root of dissent, and therefore proposed sending preachers to the north 'to instruct the people in the truth and to teach and preach the word of God sincerely to them'.[108] The shock did not, however, produce convincing evidence that Henry was deflected from his chosen religious course. The pace of monastic dissolution slowed, but perhaps only because there was policy uncertainty after the closure of the lesser houses. Cromwell's role as vicegerent was strengthened during the summer of 1537. At most the 'ignorance' of the rebels may have encouraged Henry to insist that his leading churchmen produce a more comprehensive statement of belief than the short Ten Articles issued the previous year.[109]

The third problem the king faced, that of conflicting advice, is usually seen as the most critical. Even if we posit a king who was closely engaged in the making of his own settlement, debating its doctrine, overseeing its legislation, confronting its opponents, we cannot present him as an isolated maker of policy. Cromwell, Cranmer, the collectivity of the bishops, and the council, all played official roles in the construction of Henry's church. Many others seized the opportunities of a relatively open and faction-ridden court to exert influence. The king may not have depended on any of these individuals or groups as he had done upon Wolsey. But Anne Boleyn, Cromwell, and Cranmer did manage much of the religious agenda between 1532 and 1539, and Gardiner, Cranmer, Norfolk, and some of the gentlemen of the Privy Chamber amongst others exercised influence in the last years of the reign.[110] Was Henry manipulated into choices that he subsequently came to regret by these other policy-makers? The case for Cromwell and his reform-minded supporters is the strongest. Cromwell was represented by his adherents as a leader: a warrior who

---

[107] On Henry's reaction to the Pilgrimage see Bernard, 'Making of religious policy', 336–7; Scarisbrick, *Henry VIII*, 342–6.

[108] The duke of Norfolk also diagnosed the crisis as arising from lack of preaching: 'if three or four loyal preachers had continually been in these parts, instructing the unlearned people, no such follies had been attempted as hath been': *LP* xii. i. 1158.

[109] MacCulloch, *Cranmer*, 185.

[110] On the role of faction in policy-making see Starkey, *Henry VIII*; Ives, *Anne Boleyn*; and, much less convincingly, J.S. Block, *Factional Politics and the English Reformation, 1520–1540* (Woodbridge, 1993). Block has interesting evidence on the evangelical networks but presents altogether too programmatic a view of Cromwell as leader of the reforming faction, to the virtual neglect of his flexible persona as the king's man.

fought boldly for the truth, by implication more boldly than his monarch. For Latimer he was God's chosen 'instrument'; for the Scot Alesius a great defender of the 'pure doctrine of the gospel'.[111] There is much evidence to support this view. Cromwell became the key broker of royal patronage, especially after the fall of Anne Boleyn, and he used that patronage to secure reformers in vital posts in church and state.[112] His most critical promotions for the long-term survival of the evangelical cause were those made to the king's privy chamber in the aftermath of the Boleyn debacle. Through the promotion of Anthony Denny, Thomas Cawardine, John Gates, and others, he ensured that the king had evangelicals as his immediate companions in his declining years.

Cromwell's influence appears ubiquitous in the later 1530s: he oversaw the production and dissemination of the English Bible, the dissolution of the monasteries, the attack on shrines, the enforcement of the royal injunctions. Henry more than acquiesced in these changes: the destruction of shrines, for example, had been driven partly by his determination to destroy the memory of Becket, and after Cromwell's fall the king reiterated the proclamation against them. For all the king's doubts about permitting the ordinary laity to debate the scriptures, he reinforced the order to have the English Bible in parish churches a year after Cromwell's execution. But the familiar assumption is that Henry slowly recognized that his minister was supporting too wide a range of reform causes. The very proclamation of November 1538 that finally outlawed the Becket cult also regulated the import of English books and Bibles and defended ceremonies such as creeping to the cross on Good Friday.[113] The king took the unusual step of correcting the draft of this proclamation himself, not wholly trusting his adviser to ensure the middle path. Though Cromwell adjusted his religious politics deftly in the difficult year of the Six Articles and the Cleves marriage, Henry remained conscious of his interest in reform.[114] And ultimately he found in his minister's protection of radicals a justification for his fall. Cromwell's suppression in 1539 of Lord Lisle's complaints about the nest of sectaries in Calais became one of the king's dominant grievances against him.[115]

---

[111] G.E. Corrie (ed.), *Sermons and Remains of Hugh Latimer* (PS, Cambridge, 1845), i. 411. *LP* xii. i. 790.

[112] A.G. Dickens, *The English Reformation*, 2nd edn. (1989), 130 ff.

[113] *TRP* i. 270–6.

[114] S. Brigden, 'Thomas Cromwell and the "brethren"', in Cross *et al.*, *Law and Government*, 31–49.

[115] The significance of the Calais revelations for Cromwell's fall is controversial. See A.J. Slavin, 'Cromwell, Cranmer and Lord Lisle: a study in the politics of reform', *Albion* 9 (1977), 316–36; Redworth, 'Act of Six Articles', 51–3; Ward, 'Politics of religion', 164–71, makes an interesting case for Cromwell's lack of grasp on the religious politics of Calais, though he takes at face value statements from Cromwell that seem likely to be disingenuous.

There are dangers, however, in asserting that Cromwell, or indeed any other councillors to the king, consciously risked pushing policy beyond the boundaries of the royal will. The Lord Privy Seal famously told the Lutheran envoys that though he sympathized with their religious views, 'the world standing now as it does, whatever his lord the King holds, so too will he hold'.[116] He would say so, of course: these were foreign envoys. But Henrician advisers succeeded by not making martyrs of themselves and there are ample examples of policy governing ideological preference in the behaviour of Cromwell, or, on the conservative side, of Bishop Gardiner. Perhaps what needs to be emphasized most strongly is not the ideological commitments or factional manoeuvring of these men, rather the complexity of making policy, of guiding the king in the unfamiliar world of the *ecclesia Anglicana*, and of enforcing change in a culture wedded to belief in continuity. This complexity is best explored through a more systematic case study: the dissolution of the monasteries, the 'capital event' of the later 1530s.[117]

The Monastic Dissolutions

Writing to the Scottish regent the earl of Arran in 1543, Henry gave helpful do-it-yourself advice on the abolition of monasticism. His comments read as though drawn from a Machiavellian handbook for princes: 'the enterprise ... requireth politic handling, ... commissioners must have secret commission ... [to] get knowledge of all their [the monks] abominations ... he [the ruler] agreeing with them [the nobility] for the distribution of the lands of the abbeys ...'.[118] From the perspective of 1543 the dissolution appears to the English king as a rational, fully planned, and clinically controlled operation, whose objective was the extension of the power of the crown and the distribution of a portion of the wealth to the laity. The partial truth of this tale, however, does little justice to the complexities and confusions of policy formation and execution that led to the end of the monasteries. There was, of course, from the beginning of the Reformation parliament some expectation that the revenues of the Church would be vulnerable to lay attack. 'The temporality', as one commentator wrote in the early 1530s, 'scan the possessions of the spirituality, thinking verily that they may have acquired a great deal more than reason would require.'[119] Already in 1529 a parliamentary petition had

---

[116] R.B. Merriman, *Life and Letters of Thomas Cromwell*, 2 vols. (Oxford, 1902), i. 279.

[117] The phrase is J.J. Scarisbrick's in *The Reformation and the English People* (Oxford, 1984), 68.

[118] *LP* xviii. i. 364, quoted in D. Knowles, *The Religious Orders in England*, vol. iii: *The Tudor Age* (Cambridge, 1959), 204.

[119] BL Cottonian MS Cleo. EIV, fo. 212.

revived Lollard attacks on ecclesiastical possessions, arguing that the clergy must be returned to their true purity and their property given to the crown, which would use them to reverse the 'decay of the nobility' and, with their assistance, to fight the Great Turk. Hoyle has plausibly suggested that this proposal, which did not gain official sanction, may have originated in court circles, where the dukes of Norfolk and Suffolk were bent upon the destruction of Wolsey.[120] The first dissolution proposal in Ireland, from the pen of Baron Finglas in the early 1530s, followed a similar line of thought. Border monasteries could be suppressed to finance 'young lords and gents out of England', who would colonize the contested territories to the military and financial benefit of the crown.[121]

The 1529 petition revived old complaints against the clerical estate, but also pointed to some possible motives for reform. Wolsey himself had already set the precedent in the case of the monasteries by his 1525–6 dissolutions designed to finance his new educational foundations at Oxford and Ipswich.[122] Moreover, in 1529 he received papal permission to convert abbacies into bishoprics, suppress some monastic houses to endow colleges at Windsor and Cambridge, and to unite those unable to support more than twelve members.[123] Events overtook the latter grand plan, but it represented a good example of the clerical and humanist view of how wealth might be redistributed to the benefit of the Church as a whole. It would be difficult to identify consistent clerical views on the wealth of the monasteries as the 1530s unfolded, but a common position (held by traditionalists and some reformers alike) was that while recycling of resources within the Church was acceptable, the loss of the monasteries to lay greed was not. For example, the drama 'Godly Queen Hester' (*c.*1529–30) defends the monasteries from a traditional perspective, as givers of good hospitality, looking both backwards to criticize Wolsey's suppressions and forwards to the potential threat from the crown.[124] Thomas Starkey, occupying a middle ground in his *Dialogue of Pole and Lupset*, argued for reform of the monasteries, not their destruction.[125] Much later in the decade Latimer's plea for the Benedictine house of Great Malvern to be preserved 'not in monkery...but to maintain teaching, preaching, study with praying and...good housekeeping', is the most

---

[120] The 1529 petition was discovered by Richard Hoyle and is printed and discussed in his important article on the dissolution to which the ensuing section is much indebted: Hoyle, 'Origins of the dissolution', 275–305. The original 1410 Lollard petition is printed in J. Youings, *The Dissolution of the Monasteries* (1972), 135.

[121] B. Bradshaw, *The Dissolution of the Religious Orders in Ireland under Henry VIII* (Cambridge, 1974), 44–5.

[122] *LP* iv. iii. 5607.　　[123] Gwyn, *King's Cardinal*, 464–9. *LP* xiii. ii. 1036.

[124] Walker, *Plays of Persuasion*, 108–22.

[125] T. Starkey, *A dialogue between Pole and Lupset*, ed. T.F. Mayer, CS, 4th ser. 37 (1989), 103–4.

distinctive of a range of reformers' views.[126] The problem for the clergy was that they had little autonomous voice in a matter so closely touching the regality and purse of the crown. It is striking that even Henry's favoured new archbishop played only a limited role in the dissolution saga, and cannot be shown to have had any significant effect on policy. Once disendowment of the Church became an established practice, the bishops began to protest, though even then it was most usual for them to engage in the cautious defence of their own lands. John Stokesley, for example, invoked some of that historical evidence supposedly so dear to his monarch, when he opposed a manorial grant because the land concerned had been given to the see of London by St Ethelbert and King Offa and hedged with 'strange imprecations *contra alienatores*'.[127] Meanwhile Gardiner adopted another ploy, pressing for the establishment of the new bishoprics that had been another of Wolsey's schemes, thereby saving something from the final wreckage for the cause of ecclesiastical order.[128]

The clergy had some fellow-travellers among laymen with a voice at court: most remarkably it has been argued that Anne Boleyn and Jane Seymour were hostile to dissolution, or at least to secularization that would not benefit godly causes. On Passion Sunday 1536 Anne's almoner, John Skip, preached a sermon containing a swingeing attack on lay greed, using the Old Testament story of Ahasuerus, who was deceived by his adviser Haman into proscribing the Jews. Haman, in Skip's description, is a scarcely disguised Cromwell.[129] Later the same year Jane seems to have trespassed less publicly on the same territory when she pleaded with the king for the restoration of the lesser monasteries after the Pilgrimage of Grace.[130] As the process against the monasteries advanced there were strong voices in defence of particular houses from the commissioners for visitations and from individual nobles and courtiers who, like their clerical counterparts, saw merit in conformable and hospitable monks.[131] Lord Chancellor Audley pleaded for the preservation of St John's, Colchester, and St Osyth's as colleges if not as monasteries since 'little hospitality shall

---

[126] T. Wright (ed.), *Three Chapters of Letters Relating to the Suppression of the Monasteries*, CS OS 26 (1843), 149.

[127] *LP* xiii. i. 1500. F. Heal, *Of Prelates and Princes* (Cambridge, 1980), 109–25.

[128] Papal bulls for the establishment of six new sees had actually been issued in 1532, only to be overtaken by events.

[129] E.W. Ives, 'Anne Boleyn and the early Reformation in England: the contemporary evidence', *HJ* 37 (1994), 395–400. The evidence that Anne approved of the content of Skip's controversial sermon is circumstantial, but is presented very convincingly in Ives's article.

[130] *LP* xi. 860. E. Hallam, 'Henry VIII's monastic refoundations of 1536–7 and the course of the dissolution', *BIHR* 51 (1978), 129.

[131] See J.J. Scarisbrick, *The Reformation and the English People* (Oxford, 1984), 70–4, for a summary of pleas to the crown for particular houses.

be kept' in that part of Essex if they were dissolved.[132] None of this can be said to have had a long-term effect on royal policy: and indeed Henry must have taken the anticlerical attitude of the court both before and during the dissolution as one sign that it was safe to proceed.

The king had intended action against at least some of the regulars from an early stage of the divorce crisis. In March 1533 Henry informed Chapuys that one of his objectives was to reunite to the crown all church goods held directly of it, asserting his right as founder and benefactor.[133] The next year rumour had it that this rather circumscribed plan was to be superseded by one to remove all ecclesiastical temporalities. John Husee, the Lisles' London agent, reporting this added 'whereof many be glad and few bemoan them'.[134] The parliamentary session that followed saw major changes, notably the introduction of the first fruits and tenths legislation, but nothing as drastic as Husee had indicated. He may, however, have been aware of a proposal entitled 'Things to be moved for the Kings highness for an increase and augmentation of his most royal estate and for defence of the realm, and necessary to be provided for taking away the excess which is the great cause of the abuses in the church.'[135] Hoyle has suggested that this set of proposals may actually have been presented in Parliament late in 1534: if so it left few legislative traces, though a comment by Chapuys indicates that the king may have tried to present an ambitious project for expropriation, only to retreat back to his demands for first fruits.[136] The key pressure behind 'Things to be moved...' was the Kildare revolt, and the governmental quest for an army to suppress it, and there is an emphasis on the king's rights to goods for public use.

From the beginning of 1535 it might be assumed that Cromwell would have established a clearer trajectory for dissolution. That January, letters patent appointed commissioners to survey church wealth, the end product being the *Valor Ecclesiasticus*, and in the same month the minister's elevation to the vicegerency enabled him to establish monastic visitations under the terms of the Act of Supremacy. But even the planning of the visitations does not indicate great clarity of purpose by the king and Cromwell. The question of founders' rights in the monasteries, raised by Henry

---

[132] Wright, *Three Chapters*, 246–7.

[133] Hoyle, 'Origins of the dissolution', 281.

[134] *LP* vi. 235.

[135] Heal, *Prelates and Princes*, 103–4. BL Cottonian MS Cleo. EIV, fos. 207–208ᵛ: 'Things to be moved...' is printed in J. Youings, *The Dissolution of the Monasteries* (1969), 145–7.

[136] Hoyle, 'Origins of the dissolution', 282 ff., argues strongly for this as an official document, the basis of government initiative in Parliament. It may be more 'official' than I allowed in 1980, but there are still problems with the text, especially the sense that it is a draft proposal with little evidence of how it would have been worked into legislative form.

to Chapuys, remained pertinent.[137] One of the questions that the visitors were asked to answer was who held original rights over a particular house. There may also have been some interest in the idea of voluntary surrenders, not so unrealistic in the light of Continental experience. And all of this may reflect conflicting conciliar advice to the king. The late sixteenth-century chronicle found among the papers of George Wyatt has Cromwell recommending that it might be best to proceed piecemeal 'little by little and not suddenly by parliament'. It also describes a group led by Lord Chancellor Audley and Richard Rich as finally prevailing and drafting the 1536 Suppression Act. There are certainly indications that the last series of visitors' returns, for the Northern Province, were redrafted, possibly to persuade MPs of the need for action.[138]

Other European states that took the road to Reformation faced the same difficulty and produced rather different answers. Some of the German princes moved to direct and complete appropriation: Duke Ulrich of Württemberg, for example, secularized the monasteries in the period after 1534 and used most of the proceeds to fund his government and war debts.[139] Christian II and Christian III of Denmark proceeded more slowly, with piecemeal attacks on the friars in the 1520s and encouragement to others to abandon their cloisters and wealth to the crown in the 1530s. In Sweden Gustavus Vasa proceeded somewhat cautiously under the Recess of Vasteras of 1527.[140] Founders' rights were used as a way of seizing land donated to the Church after 1454, but the monasteries were to die quietly: there was no general expulsion of the monks. Was this the type of solution canvassed between 1534 and 1536 as the political and logistic cost of dissolution was weighed?

If so, it was rejected. Founders' rights would always have been awkward to exploit because of the direct interest they offered to nobles and other laymen who were properly descendants of those who had established houses.[141] Henry's own conviction of his complete authority over the Church would probably not have brooked such a partial approach to the problem. And Cromwell himself is likely to have weighed political

---

[137] Youings, *Dissolution*, 36–42. Evidence for Cromwell's interest in a piecemeal settlement is also found in the advice he was given by counsel early in 1536 that the king could gain land for the crown worth £40,000 per annum if he exercised founders' rights—*LP* x. 242.

[138] D.M. Loades (ed.), *The Papers of George Wyatt Esquire*, CS 4th ser. 5 (1968), 159. I am grateful to Tony Shaw, who is currently working on the visitors' returns, for this information.

[139] Knowles, *Religious Orders*, iii. 165–72.

[140] Heal, *Prelates and Princes*, 15–19. In 1533 Chapuys had feared that a Lutheran embassy was coming to England to advise on expropriating church property: *CSP Sp* iv. ii. 6107. Direct knowledge of Scandinavian experience may not have been great, but it is of interest that Thomas Legh, one of Cromwell's visitors, had been on embassy to Denmark in 1532.

[141] Hoyle, 'Origins of the dissolution', 296–7.

caution against the crown's need for revenue, his own usual preference for statute, and perhaps a real reforming sense that the deficiencies of monasticism must be exposed. In his remembrances before the 1536 parliament the minister noted 'the abomination of religious houses throughout this realm and a reformation to be devised therein'.[142] It is usual to argue that the 1536 Act suppressing the smaller houses simply paid lip-service to the reform that would be achieved by legislation. But the visitors do seem to have shown that there were proportionately more problems in the lesser than the greater houses and the parliamentary draftsmen seem to have believed that they had a powerful rhetorical device when they separated the small monasteries worth less than £200 per annum, sunk in vice and immorality, from the great houses in which religion was 'right well kept and observed'.[143]

The Dissolution Bill came before the Commons in March 1536, perhaps supported by carefully managed extracts from the reports of the monastic visitors. Nicholas Harpsfield later recalled that Cranmer had also preached a sermon during parliament time, assuring the people that the king would now gain so much treasure 'that from that time he should have no need, nor put the people to...any charge for his or the realm's affairs'.[144] The rhetoric of reform and of self-interest seem to have won the government's case: no record of parliamentary opposition survives.[145] Then there was delay, which Ives has plausibly attributed to the court conflict between Cromwell and Anne Boleyn over the proper use of monastic resources. The fall of Anne coincided with the issue of commissions for the dissolution. With the process now successfully launched the language of reform was gradually abandoned, or rather it reverted to the domain of would-be reformers and ecclesiastics. Even these had to accept realities: in about June 1536 Thomas Starkey wrote to Henry accepting the diversion of monastic resources, and, in addition to concern for charitable works, pleading the cause of younger sons and lesser men as suitable beneficiaries of the king's new-found wealth.[146] When the Irish Reformation parliament had a Dissolution Bill for eight Irish houses before it in

---

[142] *LP* x. 254.

[143] The legislation is 27 Henry VIII, c. 28. Tony Shaw's research on the surviving *compendium compertorum*, made from the visitors' reports, will argue that historians have underestimated the complexity of these documents, which could have served a variety of purposes and should not simply be seen as providing the scandalous ammunition for the government's attack on the monasteries.

[144] Quoted in MacCulloch, *Cranmer*, 151.

[145] Though Latimer later claimed that the Commons were presented with scandalous evidence from the visitations and that Henry had been present when the Dissolution Bill was introduced, presumably for fear of opposition: Lehmberg, *Reformation Parliament*, 225–7.

[146] S.J. Herrtage (ed.), *Thomas Starkey's Life and Letters*, EETS ES 32 (1878), pp. liii–lviii.

September of the same year there seems to have been no argument for the improvement of monasticism, simply its extirpation. Once again, Irish policy revealed political attitudes at their most stark. Conflict over the bill delayed its passage until late in 1537, but this was caused not by commitment to the monasteries but by patronage conflicts and concerns about vested interests in the existing estates.[147] By the time the Irish legislation was finally passed in September 1537, the focus in both territories was shifting to the issue of who would benefit from the king's actions, not of the future of monasticism itself.[148]

The eclectic approach to policy on the monasteries nevertheless continued well beyond the 1536 Act. Anywhere between a quarter and a half of those houses due for closure under the legislation gained exemptions, though how selection was made remains obscure.[149] Even more puzzling is that Henry still seems to have had no absolute commitment to extirpation, as his refoundation of the abbey of Chertsey at Bisham in December 1537 suggests.[150] It is possible to believe that there was an elaborate Machiavellian plan to move immediately from the small to the great houses, but the weight of evidence suggests that the crown proceeded opportunistically, driven in part by a fear that further grand gestures would provoke a recurrence of the Pilgrimage of Grace. Cromwell had the powers of the vicegerency to exercise control over the remaining houses, and relied on a mixture of internal conflict, demoralization, and lay pressure to bring about surrenders. Only in 1538 was pressure increased with a further round of visitations, in an atmosphere coolly evoked by one of Lisle's agents, George Rolle. 'The abbeys', he wrote in February of that year, 'go down as fast as they may... I pray God send you one among them to your part.'[151]

But the moment that is most telling in this second phase of dissolution is the appointment of Richard Ingworth as visitor general to the four orders of friars in February 1538. Ingworth was initially uncertain of his brief—was dissolution always required—so in May Cromwell wrote him an explicit letter requiring disbandment and complaining that he had changed his habit 'but not his friar's heart'.[152] By now the direction of the minister's policy seems clear: the existence of the mendicants was a threat

---

[147] Bradshaw, *Dissolution*, 47–65.

[148] Hoyle points out that Henry himself abandoned the language of reform between his defence of his actions to the Lincolnshire rebels in October 1536 and his letter to the Yorkshire rebels a short time later: Hoyle 'Origins of the dissolution', 280.

[149] Knowles, *Religious Orders*, iii. 315–16 gives the lower estimate; S. Jack, 'Dissolution dates for the monasteries dissolved under the act of 1536', *BIHR* 43 (1970), 161–81, gives the higher, but qualifies by pointing out that much of the relevant documentation, especially the Augmentation Order Books, is missing.

[150] Hallam, 'Henry VIII's refoundations', 125–7.   [151] *LP* xiii. i. 235.

[152] Knowles, *Religious Orders*, 360–6.

and an anomaly and they must go. The logic would now have been a full dissolution statute. However, Parliament was not in session, and its assent would by no means have been assured: instead the policy of surrender was continued until the 1539 session was left with nothing to do except give retrospective confirmation to the debacle. Only in Ireland, where there had been limited change after 1537, did the dissolution commission of May 1539 initiate a further major round of closure.[153]

What were the plans for the land and wealth acquired between 1536 and 1540? Cromwell, writing to the king from imprisonment in 1540, claimed somewhat ambiguously, 'if it had been or were in my power to make you so rich as you might enrich all men, God help me as I would do it'.[154] Since even the entire wealth of the Church would have offered no such freedom, the crown's financial needs were obviously his first priority. Secondly, political support for royal policy had to be purchased, and the inner circle of nobles and courtiers were therefore necessary beneficiaries. Augmentations policy in 1536/7 was to maintain existing levels of rent, protect tenancies, and favour leases to local men.[155] As the process of alienation gathered momentum such political calculations were of less obtrusive importance. The English elites, by their very enthusiasm for the benefits on offer, showed the crown that they were unlikely to need careful calculation of *douceurs*. It is easier to see this kind of calculus at work where the issue of political control hung in the balance: in the case of Ireland. The Irish dissolutions were effected in an environment of conflict—the Geraldine rising—and of political experimentation with the coming of St Leger. While those in the Pale and Ormond essentially conformed to the English pattern, it was clear that in many cases economic advantage and ideological distaste for monasticism would have to be traded for a measure of political control. Even in the core area of English jurisdiction there are examples of this process: in Ormond three houses were transmuted into secular colleges because the monks were Gaelic and were closely controlled by leading local families whose allegiance to the crown was sought. Once the policy of surrender and regrant was in train in Gaelic territory it became common to allow the local chiefs to retain a measure of control of monastic suppression and any resulting property. The dissolution became, in Bradshaw's words, 'a practical experiment' in persuading the native Irish to co-operate in government under the English crown. For a time at least, this seemed a far more significant objective than that of raising additional revenue from monastic sources.[156]

---

[153] Bradshaw, *Dissolution*, 110–37. [154] *LP* xv. 776.
[155] Youings, *Dissolution*, 113–15. [156] Bradshaw, *Dissolution*, 110–80.

The narrative of the dissolution indicates no master plan for the expropriation of church wealth, but rather an experimental, opportunistic, response to novel circumstances. We can hazard that there were certain consistencies in the story: the pressures of royal finance and the needs of defence—Ireland and Kildare in 1534; the friendship of France and the Empire in 1538—dictated that wealth would be expropriated. Anxieties about parliamentary opposition and popular dissent meant that any governmental initiative had to be carefully managed. And royal gains had to be matched by some assurance that profit would also be available to the politically influential. Although the lands passing into Augmentations were initially largely retained, there were sufficient gifts and permissions to purchase to reward the inner circles of Henrician government. But the surprising aspect of a return to close examination of the politics of dissolution is the pervading sense of improvisation in policy-making, of a lack of certainty about means and even about ends.[157] It seems likely that there was more internal debate about these issues than now survives, and that, while Cromwell's managerial role is not in question, he may well have been constrained by the actions of others—Anne Boleyn, Audley, Rich. Above all, he must have had to be responsive to the king, who seems to have combined a continuing belief in some of the functions of the monks with an absolute determination to extract maximum profit and political advantage from his new *ecclesia Anglicana*. And it is symptomatic of Henry's priorities that the very last of the closures, the suppression of the order of the knights hospitaller of St John of Jerusalem in 1540, was justified, not by the fact that it was an anomaly, but by the argument that it had upheld the authority of Rome.[158]

The End of Henricianism

The last years of Henry's reign were marked by intermittent bouts of ideological and factional turmoil: the aftermath of the Act of Six Articles; the upheavals of 1543 which are subsumed under the label the Prebendaries' Plot; the last year as the problems of succession began to become acute. The debate about whether the king was manipulated or manipulator in these years is perhaps less interesting than the observation that the monarch had to move between apparently opposing policies in order to represent royal control to his subjects.[159] The inwardness of his actions is difficult to

---

[157] Hallam, 'Henry VIII's refoundations', 130–1.   [158] 32 Henry VIII, c. 24.

[159] On factionalism in these years see the references above at n. 110, and L.B. Smith, *Henry VIII: The Mask of Royalty* (1971). A. Ryrie, 'English Evangelical Reformers in the Last Years of Henry VIII', University of Oxford D.Phil. (2000), offers a major reinterpretation of these years, which emphasizes that evangelicals lived in hope of royal sympathy for reform until 1543, when Bible-reading was restricted.

penetrate, dependent as we are on commentators who were often themselves mystified (the ambassadors) or *parti pris*, like Ralph Morice who
provided John Foxe with much of his account of this period.[160] In the
years before 1543 it is plausible to suggest that the king remained deeply
interested in the form of his religious settlement, and was eager to promote
a return to stability after the oscillations associated with the Six Articles, the
international crisis, and the fall of Cromwell. His prime instrument for the
reordering of his church was to be the doctrinal statement the *Necessary
Doctrine and Erudition for any Christian Man* (1543), usually known as the
King's Book.[161] Henry gave much time and attention to this revision of
doctrine, seeing it as the 'means to stay controversy', and arguing vigorously with Cranmer on key doctrinal tenets such as justification.[162] His
confidence in its efficacy is indicated by his recommendation that Regent
Arran in Scotland made no attempt to alter statements of faith north of the
border until he had had a chance to see the English confession.[163] The
contrast between Henry's active approach to these issues and his response
to the Prebendaries' Plot is illuminating. The attempt to unseat Cranmer
and to challenge the evangelical interest in the Privy Chamber involved
many people, and is a striking indication of the polarity of late Henrician
religious politics. Charges were accumulated, co-ordinated by Gardiner,
and laid before Henry, who proceeded to do nothing with them for five
months, while plots and counter-plots swirled around him. Then he appointed the archbishop to head the commission to investigate his alleged
misdeeds. Such behaviour can be read as an impressive example of control,
a waiting on events before striking the warring parties, but the conflicts of
that year were yet another example of the damage being done to the king's
cherished unity, and Henry had some responsibility in allowing dispute to
unfold in so comprehensive a way.[164]

Some of the same questions occur in the case of the appointment of
royal tutors for Prince Edward in 1543–4: one of the critical determinants
of the future religious direction of the realm. First Richard Cox, already
known for his reformist sympathies, and then John Cheke, who must at
least be labelled an evangelical humanist, were installed to guide the future
ruler of England along the paths of knowledge.[165] The result was a nine-
year-old monarch who was already a priggish reformer when he ascended
the throne. Did Henry know this might be the outcome? Did he consciously will it? Since no firm evidence on this survives historians have

---

[160] J.G. Nichols (ed.), *Narratives of the Days of the Reformation*, CS os 77 (1859).
[161] Lloyd, *Formularies of Faith*, 373 ff.   [162] MacCulloch, *Cranmer*, 343–7.
[163] *LP* xviii. i. 364.   [164] MacCulloch, *Cranmer*, 295–323.
[165] On the royal tutors see MacCulloch, *Cranmer*, 325–6, and Rex, *Henry VIII*, 169–70. The
latter is firmly convinced of Henry's ignorance of the significance of his choices.

focused on the second-order question: who could have recommended these men to Henry? The most convincing answer is that the privy chamber men, led by Anthony Denny and abetted by the evangelical physician William Butts, presented Henry with these names, though Cranmer may have promoted Cox, who was his chaplain.[166] Henry trusted these men, but by 1544 had plenty of experience of their cautious reformism. If he did recognize the import of his actions, he may have been engaged in a rebalancing of religious politics after a period the previous year when conservative interests seemed to have been ascendant. Cox and Cheke would also inculcate his heir with a proper concern for the royal supremacy, a theme on which the conservatives could never quite be trusted. It seems unconvincing to proceed beyond this to argue that Henry willed a radical religious order upon his heir: the outcome owes more to deft manoeuvring by his intimates, who in their turn were no doubt driven in part by a concern for survival and the prospect of escape from the vicious cycles of conflict that marked the late Henrician court. Most striking in all of this is the sense that Henry played a relatively passive role in a policy decision that had vast implications for the future of his church and state.

Henry VIII remained convinced to the end that he was establishing a 'middle way' in religious politics. His famous denunciation before the parliament of 1545 of those clergy who were 'too stiff in their old mumpsimus' and others who were 'too busy and curious in their new sumpsimus', is only the most colourful rhetorical representation of his views.[167] In the process of jettisoning traditionalism he had grounded himself in an Old Testament kingship which legitimated attacks on some fundamental Catholic beliefs—love of images, the essential mediatory role of the priesthood, and, probably, after 1543 the doctrine of purgatory.[168] In his refusal to follow Luther's path he had tenaciously upheld the Catholic view of the Eucharist, and denied justification by faith alone. He had also made the life of some of his reformist clergy wretched by his profound opposition to clerical marriage. Many of these positions had been reached through his own enthusiastic study of theology and Scripture. His ideas had evolved, or sometimes revolved, in response to debate among his clergy and discussion with key advisers like More, Anne Boleyn, and

[166] P.C. Swensen, 'Noble Hunters of the Romish Fox: Religious Reform at the Tudor Court, 1543–1564', University of California at Berkeley Ph.D. (1981), 105–80. Starkey, *Henry VIII*, 125–45, offers the most convincing account of factional crises in these years. Butts had been Cheke's patron from an early date: J. Strype, *Life of the learned Sir John Cheke, knight* (Oxford, 1821), 27–30.

[167] Hall, *Chronicle*, ii. 356.

[168] On Henry and purgatory see A. Kreider, *English Chantries: The Road to Dissolution* (Cambridge, Mass., 1979), 151–3.

Cromwell. He rarely appeared deflected from his chosen path by internal dissent: foreign pressures were another matter, especially when England was exposed to the threat of crusade. In the last years of his reign factional conflicts forced a wavering policy upon Henry, and the middle way was all too easily lost in the thickets of court intrigue. It is indicative of the confusions of these late years that the final triumph of the evangelicals, and defeat of Norfolk and Gardiner in the last six months of the reign, can be read by Haigh as the merest accident.[169] Abrupt swings of royal mood were certainly a key feature of these months: the most dramatic evidence of the different direction that might have been taken being the king's acceptance in August of discussions with a papal contact, Gurone Bertano, indicating the faintest possibility of a return to Rome. But the political balance was probably already weighted in favour of the reformers on the council, the best guarantee of Edward's security. By November 1546 the political miscalculations of Stephen Gardiner, and the self-destructive folly of the earl of Surrey, then set the seal on this final change of regal direction.[170]

Scotland and England, 1542–1550

In the Scottish parliament of 1541 James V made the most public and explicit of his gestures in defence of the Church Catholic. Nine acts were passed, beginning with a general affirmation of the crown's support of the freedoms of the 'holy kirk', and embracing due reverence of the sacraments, proper support of the papacy, the honour of the Virgin, and a raft of measures against heresy.[171] The legislation represented a triumph for Cardinal David Beaton, who, since his elevation two years previously, had been using the various instruments of politics to assail heterodox beliefs.[172] In 1539 there had been a cluster of burnings of clerical and plebeian heretics and in the subsequent year the greater threat of 'Lutherans' within the royal court had been confronted with the exiling of Sir John Borthwick. But these victories for Scotland's Wolsey were not quite all that they

---

[169] Haigh, *English Reformations*, 166–7.

[170] MacCulloch, *Cranmer*, 356–60. The earl of Surrey's downfall was a consequence of his political ambitions, rather than of any conservative religious sentiments. While his religious views cannot be definitively identified with the reformed cause, the cumulative evidence of his poems and the company that he kept in the last years of Henry's reign suggest that he was sympathetic to religious change. In politics, however, he was hostile to the ambitions of the Seymour circle: S. Brigden, 'Henry Howard, earl of Surrey, and the "conjured league"', *HJ* 37 (1994), 507–37.

[171] *APS* ii. 370.

[172] M.B. Sanderson, *Cardinal of Scotland: David Beaton, c.1494–1546* (Edinburgh, 1986), 74–8, 88–90.

seemed. James was usually only seized by a fit of devotion to the Catholic Church when it could serve his interests. In 1533–4 his first heresy hunt coincided with a request to Rome for the sanction of his college of justice; in 1539 he was seeking the further promotion of Beaton to the legateship *a latere* (finally achieved only in 1544); in 1541 he was engaged in that most characteristic of monarchical activities, seeking papal sanction for a clerical tax.[173] The king would usually reaffirm his devotion to Rome when it suited his purposes. When the papacy, or his own kirkmen, proved threatening it was another story. In 1540 Beaton apparently wished to move against a list of 'heretics' with good courtly connections: James flatly refused to move beyond the one sacrificial victim of Borthwick.[174]

James Beaton led the Scottish bishops firmly in an orthodox, pro-papal policy anchored politically in support of the crown's maintenance of the 'auld alliance' with France. His opponents were a heterogeneous group of ousted nobles, humanist and reform-minded courtiers and administrators, and radical clergy. Some, though by no means all, saw Henrician England as their salvation. Henry's ambassador, Ralph Sadler, in a rare moment of perceptive observation in 1540, remarked that there were a number of those who favoured the gospel, and by implication closer links with England, 'but the noblemen be young', and there was a lack of potential leaders to counter the clerical faction.[175] While James lived these 'favourers' made little headway against his proclaimed orthodoxy, and the French alliance, so valued by Beaton, was the cornerstone of policy. However, the defeat at Solway Moss in December 1542, followed almost immediately by the king's death, led to a dramatic shift in the nature of Anglo-Scottish politics and in the religious relationship between the two realms. Henry VIII was presented with a compelling opportunity to determine the direction of the Scottish realm as a week-old female child ascended the throne and the regency council faced disarray and military defeat.[176]

[173] Although Beaton was not made *a latere* until 1544 the 1539 negotiations paid off in the form of a papal grant to him of the right to present to benefices previously reserved to Rome: Sanderson, *Cardinal of Scotland*, 108. C. Edington, *Court and Culture in Renaissance Scotland: Sir David Lindsay of the Mount* (E. Linton, E. Lothian, 1995), 53–5.

[174] The 'black list' is only described after James's death in 1543, and could be simply a construct of the enemies of the clergy, but James's willingness to manipulate opposing groupings at his court is well-attested.

[175] A. Clifford (ed.), *The State Papers and Letters of Sir Ralph Sadler*, 2 vols. (Edinburgh, 1809), i. 47. For a very interesting discussion of the nature of religious attitudes at James's court see Edington, *Court and Culture*, 45 ff.

[176] Henry's incursions into Scotland in 1542, probably designed to assuage his offended sense of honour after James had failed to meet him at York the previous year, involved the revival of the Edwardian claims to suzerainty over Scotland in his printed *Declaration conteynyng the just causes and consideratyons of this present warre*. This is published as an appendix to J.A.H. Murray (ed.), *The Complaynt of Scotlande*, EETS ES 17 (1872), 191–206.

Henry's approach to this crisis is usually presented by historians as indicative of his lack of an imperial vision in his dealings with Scotland.[177] He had an objective, in the marriage of the infant Mary to his own son, but no will to achieve it by full military intervention. Rather he preferred to rely on pro-English nobles such as the earl of Angus, and on the return to Scotland of a group of men captured after Solway Moss who had become 'assured' to the English crown, promising to defend its interests and promote the marriage.[178] The king and his advisers linked this to a religious policy of sorts: Angus and the earl of Lennox had to swear to support the preaching of the 'Word of God' and to renounce the French alliance. It was nevertheless something of an uncovenanted bonus that the new heir to the Scottish throne, the earl of Arran, who emerged as victor from the initial power-struggles of the regency council, chose to represent himself as 'a good soft God's man'.[179] Beaton was ousted in January 1543 and temporarily imprisoned. Arran ostentatiously employed two radical friars, Rough and Guilliame, as his chaplains, and had them preach at Holyrood and St Giles, Edinburgh. More significantly, he called a parliament in March 1543 and, after some conflict and against the will of the first estate, forced through a measure legitimizing the use of the New Testament in English.[180] When Sadler arrived back in Edinburgh hard on the heels of this parliament, he was most impressed by Arran's devotion to the scriptures, and his desire to have the sacred books shipped from England for dissemination. It was on hearing this report that Henry followed up with the sound advice on how to strip the kirkmen of their remaining wealth.[181]

Neither the 'assured Scots' nor Arran proved adequate allies in England's attempts to secure the person of Mary Queen of Scots or the destruction of the French connection. The trouble with Arran is memorably described by Margaret Sanderson. It was 'not that he could not be moulded but that he would not stay set'.[182] Henry VIII was powerful, but distant; Beaton was powerful and present, and before the summer of 1543 had resumed much of his former influence over Scottish politics. The return from exile of Arran's natural brother John Hamilton, the future archbishop of St Andrews, seems to have persuaded the governor to return to orthodoxy.[183] Before the end of that year the marriage negotiations had collapsed, the French alliance had been revived and the brief moment of 'gospel freedom' was lost. Those Scots who had 'taken new opinions of the Scripture' were doubly condemned as heretics and Anglo-

---

[177] D.M. Head, 'Henry VIII's Scottish policy', *SHR* 61 (1982), 1–24.

[178] M. Merriman, 'The assured Scots: Scottish collaborators with England during the Rough Wooing', *SHR* 47 (1968), 10–34.

[179] *SP HVIII* v. iv. 410.　　[180] *APS* ii. 415.　　[181] *LP* xviii. i. 161, 324, 348, 364.

[182] Sanderson, *Cardinal of Scotland*, 154.　　[183] Edington, *Court and Culture*, 59.

philes.[184] Such individuals were placed in an even more untenable position by Henry's response to the crisis. It is difficult to characterize this as
anything other than a quest for revenge upon the troublesome Scots, who
had thwarted his dynastic ambitions and refused to be quiescent while he
sought political glory in France. The brutal campaigns of 1544 and 1545,
which damaged Edinburgh, and devastated so many of the Border abbeys,
did nothing to resolve relations between the two realms, and led to one
English defeat, when the earl of Angus was so incensed at the desecration
of his family tombs that he led a successful attack on Henry's troops at
Ancrum. Head even suggests that 1544, by foreclosing any serious possibility of Anglo-Scottish co-operation, represents a more significant
turning point than the death of James V.[185]

It might be more appropriate to suggest that the very negativity of
Henry's response gradually forced a further rethinking of Scottish politics
on the English leadership, especially on the earl of Hertford. Hertford
made his military reputation in the Scottish campaigns and became that
unusual phenomenon, an English political leader more concerned with
resolving relations with Scotland than with France or the Empire. The
policy of assurance, begun to sway events at the heart of the northern
regime, was now extended more systematically to become a method of
identifying ordinary Scots with English interests. Hertford looked to a
policy of conquest and stabilization with local support, as against the intermittent raiding conducted in the aftermath of the 1543 debacle.[186] Moreover, it seems likely that even before Henry's death, Hertford saw the
merits of reviving earlier emphasis upon English concerns for anti-papalism
and the gospel, and the importance of appealing to an evangelical alliance
against France. Henry's promotion of the Word, both at home and abroad,
had been tempered by his concern for good order. Sadler had been instructed in 1543 to tell Arran that the dissemination of the scripture must
be treated cautiously, ensuring that the people did not succumb to confusion and dispute.[187] Hertford and his followers, on the other hand, were in
favour of dispensing the Word to all and sundry: the town of Dundee, for
example, requested Bibles in 1547 and was given them.[188] Meanwhile the
oath taken by the 'assured' was amplified to include a clause by which they
renounced 'the usurped power of the Bishop of Rome'.[189]

---

[184] *APS* ii. 443.   [185] Head, 'Henry VIII', 22–3.
[186] The best general account of Hertford's preoccupation with Scotland is M.L. Bush, *The
Government Policy of Protector Somerset* (1975), 7–39, though Bush underestimates the importance
of religious factors in the campaigns and garrisoning policy. Merriman, 'Assured Scots', 13–16.
[187] *LP* xviii. i. 364.
[188] *CSP Sc* i. 129. D. Davidson, 'Influence of the English printers on the Scottish Reformation', *RSCHS* 1 (1923–4), 79–81.
[189] Merriman, 'Assured Scots', 14.

Events in Scotland in the year before Henry's death had given understandable hope to Hertford and his colleagues. The murder of Cardinal Beaton and the holding of the Castle of St Andrews against Arran seemed to point to the growing strength of the Scottish gospellers, just as it constituted a major blow to the Francophile party. Loyalty to England, or at least to some sort of union to protect the gains of the reformers, began to make sense once again. The hopes of the Castilians that they would gain sufficient English aid to maintain St Andrews proved false, but the French victors (a group of galleys that assailed the Castle under Peter Strozzi) offered only short-term assistance, and the Scottish council could not depend upon adequate French aid until 1548.[190] The death of Henry VIII freed Hertford, now made duke of Somerset, to pursue a more vigorous policy of pressure north of the border, combining a major military campaign with stabilization of strongholds. It is in these circumstances that the English created an 'Edwardian moment' of high expectation about union between the two realms underpinned by godly reformation.[191] The propaganda offensive begun by Henry to win hearts and minds north of the border was now intensified. Somerset's 1547 proclamation justifying intervention in Scotland was widely circulated, and spoke of the advancement of 'the glory of God and his Word' as well as the need to abolish the 'bishop of Rome's corrupted jurisdiction'.[192] This was followed by the *Epistle Exhortatorie*, which urged the Scots to seize their providential moment and throw off the yoke of both Rome and France. Such a course was divinely ordained because Scotland and England were logically one, 'having the sea for a wall, the mutual love for garrison and God for defence'. The *Epistle* is sometimes attributed to Somerset's secretary Sir Thomas Smith, but it may have been written, or at least influenced, by a remarkable propagandist, James Henrisoun, who had accompanied Hertford to England after the attack on Edinburgh in 1544.[193]

---

[190] Knox, i. 174–207.

[191] John Hooper, the future bishop of Gloucester, had also shown a discerning eye for Somerset's obsession with Scotland when, still in exile in Switzerland, he dedicated his 1547 tract, 'A Declaration of Christ and his Office', to the Lord Protector, who would ensure the creation of 'one realm and island, divided from all the world by imparking of the sea', would now be joined in spiritual amity: S. Carr (ed.), *The Early Writings of John Hooper* (PS, Cambridge, 1843), p. xii.

[192] The 1544 proclamation of war had already invoked some of this language: A.I. Cameron and R.S. Rait (eds.), *The Warrender Papers*, 2 vols., SHS 3rd ser. 18 (Edinburgh, 1931), i. 17.

[193] Some of Henrisoun's arguments had already been anticipated in a tract addressed to Henry VIII by John Elder, a Gaelic Scot urging union for religious reasons: 'A Proposal for uniting Scotland with England', *Bannatyne Miscellany* 1 (Bannatyne Club, Edinburgh, 1827), 1–18. M. Merriman, 'James Henrisoun and "Great Britain": British Union and the Scottish Commonweal', in R.A. Mason (ed.), *Scotland and England, 1286 to 1815* (Edinburgh, 1987), 85–112. R.A. Mason, 'The Scottish reformation and the origins of Anglo-British imperialism', in Mason (ed.), *Scots and Britons: Scottish Political Thought and the Union of 1603* (Cambridge, 1994), 161–86.

Henrisoun, an Edinburgh merchant and committed reformer, was certainly responsible for the tract *An Exhortacion to the Scottes to conforme themselves to the honourable, expedient and godly unione betweene the realmes of England and Scotland* (1547). Henrisoun appealed to history, geography, and ideology. The two realms were of one blood, and boundary. Now, as a personified Britannia expresses it:

as these two realms should grow into one, so should they also agree in the concord and unity of one religion, and the same the pure, sincere and incorrupt religion of Christ, setting a part all fond superstitions, sophistications & other thousands of devilries brought in by the bishop of Rome and his creatures, whereby to give gloss to their things & darkness to Gods true word.[194]

For Henrisoun this unionist ideology was not intended to indicate imperial domination by one realm over the other, and when he established that that was the precise trajectory of English governmental thinking he became disillusioned, eventually retiring back to his native land.[195] A more explicitly English perspective on the Edwardian moment is the tract written by William Patten, one of Somerset's men who travelled north with the army to Pinkie. In his narrative, written in 1548, he assured the Scots that the English sought no dominion, but could barely conceal his contempt that they had so far failed to throw off the French yoke and their bondage 'under that hideous monster, that venomous *aspis* and very ANTICHRIST the BISHOP of ROME'.[196] The problem was that a majority of the Scottish elite not directly under English control had accepted the necessity of upholding the old order so that they did not become bound to their southern neighbour. By the time Patten wrote major French assistance was reaching Scotland and the tide of war was turning against Somerset. The bishops traded repeal of the articles on Bible reading for financial support in the war.[197] As the English ability to control the Borders and parts of the Lowlands diminished, their following among the 'assured men' also began to melt away. There were exceptions: in 1548 Lord Methven argued to the Queen Dowager, Mary of Guise, that affection for the scriptures meant that 'Englishmen were [still] favoured' by many.[198] James Lockhart more realistically saw this as the

---

[194] Henrisoun's tract, like the other pieces mentioned, is printed in Murray, *Complaynt of Scotlande*, 207–36; the quotation is at p. 234.

[195] Merriman, 'James Henrisoun', 97–9. Henrisoun remained influenced by English ideas, however, see his social reform tract, 'A Godly and Golden Book' (1548), summarized in *CSP Sc* i. 140–5.

[196] W. Patten, 'The expedition into Scotland', in A.J. Pollard (ed.), *Tudor Tracts, 1532–88* (1903), 70.

[197] *CSP Sc* i. no. 10.

[198] M.H.B. Sanderson, *Ayrshire and the Reformation* (E. Linton, E. Lothian, 1997), 64.

stand of a minority, while most had favoured union 'only for their own profit'.[199] Although Somerset could never bring himself wholly to abandon the Scottish policy, the 'rough wooing' was effectively over by 1549. Mary was in France, the garrisons largely abandoned and the reformers at a low ebb. In the propaganda wars the publication of *The Complaynt of Scotlande* (1549) reinforced the links between reform and treasonable association with the old enemy. Dame Scotia warned the three estates that none of them could expect any mercy if there was an English victory: the clergy in particular could judge from precedent that their lands would be annexed and that they would be driven out to be 'labourers', 'cordwainers', or 'tailors'.[200] English policy had made it easy for such propaganda to carry conviction: Henry's imperious handling of the 'rough wooing', and the general sense that even Somerset wanted dominance not unionist accommodation, gravely weakened the cause of reform with an English face. In the succeeding years though the 'privy kirks' would be happy enough to utilize the written instruments of Protestantism from south of the border, it became difficult to envisage that the political triumph of reform could possibly rest on English support.[201]

The Reign of King Josiah

The crowning of England's child-king was an event heavily freighted with political anxiety, but also with a sense of expectation. Somerset's regime had already survived the first fraught days after Henry's demise: Hertford had been elevated to his dukedom and made Lord Protector, other leading councillors had also been rewarded with titles, and the basic pattern of the regency council established by royal will had been affirmed. Edward's coronation was, like all such events, laden with symbolism, much of it in this case intended to bolster the young ruler's claim to the powerful status of his dead father. But the exercise of strengthening royal authority was not merely protective and conservative. There were deliberate signals that Edward should take his father's mantle in religious affairs, and perfect the work of reformation begun in the previous decades. The city pageant that preceded the coronation included a representation of Truth, 'which long time was suppressed/with hethen rites and detestable idolatrye', until freed by Henry as King David.[202] At the ceremony itself Archbishop Cranmer preached a short sermon: this unequivocally affirmed

---

[199] Merriman, 'Assured Scots', 34. [200] Murray, *Complaynt of Scotlande*, 162.

[201] J. Kirk, *Patterns of Reform: Continuity and Change in the Reformation Kirk* (Edinburgh, 1989), 11.

[202] The description of the coronation pageants is printed in full in J.G. Nichols (ed.), *The Literary Remains of King Edward VI*, 2 vols. (1857), i, pp. cclxxix–ccxci.

the royal supremacy, making it clear that the monarch's power derived directly from God, and then reminded the king to follow the example of his 'predecessor Josiah'. He must see God truly worshipped, assail the papacy and, most distinctively, remove images as part of the attack on idolatry.[203] An agenda was articulated: one in which 'deviating neither to the right hand nor the left' was to mean the vigorous pursuit of righteous reform rather than a quest for balance and the middle way.[204]

A nine-year-old monarch could scarcely, of course, initiate personally any attack upon the Church bequeathed him by his father. Policy-making lay with his council: after the fall of Thomas Wriothesley in the immediate aftermath of the coronation this was collectively disposed to a measure of reform. In practice the direction of religious change was determined by an even narrower grouping: the Lord Protector, with the intermittent assistance of William Paget and the more routine help of his own secretariat, and Cranmer and his reform-minded colleagues on the episcopal bench.[205] These committed individuals operated in an environment in which the competing ideological pressures of Henry's court were but a recent, though threatening, memory. Bishop Gardiner, the only effective leader of an ideological conservatism, was separated from the means of power: the duke of Norfolk, having escaped execution by Henry's providential death, was imprisoned in the Tower: the king's court was essentially an educational institution, Edward being surrounded by zealous godly tutors, rather than by vociferous courtiers.[206] Somerset may have operated from a narrow power-base: he faced little challenge until he began to alienate those within the council itself.

Stephen Gardiner, from his position in 1547 as an anxious spectator of the government's moves, sharply identified the strengths and weaknesses of the Protector's position. All responsibility, he wrote in late February, lay on Somerset's shoulders, 'and what so ever shall happen amiss by the faults of other, shall be imputed to your grace'. Since these 'faults' would eventually be accounted before God and before an adult monarch, Gardiner made a powerful plea for caution, for the maintenance of Henry's settlement, and for the fulfilment of the Protector's verbal assurance that he 'would suffer no innovation'.[207] The realm should be delivered to the king at his majority as

---

[203] The sermon is printed in J. Strype, *Memorials of . . . Thomas Cranmer*, 2 vols. (Oxford, 1840), i. 203–7. See also M. Aston, *England's Iconoclasts* (Oxford, 1988), i. 249–50.

[204] MacCulloch, *Cranmer*, 364–5.

[205] W.K. Jordan, *Edward VI: The Young King* (1968), 69 ff. D. Hoak, *The King's Council in the Reign of Edward VI* (Cambridge, 1976), 165 ff.

[206] For Edward's court see J. Murphy, 'The illusion of decline: the Privy Chamber 1547–1558', in D. Starkey (ed.), *The English Court from the Wars of the Roses to the Civil War* (1987), 119 ff.

[207] Muller, *Letters of Gardiner*, 265–6, 278.

his father had left it to him. Somerset's response was a lengthy summary of his particular proceedings in relation to images (the issue contested between them in the late spring), which disingenuously referred back to Henry VIII's mean: some 'can abide no old abuses to be reformed' while others 'too rash . . . headlong will set upon everything'.[208] But there is little doubt that the duke was already firmly on the side of those who sought, to quote the bishop again, 'that they call "Gods Word" against "Gods truth"'.[209] The apparent hesitations and delays in the implementation of change in the first year of the reign owed far more to the external constraints of politics than to a lack of will on the part of the Protector, or any failure of accord with the evangelical establishment under Cranmer.[210]

The major structural problem of this first Edwardian year was the failure to summon a parliament until November, a failure caused principally by the complexities of foreign relations and by the delayed Scottish campaign which culminated at Pinkie in September. At the end of April Charles V had won his shattering victory over the German princes at Mühlberg and it was hardly surprising that in the next two years voices like those of William Paget and of William Thomas, later clerk of the council, urged that radical action on religion would alienate the emperor and endanger the realm.[211] While Somerset slowly prepared to march north, the domestic religious signals remained mixed. The Act of Six Articles remained in place, and was even exploited by some of the conservative bishops, but Cranmer was given the opportunity to proceed with the *Book of Homilies*, which was issued in July after acerbic correspondence between the archbishop and Gardiner.[212] By the time the Protector finally moved north of the border in August the royal visitation of the Church was also launched. Its injunctions looked back to those of Cromwell in 1538, emphasizing preaching, teaching the Word, and the reform of the chantries rather than their abolition. They also moved more firmly into the evangelical attack with its prohibition of processions and the recitation of the rosary. Further, as MacCulloch has shown, the visitation had another agenda, which freed the individual visitors to engage in more vigorous attacks on the old religion than the precise terms of the commission

---

[208] Foxe, vi. 28–30.   [209] Muller, *Letters of Gardiner*, 272.

[210] On Somerset's religious position see Bush, *Government Policy*, 102–4, 124–5; and more recently D. MacCulloch, *Tudor Church Militant: Edward VI and the Protestant Reformation* (1999), 41–52. MacCulloch highlights the insights that Somerset's letters to the 1549 rebels offer into his policy: E. Shagan, 'Protector Somerset and the 1549 rebellions: new sources and new perspectives', *EHR* 144 (1999), 34–63.

[211] B.L. Beer and S.M. Jack (eds.), 'The Letters of William, Lord Paget of Beaudesert, 1547–1563', *Camden Miscellany* 25, CS 4th ser. 13 (1974), 23. J. Strype, *Ecclesiastical Memorials* (1816), ii. ii. 385.

[212] MacCulloch, *Cranmer*, 372–5.

indicated. The result was radical preaching by the likes of Bishop Barlow and merry bonfires of 'abused' images in Shropshire and elsewhere.[213]

When Parliament was finally convened it afforded the first opportunity to set the seal on some of the activities of the reformers. But perhaps its most significant function was to remove the legislative constraint of the Act of Six Articles and to excise the 1534 Treason Law. Thereafter religious debate and reforming action were less tied by the fear of conservative reaction employing the instruments of Henrician supremacy. Positive measures, which seem to have been promoted with full conciliar agreement, were the act dissolving the chantries and the two bills on the sacrament of the altar, eventually merged as one act. Half of this latter measure sought to curb radicals who reviled the Eucharist, the other restored communion in both kinds to the laity. The tactics used in the Lords, to get this measure past enough of the conservative bishops, were to assure them of the priority the regime gave to order and conformity as exemplified by the attack on radicals.[214] A further measure not passed in this session was the first attempt to abolish clerical celibacy: approved both by the lower house of Convocation and the Commons, it foundered in the Lords, presumably from episcopal hostility. Even in 1549, when the abolition of celibacy bill was revived, it only passed the Lords after bitter conflict. The first parliament also offered the regime a reminder that even the Commons was not necessarily subservient to conciliar aims: the chantries bill encountered stiff opposition until the borough representatives were assured that no attack was intended upon the general funds of the secular guilds.[215]

The Commons' acceptance of religious change seems to have emboldened Somerset and Cranmer to proceed with the policies begun in the first year of the reign. The endorsement of communion in both kinds opened the way for the first major stage of the liturgical revolution, the Order for Communion translating that part of the service involving lay participation into the vernacular, which was used from March 1548. The lifting of the threat embodied in the Six Articles and the Henrician Treason Act freed evangelical preachers and the printing press and encouraged the vigorous articulation of Protestant sentiment. A particularly crucial moment came in February 1548 when the council finally ordered the

---

[213] MacCulloch, *Tudor Church Militant*, 65–72.

[214] There is still no full study of Edwardian parliaments, but see J. Loach, 'Conservatism, and consent in parliament, 1547–59', in J. Loach and R. Tittler (eds.), *The Mid-Tudor Polity* (Basingstoke, 1980), 9–28, and on religious issues MacCulloch, *Cranmer*, 376–80, 404–8.

[215] The representatives of King's Lynn and Coventry mounted particularly stiff resistance to the chantries bill and succeeded in initiating separate legislation to protect their urban possessions: Kreider, *English Chantries*, 189–200.

removal of all images from churches and chapels, thereby ending a year in which conflict about the veneration of icons had been the source of sharpest debate within the elite.[216] Gardiner's passionate plea that 'the destruction of images containeth an enterprise to subvert religion and the state of the world with it', that it threatened secular as well as spiritual authority, was swept aside.[217] Instead John ab Ulmis could write to Bullinger triumphantly (if not accurately) that 'images . . . are extirpated root and branch in every part of England'.[218] The purification of ceremony became the prelude for major doctrinal change.[219] Meanwhile evangelicals often proceeded as though a full reformation was already legally in place: for example, the failure to legislate in favour of clerical marriage did not deter a number of them, including Archbishop Cranmer himself, from openly acknowledging their unions.[220]

The English Reformation was also turning international for the first time. Bernardino Ochino and Peter Martyr Vermigli arrived in late 1547 by conciliar invitation.[221] They were followed by Jan Laski in 1548 and then, most significantly, by the Strasbourg refugees Martin Bucer and Paul Fagius. 1548 saw the beginning of the stranger churches in London, with the inauguration of Ochino's Italian congregation, swiftly followed by others for the French and Dutch.[222] Here Cranmer's initiative was decisive: it was he who issued most of the invitations to outsiders, and who did most to sustain them once they arrived. He also tried to woo others who would not come, most notably Philipp Melanchthon, who had already proved resistant to Henry VIII's charms. But Melanchthon did pay Cranmer the compliment of urging that the archbishop provide 'an illustrious testament of doctrine' for others to follow, and thereby revitalized his long-standing commitment to the idea of a general council which might provide the Protestant riposte to Trent.[223] Throughout the reign Cranmer maintained his concern to situate English Protestantism at the centre of the international reform movement, consulting with the best of his generation in the production of the liturgies, confession, and law code

---

[216] *TRP* i, no. 300.   [217] Muller, *Letters of Gardiner*, 274.

[218] *OL* ii. 377.

[219] On the relationship between reform of ceremony and reform of doctrine see C. Bradshaw, 'David or Josiah? Old Testament kings as exemplars in Edwardian religious polemic', in B. Gordon (ed.), *Protestant History and Identity in Sixteenth Century Europe*, 2 vols. (Aldershot, 1996), ii. 77–90.

[220] MacCulloch, *Cranmer*, 361.

[221] G.C. Gorham (ed.), *Gleanings of a Few Scattered Ears During the Period of the Reformation in England* (1857), 38.

[222] A. Pettegree, *Foreign Protestant Communities in Sixteenth Century London* (Oxford, 1986), 23–45.

[223] On Cranmer and the general council see MacCulloch, *Cranmer*, 394, 478–9, 518.

of the Church of England. This distinctive extroversion was shared by Somerset, whose self-imaging seems to have included a notion of himself as identified with the leaders of godly reform in Europe. The Protector's evangelical imperialism in Scotland has already been discussed. Calvin and Bullinger cultivated Somerset, though most of the evidence for their specific interest comes from the period after the crisis of 1549. His own willingness to be seen in company of this kind is revealed in the gesture of allowing Peter Martyr's letter to him after his fall to be translated by Thomas Norton and published.[224] In the difficult years after Mühlberg the leaders of European Protestantism were understandably eager to look to godly King Josiah and his ministers for aid, though usually less willing to abandon their own vineyards for those of the English.

The politics of reform under Somerset are remarkable partly because so much was done without much formal concern for the notion of consent or general support from existing elites. Stephen Gardiner's warnings about the need for stability during the king's minority were ignored as *parti pris*, but so were the more measured sentiments of the Protector's own svengali, William Paget. As early as February 1548, Paget was urging 'staying all things unto the parliament time', and insisting that reform should then only proceed on the advice of the body of learned men, and of the two Houses.[225] The following December Paget commented that Somerset was contemplating changing religion by proclamation if Parliament failed to co-operate. Paget's anxiety owed much to his fear of the international consequences of overt Protestantism: early in 1549 he pointed out that the emperor could perhaps be placated if changes were represented as in 'but forms and fashions of service and ministration of the sacrament which is and hath been diverse in divers places . . .'.[226] His Henrician political training also led him to mistrust any change that could not be effectively enforced. The predilection for proclamation that Somerset had displayed, while not formally outwith the crown's power in this area, risked dissent unnecessarily.[227]

Since the second Edwardian parliament (1548/9), like all those in the reign, showed a co-operative face to the government, the issue of action by the Protector's fiat never became so crucial in this area as in some others. The conservative bishops in the House of Lords were weakened by the loss of Gardiner, and even the support of four lay peers did not enable them to suppress the measure finally legitimizing clerical marriage. The introduction

[224] Gorham, *Gleanings*, 128–40. Norton was a member of Somerset's household.
[225] Beer and Jack, 'Letters of William Paget', 15, 24.
[226] B.L. Beer (ed.), 'A Letter of William Lord Paget of Beaudesert', *Huntingdon Library Quarterly* 34 (1971), 277–83.
[227] On Somerset's use of proclamations see Bush, *Government Policy*, 147–56. Shagan, 'Protector Somerset', 34–63. See below, p. 253.

of the Book of Common Prayer via the Uniformity Bill was extensively debated (and in a rare example the record of the occasion survives) before it was finally taken through the Lords, with only two of the lay peers plus the conservative bishops opposing it.[228] By the time both Parliament and Convocation had accepted the new Prayer Book, Cranmer's revolution must have seemed to have a momentum of its own. Work quickly began on other dimensions of a full Protestant settlement. The ordinal, which fundamentally redefined the role of the priesthood, was developed in debate between the archbishop and his new houseguest, Martin Bucer, who had arrived from Strasbourg in the spring of 1549.[229] Almost before the printer's ink was dry on the first Book of Common Prayer Cranmer had begun to discuss ways in which its ambiguities might be clarified. Canon law reform, another of his favoured projects, remained stalled, but was clearly planned: only the confession of faith that eventually emerged as the Forty-Two Articles in 1552 was not yet mooted systematically. In the mind of the archbishop and his closest advisers, at least, there seems to have been an awareness of the linear development needed to construct a church congruent with the best reformed tradition of Germany and Switzerland. Finally, a kind of caution in official policy was affirmed by the attack on radicals and anabaptists: there were heresy tribunals in 1548 and 1549, culminating in the trial and burning of the freewiller Joan Bocher in 1550.[230]

The political crisis of October 1549, which might have derailed the whole reforming agenda, may be seen with the advantage of historical hindsight as little more than an unpleasant glitch in the archbishop's programme. Wriothesley and his conservative sympathizers took an active part in engineering the coup, but they operated in alliance with the earl of Warwick and his supporters on the council. While the latter group may have had a less idealistic view of reform than the Lord Protector, they were already identified as evangelical.[231] Warwick's speech on the scaffold six years later laid explicit claim to a reforming pedigree dating from the 1530s.[232] Others saw him as pliant, within the parameters of loyalty to the

---

[228] BL Royal MS 17 B 39, fos. 5 ff. Detailed extracts from the narrative are given in A. Gasquet and E. Bishop, *Edward VI and the Book of Common Prayer* (1928), 128–39.

[229] MacCulloch, *Cranmer*, 504–12. B. Hall, 'Cranmer, the Eucharist and the foreign divines in the reign of Edward VI', in P. Ayris and D. Selwyn (eds.), *Thomas Cranmer, Churchman and Scholar* (Woodbridge, 1993), 217–58.

[230] MacCulloch, *Tudor Church Militant*, 141–4. J.W. Martin, *Religious Radicals in Tudor England* (1989), 43–8.

[231] The most detailed narrative of the events of late 1549 and early 1550 is Hoak, *King's Council*, 239–58. See also S. Brigden, *New Worlds, Lost Worlds: The Rule of the Tudors, 1485–1603* (2000), 191–3.

[232] J.G. Nichols (ed.), *The Chronicle of Queen Jane and Queen Mary*, CS os 48 (1850), 21. See also his own statement to Cecil in 1552: PRO sp 10/15, fo. 137.

royal supremacy, but it was acknowledged that he was usually to be found
on the side of reform. Though in the aftermath of the 1549 coup Warwick maintained an alliance of convenience with Wriothesley, the inherent instability of the arrangement led to its collapse as soon as the latter
sought to have Princess Mary appointed as regent in Somerset's stead.
There was, perhaps, nothing inevitable about the triumph of the Protestant
cause in this fluid political environment: it was simply sufficiently likely to
make John Hooper's preparations for martyrdom seem unduly melodra-
matic.[233] Our understanding of the whole affair would no doubt be greater
had Warwick shared his predecessor's interest in self-representation and
personal glorification: instead he remained unobtrusive, employing collective forms of leadership to secure his ends.[234]

It may be unnecessary to agonize upon the precise nature of Warwick's
commitment to the Protestant cause, since he had good political reasons
to advance it. The exclusion of any claim to authority by Mary and the
inclusion of himself and his family at the centre of political power up to
and beyond the moment of the king's majority, seem cause enough. And
from at least 1550 Edward's views have to be considered as influential in
the general direction of religious policy. The 'godly imp' was no figment
of the Protestant preachers' imagination. In April of that year he ordered
sermons to be preached at court every Sunday without fail, and the Spanish ambassador reported that 'there is no bishop ... so ready to argue in
support of the new doctrine as the King'.[235] As early as 1549 Edward had
composed a treatise attacking papal authority which was considered sufficiently effective to merit translation from his schoolboy French and publication at the height of the Exclusion Crisis in the 1670s.[236] And, lest this
should all confirm the image of a desperately earnest and priggish young
king, it is worth adding that Edward may have written an anti-papal
drama, and actively supported the presentation of court interludes satiriz-
ing Rome and the clergy.[237] The most important example of Edward's
intervention came in 1551, when the council decided to abandon the
relatively conciliatory policy pursued by Somerset towards Mary's practice
of her Catholic faith. Faced with absolute intransigence by the princess,
and by the threat of invasion by the emperor if she was not protected, the
council sought compromise. But Edward was deeply opposed to any
concession, citing the precedent of God's wrath to an unfaithful Israel,

---

[233] OL i. 70.   [234] Hoak, *King's Council*, 266–7.
[235] P.E. McCullough, *Sermons at Court: Politics and Religion in Elizabethan and Jacobean Preaching* (Cambridge, 1998), 56–7. *CSP Sp* 1550–52. 63.
[236] Nichols, *Literary Remains*, i. 181–205.
[237] P.W. White, *Theatre and Reformation: Protestantism, Patronage and Playing in Tudor England*
(Cambridge, 1993), 54–6.

and he succeeded in carrying his councillors with him on this occasion. With the king showing these qualities it was an unwise politician who resisted the reforms of his archiepiscopal godfather.[238]

It was in the last year of the reign that the alliance of godly king, reforming council and Protestant episcopate appeared most threatened. By then most of Cranmer's ideological and political battles had been won: the Second Book of Common Prayer had been sanctioned by Parliament; most of the conservatives on the episcopal bench had been deprived; and a confession of faith for the new, fully reformed, church had been put in place. All this had been achieved, despite the minority, the popular disturbances of 1549, and the financial and political problems of the regime. No wonder that Sir Richard Morison, looking back from Marian exile, marvelled that 'the greater change was never wrought in so short space in any country sith the world was', or that Becon could speak of the wonder of Edward and Somerset purging religion 'in so short a time'.[239] But the strain showed: it was above all visible in the breakdown of relations between the archbishop and the duke of Northumberland.[240] The dissemination of the Second Prayer Book was delayed for six months, and Cranmer's important project for the reform of canon law was decisively rejected, in this case by the duke's direct veto. The crisis was the outcome of a very public debate that had had the potential to explode ever since the dissolution of the monasteries: the question of the proper use of church wealth. In 1552 the regime, in urgent need of revenue and patronage resources, had turned to the renewed sale of chantry lands, and to an intensified attack on episcopal property, including the dissolution of the bishopric of Durham after the deprivation of Cuthbert Tunstal. These actions caused bitter debate between Cranmer and Northumberland, exacerbated by the latter supporting John Knox's opposition to ceremonial in the draft of the Second Prayer Book.[241] Finally in the winter of 1552–3 the government launched the final stages of its confiscation of the goods of parish churches, and the evangelicals responded with a vigorous preaching campaign at court and elsewhere against the covetousness of the laity. Northumberland responded in kind: Anthony Gilby later recalled a ferocious letter to Bishop Harley of Hereford in which the 'liberty of the preachers' tongues' was denounced and conciliar reprisal

---

[238] Nichols, *Literary Remains*, i. pp. ccxxiv–ccxxxiv. Foxe, v. 700–1. For Edward's own comments, especially on his interview with Mary, see W.K. Jordan (ed.), *The Chronicle and Political Papers of Edward VI* (Ithaca, N.Y., 1966), 55–6.

[239] Nichols, *Literary Remains*, i, p. ccxxxiv. T. Becon, 'A Comfortable Epistle to the Afflicted People of God', in *Prayers and other Pieces*, ed. J. Ayre (PS Cambridge, 1845), 205.

[240] For a very full narrative of the breakdown between council and bishops see MacCulloch, *Cranmer*, 497–500, 520–35. MacCulloch suggests that animosity may have sprung partly from Cranmer's and Ridley's attempts to save the duke of Somerset's life.

[241] Nichols, *Literary Remains*, p. ccxxxiv.

threatened.[242] That reprisal was the temporary halting of the clerically led revolution, and the loss of the reform of canon law. Only the larger crisis of Edward's failing health brought a cessation of hostilities in the last two months of the reign.

Policy in Edwardian and Marian Ireland

When Somerset and Cranmer began to manoeuvre their way towards a Protestant settlement in England, against a background of conflict with Scotland, the extension of their policy to Ireland was not high on the privy council's agenda. In so far as Edward VI's second realm figured in the Protector's calculations, it was as a potential source of military instability, and of aid and encouragement to the Scots. Both the initial retention of the Henrician lord deputy, Anthony St Leger, and his reinforcement by Sir Edward Bellingham, a member of the privy council, as commander-general of the army, can be explained by the quest for control in difficult circumstances. The gradualism of the religious changes at home also made it unlikely that the Irish would initially be faced with a new legislative settlement of religion of the kind they had experienced in 1536–7.[243] The only voice encouraging the export of reform in 1547 seems to have been that of George Browne, archbishop of Dublin, who visited London in the autumn and offered proposals for implementing change, including the appointment of three preachers to offer evangelical leadership.[244] Such suggestions proved premature, not only because of the regime's other preoccupations, but because Bellingham, made lord deputy on St Leger's recall in April 1548, was busy putting down a revolt in the Irish midlands until the autumn. By the latter date there was finally some evidence of active political support for religious change. Richard Brasier, dispatching the Irish financial account to Somerset, assured him that the lord deputy was doing far more than any of his predecessors 'for the setting forth of Gods word to his Honour'.[245] Meanwhile George Browne had devised a 'book of reformation', probably assimilating the 1547 English injunctions and the moves against images, which was enforced in the Diocese of Dublin over the next two years.[246]

---

[242] Knox, iii. 175–9, 280–2; iv. 566.

[243] B. Bradshaw, 'The Edwardian Reformation in Ireland, 1547–53', *Archivium Hibernicum* 34 (1976), 83–99. The ensuing account is heavily dependent on this article, which remains the only systematic investigation of this period. On the political changes of the mid-Tudor years see C. Brady, *The Chief Governors: The Rise and Fall of Reform Government in Tudor Ireland, 1536–1588* (Cambridge, 1994), 45–71.

[244] *CSP Irl* 1509–73, Edward VI, i. no. 122.   [245] Ibid., no. 133.

[246] J. Murray, 'The Tudor Diocese of Dublin', University of Dublin, Trinity College Ph.D. (1997), 149–52.

There was apparently no doubt in the mind of the English privy council that the changes introduced at home would become binding on Edward's Irish subjects. When Sir Dongan Morrice, dean of Tuskard, was sworn to English allegiance in July 1548 he had to acknowledge that he would teach the laws and ordinances set forth by the Lord Protector and the archbishop of Canterbury. These involved 'chiefly teaching the setting forth of the usage of the communion and all other godly ordinances of the church, according as it is practised in England'.[247] In the same year John Brereton, seeking patronage for a priest, assured Bellingham that he would 'minister according to the order that shall be set forth'. The lord deputies, or their temporary replacements, were required to swear to 'serve . . . our godly proceedings in matter of religion', and Bellingham at least regarded this as providing him with sweeping powers to abolish traditional ecclesiastical rites. When the royal surveyor and attorney visited Kilkenny in the summer of 1549 they were armed with a directive to abolish 'idolatry, papistry, the Mass sacrament and the like', in other words to enforce the Act of Uniformity.[248] That English act, like preceding religious legislation, had omitted specific mention of Ireland from the listed territories in which it had force: only England, Wales, and Calais were included. The privy council presumably intended that there should be an Irish parliamentary act to enforce the change, and indeed licensed a meeting in 1548 and included in its 1550 instructions to the Irish council a recommendation to call Parliament 'against such time as you shall think good'.[249] But no Edwardian parliament met. The secular reasons are to be found in the continuing military conflicts: when St Leger returned to Ireland as lord deputy in 1550 he lamented that he had never seen the country 'so far out of good order'. There may also have been religious considerations. St Leger's approach to the management of Irish politics was always gradualist and cautious, and his view of Protestant reform was unenthusiastic. While he was willing to second the dissemination of the Book of Common Prayer, it is striking that his specific contribution was the promotion of a conciliar plan to have a Latin translation for dissemination outside the anglophone areas of Ireland. This was far less of a threat to traditional lay sensibilities than the English rite. St Leger's only vigorous gesture against the old establishment was his encouragement of the plan to abolish St Patrick's Cathedral, and his motives were entirely secular. Money would be saved for the king's government and crown servants rewarded.[250]

[247] *CPR Irl* i. 171.

[248] E.P. Shirley (ed.), *Original Letters and Papers in Illustration of the History of the Church in Ireland during the reigns of Edward VI, Mary and Elizabeth* (1851), 28, 35.

[249] S.G. Ellis, *Tudor Ireland: Crown Community and the Conflict of Cultures, 1470–1603* (1985), 178. *CPR Irl* i. 220–1.

[250] Bradshaw, 'Edwardian Reformation', 86–7.

St Leger's approach to the enforcement of religious conformity also focused on persuasion: on the encouragement of key prelates like George Dowdall of Armagh to conform (here he was unsuccessful) and the removal of the really deficient, like the elderly Bishop Coyne of Limerick. Promotions, as far as possible, were of local clerics who offered assurance that they would accept the changes in religion. The English privy council was often content to allow these forms of internal management and to maintain a rather distanced approach to the details of Irish religious behaviour.[251] A nice sense of this remoteness is indicated in the letter of November 1551 sanctioning the union of the sees of Clonfert and Elphin. The council agreed that Clonfert could absorb its neighbour for financial reasons but did not even bother with the name of Elphin which 'the messenger remembreth not'.[252] When the lord deputy was again replaced in 1551 by Northumberland's protégé, Sir James Croft, the English council began to acknowledge that this 'hands off' approach was not effective. Croft was ordered to 'give good regard' that the bishops and clergy obeyed the crown in religious matters, and his intervention precipitated the flight of George Dowdall from Armagh.[253] The lord deputy saw this as the beginning of a golden opportunity to reform the Church by changing its senior personnel and persuaded the council to give attention to the appointment of candidates from England to Irish bishoprics. There are a series of conciliar memoranda and letters indicating that at least this aspect of reform was being taken seriously by Northumberland's regime.[254] Cranmer was deeply involved. In an amusing letter of September 1552 to Cecil he describes an encounter with Richard Turner, one of his Canterbury Six Preachers, who had been in trouble for preaching to the 1549 rebels and threatened with hanging by his ordinary. 'He seemed', writes the archbishop, 'then more glad to go to hanging, than he doth now to go to Armachane [Armagh]', where he would speak none of the language.[255] Others were equally cool: in the end only two were dispatched, Hugh Goodacre for Armagh and John Bale for Ossory, and the former died at Dublin before reaching his see, poisoned if Bale was to be believed.

The legacy of Edwardian religious policy in Ireland was a curious one. Delays in the implementation of English policies meant that the Second Prayer Book was never disseminated, though it was brought into use in Ossory through the determination of Bishop Bale. The lack of a full legal basis for the Reformation hampered the efforts of those few who were

[251] Ibid., 91–4.   [252] *CPR Irl* i. 286.
[253] H.A. Jefferies, *Priests and Prelates of Armagh* (Dublin, 1997), 158–60.
[254] *CSPD Edward VI*, ed. C.S. Knighton (1992), nos. 549, 627, 662, 704.
[255] H. Jenkyns (ed.), *Works of Thomas Cranmer*, 4 vols. (Oxford, 1833), i. 355.

prepared to support the Irish council's efforts at enforcement. It is most striking that, because there was no parliament, the chantries and fraternities were never dissolved, thereby providing a focus for the later revitalization of Catholicism, and placing question marks over the Edwardian regime's interest in destroying the 'remnants of idolatry'.[256] The only fiscal measures planned against the Irish church in these years of grand expropriation in England were those for taking parochial goods: St Leger's 1550 instructions include a requirement to provide inventories.[257] The attention that the rulers of England gave to Irish affairs was frankly intermittent, and the majority of that attention was directed to law and order, military management, and financial affairs. The strain of making and enforcing religious policy at home was significant, and it is scarcely surprising that the lord deputies were often left to construct their own detailed plans out of the general injunctions issuing from the court. The key, in the eyes of both Somerset and Northumberland, seems to have been the appointment of a trustworthy lord deputy from within their own clientage, with the fall-back position that St Leger could always be recalled if factions within the Irish council made government by outsiders untenable. It is scarcely surprising in the circumstances that the reforming efforts of the Irish council were so fragmentary and ineffectual.

The political uncertainties of Marian Ireland were almost as marked as those of the preceding reign.[258] The lord deputyship was retained by St Leger until he was displaced by the earl of Sussex in 1556, the latter arguing that he could bring more order to the warring Gaelic factions and to the management of the queen's finances. But in matters of religion Mary could better afford the non-interventionist policies that had intermittently been pursued by Edward's council. Since neither Edwardian Prayer Book had been supported by local legislation, and the clergy seem to have been universally hostile to major religious innovation, the queen and the lord deputy could afford to allow the resumption of the old faith to occur with little governmental input. However, the queen chose, through careful public actions, to signal very explicitly her support for the return to the old order. George Dowdall, returned from exile and incontestably in possession of the see of Armagh since his successor had died,

[256] C. Lennon, *The Lords of Dublin in the Age of Reformation* (Dublin, 1989), 128–31. Archbishop Browne had suggested dissolution at the end of the 1540s to fund a new college, but he was ignored: M.V. Ronan, *The Reformation in Dublin, 1536–58* (Dublin, 1926), 327.

[257] Shirley, *Original Letters*, 40–1.

[258] There has been little detailed study of religion in Marian Ireland, and the following must therefore be regarded as provisional. The best of earlier narratives are Ronan, *Reformation in Dublin*, and R.D. Edwards, *Church and State in Tudor Ireland* (1935). The following account has been influenced by important new arguments in Murray, 'Tudor Diocese of Dublin', 162 ff.

was reinstated in his temporalities and given royal assistance to compensate for his losses with the gift of the priory of Ardee. And in February 1555 Mary ordered the re-erection of St Patrick's Cathedral, Dublin, 'for the glory of God and the advancement of his service'. Much of this seems to have been prompted by Dowdall's own determination to restore the old order and canonical tradition.[259]

The most interesting policy problem encountered by the Marian regime was that of jurisdiction. The issue was two-fold: first Mary, as supreme head of the Church in Ireland as in England, promoted bishops and ordinary clergy during the first year of the reign without reference to the papacy. This caused some searching of conscience in Ireland. For example, William Walsh, elected bishop of Meath in succession to the deprived Bishop Staples, was reluctant to accept consecration 'not having lawful confirmation from the universal Catholic Church', and sought his restitution of his temporalities as a temporary measure until confirmation was possible.[260] Secondly there was the more distinctively Irish issue that the crown feared a recurrence of 'Rome-running', as a challenge to its jurisdictional control. In December 1553 the oath of fealty sworn by the Gaelic chief Eugene Magennesse included the promise not to admit any provisors from the Roman court.[261] Early in the reign Conogher McCarthy sought dispensation to apply to Rome for 'certain poor bene-fices', rightly suspecting that without sanction he might be found guilty of *praemunire*.[262] No response survives in this case, but in 1558, when the earl of Tyrone's chaplain obtained papal bulls for the priory of Down Cath-edral, the queen responded sharply that she 'intended to maintain our prerogative left unto us by our progenitors in that behalf'.[263]

Ireland reveals particularly acutely the delicate balancing act in which Mary was engaged. On the one hand she affirmed her commitment to Rome as strongly there as she did in England. Her instructions to the Irish council in 1556 insisted that they 'set forth the dignity of the Pope and of the see of Rome' as well as being willing to support the clergy in the quest for heretics.[264] Pole's legatine jurisdiction, which represented the reconciliation between crown and papacy, extended to Ireland. On the other hand, the queen's loyalty to Rome stopped short of any ques-tioning of her divine right to rule. In the case of Ireland the question was raised because Henry VIII had assumed the title of King of Ireland during the schism, a title that in theory only the papacy could confer. Cardinal Caraffa, on his elevation to the papal see as Paul IV in June 1555, accepted

[259] *CPR Irl* i. 301–2, 327–35.

[260] *CPR Irl* i. 337.

[261] *CSP Carew*, 1515–74, no. 201.

[262] Shirley, *Original Letters*, 78–9.

[263] *CSP Irl* Mary, ii. nos. 56, 58.

[264] *CSP Carew*, 1515–74, nos. 206, 205.

that the bull absolving the English realm from all ecclesiastical censures because of the schism should also confer the title to Ireland on Philip and Mary. The Irish patent rolls, interestingly, registered this merely as a bull 'purporting' to erect the kingdom.[265] The oath sworn by Irish prelates continued to contain a very clear clause on upholding the statutes and ordinances of the realm. It may be partly because of the need for jurisdictional clarity that Mary's council firmly steered Sussex towards the holding of a parliament, which met in June 1557. Its legislation confirmed Mary's legitimate title by repealing the Henrician succession acts, revived the anti-heresy laws, and repealed all the anti-papal statutes made since 1528.[266]

The more specific definition of objectives for restored Catholicism was left in the hands of Archbishop Dowdall, under the general guidance of his friend Cardinal Pole, who received full authority to visit the Irish church in July 1555. By then the Irish were already regularly turning to him for the dispensations and licences that they otherwise had to seek directly from the papacy. Pole's register reveals that the habit of Rome-running was alive and well in Ireland after the years of schism, and indicates the potential influence that an English cardinal could exercise over the island.[267] But Pole had barely two years to exercise the plenitude of his power before Paul IV's quarrel with King Philip led to its revocation. In that time he proposed a similar reform programme to that initiated in England. The Irish council was told in April 1556 that Pole intended to dispatch commissioners to visit the clergy of Ireland.[268] He would presumably have endeavoured to follow the vision of renewal articulated in the synodal decrees of Archbishop Dowdall of Armagh of 1554. Dowdall was part of Pole's circle: he, William Walsh, and another new prelate, Thomas Leverous, had all had contact with Pole in Italy, the last two as part of the cardinal's household. His decrees followed a predictable pattern

---

[265] *CPR Irl* i. 339, 340. Murray argues that the initiative for the papal confirmation of the royal title to Ireland came from the local Catholic leadership under Dowdall. Dowdall certainly seems to have been a moving force behind the appointment of Hugh Curwen to Dublin a few months earlier. He also had general views on the renewal of the Church in English Ireland, which included the restoration of St Patrick's, and the revival of traditional canonical jurisdiction under royal protection. Thomas Thirlby, bishop of Ely, was both the queen's representative in the planning of the revival of St Patrick's and her leading diplomat in Rome when the papal bull was procured. Murray, 'Tudor Diocese of Dublin', 179–85.

[266] Edwards, *Church and State*, 165–9.

[267] Bibliothèque Municipale Douai MS 922 [microfilm copy held by LPL]. The register shows that regular dispensations were being issued from March 1555: Douai MS 922, Tome 2, fos. 97 ff. Irish entries from well beyond the Pale, for example the diocese of Cashel, become frequent thereafter. The Irish acts in the legatine register are analysed in T.F. Mayer, *Reginald Pole, Prince and Prophet* (Cambridge, 2000), 268–72.

[268] *CSP Carew*, 1515–74, no. 206. *CSP Irl*, Mary, i. no. 63.

of reconstruction and discipline, with an emphasis on clerical residence and the need for preaching.[269] In the following year Hugh Curwen introduced similar decrees in his Dublin provincial synod.[270] It seems in the event that all that Pole initiated was an inquiry (under royal commission) in 1557 into impropriated parsonages and other ecclesiastical revenues and ecclesiastical goods. This, however, was far less than the full visitation the legate had envisaged, and left the Irish church to continue in customary ways.[271] The Gaelic dioceses appear essentially untouched by religious renewal. It has been suggested, however, that it was precisely this leaving of the church of the Pale to its own devices that provided it with much of its strength to face the coming onslaught of Protestantism. Dowdall and Curwen renewed the old instruments of religious rule, strengthened the clerical elite, and reaffirmed the spiritual superiority of the Anglo-Irish which they now identified ever more closely with the cause of canonical Catholicism.

Restoring Catholicism: England, 1553–1558

Tudor governments, in the words of one recent historian, did not approach 'the matter of policy-making with much enthusiasm'.[272] Policy initiatives, especially in the domestic sphere, encouraged dispute and faction and presented the threat of a popular response to the royal will. Since the break with Rome, however, successive Tudor regimes had had little alternative to policy-making in religion and men who were prepared to 'ride the tiger' of change—Cromwell, Somerset, probably Edward VI himself—stood in sharp contrast to those—Gardiner, Paget, and often Henry VIII—who regretted the need to embrace new political strategies. Mary Tudor in many ways offers an extreme case of the denial of the merits of policy-making. Not only did she emerge from the dynastic crisis of 1553 fully determined to restore the old faith as she had known it in her youth: her instincts were entirely in favour of doing so with the least possible invocation of political debate or any significant exercise of the arts of persuasion. The return to Rome was incontestably the only true path and would have been pursued by the queen whatever the views of her

---

[269] Jefferies, *Priests and Prelates*, 165–8. Pole's favour towards Walsh is suggested by the fact that he was confirmed in his rights to the spiritualities and temporalities of the see of Meath in one of the acts of the cardinal while he was still waiting to cross to England in the autumn of 1554: Douai MS 922, Tome 1, fos. 18–19ᵛ.

[270] Ronan, *Reformation in Dublin*, 434. Murray, 'Tudor Diocese of Dublin', 205–7.

[271] Mayer speculates that Pole could have visited the Irish church, since the register is missing for the first half of 1556, but there is no positive hint that he did so; Mayer, *Reginald Pole*, 271–2.

[272] Brady, *Chief Governors*, 55.

subjects.[273] Fortunately for her, subjects appeared providentially in favour of her way, both in their support of the Tudor inheritance, and in their opposition to the one serious rising of the reign, that of Thomas Wyatt in January 1554.

It would be more appropriate to describe Mary as knowing her royal mind, rather than making policy, on the issue of religion. Her clear desire to return to Roman jurisdiction, as well as to reinstate Catholic worship, led her, at the end of 1553, to abandon the title of Supreme Head of the Church, which had become an intolerable burden to her conscience. This action created some legal uncertainty about royal authority in the Church, which was to endure until the full reconciliation with Rome twelve months later. This did not prevent the queen from continuing to act as though she was still supreme head, for example in initiating action to deprive married priests of their benefices.[274] Her passionate commitment to undoing the work of her brother's regime led her at times into dangerously illegal behaviour, most notably when, faced with her first parliament's refusal to restore the bishopric of Durham that had been legally dissolved in 1552, she simply acted on royal initiative to give his possessions back to Cuthbert Tunstal by letters patent.[275] This remarkable example of Tudor denial of the validity of statute was quickly resolved in the second parliament of the reign, but stands as a dramatic example of the queen's attitudes and priorities. However, it is important not to exaggerate Mary's political naivety. Her abandonment of the title of Supreme Head, for example, was followed by consultation of the judges to ascertain that she had acted legally.[276] She does not seem to have needed the prompting of Gardiner as her lord chancellor to recognize that the key religious change of reconciliation with Rome had to be achieved with political consent, and that it therefore had to wait upon the appropriate time. Her contacts with Cardinal Pole, appointed legate to England by Julius III as soon as he heard of her successful coup, are full of yearning for his arrival, but of measured caution about its timing. In August 1553 she had told the papal emissary Commendone that though she longed to show herself obedient to the Holy See 'it was first necessary to repeal and annul by Act of Parliament many perverse laws made by those who ruled before her'.[277]

---

[273] On Mary's attitudes to religious policy and government see D. Loades, *Mary Tudor: A Life* (Oxford, 1989), 193–4, 240–5, 323–7.
[274] D. Loades, *The Oxford Martyrs* (1970), 106–11.
[275] Heal, *Prelates and Princes*, 152–5.
[276] J. Loach, *Parliament and the Crown in the Reign of Mary Tudor* (Oxford, 1986), 174.
[277] Mayer, *Reginald Pole*, 206. CSP Ven v. 429.

It was left to others to make policy, though always in broad accordance with Mary's wishes. In the first part of the reign Gardiner took the primary initiative. The lord chancellor had not shed all of his Henrician pragmatism and political caution, and he was far more fully aware than the queen of the significance of parliamentary endorsement of the government's proceedings.[278] But his sense of urgency about the full restoration of Catholicism matched that of Mary. In both the early parliaments of the reign he endeavoured to revive the authority of Rome by stealth, only to be thwarted by other interests. It seems pointless to speculate on the precise nature of the bishop's recovered identity with Rome: what the Edwardian experience had clearly taught him was that there could be no secure defence of the truths of the Catholic faith without a commitment to the universal Church. The powerful sermon that he preached at Paul's Cross on the eve of the final reconciliation is testimony to his belief that the coming of Pole represented the end of a nightmare of deep error and profound confusion of policy. On the text *Now it is time to awake out of sleep*, it made the Marian awakening seem an ending to 'policy', an establishment of harmony and peace and emergence to calm after storm.[279]

Gardiner's images impressed Cardinal Pole, who thought no sermon had ever pleased him better. They resonated with his own sense of mission, which was primarily to reconcile; to calm troubled consciences and to restore that order and discipline that England had so sadly lacked in the intervening twenty years. Pole believed that without true reconciliation and penitence the realm could never be healed. He therefore devoted much time and thought to providing dispensations, offering 'comfort' to the laity and giving personal attention to the schismatic clergy.[280] There was undoubtedly a conservatism about this approach, as about the cardinal's insistence on the return to customary ceremonial as a key to faithful behaviour. All of this was to be sustained by a return to the natural arch of authority: the clergy must be honoured, he told a London congregation, 'both the order instituted of God, and the persons for order's sake'.[281] It was in this spirit that Pole's famous concerns about contentious preaching

---

[278] G. Redworth, *In Defence of the Church Catholic: The Life of Stephen Gardiner* (Oxford, 1990), 311–29.

[279] The sermon is quoted by J.A. Muller, *Stephen Gardiner and the Tudor Reaction* (1926), 384–5.

[280] Rex Pogson argued powerfully for Pole's qualities as an administrator and reconciler in a series of articles: 'The legacy of the schism: confusion and change in the Marian clergy', in Loach and Tittler, *Mid-Tudor Polity*, 116–36; 'Revival and reform in Mary Tudor's church: a question of money', *JEH* 25 (1974), 249–65; 'Reginald Pole and the priorities of government in Mary Tudor's church', *HJ* 18 (1975), 3–20. Mayer, *Reginald Pole*, 252–68, accepts most of Pogson's argument on administration, but emphasizes innovation more strongly.

[281] Strype, *Ecclesiastical Memorials*, iii. ii. 484–5.

were expressed. England, and especially London, had suffered from an excess of dispute, what was now needed was a period of calm, eventually to be followed by a renewed growth in Catholic understanding.[282] But the calm of reconciliation did not preclude deliberate policies of renewal. The legatine synod of 1555, whose consequences will be considered in detail in a later chapter, identified key areas in which reform was necessary. Several covered traditional disciplinary concerns: residence, simony, presentation to benefices. One returned to the issue of church lands, reserving harsh language for those who had appropriated the goods of the Church. The canons also included a major educational initiative, the proposal to found seminaries, and an insistence on the importance of preaching in the decree on the residence of bishops. A direct riposte to Protestantism, in the idea of providing an orthodox translation of the New Testament into English, was mooted at the synod but never reached the decrees. In these initiatives he had the queen's active support, most practically displayed in her surrender of the crown's first fruits and tenths, and in the individual restorations of monastic houses.[283]

Gardiner, and Pole following him, saw the policy of reconciliation as also offering resolution to the problem of heresy. While their particular understanding differed, both seem to have regarded heretical depravity as an acute, but small-scale problem, to be solved by determined action against the leaders of Protestantism. Their followers, once separated from this corrosion, would then be reconciled to Catholicism. Gardiner adopted a dual policy in his period of influence early in the reign. He endeavoured to frighten reformers into leaving the realm, or in the case of those stranger congregations that had been welcomed to London under Edward, specifically expelled them. On the other hand he was determined to revive the heresy laws as a more direct challenge to the canker of reform. This became a personal crusade, though one that was thwarted in the second parliament of the reign as a result of his conflict with Paget.[284] When, in the third parliament, the regime finally acquired the power to burn heretics, Gardiner ensured that the power was swiftly used against some of the clerical leaders of Edwardian Protestantism. But the

---

[282] Mayer, *Reginald Pole*, 247–50.

[283] The decrees of the synod are printed in Wilkins, *Concilia*, iv. 121–6. On the synod and the problems of its documentation see Mayer, *Reginald Pole*, 235–45. The seminary decree is usually isolated as most distinctive because of its subsequent influence on Tridentine legislation: J.A. O'Donohoe, *Tridentine Seminary Legislation: Its Sources and Formation* (Louvain, 1957). Knowles, *Religious Orders*, iii. 421–43.

[284] On the failure to pass the heresy bill in the parliament of April 1554 see Loach, *Parliament and Crown*, 97–102. K.W.T. Carleton, *Bishops and Reform in the English Church, 1520–1559* (Woodbridge, 2001), 153. Redworth, *Stephen Gardiner*, 330–1. D.M. Loades, *The Reign of Mary Tudor* (1979), 331.

first crop of public executions failed to have the predicted deterrent effect and there is no reason to doubt Foxe's statement that 'seeing thus his device disappointed,... [he] gave over the matter as utterly discouraged'.[285]

Pole's view of heresy did not include such pragmatic calculations as deterrence. The horror of heresy was such that 'there are no thieves, no murderers...nor no kind of treason to be compared' with it.[286] And on this, as on so many issues, the queen his cousin actively concurred. In other circumstances Pole had seen the merits of the policy pursued by the Henrician bishops before the breach with Rome—counsel and debate with learned heretics but always hold the threat of *potestas* for the arrogant and wilfully disobedient. But the years of disputation in Rome seem to have stiffened his resolve, and he did little to counsel the learned Protestants in England.[287] On the other hand Pole tended to detach himself from the everyday pressures of the policy of persecution and was criticized both by Bishop Bonner and by Bartolomé Carranza for his lack of fervour in the attack on individual Protestants.[288]

The continuing persecution, which showed no sign of remission even in the last year of Mary's reign, cannot be identified as the policy of any one individual, but the privy council undoubtedly supplied much of the impetus, and behind the council Mary must have positively approved in order to sustain its action. Early in these grizzly proceedings the queen had made her own commitment clear in her letter to her council advising that there should be punishment for those who seduced the simple and 'the rest so to be used that the people might well perceive them not to be condemned without just occasion'.[289] One other possibility is often discussed, at least at the inception of the policy: King Philip. Philip's own attitudes are not easily identified: he would have taken no principled stand against the burnings, but like Gardiner he was likely to weigh mundane as well as divine consequences of retribution. His confessor Alphonsus de Castro preached against the death penalty imposed on the first six Protestants tried for heresy, perhaps believing that re-education would be more effective than exemplary punishment. On the other hand, the influential Bartolomé Carranza favoured some exemplary burnings so that the faith should not be brought into disrepute: for example, he may have per-

---

[285] Gardiner tried to persuade the imprisoned preachers in London to recant between the passage of the Heresy Act and the first burnings in February 1555. Foxe, vi. 704.

[286] Pogson, 'Reginald Pole', 7–8.   [287] Dickens, *English Reformation*, 294–5.

[288] Mayer, *Reginald Pole*, 277–80, seeks to detach Pole from any sustained commitment to persecution, but the evidence is largely circumstantial and not wholly convincing. G. Alexander, 'Bishop Bonner and the Marian persecutions', *History* 60 (1975), 378.

[289] G. Burnet *History of the Reformation* ed. N. Pococke, 5 vols (1865), 5, 440.

suaded the monarchs of the necessity of burning the former monk William Flower.[290]

Mary's assumption that her restoration of Catholicism, and the return to Rome, would not in the long run be opposed by the political nation proved correct, though she may have been deluded about the strength of their ideological commitments. Jennifer Loach has shown how infrequently Parliament opposed the royal will, and how limited is the evidence of it resisting the queen for doctrinal reasons.[291] The one issue on which the crown can have entertained no doubts about the strength of political feeling was that of the lands formerly belonging to the Church. It was the question of property rights that stalled, and then threatened to wreck, the legatine mission of reconciliation. On this crucial topic Mary and Pole were not wholly in accord. Both saw the laity's retention of ecclesiastical property as a sin, and the queen made her own very public attempts to free her conscience by the restoration of lands to bishops and monasteries. But, with Philip's support, she was partially reconciled to the need to secure landed title by gaining papal dispensation for England: Pole, though forced to yield in order to gain access for his mission, never ceased to proclaim that no true peace could be established until the lands were returned.[292] On this issue policy was made by the council and Parliament, with the lawyers playing prominent roles in the drafting of the crucial statute. The final Act to Unify England to Rome included the dispensation to retain church goods clearly stated to be part of the law of the land and claiming that title to property was secured as part of the authority of the 'crown imperial'.[293] This was, of course, a triumph of material greed over ideology, but the form of the language showed the success of at least one aspect of Henry's revolution. Pole was simplifying too readily when he accused the Commons of 'returning to the obedience of the church, not moved by your duty to God, but for more surety to keep your spoil'.[294] Mary, willing or otherwise, was identified with a more complex protection of lay interests against those of the Catholic hierarchy. And an atmosphere of uncertainty continued to prevail on matters of land that showed itself in very jittery behaviour in Parliament: most notably in the Commons resolute opposition to the attempt to seize

---

[290] On Philip's role, and especially that of his confessor Carranza, see Redworth, *Stephen Gardiner*, 324–5. J.I. Tellechea Idigoras, *Fray Bartolomé Carranza y el Cardinal Pole* (Pamplona, 1977), 47–53. I am most grateful to Dr Redworth for showing me unpublished material in which he discusses the roles of Carranza and Castro.

[291] Loach, *Parliament and Crown*, 108–15, 173–9.

[292] Mayer, *Reginald Pole*, 222–4. R. Schenk, *Reginald Pole, Cardinal of England* (1950), 130.

[293] 1 & 2 P. & M., c. 8.

[294] Loach, *Parliament and Crown*, 109–10.

the property of those who had gone into exile. The possessioners were in their turn very dependent on the goodwill of the crown: with the lurking fear that a pope might always rescind the privilege of the English, as Paul IV threatened to do in 1555. Property fears do not explain the Commons' support for Elizabeth and Protestantism in 1559: however, they provide one element in the story of her welcome.

Mary I was not given to excessive interest in the imaging of monarchy. In the first year of her reign her court poets sang of her virginity, and her purity, and situated her as a type of the Blessed Virgin.[295] Cardinal Pole, in his speech of reconciliation before Parliament, expressed amazement that the queen, 'yet...being a virgin, helpless, naked and unarmed' had prevailed over her tyrannical foes, attributing her victory to divine providence.[296] Philip, on the other hand, he described as the type of the wise ruler Solomon. It is perhaps not surprising that when Mary did address the issue of self-imaging she favoured the view that she was Truth, the daughter of Time, the restorer of the integrity of her royal line.[297] The most inadvertently ironic representation came from the author of the court drama *Respublica*, in which the queen is described as 'our most wise and most worthy Nemesis' divinely appointed 'to reform th'abuses which hitherto hath been'. The goddess of revenge was invoked by an author who saw Mary as the restorer of true commonwealth and godliness, re-establishing, as Gardiner had hoped she would, the peace of the realm.[298] In the difficult struggle against heresy the queen already risked disappointing some of these hopes. But in the last years of the reign fate intervened more decisively by sweeping her up into the quarrel between the papacy and Philip, which left Pole bereft of legatine jurisdiction in the last eighteen months of the reign. Policy changed little in these last years, and indeed Mary showed a Tudor disposition to swallow her ultramontane loyalties in order to protect Pole and her church, but the vigour of 1554 and 1555 was lacking, both in cardinal and queen.[299] The irony was, of course, that Mary in the end was the destroyer of Catholic harmony and peace, not so much in her policies as in her person, through her failure to reproduce, and her early death.

---

[295] H. Hackett, *Virgin Mother, Maiden Queen* (Basingstoke, 1995), 34–6. J.M. Richards, 'Mary Tudor as "Sole Quene": gendering Tudor monarchy', *HJ* 40 (1997), 895–924.

[296] Foxe, vi. 570.

[297] J.N. King, *Tudor Royal Iconography* (Princeton, 1989), 184–200.

[298] The *Respublica* text is attributed to Nicholas Udall by its modern editor; Greg, *Respublica*, 2–3.

[299] On the last years of religious policy and the crisis with the papacy see Mayer, *Reginald Pole*, 302–20, and Loades, *Reign of Mary Tudor*, 428–52. Mary refused to surrender Pole to Rome, and at one stage was reported to have ordered her ambassador Carne to inform all the cardinals individually that England did not feel compelled to obey Paul IV on the issue. *CSP Ven* vi. 1248.

5

THE CLERGY IN THE YEARS OF CHANGE, 1530–1558

Prelates and Councils

In 1535 Charles Booth, bishop of Hereford, bequeathed his books to his cathedral library. Among them was a copy of Antonio of Florence's *Repertorium totius summe*, which included a chapter on the pastoral duties of bishops and clerics. Booth's text has a sentence underlined (one is tempted to think by the bishop himself): '*non est facile stare in loco petri et pauli*'.[1] The next decades were to show just how difficult it was for English and Scottish prelates to follow in the Apostles' footsteps. In 1537 the gathering of English bishops and theologians preparing the text that became the Bishops' Book, the second doctrinal confession of the fledgling Church of England, produced a defence of episcopal powers and priestly orders. It upheld the sacrament of orders, as a divine gift and grace, while insisting that it conferred upon the priesthood a moderate, rather than a tyrannical, power over the laity. In the case of the prelates that power included 'special . . . authority and commission under Christ to preach and teach the word of God unto his people'; to bind and loose; to display Pauline hospitality and 'to order and consecrate others in the same room, order and office'.[2] The language is confident: only the final caveat that the New Testament makes no distinction of degrees in orders or insists on any more ceremonial than prayer and the laying on of hands, points to the ideological divisions the Reformation was already opening up among the English clerical elite.

---

[1] K.W.T. Carleton, *Bishops and Reform in the English Church, 1520–1559* (Woodbridge, 2001), 30.

[2] Wilkins, *Concilia*, iii. 832–4. The lengthy discussion of the sacrament of Orders in the Bishops' Book uses the language of this document, but adds a section on the power of Christian princes within the Church. C. Lloyd (ed.), *Formularies of Faith put forth by authority during the Reign of Henry VIII* (Oxford, 1825), 101 23.

The response of the Catholic bishops to this period of crisis can best be seen in the series of Scottish, English, and Irish councils and synods convened between 1529 and 1559. When the first of the reforming Scottish provincial councils met in 1549 it claimed as its objective precisely this pursuit of consensus: the restoration of tranquillity and the preservation of 'complete unity in the ecclesiastical estate'. The maladies of churchmen had to be healed, so that in turn the wounds being inflicted by heresy could be cauterized. Archbishop Hamilton introduced an extensive set of statutes aimed primarily at the renewal of the clerical estate in the face of lay hostility. Two further councils followed in 1552 and 1559: each had a specific reforming focus—the catechism in 1552, the definition of uniformity of doctrine in 1559—but each reiterated the central importance of strengthening the clerical estate.[3] In England episcopal schemes for renewal unmediated by royal authority can be seen in Archbishop Warham's convocation decrees of 1529–31 and in those of Pole's legatine synod more than two decades later.[4] There is no Irish equivalent of Warham's initiatives, but Pole's lead was, as we have seen, paralleled by those of the synods of the two Irish provinces *inter Anglicos*.[5]

When the provincial and legatine statutes of the reforming Catholic assemblies are read together, they often display a strikingly traditional approach to the clergy's problems. The 1549 Scottish statutes, for example, commenced with the reiteration of the Council of Basel's attack on concubinage, and proceeded through such well-worn themes as sobriety in clerical dress, temperance in clerical living, the inappropriateness of secular occupations, and the need for proper behaviour within the parish. Another group of statutes cast in traditional language addressed the exercise of discipline by the bishops, and such potential abuses as non-residence, pluralism, and simony. Warham's statutes covered similar issues, though with a particularly strong emphasis on clerical residence and the proper service of cures. Even Pole's twelve legatine decrees included five directed to these standard issues of moral and institutional regulation of the clergy. The reiteration of these customary decrees cannot necessarily be labelled pre-Tridentine: the 1549 Scottish legislation, for example, quoted directly from the decrees of the first session of Trent when ad-

---

[3] D. Patrick (ed.), *Statutes of the Scottish Church*, SHS 54 (Edinburgh, 1907), 84–186. For the background see I.B. Cowan, *The Scottish Reformation* (1982), 77–83; T. Winning, 'Church councils in sixteenth-century Scotland', in D. McRoberts (ed.), *Essays on the Scottish Reformation* (Glasgow, 1961), 332–58.

[4] Wilkins, *Concilia*, iii. 717–24, 746–7; iv. 121–6. T.F. Mayer, *Reginald Pole, Prince and Prophet* (Cambridge, 2000), 235–45.

[5] H.A. Jefferies, *Priests and Prelates of Armagh in the Age of Reformations, 1518–1558* (Dublin, 1998), 166–9.

dressing non-residence, and the holding of livings in commendation. Pole gave considerable emphasis to residence not only for ordinary incumbents but also for archbishops and bishops, another Tridentine requirement, though one that in this case used a traditional concern to achieve a radical end. The vision is rather that expressed in one of the statutes addressed to the ordinaries, pleading with them 'in the bowels of Christ' to amend their own lives and morals so they could correct others.[6]

The preoccupations of the Catholic reformers are, however, more sharply revealed in the decrees that do not follow long-established patterns for the regulation of the clergy. For Warham, the attack on heresy was the obverse of the attempt to purify the parish clergy. The 1529 session of the Convocation of Canterbury was presented with a long list of heretical books, and heard a sermon denouncing heresy by Warham: the inventory of heretical texts eventually became part of the 1532 canons presented to Henry VIII for approval.[7] Scottish reforming councils all denounced heresy, and once again unorthodox books were one of the key targets. Archbishop Dowdall's Armagh decrees of 1554 insist that heretical texts must be burned. Pole's legislation, on the other hand, dealt with unorthodox belief only indirectly, as that which had to be countered by orthodox preaching and teaching. The involvement of the Tudor state in the pursuit of heresy had by this time done much to remove the legislative control over this aspect of discipline from the hands even of the Catholic clerical establishment.[8]

All the reforming statutes of these councils are also identified with the positive response to the challenge of heresy: a concern for understanding orthodox Catholic belief. The canonical requirement that incumbents with cure of souls preach at least four times yearly formed the starting-point for Warham, Hamilton, and Pole. Each council then sought to amplify provision of instruction. Canterbury Convocation in 1532 focused on the provision of uniform grammar texts for schoolmasters and on the importance of study for those with cure. Hamilton was more ambitious,

---

[6] Patrick, *Statutes of the Scottish Church*, 89–97, 113–14, 124. Mayer, *Reginald Pole*, 241.

[7] Wilkins, *Concilia*, iii. 717–22, 746–7, though Wilkins misdates the general reform proposals to 1529: M.J. Kelly, 'The submission of the clergy', *TRHS* 5th ser. 15 (1965), 97–102. Although a form of anti-heretical canon was among those presented in 1532, much of the initiative in the pursuit of heretics and their texts had passed from Convocation as early as May 1530 when a royal commission required a group of the bishops and 'learned men' to read these texts and inform the king whether they were 'expedient and profitable for his people'. Scarisbrick sees this as a royal initiative, though Craig D'Alton has now demonstrated that it is Warham's policy that is being pursued here: C.W. D'Alton, 'The Suppression of Heresy in Early Henrician England', University of Melbourne Ph.D. (1999), 247–53.

[8] On crown control over heresy proceedings under Mary, and especially the use of ecclesiastical commissions, see D. Loades, 'The enforcement of reaction, 1553–1558', *JEH* 16 (1965), 59–66.

especially in the 1552 decrees. In 1549 the Tridentine decree on the maintenance of lecturers in theology in cathedrals and monasteries was introduced, and very explicit guidance on the form of preaching was articulated. Three years later, in decrees far more directly concerned with the well-being of the laity than those of 1549, the new catechism was introduced, and detailed explanations of how it should be used were offered to the clergy. In 1559 the clergy were supplied with a list of orthodox doctrines to be used in preaching, and with the text of a homily to precede communion. These last two initiatives anticipated similar provisions made by the Council of Trent in its later sessions.[9] Pole, as we have seen, also anticipated Trent by ordering the establishment of seminaries for the training of clergy in each English diocese, by urging the provision of a catechism, and, in the synod but not the decrees, by considering an orthodox translation of the New Testament.[10]

The objectives of the reforming Catholic bishops, while not completely uniform across time or across the three realms, are remarkably similar.[11] Strong leadership was to be achieved by the clergy, who should be 'the mirror and lantern to the rest', as a Scottish petition expressed it in 1559.[12] Clerical renewal depended on traditional moral and spiritual discipline, and on the pursuit of learning to promote orthodoxy among the laity. It was to be upheld by regular visitation and episcopal intervention—the importance of which had to be underlined to the Scottish, if not the English, bishops. All this had to be achieved without significant lay support: the laity were represented in the canons and statutes largely as receptors of preaching and proper liturgy or as threats to church property. The legislative programmes were in themselves admirable: the problem as ever lay in enforcement. The first two Scottish councils took place in reasonably secure circumstances, towards the end of the Anglo-Scottish conflict

---

[9] Patrick, *Statutes of the Scottish Church*, 98–102, 108, 125, 143–5, 172–6. Winning, 'Church councils', 356–7. These reforming aspects of the councils, especially 1549 and 1552, have been shown to have connections with the Cologne reform programme of Hermann von Wied. J.K. Cameron, '"Catholic Reform" in Germany and in the pre-1560 church in Scotland', *RSCHS* 20 (1979), 105–17.

[10] Wilkins, *Concilia*, iv. 125. Only the first part of the publication programme, the need to produce homilies, was specifically addressed in the 12 Decrees. The convocation of January 1558 determined that there should be a catechism and homilies. J. Loach, 'The Marian establishment and the printing press', *EHR* 101 (1986), 138–9.

[11] A further possible comparison, of Hamilton's Scottish reforms with those of Cranmer in England, has been proposed by Clare Kellar. There are some obvious parallels, especially in concerns for education and catechizing and renewal of the clergy, but it seems difficult to regard the general approach to reform of the two clerical establishments as similar: C. Kellar, '"To Enrich with Gospel Truth the Neighbour Kingdom": Religion and Reform in England and Scotland, 1534–1561', University of Oxford D.Phil. (1999), 125–33.

[12] Patrick, *Statutes of the Scottish Church*, 156.

and before radicals had fully recovered from the setbacks of the earlier 1540s. Here the difficulty was that the reach and diversity of the decrees outstripped the control of the bishops: they acknowledged themselves in 1552 that the preaching legislation of 1549 had not been enforced, and that vicars and curates had not been examined on their knowledge of Scripture.[13] There were successes: several monasteries appointed theologians; diocesan preachers were promoted in St Andrews.[14] In the absence of visitation records it is impossible to be sure how much was achieved, but there seems to have been no instant conversion of the Scottish bench into painful superintendents. The last of the councils took place in the months of growing crisis before the full revolt of the Lords of the Congregation. This time the call to reform was taken up in the Dioceses of Glasgow and Aberdeen at least: too late for much implementation.[15] Some of the same sense of *fin de siècle* pervades Warham's reforming efforts: a worthy concern with simony and clerical dress, or even good teaching and clerical learning, pales into insignificance at the moment when the clergy were asked to accept that their whole jurisdictional power depended on the royal will.[16]

Only under Mary did the Catholic hierarchy, dominated by Pole, have some freedom to implement its legislative programme. Here the consequences are instructive. One of the best-enforced statutes appears to be that requiring episcopal residence. With the exception of the three politician-bishops, Gardiner, Heath, and Thirlby, most prelates whose movements can be traced resided in their sees, and were conscientious about visiting and ordaining in person.[17] The legate's own register shows that he took the standards established by the synod seriously: dispensing clergy for pluralism, for example, was only done after careful checking of circumstances.[18] Pole's anxiety for the protection of church goods became one small element in his major struggle to improve ecclesiastical finance. Some limited success was also achieved on schools: York, Wells, and Lincoln gained new schools, though scarcely the full-blown seminaries envisaged in 1555. On vernacular scriptures there is silence, and the full revision of the 1543 King's Book as a statement of faith proceeded no further than its sectioning for discussion by the 1555 synod.[19]

---

[13] Ibid., 149, 171.   [14] Cowan, *Scottish Reformation*, 80–1.   [15] Ibid., 86–7.

[16] Kelly, 'Submission of the clergy', 97–102.

[17] S. Thompson, 'The Pastoral Work of the English and Welsh Bishops, 1500–1558', University of Oxford D.Phil. (1984), 1–9 and Apps., but note the problems of evidence discussed there, and the difficulty of distinguishing mere residence from active participation in diocesan affairs. It should be stressed that English precedents for episcopal residence were already good. See above, ch.1, pp. 33–4.

[18] Douai MS 922, Tome 2, fos. 97 ff.   [19] Mayer, *Reginald Pole*, 244–5.

On the other hand, the basic concerns for the instruction of the laity were met. Bonner's short but important *Profytable and necessary doctryne* (1555) served as the catechism for the rest of the reign, though the synod had been more ambitious and commissioned Bartolomé Carranza to produce a full catechetical confession, produced in Castilian in the year of Mary's death. For general congregations there were the thirteen *Homilies* (1556) produced by Bonner's chaplains, John Harpsfield and Henry Pendleton, in a deliberate effort to supplant the 1547 edition and Thomas Watson's *Holsome and Catholyke Doctrine* (1558).[20] Enforcement was patchy, as a consequence both of the range of institutional problems Pole and his bishops faced and his own care in proceeding slowly with reform. However, the legate came closer than either his predecessors or his Scottish counterpart to reordering the Church according to his clerical priorities. The beneficiaries were his fellow clergy in Europe rather than England: elements of the London synod became a model for Catholic reformers in other Tridentine lands.[21]

The late Henrician and Edwardian prelates had far less of an ability to control their institutional destiny than Pole and his colleagues, or even their Scottish counterparts. The jurisdictional control that Henry assumed over the Church after 1532 recast the bishops and their assemblies in the role of spiritual advisers, rather than quasi-autonomous legislators in defence of the Church Catholic. The Bishops' Book spoke of kings as having a duty to be 'chief heads and overlookers' ensuring the proper execution of their office by priests and bishops: an oversight that for Henry in practice comprehended everything but performance in the sacerdotal office himself.[22] Power shifted from Convocation to Parliament and from bishops to court and king. The institutional structures of the Canterbury and York convocations were not permanently affected by the upheaval. However, in the late 1530s Cromwell's exercise of the vicegerency provided an additional level of authority, and a synod that overrode the customary assemblies of the two provinces.[23] During Henry's reign

---

[20] E. Duffy, *The Stripping of the Altars* (1992), 534–7. E.J. Baskerville, *A Chronological Bibliography of Propaganda and Polemic published in English between 1553 and 1558* (American Philosophical Society, 1979), 58–9. Loach, 'Marian establishment', 140–2. *Homelies sette forth by the right reverend Father in God* (1555). I am grateful to Dr Glyn Redworth for information on Carranza and the catechism. T. Watson, *Holsome and Catholyke doctyrne concurringe the seven sacramentes* (1558).

[21] J.A. O'Donohue, *Tridentine Seminary Legislation: Its Sources and Formation* (Louvain, 1957), 98–119. Mayer, *Reginald Pole*, 245.

[22] C. Lloyd, *Formularies of Faith put forth by Authority during the Reign of Henry VIII* (Oxford, 1856), 121.

[23] Carleton, *Bishops and Reform*, 65–6. Wilkins, *Concilia*, iii. 756–76, 802–32, 860–8; iv. 15–16. It is unfortunate that no good modern institutional study of the convocations of Canterbury and York has been undertaken, though see D.B. Weske, *Convocation of the Clergy* (1937).

the customary pattern of consultation of the convocations during parliamentary sessions also maintained its outward forms, though crucial issues of doctrine and discipline were often hammered out elsewhere, leaving the Church's parliament with little to do except assent. After bitter wrangling about the Ten Articles in open session in 1536 the crown turned to smaller committees of bishops and theologians to debate doctrinal statements before they were presented.[24]

By the beginning of Edward's reign the loss of institutional power was a matter of acute anxiety to some of the representatives of the clergy in the lower house of the Canterbury convocation. In 1547 they petitioned that they should be given representation in the House of Commons, since legislative sovereignty now lay in Parliament's hands, 'or else that all such statutes and ordinances as shall be made concerning all matters of religion . . . may not pass without the sight and assent of the said clergy'.[25] Their chances of success were slender: the one group of lesser clergy who had had this parliamentary access—the proctors of the Irish clergy who traditionally sat as a third house—had lost their position as a result of their opposition to the dissolution of the monasteries in 1537.[26] The clergy's fears were justified: during Edward's reign it is not clear that Convocation even met regularly to endorse the fundamental religious changes being driven through by the regime.

The bishops were in some measure complicit in this loss of institutional power, not merely its victims. Neither reformers nor traditionalists could guarantee the upper hand in all public arenas, though under Henry the convocations usually acted as a barrier to change. Public debate of doctrinal and liturgical initiatives rendered them vulnerable to challenge and alteration, as in the clashes about the Ten Articles, which apparently forced royal intervention 'to put our own pen to the book'. It was constantly tempting to use the new mechanisms of royal power, and the informal networks of court influence, to change the nature of the religious settlement. And when agreement was essential, prelates of both persuasions seem to have been willing to struggle for it in small committees assembled under royal aegis, rather than to approach the representatives of the wider clergy. The committee assembled at Chertsey to debate the first Book of Common Prayer in September 1548 offers an excellent example of the process. A group of approximately ten to twelve bishops and theologians, including at

---

[24] A partial exception should perhaps be made for the 1542–3 Convocation of Canterbury, which involved substantial debate and work on The King's Book. D. MacCulloch, *Archbishop Cranmer* (1996), 121–2, 164–6, 289–95, 377–80, 504–5.

[25] J. Strype, *Memorials . . . of Thomas Cranmer*, ed. P.E. Barnes, 2 vols. (1853), 220–2.

[26] B. Bradshaw, 'The opposition to the ecclesiastical legislation in the Irish Reformation parliament', *IHS* 16 (1968–9), 285–303.

least four conservatives, hammered out an agreement that could be taken directly to the House of Lords, which debated Eucharistic doctrine in December.[27] As so often agreement was not ideal: Bishop Thirlby was able to oppose aspects of the document to which he had assented because of ambiguities of language and purpose.[28] The use of committees made explicit the weakness of the position of the English episcopate: deeply divided throughout these decades on ideological grounds, they perforce accepted what mechanisms could best achieve their goals. Consent and assent remained fundamental political norms for bishops as for king, but in practice the prelates and their specialist advisers moved hesitantly into a world in which ideology often took precedence over all other considerations.

The confessionalization of the English bench was, however, a slow and painful process. All those who followed Henry in his renunciation of Rome had constantly to adjust their own belief patterns to the prevailing concerns of the monarch. There can have been few prelates who did not suffer some agonies of conscience when required to support and enforce either the Bishops' Book (1537) or the King's Book (1543). Yet only Latimer and Nicholas Shaxton took so trenchant a stand against royal initiatives that they were persuaded into resigning after the passage of the Act of Six Articles. For most the theology of obedience to the crown sufficed, especially as Gardiner demonstrated that an idea so Lutheran in origin could be hijacked to conservative ends.[29] Obedience to the law became part of the obedience of the faith, following traditional precepts with the aid of divine grace. There was also the secondary argument that in matters not directly essential to faith the will expressed in Parliament might suffice. 'Why do you not', Henry asked Cuthbert Tunstal in 1531, 'conform your conscience to the conscience and opinion of the great number?'[30] And indeed Tunstal did conform, while like others among the conservative leadership he engaged in what MacCulloch has appropriately called 'bush warfare' whenever traditional elements of faith were threatened. Henry was moved to assail Tunstal again, denouncing his 'obstinacy' and 'allegations . . . so little to your purpose' when he defended auricular confession in Convocation in 1536.[31]

Conformity was aided by the awareness that the composition of the bench was subject to the vagaries of court politics as well as royal control. In the 1530s the patronage efforts of Anne Boleyn and Cromwell, plus

[27] G. Burnet, *History of the Reformation of the Church of England*, 3 vols. in 6 (1820), i. ii. 515. MacCulloch, *Cranmer*, 396–7.

[28] J. Muller (ed.), *Letters of Stephen Gardiner* (1930), 268.

[29] R. Rex, 'The crisis of obedience: God's word and Henry's Reformation', *HJ* 39 (1996), 885–7.

[30] BL Cottonian MS Cleo. EVI, fo. 216.   [31] BL Cottonian MS Cleo. EV, fo. 132.

Henry's enthusiasm for those who hated the pope, led to a bench on which at the most eight reformers confronted at least ten leading conservatives. By the end of the reign deaths and deprivations had thinned the reformers' ranks, while slightly increasing the number of those strongly committed to traditional Catholicism.[32] Cranmer's determination to remain in post through all the crises of the early 1540s is testimony to one approach: waiting and hoping that the king or his heir would have their 'eyes opened' to the light of the gospel.[33] The tenacity of Gardiner, Tunstal, Heath, and Bonner, and their disposition to play roles in factional politics, is witness to a conviction that all would be well if the king would move with sufficient vigour against heresy.[34]

The full crisis of episcopal authority for the conservatives was postponed until the beginning of Edward's reign. Under Henry their doctrinal advice had been valued, if not always accepted, by the crown. Moreover it was possible for them to maintain a relatively traditional view of episcopal power. The Bishops' Book, for example, claimed that the prelates could 'by the authority of God' ordain canons on such matters as holy days and the proper ceremonies at the administration of the Eucharist. They could also legislate on those matters that pertained to their sacerdotal role. These included the *potestas ordinis*, the transmission of priestly function through the laying on of hands 'by the authority of the Gospel'.[35] In an important sermon before the king in 1539, Cuthbert Tunstal spelled out the theological consequences of any attack on orders. To challenge the sacrament was not only to assail the ecclesiastical hierarchy, it was to subvert the mediatory role of the priest, especially his power to shrive.[36]

Yet already at the end of the 1530s Cranmer was contemplating a world in which the supreme head had the right to determine forms of consecration and the transmission of spiritual authority. Nothing in God's law, he wrote in 1540, would prevent the king or prince from making bishops and priests if all the existing clergy of a region were dead.[37] That contemplation became a reality when in February 1547 the archbishop led his

---

[32] L.B. Smith, *Tudor Prelates and Politics, 1536–1558* (Princeton, 1953), 305–8. Smith's classification of bishops, with a generous estimate of seven reformers, is not without problems, but he is careful to exclude from his count prelates whose views are completely opaque.

[33] MacCulloch, *Cranmer*, 189.

[34] A good case-study of a conservative bishop engaged in exactly this warfare in the 1530s is provided by A.A. Chibi, *Henry VIII's Conservative Scholar: Bishop John Stokesley and the Divorce, Royal Supremacy and Doctrinal Reform* (Berne, 1997), 104–9, 151 ff.

[35] Lloyd, *Formularies*, 106–8. P. O'Grady, *Henry VIII and the Conforming Catholics* (Collegeville, Minn., 1990), 91–3.

[36] C. Tunstal, *A sermon . . . made upon Palme sondaye laste past* (1539), sig. cv^r–cvi^v.

[37] H. Jenkyns (ed.), *The Works of Thomas Cranmer*, 4 vols. (Oxford, 1833), ii. 117. For Cranmer the validity of orders lay in proper calling, by the prince or the community: MacCulloch, *Cranmer*, 278–9.

colleagues in petitioning the crown for new commissions for the exercise
of their authority. The council at the same time swept away the fig-leaf of
autonomy in the election of bishops, the *congé d'élire*, by which chapters
had been authorized to proceed to the ratification of the royal candidate.[38]
Gardiner quickly perceived these bureaucratic moves as a fundamental
challenge to the nature of the episcopate, effectively ensuring that bishoprics were held only at the king's pleasure. He wrote to Paget in March,
strongly objecting to the word 'delegate' included in the new commissions, 'for we be called ordinaries of the realm, and there should be a
request on our part to make ourselves delegates'.[39] When this denigration
of episcopal power was combined with the growing challenge to Catholic
doctrine, the compromises that had worked for the conservatives under
Henry were no longer valid. There were still attempts by most of the
survivors to show obedience: Nicholas Heath of Worcester, for example,
examined about his attitude to the new ordinal of 1550, argued that he
would enforce it for obedience's sake, though he would not subscribe his
name to the order.[40] In this case, as in those of Gardiner, Bonner, and
Day, there came a moment at which the challenge to Catholic conscience
could no longer be borne, and the council was provided with an opportunity to initiate deprivation proceedings.[41]

Edward's reforming bishops, led by Cranmer, had no initial difficulty in
accepting the delegated authority of the prince. They defined their tasks as
the painstaking teaching of the Word and maintenance of true doctrine.
For a radical like Hooper these were the only true functions of episcopacy: 'There is no more required of the bishop, but that he be faithful and
diligent in the execution of God's word.'[42] Prelates might be spiritual
counsellors to the supreme head, but their power was essentially that
of execution within the religious sphere. 'The spiritual sword', said Latimer, 'is in the hands of ministers and preachers...but the preacher
cannot correct the king, if he be a transgressor of God's word, with the
temporal sword; but he must correct and reprove him with the spiritual
sword.'[43] When trenchant views of this kind came into conflict with the
tough realities of Edwardian politics and godliness was not always triumphant, radicals retreated into the consoling sentiment that the Church
militant here on earth was always nourished 'by the bread of adversity

[38] D.M. Loades, *The Oxford Martyrs* (1970), 48–9. F. Heal, *Of Prelates and Princes* (Cambridge,
1980), 126–7.
[39] J.A. Muller (ed.), *The Letters of Stephen Gardiner* (Cambridge, 1933), 268.
[40] *APC* iii. 361.
[41] Smith, *Tudor Prelates*, 251–81.
[42] S. Carr (ed.), *Early Writings of John Hooper* (PS, Cambridge, 1843), 142.
[43] G.E. Corrie (ed.), *Sermons of Hugh Latimer* (PS, Cambridge, 1844), 86.

and the water of affliction'.[44] Indeed it sometimes appears that the leaders of Edwardian Protestantism had not fully reconciled themselves to the burdens of government rather than the doctrinal purity of opposition.

Nevertheless, under the determined direction of Cranmer, the episcopal leaders of Edwardian England accepted an essentially erastian view of the Church. Through collaborative action with lay authority they were able to put in place the components of the Protestant settlement: the new liturgy and ordinal, the confession of faith, the draft of a revised ecclesiastical law. Parliament provided a crucial forum for change, and key actors like Ridley, Ferrar, Coverdale, and Ponet were assiduous in their attendance.[45] Cranmer and his immediate confidants on the bench and in the ranks of the leading theologians had an agency which enabled them to acquiesce in all but the most brutal forms of governmental intrusion into the control of the Church. They could (usually) convict themselves that the task of building Solomon's temple was being actively pursued. The passage of the key documents still involved profound debate among the bishops, but the process was made easier than in the previous reign by the gradual exclusion of conservative voices. The last occasion on which a substantial challenge to Protestant pressure was mounted was the debate on the First Prayer Book: eight of the conservatives offered trenchant opposition in the Lords.[46] Within the next few years the bench was slowly transmuted into something more recognizably Protestant. The Henrician reformers were reinforced by eight new promotions, a number of them the consequence of the determination shown by Northumberland's regime in pushing through the deprivation of conservatives. By 1553 the English and Welsh bench finally had a clear majority of reformers: between fourteen and sixteen out of a total of twenty-three prelates.[47] Even then, the survival of Thirlby, along with such ambiguous figures as Salcot of Salisbury and Aldrich of Carlisle, indicates that Edward's regime had not proceeded with any general ruthlessness in the construction of a reformed prelacy. Some prelates responded to the fluctuations of religious policy by retreating into total silence—it is impossible to attach a

---

[44] Carr, *Early Writings of Hooper*, 79–80. C. Davies, '"Poor persecuted little flock" or "commonwealth of Christians": Edwardian Protestant concepts of the Church', in P. Lake and M. Dowling (eds.), *Protestantism and the National Church in Sixteenth-Century England* (1987), 78–95.

[45] B.L. Beer, 'Episcopacy and reform in mid-Tudor England', *Albion* 23 (1991), 231–52. M.A.R. Graves, *The House of Lords in the Parliaments of Edward VI and Mary I* (Cambridge, 1981), 34, 219–27.

[46] MacCulloch, *Cranmer*, 404–8.   [47] Smith, *Tudor Prelates*, 149, 307.

convincing ideological label to Bulkeley of Bangor, and Wakeman of Gloucester.[48]

Policy-making became the prerogative of a coterie in these mid-Tudor decades. Yet the bishops retained considerable agency in the enforcement of that policy, through visitation, ecclesiastical discipline, and preaching. Both Henry and Edward challenged episcopal control with the use of royal visitations, the vicegerency, proclamations, and injunctions. After the 1530s these did not, however, constitute a means of supplanting routine episcopal control. The choices made by particular bishops therefore remained of significance in the implementation of religious change. Thus John Longland's tenure of the great Diocese of Lincoln before 1547 enabled him to do much to insulate central England against reforming pressures from the centre. For example, only under direct pressure from Cromwell in 1540 were the Lincoln shrines of St Hugh and John Dalderby destroyed.[49] A parallel instance on the reformist side would be that of Hugh Latimer, whose few years in charge of Worcester raised a religious storm compounding his earlier energetic attack on traditional beliefs in Bristol.[50] The two most dynamic examples are those of Hooper at Gloucester and Worcester under Edward and Bonner at London under Mary.[51] Both were ideologically committed; both saw the need to educate as well as discipline; both applied traditional methods of control with flexibility and imagination. Hooper issued articles and injunctions of great ambition and depth, presided in person over his consistory court at Gloucester, toured the diocese informally as well as at visitation, opened his household to the needy, constantly preached, and conducted a well-known campaign to uncover and remedy the ignorance of his clergy. His episcopal model was Pauline: his objective expressed in a letter to William Cecil, 'doubtless it is a great flock that Christ will save in England...there lacketh nothing among the people but sober, learned and wise men'.[52]

---

[48] The temptation is to attach the label 'time server' to these last bishops, and several of their colleagues, but at least in the case of Wakeman his preoccupation with the needs of a new diocese may partially explain his silence at the centre of affairs: C. Litzenberger, *The English Reformation and the Laity: Gloucestershire, 1540–1580* (Cambridge, 1997), 44–6. Bulkeley and the other 'silent' Welsh bishops are unlikely to have been other than conservatives reluctant openly to oppose the crown: G. Williams, *Wales and the Reformation* (Cardiff, 1997), 171.

[49] M. Bowker, *The Henrician Reformation: The Diocese of Lincoln under John Longland* (Cambridge, 1981), *passim* and 93–5.

[50] R. O'Day, 'Hugh Latimer, prophet of the kingdom', *HR* 158 (1992), 258–76. M.C. Skeeters, *Community and Clergy: Bristol and the Reformation, c.1530–c.1570* (Oxford, 1993), 38–46.

[51] MacCulloch, *Cranmer*, 204–5. Litzenberger, *Gloucestershire*, 68–75, gives the best recent account of Hooper in his diocese. See also F.D. Price, 'Gloucester diocese under Bishop Hooper', *Transactions of the Bristol and Gloucestershire Archaeological Society* 60 (1938), 51–151. Foxe's account of Hooper in his diocese has obvious hagiographical elements, but covers many of the issues that seem to have been important for the bishop: Foxe, vi. 610.

[52] HMC Salisbury, i. 107.

His mature thoughts on the organization of his flock included a belief that there must be lesser superintendents to aid the bishops, ideally one for every ten parishes to 'oversee the[ir] profiting'.[53] We have already encountered Bonner's catechetical and homiletic efforts. His 1554 visitation articles and injunctions are models of care and ambition, and the visitation itself was wide-ranging and thorough, much of that thoroughness being directed to seeking out heresy.[54] Like Hooper he was constantly active in his own courts, and always willing to follow up cases of discipline. Unlike Hooper he was not a great preacher, but he ensured that his chaplains and others undertook these duties for him with equal vigour.[55] Both prelates made great short-term impact upon their dioceses: each had the misfortune to be imposing discipline at odds with the views of a significant part of their flock. In Hooper's case he battled with a conservative clerical establishment and laity; in Bonner's the resistance of London Protestants earned him the infamy of presiding over more than eighty heresy trials.

Among the records of the mid-Tudor episcopate one can find examples of surprising initiative in the face of royal control. For example, Bishop Ridley's 1550 visitation injunctions for London anticipate the official policy of abolishing the altar by several months.[56] Even when the crown had sanctioned action, the prelates could exercise some latitude in enforcement. In 1541 Bishop Goodrich issued a set of four injunctions against images that had their basis in a royal order, but went far beyond the crown in insisting certificates about the destruction were provided to him by each parish.[57] However, not all bishops showed the initiative of a Ridley or Cranmer, or the zeal of a Hooper or Bonner. Most surviving visitation articles and injunctions of the 1540s and 1550s, for example, followed dutifully upon the royal sets of orders, or occasionally picked up those issued by energetic colleagues. This could have curious effects: Bishop Bulkeley's 1551 enquiries for Bangor are derived almost verbatim from Ridley's London series. This meant that the clergy were being asked whether the *pater noster*, creed, and so on were being taught and recited in English: this in a diocese which was overwhelmingly monoglot Welsh. The enquiry is all the more curious because in the previous reign Bulkeley had shown himself sensitive to the needs of his flock, ordering that the *pater noster, ave*, creed and Ten Commandments be taught in English or

---

[53] C. Nevinson (ed.), *The Later Writings of Bishop Hooper* (PS, Cambridge, 1852), 132. Foxe, vi. 610. P. Collinson, 'Episcopacy and reform in England in the later sixteenth century', in his *Godly People: Essays on English Protestantism and Puritanism* (1983), 171–2.

[54] G. Alexander, 'Bonner and the Marian persecutions', reprinted in C. Haigh (ed.), *The English Reformation Revised* (Cambridge, 1987), 157–75.

[55] S. Brigden, *London and the Reformation* (Oxford, 1989), 557–8, 562–70, 578–9.

[56] *VAI* ii. 241, 67–9, 262–6.

[57] *VAI* ii. 68–9. Ely Diocesan Records, G/1/7, fo. 141.

Welsh according to the understanding of congregations.[58] The later orders seem likely to reflect an indifference to the dissemination of the Edwardian settlement rather than a conscious campaign in favour of English.

The Irish episcopate stood in a curious relationship to its Henrician and Edwardian counterpart. If the English and Welsh bishops often lacked agency, their Irish counterparts found themselves without any effective say in the direction of the Church. A majority of the Irish, especially in the Gaelic sees, were still papal nominees in the 1530s, and integrated only to the extent that they were confirmed in office by the crown. Henry VIII gained some recognition in twenty-four of the thirty-two dioceses, but this often involved little more than gestural politics.[59] In at least eight Gaelic sees the crown did not make any attempt to nominate in competition with the papacy, while the papacy tried to maintain succession in most sees except Dublin. Only the dioceses of the provinces of Dublin and Armagh *inter Anglicos* were likely to be led by men more than formally obedient to the supreme headship. In practice the only significant reformers, before Edward's last years, were George Browne, Cromwell's chosen agent to bring change to Dublin, Edward Staples of Meath, and the Irish Augustinian provincial Richard Nangle, who was intruded into Clonfert.[60] Such men had no ability to control policy: for example the 1538 injunctions were simply extended to Ireland by vicegerental fiat.[61]

Yet paradoxically the tiny group of reformers was forced to reflect more deeply than their English counterparts on how religious changes could be enforced at such a remove from royal authority. The ensuing debate has been defined by Brendan Bradshaw as a watershed in Irish constitutional history.[62] The central question for the Irish, says Bradshaw, was the degree of coercion that should be used in introducing reform to a largely resistant population. George Browne, Cromwell's catalyst in Dublin, saw the vigorous use of disciplinary visitations on the English model plus strong support from the secular arm as the way to enforce religious change.[63] Staples on the other hand believed this approach indicated that 'the supremacy of our sovereign lord is maintained only by power and not reasoned by learning': hence in a political context his argument for making Henry king of Ireland. Browne on the whole reflected an English belief in the imposition of discipline as a necessary

---

[58] *VAI* ii. 230–40, 262–6. Williams, *Wales and the Reformation*, 145, 181.

[59] B. Bradshaw, 'Sword, word and strategy in the Reformation in Ireland', *HJ* 21 (1978), 475–502.

[60] R.D. Edwards, *Church and State in Tudor Ireland* (1935), 101 ff.

[61] S. Ellis, *Tudor Ireland: Crown, Community and Conflict of Cultures, 1470–1603* (1985), 197–8.

[62] Bradshaw, 'Sword, word and strategy', 475–8.

[63] B. Bradshaw, 'George Browne, first Reformation archbishop of Dublin, 1536–1554', *JEH* 21 (1970), 301–26.

accompaniment to evangelization: in his first visitation he tried to promote the settlement among his clergy with a mixture of 'gentle exhortation, evangelical instruction', and 'threats of sharp correction'.[64] In 1538 he urged Cromwell to give the chief judicial officers of the Irish state control over conformity.[65] Staples looked rather to a slow process of re-education, though it is often difficult to disentangle how far this led him in a Protestant direction: the language of erasmian humanism often seems more characteristic of his observations.[66] Meanwhile most Irish bishops probably followed Archbishop Cromer of Armagh and implemented the royal will in a 'resolutely minimalist manner'.[67]

The Higher Clergy

Tudor bishops, like modern politicians, frequently had 'education, education, education' as the vision for their clergy. This involved training the ordinary incumbent in such a way that he could defend his faith more effectively and pass on his knowledge to his flock. For that minority which assumed leadership within the Church, it involved providing a university environment that would secure orthodoxy and offer appropriate career structures for the learned. But the unsettled conditions of the English church between the break with Rome and Elizabeth's accession failed to provide the stability at Oxford and Cambridge that would have nurtured growth and vitality. Latimer famously complained that 'few do study divinity, but so many as of necessity must furnish the colleges', and Roger Ascham told Cranmer that 'the university [of Cambridge] was then in so depressed and drooping a condition that very few had hope of coming thither at all, and fewer had any comfort to make long tarrying when they were'.[68] These comments are more revealing of the rhetorical style employed by their authors than of objective reality, but both Oxford and Cambridge do seem to have contracted during the disturbed years of the mid-century. All figures are tentative, but Oxford calculations suggest approximately 1,700 members at the end of the fifteenth century, declining to perhaps 1,150 at the end of Edward's reign.[69] Some, but by no

[64] J. Murray, 'Ecclesiastical justice and the enforcement of the Reformation: the case of Archbishop Browne and the clergy of Dublin', in A. Ford *et al.* (eds.), *As by Law Established: The Church of Ireland since the Reformation* (Dublin, 1995), 33–51.

[65] *SP HVIII* ii. 539–40.

[66] *LP* xii. ii. 760–1.

[67] Jefferies, *Priests and Prelates*, 146–7.

[68] Corrie, *Sermons of Latimer*, 179. J. Strype, *Memorials of . . . Thomas Cranmer*, 2 vols. (Oxford, 1840), vol. ii. c. 6.

[69] J. McConica (ed.), *The History of the University of Oxford*, vol. iii: *The Collegiate University* (Oxford, 1986), 152–4.

means all, of this shrinkage is attributable to the loss of the regulars after 1538. Even more significant for the leadership of the Church was the better-documented decline in those proceeding to higher degrees, which in the decade after 1530 dropped at Oxford from almost 40 per cent of known alumni to around 20 per cent. At Cambridge in the same period the overall number of degrees dropped from an average of 93 to 78.[70]

Some perspective on the English universities in the early Reformation years can be gained by comparing them with those of Scotland. The 1540s and 1550s were difficult decades politically for the northern kingdom, but there was as yet no major religious crisis to perturb applicants, and no significant loss of ecclesiastical benefices to provide employment disincentives. And yet the universities still encountered some of the same difficulties as those south of the border. Glasgow, the extreme case, attracted only fifty-three students in the 1550s; Aberdeen had problems and even St Andrews, with its newly founded St Mary's College and lively intellectual environment, barely maintained its pre-1530s numbers, though it showed signs of recovery in the 1550s.[71] It would therefore be rash to attribute the problems of Oxford and Cambridge exclusively to religious upheaval. The other comparison, between the late Henrician and Edwardian years on the one hand, and those of Mary on the other suggests, however, that religious crisis is pertinent. Though there was no obvious improvement in English economy or society the universities, and especially Oxford, showed clear signs of recovery between 1553 and 1558. Two new colleges at Oxford, St John's and Trinity, automatically helped to increase matriculands, and the numbers of bachelors determining annually increased by about 50 per cent. By the next detailed estimate of Oxford numbers, at Queen Elizabeth's visit in 1566, they appear to have recovered to their 1500 figure.[72]

The difficulties of the universities were certainly not the consequence of political neglect. By the accession of Elizabeth they had, to quote Claire Cross, 'capitulated to state control' 'to a quite unprecedented degree'.[73] Successive regimes, including Mary's, were determined to produce an orthodox higher clergy willing to follow the crown's lead in

---

[70] In both cases the abolition of the degree in canon law provides the most immediate explanation for dramatic change. M. Bateson (ed.), *Grace Book B, part ii* (Cambridge Antiquarian Society, 1905), pp. vii–viii. J.B. Mullinger, *The University of Cambridge from the Royal Injunctions of 1535 to the Accession of Charles I* (Cambridge, 1884), 192–214.

[71] J. Durkan and J. Kirk *The University of Glasgow, 1451–1577* (Glasgow, 1977), 239–40. J.M. Anderson (ed.), *Early Records of the University of St Andrews* (SHS, Edinburgh, 1926), 250–53. D. Stevenson, *King's College, Aberdeen 1560–1641* (Aberdeen, 1990), 12. A.I. Dunlop (ed.), *Acta Facultatis Artium Universitatis Sanctiandree, 1413–1588*, 2 vols. (SHS, 1964–5), vol. i, pp. lvi–lxvi.

[72] McConica, *Collegiate University*, 154–5.

[73] C. Cross, 'Oxford and the Tudor state', in McConica, *Collegiate University*, 149.

matters of faith. Royal and legatine commissions regularly punctuated the life of the communities; office-holding was closely controlled by crown and ministers; the chancellorships became more explicitly political appointments than they had been before the Reformation. Every shift of policy was likely to be reflected in more vigorous enforcement in the universities than elsewhere.[74] For example the Edwardian 42 Articles, sanctioned barely two months before the king's death, were enforced in Cambridge by Thomas Goodrich and two other commissioners. They required all theologians and masters of arts to take an oath to 'defend them as agreeable to the Word of God' and attack 'opposing articles in the Schools and in pulpits'.[75] The well-known moments of high drama— Peter Martyr's Oxford disputation of 1549, the destruction of books by the Henrician and Edwardian commissioners, the exhumation and burning of the remains of Bucer and Fagius at Cambridge in 1556—were only the tip of a very uncomfortable iceberg. If there is any truth in Aschan's claim that it was as difficult to retain men in the universities as to recruit them, part of the explanation must surely lie in the dangerous exposure of those who chose to stay within the system.

We can illustrate the vulnerability of the academic generations active in the universities between the 1530s and the 1560s through two case studies. First, take those who occupied chairs of theology, languages, and law at Oxford, with a concluding date around 1570. The two theology chairs were occupied by nine men: two distinguished foreigners, Peter Martyr and Juan de Villa Garcia; two Protestants, Christopher Goodman and Laurence Humphrey, who spent time in exile rather than compromise their beliefs; two Catholics, Richard Smith and Francis Babington, who did the same. Of the three others, one was apparently excluded in 1551, but did not flee, one was Herbert Westfaling, later bishop of Hereford, too young to be fully visible under Mary, and one, John Smith, managed to survive all the religious changes in a low-key career at Oriel.[76] Even the linguists and lawyers often suffered disastrous interruptions to their careers. Among the eleven individuals involved, two, Thomas Harding and John Story, fled abroad under Elizabeth, and four others suffered deprivation at Oxford, or otherwise lost office because of their religious beliefs. A second sample is provided by those senior clerics who appear in the *Dictionary of National Biography*, reaching their fortieth birthdays

[74] Even in such disturbed times, there was some relief, for example in the late years of Henry's reign, when, as Claire Cross's article indicates, Oxford was relatively undisturbed: McConica, *Collegiate University*, 132–3.

[75] P. Ayris, 'Continuity and change in diocese and province: the role of a Tudor bishop', *HJ* 39 (1996), 309.

[76] McConica, *Collegiate University*, 350–61.

between 1540 and 1560, exactly that generation which would have been expected to lead the mid-Tudor church. If we exclude those men who became bishops, of twenty others who reached influential positions in university and church almost all suffered for their beliefs. Most were part of the Catholic generation swept away in the early 1560s: a few like Chedsey and Bullock having already been imprisoned or fled abroad under Edward. Among the twenty there is only one clear case of constant conformity: that of Henry Siddall, who was a lively Protestant in Edwardian Oxford, a Catholic active in persuading Cranmer to recant, and a quiet conformist, still in the university, under Elizabeth.[77]

Though the universities could no longer protect their privileged members as they moved comfortably from academic training to high ecclesiastical office, we should be careful not to read the experience of the elites in wholly negative terms. The criticism of Scottish universities in these years (St Andrews sometimes excepted) was that they provided a low standard of education, not having kept sufficiently in contact with the mainstream of European thought. When a generation later Andrew Melville reluctantly returned from Geneva to Glasgow, he did so with the objective of transforming its teaching.[78] The Reformation crisis in England also severed some intellectual contacts, especially those of Oxford with Paris and Louvain.[79] Yet religious debate, only imperfectly controlled by the authorities, stimulated another form of contact with Continental scholarship, and changed the nature of higher study from a law-dominated to a theology-dominated culture. The centrality of Bible study, first for Protestants, and then in response for Catholics, encouraged that growth of linguistic scholarship that had been initiated by the humanists. Those who did survive the vagaries of royal policy, to emerge as the group from whom the next generation of the episcopate would largely be drawn, were more likely to be theologians, preachers, and authors than they had been in the early Henrician years. The confessionalization of the universities ensured intellectual vitality as well as bitter conflict. Even the

---

[77] *DNB.* Most of the group indicate at least a general disposition to Catholicism or Protestantism throughout their mature careers, though there are some interesting examples of conversion. Henry Cole, dean of St Paul's under Mary, seems to have shown commitment to reform until about 1548, and Francis Mallett, Marian dean of Lincoln, was reconverted to Catholicism by the example of Princess Mary, whose chaplain he became.

[78] Durkan and Kirk, *Glasgow*, 275–6.

[79] Some of Oxford's international reputation was already vulnerable before the Reformation: the greatest days of the arts school, for example, were over by the mid-fifteenth century. J. Catto and T.A.R. Evans (eds.), *The History of the University of Oxford*, vol ii: *The Later Middle Ages* (Oxford, 1992), 338–42. McConica, *Collegiate University*, 394–5, 314–20. It is interesting to note that, although the religious divide formally separated Oxford and Louvain, the latter formed a very attractive haven for deprived Catholics after Elizabeth's accession.

esoteric battle at Cambridge about the correct pronunciation of Greek ranged over the map of contemporary ideology, helping to define the views of the youthful auditors of John Cheke and his conservative opponents.[80] And under Henry and Edward some of the theologians found themselves in the heady position of acting as professional advisers to the crown. From the moment that Henry assembled his first team to consult on the divorce proceedings men like Richard Cox, John Redman, William May, and William Buckmaster were in regular demand to contribute to the fundamental documents of the English Reformation.[81]

Those theologians and other senior graduates who were in sufficient conformity with royal policy to be appointed to high office emerged into an institutional world even less comfortable than that of the universities. The situation of the English prelates was uncertain enough, but in the age of the dissolutions secular cathedrals were perilously close to total redundancy.[82] Archbishop Cranmer had no great love for deans and prebendaries: in so far as he was prepared to tolerate Henry's continued interest in their existence it was as a basis for learning and evangelization. In his view the prebendary had normally been 'neither a learner, nor teacher, but a good viander'.[83] He hoped to make Canterbury, refounded as a secular cathedral after the dissolution, into a full-scale university college, with lecturers in languages and forty students. This was never likely. Henry favoured the traditional pattern of cathedral worship, and was enthusiastic in encouraging Gardiner in his reconstruction of six ex-religious houses as the basis of new dioceses and cathedrals. But the Enabling Act for the New Foundations (1541) did envisage the education of the young as a prime purpose for the cathedrals. Schools were established and scholarships instituted at the universities.[84]

For a brief time it appeared that cathedrals might become one of the revivifying forces in Tudor religion. However, only part of that hope was fulfilled: the schools became an enduring part of the new establishments,

---

[80] W.S. Hudson, *The Cambridge Connection and the Elizabethan Settlement of 1559* (Durham, N.C., 1980), 43–57. The vitality of late Henrician Cambridge, and its 'stubborn reformism', has recently been illuminated by A. Ryrie, 'English Evangelical Reformers in the Last Years of Henry VIII', University of Oxford D.Phil. (2000), 215–37.

[81] Wilkins, *Concilia*, iii. 834. BL Cottonian MS Cleo. EV, fos. 75 ff.

[82] S.E. Lehmberg, *The Reformation of Cathedrals: Cathedrals in English Society, 1485–1603* (Princeton, N.J., 1988), 38–66, 101–22. C. Cross, 'Dens of loitering lubbers: Protestant protest against cathedral foundations, 1540–1640', in D. Baker (ed.), *Schism, Heresy and Religious Protest*, SCH 10 (1972), 231–2.

[83] J.E. Cox (ed.), *Cranmer's Miscellaneous Writings* (PS, Cambridge, 1846), 396–7. MacCulloch, *Cranmer*, 264–5.

[84] C.S. Knighton, 'The provision of education in the new cathedral foundations of Henry VIII', in D. Marcombe and C.S. Knighton (eds.), *Close Encounters: English Cathedrals and Society since 1540* (Nottingham, 1991), 18–42.

sometimes even performing the role of training 'poor men's sons'. It was typical of the regime that the scholarships to universities were cancelled, and the lands provided to endow them removed in 1546.[85] This is paradigmatic of the situation of the later 1540s. The cathedrals were under constant financial and patronage pressures from the crown and laity, and ideological divisions split some of the establishments. Both Canterbury and the new foundation of Osney next to Oxford became deeply enmeshed in the complex events known as the Prebendaries' Plot (1543), which further alienated Cranmer and made Henry mistrustful of those he had formerly favoured.[86] Edward's reign saw some revival of Protestant ambition for the cathedrals: Holgate's injunctions for York Minster, for example, stress preaching as the prime function of the institution, and there is evidence of lecturers being employed at Winchester and Lichfield.[87] Yet the new wine did not readily fit the old bottles: the destruction of organs, abolition of the daily offices, and attack on 'confabulation' in music must have left many of the cathedral personnel with little clear sense of function.[88]

The survival of the cathedrals and their 'vianders' owes much to their advantages as sources of patronage for the crown. They also had obvious utility as environments in which to display government religious policy.[89] Every visual change from the first attack on images, through the removal of altars, to the grandeur of Mary's restoration of the Mass, could be exemplified in the mother churches of the dioceses. The Worcester chronicler John Steynor kept a detailed record of the changes to his cathedral which convey some sense of the impact of government fiat. In 1550–1, for example, he noted that Dean Barlow, brother of the bishop of Bath and Wells, 'pulled down Our Lady's chapel... and also the altar of Jesus made in white stone, and a chapel of St Edmund wherein was a pair of organs and a Chapel of St George made of timber...'. He also noted the order to have a table 'of tree' at which Mass would be said and communion administered in English. Six years later the same chronicler was recording the elaborate Marian restoration of the chapels, but particularly of the choir with double stalls, organs, and 'a goodly loft wherein the gospel is read'.[90] An extreme case of the symbolic significance of the

---

[85] MacCulloch, *Cranmer*, 264–7.

[86] Jenkins, *Works of Cranmer*, i. 291–4.

[87] J. Fines, *A Biographical Register of Early Protestant Reformers* (Bodleian typescript) under Saunders.

[88] *VAI* ii. 310–21. The word 'confabulation' is Holgate's.

[89] D. Marcombe, 'Cathedrals and Protestantism: the search for a new identity, 1540–1660', in Marcombe and Knighton, *Close Encounters*, 50–3.

[90] D. MacCulloch, 'Worcester: a cathedral city in the Reformation', in P. Collinson and J. Craig (eds.), *The Reformation in English Towns, 1500–1640* (Basingstoke, 1998), 94–112.

cathedral in the display of royal authority is that of St Patrick's, Dublin. St Patrick's exercised a political influence in the management of the Irish church far greater than any of its English counterparts. Yet, since there were two Dublin cathedrals, it was suppressed in 1547, primarily to serve the financial interests of the crown, but partly because the local patriciate pressed the Irish council to spare Christ Church.[91] Under Mary, St Patrick's became one of only two Irish foundations to be restored by the crown. The statutes presented Philip and Mary as committed to 'the glory of God and the advancement of his service and holy word', the last served partly by the educational arrangements that were part of the restoration.[92] Marian statutes for a number of the English cathedrals, including Durham, also continued what Henry's legislation had begun: residence was more strictly enforced than in the past, and preaching and instruction of the laity became an integral part of the obligations of prebendaries.[93]

If the cathedrals were made vulnerable by religious change, those other centres of clerical power and administration, the church courts, were even more insecure. There are a variety of explanations for the decline of ecclesiastical jurisdiction in the decades after the Reformation.[94] The uncertain status of ecclesiastical law, controlled by the crown and yet still largely employing Roman canon law forms, is a key reason. The failure of Cranmer's great project for the reform of canon law left the church courts using a system of justice that had no logical place in a Protestant polity.[95] The period in the mid-1530s when the vicegerent appropriated ecclesiastical jurisdiction left a legacy of uncertainty. Moreover Cromwell's abolition of canon law as a higher degree meant that the courts had now to be staffed by civilians. Then there are the broader contextual issues: a decline in the popular respect for the authority of the Church that was a consequence both of hostility to new doctrine and a general suspicion of change; the economic and social dislocation of the mid-Tudor decades; and the structural difficulties created by the dissolutions, especially by the

---

[91] J. Murray, 'The Tudor Diocese of Dublin', University of Dublin, Trinity College Ph.D. (1997), 149–53. Ellis, *Tudor Ireland*, 201, 204.

[92] *CPR Irl* i. 327–8.

[93] D. Marcombe, 'The Durham dean and chapter: old abbey writ large?' in R. O'Day and F. Heal (eds.), *Continuity and Change: Personnel and Administration of the Church in England, 1500–1642* (Leicester, 1976), 129–30.

[94] The most important study of the work of the church courts in these mid-Tudor years remains R. Houlbrooke, *Church Courts and the People during the English Reformation: 1520–1570* (Oxford, 1979). See also his 'The decline of ecclesiastical jurisdiction under the Tudors', in O'Day and Heal, *Continuity and Change*, 239–58.

[95] R. Helmholz, *Roman Canon Law in Reformation England* (Cambridge, 1990), 28–40. On Cranmer's project see the edition of the *Reformatio* by G. Bray, *Tudor Church Reform: The Henrician Canons of 1535 and the Reformatio Legum Ecclesiasticum*, Church of England Record Society 8 (2000).

sale of appropriated rectories to the laity. The courts' sphere of jurisdiction was also slowly circumscribed by parliamentary action. For example, control of tithes was limited, especially by two statutes of 1536 and 1549, the latter of which effectively fixed the monetary value of personal tithe, and allowed plaintiffs to turn to the common law for redress.[96]

Archdeacons, chancellors, and other episcopal deputies, whose duty it was to manage the discipline of the Church on a daily basis, were understandably demoralized by the dramatic changes of these years. Such men could not wholly escape the upheavals of the mid-century: of seventy-nine English archdeacons listed in Le Neve as holding office between 1541 and 1558, twenty-three were deprived or forced to resign.[97] The survivors were tenacious, but not necessarily enthusiastic. Some of those who had begun their careers before the break with Rome assisting the Henrician prelates often seem to have lost heart by the 1540s. At Chichester Robert Sherburne's key administrators, the chancellor John Worthial and the dean William Fleshmonger, both outlived their master, Worthial not dying until 1554. But the vigour of the latter's early jurisdictional activity—holding for example peripatetic sessions of the commissary court—vanished as the internal affairs of the cathedral absorbed more and more of his time.[98] Worthial seems characteristic of mid-Tudor chancellors, both in his loss of heart and in his longevity. Although it was theoretically possible for a prelate to remove his chancellor, there was a reluctance to do so, presumably because of the accumulated expertise acquired in the post, perhaps also by the Edwardian years because of the difficulty of finding men with the correct training. Continuity in many ways served the Church well: John Rokeby, for example, who served at York from the late Henrician years into the reign of Elizabeth, was famed because only once in thirty-two years' service was a judgement for which he was responsible overturned on appeal.[99] But continuity usually also meant conservatism, either of the trenchant or the foot-dragging kind. Edmund Stuarde, Gardiner's long-serving chancellor at Winchester, was actually imprisoned for a time under Edward, and only reinstated in 1553. More common was survivalism like that of Miles Spenser, archdeacon of Sudbury and chancellor of Norwich, who remained in office through all the changes as the head of a family that became church papist and recusant under Elizabeth.[100] When a new generation had to be recruited it was

---

[96] Houlbrooke, *Church Courts*, 117–50.   [97] Le Neve, *Fasti, 1541–1830*.
[98] S. Lander, 'Church courts and the Reformation in the diocese of Chichester', in O'Day and Heal, *Continuity and Change*, 215–38.
[99] R.A. Marchant, *The Church under the Law: Justice, Administration and Discipline in the Diocese of York, 1560–1640* (Cambridge, 1969), 41–2.
[100] Houlbrooke, *Church Courts*, 24–5.

painfully obvious that ecclesiastical lawyers were not natural adherents of reform. Only a few are remarkable because of a sympathy with evangelical change: Roger Townshend, for example, who became Cranmer's commissary in his faculty office, or William May and Edward Leedes, who served Goodrich at Ely as vicars-general.[101] The Church of England experienced a crisis of middle management that was not resolved until long into Elizabeth's reign.

Wealth and Expropriation

Fundamental to the problems of the mid-Tudor bishops and the rest of the higher clergy was the issue of wealth. The Henrician Reformation removed such prohibitions as had existed against the secularization of church property and the crown often appeared to sanction a wantonly anti-clerical attitude towards the possessions of bishops and cathedrals, as well as monasteries and chantries. In one sense the full-tide of lay greed never washed against the secular clergy: after the debates of the 1530s the possibility of systematic expropriation was never fully articulated.[102] The closest that the crown came to a broad alienation of episcopal property was probably under the duke of Northumberland. Then, as the Catholic prelates were deprived one by one, a golden opportunity was opened for the crown. The imperial ambassador Scheyfve commented at the time of Gardiner's deprivation that his temporalities, and those of others, would be given to the crown and that 'hereafter the government will treat all bishops alike, and assign them pensions of one or two hundred pounds sterling for their maintenance'.[103] Nothing like this occurred, though Edward himself seems to have thought along these lines, commenting at Bishop Ponet's elevation to Winchester that he had '2000 marks of land appointed to him for his maintenance'.[104] The complex plan to dissolve Durham after Tunstal's deprivation had embedded within it a calculation that the new see would need 2,000 marks, and the proposed bishopric of Newcastle 1,000 marks. All of this followed logically enough from the premise that bishops, and other senior officers of the Church, held office at the crown's pleasure, rather than by some divine ordination. These were views in which the reformers were often complicit: Hooper

---

[101] MacCulloch, *Cranmer*, 117. F. Heal, 'The Bishops of Ely and their Diocese, 1515–ca.1600', University of Cambridge Ph.D. (1972), 76–7.

[102] Heal, *Prelates and Princes*, 101–50.

[103] *CSP Sp* x. 215.

[104] W.K. Jordan (ed.), *The Chronicle and Political Papers of Edward VI* (Ithaca, 1966), 58.

argued that the 'fourth part' of the bishop's income should suffice for a preaching minister and Latimer's sermons contain a litany of complaints against worldliness and wealth that turned prelates from their true vocations.[105]

But the crucial problem for bishops and for cathedrals was not so much the planned transmutation of the higher clergy into paid crown servants, as the quotidian pressure of lay demands upon their property. The crown was the first beneficiary, beginning with Henry VIII's appropriation of a series of attractive estates within distance of London, largely from the archbishop of Canterbury.[106] Cranmer did little to help himself, or take any stand of principle against unfavourable terms of recompense: 'forsomuch as I am a man that hath small experience in such causes, and have no mistrust at all in my prince on that behalf'.[107] Not all, even among the reformers, shared the archbishop's optimism, and as the list of manors appropriated grew there was 'grudging' though few explicit denials. The dangers of direct refusal are well-indicated by Bishop Gardiner's political disgrace in 1546, which owed something to his refusal of an exchange of lands with the king. The prelates were less inhibited on the subject of lay greed in general: a majority of the estates they lost in these years went to courtiers or their clients. The process by which the London inns of the prelates passed to courtiers is typical: Charles Brandon, duke of Suffolk, gained Norwich Place in 1536, the inn of the bishops of Coventry and Lichfield went to Lord Beauchamp in 1537, and Bath and Wells lost its inn to the earl of Southampton in 1539. The apogee, but by no means the end, of this process came when the duke of Somerset swallowed the London residences of Worcester, Llandaff, and Carlisle to clear space for his great palace in the Strand.[108] There could scarcely have been a more compelling representation of the shift of power from church to laity. Almost all the manors taken had some recompense, usually in the form of appropriated rectories. The clerical author of *Respublica* (1553) offered a stinging indictment of this policy. Oppression rejoices that he has seized most of the bishops' houses and in return given:

[105] Carr, *Early Writings of Hooper*, 397. Corrie, *Sermons of Latimer*, 65, 69–70, 100, 176, though it should be emphasized that Latimer was more preoccupied by the misdirection of episcopal energies into secular tasks than with their wealth.

[106] MacCulloch, *Cranmer*, 200–2.

[107] Jenkins, *Works of Cranmer*, i. 203, though even Cranmer tried to preserve some of his properties: according to his secretary Ralph Morice he tried to downplay the charms of Knole in order to divert Henry's interest: J.G. Nichols (ed.), *Narratives of the Days of the Reformation*, CS os 57 (1859), 266.

[108] Heal, *Prelates and Princes*, 113–14, 137.

Bare parsonages of appropriations,
Bought from Respublica, and first emprowed;
Then at the highest extent to bishops allowed,
Let out to their hands for fourscore and [nineteen] year.

(III. v)[109]

The economic reality was not quite so dire, but bare calculations of rough parity in the rents in these exchanges concealed the major problem: that the prelates were being provided with recompense at the expense of the rest of the Church.[110]

Lay expectations of all kinds had been aroused by the break with Rome and the dissolution of the monasteries, and in their turn the clergy had limited incentive to protect the possessions of a church that might at any time be subject to further appropriation. Bishops, chapters, and other clerics granted long leases of lands in order to provide immediate security for themselves and their dependants, though also perhaps to make their possessions less attractive to ambitious laymen.[111] An example of the latter comes from Lincoln, where Bishop Longland encouraged the leasing of most of the prebendal land in the 1530s and 1540s, apparently as a protective device against spoliation.[112] Such strategies did not always succeed: an extreme capitular case comes from Chester, where in 1553 the dean and two prebendaries were imprisoned in the Fleet, allegedly for taking lead from the cathedral roof, but actually as a way of persuading them to lease Sir Richard Cotton, comptroller of the king's household, most of the lands of the cathedral in fee farm.[113] Nor were churchmen themselves always scrupulous: Bishop Barlow of St David's, for example, created grave difficulties for his Protestant successor Robert Ferrar, by his alienation of property, mortgaging, and leasing at low rents. When relations between Ferrar and significant sections of the local community broke down in 1549 a major explanation was the bishop's determination to reverse the actions of his predecessor. The complex legality of his various actions is less pertinent than the very fact that a prelate should refuse to accept the prevailing ethos of acquiescence in lay demands. His enemies complained that he was obsessed with the business of his property rather than applying himself to 'his chief and principal vocation, his book and preaching'.[114] Even an

[109] W.W. Greg (ed.), *Respublica*, EETS os 226 (1952).

[110] A careful study of the York exchanges and the value of the appropriated rectories is W.J. Sheils, 'Profit, patronage, or pastoral care: the rectory estates of the archbishopric of York, 1540–1640', in R. O'Day and F. Heal (eds.), *Princes and Paupers in the English Church, 1500–1800* (Leicester, 1981), 91–110.

[111] On the leasing policies of the bishops see Heal, *Prelates and Princes*, 180–93.

[112] Bowker, *Henrician Reformation*, 96–8.   [113] Lehmberg, *Reformation of Cathedrals*, 178–9.

[114] A.J. Brown, *Robert Ferrar, Yorkshire Monk, Reformation Bishop and Martyr in Wales, c.1500–1555* (1997), 127–38.

effective bishop like Ridley felt deep frustration at his inability to control
his own property. In 1551 he complained that some of his sub-tenants
were rack-renting despite their own fixed rents, something that was 'to the
great slander of all Bishops . . . [to] suffer their poor tenants so to be pilled
and polled . . . [to the] very destruction of the commonwealth'.[115]

For the ordinary parish incumbent, who might lease out glebe or the
collection of tithe, this 'pilling and polling' by lay farmers was frequently
one of the ways in which his flock was alienated. Tithe disputes in particular
grew sharply in number in most of the ecclesiastical courts in the mid-
century. After the statute of 1540, which empowered lay owners or lessees
of tithes to sue in the ecclesiastical courts, a substantial percentage of these
cases were initiated by laymen.[116] In the Diocese of Lincoln over a third of
the cases before the church courts in the 1540s were initiated by farmers.[117]
Tithe was treated as simply another kind of income for the lay owners,
albeit one that had to be pursued through the church courts. The aggression
which some of these owners and farmers displayed in the pursuit of claims is
indicated in the demand of Kett's rebels in 1549 that knights and gentlemen
should not 'have or take in farm any spiritual promotion'.[118]

But lay manipulation of clerical resources is only one part of the story.
Rectors and vicars remained the largest group of litigants in tithe disputes.
Their tendency to resort more routinely to the courts to secure their rights
can be explained in a variety of ways. The legislation already mentioned had
facilitated their behaviour, and the declining authority of the Church
weakened their customary hold upon their congregations. The 1536 act
specifically complained that men were now unusually bold in withholding
tithe.[119] Religious change may have removed some of a cleric's power of
moral persuasion. Later in the century one Saffron Walden parishioner commented that 'privy tithes' were no longer paid because auricular confession
once moved men's consciences 'more than good preaching can do now'.[120]
Then there were the economic crises of the mid-century and property
dislocation caused by the dissolution. These inflicted severe strain on the
rural economy, producing resistance in paying customary dues and (sometimes) unusual aggression on the part of the clergy. Economic conflict

---

[115] Kent Record Office, Rochester DC, Egz. 2.
[116] Houlbrooke, *Church Courts*, 117–50. J.S. Purvis (ed.), *Select Sixteenth Century Causes in Tithe
from the York Diocesan Registry* Yorkshire Archaeological Society Record Series 94 (1949), p. viii. In
the York case it appears (unusually) that lay impropriators may be the largest category of litigants.
[117] Bowker, *Henrician Reformation*, 135.
[118] A. Fletcher and D. MacCulloch, *Tudor Rebellions*, 4th edn. (1997), 140.
[119] Houlbrooke, *Church Courts*, 121.
[120] M. Byford, 'The Price of Protestantism: Assessing the Impact of Religious Change on
Elizabethan Essex: The Case of Heydon and Colchester, 1558–1594', University of Oxford
D.Phil. (1988), 86.

soured relations between clergy and laity and provided one justification for a withdrawal of loyalty that might also have ideological roots.[121]

The levels of actual economic deprivation among the mid-century parish clergy are difficult to determine. As we have seen in an earlier chapter there was probably an over-supply of clergy in the immediate pre-Reformation period, making the labour of the unbeneficed cheap. As the crisis of church and state unfolded a declining number of ordinands eventually led to a shortage of labour and difficulty in filling poorer benefices.[122] Price rise put pressure on those who remained, though its impact was not consistent.[123] Those clerics who retained glebe, or had effective control of a rectory or vicarage with no commutation of tithes, could prosper: in Warwickshire, for example, where 87 per cent of the rectories and 40 per cent of the vicarages had substantial glebe lands, there must have been many incumbents who survived the mid-century relatively unscathed.[124] For many their greatest problem would have been the crown's demands for clerical taxation: the requirement to pay first fruits and tenths for the beneficed, and subsidies for all the clergy, which bore particularly heavily upon individuals during the war years from 1542 to 1550. The tax-burden had increased approximately four-fold from the pre-Reformation figures.[125] Those with the luxury of grumbling, but paying tax, must be contrasted with a substantial group who were impoverished *tout court*, holding benefices that were inadequately endowed, or living on fixed money payments that failed to keep pace with inflation. The urban clergy were particular sufferers: after 1549 they virtually abandoned hope of collecting personal tithes, and usually depended on a series of commutation payments, plus such fees as could be raised for specific services.[126] York

---

[121] Purvis, *Select Causes in Tithe*.

[122] M. Zell, 'Economic problems of the parochial clergy in the sixteenth century', in O'Day and Heal, *Princes and Paupers*, 19–44.

[123] This was as true in Scotland as in England, where Kirk points out that poverty and relative ease existed side by side in parishes all over the country at the beginning of the Reformation: J. Kirk (ed.), *Books of the Assumption of Thirds* (British Academy Records in Social and Economic History, 1995), pp. xliv–xlvi.

[124] D.M. Barratt (ed.), *Ecclesiastical Terriers of Warwickshire Parishes*, Dugdale Society 22 (1955), intro.

[125] J.J. Scarisbrick, 'Clerical taxation in England, 1485–1547', *JEH* 11 (1960), 41–54. F. Heal, 'Clerical tax collection under the Tudors: the influence of the Reformation', in O'Day and Heal, *Continuity and Change*, 97–9, 104–10. P. Carter, 'Economic problems of provincial urban clergy during the Reformation', in P. Collinson and J. Craig (eds.), *The Reformation in English Towns, 1500–1640* (Basingstoke, 1998), 147–58.

[126] Skeeters, *Community and Clergy*, 98–109. However, in her important article on urban clergy Claire Cross points out that poor livings did not automatically make poor clergy. Through pluralism and exploiting other sources of revenue her urban clergy often left quite adequate estates, even in the mid-century: C. Cross, 'The incomes of provincial urban clergy, 1520–1645', in O'Day and Heal, *Princes and Paupers*, 68–75.

offers an extreme case. There the large number of small parishes registered an average income of only £4. 5s. in the 1535 *Valor Ecclesiasticus* and drastic action had to be taken in 1547 when the Union of Churches Act described York livings as 'much decayed by the ruin and decay of the said City'.[127]

The case of the struggling urban clergy serves to remind us, however, that we should not automatically construct relations between clergy and laity during the Reformation in terms of the greed of the latter and weakness of the former. Townsmen often responded to the difficulties with local arrangements to protect those who served them, paying directly from the parish chest, as at St Ewan's, Bristol, or managing the benefice for a cleric, as at St Aldate's, Gloucester.[128] Or a more structured solution might be sought as in the York example of union of benefices, which was followed by Lincoln and Stamford. In York fifteen churches were closed, or combined, by 1551, despite some opposition from Archbishop Holgate.[129] Colchester drafted a similar bill for unions in 1549, but it never reached the statute book.[130] Just as guilds and fraternities took responsibility for much of the religious life of pre-Reformation towns, so councils and groups of parishioners began to assume that duty in the new and confused world of mid-Tudor religion. The beginnings of Elizabethan urban religion can be faintly discerned. That what was done was so fragmentary is a consequence both of the shortage of time under Edward, and of the fundamental fixity of the financial structures of the Tudor church. There is no evidence that either the politicians or the bishops, with the exception of Hooper, established any clear view of an alternative to the inherited and profoundly inequitable forms of ecclesiastical wealth.

While a careful analysis of the economic situation of the mid-Tudor clergy reveals a mixed picture, it is not surprising that the Catholic hierarchy under Mary identified clerical poverty and lay greed as prime targets for action. The author of *Respublica* was only one of those who saw the chaos of the previous years as a triumph for avarice. The sins of the schism demanded restitution, and while Mary and Pole were powerless to compel the laity to atone, they could work towards a cleansing of the royal conscience.[131] The queen's episodic gestures towards monastic restoration are less germane here than her actions in the secular church. Her initial moves, before she had the presence of the cardinal to guide her, consisted of the sacrifice of crown patronage in the cathedrals, the restoration of the

[127] D. Palliser, *Tudor York* (Oxford, 1979), 229.   [128] Carter, 'Economic problems', 154–7.

[129] Palliser, *Tudor York*, 240.

[130] M. Byford, 'The birth of a Protestant town: the process of Reformation in Tudor Colchester, 1530–1580', in Collinson and Craig, *English Towns*, 27–8.

[131] Heal, *Prelates and Princes*, 150–61.

see of Durham, a cause of conflict in Parliament, and the release of some bishops from the burden of first fruits. Some expropriated estates were restored: most notably the great manors taken from Cranmer in the 1530s were given to Pole, though for his lifetime only.[132] Among the individual gifts made by the queen, the grant of a set of Leicestershire and Cumberland rectories to the University of Oxford has particular significance, signalling in the words of the grant the 'raising up of the university' so that it might defend the orthodox faith against heresy.[133]

The changes guided by Pole from 1555 onwards had much greater potential significance for the clergy at large. By legislation of that year first fruits and tenths were no longer paid to the crown, instead they were to be passed to the bishops. After the payment of the remaining monastic pensions the latter were to use the surplus to provide for the poorest of the parochial clergy. Rex Pogson has traced in detail the painstaking process by which Pole and his deputies began to collect the necessary information to make good this legislation, and the way in which a limited number of poorer clerics began to benefit for the first time in 1558.[134] The bishops were required to accumulate records in a systematic manner. In that last year of the reign Mary also fulfilled her declared intention of returning crown impropriations to the Church: not in time to make much practical difference, but offering a model which her successors managed sedulously to ignore until the time of Queen Anne's Bounty a century and a half later. Many questions remain about Pole's capacity to execute the ambitious fiscal policies he had defined: not least whether the Church, after its period of dependence upon state authority, could once again enforce its own control over the lesser clergy and over the laity whose interests had become so inextricably wound into its fabric. The ambition of Pole's approach can be underlined by comparison with the reforming councils in Scotland. The Scottish bishops had not yet lived through a Reformation that legitimated direct expropriation of church property: however, they had plenty of experience of every other form of economic pressure, and impoverished clergy aplenty. In both 1549 and 1559 there were decrees endeavouring to halt the exploitation of glebe lands and the practice of feu-farming: in 1559 a more systematic decree on the direct collection of teinds by clerics was added.[135] One of the recent

[132] *CPR Philip & Mary*, iii. 69–72; i. 165–6.

[133] G. Philip, 'Queen Mary Tudor's benefaction to the university', *Bodleian Library Record* 5 (1954), 27–37.

[134] R. Pogson, 'Revival and reform in Mary Tudor's church: a question of money', *JEH* 25 (1974), 249–65. P. Carter, 'Mary Tudor, Parliament and the renunciation of first fruits, 1555', *HR* 69 (1996), 340–6.

[135] Patrick, *Statutes of the Scottish Church*, 84–188. The 1559 decrees still dealt with an aspect of lay grievance against clerical exaction—demands made for Easter offerings and mortuaries; Ibid., 185.

historians of the councils says bluntly that these limited attempts to halt lay attacks on property were unsuccessful. In Scotland it was the reformed church that painfully learned the lesson of the importance of providing a more systematic way of funding the clergy.[136]

The Parish Clergy

William Sheppard, rector of the small community of Heydon in Essex, has in recent years become one of the most remarked of English clerics. Mark Byford discovered his extraordinary 'Epitome' among the records of the parish: a document which details his benefactions and his dealings with his flock over an extensive period of ministry that lasted from 1541 to 1586.[137] Sheppard was an Augustinian canon of Leeds Priory, Kent, before his appointment to Heydon, and were it not for his text he would inevitably be labelled as a quiet conformist, a vicar of Bray who adhered with probable reluctance to royal policy in order to avoid being dismissed from his second lodging place. In fact Sheppard was a model pastor, and not only in his own estimation: in the collective memory of the community his reputation was still alive well into the seventeenth century. He cared for the poor, rebuilt significant parts of the church, and engaged in local public works. He also preached in his own cure and, despite perhaps some conservative instincts, was a strong adherent of the religion ordained by 'the Queen's Majesty's injunctions', as he put it, under Elizabeth. By the 1580s he seems to have turned a significant section of his congregation into sermon-going Protestants. Though we know less of his doings under Edward and Mary than in the subsequent reign, there is no reason to suppose that he did not lead his flock steadily where the crown demanded it should go. When required to describe his ministry in a Chancery suit in the 1580s he talked of his 'integrity of life' and 'honest and godly conversation'.

One cannot assume that the pastoral devotion sustaining Sheppard's ideological accommodation is characteristic of those clergy who had to live through the dangerous years of the mid-sixteenth century. Two other clergy who survived and, most unusually, commented on their lot— Robert Parkyn of Adwick le Street, Yorkshire, and Christopher Trychay of Morebath, Devon—were both deeply conservative, and only reluctantly conformist to the Edwardian changes.[138] Parkyn, from the relative safety of Mary's reign, spoke of the 1552 parliament as one 'wherein no

---

[136] Winning, 'Church councils', 344. See below, pp. 408–11.

[137] Byford, 'Price of Protestantism', 15–87.

[138] A.G. Dickens (ed.), 'Robert Parkyn's narrative', in his *Reformation Studies* (1982), 287–312; 'South Yorkshire letters, 1555', in his *Late Monasticism and the Reformation* (1994), 191. J. Erskine Binney (ed.), *The Accounts of the Wardens of the Parish of Morebath, Devon, 1520–1573*

goodness towards holy church proceedeth, but all things contrary'. His mental world, as exemplified in his commonplace book, included an interest in the mysticism of Richard Rolle, in the moralizing poetry of Lydgate, and in the piety of Thomas More. Trychay recorded in 1558 the return of many of his beloved church goods after the years of King Edward's reign when the Church 'ever decayed'. In much of the recent literature it is Parkyn and Trychay who are taken to represent the default position of the reflective and conscientious parish clergy. They did not want change, were profoundly disturbed by the loss of traditional liturgy, and were sufficiently doctrinally aware to understand that the ideological underpinnings of their faith were threatened. As for the less acute, or able, probably the vast majority of ordinary incumbents and their deputies, the assumption is that their accommodation to the new order was almost as reluctant: spontaneous enthusiasm for reform, or the general proceedings of Henry and Edward, was, it is argued, unusual in the pulpit. Even in London, most of the City clergy hated the new ways, 'wishing that all things was now as it was twenty years since'.[139]

It is certainly true that those parochial clergy who can be counted as taking a clear stand for reform are in a small minority in the English parishes, almost non-existent in Wales, and wholly so in Ireland. Fines's listing of early known Protestants includes approximately 170 men serving English cures or at Calais who could be described as vigorously reformist, this spread over thirty years and about 9,000 parishes.[140] The closer analysis of London evidence conducted by Susan Brigden traces more than fifty reforming clergy in Henry's last years, distributed among the hundred parishes and other institutions.[141] Only in London was there a critical mass of active reformers: though Kent, Suffolk, and Essex had a generous scattering of such clergy from the 1530s onwards.[142] The identified clergy run the predictable gamut of the reform-minded: from Thomas Forman

---

(Exeter, 1904). E. Duffy, *Voices of Morebath: Reformation and Rebellion in an English Village* (New Haven, Conn., 2001), 165. A third traditionalist record-keeper was Sir Thomas Butler, vicar of Much Wenlock, who noted religious changes in his register, with occasional resentful comments: W.A. Leighton, 'The register of Sir Thomas Butler, vicar of Much Wenlock', *Transactions of the Shropshire Archaeological and Natural History Society* 6 (1883), 93–132.

[139] Brigden, *London*, 396–7.

[140] Fines, *Biographical Register*. It must be stressed that this counts individuals, not the number of parishes they influenced. Many moved from one benefice to another, or undertook itinerant preaching. There are interesting parallels in Scotland, where the leadership for reform was often clerical, but rarely found among the parochial clergy: Kirk lists nine instances in the 1530s and 1540s: J. Kirk, *Patterns of Reform* (Edinburgh, 1989), 7.

[141] Brigden, *London*, 398–404.

[142] D. MacCulloch, *Suffolk under the Tudors* (1988), 162–3, 177–8. Other recent local studies sometimes add to Fines's figures, though not substantially. See for example the small group of Marian exiles from West Wales identified by Glanmor Williams, *Wales and the Reformation*, 208–9.

and the Lollard sympathizers of the 1520s; through Foxe's learned heroes
of the Protestant Reformation, Rowland Taylor at Hadleigh, or John Bale
at Bishopstoke; to curates accused of non-conformity because they were
at odds with the parish on a range of issues, many of them of the traditional kind. Among this minority were men who burned with an ardour
to convert at all costs, to bring if necessary a sword not peace to their
parishes. Like Rowland Taylor they believed that 'preachers must be bold
and not milk mouthed' or like Thomas Hancock, curate of Poole, and
preacher at Southampton, they were prepared to risk division and conflict
to plant the gospel in a new corner of England.[143]

On the Catholic side those who were sufficiently vocal to bring themselves to the attention of the government and be perceived as a threat were
also a small minority. In the period of most determined political enforcement of the Reformation, under Cromwell in the 1530s, 187 secular clergy
were denounced to the regime as potentially traitorous.[144] This figure excludes those involved in major rebellion, but includes a number of accusations that seem to have had little basis beyond malice and local conflict.
Only 13 per cent of this group suffered death under the harsh Treason Law
of 1534. Conservative clergy were, of course, also deeply implicated in the
two major uprisings of 1536 and 1549. The Lincolnshire Rising was initiated
by the preaching of Thomas Kendall of Louth, and nurtured by a network of
at least thirty local clerics.[145] Parish clergy were active in most areas affected
by the Pilgrimage of Grace: for example at least six benefice-holders were
involved in the Cumberland rising. The complex nature of priestly involvement in these risings is indicated in Sir John Bulmer's deposition that he had
sent out his chaplain to enquire if the commons would rise, which the local
clergy 'should know by men's confessions'.[146] The Edwardian council was
looking for simple answers when it attributed the Western Rising to
'the provocation only of certain popish priests', but the latter were a significant element in the leadership of the revolt.[147] At least nine incumbents
were executed in the aftermath, and others were deprived: the vicar of
St Thomas's, Exeter, who had 'persuaded the people to the condemning of the reformed religion', was hanged in chains from his church

---

[143] J. Craig, 'Reformers, conflict and revisionism: the Reformation in sixteenth-century
Hadleigh', *HJ* (1999), 1–23. J.G. Nichols (ed.), *Narratives of the Days of the Reformation*, CS os
57 (1859), 76–7. Somerset himself stopped Hancock preaching at Southampton for fear of
divisions.

[144] G.R. Elton, *Policy and Police: The Enforcement of the Reformation in the Age of Thomas
Cromwell* (Cambridge, 1972), 398–9.

[145] Bowker, *Henrician Reformation*, 152–5.

[146] M.J. Bush, *The Pilgrimage of Grace* (Manchester, 1996), 355–6.

[147] S.L. Jansen, *Dangerous Talk and Strange Behaviour: Women and Popular Resistance to the
Reforms of Henry VIII* (Basingstoke, 1996), 12.

tower.[148] Such behaviour was predictably rare: not only did most traditionalists continue to serve silently through the Edwardian years, the great majority who survived into Elizabeth's reign also acquiesced and subscribed to
the supremacy. While after 1559 the higher clergy often followed their
bishops' example and refused subscription, all but between 200 and 400 of
the beneficed men remained in place, though it seems that many may have
evaded actual signature.[149] Even this, of course, could have serious effects in
some localities: it has been estimated that 10 per cent of West Country
clerics lost their posts in the first twelve years of Elizabeth's reign.[150]

   The majority of these dutiful clerical followers of royal policy seem unlikely to have harboured any profound enthusiasm for Protestantism. Even
in London clerical wills for the last years of Henry's reign show an almost
complete absence of reformist sentiment, and the majority, through traditional intercessory forms and specific bequests, indicate their identity with
Catholic belief.[151] In Suffolk the clergy were far slower than the laity to
abandon the traditional form of spiritual commendation in their wills, and
readopted it more rapidly under Mary.[152] Reformers could find themselves
ostracized within their localities: the vicar of Yoxford, Suffolk, who wrote
evangelical dramas, complained to Cromwell that the clergy would have no
dealings with him.[153] There are examples of clerics who acknowledged
their shifting behaviour as a simple consequence of *force majeure*. An Exeter
cleric who had sworn not to return to the Mass did so under Mary, defending himself to his friend Mayor Midwinter, 'It is no remedy, man, it is no
remedy.'[154] In other cases priests tried to replicate the old services within the
new, or simply abandoned the struggle to their curates, as did John Thack-
wray of East Retford, who settled with a local gentry family in order to
escape the demands of Reformation.[155] Other forms of retreat were

---

[148] R. Whiting, *The Blind Devotion of the People: Popular Religion and the English Reformation*
(Cambridge, 1989), 230. J. Vowell alias Hooker, *Description and Account of the City of Exeter*
(Exeter, 1765), 82.

[149] H. Gee, *The Elizabethan Clergy and Settlement of Religion* (Oxford, 1898), 236–47.

[150] C.A. Haigh, *English Reformations: Religion, Politics and Society under the Tudors* (Oxford,
1993), 243–4.

[151] Brigden, *London*, 396–7.

[152] MacCulloch, *Suffolk*, 161–2; though the small sample for the diocese of Ely in the same
period shows more movement: the group that have rejected some aspect of traditional will-
making outnumber the full conservatives by 1547: F. Heal, 'The parish clergy and the Reformation in the Diocese of Ely', *Proceedings of the Cambridgeshire and Huntingdonshire Archaeological
Society* (1974), 152–3. For good examples of conservatism in practice see Haigh, *English Reformations*, 178, 248 ff. P. Marshall, *The Face of the Pastoral Ministry in the East Riding, 1525–1595*,
Borthwick Papers 88 (York, 1995).

[153] *LP* xii. i. 529. For an interesting discussion of the letter see Ryrie, 'English Evangelical
Reformers', 9–14.

[154] W.T. MacCaffrey, *Exeter, 1540–1640* (Cambridge, Mass., 1958), 191–2.

[155] D. Marcombe, *English Small Town Life: Retford 1520–1642* (Nottingham, 1993), 167–8.

possible: the Winchester vicar and minor canon Thomas Dackcomb, who was a zealous book collector, seems to have used his intellectual interests as a means of expressing a traditionalism that was otherwise inadmissable.[156]

One of the most accessible explanations for this resistance to change is the pattern of recruitment to the English church in these disturbed decades. On the eve of Henry's break with Rome the Church was, if anything, overstaffed. The 1520s had been a particularly significant decade for recruitment in a longer period of considerable growth in the number of ordinands. These were the men who were to fill the parishes for the next generation, either because they had moved directly into benefices and curacies, or because they were regulars, or chantry chaplains, and then sought places in the parochial church after the dissolutions. Meanwhile, the number coming forward for ordination declined, at first slowly and then precipitately in the Edwardian years.[157] Some of the decline must be attributed to ideological resistance to change: in the Diocese of Oxford, in which many of those emerging from the university would normally be ordained, there were no ordinations between 1551 and 1554, precisely the years when the new Edwardian ordinal was in use. In Chester, Lincoln, and Durham there seem to have been no ordinations between 1547 and 1554 or later.[158] Where the fall in recruitment occurs from the 1530s onwards, as it does in Exeter and Winchester, it must be presumed that the insecurity of the Church and competition from the regulars, as well as changed ideology, had disrupted ordination. The consequences were the same in any case: a high dependence on pre-Reformation clerics to service the parishes and too few new recruits who might have had exposure to reform through education or would be entering the Church because of a vocation to Protestant ministry.[159] 'It seems unlikely', says Margaret Bowker, 'from the evidence of the ordination lists that the religion of the statute books became the religion of men's hearts.'[160]

Declining numbers of ordinands eventually resulted in structural difficulties for the parishes, though the worst effects of the gaps in manpower did not reveal themselves until Elizabeth's reign. Kentish parishes were still able to muster an average of 1.17 clerics per parish in 1550, a marked decline from a pre-Reformation figure of almost 2 but not catastrophic.[161] In the

---

[156] F. Bussby, *Winchester Cathedral, 1079–1979* (Southampton, 1979), 110.
[157] M. Bowker, 'The Henrician Reformation and the parish clergy', in C. Haigh (ed.), *The English Reformation Revised* (Cambridge, 1987), 78–84, 92.
[158] Thompson, 'Pastoral Work', 179–85.
[159] C. Cross, 'Ordinations in the Diocese of York, 1500–1630', in C. Cross (ed.), *Patronage and Recruitment in the Tudor and Early Stuart Church* (Borthwick Studies in History, York, 1996), 8–12.
[160] Bowker, 'Parish clergy', 92.
[161] M. Zell, 'The personnel of the clergy in Kent in the Reformation period', *EHR* 89 (1974), 517–24.

Marian period the combination of the dislocation caused by deprivations for marriage and the high mortality of 1557 to 1558 rapidly worsened the situation. As numbers contracted, the inflexibility of the parochial structure began to reveal itself more sharply. The smaller clerical proletariat of Kent did not always serve the most urgent parochial need, and in some cases turnover was high and vacancies inevitable. At the other end of the country the loss of the regular clergy proved critical in the Scottish Borders, where friars had provided much of the manpower in areas like Annandale.[162] In the first few post-dissolution years the ex-religious seem to have stayed with their flocks. By the beginning of Elizabeth's reign few Englishmen were coming forward to supply the gaps created by death, and many parishes and chapelries came to depend on Scottish clerics, who were often fleeing the effect of religious change in their own land. The other structural change produced by the dissolutions, the displacement of benefices into the hands of the laity and higher clergy, was yet another form of difficulty, particularly in the early years when ownership could shift rapidly. The additional patronage received by the bishops in the course of exchanges with the crown was of long-term significance in enabling them to influence the parishes ideologically. But the much more numerically dominant translation of benefices into lay hands had ambiguous consequences. Several dioceses saw a decline in the proportion of graduates recruited to parish livings—from 39 per cent for Canterbury under Warham to 25 per cent in the post-Reformation years, from 53 per cent to 48 per cent in the fortunate diocese of Ely—and lay patronage was probably as important an explanation as declining graduate numbers.[163] In Bristol, where the problem has been studied at community level, the transfer of the patronage of a significant number of city churches to the Brayne family certainly contributed to the decline in the educational quality of the parish clergy identified by Skeeters.[164]

The argument has at this point lost sight of the vision of conformity embodied by William Sheppard. But positive aspects of conformity must surely be invoked if we are not to read the English and Welsh clergy as all living their lives in profound alienation from the church to which they had been recruited. For Sheppard, at least in the Elizabethan years, the sustaining structures of his ecclesiastical universe were divine commandment, royal injunction, and 'the decent rites of the Church of Christ'.[165]

---

[162] S.M. Keeling, 'The Reformation in the Anglo-Scottish borders', *Northern History* 15 (1979), 28–9.

[163] Heal, 'Bishops of Ely', 86. Bowker's figures for Lincoln, which stop in 1547, combine ordination and vacancy calculations to indicate that the situation must have rapidly become worse under Edward, Bowker, *Henrician Reformation*, 121–6.

[164] Skeeters, *Community and Clergy*, 94–8, 117–20.

[165] Byford, 'Price of Protestantism', 42–5.

It needed a full focus on the middle of these three to help reconcile the conscience to changes in the last, something that must have occurred in many parsonages in these years. The clergy of Hooper's Gloucestershire proved very deficient when interrogated: 168 of the 312 investigated in 1551 could not repeat the Ten Commandments; using the English Bible, thirty-nine could not locate the Lord's Prayer; but even some of the least secure had assimilated the importance of the royal supremacy. Three attributed the Lord's Prayer to 'Our Lord the King'.[166] If such adherence to the royal will proved an imperfect justification for turning, then there was always the pastoral virtue of continuity to ensure the proper cure of souls and the resolution of local conflict. Even Christopher Trychay emerged into the Elizabethan era as a conformist who was 'more than a grudging' minimalist: continuing to preach and care for his flock.[167]

The most profound social change experienced by the mid-Tudor clergy—the possibility of marriage—may perhaps most usefully be read in the light of the reconciliation of the reluctant to the new order of things.[168] There were a few cases of clerical marriage that long preceded the grudging legislative permission of 1549. In the 1530s reformers anticipated that Cranmer and Cromwell would move Henry VIII towards the acceptance of marriage, little comprehending his deep antipathy, suddenly made visible in the Six Articles. At this stage the deliberate choice of marriage cannot be separated from evangelical sentiment. To take just two examples, the vicar of Mendlesham, Suffolk, who was in trouble for marrying in 1537, was from a community deeply identified with radicalism, and William Turner wed at the time of the Six Articles as a part of his renunciation of Henricianism before departing for exile.[169] The most dramatic case comes from Scotland in 1539, where a group of reforming priests attended the wedding of their colleague the vicar of Tullibody, breaking the Lenten fast in order to do so. Three regulars and one secular, plus one layman, were burned at Edinburgh for this offence.[170] After Edward's accession it became clear that clerical marriage was likely to be permitted, though attempts to gain parliamentary

[166] Litzenberger, *Gloucestershire*, 70–1. K.G. Powell, 'The beginnings of Protestantism in Gloucestershire', *Transactions of the Bristol and Gloucester Archaeological Society* 90 (1971), 141–57.

[167] Duffy, *Morebath*, 175–6. Both Zell and Bowker also emphasize that the relative security of benefices in comparison with all other forms of clerical employment must be seen as a major element in the immobility of parochial clergy.

[168] For good summaries of the issue of clerical marriage see P. Marshall, The *Catholic Priesthood and the English Reformation* (Oxford, 1994), 163–73; E. Carlson, 'Clerical marriage and the English Reformation', *JBS* 31 (1992), 1–31. By far the most thorough investigation of the phenomenon is by H. Parish, *Clerical Marriage and the English Reformation* (Aldershot, 2000).

[169] MacCulloch, *Suffolk*, 178–9. E. Carlson, 'The marriage of William Turner', *HR* 65 (1992), 336–9.

[170] R. Pitcairn (ed.), *Ancient Criminal Trials of Scotland*, 3 vols. (Bannatyne Club, Edinburgh, 1829–33), i. 216–17.

sanction in 1547 failed and only in 1549 were such unions made legal, even then with the less than ringing endorsement that they were the remedy for sin.[171]

Thereafter the clergy began to marry in considerable numbers, though with wide variations between dioceses. Historians have calculated rates of married clergy using the somewhat difficult records for deprivations under Mary.[172] It is estimated that one in three clergy married in London and Essex, one in four in Norwich diocese, but one in ten or less in Exeter, Coventry and Lichfield, and Winchester. Among English areas that have been studied in detail Lancashire is the outlier, with only seven of its over 250 clergy apparently married at the beginning of Mary's reign.[173] Only two Welsh sees, St David's and Bangor, can be calculated, and they produce figures of one in six and one in eight respectively.[174] As for Ireland, although several of the bishops and higher clergy lost benefices at the beginning of Mary's reign because of marriage, there is very limited evidence on those holding parochial livings. Only two parochial clergy seem to have been deprived in the Diocese of Dublin, though as usual the situation was made complicated by concerns to assail concubinage as well as marriage.[175] These marked disparities have long led historians to associate sympathy with reform among the clergy with a propensity to marry, especially since it has become clear that there was a considerable weight of lay opinion against the marriage of priests. Why risk social ostracism, runs the argument, unless there was an ideological as well as a practical incentive to marry?

Reformers often married, and congregations that had some sympathy with change may have offered some encouragement. Robert Parkyn argued that those who married showed their true identity by refusing to elevate the host at Mass even before the 1549 Prayer Book was enforced.[176] A linkage between clerical marriage and Protestant sympathy is indicated by the complaint from Kent in 1554 that there were no priests to serve at Sandwich, a reform-minded community, because of depriv-

---

[171] 3EVI c. 17.

[172] The English sources are marshalled in E.J. Carlson, *Marriage and the English Reformation* (Oxford, 1994), and in Parish, *Clerical Marriage*.

[173] The Lancashire figures, unusual in including parochial assistants as well as incumbents, are included in Haigh's calculations: C.A. Haigh, *Reformation and Resistance in Tudor Lancashire* (Cambridge, 1987), 180–2.

[174] The Welsh figures have only recently been calculated in Williams, *Wales and the Reformation*, 195–7.

[175] M.V. Ronan, *The Reformation in Dublin, 1536–1558* (1926), 428–9. Jefferies, *Priests and Prelates*, 166, indicates that deprivations in Armagh are very unlikely, but the firm evidence is missing. Murray, 'Tudor Diocese of Dublin', points to the embarrassment caused to the revived cathedral of St Patrick's in late 1555 when it was revealed that Richard Johnson, one of the prebendaries, had been married: p. 209.

[176] I am indebted to Dr Parish for the ensuing analysis. Parish, *Clerical Marriage*, 180 ff.

ation for marriage.[177] It is also implied by the fact that in the same year Ipswich had only two priests to serve the parishes.[178] In many cases, however, the alacrity with which clerics disposed of their spouses in 1554 and were prepared to accept other benefices after deprivation suggests a lack of commitment to either marriage or reform. And in some extreme cases marriage was the only change that the cleric embraced. Philip Stanlake of Little Cheverell in Salisbury diocese had a wife, yet was in trouble at the 1553 visitation for failing to preach in a parish where the high altar had not been destroyed.[179] There is some evidence from the Dioceses of Chichester and Winchester that other inducements to marriage may have been significant, especially the behaviour of near neighbours among the clergy. Clusters of parishes with married priests can be identified in Sussex, not only in the Rye and Winchelsea area, which was radicalized under Edward, but in the Weald and in the extreme west of the county, which seem to have been thoroughly conservative in other ways.[180] At most the association between clerical marriage and Protestantism can only be argued in the negative: strong Catholic identities were not compatible with taking a wife, since the unchaste priest polluted the sacraments. For the rest it might be most useful to regard marriage as one of those elements that helped to create a certain loyalty to the Protestant regimes among a drifting and often disorientated body of clergy. As John Foster had argued to Cromwell as early as 1538, had Henry allowed marriage he would have found doubly loyal priests, 'first in love, secondly for fear that the bishop of Rome should set on his power unto their desolation'.[181] The predisposition to marriage, which once again revealed itself rapidly after Elizabeth's accession, does something to prove his case. Few clergy would martyr themselves before a determined regime on this issue: given choice, however, many of them embarked once again on what was inevitably a contract with the crown against Rome. The bad news for the Edwardian reformers was that only a minority entered this contract in the years of uncertainty: even on this weak test of loyalty to the new order of things the parish clergy were found wanting.

---

177 Zell, 'Clergy in Kent', 530.   178 MacCulloch, *Suffolk*, 174–5.
179 Parish, *Clerical Marriage*, 209.   180 Ibid., 217–19.
181 BL Cottonian MS Cleo. EIV, fo. 140.

6

RESPONSES TO CHANGE: THE LAITY AND THE CHURCH

The Defence of Tradition

Seldom can the 'bare ruined choirs' of lost Catholicism have been evoked so powerfully as in Eamon Duffy's *The Stripping of the Altars*. His study of the process of desacralization is introduced with a haunting lament for the loss of the shrine of Our Lady at Walsingham, possibly written by the Elizabethan earl of Arundel. Its concluding stanzas express a bitterness that departs from the elegiac quality of Shakespeare's lament for the loss of the 'sweet birds':

> Weep, weep, O Walsingham,
> Whose days are nights,
> Blessings turned to blasphemies,
> Holy deeds to despites.
> Sin is where Our Lady sat,
> Heaven turned is to hell.
> Satan sits where Our Lord did sway;
> Walsingham, O, farewell.[1]

A world lost, and sins felt with an intensity that shakes the historian's tendency to analytical complacency. Few were able to say anything so explicit in the England of Elizabeth, but we must accept with Duffy that the sentiments were still felt by many. They were alive in Bartholomew Hussey, who scribbled in a Winchester service book, 'I pray God I may live to see the Mass to be said in England again, for that to see it would glad my heart so much as anything in the world.'[2]

---

[1] E. Jones (ed.), *The New Oxford Book of Sixteenth Century Verse* (Oxford, 1991), 551. E. Duffy, *The Stripping of the Altars: Traditional Religion in England 1400–1580* (New Haven, Conn., 1992), 377–8.

[2] F. Bussby (ed.), *Winchester Cathedral, 1079 1979* (Southampton, 1979), 110.

Powerful evocation of traditional belief still, however, begs questions about the nature of 'traditional' religion in the age of crisis. The first is whether the popular Catholicism of the 1520s was significantly changed by the experience of conflict and persecution. The second, and far more intractable, question concerns the quality and quantity of commitment to the old ways. In both areas there is now a rich secondary literature, which may justify some rather summary generalizations, before we turn to the exponents of change.

Any consideration of alterations in the nature of Catholicism between the 1520s and Mary's reign must first assume that it was continuities with the old world that the laity valued.[3] Several years before Mary was restored John Ponet had complained that men urged one another to 'believe as your forefathers have done before you...follow ancient customs and usages'.[4] The most popular of the Marian polemicists, Miles Hogarde, looked back to a time when England lived in 'marvellous love and amity, in true dealing and honest simplicity'.[5] The Mass had been at the heart of English religious experience then, and it seems abundantly evident that it was the promise of the restoration of the Mass that galvanized support for Marian religious policy long before the full range of her intentions became visible. In July and August 1553 there were many examples of clergy and ordinary parishioners anticipating government action by setting up altars and returning to the old service, especially after Mary's ambiguously worded proclamation of 18 August seemed to sanction their behaviour. By the beginning of September Robert Parkyn was reporting triumphantly that 'very few parish churches in Yorkshire but mass was song or said in Latin'.[6] In Ireland a horrified Bale observed how the clergy and laity rushed to set up the Mass again: 'they brought forth their copes, candlesticks, holy water stock.... They mustered forth in general procession most gorgeously all the town over'.[7] The wardens of Stanford-in-the-Vale, Oxfordshire, went one stage further by immediately selling their communion table, the symbol of the 'wicked time of schism'.[8] But even in the heartland of reforming influence there were similar demonstrations: Mass was being sung in London as early as 6 August, and after the proclamation it began in four or five of the city churches 'not by commandment but of the people's devotion'.[9] By Sep-

---

[3] See discussion and examples in Duffy, *Stripping of the Altars*, 524 ff., C. Haigh, *English Reformations*, (Oxford, 1993), 205–12 and D. Loades, *The Reign of Mary Tudor* (1979), 98–102.

[4] A. Gasquet and E. Bishop, *Edward VI and the Book of Common Prayer* (1928), 257–8.

[5] M. Hogarde, *The displaying of the Protestantes* (1556), fo. 92.

[6] 'Robert Parkyn's Narrative', in A.G. Dickens, *Reformation Studies* (1982), 309.

[7] P. Happé and J. King (eds.), *The Vocacyon of John Bale* (Binghamton, N.Y., 1990), 62.

[8] R. Hutton, 'The local impact of the Tudor reformations', in C. Haigh (ed.), *The English Reformation Revisited* (Cambridge, 1987), 128.

[9] S. Brigden, *London and the Reformation* (Oxford, 1989), 528–32.

tember a hostile witness was reporting the Mass as 'very rife' in London.[10] At Poole the zealous Thomas Hancock prevented his congregation from saying Mass in church, only to find that a powerful group had begun the traditional service in the house of Thomas White.[11]

Since the Marian regime was in accord with these enthusiasts about the urgency of restoring the Mass, it is not surprising that the evidence of the churchwardens' accounts is of sustained effort to recover the impedimenta of traditional worship. Altars and altar-cloths, Mass vestments, chalices, pyxes, censors and sacring bells are recorded as purchased or retrieved in parish after parish.[12] The accounts, and following them surviving visitation returns, suggest that much of this kind was done quickly and effectively, though structural work to replace altars and rebuild roods, and the accumulation of proper texts for worship, sometimes lagged behind the more strictly ceremonial items. Pole, as we have seen, deliberately encouraged this sense of the renewal of tradition since 'the observation of ceremonies, for obedience sake, will give more light than the reading of the scriptures'.[13] Other elements in the old religion that lent support to this basic restoration of ceremony were also taken up with enthusiasm in the localities. The Corporation of York restored the Marian plays that had been excluded under Edward from the Corpus Christi mystery cycle; and a host of communities that had actually suppressed their religious drama revived it under royal encouragement.[14] Other feasts and processions, Whit Monday in Leicestershire, Becket's feast in Canterbury, Palm Sunday processions, can be traced in the surviving records.[15]

When Marian Catholicism did not revert fully to its early Henrician past, it was often because some institutional change was almost irreversible, or because economic considerations made it impossible.[16] Time was short and continuing political and religious uncertainties made givers cautious. Will-makers sometimes hedged their provisions for obits and chantries with the caveat 'if the law will suffer it'.[17] And where, as in Gloucester diocese, systematic studies of wills have been undertaken for the Marian period, they show a decline both in structured provision

---

[10] BL Harl. MS 353, fo.143[v].

[11] J.G. Nichols (ed.), *Narratives of the Days of the Reformation*, CS OS 57 (1859), 82–3.

[12] Haigh, *English Reformations*, 210–13. Hutton, 'Local impact', 128–31.

[13] J. Strype, *Ecclesiastical Memorials*, 3 vols. in 7 (1816), iii. 2. 503.

[14] D. Palliser, *Tudor York* (Oxford, 1979), 242. D. Galloway (ed.), *Norwich 1540–1642* (Records of Early English Drama, Toronto, 1984), 343–4. M. McClendon, *The Quiet Reformation: Magistrates and the Emergence of Protestantism in Tudor Norwich* (Stanford, Calif., 1999), 167.

[15] R. Hutton, *The Rise and Fall of Merry England: The Ritual Year, 1400–1700* (Oxford, 1994), 98.

[16] Hutton, 'Local impact', 131–3.

[17] P. Collinson, *The Birthpangs of Protestant England* (1988), 40.

for the soul's health and in the donation of small, ritualistic gifts to the Church.[18] Each could be explained by lingering doubts about the good sense of such donations in the circumstances. However, it is possible to argue that wills point the historian towards slow changes in the nature of traditional religious behaviour. The two areas of pre-Reformation giving that appear less significant in Marian wills are those for prayer for the dead and support for the saints. Confidence in the contract between the living and the dead, with its mutuality of benefit, seems to have been shaken by the attack on the chantries. The paraphernalia of obits, bede-rolls, and provision for individual intercessory prayers did not return at pre-Reformation levels. And within the body of the Church the restoration of the rood took priority over the renewal of saints' images.[19]

The difficult evidence of will preambles, which do not automatically express the sentiments of individual testators, also suggest a diversification away from the traditional invocation of saints and towards more Christocentric forms of devotion. The latter, as Duffy indicates, were nothing new, but they appear somewhat more regularly in this period, perhaps in response to the challenge of reform.[20] When Joan Holder, or her scribe, wrote in 1556 that she bequeathed her soul to 'God my creator and redeemer unto whose mercy I commit myself unto, trusting by the merits of his passion to inherit the kingdom of heaven and also desiring our blessed Lady with all the whole company of heaven to pray for me', she

[18] C. Litzenberger, *The English Reformation and the Laity: Gloucestershire, 1540–1580* (Cambridge, 1997), 91–8.

[19] Haigh, *English Reformations*, 215. Duffy, *Stripping of the Altars*, 563–4.

[20] Duffy, *Stripping of the Altars*, 518–22, emphasizes the diversity and the Christocentric quality of Marian wills, but is perhaps too keen to argue that these are continuities. I do not propose to dilate in detail on the battle on the meaning of wills which has preoccupied historians of the Reformation period for the past thirty years. Much sound and fury, and some light, have been directed to the evaluation of will preambles as a source of evidence for belief. The literature is well-summarized in appendix A of Litzenberger's study of Gloucester. There is also a systematic discussion in a thesis by M.D. Lucas, 'Popular Religious Attitudes in Urban Lincolnshire during the Reformation: The Will Evidence 1520–1600', University of Nottingham Ph.D. (1998). One of the best of the summaries is C. Marsh, 'In the name of God? Will-making and faith in Early Modern England', in G.H. Martin and P. Spufford (eds.), *The Records of the Nation* (Woodbridge, 1990), 215–49. There is still no consensus on exactly how much weight can be put upon this evidence, but the following points have emerged relatively clearly from the debate. (1) Will-makers in early modern England normally drew up their testaments only shortly before death. (2) Most wills were actually prepared by scribes, and the opinion, or training, of those scribes often played a part in determining the formulae used. (3) Will-makers and their advisers had reason to be cautious in the expression of unorthodox views lest these failed to pass the process of probate in the ecclesiastical courts. (4) For devout testators the bequest of the soul remained of great significance and was unlikely wholly to be surrendered to a third party. Litzenberger adds the important point that the samples taken by historians to demonstrate points from wills have often been too small, or too imprecisely used, to yield any valid results. Although will evidence is used in this and other chapters I wish to avoid placing great trust in the quantitative findings of historians.

was reflecting an orthodox Catholic consciousness that had surely been honed somewhat by the experiences of a world lost.[21]

The second issue, that of the scale of adhesion to traditional and Catholic beliefs and practice, is difficult and controversial. It remains easiest to approach via negation: that for the laity, as for the clergy, there is only limited evidence of the committed acceptance of the new. Even though the approximately 3,000 visible reformers whom Fines was able to count are only a section of those who worked for change under Henry and Edward, even calculating to the largest iceberg would only produce a small minority in a population of 2.5 to 3.0 million. The question is whether the bulk of the rest should be identified as Catholic, or should be assimilated under that useful, but inherently ambiguous, term 'neuter'. Neuters were the uncommitted and indifferent: they were also the confused, and the outwardly conformist who might inwardly believe differently, three categories that are themselves somewhat distinct. When, early in Elizabeth's reign, the bishops were asked to categorize the JPs into three groups, their neuters, roughly a third of the whole, were essentially those who would probably conform, but would do little to enforce the new settlement.[22] The ideologically committed, both Protestant and Catholic, were prone bitterly to denounce such men as *nullifidians*, 'not regarding any doctrine, so they may be quiet to live after their own wills and minds'.[23] And there are examples of laymen who respond to religious upheaval by plaguing all houses. On the other hand, the church papist that emerged in the later sixteenth century has obvious antecedents in the grudging conformist under Edward.[24]

None of the materials historians can use to evaluate lay opinion—wills, church court records, churchwardens' accounts, material accumulated by the government at times of civil disturbance—come near to offering us a full opportunity to assess the views of the silent majority. The attempts to calculate the part of the population that was resistant to organized religion has often taken the form of trying to estimate church attendance.[25] But this is impossible for the mid-century since the ecclesiastical authorities became interested in attendance as a test of orthodoxy only after 1559. Of

---

[21] Litzenberger, *Gloucester*, 93.

[22] M. Bateson (ed.), 'A collection of original letters from the bishops to the Privy Council', *Camden Society Miscellany* 9, CS NS 53 (1895), pp. iii–iv.

[23] S. Bateman, *A christall glasse of Christian reformation* (1569), sig. G4.

[24] A. Walsham, *Church Papists: Catholicism, Conformity and Confessional Polemic in Early Modern England* (1993), 73 ff.

[25] K. Thomas, *Religion and the Decline of Magic* (1971), 190, 204. Some generalizations by historians about church attendance are set out in C. Marsh, *Popular Religion in Sixteenth-Century England* (Basingstoke, 1998), 43–4. Most of the valuable estimates are for the later sixteenth century: see particularly M. Ingram, 'From reformation to toleration: popular religious cultures in England, 1540–1690', in T. Harris (ed.), *Popular Culture in England, c.1500–1850* (Basingstoke, 1995), 111–12. See below, pp. 465–7.

'The nullifidians' watch the priests attacking the preacher. Stephen Bateman,
A Christall Glasse (1569). Permission of the Bodleian Library

much more significance was the general insistence on obedience, the dominant ethos, it has been suggested, of the early Church of England.[26] Obedience was constantly tested for those in any authority: among the laity in the
parish it was most demanded of the churchwardens. Their response, in so
far as it can be traced through the fragmented records, was generally consistent. When the royal will was clear (by no means always the case as in the
first year of Edward's reign) the work of destruction in the churches was
carried out obediently, even though the importation of new materials like
Bibles was much less consistent. Indeed, a recent study of East Anglia concludes that only in the 1560s did the vast majority of parishes have access to
the key texts of Protestant Reformation.[27] The most important investigation of the body of material left behind by the wardens concludes that the
most remarkable feature of the record is the capacity of the Tudor regimes

[26] R. Rex, 'The crisis of obedience: God's Word and Henry's Reformation', *HJ* 39 (1996),
863–94.
[27] I am grateful to Greg Duke for this information.

to compel obedience from their subjects. That obedience moreover, while sometimes grudgingly given, especially under Edward, appears more than simply a yielding to power: it is as though, says Hutton, the English and Welsh had 'a limited capacity to sustain any beliefs attacked by both leading churchmen and by the Crown'.[28] This can be contrasted interestingly with the situation in Ireland, where a measure of political obedience was not necessarily associated with religious conformity, even in the case of many of the leaders of the Old English community.[29]

Above the parish and its wardens the interests of lay rulers in town and countryside was more often served by acquiescence in the royal will than by challenge to it. Once again, however, conformity conceals a very wide range of detailed responses and known sympathies. If we take the example of some of the English cities that have been studied in detail an interesting gamut of behaviour emerges. York remained an essentially conservative city, and was the only one exposed to the charge of disobedience for the distinctly ambiguous role that some of its aldermen played in 1536 when the Pilgrims of Grace occupied it. Thereafter, it made an ostentatious duty of following the crown, while still revealing, in, for example, the celebrations at the accession of Mary, where its sentiments lay.[30] Bristol was another city that learned, painfully, to make a virtue of neutrality and caution. For much of the 1530s it was caught up in the ideological conflicts generated by Latimer's preaching campaigns: the corporation at odds with many of its clergy. After several bruising incidents, in which governmental support for local initiative was at best ambiguous, the city fathers adopted an explicit policy of following the royal will as closely as possible. In February 1540, for example, they were calculating what course to steer in the aftermath of a visitation by Latimer's successor at Worcester, John Bell, and decided to ask Cromwell to send a representative to Bristol to 'reform certain points'.[31] Norwich's conformity, on the other hand, took the form of avoidance of trouble from the outset, prompting its historian's labelling of its 'quiet Reformation'. Divided religious sentiment was largely contained within the boundaries of the city and its courts. The external face that Norwich chose to present to the world, except during the crisis of Kett's rebellion, was one of studied acceptance of the providential wisdom of Tudor regimes.[32]

---

[28] Hutton, 'Local impact', 138.

[29] C. Lennon, *The Lords of Dublin in the Age of Reformation* (Dublin, 1989), 128–34, 141.

[30] Palliser, *Tudor York*, 234–44.

[31] M.C. Skeeters, *Community and Clergy: Bristol and the Reformation, c.1530–c.1570* (Oxford, 1993), 34–56. K.G. Powell, *The Marian Martyrs and the Reformation in Bristol* (Bristol, 1972).

[32] McClendon, *Quiet Reformation*, 61 ff. Similar contrasts emerge in smaller urban centres: Lucas shows convincing will evidence of early sympathy for reform among the lay leaders of Grantham and Boston, while Grimsby remained largely immune to change until the second generation of Elizabeth's reign. Lucas, 'Popular Religious Attitudes', 68 ff.

That calm, studied, or sullen, acceptance of the demands of the powers that be routinely prevents historians from reading the actuality of popular sentiment.[33] Those who, in the words of Sir Thomas Smith, had no part in rule, could usually evade the intrusive eye of governors lay and clerical.[34] It was common for commissioners and JPs to comment that the people were 'quiet and conformable', the equivalent of that bland *omnia bene* with which so many churchwardens repelled episcopal interrogators and subsequent historians.[35] But the indications of a reluctance to change the customary patterns of faith remain widespread in these years, almost certainly justifying the comment of the French ambassador in 1539 that the people were 'much more inclined to the old religion than to new opinions'.[36] For example, will makers in many parts of the country returned more rapidly to traditional formulae on Mary's accession than they jettisoned such patterns under Henry and Edward. We have already noted the evidence of enthusiasm for the return of the Mass ahead of official Marian pronouncements. The language of conformity could itself contain firm expressions of orthodoxy, as in the two parishes of the divided community of Marian Colchester that pronounced their devotion to 'the laws of the Catholic Church and of the King and Queen', when simply asked if the parishioners attended divine service.[37] It is rare for historians to study a community like Colchester and not to find that it contained committed Catholics resisting Protestant preaching. Even Hadleigh, a 'University of the learned' under the godly Rowland Taylor, still harboured traditionalists among its leading clothiers, and its churchwardens showed a distinct reluctance to turn their church into a preaching house.[38]

Sustained and militant resistance to religious changes ordered by authority was uncommon for the laity as for the clergy. What can be adduced, especially in the evidence forwarded to Cromwell in the 1530s, is a widespread resentment at the attack on images and other supports of the traditional faith. Parishioners, like their clergy, were often angered by the changes. A fine example comes from Chilham in Kent in the difficult days of 1543. The vicar, Dr John Willoughby, a known and articulate traditionalist, was ordered to destroy his rood, targeted by the diocesan authorities as a monument of superstition. He assembled the leaders of the

---

[33] R. Whiting, *Local Responses to the English Reformation* (1997), 117 ff.

[34] Sir Thomas Smith, *De Republica Anglorum*, ed. M. Dewar (Cambridge, 1982), 76.

[35] Marsh, *Popular Religion*, 201–2.

[36] *LP* xiv. i. 1092.

[37] L.M. Higgs, *Godliness and Governance in Tudor Colchester* (Ann Arbor, Mich., 1998), 172.

[38] J. Craig, 'Reformers, conflict and revisionism: the Reformation in sixteenth-century Hadleigh', *HJ* 42 (1999), 18–20.

parish, and with their assent devised a response invoking The King's Book to protect the images, thereafter locking the church against the ecclesiastical officials. In this case Willoughby escaped the consequences of disobedience through the protection of conservative Kentish JPs.[39] A more normal result in the years of reformist ascendancy would have been the loss of the rood, its images possibly secreted away against better times. When priests conformed and sought to enforce the royal will laymen, unconstrained by deference to their spiritual authority, often protested vigorously. The curate of Beverley read the royal injunctions for the abrogation of saints' days in 1536 but the parishioners collectively insisted 'they would have their holydays bid and kept as before'.[40] In St David's at the end of the decade Bishop Barlow complained that the people were 'wilfully solemnizing' the feast of their patron saint and continuing to venerate his relics.[41] The catalyst for the 1549 Prayer Book Rebellion was the reading of the new liturgy by the vicar of Sampford Courtenay: resistance by a small group of parishioners was then emulated by the whole congregation.[42] Habits of deference and obedience were not necessarily proof against strongly held religious principles and the fact that the laity had long been organizing much of their own local religious lives. But to resist was to rebel. One of the most painful of learning experiences for the ordinary parishioner committed to the old faith was that communal autonomy in matters of religion was now challenged by the power of the crown. The power of the saints, like so much else, now deferred to that of the supreme head of the *ecclesia Anglicana*.

When ordinary laymen did take the fatal step of rebellion for the sake of religion their most clearly articulated motives were the protection of parochial worship.[43] The Lancashire pilgrims in 1536 saw the defence of their local churches, and the promotion of good priests, as prime reasons for protest.[44] The Lincolnshire rising which preceded the main pilgrimage undoubtedly drew much of its early support from the belief that the king was about to suppress local churches as well as the monasteries.[45] Less usually, there is the case of the group of women who terrorized the

---

[39] *LP* xviii. ii. 303, 319, discussed by Duffy, *Stripping of the Altars*, 441–2.

[40] *LP* xii. i. 201, this incident immediately preceded the Pilgrimage of Grace, and may help to explain Beverley's involvement in it.

[41] *LP* xiii. i. 604.

[42] J. Vowell alias Hooker, *The Description and Account of the City of Exeter* (Exeter, 1765), 34–5.

[43] The debate on motives for revolt is extensive and need not be trawled here. See the good summary in A. Fletcher and D. MacCulloch, *Tudor Rebellions*, 4th edn. (1997), esp. 117 ff.

[44] C.S.L. Davies, 'Popular religion and the Pilgrimage of Grace', in C.S.L. Davies and J. Stevenson (eds.), *Order and Disorder in Early Modern England* (Cambridge, 1985), 58–88.

[45] M. Bowker, 'Lincolnshire in 1536: heresy, schism or religious discontent', in D. Baker (ed.), *Heresy, Schism and Religious Protest*, SCH 9 (1972), 227–43.

workman seeking to demolish the rood of St Nicholas Priory, Exeter, in 1536. They presumably saw a monastic house as the focus of their religious practice.[46] The Helston revolt of 1548 in Cornwall was, as far as can be discerned, another attempt to resist the destruction of images in the parish church.[47] But the laity who rose were at the least persuaded by their leaders of the necessity of appeal to wider religious principles: the return of the spiritual power of the papacy in the case of the Pilgrimage of Grace; a moratorium on further religious change during the minority for the Helston rebels; the rejection of Prayer Book innovation in 1549. The evidence is too slender to talk of a more informed popular Catholicism emerging from the mid-Tudor decades. Yet we might suggest that traditionalists, like their Protestant opponents, began to understand that a greater confessional awareness was a necessary consequence of crown behaviour.

Evangelical Environments

The coming of Reformation in England and Scotland has thus far been explained largely in political terms, as the consequence of decisions taken within a circumscribed environment by councillors and clerics driven principally by royal choice. Yet even if a state-centred view of religious change is deemed most appropriate, the response of those who had to enforce reform remains crucial, and the leaven of men who were committed to the new evangelism essential. For Protestantism to gain sufficient control in either realm it needed committed nobles, gentlemen, and magistrates to enforce the royal will, or to stand against it in the case of Scotland, and determined preachers to disseminate the new ideology. It also needed foot soldiers, to provide the beginning of engagement in the parishes and, as it transpired, to show the fidelity to the new truth that produced a significant band of martyrs. Where all these elements were present, as they were at different times north and south of the Anglo-Scottish border, a Reformation could be made. Where they were lacking, as in Ireland, the royal will alone could make little headway.

There were, of course, a myriad of individual routes away from Rome and towards Protestantism, many of them impenetrable to the historian. But it is possible to consider what Haigh calls the 'formation of a minority' in structural terms, and especially to look at the environments that facilitated the ideological transactions that could lead to conversion. The

---

[46] W. MacCaffrey, *Exeter 1540–1640* (Cambridge, Mass., 1975), 182.

[47] R. Whiting, *The Blind Devotion of the People: Popular Religion and the English Reformation* (Cambridge, 1989), 76, 118.

environment that is most immediately significant is that of the royal court. The Henrician court offered a critical focus for forms of religiosity that migrated between Erasmian pietism, biblical evangelicalism, and outright rejection of Catholic belief.[48] In Scotland, where James V's insistence on orthodoxy made it dangerous to stray too far from Catholicism, sections of the court embraced both humanist ideas and evangelical concerns.[49] In both courts the background to new forms of devotion was on the one hand the well-established tradition of aristocratic pietism, with its concern for the inward life, and on the other the growing heterodoxy of the French court. Anne Boleyn may have 'fetched her evangelism' from France, and the Scottish nobility were also exposed to some of the cultural influences of the new French pietism.[50]

Courtiers were not necessarily constructed into piety, nor were the pious necessarily led to question orthodox beliefs. Most of the leading humanists of Henry's early court remained in some degree Catholic when crisis came in the 1530s.[51] But a milieu which placed great emphasis on education, for women of high status as well as men, and that offered the time for intellectual debate, proved very fruitful for the promotion of new ideas. The Boleyn circle, especially her brother George, Lord Rochford and the poet Thomas Wyatt, exemplify the evangelicalism of the Henrician court.[52] Wyatt's guarded translations of the penitential psalms reveal enough awareness of solifidianism to be more than an orthodox devotional cycle. Rochford's more explicit commitment is summed up in his scaffold speech in which he expressed proper penitence, not in usual forms but because he had not 'in very deed kept God's holy word even as I read it and reasoned about it'.[53]

[48] On the theme of court and reform see M. Dowling, 'The gospel and the court: reformation under Henry VIII', in P. Lake and M. Dowling (eds.), *Protestantism and the National Church* (1987), 36–77; J.K. McConica, *English Humanists and Reformation Politics under Henry VIII and Edward VI* (Oxford, 1968).

[49] C. Edington, *Court and Culture in Renaissance Scotland: Sir David Lindsay of the Mount* (E. Linton, E. Lothian, 1995).

[50] E. Ives, *Anne Boleyn* (Oxford, 1986), 42, 317–24, though Ives warns that the timing of Anne's contacts with the Margaret of Angoulême circle is such that it makes this an unlikely source of immediate religious influence. For Scotland see Edington, *Court and Culture*, 164–6.

[51] L.E.C. Wooding, *Rethinking Catholicism in Reformation England* (Oxford, 2000), 16 ff., emphasizes, however, the degree to which humanist Catholicism remained reformist in the 1530s. McConica, *English Humanists*, though this tends to emphasize the continuity between earlier humanism and the 1530s at the expense of new influences from France.

[52] Dowling, 'Gospel and court', 52–6. The current researches of James Carley into the library of Henry VIII will also throw further light on the reforming texts owned by the Boleyn circle.

[53] R.A. Rebolz (ed.), *The Complete Poems of Thomas Wyatt* (1978), 195–216. Ives, *Anne Boleyn*, 306.

From a few key sympathizers with the gospel in the court at the beginning of the 1530s—the example of William Butts can be added to that of Anne and her allies—new ideas circulated outwards through the networks of patronage and political contact. Sympathetic chaplains and tutors were employed, and through scripture reading and debate the merits of reform were laid before key sections of the elite.[54] Two vignettes exemplify this cycle of exchange: Nicolas Bourbon, a French reformer who had to flee for his beliefs in 1535 approached Butts, who turned to Anne Boleyn for support. She employed him, amongst other things putting him to tutor three children of courtiers. He was drawn by Holbein and dedicated verses, his *Nugae*, to like-minded courtiers.[55] A decade later another set of verses, John Parkhurst's *Ludicra sive Epigrammata* weaves within its pages compliments to a wider evangelical network based upon the court: the Brandon, Dudley, and Grey families, Edward Bainton and William Butts, Cranmer, Cox, Cheke, and Sir Anthony Cooke as Edward's tutors, Sir Anthony Cope and Anne Carew from Catherine Parr's household.[56] Many of these shared in the vicissitudes of the reform cause in the last lethal months of Henry's reign. This was a world which in its most exaggerated manifestation produced a self-confident autodidact like Sir John Gates, who on the scaffold in 1554 described himself as 'the greatest reader of scripture that might be of a man of my degree' while formally regretting that he had interpreted it 'after my own brain and affection'.[57]

The courtly world offered access to new ideas and debates not only to the elite of the household of magnificence. Fragmentary evidence reveals evangelicals, and even radical Protestants, within the bourg of court. Edward Underhill, one of the gentlemen pensioners, wrote the story of his imprisonment under Mary for Foxe, and claimed with confidence that there was 'no better place to shift the Easter time', that is to avoid partaking of the sacrament, than the queen's court. He identified 'favourers of the gospel' among the guard, including the lieutenant Sir Humphrey Ratcliffe, who ensured that his wages were paid to him though he was a known Protestant.[58] Even more remarkable is the case of Robert Cooch, one of the most articulate of the mid-century radicals, who began his career as wine steward to Catherine Parr. Bishop Parkhurst described him to the Swiss Rodolph

[54] Dowling, 'Anne Boleyn as patron', in D. Starkey (ed.), *Henry VIII: A European Court in England* (1991), 107–11.

[55] M. Dowling (ed.), 'William Latymer's Chronickille of Anne Bulleyn', *Camden Miscellany* 30, CS 4th ser. 39 (1990), 56.

[56] J. Parkhurst, *Ludicra sive Epigrammata Juvenilia* (1573). Parkhurst was later Elizabethan bishop of Norwich.

[57] P.C. Swensen, 'Noble Hunters of the Romish Fox: Religious Reform at the Tudor Court, 1542–1564', University of California, Berkeley, Ph.D. (1981), 174.

[58] J.G. Nichols (ed.), *Narratives of the Days of the Reformation*, CS os 57 (1859), 149, 161.

Gualter as an accomplished man and skilled musician who 'very frequently troubled Coverdale and myself by controversies' and was always eager to argue with any visiting divines such as John Jewel.[59] Cooch became a gentleman of the chapel royal and may have organized gathered meetings within the court. He was forced to recant once in the 1570s in order to retain his post, but seems to have returned to his radicalism, and may well have been associated with sectarians of the Family of Love who had some hold among the yeomen of the guard in that decade.[60]

There are marked parallels between the development of evangelical sentiment at the Scottish and English courts. James V's court also had its humanists who turned evangelical, most notably David Lindsay of the Mount and the young George Buchanan, and its evangelicals already sympathetic to Luther, especially Sir John Borthwick; James Kirkcaldy of the Grange, the Royal Treasurer; James Learmouth of Dairsie, the Master of the Household; Henry Balnaves, the Treasurer's Clerk; and Thomas Bellenden, the Justice Clerk.[61] Like their English counterparts these men seem to have reinforced one another through patronage, and by showing what support they could for clergy of a reforming disposition. They shared an interest in the vernacular scriptures that came briefly to fruition when Balnaves was one of the sponsors of the parliamentary bill of 1543 permitting the English Bible. They used the medium of drama to disseminate anti-clerical and reforming ideals.[62] The existence of a reform movement at the centre of the English court gave them the confidence to press for change at home, something that is most directly visible in Borthwick's attempts to 'Cromwellianize' Scotland. What they lacked was any ability to capture influence over the Church, where the monarch's consistent refusal to contemplate reform stood against them. Borthwick was made a sacrificial victim to demonstrate James's orthodoxy, though he escaped final punishment by fleeing to England.[63] Yet despite the king's antipathy the influence of the reformers depended on the continuing existence of a strong court, and the crises of the regency weakened central structures in sharp contrast to the situation in England. The conflicts of the 1540s dispersed a number of them to exile, but also ensured that they and their families became important adherents of reform after 1559.

---

[59] G.C. Gorham (ed.), *Gleanings of a Few Scattered Ears during the Reformation*, 2 vols. (1857), i. 481–2.

[60] C.J. Clement, *Religious Radicalism in England, 1535–1565* (Carlisle, 1997), 237–59.

[61] Edington, *Court and Culture*, 44–57, 163 ff.

[62] J. Durkan, 'The cultural background in sixteenth-century Scotland', in D. McRoberts (ed.), *Essays on the Scottish Reformation, 1513–1625* (Glasgow, 1962), 274–331.

[63] J. Durkan, 'Scottish "evangelicals" in the patronage of Thomas Cromwell', *RSCHS* 21 (1983), 127–56.

The mobility of courts provided opportunities for their denizens to influence others by contact and example. The young George Buchanan, for instance, seems to have forged links with men in Stirling later executed for heresy when visiting the area with the king at Easter 1538. He also later claimed to have been influenced by anti-papal *picturae* brought to the Jacobean court by Henry's ambassador, William Barlow.[64] That these were life and death issues, part of the deadly struggle for the future of the Church, does not preclude an element of fashion in the behaviour of the English or Scottish court. For example, elite sponsorship of drama proved to be one of the most attractive means of reaching out to a wider audience. In the 1530s Cromwell set the example by his patronage of John Bale, and several others like George, Lord Rochford had their own 'men' who played interludes on evangelical themes.[65] So fashionable were 'scripture interludes' in this decade that even Lady Lisle, a great bulwark of traditional religion at Calais, wanted her agent John Husee to find her a scriptural play for the Christmas festivities of 1538. Husee responded that he would try to do so, 'but these new ecclesiastical matters will be hard to come by'.[66] Later, when conservatism once again seemed triumphant, the key office of Master of the Revels was held by Sir Thomas Cawarden, one of the reform-minded members of the Privy Chamber, who continued to promote the new drama whenever he was able to do so. The same combination of deadly earnest desire for reform, and the ability to use the fashionable court medium of drama for its exposition, lies at the heart of the impact of Sir David Lindsay in Scotland. Like Cawarden he kept alive a critical drama in difficult times, producing the *Tragedie of Cardinall Betoun* in 1547 and his masterpiece *The Thrie Estates* in the early 1550s. The performance of the latter in August 1554 on the slopes of Carlton Hill, Edinburgh, brought together the court and nobility, with a 'great concourse of people', who watched the spectacle for the whole day.[67]

Given the vitality of reforming ideas at the English and Scottish courts it is tempting to pose the counter-factual question: what if Ireland had possessed an equivalent cultural and political centre? So acutely different were the circumstances of Henry VIII's second realm that the question is unanswerable. However, it is worth noting that those Irish nobles who

[64] I.D. McFarlane, *Buchanan* (1981), 50, 68–70.

[65] P. Whitefield White, *Theatre and Reformation: Protestantism, Patronage and Playing in Tudor England* (Cambridge, 1993), 15–46.

[66] *LP* iv. 4942. S. Baker House, 'Literature, drama and politics', in D. MacCulloch (ed.), *The Reign of Henry VIII* (Basingstoke, 1995), 15–16.

[67] R. Lyall (ed.), *Sir David Lindsay of the Mount: Ane Satyre of the Thrie Estaitis* (Edinburgh, 1989), introduction. Brother Kenneth, 'The popular literature of the Scottish Reformation', in McRoberts, *Scottish Reformation*, 173.

were exposed to the English court occasionally responded positively to the atmosphere of change. James Butler, heir to the earl of Ormond, knew the court in the 1520s, but maintained his contacts through intermarriage with the Boleyns, and in 1538 wrote to the king with an enthusiasm for the 'set[ting] forth the word of God to the people', which is only partially explained by the political advantage such a stand offered his family in Irish politics.[68] He corresponded with Latimer, from whom he requested some 'good works'.[69] A generation later the well-known intimacy between Edward VI and his school-fellow Barnaby Fitzpatrick, later second baron of Upper Ossory, produced an Irish loyalist who, while no determined Protestant, identified strongly with the intellectual world of his upbringing.[70] The later training of Donough O'Brien, fourth earl of Thomond, at the Elizabethan court was a more marked success story in the inculcation of Protestant values, surprising even the privy council by the unwavering loyalism it produced.[71] But these were isolated cases: the Irish magnates lacked any domestic environment in which to assimilate new ideas or to pursue the political benefits of Protestantism.

While courts offered the most significant opportunity for the exposure of the lay elites to new beliefs, the leading clergy of the reformed movement were principally nurtured in the scholastic environment of the universities. John Foxe's well-known description of the White Horse tavern meetings at Cambridge, at which the 'godly learned' of seven colleges met in the 1520s to debate the gospel, may read Protestantism into intellectual debate *avant la lettre*.[72] Yet there is no doubt that the university was the breeding-ground for radical questioning of the existing order of the Church. From the Cambridge in which Robert Barnes is said to have planned his first explicit challenge to the Church of 1525 in the company of Bilney, George Stafford, and Latimer, heresy spread to Oxford by the unlikely medium of Wolsey, who imported a subversive group of scholars to his new foundation of Cardinal's College. The arrest in 1528 of the Lutheran student and bookseller Thomas Garrard began an investigation that revealed that many 'inexpert youth' had been exposed to the poison of heterodox ideas.[73] For a time

---

[68] *SP HVIII* ii. 563. R.D. Edwards, *Church and State in Tudor Ireland* (1935), 33–5, though Edwards is dismissive of Butler's Protestant credentials.

[69] *SP HVIII* iii. 32.

[70] *DNB*.

[71] Ellis, *Tudor Ireland*, 288.

[72] Foxe, v. 415. Gardiner was being somewhat disingenuous about his own early flirtation with this academic debate when in 1545 he described how he was 'familiar with such sort of men' because 'there was not in them malice, and they maintained communication having some savour of learning'. J.A. Muller (ed.), *The Letters of Stephen Gardiner* (Cambridge, 1933), 166.

[73] J. McConica (ed.), *The History of the University of Oxford*, vol. iii: *The Collegiate University* (Oxford, 1986), 123–4.

Oxford succeeded in closing its doors upon the danger: at Cambridge, on the other hand, religious controversy had a continuous history, never fully dislocated by the growing vigour of episcopal persecution. Even in the more conservative Oxford MacCulloch has found it possible, using Fines's figures, to identify 189 graduates of the pre-Elizabethan era who held evangelical opinions.[74] In the case of Scotland St Andrews seemed destined to play a role similar to that of Cambridge. Patrick Hamilton's return from Germany to the university in 1528 and his trial and execution there created religious conflict.[75] Alexander Alesius was converted by Hamilton's example, having been an academic opponent earlier in the decade. Among its constituent colleges St Leonard's was thereafter thought to be heterodox: those sympathizing with religious change were said to have 'drunk at St Leonard's Well'.[76] But Scottish politics did not allow sustained dissent within an institution so close to the control of the archbishops. Even after the burning of Wishart in 1544 and the murder of Cardinal Beaton, Knox and his followers did not meet with unqualified success in preaching reform within the university. It is difficult to argue that any of the Scottish universities provided a critical environment for reform before 1558.[77]

Universities also offered crucial opportunities for the interaction of clergy and laity: those who could influence the state as well as ruling the church. The Cambridge of the later 1530s and 1540s demonstrates this process most significantly. Among those leading lay evangelicals who emerged at the centre of power under Edward and especially under Elizabeth there were key figures who had spent some time in higher education. William Cecil established himself at the heart of what Hudson has rightly called the Cambridge connection.[78] Seven members of Elizabeth's privy council had been at Cambridge, as had many of the second-rank administrators who sustained the Protestant establishment. Beneath this key political elite there is already the beginning of signs of the universities influencing those sons of gentlemen sent to them for a humanist training in ideological directions. Among those who went into exile under Mary, for example, were Thomas Dannett, gentleman, a student of St John's and friend of John Aylmer, future bishop of London. Another gentleman was

---

[74] D. MacCulloch, *Tudor Church Militant: Edward VI and the Protestant Reformation* (1999), 111.

[75] Foxe, v. 421–9.

[76] H. Ellis, *Original Letters Illustrative of English History*, 3rd ser. (1827), i. 240.

[77] I.B. Cowan, *The Scottish Reformation: Church and Society in Sixteenth-Century Scotland* (1982), 94, 102–3. It is, however, important to note that both St Andrews and Aberdeen sustained the type of advanced humanism that could issue in reformed ideology: J. Kirk, 'The religion of early Scottish Protestants', in J. Kirk (ed.), *Humanism and Reform: The Church in Europe, England and Scotland, 1400–1643*, SCH Subsidia 9 (Oxford, 1991), 363–5.

[78] W.S. Hudson, *The Cambridge Connection and the Elizabethan Settlement of 1559* (Durham, N.C., 1980), 34 ff.

Christopher Hales, again trained at St John's, who was to have a future as an active supporter of non-conformity.[79] Parallel developments can be traced among committed Catholics, with the networks established under Mary often sustaining religious exiles during and after the 1560s.

In the case of England, the universities, and especially Cambridge, played key roles as environments for nurturing religious change. One of the problems for those seeking the conversion of Ireland was the absence of any institutions of higher education that might have provided access open to new theories circulating in texts. There were certainly plenty of internal critics of Irish education who argued that ignorance and barbarism continued partly because there was no indigenous university to raise men in civility.[80] The project for an Irish university, quite regularly debated during the sixteenth century, acquired a new urgency when religious change was at issue. In 1547 Archbishop Browne produced a detailed scheme for the erection of a college financed by the dissolution of St Patrick's Cathedral, with the guilds and chantries. Its objectives were 'the unspeakable reformation' of the kingdom, and the education of youths in the knowledge of God and obedience to the king.[81] Since the plan for a university was not implemented until 1591 we cannot judge whether Browne's college would have changed the commitment of the Irish clergy to reform. The evidence of Scotland, and indeed of Oxford for much of the century, suggests that we should not be too ready to equate higher education with vigorous support for Protestantism. It may be more appropriate to argue that when a critical mass of intellectual support for change had developed, as at Cambridge, the university was peculiarly suited to the task of consolidating new knowledge and belief in its members.

When intellectuals did not learn their evangelism exclusively from the universities or the printed word, they usually assimilated it from Protestant environments in Germany and the Low Countries. A small but crucial number of the clerical reformers developed or enlarged their heterodox views as a consequence of study abroad. Tyndale, Frith, George Joye, Lambert, and Coverdale all fled abroad and acquired their full reformed

---

[79] C. Garrett, *The Marian Exiles* (Cambridge, 1938), 139, 171.

[80] See for example the famous speech of James Stanyhurst in the 1570 Irish parliament on the need for education and English civility: E. Campion, *Two Bokes of the Histories of Ireland*, ed. A.F. Vossen (1963), 180–1.

[81] *CPR Irl* i. 327–35. Printed in full in M.V. Ronan, *The Reformation in Dublin, 1536–1558* (1926), 322 ff. J. Murray, 'The Tudor Diocese of Dublin: Episcopal Government, Ecclesiastical Politics and the Enforcement of the Reformation, 1534–90', Trinity College Dublin Ph.D. (1997) argues that Browne's 'Device' was largely a protest against the plan to dissolve St Patrick's, which was destroying his capacity to administer his diocese. Later projects for the Irish university usually foundered on the problem of its finance, and also on the question of who would control its curriculum. Murray, 'Tudor Diocese of Dublin', 331–62.

theology only after they had experienced conversion in England.[82] Of
that first generation Robert Barnes was probably the only one who developed his initial critique while on the Continent, studying at Louvain.[83]
Equally striking is the number of this generation who had little or no
direct contact with what was happening overseas. Thomas Bilney is the
extreme case of a radical who depended very little on European example:
Latimer, Hilsey, and Ridley are among those bishops who never travelled
abroad: Barlow and Ferrar went no further than Scotland, until the former
was propelled into exile under Mary.[84] Even Cranmer, whose early
German travels for the crown were of great significance in his growing
understanding of the reform movement and for the structuring of his
networks of evangelical support, perforce developed his vision of Protestantism at home, without immediate experience of 'the best reformed
churches'. His enthusiasm for summoning aid from learned Continental
divines under Edward shows his awareness of the dangers of inexperi-
ence.[85] It took the Marian exile systematically to break down insularity in
the attitudes of the leaders of English Protestantism.

The contrast with Scotland is striking. The Scottish intellectual elite
entered the period of reformation with a far greater acceptance of the
internationalism of learning than that which characterized the English.
Students no longer had to leave Scotland to study: however, it was considered entirely normal that they should do so. Some of the earliest reformers were converted abroad, not at home. Patrick Hamilton, the
proto-martyr, learned his basic ideas in Paris and Louvain, though, like
his English counterparts, his developed Lutheranism was the product of
his period of exile after 1527.[86] Buchanan was launched into his long
quest for religious truth by his early experience of Paris. John Gau, the
publisher of one of the first Scots Lutheran texts, lived in Malmo and
probably absorbed his Lutheranism there. John MacAlpine and John Macdowell were graduates of Cologne in the heady days of German reformation.[87] All those clergy who made any stand for reform in the
mid-century were forced to choose exile, sometimes for a second time, or
risk execution. Hence the leading Scottish reformers became part of a far
longer diaspora than their English counterparts: Alesius ended in Leipzig
and never returned to his native land; MacAlpine became professor of

[82] W.A. Clebsch, *England's Earliest Protestants 1520–35* (New Haven, Conn., 1964), 78 ff.
[83] C.R. Trueman, *Luther's Legacy: Salvation and the English Reformers 1525–1556* (Oxford,
1994), 18–19.
[84] *DNB.*
[85] MacCulloch, *Cranmer*, 380 ff.
[86] J.E. McGoldrick, *Luther's Scottish Connections* (1989), 36.
[87] Ibid., 42 ff. Kirk, 'Early Scottish Protestants', 379–81.

theology at Copenhagen.[88] For those, like Knox, who eventually made the return after long exile there were both advantages and disadvantages in the separation from their native land. Their thorough understanding of the 'best reformed churches' was of great benefit in structuring the new kirk: but it created a yearning for the 'Calvinist international' and could lead to tensions with those, like Erskine of Dun, who had endeavoured to work quietly for reform within Scotland.[89]

An alternative or complementary context for the assimilation of reformed ideas by the clergy was the religious community. Robert Barnes made the Augustinian house at Cambridge 'flourish with good letters' and ideological debate in the 1520s.[90] In Scotland some of the most vigorous conflicts between the old and the new must have been fought out in the friaries of Perth, Dundee, and St Andrews, from which came a number of the key exiles of the 1530s and 1540s. The Dominicans, in particular, divided upon reform. Black friars were executed at Edinburgh in 1539, and were in the forefront of the preaching campaigns that flourished during the brief reforming phase of Arran's regency. The Augustinians also played a significant role in the early debates about reform.[91]

Beyond court and universities the environments that might nurture reform were heterogeneous. Since trade with the Low Countries was of great importance for both England and Scotland, men, books, and ideas constantly filtered into the ports from the imperial territories. One could list evidence of men suspected of heresy, or books seized, for most of the larger ports of the eastern and southern seaboards.[92] As early as 1525 it was reported around Aberdeen that 'sundry strangers and others...has books of that heretic Luther'. A decade later at Leith two Scots, a sea-skipper and a shipwright, were accused of heresy.[93] In Yorkshire the earliest heresy trials are of 'Dutchmen' in York and traders in Hull, and a number of prosecutions of outsiders continued into Mary's reign.[94] In the 1520s Tunstal's heresy investigations picked up Dutch sacramentarians in Colchester

[88] J. Dawson, 'The Scottish Reformation and the theatre of martyrdom', in D. Wood (ed.), *Martyrs and Martyrology*, SCH 30 (Oxford, 1993), 259–61.

[89] On Knox and exile see R. Greaves, 'The Knoxian paradox: ecumenism and nationalism in the Scottish Reformation', *RSCHS* 18 (1972), 85–98.

[90] Foxe, v. 415.

[91] Kirk, 'Early Scottish Protestants', 379–81.

[92] The detailed process of transmission is nicely exemplified in a case before Tunstal in 1528, in which John Hig, who may have been Dutch, was charged with translating from a 'Dutch' Gospel, and reading the book out loud to a London congregation during the elevation of the host. *LP* iv. 4038 (1).

[93] Knox, i. 56–8. Pitcairn, *Trials*, i. 321. Cowan, *Scottish Reformation*, 93, 97. The patterns of Anglo-Scottish trade may be another form of such exposure, especially in the case of Ayr, with its precocious Lollard community.

[94] A.G. Dickens, *Lollards and Protestants in the Diocese of York* (Oxford, 1959), 17–23.

and London, and Lutheran heretics among the merchants of the London Steelyard.[95] In 1530 Bishop Nykke of Norwich commented to the duke of Norfolk that only merchants and those living near the sea were infected with erroneous doctrines.[96] 'The Germans and Saxons', said Roger Edgeworth of the 1530s with visible distaste 'bring in their opinions'.[97] The key texts of reform, especially Tyndale's New Testament, were disseminated via the trading networks of Antwerp and London. The list could be continued and enlarged for both countries: especially important in London was the construction of the stranger churches under Edward, representing to the host community the best-reformed congregation.[98] But foreign individuals and groups were an equivocal model for the Scots and English. Xenophobia, especially among the latter, meant constraints upon the circulation of ideas: in 1551 the Spanish ambassador thought that the hostility of Londoners to outsiders was reinforced by the sight of large congregations at their church of Austin Friars.[99] And the religion that they brought with them did not necessarily accommodate itself to a well-defined mainstream Protestantism: radicals of many hues found it advantageous to escape to England from Continental persecution.[100]

The contexts in which most laymen gained access to evangelical ideas must have been the quotidian ones of parish, market-place, ale-house, and family. Here favourable conjunctions of circumstance were a necessary prelude to conversion. Areas of old heresy, in which families and individuals were attuned to the importance of the Bible and to anti-clericalism, provided one supportive environment.[101] The historical debate about continuities between Lollardy and Protestantism has recently been revived by valuable evidence of long-term continuities of dissent in the Chiltern heartland. It is now possible to give some genealogical flesh to the theory: Bartlets, Butterfields, Hardings, and others were suspect heretics in the early sixteenth century, their descendants were Baptists and Quakers in the mid-seventeenth century.[102] Such precision is unusual, but Essex and

---

[95] *LP* iv. i. 1962; ii. 1481, 4038. A.G. Chester, 'Robert Barnes and the burning of books', *Huntingdon Library Quarterly* 14 (1951), 216–19.

[96] R. Houlbrooke, 'Persecution of heresy and Protestantism in the Diocese of Norwich under Henry VIII', *Norwich Archaeology* 35 (1970/73), 313.

[97] J. Wilson (ed.), *R. Edgworth, Sermons very fruitfull, godly and learned* (Woodbridge, 1993), 197.

[98] A. Pettegree, *Foreign Protestant Communities in Sixteenth-Century London* (Oxford, 1986), 46 ff.

[99] *CSP Sp* x. 278–9.

[100] J.W. Martin, *Religious Radicals in Tudor England* (1989).

[101] A.G. Dickens, *The English Reformation*, 2nd edn. (1989), 56–60, summarizes the argument in favour of continuity. J.F. Davis, *Heresy and Reformation in the South-East of England, 1520–1559* (1983). For a sceptical view of Lollard influence see Haigh, *English Reformations*, 54–5.

[102] N. Evans, 'The descent of dissenters in the Chiltern Hundreds', in M. Spufford (ed.), *The World of Rural Dissenters, 1520–1725* (Cambridge, 1995), 288–308.

Suffolk have communities and areas in which the emergence of commitment to reform seems connected to older networks of Lollardy. The Stour valley and Mendlesham in Suffolk, Colchester, and Steeple Bumpstead in Essex seem to represent such continuities. A similar pattern is shown in London in groups who focused in families rather than parishes, and on conventicles like the one in Coleman Street uncovered by Tunstal, but gradually emerging into identity with the new faith. A good example is that of John Tewkesbury, a leatherseller, who had been a member of the Coleman Street group, and then was converted to Lutheran ideas by the texts given him by London evangelicals. He recanted once, was caught up in the persecution of 1531, and was burned.[103] The most remarkable evidence of continuity comes from south-west Scotland, where the small and isolated Lollard group of the 1490s does appear to have fed Ayr's growing reputation for radicalism half a century later. Again it is families who provide the inferential evidence of continuity: Campbells, Fullartons, and Reids were among those arrested in 1494: the same names are to be found in support of the campaigns leading to the Reformation.[104]

Urban environments were those most likely to offer access to reforming ideas where specific kin or trade networks were lacking. The complaint against Anthony Ward of Oundle in the 1530s reveals a process of transmission that must have been common. Ward told a group of friends in the local hostelry, the *Lion*, that on his recent visit to London he had heard a sermon against the reserved sacrament, and had attended a play, at which one of the actors appeared to challenge the real presence.[105] London's Protestant minority survived under Henry VIII, grew under Edward, and maintained a tenuous existence under Mary because it was nurtured by preaching, had ready access to the circulation of ideas in print and otherwise, and could network through the complex social structures of the city. Henry VIII's fears about the 'rhyming and jangling' of the scriptures in ale-houses resonate with our knowledge of heterodox views discussed in Colchester taverns under Mary. Thomas Tye, writing to Bonner from Colchester in 1556, lamented that 'the blessed sacrament of the altar is blasphemed and railed upon in every alehouse and tavern'.[106] Bristol citizens in the 1530s could scarcely avoid being caught up in the battle of

---

[103] Brigden, *London*, 86–106, 191.

[104] M.H.B. Sanderson, *Ayrshire and the Reformation* (East Lothian, 1997), 39–45. It is, of course, more problematic to be sure of immediate connection in the Scottish clan structure than in the nuclear families traced by Evans.

[105] P. Collinson and J. Craig (eds.), *The Reformation in English Towns, 1500–1640* (Basingstoke, 1998), introduction. A.G. Dickens, *Late Monasticism and the Reformation* (1994), 143.

[106] M. Byford, 'The birth of a Protestant town: the process of reformation in Tudor Colchester, 1530–1580', in Collinson and Craig, *English Towns*, 32. Higgs, *Godliness and Governance*, 146–81.

the pulpits.[107] The effects on community worship are vividly evoked by the conservative preacher Roger Edgeworth: men mock 'the divine service' which 'letteth and hindereth other men from their prayers, and from attending and hearing God's service'.[108] In Norwich, where the pulpits 'jangled' less aggressively, the cases investigated by the mayor's court indicate the way in which new ideas were spread within the face-to-face society of the city. Hand-bills and songs, both for and against religious change, were common, the spread of rumours through market-place and ale-house were reported, and the public stand of priests for or against change was much discussed. Demonstrations of a purely symbolic kind—a group eating meat in an ale-house during Lent—or a more violent kind— a priest and his adherents tearing down the altar of St Augustine's in 1549—were presumably intended to sway public opinion.[109] We know less in detail of the Scottish towns, but at least in Perth, Dundee, and Ayr the aggression of iconoclastic mobs must have depended in some degree on the circulation of reformed ideas and the emergence of a critical mass of townsmen who responded to them.[110]

Finally, there is the significance of the town as the arena in which the 'theatre of martyrdom' was presented.[111] Exemplary execution was not, of course, an exclusively urban phenomenon: Tudor and Stuart regimes punished wherever they believed the effects would be most powerfully felt, sometimes with faint regard to judicial convenience. But on the whole the monarchs and their agents pursued the principle that the larger the crowd of witnesses the better, and their subjects often concurred. Thomas Mountain, one of the Protestant clerics who narrowly escaped execution under Mary, describes how men and women had come to Cambridge from as far afield as Lincoln to witness his death only to be disappointed by the absence of a warrant.[112] The authorities carefully placed Henry Forrest's pyre in St Andrews so that it could be seen not only by the townsfolk but across the

---

[107] Skeeters, *Community and Clergy*, 57.

[108] J.M. Wilson, 'The *Sermons* of Roger Edgeworth: Reformation preaching in Bristol', in D. Williams (ed.), *Early Tudor England* (Woodbridge, 1989), 223–40.

[109] McClendon, *Quiet Reformation*, 138–41.

[110] Kirk, 'Early Scottish Protestants', 378 ff. Sanderson, *Ayrshire*, 61 ff.

[111] J.E.A. Dawson, 'The Scottish Reformation and the theatre of martyrdom', in D. Wood (ed.), *Martyrs and Martyrologies*, SCH 30 (Oxford, 1993), 259–70. The use of persecution as dramatized punishment has been considered most fully for France: D. Nicholls, 'The theatre of martyrdom in the French Reformation', *PP* 121 (1988), 49–53. Nicholls suggests that if the dramatized punishment is to work in favour of the authorities there has to be near unanimity of view against the victims in the community. This may explain why, as a rough generalization, the exemplary punishment of rebels worked more effectively for the state than that of heretics. See also S. Byman, 'Ritualistic acts and compulsive behaviour: the pattern of Tudor martyrdom', *AHR* 83 (1978), 625–43.

[112] Nichols, *Narratives of the Reformation*, 202–3.

Tay estuary.[113] There may have been occasional doubts: for example the city fathers of Exeter declined the pleasure of burning Thomas Bennet in 1531 and the sheriff had to move the execution to a nearby parish.[114] After Rowland Taylor's execution at Hadleigh his successor complained that 'it moveth many minds to see an heretic constant and to die'.[115] And while individual burnings might produce a variety of responses, the Marian holocaust proved too much in some towns: in Colchester in the last year of the reign the burnings became more furtive events, no longer triumphant affirmations of the return of the community to spiritual purity.[116]

Studies of German cities during the Reformation have shown that any discussion of the responsiveness of urban populations to religious change needs to be carefully nuanced. Some literacy and access to preaching may have been necessary conditions for reform to gain hold; they were rarely sufficient in themselves. It required social or political groups, or kin or neighbourhood networks to acquire a deep investment in new ideas for the tenor of urban behaviour to be altered.[117] Much of that investment was in the long run to come from the magistracy: by 1600 many Scottish and English communities had been led firmly in the direction of religious and moral reform by their corporations, representing themselves as 'Jerusalem...that is compact together in itself'.[118] In the troubled decades before 1560, however, few local regimes had begun to contemplate such reformation from above, when political survival seemed the main duty of the burghers. A recent historian of Reformation towns argues that preoccupation with the material consequences of monastic and chantry dissolutions is the defining feature of many local oligarchies.[119] Only a few towns—Canterbury and Sandwich in Kent, Rye in Sussex, and perhaps Ipswich—show clear signs of being driven by a powerful section of their elites towards godly reformation in the mid-Tudor years.[120] The situation

---

[113] Dawson, 'Theatre of martyrdom', 262.　　[114] MacCaffrey, *Exeter*, 186.

[115] BL Harl. MS 425, fo. 119ᵛ.

[116] Byford, 'Tudor Colchester', 31–3 and notes: the Marian persecution seems to have played a major role in Colchester in turning it into a strongly Protestant community. There are major problems in evaluating the collective reaction of the ordinary laymen who observed the gruesome deaths of the Scottish and English martyrs, both Protestant and Catholic, because the nature of the hagiographical narratives of these events is intended to conceal as much as reveal.

[117] There is, of course, a vast literature on the Reformation in the German cities. Reference to the valuable range of local and regional studies can be found in E. Cameron, *The European Reformation* (Oxford, 1988), ch. 15.

[118] Collinson, *Birthpangs*, 28–59.

[119] R. Tittler, *The Reformation and Towns in England* (Oxford, 1998), 59–136.

[120] P. Clark, 'Reform and radicalism in Kentish Towns *c*.1500–1553', in W.J. Mommsen (ed.), *Stadtbürgertum und Adel in der Reformation* (Stuttgart, 1979), 107–27. G. Mayhew, *Tudor Rye* (Brighton, 1987), 64–72. Ipswich had a 'common preacher' as early as 1551: P. Collinson, *The Religion of Protestants* (Oxford, 1982), 172.

of Exeter, where the 1549 Rebellion exposed a divided magistracy and a
majority opinion in favour of tradition, is probably more characteristic.
Fear of the consequences of rebellion compelled loyalty in the magistracy,
but the Protestant chronicler Hooker admits that there were those who
wanted to make alliance with the 'good and religious men' besieging
the city.[121] Finally the Irish trading cities—Cork, Galway, Waterford,
Dublin—should remind us that there was no deterministic connection
between an open urban environment and sympathy to reform. In Ireland
the story was reversed, and it was Catholic books and preachers that were
able to employ the networks of the towns in the interest of Counter-
Reformation proselytizing.[122]

In the light of recent research we might tentatively suggest that kin
networks among those who had some influence in their communities may
have been a more important agency for religious change. One important
example is Haigh's demonstration that Protestantism was planted in the
southern Lancashire towns by a network of Cambridge reformers supported by their families and friends.[123] Such kin networks proved crucial
to the diffusion of new ideas in the decentralized environment of Scotland.
The Campbell affinity is the best-known; but Ayrshire and Angus and the
Mearns, the early territories of reform, also reveal the centrality of a
number of less powerful lairds and their men in the process.[124] One interesting consequence, observed by the historian of Reformation Ayrshire, is
that religious change reversed the anticipated pattern and moved from
countryside to town.[125]

In England neighbourliness and friendship were likely to supplement
familial bonds. Early reform in Halifax was indebted to a group of substantial families, bound together by identity with their curate, rather than by a
particular trade or craft.[126] Some of the narratives of those who survived
the Marian persecution tell the same tale. Rose Hickman's reminiscences
of her family's experiences during the Marian persecution provide an excellent example of a Protestant network of this kind. Rose was the daughter of Sir William Locke, a London mercer involved in the importation of

---

[121] J. Hooker, *Description and Account of the City of Exeter* (Exeter, 1765), 71–2.

[122] B. Bradshaw, 'The Reformation in the cities: Cork, Limerick and Galway, 1534–1603',
in J. Bradley (ed.), *Settlement and Society in Medieval Ireland* (Kilkenny, 1988), 445–76.

[123] C. Haigh, *Reformation and Reaction in Tudor Lancashire* (Cambridge, 1979), 159–74.

[124] J. Dawson, 'Clan, kin and kirk: the Campbells and the Scottish Reformation', in N. Scott
Amos, A. Pettegree, and H. Van Nierop (eds.), *The Education of a Christian Society* (Aldershot,
1999), 211–41. Sanderson, *Ayrshire*, 64–80. F. Bardgett, *Scotland Reformed: The Reformation
in Angus and the Mearns* (Edinburgh, 1989), 42 ff.

[125] Sanderson, *Ayrshire*, 141.

[126] W. and S. Sheils, 'Textiles and reform: Halifax and its hinterland', in Collinson and Craig,
English Towns, 130–46.

Bibles in the early 1530s, who became an influential city trader. The family largely leaned to the new faith, though not always vigorously enough in the view of Sir William's daughter-in-law Anne, who became the close confidante of John Knox. By the beginning of Mary's reign Rose was married to another mercer, Anthony Hickman, and he and her brother played active roles in sustaining the imprisoned Protestants. This led to their imprisonment, where they in turn were assisted by a group of merchant friends themselves imprisoned for their misdemeanours as jurors in not finding Sir Nicholas Throckmorton guilty of treason in 1554. In the end the brothers purchased their liberty and Rose and her husband decamped to Antwerp until the end of Mary's 'tyrannous reign'. After her first husband's death in 1573 Rose remarried a Throckmorton, one of the Protestant branch of that ideologically divided family.[127]

The solidarities that constructed reform also derived on occasions from shared trade or profession. These can be glimpsed in Perth, where the *Perth Craftsmen's Book* reveals defence of craft liberties becoming enmeshed with reforming language from the 1540s onwards. This culminated in the remarkable 1558 document announcing the conversion of the community: 'God stirred up our whole community of merchants and crafts by the assistance of His Holy Spirit to be joined in one congregation of Christ...'[128] In London several of the City companies, including the Drapers, Grocers and Mercers, had cells of dissidents well before the 1530s.[129] General fellowship may explain as much here as shared economic interests, and historians are rightly suspicious of any determinist link between particular trades and religious change. The clothing industry is, however, usually identified as the most explicit example of this possible interconnection.[130] Weavers and tailors were disproportionately represented among the Essex Lollards, and once more among those persecuted under Mary.[131] Again and again it is the clothing towns of southern England that produce early examples of Protestant affinities, often amid a vigorous religious traditionalism.[132] John Careless, the Coventry weaver, was at the heart of a network bound together by

---

[127] M. Dowling and J. Shakespeare (eds.), 'The recollections of Rose Hickman', *BIHR* 55 (1982), 97–102.

[128] M.B. Verschaur, 'The Perth Craftsmen's Book', *RSCHS* 23 (1988), 157–74, 168.

[129] Brigden, *London*, 121–2. Of course, in general, the livery companies, like many other corporations, proceeded by slow adaptation to religious change, rather than some precocious turn to radicalism. Only by the 1570s was the new world firmly established in these essentially traditionalist organizations: J.P. Ward, 'Religious diversity and guild unity in early modern London', in E.F. Carlson (ed.), *Religion and the English People, 1560–1640* (1998), 77–97; N. Jones, *The English Reformation: Religion and Cultural Adaptation* (Oxford, 2002), 111–15.

[130] Martin, *Religious Radicals*, 133.

[131] J.E. Oxley, *The Reformation in Essex* (Manchester, 1965), 6–9, 216–37.

[132] A.D. Brown, *Popular Piety in Late Medieval England* (Oxford, 1995), 224 ff.

trade, to whom he wrote letters of exhortation during his King's Bench imprisonment.[133] Yet it is equally true that a number of the cloth manufacturing towns, even those like Lavenham in Suffolk that had some tradition of popular political dissent, were not centres of radical religion.[134]

There is a danger in focusing too explicitly on social networks and structures in seeking to explain early evangelical success. Access to the scriptures, for example, may have depended on favourable environment: the *intensity* with which they were experienced was essentially an individual matter. When James Bainham, husband of Simon Fish's widow, rejoiced that 'the truth of Holy Scripture' was now revealed after being hidden for 800 years, he gave voice to a very personal kind of wonder at God's providence.[135] John Porter read from the Bible placed in St Paul's in the late 1530s and proclaimed that Christ 'hath left the eternal life by his Word here amongst us'.[136] Conversion could be based directly on an assimilation of the vernacular scriptures as Bainham's story and many other narratives from the first generation of English Protestantism make clear. Rose Hickman described how her mother gained access to reformed ideas through books sent her from the Continent in the 1540s.[137] The Worcester apprentice John Davis claimed that he began to read the New Testament at the age of twelve and, partly out of fear of prosecution in Henry VIII's last years, kept his conversion secret until a friend manipulated the truth out of him and betrayed him.[138] There are also a number of Scottish examples of the intensity with which Scripture was experienced, like that of the five Dundee men and women executed in 1543 for, amongst other things, 'conferring and disputing...upon the holy scripture'.[139] David Straiton, executed in 1534, seems to have moved from anti-clericalism, and denying his teinds, to personal study of the New Testament, read to him by his nephew since he was illiterate, in a 'quiet place'.[140] Adam Wallace, of Ayrshire, burned in 1550, also appears as an autodidact, though he was not content with concealed faith, and evangelized 'at the table and sometimes in other privy places'.[141]

---

[133] Foxe, viii. 176–200, though it should be noted that he wrote to a very wide range of other individuals as well.

[134] D. McCulloch, *Suffolk and the Tudors: Politics and Religion in an English County, 1500–1600* (Oxford, 1986), 176–9, 291–8.

[135] Foxe, iv. 698–700: Bainham was one of the most committed of the Bible-men of pre-Reformation London, and was burned for his views in 1532.

[136] Brigden, *London*, 332–3.

[137] 'Recollections of Rose Hickman', 97.

[138] Nichols, *Narratives of the Reformation*, 60–3.

[139] D. Calderwood, *History of the Kirk of Scotland*, 8 vols. (Wodrow Soc., Edinburgh, 1842–9), i, 171–2.

[140] T. Thomson (ed.), *Diurnal of Remarkable Occurrents* (Edinburgh, 1833), 18–19.

[141] Kirk, 'Early Scottish Protestants', 382. Sanderson, *Ayrshire*, 50–1.

Taxonomies of Reform

Most inhabitants of England and Wales were neither James Bainham nor John Careless, and not only because the impulse to martyrdom was the prerogative of the few. The fluidity of the religious settlements destabilized most attempts to stand firmly upon an ideology which was nevertheless politically acceptable. In some ways the situation was more comprehensible north of the border than in the territories of the English king. There the clear intention of the crown and its advisers to remain within the Roman fold imposed certain limits upon challenges to the Church: to move beyond these was to make an explicit statement of opposition to royal policy. After 1542, when English intervention helped to crystallize the connections between politics and religious change, attitudes to the Church began to be used to identify groupings and parties. This only became fully visible in England, Wales, and Ireland under Mary: though we might also argue that the process of confessionalization was sufficiently developed in Edward's last years to increase the necessity of a firm response from faithful laymen of any religious persuasion.

What, in these circumstances, did maps of Scottish and English reform look like in 1558 and 1553 respectively and how did they compare? Scotland seems to have possessed scattered cells of reformed belief and behaviour, focused partly in the burghs, and in the universities, but increasingly dependent on the patronage of a section of the nobility and the lairds. The latter offered crucial protection that allowed the intermittent preaching campaigns and meetings with clerical reformers that were essential to the consolidation of Protestant sentiment. The process was iterative. Support for George Wishart in the 1540s, when for example he preached before the Earl Marischal and other nobles at Dundee, failed to protect him from the wrath of the bishops.[142] Ten years later the networks were sufficiently strong for Knox to travel and preach throughout Ayrshire and a significant part of the East Coast.[143] Success of this kind, however, depended upon secrecy rather than direct confrontation. Knox himself observed that the Protestants 'kept their conventions and held councils with such gravity and closeness that the enemies trembled', but it was the closeness that was most visible in 1555.[144] Networks of the 'privy kirks' can be faintly discerned in the years before the revolt of the Lords of the Congregation. They met in many of the larger burghs: and not only those that had produced early martyrs or shown overt aggression to the old church. Edinburgh, the only city for which detailed information has survived, had congregations that

---

[142] Cowan, *Scottish Reformation*, 101–4. Kirk, 'Early Scottish Protestants', 394–405.
[143] Bardgett, *Scotland Reformed*, 34–6. Sanderson, *Ayrshire*, 80–2.
[144] Knox, i. 256.

met in merchants' houses in the winter and the fields in summer. They elected elders and deacons, and chose individuals to exhort and read.[145]

Outside the burghs the houses of nobles and lairds provided the obvious focus for Protestant worship. Before 1555 this was perhaps no more than Bible-reading and discussion within the household. This can occasionally be described precisely, as in the case of the household of Robert Campbell of Kinzeancleuch, whose later chaplain John Davidson talked of the readings and prayers conducted there while the Church was 'under the cross'.[146] After 1555/6 Knox, in his own narrative, persuaded significant groups of lairds in Ayrshire and Angus and the Mearns to break with the old church and reject the Mass as idolatry.[147] In the Mearns John Erskine of Dun led this withdrawal, probably supported by a majority of the local landowners. In Ayrshire, a similar departure was led by John Lockhart and the earl of Glencairn, though there may have been more division of view among the lairds. Allegiance in both areas has to be understood in terms of local power structures, especially, as noted above, those of kin.[148] Kin-based authority was essentially contractual: a 'surname' or clan might be mobilized by the likes of the earls of Glencairn, but only in return for appropriate reward, and influence beyond the immediate kin group was limited. Thus in Kyle, or the Mearns, the lairds had some flexibility in the construction of religious identities because they were not closely tied to one or two great names. In other areas of Scotland, especially the north-east, as well as the majority of the Highland zone, the political elites seem to have remained untouched by reform until the crisis of 1558–9. The crucial conversion of the fourth earl of Argyll in the mid-1550s stands out in these circumstances as a defining moment for the broadening of Protestant support outside the heartlands.[149]

When a Protestant enthusiast in 1559 described 'the greatest fervency' for the movement as lying in the Mearns, Angus, Kyle, Fife, and Lothian, with Dundee as the outstanding example of a faithful burgh, he probably summarized the geographical extent of its impact.[150] As for the scale of

[145] J. Kirk, *Patterns of Reform* (Edinburgh, 1989), 9–15. M. Lynch, *Edinburgh and the Reformation* (Edinburgh, 1981), 31–2, 38–9, 83–5.

[146] Sanderson, *Ayrshire*, 108–9. Cowan, *Scottish Reformation*, 107.

[147] Bardgett, *Scotland Reformed*, 46–53. Knox, i. 120–2.

[148] On the need to fit an understanding of religious change into the study of local power structures see J. Wormald, '"Princes" and the regions in the Scottish Reformation', in N. MacDougall (ed.), *Church, Politics and Society* (Edinburgh, 1983), 65–84.

[149] Dawson, 'Clan, kin and kirk', 211–41.

[150] It is important not to divide burghs too sharply from nobles and lairds. All Scottish burghs were influenced by their hinterlands, and links can often be made explicit in the early history of the Reformation, for example in the case of Erskine of Dun's involvement in the establishment of the 'privy kirk' in Edinburgh: Knox, i. 119.

reformed influence: it can only be judged, and then very imperfectly, by the support offered in the initial period of the revolt of the Lords of the Congregation. Dundee, Ayr, Montrose, and (less clearly) Perth moved rapidly to establish reform. In Dundee even before the crisis the preaching of John Willock and Paul Methven strengthened the faithful who 'exceeded all the rest in zeal and boldness'.[151] Ayr town council dismissed its chaplains and banned private Masses in May 1559, long before any outcome of the armed revolt of the Lords of the Congregation could have been known.[152] James and George Bannatyne were also paid for riding to Edinburgh and 'bringing home a preacher'.[153] It is interesting that only slightly earlier the burgesses of Peebles had prevented a preacher from using 'any new innovations of common prayers or preaching'.[154] Popular support for reform, and hostility to it, undoubtedly existed in the Scotland of 1559. As usual, however, much is concealed from historical record. There was, for example, some sympathy for reform in St Andrews before 1559. But what are we to make of the attitudes of the good citizens who woke up on Sunday 11 June 1559 as Catholics and went to bed as Protestants by the will of the Lords of the Congregation? Their later pride in possessing one of the 'best reformed kirks' in Scotland is no substitute for evidence about their earlier engagements.[155]

It is difficult to find a precise moment at which to compare the taxonomy of the English Reformation with that of Scotland. The 1530s and the reign of Edward VI had legitimated reformed activity, and offered it partial state support in a way that did not occur north of the border until 1560. The textual instruments of the Protestant revolution—Bible, Prayer Book, and catechisms—had been placed in the hands of most of the clergy and some of the people. The economic interests of large sections of the elite had been linked to the rejection of Rome through the dispersal of the monastic and chantry lands, and the theology of obedience to the wishes of the crown had been articulated with all the rhetorical power at the disposal of the state. The taxonomy of Protestantism on the eve of Mary's accession therefore perforce included a large percentage of the population who sat in the pew week in and week out listening to the new messages of sermons and homilies, and not actively resisting whatever their inward beliefs. The fact that they remained in their places under

---

[151] R. Pitcairn (ed.), *Ancient Criminal Trials of Scotland*, 3 vols. (Bannatyne Club, Edinburgh, 1829–33), ii. 406–7. Knox, i. 300–1.

[152] Sanderson, *Ayrshire*, 90.

[153] G.S. Pryde (ed.), *Ayr Burgh Accounts, 1534–1624*, SHS 3rd ser. 28 (1937), 130.

[154] The preacher was John Willock. Cowan, *Scottish Reformation*, 113–14.

[155] J. Dawson, '"The Face of the Perfyt Reformed Kyrk": St Andrews and the early Scottish Reformation', SCH Subsidia 8 (Oxford, 1991), 413–55.

Mary has already been discussed. It would be attractive to think that we could penetrate the silence of these pews by examining wills, but we must conclude reluctantly that a gradual shift towards neutral and cautious formulae in testaments tells us little more than that it was desirable to be cautious under the male Tudors.

However, a taxonomy of a kind emerges from the ecclesiastical and other records of the mid-Tudor decades. Most Protestants who ran into trouble, or were at least noted by the authorities, were from London and the South-East. MacCulloch has calculated from Fines's records that 17 per cent came from London itself, 14 per cent from Essex, 12 per cent from Kent, and a further 15 per cent from Suffolk and Norfolk, the former predominating.[156] Within these figures there is a preponderance of urban dwellers, even if London is excluded. Approximately a third of those that can be identified by profession are drawn from the ranks of skilled craftsmen or traders. Beyond the confines of the South-East, only the Bristol hinterland and Thames Valley yield large numbers: only 2.5 per cent are drawn from the South-West, and only twenty-six lived in Wales. There are obvious dangers in focusing on the highly visible and dissident, notably that we are often gaining more access to the views of the prosecutors than the prosecuted. London's dissent immediately registered with regimes for whom internal security was of paramount importance. Evangelical activity in farthest Wales might well have escaped observation. Many, no doubt most, devout evangelicals managed to avoid particular notice under Henry and Edward, and conformed under Mary for fear and in hope of better times. Even the noisy might survive if they were part of a sympathetic community. But with all allowances made, the particular geographical nature, and the often cellular quality, of early Protestantism seems well articulated by the head-count. Even in the South there were areas that seem virtually untouched by more than a narrow conformity before Elizabeth's reign: Hampshire and West Sussex for example. Traditionalist bishops; patronage from gentry who remained overwhelmingly conservative; the absence of an indigenous Lollard tradition; few clothing centres and few large towns might be some of the environmental explanations. Yet it remains difficult to offer convincing reasons why Southampton or Portsmouth should not have followed the pattern of other coastal areas. John Bale, marooned in his Hampshire parish, felt alienated and complained that he had not seen 'blasphemy' like that of the

---

[156] MacCulloch, *Tudor Church Militant*, 109–11. For a detailed survey, calculating Fines's figures slightly differently and expressing more optimism about geographical spread, see Dickens, *English Reformation*, 325–30.

local 'frantic papist': this before he had been sent to Ireland as bishop of Ossory.[157]

Our taxonomy must include acknowledgement that active Protestants were in a minority even in those areas that showed their greatest numerical strength. It is possible to make some sort of appeal to the evidence of wills to argue that numbers of the committed were increasing, albeit slowly. In a series of studies, not always measuring exactly the same thing, historians have concluded that even in the high years of Edwardian Protestantism will-makers did not necessarily follow official lines.[158] Thirteen per cent of Londoners had unequivocally evangelical will formulae in the last years of Henry's reign; in the following reign between a third and a half adopted a formula that was explicitly Protestant.[159] The small group of wills available for the town of Boston, Lincolnshire, shows 51 per cent with solifidian preambles under Edward.[160] These look remarkably high percentages, when compared to Kent, which is said to have only 7 per cent Protestant wills in Edward's reign.[161] Seventeen per cent from Northamptonshire and Rutland, and 12 per cent from East Sussex approximate more closely to what might be anticipated.[162] The Diocese of York apparently has less than 5 per cent of wills with Protestant dedications of the soul during Edward's reign, though this from a starting-point before 1547 when there were none.[163] In Gloucestershire, the subject of by far the most thorough study of wills thus far undertaken, a large sample shows that under Edward 23 per cent of gentry wills were expressed in clearly Protestant terms, but only 6 per cent of non-elite wills were so unambiguous.[164] Norwich, which has a relatively high percentage of unambiguously Protestant wills under Edward—37 per cent—also shows a distinction between the small group of aldermanic wills, almost all reformist, and

---

[157] J. Bale, *Expostulation or complaynte agaynste the blasphemyes of a frantike papyst of Hamshyre* (?1552). The occasional Protestant in Hampshire seems worthy of very distinctive comment. See R. Fritze, '"A Rare Example of Godlyness amongst Gentlemen": the role of the Kingsmill and Gifford families in promoting the Reformation in Hampshire', in Lake and Dowling, *Protestantism*, 144–61. Fritze places the Kingsmills at the centre of a Protestant network, which did indeed begin to influence Hampshire politics after the first few years of Elizabeth's reign, but held precious little power between the fall of Cromwell and that period.

[158] For discussion of the problems of using wills as evidence, especially in any quantitative way, see above, p. 220.

[159] Brigden, *London*, 384, 486.

[160] Lucas, 'Popular Religious Attitudes', 113.

[161] P. Clark, *Reform and Revolution* (Hassocks, 1977), 58, 67.

[162] W.J. Sheils, *The Puritans in the Diocese of Peterborough, 1558–1610* (Northamptonshire Record Society, 1979), 15–16. Haigh, *English Reformations*, 200.

[163] A.G. Dickens, *Lollards and Protestants in the Diocese of York* (Oxford, 1959), 215, 220.

[164] Litzenberger, *Gloucestershire*, 75–9.

those of the rest of the population.[165] The figures have to be treated with the utmost caution, but they remain one of the few forms of evidence to offer indication of when, where, and by whom the new ideas were accepted positively.

Protestantism was in its inception a religion of protest, and it continued in this role in England and Wales for most of the Henrician period as well as under Mary. Even under Edward, as we have seen, committed Protestants often found it difficult fully to identify themselves with an establishment role. In Scotland protest was the inevitable mode until political victory in 1559. Hence there was always some tendency to attract those who had little to lose by challenging 'natural' hierarchy. The group usually emphasized here is the young.[166] This is partly because their elders consistently assumed that they would be delinquent, and therefore pounced upon supporting evidence of rebellion. Lucubrations such as Catholic complaints that 'lewd lads' were spreading heresy need to be treated with predictable caution. Footloose apprentices might bait Marian priests in London just for the pleasure of anarchy. Examples of schoolboy conflict— a fight between the old and the new religion at Bodmin School in 1549 and a mock battle in Finsbury fields between the 'troops' of Wyatt and Prince Philip in 1554—probably tell us more about the need to handle civil violence by re-enacting it than about the faith of youths.[167] There are, however, plenty of instances of confrontation between generations about beliefs. One of the best is Dickens's discovery of William Bull, an apprentice clothworker who learned his Protestantism in Ipswich in the 1540s and returned to Dewsbury to try to convert parents and neighbours, only to come to the attention of the authorities because of his trenchant evangelism. Eighteen-year-old John Tudson, also from Ipswich, was apprenticed in London and burned under Mary. The diarist Machyn says

---

[165] E.M. Sheppard, 'The Reformation and the citizens of Norwich', *Norfolk Archaeology* 38 (1983), 52–5. The smaller-scale studies that have been undertaken on individual communities show the dangers of generalization. Rye conforms to expectation, with at least a third of its Edwardian wills firmly Protestant and a complete elimination of the full Catholic formulae, but Hadleigh only produces five out of twenty-two, and one of the twenty-two is traditional. On the other hand Havering, Essex, where there was a distinct lack of effective clerical leadership, produces 26 per cent Protestant wills in the late Henrician period, and 43 per cent in the reign of Edward. Numbers in all cases are of course small and, in principle, individual scribal influence could therefore be particularly distorting, though it does not seem to be particularly evident in either Hadleigh or Havering. Mayhew, *Tudor Rye*, 63; Craig, 'Hadleigh', 17–19. M. McIntosh, *A Community Transformed: The Manor and Liberty of Havering, 1500–1620* (Cambridge, 1991), 188–90.

[166] S. Brigden, 'Youth and the English Reformation', *PP* 95 (1982), 37–67. Dickens, *English Reformation*, 334–8.

[167] A.L. Rowse, *Tudor Cornwall*, 2nd edn. (1969), 262. A.G. Dickens, 'The Battle of Finsbury Fields and its context', in *Late Monasticism and the Reformation* (1994), 177–90.

that all the young were banned from his burning.[168] He was in good, if tragic, company: Foxe's martyrs include a significant scattering of apprentices, serving maids, and 'young men', the age group to have learned their Protestantism under Edward.[169]

Protestant art both imitated and sought to mould the response of the young. Since the instruction of youth was a prime objective of the reformers it is not surprising to find that they often dramatized the experience of conversion. In *Nice Wanton* the Edwardian court was treated to a solemn study in the need to educate wayward youth.[170] William Baldwin's *Beware the Cat* has one cat tell a satirical tale of the old couple rooted in their faith in the Mass, which led their sons 'to be the more earnest to persuade them' to the new ways.[171] Lewis Wager's *Mary Magdalene* presents Mary as a young gentlewoman of the court, blaming her Catholic parents for the profligate lifestyle she had pursued.[172] Her counterpart in the real world, shorn of the profligacy, was Lady Hoby, who sententiously tried to convert her father, Sir Walter Stonor, from the Catholicism and fornication in which he was mired.[173] The drama which most obviously presents a *topos* closer to the life of ordinary Englishmen is *Lusty Juventus*, in which a youthful Everyman is tossed between vice and virtue, in the newer guises of the Old and the New Law. Juventus's conversion by Knowledge to an understanding of scriptural truth—'my elders never taught me so before'—must surely have resonated with at least some of the interlude's audience. So must the dramatic inversion in which the vice Hypocrisy is given lines of lamentation about the decay of natural obedience:

> The world was never mery
> Since children were so bolde;
> Now every boy wyl be a teacher,
> The father a foole, and the chyld a preacher....
> *Lusty Jurentus* (ll. 651–4)

---

[168] J. Nichols (ed.), *The Diary of Henry Machyn*, CS os 42 (1848), 99–100.

[169] Haigh, *English Reformations*, 190–1, notes eight who are identified by Foxe as nineteen or twenty, and a larger group in their early twenties, but there are many for whom no specific years are given. For a more questioning view of the engagement of youth in the Reformation see P.Griffiths, *Youth and Authority: Formative Experiences in England, 1560–1640* (Oxford, 1996), 178–9. See below, ch. 10, p. 466.

[170] White, *Theatre and Reformation*, 100–23.

[171] W.A. Ringler and M. Flachmann (eds.), *Beware the Cat by William Baldwin. The First English Novel* (San Marino, Calif., 1988), 37–9.

[172] J.N. King, *English Reformation Literature* (Princeton, N.J., 1982), 312–15.

[173] S. Brigden (ed.), 'The Letters of Richard Scudamore to Sir Philip Hoby, September 1549–March 1555', *Camden Miscellany* 30, CS 4th ser. 39 (1990), 100–1. For other examples see Jones, *English Reformation*, 35–8.

'God's word', moans the Devil, 'is...greatly sprung up among youth'.[174]
It seems likely that the Kilkenny boys who played John Bale's interludes
while he was bishop of Ossory were equally encouraged to rebel against
the old order.[175]

Evangelicals and Protestants remained a minority in all English and
Scottish environments before 1558: this was even more obviously so in
Wales, and Ireland seems virtually untouched by the new ideologies. The
minorities themselves are not always easily labelled, since reforming ideas
had arrived and been disseminated in a variety of forms. Moreover, the
clergy themselves were constantly grappling with changing official dogma.
In this world it is scarcely surprising that the range of the beliefs articulated by Edwardian Protestants and Marian martyrs do not conform tidily
to the mainstream solifidianism of Wittenberg, Zurich, or Geneva. The
taxonomy of popular Protestantism has to include those who John Foxe as
martyrologist preferred to exclude from his story, or to redefine into
orthodoxy.[176] The best-known group are the freewillers who met at
Faversham in Kent and Bocking in Essex in the mid-Edwardian years.
Their depositions in 1551 reveal a hostility to predestination and to established churches and their learning that could represent some descent from
radical Lollardy, or exposure to radical ideas imported into the South-East.
Their leader, Henry Hart, was sufficiently doctrinally confident to engage
in formal debate with John Bradford while both were imprisoned under
Mary. Antinomianism is more visible in the case of John Champnes, tried
in London in 1548, who argued that a man regenerate in Christ cannot
sin, a view surely drawn from the Dutch libertines. The following year
Michael Thombe, a London butcher, abjured what appear to be anabaptist
beliefs. Most famously Joan Bocher, who had a history as a sacramentarian
in Kent under Henry VIII, was tried and burned in 1550 for a remarkable
mixture of anabaptist and spiritualist beliefs on the nature of Christ's humanity.[177]

---

[174] S R. Wever, *Lusty Juventus*, ed. H. Thomas (New York, 1982). For another example of
Shepherd's encouragement of challenge to authority, this time a simple countryman questioning
his priest, see J.C. Devereux, 'Protestant propaganda in the reign of Edward VI: a study of Luke
Shepherd's "Doctour Double Ale"', in E.J. Carlson (ed.), *Religion and the English People,
1500–1640* (Kirksville, Mo., 1998), 121–46.

[175] Happé and King, *Vocacyon of John Bale*, 59.

[176] There is a large secondary literature on the radicals. See especially, Davis, *Heresy and
Reformation*; Martin, *Religious Radicals*; I.B. Horst, *The Radical Brethren* (Nieuwkoop, 1972);
D.A. Penny, *Freewill or Predestination: The Battle over Saving Grace in mid-Tudor England*, Studies
in History 61 (1990). The most recent study is C. Clement, *Religious Radicalism in England,
1535–1565* (1997), but this adds little to previous analyses.

[177] The best study of the doctrinal beliefs of the mid-century radicals is Penny, *Freewill or
Predestination*.

In the general taxonomy of reform Henry Hart, his small conventicle, and the heterogeneous individuals who spoke with radical tongues should not be given exaggerated attention. Their capacity to embarrass Protestant leadership and alarm Tudor governments seems out of all proportion to their known numbers. Particularly striking is the prominent place an attack on radical beliefs was given in the Forty-Two Articles.[178] There anabaptism and libertinism are to be solemnly forsworn, though neither had shown significant signs of influencing the English clergy. The explanation lies primarily in the convolutions of the stranger congregations in London, especially the Dutch, where Martin Micron battled to keep radicalism at bay.[179] The militancy of the radicals was not confined to this environment: in 1549, for example, they had attended the lectures of the new Protestant star John Hooper, and challenged his views. The burning of Bocher and rounding-up of the Hart group drove sympathizers underground, and the council ensured that they remained there by commissioning Cranmer to search out heresy in Kent at the end of 1552.[180] Undeterred the freewillers re-emerged under Mary to play striking roles in the period of persecution. In London, Kent, and Essex at least some of those condemned expressed radical views on the nature of the Godhead, on free will, and on baptism that Foxe, who accumulated the material, subsequently suppressed in his printed martyrology. A few would not have been misplaced in radical Munster: five men burned at Smithfield in April 1557 argued for the community of wives.[181]

In sharp opposition to these blunt forms of radicalism we might locate in the taxonomy of reform those who were at some point explicit evangelicals, but whose experiences led them to forms of equivocation about their faith. There were, of course, direct conversions back to Catholicism, most famously that of Nicholas Shaxton, bishop of Salisbury until the Act of Six Articles, who recanted in 1546 while curate of Hadleigh and ended his career as suffragan of Thomas Thirlby, the Marian bishop of Ely.[182] If Shaxton provided one model for those experiencing persecution, Edward Crome, the equivocator *par excellence*, offered another. His three recantations under Henry were all so structured as to signal his true reformist beliefs, but they produced an ambivalent response in the community of

---

[178] The Articles attack millenarianism, mortalism, and the belief in universal salvation: G. Bray (ed.), *Documents of the English Reformation* (Cambridge, 1994), 309–40.

[179] Pettegree, *Foreign Communities*, 62–3.

[180] MacCulloch, *Cranmer*, 530–1. It is interesting that one of the free-willers of 1551, Thomas Cole, had by 1553 been ordained and turned orthodox, preaching a sermon against his erstwhile colleagues in Maidstone at the end of Cranmer's campaign.

[181] Penny, *Freewill or Predestination*, 68 ff. Foxe, viii. 310–13. Davis, *Heresy and Reformation*, 147.

[182] Craig, 'Hadleigh', 8–11.

the godly and left behind him an uncertain reputation. Yet, as Ryrie indicates, in the late Henrician years a 'low-key, pragmatic attitude' to recantation was common among English evangelicals.[183] Many of the other stars of Edwardian Protestantism had had to compromise in varying degrees in the difficult 1540s. The gravest test for committed Protestants, the beginning of persecution under Mary, saw these and other responses, to the deep anxiety of those who had gone into exile. One of the prime objectives of the polemical literature that the exile communities began to publish was an assault upon nicodemism: the belief that those who remained faithful to the gospel in spirit could conform in bodily practice when required to do so by the magistrate.[184] 'The body goeth not to Mass without the company and consent of the soul', argued John Olde. Bodies were temples of the Holy Ghost, and to take them to church was to contaminate them by contact with idols.[185] This was precisely what the equivocators of Henry's reign had done but, the clerical reformers did not add, it was also what had been sanctioned within the indigenous heresy, Lollardy.

In practice the survival of Protestantism under Mary as any sort of popular movement depended as much on compromise as confrontation. When Ralph Allerton told Bishop Bonner in 1557 that there were many who observed his outward command but had 'their hearts set wholly against the same' he was surely identifying an important aspect of popular sentiment, though one which neither he nor his interrogator could endorse.[186] Survivalism, to use a term more often employed in a Catholic context, ensured a measure of sympathy for the next great change of governmental policy at Elizabeth's accession. Sympathizers might and did provide a network of informal support for the exiles, and for the prisoners who had made a stand in England, and powerful laymen who chose to compromise, most notably William Cecil, could on occasion make more public gestures of defiance. Cecil and other parliamentarians were able to destroy a bill aimed at depriving the exiles of their rights to their English property.[187] And lesser men like the burghers of Rye could at least signal

[183] S. Wabuda, 'Equivocation and recantation during the English Reformation: the "Subtle Shadows" of Dr Edward Crome', *JEH* 44 (1993), 224–42. For Dr Richard Smith as a comparable Catholic equivocator see P. O'Grady, *Henry VIII and the Conforming Catholics* (Collegeville, Minn., 1990), 130–3. See also the valuable discussion in A. Ryrie, 'English Evangelical Reformers in the Last Years of Henry VIII', University of Oxford D.Phil. (2000), 97–122.

[184] A. Pettegree, 'Nicodemism and the English Reformation', in his *Marian Protestantism* (Aldershot, 1996), 85–117.

[185] J. Olde, *Confession of the true Catholic Old belief* (Emden, 1555), sig. E3. R. Horne, *Whether Christian faith may be kept secret in the heart without confession thereof openly to the world* (1553), sig. A4.

[186] Foxe, viii. 407.   [187] Pettegree, 'Nicodemism', 104–5.

their unhappiness with Mary's regime by returning a Member of Parliament known for religious non-conformity.[188] The equivocating Protestant, like the later church papist, was an inevitable product of the religious circumstances of mid-Tudor England. Like the church papist, he or she would in the very long term have had to identify with one or other faith in a more confessionalized land. Like them, the conformist could well have had an extended afterlife of reluctant adjustment to the norms imposed by the ecclesiastical establishment.[189]

Confusion, taciturnity, nicodemism: it might be logical to conclude that these were the significant responses of the majority of the English laity to Reformation crisis. But there are occasional signs of a shift in consciousness that indicate a firmer recognition of the need to adapt to change. When the eastern counties were destabilized by rebellion in the summer of 1549 the duke of Somerset chose to temporize and negotiate as a means of dispersing the camps of the men of Norfolk, Suffolk, and Essex. The duke's behaviour is of less interest here than his use of language, or rather what his letters reveal about the petitions he had received from the 'camps' of Norfolk, Suffolk, Essex, and Oxfordshire. The first three had all couched their appeals in the discourse of the new Protestant establishment, alleging 'sundry texts of scripture', 'professing Christ's doctrine in words', and claiming to 'greatly hunger' for the gospel. The Essex rebels, in particular, had perturbed the duke by 'a recital of texts to make for your present purposes': in other words the manipulation of the Protestant's own device in defence of their grievances. This provoked a severe lecture upon the centrality of the doctrine of obedience: that it had no meaning to embrace God's word if his truth was not followed in proper social or political conduct.[190] We have no independent evidence through which to test the veracity and sincerity of the Essex men, but at the least they reveal a capacity to engage in a new rhetoric and deploy it for their purposes. The petitions of 1549 indicate that the 'years of confusion' in religious policy did not automatically leave ordinary laymen alienated, apathetic, or shorn of all agency. Rather they are a faint sign of the process of assimilation, by which a new language and ideology were to become normative, the stuff of everyday experience and exchange.

---

[188] Mayhew, *Tudor Rye*, 73, 75.   [189] Walsham, *Church Papists*.
[190] E. Shagan, 'Protector Somerset and the 1549 rebellions: new sources and new perspectives', *EHR* 114 (1999), 58–62.

PART III

WORD AND DOCTRINE

7

THE WORD DISSEMINATED

The English Reformation did not produce a strong iconographic tradition to counter the suasive power of traditional Catholic imagery.[1] However, there are two images that do recur in official and popular texts. They are of the monarch disseminating the Word, and of the preacher preaching it. The first famous visual expression of the two images conjoined is that of the frontispiece of the Great Bible (1539), in which Henry VIII offers the scriptures to Cromwell and Cranmer, as representative of the lay and clerical orders, while at the bottom of the page the priest preaches to seated men and women who praise the magnanimity of the prince. But this is a vision not so much of authoritative monarchical statement of identity with Scripture as a plea from the evangelical promoters of the Word for royal support. The preacher *ad plebes* does not quote Scripture explicitly: instead he enjoins all men to pray for the king and those in authority.[2] Later evangelical Protestants could be more direct. Both the representation of the monarch and that of the preacher were regularly used, each reiterating the idea that the prince gave the gift of the Word to his people, and that the preacher expounded it to an informed laity. By the Elizabethan period, however, there is an interesting parting of the ways: the queen and her advisers rarely employed the image of the crown

---

[1] This is a more contentious statement than it would have appeared a few years ago. In his *Birthpangs of Protestant England* (1988), Patrick Collinson provided a powerful argument on Protestant iconophobia, based on the traditional view that there was a flight from the image by godly Protestants under Elizabeth. This has now been challenged by both Tessa Watt, in *Cheap Print and Popular Piety* (Cambridge, 1991), and Alex Walsham, in *Providence in Early Modern England* (Oxford, 2000), both arguing that English Protestant printing, broadly defined, remained concerned with the visual through into the seventeenth century. It remains true, however, that religious texts were rarely richly engraved after the 1560s: Foxe's *Acts and Monuments* being the exception that proves the rule.

[2] The most recent and interesting analysis is G. Walker, *Persuasive Fictions: Faith, Faction and Political Culture in the Reign of Henry VIII* (Aldershot, 1996), 85–8, 92–5. The point about royal authority was reinforced by the presence of a prison on the bottom right corner of the title page—no toleration of dissent from the royal will. Professor MacCulloch points out that in the painted copy of the Great Bible now in St John's Library, Cambridge, said to have belonged to Cromwell himself, the prison is omitted: D. MacCulloch, *Thomas Cranmer* (New Haven, Conn., 1996), 239.

Title-page of the Great Bible (1539). Permission of the Bodleian Library

offering the Word: the representation of the faithful congregation retained its vitality, surfacing as late as the Jacobean period in very traditional forms. The congregation with its preacher appears, for example, at the foot of the title page of the 1569 Bishops' Bible, deriving from an image of Archbishop Parker delivering a sermon.[3] The iconic structure of the godly congregation hearing its preacher had been established by Cranach and the German engravers of the first Reformation generation and varied little in English reproductions. The essence of the scene was a combination of intimacy and intellectual engagement, the preacher placed above, but not too far above, his auditors, they grouped informally beneath the pulpit, women seated with open books, children sometimes on the floor, men standing in rapt attention, and once again often holding texts in their hands. In the woodcut in Thomas Williamson's *The Sword of the Spirit* even the child on the floor holds open his book.[4]

The ideal was of the rapt congregation, unmoved by cold, or other physical discomfort, 'turning up [their] eye, and turning down the leaf in [their] book, when [they] hear chapter and verse'.[5] This diametrically opposed another topos routinely invoked by Reformation preachers who complained that the laity preferred the alehouse to the church or allowed

Title-page, lower left. John Foxe's Book *of Martyrs* (1583 edn.). Permission of the Bodleian Library

---

[3] The detail is interesting here because it shows the preacher with his hour-glass before a congregation that is all seated. The image was used again in an early seventeenth-century madrigals text, and in the 1634 edition of the Welsh Book of Common Prayer: R.B. McKerrow and F.S. Ferguson (eds.), *Title-Page Borders used in England and Scotland, 1485–1640* (1932), pl. 127.

[4] T. Williamson, *The sword of the spirit to smite in pieces that antichristian Goliath* (1613), 61.

[5] J. Earle, *Microcosmographie* (Leeds, 1966, facsimile), 117.

Frontispiece, 'Matthew Parker preaching'. The Bishops' Bible (1577 edition)
Permission of the Bodleian Library

'Preacher and congregation'. Thomas Williamson, *The Sword of the Spirit* (1613).
Permission of the Bodleian Library

their thoughts to be elsewhere 'like the birds which fly about the church'.[6] Neither is likely to embody the whole truth, but it is the ideal from which we need to begin in order to understand the processes of evangelism in the Reformation. The watchword of the evangelists was preaching—preaching and more preaching—with Scripture as the sole authority for the Word spoken. It was the conjunction of the text and the word of Scripture that was critical: hence the representations of Protestant and Catholic preaching are distinguished iconographically by the presence of the Scripture in the former. The message that the godly preachers conveyed was one of sustaining simplicity. William Lauder, minister of the reformed church in Perth, rhymed it thus in advising that the king must protect God's word:

> Itt suld be precheit to all does seik it;
> Itt nother suld be paird nor ekit,
> Saif Scripture with Scripture ye expone
> Conforme unto the trewtwiche stone,
> Quhilk is the auld and new Testament,
> Quhilk suld be taught most deligent
> Be faithfull Pastors that preche can
> But feir of ony erthlie man.[7]

The Perils of Idolatry

The impediments to the fulfilment of this simple vision were legion. Some, those of a specifically political nature, have already been considered: those that are part of the detailed pattern of clerical organization and parochial behaviour remain to be discussed in later chapters. Here we are concerned with the barriers to effective communication that were conceptual and structural. An appropriate starting-point is Margaret Aston's observation that the reformers aimed not to re-educate, but to re-convert, the world.[8] The edification that is represented in the preaching images is an opening of the spirit to the inner workings of God's grace as well as an exposition of true doctrine. This could only be effective when men's minds had been emptied of false beliefs, and their vision purged of corroding icons. The destruction of Milton's 'new vomited paganism of sensual idolatry', the images and sacramentals that enveloped Catholic worship, became for most zealous Protestants the essential ground for conversion. The vehemence of the *Homily against the Peril of Idolatry*, by

---

[6] M. Maclure, *The Paul's Cross Sermons, 1534–1642* (Toronto, 1958), 300.

[7] W. Lauder, *Ane Compendious and Breve Tractate concernyng ye Office and Dewtie of Kyngis, Spirituall Pastoris and Temporall Iugis (1566)*, ed. F. Hall, EETS os 4 (1864), 1.

[8] M. Aston, *England's Iconoclasts: Laws against Images* (Oxford, 1988), 9.

far the longest of the second set issued early in Elizabeth's reign, summarizes the strength of reformed feeling on this issue.

The church or house of God is a place appointed by the Holy Scriptures, where the lively word of God ought to be read taught and heard . . . [but] . . . corruption of these latter days hath brought into the church infinite multitudes of images . . . thereby [the priests] greatly hurt the simple and unwise, occasioning them . . . to commit most horrible idolatry . . .[9]

The attitude of the Scots was more direct and more trenchant. The Scottish Kirk after 1559 saw the destruction of images as the essence of its role in reconverting the ungodly.[10] The Scottish Reformation had from its outset been marked by vigorous outbursts of iconoclasm, like the attacks on the Perth and Dundee houses of friars in 1543. 'Casting down', a piece of language applied to assaults both on buildings and on their contents, became a test of firm commitment to reform in the dark years of the 1540s and 1550s.[11] Heinrich Bullinger, seeking to strengthen Knox's resolve when he was in exile, insisted that death was preferable 'to the admission of idolatry'.[12] He need not have worried: as early as 1556 Knox's obsessive fear of idolatry was fully fixed. He believed that idolaters should suffer the penalty of death, a sentiment that by 1558 had enlarged itself into a call for the death of Mary Tudor and other idolatrous queens.[13] This was not an immediately practicable possibility, but it established the tone for the Scottish Reformation. As the reformers swept forward in 1559 Kirkaldy of the Grange assured Cecil that 'open defiance is now given to all who maintain idolatry', and the 'images and monuments of idolatry' became a major focus of attack in the Reformation parliament.[14] Robert Bruce, Knox's successor in Edinburgh, spoke with the true voice of the ministers when he denounced 'idolatry and blood; for under there I comprehend all the sins committed against the Two Tables'.[15]

The linearity of the Scottish attack upon images was not matched by the English experience because of the vagaries and ambiguities of official policy, but this does not mean that the leaders of reform felt less keenly

[9] J. Griffiths (ed.), *The Two Books of Homilies Appointed to be Read in Churches* (Oxford, 1859), 167–8.

[10] J. Kirk, 'Iconoclasm and Reformation', *RSCHS* 24 (1992), 366–83.

[11] D. McRoberts, 'Material destruction caused by the Scottish Reformation', in D. McRoberts (ed.), *Essays on the Scottish Reformation, 1515–1625* (Glasgow, 1962), 420–3, 428.

[12] Knox, iv. 224.

[13] J.E.A. Dawson, 'Trumpeting resistance: Christopher Goodman and John Knox', in R.A. Mason (ed.), *John Knox and the British Reformations* (Aldershot, 1998), 141–5.

[14] J. Kirk, *Patterns of Reform* (Edinburgh, 1989), 104.

[15] W. Cunningham (ed.), *Sermons of Revd Robert Bruce* (Wodrow Society, Edinburgh, 1843), 192. *The First Book of Discipline* asked for the death penalty for idolaters and blasphemers: J. Cameron (ed.), *The First Book of Discipline* (Edinburgh, 1972), 204–7.

about the issue. Among those who actively pressed for religious change there were few Luthers, few who were prepared to say that although they did 'not love images very much' eradicating imagery from the church came second to eradicating idolatry from the heart.[16] Instead there was such spiritual anxiety about the issue that Luther's lukewarmness on icono-clasm had to be explained away, by Foxe among others, as being a conse-quence of time and circumstance, not conviction.[17] Time and circumstance certainly constrained those who in the 1520s and 1530s saw the abolition of idolatry as an essential prelude to the proper preaching of the gospel. Wil-liam Roye's *Brief Dialogue between a Christian Father and his Stubborn Son* (1527) has the father urging that images are idols and that the prince should cleanse them, following the example of the good king Josiah.[18] Tyndale was not quite so sweeping in his condemnation, but concluded in his answer to More that since images had been so abused they must be re-moved.[19] Latimer developed from a moderate critique of image abuse to leadership of the official iconoclastic movement by the later 1530s. His appeal to the 'brethren and fathers' of Convocation in 1536 to 'take utterly away these deceitful and juggling images' heralded the first serious attempt to precipitate the crown into action against idolatry.[20]

The partial success of the assault on images in the late 1530s both en-couraged and frustrated those like Latimer, Cranmer, Hilsey, and Goodrich who had made their total opposition to icons explicit.[21] Foxe's judgement was that 'idolatry and superstition [were] somewhat repressed'.[22] William Turner, writing from exile in Zurich, was able to express a more trenchant view than the bishops who had been left discomforted at home: 'the Scripture forbiddeth to make images, and to have images, then much more it forbiddeth to worship them'.[23] It was presumably this experience that made the leaders of reform so determined to confront the issue directly

---

[16] J. Pelikan (ed.), *Luther's Works* (St Louis, Mo., 1960), ix. 82. M. Stirm, 'Die Bilderfrage in der Reformation', in G.A. Benrath (ed.), *Quellen und Forschungen zur Reformationsgeschichte* 45 (Gutersloh, 1977), 36–7, 41, 69.

[17] Foxe, iv. 315–16. Aston, *England's Iconoclasts*, 41–3.

[18] A. Wolf (ed.), *William Roye's Dialogue between a Christian Father and his Stubborn Son* (Vienna, 1874), 37, 79.

[19] H. Walter (ed.), *Willliam Tyndale's Answer to Sir Thomas More's Dialogue* (PS, Cambridge, 1850), 88, 125.

[20] G.E. Corrie (ed.), *Sermons of Hugh Latimer* (PS, Cambridge, 1844), 55. For Latimer's earlier position see Aston, *England's Iconoclasts*, 169–72.

[21] The King's Book (1543) shows Henry's own intervention in favour of a moderate support of images 'we be not forbidden to make or to have similitudes or images, but only we be forbidden to make or have them to the intent to do godly honour unto them'. C. Lloyd (ed.), *Formularies of Faith put forth by Authority during the Reign of Henry VIII* (Oxford, 1825), 299.

[22] Foxe, iv. 167.

[23] W. Turner, *The Huntyng and Fyndyng out of the Romishe Foxe* (Bonn, 1543), sig. C vii[r].

once 'the godly Josiah' had succeeded his father. Cranmer's call at Edward's coronation to see 'idolatry destroyed; the tyranny of the Bishops of Rome banished from your subjects and images removed' was echoed by Ridley and Latimer, and applauded from afar by John Hooper.[24] Between the issuing of the royal injunctions of 1547 and the 1550 statute for 'the abolishing and putting away of divers books and images' a radical extirpation had taken place, even if it was not as exhaustively enforced as the leadership would have wished. The vision that they sought to realize is powerfully exemplified in John Foxe's famous page prefacing the ninth book of the *Acts and Monuments*. There the papists flee to the ship of the Romish church, carrying their 'trinkets' and 'paltry', while the godly assemble in the purified temple, beneath the communion table and the baptismal font, to hear the words of their preacher unencumbered.[25]

Yet the cleansing of the temple was not secured. Morebath still mourned for its saints.[26] The return of Catholicism under Mary was marked by a particular parochial enthusiasm for the re-embellishment of the churches. It may be that the saints were not the primary focus of this commitment, but it must have been clear to reformers that the battle to purge false image worship and visual sensuality had thus far been lost. This sense of defeat, coupled with a justified anxiety about the new queen's attitude to images, lent the early Elizabethan attack on icons an urgency even greater than that of the Edwardian years. The political battle focused on the problem of the chapel royal, with its candles and crucifix, though Elizabeth believed more generally that images were not proscribed by the second commandment. As Edwin Sandys wrote to Peter Martyr in 1560:

The queen's majesty considered it not contrary to the word of God, nay, rather for the advantage of the Church, that the image of Christ crucified, together with Mary and John, should be placed, as heretofore, in some conspicuous part of the church, where they might more readily be seen by all the people.[27]

The queen sought to circumscribe the attack on idolatry, but at the public level she had to accept that the returning exiles who manned her church were deeply iconophobic and that the articles administered by the royal visitors in 1559 legitimized wholesale image destruction.[28] This, and the continuing conflict about the chapel royal, is the context for the lengthy

---

[24] J.E. Cox (ed.), *Miscellaneous Writings and Letters of Thomas Cranmer* (PS, Cambridge, 1846), 127. J.A. Muller (ed.), *Letters of Stephen Gardiner* (Cambridge, 1933), 255–9. S. Carr (ed.), *Early Writings of John Hooper* (PS, Cambridge, 1843), 203.

[25] Aston, *England's Iconoclasts*, 254–70. J. Phillips, *The Reformation of Images: The Destruction of Art in England, 1535–1660* (Los Angeles, 1973), 82–100.

[26] E. Duffy, *The Voices of Morebath: Reformation and Rebellion in an English Village* (New Haven, Conn., 2001), 162–3, shows the parishioners bringing preserved images out of hiding.

[27] *ZL* i. 73–4.   [28] *VAI* iii. 1.

homily against the perils of idolatry, which was one of the set presented to the convocation of 1563. As Aston has shown, the final authorized version of the homilies toned down the vigour of the anti-image polemic, and in particular sought to ensure that its lengthiest section was not assumed to be public reading but was for 'the curates themselves, or men of good understanding'.[29]

It was in this last section of the homily that a specific, inverse correlation between image worship and preaching was outlined. Why, asked the author, might images not be allowed to exist alongside 'diligent and sincere preaching of God's word', which would rob them of their 'poison'? The answer was in part practical; since the harvest was plentiful but the labourers few, preaching could not immediately substitute for the constant presence of, and familiarity with, the graven image. Icons 'last for many hundred years' cheaply, while preachers must be maintained at high cost. But the power of the image extended beyond familiarity and ease, it poisoned even the best evangelical challenge. 'Those blind books and dumb school-masters, I mean images and idols . . . . prevailed against all [the Fathers] written books, and preaching with lively voice, as they call it.' If images remained in the churches 'ye shall in vain preach and teach them against idolatry' since men were as prone to 'spiritual fornication' as to its secular equivalent.[30] Here indeed in the mouth of the established church was bitter hostility to even moderate icondulia since it was the chief stumbling-block to conversion. It was apparently the intense hostility to images in the 1560s, a hostility largely shared by the first generation of Elizabeth's bishops and their more radical clerical colleagues, that produced the famous painting of Edward VI trampling the pope underfoot, watched by his father on his death-bed and the council, while the destruction of 1548 was recorded in a window at the back of the canvas.[31] When church paintings often remained 'slubbered over with a white wash that in a house may be undone, standing like a Dianas shrine for a future hope and daily comfort of old popish beldames and young perking papists . . .' there was need for perpetual vigilance.[32] And, as a Paul's Cross preacher remarked in 1577, even damaged images could retain their sway: 'though their heads be off, yet can they make somewhat of their bodies . . .'.[33]

---

[29] Aston, *England's Iconoclasts*, 321–5. Griffith, *Homilies*, pp. xxix–xxxii.

[30] Griffiths, *Homilies*, 266–72.

[31] M. Aston, *The King's Bedpost: Reformation and Iconography in a Tudor Group Portrait* (Cambridge, 1994), has fundamentally changed our understanding of this important painting, which had previously been dated to the Edwardian era that it represents. She suggests a date between 1569 and 1572.

[32] A. Peel (ed.), *The Seconde Parte of a Register* (Cambridge, 1915), i. 190–1.

[33] J.W. Blench, *Preaching in England in the Late Fifteenth and Sixteenth Centuries* (Oxford, 1964), 299.

Later in Elizabeth's reign the preoccupation with the purification of image entered a new phase as the focused concern with the public space of the church was enlarged to encompass a debate about broader problems of religious representation. Puritan perceptions of the corroding danger of the image evolved through the vestarian controversy into a rooted opposition to the seductive power of the visual.[34] The church remained the first line of conflict, with the orthodox Calvinist position being articulated by William Perkins. Histories of the Bible, he argued, might be painted, but not in the church, where they might nurture idolatry; instead they could be presented 'in private places'. Even then, this seemed more concession than positive acceptance for 'it is not meet that a Christian should be occupied by the eyes but the meditation of the mind'.[35] Within the church stained-glass windows became a particular focus of contest if only because, as William Harrison noted in the 1570s, they were often left in place for 'want of sufficient store of new stuff'.[36] Beyond parochial buildings there were other contentious public spaces containing images—market and churchyard crosses being the most obvious. And there was the far greater challenge represented by both the theatre and fictive writing, where the arts of preaching were too often pre-empted by others and led either directly or implicitly back to loathsome idolatry. The attack on the old mystery cycles of drama, and the subsequent pursuit of the metropolitan theatre by zealous authors like Northbrooke, is beyond our immediate purposes here. However, it is important to note that it was the stage representation of Christ, and eventually more generally of biblical material, that incurred godly wrath. The divine could no longer be counterfeited and humanized in the old way without the danger of blasphemy. It was the displacement of religious meditation from its proper locations in church and text that proved unacceptable to those who believed that godly reformation was still imperfectly achieved in Elizabethan England.[37]

Hostility to the drama, as recent studies have been at pains to argue, cut across any simple divide between the godly and the conformist. While many of the hotter sort of Protestant continued to find play-going

---

[34] Collinson, *Birthpangs*, 115–21, though see above at n.1.

[35] W. Perkins, *A Reformed Catholicke: Or a Declaration shewing how neer we may come to the present Church of Rome in sundrie points of Religion* (Cambridge, 1598), 172. Phillips, *Reformation of Images*, 173–5. M. Aston, 'Puritans and Iconoclasm, 1560–1660', in C. Durston & J. Eales (eds.) *The Culture of English Puritanism, 1560–1700* (Basingstoke, 1996), 92–105. John Hooper had already made a very similar point: 'to have the picture or image of any martyr or other, so it be not put in the temple of God or otherwise abused, it may be suffered': *Early Writings*, 44.

[36] G. Edelen (ed.), *William Harrison: A Description of England* (Ithaca, N.Y., 1968), 35–6.

[37] P.W. White, *Theatre and Reformation: Protestantism, Patronage and Playing in Tudor England* (Cambridge, 1993), 166–74. M. O'Connell, 'The idolatrous eye: iconoclasm, anti-theatricalism and the image of the Elizabethan theatre', *Journal of English Literary History* 52 (1985), 279–310.

tolerable, men like Philip Stubbes and Anthony Munday, who were not particularly identified with Puritanism, saw in the shape-changing and delusion of the professional stage the very model of that idolatry that the Church was struggling to banish from its bounds.[38] Players mixed 'scurrility with divinity' and seduced men with the 'idolatrous eye'. Once again they raised the spectre that the Word could not compete with the assault upon the eyes and ears that was embedded in the old faith and now in the new drama. 'How wary,' said Gosson, 'ought we to be, that no corruption of idols, enter by the passage of our eyes and ears into the soul?'[39] At a more mundane level plays and players also represented unfair competition to the labour of the preachers seeking to convert the realm for 'will not a filthy play, with the blast of a trumpet, sooner call thither a thousand than a hours tolling of a Bell, bring to the Sermon a hundred?'[40]

While the assault on plays and all images as a source of idolatry seems strongly identified with an obsessive minority, their angst makes sense when placed in the broad context of the forms of cultural perception that they confronted. There was an 'incarnational logic' about the way in which the divine was experienced in traditional Catholic worship, in which the boundaries of the sacred were permeable, and saints' cults, liturgy, the sacrifice of the Mass, religious art, music and drama all embodied a part of the holy.[41] This was shown most clearly in a culture that did not surrender the traditional, or abandon the image, that of Ireland. In the late 1530s there had been an attack on the great pilgrimage images similar to that experienced in England. Commissioners toured the Pale in the winter of 1538–9, netting a modest return of wealth from shrines for the crown, and confirming the slightly earlier attacks on the great shrines of the Virgin at Trim, the *Baculus Jesu* in Christ Church, Dublin, and the Holy Cross at Ballyboggan, County Meath. The evidence on the fate of the images is ambiguous, but Brendan Bradshaw has shown that there was every incentive for the Dublin regime to proceed with caution, and it seems likely that even the greater images were often stripped rather than destroyed.[42] If Our

---

[38] A. Walsham, '"a Glose of Godlines": Philip Stubbes, Elizabethan Grub Street and the invention of Puritanism', in S. Wabuda and C. Litzenberger (eds.), *Belief and Practice in Reformation England* (Aldershot, 1998), 177–206. Collinson, *Birthpangs*, 112–15. P. Stubbes, *The Anatomie of Abuses* (1583), sig. L vi. A. Munday, *A Second and Third Blast of Retrait from Plaies and Theater* (1590), 95–6.

[39] S. Gosson, *Playes Confuted in five actions* (1582?), sig. B 8ᵛ.

[40] J. Stockwood, *A Sermon Preached at Paules Crosse* (1578), 23–4.

[41] S.A. Meigs, *The Reformations in Ireland: Tradition and Confessionalism, 1400–1690* (Basingstoke, 1997), 28–40. E. Duffy, *The Stripping of the Altars* (New Haven, Conn., 1992), 91 ff.

[42] B. Bradshaw, *The Dissolution of the Religious Orders in Ireland under Henry VIII* (Cambridge, 1974), 100–9. R. Gillespie, *Devoted People: Belief and Religion in Early Modern Ireland* (Manchester, 1997), 1 – the *Bachulus Iesu* was a staff given to St Patrick by Christ.

Lady of Trim was destroyed, as the *Annals of Loch Cé* suggest, it seems to have been in the minority of 'abusive' images that could not be ignored.[43] Neither this commission, nor the later Edwardian one, had the ability, or perhaps the inclination, to engage in the sort of vigorous cull that would have cleared those churches outside the most immediate range of government supervision. The triumph of the saints is vividly suggested in Bishop Bale's description of the speed with which the clergy 'suddenly set up all the altars and images in the cathedral church' of Kilkenny on the very day that the restored Mass was proclaimed.[44] Three years later the lord deputy, Fitzwalter, thought that it was this return of the visual environment of worship that sustained Irish devotion:

> their churches [are] so kept and adorned as the sight thereof may bring reverence ...the hearts of the people more being daily put in remembrance of their eye than the words of a rare preacher which for the time commonly feedeth the ear and after falleth from the remembrance of the ignorant.[45]

The power of the image, and its ability to sustain the old symbolic understanding of the faith, is constantly attested in the later sixteenth century and beyond. Religious statues were common in Waterford houses in the 1580s, and by the turn of the century the churches of New Ross were 'full of the most miserable idols', who stood in place of adequate Protestant incumbents.[46] Although the evidence is, as usual, very fragmentary, there seems no reason to suppose that the Irish experience of the saints as a prime form of access to the holy changed significantly during the course of the Reformation century. Peter Lombard, an Irish theologian writing in 1601, claimed that early Elizabethan Irish Catholics had attended heretic services, but had used 'the crucifix, with the image of our Saviour...and pictures of the saints' as devotional defence against the Protestant Latin liturgy. Such continuity, the reformers would have assured themselves, would of itself have been enough to close the ears of the worshipper against the pure message of the gospel relayed through the new ritual.[47]

---

[43] W.M. Hennessy (ed.), *Annals of Loch Cé*, 2 vols. (London, 1871), ii. 314. The *Annals of Connaught* and the *Annals of Ulster* also dwell on the losses at Trim, though with inaccurate dating, Meigs, *Reformations in Ireland*, 58–9.

[44] P. Happé and J.N. King (eds.), *The vocacyon of Johan Bale* (Binghamton, N.Y., 1990), 67.

[45] E.P. Shirley (ed.), *Original Letters and Papers in Ilustration of the History of the Church in Ireland during the Reign of Edward VI, Mary and Elizabeth* (London, 1851), 76–7. Fitzwalter, however, was a Catholic of a rather different stripe, since he urged the council in London to provide the best priests and ministers to be sent out to instruct the ignorant people.

[46] Gillespie, *Devoted People*, 20, 68–78. *CSP Irl* 1606–8. 15: this is part of an extended report on his Irish activity to the earl of Salisbury by Sir John Davies.

[47] Meigs, *Reformations in Ireland*, 70.

Sola Scriptura

'Alas, Gossip,' says the imagined goodwife in the *Homily of the Place and Time of Prayer*, 'what shall we now do in church, since all the saints are gone, since all the goodly sights we were wont to have are gone?' The answer was, of course, to attend and to learn: to resort to the church on Sunday to 'be partakers of his holy sacraments, and be devout hearers of his holy Word'.[48] Men must learn to assimilate the evangelical message and to do so not in a formulaic or thematic way—those patterns of understanding that Walter Ong identifies as characteristic of an oral culture—but as the Word individually experienced.[49] Reformers would have put it more vigorously: Christians must turn from the dead image to the living Word. When William Bill, later dean of Westminster, praised Hutchinson's work on the *Image of God* in 1550, he did so in precisely these terms:

> Images are made to put us in mind
> Of that which is dead or far absent;
> But God is neither, as we do find,
> But aye living, and each where present.
>
> Images are cursed, graven by man's wit,
> In place that are set for any religion;
> But an Image made out of holy writ
> Is not forbidden, in mine opinion.[50]

The hearing of the Word meant ideally its lively preaching, for only so could conversion be secured. But underpinning the edifice of instruction was Scripture itself—the Word made present in text, read from the lectionary week by week, even, in the appalled observation of Henry VIII in 1545, 'rhymed ... and jangled in every ale-house'. It is no longer fashionable to credit J.R. Green's ringing sentence that by the time of the meeting of the Long Parliament 'England became the people of a book, and that book was the Bible'.[51] However, the failure of the grandest of the reformers' designs should not be employed, as too often they are in current debate about religious change, as a means of displacing the major ideological

---

[48] Griffiths, *Homilies*, 349–50. Pilkington also characterized the horror of the gossips at the bareness of worship: 'What shall I do at the church? ... there is no images nor saints, to worship and make curtesy unto: little god in the box has gone: there is nothing but a little reading and preaching, that I cannot tell what it means ...' J. Scholefield (ed.), *The Works of Bishop Pilkington* (PS, Cambridge, 1842), 156.

[49] W. Ong, *The Presence of the Word* (New Haven, Conn., 1967), 27–30.

[50] J. Bruce (ed.), *The Works of Roger Hutchinson* (PS, Cambridge, 1842), 10.

[51] J.R. Green, *History of the English People* (1876 edn.), 447. C. Hill, *The English Bible and the Seventeenth-Century Revolution* (Penguin edn., 1994), 4–44.

and cultural shift that the cry *sola scriptura* generated.[52] Scottish, Welsh, and English Protestantism was constructed upon the work of the translators, that succession of learned evangelicals stretching from Tyndale, through Whittingham and his Geneva colleagues and William Morgan for the Welsh, to the staid uplands of the committee that arrived at the literary masterpiece that is the Authorized Version.[53] It is an intriguing consequence of the long march from a Whig view of the triumph of Protestantism that only Welsh and Scottish historians still feel comfortable with traditional emphases on the centrality of scriptural translation.[54]

Tyndale's assumption that conversion had to be posited on an understanding of scripture drew little distinction between the written and the preached word: the urgency of the message transcended any specific concerns about the medium. 'God is not man's imagination; but that only which he saith of himself. God is nothing but his law and his promises; that is to say that which he biddeth thee to do, and that which he biddeth thee believe and hope.'[55] This was essentially the position adopted by the first generation of biblical translators. Access to the Word demanded a sustained effort at promulgation of the written text: without this the clergy would be unlikely to preach from the Scripture and would resort to 'silly fables' and other 'feigned narratives'; without this the literate laity could not check upon the truth of their priests' words. Hence the anger of the evangelical preacher Michael Dunn, when Henry VIII restricted the reading of Scripture in 1543: he denounced those who 'went about to pluck Christ's words and the Holy Ghost's from the people'.[56] It was an article of faith that men must be given access to the text and that trust in God's message was what demarcated the true from the false Church. 'We allure the people to read and to hear God's word,' said Jewel, 'We lean unto knowledge, they [the Catholics] unto ignorance.'[57] The high-water

---

[52] It is difficult, for example, to imagine that by the seventeenth century a devout woman could have articulated such an undifferentiated view of texts as did Margery Kempe when she described her reading, eliding the Bible and the commentaries on it with Bonaventura, Hilton's *Ladder of Perfection*, and other devotional tracts: S.B. Meech and H.E. Allen (eds.), *The Book of Margery Kempe*, EETS os 212 (1940), 143.

[53] P. Collinson, 'The coherence of the text: how it hangeth together: the Bible in Reformation England', in W.P. Stephens (ed.), *The Bible, the Reformation and the Church*, Journal for the Study of the New Testament Supplement Series 105 (1997), 84–108. S. Greenslade (ed.) *The Cambridge History of the Bible*, 3 vols. (Cambridge, 1965), iii. chs. 4 and 5.

[54] G. Williams, *Wales and the Reformation* (Cardiff, 1997), 338–60. D.F. Wright, '"The Commoun Buke of the Kirke": The Bible in the Scottish Reformation', in D.F. Wright (ed.), *The Bible in Scottish Life and Literature* (Edinburgh, 1988), 155–78.

[55] H. Walter (ed.) *William Tyndale, Doctrinal Treatises etc.* (PS, Cambridge, 1848), 160.

[56] *LP* xviii. ii. no. 546.

[57] J. Ayre (ed.), *Jewel, The Apologie for the Church of England*, in *Works*, 4 vols. (PS, Cambridge, 1848), iii. 92–3.

mark of this enthusiasm for the unmediated dissemination of Scripture in official Protestant thinking is once again the Homilies, this time in their Edwardian form. There, in the first homily almost certainly written by Cranmer, is a most powerful and unequivocal call to the reading of the Word:

Unto a Christian man, there can be nothing either more necessary or profitable than the knowledge of holy Scripture: forasmuch as in it is contained God's true word, setting forth his glory, and also man's duty....Therefore forsaking the corrupt judgement of fleshly men, which care not but for their carcase, let us reverently hear and read Holy Scripture, which is the food of the soul....These books, therefore, ought to be much in our hands, in our eyes, in our ears, in our mouths, but most of all in our hearts... For that thing, which by continual use of reading of Holy Scripture, and diligent searching of the same, is deeply printed and graven in the heart, at length turneth almost to nature.

As for the complexity of scriptural exegesis, Cranmer boldly dismissed the idea with the assertion that those things that were necessary for salvation would be made plain by God.[58]

This powerful confidence in the pellucid quality of the scriptures and the accessible truth of their fundamental message was assailed during the Reformation century from a variety of positions. The first, usually held by conservative humanists, such as Thomas More, John Longland, and Stephen Gardiner, gradually abandoned the old establishment hostility to the vernacular scriptures, but insisted that it was the nature of translation and the nature of what could be read that was at issue.[59] It was advantageous to have Scripture in the mother tongue, said the preacher Roger Edgeworth, 'if we could get it well and truly translated, which will be very hard to be had'.[60] Hostility to the Tyndale/Coverdale Bible surfaced at the level of official debate in 1542, when Gardiner campaigned in Convocation to revise the text, and only Cranmer's deft manoeuvre in persuading the king that the matter be referred to the two universities prevented further challenge.[61] Behind the disputes about language lay deep reservations about unrestricted access to the scriptures, since their profundity demanded interpretation of the kind only truly provided by

---

[58] Griffiths, *Homilies*, 7. On the authorship of the homily see D. MacCulloch, *Thomas Cranmer* (1996), 372. Cranmer's preface to the 1540 edition of the Great Bible made a similar case, though there he warned of 'some... that be too slow, and need the spur: some other seem too quick, and need more of the bridle'.

[59] L.E.C. Wooding, *Rethinking Catholicism in Reformation England* (Oxford, 2000), 32, 76, 80. This important study emphasizes that such reformist impulses were widespread, and seeks to minimize the negative views of translation expressed by clerics like Standish.

[60] J. Wilson (ed.), *Sermons very fruitfull, godly and learned: Roger Edgeworth Preaching in the Reformation, c.1535–c.1553* (Woodbridge, 1993), 137.

[61] MacCulloch, *Cranmer*, 290–1, 311.

the learned. The laity, thought More, might read and mark the 'ordinances of God' and the example of Christ's life but could scarcely be
unleashed on such texts as the Psalms and 'should leave all these things to
them whose holy study is beset thereupon and to the preachers appointed
thereunto'.[62] Henry's curious restrictions upon the open reading of the
Bible, while they seem to reflect partly his own idiosyncratic vision, also
lent credence to this timorous view of the dangers of the text. After
Edward's reign the controversialist John Standish took a more trenchant
stand: the common people he complained had been babbling about the
mysteries of faith, 'both at drinking and eating, as though it were but a
Canterbury tale'.[63] Even a woman, as the conservative Roger Edgeworth
bemoaned in 1539, 'studieth the scriptures [and] teacheth it and disputeth
it'.[64] Cardinal Pole, reflecting in his homilies on the consequences of this
intemperate enthusiasm, concluded that the thirst for Scripture 'must be
directed, and the wit of man that seeketh, and coveteth knowledge must
be limited; which, because it is not, all these disorders and inconveniences
doth follow that we daily do see'.[65]

The other, more explicitly Catholic, assault on the vernacular scriptures
concerned the fundamental principle of the sufficiency of the text as the
embodiment of all revealed truth. More's crucial challenge to Tyndale was
that the latter prove that there were no 'unwritten verities' to which the
Church could lay claim through Christ's promise of the Holy Spirit.[66]
The Apostles had 'beside the scripture preached gods word unwritten as
long as they lived', and when even learned men found that the 'plain text
of scripture seem to speak for both the sides' of an argument, then the only
resort was to the guidance of the Holy Spirit, articulated through the
customs of the Church. Later Catholic controversialists developed the
theme of unwritten verities, and much of the obsessive Protestant insistence on the plainness of Holy Writ must be seen in the context of these
polemical encounters. Roger Hutchinson and Thomas Becon in the mid-
Tudor generation, William Fulke and William Whitaker in the Elizabethan, all found themselves in this position of defence. They also
struggled against the charge that Protestant insistence on *sola scriptura* elevated the letter of the law at the expense of its spirit. 'The papists', said
Hutchinson, 'seek by all means to spoil the people of their sword, which

---

[62] *CWTM* vi. 335.

[63] J. Standish, *A Discourse wherin is debated whether it be expedient that the Scripture should be
in English for al men to reade that wyll* (1554), sig. A vii.

[64] S. Wabuda, 'The Provision of Preaching during the Early English Reformation, with
special reference to Itineration, c.1530 to 1547', University of Cambridge Ph.D. (1991), 12.

[65] Ms. Vat. Lat. 5968, fo. 416ʳ [Bodley microfilm].

[66] *CWTM* viii. 150–62, 397.

is God's word saying…"The letter killeth, and the spirit quicke-
neth"…Is God's word the letter ?': to which the answer was Tyndale's
emphatic insistence that the gospel was the *evangelion*, the good news of
the Spirit.[67]

The case for 'unwritten verities' was one that no Protestant could
concede to the Catholic controversialists. But the dangers of allowing the
text of Scripture to appear as the dead law rather than the living truth of
Christ's redemptive power was one which engaged at least some of those
who regarded the English church in the later sixteenth century as 'but
halfly reformed'. Their animus was directed not against Bible-reading *per
se*: rather against the public use of the Word in liturgy as a substitute for
preaching; those readings from Scripture which were, in the words of the
Admonition to the Parliament (1572) 'not feeding' of the flock, but 'silly
reading'.[68] In the subsequent Admonition controversy Thomas Cartwright
elaborated the point, insisting that 'the bare reading of the Scriptures without the preaching cannot deliver so much as one poor sheep from destruction'.[69] The Scots had already moved in this direction: the First Book
of Discipline defined the reading of Scripture in the public service as
'profitable', but preaching as 'utterly necessary'. In particular there was
explicit hostility to the division and fragmentation of scriptural reading.
Congregations were to hear each book of Scripture read in whole, and
expounded by the minister, with no 'skipping and divagation from place
to place' as in the old lectionary.[70] 'No pistling [and] gospelling after the
Popes fashion', was the equivalent demand in England.[71] This prompted
Whitgift's suave response that 'I marvel that you, professing the Gospel,…speak so basely of reading the word of God, being a thing so
precious, and so singular a means of our salvation.'[72] Puritan polemicists
did not go quite so far: however, the godly in both realms took a firm
stand on the need to approach the scriptures systematically and always to
support reading with exposition.

While the controversialists might assert the plain truth of Scripture in
the face of their Catholic opponents there was a constant acknowledgement that the latter could make compelling points about the complexity
and opacity of the Word. There was indeed a need for interpretation and

---

[67] Bruce, *Works of Hutchinson*, 15–16.
[68] W.H. Frere and C.E. Douglas (eds.), *Puritan Manifestoes* (1954 edn.), 22.
[69] Ibid., 102.
[70] Wright, 'Bible in the Scottish Reformation', 169, 173.
[71] A. Peel (ed.), *The Seconde Parte of a Register*, 2 vols. (Cambridge, 1915), i. 95, 151.
[72] J. Ayre (ed.), *Works of John Whitgift*, 3 vols. (PS, Cambridge, 1851), iii. 38, 50, 53. The
most powerful criticism of the Puritan position came, as so often, from Hooker, who in Book V
of *The Laws of Ecclesiastical Polity* demonstrated the illogicality of separating scriptural reading
from preaching: R. Hooker, *Laws of Ecclesiastical Polity*, v. 21. 1–22:20.

the exegetical skills that derived from learning in the ancient tongues and in formal philosophical understanding. William Fulke's peroration to the biblical translators at the end of his *Defence of the . . . Translation of the Holy Scriptures into the English Tongue* (1583) summarizes the significance of such learning for English and Scottish Protestantism:

Happy and thrice happy hath our English [*sic!*] nation been, since God hath given learned translators, to express in our mother tongue the heavenly mysteries of his holy word, delivered to his church in the Hebrew and Greek languages.[73]

All the sixteenth-century translators recognized that exposition of the text was a part of their duty. Even the Bishops' Bible (1568) retained limited explanatory marginalia, a technique only finally eliminated in the Authorized Version of 1611. The notoriety and controversial nature of both the Tyndale and Geneva translations lay largely in their exegetical material.[74] Exposition of thorny and contentious passages of Scripture in sermons and tracts was also of the essence of godly ministerial labour, and the necessary accompaniment to the basic presentation of the text. Since the papists made scriptures 'nose of wax and a tennis-ball, wresting them unto every purpose', Protestants had to use all the resources of true learning to affirm God's purposes.[75] But even as in the second and third generations of Protestantism the labour of scriptural exposition spawned a vast literature, so there remained an insistence on the difference between human knowledge and faith in the process of understanding. William Whitaker put the case powerfully in his 1588 tract:

We say that the Holy Spirit is the supreme interpreter of scripture because we must be illuminated by the Holy Spirit to be certainly persuaded of the true sense of Scripture; otherwise although we use all means, we can never attain to that full assurance which resides in the minds of the faithful.[76]

Whatever the reservations about the need for interpreters, all Protestant evangelists saw it as a prime task to make the Word available and accessible to the people. The English could, as Fulke indicated, afford to be complacent about the endeavours of their translators. Tyndale provided the essential framework, both in terms of formal humanist learning and of an appropriate vitality in the use of the English language. Coverdale was

---

[73] W. Fulke, *A Defence of the Sincere and True Translation of the Holy Scriptures into the English Tongue*, ed. C.H. Hartshorne (PS, Cambridge, 1843), 591.

[74] Greenslade, *History of the Bible*, iii. 150–61.

[75] Bruce, *Works of Hutchinson*, 15. The idea of the 'nose of wax' is derived from the Dutchman Pighius: see H. Porter, 'The nose of wax: Scripture and the Spirit from Erasmus to Milton', *TRHS* 5th ser. 14 (1964), 155–74.

[76] W. Whitaker, *A Disputation of Holy Scripture*, trans. W. Fitzgerald (PS, Cambridge, 1848), 415.

deficient in the first respect, but followed the rhetorical skills of his predecessor.[77] Although the upheavals of the later Henrician years did not lend themselves to further Protestant translation, Cranmer remained aware that there were contentious issues of translation still to be resolved, and in 1549 made an abortive attempt to produce a new standard of Latin text that would have provided an authoritative basis for future vernaculars.[78] The Geneva translators remedied some of the deficiencies in earlier translations, and even the Bishops' Bible added some stylistic felicities.[79] One acknowledgement of the significance of this work lay in the Catholic response. Even though, as we have seen, there had long been Catholic interest in the vernacular scriptures, it was only slowly that the urgency of orthodox translation was accepted. In 1565, in his attack on John Jewel, Thomas Harding was still relatively hostile to translation: by 1567 he was associating himself with Nicholas Sanders in an appeal to Cardinal Morone to support at least some of the Bible in the vernacular to aid the faithful.[80] Nothing came of this scheme, but a decade later William Allen took up the cause, and eventually in 1582 the Rheims New Testament was published. Its purposes were explicitly polemical: to counteract 'the corruptions whereby the heretics have so long lamentably deluded almost the whole of our countrymen'.[81] The new Catholic attitude is reiterated in an interesting manner by the Jesuit missioners in Scotland. In 1582 they argued that there should be a Scots translation of the New Testament, since this would greatly aid their work.[82]

The precise forms of translation remained matters of dispute—at least across the religious divide—but in many ways they pale into insignificance when compared to the institutional difficulties the vernacular scriptures encountered. These included the hostility of the conservative bishops in Henry VIII's reign; the distaste for the Geneva translation by sections of the clerical establishment under Elizabeth; the relatively limited royal support for the dissemination of scriptures except for a brief period in the 1530s and during Edward VI's reign; and responses ranging from lack of

---

[77] P. Collinson, 'William Tyndale and the course of the English Reformation', *Reformation* 1 (1997), 72–97. J.E. Mozley, *Coverdale and his Bibles* (1953), 78–109.

[78] MacCulloch, *Cranmer*, 426–9.

[79] B. Hall, 'The Geneva version of the English Bible: its aims and achievements', in Stephens, *Bible, Reformation and Church*, 124–9. G. Hammond, *The Making of the English Bible* (Manchester, 1982). D.G. Danner, 'The contribution of the Geneva Bible of 1560 to the English Protestant tradition', *C16J* 12 (1981), 5–18.

[80] T. Harding, *An Answere to Maister Juelles Chalenge* (Antwerp, 1565) Facsimile, English Recusant Literature 229 (1975), fos. 197ᵛ, 200. A.O. Meyer, *England and the Catholic Church under Queen Elizabeth* (New York, 1967), 475–8.

[81] T.F. Knox (ed.), *The First and Second Diaries of the English College, Douay* (1887), 145.

[82] T. McCoog, *The Society of Jesus in Ireland, Scotland and England, 1541–1588* (Leiden, 1996), 212.

enthusiasm to outright fear of heresy and sedition from the parishes. These complications have provoked vigorous, but rather inconclusive, debate among historians of the English Reformation about the impact of the vernacular scriptures upon the man in the pew.[83] The first difficulty is that of understanding the sheer logistics of the dissemination of the Bible under Henry VIII and Edward VI. It is a relatively easy task to estimate levels of production of the scriptures, provided that we do not demand too much precision of the figures. About a hundred editions of the whole Bible can be identified between 1525 and 1599, plus 116 versions of one or other of the testaments and 37 psalters. The great weight of this production occurred during Elizabeth's long reign, but 24 complete Bibles and 60 testaments were imprinted before 1553.[84] Although print runs are never easy to estimate for the early modern period, it may be valuable to note that in the 1640s Michael Sparke, attacking the Stationers' Company monopoly, repeatedly used 3,000 as the usual figure for an impression of the Bible.[85] This was in the period when folio texts were falling from fashion, and they almost certainly had shorter print runs but, argue the bibliographers, probably not much less than 2,000. When Richard Grafton, charged with overseeing the printing of the Great Bible in Paris in 1538, had all his printer's stock and the prepared quires seized by the inquisitor general, he complained that 2,500 had been lost. These were eventually retrieved, and became part of an extended English printing effort that is usually estimated by 1540 to have provided enough texts for the nearly 9,000 parishes of England and Wales.[86]

It was, however, one thing to have enough Bibles, another to ensure that they were purchased. One of the consequences of a shift in historical thinking about the speed of popular reformation has been an acknowledgement that churchwardens did not necessarily share the logophilia of the evangelists. The Great Bible was expensive, £1. 5s., of which incumbents were supposed to contribute half, and for the first two years after the 1538 injunctions had ordered it to be set up in every parish church, it seems certain that only a minority had obeyed.[87] The proclamation of

---

[83] See A.G. Dickens, *The English Reformation*, 2nd edn. (1989), 154–60; C.A. Haigh, *English Reformations: Religion, Politics and Society under the Tudors* (Oxford, 1993), 157–8, 250–1; R. Rex, *Henry VIII and the Reformation* (Basingstoke, 1993), 123–6. Duffy, *Stripping of the Altars*, 420–3.

[84] I. Green, *Print and Protestantism in Early Modern England* (Oxford, 2000), 50–6. Green's calculations essentially agree with those in T.H. Darlow and H.F. Moule, *A Historical Catalogue of Printed Editions of the English Bible, 1525–1901*, revised by A.S. Herbert (1968).

[85] C.J. Sommerville, 'On the distribution of religious and occult literature in seventeenth-century England' *The Library* 29 (1974), 222–3.

[86] Greenslade, *History of the Bible*, iii. 151. A.J. Slavin, 'The Rochepot Affair', *C16J* 10/1 (1979), 3–20.

[87] Haigh, *English Reformations*, 157–8.

May 1541 that gave parishes six months to comply under penalty of a fine of £2 undoubtedly clarified minds, and the general instinct for conformity among Tudor officials did its work in many cases.[88] However, recent investigation of East Anglian parishes, which were scarcely located in a 'dark corner' of the land, has indicated that compliance often occurred only in 1547 when the Edwardian commissioners insisted on Bible ownership and when some sale of church plate was permitted in order to purchase the necessary equipment for Protestant worship.[89] In Lancashire even in 1552 only six churches out of eighty-eight claimed to have Bibles, a figure that Haigh argues may be a consequence of poor record-keeping, but which nevertheless must include some actual gaps in ownership.[90] The archdeaconry of Derby may offer a more realistic, if still not encouraging, figure: there in 1552 nine out of twenty-two parishes claimed a Bible among their church goods.[91] These logistic problems were no longer such a major issue in the Elizabethan church, although visitation *comperta* still reveal cases of missing Bibles, and of a lack of the necessary supporting text, Erasmus's *Paraphrases*. Sometimes failures of episcopal visitation can conceal problems for a surprisingly long time: in Gloucester diocese, for example, it was only when a reasonably energetic archiepiscopal visitation was conducted in 1576 that a significant minority of parishes reported they had no Bible.[92] So it seems that the booksellers had to be patient in marketing their folio Bibles: they could be sure of some level of compliance and hence sales, but not of all churchwardens beating a path to their doors unprompted.

The public presentation of the scriptures, making them available for the services of the Church and visible to the laity, was only one step on the road to the vision of a godly, Bible-dominated, society. Private possession of the text, which would enable the congregation to read, mark, and follow as in the woodcuts, was the appropriate ambition of the reformers. This was made explicit for the Scots when in 1579 an Act of Parliament ordered every householder, yeoman, and burgess of substance to have a copy of the Geneva Bible and a Psalter on pain of fine.[93] In England it is necessary to use the indirect evidence of print history to guess at dissemination. The

---

[88] *TRP* i. 296–8.

[89] I am grateful to Gregory Duke for allowing me to cite this material from his research on East Anglia.

[90] C. Haigh, *Reformation and Resistance in Tudor Lancashire* (Cambridge, 1975), 115–16.

[91] J. D'Arcy, 'Late Medieval Catholicism and the Impact of the Reformation in the Deanery of Derby, c.1520–1570', University of Nottingham Ph.D. (1996), 141.

[92] C. Litzenberger, *The English Reformation and the Laity: Gloucestershire, 1540–1580* (Cambridge, 1997), 138–9. The same may be true in Scotland after 1560, though the evidence is even more patchy, Wright, 'Bible in the Scottish Reformation', 161.

[93] Ibid., 162.

decisive decade was that of the 1560s, when both the Geneva Bible and the Bishop's New Testament were printed in octavo form, providing a portable text, at a price that could in principle be afforded by many of the literate laity. But the earlier print history of the production of individual testaments, in addition to whole Bibles, is one indication of a demand that went beyond the official requirements of church and state—those sixty imprints constituting a formidable bulk of Scripture.[94] Yet only a tiny percentage of lay inventories and wills record Bible-ownership, and even if we attribute some of this to the vagaries of appraisal practice, it seems unlikely that we have a scripture-owning literate population before the turn of the sixteenth century.[95] Even late in the century it is only on very rare occasions that there is effective evidence of congregations that behave like those in the preachers' woodcuts, bringing their private Bibles into the public forum of the church and using them. The most famous is William Weston's description of the Puritan fasts at Wisbech, witnessed from the Castle where he was imprisoned during the Armada crisis. There the godly all brought their Bibles and searched for the appropriate texts and disputed their meanings 'all of them, men and women, boys and girls, labourers, workmen and simpletons'.[96]

Was the process of dissemination any easier in Scotland than in England? The Scots laboured under the disadvantage that they were dependent on the work of the English translators and had to receive a text that was in some measure alien. As Gordon Donaldson remarked, 'it is one of the most important facts in their history that the Scottish people never had a printed Bible in their own tongue'.[97] The Great Bible was the text of clandestine Scottish Protestantism before 1560, thereafter the Geneva text superseded it and remained dominant until the end of the century. Whitaker among others noted the importance of this importation, but assumed, with some complacency, that it scarcely mattered: 'the Scots read the English version of the scriptures in their churches, and the people understand it'.[98] Perhaps it did matter little when compared to the urgency felt by the reformers about making the scriptures accessible. Even

[94] Darlow and Moule, *English Bible*, 84–5, 90, 94. Of course, the New Testament was already being produced in octavo form during the 1530s and 1540s: Green, *Print and Protestantism*, 57–62.

[95] Whiting, for example, found only four examples of Bible-ownership by the laity in the South-West before 1570, one of these being of a Latin New Testament. R. Whiting, *The Blind Devotion of the People: Popular Religion and the English Reformation* (Cambridge, 1989), 190.

[96] W. Weston, *The Autobiography of an Elizabethan*, ed. P. Caraman (1955), 164–5.

[97] G. Donaldson, 'The foundations of Anglo-Scottish Union', in his *Scottish Church History* (Edinburgh, 1985), 145. It is interesting that it was the Jesuits, rather than the official Kirk, who considered remedying this: see above, n. 82.

[98] Whitaker, *Disputation*, 215.

when the Scots began to show some independence of the London printers after 1579 there was no attempt to concede to the spoken language. The reverence for the text of Scripture as the starting-point of true reformation was more explicit in Scotland than in England. There is a wonderfully evocative description by Knox of the situation in 1543, when the temporary lifting of a ban on the reading of the vernacular scriptures led to 'the Bible lying almost upon every gentleman's table. The New Testament was borne about in many mens hands...'[99] This no doubt tells us more about the imagination of the reformer than the objective situation of the texts, but it was the Word of God that provided the rallying-cry for the small groups of evangelicals who had to struggle for so long to establish reform. Hence in part the intense affirmation of *sola scriptura* when the Lords of the Congregation triumphed in 1559. Scripture became the badge of identity for a radical movement that rejected intermediary forms of authority far more decisively than its English counterpart.

There is one further test of the importance of the vernacular scriptures for the leaders of English and Scottish Protestantism. In each of the realms, and of course in the separate realm of Ireland, there were substantial minorities (or majorities) who did not speak any form of English. The needs of the Welsh, and of Irish and Scottish Gaelic speakers, posed a significant challenge for committed evangelists.[100] Erasmus saw the Gaelic lands as one of Europe's ultimate linguistic frontiers. 'Would', he wrote in the 1516 exhortation to the reader of the New Testament, 'that these [words] had been translated into the languages of all men, so that they could be read and studied by Scots and Irishmen, by Turks and Saracens.'[101] The challenge was more complex than it might at first appear. It involved first and foremost the formation of a view on the role of language in the process of conversion, and on the relationship between authority and evangelism rather different from that which was the centre of English debate. This can be seen from a brief consideration of the role of Thomas Cromwell in the promotion of Scripture. Cromwell's credentials as the key agent for the dissemination of the official English Bible are no longer in doubt, and few historians would question his evangelical concerns. But in the historiography of Wales Cromwell features largely as

---

[99] Knox, i. 100.

[100] R. Wardhaugh, *Languages in Competition* (Oxford, 1987), ch. 4. In his work on British history Pocock stresses the long-term significance of language as a way of maintaining cultural hegemony. 'The dominant culture maintains rules, speaks a language and preserves a history so powerfully effective that it obliges others to act in the same way.' J.G. Pocock, 'British history: a plea for a new subject', *Journal of Modern History* 47 (1975), 610–11. This may have been the consequence of the use of English for the scriptures; it was not the purpose of the evangelists.

[101] Erasmus's preface to the New Testament, trans. W. Roye, *An Exhortation to the Diligent Study of the Scripture* (Antwerp, 1529), sig. Bi^v–ii^r.

the instrument of an Anglocentric political regime that sought to extirpate cultural difference, to identify Welsh elites with the Tudor regime, and to eliminate the Welsh language from official and legal proceedings.[102] Does this indicate therefore that Cromwell would have seen English as the appropriate language in which to make the scriptures available to a population estimated to have been 80 per cent monoglot Welsh? The question is more difficult to answer than some of the secondary sources imply. There was scarcely time for Cromwell to oversee the production of the Great Bible before his fall, and certainly none for him to give sustained consideration to the needs of the Welsh and the Irish.[103] It seems dubious to infer from a policy of anglicizing the political elites that Cromwell would necessarily have rejected a role for the vernacular in religious instruction. Rather it seems likely that Cromwell would have turned to the advice of his regional governors, and to the episcopate whose duty it was to introduce the Reformation into the Celtic lands. In the 1530s, as later, it often appears that the failures of evangelical impulse from the centre were more failures of political and administrative will than of any resistance to the translation of the scriptures. The Scots came to this problem far later, and via a very different form of reformation: the relative weakness of royal control in the Highlands left the Kirk in practice to make the necessary decisions about communication and conversion.[104] It is difficult to see that James VI's famous views on the barbarity of the Highlanders and their language made much difference in practice to the spread of Protestantism in Gaelic.[105]

The attitudes of both local elites and of those appointed from London were complex. In the case of the Welsh the bilingual gentry were usually sympathetic to the use of their 'mother tongue' but rarely interested in Protestant evangelism until late in the sixteenth century. The minority of the clergy who did see the Bible as the cornerstone of true conversion were themselves divided. Some saw the advance of civilization, religious reform, and the English language as an integrated experience: others quickly recognized that they had a prime responsibility to translate for their congregations.[106] William Barlow, bishop of St David's from 1536 to 1548, was the leading exponent of anglicizing evangelism. As early as

---

[102] Williams, *Wales and the Reformation*, 105–7. P. Roberts, 'The Welsh language, English law and Tudor legislation', *Transactions of the Honourable Society of Cymroddorion* (1989), 19–76.

[103] R.D. Edwards, *Church and State in Tudor Ireland* (Dublin, 1935), pp. xlii–xliii. A.L. Rowse, *Tudor Cornwall* (1941), 21–5.

[104] Kirk, *Patterns of Reform*, 483–5.

[105] Though the contrary view is expressed by Meek, who blames much of the delay in evangelizing on government hostility to Gaelic. D. Meek, 'The Gaelic Bible', in Wright, *Bible in Scottish Life*, 10.

[106] Williams, *Wales and the Reformation*, 63–4.

1535, when he was prior of the Augustinian house of Haverfordwest, one of his servants had a copy of the prohibited English scriptures.[107] Once he was well established in his see he devoted his considerable energies to denouncing Welsh superstition and idolatry, to fighting his cathedral clergy, and to establishing English preaching and schooling. When, in 1538, he instructed the clergy of Cardigan to declare the gospel and epistle in 'the mother tongue' it seems likely that he meant English.[108] Barlow's successor, Robert Ferrar, an enthusiast for evangelical preaching, offered equally little support to Welsh speakers.[109] One should not automatically assume, however, that Barlow's attitude was shared by all outsiders. Bishop Parfew of St Asaph seems to have been aware of the desirability of communication in Welsh, while in neighbouring Cornwall Bishop Voysey made it clear after the 1538 Injunctions that the gospel and epistle should be declared in Cornish 'where the English tongue is not used'.[110]

The case of Ireland is yet more complicated, because the assumption of the 'New English' that it was obviously desirable to function entirely in that language was seconded by the belief of the 'Old English' that English was the demarcator between civility and barbarism. Although the linguistic boundaries were in practice very fluid, and by the 1530s the use of Irish was common even in the southern trading towns and in the Pale, there was still a political impulse in favour of the metropolitan language.[111] Hence there is the promotion in the 1537 parliament of English-speaking parochial schools, and the acceptance of the requirement that those appointed to Irish benefices should 'endeavour... to learn the English tongue and language and use English order [and] fashions if you may...'.[112] These assumptions by the Old English community might in theory have simplified the reception of the Great Bible, and made the scriptures an instrument of coercive control as well as evangelism in a benighted land. In 1538 James Butler, heir to the earl of Ormondy, wrote to Henry VIII urging that 'the word of God' should be 'set forth' as a means of bringing the people to civility.[113] But the association of the metropolitan language with religious change had the opposite effect, div-

---

[107] *LP* x. 1091.

[108] *LP* xi. 1428. T. Wright (ed.), *Three Chapters of Letters on the Suppression of the Monasteries*, CS os 26 (1843), 187. Williams, *Wales and the Reformation*, 118–25.

[109] A.J. Brown, *Robert Ferrar* (1997), 100–1, 171–4.

[110] P.B. Ellis, *The Cornish Language and its Literature* (1974), 59.

[111] S. Ellis, *Tudor Ireland: Crown Community and the Conflict of Cultures, 1470–1603* (1985), 183–225. N. Canny, *Kingdom and Colony: Ireland in the Atlantic World* (Baltimore, 1988), 11–12.

[112] H.A. Jefferies, *Priests and Prelates of Armagh in the Age of Reformation, 1518–1558* (Dublin, 1997), 145, shows that the order to function in English had the support of the Old English elite in County Louth.

[113] R.D. Edwards, *Church and State in Tudor Ireland* (1935), 33–4.

iding the settler communities, and leading to profound debate about how reform might be established.[114] In the absence of clear policy from the crown such divergent opinions could flourish and impede evangelism in the indigenous tongue.[115] The later history of the translation of Scripture into the other languages of the British Isles largely confirms the importance of regional initiative, and individual commitment, against any sustained engagement by the metropolitan leaders of church and state.

Although the reformers cried *sola scriptura*, in practice the Bible was not always the first priority for translation and printed dissemination. The first full text of the reform printed in Welsh was the 1549 Book of Common Prayer, translated by William Salesbury, which had been preceded by a printing of the Epistles and Gospels used in the liturgy.[116] In Irish the catechism long preceded the printing of the New Testament, while in Scottish Gaelic the Form of Common Order was printed in 1567, the full Bible not until 1801.[117] Manx Gaelic had no Bible until the eighteenth century: the first attempt at a local version of the Prayer Book came in the early seventeenth century.[118] In Cornish it was felt by the bishops that the most necessary use for the local language was in catechizing, though Nicholas Udall also advocated the translation of the liturgy.[119] Much of this contrast is, of course, to be explained by the difficulty of translating and printing the full text of the Bible—the form of the languages in which to print was initially uncertain; neither orthography nor typography were necessarily fully agreed; the cost of production and the limited market made the product expensive; there were difficulties in finding printers.[120] The Welsh reformers, in particular, had no doubt about the critical importance of the Word, and laboured with formidable energy to overcome these practical difficulties to make scriptural translation a practical reality.

---

[114] B. Bradshaw, 'Sword, word and strategy in the Reformation in Ireland', *HJ* 21 (1978), 475–502.

[115] H.A. Jefferies, 'The early Tudor Reformation in the Irish Pale', *JEH* 52 (2001), 34–62.

[116] W. Salesbury, *Kynniver Llith a Ban*, ed. J. Fisher (Cardiff, 1931).

[117] D. Meek, 'The Gaelic Bible', in Wright, *The Bible in Scottish Life*, 9–23.

[118] A.W. Moore (ed.), *The Book of Common Prayer in Manx Gaelic* (Manx Society, 1895), pp. xxi–xxii.

[119] Ellis, *Cornish Language*, 62–4.

[120] For example, the orthography of Manx was so fluid that one of those clerics asked to review Bishop Phillip's Prayer Book alleged that he could not understand it at all: Moore, *Manx Gaelic*, p. xi. One of the many problems in the Scottish case was that Carswell translated into a modified form of the literary language—Classical Common Gaelic—rather than the Common Vernacular used by the ordinary population. J. Dawson, 'Calvinism and the Gaidhealtachd in Scotland', in A. Duke, G. Lewis, and A. Pettegree (eds.), *Calvinism in Europe* (Cambridge, 1994), 231–53. J. Bannerman, 'Literacy in the Highlands', in I.B. Cowan and D. Shaw (eds.), *The Renaissance and Reformation in Scotland* (Edinburgh, 1983), 221–8.

But in both the Welsh and the Scottish case another explanation for the slowness of translation can be advanced. These Celtic and Gaelic cultures were primarily oral, dependent on elite bardic traditions for the transmission of knowledge. To become logocentric—to experience at first or at second hand that reverence for the 'word-in-space' that Ong identifies as the characteristic of print cultures—required an even greater change than it did in England or lowland Scotland.[121] So approaches to the scriptures were modified to suit local conditions. The case can be made best in the Scottish Gaidhealtachd, since there the appearance of the full printed scriptures long post-dated conversion to Calvinism. The pattern established in the reformed churches of the Highlands was that the readers, who assisted the ministers, were supposed to translate directly from the English text into the Scottish Vernacular Gaelic, while clergy made their own translations of texts and passages for sermons.[122] This enabled individuals to overcome the problems of dialect and the divergent forms of the vernacular, and to modify language to render it accessible. It may be that in Wales the anonymous translation of part of Tyndale's New Testament made in 1543 was a similar exercise, intended to act as an aid to preaching and 'declaring' the epistles and gospels. Glanmor Williams identifies its prose style as a mixture of the literary and colloquial, with a South Welsh origin, precisely the sort of tool to verbal evangelizing that the Scots later used.[123]

The success of oral forms of the transmission of the Word should caution us against too ready an acceptance of the centrality of print culture in the dissemination of Protestantism. The enthusiasm of a small number of Welsh reformers for a proper and established text of the Bible was certainly focused upon its importance as a tool of evangelism. It also concerned the intellectual status of the Welsh language: its coming of age in a period of philological learning.[124] The story of the triumph of William Salesbury, Richard Davies, and William Morgan is so well known as to need little repetition, especially as the evidence has been elegantly assembled by Glanmor Williams.[125] But it is important to emphasize the extent

---

[121] Ong, *Presence of the Word*, 272–4.

[122] On this issue see Jane Dawson's crucial article, 'Calvinism and the Gaidhealtachd', 238–41.

[123] Williams, *Wales and the Reformation*, 146–7.

[124] There is a danger here of privileging Ong's transition from oral to literate culture as being the essential explanatory tool for the discussion of the transmission of the religion of the Word. The work of Dawson and others is an important correction, and reminds us of the greater significance of the oral in some environments. In the Isle of Man, for example, apparent conformity to the Elizabethan Settlement was achieved by bilingual clergy using entirely oral modes for their congregations. W.J. Ong, *Orality and Literacy: The Technologizing of the Word* (1982). Moore, *Manx Gaelic*, pp. xii, xxi.

[125] Williams, *Wales and the Reformation*, 235–44, 338–60.

to which regional initiative drove the project, and also to note those
moments at which the intervention of the centre proved critical as well.
William Salesbury was profoundly convinced that until translated into
Welsh the scriptures were 'bound in fetters' for his countrymen.[126] And
when the Elizabethan Settlement offered new hope for Protestantism he
and Richard Davies, the new bishop of St Asaph, began to press for a
translation. The key for these men was not simply a translation, but an
authorized text for churches, hence the need to engage the political centre
and the interesting choice of parliamentary legislation as the route taken.
The 1563 Act for the rendering of the Bible into Welsh was a private
initiative, sponsored by Davies and Humphrey Lluyd, but the sympathy
displayed by Archbishop Parker and William Cecil must have been of
significance.[127] Williams suggests that Cecil's interest was engaged partly
because he saw Wales as a possible 'back door' to England for Catholic
traitors. It is certainly the case that political and religious threat focused
minds in England on Welsh evangelism: in 1587 John Whitgift gave Morgan vital support in the last stages of production under the spur of the
radical challenge from John Penry and the Mary Stuart crisis.[128] The result
of Morgan's labours, the 1588 Bible, was ordered to be held in all Welsh
churches from Christmas of that year and, with some of the usual delays,
it seems the parishes complied.[129] As for private reading: the poet-parson
Thomas Jones was already writing that Christmas that men should 'go, sell
[their] shirt' in order to have this 'treasure beyond price'. It is unlikely
that they did, but it may be that because the Welsh Bible came into a
world already partially Protestantized, its impact was felt more swiftly than
that of its English counterpart.[130]

The Irish experience of scriptural translation differs as markedly from
that of the Welsh and Scots as does their general religious circumstances.
The most obvious contrast was that there was no strong indigenous pressure for translation: the key social group that might have generated such a
demand, the bardic learned orders, having consistently resisted any religious change. The surviving poetry of the learned elites suggests that the
bards were deeply content with traditional Catholicism and saw any challenge to it as alien imposition.[131] English Bibles, already circulating in

---

[126] Salesbury, *Kynniver*, dedication.
[127] R. Flower, 'William Salesbury, Richard Davies and Archbishop Parker', *National Library
of Wales Journal* 2 (1941), 7–14. 5 Elizabeth, c. 28.
[128] Williams, *Wales and the Reformation*, 350–1.
[129] *APC* 1588. 283–4.
[130] Jones, a poet-parson of Llandeilo Bertholau, Monmouthshire, wrote his verses in praise
of Morgan's translation as early as Christmas 1588, a few weeks after its publication: Williams,
Wales and the Reformation, 358.
[131] Meigs, *Reformations in Ireland*, 60–5.

Ireland from the 1530s, were just such an imposition. Therefore, any translation of the scriptures had to be undertaken as missionary endeavour, mission which was often viewed as an exercise in civilizing control rather than the *evangelion* of Tyndale's vision. In a few enthusiasts these elements were indeed combined. There is a fascinating example in the presentation of an old Irish text containing scriptural extracts made by Laurence Humphrey to Queen Elizabeth on her visit to Woodstock in 1575. In his speech he prayed that 'by this Word may the English be more and more strengthened; by this Word may the wild Irish be tamed'.[132] For the councils in London and Dublin 'taming' often took precedence over evangelizing. In 1563, when Cecil was apparently worrying about the threat of Catholic invasion, the Privy Council in London arranged for the payment of the large sum of £66. 13s. 4d. to Archbishop Loftus and Bishop Brady, for the printing of an Irish New Testament.[133] Loftus and Brady were considered the only reliable leaders of the Protestant church in Ireland, and the latter, at least, had already showed himself concerned to evangelize in Irish. Yet, given the notable fiscal caution of Elizabeth's regime it seems unlikely that this sum would have been paid unless it was thought that it would purchase political stability. The council followed this initiative by arranging for the cutting of fount for Irish letters, probably by John Day, who undertook the cutting of the fount for Archbishop Parker's Anglo-Saxon text.[134] It seems that nothing was done with the money in Ireland, for three years later the council was demanding its money back, and the only serious translator beneficed in the Irish church, John Kearney, was turning his attention to the more modest task of the catechism.[135]

When the New Testament was finally produced in 1602–3 it was as a result of the combined efforts of several men from the learned Gaelic orders who had by then become converts to Protestantism, and the funding came largely from Anglo-Irish families.[136] By then, what might have been a major official initiative was dissipated, and there was no sustained attempt to place the New Testament officially in the churches. Neither London nor Dublin was really committed to the work of mission among the Irish. There were occasional attempts by the crown to do something more, as in James I's comments on Trinity College's obligations

---

[132] J. Nicholls, *The Progresses of Queen Elizabeth*, 3 vols. (1810), i. 583–99. Sir William Croft, *Croftus sive Hibernia Liber*, ed. A. Keaveney and J.A. Madden (Dublin, 1992), 99.

[133] M. Ronan, *The Reformation in Ireland under Elizabeth, 1558–1580* (1930), 360–1.

[134] E.W. Lynam, 'The Irish character in print, 1571–1923', *The Library* 4th ser. 4 (1924), 288–92. B. Dickins, 'The Irish broadside of 1571 and Queen Elizabeth's types', *Transactions of the Cambridge Bibliographical Society* 1/1 (1949/53), 48–60.

[135] *CSP Irl* i. 356.

[136] See below, p. 439.

in 1620. The Irish church went its own way, creating an anglicized ministry. And Bishop Bedell's later passionate efforts to provide an Irish Bible
met with a cool response from the great James Ussher, apparently on the
grounds that it would merely encourage the separatist tendencies of a
hostile people.[137]

Preaching and Teaching

The Word had to be illuminated by the labour of preaching. 'The gospel
sincerely preached' was from the beginning of the Reformation one of
the defining marks of the true Church, one of the only two marks agreed
by all the magisterial reformers. 'When the Bible and true preachers
thereof be restored into the Church,' said Hooper in his answer to Gardiner's defence of the sacraments, 'God shall restore likewise such light as
shall discern everything aright.' Preaching could not, of course, construct
faith, which was the sole gift of divine grace, yet it was 'of all things in
this world most necessary for the people'.[138] Richard Rollock, preaching
on Corinthians to his Edinburgh auditors, spoke of two revelations: 'the
first be Word, when it is preached: the second be the spirit when that
holy spirit concurs with the Word'.[139] 'We cannot be saved without faith,
and faith cometh by hearing of the Word,' thus Latimer in one of his
sermons before Edward VI, 'there must be preachers if we look to be
saved'.[140] Such arguments were constantly articulated throughout the
English and Scottish Reformations.[141] Even when they had become commonplaces to the second and third generation of Protestants, and when
the practice of preaching had become a bitterly contested issue, there was
still little dissent among divines that the duty of preaching was the first call
upon a minister. The duty of the pastor, said Laurence Chaderton, was to
'listen unto the voice of Christ "feed, feed, feed"'.[142] Few put the matter
as passionately as Edward Dering, that key link between the first generations of Protestant preachers and their Puritan successors: 'we cannot
believe except we hear, nor we cannot hear without a preacher'.[143] The
importance of preachers was such that, if their duty was properly discharged:

---

[137] A. Ford, *The Protestant Reformation in Ireland, 1590–1641* (Dublin, 1997), 124–5. R. Buick
Knox, *James Ussher, Archbishop of Armagh* (Cardiff, 1967), 88–90.
[138] Carr, *Early Writings of Hooper*, 205.
[139] R. Rollock, *Certain sermons upon severall places of the epistles of Paul* (Edinburgh, 1599), 155.
[140] Corrie, *Sermons of Latimer*, 200.
[141] Kirk, *Patterns of Reform*, pp. xii–xiii.
[142] L. Chaderton, *A Fruitfull Sermon, upon the 3, 4, 5, 6, 7, and 8 verse of the 12 chapter of the
Epistle of St Paule to the Romanes* (London, 1584), 72.
[143] E. Dering, *A Briefe and Necessarie Catechisme*, in *Workes* (1614), sig. A3ᵛ.

the sword of the spirit which God hath given them would vanquish Satan and destroy the power of darkness, till the knowledge of God were plentiful upon earth, and all the joys of heart were sealed unto men in perfect beauty.[144]

The sword was the Word of God: *sola scriptura*. 'All truth', argued John Knox's Edinburgh successor Robert Bruce, 'is contained in the Scriptures, there can be no interpretation but that which floweth therefrom.'[145] The early generations of Protestant preachers had to clear away what they saw as the thickets of error in popish preaching, especially the stories of 'bears or apes . . . gesta romanorum, legenda aurea, . . . [or] such other lies'.[146] But though truth flowed from Scripture it was notoriously difficult to arrive at an uncontested reading of the Word, which required the lively interpretation of the learned minister. Every minister must in Chaderton's view 'teach sound doctrine by the true interpretation of the word and . . . confute all contrary errors by unanswerable arguments and reasons'.[147] When Kentish ministers agreed articles for the prophesying conferences held in 1572, they urged that speakers upon scriptural texts should 'open the literal sense and meaning of the Holy Ghost and digress not into exhortation, and especially into invectives'.[148] Even this strict insistence on a literal reading of Scripture, which became the hallmark of the Calvinist divine, allowed some scope for stages of exposition: explaining the words of Scripture, trying different and 'contrary' readings, adding comparative texts, and offering a context for the words. The process sounds, and often no doubt was, austere and demanding, but some concession could be made to 'popularity'. William Perkins, in his *Art of Prophesying*, identifies Bruce's fourth heading as 'to apply . . . these doctrines rightly collected to the life and manners of men in simple and plain speech'.[149] Bruce himself put this even more directly: 'unless you hear Christ in a familiar and homely language, you cannot understand, and unless you understand it is not possible for you to believe'.[150]

---

[144] BL Lans. MS 17/90, fo. 198ʳ. On Dering and preaching see P. Lake, *Moderate Puritans and the Elizabethan Church* (Cambridge, 1982), 16–24; P. Collinson, 'A mirror of Elizabethan Puritanism: the life and letters of "Godly Master Dering"', in his *Godly People: Essays on English Protestantism and Puritanism* (1983), 10–11.

[145] W. Cunningham (ed.), *Sermons of the Reverend Robert Bruce* (Wodrow Society, Edinburgh, 1843), 375–6.

[146] Wabuda, 'Provision of Preaching', 54, quoting Robert Wisdom.

[147] Chaderton, '*Fruitfull Sermon*', 61.

[148] P. Clark, 'The prophesying movement in Kentish towns in the 1570s', *Archaeologia Cantiana* 93 (1978 for 1977), 85.

[149] W. Perkins, *Works*, 3 vols. (Cambridge, 1631), ii. 259. On forms of preaching see J.W. Blench, *Preaching in England in the Late Fifteenth and Sixteenth Centuries* (Oxford, 1964), 71–112.

[150] R. Bruce, *Sermons on the Sacrament preached in Edinburgh, 1589*, ed. T.F. Torrance (1958), 112–13.

Plain speaking, being able to translate the literal meanings of Scripture into the hearts of men, was the ambition of those godly divines who preached *ad plebes*. Although they themselves needed to be well founded in biblical learning they should not disturb their auditors with Latin and Greek, lest, says Perkins, 'they cannot fit those things which went before with those that follow after'.[151] Such prescriptions seem to have been followed more systematically in Reformation Scotland than in contemporary England, where forms of preaching remained markedly pluralistic throughout the sixteenth century.[152] It often seems that the only discernible consistency among Protestant preachers is the use of scriptural material as a ground for preaching. Even then defences of the royal supremacy early in the period, or the growing genre of sermons for public occasions under Elizabeth, could readily depart from this defining core.[153] The Edwardian preachers were particularly committed to the use of plain style, with Latimer offering a particular sub-set of colloquial and anecdotal techniques in the presentation of Scripture, but late Elizabethan conformist preachers like John King and John Bridges still used very similar methods. Plenty of godly Protestant preachers adopted a more ornate approach to their material, and did not hesitate to use allegorical ways of interpreting Scripture when it suited their purposes. Nor was elaborated oratory necessarily reserved for a courtly audience: men like Paul Bush and Thomas Playfere were quite capable of taking their formal rhetoric to Paul's Cross congregations who might be thought in need of direct and explicit edification.[154]

This diversity must be partly explained by the need to regard the sermon as performance. As Patrick Collinson has recently observed, this elusive aspect of evangelizing is too easily overlooked in concentration upon the printed word, but the 'quickening of the spirit' that was seen as the purpose of preaching demanded the stimulus of lively presentation.[155] Thomas Wilson in his *Arte of Rhetorique*, that popular work that provided much of the practical guidance for preachers, observed, 'except men find delight, they will not long abide . . . Therefore even these ancient

---

[151] Perkins, *Works*, ii. 670–1.

[152] D.G. Mullan, *Scottish Puritanism 1590–1638* (Oxford, 2000), 57–62. Blench, *Preaching in England*, *passim*.

[153] MacLure, *Paul's Cross Sermons*, 14 ff., 69–70; *Register of Sermons Preached at Paul's Cross, 1534–1642*, revised by P. Pauls and J.C. Boswell (Ottawa, 1989). The listings of the known sermons at the Cross for the 1530s is so remorselessly political that it is quite a surprise to find Wriothesley's Chronicle remarking on Bishop Hilsey as 'a great setter forth of the sincerity of Scripture': C. Wriothesley, *A Chronicle of England during the Reigns of the Tudors from AD 1485 to 1559*, ed. W.D. Hamilton, 2 vols. CS NS 18 *and* 20 (1875–7), i. 104.

[154] A.F. Herr, *The Elizabethan Sermon: A Survey and Bibliography* (Philadelphia, 1940).

[155] P. Collinson, 'Elizabethan and Jacobean Puritanism as forms of popular religious culture', in Durston and Eales, *Culture of English Puritanism*, 46–8.

preachers must now and then play the fools in the pulpit... or else they are like some time to preach to bare walls'.[156] The concept of entertainment presumably embraced a spectrum of behaviour from sheer spiritual eloquence—'as every sound is not Music, so every sermon is not preaching' says the editor of Rollock's sermons—to the violence of delivery that allowed Foxe to mock Latimer's opponent Hubberdine for 'dancing' his sermon until in his zest he landed among his auditors and broke his leg.[157] A rather more acceptable Protestant performance was described by Sir John Harington, who recalled the court sermons of Matthew Hutton: 'I hear him out of the Pulpit thundering [his] text.'[158] The competing colloquial narratives of Latimer and Roger Edgeworth presumably offered specific opportunity to perform within the pulpit: Edgeworth, says his recent editor, sometimes used the language and dialect of his Bristolian audience to enhance narrative and engage attention.[159] Later in the century the habit of preaching on the moral and spiritual lessons to be drawn from prodigies and sensational events provided some of the same entertainment value from the pulpit.[160]

This need to entertain and to arrest the attention of auditors seems to confirm the pessimism of the godly about the populace and its reluctance to hear the Word. Arthur Dent, George Gifford, and other zealous Protestants who concerned themselves with the attitudes of the plebeians were convinced that they did not wish to hear the preacher. Most ordinary men, complained William Harrison of Lancashire, were deaf adders who closed their ears to God's Word.[161] It is unlikely that all Tudor laymen, or even their Scottish counterparts, had a desire to run 'to sermons' and prattle 'of the scriptures', which even at their most stimulating were lengthy and demanding of concentration of a very different kind from the ordinary routines of the liturgy.[162] But the evidence of the popularity of Paul's Cross sermons should perhaps not be regarded as completely atypical, or the words of sharp critics of popular behaviour as gospel truth. It will never be possible to judge fully what the ordinary man and woman in the pew thought of the fare that was provided for them from the growing number of pulpits in the parish churches in the late years of the sixteenth

---

[156] T. Wilson, *The Arte of Rhetorique*, ed. G.H. Mair (Oxford, 1909), 3–4.

[157] Rollock, *Sermons on Paul*, preface.

[158] Harington, quoted in P. McCullough, *Sermons at Court: Politics and Religion in Elizabethan and Jacobean Preaching* (Cambridge, 1998), 30.

[159] Wilson, *Sermons by Edgeworth*, 75–6.

[160] A. Walsham, *Providence in Early Modern England* (Oxford, 2000).

[161] A. Dent, *A Plaine mans path-way* (1601). G. Gifford, *A briefe discoures of certaine points of the religion which is among the common sort of Christians, which may be termed the countrie divinitie* (1583). W. Harrison, *The difference of hearers. Or an exposition of the parable of the sower* (1614), sig. A7ᵛ.

[162] Dent, *Plaine mans path-way*, 151.

century. What is clear is that, in the towns in particular, there was ample opportunity to gad to sermons, and that men and women did so in numbers.[163]

For the committed evangelicals considerations about the precise structural and literary forms of preaching were often otiose. The problem was always that there was too little preaching of any kind; too little presentation of the truths of Scripture to ordinary laymen. 'How should the people be saved without teachers?', thus asked Bishop Sandys, but the Pauline question echoed throughout the English and Scottish Reformations.[164] We shall return to the problem and the attempted institutional solutions in a later chapter. Here we may just briefly note some of its parameters: only nine preachers, for example, among 166 clergy in the Diocese of Peterborough in 1560, or thirty-three between 135 West Sussex parishes in 1579.[165] Only at the very end of our period do the 1603 episcopal returns suggest that a preaching ministry was securely established in much of England.[166] In Wales the process was even slower; the bishops of St David's could muster only ten and fourteen preachers in 1570 and 1583 respectively, lending some credence to John Penry's charge that not one in twenty parishes had adequate preaching.[167] Ireland, as ever, presents the extreme case, both because of a desperate shortage of properly qualified preachers and because of the divided opinions of its Protestant leaders about how best to evangelize. Bishop Loftus of Dublin, responding to a complaint of Burghley's about lack of preaching, pointed out that sermons would be nugatory without the sword to force men to conformity: 'unless they be forced they will not once come to hear the word preached'.[168] At the other extreme William Herbert was unique in his evangelical zeal in the lands of North Kerry, seeking out bilingual men for local parishes and advising them on preaching from the scriptures.[169] Only in Scotland, where the fledgling Kirk invested its greatest energy in the quest for a preaching ministry, did most populous parishes have access to a preacher by the 1580s.[170]

---

[163] P. Seaver, *The Puritan Lecturerships: The Politics of Religious Dissent 1560–1662* (Stanford, Calif., 1970), 88–117.

[164] J. Ayre (ed.), *The Sermons of Edwyn Sandys* (PS, Cambridge, 1842), 154.

[165] W.J. Sheils, *The Puritans in the Diocese of Peterborough, 1558–1610* (Northamptonshire Record Society, 1979), 20. Haigh, *English Reformations*, 269.

[166] R.G. Usher, *The Reconstruction of the English Church*, 2 vols. (New York, 1910), i. 241.

[167] Williams, *Wales and the Reformation*, 300–1. D. Williams (ed.), *J. Penry: Three Treatises concerning Wales* (Cardiff, 1960), 36.

[168] Bradshaw, 'Sword, word and strategy', 487.

[169] *CSP Irl* iv. 189, 192.

[170] Kirk, *Patterns of Reform*, 147–8.

In the absence of sufficient preachers the Protestant churches resorted to other means to disseminate the Word: most notably in England the official homilies, first published in 1547.[171] The homily as a read sermon had a long history: late medieval cycles such as Mirk's *Festial* were part of the genre, in so far as they could be delivered verbatim on appropriate Sundays and festivals, though they could also form the source material from which independent sermons could be preached.[172] Archbishop Warham urged John Longland to print some of his sermons so that they could be 'read for the common profit', implying that this was common practice.[173] Preaching from a cleric's own resources must always have been a daunting business, but it acquired both a new urgency and new challenge when he was required, as in Cromwell's Royal Injunctions, to 'purely and sincerely declare the very gospel of Christ'. The reformers set their faces clearly against the 'legendary' tradition of edifying stories represented by Mirk or the *Legenda Aurea*. Even Bishop Bonner acknowledged that his London clergy should not be preaching 'fable or other histories' and should avoid sermons written within the last two or three hundred years.[174] The need, as Cranmer perceived from a very early moment in the Henrician Reformation, was for authorized texts based on Scripture that could be offered verbatim to congregations by even the most ignorant curate. Richard Taverner, who anticipated the official homilies in his *Epistles and Gospels with a brief Postyll upon the same* (1540), wrote in his preface of the 'singular help and benefit' incumbents would receive from the commentaries for the 'edification of Christs Church'.[175] These sentiments were echoed in more authoritarian tones in the Preface to the official English homilies which spoke of ministers who lacked the gift of preaching 'whereof great inconveniences might rise, and ignorance still be maintained' if the crown had not provided appropriate instructional material.[176]

But from the beginning the Reformation homilies had a dual purpose, best expressed by the convocation order of 1542 that sermons should be compiled 'to make for stay of such errors as were then by ignorant preachers sparkled among the people'.[177] The homilies were to become

---

[171] S. Wabuda, 'Bishops and the provision of homilies, 1520 to 1547', *C16 J* 25/3 (1994), 551–3.

[172] T. Erbe (ed.), *Mirk's Festial: A Collection of Homilies, by Johannes Mirkus*, EETS ES 96 (1905).

[173] Wabuda, 'Provision of homilies', 551.

[174] *VAI* ii. 89–90.

[175] R. Taverner, *The Epistles and Gospelles with a brief Postil upon the same from after Easter tyll Advent* (? 1545).

[176] Griffiths, *Homilies*, 3–4.

[177] Muller, *Letters of Gardiner*, 296.

the exposition of the faith of the new Church, securing orthodoxy in the pulpit. Already by this date the Bishops' Book had been presented in homiletic form, designed to be read as sermons, and the 1542 project atrophied partly because the King's Book was presented in similar structure the following year.[178] When Cranmer finally had his way with the publication of the *Book of Homilies* in 1547 he began with his ringing affirmation of the necessity of Bible-reading and then proceeded to the clearest possible articulation of the relationship between faith and works. There was some attempt to accommodate more traditional attitudes in the 'good works' sections of the text. In two cases these were written by Bishop Bonner and by his chaplain John Harpsfield, but the doctrinal agenda was firmly established by the archbishop himself. 1547 was not an ideal moment at which to articulate the full confessional stance of the Church of England, and the pressures of the later years of Edward's reign did not allow Cranmer time to return to the project.[179] It was therefore left to the first generation of Elizabeth's bishops, and particularly to John Jewel, to produce the revised homilies that became the staple of the late Tudor parish.

The value of the official homilies in the process of evangelizing is most explicitly indicated by the work of Bishop Bonner during the Marian period. Bonner supervised the production of two sets of instructional literature during 1555: *A Profitable and Necessary Doctrine*, which was a revised and enlarged version of the King's Book, and *Homelies Set Forth*, a group of thirteen sermons designed for reading by clerics to their congregations.[180] In the latter particular attention was paid to the Eucharist and papal supremacy. In the following year Cardinal Pole followed the example of the Edwardian regime and ordered that every parish acquire the volume.[181] It seemed that the homilies were being established in a role as core doctrinal documents of the religious settlements. It can be argued, however, that that role was somewhat weakened by the amended form of the Elizabethan homilies, which gave a disproportionate role to the moral and social dimensions of faith. The point was beautifully exemplified in the hostile question of the authors of the *Admonition to the Parliament* (1572), 'are not the people well modified think you, when the homily of sweeping the church is read unto them?'[182] The godly were, of course, dissatisfied not only with such trivia, but even with Cranmer's

---

[178] Ibid., 306, 311–15.   [179] MacCulloch, *Cranmer*, 206, 224, 293–4.

[180] E. Bonner, *A Profytable and Necessarye Doctryne* (1555). *Homelies sette forth by the right reverende Edmunde bishop of London* (1555).

[181] Haigh, *English Reformations*, 216–17.

[182] Quoted in P. Collinson, 'The Elizabethan church and the new religion', in C. Haigh (ed.), *The Reign of Elizabeth I* (1984), 179.

austere and sound prose on faith and justification. The bare reading of text, cut up as it usually was into manageable lengths for accessible reading, could in no way edify as did preacher moved by the spirit. Thomas Cartwright adopted the purist position that homilies, like the Apocrypha, had no place in the Church.[183] But other sound Calvinists were not so sure: a bad sermon, said Richard Rollock's editor, might be worse than 'if one should stand up and read a Homily'.[184] So homilies might be tolerated, as they were in the Scottish church for much of the first Reformation generation. There the English text was used by readers, that order of ministers who had no call to independent preaching.[185] Yet they were not often given pride of place as instruments of instruction or evangelization. An interesting test here is the absence of translations into the other tongues of the British Isles, for Ireland, Gaelic Scotland, and Wales, where it might be thought there was urgent need for preaching assistance. There was eventually a Welsh translation, printed in 1606, though Siôn Dafydd Rhys claimed that he had been engaged on one for the previous twenty-five years. It was one of the handful of texts that defined Welsh religious prose-writing, but its impact is likely to have been limited, only one edition appearing before the 1640s.[186] The only other Celtic tongue to have a set of homilies is, intriguingly, Cornish. There the inspiration was Catholic, not Protestant, and the translation from Bishop Bonner's *Homelies* was presumably designed to sustain traditional religious beliefs.[187]

The defence of official homilies by the English establishment also seems curiously lack-lustre. The main point that both Whitgift and Hooker adduced against Cartwright's attack was the obvious one that homilies were merely written sermons, as likely to be divinely inspired as the spoken word from the pulpit.[188] Hooker displays little of the loving affection for them that he lavishes on the liturgy or the reading of the scriptures. The ambivalence of contemporaries is often echoed by historians, who treat the homilies as an important source of evidence of the concerns of the Tudor church while ignoring their possible influence on the man in the pew. It is in the nature of this type of official text that we know more about the failures to employ it, expressed in complaints before the church court, than we do about its positive effect. Some compensation for this deficiency is supplied by William Harrison's famous commentary on Protestant worship,

---

[183] Ayre, *Works of Whitgift*, iii. 53. [184] Rollock, *Sermons on Paul*, preface.

[185] G. Donaldson, *The Scottish Reformation* (Cambridge, 1960), 83.

[186] Williams, *Wales and the Reformation*, 341, 386, 393.

[187] Ellis, *Cornish Language*, 64–5. The translation was undertaken by a local priest, John Tregrar, but it indicates the difficulties of providing a proper translation into Cornish by leaving Latin terms in the original on occasions and sometimes adding English terms.

[188] Ayre, *Works of Whitgift*, iii. 339. Keble, *Hooker: Works*, ii. 110–12.

in his *Description of England*. Harrison was hostile to 'dumb dogs', those who failed to preach, but he argued that the homilies were a major help to those who lacked the training to offer independent sermons.[189]

The Elizabethan hierarchy was even more indifferent to the other aid to exposition of the scriptures widely promoted by the Edwardian regime. At the 1547 royal visitation the English and Welsh parishes were ordered to acquire, in addition to the *Homilies*, copies of Nicholas Udall's translated edition of Erasmus's *Paraphrases* on the New Testament. The order was repeated and pursued in later Edwardian episcopal injunctions and again became the official policy of the Church in 1559.[190] There were, as usual, practical problems. The printed editions of the first tome, covering the Gospels and Acts, did not emerge from the presses until 1548, and the commentary on the rest of the New Testament was not available until 1551. Richard Whitchurch, the printer, seems to have used at least five presses in 1548 to produce sufficient copies, but there were only two editions in 1551 and, remarkably, no Elizabethan reprinting to satisfy an apparently huge market.[191] Yet the evidence of the churchwardens' accounts is that parishes often purchased dutifully, and replaced in Elizabeth's reign, having presumably returned their copies to the authorities under Mary.[192] The *Paraphrases* were an unusual evangelical tool to be placed in this compulsory way at the disposal of all parishioners. Not only did they emanate from a Catholic source, however sound; they were of a relatively demanding intellectual standard, not always the plain fare offering easily attained 'understanding of the Gospel' that Udall claimed in his preface.[193] Indeed that preface is striking because of its reiterated insistence that the text would benefit the 'gross and rude multitude' of curates and teachers. Udall at least seems to have seen the work as a way of educating the clergy in the scriptures: the laity were not excluded, but the assumption is that they were most likely to benefit at second hand.[194] Acquiring Erasmus became yet another test of parochial conformity: as an educational tool for the laity there is deafening silence about its impact.

---

[189] Edelen, *Harrison: A Description of England* 36. See below, p. 427.

[190] *VAI* ii. 117–18, 180, 235, 289–90; iii. 10, 88, 210.

[191] Pollard and Redgrave, *Short Title Catalogue of English Books Printed 1475–1641*, publishing history under New Testament. Darlow and Moule, *English Bible*, 38–40.

[192] See, for example, Whiting, *Blind Devotion*, 160, 191–2. There are examples of copies held by the Marian authorities being retrieved, as in the Exeter parish that paid 2d. for 'fetching home of the Paraphrases' in 1560. A glimpse into the mechanisms by which copies were disseminated is given in Bishop Ferrar's accusation that one of his officials was withholding copies of the *Paraphrases* for profit: A.J. Brown, *Robert Ferrar* (1997), 101. The forthcoming article by John Craig should illuminate the Elizabethan history of the *Paraphrases*.

[193] N. Udall, *Preface to the Paraphrases on the New Testament: tome 1* (1548), sig. B7[v].

[194] Ibid., sigs. B2[v], B7[v].

Hooker ignored the *Paraphrases*, but he was keen to emphasize another evangelical tool: catechizing. This was 'a kind of preaching...[which is] public performance...in the open hearing of men'.[195] His Puritan opponents might have been unhappy to hear catechizing described as preaching, since they saw it as essentially a means of training the layman to give an account of his or her faith, but they would have endorsed his argument for the centrality of this form of exegesis. Indeed catechizing can be seen as the most fashionable of all the means by which the faith was disseminated in sixteenth-century Europe. Catholics and Protestants, Conformists and zealous Puritans, all placed the training of the laity by catechetical means at the heart of their activities. In this field as in others historians of the late medieval Church have recently warned their colleagues not to exaggerate the uniqueness of the Reformation experience: there was an abundance of aids to Christian understanding in fifteenth-century England.[196] But both the intensity of concern for the education of the laity, and the forms of tract that emerged in the aftermath of the Reformation, are qualitatively different from the ploughman's learning of his *pater noster*. In England the period between the 1530s and the death of Edward saw ambitious experimentation with both primers and catechisms, providing among others things what Philippa Tudor has called 'an ambitious programme of religious instruction for children and adolescents... planned on a nation-wide basis'.[197] During these uncertain years experimentation was not confined to evangelicals: primers, or books of devotion, were issued using the full panoply of the Sarum Use, pointing the laity to a better understanding of the offices and articles of faith in English.[198] During Mary's reign Bonner used his publications as forms of catechesis as well as homily, and under Elizabeth Catholic writers established a genre of Tridentine writing that was to have significant impact within the recusant community.[199] The provision of proper tools for guiding the laity was also a priority of the Catholic missions within the Celtic lands of the British Isles. One of the first Gaelic texts of the Irish Franciscans based

---

[195] Hooker, *Laws of Ecclesiastical Polity*, v. 18. 3. This and the ensuing paragraphs are heavily indebted to Ian Green's magisterial study of English catechisms, *The Christian's ABC: Catechisms and Catechizing in England, c.1530–1740* (Oxford, 1996).

[196] On pre-Reformation education for the laity see above, ch. 3, and Duffy, *Stripping of the Altars*, 53–68.

[197] P. Tudor, 'Religious instruction for children and adolescents in the early English Reformation', *JEH* 35 (1984), 391.

[198] C.C. Butterworth, *The English Primers, 1529–1545* (reprint, New York, 1971), 87–103, 131–9.

[199] Bonner, *Profitable and Necessarye Doctryne*. The most important of the English Catholic catechisms was that of Laurence Vaux, first printed abroad in 1568, and extensively reprinted up to the 1620s [RSTC 24625.5–27a.4].

at Louvain was the metrical catechism of Bonaventura O Hussey, a bard turned priest, and the only Catholic work printed in Welsh during Elizabeth's reign was Morys Clynnog's *Athravaeth Grostnogawl* (1568), a translation of the catechism of Father Juan Alfonso de Polanco.[200]

Protestants could therefore in no sense claim exclusive rights either to the invention of vernacular training in the faith for the laity or for the development of catechism as a tool of confessional identity. Polemical claims that the accession of Mary Tudor pushed the unlearned back into a dark world of unmediated religious images were merely grist to the mill of ideological controversy.[201] But Protestants did invest unusual resource and energy in the provision of printed catechisms. Ian Green's calculations indicate that nearly 200 new or translated catechisms or catechetical works were published in England between 1530 and the turn of the century, and to this can be added a few imprints on the Continent, plus a number of Scottish printings of Calvin's catechism as part of the Book of Common Order. It was the second half of Elizabeth's reign that saw rapidly growing numbers of texts, and this period too that witnessed sufficient reprints of the key Prayer Book catechism through the editions of the Book of Common Prayer, the *ABC with the Catechisme* and the *Primer and Catechism* for it to be reasonable to assume that all parishes and most individuals could have multiple copies cheaply available.[202] We can observe some of the significance attached to the provision of the formal tools for training the young among Protestants through the process of translation. In the case of Welsh the famous first published book was Sir John Price's primer, which included the Creed, Ten Commandments and Pater Noster, for the benefit of the rude and unlearned, and later in the century Siôn Dafydd Rhys translated the more advanced catechisms of Alexander Nowell and Gervase Babington.[203] In Ireland the first focus for crown investment in translation was Kearney's rendering of the Prayer Book catechism, published in 1571.[204] For the Scottish Highlands John Carswell's translation of the Book of Common Order included Calvin's catechism, though it was not until the 1650s that a fully popular form was printed in the Scottish Vernacular.[205]

---

[200] Meigs, *Reformations in Ireland*, 81–2. C. Mooney, *Devotional Writings of the Irish Franciscans, 1224–1950* (Killiney, 1952), 16–17. Williams, *Wales and Reformation*, 252–3.

[201] Tudor, 'Religious instruction', 392.

[202] Green, *The Christian's ABC*, 51, 63–8.

[203] J.H. Davies (ed.), *Yny Lhyvyr Hwnn*... (Bangor, 1902). Williams, *Wales and the Reformation*, 341.

[204] J. O'Kearney, *Aibidil Gaoidheilge & Caiticiomsna* (Dublin, 1571). C. O'Hainle, 'The *Pater Noster* in Irish: Reformation texts to *c.*1650', *Celtica* 22 (1991), 146–7. Kearney exceeded Sir John Price's rhetoric by referring to the Irish in his preface as 'more savage and more barbarous' than any other Western race.

[205] Dawson, 'Calvinism and the Gaidhealtachd', 238–41.

From 1552 all children within the English and Welsh church were supposed to receive regular instruction in the basic catechism of the Prayer Book, every Sunday and holy day in the parish church.[206] After 1560 their Scottish counterparts were also expected to attend regular Sunday instruction, usually in the afternoon after the main service.[207] Both churches had by this time fully adopted the distinctive question-and-answer form that marked out Protestant catechisms from their pre-Reformation models. At the simplest level, in the learning of the basic texts of the faith, this change of form may not have signified greatly, the process of assimilation was that of rote learning and repetition that inevitably characterized an oral society. Cranmer's catechism, which was only four pages long, did little more than provide a new dialogue form to embrace the basic profession of faith, with the shortest of expositions of his or her understanding by the catechumen. It was perhaps characteristic of the nature of the emerging Church of England, that there was initially little between this simple training in faith, preparing children for confirmation, and rather more demanding texts suitable for 'scholars', the most popular of which was Alexander Nowell's 1570 compilation. It was also characteristic of Scottish Protestantism that it should adopt Calvin's catechism, not only because of the stature of its author, but because it was a lengthy and full exposition of belief, comprehensively supported by scriptural reference. Later English editions of Calvin divided the text into short components, with approximately two pages to be absorbed each Sunday, which suggests the level of demand that was being made upon ordinary Scottish congregations.[208]

In England there was a growing tendency to generate texts which would exist in what Green describes as an intermediate ground.[209] These were often, though not exclusively, produced by the godly, for both the young and for older parishioners who had mastered the Prayer Book basics and were now to be led to a more explicit understanding of the faith. This underlines a difference of emphasis in the use of catechizing, certainly between Protestant and Catholic and perhaps also between different types of Protestant. For the Catholic the principal purpose of training was preparation for participation in the life of the Church, especially preparation for confession and communion. This was, of course, also of significance in the reformed churches: for the Scottish Kirk admission to communion, and also to baptism and marriage, was contingent on

---

[206] J. Kettley (ed.), *The Two Liturgies of Edward VI* (PS, Cambridge, 1844), 300–1: the 1549 Book had simply required instruction for the six weeks preceding confirmation.
[207] Knox, iv. 343.　　[208] Green, *The Christian's ABC*, 68–78, 102 ff.
[209] Ibid., 68 ff.

knowledge of the catechism. But the Protestant was also required to give an account of the reasons for faith, argued from biblical example, and this is what the question-and-answer form and the enlarged catechisms were designed to elicit.[210] As so often, George Herbert seems to see the essential value of the medium: 'at sermons and prayers', he observes, 'men may sleep and wander; but when one is asked a question he must discover what he is'.[211] The catechism could also 'edify', in the formal sense of stirring up the spirit and aiding the work of conversion: something at which the unofficial texts seem particularly to have aimed.[212]

Another crucial medium for the dissemination of the Word was, somewhat paradoxically, music. Liturgy had always been sustained by the musical traditions of the Church that, in pre-Reformation England in particular, reached new heights of polyphonic splendour. It was precisely the elaboration of Catholic music that made it in the eyes of many reformers an inappropriate vehicle for the new churches. The composers and choirs of Reformation England showed that much could be done to adapt both to the new language of liturgy and to the requirement that the meaning of the words took precedence over musical complexity. Cranmer, who showed little enthusiasm for any demanding music to support the liturgy, wrote to Henry VIII in 1544 about processional singing that it should 'not be full of notes but, as near as may be, for every syllable a note'.[213] The 1552 Prayer Book virtually abandoned even this concession to the old ways, and it seems likely that if Elizabeth had not been a passionate supporter of music within the liturgy the professional cathedral choirs and their adaptations of the service would not have survived.[214] But ordinary congregations assembled in their Scottish kirks, and English parishes must often have been almost unaware of this withering of the great tradition of polyphonic music. While a few parishes had been able to muster choirs to sing the offices, in most instances there can have been little more than the voices of clerks and the most basic manipulations of plainsong.[215]

---

[210] I. Green, '"The necessary knowledge of the principles of religion": catechisms and catechizing in Ireland, c.1560–1800', in A. Ford, J. McGuire, and K. Milne (eds.), *As by Law Established: The Church of Ireland since the Reformation* (Dublin, 1995), 70–2.

[211] F. Hutchinson (ed.), *The Works of George Herbert* (Oxford, 1941), 257.

[212] E. Duffy, 'The Long Reformation: Catholicism, Protestantism and the multitude', in N. Tyacke (ed.), *England's Long Reformation: 1500–1800* (1998), 42–4.

[213] *LP* xx. ii. 539. MacCulloch, *Cranmer*, 330–1.

[214] N. Temperley, *The Music of the English Parish Church* (Cambridge, 1979), 1–16.

[215] There were some notable exceptions: at Ludlow, for example, there was not only a full musical tradition before the Reformation, but the choir was still singing Latin motets as late as 1597: A. Smith, 'Elizabethan church music at Ludlow', *Music and Letters* 49 (1968), 108.

It was into this world that the reformers introduced congregational singing, one of the most important cultural experiences of the sixteenth century. Luther's 'vernacular psalms', or what he described in a letter to Spalatin as 'spiritual songs so that the Word of God even by means of song may live among the people', began a major tradition of the writing of hymns, metrical psalms, and sacred ballads.[216] In England and Scotland the intentions of the early translators were at once didactic and relatively eclectic. Coverdale, who published *Goostly psalmes and spirituall songes* in the mid-1530s, expressed his hope that 'our minstrels had none other thing to play upon, . . . save psalms, hymns and such godly songs as David is occupied withal'.[217] In practice this meant largely the translation of Luther's hymns, which were themselves drawn from a variety of sources, the psalms, the liturgical hymns of the Church and even the elements of the catechism to be sung. The closest Scottish parallel, *The Gude and Godlie Ballatis*, published in 1567, but put together in the 1530s by John and Robert Wedderburn, was even more diverse, translating some of the psalms, and many of Luther's 'ditments'. It also, says Calderwood, turned 'many bawdy songs and rhymes into godly rhymes'.[218] The work of both Coverdale and the Wedderburns fitted well into the general endeavours of the first reforming generations to use all possible media for the transmission of the evangelical message.[219]

The metrical psalms that were to become the dominant element in congregational singing also emerged from this pluralistic world of mid-Tudor translation. Thomas Sternhold, the key figure, seems to have been less obsessively didactic in his approach than Coverdale.[220] His psalms were, according to William Baldwin, 'sung openly' before the young Edward VI, and his writing seems closely linked to the English and French courtly traditions of devotional translation. But Sternhold did intend his psalms to be sung, and it was probably he who popularized the so-called common metre that made the verses accessible and memorable.[221] The psalms were already afforded a high and privileged place in Protestant thought, 'for it containeth', said Becon, 'what so ever is necessary for a Christian man to know'.[222] The logic would therefore have been to

---

[216] G.G. Krodel (ed.), *Luther's Works: Letters II*, vol. il (Concordia, Pa., 1972), 68.

[217] R. Leaver, '*Goostly Psalmes and Spirituall Songes*': *English and Dutch Metrical Psalms from Coverdale to Utenhove, 1535–66* (Oxford, 1991), 3, 62–81.

[218] A.F. Mitchell (ed.), *A Compendious Book of Godly and Spiritual Songs commonly known as 'The Gude and Godlie Ballatis' (1567)*, STS 1/39 (Edinburgh, 1897), introduction.

[219] J.N. King, *English Reformation Literature: The Tudor Origins of the Protestant Tradition*, (Princeton, N.J., 1982), 209–25.

[220] Leaver, '*Goostly Psalmes*', 117 ff.

[221] R. Zim, *English Metrical Psalms: Poetry as Praise and Prayer, 1535–1601* (Cambridge, 1987), 31, 121–5.

[222] T. Becon, *David's harpe, ful of moost delectable armony* (1542), sig. A7ᵛ.

employ Sternhold's work in church, especially once the 1552 Prayer Book
had emphasized the significance of congregational participation in worship. This was, however, a logic that was only slowly recognized. In
Edward's reign official psalm-singing was confined to the stranger
churches where, in the words of the *Forma ac ratio*, 'there is a psalm sung
in the vulgar tongue of the whole congregation'.[223] In exile the English
and Scots finally discovered the merits of communal singing, and not only
at Geneva, though it was there that many extra translations were added to
the Sternhold and Hopkins originals by Whittingham, Kethe, and others.
The Frankfurt congregation, from which Knox and the Genevans were
expelled, also used the metrical psalms, linking them with the 1552 Prayer
Book to which they were committed.[224]

Though godly ballads and psalms were making some inroads into the
Protestant culture of England and Scotland in the mid-sixteenth century, it
was the years after 1559 that witnessed the development of congregations
into singers of what became known opprobriously as Geneva jigs.[225]
Even then this was not necessarily a change high on the agenda of those
seeking to make good Protestants out of the Catholic masses. The first
Book of Discipline encouraged the use of the psalms, while acknowledging without apparent anxiety that singing might not be possible in some
churches.[226] But the Scots were at least sufficiently eager to break older
traditions of church music, and the revised metrical psalter was made an
integral part of the Book of Common Order after 1560.[227] The 1559 Royal
Injunctions in England made more oblique gestures towards congregational
music. It was made permissible to sing 'an hymn or suchlike song' at
the beginning and end of public prayer, provided that the music made the
meaning of the words clear.[228] This weak form of liturgical advice seems
to have been intended partly to deflect the queen's attention from anything that smacked of Genevan practice. Elizabeth managed to show her
distaste for metrical psalms in characteristic fashion, deliberately leaving
the opening of the 1562 session of Parliament when one was sung. Her
subjects seem to have felt differently: psalms 'in the Geneva fashion' began
to be sung at Paul's Cross sermons in 1559, and quickly became associated
with preaching occasions. Jewel described 'six thousand persons, old

---

[223] Bodl. MS Barlow 19, fo. 151. This is the translation of *Forma ac ratio*, probably prepared
with Cranmer's approval.

[224] Temperley, *Music of the English Parish Church*, 18.

[225] Leaver, '*Goostly Psalmes*', 238ff.

[226] Cameron, *First Book of Discipline*, 180.

[227] The Genevan version of the metrical psalms used in Scotland excluded the hymns added
to Day's English text. It is interesting that the only formal addition of metrical psalms to
the English liturgy came in 1578.

[228] *VAI* iii. 23.

and young, of both sexes, singing together and praising God'.[229] The popularity of the new form of worship is attested by the publishing history of the revised Sternhold and Hopkins printed by John Day after 1562. *The Whole Booke of Psalmes* went through almost 500 editions in the following century and a quarter, and by the mid-Elizabethan period every congregation must in principle have had ready access to the text.[230] By 1578 the ecclesiastical establishment had decided that congregational singing must be embraced wholeheartedly, and metrical psalms and hymns were ordered to be sung at the Accession Day celebrations.[231]

The evangelical potential of psalm-singing is suggested by the Scottish commentator who described the collective knowledge of words and tunes as so good that ministers were 'able to direct a psalm to be sung agreeable to the doctrine to be delivered, so he that taketh up the psalm is able to sing any tune, and the people for the most part to follow him'.[232] In rural Essex William Harrison prided himself on singing so plain 'that each one present may understand what they sing'.[233] But congregational psalm-singing was probably an ambivalent tool for the construction of godliness. Its very popularity suggests more about traditions of singing and the pleasure it offers than about enthusiasm for the message of the psalms. The translation of ballad tunes and vigorous musical rhythm into a sacred context presumably produced its own excitement, though this did not necessarily last as years of exposure to this type of unaccompanied singing reduced Geneva jigs to slow-tempoed dirges. A set of common tunes based on more formal principles of mid-Tudor church music became normative, and by the early seventeenth century Temperley estimates that a psalm note could last for two seconds.[234] The other ambiguity of godly singing was the relationship between those scriptural texts of uncontested probity employed in church, and the wider pattern of godly ballad-making. The latter existed outside a formal liturgical context and was less susceptible to clerical control than the former. Here, as Tessa Watt has shown, English Protestantism developed a strong godly and popular ballad tradition, which began, like so many other cultural manifestations of evangelism, to falter after the 1570s. Thereafter the self-styled godly were less likely to want what William Samuel had sought with his rhyming

---

[229] ZL i. 71. [230] Temperley, *Music of the English Parish Church*, 46–55.

[231] Later services of thanksgiving etc. prescribed psalms but did not specify their metrical form: W. Keatinge (ed.), *Liturgies and Occasional Forms of Prayer set forth in the Reign of Queen Elizabeth* (PS, Cambridge, 1847), 558–61.

[232] Quoted in I.B. Cowan, *Scottish Reformation* (1982), 158.

[233] Edelen, *Harrison: A Description of England*, 33. G.R.J. Parry, *A Protestant Vision: William Harrison and the Reformation of Elizabethan England* (Cambridge, 1987), 150–1.

[234] Temperley, *Music of the English Parish Church*, 64–7.

Pentateuch in the mid-century: to 'have my country people able in a small sum to sing the whole contents of the Bible'.[235] The medium became suspect, and there was a tendency to revert to more formal tools such as catechisms and primers. But godly ballad-making, as well as psalm-singing, survived as forms of cultural expression that possessed genuine popularity beyond the ranks of the zealous.[236]

Idols, Words, and Texts

The 'Genevans', that small band of clerical brothers who became 'public enemies number one' to Elizabeth I, believed fervently that there must be 'full and plain' reformation 'according to Gods holy will and work without addition'.[237] 'Consider', wrote one of their leaders, Christopher Goodman, to Cecil in 1559, 'the danger to us all if we proceed not with more ferventness'.[238] Goodman, with Anthony Gilby and John Knox, formed a trio passionately committed to the most austere form of radical religious change. Idolatry, monuments of superstition, lay avarice, and popular superstition were to be swept ruthlessly aside by the pure light of the gospel. The only true instruments of evangelism were the Scripture and preaching: catechizing and psalm-singing might be conceded, but they were of secondary value in the pursuit of the victory of the true Church. And at the end of the 1550s that victory was to have explicitly British dimensions. Gilby wrote of the need for 'earnest travail' in the 'Lord's vineyard', while Goodman followed Knox to Scotland and served the fledgling kirk at Ayr and St Andrews. He also undertook a preaching tour to the Isle of Man, and in the mid-1560s went to Ireland as chaplain to Sir Henry Sidney in the hope of further conversions (and promotion).[239] Knox constantly prayed that both the realms and Scotland would experience full reformation.[240]

The vision of Christ's Church made wholly anew by preaching and teaching was always a chimera, as was the hope of spiritual unity within 'Great Britainy'. In Scotland circumstances made it possible for some acute confrontation between the old and the new: though even there at the level of the congregation radical reform had to be made acceptable by

---

[235] W. Samuel, *The abridgements of Goddes statutes in myter* (1551), sig. A2.

[236] Watt, *Cheap Print*, 42–57, 115.

[237] A. Gilby, 'An admonition to England and Scotland to call them to Repentance', in Knox, vi. 562.

[238] *CSP Sc* i. 257.

[239] J. Dawson, 'Anglo-Scottish Protestant culture and integration in sixteenth-century Britain', in S.G. Ellis and S. Barber (eds.), *Conquest and Union: Fashioning a British State 1485–1725* (1995), 92–105. *DNB*

[240] See below, p. 366.

a measure of integration with old forms and values.[241] In Ireland, as we have seen, even the preliminary work of cleansing the idols was barely undertaken, and the crucial dissemination of the Word was hampered by lack of resources and lack of will. The story is more complex in England: the extirpation of the idols proceeded with apparent vigour: yet it was never complete. Almost a century after Edward's godly rule William Dowsing was able to uncover dramatic evidence of the survival of images throughout East Anglia.[242] More important than this survivalism is the sense that the cleansers of the Temple always had to contend with alternative cultural visions that were not swept aside by their zeal. The 'idols in the frontispiece', images directly or indirectly religious, that have been so vividly described by Tessa Watt, show the existence in post-Reformation England of a continuation of mixed modes of expression of religious ideas.[243] The eye continued to be distracted and seduced from the purest forms of hearing the Word.

Words and texts were also less than amenable to the highest demands of Knoxian Protestantism. Not only did the godly preachers have to contend with those literary manifestations of a pluralistic culture like Guy of Warwick and Robin Hood denounced by Edward Dering as 'childish folly', and 'witless devices': they had to persuade their auditors that the way of Christ was to be preferred to these secular tales.[244] The rigorous response to the unregenerate multitude was to compel them to conformity through discipline: to construct the captive congregation that might then become obedient to the Word. This was Archbishop Loftus's argument in Ireland: first force your recusants onto the church bench, then constrain them to listen to the sermon.[245] But even rigorous Calvinists recognized that coercion was an imperfect tool for the regeneration of Christian society: discipline and evangelism were two sides of one coin. And the persuasion that was essential to true evangelism was also a process of negotiation with auditors and readers. Negotiation involved the accommodation of the Protestant message to congregational needs, and more broadly the adjustment of wider cultural norms to meet new circumstances. It was characteristic of Elizabethan England that absolute prohibitions on forms of religious representation or argument were unusual unless they threatened the security of the state. But what was acceptable did slowly change—in visual terms, saints were replaced in print and paint by Old Testament figures and eventually by allegorical or classical figures; in text, Bible

---

[241] On this theme see below, ch. 10.
[242] T. Cooper (ed.), *The Journal of William Dowsing* (Woodbridge, 2001).
[243] Watt, *Cheap Print*, 131–68.
[244] Dering, *A briefe and necessary Catechisme* sig. A2ᵛ.
[245] *CSP Irl* iv. 365 ff.

stories superseded those of medieval legendaries.[246] Prints of providential deliverances and images of martyrs or reformers affirmed a stronger visual identity with the new faith: one that even Knox would have found it difficult to dispute.[247] The success of the evangelists depended upon an ability to work with the grain of the culture. If a logocentric faith was to be constructed in Reformation Britain, it had to engage with a predominantly oral and visual environment, and not one in which either written text or formal preaching had easy access to the people. The world could sometimes be made anew: more often it had to be renewed painfully in accommodation with the very culture that the exponents of godliness despised.

[246] Watt, *Cheap Print*, 178 ff. But Walsham gives interesting examples of old narratives embedded in new texts: for example, medieval exempla of the punishment of lecherous priests by zealous saints survive little adapted, Walsham, *Providence*, 90–1.

[247] Walsham, *Providence*, 252–3.

8

THEOLOGY AND WORSHIP

Confessions

Reformed churches required confessions. They were obliged both to situate themselves within the communities of the Protestant faithful and to offer a standard of orthodoxy to their own people. Definitive English, Scottish, and Irish formularies of faith were all promulgated within a decade in the 1560s. The Thirty-Nine Articles, though strictly speaking Thirty-Eight since one was removed for political reasons, were approved by Convocation in 1563. Their final form was endorsed by Parliament in 1571.[1] The Scots Confession was devised and ratified in 1560.[2] Then in 1567 the Irish acquired a partial confession in the Twelve Articles, agreed by the bishops and Lord Deputy Sidney.[3] Of course the history of statements of faith was far longer, stretching in the case of sixteenth-century England from the Ten Articles of 1536 to those of Lambeth in 1595, and in that of Ireland having a terminus only in the articles issued by the Irish convocation of 1615.[4] However, the 1560s provides a useful vantage point from which it is possible to examine the doctrinal influences that led to the articulation of a particular form of confession, and to look forwards to the responses of mature Protestantism in the last decades of the century.

Labelling the confessions of faith with the badge of identity of one of the great Continental reformers has long been a hobby of theologians and historians. In the case of Scotland there has been a comfortable consensus that the Confession is strongly Calvinistic. The English Articles have always presented more problems because of their evolutionary nature, based as they are on Cranmer's 1553 Forty-Two Articles but incorporating

---

[1] For the Thirty-Nine Articles, Cranmer's Forty-Two Articles that preceded them, and the Irish Articles, the standard text is C. Hardwick, *A History of the Articles of Religion*, 3rd edn. (1895). There is a useful comparative text of the two forms of the English Articles in G. Bray (ed.), *Documents of the English Reformation* (Cambridge, 1994), 284–311.

[2] For the Scots Confession see Knox, ii. 95 ff., and in *APS* ii. 526 ff. For textual problems, see M. Robinson, 'Language choice in the Reformation: the Scots Confession of 1560', in J.D. McClure (ed.), *Scotland and the Lowland Tongue* (Aberdeen, 1983), 59–78.

[3] Hardwick, *Articles of Religion*, 120–3, 327–9.

[4] A. Ford, *The Protestant Reformation in Ireland, 1590–1641* (Dublin, 1997), 156–78.

the ideas of Archbishop Parker and his fellow bishops. They are also problematic because Cranmer's own theology evolved, and is not easily frozen in a moment of time.[5] Both English and Scottish formularies certainly borrowed freely linguistically and conceptually from Continental sources.[6] However, it is important to consider them as organized statements of the beliefs of their immediate authors, and the distillation of those aspects of faith that were thought to be essential for their national churches. And since we are comparing neighbour kingdoms articulating their beliefs in close physical and temporal proximity it may be valuable to focus upon similarity and difference largely in a British context.

The briefest of schematic summaries indicates both similarity and difference. Each confession begins from the principle that articles of faith should follow medieval precedent in that they should serve as an exposition of the Creed, the Paternoster and the Decalogue. The Scots Confession moves through twenty-five articles essentially under six category headings. Beginning with theology, the doctrine of God, it moves through anthropology, Christology, and ecclesiology to end with the rewards of faith, or eschatology. Its closest focus is on the cycle of justification, sanctification, and regeneration, which occupy articles twelve to fifteen. The English Articles also begin with theology, and Christology, but then appeal to the authority of Scripture, before turning to anthropology. Once again the central articles, ten to eighteen, are on justification and election, followed by ecclesiology, that is articles on the visible and catholic Church. The concluding articles contain no eschatology, though this had been present in Cranmer's earlier version. Instead they return to ecclesiology and the English church's relation to civil society. Thus expressed the similarities of organization and concern seem clearly to outweigh the differences. Only the greater preoccupation of the English text with the particularities of ecclesiastical affairs, and its silence on eschatology, immediately offers contrast.

Much the same could be argued about the content of many of the individual sections of the confessions. The two churches share in general Catholic dogma on the persons of the Trinity, and of Christology, and they participate equally in the reformed concerns for a proper account of

---

[5] There is a large literature on the Thirty-Nine Articles, much of it reflecting confessional concerns within modern Anglicanism. Of continuing value are E.C.S. Gibson, *The Thirty-Nine Articles of the Church of England*, 2 vols. (1910); E. Bicknell, *A Theological Introduction to the Thirty-Nine Articles*, revised edn. (1955). The liveliest theological discussion, mercifully unburdened with too many concerns for labelling, is O. O'Donovan, *On the Thirty-Nine Articles* (Exeter, 1986).

[6] The Scottish Confession has not produced quite such controversy, though considerable disagreement remains about influences: there are good discussions in W.I.P. Hazlett, 'The Scots *Confession* of 1560: contexts, complexion and critique', *ARG* 78 (1987), 287–320; and briefly J.T. McNeill, *The History and Character of Calvinism* (New York, 1967), 298–300.

justification, grace, and redemption. Both follow the common Protestant belief in solifidianism, in the inefficacy of works for salvation, and in predestination, the latter term interestingly not used by the Scots. Both, it has been suggested, reveal a vigorous negative response to the decrees of the first session of the Council of Trent on grace, justification, Scripture, and tradition. They accept the existence of only two sacraments explicitly enjoined by Christ and offer very similar statements about the nature of Christ's presence in the Eucharist. 'The mean', says the English Article 28, 'whereby the Body of Christ is received and eaten in the Supper is Faith.' 'The Holy Ghost', says Article 21 of the Scottish Confession, 'makes us to feed upon the body and blood of Christ Jesus...which now is in the heaven.' Both affirm the importance of the visible Church militant here on earth, and both acknowledge that true churches can adopt local custom while being identified at least by the two 'marks' of proper preaching and administration of the sacraments. Indeed it would be difficult to identify fundamental doctrinal issues that separate the two, or collectively divorce them from the mainstream of Continental reformed thought.[7]

It is not difficult, however, to discern the seed of future division in both the substance and the rhetoric of the confessions. The famous English Article 17 on predestination is not wholly incompatible with its Scottish counterpart: neither at this stage offers a full and stark formulation of the double decree, the predestination to election or reprobation, which is found in later Calvinist confessions. Yet the Scots begin from God's 'eternal and immutable decree', and then turn to election as a part of the chapter on Christology.[8] Cranmer and his revisers move rapidly from the divine purpose to an equally Christological view of election, one in which men are chosen 'in Christ' out of mankind. The difference lies in a stronger, Godward emphasis in the Scottish text, as against an anthropological concern in the English Article. Here, as elsewhere, forms of language seem particularly important in marking difference. The English predestinarian decree dwells upon the knowledge of election as 'full of sweet, pleasant and unspeakable comfort to godly persons, and such as feel in themselves the working of the spirit of Christ': the Scots gives far greater weight to the objective theology of Christ's atonement, and man's depravity, emphasizing the 'darkness' of men's minds and the grace of the Creator, wholly unmerited by his creatures. Although the Scots Confes-

---

[7] It is interesting, however, that the most direct connection between the English and Scottish articles comes from the use that the latter make of Cranmer's condemnations of works of supererogation, of transubstantiation, and of the sleep of the soul after death, the last of which did not survive into the revised 1563 English text.

[8] The Scots actually avoid the term predestination, and the full exposition of election is subsumed under Christology.

sion was the work of six hands, the six Johns, it is difficult not to associate some of its gloomier passages with that purveyor of moral Calvinism, John Knox.[9] Chapter 13, on the cause of good works, is particularly trenchant, denouncing 'murderers, oppressors, cruel persecutors, adulterers, whore-mongers, filthy persons, idolaters, drunkards, thieves and all workers of iniquity' as excluded from the possibility of sanctification. The fact that in 1 Corinthians 6 hope is held out to exactly these sinners appears not to have troubled the writers. The positive side of this language is a concern for evangelical activism in the defence of faith that is lacking in the English Articles. 'The sons of God does fight against sin, . . . and if they fall, they rise again with earnest and unfeigned repentance.'[10]

And with a distinction of language came some separation of doctrinal emphasis. The Scots followed Calvin in an explicit insistence that regener-ation and renewal, following upon election, led to a continual battle between flesh and spirit. Justification is the beginning of a process of sanctification.[11] Cranmer and Parker engaged in some denials and affirm-ations that seemed far less relevant to the Scots: attacking purgatory and the five non-dominical sacraments; explicitly upholding sacramental effi-cacy when the minister proved unworthy; and offering a very precise definition of the canonical books of Scripture. A belief in covenant the-ology is sketched in the Scots Confession: Chapters 4 and 5 can be read as a narrative of the promises made between God and man from Adam to Christ. But it is, as already indicated, in ecclesiology that the two texts most clearly diverge. The English Articles maintain a remarkable silence about the invisible Church of the elect: though their predestinarian views argue for its necessity. The Scots, while acknowledging the visible, cath-olic Church, are driven by their understanding of the Church of the saints, 'citizens of the heavenly Jerusalem', the 'Kirk . . . invisible, known only to God'. In consequence they are concerned to separate the true and false Church in this world and to seek out the marks of the former. The addition of discipline, as a third mark of the true Church, can be ex-plained by the influence on the Confession of the earlier *Forma ac ratio* of Jan Laski, which became the model for reformed texts from the 1560s.[12] It also expresses a clear dualistic theology, in which the wheat and chaff of

---

[9] The six authors of the Confession were John Knox, John Willock, John Winram, John Spottiswoode, John Douglas, and John Rowe. Apart from Winram, all had studied abroad and were familiar at first hand with reformed practice. Knox, ii. 128, 105.

[10] Hazlett, 'Scots Confession', 295–7.

[11] Ibid., 314.

[12] I am grateful to Professor MacCulloch for pointing out the influence of Laski. See his article 'The importance of Jan Laski in the English Reformation', in C. Strom (ed.), *Johannes a Lasco, 1499–1560* (Emden, 2000), 315–45.

the visible Church must be separated as far as it lay within human capacity to perform God's will. On the other hand, the ordering of the visible Church and its relationship with the state was a dominant concern of the English Articles. The doctrine of the Church was established briefly: its traditions, ceremonies, and texts were accorded much attention.

Since the Scots Confession and the Thirty-Nine Articles became established as the founding doctrinal statements of their respective churches there is a tendency to accord them a status equivalent to the Catholic *magisterium* at the moment of their production. But their contemporary standing was less assured. Their authors were indeed seeking to articulate definitive beliefs, but in circumstances that they acknowledged were imperfect. At the deepest level imperfection was a consequence of man's inherent depravity and incapacity. Thus the preface to the Confession followed the example of some of its Continental models by appealing to the spiritual verification of Scripture, and by requiring that anyone who doubted its consistency with the Word should 'admonish us of the same in writing' so that the authors might endeavour to give satisfaction.[13] To this must be added the legitimation for adaptation and change, at least in the areas of pure worship and Christian life, provided by an understanding of ecclesiology that emphasized the 'marks' of the true Church rather than the full corpus of dogma. Thus Parker apparently felt free to abandon Cranmer's specific condemnations of millenarianism and other radical doctrines that appeared by 1562 to be less than central to the interests of the English church.[14] The Scottish Kirk was more radical in replacing the Confession for a time with the closely parallel statement of the Genevan exiles of the 1550s: this was the printed version that appeared in the Book of Common Order after 1564.[15]

The formulation of the texts also has to be understood in terms of audience. This is particularly true in England, where the Thirty-Nine Articles happened to represent the end of an extraordinarily complex struggle to establish a confession of faith. Cranmer had spent much of his archiepiscopate wrestling with doctrinal statements.[16] Both the major formularies of the Henrician church and the endless negotiations with Lutherans in the same reign had developed in him acute confessional antennae as well as providing a stock of language that he was able to recycle into his final Articles.[17] Debates with the Lutherans led him into a

---

[13] Knox, ii. 96. P. Schaff, *The Creeds of the Evangelical Protestant Churches* (1877), 437–79.

[14] W.P. Haugaard, *Elizabeth and the English Reformation* (Cambridge, 1968), 247–51.

[15] Hazlett, 'Scots Confession', 295. Knox, ii. 169–73.

[16] D. MacCulloch, *Thomas Cranmer* (New Haven, Conn., 1996), 30–1, 161–6, 206–8, 520–38.

[17] The articles drafted for agreement with the Lutherans in 1538 proved a major linguistic influence on the Forty-Two Articles.

pattern of balancing the need for an explicit statement of the faith of the
Church of England, against his profound belief in the need for unity
among 'true' churches, and these two against the political exigencies of
Protestant alliance. It is striking that when Cranmer was in a more powerful position under Edward he chose to focus upon pure worship and the
purified Church before he returned to the articulation of England's confessional identity. MacCulloch has suggested that the delay is to be explained by the archbishop's ecumenical concerns. In March 1552 he wrote
to Calvin urging that the Protestant churches should convene a meeting
that might 'handle all the heads of ecclesiastical doctrine', and propagate
the truth, in opposition to the work of the first session of Trent.[18] At the
same time he approached Bullinger and Melanchthon. All was to little
effect, so the archbishop began to collate work begun long before to
ensure that at least England had its own confession.

A second explanation can be offered for Cranmer's ordering of his
religious changes, if not their precise timing. Doctrine taught through
liturgy, and expressed in new church discipline, was a more powerful
evangelical weapon than the theological statement. The notion of the
'edification of the members of Christ' embraced all these levels of exposition, but might in certain circumstances prioritize the first two over the
last. It is revealing that in the contracted timetable available to the Scots in
the first year of their Reformation the preparation of the Book of Discipline was given precedence over the Confession.[19] Moreover the divines
who prepared the statements of belief always worked against a background
of secular political need and expectation. In 1560 the Scots were deeply
dependent upon English aid, and were constrained by English interests.
The Confession became one of the elements in the pursuit of 'how a
uniformity might be had in religion in both realms', and Maitland of
Lethington was anxious to assure Cecil that if the document gave offence
it could either be changed or 'at least in some thing qualified'.[20] The
Elizabethan Articles were caught up in conflicts which may have been
partly internal debates about ideology, but which also had an eye to the
need to remain in harmony with the Lutherans.[21] After the bishops had
actually subscribed to the Articles following considerable debate and
redrafting in the 1563 convocation, Article 29 on the wicked at the Lord's

---

[18] OL i. 24–5.
[19] Knox, ii. 183–4. Cameron, in his edition of the First Book of Discipline, prefers the view
that ecclesiastical policy, rather than doctrine, was still undecided: J.K. Cameron (ed.), *The First
Book of Discipline* (Edinburgh, 1972), 8–9.
[20] *CSP Sc* i. 471, 479.
[21] H. Horie, 'The Lutheran influence on the Elizabethan Settlement, 1558–1563', *HJ* 34
(1991), 519–38.

Supper was abruptly omitted. This must have been on royal initiative: the tone of the article was anti-Lutheran, and it also offended the sensibilities of those who sought a strengthening of the idea of the real presence in the Eucharist. Elizabeth probably disliked it on both counts, though not sufficiently to oppose its restoration in 1571 when the diplomatic situation had altered.[22]

The 1567 Irish Articles offer a particular instance of this need to respond to political expediency. While the English hierarchy wrestled with the final formulation of a full doctrinal position the Irish were left in limbo, a situation which the small number of committed Protestants among the clergy began to exploit to avoid the full consequences of English conformity. There was a political interest, both from the Irish bishops and from the English governors, in doing as little as possible further to destabilize the local situation, and so Parker's Eleven Articles of 1561 were adapted to an Irish environment.[23] Parker's Eleven Articles, one of several formularies proposed before 1563, were cautious and general, avoiding precise definitions of the most controversial issues of Reformation doctrine—the sacraments, justification, and sin against the Holy Spirit. The Irish were left with an 'imprecise and undifferentiated Protestantism', rather than any thorough articulation of faith.[24] In the event this political caution served the fledgling Protestant church rather well, since it allowed it to develop with less constraint than the full Church of England *credo* might have done. The Irish case also reinforces the point that full confessional documents were not necessarily essential to the development of a church. By the time the Irish Protestants did acquire such a document in 1615 they had lived for half a century with only a sketchy account of their faith.

Doctrine Before the Confessions: Henry VIII's Reign

More than forty years of doctrinal crisis and conflict lay behind the final formulation of the English and Scottish confessions. This was never contained within national boundaries, since it found expression in the debates of theologians in the universal language of Latin and the universal medium

---

[22] Haugaard, *Elizabeth and Reformation*, 253–4, stresses Elizabeth's own tastes as against the issue of Lutheran diplomacy.

[23] Hardwick, *Articles of Religion*, 327–9. The Eleven Articles became Twelve by the simple expedient of splitting one into two parts. A. Clarke, 'Varieties of uniformity: the first century of the Church of Ireland', in W.J. Sheils and D. Wood (eds.), *The Churches, Ireland and the Irish*, SCH 25 (Oxford, 1989), 107.

[24] A. Ford, 'The Church of Ireland, 1558–1634: a Puritan church?' in A. Ford, J. McGuire, and K. Milne (eds.), *As by Law Established: The Church of Ireland since the Reformation* (Dublin, 1995), 57–8.

of the printed text. It was also structured by the specific circumstances of the reforming generations: the roles they were able to play within the universities; the common experience of exile; ultimately the tragedy of martyrdom. Analysis of the shifting beliefs of the reformers has to remain sensitive to these external influences. They provided the matrix within which doctrine was articulated: they also at times profoundly influenced the nature of dogma itself.

The first generation of reformers in both England and Scotland fell first and foremost under Lutheran influence. There are predisposing influences within the universities, above all of course the growing interest in humanist ideals and the study of languages. The beginning of direct biblical exegesis in university lectures, when added to the key contribution of Erasmus's *Novum Testamentum*, provides much of the ground on which the reformers were to build. Bishop Fox's instructions for his theology reader (1517) clearly broke with the medieval tradition of biblical commentary.[25] At Cambridge, in particular, Augustinian scholarship still possessed influence, sustaining some areas of doctrinal debate that were to be of great significance for the Lutherans.[26] The internationalism of all the universities, but especially of the Scottish ones, made access to advanced humanist scholarship, and later to the earliest reformed ideas, a natural progression for a minority. Finally, there is the paradox that both St Andrews and Cambridge had towering intellectuals who, by their very engagement on the side of tradition in the first stages of the European crisis, brought an awareness of new ideology home to the British Isles. John Major, the great reviver of the nominalist position, found himself under direct attack by Melanchthon, and may have contributed to the earliest debates on reform when he taught at St Andrews from 1523 to 1526. John Fisher, even more clearly, did much to disseminate knowledge of Lutheran beliefs when he published in *Assertionis Lutheranae Confutatio* (1523) the most systematic doctrinal defence of the Catholic position in the generation before the Council of Trent.[27]

But it was essentially Lutheranism that seduced away the liveliest British theologians of the 1520s and early 1530s. A number, like Robert Barnes, William Tyndale, and Patrick Hamilton, moved from a formal humanist

[25] S.L. Greenslade, 'The faculty of theology', in J. McConica (ed.), *The History of the University of Oxford*, vol. iii: *The Collegiate University* (Oxford, 1986), 304, 313–14. One can sometimes see a largely inadvertent link between the arts and reform, as in the Oxford requirement in 1527 that lectures be given on Melanchthon's Logic: ibid., 179.

[26] R. Trueman, *Luther's Legacy: Salvation and the English Reformers 1525–1556* (Oxford, 1994), 18–19.

[27] G. Wiedermann, 'Martin Luther versus John Fisher: some ideas concerning the debate on Lutheran theology at the University of St Andrews, 1525–30', *RSCHS* 22 (1984–6), 13–34.

training into heresy, and it is often difficult to identify a precise moment when they themselves fully rejected the Church. But none, except perhaps the eclectic Bilney, escaped the dominance of Luther's theology as it began to circulate in a series of key texts from 1520 onwards. The consequences of full commitment were usually flight into exile. Tyndale, the first to take this path, left England in 1524, closely followed by William Roye, from the Observant Franciscans at Greenwich. George Joye escaped in 1527 at the time of the trial of Bilney and Arthur, and John Frith in the next year.[28] Hamilton fled to Marburg from St Andrews in 1527. Robert Barnes spent two years under house arrest in his Augustinian order after 1525 and probably left for the Continent in 1528. Slightly later, Alexander Alan, subsequently known as Alesius, fled from St Andrews after making clear his conversion in the aftermath of the burning of Hamilton.[29] The exiles were all more directly exposed to Lutheran ideas once on the Continent, and several, including Barnes, studied at Lutheran universities. If they were not fully Protestantized before departure, they swiftly became so.

As men of the 'new learning' this generation took seriously Luther's injunctions that correct understanding of the divine will was essential to the Christian life.[30] None, except perhaps Frith, seem to have been theological systematizers by vocation: they were rather translators, evangelists, and controversialists, and in consequence they often appear in their doctrinal writings primarily as conduits for Continental ideology.[31] Robert Barnes, the most explicitly Lutheran of the English reformers, saw his *Supplication* (1531) as a way of making the range of German thought available in English. After defending himself against the charges of heresy that had been levelled against him he offered ten theological commonplaces. By far the most significant of these was the insistence that works played no part in justification. This, for Barnes, was the heart of the Pauline message, and therefore the central organizing principle of the scriptures. The vision was strongly Christocentric: He is the all-sufficient redeemer and 'we need of nothing but of him only'.[32] Barnes, following

---

[28] There are useful short biographies of this generation of English reformers in W.A. Clebsch, *England's Earliest Protestants, 1520–1535* (New Haven, Conn., 1964). Also D. Daniell, *William Tyndale: A Biography* (New Haven, Conn., 1994); C.C. Butterworth and A.G. Chester, *George Joye: 1495–1553* (Philadelphia, Pa., 1962); J.P. Lusardi, 'The career of Robert Barnes', in *CWTM* viii. 1365–415.

[29] For Hamilton see Wiedermann, 'Martin Luther versus John Fisher', 15–18; for Alesius, Wiedermann, 'Alexander Alesius, Scottish Lutheran (1500–1565)', *ARG* 55 (1964), 161–91.

[30] J.E. McGoldrick, *Luther's English Connection* (Milwaukee, 1979).

[31] This, and the following paragraph, are strongly indebted to Trueman, *Luther's Legacy*.

[32] R. Barnes, *A Supplicatyon made by Robert Barnes doctoure in divinite unto the most excellent and redoubted prince henrye the eyght* (Antwerp, 1531), fo. 38[v].

Luther, stressed man's passivity in the process of justification, and his dependence upon divine grace for the gift of faith. Works were not denied, but they were placed firmly within the context of the believer's grateful response to justification as the fruits of faith. It has been suggested that in the second edition of *A Supplication*, written in 1534 after he had returned to England, Barnes may have diluted his strong defence of the Lutheran view of justification and works by accepting the controversial Letter of James as canonical.[33] But at most this seems directed to emphasizing that abiding concern of the reformers, the moral results of solifidianism.

Tyndale and Frith display rather more distinctive doctrinal positions on grace, justification, and works, under the broad influence of Luther's thought. Tyndale's vision of man's redemption focused explicitly on the latter's bondage to sin, and the role of justification in freeing man to fulfil the law. He was concerned with the ethics of works and the possibility of regeneration through them after justification.[34] Through Christ's promises 'the elect were then justified inwardly before God, as outwardly before the world by keeping of the laws and ceremonies'.[35] The Old Testament provided Tyndale with much of his account of the proper keeping of law and ceremonies. While clearly starting from a Lutheran view of grace and justification during his years of work on the New Testament, Tyndale moved via study of the Pentateuch towards the concerns of writers in the reformed tradition, especially Bucer. Clebsch sees this as part of a movement away from the theocentrism of early Lutheran thought, and towards the beginning of covenant theology; and Tyndale is indeed a proponent of the idea that God and man are bound together by mutual promises.[36] As he explained in *A Fruitful and Godly Treatise expressing the Right Institution and Usage of the Sacraments* (1536), 'by baptism we be bound to God and God to us, and the bond and the seal of the covenant is written in our flesh'.[37] But for Tyndale, unlike many later covenant theorists, the bond between God and man is not that of contract, it is rather one of family loyalty founded in love. Frith moved closer in sentiment to Luther with his concern for God's righteous wrath against man and his emphasis on the atonement, though he stressed that faith in Christ must be associated

[33] Trueman, *Luther's Legacy*, 169–71, 194–6.

[34] In the case of both Tyndale and Frith Trueman argues convincingly against Clebsch that there is a basic consistency in their approach to soteriology.

[35] H. Walter (ed.), *William Tyndale's Doctrinal Treatises and Other Works*, 4 vols. (PS, Cambridge, 1848–9), i. 417.

[36] Clebsch, *England's Earliest Protestants*, 181–204. M. McGiffert, 'William Tyndale's Concept of Covenant', *JEH* 32 (1981), 167–84.

[37] T. Russell (ed.), *The Works of the English Reformers: William Tyndale and John Frith*, 3 vols. (1831), iii. 517.

with the cross of suffering and that assurance depended upon a single-minded commitment to faith. Much of his vision of the righteousness of God emerged from his most significant polemical work, his attack on purgatory, in which the false purgatory of the papists was contrasted with the true purgatories of faith and the cross. Frith was also the translator of *Patrick's Places*, the tract based on Patrick Hamilton's disputes at his trial in 1528.[38] These are strongly identified with Lutheran soteriology, especially on the antithesis between the law and the gospel that was a paradigmatic assumption of the German. And when Alesius came to lecture on the Psalms in Cambridge in 1536 he followed Luther and Melanchthon in insisting that the Psalter provided the *loci communes doctrinae Christianae*: the major exegetical tool through which the Pauline opposition of law and gospel could be made manifest.[39]

While Luther's soteriology was of central importance to this generation of reformers, his views on the other key area of doctrine disputed with the Roman church, the sacraments and especially the sacrament of the altar, were never so fully accepted. The dilemma of the nature of Christ's presence in the elements was resolved by Lutherans with an insistence on the reality of the body and blood, underpinned by a belief in the ubiquity of Christ's risen body. This specific solution, defended by Luther at Marburg in 1529, seems to have elicited little enthusiasm from the English, though Barnes appears to have held it.[40] Other theologians, in contact with a range of Protestant beliefs, were already looking to the Swiss for a more compelling theology of the Eucharist. George Joye published a tract (anonymously) called *The Supper of the Lord*, in which he attacked the sacrifice of the Mass, but also questioned the nature of the real presence.[41] Frith is the best-known anti-Lutheran: after his return to England in 1532 he was imprisoned, tried, and ultimately burned for sacramentarianism. In two tracts *A Christian Sentence* and his *Answer to More* he had rejected transubstantiation on the grounds that Christ's presence in the heart, not the bread, is salvific. He was less interested in the precise nature of Christ's relationship to the bread and wine, though ultimately he argued that spiritual feeding by the faithful was the only true form of communion. At his trial he argued that he could not swear that 'our Prelates opinion of

---

[38] Knox, i. 19–35, prints Frith's translation.

[39] G. Wiedermann, 'Alexander Alesius' lectures on the Psalms at Cambridge, 1536', *JEH* 37 (1986), 22–3.

[40] This, at least, is what Tyndale believed, when he advised Frith not to meddle with the presence of Christ in the sacrament since 'Barnes will be hot against you'. Walter, *Tyndale's Works*, vol. i, p. liiii.

[41] Butterworth and Chester, *George Joye*, 93–6. W.D.J. Cargill-Thompson, 'Who wrote "The Supper of the Lord"?', in his *Studies in the Reformation: Luther to Hooker*, ed. C.W. Dugmore (1980), 83–93.

the sacrament', that is that Christ was corporally present, 'is an undoubted article of faith'.[42] Cranmer, still orthodox in his adherence to a view of the corporal presence, identified Frith's position with that of Oecolampadius.[43]

In the years after Henry's break with Rome the experience of English and Scottish theologians was inevitably different. The Scots who adopted the new faith continued to face the harsh necessity of exile or execution. The most important of them remained a part of the Protestant diaspora, sometimes until death. Their need for patronage led a number to England, where the support of Cromwell and Cranmer was of crucial importance in providing livings and security. Alexander Seton, John MacAlpine, John MacDowell, and John Willock were the most distinguished of a group that escaped south of the border from James V's intermittent persecution.[44] Others, like George Wishart and John Wedderburn, chose European refuge instead. The choice of exile was obviously painful, yet it brought with it the opportunity to pursue gospel truth unimpeded by the need to consider the construction of a church. Hence Cranmer found the Scots in England an uncompromising group; worthy predecessors to that most famous exile John Knox. When Alesius lectured on the Psalms at Cambridge his Lutheran message was harsh. The true church was distinguished by the Word and the Cross, the company of saints justified and unified by Christ but suffering under the Cross. In a sharply dualistic image the prosperity of the false Church was compared to the pains of the true, experiencing weakness and persecution for Christ's sake. There was little reflection on the building of the visible Church for these battered Christians.[45] Alesius was equally unbending on the sacraments. Having been run out of Cambridge by the university authorities he was offered the opportunity by Cromwell to participate in the debate on the Ten Articles (1536). He did so with a trenchant speech on the dominical status of only two sacraments, and was eager to continue in this vein until told firmly by one of Cranmer's aides that he could no longer, as a stranger, be admitted to the disputation.[46]

---

[42] Clebsch, *England's Earliest Protestants*, 122–7.

[43] J.E. Cox (ed.) *The Works of Thomas Cranmer, Archbishop of Canterbury, Martyr, 1556*, 2 vols. (PS, Cambridge, 1844–6), i. 32. D. MacCulloch, *Thomas Cranmer* (1996), 101.

[44] J.E. McGoldrick, *Luther's Scottish Connections* (1989), 36 ff. J. Durkan, 'Scottish "evangelicals" in the patronage of Thomas Cromwell', *RSCHS* 21 (1982), 127–56.

[45] Wiedermann, 'Alexander Alesius' lectures', 37–41.

[46] Alesius himself tells this tale in A. Alesius, *Of the authorite of the word of God agaynst the bisshop of London* (?Leipzig, ?1537), sigs. A v–B viii. Wishart encountered similar problems at Bristol with his uncompromising preaching: M. Skeeters, *Community and Clergy: Bristol and the Reformation c.1530–c.1570* (Oxford, 1993), 51–6.

The shadow of exile had not wholly lifted for English theologians and polemicists, but from the early 1530s onwards they encountered the possibility of change sanctioned by the prince. This stimulated a struggle to build a godly visible Church that tended to overshadow more abstract doctrinal speculation. Indeed even before Henry VIII had contemplated a breach with Rome Tyndale's two 1528 publications, *The Parable of the Wicked Mammon* and *The Obedience of a Christian Man*, had signalled clearly that the reformers were committed to building a new order within the English polity.[47] Two interconnected forms of their struggle are particularly important for an understanding of religious change. First, the reformers met vigorous ideological opposition from their conservative colleagues. The tradition of polemical debate begun by Fisher and so powerfully developed by More was continued by Tunstal, Gardiner, and Bonner, as well as lesser figures like John Standish, Richard Smith, and the artisan Miles Hogarde.[48] These conflicts moulded Protestant response, most obviously in focusing upon certain issues, the authority of the Church, vernacular Scripture, clerical marriage, and the nature of the presence in the Mass that were central preoccupations for Catholics.[49] Secondly, much reforming thought had to be directed to issues of ecclesiology, church building, and the role of the godly prince that were a consequence of the political opportunities of the 1530s. The limits of obedience became, for obvious reasons, one of the most deeply experienced ideological debates of the mid-Tudor decades.[50]

The polemical thrust of Thomas More's work was sufficiently wide-ranging and ambitious to force response from the reformers across almost the whole of the controverted theological landscape. He had, after all, begun the challenge to Luther, with his support for Henry's *Assertio Septem Sacramentorum*, and his own contribution in the *Responsio ad Lutherum* (1523). This, however, was part of the international campaign, keeping the debate within the parameters of European learned discourse, and in Latin. From 1529 onwards the theological controversy was brought into an English environment with the publication of the *Dialogue concerning Heresies*.[51] More became, in Cuthbert Tunstal's famous phrase, 'a rival [to] Demosthenes in our native tongue'.[52] The purpose was not a narrow assertion of

---

[47] Daniell, *William Tyndale*, 155–249.

[48] R. Pineas, *Thomas More and Tudor Polemics* (Bloomington, Ind., 1968). Clebsch, *England's Earliest Protestants*, 286–90. P. O'Grady, *Henry VIII and the Conforming Catholics* (Collegeville, Minn., 1980).

[49] H.L. Parish, *Clerical Marriage and the English Reformation: Precedent, Policy and Practice* (Aldershot, 2000), 115–79.

[50] *CWTM*, viii. 1137–1268.

[51] A. Fox, *Thomas More: History and Providence* (Oxford, 1982), 128–66. *CWTM* vi. i. 1–435.

[52] E.F. Rogers (ed.), *The Correspondence of Sir Thomas More* (Princeton, N.J., 1947), 387.

doctrinal orthodoxy: rather a powerful act of persuasion directed at the spiritually faint-hearted utilizing every form of attack upon heresy and its writers. Tyndale's *Answer unto Sir Thomas More's Dialogue* (1531) is more overtly doctrinal, focusing upon the nature of the Church, the centrality of Scripture, and the problem of authority.[53] This established the tone for the later stages of More's confrontations not only with Tyndale, but with Frith and Joye: the reformers on the whole sought to focus on doctrinal issues; More on the rhetoric of persuasion in defence of the established Church.[54] Diatribes there were on the Protestant side, but they tended to come from individuals like William Barlow and Simon Fish, more interested in trading in old-style anti-clerical abuse than in the theology of reform.[55]

In the aftermath of the break with Rome the polemical energies of English theologians were for a time caught up in the defence of Henry's settlement. The main audience was once again international, and diatribes against Rome provided the most lively rhetorical material. But the struggle to establish the doctrinal nature of the new church quickly provided the forcing-ground for another cycle of internal polemical conflict. The 1530s saw the first two attempts at English formularies, the Ten Articles and the Bishops' Book, the first partially based on the agreements reached with the Lutherans known as the Wittenberg Articles. The Ten Articles followed Wittenberg in identifying only three sacraments, penance as well as baptism and the Eucharist, and in arguing that the 'only sufficient and worthy causes' of justification were God's grace freely promised through the merits of Christ's blood and passion. Otherwise they represented a series of compromises between conservatives and reformers in which the tone of commentary, for example on the saints, is often evangelical, but the substance would scarcely have satisfied any Lutheran. The Bishops' Book resuscitated all seven sacraments, but in other ways it pushed further in the direction of the Articles, articulating a sacramental theology that was explicitly Lutheran. It perhaps owed most to Melanchthon's *Loci Communes*, which had been dedicated to Henry in 1535. The Bishops' Book was produced after a series of bruising encounters between conservatives and reformers: the former, for example, failed to get a strong defence of shrines and pilgrimages inserted into the text.[56]

---

[53] *CWTM* viii. i. and ii. W. Tyndale, *An answere to Sir Thomas More's Dialogue*, ed. H. Walter (PS, Cambridge, 1850).

[54] Daniell, *William Tyndale*, 250–80.

[55] On the contribution of Barlow and Fish see Clebsch, *England's Earliest Protestants*, 229–51. His third 'minor' figure Roye is also a popularizer, but has what appears to be an interest in more advanced reforming theology in his work of translation.

[56] C. Lloyd (ed.), *Formularies of Faith put forward by Authority during the Reign of Henry VIII* (Oxford, 1825), 3–211. The account given here follows closely that of MacCulloch, *Cranmer*, 161–6, 185–97.

Such compromises failed to please the zealous, and years later Alesius recalled bitterly to Elizabeth that 'as soon as the King began to hate [your mother], laws hostile to the purer doctrine of the Gospel appeared'.[57] The continuing negotiations Cromwell conducted with the Lutherans persuaded conservative theologians that confrontation was once again necessary.[58] The opportunity came in 1540, when after the passage of the Act of Six Articles and the debacle of the Cleves marriage Gardiner was able to attack Cromwell through that most determined of spokesmen for Lutheranism, Robert Barnes. Gardiner's sermon for the first Sunday in Lent deliberately challenged Barnes on the key tenet of justification and faith. Faith and works were both necessary for justification by God.[59] John Standish, responding to Barnes's protestation at the stake, denounced him on the key grounds that he had taught 'that God is the author of sin, and that works do not profit, and that Christ's death is sufficient'.[60] And indeed not only Barnes, but Jerome and Garret who were burned with him all presented faith in Christ's merits and a denial of meritorious works at the heart of their profession of faith.

The Act of Six Articles, followed by the fall of Cromwell and the burning of Barnes, Jerome, and Garret, once again changed the ideological landscape. The next few years produced a second Protestant diaspora, driving key reformers, John Bale, William Turner, John Philpot, John Rogers, and the young John Hooper, overseas, and ensuring that survivors like Miles Coverdale and George Joye were sent on their travels again.[61] Their places of exile are significant: by now the magnets were the reformed cities of Strasbourg and Basel, along with the great centre of Swiss Protestantism, Zurich. Antwerp, of course, remained attractive because of its proximity to England, its printing industry, and its political environment. While some of the Scots still chose a Lutheran environment—MacAlpine went to Copenhagen and John Lyn to Wittenberg—this was very unusual for English refugees of the 1540s.[62] The Henricians had fled from the power of a visible Church that constrained their con-

---

[57] *CSP For* Eliz. I, no. 1303, pp. 532 ff. [58] O'Grady, *Conforming Catholics*, 98–102.

[59] On Gardiner's role in these controversies see G. Redworth, *In Defence of the Church Catholic* (Oxford, 1990), 106 ff. See also L.E.C. Wooding, *Rethinking Catholicism in Reformation England* (Oxford, 2000), 62–81, though this constructs Gardiner as far too sympathetic to some of the ideas of the reformers.

[60] Foxe, v. 434–8.

[61] Ryrie has traced thirty men and women who spent time abroad between 1539 and 1547 at least partly for their faith: A. Ryrie, 'English Evangelical Reformers in the Last Years of Henry VIII', University of Oxford D.Phil. (2000), 123–46.

[62] J. Kirk, 'Early Scottish Protestants', in J. Kirk (ed.), *Humanism and Reform: Essays in Honour of James K. Cameron*, SCH Subsidia 9 (Oxford, 1991), 379–80. J. Durkan, 'Heresy in Scotland: the second phase, 1546–58', *RSCHS* 24 (1992), 329, 333–4.

sciences primarily on three issues: the nature of the Eucharist, free access
to the vernacular scriptures, and the marriage of priests. On the last two
Lutherans were thoroughly sound; on the former they often appeared
little better than the 'Act with Six Strings'. The works that this group
produced in exile reflect their preoccupations: attacks on the false Church
and the clergy, defence of clerical marriage, and the beginning of the great
English debate on the real presence. The tracts from this period attributed
to George Joye give some flavour of exile attitudes. He did continue the
debate about faith and works, bitterly charging Gardiner as the agent of
Barnes's downfall, thereby provoking another round of polemical tracts
on justification, and predestination.[63] But he also translated Melanchthon's
Defence of Priests' Marriage, originally sent to Henry VIII, and produced his
own defence of matrimony; he seems to have been responsible for translating Zwingli's *Christianae Fidei Exposito*, and possibly for a text on *Bap-
tysme and the Lordis Souper*, which gives a broadly reformed view of the
Eucharist.[64] Finally, in a curious and rambling commentary on Daniel,
incorporating a translation of Osiander's reflections on the ending of the
world, he points forward to the preoccupation with eschatology that was
to become so important a feature of English Protestant thought.[65]

It was scarcely surprising that a persecuted minority should turn to the
prophetic books, and particularly to Revelation, as a way of providing
meaning and purpose for Christ's people suffering under the cross.[66] In
his first sermon after his conversion in 1547 John Knox was already identifying the Roman church with the Antichrist and contrasting this with
the true Church, which 'heard the voice of the one pastor, Jesus Christ'.[67]
Heinrich Bullinger, in a commentary on the Apocalypse that deeply influenced English Protestants, spoke of the prophecies as indicating the
working out of God's purposes in history, and his just rule over everything in this world. The sealed book of Revelation 5. 1 contained 'all the
counsels of God, all his works and judgements' which, though hidden
from the world, could be understood by the elect who knew Christ.[68]
This accorded well with the reformers' general insistence on the need for
faith in Christ's hidden glory, and the hope in his promise that would be
made manifest at the End. Traheron, in a tract partly based on Bullinger,

---

[63] Joye wrote against Gardiner in 1543; Gardiner responded in 1546 with *A Declaration of such true articles as George Joye hath gone about to confute as false* (1546), and Joye countered with *The refutation of the byshop of Winchesters derk declaration of his false articles* (1546).

[64] G. Joye, *A frutefull treatis of baptyme and the lordis souper* (? Antwerp, 1541). Butterworth and Chester, *George Joye*, 205–44.

[65] K.R. Firth, *The Apocalyptic Tradition in Reformation Britain, 1530–1645* (Oxford, 1979), 61–5.

[66] R. Bauckham, *Tudor Apocalypse* (Appleford, Oxon., 1976), 113–24.

[67] Knox, i. 190.

[68] H. Bullinger, *A hundred Sermons upon the Apocalips of Jesu Christe . . .* (1561), 156.

written during the Marian exile, explicitly linked the coming of Antichrist with this dependence upon God's providence:

the decay and ruin, the afflictions, and persecutions of the Church in this latter time, whatsoever is done in the world by Antichrist and his members, is not tossed at adventure by hap, but governed by the hand and certain providence of God.[69]

The most vigorous of this generation's contributors to the debate about the role of Antichrist and the theology of Last Things was John Bale, whose *Image of bothe churches* was constructed in three phases during his Henrician exile.[70] Bale was less a theologian than historian and polemicist, though he was thoroughly steeped in reformed theology and passionately committed to *sola scriptura*. Scripture had primacy in the understanding of divine purposes, but Scripture had to be used carefully to read the story of God's actions from chronicle. There was a continuing history of the true, as of the false, Church: in any age men could determine whether they 'are citizens in the new Jerusalem with Jesus Christ, or...in the old superstitious Babylon with antichrist the vicar of Satan'.[71] The text of Revelation provided Bale with the structure of his commentary on the history of the two churches, not only in the specific identifications of, for example, the pope with the whore of Babylon, but in the historic scheme which correlated the seven seals with the seven ages of the Church's history. The Reformation, the time of the seventh seal, was to be the fulfilment of prophecy.[72] Bale shared his concern for the proper doctrinal and moral understanding of the pattern of history with Bullinger, Osiander, and the Magdeburg Centuriators. However, his popular text, which went through four editions in the reigns of Edward VI and Elizabeth, formed the basis for a very strong and distinctive English engagement in the struggle between Christ and Antichrist, and in the narrative of history as revelation. It exerted a powerful influence over John Foxe, whose *Acts and Monuments* shed Bale's lurid language, and his insistence on the magisterial voice of the author, while sharing his basic understanding of the relationship between prophetic Scripture and the history of the true Church.[73]

The 'persecuted remnant' also took up a polemical theme that was particularly close to many of their hearts: the defence of clerical mar-

---

[69] B. Traheron, *An Exposition of the 4. Chapter of St. John's Revelation* (1573), sig. Aiii.

[70] Firth, *Apocalyptic Tradition*, 32–68. Bauckham, *Tudor Apocalypse*, 68–91.

[71] J. Bale, 'The Image of Both Churches', in *Select Works*, ed. H. Christmas (PS, Cambridge, 1849), 252.

[72] Parish, *Clerical Marriage*, 61–81, 151–2.

[73] T. Betteridge, *Tudor Histories of the English Reformation, 1530–1583* (Aldershot, 1999), 80–8, 175–89.

riage.[74] While the principle of marriage for priests had been espoused with
vigour by most of the magisterial reformers, circumstances in England
ensured that the controversy would be particularly prolonged and bitter.
Henry VIII's profound hostility to married priests, the curiously reluctant
acquiescence of Edward's regime, and Mary's deliberate policy of depriving married clergy, all fuelled the controversy. But so did an awareness by
the major protagonists that the dispute about celibacy and marriage
touched many of the key doctrinal issues of the reformed faith. As in the
case of revelation, prophecy, and the history of the churches, no-one
enlarged on this issue so fully as Bale. It was he who most explicitly
identified clerical celibacy, with its inevitable concomitant of 'whoredom
and hypocrisy', as being the mark of Antichrist. He linked together history and his loathing of the 'whoring clergy', by showing that the popes
Sylvester II and Gregory VII had poisoned the Church with their insistence that 'none should be admitted to holy orders unless he forswore
marriage for the term of his life'. Bale also assailed the falsity of vows by
the celibate clergy, and the pollution of the sacraments that came from
clerical concupiscence. A vow of chastity, especially one made in a monastic context, was inherently idolatrous, because it was a form of will-
work, claiming the capacity to be virtuous, and to elevate the Rule in the
place of the more visibly idolatrous graven image. And for Bale and others
who wrote in the same vein the impossibility of a chaste priesthood
subverted all claim to a mediatory role in the Eucharistic sacrifice. God,
wrote Anthony Gilby, 'will not be changed into any new forms by the
mumbling and breathing of a whoremonger or sodomitical priest'.[75]

The debate about clerical marriage had wide doctrinal implications,
but, more than almost any other aspect of Reformation polemic, it also
had a tendency to be conducted at a level of cheap jibes and scurrilous
innuendo. On the Catholic side Thomas More in the first generation and
Miles Hogarde and Thomas Martin thereafter were as willing to be venomous as Bale, Gilby, and William Turner were among the reformers.[76]
The battle was in part being fought for an influence over the hearts and
minds of the laity, but the more immediate targets were the clergy themselves, who might be won or lost for the wider cause of Reformation by

[74] I am indebted to the work of Dr Parish, cited above, for this and the ensuing paragraph.
[75] A. Gilby, *An Answere to the devillish detection of Stephane Gardiner* (1547), fo. 56ᵛ.
[76] At least sixteen of Bale's writings engage in the debate about marriage and celibacy. No-
one else approximates to this figure, though six of More's polemics have some mention of
marriage and celibacy, as do the same number of William Turner's. Apart from Bale, the fullest
texts are George Joye, *The Defence of the Mariage of Preistes Agenst Steven Gardiner* (1541); Thomas
Martin, *A treatise declaring and plainly Provyng that the pretensed marriage of prestes . . . is no mariage*
(1554); and John Ponet, *A defence of the mariage of Priestes by Scripture and Auncuiente Wryters*
(1549).

the persuasion of the pamphleteers on this issue. This was practical divinity with a vengeance: the subduing of the flesh promising 'double honour' to the clergy in the view of the Catholic polemicists, the sober choice of marriage being an indication of election for the Protestant. And while the political issue hung in the balance it seems that more energy was employed in this ideological confrontation than in any other except the profound divisions of the Eucharistic debate.

The Eucharistic Debate and Cranmerian Liturgy

Early English Reformation polemical debate ranged widely over the intellectual and spiritual landscape in contention between Catholics and reformers. Yet it had an unerring tendency to return to the deepest source of Catholic distress: the challenge to the nature of the Mass. To take Gardiner's work as exemplary of traditional beliefs: he turned to a public defence of the Mass in 1546 in his *A Detection of the Devil's Sophistrie*, which urged the unlearned not to reject the central mysteries of the Eucharist because of the complexity of the arguments being presented to them. Under Edward, while challenging Bucer on clerical marriage, he reserved his most powerful debating skills for the defence of the Mass against Cranmer's attack. Though Gardiner could acknowledge that Catholic understanding of transubstantiation had changed over time he grounded his faith most passionately upon a belief in the reality of Christ's miraculous presence in the mutation of bread and wine into body and blood.[77] The defence of the Mass was also a defence of the sacrificing priesthood, set apart to re-enact Christ's redemptive offering upon the cross: it touched the heart of traditional conviction that the sacralized, mediatory role of the clergy was central to the process of salvation. In comparison, justification by faith alone, though 'a terrible speech', as Gardiner described it when discussing Cranmer's 1547 homily on the subject, was opposed not so much for itself as for its threat to the supremacy of the Eucharistic sacrifice.[78] The Scottish hierarchy displayed some of the same horror of sacramentarian heresy above all others. The 1549 provincial council proposed to proceed against heretics and sacrament-

[77] Redworth, *Church Catholic*, 235–6, 260–1. In all Gardiner produced six volumes of polemics during his enforced stay in the Tower under Edward. The immediacy of *A Detection* is indicated by the fact that Gardiner seems to have written in response to the sacramentarian views of the martyr Anne Askew.

[78] Gardiner was most familiar with the complexities of the debate on justification through his attendance at the diet of Regensburg in 1541. Apart from Gardiner, the most significant defence of the Catholic position was provided by Tunstal in 1551: *De Corporis et Sanguinis Domini in Eucharistia*, published in Paris in 1554: H. Davies, *Worship and Theology in England from Cranmer to Baxter* (Princeton, N.J., 1970), 88–90.

arians 'and chiefly against those who inveigh against the sacrament of the Eucharist'.[79]

The intensity of Catholic commitment to the Mass was more than matched by the vigour of reformed opposition. Once Henry VIII's constraining hand had been lifted there was an outpouring of polemical literature against 'Mistress missa'. 1548 alone saw thirty-one hostile tracts published, ranging from simple negative polemics to sophisticated treatises preparing the ground for the debate on the First Prayer Book.[80] Both sides acknowledged that, in terms of practical divinity, the most critical task of a new liturgy would be the proper definition of the central act of Christian worship. Hence the overwhelming importance of a proper understanding of Cranmer's doctrine of the Eucharist, and of the ways in which he sought to represent it liturgically. Each phase of the archbishop's evolving understanding of Eucharistic theology has been sharply debated by theologians and historians.[81] What has seemed generally clear since the work of Peter Newman Brooks a generation ago is that Cranmer rejected full Catholic dogma in the early 1530s and adopted a position not far removed from that of the Lutherans, insisting on a true and corporal presence of Christ in the elements while moving away from an explicit emphasis on transubstantiation.[82] Then sometime between Henry's last regnal year and 1548 Cranmer moved decisively away from the idea of the real presence, and we have his own word that the main agent for this change of heart was Nicholas Ridley. Ridley 'by sundry persuasions and authorities of doctors', and in particular through his reading of the ninth-century theologian Ratramnus of Corbie, persuaded the archbishop to accept that Christ's words at the Last Supper should be interpreted in a spiritual sense.[83]

Ridley's mature view of the Eucharist, articulated in his prison treatise *A Brief Declaration of the Lord's Supper* (1554), included praise of Ratramnus's figurative interpretation of Christ's presence, but focused on the spiritual feeding that was accessible to those who apprehended that presence through faith. His people were sealed in a unity with his mystical body.[84] As bishop of London Ridley's most powerful contribution to the reform movement was his fierce hostility to altars, with their implication of sacrifice. A table was the appropriate board at which 'spiritually to eat

---

[79] D. Patrick (ed.), *Statutes of the Scottish Church 1225–1559*, SHS 54 (1907), 123–4.

[80] J.N. King, *English Reformation Literature* (Princeton, N.J., 1972), 89. At the other end of the debate, Peter Martyr was still writing in answer to Gardiner in 1556: A. Pettegree, *Marian Protestantism* (Aldershot, 1996), 120–1.

[81] C.W. Dugmore, *The Mass and the English Reformers* (1958), 117. MacCulloch, *Cranmer*, 278, 399–403.

[82] P.N. Brooks, *Thomas Cranmer's Doctrine of the Eucharist* (1965).

[83] MacCulloch, *Cranmer*, 382–3.   [84] Davies, *Worship and Theology*, 103–6.

his body and spiritually to drink his blood'.[85] Cranmer arrived at much the same conclusion, through complex paths, exposed to a diversity of influences. Among those influences prior to the full construction of the First Prayer Book were two of the greatest Continental reformers to engage themselves with the English Reformation: Martin Bucer and Peter Martyr Vermigli.[86] Bucer corresponded with Cranmer in 1547 and 1548, expressing his own Eucharistic views: complete hostility to transubstantiation and adoration of the elements, with a form of receptionism in which the faithful were drawn up to heaven and receive their 'own Christ, as celestial food'.[87] Peter Martyr brought to England on his first visit a text of John Chrysostom, which apparently asserted the unchanging nature of the bread and wine at the Eucharist.[88] Armed with these guides and his own wide reading in the scriptures and Fathers Cranmer set out to translate the liturgy and steer his revised Eucharist through Parliament. This, as we have seen, demanded political skill to arm theological rectitude: as Martyr observed at this crucial juncture, 'I see there is nothing in the world more difficult than to found a church.'[89]

Parallel developments in Scotland obviously lacked the formality of doctrinal debate that characterized Edwardian England, but the nature of the Eucharist was also a central preoccupation. The most articulate of the Castilian exiles, Henry Balnaves, still concentrated on the core Lutheran doctrine of justification in his 1548 tract *The Confession of Faith*, written in his Rouen prison.[90] But George Wishart, the leading martyr of the 1540s, had already used his preaching mission in new ways, introducing his fellow Scots to a modified Swiss position on the sacraments, and translating the First Helvetic Confession of 1536 for their benefit. The Lord's Supper was commemorative: the bread and wine were also signifiers of the spiritual presence of the body and blood in the souls of the faithful. Thereafter the Scottish reformers regarded it as normative to oppose Catholic doctrine with a version of the spiritual presence.[91] By the time

---

[85] H. Christmas (ed.), *The Works of Nicholas Ridley* (PS, Cambridge, 1843), 322. Though note that Ridley was not the first to attack the altars: Cranmer's visitors in Norwich diocese initiated the campaign at the end of 1550. R. Houlbrooke, *Church Courts and People during the English Reformation, 1520–70* (Oxford, 1979), 165–6; MacCulloch, *Cranmer*, 438.

[86] MacCulloch, *Cranmer*, 381–3.

[87] B. Hall, 'Cranmer, the Eucharist and the foreign divines in the reign of Edward VI', in P. Ayris and D. Selwyn (eds.), *Thomas Cranmer, Churchman and Scholar* (Woodbridge, 1993), 217–58.

[88] M. Anderson, 'Rhetoric and reality: Peter Martyr and the English Reformation', *C16J* 19 (1988), 456–61.

[89] G.C. Gorham (ed.), *Gleanings of a Few Scattered Ears during the Period of the Reformation in England*, 2 vols. (1857), i. 74.

[90] H. Balnaves, *The Confession of Faith* (Edinburgh, 1584): it was Knox who rescued this text, intending it to be printed. Knox, i. 250.

[91] Kirk, 'Early Scottish Protestants', 394–6.

Knox returned from his period of Continental exile to preach to the 'privy kirks' in 1555 his form of presentation of the sacraments was emphatically reformed: he ministered to the gentlemen of the Mearns, for example, at 'the Table of the Lord Jesus'.[92]

The debate about the First Prayer Book showed Cranmer's clear identity with reformed views, especially in his insistence that only those who are 'members of his body' truly receive Christ. In Cranmer's revision of the Mass the adoration of the elements was firmly suppressed; Christ's sacrifice upon the cross was located at a once-for-all historical moment and was uncoupled from any re-presentation of the atonement; and all idea of offertory was detached from the elements.[93] In the homily that preceded the reception of the elements, the spiritual form of feeding was made explicit: 'if with a truly penitent heart and lively faith we receive that holy Sacrament;...then we spiritually eat the flesh of Christ and drink his blood; then we dwell in Christ and he in us'.[94] Cranmer's surviving canon of the Mass was intended to substitute for the Latin sacrifice a clear statement denying all material oblation.[95] But the language and structure of the book itself was often conciliatory to conservative opinion, and was already envisaged by Bucer as 'only to be retained for a time' while 'the people...may be won over'. Hooper famously complained that he was so offended by the book that 'if it be not corrected, I neither can nor will communicate with the church in the administration of the supper'.[96] The words of administration remained ambiguous, and the wafer was still broken: some sense of corporeal presence might still be read into Cranmer's words. Gardiner's on/off response to the text, claiming that on Christ's presence in the sacrament 'there was as much spoken in that book as might be desired', may have been merely tactical, or a desire to stretch obedience to the limits.[97] However, it underlined the need, already detected by the archbishop's foreign advisers, to produce an unambiguous text.

The interval between the two Prayer Books was occupied by continuing intense debate about the nature of the Eucharist, now driven much more explicitly by the contributions of Cranmer's foreign advisers. Peter Martyr's most visible offering was his role in the debate on the nature of

---

[92] F. Bardgett, *Scotland Reformed: The Reformation in Angus and the Mearns* (Edinburgh, 1989), 47.

[93] F.A. Gasquet and E. Bishop, *Edward VI and the Book of Common Prayer* (1890), 404–5, 442.

[94] J. Ketley (ed.), *The Two Liturgies*, AD 1549 *and* AD 1552 . . . *in the Reign of Henry VIII* (PS, Cambridge, 1844), 79.

[95] E.C. Ratcliff, 'The liturgical work of Archbishop Cranmer', *JEH* 7 (1956), 197–8.

[96] *OL* i. 535–6, 79.

[97] Foxe, vi. 14. W.K. Jordan (ed.), *The Chronicle and Political Papers of King Edward VI* (Cornell, 1966), 36.

the Eucharist in the Oxford disputation of May/June 1549. The Oxford disputation showed Martyr at his most vigorous in the attack on transubstantiation, and in his use of patristic sources to demonstrate that bread and wine continued to be so described after consecration. Although he was himself dissatisfied with his performance, Martyr seems to have expounded the basic nature of the reformed position sufficiently clearly.[98] In the parallel Cambridge disputations there was not the same sense of a solo performance by a great divine: Madhew, Ridley, Grindal, Guest, Pilkington, and Perne all spoke against the Catholic position: Bucer seems to have been present in Cambridge but content for others to lead. There were some differences of emphasis between Cranmer's two great advisers: Martyr's position on the presence being nearer to what Gerrish has called 'symbolic parallelism' than Bucer, whose view, like that of Calvin, was that the signs of the elements produce actual spiritual experience for the faithful.[99]

Bucer was alarmed that Martyr's propositions for the Oxford debate might lead men to assume that Christ was absent from the Supper. But they were agreed on the essence that had to be conveyed to the faithful through liturgy. This can be summarized under four headings: Christ's body and blood are spiritually present in the sacrament; their presence is only apprehended through faith; the Holy Spirit stirs up such faith; and a conjunction is effected between believers and the body of Christ.[100] All of this demanded an absolutely explicit separation between the signs and the things signified. Martin Bucer in his *Censura*, a thoroughgoing critique of the 1549 Prayer Book text, insisted, for example, that bread rather than communion wafers should be used in the service, and that any remainder of the elements should be taken home and used by the celebrant.[101] Two other theologians also influenced Cranmer: the 'Zurichers' John Hooper and Jan Laski. Laski, at Cranmer's prompting, endeavoured to orchestrate an agreed statement among the exiles about the nature of the Eucharist; this failed largely because Bucer was concerned that the language of Zurich remained too symbolist.[102] Hooper offered his own trenchant

[98] Foxe, vi. 297–335. P. McNair, 'Peter Martyr in England', in J.C. McLelland (ed.), *Peter Martyr Vermigli and the Italian Reformation* (Waterloo, Ont., 1980), 85–105.

[99] Anderson, 'Rhetoric and reality', 454 ff. Hall, 'Cranmer and the foreign divines', 227–33, though this is misleading in minimizing Martyr's influence and exaggerating that of Bucer. B.A. Gerrish, *Grace and Gratitude: The Eucharistic Theology of John Calvin* (Minneapolis, 1993), 166–7. Cranmer's relationship to these positions is discussed by MacCulloch, *Cranmer*, 614–16.

[100] C. Hopf, *Martin Bucer and the English Reformation* (Oxford, 1946), 41–51.

[101] B. Hall, 'Martin Bucer in England', in D.F. Wright (ed.), *Martin Bucer: Reforming Church and Community* (Cambridge, 1994), 152–4. Davies, *Worship and Theology*, 107–11.

[102] Jan Laski contributed a 'memorialist' tract to the Eucharistic debate: *Brevis ac dilucida de sacramentis ecclesiae Christi tractatio* (1552). MacCulloch, 'Jan Laski', 328–9.

contribution to the debate with his *Answer* to Gardiner's polemic and underscored the memorialist qualities of the rite: 'as for the sacramental eating...there is nothing but a memory of this death, whereof Christ altogether spoke in the sixth of John, and interpreteth many times this word "eat" for "believe"'.[103]

While Cranmer was advised and supported by his theological specialists, his own full exposition of Eucharistic doctrine, set out in the *Defence of the True and Catholic Doctrine of the Sacrament of the Body and Blood of our Saviour Christ* (1550), showed no slavish dependence upon the formulations of others.[104] Patristic sources were marshalled with great confidence to sustain a case that there must be a complete break from Catholic concepts of the Mass, the repeated sacrificial offering of Christ, the adoration and oblation, the belief that the wicked can eat and drink Christ's body, and the notion that the elements can be in any sense transmuted. These were themes of far greater import to the archbishop than the precise definition of the form of reception of the elements, though on the latter he was insistent that Christ truly dwelt in faithful communicants and they in him. This proceeded beyond any memorialist or metaphorical definition of the nature of reception, and yet Cranmer tended to eschew any implication of a substantial presence of Christ in the Eucharist, which he saw as articulated in Bucer's emphasis upon the organic unity of the faithful in the body of Christ. A characteristic Cranmerian observation is that 'Christ is present in the sacrament, as they [Scripture and the fathers] teach also that he is present in his word, when he worketh mightily in the hearts of the hearers.'[105]

The actual Eucharistic changes of the Prayer Book of 1552 assimilated Cranmer's own views, those of his advisers, and the need to respond to critics, especially Gardiner.[106] The canon of the Mass was dramatically broken: for example, the Lord's Prayer was removed to the post-communion phase of the liturgy lest it should be seen in its petition for daily bread as having Eucharistic reference, and the Benedictus was deleted for the same reason. The memorialist form of the administration of the elements, 'Drink this in remembrance that Christ's blood was shed for thee and be thankful', was emphasized, though the notion of partaking of the body and blood was not wholly lost. There was a sustained attempt to remove any implication of consecration, and the symbolic elevation of bread and

---

[103] S. Carr (ed.), *Early Writings of John Hooper* (PS, Cambridge, 1843), 156.

[104] The most compelling discussion of Cranmer's writings is in MacCulloch, *Cranmer*, 462 ff. See also Davies, *Worship and Theology*, 111–20.

[105] J.E. Cox (ed.), *The Works of Thomas Cranmer, Archbishop of Canterbury, Martyr, 1556*, 2 vols. (PS, Cambridge, 1844–6), i. 11.

[106] MacCulloch, *Cranmer*, 504–12.

cup by the minister during the recitation of the words of institution was also abolished.[107] And, although the changes to the Eucharistic rite were of central importance, the ending of prayers for the dead was of almost equal significance. The use of the communion service at funerals, still sanctioned in 1549, was abolished, as was the commendation of the soul of the dead person to the Father. The intermediary role of the priest, linking the living and the dead, and the possibility of offering sacrifice to influence the fate of the departed, were both swept aside as part of the denial that the Mass could be made efficacious through human agency.[108]

The radicalism of Cranmer's 1552 liturgy was also marked in its final removal of all suggestion of veneration of the saints and its final denial of processions as a part of worship. But while its doctrinal position was now unambiguous, and its denial of any association with the old canon abundantly clear, it remained something very different from the reformed liturgies which were being developed in the cities of Switzerland and southern Germany. It may be, as MacCulloch has suggested, that the archbishop himself wished to go further. Peter Martyr told Bucer in 1551 that 'if the business had been committed to his individual hand, purity of ceremonies would without difficulty have been attained', but that he was constrained by others.[109] On the other hand, when Cranmer did battle with John Hooper about the ordinal and the wearing of vestments he revealed a dimension of his beliefs that militated against rapid change or the purity of Switzerland.[110] At the core of the conflict about whether the bishop-elect of Gloucester should be consecrated according to the ordinal was an attitude to authority, meshed with a belief in co-operation and political pragmatism. 'The general consent of the whole kingdom' had established the ordinal, with its insistence on proper clerical dress, and only a change in such consent could alter the need for obedience to a requirement that was not repugnant to God's Word. Here the future battle-lines separating conformists and non-conformists, with their conflicting views of *adiaphora*, things indifferent, are already discernible.[111]

And the ordinal itself also sheds some light on the cautious, even conservative, aspects of Cranmer's beliefs. It basically followed proposals made by Bucer in 1549, which torpedoed the old view of a sacrament of orders,

---

[107] F.E. Brightman, *The English Rite*, 2 vols. (1915), vol. i, pp. cxliv–xvi; ii. 849–77.

[108] A.H. Couratin, 'The service of Holy Communion, 1552–1662', *Church Quarterly Review* 163 (1962), 431–42.

[109] Gorham, *Gleanings*, 232.

[110] MacCulloch, *Cranmer*, 460–1, 471–85.

[111] When Martyr was asked by Cranmer to comment on the dispute with Hooper he did so (though perhaps reluctantly) in terms of the importance of public authority and the concept of *adiaphora*: OL i. 486–90.

situating the ministry firmly amidst the body of the faithful people.[112] Yet, while Bucer suggested no marked contrast between the calling of bishops, priests, and deacons, the official ordinal differentiated them by providing different services, and the giving of different symbols. A priest still received chalice and paten, a bishop his crozier, until a revision of 1552 deleted these.[113] Once again, Cranmer seemed content to allow a measure of customary behaviour, which was open to traditionalist misinterpretation, while himself holding a thoroughly revised view of the ministry.

Forms of Protestantism: The Second Generation

The doctrinal debates of the later 1540s and 1550s took place in a very different environment from those of their predecessors. For the English there was the overwhelming importance of building a visible Church, and then rescuing its shadow from the debacle of Mary's succession. Internationally the Protestant churches were swayed to and fro by the changing fortunes of the German princes and the emperor. The 1548 Interim, agreed after Charles's crushing defeat of the Schmalkaldic League at Mühlberg, represented the low point for reformed fortunes, while the emperor's defeat at Innsbruck in 1552 did something, belatedly, to restore them.[114] The Interim shifted the balance of influence within the reformed churches decisively away from Strasbourg and towards the Swiss, underlining the growing influence of Geneva as well as securing Bullinger's role at Zurich. The *Consensus Tigurinus* of 1549, in which the major reformed churches agreed to compromise their differences upon the Eucharist, was as much a consequence of political threat as of the eirenical efforts of Calvin. And it was the Interim that helped to produce a flood of religious refugees in England, providing Cranmer with his advisers, and London with its fledgling stranger churches.[115]

These circumstances stimulated debate on issues other than the Eucharist: issues which were to assume central significance once the broad contours of sacramental theology had been resolved within magisterial Protestantism. The first took its participants back to the Ur-themes of justification and grace, but now began to add a far more specific preoccupation with the nature of predestination.[116] The second addressed ecclesi-

---

[112] P. Collinson, 'The reformer and the archbishop: Martin Bucer and an English Bucerian', in his *Godly People: Essays on English Protestantism and Puritanism* (1983), 27–9.

[113] Brightman, *English Rite*, ii. 928–1017.

[114] E. Cameron, *The European Reformation* (Oxford, 1991), 347–9.

[115] A. Pettegree, *Foreign Protestant Communities in Sixteenth-Century London* (Oxford, 1986), 23–38.

[116] Trueman, *Luther's Legacy*, 243–88.

ology, the nature of the Church and its ministry. Predestination was, of course, one of the rocks on which the reformers founded their faith in the divine purposes of God towards his faithful people. As such it is to be found in the thinking of Cranmer, of Peter Martyr, and of Bucer throughout the 1540s.[117] Bucer, in particular, saw predestination as of central doctrinal importance, and it must have been one of the themes on which he lectured at Cambridge, drawing his material from his commentary on Ephesians. For Bucer predestination was both a necessary affirmation of God's glory and an assurance to the man of faith that he was secure in his election.[118] It was the second of these themes which, as an ideal tool of spiritual counsel and practical divinity, was taken up by John Bradford, in his confrontation with the 'free-will men' when they were imprisoned together in King's Bench in 1554. Bradford affirmed a version of absolute predestination, and in a rather unsystematized form points forward towards a doctrine of double predestination, though the implications of the doctrine for the assured Christian life always remain uppermost in his writing.[119]

A few years earlier another of the Marian martyrs, John Hooper, had had a dispute with Bartholomew Traheron on the issue of the divine decree.[120] John ab Ulmis, writing to Bullinger in 1550, noted that it 'is wonderful how very far they disagree respecting God's predestination of men'.[121] This is interesting partly because Traheron was one of the first of the Edwardian generation to acknowledge the growing influence of Calvin in this field, and to identify clearly with his views.[122] John Knox also seems to have touched on a Calvinist form of predestination in his English sermons before he was exposed to direct Genevan influence. On the other hand the 'proto-Puritan' Hooper was deeply disturbed by the implications of the doctrine because of the danger that it made God the author of sin and because it seemed to lift from the individual Christian

---

[117] MacCulloch, *Cranmer*, 405–6, 615–16, places great emphasis upon Cranmer's commitment to predestinarian theology. D.D. Wallace, *Puritans and Predestination: Grace in English Protestant Theology, 1525–1695* (Chapel Hill, N.C., 1982), 15–19. Ochino was another of the Edwardian exiles who wrote on the theme, asserting incautiously that even Christ cannot 'save a reprobate nor damn an elect': *Certayne Sermons of the ryghte famous and excellente Clerke Master Bernardine Ochine* (1550), sig. M i.

[118] W.P. Stephens, 'The Church in Bucer's commentaries on the Epistle to the Ephesians', in Wright, *Martin Bucer*, 45–60.

[119] A. Townsend (ed.), *The Writings of John Bradford*, 2 vols. (PS, Cambridge, 1844, 1855), i. 307–30; ii. 194–8.

[120] Trueman, *Luther's Legacy*, 205–42.

[121] *OL* ii. 406.

[122] In 1552 Traheron wrote to Bullinger asking for his views on predestination and asserting that he and others 'embrace the opinion of John Calvin as being perspicacious and most agreeable to holy scripture': *OL* i. 426.

the obligation to struggle to shun sin and love the gospel after he or she is saved. Hooper followed Tyndale in his affirmation of the importance of a covenant centred upon Christ, and upheld through law, and he clearly feared the antinomian possibilities of the full 'Calvinist' position.[123] Trueman has shown that Hooper was here particularly indebted to Melanchthon's *Loci Communes*, a circumstance which underlines the danger of trying to 'pigeon-hole' English reformers too neatly in these early decades of change.[124]

In the event Hooper lacked successors, and as English and Scots reformers fled abroad after 1553 they were increasingly exposed to Calvin's views on this most critical of doctrines. Anthony Gilby, William Whittingham, and John Knox all wrote or translated on predestination under Genevan influence. Whittingham translated a short tract by Beza on the subject, and Gilby wrote *A Briefe Treatyse of Election and Reprobacion*. John Knox wrote a tract in 1558 against that 'anabaptist' denier of predestination encountered in an earlier chapter, Robert Cooch.[125] It is characteristic of Knox at this stage of his career that his eyes should partly be fixed on a debate with an English antagonist rather than directed towards Scotland. But Knox also addressed his reforming message north of the border, in 1557 advising his 'brethren in Scotland' that with or without the aid of the established authorities they must ensure that 'Christs Evangel may be truly preached and his holy sacraments rightly ministered'.[126] The most interesting case is that of John Scory, the Edwardian bishop of Chichester, who translated Augustine on election, predestination, and perseverance while in exile. Scory did visit Geneva, but apparently spent most of his exile in Emden and cannot be accounted one of those who fell wholly under Calvin's spell. His main objective seems to have been a demonstration that the Church of England was a true, Catholic church that had inherited proper doctrine from the scriptures and fathers. His emphasis on the importance of the divine decree nevertheless is indicative of the particular issues that he and his contemporaries regarded as central to that tradition.[127]

John Hooper may have had doubts about the more absolutist forms of predestinarian belief to be found in the 'best reformed churches', but he was clear that the latter's separation of church and state was the ideal to which the English church should aspire. 'It is not', he wrote early in his

---

[123] C. Nevinson (ed.), *The Later Writings of Bishop Hooper* (PS, Cambridge, 1852), 26–7.
[124] Trueman, *Luther's Legacy*, 223–6.
[125] Wallace, *Puritans and Predestination*, 24–8.
[126] Knox, iv. 285. J.A. Dawson, 'The two John Knoxes: England, Scotland and the 1558 Tracts', *JEH* 42 (1991), 567.
[127] Pettegree, *Marian Protestantism*, 23–4.

career, 'the office of the bishop to play the king and lord, nor the king's part to play the bishop.'[128] His clash with Ridley and Cranmer over conformity to the requirements of the ordinal marks fundamental difference about the role of the state in the affairs of the Church; difference that was only partially compromised when he finally conceded and was elevated to the Diocese of Gloucester.[129] For the other leaders of the English reform movement ecclesiological doctrine remained essentially as it had been under Henry, with the royal supremacy at its heart. The application of this principle, however, became a source of intense division within the exile churches under Mary, and did more than anything else to open up a gulf between the English and Scots on the eve of their final reformations. The troubles at Frankfurt, separating Coxians and Knoxians, were sustained by different beliefs in the nature of the Church; in the degree to which it must replicate 'the grave and godly face of the primitive Church' and the nature of magisterial intervention in its fortunes.[130] The English could no longer so readily take a sanguine view of royal authority after the triumph of Mary; yet many of them were unwilling to surrender the perception of a visible Church defined by the mark of loyalty to devotional forms established by law.

On the other hand, exile allowed many to experience 'purer' forms of worship and organization at first hand, not only Genevan structures but those which Jan Laski had already employed in the London stranger congregation.[131] Such groups more readily approximated to the faithful brethren of the invisible Church than to the flawed society of the visible Church of Edwardian England.[132] This, more perhaps than any immediate insistence that church organization should conform to a Genevan understanding of New Testament models, explains the mixed emotions with which the Continental wanderers greeted Elizabeth's restoration of the Protestant Church in England. And the Scots, who were unencumbered by the complex history of a state reformation, were able to assimilate lessons for their own revolution from that 'city on a hill' that gave refuge to their future leader. When in 1560 Thomas Randolph, as Elizabeth's ambassador, was negotiating with the Scots about their religious

[128] Carr, *Early Writings of Hooper*, 566–7.

[129] D. MacCulloch, *The Later Reformation in England, 1547–1603*, 2nd edn. (2001), 14–16.

[130] J. Petheram (ed.), *A brieff discours off the troubles begonne at Franckford* (1846). P. Collinson, 'The authorship of "A Brieff discours off the troubles begonne at Franckford"', *JEH* 9 (1958), 188–208.

[131] MacCulloch, 'Jan Laski', 326–30.

[132] Pettegree, *Marian Protestantism*, 19–36. The most trenchant view came from Anthony Gilby, who described Henry's Reformation as a 'deformation' and the Book of Common Prayer as 'an English matins, patched forth of the Popes portasse': Gilby, 'An admonition to England and Scotland to call them to repentance', in Knox, iv. 563–4.

settlement he found their ministers uncompromising in their commitment to their new doctrinal purity. They were 'so severe in that they profess [the Confession], and so loath to remit any thing of that that they have received, that I see little hope [of agreement with England]'.[133]

Doctrines of the Church in the Later Sixteenth Century

The sound and fury of the conflict between the godly and the conformists in Elizabethan England can easily be displaced into the category of a crisis about church governance and ceremony within an essentially shared view of doctrine. On this reading the main contrast between English and Scottish Protestants was that the latter had been able, by virtue of their freedom from the constraints of the magistrate, to develop a system of governance and worship that accorded fully with the 'best reformed principles' espoused in both countries. The argument for an essential community of doctrinal view on the Church, as on other aspects of reformed theology, has something to commend it. The Scottish Confession, the Thirty-Nine Articles and the subsequent contributions to English doctrinal debate, especially in the Admonition controversy, all emphasized the critical importance of the visible Church, and of its first two defining marks, the preaching of the Word and the proper administration of the sacraments. All accepted the fundamental distinction between the visible and invisible Church and, in accordance with reformed teaching on election and reprobation, saw the latter as the universal Church of the elect in all ages. All saw the visible churches as containing the regenerate and unregenerate, as ordained partly for the regulation of man's sin, and as subject to national regulation, structure, and discipline. All accepted that there were areas of ecclesiastical behaviour in the visible Church that were indifferent, that is that were not precisely prescribed by Scripture, which therefore had to be ordered by human agency.[134] This *might* include ceremonies or even vestments not wholly attractive to all the godly: for as the Genevan ministers themselves argued, many 'things...ought to be borne and tolerated, which are...not justly commanded'.[135] The contrast between the godly and conformists in England was more one of temperature, of the intensity of commitment to spiritual regeneration, than of doctrinal substance.

---

[133] *CSP Sc* i. 479.

[134] P. Collinson, *The Elizabethan Puritan Movement* (1967), 101–21. P. Lake, *Anglicans and Puritans? Presbyterian and English Conformist Thought from Whitgift to Hooker* (1988), 13–52.

[135] Petheram, *A brieff discours*, 205.

Yet from the earliest years of Protestant triumph in the two realms an ideological division between views of the Church was already implicit, wanting only the circumstances of the Admonition controversy to reveal it fully. The Scots Confession, as we have seen, had developed a particular strain of the reformed tradition in its insistence that discipline should be construed as the third mark of the true Church. While Knox's own interpretation of the nature of the Church shifted in emphasis during the years following 1560, he was consistent in maintaining that the use of proper discipline in the visible Church was the means of making it holy, and ensuring that it was a proper vessel to serve the invisible Church of the elect.[136] In his late work *An Answer to James Tyrie*, completed in 1568, he answered taunts about the invisibility of the Scottish Kirk with the confident assertion that 'the true Kirk of Jesus Christ is as visible ... within the Realm of Scotland, as ever she was in Corinth, Galatia, Philippi (yea or yet in Rome itself)'.[137] Knox was confident that the visible Kirk was seeking to conform itself not just to best Continental practice, but to the scriptural standards of the early Church. Failure, when it occurred, was a consequence of individual sin, not of a lack of doctrinal purity.[138]

Zealous English reformers had no such consolation. They shared with Knox and his colleagues a conviction that the visible Church would never be regenerate unless it was made subject to what Thomas Cartwright was routinely to call 'the Discipline'.[139] For many this meant a full presbyterian system of church government based on the scriptural model increasingly endorsed by the European reformed churches. But even those who did not focus their attention on a particular ecclesiological structure shared beliefs about the nature of the Church that were not readily integrated into Elizabeth's settlement. These beliefs are most fully explored in Cartwright's discursive contributions to the controversy with Whitgift.[140] At the heart of Cartwright's arguments lies an insistence that the visible Church can become an effective vessel of the regeneration of the Christian society, which in its turn will serve to sustain and advance the invisible Church of the elect.[141] It was the duty of the Church to provide for the 'edification' of the community of true believers, for it, as a spiritual

---

[136] R. Kyle, 'The nature of the Church in the thought of John Knox', *Scottish Journal of Theology* 37 (1984), 485–501.

[137] Knox, vi. 494.

[138] R. Greaves, *Theology and Revolution in the Scottish Reformation* (Grand Rapids, 1980), 50–6.

[139] Lake, *Anglicans and Puritans*, 28–31.

[140] The Admonition controversy is printed in J. Ayre (ed.), *The Works of John Whitgift*, 3 vols. (PS, Cambridge, 1851–3), i–iii.

[141] J.S. Coolidge, *The Pauline Renaissance in England: Puritanism and the Bible* (Oxford, 1970), 38–9. T.D. Bozeman, 'Federal theology and the "national covenant": an Elizabethan Presbyterian case-study', *Church History* 61 (1992), 400–6.

body, to be 'fitly joined together... unto the edifying of itself in love'.[142] The task of its leadership must therefore be the ambitious one of constructing a discipline and a pattern of offices approximating as closely as possible to the precepts of scripture in order to secure the collective growth of Christians in grace.

The Church of the elect could never fully be known, but for Cartwright and his colleagues its visible form was focused upon a community of the godly, called together by the spirit, whose worship must be facilitated and enhanced by proper discipline, organization, and constant access to preaching. Regeneration had to be achieved by public policy, so that God's promise to his people as individuals that they would be given the gifts necessary to salvation could be enlarged. Christ would rule 'not alone in the hearts of everyone by his spirit, but also generally, and in the visible government of his Church, by those laws of discipline he hath prescribed'.[143] The association between the edification of the spiritual body of Christians and the reconstruction of the visible Church was clearly a difficult one, since the latter operated in the wider unregenerate society, but a passionate belief that God intended the edification of his people through the rebuilding of his Church sustained the practical divinity of the godly preachers.[144]

A corollary of this emphasis upon the doctrine of spiritual regeneration through the visible Church was a growing commitment to covenant or 'federal' theology.[145] The Scots Confession already revealed a narrative of redemption that was cast in these terms, pointing towards the covenant of grace established between God and his people as the road to salvation for the latter. As covenant theology developed on the Continent, especially through the work of the Heidelberg Calvinist theologians Zacharias Ursinus and Hieronymus Zanchius, it was of most significance as a form of assurance that the elect were given faith.[146] Just as Abraham had been given the unconditional covenant of grace and blessing by God, so the elect were now made a part of the same covenant. It was a doctrine that could also be invoked in the public sphere. For Knox and his generation of the Scots the covenant that God established with Israel was part of a theology of history.[147] Their perception was identical with that which one of the fathers of

---

[142] Ayre *Works of Whitgift*, ii. 113–14.

[143] Ibid., iii. 315.

[144] P. Lake, 'Presbyterianism, the idea of a national church and the argument from divine right', in P. Lake and M. Dowling (eds.), *Protestantism and the National Church in Sixteenth Century England* (1987), 199–202.

[145] Coolidge, *Pauline Renaissance*, ch. 5. Bozeman, 'Federal theology', 394–407.

[146] M. McGiffert, 'From Moses to Adam: the making of the covenant of works', *C16J* 19 (1988), 132–6. D. Visser, 'The covenant in Zacharius Ursinus', *C16J* 18 (1987), 532–5.

[147] R. Greaves, 'The Knoxian paradox: ecumenism and nationalism in the Scottish Reformation', *RSCHS* 18 (1972), 96–7.

covenant theology, Zwingli, had articulated: 'the same covenant which he entered into with Israel he has in these latter days entered into with us, that we may be one people with them, one church and may also have one covenant'.[148] God made his covenant with 'every city, realm, province or nation' and each had to bind themselves collectively to that agreement, renewing the commitment if apostasy occurred, as it had done for England under Mary. When a covenanted nation had accepted the true religion and then lapsed into idolatry it must be cleansed at all costs: which in political terms led to the radicalization of resistance theory at the hands of Knox and Goodman.[149] More generally, where covenant had been established as in Scotland after 1560 there was a common obligation within the visible Church to act under the covenant for the regeneration of the society.

The single covenant of grace, manifesting God's unconditional gift to the Church and to the individuals within it, was a regular feature of Elizabethan theological writing. In ecclesiological terms the historicized view of the covenant could be used to justify either God's gift to the whole visible Church, or more specifically validating the faithful remnant who were the direct descendants of Abraham.[150] But it was from the 1580s, with the publication of Dudley Fenner's treatise of systematic theology, *Sacra Theologia*, that covenant theology began to exercise major influence within English Protestant thought. Fenner, and following him Perkins and most of the other Puritan divines, distinguished the covenants of law and grace, making the former the conditional, moral contract into which 'all men at all times' were presumed to have entered freely.[151] Meanwhile the covenant of grace was preserved in the compact 'made between God and man touching reconciliation and life everlasting in Christ'.[152] The two covenants were of a fundamentally different order, but the distinction was not between an individual covenant of grace and a collective one of law. Puritan thinkers were clear that the people as a whole could be covenanted under grace: we are, says John Field, of the English, 'his people adopted, assured in a new covenant, sealed in the blood and obedience of Jesus Christ'.[153]

---

[148] Kyle, 'Knox on the Church', 494–5.

[149] There is an extensive literature on covenanting and the political thought of the Genevan exiles, well surveyed in R.A. Mason, 'Covenant and commonweal: the language of politics in Reformation Scotland', in N. Macdougall (ed.), *Church, Politics and Society: Scotland, 1408–1929* (Edinburgh, 1983), 97–126. See also Dawson, 'Two John Knoxes', 555–76.

[150] Bozeman, 'Federal theology', 394–400.

[151] M. McGiffert, 'Grace and works: the rise and division of covenant divinity in Elizabethan Puritanism', *Harvard Theological Review* 75 (1982), 463–502. J. Møller, 'The beginnings of Puritan Covenant Theology', *JEH* 14 (1963), 46–67.

[152] *The Workes of that Famous and Worthy minister of Christ . . . Mr William Perkins*, 2 vols. (Cambridge, 1608–9), i. 167.

[153] Quoted in Bozeman, 'Federal theology', 401. Bozeman makes absolutely clear that the covenant of grace was understood to be both individual and collective.

The full ecclesiological and political consequences of the doctrine of the two covenants belong more properly to the seventeenth than to the sixteenth century. In the case of Scotland the new period begins from 1596 when Richard Rollock, the first principal of Edinburgh University, led the General Assembly of the Kirk to the 'renewal of the covenant with God'.[154] The Church and the nation were bound together in a promise of moral renewal that pointed forwards to the covenanting movement of the next century. Meanwhile English Puritans of Perkins's generation began to wrestle with the consequences of a belief that the nation could be elect, and under the covenant of grace. How could this be reconciled with the reprobation of the majority? Was judgement and death the inevitable fate of most of the children of Israel and England, part of an elect nation and church only in the sense that it provided the proper environment for the sanctification of the few?[155]

The conformist understanding of the doctrine of the Church anticipated many of the dilemmas faced by the Puritans of Cartwright's generation. For Whitgift, the key doctrinal issue was the clearest of possible separations between the visible and invisible Churches. His understanding of the latter was congruent with that of his opponent, but the visible Church was inevitably marked out by both good seed and tares, and must therefore be under law 'to maintain peace and unity'. The invisible Church of the elect was a reality known only to God in Christ, and its members were reunited with him steadily throughout the pattern of Christian history. The visible Church could not, in a series of dramatic disciplinary gestures, be made the agent for the perfectibility of the saints: that way lay anabaptism. A measure of collective spiritual growth might be the consequence of the right administration of sacraments, and as much preaching as was compatible with external order, but regeneration for Whitgift, as for many conformists, was often a matter of individual piety rather than the general sanctification of the members of the visible Church.[156] The latter was both temporal and spiritual, but practical considerations as much as doctrinal ones led the conformists to emphasize the temporal aspect of the Church under a godly prince. 'I am fully persuaded', claimed Whitgift in an important passage, 'that there is no such

---

[154] S.A. Burrell, 'The covenanting idea as a revolutionary symbol: Scotland 1596–1637', *Church History* 27 (1958), 338–50. Though it should be noted that, in the latest study of covenanting theology in Scotland, Mullan is less impressed by 1596 as a turning-point, seeing no powerful connection between earlier interest in federal theology and the developments of the 1630s: D.G. Mullan, *Scottish Puritanism, 1590–1638* (Oxford, 2000), 171–207.

[155] P. Collinson, *The Birthpangs of Protestant England* (Basingstoke, 1988), 18–24. Collinson points to a large number of printed sermons of the early seventeenth century on the Hosea text: 'Then said God . . . ye are not my people, and I will not be your God.'

[156] Lake, *Anglicans and Puritans*, 28–42.

distinction between the church of Christ and a Christian commonwealth as you and the papists dream of.'[157]

Later Elizabethan conformist positions deviated from Whitgift's principally in the doctrinal legitimation offered for the existing form of governance of the Church. Presbyterian claims for the divinely ordained nature of 'the Discipline' were slowly countered by a growing emphasis on the significance of episcopacy, not just as a lawful form of government sanctioned by the crown for the maintenance of good ecclesiastical order, but as *iure divino*.[158] 1590 saw the publication of two important tracts that underpinned the new claims: Hadrian Saravia's *Diverse degrees of the ministers of the gospel* and Matthew Sutcliffe's *Treatise of ecclesiastical discipline*.[159] Saravia and Sutcliffe began from the principle that there had always been inequality within the ministry, sanctioned not just by the New, but also the Old Testament, with its priestly hierarchy. Christ chose the apostles as his particular stewards, bequeathing to them not only the obligation to preach and minister the sacraments properly, the duty of all priests, but the power of the keys and discipline for the building of the visible Church and the Christian community. Saravia concluded that this was 'the form of government which was ordained by God, and delivered of the apostles'.[160]

The protagonists of divine right episcopacy did not yet, however, fundamentally challenge the view that the Continental Protestant churches, with their alternative discipline, were true churches. The most powerful effect of a revival of confidence in the spiritual legitimacy of the form of government espoused by the English church was rather to refocus intellectual attention upon the Catholic past, and on a reconsideration of the Church's relationship with Rome. The apocalyptic tradition, with its sharply dichotomous depiction of the true and false Churches had left scarcely any scope for the idea that the visible Church of Rome might simply have strayed from its primitive purity rather than being the embodiment of Antichrist.[161] But there was always a more cautious doctrinal position, which acknowledged that the Roman church was a church of Christ *secundum quid*, in some sense despite the accumulation of error.[162] Jewel, in his *Apology*, talked of the 'rueful state' and 'lamentable form' of the Church of Rome without directly denying its title, and the continu-

---

[157] Ayre, *Works of Whitgift*, iii. 160.

[158] W.D.J. Cargill Thompson, *Studies in the Reformation* (1980), 94–130.

[159] H. Saravia, *Of the diverse degrees of the ministers of the gospel* (1590). M. Sutcliffe, *A treatise of ecclesiastical discipline* (1590).

[160] Saravia, *Diverse degrees*, 41.

[161] P. Lake, 'The significance of the Elizabethan identification of the pope as Antichrist', *JEH* 31 (1980), 161–78.

[162] A. Milton, *Catholic and Reformed: The Roman and Protestant Churches in English Protestant Thought, 1600–1640* (Cambridge, 1995), 128–40.

ing acceptance of the Roman sacrament of baptism was an affirmation of the need to affirm her as a church, however unsound.[163]

From the 1580s onwards this minimalist acceptance of Rome began to be subject to intermittent questioning from English theologians. The first concern was that the pre-Reformation Church could be regarded as a true visible Church, thus ensuring that the forefathers of the Protestants were embraced within Christ's scheme of salvation. Men as diverse as Richard Hooker and the Calvinist polemicist Robert Some pursued this line of thought.[164] But Hooker went much further. In response to the Puritan vision of a Church marked by true preaching, sacraments, and discipline he posited one founded upon reason and law, articulating in its visible form the worshipping community.[165] In the light of this basic position the Church of Rome might be misguided and its doctrinal errors manifest, but it was scarcely to be denied a place as 'of the family of Jesus Christ' or 'a part of the house of God, and a limb of the visible church of Christ'.[166] This was a shift of understanding that immediately provoked an alarmed response from among the godly. Andrew Willet, for example, insisted that it was essential to return to the earlier Protestant understanding of the 'true Church', in which it was the apostasy of Rome that excluded her from the company of the visible Church. Thus Hooker began a new and very intense debate on the theological nature of the relationship between the English and the Roman church that was to be deeply divisive in the early years of the seventeenth century.[167]

Calvinist Consensus?

The Scottish Confession and the Thirty-Nine Articles proclaimed the centrality of a reformed theology of grace that became the heart of Protestant doctrinal identity in the succeeding generations. It was, says Wallace, a pattern of belief that 'sought above all to magnify the role of divine grace in the process of salvation by stressing gratuitous regeneration and sanctification as well as predestination'.[168] The precise nature of that theology has been the subject of deep and prolonged controversy among historians. The disagreements may be summarized baldly as focusing first upon the degree of doctrinal consensus on predestination that existed in the late sixteenth-century Church and secondly the extent to which any

---

[163] J. Jewel, *An Apology of the Church of England*, ed. J.E. Booty (Ithaca, N.Y., 1983), 99.

[164] R. Bauckham, 'Hooker, Travers and the Church of Rome in the 1580s', *JEH* 29 (1978), 44–7.

[165] Milton, *Catholic and Reformed*, 146–50.

[166] R. Hooker, *Of the Laws of Ecclesiastical Polity*, iii. 1.10; v. 28. 1.

[167] Milton, *Catholic and Reformed*, 128, 140.   [168] Wallace, *Puritans and Predestination*, 29.

such consensus should be labelled with Calvin's name, or with that of his followers such as Beza and the Heidelberg theologians. The intensity of this debate, much of which is directed to the problem of the breakdown in the Caroline church in the 1630s, has sometimes obscured the reflective contributions of the historians of theology. It is on their work that the ensuing analysis is essentially based.[169]

English and Scottish theologians rarely sought to question the divine decree: or to deny the existence of the elect 'chosen in Christ before the beginning of the world' (Eph. 1.4). Their profound engagement with Scripture led them to a sufficiency of texts to confirm this belief. Scripture also indicated the reasons for the exclusion of the non-elect that, for some, amounted to an affirmation of the double decree to reprobation. There was wide assent for the idea that there was a close causal connection between lack of faith and reprobation. Many of those who were influenced by Genevan theology insisted clearly that there was an immutable decree of double predestination by which God had created some men for damnation as well as others for salvation. It was this fundamental issue that was felt to have been left in some ambiguity by the Thirty-Nine Articles, which failed to discuss reprobation and implied, in Article 16, that men could fall permanently from grace after they had received the Holy Spirit. In 1595 Archbishop Whitgift was persuaded to intervene in the Cambridge controversies about the nature of grace and, in the Lambeth Articles, to give the imprimatur to a more comprehensive predestinarian position. 'From eternity', the first Article states baldly, 'God has predestined some men to life and reprobated some to death.'[170]

While some divines insisted that this was as far as men should seek to penetrate the mysteries of faith, speculative theologians, especially those influenced by Beza, pursued the consequences of predestinarian belief

---

[169] For key contributions to the 'consensus' debate see N. Tyacke, *Anti-Calvinists: The Rise of English Arminianism, c.1590–1640* (Oxford, 1987); P. White, *Predestination, Policy and Polemic: Conflict and Consensus in the English Church from the Reformation to the Civil War* (Cambridge, 1992), P. Lake, 'Calvinism and the English church, 1570–1635', *PP* 114 (1987), 38–59, and 'Predestinarian propositions', *JEH* 46 (1995), 110–23. Crucial doctrinal analyses are provided by J.T. Kendall, *Calvin and English Calvinism to 1649*, 2nd edn. (Carlisle, 1997) and Wallace, *Puritans and Predestination*. See also the important contribution of R. Muller, *Christ and the Decree: Christology and Predestination in Reformed Theology from Calvin to Perkins* (Durham, N.C., 1986), which questions the centrality of the Bezan position. There is a danger that the debates about theology in their turn underestimate the importance of the pastoral implications of belief. There is a detailed consideration of the pastoral implications of the doctrines of grace in I. Green, *The Christian's ABC* (Oxford, 1996), 350–422. See also K.L. Parker and E.J. Carlson, '*Practical Divinity': The Works and Life of Revd Richard Greenham* (Aldershot, 1998), 104–22.

[170] Bray, *Documents of the English Reformation*, 399–401. On the Lambeth Articles see H.C. Porter, *Reformation and Reaction in Tudor Cambridge* (Cambridge, 1958), 344–90. Porter takes the view that Whitgift's objective was to rein in conflict. For the alternative view followed here, see P. Lake, *Moderate Puritans and the Elizabethan Church* (Cambridge, 1982), 218–42.

more explicitly. Beza argued that the fixed decree of election, which took precedence over all other divine decrees, meant that Christ died only for those determined for salvation.[171] This had been established before the Fall, and was 'supralapsarian': atonement was limited, not universal. This is marked out from the 'infralapsarian' position espoused by a majority of sixteenth-century English divines, which accepted the possibility of universal atonement, and gave no automatic precedence to God's determining purposes before the Fall.[172] Instead they understood that some are predestined not to accept the redemptive act of Christ's death. The latter was a sufficient payment for the sins of all mankind: it was an efficient payment only for the elect. Christ's sacrifice was therefore understood above all as an effectual form of salvation for those chosen. This was, said Christopher Shutte, 'only proper to the elect, whereby through faith .... [they were] assured that [their] salvation is wrought by Christ'.[173]

From the debate about limited atonement followed that about the irresistibility of grace. How far was the human will, corrupted by sin, capable of withstanding the grace offered freely to the elect?[174] This was one of the questions that most bitterly divided the delegates to the 1618 Synod of Dort, where irresistibility was eventually affirmed.[175] Those sixteenth-century theologians who linked predestination to the divine attributes were most likely implicitly or explicitly to accept irresistibility and the indefectibility of God's gift to men. The elect were destined to persevere in faith, by the *ordo salutis* or process of salvation, which by 'degrees and means' led them finally to God. Consideration of salvation as process, but one from which the elect could not finally fall away, had begun in the work of Bucer and Martyr.[176] Both argued that there were a series of sequential steps proceeding from predestination to calling, justification, sanctification, and glorification. Martyr added the crucial idea that perseverance in this *ordo* depended on God's election, and that the chosen could have comfort and assurance in their calling.[177] These were interpretations of the divine order that assumed great significance in Elizabethan pastoral

---

[171] On Beza see Kendall, *Calvin*, 29–41.

[172] For the varieties of 'infralapsarian' view that can be traced by the time of the Synod of Dort see S.F. Hughes, 'The problem of "Calvinism": English theologies of predestination *c.*1580–1630', in S. Wabuda and C. Litzenberger (eds.), *Belief and Practice in Reformation England* (Aldershot, 1998), 229–49.

[173] C. Shutte, *A Compendious forme and summe of Christian doctrine* (1584), sig. B2ᵛ.

[174] A. McGrath, *Iustitia Dei: A History of the Christian Doctrine of Justification*, 2 vols. (Cambridge, 1986), ii. 15–16, 28–30. White, *Predestination*, 53–5, 192–4.

[175] For Dort see Schaff, *Creeds*, 589–90. Wallace, *Puritans and Predestination*, 43–55.

[176] W.P. Stephens, *The Holy Spirit in the Theology of Martin Bucer* (Cambridge, 1971), 42, 46, 49 ff.

[177] J.C. McLelland, 'The reformed doctrine of predestination according to Peter Martyr', *Scottish Journal of Theology* 8 (1955), 261, 267.

writing and preaching, since they offered hope to the afflicted conscience, and guidance to those who sought to persevere in righteousness. As Anthony Maxey put it: 'predestination, calling, justifying and glorifying are so coupled and knit together, that if you hold fast one link, you draw unto you the whole chain; if you let go one, you loose all'.[178]

Elements of the doctrines of irresistibility, and of a concern to articulate the *ordo salutis*, can be found in many late sixteenth-century divines. But its full development is identified with what is sometimes labelled Protestant scholasticism, which influenced both Cambridge and Oxford in the 1580s and 1590s.[179] The prime Continental influences were those of Beza and Zanchius: the latter was particularly important for his detailed treatment of the process of assurance, dividing the relative simplicity of Bucer's scheme into thirteen sections, each contributing to the process of salvation. While Oxford produced a generation who responded to these scholastics largely through preaching, Cambridge, in the persons of William Whitaker, Robert Some, and above all William Perkins, had theologians capable of making distinctive contributions to the development of predestinarian thought.[180] They added to later Calvinist doctrinal thinking the use of Ramist logic, clarifying division by sharp dichotomies, which were perceived as the proper reflections of the working of human rationality.[181] One of the most marked preoccupations of these Cambridge theologians was the doctrine of perseverance, and the question of whether grace can ever be lost. Their clear answer was no, since when God wills regeneration 'His work cannot be resisted', but the knowledge of this process was more difficult since it had to be linked to a justifying faith 'whereby a man is persuaded in his conscience' of his true calling. The obverse of this true experience was the delusion of faith, or the experience of temporary faith, that could be felt by the reprobate. Those condemned by the double decree could still acknowledge God, desire salvation, and 'confusedly believe the promises of God'. But the eternal decree was immutable and the experience of regeneration illusory.[182] All of this Perkins expressed most vividly in the famous table that accompanied his *A golden chaine*, which allowed even the illiterate by tracing the lines with their fingers 'sensibly [to] perceive the chief points of religion, and the order of them'.[183]

---

[178] A. Maxey, *The Golden Chaine of Mans Salvation* (1610), sig. A 3.

[179] C.M. Dent, *Protestant Reformers in Elizabethan Oxford* (Oxford, 1983), 98–102.

[180] Lake, *Moderate Puritans*, 96–103.

[181] L. Jardine, 'The place of dialectic teaching in sixteenth-century Cambridge', *Studies in the Renaissance* 21 (1974), 31–62.

[182] *Workes of Perkins*, i. 716; ii. 29. Kendall, *Calvin*, 51–76.

[183] R.A. Muller, 'Perkins' *A Goldene Chaine*: Predestinarian system or schematized *Ordo Salutis?*', *C16J* 9 (1978), 70–7. The table reproduces and elaborates one by Beza.

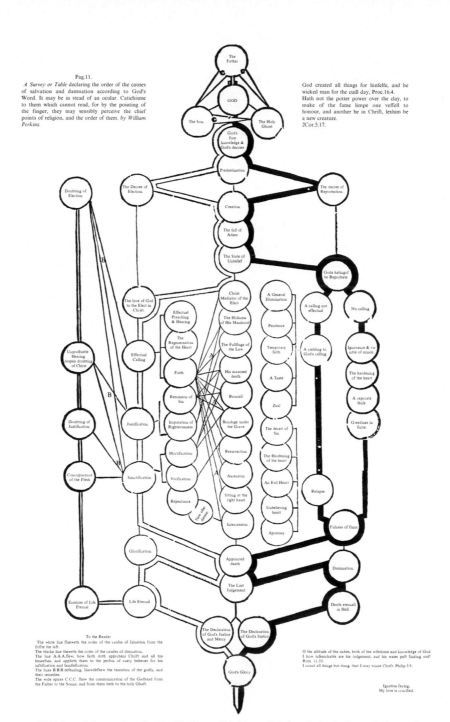

A Survey or Table declaring the order of the causes of salvation and damnation according to God's Word. It may be in stead of an ocular. Catichisme to them which cannot read, for by the pointing of the finger, they may sensibly perceive the chief points of religion, and the order of them. *by William Perkins.*

God created all things for hinfelfe, and he wicked man for the cuill day, Proc.16.4.
Hath not the potter power over the clay, to make of the fame limpe one veffell to honour, and another be in Chrift, lexhim be a new creature.
2Cor.5.17.

To the Reader

The white line flueweth the order of the caufes of faluation from the firfte the laft.
The blacke line theweth the order of the caudes of dimuation.
The line A.A.A.flew, how faith doth apprehend Chrift aud all his beuefeus, aud applieth them to the perfon of euery beleeuer for his iuftificatiou aud fandlefication.
The lines B.B.B.defeudiug, like wiefhew the teutation of the godly, and their remedies.
The wide fpices C.C.C. fhew the communication of the Gadhead from the Faiber to the Sonne, aud from them beth to the holy Ghaft.

O the altitude of the riches, both of the wifedome and knowledge of God
I how infearchable are his iudgement, aud his waies paft finding out?
Rom. 11.33.
I count all things but dung, that I may winne Chrift. Philip.3.9.

Ignatius faying,
My love is crucified.

'Table of the *ordo salutis*'. William Perkins, *Workes* (1630). Permission of Christ Church, Oxford

The Cambridge theological stirs of the 1590s came out of the world of scholastic Protestantism. William Barrett, who in 1595 assailed the prevailing predestinarian orthodoxy, was bent on a denial that assurance of salvation was possible for the ordinary Christian.[184] The spectre of antinomianism, of a Calvinist theology that located reprobation not in sin but in the divine will, had been raised by the unyielding style of Cambridge Protestant polemic. Now Barrett, and seconding him Peter Baro and John Overall, went on the offensive against this apparent consensus.[185] One possible reading of the outcome of the crisis is that, once the implicit acceptance of a 'Calvinist' orthodoxy by most Protestants was enshrined in the Lambeth Articles, it was inevitable that they should become the focus for outright dissent. In 1596 when Baro found himself isolated from the university and church establishment, he cast around for support, contacting Lancelot Andrewes and such Continental divines as the Danish Lutheran Hemmingius. Richard Hooker, who in *The Laws of Ecclesiastical Polity* had trodden very cautiously on the issue of predestination, moved in a draft pamphlet of 1600 towards Baro's position, emphasizing God's general will to save all men. The beginnings of a new doctrinal identity were being sketched.[186]

There are alternative readings of the Calvinist 'consensus' and its decline. White has stressed the thread of continuity linking together those theologians who never assented fully to predestinarian views, still less enthused about their refined forms articulated by Perkins and his colleagues.[187] Many of this generation had been reared in an intellectual environment in which Lutheran texts were some of the most readily available Protestant works.[188] The favoured volume for training in practical divinity was the *Common Places* of the moderate Berne reformer Wolfgang Musculus.[189] There were always a few who refused to subscribe to the prevailing reverence for Calvin, even though they proclaimed their orthodox acceptance of the Church of England and its doctrine. Everard Digby, who fell foul of Whitaker as master of St John's, Cambridge, was one of these curious sorts of Protestant. He seems to have believed in human ethical choice as contributing to salvation, while asserting the merits of the traditions of the medieval Church as continued by Elizabeth.[190] At Oxford it was the alien presence of Antonio de Corro in the

---

[184] Lake, *Moderate Puritans*, 201–42. [185] Tyacke, *Anti-Calvinists*, 29–37.
[186] Lake, *Anglicans and Puritans*, 182–97. [187] White, *Predestination*, 83–7.
[188] Even Emmanuel College, Cambridge, had twice as many Lutheran as Reformed texts in the 1590s: S. Bush and C.J. Rasmussen, 'Emmanuel College Library's first inventory', *Transactions of the Cambridge Bibliographical Society* 8 (1985), 516. But note Pettegree and Higman, below nn. 192 and 193 on the pattern of book ownership and translation in England.
[189] W. Musculus, *Common places of the Christian Religion* (1563).
[190] Lake, *Moderate Puritans*, 172–80.

1570s that threatened doctrinal consensus. Corro, a Spanish-born Protestant who had been in England for much of the previous decade, sought a degree and access to Oxford to publicize his view that salvation depended on moral improvement and co-operation with the divine will. The charge of Pelagianism was inevitably raised against him by such leaders of Oxford Calvinism as John Reynolds. It may have been Corro's position that encouraged his friend Peter Baro to first air his own anti-predestinarian views in 1579.[191]

A few determined critics of Calvinist positions, however, scarcely dispose of the thesis that there was a broad consensus on matters of doctrine. What is perhaps more significant is that this consensus depended as much on an unwillingness to probe high theological mysteries as on a systematic set of beliefs, rigorously analysed. There is, of course, little doubt that the works of Continental reformed Protestantism, in which such doctrines were fully analysed, were prized and popular in Elizabethan England. Despite those Lutheran library holdings, Pettegree's recent investigation of Cambridge academic wills shows that Calvin's writings were by far the most generally owned, followed by those of Beza and Martyr.[192] On most tests that can be applied—numbers of English translations, or editions of works, for example—Calvin reigns supreme, especially by the 1580s.[193] But when we turn from imported works to English productions the story changes. Only in the 1590s, when Perkins's work began to reach print, did any English doctrinal writing achieve any great influence. The usual explanation is that the theologians were so enmeshed in the ecclesiological conflicts of the reign that they had little resource left for debates upon soteriology or doctrines of grace. An alternative reading, suggested by Green's study of catechisms and by the recent analysis of the career of Richard Greenham, is that the predominant concern of contemporary divines was pastoral care and guidance, a process not aided by the spelling out of contentious doctrines such as limited atonement or the fate of the reprobate. 'I am rather to thank God that I do believe', said Greenham, 'than to search out the reason, why others do not believe.'[194]

---

[191] Dent, *Protestant Reformers*, 110–25.

[192] A. Pettegree, 'The reception of Calvinism in Britain', in W.H. Neusner and B.G. Armstrong (eds.), *Calvinus sincerioris religionis vindex*, Sixteenth-Century Essays and Studies (36, 1997), 267–89.

[193] F. Higman, 'Calvin's works in translation', in A. Pettegree, A. Duke, and G. Lewis (eds.), *Calvinism in Europe* (Cambridge, 1994), 82–99. Dent comes to rather different conclusions on the basis of Oxford material, where the Zurichers retained much influence until at least the 1580s: Dent, *Protestant Reformers*, 93–4.

[194] Green, *Christian's ABC*, esp. 564–70. Parker and Carlson, *Practical Divinity*, 114. Mullan's study of Scottish divines suggests that a similar argument might be applied north of the border: *Scottish Puritanism*, 45 ff.

Conclusion

There are very striking generational shifts in the engagements of English theologians during the sixteenth century. The pre-Reformation Catholic theologians, led by John Fisher, had addressed themselves primarily to issues of authority, scriptural exegesis, and translation, turning under the influence of the conflict with Luther towards the profound debates about faith and justification. The first Protestant generation focused above all on these same problems, especially on *sola scriptura* and *sola fide*. By the 1540s the Eucharistic debate assumed overwhelming importance, while for zealous Protestants the attack on idolatry became the essential precursor to the establishment of the true visible Church. After the accession of Elizabeth, and the Scottish Reformation, two themes above all generated debate in the universities: the nature of the visible Church, its structure and authority, and the theology of grace and election. Towards the end of the century the challenge of Rome began to evoke a new and complex doctrinal response about the nature of the Church. This sense of movement within the broad parameters of Christian doctrine may, however, be somewhat illusory. The 'hot spots' of controversy have to be accommodated within the growing body of literature, catechetical, expository, even systematic divinity, which endeavoured to present a broad analysis of Protestant belief. If neither the English nor the Scots were initially disposed to systematic theology, we can at the end of the century begin to see attempts in England to remedy this deficiency. Fenner's *Sacra Theologia* was followed by William Barlow's *A Defence of the Articles of the Protestants Religion* (1601). Andrew Willet's *Synopsis Papismi* (3rd edn. 1600) can be characterized as a systematic exposition of belief arising from anti-Roman controversy.[195] The internal conflict between Puritans and conformists also produced its own form of systematized defence of the Church of England in Hooker's *Laws of Ecclesiastical Polity*. Hooker's theoretical ambition took the existing debate beyond its Whitgiftian forms and offered a very different understanding of the relationship between the Christian community, authority, and belief. The possibility of an integrated mode of thought and behaviour called Anglicanism was thus signalled at the very end of our period.[196]

A rapid glance at Fenner and Willet serves to indicate those areas of belief too easily swept aside by the intensity of doctrinal dispute on the key issues identified above. Christology, though of great significance for Cranmer and for Calvin, among others, proved less than central in mature

---

[195] Milton, *Catholic and Reformed*, 10–30.
[196] On Hooker see Lake, *Anglicans and Puritans*, 145–230.

Protestantism. The knowledge of Christ's personal sacrifice, and the anthropological understanding of the nature of redemption that often accompanied it, yielded to a greater emphasis on the majesty of God and a
theocentric understanding of the atonement. Reflection about the nature
of the afterlife, as opposed to the possibility of attaining it, suffered from
the death of purgatory, and the reluctance of Protestant divines to speculate on the destinations of the dead.[197] The so-called 'Descensus Controversy', on the nature of Christ's descent into hell, forced some thought on
these issues, but scarcely made them central to debate.[198]

There was also a curious gap in the output of sixteenth-century English
Protestants, in that they rarely published systematic biblical commentaries.
Most of the great Continental founders of Protestantism had felt it mandatory to embark upon such commentaries. Among the English reformers of
the first generations only John Hooper, that faithful imitator of Continental models, and Anthony Gilby published on the prophets.[199] By the
1560s it was more common, as witness for example Bishop Pilkington's
commentaries on the Prophets, or Edward Dering on the Epistle to the
Hebrews.[200] Sermon series and lectures on the Bible became a regular
feature of Elizabethan Oxford and Cambridge. Few, however, found their
way into print before the mid-Jacobean years. Among William Bradshaw's
large output, for example, there was only one expository work, on the
second epistle to the Thessalonians.[201] The best explanation is that English
divines deferred to the great work of Bucer, Bullinger, Martyr, and Calvin
in biblical interpretation as in much else.[202] The Scots also 'supped their
learning' from Geneva, but in the particular matter of commentaries they
showed more ambition. Their surviving sermons usually take the form of
extended biblical commentaries. Robert Rollock gave an important series
of sermons on Corinthians in Edinburgh in the 1590s that helped to
establish the genre. They were almost immediately put into print. Beza

---

[197] P. Marshall, '"The map of God's word": geographies of the afterlife in Tudor and early
Stuart England', in B. Gordon and P. Marshall (eds.), *The Place of the Dead: Death and Remembrance in Late Medieval and Early Modern Europe* (Cambridge, 2000), 110–30.

[198] D.D. Wallace, 'Puritan and Anglican: the interpretation of Christ's descent into hell in
Elizabethan theology', *ARG* 69 (1978), 248–87.

[199] Carr, *Early Writings of Hooper*, 431–560, for his commentary on Jonas. Gilby published
commentaries on Malachi and Micah: A. Gilby, *A Commentarye upon the Prophet Malaky* (1553);
A Commentarye upon the prophet Mycha (1551).

[200] J. Scolefield (ed.), *The Works of James Pilkington, B.D.* (PS, Cambridge, 1842), 1–496.
E. Dering, *Workes* (1614), no. 3.

[201] W. Bradshaw, *A plaine and pithy exposition of the second epistle to the Thessalonians* (1620). In
the earlier generation Udall, Wilcox, and Fulke each published one biblical commentary.

[202] The central texts of Elizabethan theology and religious learning were all foreign: Musculus's *Commonplaces*, Martyr's *Commonplaces*, Bullinger's *Decades*, and Calvin's *Institutes*.

was fulsome in his praise of Rollock's other published commentaries on Romans and Ephesians.[203]

The limited output of the printing presses in the area of biblical exegesis may underscore the problem of interpreting doctrinal change from the surviving polemical texts. The Church of England was, from its inception, embattled ideologically, first and foremost against Rome, but secondly against itself as its leaders wrestled with the ways in which a reformed Church might be constructed within the parameters defined by the crown as supreme head and governor. The internal debate contrasted sharply with the experience of the Scots, who after 1560 were able to direct most of their debates outwards, against the hostility of the Catholics and the ignorance of the people. English circumstance produced a lively, strongly committed, theology, whether expressed in the scurrilous polemics of John Bale or the measured prose of Richard Hooker. It did not isolate itself completely from the European reformed mainstream: there were, we now know, more translations of Calvin into English than into any other language.[204] Indeed, after a period in the first half of Elizabeth's reign when the intellectual challenge of Continental Protestantism sometimes appeared lost in the heat of exchanges on the governance of the Church, mature Elizabethan reform once again looked outwards to Geneva and (negatively) to Rome. There always remained, however, the complicated sense, as Cox had once famously insisted to Knox, that he and his colleagues would have 'the face of an English Church'.[205] Even the most fundamental doctrinal debate was liable to be coloured by that sense of Englishness.

---

[203] R. Rollock, *Certain sermons upon severall places of the epistles of Paul* (Edinburgh, 1599). Mullan, *Scottish Puritanism*, 19. Rollock also published on the Psalms.

[204] Higman, 'Calvin's works in translation', 82–99.   [205] Petheram, *A Brieff Discours*, 38.

PART IV

REFORMATIONS ESTABLISHED
AND CONTESTED

9

CUIUS REGIO, EIUS RELIGIO? THE CHURCHES, POLITICS, AND RELIGIOUS IDENTITIES, 1558–1600

Making Two Reformations

John Knox occupies an honourable place among the lengthy catalogue of great historical blunderers. Determined after his successful Scottish preaching tour of 1555–6 to exercise a direct influence over the religious fate of the British Isles, Knox returned to the Geneva congregation to which he had been elected as minister at the end of 1555. There he and his fellow minister Christopher Goodman moved to increasingly radical sentiments, starkly justifying the process of resistance to idolatrous regimes. France and Scotland were of growing significance in Knox's vision, but his passions were still most fully engaged by the horrors of English apostasy from the covenant, and by the need to recall the people from their sins. Yet England failed to act, and therefore had to be roused from its slumber by that memorable treatise *The First Blast of the Trumpet against the Monstrous Regiment of Women*, which emerged from the printing press just in time for the accession of Elizabeth.[1] No one man did more, by gross miscalculation, to determine that Genevan reform should be anathema to the princess to whom the reformers had to turn as the agent of the kingdom's spiritual renewal. Among the earliest acts of the Elizabethan regime were a vigorous hunt for copies of the offending text, and the encouragement to John Aylmer to construct his counter-blast *A harborowe for faithfull and*

---

[1] Knox, iv. 349–422, also printed in R.A. Mason (ed.), *John Knox, On Rebellion* (Cambridge, 1994), 3–47. There is a large literature on Knox's views of revolt: see especially R.A. Mason, *Kingship and the Commonweal: Political Thought in Renaissance and Reformation Scotland* (East Linton, 1998), 139–64, expanding his introduction to *John Knox, On Rebellion*; J.A. Dawson, 'Revolutionary conclusion: the case of the Marian exiles', *History of Political Thought* 11 (1990), 257–72; 'The two John Knoxes: England, Scotland and the 1558 Tracts', *JEH* 43 (1991), 555–76 and 'Trumpeting resistance: Christopher Goodman and John Knox', in R.A. Mason (ed.), *John Knox and the British Reformations* (Aldershot, 1998), 131–53.

trewe subjects agaynst the late blowne blaste concerninge the government of wemen.[2] As late as 1561 Knox was attempting to exculpate himself, claiming that he had 'mitigated somewhat the rigour of his book, referring much unto the time that the same was written'.[3] It did no good: he was forever anathema to Elizabeth, along with his zealous Genevan allies.

Knox's second 1558 attempt to change the world met with better success. His *Appellation . . . to the Nobility and Estates of Scotland* was disseminated in an environment already receptive to his calls for the punishment of idolatry and the reform of religion.[4] Since Scotland was still an uncovenanted nation Knox's main concerns were the protection of the fledgling 'privy kirks' and their purity of worship against the malice of the idolatrous Catholic clergy. Implicit in his appeal to the nobility to act in this cause was permission to them to oppose the civil authority if it impeded godly change.[5] The key to the contrast between Knox the blunderer and Knox the voice of religious revolution lies more within the two British realms than within the man himself. It can be expressed simply in the notion that we can date the beginning of the second phase of the English and Welsh Reformation to 17 November 1558, Elizabeth's Accession Day. The Scottish Reformation has no such precise origin date, though later, in the usual search for beginnings, various dates between the signing of the Band of the Lords of the Congregation in December 1557 and the calling of the Reformation parliament in August 1560 were canvassed.[6] The contrast is, of course, too simplistic, since the English settlement was a long, complex, and contested process and the Scottish Reformation slowly established itself with full legal foundations.[7] Yet in essence the first was founded on monarchical choice and order, the second on the radical rejection of existing authority in church and state.

Scottish reformers, like many of their kind, started with little disposition to revolution. Their objective, to secure their own worship within 'the privy kirks', must in 1557 have seemed a possible goal, because the regent Mary of Guise still retained a strong vested interest in religious concili-

---

[2] The observation on house-to-house searches comes from Anthony Ashe, a former member of the Edwardian stranger church who came from Emden to try to re-establish its privileges in London in 1559. He attributed the difficulties he encountered to official hostility to Knox. A. Pettegree, 'The Marian exiles and the Elizabethan Settlement', in his *Marian Protestantism* (Aldershot, 1996), 144–5.

[3] *CSP Sc* i. 533 [no. 983].

[4] Knox, iv. 461–520.

[5] Mason, *Knox on Rebellion*, 72–114. J.H. Burns, *The True Law of Kingship: Concepts of Monarchy in early Modern Scotland* (Oxford, 1996), chs. 4–5. R.A. Mason, 'Knox, resistance and the royal supremacy', in Mason, *Knox and the British Reformations*, 154–75.

[6] J. Wormald, *Court, Kirk and Community: Scotland 1470–1625* (1981), 111–13.

[7] C. Cross, *The Royal Supremacy in the Elizabethan Church* (1969), 19–37.

ation as a route to political stability. The First Band of Association of the Lords of the Congregation, signed by the fourth earl of Argyll, the earl of Morton, the earl of Glencairn, and John Erskine of Dun, among a limited group of others, might seem the initial break with a policy of co-operation from the Protestant perspective. In fact it was followed by a period in 1558 when collaboration was at its height and when Mary, in order to secure political support for the marriage of her daughter to the Dauphin Francis, allowed public Protestant assemblies outside the capital.[8] The regent was praised in letters from Calvin 'for excellent knowledge of God's word and goodwill towards the advancement of his glory'.[9] The language is significant: there was as yet no break with the magistrate, but the objective was reform on Protestant terms. The leaders of the Band acted in concert, supporting direct action as well as negotiation with the regent. In the November parliament of 1558 the pressure was increased with a direct petition from the Lords for freedom of worship: Mary stalled, offering some reassurance in return for support on the marriage treaty. When, in December 1558, Archbishop Hamilton summoned preachers before the church courts it was the Congregation that protested, appealing the case to the regent 'to be tried most justly according to the holy scriptures'.[10]

By the latter date the possibilities of political compromise were diminishing, both for the regent and for those committed Protestants who sought reform through the mechanisms of state. The most critical moment, for Scotland as for England, was the death of Mary Tudor. With the accession of Elizabeth came the very real threat of a reversion to the politics of the 1540s, in which a reforming minority in Scotland sought English support to counter the 'auld alliance'. Mary of Guise could no longer pursue toleration; radical Protestants awoke to the possibility of a double reformation, and the Lords of the Congregation indeed began to reflect on English aid.[11] Meanwhile the *de facto* toleration of preaching and propagandizing had facilitated the hardening of religious attitudes, most clearly demonstrated on the Protestant side by the publication of the 'Beggars' Summons' of January 1559, warning the friars to 'flit and quit' their hospitals by the following Whitsunday.[12] On the Catholic side, Archbishop Hamilton's summoning of a provincial council of the Church

---

[8] Calderwood, i. 326–8, 416–17, 420–1. I.B. Cowan, *The Scottish Reformation* (1982), 111 12.

[9] Calderwood, i. 421–2.

[10] Knox, i. 256–66, 274–5. F.D. Bardgett, *Scotland Reformed: The Reformation in Angus and the Mearns* (Edinburgh, 1989), 66–70.

[11] Wormald, *Court, Kirk and Community*, 114–16.

[12] Knox, i. 320–1. Brother Kenneth, 'The popular literature of the Scottish Reformation', in D. McRoberts (ed.), *Essays on the Scottish Reformation, 1513–1625* (Glasgow, 1962), 179.

for March is equal evidence of a determination to act.[13] The regent made her own position abundantly clear by a very public celebration of the Easter communion, and by Lenten proclamations threatening death to those who attacked Catholic worship in the 'communion-season'.[14] Meanwhile the signing of the treaty of Cateau-Cambresis, and the subsequent death of Henri II of France, opened up the possibility of a Catholic league against the Protestants in Scotland, and of a jurisdictional claim to the throne of England as well as Scotland by Mary Queen of Scots and her husband, now Francis II.[15]

The immediate trigger for the Scottish revolt was the attempt by the regent in early May 1559 to enforce the Lenten proclamations and to discipline the intransigent preachers, led by Paul Methven. She drew back briefly when petitioned to do so by Erskine of Dun, but her final decision to put the ministers to the horn led to full-scale military action by the Lords of the Congregation, who occupied Perth and enforced reformation.[16] The coincidental (or providential) arrival of Knox in the same month reinforced the preachers, and helped to foster popular reformations in Dundee and Ayr. A number of burghs—Perth, Brechin, Montrose, Stirling, St Andrews, and Edinburgh—were occupied by forces of the Congregation in the following months, and were rapidly opposed by the regent's forces, backed by French troops.[17] The speed of descent into civil war after a long period of negotiation and apparent compromise is striking, and indicative of the fact that both sides had been made vulnerable by the rapid shifts in international events in the first half of 1559. Despite its popular dimension, the war of the Congregation has to be seen largely as a political battle for survival by a beleaguered elite, whose commitment to religious change had led them far further down the path to radical opposition to the monarchy than they had originally intended. They were constantly to be reinforced by those who feared the newly ascendant power of France, and saw in the crisis the opportunity to rid Scotland of foreign dominance.[18] It was no doubt fortunate that John Knox was available to provide this heterogeneous alliance with a justification for their actions. Idolatry must be punished, and men had a general duty to enforce God's laws against the rulers. By 1564 Knox was spelling out clearly a position he seems to have

---

[13] D. Patrick (ed.), *Statutes of the Scottish Church, 1225–1559* (SHS, Edinburgh, 1907), 160–1.

[14] Bardgett, *Scotland Reformed*, 70–1.

[15] On the broad significance of Cateau-Cambresis see S. Alford, *The Early Elizabethan Polity: William Cecil and the British Succession Crisis, 1558–1569* (Cambridge, 1998), 53–5. Henry had requested aid from Philip II to restore Catholicism and French authority in Scotland.

[16] Calderwood, i. 437–9.

[17] Knox, i. 317–82; ii. 452.

[18] J. Leslie, *The History of Scotland* (Edinburgh, 1830), 271–9. Cowan, *Scottish Reformation*, 115–19.

adopted from the time of his return to Scotland: 'subjects may not only lawfully oppose themselves to their kings... but also they may execute judgement upon them according to Gods law'.[19]

By the time that the forces of the Lords of the Congregation temporarily occupied Edinburgh in July 1559 the Elizabethan settlement was already a legislative fact. The parliament which had re-established Protestantism had been dissolved on 8 May; commissions for the royal visitation to enforce religious change were issued in June and the first coterie of reformed prelates were about to be nominated to their sees.[20] The settlement was indubitably orchestrated by the queen and her advisers and, the returning exiles convinced themselves, was indication of Elizabeth's true commitment to the reformed religion. 'We have', Jewel wrote to Bullinger, 'a wise and religious queen, and one too who is favourably and propitiously disposed towards us.'[21] Historians have not always been so confident about Elizabeth's motives. The opacity of her personal religious views and the fragmentary nature of the evidence for the decisions that produced the settlement have been a fruitful ground for controversy. Yet the broad public outlines of policy both before and after the 1559 parliamentary session are reasonably clear. Although the queen moved with caution, not even significantly changing the nature of worship within her own chapel royal in advance of parliamentary sanction, she employed calculated public gesture to signal her hostility to Catholicism. Famous moments include her dismissal of the taper-carrying monks of Westminster, her insistence that the Host should not be elevated in her chapel, and her kissing of the Bible during the coronation pageants provided by the city of London.[22] Less frequently remarked is the proclamation of December 1558 licensing churches to read the Epistle and Gospel at Mass in English.[23]

At the end of the parliamentary session an explicitly Protestant settlement had indeed emerged. The Acts of Supremacy and Uniformity had restored the royal supremacy, in its modified form of royal governorship, and the 1552 Edwardian Prayer Book in all its essentials. The royal injunctions spoke apparently unambiguously of the 'suppression of superstition' and the need 'to plant true religion to the extirpation of all hypocrisy, enormities and abuses'.[24] While the settlement was liturgically driven,

---

[19] Mason, *Knox on Rebellion*, 203. Dawson, 'Goodman and Knox', 145.

[20] N.L. Jones, *Faith by Statute: Parliament and the Settlement of Religion 1559* (1982). W.S. Hudson, *The Cambridge Connection and the Elizabethan Settlement of 1559* (Durham, N.C., 1980). Pettegree, 'Marian exiles', 129–50.

[21] *ZL* i. 33.

[22] A.F. Pollard (ed.), *Tudor Tracts 1532–1588* (1903), 376. C.G. Bayne, 'The coronation of Queen Elizabeth', *EHR* 22 (1907), 662.

[23] *TRP* ii. 102–3.   [24] *VAI* ii. 176–89.

rather than espousing the 'best reformed model' of a confession as the essential preliminary to spiritual renewal, there was an expectation that the rest would quickly follow. It may be that the new leaders of the Church hoped that something like the 'Declaration of doctrine' offered to the queen in April 1559 by a group of the Marian emigrés, which followed the pattern of the Edwardian Forty-Two Articles, would be adopted.[25]

The months between the coronation in January 1559 and the end of the parliament are fraught with interpretative difficulty. A frame is provided by the two parliamentary sessions, with a break over the Easter period, and by the signing of the Treaty of Cateau-Cambresis, news of which reached England at the end of the first week in April. The latter event was as crucial politically for the English as for the Scots, but as Norman Jones has shown it came too late fundamentally to influence the direction of the settlement.[26] As for the struggle for settlement itself: the major competing interpretations turn on the intentions of the regime and on who provided the parliamentary opposition. For J.E. Neale the queen was a very tepid sort of Protestant, seeking a return to Henrician values or at worst the revival of the 1549 Prayer Book. She and her ministers were opposed by a determined pressure group in the Commons, who forced her into the acceptance of the 1552 Prayer Book with its unequivocal commitment to the Protestant cause.[27] Jones's challenge to this thesis displaced opposition to the Lords and the refusal of the prelates to accept any movement away from Catholicism, and sought to prove by a careful reconstruction of the texts, that Elizabeth and her advisers achieved the settlement that they always intended.[28]

Jones's thesis has won wide acceptance, and in its interpretation of the oppositional forces faced by the new regime carries great conviction. But it is less clear that Neale's reading of the queen herself has been fully displaced. Much of Elizabeth's later behaviour towards her church was so idiosyncratic, ambiguous, or, in the view of the godly reformed, downright erroneous, that it is difficult to see her as driven by the pure light of the gospel in the early months of 1559.[29] A recent insight into the queen's

---

[25] W.P. Haugaard, *Elizabeth and the English Reformation* (Cambridge, 1968), 238–9.

[26] Jones, *Faith by Statute*, 83–159.

[27] J.E. Neale, 'The Elizabethan Acts of Supremacy and Uniformity', *EHR* (1950), 304–32.

[28] N.M. Sutherland, 'The Marian exiles and the establishment of the Elizabethan regime', *ARG* 78 (1987), 253–84, essentially supports the Jones thesis, as does Pettegree, 'Marian exiles', in *Marian Protestantism*.

[29] For valuable reflections on the ever-vexed topic of Elizabeth's religious convictions see P. Collinson, 'Windows in a woman's soul: questions about the religion of Queen Elizabeth I', in his *Elizabethan Essays* (1994), 87–118. Also, S. Doran, 'Elizabeth I's religion: the evidence of her letters', *JEH* 51 (2000), 699–720. Both authors see the queen as Protestant doctrinally, but traditionalist in her religious behaviour.

views as she pondered the settlement of religion has come from Roger Bowers's study of music prepared for the chapel royal in the early months of the reign.[30] Compositions by Sheppard, Mundy, Parsons, and Tallis, which can be assigned with some confidence to the early years of the reign, set texts from the 1549 Prayer Book. It is also possible that a letter from Edmund Guest, later bishop of Rochester, to Cecil, commenting adversely on proposed amendments to the 1549 Prayer Book, dates from this period.[31] Guest resisted suggestions that processions should be revived, the cross used, and prayer for the dead reincorporated into the communion service. He also opposed the reintroduction of ceremonies, and insisted on the lawfulness of kneeling or standing for communion. This reads as a firm response to Elizabeth's preoccupations and suggests that we should take seriously once again the suggestion that Elizabeth would have preferred the first to the second Edwardian text and would have liked to give it an enhanced ceremoniousness. The details here are significant both because of the later history of the Elizabethan church and because, if true, they raise the question of who or what persuaded the queen away from her early preference.

While it would be possible to resuscitate the zealous in the Commons as a source of influence on the settlement, the fragmentary evidence points more consistently towards the inner conciliar circle, and above all to William Cecil. Although Cecil, like the queen herself, and like Matthew Parker, had chosen to be a nicodemite and to conform under Mary, his Protestant instincts are not in serious doubt.[32] There is nothing in his later behaviour that suggests that he had any interest in processions, crucifixes, or vestments, and in his previous existence under Edward he had been identified fully with the reformed. In 1559 the queen's cause was his cause, but within a few months he was to show how effectively he could manoeuvre his mistress when both the gospel and national security were threatened in the case of Scotland. It is impossible to be sure

---

[30] R. Bowers, 'The chapel royal, the first Edwardian Prayer Book and Elizabeth's settlement of religion, 1559', *HJ* 43 (2000), 317–44. I am very grateful to Dr Bowers for allowing me to see a copy of his paper in advance of publication, and for conversations about the settlement.

[31] The text of the Guest revision is in H. Gee, *The Elizabethan Prayer Book and its ornaments* (1902), 215–24. Gee argues forcefully, against Strype, that the document dates from 1552 and is associated with the preparation of the second Edwardian Prayer Book. Most modern commentators have accepted this dating, but the internal evidence of the topics discussed is more compatible with 1559. Above all, the covering note, addressed apparently to Cecil, who much later forwarded it to Parker, talks of 'some causes of the order taken in the new service', language which from Guest fits better with 1559; Gee, *Elizabethan Prayer Book*, 31 ff. Bowers, 'Chapel royal', 330–2.

[32] Alford, *Early Elizabethan Polity*, 25–7. Hudson, *Cambridge Connection*, 100–2. On nicodemism under the Marian regime see Pettegree, 'Nicodemism and the English Reformation', in *Marian Protestantism*, 86–117.

whether Cecil was able to deflect the queen from the 1549 Prayer Book before it reached Parliament. Two differently labelled bills for the uniformity were introduced into the Commons in mid-February 1559: they may have been promoting competing versions of the Edwardian book, with the regime initially sponsoring 1549, or, as Jones suggests, simply different labels for the same bill, sponsoring 1552.[33] If there were moves towards the 1549 rite it seems likely that they were suppressed by Cecil and his allies.[34] Much later the royal secretary defensively reminded Edward Dering of how he had been active 'above all others in propagating religion in the beginning' of the reign, 'enduring great contestation in it'.[35] A number of others no doubt contended in support of Cecil: his brother-in-law Nicholas Bacon, Anthony Cooke, and Francis Knollys. And in the shadowy world of spiritual advisers there were men like Richard Cox and Edmund Grindal, the latter recalling in after years that they had struggled long and earnestly for further reform but were 'unable to prevail'.[36] Cecil and his network of friends and allies were certainly those best equipped to persuade the queen of the position that the House of Commons seems to have supported throughout, that the restitution of the 1552 Prayer Book was the mark of a true Protestant settlement.

In achieving her settlement Elizabeth had been forced to abandon the hope of persuading even the most *politique* of her Catholic bishops to endorse religious change. The most that was in the end offered as gestures to conservative opinion within the legislative settlement was the so-called 'ornaments clause' inserted in the Act of Uniformity, permitting chancel ornaments and vestments according to the 1549 use, and the amplification of the sentences of reception in the communion service.[37] The latter married the 1552 formula, 'take and eat this in remembrance that Christ died for thee and feed on him in thy heart by faith with thanksgiving', to that of 1549, 'the body of the Lord Jesus Christ which was given for thee, preserve thy body and soul unto everlasting life'. It can be argued that no change of doctrine was involved, merely a move away from an overly blunt statement of Swiss memorialism in 1552 to the more nuanced articulation of Christ's spiritual presence in the Eucharist that was the mature reformed position.[38] Since no evidence of controversy about this

---

[33] Jones, *Faith by Statute*, 90–5.

[34] *CSP Sp* 1558–67. i. 25, 33, for the assumption of the Spanish ambassador Feria that Cecil was driving change.

[35] J. Strype, *Annals of the Reformation* (Oxford, 1824), i. i. 119.

[36] P. Collinson, *Archbishop Grindal, 1519–83: The Struggle for a Reformed Church* (1979), 85–9.

[37] 1 Eliz. I c.2: the ornaments proviso was the last to be added to the text, suggesting that it was possibly a late insertion.

[38] D. MacCulloch, *The Later Reformation in England, 1547–1603* (1990), 30–1.

change survives it may be assumed to have been acceptable to Protestants: at the most among Catholics it could have appealed to those who were already actively seeking a way of accommodating their consciences to the demands of the new regime. For the queen, on the other hand, both provisions opened the way for an emphasis on devotion to the sacraments, and to the forms of ritual and prayer which she had valued in her youth. The determination with which she subsequently maintained the crucifix and candles in her private chapel, and her clear preference for a formal, sung liturgy rather than an excess of sermons, were already given a type of legitimation in the gestures of the settlement.[39]

The years that followed the end of the 1559 parliament saw the most critical stages of struggles to appropriate its meaning as a Protestant settlement.[40] The new bench of bishops was slowly appointed, the royal visitation was completed, and the first confessional statement, the Eleven Articles, was produced. Through all of this the assumption was that 1559 marked the beginning of a process of building a reformed church, not its apotheosis. Even Cecil, far better placed than most of the new church leaders to recognize the difficulty of moving Elizabeth, seems to have proceeded on the assumption that further change was a practical possibility. In his lists of proposals for filling the vacant bishoprics Cecil consistently favoured active reformers, many of them drawn from his networks of connection from Edwardian and Cambridge days. He may also have hoped for a modified episcopate, closer to Lutheran superintendency than to old lordly prelacy.[41] When Edmund Grindal was given charge of the stranger congregations in London he was made their superintendent at the secretary's insistence.[42] Ultimately Cecil met with much success in his nominations for the bench, though he was thwarted both by clerical opposition to plans to reduce the value of bishoprics and by Elizabeth's unwillingness to unbalance her bench with an excess of exiles, especially any with the slightest taint of Geneva. The interminable slowness with which the sees were filled, not really completed until 1561, led the

---

[39] The controversy between Elizabeth and her Protestant bishops about crucifix and candlesticks has frequently been narrated: see Haugaard, *Elizabeth and the English Reformation*, 185–200. On the services in the chapel royal under Elizabeth see P. McCullough, *Sermons at Court: Politics and Religion in Elizabethan and Jacobean Preaching* (Cambridge, 1998), 76–8.

[40] Much of the interpretation in this paragraph draws on the work of Brett Usher on Cecil and the appointment of the first Elizabethan episcopal bench. I am grateful to Mr Usher for allowing me to see a part of his text in advance of publication.

[41] See F. Heal, *Of Prelates and Princes* (Cambridge, 1980), 200–10; 'The bishops and the Act of Exchange of 1559', *HJ* 17 (1974), 227–46. Cecil recommended Danish-style superintendency and the taking of episcopal wealth to the Lords of the Congregation in 1559: *CSP For 1558-9*. no. 1086.

[42] A. Pettegree, *Foreign Protestant Communities in Sixteenth-Century London* (Oxford, 1986), 136–8.

secretary into intermittent hand-wringing about the failure of true settlement. In March 1560 one of his memoranda reads: 'to see the realm set in
order with a clergy, that the Ire of God light not upon the people of the
realm'.[43]

The new bishops and their supporters among the Protestant clergy also
saw the settlement as a crucial new beginning. Despite bruising encounters with the queen about her cross and candlesticks—those 'great grief[s]
to the godly'—clerical marriage, and episcopal lands, the prelates anticipated a fuller reformation. Looking north of the border they saw what
could be achieved: the Scots, John Parkhurst told Bullinger in 1560, 'have
made greater progress in true religion in a few months than we have done
in many years'.[44] The royal visitation of 1559 provided the returning
exiles with a major opportunity to make clear statements of faith, preaching extensively on their circuits and deliberately circumventing Elizabeth's
cautious injunction on the removal of 'monuments of feigned miracles,
pilgrimage, idolatry and superstition' by encouraging a return to wholesale
Edwardian iconoclasm.[45] But the most important opportunity came in
1562-3 when, with the new personnel of the Church firmly in place, the
calling of Parliament opened the way for the first convocation of the new
reign.[46] That convocation once again restored England's full confessional
status with the passing of the Thirty-Nine Articles, but it sought more,
including reform of canon law and alterations to the liturgy. Issues raised
included some that were to become familiar battle-ground between
Puritans and conformists over the ensuing decades: ministerial dress,
kneeling at communion, forms of music in church, the sign of the cross in
baptism. The careful reconstruction of the surviving documents of the
convocation by David Crankshaw suggests that the bishops were responsible for the preparation and promotion of these reforming proposals.
From this convocation came the so-called 'Alphabetical bills' with which
the bishops sought in the next two parliaments to promote further reform
in the Church.[47] But by then the world had changed: hopes focused on
Elizabeth had dimmed, and the problem of order and authority in church
and state had been opened up by the beginnings of the conflict over
vestments.

[43] PRO sp 12/11/35.   [44] ZL i. 91.

[45] *VAI* ii. 176–89. M. Aston, *England's Iconoclasts: Laws against Images* (Oxford, 1988),
298–303.

[46] The fullest account of the 1563 convocation is in Haugaard, *Elizabeth and the English
Reformation*, 52–78, but its interpretation needs fundamental amendment in the light of the
following. D. Crankshaw, 'Preparations for the Canterbury provincial convocation of 1562–3: a
question of attribution', in S. Wabuda and C. Litzenberger (eds.), *Belief and Practice in Reformation England* (Aldershot, 1998), 60–93.

[47] G.R. Elton, *The Parliament of England, 1559–81* (Cambridge, 1986), 205–12.

Despite the initial success of the parliamentary settlement, Cecil's memoranda in the second half of 1559 are filled with foreboding about the dangers to the realm within and without. Within men suffered 'for lack of good government ecclesiastical' and were not taught 'to live in obedience to the laws established'; without there were threats from Catholic powers in general, and above all from France and from Mary Queen of Scots' claim to the English throne.[48] In these strained circumstances the 'Protestants of Scotland', as Cecil swiftly came to label the Congregation, could offer the opportunity to counter French threat. From June 1559 Cecil's agents, especially Sir Henry Percy, were in deep negotiation with the Scottish lords, and the language of the 1540s was being resurrected to meet the new circumstances.[49] In July Cecil wrote to the earls of Argyle and Glencairn, and other lords, presenting the English settlement with a clarity he could not always muster at home. The country had abandoned 'idolatry and brought [in] our saviour Jesus Christ', and Cecil prayed that the same would happen to the Scots, 'thereby this terrestrial kingdom of Christ may be dilated through this noble Isle'.[50] This is not quite the crude unionism of the 1540s, partly because the regime was not ready for direct intervention, partly because, if we are to take Cecil at his word, it was a common amity of religion and politics binding two realms that seemed to him the desirable outcome. The implications of this amity for the governance of Scotland were spelled out in the secretary's 'memorial of certain points' at the end of August. This endorsed the militant purging of the kingdom, the authority of the estates, and, most radically of all, the possibility of deposing a tyrannous monarch.[51]

Fine sentiments were no substitute for big battalions. In the autumn of 1559 England was not backing its rhetoric with direct support, despite the Congregation's requests for aid. Like Cecil, the Lords cast their rhetoric partly in religious, indeed apocalyptic, language, asking for a 'league made in the name of God' seeking 'rather the heaven than the earth'.[52] In reality, the situation in Scotland was somewhat less apocalyptic, and when it became essential to secure English support the Lords turned to a more directly political form of appeal. The Congregation had remained largely in the ascendancy in these months, and there were dramatic moments, notably the 'suspension' from power of the regent in October, an action which had little practical effect. The Scots had reached something like stalemate, a

---

[48] PRO SP 12/4/40.   [49] Alford, *Early Elizabethan Polity*, 55–8.
[50] PRO SP 52/1, fos. 147–8, calendared in *CSP For 1558–9*. 424 [no. 1086].
[51] BL Lans. MS 4, fos. 26ᵛ–27, printed in Alford, *Early Elizabethan Polity*, 223–4. See also J. Dawson, 'William Cecil and the British dimension of early Elizabethan foreign policy', *History* 74 (1989), 196–216.
[52] *CSP For 1558–9*. 396 [no. 1028], 431 [no. 1097]; *CSP Sc* i. no. 903.

situation in which it was expected that only the vigorous intervention of England or France would finally shift the balance of power. In the winter of 1559 it looked as though the role of the latter would be crucial: Congregation forces had to retreat from Edinburgh and were losing to French forces around Stirling and St Andrews. Eventually, under the pressure of a formal delegation from the Congregation and growing fears of French intentions, Cecil became a fervent advocate of direct intervention and in turn persuaded a reluctant queen to action. By spring 1560 Lord Grey's army had made sufficient impact on the French at Leith for the parties to accept a negotiated settlement. This proved extremely difficult to achieve, though the practical need of all parties for compromise and the death of Mary of Guise in June 1560 finally opened the way for the signing of the Treaty of Edinburgh on 6 July. Cecil himself travelled to Scotland to sign the accord and take the measure of the Scottish political leadership.[53]

The most curious feature of the treaty was that it did not resolve the religious issue, which had proved 'too hot for the French to meddle withal', as Cecil reported to Elizabeth.[54] Even the English commissioners were taken aback by the commitment of the Scots, 'so deeply persuaded in the matter of religion, as nothing can persuade them that may appear to hinder it'.[55] It was certainly true that the Scottish leadership had no intention of waiting on the judgements of the French king and queen as the treaty had proposed. The extended nature of the revolt against Catholicism had given congregations in Ayrshire, Angus and the Mearns, and Fife the opportunity to expel their old ministers and appoint reformers. Those involved in military action had taken a second band in April 1560 to 'set forward the reformation of religion' and to welcome English military assistance.[56] By the time of the signing of the Treaty of Edinburgh the Protestant leadership was ready to act, and the parliament that met in August 1560 proceeded at a pace that put English endeavours to shame. Papal authority was annulled, the Confession of Faith was accepted and the Book of Discipline was commissioned.[57] Randolph, the English ambassador, reporting to Cecil, remarked that 'I never saw so important matters, sooner dispatched, or agreed to with a better will.'[58] It was as

---

[53] Alford, *Early Elizabethan Polity*, 64–5. C. Kellar, '"To Enrich with Gospel Truth the Neighbour Kingdom": Religion and Reformation in England and Scotland, 1534–1567', University of Oxford D.Phil. (2000), 210–12.

[54] S. Haynes (ed.), *A Collection of State Papers relating to Affairs in the Reigns of King Henry VIII, King Edward VI, Queen Mary and Queen Elizabeth*, 2 vols. (1740), i. 352.

[55] Ibid., 333.

[56] Bardgett, *Scotland Reformed*, 70–83. M.H.B. Sanderson, *Ayrshire and the Reformation* (E. Linton, E. Lothian, 1997), 97–8.

[57] *APS* ii. 526–35. Knox, ii. 61.   [58] *CSP Sc* i. 466–7 [no. 886].

though the Scots, having come so tardily to public reformation, now intended to compensate for decades lost.

But appearances can be somewhat deceptive, and the contrast between the tense and cautious English parliament of 1559 and the vigorous Scottish response to the clarion call of reformation should not be exaggerated. In the Scots parliament itself opposition was certainly muted: laymen who were not convinced wisely remained silent, though two of the three bishops present offered cautious resistance to the Confession.[59] The Book of Discipline aroused more controversy: its first version was not presented in Parliament and a group of divines was commissioned to work on a second version in the autumn of 1560. The finished product was approved by the first General Assembly of the Kirk in December and then presented to a Convention of the Estates for approval. It won informal approval from a group of signatories, but among the stars of the reformed firmament who refused to sign were Maitland of Lethington and Erskine of Dun.[60] While there seems to have been very little ideological opposition to the introduction of a firm Calvinism, and the accompanying disciplinary framework, the problems presented by the need to finance the new kirk proved deeply contentious. Knox remarked darkly that those who opposed the Book were wholly taken up with their 'worldly commodity'.[61] The Book was eventually accepted by the Convention of Estates and the Privy Council, but was given no general parliamentary sanction.[62] It was scarcely surprising that, after many further vicissitudes, the General Assembly seized a favourable moment in the 1570s to 'set down a constant form of church-policy and present the same to be allowed by the council'.[63]

Relations with England were equally uncertain, despite the general gratitude expressed by the reformers for the decisive military intervention of 1560. There were those, most notably Maitland of Lethington, who saw in the English alliance a possibility of bringing the kingdoms into closer union. The Lords of the Congregation had optimistically proposed to Elizabeth that a marriage alliance with the young earl of Arran was the best way to achieve this.[64] The project was killed by the queen's lack of enthusiasm in 1559, but renewed with much greater formality towards

[59] Kellar, 'Gospel Truth', 215–16. G. Donaldson, *The Scottish Reformation* (Cambridge, 1960), 66–8.

[60] J.K. Cameron (ed.), *The First Book of Discipline* (Edinburgh, 1972), 3–14, 70–5. It should be noted that the drafters of the First Book confidently followed Calvinist practice in *requiring* the civil powers to enforce the Kirk's will, not *petitioning* for state support.

[61] Knox, ii. 297.

[62] The whole Reformation settlement, indeed, remained in an ambiguous legal position because of Mary's refusal to endorse its proceedings.

[63] J. Kirk (ed.), *The Second Book of Discipline* (Edinburgh, 1980), 41–2.

[64] *CSP Sc.* i. 465, 495 [nos. 885, 926].

the end of 1560.[65] Any personal preference apart, it does not seem that Elizabeth took any great interest in British unionist projects of the kind that underlay these proposals. By this time she may also have begun to understand a little of the nature of the Scottish religious settlement, not only its detachment from its sovereign, but its Calvinist nature. Even if John Knox was less central to the drama for contemporary Englishmen than for the later readership of his *History of the Reformation*, he was clearly established as a leading preacher, and was seconded by that other hated Genevan, Christopher Goodman. As for Knox himself: he held to a passionate vision of religious unity between the realms he loved, and was a more intense unionist than most of his contemporaries, but his view of that bond was unyielding. The English, like the Scots, must profess the purity of the gospel, officially if possible, but if not, little by little as the Scots had done.[66] It was the view that had been articulated most clearly by Anthony Gilby while the Genevans still remained in exile in 1558: both nations must repent and 'return into the vineyard', winning God's favour with complete victories over their enemies. There could be no union between those who failed to do the Lord's work unequivocally.[67]

Any triumphalism felt by Scottish Protestants in the months after the Treaty of Edinburgh and the Reformation parliament was to be short-lived. Fate intervened and cast up Mary Queen of Scots as a widow on the shores of her kingdom.[68] In August 1561, barely a year after the meeting of Parliament, an adult queen of Catholic persuasion had returned to rule. The few articulate Catholic divines who were confronting Calvinism, notably Quintin Kennedy and Ninian Winzet, were encouraged, as were those nobles who had no Protestant commitment and no enthusiasm for the English alliance. Mary could not return to the principle of *cuius regio, eius religio* in the absence of military backing from France, but her commitment to private Catholic worship was sufficient to destabilize the settlement, and incidentally to destabilize Knox, who desired direct confrontation with the Antichrist. He was constrained by Moray and Maitland, who were insistent that compromise was necessary for political stability, and so it proved for a few years. Mary, however, was

[65] Haynes, *State Papers*, i. 364.

[66] Alford, *Early Elizabethan Polity*, 88–9. Kellar, 'Gospel Truth', 218–20.

[67] A. Gilby, *Admonition to England and Scotland, to call them to repentance*, reprinted in Knox, iv. 553–71. J. Dawson, 'Anglo-Scottish Protestant culture and integration in sixteenth-century Britain', in S.G. Ellis and S. Barber (eds.), *Conquest and Union: Fashioning a British State, 1485–1725* (1995), 99–110. G. Donaldson, 'The foundations of Anglo-Scottish union', in his *Scottish Church History* (Edinburgh, 1985), 142.

[68] Alford, *Early Elizabethan Polity*, 86–7, stresses how critical Mary's return was to Anglo-Scottish relations.

to demonstrate that even in a Scotland reformed without royal fiat sovereigns could still count.[69]

Securing the Settlements: Scotland and England Before the mid-1580s

The *annus mirabilis* of the Scottish Reformation was not succeeded by any secure settlement of religion: indeed the Kirk had to wait another thirty years before it could claim its place in the structure of the Scottish state with full confidence. Calvinist ecclesiology not only enabled it to survive in this uncertain climate, it helped positively to affirm the separation of the Kirk from lay authority.[70] The magistrate was confined to authority over those 'whom they govern civilly': the spiritual governance of the Church given to Christ alone. The 'two kingdoms theory', adumbrated by the Lords of the Congregation as early as 1559, ensured that it was the ministry that possessed the power of the keys 'which our Master gave to his disciples and their true successors'.[71] Only the clergy could preach, teach, administer the sacraments, and bind and loose in disciplinary judgement. Admittedly, in an ideal Calvinist polity the civil authorities were to co-operate with the ministry, but initiative incontestably lay with the spiritual arm.[72] In the real political world, however, the Kirk had constantly to confront the mutability of power and its uncertain impact on religious organization. The cycle of events began with the personal rule of Mary, which until 1565 was marked by uneasy manoeuvring between the queen and the Protestant lords.[73] The breathing-space provided allowed the Protestant church to gain support. It did not permit it to establish itself with full legality or to solve its pressing financial problems. Then in 1566 there was crisis when in the aftermath of her marriage to Darnley and Moray's rebellion Mary made a bold bid to restore Catholicism through Parliament. Not only the reformed Kirk, but the whole structure of Anglo-Scottish Protestant alliance was threatened. At this the queen's world famously collapsed.[74]

Mary's deposition in 1567 offered the Kirk the opportunity for better collaboration with the state: the earl of Moray as regent for the infant

---

[69] Knox, ii. 142–3. J. Wormald, 'Godly Reformer: Godless Monarch: John Knox and Mary Queen of Scots', in Mason, *Knox and the British Reformations*, 231–2.

[70] Donaldson, *Scottish Reformation*, 53–75.

[71] J. Kirk, *Patterns of Reform* (Edinburgh, 1989), 232–40. Cameron, *First Book of Discipline*, 99, 103.

[72] Mason, 'Knox, resistance and the royal supremacy', in *Knox and the British Reformations*, 154–8, 172–5.

[73] J. Wormald, *Mary Queen of Scots: A Study in Failure* (1988), 103–28.

[74] G. Donaldson, *All the Queen's Men: Power and Politics in Mary Stewart's Scotland* (1983), 74–82.

James being the closest approximation to a 'godly prince' that was to be experienced in this disturbed period.[75] The parliament that met in December of that year ratified the legislation of its predecessor in 1560, and added some of those public affirmations of the status of the new faith that were necessary in the confessional state. Public office was restricted to Protestants, the Kirk was given the right to examine all those promoted to benefices, and had its control over preaching, discipline, and the administration of the sacraments proclaimed. With the exception of a full financial settlement it seemed to have gained all that it desired. This did not mean, however, that the leaders of the reform movement had broken faith with the 'two kingdom' ideal. In 1568 the printer John Bassenden was in trouble for a book title that described James VI as 'supreme head of the primitive Kirk'.[76] Four years later the Scottish Oath of Supremacy described him only as 'governor of this realm as well in things temporal as in the conservation and purgation of religion'.[77]

The conservation of religion proved difficult in the 1570s. The assassination of Moray in 1570 was followed by a brief English military intervention. This led to full-scale civil conflict, only gradually resolved after the appointment as regent of the earl of Morton. Morton's early history as a signatory of the First Band of Association did not automatically make him a friend of the ministers, and from 1572 onwards he endeavoured to enhance the authority of the crown over the ecclesiastical structure by supporting the continuance of bishops. By the time that the Kirk drew up the Second Book of Discipline in 1578, the crown's advisers were firmly committed to the episcopate, a major moment of conflict being Morton's attempt to appoint Patrick Adamson as archbishop of St Andrews in 1576.[78] Morton's hold on power was subsequently weakened when he was stripped of the regency in 1578, and then further damaged by Esmé Stewart, duke of Lennox, whose pro-French interests and ascendancy over the young king threatened to destabilize the whole Protestant settlement. Morton was executed in 1581 after a trial controlled by his enemies.[79] Stewart was displaced in 1582, but there followed the capture of the king by the 'Ruthven raiders'. The Ruthven lords were supposedly sympathetic to the Kirk. However, they showed erastian tendencies and

[75] A.R. MacDonald, *The Jacobean Kirk, 1567–1625: Sovereignty, Polity and Liturgy* (Aldershot, 1998), 6–8.

[76] Mason, 'Knox, resistance and royal supremacy', in *Knox and the British Reformations*, 154, 174.

[77] The oath can be compared with its English counterpart in W.C. Dickinson, G. Donaldson and I.A. Milne (eds.), *A Source Book of Scottish History*, 3 vols. (Edinburgh, 1952–4), iii. 12–13.

[78] Donaldson, *Scottish Reformation*, 183–216.

[79] For the best full narrative of these events see G.R. Hewitt, *Scotland under Morton* (Edinburgh, 1982).

an unwillingness to commit further resources to the ministry.[80] In a final twist in 1583 James escaped from the influence of the Ruthven lords, only once again to promote the Stuart, pro-French interest in the person of the earl of Arran. The Kirk's support for the ousted regime led directly to one of the greatest moments of crisis in its chequered first half-century of existence. In the ensuing factional struggles a group of ministers led by Andrew Melville fled to England, while others resisted the Arran regime at home. Only James VI's assumption of power in November 1585 produced some semblance of calm.[81]

The Kirk therefore developed its identity partially in independence from an insecure and unsettled monarchy. From the moment of the First Book of Discipline onwards the essential features of church organization were put in place. Local congregations, guided by their elders and deacons, called ministers to their service, though the process of vetting for the clergy in practice lay in the hands of the wider pastorate.[82] Individual churches had kirk sessions as their focal assemblies 'for treating of things concerning the Kirk and pertaining to their charges'.[83] Broader ecclesiastical policy was to be decided by the General Assembly, which met for the first time at the beginning of 1561.[84] It is the intentions of Knox and his colleagues in regard to the levels of organization that were intermediate between congregation and general assembly that have sparked most controversy among historians.[85] The structures that served a city-state quickly had to be modified in Scotland as in France to create at least the skeleton of a national church. It may be that, as James Kirk has forcefully argued, the logic of the Scottish system was presbyterian, disposed towards a cellular hierarchy of assemblies in which the ministry and eldership governed without need for an episcopate of any kind. The general

---

[80] MacDonald, *Jacobean Kirk*, 18–29.

[81] James Melville, Andrew's nephew and a fellow minister, vividly evokes the 'dark and heavy winter to the kirk of Scotland', and his own later flight into exile, R. Pitcairn (ed.), *The Autobiography and Diary of Mr James Melvill* (Wodrow Society, Edinburgh, 1843), 139–72.

[82] Cameron, *First Book of Discipline*, 168–79. Kirk, *Second Book of Discipline*, 57–73.

[83] Knox, i. 333.

[84] D. Shaw, *The General Assemblies of the Church of Scotland, 1560–1600* (Edinburgh, 1964). It is important to note that in its early years the General Assembly did not conform at all neatly to a Calvinist vision. It contained the secular nobility, at least until James's period of majority, the superintendents, bishops, and commissioners appointed by the Kirk, representatives of the clergy chosen in rather traditional ways from the diocesan synods, and representatives of the burghs, shires, and universities.

[85] The controversy over the nature of the early reformed Kirk was conducted between the late Gordon Donaldson and James Kirk. The former wished to demonstrate continuity with the past, and above all with contemporary English experience: Donaldson, *Scottish Reformation*, 130–5; 'Foundations of Anglo-Scottish Union', in his *Scottish Church History*, 137–63. The latter challenges these arguments, looking above all to the Genevan influence on the Reformation: J. Kirk, *Patterns of Reform* (Edinburgh, 1989), esp. 70–95, 334–67.

determination of the first generation of ministers to conform to the 'polities of the best reformed kirks' in the areas of doctrine and worship certainly extended to matters of discipline and church order. From the very beginning a system of diocesan and regional synods, similar to those of the old church, supplemented the work of the kirk sessions and acted as courts of appeal.

Within this graded system there remained space for the exercise of individual authority, though not for traditional prelacy. In 1561, as a late addition to the Book of Discipline, a plan for superintendency was introduced. It was proposed that there should be ten reorganized provinces or dioceses, each of approximately 100 parishes, each cared for by a superintendent 'to plant and erect kirks, to set, order and appoint ministers'.[86] The proposal was only partially implemented, because the return of Mary and the acceptance of reform by three of the established bishops created major complications. But in Fife, Angus and the Mearns, Galloway, Glasgow, and Lothian, superintendency became a reality. The individuals who held these posts were not bishops with property, secular power, or exclusive jurisdictional rights, though they did exercise power over appointments and visitatorial discipline that seems at odds with a presbyterian view of parity of ministry. A superintendent was an overseer, subject to the discipline of his own ministers, and not necessarily endowed with permanent power, yet possessed in practice of considerable influence should he choose to exercise it.[87]

Only after the difficult Marian years did the issue of authority in the Church begin to become critical. In 1569 the General Assembly expressed its commitment to the system of superintendency by asking the Privy Council to make proper financial provision so that the office might be extended. Meanwhile there was a pressing need to replace the bishops of the old church who had retained their benefices.[88] In 1571 John Douglas, rector of St Andrews University and a kinsman of the earl of Morton, was nominated to the archbishopric against fierce opposition from the General Assembly. The issue was compromised in the 'Concordat of Leith' of the following year, by which it was agreed that bishops should be appointed, but that they should hold a parish like other ministers and be subject to the General Assembly in matters spiritual. The principles of oversight embodied in the superintendency were upheld but, ominously, the crown

---

[86] For a thorough, but rather negative, interpretation of superintendent power see Kirk, 'The superintendent: myth and reality', in *Patterns of Reform*, 154–231.

[87] For a good recent study of the early operation of superintendency in Fife see L.J. Dunbar, 'Synods and superintendence: John Winram and Fife, 1561–72', *RSCHS* 27 (1997), 97–125.

[88] D.G. Mullan, *Episcopacy in Scotland: The History of an Idea, 1560–1638* (Edinburgh, 1986), 33 ff.

retained rights of appointment subject to vetting by the Kirk.[89] The Leith settlement survived for a few years, at the cost of organizational confusion, particularly on the issue of disciplinary responsibility.[90] By 1574 the Kirk was eager to look for a more permanent structural solution, and the providential return from Geneva of Andrew Melville offered the opportunity for such a re-evaluation.[91] The General Assembly established a committee to enquire 'whether . . . the bishops, as they are now in the Kirk . . . have their function of the word of God or not'.[92]

The answer, for most kirk-men, was that a reformed polity had no place for lordly prelates. The Second Book of Discipline, which was the end product of the 1570s debates, made it abundantly clear that all ministers were of equal standing, and that bishops were explicitly excluded from exercising the disciplinary functions associated with diocesan visitation.[93] Bishops slowly ceased to attend meetings of the General Assembly. The sentiments of Melville on godly discipline prevailed, even though we can no longer describe the Second Book as his personal handiwork.[94] But while the disciplinary structure of the Church was tightened and moved more firmly in a Genevan direction, the political problem remained. Morton as regent was determined to continue to exercise royal patronage and to sustain episcopacy, beginning in 1576 a protracted battle with the General Assembly about the nomination of Patrick Adamson to the archiepiscopal see of St Andrews. In this Morton eventually prevailed and he also thwarted the Kirk in its attempts to have the Book of Discipline sanctioned by Parliament.[95] Although no clear statement of his motives survives, the Kirk's response that 'it became not the prince to prescribe a policy for the Kirk', makes the fundamental issue clear. Episcopal power was now deeply identified with princely meddling, and fundamentally incompatible with the separation of spiritual power on which the Kirk was bent. When Morton was ousted and Lennox achieved ascendancy the General Assembly, despairing of royal sanction, formally adopted the Second Book of Discipline, and argued that it was resolved 'wholly to condemn the estate of bishops as they are now in Scotland'. In 1581 the 600 parishes were divided into fifty presbyteries, and thirteen were launched as pilot organizational units.[96] Fear of Lennox's Catholic leanings

---

[89] MacDonald, *Jacobean Kirk*, 8–14.   [90] Kirk, *Patterns of Reform*, 353, 355.

[91] T. McCrie, *The Life of Andrew Melville*, 2 vols. (Edinburgh, 1819), i. 158–9.

[92] *BUK* i. 331, 336–7.

[93] Kirk, *Second Book of Discipline*, sections 176 and 183, on ministers, section 196–7 on visitation.

[94] On Melville see Kirk, *Second Book of Discipline*, intro., 47–52. McCrie, *Life of Melville*, i. 172–4.

[95] MacDonald, *Jacobean Kirk*, 16–22. Calderwood, iii. 413–16, 619–20.

[96] *BUK* ii. 474–5, 480–7.

intensified the determination of the assembly to resist state intrusion and episcopal nomination.[97] Conflict about the promotion of Robert Montgomery to the see of Glasgow led to a special assembly that warned James that 'in your graces person some men propose to erect a new popedom'.[98]

Such trenchant behaviour offered its own moral rewards, yet the Kirk had to exist in the real political world, hence the enthusiasm of the ministers for the overthrow of Lennox and the victory of the 'Ruthven raiders'. James Melville hailed the event in his diary as 'a great relief to the Kirk'.[99] The Ruthven leaders were certainly sound Protestants, but their insecure political position scarcely justified the faith that Melville and others placed in them. The Second Book of Discipline remained unratified, and while the Ruthven Council acknowledged kirk sessions, synods, and the General Assembly, it avoided pronouncements on either bishops or presbyteries.[100] When the Stuart faction regained the initiative Archbishop Adamson saw an opportunity for influence and quickly became an adviser to the crown. In December 1583 he went to England and had meetings among others with the new archbishop of Canterbury, John Whitgift.[101] Thus the seeds of an anti-presbyterian campaign in Scotland were sown. Meanwhile, the ministerial support for the Ruthven faction led inexorably to the disgrace of their leadership, culminating in the flight to England of Andrew Melville and a coterie of ministers who were under suspicion of treason. In May 1584 the Scottish parliament passed the so-called 'Black Acts'. These claimed royal authority over all matters spiritual and temporal and outlawed 'all jurisdictions and judgements not approved by parliament', this of course including the whole presbyterian system.[102] Ministerial protest was in vain, and merely led to a further flight to England by threatened clerics. It appeared that the crown's advisers had won a notable victory and that episcopacy was secured, though, as so often in Scottish politics, the drama proved no permanent indicator of royal success.[103]

---

[97] The Kirk's fears about Lennox's Catholicism seem thoroughly justified in the light of the grand Jesuit plot of 1582 for the conversion of James, armed intervention in Scotland, and perhaps Ireland, by the duke of Guise, and the overthrow of Elizabeth: T. McCoog, *The Society of Jesus in Ireland, Scotland and England, 1541–1588* (Leiden, 1996), 178–89.

[98] *BUK* ii. 488–512.

[99] Pitcairn, *Autobiography of James Melvill*, 134.

[100] Donaldson famously described the Ruthven raiders as 'ultra-Protestant', a position seen by most other historians as exaggerated. G. Donaldson, *Scotland: James V–James VII* (Edinburgh, 1971), 179.

[101] G. Donaldson, 'The attitude of Whitgift and Bancroft to the Scottish Church', in his *Scottish Church History*, 164–77.

[102] *APS* iii. 292–4.

[103] J. Kirk, 'Royal and lay patronage in the Jacobean Kirk, 1572–1600', in N. MacDougall (ed.), *Church Politics and Society, 1408–1929* (Edinburgh, 1983), 135 ff. MacDonald, *Jacobean Kirk*, 25–6. *APS* iii. 292–4.

When Thomas Cartwright, the doyen of Elizabethan presbyterians, responded to John Whitgift's attack on the *Admonition to the Parliament* (1572), he spoke bluntly of the role of the magistrate in the Church:

he [Whitgift] thinketh that the Church must be framed according to the commonwealth, and the Church government according to the civil government, which is as much to say, as if a man should fashion his house according to his hangings, when as indeed it is clean contrary, that, as the hangings are made fit for the house, so the commonwealth must be made to agree with the Church . . .[104]

It was small wonder that his opponent was able to retort triumphantly that 'these words would be well considered, for they contain the overthrow of the prince's authority both in ecclesiastical and civil matters'.[105] It mattered little that this was certainly not the end at which the leaders of the presbyterian movement aimed. What sufficed was the capacity to think such thoughts and to air them in public, printed debate. Suddenly the tensions about the exact nature of ceremony and vestments, which had dominated the previous decade, paled into insignificance beside the powerfully articulated plea for the construction of a fully confessionalized church, conforming in order as in doctrine to the best reformed Continental models.[106]

Although Cartwright's lectures as Lady Margaret Professor of Divinity at Cambridge in spring 1570 are said to have begun the presbyterian debate in England, the key event was the publication of the *Admonition to the Parliament* in June 1572.[107] The timing of the onslaught was not fortuitous. In a domestic context it was the consequence both of the general alienation of the godly preachers from the episcopal leadership of the Church, which had begun before the vestiarian controversies of the mid-1560s, and of the specific quarrels of the previous year. In the latter the Privy Council and the bishops had resisted William Strickland's proposals for cleansing the Book of Common Prayer introduced into the Commons.[108] The international context was also significant. For several years Theodore Beza, Calvin's successor in Geneva, had been hardening his line on the governance of the British churches. He appears genuinely to have been shocked by the information that godly bishops had no power to exercise autonomous discipline with their fellow pastors, and in 1568 reproved Grindal for the arbitrary powers of the prelates. He welcomed

---

[104] J. Ayre (ed.), *Works of John Whitgift*, 3 vols. (PS, Cambridge, 1843), iii. 189–90.

[105] Ibid., 190.

[106] P. Collinson, *The Elizabethan Puritan Movement* (1967), 112 ff.

[107] Collinson, *Puritan Movement*, 112–13. Note his caution that we know only a limited amount about the detail of Cartwright's lectures.

[108] N.L. Jones, 'Religion in Parliament', in D.M. Dean and N.L. Jones (eds.), *The Parliaments of Elizabethan England* (Oxford, 1990), 122–4.

Cartwright to Geneva when the latter was banished from Cambridge in 1571, and in the next year warned Knox of the dangers to Scotland of '*pseudoepiscopi*'.[109] Although this last letter, with other Bezan correspondence, was not published until 1573, Genevan views were well known in English radical circles. And the publication of the papal bull *Regnans in excelsis*, excommunicating Elizabeth, provided a further context for the urgency of Puritan demands. The conflict with the Counter-Reformation Church was now intensified and that binary division of the world into the forces of light and darkness that characterized godly thought found one outlet in an insistence on the need for biblical purity in church governance.

In the early years of Elizabeth's reign godly Protestants were encouraged to believe that further changes would be acceptable to the crown. The support of the Scots and of the Huguenots at Le Havre bred a conviction that 'full reformation' at home could not long be delayed. The English garrison at Le Havre, with the radical Genevans William Whittingham, Christopher Bradbridge, and the Scot William Kethe as its chaplains, saw the 'marvellous conjunction' they had established with the Huguenots as the beginning of a new era at home.[110] The fact that the crown's representatives in the Channel Islands acquiesced in the establishment of Calvinist congregations led by Huguenots as a way of converting the conservative islanders, also indicated the possibilities for 'other of your Majesty's dominions and countries'. That the Channel Islanders were carefully treated as a breed apart for religious purposes does not appear to have troubled the godly. It is, however, striking that there was no effort to enforce the Prayer Book or the Act of Supremacy in the islands and that when individuals from Guernsey or Jersey visited the mainland they were treated as part of the stranger churches.[111] In practice the Elizabethan regime showed itself far more concerned with the strategic circumstances of the Channel Islands than with the nuances of their religious position. It was essential that their Protestant loyalty was secured, and in practice this could only be done by evangelization from France.[112] What the godly

---

[109] T. Beza, *Epistolae*, 2nd edn. (Geneva, 1575), no. lxxix: this was to Knox in 1572; to Grindal four years earlier he had been more circumspect: ibid., no. xxiii. Donaldson, *Scottish Reformation*, 187–9.

[110] C.S.L. Davies, 'International politics and the establishment of Presbyterianism in the Channel Islands: the Coutances connection', *JEH* 50 (1999), 505–22.

[111] D.M. Ogier, *Reformation and Society in Guernsey* (Woodbridge, 1996), 62–9. A.J. Eagleston, *The Channel Islands under Tudor Government, 1485–1642* (Cambridge, 1949), 55–8.

[112] Davies shows that, though the acceptance of Huguenot conversion by the crown and its island representatives was probably based on strategic considerations in the early 1560s, royal power was too weak to manage the subsequent reformation. By about 1570 when the last dean, John Aster, left the islands, there was no effective English control, although Robert Horne, bishop of Winchester, had nominal authority.

were observing was a pragmatic response to a political threat, not a signal about the possibilities of further structural change at home.

In 1563, when Convocation and Parliament were dissolved there was still the optimistic expectation that the Elizabethan settlement would be completed with a disciplinary and organizational structure appropriate to a fully reformed polity. The business of isolating those Catholics who overtly defied the settlement continued, though in the most cautious manner. After the passage of the Treason Act of 1563 the supremacy oath was administered to all office-holders and, despite the queen's determination to apply it moderately, deprivations followed and the Catholic exile community increased rapidly.[113] In the 1566 parliament, and again in that of 1571, the bishops promoted measures to strengthen the Church through the so-called alphabetical bills.[114] These would have given parliamentary sanction to the Thirty-Nine Articles, and would have attacked a variety of weaknesses in the existing disciplinary structure of the Church. None succeeded in 1566, and even in 1571 only the bill for the Articles finally became statute. The story is complex, and not always adequately described in the secondary sources, but the essential point is not in doubt: that it was the queen who opposed initiatives from the prelates and their parliamentary supporters. For Elizabeth the settlement was established: any necessary adjustments must be undertaken by the prelates on their own authority, perhaps supported by the royal prerogative. When Elizabeth refused to accept the 1566 bill providing statutory sanction for the Articles of Faith Archbishop Parker acknowledged the nature of the problem: 'Her Majesty is not disliking of the doctrine of the book which she doth openly profess, but the manner of putting forth the book.'[115]

The bishops sometimes appeared equally the victims of circumstance in the major ecclesiastical crisis of the 1560s: the controversy over vestments.[116] Elizabeth willed conformity to the essential standards of clerical dress established in the 1559 settlement, and regarded her royal orders to the archbishop and his colleagues as sufficient authority for them to act. She consistently refused to offer her explicit support for Parker's efforts to provide a full standard of discipline through the Advertisements. 'The Queen', complained Parker in March 1566, 'will needs have me assay

---

[113] N.L. Jones, *The Birth of the Elizabethan Age: England in the 1560s* (Oxford, 1993), 72–8.

[114] Elton, *Parliament of England*, 205–12.

[115] T. Perowne (ed.), *The Correspondence of Matthew Parker* (PS, Cambridge, 1853), 291–2. The queen's refusal to allow parliamentary sanction of the Articles in 1566 prompted a general letter from the bishops pleading for endorsement, but to no avail: Perowne, *Correspondence of Parker*, 292–4.

[116] The story of the vestiarian controversy has often been told; nowhere more effectively than in Collinson, *Puritan Movement*, 59–100.

with mine own authority what I can do for order.'[117] This was more than
a year after Elizabeth herself had apparently precipitated the crisis with a
letter complaining of 'open and manifest disorder' in the Church, and
episcopal connivance therein. The prelates appeared ground between the
upper millstone of royal anger and the nether stone of godly non-
conformity. For divines like Thomas Sampson and Laurence Humphrey,
respectively dean of Christ Church and president of Magdalen, the wearing of the surplice and square cap were bitter reminders of popery. For in
Queen Mary's time, said a contemporary commentator, 'all shavelings,
known tormentors and massing priests wore such cap'.[118] Such things
were not to be tolerated in the new Church. To the regular episcopal
argument that these things were indifferent and should be borne 'for
order's sake and obedience to the prince', the divines responded that
tender consciences should not be forced.[119] A number of the prelates,
most notably Bishop Grindal in London, were indeed deeply reluctant to
force consciences. Such bishops took an uncompromising stand on conformity only when faced with the inevitability of royal demands.[120]

But it would be a mistake to present Parker and his fellow bishops as
mere victims of a confrontation between the queen and her intransigent
clerical subjects. Much of the initiative to secure conformity came from
the archbishop himself and it was he who requested the queen's letter to
provide support in his campaign. In the crisis of 1566 Parker reflected
bitterly that those like Grindal who had winked at those not using the
surplice had perpetuated the problem of indiscipline which otherwise 'had
been suppressed for five or six years ago, and had prevented all this un-
quietness now taken'.[121] Parker was firmly backed by Richard Cox of
Ely, who insisted that if London was disciplined the whole realm would
easily follow. There was here a strain of thought that led from Cox's own
experiences in the troubles of Frankfurt through to Whitgift's campaign
against non-conformity in the 1580s.[122] Obedience, order, and a disciplined hierarchy were not only the requirements of the Supreme Governor,
they reflected the nature of the Church itself as seen by these prelates.
Parker had always feared what he called 'popularity'. As early as 1559 he
had prayed fervently 'God keep us from such visitation as Knox have
attempted in Scotland; the people to be the orderer of things.'[123] He may
have been in a minority among his colleagues, but internal convictions

---

[117] Perowne, *Correspondence of Parker*, 272, 223–7.   [118] Bodl. Tanner MS 79, fo. 16.
[119] Jones, *Elizabethan Age*, 54–8.   [120] P. Collinson, *Archbishop Grindal* (1979), 168–78.
[121] Perowne, *Correspondence of Parker*, 284, 270.
[122] F. Heal, 'The Bishops of Ely and their Diocese during the Reformation Period,
ca.1515–1600', University of Cambridge Ph.D. (1972), 26–38.
[123] Perowne, *Correspondence of Parker*, 105.

about the spiritual virtues of order and discipline seem to have sustained a number of them in these troubled decades when laymen and godly clerics alike dealt contemptuously with them.

The crisis provoked by Parker's disciplinary action on clerical dress evolved into a wider conflict in London that uncovered overt defiance of episcopal order and led to the suspension of thirty-seven ministers. That was in 1566: in the following year about a hundred godly Londoners were arrested at Plumbers' Hall, for conducting separatist worship in what appears to have been a conscious revival of the pure Marian 'underground church', but now with the Geneva form of discipline and worship.[124] Their primary purpose seems to have been a refusal to compromise with those they called the 'traditioners', and they already possessed that impatience with 'tarrying for the magistrate' that was the hallmark of later Elizabethan separatism. Moreover, they believed that they had models closer than Geneva that they could emulate: the French and Dutch stranger congregations in London, and the pure Kirk established north of the border.[125] They wrote boldly to John Knox seeking Scottish support, and urging that 'we desire no other order than you hold'. In this last instance the hard-core separatists got more than they bargained for: in 1569 Grindal sent a group of them to Knox for 're-education'.[126] They found the Scots hostile enough to surplices and Prayer Book, but refusing to countenance even semi-separation, and 'not pure enough for our men'. By 1570 the group had been broken and dispersed and the energies of the godly clergy were being refocused upon the construction of a revised discipline within the Church.[127]

Paradoxically, the series of challenges that the English church encountered after 1570 provided some clarity of focus to its leadership. The political landscape was more stable, the threat of international Catholicism had been made explicit, and within the Church conflict became concentrated largely upon the issue of ecclesiastical structure. None of this offered much consolation to Matthew Parker, whose declining years were made weary by the (correct) belief that his sovereign would never provide him with full support, and by irrational conspiracy theories.[128] On the other hand, the fledgling Church began slowly to stabilize its personnel, and to define itself over and against 'recusancy', both from Catholics and

---

[124] Collinson, *Puritan Movement*, 84–91.   [125] Collinson, *Archbishop Grindal*, 177–82.
[126] W. Nicholson (ed.), *The Remains of Edmund Grindal* (PS, Cambridge, 1843), 295–6.
[127] J.P. Lorimer, *John Knox and the Church of England* (1875), 298–300.
[128] V.V.K. Brooks, *A Life of Archbishop Parker* (Oxford, 1962), 314–40. The substantive basis for Parker's late conspiracy obsession was the claim of the confidence trickster Humphrey Needham that the earl of Bedford planned to murder Burghley, Hatton, and the bishop of Winchester: Perowne, *Correspondence of Parker*, 461–5. APC viii. 261, 319, 322, 340.

from the small minority of sectaries. After 1571 Parliament ceased to be used by the bishops as a means to re-ordering the Church: such limited changes as were made were undertaken through Convocation with the assent of the queen, as in the canons of 1576, which essentially reaffirmed the status quo.[129] Meanwhile the challenge of presbyterianism was initially met by what Collinson, with some exaggeration, called a witch-hunt: the imprisonment of Field and Wilcox as authors of the *Admonition*; the suspension of a number of ministers in Northamptonshire, Warwickshire, and elsewhere, who refused to subscribe to articles defining church law on authority; and the vigorous pursuit of 'Puritan' publications in London. But the drive was less systematic than in the vestiarian controversy, and with Parker's death and Grindal's promotion to Canterbury the relationship between the prelates and their critics ceased for a time to be so acrimonious.[130]

The 'Grindalian moment' in the Church of England is the stuff of much subsequent myth-making. From the later perspective of the godly it appeared as an opportunity to set the Church on the true path to full reformation. 'Such bishops', Richard Baxter famously remarked, 'would have prevented our contentions and wars.'[131] Edmund Grindal certainly possessed advantages over his predecessor: he inherited a church which, internal conflict and Catholic threat notwithstanding, was more stable than that of the 1560s. His strong reputation as a zealous Protestant won him the affection of many so-called 'moderate Puritans', and for the same reason he had active support within the Privy Council. Sir Walter Mildmay and others made it clear that they believed his views made him very popular among the devout laity. The problem is that there was so little time to test Grindal's abilities as a leader, since within a few months of his elevation to Canterbury in 1576 he was in deep conflict with the queen about prophesyings, and was suspended, leaving a power-vacuum at the heart of the Church.

Elizabeth's hostility to the clerical meetings at which collective edification was sought through preaching and biblical study probably owed much to her general frustration at the behaviour of the godly over the previous ten years. Perhaps, like Cox who was one of the few bishops to oppose the meetings, she resented a world 'full of new fangles and fancies'.[132] She certainly felt no great affinity for the type of earnest biblical exegesis that was the stuff of the assemblies held in a wide range of

---

[129] Elton, *Parliament of England*, 215–16. Wilkins, *Concilia*, iv. 284–5.

[130] C. Litzenberger, 'Defining the Church of England: religious change in the 1570s', in Wabuda and Litzenberger, *Belief and Practice*, 137–53.

[131] Collinson, *Archbishop Grindal*, 283–93, quotes Baxter at 283.

[132] LPL MS 2003, fo. 7.

dioceses. But the issue between herself and her archbishop almost immediately became one of authority. When Grindal felt that he had to defend
the practice of edification at the cost of refusing to circulate the royal
order to suppress prophesyings he acknowledged, for all his deference, a
higher duty. 'Where preaching wanteth obedience faileth.'[133] He played,
as Collinson has vividly demonstrated, St Ambrose to the queen's Theodosius: like Ambrose, whose words he used, he expected God's judgement to light on a prince who behaved unrighteously, even if he did not
expect to follow this to the saint's logical conclusion of excommunication.[134] Elizabeth's retribution was her six-year suspension of her prelate.
At least twice she endeavoured actually to proceed to his deprivation,
only to be restrained by wiser counsels. Nothing conveys more vividly
the queen's understanding of her authority than her assumption that she
could deprive Grindal with the merest fig-leaf of legal precedent. However, the limits to her capacity are equally striking. Her ministers wrung
their hands, 'these proceedings cannot but irritate our merciful God'
lamented Burghley. They also circumvented her will until calmer counsels
prevailed. And even prophesyings, though dramatically suppressed in
1577, re-emerged under the more circumspect title of 'exercises' during
the next decade. Before the end of Elizabeth's reign many of these had
merged into the lectures by combination that were commonplace in English market centres.[135]

By the beginning of the 1580s the structural paralysis created by Elizabeth's exclusion of Grindal had been partially resolved by the labour of
John Aylmer, bishop of London and president of High Commission, and
of the rising star of the episcopal bench, John Whitgift.[136] Neither was a
friend of forward Protestants, and those who resisted conformity to Prayer
Book and surplice now began to find themselves 'horsed up to London'
to face disciplinary proceedings before the bishops in Commission.[137] But
the years preceding Whitgift's elevation to Canterbury in 1583 were more
conspicuously marked by fears of Catholic threat than by internal Protestant conflict. In 1578 Sir Francis Knollys had associated the possible deprivation of Grindal with that threat: 'if the bishop of Canterbury shall be
deprived, then up starts the pride and practice of the papists'.[138] The

---

[133] Nicholson, *Remains of Grindal*, 376–90.

[134] On Ambrose and Theodosius see P. Collinson, 'If Constantine, then also Theodosius:
St Ambrose and the integrity of the Elizabethan *Ecclesia Anglicana*', in his *Godly People: Essays on
English Protestantism and Puritanism* (1983), 109–33.

[135] Collinson, 'Lectures by combination: structures and characteristics of church life in
seventeenth-century England', in *Godly People*, 467–98.

[136] J. Strype, *Life of Aylmer* (Oxford, 1821), 60–4. Aylmer also presided over the convocation of
1581.

[137] Collinson, *Puritan Movement*, 204–6.   [138] BL Harl. MS 6992, fo. 89.

prospect in the following year of the queen's marriage to the duke of Anjou must have confirmed his fears. Protestant opinion rallied against the match. The attack was led by the passionately ideologically committed, most famously John Stubbs, Cartwright's brother-in-law, who lost his hand for his publication of *The discoverie of a gaping gulf*. The crisis passed, and in the next years there was a rare measure of accord between the queen and her godly subjects on the need for defence against Catholicism. Papal intervention in Ireland and the arrival of the first group of Jesuit missionaries in England led to the passage of the 1581 Treason Act, a measure that may not wholly have pleased any of its makers, but which gave clear signals of the realm's determination to resist Catholic incursion.[139]

Ireland and the Elizabethan Settlement

In May 1559 Thomas Radcliffe, earl of Sussex, and Mary's erstwhile lord deputy of Ireland, drafted a comprehensive proposal for settlement in Ireland. It included an insistence that there must be careful planning for the first parliament of the reign to ensure that Elizabeth's legislative programme was successful. The crown must construct a strong party in the Commons; the membership of the Lords should be vetted; and potential opponents of religious change, such as the bishops of Kildare and Meath, should be called to London on 'matters of state' and held there for the duration of the session.[140] Sussex brought a cool head and a sense of *realpolitique* to address metropolitan concerns that any attempt at reformation in Ireland would produce turmoil 'by reason of clergy that is so addicted to Rome'.[141] The new queen accepted that he was likely to be the most able and knowledgeable of those whom she could choose as her deputy, and Sussex returned to Dublin in August 1559. Bills modelled on the English statutes were prepared in October of that year and Parliament assembled at the beginning of 1560.[142]

The sparse documentation on the 1560 parliament has led to a variety of theses on the reasons for the success of the government's legislative programme. Brendan Bradshaw, taking his cue from Sussex's forceful arguments, has suggested extreme coercion, and a meeting bristling with

---

[139] Elton, *Parliament of England*, 186–7, for a careful consideration of the bill's passage, and a suggestion that the major divisions about its provisions may have come from within the Privy Council.

[140] HMC Salisbury MSS, vol. iii, no. 968.

[141] The comment on Irish religion is from the very cautious 'Device for alteration of religion', BL Cottonian MS. Julius FVI, fo. 167.

[142] H.A. Jefferies, 'The Irish parliament of 1560: the Anglican reforms authorised', *IHS* 26 (1988), 128–9.

'armed government troops'.[143] Others believe that the settlement never passed the Upper House, despite the fact that all parties in Elizabethan Ireland seem to have accepted its full legal status.[144] The most recent attempt at reconstruction is disposed to the view that opposition to the Acts of Supremacy and Uniformity was not necessarily vociferous, and that the government was able to gain a measure of support, albeit at some cost.[145] The cost was the addition to an Act of Uniformity otherwise virtually identical to English legislation of a clause permitting the use of a Latin version of the Book of Common Prayer 'in every such church or place where the common minister or priest had not the use or knowledge of the English tongue'.[146] This book, unlike its Edwardian predecessor, was not necessarily envisaged as a stop-gap made available only until an Irish version could be produced, and when it was printed in 1560 the *Liber precum publicarum* perpetuated many of the most doctrinally conservative elements of the 1549 English Prayer Book. It was a text that proved popular among the Anglo-Irish population of the Pale, who had no reason not to use the English version.[147] With this concession to conservative opinion the lord deputy was able to put through his legislative programme. Even the bishops took no general stand against the rejection of Rome. Of the three who seem to have opposed the parliamentary changes, Archbishop Bodkin of Tuam, Bishop Walsh of Meath, and Bishop Leverous of Kildare, only the last two explicitly refused to take the oath of supremacy and were subsequently deprived. Thomas Leverous appears to have refused obedience on the interesting grounds that women were by nature excluded from the exercise of any authority in the Church.[148]

Thus Sussex achieved an initial success in establishing the queen's settlement that is in some ways more remarkable than its English counterpart. When the Act of Uniformity came into effect in June 1560 it did so without any serious evidence of conflict or protest.[149] Most sees remained filled

---

[143] B. Bradshaw, 'The beginnings of modern Ireland', in D. Farrell (ed.), *The Irish Parliamentary Tradition* (Dublin, 1973), 80–1.

[144] R.D. Edwards, *Church and State in Ireland: A History of the Penal Laws against Irish Catholics, 1534–1603* (Dublin, 1935), 170–91.

[145] Jefferies, 'Irish parliament', to which this paragraph is much beholden.

[146] *The Statutes at Large: Ireland*, 20 vols. (Dublin, 1786–1801), i. 275 ff. Jefferies suggests that the Prayer Book clause was added late, during the passage of the uniformity bill through Parliament.

[147] The Latin liturgy was used regularly into the 1580s and was still being used in at least one parish of the deanery of Ballymore as late as 1615: J. Murray, 'The Tudor Diocese of Dublin', University of Dublin, Trinity College Ph.D. (1997), 220.

[148] M.V. Ronan, *The Reformation in Ireland under Elizabeth, 1558–1580* (1930), 30.

[149] A. Clarke, 'Varieties of uniformity: the first century of the Church of Ireland', in W.J. Sheils and D. Wood (eds.), *The Churches, Ireland and the Irish*, SCH 25 (Oxford, 1989), 109–11.

and few clergy seem to have thought in the first instance of any direct appeal to Rome against Elizabeth. But the obverse of this success was that enforcement, even of the most conservative form of the new faith, was possible only in those areas over which an effective jurisdiction could be exercised. This still meant primarily the Pale, and some of the southern towns with an English-speaking population. Beyond this circuit were lord-ships where a measure of political influence could be exerted: Munster and Connacht for example, where occasionally a conformist lord like the earl of Clanrickard would support government initiative. Elsewhere in Gaelic territory, most notably in Ulster, any amendment of religious behaviour was likely to have to wait on political change. It was preoccupation with the political problems of Ireland, as well perhaps as a certain innate conservatism, that led Sussex to do little to enforce the religious order he had helped to construct.[150]

Although the oath of supremacy was administered to some of the bishops of English Ireland it was otherwise virtually neglected as an instrument of conformity.[151] In the Pale moreover, even when a bishop like William Walsh of Meath was deprived, there was no attempt at this stage to remove him from the diocese in which he had previously ministered. The survival of Hugh Curwen at Dublin in the early years of the reign also provided a significant impediment to change, something that may have influenced his decision in accepting the oath of supremacy.[152] Sussex dutifully followed the English model in establishing local ecclesiastical commissions, in 1561 and 1562, and a national commission followed in 1564, but little action seems to have ensued. For the first few years it must have appeared to the Palesmen that, whatever their other disagreements with the lord deputy, they were unlikely to be pressed into greater Protestant commitment than they had been under Edward. And the policy of the Privy Council in London also remained more preoccupied with strategic political issues than with the labour of conversion. William Cecil certainly held the Protestantization of Ireland as a serious objective, but in 1560 he saw his goal substantially in military terms, articulated through the alliance forged with the fifth earl of Argyle, who after the Treaty of Berwick forged a 'mutual and reciprocal' agreement with Sussex to counter the papist Ulstermen.[153]

---

[150] On the political policy of Sussex see C. Brady, *The Chief Governors: The Rise and Fall of Reform Government in Tudor Ireland, 1536–1588* (Cambridge, 1994), 72–101, 179–80.

[151] W.N. Osborough, 'Ecclesiastical law and the Reformation in Ireland', in D. Helmholz (ed.), *Canon Law in Protestant Lands* (Berlin, 1992), 233–4.

[152] On the choices made by Curwen see Murray, 'Tudor Diocese of Dublin', 216–20.

[153] Alford, *Early Elizabethan Polity*, 75–6. J.A. Dawson, 'Two kingdoms or three? Ireland in Anglo-Scottish relations in the middle of the sixteenth century', in R.A. Mason (ed.), *Scotland and England 1286–1815* (Edinburgh, 1987), 119.

In 1564 the earl of Sussex was finally recalled to London after a series of disastrous and costly campaigns against Shane O'Neill. Objective failure in Ireland was compounded by the fixed hostility of Robert Dudley at court. Dudley chose to invest considerable political capital in Ireland in the early 1560s, first campaigning to unseat Sussex, then to replace him with his chosen agents Sir Nicholas Arnold and Sir Thomas Cusack, and finally, when they failed, to promote the popular Sir Henry Sidney. Sidney assumed the viceroyalty in 1565 and was the dominant figure in Irish politics for much of the next twelve years.[154] His instructions on assuming office were comprehensive and detailed, and included a commitment to the active promotion of religious reform, with the words 'the principal and first care which her Majesty committeth to the...Lieutenant and Council'. The language closely resembled that of the orders to Sussex when he resumed power in 1559, but Sidney seems to have started out in the sincere belief that something must be done to make his own Protestant faith viable in the new land. His instructions, which conformed to his own interests, placed great emphasis on the erection of a college to be funded out of the revenues of St Patrick's Cathedral. This would both be of more 'public benefit for the service of God' and ensure an increase of 'knowledge and civility...where now nothing but barbarous and savage conditions remaineth'.[155]

Two years after his elevation Sidney appears to have been the driving force behind the publication of the Twelve Articles, derived from Archbishop Parker's first doctrinal formulation, and a cautious enough statement of belief to be reasonably inclusive.[156] The next year he hailed the promotion of Archbishop Loftus to Dublin with the words 'the hour has now come for reforming the church'.[157] Sidney may have helped Loftus to evade the pressures of the vestiarian crisis: the Zurich divines heard from some of the former English exiles that the churches in Ireland had been permitted to 'live in the greatest tranquillity' on this issue.[158] The hour of reform passed, but throughout the later years of his viceroyalty Sidney repeatedly called for a preaching ministry. He also sought the establishment of proper educational facilities to inculcate Protestantism, and looked for help from any source, including Scotland, to add to the woefully inadequate clerical personnel available to the bishops. As late as

---

[154] For contrasting views of the significance of Sidney's 'new start' see N. Canny, *The Elizabethan Conquest of Ireland: A Pattern Established 1565–1576* (Hassocks, Sussex, 1976), 45 ff., and Brady, *Chief Governors*, 113–58.

[155] E.P. Shirley (ed.), *Original Letters and Papers in Illustration of the History of the Church in Ireland during the reigns of Edward VI, Mary and Elizabeth* (1851), 206–9.

[156] Clarke, 'Varieties of uniformity', 107. See above, p. 311.

[157] Shirley, *Original Letters*, 292.   [158] ZL ii. 167.

1576, submitting Hugh Brady's visitation of Meath to the Privy Council in London, Sidney urged that Elizabeth write to the Scottish regent to send some 'honest, zealous and learned men' who spoke Irish to aid in the work of conversion.[159] These aspects of Sidney's behaviour offered some encouragement to those who believed that the work of reform in Ireland must be undertaken by persuasion. Irish-born reformers like Brady, Lord Chancellor Cusack, and Chief Baron Dillon espoused these views, but so did some of the incomers like Archbishop Lancaster of Armagh and Lord Chancellor Weston.[160] Weston gave active support to the proposal finally passed by the Irish parliament in 1570 for the establishment of free diocesan schools and was a convinced proponent of a bilingual clergy that should persuade through preaching as the route to conversion.[161]

Sidney's moderate reformism was, however, far from the forefront of his priorities. Political survival depended upon success in pursuing the queen's goals and demonstrating his capacity to order a disordered province at a price that Elizabeth was willing to pay. His plans included using colonization and the necessary force to secure control. Among the officials who served him there was a far more intense debate about how to enforce the rule of law than about the need to stabilize the Reformation.[162] And as revolt followed upon revolt with scarcely a few years of calm between, a growing number of observers concluded that the civilizing mission of the English must precede any sustained attempt to convert the native Irish. The lord deputy himself expressed horror when, on his grand tour of Munster in 1567, he found no one to instruct the barbarous people 'in the rules of a Christian, or if they were taught...no grace in them to follow it'.[163] Fitzwilliam, who temporarily succeeded Sidney in the early 1570s, was more directly brutal: 'this people...hath been long nursled in beastly liberty and sensual immunity so as they cannot abide to hear of correction, no not for the horriblest sins they can commit'.[164]

The development during Sir Henry Sidney's deputyship of debate about how to manage conquest has often been conflated with the more immediately pressing issue of how to ensure a measure of conformity in the Pale and among the settled Old English.[165] There the issue was not one of civility, but of the degree of disciplinary pressure that should be applied to the local elites to ensure their attendance at the liturgy and their overt acceptance of the new order. In the first two decades of Elizabeth's

[159] *CSP Irl* 1574–85. 92–3.
[160] B. Bradshaw, 'Sword, word and strategy in the Reformation in Ireland', *HJ* 21 (1978), 484–5.
[161] Ronan, *Reformation in Ireland*, 280–1. Canny, *Elizabethan Conquest*, 128.
[162] Brady, *Chief Governors*, 113 ff.　　　[163] PRO SP 63/20/66, fo. 138[v].
[164] PRO SP 63/37/60.　　　[165] Bradshaw, 'Sword, word and strategy', 485–7.

reign there is evidence that in Dublin and other major population centres the church papist was a characteristic figure, appearing at Protestant services, albeit reluctant to take communion and willing to turn to the support of Catholic chaplains in private. Even the papal agent David Wolfe conceded that the policy had some success: he reported of the Dubliners, 'they go perforce to the communion and sermons of the heretics'.[166] Outside these centres the ecclesiastical commissioners found that the Mass was still routinely said, and that the new form of public prayer was poorly established. A major problem for the new church was that at its heart, in the cathedral establishment of St Patrick's and the ecclesiastical administration in Dublin, there was profound resistance to change. For a time at the end of the 1560s Archbishop Loftus and Lord Chancellor Weston worked in harmony to manoeuvre these conservatives out of positions of influence. They did so by 'canonical' means, using the weapons of visitation and traditional discipline to change some personnel and scare others into conformity.[167]

In the years preceding Weston's death in 1573 there was some hope that gradualist pressure on the clergy of the Pale might begin the process of true reformation. But politics once again intervened, and in his final period in office Sidney swept aside the policy he had earlier espoused and began to argue for a greater coercion in the establishment of religious conformity.[168] Eventually Loftus accepted compulsion as the only route to conformity. By the late 1570s he was once again a vigorous advocate of using the ecclesiastical commission for this purpose.[169] In the 1590s, when the elites of the Pale had moved decisively towards recusancy, Loftus wrote gloomily to Burghley that there was little point in the encouragement of preaching unless men were forced into attendance at worship.[170] Yet in practice the commission seems to have done little in any routine way to compel such obedience. The network of the Pale gentry was too close for effective penetration: 'they are so linked in friendship and alliance one with the other that we shall never be able to correct them by the ordinary force of statute', Loftus had written to Elizabeth as early as 1565.[171] The London regime's extreme caution even in the administration

---

[166] C. Lennon, 'The Counter-Reformation in Ireland, 1542–1641' in C. Brady and R. Gillespie (eds.), *Natives and Newcomers: Essays on the Making of Irish Colonial Society, 1534–1641* (Dublin, 1986), 75–86.

[167] Murray, 'Tudor Diocese of Dublin', 229–55.

[168] Ronan, *Reformation in Ireland*, 480, 139–40.

[169] Murray, 'Tudor Diocese of Dublin', 270–3.

[170] *CSP Irl* iv. 1588–92. 366. As early as his elevation to Armagh Loftus gained a commission to enforce penal legislation in his jurisdiction *Fiants (Ireland) Elizabeth*, nos. 462, 547.

[171] PRO SP 63/13/42.

of the oath of supremacy is indicative of a fear that pressure might be detrimental to the political interests of the crown.[172]

It was those political interests that contributed significantly to the withdrawal of the Pale gentry and the Dublin merchant community from their limited conformity of the early Elizabethan years. Problems of resources and personnel conspired to ensure that the Protestant episcopate could do little to transcend the survivalist environment of these early years: the failure to establish a Dublin college was emblematic of far wider difficulties. But the militant denial of the new faith which contemporaries began to identify from 1580 onwards was linked both to a growing assertion by the Palesmen of their separate identity and to a conviction that they had to confront coercive colonial government directly.[173] The turning-point has often been taken to be the Baltinglas conspiracy of 1580, in which a group of sons of gentry and merchant Palesmen rose in a militant attempt to overthrow the established religion and challenge English power.[174] It is, however, the subsequent policy of repression within the Pale that seems most deeply to have alienated local rulers. They also resented the taxation burdens imposed by Sidney and the general costs of the enlarged administrative establishment constructed by the lord deputies.[175] By the time of the parliament summoned by Lord Deputy Perrot in 1585 the Palesmen managed not only to oppose anti-Catholic legislation, but explicitly to assert their claim to an alternative faith.[176] The lawyer Edward Nugent said openly in Parliament that 'things prospered in Henry V's and other kings' times when mass was up'.[177] From this moment, as Archbishop Loftus noted, an early 'general disposition to popery ... [became] ... this general recusancy'.[178]

Defining the Reformations: Authority and History

'You know,' wrote George Gifford in 1596, 'it is the question which every papist propoundeth, where was your Church an hundred years

---

[172] H.C. Walshe, 'Enforcing the Elizabethan settlement: the vicissitudes of Hugh Brady, bishop of Meath, 1563–84', *IHS* 26 (1989), 352–74.

[173] C. Brady, 'Conservative subversives: the community of the Pale and the Dublin administration, 1556–1586', in P.J. Corish (ed.), *Radicals, Rebels and Establishments*, Historical Studies 15 (Belfast, 1985), 11–32.

[174] H.C. Walshe, 'The rebellion of William Nugent, 1581', in R.V. Comerford *et al.* (eds.), *Religion, Conflict and Coexistence in Ireland* (Dublin, 1990), 26–52: Walshe stresses the essentially localist aims and consequences of the Nugent revolt.

[175] S.G. Ellis, *Tudor Ireland: Crown Community and the Conflict of Cultures, 1470–1603* (1985), 286–7.

[176] V. Treadwell, 'The Irish parliament of 1569–71', *Proceedings of the Royal Irish Academy* 65 C (1966–7).

[177] PRO SP 63/154/37.   [178] Ibid.

past?'[179] Catholic controversialists certainly exploited the vulnerability of the Protestant churches to the charges of contempt of authority and of a denial of the continuity of the visible Church Catholic.[180] The responses of English and Scottish divines to this challenge were diverse and complex, and often very revealing of wider assumptions about the nature of the Protestant churches. Although Gifford's question had already been posed in the mid-Tudor years, it assumed full polemical significance only after 1559, when John Jewel tried to pre-empt critics in his *Apology of the Church of England*. Jewel was determined to show that the essential historical foundations for the Church of England were to be found in Scripture and in the authority of the early Church Fathers.[181] He is worth quoting in detail for his key positional statement on authority:

We have searched out of the Holy Bible, which we are sure cannot deceive, one sure form of religion, and have returned again unto the primitive church of the ancient fathers and apostles, that is to say, to the first ground and beginning of things, as unto the very foundations and headsprings of Christ's Church.[182]

For John Foxe the true Church was founded on a form of doctrine 'planted by the apostles, and taught by true bishops; afterward decayed and now reformed again'.[183] Provided that Protestants could claim to derive their doctrines and practices from the earliest Church it mattered little that the Catholics could display longevity: 'Priority', said John White, 'is the first and best antiquity.'[184]

Appeal to the primitive Church of the Fathers as the validating authority, after Scripture, of the English church permitted some interpretative flexibility in relation to two other key elements in the story, the power of councils and the role of secular authority. One of Jewel's major objectives was to assail the credentials of Trent as a true council, and he succeeded in marrying true councils to secular authority by arguing that the councils of the first five hundred years of the Church had been summoned by emperors. Trent had denied the emperor his right.[185] Moreover, since these early emperors were part of the primitive Church they must be true Christians, wielding legitimate authority, unlike their papalist successors.

---

[179] G. Gifford, *Sermons upon the Whole Book of the Revelation* (1596), 168, quoted in R. Bauckham, *Tudor Apocalypse* (Sutton Courtenay, 1978), 118.

[180] A. Milton, *Catholic and Reformed: The Roman and Protestant Churches in English Protestant Thought, 1600–1640* (Cambridge, 1995), 270–3.

[181] W.M. Southgate, *John Jewel and the Problem of Doctrinal Authority* (Cambridge, Mass., 1962), 174–91.

[182] J. Ayre (ed.), *The Works of John Jewel*, 4 vols. (PS, Cambridge, 1845–9), iii. 106.

[183] Foxe, iv. 217.

[184] J. White, *A Defence of the Way of the True Church* (1614), sig. **4ᵛ.

[185] Ayre, *Works of Jewel*, i. 62, 68, 205, 231.

John Foxe's narrative of the early Church enlarged the issue by making Constantine a model of Christian authority whose lifting of persecution foreshadows God's providential delivery of the Church of his own day. The early editions of *Acts and Monuments* include flattering comparisons between Elizabeth and her great Roman predecessor; these, however, give way after the 1570s' edition to a conspicuous silence on such parallelism. Foxe did not abandon Constantine, or the notion that he pointed the way to true godly magistracy in the Church; he certainly came to doubt whether Elizabeth would emulate her great predecessor.[186] Others within the godly mainstream were more directly critical of Constantine and, by implication, of Elizabeth. For William Harrison the emperor's willingness to trust his own spiritual judgement led to the recall of Arian heretics and hence showed how dangerous it was 'for a civil magistrate to lean unto his own wisdom in cases of doctrine'.[187]

Jewel's appeal to the primitive Church as that which validated current Protestant practice seems to have satisfied his polemical needs. The Church of Rome had subsequently descended into error, from which Protestant Christians were now being rescued. For Foxe this approach must have begged as many questions as it answered. He was at one with Jewel on the primitive Church, but early Christianity was only one stage in the providential process of the realization of God's purposes in history. The particular churches that had emerged from the Reformation were manifestations of that true Church which had constantly battled against the false Church of the Antichrist of Rome.[188] Elizabeth's church was the heir both of the pure Christianity of the early centuries and of those who 'under the cross' had battled against Rome throughout the intervening millennium. As a result the most unlikely and disparate of individuals and groups were invoked to sustain the true faith: Waldensians and Albigensians, Lollards and Hussites were heaped together. They were joined in Foxe, as in related apocalyptic narratives, as part of the invisible Church of the elect in all ages. The establishment of the Elizabethan

---

[186] M.S. Pucci, 'Reforming Roman emperors: John Foxe's characterization of Constantine in the *Acts and Monuments*', in D. Loades (ed.), *John Foxe: An Historical Perspective* (Aldershot, 1999), 29–51. Archbishop Adamson endorsed this view of Constantine from the Scottish perspective: the Christian Kirk had flourished under 'the best Emperor, Constantine'. Mullan, *Episcopacy in Scotland*, 55–6. George Buchanan, on the other hand, was always contemptuous of Constantinian kingship, precisely because of its imperialist, caesaropapist, and English implications: the emperor was dismissed as the bastard son of a general's concubine: J. Aikman (ed. and trans.), *George Buchanan's History of Scotland* (Glasgow, 1827), i. 199.

[187] G.J.R. Parry, *A Protestant Vision: William Harrison and the Reformation of Elizabethan England* (Cambridge, 1987), 240.

[188] J. Facey, 'John Foxe and the defence of the English church', in P. Lake and M. Dowling (eds.), *Protestantism and the National Church in Sixteenth-Century England* (1987), 162–92.

church under its Constantine had supposedly resolved any tension between this invisible Church and the visible church of the national community: history was fulfilled and justified. But the privileging of those few who had opposed Catholic power, and who had also often resisted the lay 'powers that be', was an awkward process that opened the possibility of a dissenting ancestry for the established church. By the end of the century those who followed Foxe from within the moderate Puritan tradition were eager to stress the relative visibility and respectability of his 'heretic' groups.[189]

While Jewel was defending the Church with the aid of the Fathers, and Foxe was elaborating the cosmic pattern of Christian history, Matthew Parker and his circle sought to confront the question of Protestant identity in a more parochial manner. Since Henry VIII's break with Rome it had been recognized that it was important to offer an English, or rather a British, history of the Church that detached it from papal influence as completely as possible.[190] The one general point of agreement was that the conversion of the British long pre-dated Augustine's Roman mission to Kent. The legends of Joseph of Arimathea and Simon Zelotes were invoked as indicators of very early evangelization, but the favoured narrative rapidly became that of Geoffrey of Monmouth's story of King Lucius and Pope Eleutherius.[191] King Lucius supposedly ruled the Britons in the late second century, and in AD 187 wrote to Rome seeking guidance on the best method of converting his people. Eleutherius responded by sending missionaries but, crucially, assured the king that he needed no further authority for conversion than that already contained in the scriptures. From these sound beginnings the British were converted to Christianity and never again lost the faith.[192] This is the aspect of the story that interested the Henrician apologists: the compilers of the *Collectanea satis copiosa* used King Lucius to demonstrate that the crown could act autonomously in religious matters. Parker's circle employed an extended narrative for rather different purposes. This included an attack on Augustine, using the more respectable Bede as well as Geoffrey. Bede's account of Augustine's inability to work with the British bishops was emphasized, and his story of the massacre of 1,200 monks of Bangor by Ethelfrid was transmuted into a claim that Augustine had sanctioned this.[193]

---

[189] Milton, *Catholic and Reformed*, 281–3.

[190] G. Williams, *Reformation Views of Church History* (Richmond, Va., 1970).

[191] G. Williams, 'Some Protestant views of early British church history', in his *Welsh Reformation Essays* (Cardiff, 1967), 207–19. Geoffrey derived a brief version of the Lucius legend from Bede.

[192] A. Fox and J. Guy, *Reassessing the Henrician Age* (Oxford, 1986), 158–71.

[193] A.M. Sellar (ed.), *Bede's Ecclesiastical History of the English People* (1912), 84–7. Bede quite clearly says that the monks came to pray for victory and blames the Celtic side for not defending them. Augustine is not blamed. M. Parker, *De Antiquitate Britanniae Ecclesiae* (1572), ii. 4.

The archbishop's engagement with the early British narratives may in part have been stimulated by Abbot Feckenham's provocative contribution to the staged debate on religion that preceded the Elizabethan settlement. Feckenham chose as his main polemic an attack on the novelty of Protestantism. This he contrasted with the continuity and fidelity of the Catholic Church in England, which since the days of King Lucius had never wholly been lost. The true faith had been imparted by Rome, and upheld by the Holy See. The sins of the original British Christians, usefully denounced by Gildas, had led to their defeat at the hands of the Saxons and the renewal of the mission under Augustine.[194] Other Catholic polemicists also made great play of the centrality of papal mission: indeed Cardinal Pole in his speech of reconciliation before the 1554 parliament extolled Britain for being the first territory to receive the gospel 'from the Apostolic see universally, and not in parts as in other countries'.[195] Harding taunted Jewel with the same points in his debate on the *Apology*, and the latter was forced twice to deviate from his concerns for the primitive Church to debate the role of Eleutherius and to denounce Augustine.[196] Others such as Calfhill used the Lucius and Augustine stories to prove the English church's claim to ancient independence of Rome, and the deleterious effect of the papal mission.[197] But it was left to Parker in his *De Antiquitate Britanniae Ecclesiae* (1572), to put together all the early narratives to justify his claim that the British church was indeed the most ancient of territorial churches and that it owed no significant debt to Rome beyond assistance with evangelism.[198]

While Parker's overwhelming concern was to prove that the Church of England had a history independent of Rome, the narrative of early Christianity also focused controversialists on the relationship between the churches of the British Isles. Could all claim pre-papal origin? If so, were all foreordained to share a common opposition to Rome, and was an institutional bond thereby created between them? The claim that the British churches were at the inception of a continuous tradition of Christianity more significant than papal authority inevitably made the Welsh church, in Richard Davies's words, the senior sister of its English counterpart. In his introduction to the Welsh translation of the New Testament Davies constructed an ecclesiastical history that made Protestantism both ancient and Welsh, the 'once most glorious heritage' of his nation.[199] It was probably more significant to this generation of Welsh Protestants to

---

[194] Gee, *Elizabethan Prayer Book*, 229–30.   [195] Foxe, vi. 569.

[196] Ayre, *Works of Jewel*, i. 300–6; iii. 164–5.

[197] J. Calfhill, *Answer to John Martiall's Treatise of the Cross*, ed. R. Gibbings (PS, Cambridge, 1846), 305–7.

[198] Parker, *De Antiquitate*, sig. ii^v, 2–7.

[199] Williams, 'Early British church history', 212–13.

make their faith congruent with their own cultural identity than to link it with England: in practice it was of course possible to do both, because the English church needed its pre-Saxon ancestry so urgently.

The story was very different in the case of Ireland and of Scotland. For Ireland in the late Tudor period there was really no strong indigenous Protestant church whose historical roots yet needed to be purged of Roman corruption. Only in the early seventeenth century, when Protestantism had begun to establish its position as the religion of the minority, did the Anglo-Irish begin to address this issue.[200] The key figure is James Ussher, who in 1613 began his contribution to the history of Protestant controversy with *Gravissimae quaestionis*. This essentially followed Foxe in identifying a true Church that had over the centuries maintained its integrity amid the decline and corruption of papal power. This was later followed by his much bolder confrontation of Catholic claims to purity of Irish descent from the papally inspired conversion by St Patrick. He denounced the errors of Edmund Campion, who had believed that the Irish gave themselves to Rome in temporalities as well as spiritualities. Instead he succeeded in proving, to his own satisfaction, that the original Irish church had been pure, biblical, and largely out of the control of Rome.[201] Ussher performed the interesting feat of making the Irish church both autonomous and closely integrated with its Protestant neighbours. He used the evidence of Bede to affirm that the five peoples of the islands in his day 'confess one and the same knowledge of the highest truth', with scriptures available to all. But the Irish church, as converted by Patrick, was clearly separate unto itself, and, by implication at least, must so remain.[202]

The Scottish understanding of the 'early British church' was complicated by contested histories that reflected the complex relationships between northern and southern neighbours.[203] One reading, essentially English, had King Lucius as ruler over the whole island, converting all its peoples. Another, equally favoured by the English, identified Constantine as a pan-British monarch, upholding a unified and Christian island society. The Scots had an alternative in the medieval invention of a conversion by missionaries sent by Pope Victor to King Donald in AD 190. However, the

---

[200] A. Ford, ' "Standing one's ground": religion, polemic and Irish history since the Reformation', in A. Ford, J. McGuire, and K. Milne (eds.), *As by Law Established: The Church of Ireland since the Reformation* (Dublin, 1995), 2–3.

[201] J. Ussher, 'Gravissimae quaestionis', in C.R. Elrington (ed.), *The Whole Works of James Ussher*, 17 vols. (Dublin, 1864), ii. 1 ff.; and 'A discourse of the religion anciently professed by the Irish and British', ibid., iv. 238–9.

[202] Elrington, *Works of Ussher*, iv. 243.

[203] R.A. Mason, ' "Scotching the Brut": the early history of Britain', in J. Wormald (ed.), *Scotland Revisited* (1991), 49–59. A.H. Williamson, *Scottish National Consciousness in the Age of James VI* (Edinburgh, 1979), 117 ff.

reformers seem understandably to have been reluctant to adapt this story, 'from the time of blindness', to Protestant needs. Instead when they reflected on the historical origins of their faith they were most likely to think of a diffusionist model, acknowledging the priority of British Christianity, but seeing the conversion of Scotland as being the work of small groups fleeing from the persecution of Diocletian.[204] This had the double advantage of denying the significance of papal mission, and of detaching Scottish Christianity from any taint of monarchical or imperialist conversion. Thus Calderwood, building on the original work of Buchanan, argued, 'it is probable . . . that the Christian Britons were the first teachers of the Christian faith to the Scots'.[205]

Both the importance and the plasticity of the early history of the British churches are suggested by the example of one of the few English controversialists who denied the King Lucius story. Thomas Cartwright did so in his disputes with Whitgift, taking pleasure in assailing the 'false Geoffrey'. Instead he reverted to Gildas to argue that the faith had been received slowly from the time of Tiberius onwards, by groups of individuals 'some boldly . . . some soundly'.[206] Like the Scottish reformers, English Presbyterians had no desire to 'stand their ground' on a church that claimed its birth from royal fiat and was articulated in a hierarchy of bishops, the inheritors of the Lucian titles 'flamines' and 'archiflamines'. Zealous reformers were anyway more likely to be concerned with the providential and apocalyptic justifications for the true Church than with its historical roots. The inception of Knox's *History of the Reformation in Scotland* is characteristic of this approach. God has 'caused light to shine out of darkness, in the multitude of his mercies' and has 'made his truth so to triumph among us that, in despite of Satan, hypocrisy is disclosed'. The struggle for truth had its own history for Knox: a drastically foreshortened narrative, in which only the immediate 'morning-stars of Reformation' signified. Future generations studying his contemporary history could be taught 'how wondrously hath the light of Christ Jesus prevailed against darkness in this last and most corrupted age'.[207] A Foxeian vision of the cycles of Christian history was implicit, but Knox's Church needed no legitimation beyond its appeal to God's providential judgement in favour of those who had struggled against the Antichrist.[208]

The *Acts and Monuments*, for all its profound and complex historical understanding, could readily be used as a text for an intensely dualistic and

---

[204] Aikman, *Buchanan's History of Scotland*, i. 188, 199.   [205] Calderwood, i. 37.

[206] T. Cartwright, *The Second Replie of Thomas Cartwright against Maister Doctor Whitgifts Seconde Answer touching Churche Discipline* (Heidelberg, 1575), 472–5.

[207] Knox, i. 3–5.

[208] K.R. Firth, *The Apocalyptic Tradition in Reformation Britain* (Oxford, 1979), 125–8.

separatist reading of the history of the Protestant churches. The appropriation of Foxe by a diverse group of radicals from Henry Barrow onwards indicated the possibilities of the text and perhaps justified some of the anxieties articulated by the second and third generation of Elizabeth's bishops. Whitgift gave serious consideration to the possibility of an alternative history of the Church, one which would build on Parker's researches and look explicitly to the justification of the Elizabethan settlement.[209] Nothing came of this, but the archbishop was later offered an opportunity to 'manage' subversive interpretations of Foxe by supporting the abridgement of *Acts and Monuments* by Timothy Bright. Bright cut and pasted in ways which directed the reader in no uncertain terms. He made much of the King Lucius story, which Foxe had doubted though ultimately accepted, and he directly linked the establishment of episcopacy with that monarch's efforts at conversion. In his preface Bright spoke with extraordinary confidence of England as 'the first that embraced the Gospel: the only establisher of it throughout the world: and the first reformed'.[210] In 1589 when it was published this was, at one level, an example of the shift, in the celebratory aftermath of the Armada, from Foxe's cautious acceptance of England as 'an elect nation' to the triumphalism that God was English. Yet for the bishops it should probably be seen as a particularist affirmation of the integrity and historicity of their church, a defence against Puritan charges that it was 'but halfly reformed'.[211]

At the end of the century the debate about the nature of the Protestant churches and their origins was again shifted by Hooker in his *Laws of Ecclesiastical Polity*. Hooker accepted both the Jewel arguments for the congruence of the practice and belief of the Church of England with that of the primitive Church, and Parker's insistence on the importance of the foundation myths of British Christianity. However, his primary objective was to affirm the catholicity and the rationality of the Church of England: to situate it once again within a more universalist framework of law and faith. Men were endowed with reason so that they could apprehend the divine will as articulated through Scripture, and it was through the 'authority of God's church' that those reasoning processes were exercised.[212] The visible Church that interpreted Scripture had, for Hooker, to be a

[209] D. Nussbaum, 'Whitgift's "Book of Martyrs": Archbishop Whitgift, Timothy Bright and the Elizabethan struggle over John Foxe's legacy', in D. Loades (ed.), *John Foxe* (Aldershot, 1999), 135–53.

[210] T. Bright, *An Abridgement of the Booke of Acts and Monuments* (1589), preface, 68–9.

[211] Parry, *William Harrison*, 189–92. On the Englishness of God in the 1580s see below, ch. 10, pp. 481–2.

[212] R. Hooker, *Laws of Ecclesiastical Polity*, iii. 1. 3. Citations from J. Keble (ed.), *The Works of Richard Hooker*, 3 vols. (Oxford, 1841).

continuous entity 'from the first beginning of the world to the last end', though it could take particular shapes in different environments.[213] There could scarcely have been a sharper break from the Foxeian vision of the historical Church. Hooker explicitly denied that the test of the true Church was the witness of faithful believers in the succession of underground congregations or individual witnesses.[214] Instead he insisted that the popish church must be part of the true Church, albeit one that had become corrupted in its beliefs and practices. The Church of England was a reformed continuation of the one visible and Catholic Church. Suddenly it became easy to answer the 'where was your church?' question.[215] 'In the church', averred Hooker, 'we were, and we are so still.' The affirmation might be easy: the consequences of this profound rereading were to haunt the Church for the next century and far beyond.[216]

Hierarchy and Discipline

When the kirk of St Andrews recorded the institution of its superintendent John Winram in 1561 it noted that 'without the care [of] superintendents neither can the kirk be suddenly erected, neither can th[ey] be retained in discipline and unity of doctrine'.[217] Order and godliness were to be achieved in this unregenerate world through a hierarchical structure and discipline. Calvin's description of discipline as the 'sinews' of the Church was affirmed in the Scots Confession and in the Book of Common Order.[218] It was also a view that found favour with the first generation of Elizabeth's divines, especially those who had experienced exile. Jewel talked about discipline as the entity which strengthened the Church, joining and knitting its parts together, and years later Sandys called it the church's third net in which to take 'the little foxes which destroy the vines'.[219] In the high years of Protestant anticipation of full reform the claim that discipline was the third mark of the true Church had even crept into the official catechism of 1553.[220] Whether or not it became an

---

[213] Hooker, *Laws of Ecclesiastical Polity*, iii. 1. 10.

[214] P. Lake, *Anglicans and Puritans? Presbyterianism and English Conformist Thought from Whitgift to Hooker* (1988), 153–62.

[215] Milton, *Catholic and Reformed*, 128–72.

[216] *Laws of Ecclesiastical Polity*, iii. 1. 10, in Keble, *Works of Hooker*.

[217] D. Hay Fleming (ed.), *Register of the Ministers, Elders, and Deacons of the Christian Congregation of St Andrews*, pt. 1: *1559–82* (Edinburgh, 1889), 75.

[218] Knox, iv. 203.

[219] Ayre, *Works of Jewel*, ii. 986. J. Ayre (ed.), *The Sermons of Edwyn Sandys D.D.* (PS, Cambridge, 1841), 71–2: the metaphor continues the Protestant tradition of identifying the fox with 'Romish practice'.

[220] J. Ketley (ed.), *The Two Liturgies of the Reign of Edward VI* (PS, Cambridge, 1844), 513.

identifying mark of the true Church, the demand that a reformed church should exercise a thorough control over the people was common to all the reformers. Magistrates had, in the Prayer Book's words, a duty 'truly and indifferently [to] minister justice, to the punishment of wickedness and vice', but where sin and error abounded the Church had the responsibility for its correction.[221]

Proper discipline was a necessary objective of the Protestant churches. The question was how was it to be achieved, and by whom? John Knox's answer, bred of his Genevan experience and of his mistrust of the exercise of lay magisterial power in Edwardian England, was that control was most properly to be exercised by the congregation constituted according to the principles of Scripture.[222] Before the advent of the presbyterian system in the 1580s this meant the development of local kirk sessions, which spread unevenly through urban Scotland after 1560. The impact of these sessions will concern us later: here it may suffice to note that even in those burghs which quickly established functioning disciplinary mechanisms, progress towards Knox's goals was spasmodic. St Andrews has been much studied as a model of 'perfect reform'.[223] Aberdeen has been identified as essentially traditionalist, with its urban magistrates seeking to behave as they always had, except when required by public pressure to display a façade of godly zeal.[224] At the level of the national church Knox seems to have had no difficulty in accepting the idea of superintendency, as it was added to the First Book of Discipline, by which essentially supervisory tasks were to be assigned to ministers of particular distinction. Superintendents were to become the visitors of the Kirk, preaching, admitting ministers and readers, convening local synods, ensuring the good repair of churches. By 1565 the General Assembly had added to these powers the right of excommunication, the highest form of disciplinary power, in those areas where the Kirk had not yet established full local reformed practice. Elsewhere the power of the local sessions was upheld, though there was a *de facto* expectation that they often operated in collaboration with the superintendent in difficult cases. When disciplinary problems outran the capacity of the local community to resolve

---

[221] Ibid., 87.

[222] M.F. Graham, 'Knox on discipline: conversionary zeal or rose-tinted nostalgia', in Mason, *Knox and the British Reformations*, 268–86.

[223] J.A. Dawson, '"The face of ane perfyt reformed kyrk": St Andrews and the early Scottish Reformation', in J. Kirk (ed.), *Humanism and Reform: The Church in Europe, England and Scotland 1400–1600*, SCH Subsidia 8 (Oxford, 1991), 413–35. G. Parker, 'The "Kirk by Law Established" and the origins of "the Taming of Scotland": St Andrews 1559–1600', in R. Mentzer (ed.), *Sin and Calvinists: Moral Control and the Consistory in the Reformed Tradition* (Kirksville, Mo., 1994), 158–97.

[224] A. White, 'The impact of the Reformation on a burgh community: the case of Aberdeen', in M. Lynch (ed.), *The Early Modern Town in Scotland* (1987), 81–101.

them, the instinct of the Kirk already in the 1560s was to turn to the higher councils of synod and General Assembly.[225]

It is easy to argue that the very different nature of the Elizabethan settlement inevitably produced a very different interpretation of order for England, Wales, and Ireland. An inherently conservative political settlement sustained a traditional view of ecclesiastical order, with a hierarchy of clerics and discipline left firmly in the hands of the church courts in their unreconstructed form. But the story of the early Elizabethan years includes some hypothetical possibilities that modify this picture. The first generation of bishops, especially those who had experienced exile, were motivated by the idea that they were above all preaching pastors, leading their clergy by spiritual example and instruction. Some, like Jewel, were willing to own the title of superintendent, and to see themselves as no more than seniors among a group of preaching pastors.[226] Others, notably Grindal, seem to have been directly influenced by Martin Bucer's theories of church government in *De Regno Christi*, in which the great reformer emphasized the pastoral and supervisory role of the bishops. Discipline should be exercised in a personal, moral, and restorative framework, with other clergy assisting the bishop, and these lesser ministers, or *chorepiscopi*, should be joined together as a synod to preside over the local clergy.[227] Aylmer seems to have been attracted by something like this scheme when he responded to Knox's challenge about lordly prelates by suggesting that 'every city [may have] his superintendent'.[228] In the practice of the Elizabethan church it seemed from time to time that rural deans might become Bucer's *chorepiscopi*. Thomas Bentham, bishop of Coventry and Lichfield, ordered in 1563 that moral offences should be reported quarterly to the dean, while in the parliament of 1571 Nicholas Bacon proposed that rural deans should be given ordinary courts 'for the well executing of those laws of discipline'.[229] This last suggestion was taken up in a general proposal for making the rural deans of Norwich diocese into godly supervisors in 1578.[230]

The opportunities for change should not, however, be exaggerated. Not only did the queen, the laity, the system of patronage, and existing ecclesiastical structures militate against any major reform: elements in the

---

[225] Kirk, 'Superintendent', in *Patterns of Reform*, 182–8.

[226] Ayre, *Works of Jewel*, iv. 906.

[227] M. Bucer, *De Regno Christi*, ed. F. Wendel, Opera Latina 15 (1955), 118. P. Collinson, 'The reformer and the archbishop: Martin Bucer and an English Bucerian' in his *Godly People*, 19–44.

[228] Aylmer, *An harborowe*, sig. O4ᵛ.

[229] P. Collinson, 'Episcopacy and reform in England in the later sixteenth century', in *Godly People*, 169–75. HMC Salisbury MSS, ii. 195–8.

[230] Collinson sees the prophesyings as proving some substitute for the weakness of the rural deanery scheme, since they embraced both edification and moral discipline.

thinking even of the bishops of this first generation look very different from those of the Scottish reformers. James Pilkington was one of the exiles who believed in the essential parity of ministers and bishops and in many ways accepted that the latter were godly overseers. But the confidence with which he spoke of prelacy in 1561 is qualitatively different from anything that John Winram or Erskine of Dun might have uttered:

> The power and authority of bishops is spiritual, belonging to man's soul, as their office and ministry is; and it stands chiefly in these two points, in doctrine and discipline... God's minister [has] in his church full power and authority to teach sound doctrine, and confute the false;... to bind and loose the conscience by virtue of God's word;... to cast out of God's church, and receive again, such as he rightly judges by the scriptures meet for mercy or justice.[231]

Control lay properly in the hands of the bishops. They must indeed, as Sandys urged in a pastoral letter to Chaderton, bishop of Chester, feed the flock, but 'sin should not be allowed to burst the bonds of established law and fly abroad with impunity'.[232] There seem to have been few reservations about the exercise of power, including the power of excommunication. Bishops were pastors to their flock, and the latter were required to obey, not to participate in moral discipline and regeneration within their own congregations.[233] Even the sensitive Grindal would not brook direct challenge to his authority in London in the latter stages of the vestiarian controversy. Whitgift's generation of bishops acquiesced gladly in the monarchical and prelatical church: their predecessors did so with some heart-searching, but also with some belief in the true merits of episcopal leadership.[234]

Moderate Puritans might have tolerated a measure of pastoral assertiveness by the bishops had it been matched with a willingness to see discipline as primarily a process of moral regeneration, conducted in congregation, parish, and synod.[235] As it was they feared from the outset that the old systems of ecclesiastical courts and canon law would permit no such redemptive intimacy. 'No discipline is as yet established by any public authority,' Thomas Lever reported to Zurich at the beginning of the reign, and nothing that occurred in the next forty years would have led him to change his views.[236] When more radical Puritans finally took the risk of trying to establish 'presbytery in episcopacy' in the early 1580s,

---

[231] J. Scholefield (ed.), *The Works of James Pilkington* (PS, Cambridge, 1842), 491–2.

[232] Ayre, *Sermons of Sandys*, 440.

[233] In these early years Jewel and Alexander Nowell were prepared to consider that even the prince could be subject to ecclesiastical censure, an idea quietly dropped thereafter.

[234] P. Collinson, *The Religion of Protestants: The Church in English Society, 1559–1625* (Oxford, 1982), 10–38; *Archbishop Grindal*, 52–4.

[235] Ayre, *Sermons of Sandys*, 419.   [236] ZL i. 84.

it was the desire for proper fraternal order and discipline that proved the crucial catalyst. The Dedham conference, established in Suffolk in 1582, combined features of the earlier 'prophesyings' with a more institutionalized desire to subject its members to local, and essentially congregational, control.[237] At the national level the leaders of the presbyterian movement were deeply influenced by their, imperfect, understanding of the situation in Scotland. The *Admonition* had asked rhetorically 'Is discipline meet for Scotland? And is it unprofitable for this realm?'[238] And when Andrew Melville and his colleagues had to pass the winter of 1584–5 in exile in London they became an important influence on the construction of that most radical of presbyterian texts, the Book of Discipline. Its author, Walter Travers, provided for the first time a fully considered rejection of episcopal discipline in all its forms, and followed the Scots in their separation of spiritual and secular power. The logical outcome of fraternal discipline was the denial that the supreme governor had any role in the regulation of the Church.[239]

For the episcopate any yearning for full moral and spiritual discipline had little place in the Elizabethan polity. The quest for order meant primarily the enforcement of a basic conformity to the parameters of the settlement: moral control was left in the uncertain hands of the church courts. Although Protestant non-conformity produced some spectacular conflicts, the quotidian experience of the ecclesiastical hierarchy was far more that of ensuring obedience from alienated Catholics. The principal device for the enforcement of conformity, the ecclesiastical commission, was established by legislation in 1559, before any of the Protestant episcopate had been consecrated.[240] The commission in theory circumvented the general problem that the church courts had only one significant weapon to use to discipline the laity: that of excommunication. It was a weapon that had power only in circumstances where the Church commanded ideological assent. The ecclesiastical commission had powers to fine and imprison: as Bishop Horne expressed it vividly, the men of Hampshire feared 'punishment by the purse more than God's curse'.[241] Moreover the addition of laymen offered the possibility of strengthening clerical authority. The national commissions were slowly reinforced by

---

[237] Collinson, *Puritan Movement*, 222–39.

[238] W.H. Frere and C.E. Douglas (eds.), *Puritan Manifestoes: A Story of the Origin of the Puritan Revolt* (1954), 19.

[239] Collinson, *Puritan Movement*, 291–302. T. Fuller, *The Church History of Britain*, ed. J.S. Brewer, 6 vols. (Oxford, 1845), v. 7.

[240] For a general survey of the ecclesiastical commissions see P. Tyler's introduction to the 1969 edition of R.G. Usher, *The Rise and Fall of the High Commission*. P. Tyler, 'The significance of the ecclesiastical commission at York', *Northern History* 2 (1967), 27–44.

[241] BL Lans. MS 12, fos. 63, 74.

diocesan bodies that have left only limited archival evidence of their activities.[242]

The bishops at times spoke optimistically of the possibilities offered by the ecclesiastical commission. Parker and Sandys, inviting participation of one of their colleagues in the attack on Dering in 1573, wrote of the good their meeting could do for the 'maintenance of [the] gospel, establishing of decent and good order, to the edifying of [God's] people, and to the repressing of all gainsayers'.[243] Adam Loftus regarded the provision of a strong ecclesiastical commission as the only effective way of instituting discipline in the Irish church.[244] Bishop Horne was only one of a number of English bishops who saw a commission as the answer to the current 'want of severe discipline'.[245] But high expectations seem only intermittently to have been fulfilled. The laity who supposedly strengthened the disciplinary hands of the prelates often proved a disappointment. Catholic recusancy was a constant and intractable problem, compounded by the reluctance of gentlemen to prosecute their neighbours. Even the relative success of the central commission produced its own difficulties. 'Papistry', said Parker in 1573, 'is the chief wherein we should deal, and yet the clamorous cry of some needy wives and husbands do compel us to take their matters out of their common bribing courts, to ease their griefs in commission'.[246] Ultimately the urgent political need to combat Catholic recusancy in the 1580s displaced the commissions in favour of penal laws enforced by the state, and conflict about Archbishop Whitgift's campaign against Puritan non-conformity may have subverted the local tribunals from within. Roger Manning has even suggested that the emergence of *iure divino* views of episcopacy owed something to the bishops' inability to make the commissions serve their purposes.[247]

The commissions were never intended to replace the ordinary disciplinary controls of the church courts. Throughout Elizabeth's reign the English, Welsh, and Irish bishops had to accept that their ability to extirpate sin and ensure spiritual conformity depended on a body of legal

---

[242] By 1570 Archbishop Parker, in organizing the detail of a new ecclesiastical commission, was convinced of the significance of its local dimension: he asked Cecil to ensure that there was no administrative overlap between Winchester, Chichester, and Canterbury commissioners: Perowne, *Correspondence of Parker*, 370–1. One of the few examples of a local commission at work, and functioning quite effectively, is F.D. Price (ed.), *The Commission for Ecclesiastical Causes within the Dioceses of Bristol and Gloucester, 1574*, Bristol and Gloucestershire Archaeological Society, Records Section, 10 (Gateshead, 1972).

[243] Perowne, *Correspondence of Parker*, 435.

[244] See particularly his letters to Burghley: PRO SP 63/42/76, 63/71/9. *CSP Irl* iv. 517–18.

[245] BL Lans. MS 12, fo. 74.

[246] Perowne, *Correspondence of Parker*, 450.

[247] R.B. Manning, 'The crisis of episcopal authority during the reign of Elizabeth I', *JBS* 11 (1971), 23–5.

officials and a pattern of courts scarcely altered since the Reformation.[248]
When Richard Cosin sought to defend these bodies and their procedures
against the combined attacks of the godly and the common lawyers in his
1591 *Apologie*, he offered a clever lawyer's justification of civil law proceedings and the virtues of order.[249] Largely untouched was the fundamental issue of what law was appropriate to a reformed church.
Elizabeth's notorious reluctance to alter the settlement left the bishops
without the ability to revise canon law in significant ways, and until 1604
the law of the church was a patchwork of old Catholic practice onto
which had been grafted specific measures relevant to the new orthodoxy.[250] In 1598 the bishops collectively protested that they were assailed
by the common lawyers and given insufficient support from the crown
that should have upheld their power.[251] Individually they were also prone
to lament that their dependence on lawyers to staff their courts meant
that they were thwarted by conservatism and sometimes by outright corruption in their deputies. These laments had some justification, especially
in the first Elizabethan generation when officials inherited from the mid-
century remained in place, and inexperienced administrators like Cheney
of Gloucester had no means of managing them successfully.[252]

But it can be suggested that the bishops did protest too much, and that
historians have been too ready to take them at their word. The courts, as
Ingram and others have argued, were not necessarily unpopular with the
English people, nor were their disciplinary weapons wholly redundant.[253]
And, while the prelates portrayed themselves as ground between the
upper millstone of crown indifference and the nether millstone of lay
hostility, much could in practice be achieved by a determined bishop.[254]
For example, visitation was conducted regularly and systematically in most

[248] The best short summary of the activity of the courts remains R.A. Houlbrooke, 'The
decline of ecclesiastical jurisdiction under the Tudors', in R. O'Day and F. Heal (eds.), *Continuity and Change: Personnel and Administration of the Church in England, 1500–1642* (Leicester, 1976),
239–57. See also his *Church Courts and the People during the English Reformation, 1520–1570*
(Oxford, 1979). R.A. Marchant, *The Church under the Law: Justice, Administration and Discipline in
the Diocese of York, 1560–1640* (Cambridge, 1969).
[249] R. Cosin, *An Apologie: of, and for Sundrie Proceedings by Jurisdiction Ecclesiasticall* (1591).
Cosin's main objective was the defence of *ex officio* proceedings in High Commission: J. Guy,
'The Elizabethan establishment and the ecclesiastical polity', in J. Guy (ed.), *The Reign of
Elizabeth I: Court and Culture in the Last Decade* (Cambridge, 1995), 137–47.
[250] R. Helmholz, *Roman Canon Law in Reformation England* (Cambridge, 1990), 34 ff.
[251] J. Strype, *The Life of John Whitgift, D.D.* (1718), 521–2. BL Harl. MS 358, fo. 186.
[252] F.D. Price, 'An Elizabethan church official: Thomas Powell, chancellor of Gloucester
diocese', *Church Quarterly Review* 128 (1939), 94–112.
[253] M. Ingram, *Church Courts, Sex and Marriage in England, 1570–1640* (Cambridge, 1987). See
Helmholz on the creativity of ecclesiastical lawyers.
[254] R. Houlbrooke, 'The Protestant episcopate 1547–1603: the pastoral contribution', in
F. Heal and R. O'Day (eds.), *Church and Society in England, Henry VIII to James I* (1977), 90–4.

Elizabethan dioceses, and visitation articles attest to the wide range of issues addressed on circuit.[255] Several of the first Elizabethan generation were powerfully involved in these progresses—Grindal, Jewel, and Horne predictable names among them. Later there may have been less need to supervise officials whose religious loyalties were suspect, but it is clear from a Whitgift directive of 1591 that he still expected bishops to visit in person.[256] Bishops could, and occasionally did, sit in their own consistory courts. In particularly trying cases the bishops could attempt to circumvent their own officials, as Grindal did at York when he sent his own chaplains around the deaneries to discover the actual state of the parochial clergy.[257] The importance of these supervisory roles is revealed by the comparison with Scotland, where the exact nature of the visitatorial powers of superintendents, commissioners, and bishops was a long-running source of conflict within the Kirk. The Second Book of Discipline defined a visitor as not an 'ordinary office ecclesiastical in the person of one man', that power was held by the congregation, but in reality supervision was necessary, and its success depended on the capacities of one man and his assistants.[258]

The political and social circumstances of late sixteenth-century Britain made it difficult for the bishops to achieve their objectives of reformation combined with good discipline. In the case of Ireland these goals appear well-nigh impossible. Bishop Brady of Meath, the Irish-born reformer who had all the attributes necessary for proper Protestant leadership, certainly found it so.[259] At the other end of a spectrum one might take the episcopate of John Jewel in the reasonably manageable Diocese of Salisbury. Jewel did not escape from the frustrations of office—some of his later correspondence with Zurich sounds weary in its denunciations of non-conformity—but his energy in visitation and in personal supervision of his see seems to have been rewarded by general acquiescence to his rule.[260] In a later generation Matthew Hutton, as bishop of Durham and then archbishop of York, may be taken as another exemplar of the effective Protestant prelate, unbending in his pursuit of papists and committed to the preaching ministry.[261] But energy and reforming zeal were not sufficient to guarantee a successful episcopate, even in the relatively stable

[255] *VAI* iii, *passim*. H.G. Owen, 'The episcopal visitation: its limits and limitations in Elizabethan London', *JEH* 11 (1960), 179–85, takes a less sanguine view of disciplinary possibilities.
[256] Strype, *Whitgift*, Appendix, 168–9.
[257] J.S. Purvis (ed.), *Tudor Parish Documents of the Diocese of York* (Cambridge, 1948), 109–25.
[258] Kirk, *Second Book of Discipline*, 197. Mullan, *Episcopacy in Scotland*, 52–3.
[259] Walshe, 'Bishop Brady', 352–76.
[260] *VAI* i. 168. Southgate, *John Jewel*, 64–79.
[261] P. Lake, 'Matthew Hutton: a Puritan bishop?' *History* 64 (1979), 182–204.

dioceses of southern England. Bishop Curteys of Chichester had both in abundance in the 1570s, but failed to recognize the importance of collaboration with the local lay elites. His proceedings against the most distinguished lay conservatives in his diocese without adequate sanction from the Privy Council led to reprimand and effective disgrace before the local community.[262] Finally we might note two examples of the limited authority of prelates being used effectively in the unpromising circumstances of Elizabethan Wales. Richard Davies, successively bishop of St Asaph and St David's, is famous primarily for his translation of the New Testament into Welsh. He was also a conscientious, resident diocesan in both sees, labouring with inadequate resources to introduce the beginnings of Protestant discipline. Like Curteys, he was appalled by gentry and justices who defended 'papistry, superstition and idolatry'. However, he seems to have had a better understanding of what could be achieved within his jurisdiction.[263] A generation later Henry Rowlands, bishop of Bangor from 1594 to 1616, showed the merits of being fully integrated into local society as a native son who preached and showed outstanding piety as an example to his Protestant flock.[264]

Financing the Churches

'The temporalty', complained John Whitgift in 1575, 'seek to make the clergy beggars, that we may depend upon them.'[265] Conspiracy theory already had its attractions to the future archbishop, and there were no doubt those among the laity who did indeed equate poor clerics with subservient ones. It is more convincing, however, to invert the argument and say that any display of clerical wealth was likely to attract lay hostility, that automatic reflex of anti-clericalism that was a feature of the English elite. Lord Burghley complained bitterly of the 'evil examples in covetousness, looseness of life and many other defaults' that he found among the proud prelates.[266] 'The care of this world', wrote the earl of Leicester to Bishop Scambler, 'truly hath choked you all...'.[267] 'Let the godliest man', said a friend of the Puritan Thomas Wood, 'put once a rochet on his back, and it bringeth with it such an infection that will mar him

---

[262] R.B. Manning, *Religion and Society in Elizabethan Sussex* (Leicester, 1969), 78–90.

[263] G. Williams, *Wales and the Reformation* (Cardiff, 1997), 218, 228–30, 233–4, 389.

[264] Sir John Wynn of Gwydir registered great surprise that Rowland discharged all the obligations of a good bishop 'yet died rich': Sir John Wynn, *History of the Gwydir Family* (1827), 102–6.

[265] White Kennett, *The Case of Impropriations Truly Stated* (1704), app. ix, p. 21.

[266] PRO SP 12/4/40.

[267] P. Collinson (ed.), 'Letters of Thomas Wood, puritan, 1566–1577', in his *Godly People*, 77.

forever.'[268] The lordly bishops remained the prime target for this type of criticism, but archdeacons, deans, and their prebendaries all attracted their share of contempt, and at the parochial level tithe disputes and visitation returns provide a repository of hostile comment on greedy and wealthy ministers.[269] Henry Trickett, vicar of Marston and Doveridge in Lichfield diocese, was accused by his parishioners of living 'as a layman', purchasing land, and lending money at interest; while the dreadful John Otes of Carnaby in the East Riding of Yorkshire was rightly charged with money-grubbing by his aggrieved flock.[270] The ministers of the Scottish Kirk were not immune from these criticisms: the motives of those bishops and clergy who had converted to the reform and retained their benefices were questioned, and by the end of the century the new Protestant prelates were being accused by their enemies of avarice and worldly ambition.[271]

Conversely, clerical commentators of all ideological complexions were in little doubt that the laity was a constant threat to the possessions of the Church. 'Too much dignity and authority', thought William Crashaw, '[has been taken] from our ministry and...too much poverty, contempt and baseness [laid] upon it.'[272] At the parochial level he blamed the pernicious system of impropriations, which by 'sacrilege and church robbing' impoverished livings, 'which is the source and fountain of all other evils in our church'. Whitgift agreed, in 1588 calculating the loss to the Church in England and Wales at £100,000. Grindal was bold enough to complain directly to the queen that the Church of England had been spoiled by the process.[273] Even more impressively Edward Dering denounced her in a court sermon for 'let[ting] all alone', while benefices were defiled by impropriation and patrons were given to simony.[274] The Scottish ministers felt equally bitter, denouncing the 'insatiable sacrilegious avarice' of earls, lords, and gentlemen, who deprived the clergy of proper maintenance.[275]

---

[268] Ibid., 101.   [269] F. Heal, *Of Prelates and Princes* (Cambridge, 1980), 202–22.

[270] R. O'Day, *The English Clergy: The Emergence and Consolidation of a Profession* (Leicester, 1979), 186. P. Marshall, *The Face of the Pastoral Ministry in the East Riding, 1525–1595*, Borthwick Papers 88 (York, 1995), 19, and esp. 'Discord and stability in an Elizabethan parish: John Otes and Carnaby, 1563–1600', *YAJ* 71 (1999), 185–99. W.J. Sheils, '"The right of the church": the clergy, tithe and the courts of York, 1540–1640', in W.J. Sheils and D. Wood (eds), *The Church and Wealth*, SCH 24 (Oxford, 1987), 231–55.

[271] Kirk, *Patterns of Reform*, 312; *Second Book of Discipline*, 33; *BUK* i. 166–7. Mullan, *Episcopacy in Scotland*, 127–8.

[272] W. Crashaw, *Preface to William Perkins's Of the Calling of the Ministerie* (Cambridge, 1608), 2. D.J. Lamburn, 'Petty Babylons, godly prophets, petty pastors and little churches: the work of healing Babel', in W.J. Sheils and D. Wood (eds.), *The Ministry: Clerical and Lay*, SCH 26 (Oxford, 1989), 237–9.

[273] C. Hill, *Economic Problems of the Church from Archbishop Whitgift to the Long Parliament* (Oxford, 1956), 139, 145, 14–38.

[274] E. Dering, *A Sermon Preached before the Queenes Maiestie*, in *Workes* (1614), sig. L8.

[275] Pitcairn, *Autobiography and Diary of Melvill*, 188.

The crisis was most dramatically visible in the case of the English higher clergy. Why, Abbot Feckenham asked his Protestant opponents in 1559, should he wish to join a church in which he could see nothing but spoil 'of bishops' houses and of colleges' lands'?[276] The crown duly confirmed his prejudices by promoting the Act of Exchange that took valuable episcopal estates and permitted long leases of episcopal property to be made only to itself.[277] Thereafter the story of episcopal possessions was one of constant struggle to protect them against the predatory interests of courtiers and other members of the elite who turned to the crown for material rewards. While the queen lived there was little relief, despite the conspicuous favour that she could on occasions display to individuals.

For defenders of the Elizabethan establishment threats to the wealth of the prelates were as damaging as the impoverishment of the parishes. Hooker argued that 'to make the bishops poorer than they are were to make them of less account and estimation than they should be'.[278] But here, of course, the bishops and their critics parted company acrimoniously. The general position of the godly was that the resources of the Church were its own to manage for the good of the gospel.[279] The good of the gospel was, however, defined explicitly as the good of the presbyterian church: the funding of preachers, and of the discipline. Even moderate Puritans showed no enthusiasm for episcopal wealth, arguing instead that it should largely be diverted for the benefit of the parishes. The bitterness of this division usually prevented clerics from making common cause in defence of proper funding for the Church, despite many shared assumptions. Indeed, ideological hostility could persuade polemicists to encourage the very lay voracity that most churchmen feared. John Penry sought the earl of Essex's help for the overthrow of the bishops with the words, 'I offer your lordship of her [the church's] spoil.'[280] On the other party Richard Bancroft denounced the presbyterians as threatening hierarchy and the rights of property and sought political capital by raising the old spectre that the godly aimed to reappropriate monastic land.[281] As

---

[276] Strype, *Annals*, i. i. 529.

[277] On the Act of Exchange see F. Heal, 'The bishops and the Act of Exchange of 1559', *HJ* 17 (1974), 227–46; on its consequences, *idem*, *Prelates and Princes*, 228–36. N.L. Jones, 'Profiting from religious reform: the land rush of 1559', *HJ* 22 (1979), 279–94.

[278] *Laws of Ecclesiastical Polity*, vii. 24. 19, in Keble, *Works of Hooker*.

[279] Though, as Collinson points out, the godly ministers were often reluctant to draw the logical conclusion that a prosperous ministry needed to be funded by support from the laity, as well as the redirection of resources within the Church: *Puritan Movement*, 456.

[280] A. Peel (ed.), *The Notebook of John Penry*, CS 3rd ser. 67 (1944), 93. Some of the encouragement offered to Leicester in the 1580s seems nearly as blatant.

[281] P. Lake, 'Conformist clericalism? Richard Bancroft's analysis of the socio-economic roots of presbyterianism', in Sheils and Wood, *The Church and Wealth*, 219–29.

chaplain to Christopher Hatton, Bancroft also constructed much of the lord chancellor's blunt appeal to the 1586 parliament against the presbyterian proposal for a new Prayer Book and Discipline. It should be opposed on the grounds that its attempts to use ecclesiastical wealth to support a preaching ministry threatened the property rights of the laity.[282]

While the clergy argued, the laity consolidated their gains at the expense of the bishops. An extreme case is that of the Isle of Man, where the earls of Derby continued to reign supreme. Half a century after Elizabeth I's death the seventh earl advised his son to continue the traditional practice of keeping the lands of the see on long lease, though he acknowledged that to persuade a cleric to reside it might be wise to 'give way to leasing some petty thing or other of little moment'.[283] The Irish church also produced some spectacular cases of lay intrusion, like that of Patrick Sarsfield, who managed to exchange some tithes of little value with Alexander Craike, bishop of Kildare, in the 1560s, and gain in return most of the property of the see.[284] But even in the more regulated environment of mainland England and Wales at least nineteen sees were subject to demands for leases orchestrated by the crown.[285] Meanwhile Elizabeth's regime also burdened the bishops with regular taxation and with the obligation to act as collectors of taxes in their dioceses. The resultant cries of pain echo through the records of the Elizabethan Exchequer: some bishops like Parkhurst of Norwich and Overton of Coventry and Lichfield, who failed to control the proper collection of crown funds, were driven almost to desperation by their debts.[286] Others, like Bishop Brady of Meath, found that even paying their own first fruits on entry to the see produced a 'mountain of accumulated debt'.[287] Not all bishops were in such dire straits. The situation was particularly bad at the beginning of the reign, and a few sees encountered recurrent difficulties. Others like Lincoln seem largely to have escaped through a combination of good management and good fortune.

The problems of funding the ecclesiastical hierarchy paled into insignificance beside those of providing for the parochial church. Despite the

[282] T.E. Hartley (ed.), *Proceedings in the Parliaments of Elizabeth I*, 2 vols. (1995), ii. 333–8. J.E. Neale, *Elizabeth I and Her Parliaments*, 2 vols. (1957), ii. 160–1. Collinson, *Puritan Movement*, 313–14.

[283] *The History and Antiquities of the Isle of Man*, in F. Peck (ed.), *Desiderata Curiosa* (1779), 436.

[284] Ronan, *Reformation in Ireland*, 54.

[285] Heal, *Prelates and Princes*, 233–6.

[286] P. Carter, '"Certain, continual, and seldom abated": royal taxation of the Elizabethan church' in Wabuda and Litzenberger (eds.), *Belief and Practice*, 94–112. S.M. Jack, 'English bishops as tax collectors in the sixteenth century' in S.M. Jack and B.A. Masters (eds.), *Protestants, Property, Puritans: Godly People Revisited* (Parergon, n.s. 14, 1996), 129–63.

[287] Walshe, 'Bishop Brady', 362–3.

passionate pleas of the godly, and the more measured criticism of the bishops, Elizabeth had no intention of changing a system of patronage and finance that had sufficed for her predecessors. Impropriations, the leasing of benefices, and the wide variety of forms of funding of incumbents and curates continued essentially as in the past.[288] But distinctive difficulties were added: inflation could erode the value of livings which depended on money payments or limited access to tithe; taxation became, in William Harrison's words, 'certain, continual and seldom abated'; and clerical marriage brought its own pressures in the need to provide for families.[289] None of these was uniformly negative in its effects. Clerical marriage was costly but, as the ubiquitous Harrison again had it, it ensured domestic efficiency: meat 'well dressed' and hospitality maintained.[290] Taxation was always burdensome, yet not really acutely so before the war crisis of the 1590s, and the fact that assessments were still at the *Valor Ecclesiasticus* rates offered some relief to a proportion of the clergy.[291] Above all, inflation benefited some clergy: Christopher Hill demonstrated that a sample of rectories grew more than fivefold in money value between the 1535 survey and those done by Parliament during the interregnum. Since these were also the livings most likely to have glebe land, and hence some capacity to raise revenue in kind, we may assume they survived well even in the later sixteenth century.[292] The Puritan surveys of parochial livings in Cornwall and Berkshire in 1586 show average increases over the *Valor* of between 220 per cent and over 300 per cent, suggesting broadly a capacity to keep pace with inflation.[293]

There is, however, ample evidence that parts of the English, Welsh, and Irish churches were now so poorly funded that they could attract neither incumbents nor adequate curates. At the end of the sixteenth century chapel curates in Lancashire were being paid an average of £4 per annum: not surprisingly there was difficulty in filling the posts.[294] It is a reflection on the even graver financial problems of the Scottish Kirk that at least thirty-two chaplaincies and curacies in the Border counties were filled by

---

[288] F. Heal, 'Economic problems of the clergy', in Heal O'Day, *Church and Society*, 108–18.

[289] Carter, 'Royal taxation', 95–100.

[290] G. Edelen (ed.), *William Harrison: A Description of England* (Ithaca, N.Y., 1968), 37.

[291] Whitgift's recognition of the significance of retaining the 1535 assessments is indicated in his memorandum to Burghley opposing revision: BL Lans. MS 45, fos. 184–5ᵛ.

[292] Hill, *Economic Problems*, 111. Hill's sample—525 parishes—is large but is heavily weighted to Essex, Worcester diocese, and London. 87 per cent of rectories and 40 per cent of vicarages in Warwickshire had glebe: D.M. Barratt (ed.), *Ecclesiastical Terriers of Warwickshire Parishes*, Dugdale Society 22 (1955), intro.

[293] M. Zell, 'Economic problems of the parochial clergy in the sixteenth century', in R. O'Day and F. Heal (eds.), *Princes and Paupers in the English Church, 1500–1800* (Leicester, 1981), 35–41.

[294] C. Haigh, *Reformation and Resistance in Tudor Lancashire* (Cambridge, 1975), 238–9; cf. London, where curates were often paid £20: H.G. Owen, 'Parochial curates in Elizabethan London', *JEH* 10 (1959), 69.

Scots in the 1560s and 1570s. Bishop Pilkington acknowledged baldly that this was 'because they take less wages than other'.[295] Urban livings, always vulnerable because of the need to depend on personal tithes and offerings, suffered particularly badly. In cities most acutely affected, like York, pluralism and non-residence were the rule as a means of survival for the clergy.[296] The extreme cases were, as always, Wales and Ireland. In Wales Richard Davies blamed impropriators who gave their clerics no more than starvation wages, and often made do with a cleric from another parish paid no more than £4 a year.[297] As for Ireland, the best of the evidence available is Bishop Brady's 1576 survey of Meath, which revealed that more than half the impropriated parishes were served by impoverished curates who lived on bare altar offerings. Inflation was a final blow for many of these clerics. In 1584 the prebendaries of St Patrick's, Dublin, vividly described for the Privy Council the fate of their curates who travel like 'lackeys to three or four churches in a morning' to secure enough stipend to live.[298] At these levels of absolute poverty there is no question that the structure of the Church prevented any significant religious change being initiated. Bishop Brady spoke with feeling about how his clergy were 'wont to live upon the gain of masses, dirges, shrivings and such like trumpery godly abolished'.[299]

The critical issue facing the British and Irish churches was not how to provide for 'ragged clergy' or the mere readers who plugged the worst gaps in parochial ministry after the accession of Elizabeth, but how to offer long-term endowments and incomes suitable for a learned, preaching ministry. By the later years of Elizabeth's reign the rough rule of thumb about the size of income needed to support a preaching cleric had moved from Archbishop Cranmer's £10 to £30, a figure that was used by the Irish bishops as well as by those engaged in the internal English debate about the ministry. Grindal thought that at most one parish in eight could yield enough for a preacher.[300] Whitgift, taking as always a more trenchant view, insisted that not one parish in twenty was worth £30 clear, and used this to support his argument that pluralities must continue as a means of maintaining a preaching cadre.[301] As the Puritan position became more strident, polemicists argued that ministers needed £100 or more for

---

[295] S.M. Keeling, 'The Reformation in the Anglo-Scottish Border counties', *Northern History* 15 (1979), 30.

[296] C. Cross, 'The incomes of provincial urban clergy, 1520–1645', in R. O'Day and F. Heal (eds.), *Princes and Paupers in the English Church, 1500–1800* (Leicester, 1981), 65–89.

[297] Williams, *Wales and the Reformation*, 297–8.

[298] PRO SP 63/113/56.   [299] Walshe, 'Bishop Brady', 362–3.

[300] Nicholson, *Remains of Grindal*, 383.

[301] Strype, *Whitgift*, 193. Bishop Curteys argued for a variant on Whitgift's insistence on pluralities: the unification of benefices and allowing pensions out of parishes occupied by the unlearned for the benefit of preachers.

sufficiency.[302] What all parties frequently ignored was the supply side of the issue: until at least the 1590s there were simply not enough graduates to supply the English parishes (let alone those of Wales or Ireland) with preachers at any price.[303]

The issues involved in providing proper funding for a Protestant church are revealed more starkly when Scotland is compared with the rest of Britain and Ireland. The Scottish Reformation was inevitably accompanied by a major upheaval in ecclesiastical finance, since there was a clear break between the old Kirk and the new. Since congregations provided the building-blocks of the reformed polity they might be expected, like their Continental counterparts, to provide funding for the ministry as well.[304] But the new Kirk could also from the beginning claim some measure of establishment by law: the rituals of the Catholic Church were prohibited, and therefore in principle it had a powerful claim upon the latter's resources as well. Those resources, just as in the English case, were already deeply woven into the structure of the society, both clerical and lay. Specifically, the system of feuing ensured that large sectors of the Scottish elite had a vested interest in church property, and the localist, kin-based nature of the society meant that it was extremely difficult to unskein lay and clerical interests. The revolution had been made by nobles and lairds who had a strong interest in the maintenance of the structure of the old Church.[305] Therefore much of the energy of the fledgling Kirk had to be directed to finding financial solutions that would secure support for a 'learned ministry' without compromising the wealth of their lay supporters. The belief of the First Book of Discipline that all teinds should be returned to the Church as proper spiritualities did not at this stage look likely of realization.[306]

The first, rather deft, compromise proposed by Mary's council was the agreement of 1562 that when beneficed men did not support the reform, they should have a third of their income appropriated for the shared use of the crown and the new Kirk. This produced the major survey of ecclesiastical revenues known as the Books of the Assumptions of the Thirds of Benefices, and for a brief period the division of the spoils between crown and kirk appears to have been reasonably successful.[307] This is despite

---

[302] A. Peel (ed.), *The Seconde Parte of a Register: Being a Calendar of Manuscripts . . .* , 2 vols. (1915), ii. 209.

[303] K. Fincham, *Prelate as Pastor: The Episcopate of James I* (Oxford, 1990), 181–3: Dr Fincham points out that even in the early seventeenth century the capacity of the bishops to ordain graduates remained highly area-sensitive.

[304] Donaldson, *Scottish Reformation*, 64–72.

[305] On the difficulties that church finance produced in the initial settlement see above, p. 365

[306] Cameron, *First Book of Discipline*, 30–1, 156–64.

[307] J. Kirk (ed.), *The Books of the Assumptions of the Thirds of Benefices*, British Academy Records in Social and Economic History NS 21 (1995), pp. xiv, xvii ff.

John Knox's famous observation that 'two parts [was] freely given to the Devil, and the third must be divided betwixt God and the Devil'.[308] It was, however, inevitable that an impoverished crown would be tempted to appropriate income designated for the clerical estate. The thirds were only a temporary expedient, and the General Assembly began to demand a more fundamental solution to these problems with growing vociferousness in the later Marian years. Finally in 1567 the Kirk was granted succession to all the lesser benefices of the old Church as they became vacant, and church collectors were placed in control of the thirds. This still left unresolved the problem of the major benefices—bishoprics and abbeys. In the 1572 Leith agreement there was again a rather elegant attempt at compromise in which the bishoprics were to be included in the new Kirk, and monastic resources divided between land and teinds, the latter coming to the Kirk. The General Assembly, however, remained committed to the view that all ecclesiastical resources should be returned to the Kirk, and this was the position adopted in the Second Book of Discipline. The issue was not really settled until in 1587 the Act of Annexation was passed, by which the temporalities passed to the crown, while the spiritualities were to remain with the holders, and were by this time largely available to the Kirk.[309]

The moral is that the Scottish reformers were no more successful than their English counterparts at freeing the clerical estate from the embrace of lay interest. Melville wrote bitterly to Beza in 1578 that 'those who have grown rich by sacrilege . . . deny that ecclesiastical discipline is to be derived from the word of God'.[310] And, since the aggregate resources available to the clergy had always been more limited than south of the border, the inevitable consequence was a Kirk that struggled to meet the needs of its ministry. The First Book of Discipline had recommended that ministers should be paid equitable stipends, varied mainly by marital circumstance and the logistical burdens of a parish.[311] In reality few ministers in the early years could command more than £100 Scots per annum, and there are many cases where kirks struggled to provide a bare minimum for their clerics. In the somewhat extreme case of Caithness it was not possible to offer more than £66 for a minister, or £20 for a reader in the early years.[312] The Kirk not only had problems about establishing a legal claim to the resources of the old Church, it also encountered resistance to paying from those owing teinds: a combination of opportunism born of political confusion and a demand for value for

---

[308] Knox, ii. 29.   [309] Kirk, *Second Book of Discipline*, 17–18, 23–5, 122–4.
[310] McCrie, *Life of Melville*, ii. 200–1.   [311] Cameron, *First Book of Discipline*, 108–9.
[312] Kirk, *Patterns of Reform*, 123–36, 314–22. In Angus and the Mearns, where the ministers seem to have been fairly well-placed, over half received an income in excess of £100 by 1563, but only twenty-eight out of eighty-eight clergy in the new church were ministers: Bardgett, *Scotland Reformed*, 90, 109.

money in religious services. There were problems about payment at every level within the Kirk, from conflicts about superintendents' salaries to the difficulty of recruiting readers in the Highlands because of the impossibly low stipends.[313]

Yet the early history of financing the Scottish Reformation actually provides a salutary corrective to easy assumptions that a poor church was necessarily a spiritually ineffective church. In practice the first generation of reformers resolved many of the most pressing fiscal problems by ad hoc means. In the 1560s there might be no guarantee of secure income for learned ministers, but there were a series of individual initiatives that helped to provide funding. Benefice holders who had not converted to the new Kirk often gave voluntary support to clerics, lessees sometimes funded ministers, and congregations occasionally raised their own revenue to call a minister.[314] In 1562 an Ayrshire bond was signed to 'assist the preaching' and 'maintain the ministers of the same'.[315] Congregational enthusiasm was met with reasonable supply of clerics from the old Church, so that at least at the level of readers it was relatively easy to service the new congregations. By the early 1570s there were almost 1,000 men in the ministry, close in principle to the number needed to furnish the number of Scottish parishes.[316] There is, of course, a further problem about the nature of these clerics: about 70 per cent in the figures accumulated in 1574 were readers or exhorters not full preaching ministers. Here informal solutions, especially that of giving a minister supervisory control over several adjacent parishes, were usually attempted.[317]

In the second and third generation of the Reformation the financial problems of the Kirk had a rather different impact. As more graduates were produced by the universities, and the future of the Kirk became more secure, it became possible in principle to fulfil the General Assembly's ambition of recruiting more fully learned men to the ministry. The financial expectations of such men were very different from those of readers. A minister in the 1590s still did not necessarily command a salary of more than £100, though there was a general tendency for stipend to edge upwards.[318]

---

[313] A. Macdonald (ed.), *Register of Ministers, Exhorters and Readers and of their Stipends after the period of the Reformation* (Edinburgh, 1830).

[314] Kirk, *Patterns of Reform*, 117, 122–30.   [315] Knox, ii. 55–6.

[316] Macdonald, *Ministers, Exhorters and Readers*.

[317] M. Lynch, 'Preaching to the converted? Perspectives on the Scottish Reformation', in A.A. MacDonald, M. Lynch, and I.B. Cowan (eds.), *The Renaissance in Scotland* (Leiden, 1994), 310. Bardgett, *Scotland Reformed*, 89–90.

[318] Kirk and Bardgett take a reasonably positive view of the financial progress of the 1580s to 1590s, emphasizing a slow if uneven advance for many ministers: Bardgett shows that stipends were increasing on the whole in Angus and Mearns, *Scotland Reformed*, 109. Lynch, on the other hand, emphasizes a second-generation crisis, partly created by inadequate resources: 'Preaching to the converted?', 307–13.

The leaders of the Kirk now aimed to make it possible to have such preaching ministers in every parish, while acknowledging that salaries must at least keep pace with inflation. In the 1580s the General Assembly seriously considered reducing the number of parishes to 600 to ensure proper ministerial supervision.[319] This came to nothing because in a slow and piecemeal way more of the wealth of the old Church became available to the new, and because the status, if not the income, of the ministry continued to rise. Moreover the king's serious assurances that he wished 'all the kirks of Scotland planted with ministers and sufficient livings appointed to them' led the assembly to continue in hope.[320] But not until the early seventeenth century was there a systematic attempt to improve ministerial incomes through augmentation, and then it was orchestrated not by the General Assembly, but by the crown and the much-despised bishops.[321]

Did the economic problems of the British and Irish Protestant churches make any fundamental difference to their evangelical success? It is unlikely that direct economic determinism is a particularly useful guide to the impact of Protestantism. Wealthy livings certainly attracted the well-educated and influential: poor curacies, if filled at all, would draw only the marginal. When particular inducements were available, as they were in the case of Scottish preachers persuaded to Ulster in the next century, the nature of evangelism could certainly be changed.[322] But supply, in the form of output from the universities, was probably the most critical way in which the quality of clergy was changed by the early seventeenth century. Graduates might make high claims for their financial rights: they had to settle for what the market offered, and in so doing began to spread the preaching of the Word beyond a small minority of rich parishes. The greatest significance of financial problems was that they distracted clergy, at all levels of the churches, from their primary spiritual duties. Unseemly wrangles about leases and property, and difficulties about tax collection, certainly diverted the energies of Elizabeth's bishops. Litigation about tithe; tensions with patrons, or with farmers and lessees; the need to pursue other sources of profit: all these could burden a cleric. The solution of the godly—that ministers should be relieved of worldly cares and dedicate themselves solely to their cures in return for an adequate salary—was no doubt the ideal one. Always it fell foul of the willingness of the laity to pay the true costs of such a church. In the case of England, at least, it was also a solution that violated those principles of hierarchy, which must be sustained by money. Wealth, said Hooker, 'is held in so great admiration ... in this golden age ... that

---

[319] *BUK* ii. 480–7; Kirk, *Second Book of Discipline*, 104–5.   [320] *BUK* ii. 771.

[321] On the changes of the early 17th cent, see W.R. Foster, *The Church before the Covenants: the Church of Scotland 1596–1638* (Edinburgh, 1975), 156–72.

[322] A. Ford, *The Protestant Reformation in Ireland, 1590–1641* (Dublin, 1997), 72–4.

without it angelical perfections are not able to deliver from extreme contempt'.[323] And the nature and power of that hierarchy was to become one of the defining issues of the last decades of Elizabeth's reign.

Last Decades

Two distinguished contributions to a recent study of church and politics in the 1580s and 1590s chose to title their papers 'ecclesiastical vitriol'.[324] The language reflects a paradox pertinent to both English and Scottish Protestantism. As the internal settlements of religion became more secure—in Scotland through the presence of an adult monarch willing to uphold the Calvinist faith, in England through the acceptance that the queen's faith was the faith of the majority of the nation—so the polemic of the churches became more aggressive. This is partly to be explained by intense fears about the genuine threat of resurgent Catholicism. The glorious success of the Armada, and the Protestant wind that turned back subsequent invasion attempts, were regarded only as provisional victories in the struggle against the forces of Antichrist. Ireland remained a constant reminder of the reality of the papal challenge, especially when general insurrection threatened in the 1590s after the outbreak of Tyrone's revolt.[325] The impact of the Jesuit mission in England and Scotland stirred deep horror of the enemy within, and the vacillation of official policy towards the Catholic laity of both realms generated bitter disputes between the godly and the politicians.[326] But ecclesiastical vitriol also erupted from the unresolved problems of church governance, of the authority of the prince, and of the autonomy of the churches. And lurking in the wings was the awareness that James was Elizabeth's only credible successor.

The figure that encapsulated many of these fears and conflicts was that Rottweiler of the English establishment, Richard Bancroft. Bancroft's famous sermon at Paul's Cross in February 1589, the week of the opening of the parliamentary session, managed to touch aggressively on almost every contentious issue in English and Scottish ecclesiastical politics. He remembered to give due thanks to the Almighty for the deliverance of the Armada, and for the godly rule of his sovereign Elizabeth, but his objective was to attack the 'consistorian puritans' wherever they were to be found. Taking as his text 'many false prophets are gone out into the

---

[323] *Laws of Ecclesiastical Polity*, vii. 24. 19, in Keble, *Works of Hooker*.

[324] P. Collinson, 'Ecclesiastical vitriol: religious satire in the 1590s and the invention of puritanism', in Guy, *The Reign of Elizabeth I*, 150–70; J. Wormald, 'Ecclesiastical vitriol: the kirk, the puritans and the future king of England', in *idem*, 171–91.

[325] Ellis, *Tudor Ireland*, 298–311.   [326] McCoog, *Society of Jesus*, 224 ff.

world', he denounced the zealous who assailed bishops, insisted on an equality within the ministry, gaped after episcopal property, and refused to conform to the order of Prayer Book services. He isolated in particular their refusal to subscribe fully to the Elizabethan settlement: the issue that had preoccupied his patron Archbishop Whitgift in the previous half decade.[327] Behind his anger about clerical disobedience, however, Bancroft insisted there lay a deeper fear about the consequences of Puritan behaviour for the whole structure of church and state. It was here that he raised the question of Scotland. The Scots, to his mind, revealed all too starkly what happened when the 'consistory' gained authority in the state. The king of Scots was not master in his own land: his desire to control the Kirk, expressed in the 'Black Acts', was now swept aside by the assertive ministers. But in the end 'his crown and their sovereignty will not agree together'. Scotland should act as a profound warning to England, lest things should also 'grow to extremities' south of the border. There was in the ambition of the ministers an implication of treasonous levelling when 'civil government is called into question: princes' prerogatives are curiously scanned: the interest of the people in kingdoms is greatly advanced and all government generally is pinched at and condemned'.[328]

Bancroft's denunciations of Scottish presbyters occupied only nine text pages of a long sermon, but it produced an intense reaction both from the divines themselves and from an angry James. John Davidson wrote a rebuttal, and the Edinburgh presbytery drew up a supplication to Elizabeth against her preacher, though in the end they had the sense not to send it.[329] The king, on the other hand, did protest once he had returned from his wedding visit to Denmark, and Bancroft was belatedly made by Burghley to publish a rather unapologetic submission.[330] The shared anger of kirk and king brought a rare moment of full accord and contributed to James's most public statement of identity with his ministers when he addressed the 1590 General Assembly. There he praised the Deity for the purity of the Kirk, elevating it even above that of Geneva which 'keepeth Pasche and Yule'. And, to show Bancroft that he was not the only bruiser

---

[327] R. Bancroft, *A Sermon preached at Paules Crosse the 9 of Februarie . . . Anno 1588* (1589). Quotations are at 75, 84, 87. For analysis of the sermon see W.D. Cargill Thompson, 'A reconsideration of Richard Bancroft's Paul's Cross sermon', *JEH* 20 (1969), 233–66; Wormald, 'Ecclesiastical vitriol', 174–7.

[328] Bancroft is an intriguing figure in that he also links the Irish and the English churches. He was a great-nephew of Hugh Curwen's and began his route to promotion as a prebendary of St Patrick's Cathedral, Dublin. He may have been instrumental in preventing Sir James Perrot's plans for the appropriation of St Patrick's revenues to construct an Irish university in 1585.

[329] J. Davidson, *Bancroft's Rashness in Rayling against the Church of Scotland* (Edinburgh, 1590). Mullan, *Episcopacy in Scotland*, 69–70. For James's protests see *CSP Sc* 1589–93 x. 409–10, 528.

[330] O. Chadwick, 'Richard Bancroft's submission', *JEH* 3 (1952), 58–73.

in inter-kingdom disputes, he denounced the Book of Common Prayer as 'an evil said mass in English, wanting nothing but the liftings'. As with any outstanding party political speech the result was fifteen minutes of standing ovation.[331]

Bancroft's tactless intervention in Scottish affairs, which incidentally was renewed in his pamphlet war of 1593, showed no understanding of the complexity of relations between king and kirk in the years after 1584.[332] The ministers and the General Assembly were certainly capable of overt denunciations of royal delinquency, both on moral issues and on the politics of religion. But much of this was part of the hard-bargaining necessary to secure a godly prince for the 'conservation and purgation of religion' as well as for the proper management of temporal affairs.[333] For his part James desired greater ability to command his stroppy Melvillians: given the well-entrenched nature of the Kirk's power he acknowledged, however, the need for management and negotiation.[334] His archbishop of St Andrews, Patrick Adamson, was moved by indignation against the presbyters to write *A declaration of the kings majesties intention and meaning toward the lait actis of parliament* in 1585, a tract which became one of Bancroft's prime sources.[335] James may have encouraged the publication: he did not formally endorse it. In the second half of the 1580s he therefore allowed a slow movement towards presbyterian church structures while not surrendering his claims to uphold episcopacy. After 1584 James also maintained his right to summon the General Assembly. For a time in 1586 and 1587 reorganized dioceses were overseen by bishops or newly appointed commissioners, while presbyteries were also re-established. By 1590 the latter had superseded the former in many areas of organization, culminating four years later in the right to examine appointees to benefices. In 1592 the so-called 'Golden Acts' gave legislative endorsement to the presbyterian system, though crucially the king still retained his erastian right of summons of general assemblies. There were therefore plenty of specific moments of conflict between kings and clerics in these years, though hardly enough to demonstrate that the king could not live with some version of the 'two kingdoms' theory of authority.[336]

---

[331] *BUK* ii. 771.

[332] In his 1593 pamphlet, *Dangerous Positions and Proceedings, published and practised within this Island of Brytaine under pretence of Reformation and for the Presbiteriall Discipline* (1593), bk. i, Bancroft indulged himself in a much more lengthy denunciation of the Scots.

[333] Wormald, 'Ecclesiastical vitriol', 182–6.

[334] Mullan, *Episcopacy in Scotland*, 58–9.

[335] The text of Adamson's *Declaration* was printed in the 1587 edition of Holinshed's *Chronicle of England, Scotland and Ireland*, 6 vols. (1808), v. 713–20.

[336] MacDonald, *Jacobean Kirk*, 30–49.

The major source of dispute between James and his clergy throughout the late 1580s and the early 1590s was relations with the lay elite. For the Kirk, the king's failure properly to discipline the key leaders of Catholicism, the earls of Huntly and Erroll, was a fundamental betrayal. For James, the ministers' flirtation with the earl of Bothwell after his involvement in treason and witchcraft was equally threatening. Even when, in 1594, all three nobles were banished, suspicions were not wholly allayed. Two years later the combination of a government headed by a group of men known as the Octavians, several of whom were suspected of Catholic leanings, and the secret return of Huntly and Erroll, once again stimulated denunciations from the Melvillians.[337]

It was at this point that the king's relations with the Kirk moved from chronic stand-off to acute conflict. James Melville, looking back over the years between 1596 and 1610, was to label them 'A True Narration of the Declining Age of the Kirk of Scotland', and, at least for the first of those years, his apocalyptic sentiment had some justification.[338] Faced with royal reluctance to move against the earls, local presbyteries and synods attempted their own initiative, and a standing commission of the General Assembly convened first in Cupar and later in Edinburgh without royal licence.[339] When king and ministers met in September 1596 tempers ran high. It was on this occasion that Andrew Melville memorably plucked James's sleeve, called him 'God's silly vassal', and delivered himself of a full lecture on the 'two kingdom theory'.[340] In October David Black, minister of St Andrews, deepened the crisis by preaching a sermon in which he allegedly denounced the king as treacherous, Queen Anne as unsound in religion, and, for good measure, the queen of England as 'an atheist'.[341] This was not all that remarkable as Scottish pulpit rhetoric, but in the circumstances it was too much for James. He insisted that Black be disciplined, and by the Privy Council, not the Kirk. Black, supported by the commissioners, denied the council's power in the case. By December there was confrontation in Edinburgh: the king ordered the dispersal of the commissioners and their supporters and summoned his own convention of ministers to Perth for February 1597. A riot resulted, leading James to withdraw both the royal court and the courts of justice to Linlithgow. Thereafter tempers cooled and the king began to regain the initiative. The four leading ministers of Edinburgh fled, and before the end of the year the courts had been restored.[342]

[337] Ibid., 50–73.   [338] Pitcairn, *Autobiography of James Melvill*, 505.

[339] Mullan, *Episcopacy in Scotland*, 80–3.   [340] Pitcairn, *Autobiography of James Melvill*, 37.

[341] Calderwood, v. 443 ff.   [342] MacDonald, *Jacobean Kirk*, 65–73.

Most recent accounts of the crisis at the end of 1596 have emphasized the situation-specific nature both of the ministers' behaviour and of James's response. Without the earls, and without the tactlessness of Black, no confrontation would necessarily have occurred.[343] But as Williamson has pointed out, the moment at which co-operation failed was that at which 'basic questions about the nature of authority... would surface'.[344] Buchanan's texts could be brought out of the closet and upheld or challenged by the warring parties.[345] An insistence on the right of the Kirk to try its own was a catalyst for James to campaign vigorously for a true royal supremacy. And, though it seems that many moderates among the clergy were initially indignant about royal intervention, there was a gradual acknowledgement that the Melvillians and the Edinburgh ministers had gone too far. The king held his convention at Perth in February 1597, followed by a full General Assembly at Dundee in May. Both were well attended by ministers from the north, helping to secure loyalty. A commission of the assembly was given permanent status under the king, and this began to exercise power over the local presbyteries. In the following period the possibility of reviving episcopacy was opened by the king's proposal that the Kirk should have parliamentary representation through chosen ministers. A newly compliant assembly voted in support. However, co-operation did not necessarily indicate trust. James's reaction to the events of 1596–7 appeared in his writings on monarchy, *Basilikon Doron* and *The Trew Law of Free Monarchies*. These laid Buchanan's ghost (temporarily) and enabled him to give a bitter account of the consequences of popular reformation to his older son. 'Some fiery spirited men in the ministry... finding the gust of government sweet, they began to fantasy to themselves, a democratic form of government' and fed themselves on the hope 'in a popular government by leading the people by the nose, to bear the sway of all the rule.'[346] In words that must have been music to Bancroft's ears he denounced the doctrine of ministerial parity as 'the mother of confusion and enemy to unity'. Whatever James's sentiments before 1596, thereafter he was already anticipating his Hampton Court assertion of 1604: 'no bishops, no king'.

When Bancroft preached his Paul's Cross sermon, he looked back on five years of struggle with the non-conformist godly both in the English dio-

---

[343] Wormald, 'Ecclesiastical vitriol', 180–9. MacDonald, *Jacobean Kirk*, 62–83. Lynch, 'Preaching to the converted?', 315–17.

[344] A. Williamson, *Scottish National Consciousness in the Age of James VI* (Edinburgh, 1979), 50.

[345] R.A. Mason, 'George Buchanan, James VI and the presbyterians', in R.A. Mason (ed.), *Scots and Britons: Scottish Political Thought and the Union of 1603* (Cambridge, 1994), 112–37.

[346] J. Craigie (ed.), *The Basilikon Doron of King James VI*, 2 vols. (STS, 1944–50), i. 75, 79 (quotation is from the 1603 edition).

ceses and in Parliament. At the beginning of the third parliamentary session since Whitgift's promotion to Canterbury Bancroft was also issuing a warning to those MPs who might be disposed to return to the bruising conflicts of 1584/5 and 1586/7.[347] Those, for the godly, were the heroic years when John Field orchestrated the compilation of surveys on the state of the ministry and the accompanying petitions to Parliament, Robert Beale directly challenged the archbishop, and Sir Anthony Cope promoted the 'Bill and Book' to sweep away the Book of Common Prayer. The last, described by Collinson as 'perhaps the most immoderate measure ever to come before the House of Commons', is indicative more of desperation than of any tactics likely to achieve the desired goal.[348] Other aspects of the reform programme, especially the attempt to protect ministers against pressures to conform, were more moderate and popular, but even they met with a determinedly negative response from bishops and queen. At the end of the 1587 session the queen sent a peremptory message to her MPs insisting that her religious settlement was inviolate and she 'mindeth not now to begin to settle herself in causes of religion'.[349] By 1589 it may not have needed Bancroft's monitions to reinforce this point: after thirty years the godly seem finally to have understood the message. There would be no more attempts to build a new Jerusalem through Parliament.

The bitterness of these 1580s sessions is a reflection of the extraordinary impact that the arrival of Archbishop Whitgift had had on the godly ministers and their lay supporters.[350] When Walsingham's secretary, Nicholas Faunt, reported the likely promotion six months before Grindal's death he already opined that 'the Lord is even determined to scourge his Church for their unthankfulness'.[351] Whitgift entered office committed to the imposition of order on the wayward brethren, though also, of course, to strengthening the organizational structure of the Church and reforming and improving its ministry. The notorious three articles, promulgated as part of a more general reform programme at the end of 1583, became the focus of a fundamental conflict about subscription and obedience. Of the three only the second, it should be noted, was anathema to many of the zealous ministers. This required that clerics should swear that the Book of Common Prayer and the ordering bishops, priests, and deacons 'containeth nothing in it contrary to the word of God'. Moreover they were to agree to use the form of the book in public prayer and the administration of the sacraments.[352] Proceedings for the taking of subscriptions began

---

[347] On the politics of these parliaments see Neale, *Elizabeth I and Her Parliaments*, ii. 58–83, 145–65; Jones, 'Religion in Parliament', in Dean and Jones, *Parliaments of Elizabethan England*, 124–7; Collinson, *Puritan Movement*, 273–88, 303–16.

[348] Collinson, *Puritan Movement*, 307.   [349] LPL MS 178, fo. 88.

[350] Collinson, *Puritan Movement*, 243–72.   [351] LPL MS 647, fo. 162ᵛ.

[352] Strype, *Whitgift*, app., 51.

promptly in November 1583. By the time that the majority of the southern province had been covered during 1584 between three and four hundred ministers had been suspended. The raw numbers indicate widespread and deep perturbation among the parish clergy, especially in key areas such as London, Essex, and Northamptonshire.[353] But the influence of these individuals outweighed their numerical strength, both because they were a learned section of the ministry and above all because they had such powerful lay support in court and in country. Robert Beale was the councillor who most systematically risked his career in defence of the non-conformists: he was backed by Mildmay, Walsingham, and, most noisily, by Knollys. Burghley, though as constitutionally cautious as ever, strongly opposed Whitgift in a number of specific cases. Only Sir Christopher Hatton proved a dependable friend to the archbishop.

During the latter half of 1584 Whitgift, a political realist as well as a disciplinarian, accepted that compromise was necessary to separate those of 'tender conscience' from the determinedly non-conformists and those heavily implicated in the presbyterian movement. Subscription became 'somewhat more tolerable', and in many cases less than full adherence to the second article was demanded. If there were ever any plans to extend subscription to the northern province they were shelved.[354] Before the autumn parliamentary session the archbishop had therefore been able to reduce the number of clerics who had to be deprived to a small core of 'ultras'.[355] For the rest, the later history of the reign was scarcely one of happy acquiescence in the ways of the archbishop, but involved a realistic recognition of the dangers of proceeding too far in building the 'church within a church' that was the presbyterian discipline. In the aftermath of 1584 the archbishop began to accept that diocesan bishops must also exercise a measure of discretion in the taking of subscriptions. Thus Fincham has shown that, while some bishops like Aylmer of London followed Whitgift in a strict policy of enforcement, elsewhere after the initial burst of activity subscription was not 'much urged'.[356] In a number of dioceses such as Exeter, Chichester, and Salisbury the three articles were not subscribed in the later years of the reign: often prelates accepted just the oath to the articles of religion instead. Needless to say, none of this met with

[353] For the history of the Articles in Northamptonshire see W.J. Sheils, *The Puritans in the Diocese of Peterborough, 1558–1610*, Northamptonshire Record Society 30 (Northampton, 1979), 48–51.

[354] G.W. Kitchin (ed.), *The Records of the Northern Convocation*, Surtees Society 113 (1907), lxxviii–lxxx, 354.

[355] Collinson, *Puritan Movement*, 263 ff.

[356] K. Fincham, 'Clerical conformity from Whitgift to Laud', in P. Lake and M. Questier (eds.), *Conformity and Orthodoxy in the English Church, c.1560–1660* (Woodbridge, 2000), 126–33.

Bancroft's approval: in 1593 he denounced bishops who, desiring 'to be at ease and quietness', did not require subscription of 'that factious sort'.[357]

The combination of court pressure and a dawning political realism robbed Whitgift of success in his full-frontal attack on non-conformity in 1583. Yet the crisis both gave clear notice that overt challenge to the episcopal order would not be tolerated and left the archbishop with a formidable weapon against the radical minority. The latter was the use by the revitalized High Commission of the *ex officio mero* oath. This had already been employed as a form of civil law procedure against Catholic recusants, virtually requiring them to swear to incriminate themselves and permitting the judges to proceed inquisitorially on the basis of 'notoriety' or 'common fame'. It was now used with interrogatories addressed to those like seven Cambridge ministers who refused to subscribe in May 1584.[358] Beale, trained in common law and like most of his legal colleagues deeply opposed to *ex officio* procedure, complained that commissioners acted with 'cunning dealing [which] savoureth more of a Spanish inquisition than Christian charity'.[359] Not surprisingly, the 1584 parliament demanded the abolition of the oath. On this issue Whitgift did not yield to pressure, and throughout the later 1580s non-conformists were summoned to London to be put on oath. Those who refused to swear (which became the common godly position) were proceeded against for contumacy.

It is, however, interesting that one of the contentious issues that Bancroft did not pursue in his Paul's Cross sermon was the *ex officio* oath. Only in the period immediately after his harangue did this disciplinary weapon achieve its full significance, to be defended with predictable vigour in his 1593 pamphlets. The English 'ecclesiastical vitriol' of the 1590s had obvious roots in the previous decade: it might not have developed had it not been for the conjunction of the remarkable Martin Marprelate crisis and the consequent uncovering of the Puritan 'classes'.[360] The Marprelate tracts, that extraordinary flurry of pamphlets produced by an illegal press between October 1588 and June 1589, adopted the tone and strategies of popular satire to lambast the bishops. Although there were solemn anti-Martinist responses, notably Bishop Cooper's *Admonition*, there were also answers in rhetorical kind, helping to perpetuate popular enjoyment of episcopal discomforture.[361] If, said Thomas Bright-

---

[357] R. Bancroft, *A Survay of the pretended Holy Discipline* (1593), 310–11.

[358] J. Guy, 'The Elizabethan establishment and the ecclesiastical polity', in Guy, *Reign of Elizabeth I*, 126–49. Collinson, *Puritan Movement*, 266–7, 270–1.

[359] BL Add. MS 48039, fos. 49ᵛ–50.

[360] Collinson, 'Ecclesiastical vitriol', 154–65. On the Marprelate crisis in general see L.H. Carlson, *Martin Marprelate, Gentleman: Master Job Throkmorton Laid Open in his Colors* (San Marino, Calif., 1981).

[361] On the anti-Martinist literature see Carlson, *Martin Marprelate*, 59–74.

man, the angel of the Church of England had had any credit, men 'would rather have cast those writings into the fire, than have worn them out with continual reading and handling of them'.[362] As it was, the bishops could only search for the press and, in the furious hunt, the pursuivants closed in on the circle of Job Throckmorton, John Udall, and John Penry. In the latter part of 1589, evidence was seized of the organized presbyterian *classis* in Northamptonshire: the legal attack on radicalism was resumed.[363]

Throughout 1590 and 1591 the leading non-conformist preachers were harried, silenced, and imprisoned, often for refusing the *ex officio* oath. In extreme cases the high commissioners handed men over to the secular arm.[364] John Udall was tried at Surrey Assizes for the felony of publishing the *Demonstration of discipline*, and sentenced to death, though eventually pardoned, interestingly through the intervention of James VI.[365] Eventually Thomas Cartwright himself was imprisoned for refusal to take the oath, and thirty-one articles were presented against him. Cartwright had led a charmed life, protected by significant court interests, but in 1590 even the sympathy of Burghley could not protect him from Whitgift and from the queen's 'heavy displeasure'. During the winter of 1590 Cartwright wrestled with the commissioners as he had once wrestled in written exchange with Whitgift. By the next spring it had been decided to put Cartwright and nine of the other leaders of presbyterianism on trial in Star Chamber. There much of the evidence produced against them had been unearthed by the ubiquitous Bancroft.[366] The charges against the men were essentially that they intended to put their Book of Discipline into practice, in defiance of the laws of the realm and the queen's settlement, and that they encouraged rebellion through their pamphleteering. Whether they were to be regarded as dangerous radicals or as moderate 'mainstream' reformers was very much in the eye of the beholder.

The outcome of the show trial was, to quote Collinson, a 'typically Elizabethan' story with no tidy ending. The accusations were not upheld, the ministers were offered some form of submission and were slowly released, first into house arrest and then permitted back to their counties. Cartwright ended in Guernsey in 1595. The defendants repeatedly claimed no desire to separate from the Church, only to work within a

---

[362] T. Brightman, *Workes* (1644), 150.

[363] Sheils, *Puritans in Peterborough*, 51–60.

[364] Collinson, *Puritan Movement*, 403–31.

[365] J. Udall, *A Demonstration of the Truth of that Discipline* (1588).

[366] Whitgift boasted of Bancroft's role when he recommended the latter for the bishopric of London in 1597: R.G. Usher, *Reconstruction of the English Church*, 2 vols. (1910), ii. 366–9.

system of discipline that they hoped to see legally established. It was a refusal to adopt this line which doomed John Penry, who was executed with the separatists Barrow and Greenwood in 1593. By then Whitgift had driven organized presbyterianism decisively underground and effectively silenced the seditious press. He had also, with powerful assistance from Bancroft, Hatton, and the civil lawyer Richard Cosin, managed to protect much of the interest of High Commission, and the queen's imperial prerogative, from the challenges of the common lawyers.[367] In 1591 there occurred one of the critical cases of Elizabethan constitutional law, when the judges of Queen's Bench were asked to rule on whether it had been lawful for Robert Cawdrey, a non-conformist minister, to be deprived of his benefice by High Commission. The ruling was that it was lawful, because the queen had 'plenary and entire power' to give her imperial authority to her bishops so to act. The victory, like so many in law, was less complete than it appeared, but it provided a justification for that authoritarian reading of the rights of the Church which appealed to the archbishop. And it suited a world in which the divine right of bishops was beginning to be asserted freely in polemical writings. The monarch reigned and guided the Church by imperial right. Her commission for the regulation of that body was given directly to the prelates, who formed beneath her a spiritual hierarchy divinely ordained and legitimated.

One sceptical observer of this love-fest between the bishops and Elizabeth was Lord Burghley. There is no evidence that his affection for ambitious and assertive prelates had increased during the course of the reign.[368] He seems to have been particularly troubled by the claims to *iure divino* episcopacy being canvassed at the end of the 1580s. He told Sir Francis Knollys, who pressed him to consider this matter in 1589, that he believed all bishops and ministers had equal authority under Scripture and that the superiority of the former was merely 'a positive ordinance by wisdom of men'.[369] Burghley seems to have regarded the nine ministers as moderate and Whitgift's and Hatton's obsessive pursuit of Protestant nonconformists as mistaken.[370] This is not to say that full resistance to the settlement was to be tolerated: the Martinist assault had to be suppressed and the separatists assailed. Even in these last cases, however, Burghley

---

[367] Guy, 'Elizabethan establishment', in *Reign of Elizabeth I*, 131–48.

[368] In the 1589 parliament Burghley spoke for the abolition of pluralities, denouncing the bishops for slackness and greed, and complaining, 'all the fruits are gathered and put in the purse': BL Lans. MS 396, fo. 60.

[369] BL Lans. MS 61, fo. 66. The later years of Burghley's religious policy are analysed in W.B. Richardson, 'The Religious Policy of the Cecils, 1588–98', University of Oxford D.Phil. (1994), esp. chs. 1–4.

[370] Richardson may exaggerate here the level of conflict between Burghley and Whitgift and Hatton, but he unravels a number of complex policy debates not properly evaluated elsewhere.

was reluctant to use exemplary punishment, though in the end he was unable to save Barrow, Greenwood, and Penry from their determination to oppose the religion of the state. Meanwhile, the complex parliamentary history of the 1593 Act against Seditious Sectaries may reflect Burghley's attempt to address the problem of those who rigorously refused to tarry for the magistrate, without threatening the rest of the godly. Under the Act, which was not in force when the three separatists were executed, those who dissented were to be banished: the Elizabethan regime was thereby unwittingly beginning a new and remarkable chapter in the history of religion.[371]

The key to Burghley's awkward progress through the religious politics of the 1590s was his perception that the Catholic threat outweighed all others. In particular, his dealings with the leading lay English Catholics was marked by profound mistrust, and by a desire to keep them interned when there was any external danger.[372] This could readily be justified in 1588 and again in later periods of invasion scare, but after 1590 some of the council, including perhaps Whitgift, were increasingly sceptical.[373] When Richard Rowlands denounced Burghley in his *Declaration of the True Causes* (1592) as 'violently' overruling his colleagues on the council he was no doubt scoring propaganda points.[374] Yet it was true that the minister drove the ambitious recusancy commissions of 1591–3.[375] And when, at Walsingham's death, he had to take over part of the work of the secretaryship, his long memorandum of tasks had as its first target to have care that all papists and recusants of wealth and influence 'be restrained and punished according to the laws'.[376] In pursuing these policies Burghley was proving consistent to the attitudes of the previous generation of Elizabeth's ministers. He also represented an important aspect of Protestant belief and behaviour that had not been lost despite the loud voices of the disciplinarians and the confidence of new claims for episcopacy. There were still bishops who sympathized with Dr John Reynolds's observation that they should take greater comfort in 'labouring to discover and overthrow the errors of Jesuits and papists, enemies of religion' than in assailing 'brethren professing the true faith of

---

[371] On the Act against Sectaries see Neale, *Elizabeth I and Her Parliaments*, ii. 280–97, but Richardson modifies this account with a more convincing analysis of the subtlety of Cecilian policy: Richardson 'Religious Policy', 83–120.

[372] Richardson, 'Religious Policy', 127 ff.

[373] M.C. Questier, *Conversion, Politics and Religion in England, 1580–1625* (Cambridge, 1996), 157–62.

[374] R. Rowlands, *A Declaration of the True Causes of the Great Troubles, presupposed to be intended against the realm of England* (Cologne, 1592), sig. E4ᵛ.

[375] R.B. Manning, 'Elizabethan recusancy commissions', *HJ* 15 (1972), 23–35, esp. 31–4.

[376] PRO sp 12/231/70.

Christ'.[377] Men like Matthew Hutton were consistent in their belief that the prime duty of the Christian prince was still to 'put down idolatry and punish idolaters' and pursued Catholic recusancy with vigour, while still showing tenderness towards Protestant consciences.[378] And a new generation of bishops—Anthony Rudd, Richard Vaughan, William Barlow, John King, and Arthur Lake—shared many of the same values.[379] By the turn of the century such men might be less willing than their predecessors to accept the erastian assumptions of a Burghley or a Knollys: they remained convinced that the ideological agenda of such politicians was still critical.

In both England and Scotland the last few years before the union of the crowns were periods of relative calm in the long story of religious conflict. James's initiatives against the Kirk had stilled some of the paranoid anxiety of Bancroft and his allies; the godly were living in expectation that the Scottish king would offer them a more truly reformed church than the infuriating Elizabeth had done. But inhabitants of the British Isles had only to look across the Irish Sea to perceive the vulnerability of their settlements and the limitations of the ideological control exercised by either the godly prince or the Protestant ministry. In the decade preceding the Nine-Years-War lord deputies, the ecclesiastical establishment, and the new settlers had continued to wrangle about how best to convert the island. When bold moves were made they usually foundered on local resistance, as when Lord Deputy Perrot tried to make the Pale JPs take the supremacy oath and could not then fill the commission. In 1591, when the ecclesiastical commission tried to fine seven leading recusant Palesmen not actually caught attending Mass, the queen ordered more restraint, implicitly criticizing the general direction of Archbishop Loftus's policy.[380] Thereafter the constant presence of rebellion, and the fear of invasion, offered English officials little opportunity to worry about conversion or control. But when, in 1602, Tyrone's rebellion was over, the endless discussion about who to convert and how to undertake the task resurfaced. It was now Lord Mountjoy, the most successful of Elizabeth's lord deputies, who revived the argument that persuasion was the necessary route to religious change and conformity. Meanwhile Loftus and the Dublin establishment continued to adhere to a disciplinary approach.[381] Neither party to this debate had begun seriously to address a situation in which political authority now extended over the whole island. Conversion

---

[377] P. Lake, 'The significance of the Elizabethan identification of the pope as antichrist', *JEH* 31 (1980), 161–78.

[378] Lake, 'Matthew Hutton', 189–91. [379] Fincham, *Prelate as Pastor*, 250–76.

[380] Ellis, *Tudor Ireland*, 219–20. [381] Edwards, *Church and State*, 270–80.

remained something to be achieved through those centres of 'civility', the Pale, the port towns, and a few carefully chosen areas of anglicized interest.[382]

There is a curious paradox in this continuing debate about the proper methods for the reformation of the Irish. While its terms remained largely unchanged the external realities of religious behaviour were shifting, not only among the Catholic population, but within the world of the Protestant minority. The 1590s, for all its dislocation, was a critical period in the formation of the Counter-Reformation Catholic Church and of the Protestant Church of Ireland.[383] While the Irish bishops would have rejected the notion that they were laying the foundations of a minority church, in practice their efforts at educational and pastoral reorganization were often a more effective form of spiritual activity than the arid and dispiriting attempt to sustain the Protestant royal supremacy in the world of the Pale. The evolution of separate, and clearly confessional, churches in early seventeenth-century Ireland did not dismantle the principle of *cuius regio, eius religio*, but it rendered it marginal.

So Bancroft's paranoia in 1589 had some justification. Although James VI and I was to prove a sound defender of ecclesiastical hierarchy, and a canny adherent of the principle that the prince should have the rulership of the Church under God, confessional politics were always prone to escape from monarchical control. It appeared that the English, dissenting minorities apart, were prepared to acknowledge royal claims to authority, while the Scots and the Irish did so only upon conditions. The next half-century was to show that even in England the Reformation had taught men of conscience that the king did not have binding control over their religious behaviour.

---

[382] Ford, *Protestant Reformation*, 48–55.
[383] P.J. Corish, *The Irish Catholic Experience: A Historical Survey* (Dublin, 1985). Ford, *Protestant Reformation*, 31 ff.

REFORMING PEOPLE AND COMMUNITY: CHURCH, CLERGY, AND LAITY, 1558–1600

In 1603 the congregation of the remote kirk of Kilchrist, Easter Ross, is alleged to have been imprisoned in their building and burnt alive by a rival clan, the Glengarry Macdonalds.[1] This is one of several narratives of bloody feuds in the Scottish Highlands involving attacks on rivals during Sunday worship. The significance of such tales of the Gaidhealtachd in the early seventeenth century is that they assume the regular presence of clan members in church on the sabbath: almost certainly a sharp contrast with the pattern of pre-Reformation religious observance. Then the vast Highland parishes, often focused on churches that were located on in-accessible sites such as islands off the coast or in lochs, were a major disincentive to parishioners who in theory should have observed the requirement to attend Matins, Mass, and Evensong each Sunday. In practice the critical function of these churches for the community seems to have been to act as the focus for festivals and pilgrimages. Now, in the long aftermath of the Scottish Reformation, makeshift buildings had to be pressed into action to accommodate congregations under discipline and law, who were beginning to learn the full significance of sabbatarian practice.[2]

Throughout most of the territories of the British Isles and Ireland, however, it had been feasible for parishioners to observe the requirements of weekly church attendance before the Reformation, in either their

---

[1] J. Dawson, 'Calvinism and the Gaidhealtachd in Scotland', in A. Pettegree, A. Duke, and G. Lewis (eds.), *Calvinism in Europe, 1540–1620* (Cambridge, 1994), 243–50. There is a possibility that the tradition of the Easter Ross massacre is apocryphal, but it is important as a representation of expected patterns of behaviour. Sir John Wynn tells a parallel tale for pre-Reformation Wales, where his great-grandfather built the church of Dolwyddelan in about 1512 in open country to be safer from his enemies during divine service, and then posted watchmen to stand guard while the family was at worship: J. Wynn, *The History of the Gwydir Family* (Ruthin, 1827), 93–4.

[2] I.B. Cowan, 'The medieval church in Argyll and the Isles', *RSCHS* 20 (1978), 15–29.

own church or a dependent chapelry. The great religious changes of the century meant for many of them the substitution of one form of mandatory liturgy for another, with attendance now being enforced with the support of state as well as church. The choice of language for the titles of the English and Scottish liturgies is obviously significant: the Book of *Common* Prayer, the Book of *Common* Order. There was an expectation on the part of the reformers that the population would sit in pews or on benches week in and week out for the same shared acts of worship.[3] Though for Protestants the sermon was bound to be the centre of that process, it also involved a more complex act of prayer and praise, a ritual integration of ordinary Christians into experience and knowledge of the divine. 'The whole multitude of Gods people in the parish', said the *Homily for repairing and keeping clean of churches*, 'should with one voice and heart call upon the Name of God.'[4] Resistance to the liturgy, often its outright rejection, has been a theme constantly emphasized by historians. Only in recent studies, however, has the centrality of the practice of the liturgy in the parish for the establishment of Protestant identities been more systematically explored.[5]

By the time of the union of the crowns in 1603 three generations of English, Welsh, and Scottish parishioners had been regularly participant in the reformed liturgies. That experience framed and conditioned their religious life, both positively and negatively, and needs to be understood as a prelude to any discussion of religion, community, and the individual. In his *Description of England* William Harrison provided a revealing account of the liturgical round, reflecting his own experience in the parish of

---

[3] See above, pp. 259–61.

[4] J. Griffiths (ed.), *The Two Books of Homilies* (Oxford, 1859), 275.

[5] For an excellent summary of the English evidence see C. Marsh, *Popular Religion in Sixteenth-Century England* (Basingstoke, 1998), 31–43, and '"Common prayer" in England 1560–1640: the view from the pew', *PP* 171 (2001), 66–94. S.L. Arnault, '"Spiritual and sacred actions": the Book of Common Prayer and the understanding of worship in the Elizabethan and Jacobean Church of England', in E. Carlson (ed.), *Religion and the English People: 1500–1640*, Sixteenth-Century Essays and Studies 45 (Kirksville, Mo., 1998), 25–47. J. Maltby, '"By this Book": parishioners, the Prayer Book and the established church', in K. Fincham (ed.), *The Early Stuart Church, 1603–42* (Basingstoke, 1993), 115–37. A valuable account from a literary perspective is R. Targoff, *Common Prayer: The Language of Devotion in Early Modern England* (Chicago, 2001). Above all see Judith Maltby's full development of this theme in her *Prayer Book and People in Elizabethan and Early Stuart England* (Cambridge, 1998). I.B. Cowan, *The Scottish Reformation* (1982), 139–58. G. Donaldson, 'From reformation to covenant', in D.B. Forrester and D.M. Murray (eds.), *Studies in the History of Worship in Scotland* (Edinburgh, 1984), 37–47. There is also an older pattern of liturgical study that provides excellent insight into the broad intellectual significance of the reformed liturgy: W.H. Davies, *Worship and Theology in England from Cranmer to Baxter* (Princeton, 1970). W. McMillan, *The Worship of the Scottish Reformed Church, 1550–1638* (1930).

Radwinter, Essex. The fixed core of Sunday worship was the combination of Morning Prayer, litany and ante-communion, supplemented by sermon or communion on occasions. The cycle of scriptural reading built into these services ensured that parishioners heard the Psalter every thirty days, the New Testament four times a year and the Old Testament once. The ante-communion 'of some in derision called the dry communion' noted Harrison, was followed by a homily if there was no sermon. Although he was hostile to 'dumb dogs', the non-preaching clergy, he was willing for public consumption and national pride to acknowledge the merits of the homilies. But his warmth was reserved more for the manner of the services than their matter. The minister now addressed the congregation directly, enabling even the unlearned to understand and repeat psalms and prayers. The literate followed in their books 'so that the whole congregation in one instant pour out their petitions unto the living God, for the whole estate of the church in most earnest and fervent manner'.[6]

The earliest parallel Scottish account of the practice of regular worship comes from the beginning of the next century. William Cowper, bishop of Galloway, described a Sunday service that conformed closely to the Book of Common Order. This began with the readers' service, comprised of scriptural passages, set prayers, and the singing of metrical psalms, by which 'the hearts of the people are prepared more reverently to hear the word'. The second phase of worship began when the minister entered the pulpit, a psalm was sung, a prayer offered, and then the sermon delivered. The whole was concluded with further prayer, the creed, and the benediction.[7] It is worth stressing the contrasting manner of the two rituals. The Scottish emphasis on the sermon not only displaced a number of the affective aspects of liturgical behaviour; it reinforced the idea that this was a clerically dominated act of worship. Congregational participation in the ritual was confined to the singing of psalms and the saying of the creed: other prayer was explicitly ministerial petitioning on behalf of the community. The predictability and repetitiveness of the English service, allowing collective responses in set formulae, was never the Scottish way, and the only assurances in worship were that Scripture would be

---

[6] G. Edelen (ed.), *William Harrison; The Description of England* (Ithaca, N.Y., 1968), 35–6. In fact Harrison's narrative leaves out several aspects of the obligatory cycle, especially of Morning Prayer with its collects, use of the 'Te Deum' and 'Benedictus' and general confession: W.K. Clay (ed.), *Liturgies and Occasional Forms of Prayer set forth in the Reign of Queen Elizabeth* (PS, Cambridge, 1847), 53–63.

[7] Knox, iv. 293 ff. McMillan, *Worship*, 127–9. The pattern of the reader's service still retained the basic structure of matins and ante-communion, though in a drastically simplified form.

proclaimed, psalms sung, and, when a minister was available, a long sermon given.[8] Yet the differences can easily be exaggerated: Scottish congregations were expected to be actively participant in prayer and praise: the saying of 'Amen' clearly 'declaring their consent to that which is said' and responding with their reason and spirit to the words of the preacher.[9]

Public prayer and collective worship were seen as equally crucial by English and Scottish divines. Not only were these the necessary means to inculcate spiritual obedience and understanding in individuals, they were also a most powerful weapon in gaining divine attention and blessing. Richard Hooker, following Chrysostom, reminded his readers that 'the Prince and the people of Nineveh assembling themselves as a main army of supplicants, it was not in the power of God to withstand them'.[10] But Hooker and his conformist contemporaries were more impressed by the idea that public prayer offered the opportunity for 'common consent', for the pursuit of what was 'needful and good' for the community. In a most vivid phrase Hooker asserted that the collective performance of prayer made everyone present 'earwitnesses' to the petitions and desires of each man.[11] Private prayer, and the pursuit of individual spirituality, while not of themselves condemned, could never substitute for the collective prayer of the Christian corporation, which was far from the mindless conformity or rote repetition assailed by the Puritans. Hooker, of course, sought to defend the 'due performance' of Prayer Book worship, the inward assimilation of formalized prayer, but his affirmation of the power of collective worship could stand as exemplary of the ambition of all Protestant reformers.[12]

Of course, the familiarity of worship might breed contempt as well as acquiescence. Nothing in the repetitions of the Prayer Book liturgy seems to have touched those Dublin congregations that turned from bare conformity to private Catholic devotion. Every form of dissent from outright rejection to sleeping in the pews is to be found in the ecclesiastical records. But it is still essential to emphasize that the proper performance

---

[8] Arnault, 'Book of Common Prayer', 34 ff. There is debate in Scottish historiography about how far the Book of Common Order was a guide and directory rather than a ritual: see Knox, vi. 281–3. Donaldson, 'Reformation to covenant', 41–7.

[9] Targoff, *Common Prayer*, 38–41.

[10] R. Hooker, *The Laws of Ecclesiastical Polity*, v. 24. 1. Jewel also emphasized the power of collective prayer, drawing on Chrysostom: Targoff, *Common Prayer*, 52–5.

[11] Hooker, *Laws*, v. 36. 2.

[12] Margo Todd discusses the importance of active and consensual participation in Scottish worship in *The Culture of Protestantism in Early Modern Scotland* (New Haven, Conn., 2002), 84 ff.

of worship was the bedrock on which all reformation of the parish and its people had to be grounded. Where this critical service failed, or was never fully established, there was little hope of constructing a conformist laity, let alone full Protestants. Both acculturation to the new forms of religious behaviour and gradual training in their meaning were essential for further progress. The local minister remained the key agent in both processes, and on his abilities and dedication most of the viability of the religious settlements rested. The Reformation had stripped the churches of alternatives to parish ministry: there were no post-Tridentine forms of mission to reinforce the efforts of the parson.[13] Most of the time the latter stood alone and as Edward Dering described him: 'the Minister by whom the people do believe'.[14]

The Pastoral Ministry

Richard Greenham, the godly pastor of Dry Drayton in Cambridgeshire, was said to have summed up the duties of the minister as 'none other thing, but to preach the word of God sincerely, and purely with a care of the glory of God . . . and secondly a reverent administration of the sacraments, according to the order and institution of our Saviour Jesus Christ'.[15] In reality his tasks were more complex, including catechizing and other forms of instruction, and the provision of a variety of liturgical services still expected by parishioners and sanctioned by law. And, in emphasizing the primary spiritual duties he undertook, Greenham omitted his own functions as a counsellor, and a leader of the community. He was remembered, for example, as 'a great Friend to, and promoter of peace and concord amongst his neighbours', one who often prevented recourse to litigation, and who himself avoided disputes with his parishioners.[16] Much of this pattern of godly leadership would have been seen as the function of the parish ministry both before and after the Reformation, and across different forms of churchmanship. To read the commentaries on Greenham's time at Dry Drayton is often to recall George Herbert's country parson, or even William Sheppard's ministry in Heydon.[17]

[13] On the wider choices available to the Catholic Church, and the general significance of parish ministry in England, see E. Duffy, 'The Long Reformation: Catholicism, Protestantism and the multitude', in N. Tyacke (ed.), *England's Long Reformation, 1500–1800* (1998), 33–70.

[14] E. Dering, *A Briefe and necessarie Catechisme or Instruction, very needfull to be known to all Housholders*, in *Workes* (1614), sig. A 3ᵛ.

[15] K.L. Parker and E.J. Carlson, *'Practical Divinity': The Works and Life of Richard Greenham* (Aldershot, 1998), 59.

[16] Ibid., 59–85.

[17] F.E. Hutchinson (ed.), *The Works of George Herbert* (Oxford, 1941), 244–86. On Sheppard, see above, p. 208.

Greenham's contemporary Bernard Gilpin, the 'apostle of the North', exemplified many of the traditional qualities of the parson. He was charitable, reconciled neighbours, and gave hospitality, as well as conducting powerful preaching campaigns.[18] Even the purists of the Scottish kirk were not unaware of the importance of the minister's general spiritual and social leadership of his community. William Lauder advised that clergy must be chosen who preached the true gospel, but who could also 'with example of their life/ . . . edify Man, Maid and wife', as well as providing hospitality and charity.[19]

But the prime function of the pastoral ministry was the provision of preaching and instruction in the Protestant faith. Indeed, as Collinson and others have pointed out, it would be possible to assume from much of the literature designed to guide the cleric that there were no other duties of critical importance.[20] Richard Bernard's *The Faithfull Shepherd*, one of the most important examples of the genre, devoted almost two-thirds of its length to the process of preaching, and much of the rest to the preacher's relationship with his congregation.[21] The centrality of preaching led in its turn to the dream of both English and Welsh bishops and Scottish general assemblies that the parochial clergy should become a body of graduates. They would be learned in theology and the tongues and able to convey pure doctrine with authority even to the most discerning of lay audiences. The obstacles in the way of the realization of this vision could be rehearsed at great length. As we have already seen, financial constraints contributed to the difficulties of recruiting learned clergy in all parts of the British Isles, especially in the Highland zones and in Ireland, where little was done to tackle the problems until the next century. Secondly there was the general issue of the instability of the religious settlements until well after 1560, which meant that recruitment of any kind proved to be problematic, and that the difficulties caused by the survival of a previous generation of clerics was compounded by the need to take less-

---

[18] G. Carleton, *The Life and Death of Bernard Gilpin* (1727 edn.), 29–31, 43–4. D. Marcombe, 'Bernard Gilpin: anatomy of an Elizabethan legend', *Northern History* 16 (1980), 20–39. The importance of the traditional virtues in clerics is endlessly underlined in visitation returns. Typical is the comment of Herne parishioners in 1569: 'Mr. Vicar should be a peace-maker, but is a peace breaker': A. Hussey (ed.), 'Visitations of the archdeaconry of Canterbury', *Archaeologia Cantiana* 25 (1902), 26.

[19] F. Hall (ed.), *William Lauder: Ane Compendious and Breve Tractate concernyng the Office and Dewtie of Kyngis, Spirituall Pastoris and Temporall Iugis*, EETS os 4 (1864), 12.

[20] P. Collinson, 'Shepherds, sheepdogs and hirelings: the pastoral ministry in post-Reformation England', in W.J. Sheils and D. Wood (eds.), *The Ministry: Clerical and Lay*, SCH 26 (Oxford, 1989), 185–220. N.R. Enssle, 'Patterns of godly life: the ideal parish minister in sixteenth and seventeenth century English thought', *C16J* 28 (1997), 3–28.

[21] R. Bernard, *The faithfull shepherd . . . to further young divines in the studie of divinitie. With shepherds practise in the end* (1621).

than-satisfactory successors into the ministry. Thirdly there was the question of patronage, and of lay control of key parts of the parochial ministry (less of a dilemma in Scotland than elsewhere). This meant that even when suitable men were ordained they were not necessarily those whom lay patrons wished to promote. And finally there was the question of training: how possible was it for the universities to educate enough men to fill the 9,000 English and Welsh parishes, and the 1,000 Scottish ones, let alone to leave some surplus for Ireland? Harrison certainly thought that the supply of graduates could not meet the demand: 'both our universities are never able to perform' the furnishing of 'able men' for all cures. He commended instead the planned union of benefices, especially in the towns.[22]

The output of the universities was of critical importance in the construction of the pastoral ministry, since Oxford and Cambridge and the four Scottish universities between them provided the major training ground, though they were slowly being supplemented by Trinity College, Dublin, at the very end of the century. Already in 1573 Whitgift was claiming that Cambridge had bred 450 preachers since Elizabeth's accession.[23] Twenty years after Harrison wrote, his pessimism would have been less justified: there were now sufficient graduates in parts of England to fill 80 per cent of the livings in favoured dioceses, and to supply over 50 per cent in almost all.[24] Even in Wales approximately half of those beneficed in Bangor diocese were graduates by the turn of the century.[25] From the university side the matriculation records of Oxford and Cambridge show a marked upward turn in numbers especially after the 1580s. Stone calculated admissions in excess of 400 per annum at Cambridge in the last decades of the century, with a similar but more fluctuating figure for Oxford.[26] Graduation figures were, of course, much lower—between a quarter and a third of those admitted to Oxford seem to have gained BAs in this period—though in turn the majority of this last group were undoubtedly destined for the Church. In Scotland the story was much the same: by the 1590s it was possible to contemplate staffing as many lowland parishes as could afford the cost with graduate clergy, and the steady growth of the universities sustained this trend.[27] The extreme contrast between this situation and that of Ireland did not escape contemporaries.

---

[22] Edelen, *Harrison's Description of England*, 28.

[23] J. Ayre (ed.), *Works of John Whitgift*, 3 vols. (PS, Cambridge, 1851–3), i. 313.

[24] R. O'Day, *The English Clergy* (Leicester, 1979), 135–6.

[25] G. Williams, *Wales and the Reformation* (Cardiff, 1997), 390–1.

[26] L. Stone, 'The size and composition of the Oxford student body, 1580–1910', in L. Stone (ed.), *The Universities in Society*, 2 vols. (Princeton, N.J., 1975), i. 91–2.

[27] D. Stevenson, *King's College, Aberdeen* (Aberdeen, 1990), 55–6, gives figures for average admissions at Aberdeen, Glasgow, and Edinburgh for the decade 1601–10: 19.1, 27.4, and 26.6 respectively.

Until the foundation of Trinity College in the 1590s the only hope of
providing graduates for the Irish church lay either in recruiting native-
born English or Irish clergy, or in persuading Englishmen or Scots to
serve.[28] Neither strategy proved very successful: in the Diocese of Dublin
the only graduates normally in parochial cures were the prebendaries of
St Patrick's Cathedral, and by the 1580s they were almost all imported
from England.[29] Bishop Lyon's reports on the Dioceses of Cork, Cloyne,
and Ross in the 1590s showed that none of his native-born clergy were
graduates or preachers.[30]

It is important to stress how far the mainstream Scottish and English
churches had moved in their pursuit of a learned body of parish clergy
between 1560 and the end of the century. The Scottish Kirk had the
graver problem initially, because it could not automatically depend on the
conversion of the old clergy to staff its parishes, and it had no significant
reserve of new candidates to make good the deficit. The solution was to
ensure that at least readers were recruited to every kirk, while ministers
who were approved as preachers were given the task of covering several
congregations.[31] These basic standards were met outside the Highland
dioceses by the early 1570s, though the proportion of ministers to readers
was only one to five in some places.[32] The percentage of clergy recruited
from the old Church seems to have varied quite widely: in Orkney, for
example, where the bishop, Adam Bothwell, led the way with his own
conversion, a majority of the reformed congregations were served by men
ordained under the old order. On the other hand, the Catholic clergy of
Moray seem collectively to have been unwilling to transfer their allegiance
to the new Kirk: only a handful of the 200 can be traced serving new
congregations.[33] Perhaps the situation in Angus and the Mearns is more
characteristic of lowland Scotland: there between a third and a half of
those who served the new churches in the early 1560s were drawn from
the old establishment.[34] By the 1580s even that part of the old generation
that had changed was no longer available, and the General Assembly also

---

[28] A. Ford, *The Protestant Reformation in Ireland, 1590–1641* (Dublin, 1997), 63–7.

[29] J. Murray, 'The Tudor Diocese of Dublin: Episcopal Government, Ecclesiastical Politics and the Enforcement of the Reformation, 1534–90', Trinity College Dublin Ph.D. (1997), 302–5.

[30] Ford, *Protestant Reformation*, 36–7.

[31] R.M. Healy, 'The preaching ministry in Scotland's First Book of Discipline', *Church History* 58 (1989), 339–53.

[32] T.M.Y. Manson, 'Shetland in the sixteenth century', in I.B. Cowan and D. Shaw (eds.), *The Renaissance and Reformation in Scotland* (Edinburgh, 1983), 211.

[33] C.H. Haws, 'Continuity and change: the clergy of the Diocese of Moray, 1560–74', *Northern Scotland* 5 (1983), 91–8.

[34] F. Bardgett, *Scotland Reformed: The Reformation in Angus and the Mearns* (Edinburgh, 1989), 90–3.

began to take a more rigorous attitude to the position of reader, alleging that it was not an office within the Church, and apparently prohibiting further admissions.[35] Yet readers continued to be employed into the seventeenth century, and inevitably had to be available to plug gaps in a system that still, it was claimed in the 1590s, had 400 parishes 'destitute of the Word'.[36]

While the English and Welsh churches did not experience the same sharp break with the past as did Scotland, the recruitment of clergy proved almost as problematic. In the 1560s and even into the 1570s there were simply too few men of any intellectual calibre being ordained to fill the benefices emptied by the crises of the previous decades. Only one-third of livings in the Diocese of Ely had a resident minister in 1561, and in 1563 the same proportion of Suffolk benefices had no cleric at all.[37] Two decades later parts of the North were still in as bad a condition. Bernard Gilpin, on his itinerant preaching tours of Northumberland, described the clergy as 'poor base priests' with not a preacher among them, and some congregations as 'even dispersed and destitute of pastors'.[38] The bishops were forced to take those who presented themselves, acting, to quote Rosemary O'Day, on the principle that 'an ignorant pastor was better than no pastor'. There were serious attempts to examine candidates on their doctrinal knowledge, and early attempts by Parker to become more 'circumspect in admitting any to the ministry', but circumstances forced uncongenial decisions on most of the prelates.[39]

The archbishop's temporary solution, like that of his Scottish counterparts, was to employ non-ordained readers who could take the regular Sunday service and read the homilies. The English readers never had the preponderant numerical role that they had in parts of Scotland: Grindal's 1561 visitation of London, for example, shows fifty-two readers, and thereafter there was a marked decline to only eleven at the time of Aylmer's 1574 visitation.[40] It seems clear that the leadership of the Church of England found the need to employ readers embarrassing in a way that the Scots did not, and it made every effort to curtail their role. There must, in consequence, have been a number of examples of presentations of unsatisfactory incumbents to livings, men who thereby acquired permanent

---

[35] *BUK* iii. 876.   [36] J. Kirk, *Patterns of Reform* (Edinburgh, 1989), 97–153.
[37] O'Day, *English Clergy*, 49–54, 126–34.   [38] Carleton, *Life of Gilpin*, 45.
[39] The most important example of admissions examinations conducted by the bishops in these years comes from Ely. Even in the early 1560s the archdeacon was rejecting some of those who presented themselves. By the late 1560s enquiries about scriptural knowledge were quite searching and individuals were regularly rejected: Ely Diocesan Records, A/5/1. Perowne, *Correspondence of Parker*, 120–1.
[40] B. Usher, 'Expedient and experiment: the Elizabethan lay reader', in R.N. Swanson (ed.), *Continuity and Changes in Christian Worship*, SCH 35 (Woodbridge, 1999), 185–98.

security in situations which might better have been resolved by short-term appointments until calmer times came. Nor is it entirely clear that readers, in either country, were necessarily the sweepings of the pool of ecclesiastical manpower. The Scots intended readerships as a possible route into full ministry, and in England there are examples of men of good Protestant credentials and some standing taking readers' posts and then moving to ordination and into benefices.

The reformers endeavoured to remedy the deficiencies of clerical understanding with in-service training of the kind that attracted Elizabeth's wrath during the prophesyings crisis. In both Essex and Kent the supervision of unlearned clergy, and their examination in Scripture, was an essential obligation of the prophesying, and in practice continued in one form or another after the major crisis of the 1570s.[41] Bishop Barnes of Durham was persisting steadily with his demand that the clergy give an account of the contents of St Matthew's Gospel to his commissioners in the year after Grindal's disgrace.[42] The convocation of 1587 drew up general orders for the supervision of the unlearned by 'certain grave and learned preachers'.[43] At the end of the century Bishop Howland of Peterborough among others was still enquiring earnestly whether the exercises for 'the increase of . . . knowledge in the Holy Scriptures' were being observed.[44]

None of this wholly satisfied the godly, bent as they were on a preaching ministry, and they continued to denounce 'tolerated readers and . . . newly-made ministers whose readings . . . are such that the people cannot be edified'.[45] They should perhaps have been more grateful that even this bare reading from new men might protect congregations from the worse infection of 'old popish priests', continuing to hold their livings but scarcely changing their spiritual attitudes. It was this latter group, Haigh suggests, who in the transitional generation of the 1560s and 1570s constructed the Elizabethan liturgy in ways that were acceptable to conservatives, adding Latin prayers, accepting the telling of beads during worship, or reciting facing the east end of the church.[46] Curates like William Shaw of Baddesley Clinton, Warwickshire, who 'prayeth for the dead' while administering the Eucharist according to the Protestant rite, were part of an 'army of

---

[41] P. Collinson, *The Religion of Protestants: The Church in English Society 1559–1625* (Oxford, 1982), 128–31.

[42] *The Injunctions and other Ecclesiastical Proceedings of Richard Barnes, Bishop of Durham from 1577 to 1587*, Surtees Society 22 (1850), 70–9.

[43] Wilkins, *Concilia*, iv. 321–2.

[44] W.J. Sheils, *The Puritans in the Diocese of Peterborough, 1558–1610*, Northamptonshire Record Society 30 (1979), 95.

[45] Usher, 'Elizabethan lay reader', 197: the quotation is from *A Brieff Discours off the Troubles at Franckfort* (1575).

[46] C. Haigh, *English Reformations* (Oxford, 1993), 247–9.

time-servers', whose size, precise views, and ultimate affiliation can only be conjectured.[47] In some areas, notably Lancashire, but also in parts of Yorkshire, and in the archdeaconry of Derby, such men were probably in a majority among those serving the parishes in the first years of the reign.[48]

Only in the case of Ireland can we be reasonably certain that variations on the theme of church papism and minimal conformity remained the standard norms of behaviour for the clergy throughout Elizabeth's reign. Andrew Trollope, a prebendary of St Patrick's, believed that the local curates carried with them the Latin version of the Book of Common Prayer but read 'little or nothing of it or can well read it, but they tell the people a tale of our Lady or St Patrick'.[49] One of his colleagues denounced the curates as 'a company of Irish rogues and Romish runagate priests'.[50] There were recurrent complaints of this kind: the clergy were too ignorant and worldly, but were also papists at heart.[51] It seems to have made little difference whether the Pale was being described or those border and Gaelic areas brought under more effective political control in the second half of the Elizabethan era. For example, Bishop Lyon, the conscientious prelate of Cork, Ross, and Cloyne, visited his three dioceses in the early 1590s and found both extensive church papism and the desertion of Protestant services. The clergy often led their congregations into outright recusancy. In 1595 Lyon reported that 'the priests of this country forsake their benefices to become massing priests because they are so well entreated and so much made of amongst the people'.[52] The result was a remarkable manpower crisis experienced by the Church of Ireland that was the reverse image of the situation in mainland Britain. By the turn of the century, when the parishes of England, Scotland, and even Wales were increasingly filled by trained pastors, the Irish church finally lost the remnant of its pre-Elizabethan clergy. They could not be replaced. At that point, if not before, the Protestant church in Ireland ceased to have even a tenuous claim to provide a general parish ministry to the people.[53]

---

[47] A. Walsham, *Church Papists: Catholicism, Conformity and Confessional Polemic in Early Modern England* (Woodbridge, 1993), 15.

[48] J. D'Arcy, 'Late Medieval Catholicism and the Impact of the Reformation in the Archdeaconry of Derby, c.1520–1570', University of Nottingham Ph.D. (1996), 269–75.

[49] PRO SP 63/131/64.

[50] PRO SP 63/115/27.

[51] Murray, 'Tudor Diocese of Dublin', 324–7.

[52] PRO SP 63/183/47. Bodl. MS Carte 55, fos. 580ᵛ–86.

[53] Ford, *Protestant Reformation*, 36–40. For other visitation materials for these years see H.J. Lawlor, 'Two collections of visitation reports in the library of Trinity College', *Hermathena* 31 (1905), covering Commission for Faculties material, but really just a *liber cleri*. A less formal report on religious affiliation in Thomond is printed by B. Cunningham, 'A view of religious affiliation and practice in Thomond, 1591', *Archivium Hibernicum* 48 (1994), 13–23: this pays scant attention to the parishes, focusing instead on the prelates, towns, and noble households.

The Congregation: Leadership

Zealous divines argued that, if only the pastor were worthy, the sheep would unhesitatingly follow him. The history of the Reformation parish yields ample examples to support this premise: communities that were transformed by godly preaching in such a way that lay behaviour was unequivocally altered. The vigour of the young Scottish Kirk is exemplified by the congregational leadership of men such as John Hepburn at Brechin or James Melville at Fern.[54] William Denman, deprived under Mary as rector of Ordsall, Nottinghamshire, returned at the beginning of Elizabeth's reign and for the next decade exercised a crucial influence over the development of Protestantism in his own parish and in neighbouring Retford.[55] When John Favour was appointed as vicar of Halifax in 1594 he immediately began to transform a vast parish of uncertain spiritual loyalties into one in which the principal inhabitants followed his clear lead in the enforcement of strong Protestant standards.[56] It is even easier to argue the case from its negative. Parishes that did not have strong, evangelical leadership from their clergy were frequently slow to assimilate reformed ideas. Thus Tewkesbury, with no resident incumbent and a series of non-preaching curates, did not begin to respond to the Reformation with any visible enthusiasm until the 1580s.[57] Grimsby displayed the same conservatism, born largely of the influence of the traditionalist vicar, Peter Munby, who survived into the Elizabethan era from the mid-Tudor decades.[58] Once again, examples could be multiplied and extended across the English realm, though they are less pertinent to Scotland, with its sharp break with the past.

An emphasis on the dominant influence of the clergy conceals, however, the more complex reality. Power and influence in the parish was shared between clergy and laity: the latter were patrons, wardens, elders, overseers for the poor, and the like. The views of men of weight and worth in the community on matters of religion proved critical to any effective construction of reform.[59] While some of these laymen might

---

[54] Bardgett, *Scotland Reformed*, 103.

[55] D. Marcombe, *English Small Town Life: Retford, 1520–1642* (University of Nottingham, 1993), 179–81.

[56] W. and S. Sheils, 'Textiles and reform: Halifax and its hinterland', in P. Collinson and J. Craig (eds.), *The Reformation in English Towns, 1500–1640* (Basingstoke, 1998), 141–3.

[57] C. Litzenberger, 'The coming of Protestantism to Elizabethan Tewkesbury', in Collinson Craig, *English Towns*, 86–90.

[58] M.D. Lucas, 'Popular Religious Attitudes in Urban Lincolnshire during the Reformation: The Will Evidence, 1520–1600', University of Nottingham Ph.D. (1998), 111–12.

[59] On the general theme of lay/clerical relations in the parish see P. Collinson, 'Magistracy and ministry: a Suffolk miniature', in his *Godly People: Essays on English Protestantism and Puritanism* (1983), 445–66.

tarry on the leadership of the clergy, they were equally likely to seize the initiative if circumstances permitted. When the leading parishioners of Hornchurch in Essex found their conservative vicar William Lambert not to their ideological taste in the 1580s they withdrew to other churches, protesting against his 'unsound doctrine' and failure to preach. In the next decade they went further, persuading the patrons of the benefice, New College, Oxford, to allow them the *de facto* nomination of clerics in return for a contribution to their support. Thereafter the incumbents of Hornchurch had two characteristics: they were sympathetic to Puritan views and they were related to one or other of the key families of the parish.[60] This was merely to act within a traditional parochial structure in ways that town councils behaved throughout England, as they promoted lecturers to urban pulpits and supported the disciplinary efforts of the clergy with their own court structures. While godly preachers like Percival Wiburn in Northampton, Anthony Gilby at Ashby-de-la-Zouch, or Samuel Ward in Ipswich sought to build mini-Genevas in English towns, they had constantly to be aware of the power of the magistracy and their need for its support. This was particularly true when the non-conformity of such men attracted episcopal wrath: for example, the bailiffs of Colchester were unremitting in their efforts to have the town preacher, George Northey, reinstated after he was suspended by Bishop Aylmer in the autumn of 1583. After a year of petitioning, and some braving of episcopal anger, Northey was restored to them and was once more preaching 'the sincere Word of God'.[61]

The Scottish Kirk provides particularly clear evidence of active lay initiative within the parish. Calvinist elders assumed key disciplinary and organizational roles in the kirk sessions and, within the continuing constraints of the traditional patronage system, chose and evaluated their ministers.[62] Indeed the surviving records of the sessions often convey the impression that the clergy were playing subordinate roles in the parishes, especially in those burgh churches where laymen had traditionally funded much of their own religious provision. When the burgesses of Ayr elected boldly to support the Lords of the Congregation and adopt Protestant worship they sent representatives to Edinburgh to find a minister, then casually alluded to in the accounts as 'a preacher'.[63] The only early surviv-

---

[60] M. McIntosh, *A Community Transformed: The Manor and Liberty of Havering, 1500–1620* (Cambridge, 1991), 181 3.

[61] M. Byford, 'The birth of a Protestant town: the process of reformation in Tudor Colchester, 1530–1580', in Collinson and Craig, *English Towns*, 42–5. L.M. Higgs, *Godliness and Governance in Tudor Colchester* (Ann Arbor, Mich., 1998), 323–4.

[62] Kirk, *Patterns of Reform*, 368 ff.; 'Royal and lay patronage in the Jacobean kirk, 1572–1600', in MacDougall, *Church*, 127–50.

[63] G.S. Pryde (ed.), *Ayr Burgh Accounts, 1534–1624*, SHS 3rd ser. 28 (Edinburgh, 1937), 130.

ing example of a rural register for a kirk session, that for Monifieth in Angus, shows the powerful influence of families of local lairds as elders but is surprisingly silent on the role of the clergy.[64] Later records are more ample, and do much to correct these impressions, but the intrusion of the laity into what might customarily be thought to be clerical affairs is striking. It seems, for example, that it was accepted practice for the sessions to agree on the subjects suitable for preaching: in 1598 St Andrews' session endorsed the arrangement by which the minister, George Gladstaines, would give sermons on the Second Book of Samuel, to be followed by the Book of Kings.[65]

Yet it would be naive to conclude from the last example that the ferocious ministers who led the Calvinist revolution in Scotland saw themselves as subordinated to lay interests. Gladstaines was conciliating a congregation that had been deeply polarized by a prime example of ministerial determination not to co-operate with the laity. David Black, the minister at St Andrews from 1590 to 1597, was a high clericalist who would, as one historian has noted, have gladdened the heart of Innocent III. In 1592 he refused for a time to continue his ministry on the grounds that his flock did not deserve him and he would 'disgrace his ministry no more amongst them'.[66] The only consolation for his congregation was that he despised his fellow ministers as much as the laity, calling them 'belly fellows, sycophants, gentlemen ministers, leaders of the people to hell'.[67] Black was merely the most extreme of a Melvillian coterie who denied any possibility of compromise within the local kirks. James Melville described another, Robert Bruce, as 'most comfortable to the good and godly, and most fearful to the enemies,' but the danger was that extremism lost such men as those to whom they should be 'most comfortable'.[68] The lesson learned by the end of the 1590s was that such absolutism was counterproductive: even in the white heat of religious revolution good governance of the Church depended on lay–clerical

---

[64] F.D. Bardgett, 'The Monifieth kirk register', *RSCHS* 23 (1987–9), 175–95. McMillan, *Worship*, 121. This impression of initiative is sometimes the product simply of a shortage of clergy. The image of parishioners organizing much of their own spiritual lives, because they had no preachers, emerges very clearly from visitations of the 1580s: J. Kirk (ed.), *Visitation of the Diocese of Dunblane*, SRS 11 (Edinburgh, 1984).

[65] D. Hay Fleming (ed.), *Register of the Minister, Elders and Deacons of the Christian Congregation of St Andrews*, 2 vols., SHS 4, 7 (1889–90), ii. 856.

[66] G. Parker, 'The "Kirk by law established" and the origins of "the taming of Scotland": St Andrews 1559–1600', in R. Mentzer (ed.), *Sin and the Calvinists: Moral Control and the Consistory in the Reformed Tradition* (Kirksville, Mo., 1994), 186–7.

[67] M.F. Graham, *The Uses of Reform: 'Godly Discipline' and Popular Behaviour in Scotland and Beyond, 1560–1610* (Leiden, 1996), 192–201.

[68] R. Pitcairn (ed.), *The Autobiography and Diary of James Melvill* (Wodrow Society, Edinburgh, 1842), 271.

co-operation.[69] 'If magistrates and ministers agree not,' said a Bury St Edmunds preacher in 1600, 'and the people reverence and love them both, what can come of it?'[70]

There has been much debate among historians about the status of those laymen who exercised influence over the parochial church in the later sixteenth century. The thesis sometimes advanced is that the diversity of lay office-holding before the Reformation, diffused as it was through the ranks of the guilds and fraternities, ensured participation from men of modest standing in the community. However, by the end of the century it was only the 'better sort' who could exercise control through patronage and office in England, and through the specific institution of the eldership in Scotland.[71] Parallels are remarked with the intensification of oligarchy in secular government in towns and burghs. There is evidence to support these views: the eldership in Scotland was certainly led in many rural areas by lairds. In the burghs the mercantile establishments were dominant: in Edinburgh, for example, they are described as becoming 'virtually the proprietors' of the kirk sessions, though they needed support from leading lawyers.[72] At St Andrews an equally oligarchic arrangement divided power between the leaders of the burgh and the university regents.[73] Much the same function was performed in Irish towns by the guilds that, incongruously, had been allowed to survive the Reformation. The Dublin guild of St Anne dominated the church of St Audoen's, and its masters and wardens were almost invariably drawn from the ranks of the aldermen.[74] It is indicative of the peculiar religious situation in the Irish capital that the guild was a crypto-Catholic public institution that evaded governmental attempts to change its nature. The most powerful urban initiatives in support of the English clergy usually came from town councils, as corporations strove to build new Jerusalems 'compact together'.[75] At

[69] For some interesting comparative examples of negotiations between laity and clergy in different European Reformation contexts see A. Pettegree (ed.), *The Reformation of the Parishes: The Ministry and the Reformation in Town and Country* (Manchester, 1993). The ability of Scottish elders and ministers to use the support of local secular courts also needs to be stressed: B. Lenman, 'The limits of godly discipline in the early modern period with particular reference to England and Scotland', in K. Von Greyerz (ed.), *Religion and Society in Early Modern Europe, 1500–1800* (1984), 137–9.

[70] Quoted in P. Collinson, *The Religion of Protestants* (Oxford, 1982), 156.

[71] The classic statement of the restrictive view of lay participation after the Reformation is in J.J. Scarisbrick, *The Reformation and the English People* (Oxford, 1984), 162–4.

[72] M. Lynch, *Edinburgh and the Reformation* (Edinburgh, 1981), 39–41.

[73] Graham, *Uses of Reform*, 78–82. Parker, 'St Andrews', 166–7.

[74] C. Lennon, *The Lords of Dublin in the Age of Reformation* (Dublin, 1989), 144–9, 163.

[75] P. Collinson, *The Birthpangs of Protestant England* (Basingstoke, 1988), 28–59: the quotation is from the Geneva Bible. Higgs, *Tudor Colchester*, 191–8. J. Martin, 'Leadership and priorities in Reading during the Reformation', in Collinson and Craig, *English Towns*, 125–7.

parochial level concerns for godliness and good order began to express themselves in the later years of the century in the form of 'closed' or 'select' vestries.[76]

But a case can be made for a continuing pluralism in lay service of the parish. Elders had to be seconded by deacons, and they could be drawn from a wider cross-section of the community. Churchwardens were still often chosen from the ordinary ranks of the middling sort, the 'solidly placed' rather than necessarily the wealthy or influential.[77] Beneath them the growing diversity of parochial obligations also created a diversity of offices. Sworn men, overseers of the poor, administrators of private charities, and, somewhat later, sidesmen, were added to the crucial wardens. In St Mary's, Chester, the late sixteenth and early seventeenth centuries saw a ten-fold increase in office-holders.[78] Towards the end of the century both wardens and sidesmen in Romford and Hornchurch, Essex, were drawn from the middling ranks of local society, with a strong representation from artisan groups.[79] Parochial involvement was certainly not egalitarian, since it usually demanded a measure of standing in the community, but it was often diffused more widely than is suggested by historians obsessed by the growth of oligarchy.

The Use of the Church

A prime necessity for the congregation was the provision of a proper physical environment and the supporting furnishings for Protestant worship. Neither the English nor the Scottish settlement was fully prescriptive on this matter. There was a pragmatic understanding that existing buildings would have to be adapted as best they might to the demands of the new liturgy. In the case of Scotland the basic principles for reformed worship followed from the guidance of the Book of Common Order: there was to be no division within the church, the pulpit was to be the focus of the assembly, and when communion was to be celebrated a table

---

[76] B. Kümin, *The Shaping of a Community: The Rise and Reformation of the English Parish, c.1470–1560* (Aldershot, 1996), 29–31, 236. P. Collinson, 'Cranbrook and the Fletchers: popular and unpopular religion in the Kentish Weald', in P.N. Brooks (ed.), *Reformation Principle and Practice* (1980), 171–202.

[77] E. Carlson, 'The origins, function and status of the office of churchwarden, with particular reference to the diocese of Ely', in M. Spufford (ed.), *The World of Rural Dissenters, 1520–1725* (Cambridge, 1995), 191–200. J. Craig, 'Co-operation and initiatives: Elizabethan churchwardens and the parish accounts of Mildenhall', *Social History* 18/3 (1994), 357–80.

[78] N. Alldridge, 'Loyalty and identity in Chester parishes 1540–1640', in S. Wright (ed.), *Parish, Church and People* (1988), 103–12. The Chester hierarchy within parish office-holding can be identified by age as well as status; senior offices were largely reserved for men of mature age.

[79] McIntosh, *Community Transformed*, 231–8. Marcombe, *Retford*, 235–9.

was to be set in the midst of the congregation, who were to be seated around it.[80] Even this apparent clarity left considerable scope for congregational adaptation. In the early years some chancels continued to be used for the administration of communion, as at Crail and Perth.[81] An alternative location for the table was a separate communion aisle. Much more significantly, many congregations seem in the early years to have resisted the specific requirement of the General Assembly that there should be no burials in the church. Like their English counterparts Scottish congregations continued to use their churches as a means of articulating social hierarchy: pewing became common in the new sermon-based form of worship, and pews were so ordered that 'everyone [is] entertained answerable to his quality'.[82] The placing of pulpits, decoration of the walls with scriptural texts, and the painting of lofts all reflected much local congregational choice.[83]

The Book of Common Prayer also seemed to offer firm instructions for the physical environment of worship in the parish church. The rubric before Morning Prayer ordered that chancels should remain as they had been, demarcated from the nave. The 1559 Book repeated the order of the 1552 Communion Service that the celebrant stand on the north side of the communion table, which should be located 'in the body of the Church, or in the chancel, where Morning Prayer and Evening Prayer be appointed to be said'.[84] But these orders proved open to a variety of interpretations. The Royal Injunctions of 1559, displaying Elizabeth's sympathies, actually insisted that it was of no great significance whether altars or tables were used in churches provided 'the Sacrament be duly and reverently ministered'.[85] The visitors, however, adopted the firmest interpretation of the orders, denying that the altars were matters of indifference, and upholding the principle of the moveable table, placed against the east wall only when not being used for communion. Stone altars were attacked systematically. Edwin Sandys may have exaggerated when he claimed in 1559 that 'all

---

[80] Knox, vi. 292 ff.

[81] G. Hay, *The Architecture of Scottish Post-Reformation Churches 1560–1843* (Oxford, 1957), 25–6, 179–81.

[82] The seventeenth-century pewing plan for the new church of Burntisland shows the Scottish preoccupation with status within church: D. Howard, *The Architectural History of Scotland: Scottish Architecture from the Reformation to the Restoration, 1560–1660* (Edinburgh, 1995), 175–84. P. Hume Brown, *Early Travellers in Scotland* (Edinburgh, 1891), 205.

[83] Hay, *Scottish Churches*, 216. N. Yates, *Buildings, Faith and Worship: The Liturgical Arrangements of Anglican Churches, 1600–1900* (Oxford, 1991), 28.

[84] J. Ketley (ed.), *The Two Liturgies AD 1549 and AD 1552 . . . In the Reign of King Edward VI* (PS, Cambridge, 1844), 217, 265.

[85] G. Bray (ed.), *Documents of the English Reformation* (Cambridge, 1994), 347. On the bishops' opposition to Elizabeth on the stone altars see J. Strype, *Annals of the Reformation* (1824 edn.), i. i. 237–42.

polluted and defiled altars' were down, but within a few years all but the most remote parishes had displaced their stones.[86]

Episcopal orders, the Interpretations of 1561 and the 1566 Advertisements, offered further, somewhat divergent, directions for worship. The second allowed the communion table to be moved into the nave for the celebration 'where either the choir seemeth to be too little or at great feasts of receiving'; the last permitted Common Prayer to be said 'in such place as the Ordinary shall think meet . . . so that the people may be most edified'.[87] Later episcopal injunctions tended to interpret the last comment as meaning that the service should be read in the body of the church, finally affirming the end of the separation between laity and clergy in nave and chancel. The drastic process of remodelling was completed by the replacement of the old images with the royal arms, and scriptural texts, especially Commandment boards.[88]

In practice these injunctions, like those of Scotland, left scope for congregational initiative. The communion table, for example, was normally stored at the east end of the church, but its exact positioning for the giving of the Eucharist remained unspecified.[89] The fragmentary evidence suggests that parishioners overcame any earlier aversion to moving into the chancel and gathering round the communion board.[90] However, only in 1604 did the canons finally fix the location of the table east/west in the centre of the chancel for the administration of communion.[91] Other issues, such as where the minister should stand to read the service and whether organs were retained, were largely determined by congregational choice, within broadly stated principles of decorum and audibility.[92] A traditional parish like Tewkesbury took until a decade into the seventeenth century to move its pulpit to the customary place in the nave,

[86] J. Ayre (ed.), *The Sermons of Edwyn Sandys* (PS, Cambridge, 1841), 250. R. Hutton, 'The local impact of the Tudor Reformation', in C. Haigh (ed.), *The English Reformation Revised* (Cambridge, 1987), 134–6. Parts of Wales seem to have been an exception: Bishop Middleton remained convinced in the 1580s that altars and rood lofts survived, and railed against them in his injunctions: W.M. Kennedy, *Elizabethan Episcopal Administration*, 3 vols. (1924), iii. 139 ff.

[87] *VAI* iii. 62, 174, 208–9.

[88] G.W.O. Addleshaw and F. Etchells, *The Architectural Setting of Anglican Worship* (1948), 30–6.

[89] Yates, *Buildings, Faith and Worship*, 31. G. Yule, 'James VI and I: furnishing the churches in his two kingdoms', in A. Fletcher and P. Roberts (eds.), *Religion, Culture and Society in Early Modern Britain* (Cambridge, 1994), 182–208. In an early lament about diversity of liturgical practice, Archbishop Parker complained of the endless ways in which the communion table was being stored and used: BL Lans. MS 8, fo. 16.

[90] Maltby, *Prayer Book and People*, 48–9.

[91] G. Bray (ed.), *The Anglican Canons, 1529–1947*, Church of England Record Society 7 (Woodbridge, 1998), 377.

[92] Craig, 'Co-operation and initiatives', 372. For a parochial debate on organs see H.G. Owen, 'Tradition and reform: ecclesiastical controversy in an Elizabethan London parish', *Guildhall Miscellany* 11 (1961), 63–70.

presumably thus belatedly signalling its acceptance of the centrality of sermons.[93] The survival of chancel screens, demarcating the areas of the church, was similarly a matter of local choice, and the bishops in general seem to have been willing to accept that screens were quite distinct from the roods that they had once held, in no sense a monument to superstition. Stained glass often remained, despite an attack on it in 1559 as part of the challenge to images, for the very practical reason that it was too costly to replace.[94] Like the Scots, English parishioners also retained considerable freedom to furnish their churches with pews, tombs, and the like, within the broad parameters of ecclesiastical law. Pews became an ever more important element in the hierarchical ordering of the congregation, the subject of increasingly elaborate planning by the churchwardens and a fertile source of litigation in the church courts. Burial within the church continued to be acceptable to the English bishops, and the last years of the sixteenth century became a golden age of funeral architecture.[95]

Ecclesiastical authorities were often more concerned about the state of the fabric of churches than about their precise internal layout. The 1562 homily 'For repairing and keeping clean the Church' lamented that 'the world thinketh it but a trifle to see their church in ruin and decay', and a host of visitation returns attest to the depth of the problem in England and Wales.[96] Litigiousness between churchwardens, responsible for the care of the nave, and appropriators, farmers of rectories, or clerics responsible for the chancel, enhanced the rhetoric of complaint, but the physical problems of fabric decay were very real.[97] Even so, the building stock of the English church was in better heart than that of the Scots. In Scotland the neglect of appropriators, the relative poverty of congregations, and the general weakness of the parochial structure outside the burghs meant that there was major work to be done to provide a proper physical environment for worship. This was just beginning in the last decades of the sixteenth century: fewer than a dozen new churches were built between 1560 and 1620.[98]

---

[93] Litzenberger, 'Tewkesbury', in Collinson and Craig, *English Towns*, 88.

[94] Edelen, *Harrison's Description of England*, 35–6.

[95] For a useful set of examples from the ecclesiastical records see J.S. Purvis (ed.), *Tudor Parish Documents of the Diocese of York* (Cambridge, 1948), 87–91. On tombs see N. Llewellyn, *Funeral Monuments in Post-Reformation England* (Cambridge, 2000), which supersedes all earlier work, and P. Sherlock, 'Funeral Monuments: Piety, Honour and Memory in early Modern England', University of Oxford D Phil. (2000).

[96] Griffiths, *Homilies*, 275.

[97] For example, a third of the parishes of Chichester registered defective fabric at the 1571 visitation of West Sussex, and Grindal's 1575 visitation of York produced 75 chancels and 25 churches in decay: Haigh, *English Reformations*, 250; W.J. Sheils (ed.), *Archbishop Grindal's Visitation, 1575*, Borthwick Texts and Calendars 4 (1977), vii.

[98] Howard, *Architectural History*, 177–88. Yule, 'Furnishing the churches', 204–7.

Those Scottish kirks that were constructed in the early decades of the Reformation show a very self-conscious break with the Catholic past both in physical organization and in aesthetics. Apart from the remarkable square church at Burntisland, thought to have been influenced by both Scandinavian and French examples, the rest tend to a simple rectangular, or later to a T-plan, seek to maximize open space, and use modified classical features rather than Gothic detail.[99] No semblance of a chancel was retained. These seem to be the choices of the devout laymen who paid for their construction, and they can be read as evidence of firm acceptance of clerically defined Calvinist forms of worship.[100] But Scottish kirk buildings reveal one significant deviation from the established convention of the simple open church structure: the building, or extension, of burial aisles often associated with a loft or seat above for the family of the laird. The importance of burial practices, and of the continuity between living and dead kin, could scarcely be more strongly illustrated. And this was undertaken in the face of the explicit hostility of the General Assembly.[101]

In England there was effectively no new church building in the late sixteenth century, though from the 1580s onwards there are significant examples of internal reconstruction.[102] What can be accumulated from churchwardens' accounts is evidence of adaptivity in the use of existing building space. There seems to have been quite wide acceptance of the continued partitioning of the church, and plenty of examples of the alteration of stalls in the choir to make them suitable for communicants kneeling around a table in the centre of the chancel. It is probable that a number of churches went further and, as in the surviving examples at Hailes and Deerhurst, Gloucestershire, constructed virtual communion rooms for the comfort of the parish, running the benches around the back of the east wall, as well as in the customary choir location.[103] These

[99] Though it must be said that not all simple rectangular churches derive from the post-Reformation period: this modest form with no differentiated chancel was characteristic of many small kirks in the late medieval period: Hay, *Scottish Churches*, 19, 22–3.

[100] The only new church specifically inspired by, and partly funded by, a cleric appears to be Prestonpans, where the minister was John Davidson: Howard, *Architectural History*, 184–5.

[101] A. Spicer, ' "Defyle not Christ's kirk with your carrion": burial and the development of burial aisles in post-Reformation Scotland', in B. Gordon and P. Marshall (eds.), *The Place of the Dead: Death and Remembrance in Late Medieval and Early Modern Europe* (Cambridge, 2000), 149–69.

[102] D. MacCulloch, 'The myth of the English Reformation', *JBS* 30 (1991), 13. The accumulating evidence suggests that the period from the 1590s onwards is significant for church refurbishment, with Archbishop Whitgift's survey of churches commissioned in 1602 providing the stimulus for renewal already under way: A. Foster, 'Churchwardens' accounts of early modern England and Wales', in K.L. French, G.C. Gibbs, and B.A. Kümin (eds.), *The Parish in English Life, 1400–1600* (Manchester, 1997), 86–9.

[103] Addleshaw and Etchells, *Anglican Worship*, 37–45. Yule, 'Furnishing the churches', 192–8. C. Litzenberger, 'St Michael's, Gloucester, 1540–1580: the cost of conformity in sixteenth-century England', in French *et al.*, *Parish in English Life*, 246–7.

alterations show acceptance of reformed Eucharistic practice, but also positive investment in what was only a very intermittent aspect of parish worship. Otherwise the evidence of repair and reconstruction in the years before 1600 often seems to indicate conservatism among those supplying the funds, whether patrons or congregations.[104] The survival of Gothic design for windows, arches, and the like shows that masons were not pressed to rethink their traditional ecclesiastical repertoire, even though they might be required to produce classical motifs for tombs.[105] It seems to have occurred to no one in England that clear aesthetic delineation of places of worship might signal more explicitly the separation of the Church from its popish roots. The only classical temple for worship

'The Reformed Church'. John Foxe's *Book of Martyrs*. Permission of the Bodleian Library

[104] The only wholly new buildings tend to be chapels associated with noble and gentry households, though Easton Grey in Wiltshire was built in 1591 by Edward Seymour, earl of Hertford, after the demolition of the friary church. St James, Southwick, Hampshire, was rebuilt in 1566 by John Whyte, and a new church at Risley in Derbyshire was begun by Michael Willoughby in 1592: N. Pevsner, *Buildings of England: Wiltshire* (1975), 233; *Hampshire* (1967), 604–5; *Derbyshire* (1978), 310.

[105] A. Woodger, 'Post-Reformation mixed Gothic in Huntingdonshire church towers and the campanological associations', *Archaeological Journal* 141 (1984), 269–308. The Tuscan columns identified by Pevsner at Metheringham, Lincolnshire, are a rare exception, made the more interesting because they are by John Tirrell, mason to the recusant Sir Thomas Tresham, a noted exponent of Renaissance architecture: N. Pevsner, *The Buildings of England: Lincolnshire*, 605.

remained in the visual imagination of John Day when he illustrated the
Edwardian Reformation in Foxe's *Book of Martyrs*.[106]

The drastic changes in the physical appearance of British churches in
the half-century after the Reformation raises the further question of how
far the idea of the church as sacred space was altered by religious change.
The ecclesiastical authorities in England, Scotland, and Ireland consistently
maintained that the church was territory apart, 'not for any superstition'
or veneration of a popish kind, but because it was 'God's house'.[107] After
the Reformation, as before, visitation articles asked about the decent order
of the church and churchyard and reverent behaviour during services and
at other times. And there were invariably a stream of complaints in archdeacons' courts and at kirk sessions under all these headings. Naves were
routinely in disrepair; dog-whippers had to be appointed to remove the
barking animals during divine worship; children played in the kirk and the
kirkyard; popular festivities invaded sacred territory.[108] Two examples can
stand for an infinity of others: the wardens of Goring, Berkshire, were
in trouble in the 1580s for allowing dancing and bowling in the churchyard, the latter 'in the processional way'. They also turned a blind eye
to the curate's pigs, who rooted among the tombs. Meanwhile two 'ale-
men' were cited for disturbing the minister during the service, apparently
by allowing a reveller to enter the church during Whitsun week celebrations.[109]

Much of the evidence of casual profanity of sacred space, neglect of
fabric, and promiscuous mixing of the sacred and secular is merely a
continuation of age-old peccadilloes, contested between the local agents
of the parish and their superiors. However, there are some indications of
change before 1600. The general assault upon popular festivities in both
England and Scotland had the indirect consequence of diminishing conflict about the use of sacred space: no Lords of Misrule, no invasion of the
church.[110] In so far as festivity continued to possess a sacred dimension, it

[106] Included as illus. 8.
[107] Todd, *Culture of Protestantism*, 315 ff. J. Hubert, 'Sacred beliefs and beliefs of sacredness',
in D. Carmichael, J. Hubert, *et al.* (eds.), *Sacred Sites, Sacred Places* (1994), 11–14.
[108] I owe the emphasis on dog-whippers to a paper given by John Craig at the Reformation
Studies Colloquium, Warwick, April 2000. The Scottish Kirk was also eager to exclude dogs,
McMillan, *Worship*, 157–8. On May revellers invading the church see R. Hutton, *The Rise and
Fall of Merry England* (Oxford, 1994), 116–17, citing a famous passage of denunciation by Philip
Stubbes.
[109] E.R.C. Brinkworth (ed.), *The Archdeacon's Court: Liber Actorum, 1584*, 2 vols., Oxfordshire
Record Society 23–4 (1942–6), i. 27, 43.
[110] On the slow exclusion of popular drama from the church see Collinson, 'Elizabethan and
Jacobean Puritanism as forms of popular religious culture', in C. Durston and J. Eales (eds.), *The
Culture of English Puritanism 1560–1700* (Basingstoke, 1996), 32–57.

was more likely to be marginalized and heterodox, to locate itself in such alternative venues as holy wells.[111] The notion that the whole parish was in some way sacred space was also weakened by the general attack on processions, and by official constraints on the one form of procession still permitted in the English church: the beating of the bounds at Rogation-tide. A series of injunctions sought to limit the idea of Rogation to thanksgiving for divine blessings, avoiding any implication that any form of consecration was involved. Grindal's 1560 injunctions set the tone by ordering that no banners, surplices, or lights should accompany the processions. There were plenty of complaints of neglect of the ceremony under Elizabeth, but far fewer that it had been abused for popish ends.[112]

The greatest change, however, was internal to the church, and consequential on the Protestant demolition of the sacrificial sacramental economy of the Mass. The official removal of the altar and its replacement by a formal table was deemed insufficient by the godly: they admired instead the Scottish example of tables placed temporarily in the kirk for the communion. There were therefore symbolic gestures of 'irreverence' towards the communion table by Puritans, with hats placed upon it and the like. In the Isle of Man one enthusiast ended in gaol for persisting in 'irreverently' leaning on the table.[113] Ordinary English parishioners were not necessarily moved to subvert the sacred in this way. However, they do seem to have recognized the table as spiritually distinct from the altar that had preceded it. The evidence that the parishioners of Morebath conducted their annual audit at and on the communion table is particularly revealing. It still offered a serious focus for parochial activity, but no longer one imbued with the sacred.[114] Perhaps sacred space became, for some of these parishioners, something that might more properly be called solemn space: an environment in which proper reflection on religious matters took place. But older views died hard, and the belief in consecrated ground as set apart retained efficacy in the new world. The insist-

---

[111] R. Gillespie, *Devoted People: Belief and Religion in Early Modern Ireland* (Manchester, 1997), 90–2.

[112] *VAI* iii. 164. See also iii. 14, 15, 60, 208, 264, 378. Hutton, *Merry England*, 142–3. F. Emmison, 'Tithes, perambulation and sabbath-breach in Elizabethan Essex', in F. Emmison and R. Stephans (eds.), *Tribute to an Antiquary* (1976), 183–7. R. Greaves, *Society and Religion in Elizabethan England* (Minneapolis, Minn., 1981), 427–8. Perambulation was widely neglected by the late years of Elizabeth's reign, but it is impossible to distinguish godly objections to the practice from a plethora of practical objections to going a-walking.

[113] A.W. Moore (ed.), *The Book of Common Prayer in Manx Gaelic* (Manx Society, Oxford, 1895), p.ix. The determination of the godly to desacralize the altar is understandable in the light of the type of report from New Ross, County Wexford, in 1606 that Catholics regularly made superstitious offerings at the place 'where the high altar stood': *CSP Irl* 1606–8. 15.

[114] E. Duffy, *The Voices of Morebath: Reformation and Religion in an English Parish* (New Haven, Conn., 2001), 144.

ence of Scottish congregations on kirk burial in the teeth of clerical opposition is a paradigmatic example of this sentiment.[115]

Patterns of Worship: Communion and the Rites of Passage

The Book of Common Prayer required that parishioners should take
communion three times a year, including Easter. The General Assembly
of the Scottish Kirk decreed in 1562 that communion should be celebrated four times a year in the burghs, though twice was thought sufficient in rural areas.[116] Yet in both churches committed Calvinist divines
longed for a much more regular reception. Herbert Westfaling, later
bishop of Hereford, wrote in 1582 of 'our negligence in resorting to
the Lords table' that 'giveth the adversary great advantage against us'.[117]
The ideal of a monthly, or even weekly, communion was regularly in the
minds of those godly divines who counselled on proper Christian behaviour. There is little evidence, however, that the laity of either realm felt
moved by the arguments of their clergy on this issue. The cultural norm,
inherited from the pre-Reformation world, was that of an annual Easter
communion, and even when clerics supplied three celebrations a year, or
even had begun to follow the episcopal ideal of monthly celebration, the
laity seem to have assumed that only one appearance was required of
them.[118] There are many possible explanations for this adherence to old
patterns of behaviour, including, no doubt, residual beliefs that the two
rites possessed the same meaning. But there was also the fact that it was at
least as complex to administer the Eucharist in the reformed rite as it had
been under Catholicism. The demands on the clergy were significant.
Parishioners had to be subject to some examination of their worthiness to
receive, disputants to be reconciled, and adults tested on their knowledge
of the Ten Commandments, Creed and Lord's Prayer. The burdens on
the wardens or elders included the purchase of considerable quantities of
wine, and the difficult logistics of managing large congregations, the latter

---

[115] One of the identifying marks of radical non-conformity should have been the insistence
that the church as building possessed no distinctive holiness: in practice one of the few
who makes this attack is John Penry, who in a draft letter to the earl of Essex denounces existing churches and cathedrals, which must be destroyed so 'that the land may be cleansed from
these dead bones of Gog': A. Peel (ed.), *The Notebook of John Penry, 1593*, CS 3rd ser. 67 (1944),
89.
[116] J.K. Cameron (ed.), *The First Book of Discipline* (Edinburgh, 1972), 183, for the initial
insistence on communion four times yearly. *BUK* i. 30, 58.
[117] H. Westfaling, *A treatise of Reformation in Religion* (1582), sig. 2Bi.
[118] A. Hunt, 'The Lord's Supper in early modern England', *PP* 161 (1998), 41–9. *Injunctions
of Bishop Barnes*, 13.

problem both in Scotland and England leading to the introduction of communion tokens in urban parishes.[119]

There were, therefore, practical disincentives to frequent celebrations. In Scotland and Ireland, as elsewhere in the Calvinist world, the logical development of a sacramental celebration taken so solemnly and involving such complexity was the great open-air communion service, called the 'holy fair' by Burns.[120] There are some signs that English Puritan congregations might have moved in this direction, in the communions that they associated with days of preaching and fasting, like the famous assembly of over a thousand people in the grounds of Wisbech Castle, witnessed by the Jesuit William Weston.[121] The English church courts and ordinary English parishioners continued to settle for the more modest target of regular Easter communion, though by the end of the century there is evidence of a slow movement towards more frequent celebration in some communities.[122] London parishes seem to have led the way, with quite regular conformity to the Prayer Book requirement increasing to monthly communion in some places during the early Jacobean years.[123]

The general continuance of annual celebration of communion does not point to a conclusion that the sacrament was not taken seriously by either clergy or parishioners. Many of the former saw it as an opportunity to ensure that their flocks had a proper understanding of the faith. The weapon of exclusion from communion appears to have been used sparingly, but when it was employed in England in the late sixteenth century it was most often because of alleged ignorance. The rector of Lexden, Essex, refused communion to two of his parishioners in 1580, and they were told by the church court to go to him each week to 'learn to say that catechism by heart'.[124] Elinor Awd of Elwick, County Durham, was excluded by the collective judgement of the curate and churchwardens because she had quarrelled with a neighbour, but also because 'she is not

---

[119] The classic study of the organizational demands of communion in late Elizabethan England is J. Boulton, 'The limits of formal religion: the administration of Holy Communion in late Elizabethan and early Stuart London', *London Journal* 10/2 (1984), 140–6. I.B. Cowan, *The Scottish Reformation* (1982), 144–9.

[120] L.E. Schmidt, *Holy Fairs: Scottish Communions and American Revivals in the Early Modern Period* (Princeton, N.J., 1989). Gillespie, *Devoted People*, 100–1.

[121] P. Caraman (ed.), *William Weston: The Autobiography of an Elizabethan* (1955), 164–5. See also Patrick Collinson's comments on this form of popular religious culture in his 'Elizabethan and Jacobean Puritanism', in Durston and Eales, *Culture of English Puritanism*, 52–6.

[122] M. Ingram, *The Church Courts, Sex and Marriage in England, 1570–1640* (Cambridge, 1987), ch. 3.

[123] Hunt, 'The Lord's Supper', 53–5.

[124] C. Haigh, 'Communion and community: exclusion from communion in post-Reformation England', *JEH* 51 (2000), 721–40.

diligent to learn the Ten Commandments'.[125] The test of basic catechism knowledge was also applied firmly in Scotland, where tokens were only handed out once the recipients had recited the relevant confessions.[126] From the perspective of the parishioners access to communion was likely to possess both social and spiritual connotations. It continued, as in the pre-Reformation period, to show that you were in charity with your neighbours, and therefore in good standing in the community.[127] Exclusion was an embarrassment, a challenge to status and reputation, and there are examples of individuals expressing this clearly by demanding their 'rights' to the sacrament, or even forging tokens if they were denied access. The visibility of the 'goats' excluded from grace was clearest in Scotland, where the communion tables were roped off to keep the token-less outside. But the evidence sometimes points to a rather more complex commitment to communion in the new dispensation. There were complaints against clergy who failed to provide the proper occasions for reception. John Robotham's parishioners were aggrieved that at Easter 1577 he was so preoccupied by bowls that they were 'defrauded of their intent'.[128] Or there is the admission from several of the Puritan ministers critical of popular behaviour that parishioners often regarded the day of the Eucharist as a solemn occasion when virtue and sobriety predominated. The common people, said Jeremiah Dyke, will resist temptation by their companions after the sacrament saying 'Oh fie, by no means, I have been today at the sacrament, I may not so much forget my self.'[129]

Taking the Eucharist in Elizabethan England and Jacobean Scotland showed some continuities with the Catholic past. One was the insistence on proper preparation: for the Protestant clergy primarily a matter of the congregation having appropriate understanding of the rite; for the laity it involved an insistence on 'being in love and charity with thy neighbour'.[130] Clerics were willing to forbid feuding members of the community the table, though this was not a common reason for exclusion. The records of the church courts would, however, suggest that this was the commonest excuse that the laity offered for their failure to communicate. Margaret Crosby of Chesilton, Dorset, did not receive Easter communion because of a quarrel with her neighbour in 1593, though she assured the court that she would receive at Whitsun. Some were inhibited by quarrels with their clerics, like Anne Bradbury of Wicken Bonhunt, Essex, who

[125] *Injunctions of Bishop Barnes*, 125.   [126] Graham, *Uses of Reform*, 107.

[127] Hunt, 'The Lord's Supper', 63–8.

[128] Maltby, *Prayer Book and People*, 46 and following pages for other examples.

[129] J. Dyke, *A Worthy Communicant: or, A Treatise, Shewing the Due order of Receiving the Lords Supper* (1636), 615.

[130] Haigh, 'Exclusion from communion', 738–9.

would not take communion because of 'a controversy between her and Mr Swynho, parson there'.[131] In Scotland, where feud was an integral part of the social environment, it could dislocate even well-established Calvinist congregations. In 1603 the disciplinary arrangements of the kirk of Monifieth were paralysed by the refusal of either of the local lairds to take the Eucharist because of a feud. Once the two were persuaded to return to communion, normal disciplinary life was resumed.[132] The function of communion as an instrument of reconciliation within the community survived the doctrinal upheavals of the Reformation.

The problem for the ecclesiastical authorities lay in drawing boundaries between this acceptance of communion as the ritual that defined men's relationships with their neighbours, and the manipulation of the idea of feud as a protective device by church papists and others.[133] The standard formula of the visitation returns, so-and-so 'being out of charity' did not communicate at Easter, can conceal a multitude of sins, but could obviously be a cover for non-conformity. The vehemence of some wardens' returns shows that they were conscious of the need to demarcate the non-conforming from those merely out of charity. Richard Westerdale was presented by the wardens of Bridlington, Yorkshire, in 1575 because he was not in charity 'and not of any obstinacy'.[134] Yet we know that William Shakespeare's father excused himself from communion because of debt and that in this case there was deliberate avoidance of the sacrament for conscientious reasons.[135] John Earle's later caricature of the church papist as one keen 'to shift off the Communion, for which he is never unfurnish't of a quarrel, and will be sure to be out of Charity at Easter' exemplified a type that must have become more common in the second half of Elizabeth's reign, as the pressure to use communion as a test of conformity increased.[136] Presence at communion, and the reception of the Eucharist, became the critical marks of conformity, identifying marks understood by the authorities to be meaningful precisely because they involved a denial of fellowship as well as belief.[137]

The impact of community values was felt even more directly upon the other episodic ceremonies of the reformed churches: the celebration of

---

[131] Hunt, 'The Lord's Supper', 47–51.   [132] Graham, *Uses of Reform*, 243–4.
[133] Walsham, *Church Papists*, 85–97.   [134] Sheils, *Grindal's Visitation*, 87.
[135] J.F. Andrews (ed.), *William Shakespeare: His World, His Work and His Influence*, 3 vols. (New York, 1985), i. 38–9.
[136] J. Earle, *Microcosmographie*, facsimile edn. (Leeds, 1966), 41.
[137] The insistence of Scottish reformers and English Puritans on not kneeling at the communion is primarily doctrinal, a refusal to indicate any adoration of the elements, but it also serves to emphasize the nature of communion as a love feast, breeding spiritual and social reconciliation in the community. For an important discussion of the implications of such communitarian concerns in a German context see D. Sabean, *Power and the Blood: Popular Culture and Village Discourse in Early Modern Germany* (Cambridge, 1984), 37–60.

the rites of passage. The rite of baptism provides an interesting study in the diversity of English practice and some contrast with that of Scotland. Both churches articulated the same essential doctrinal understanding of the sacrament: the baptismal water *signified* forgiveness of sin and new spiritual life, but only divine grace conferred faith and secured forgiveness. The ceremony, incorporating the child into the church, was a 'seal' of union with Christ.[138] Liturgical practice was less homogeneous. The Scottish Kirk deliberately chose to make a physical break with the past: insisting that baptism should be conducted in a basin, not in the font that was a symbol of the old Church. Baptism was always to be a public ceremony, integrated into the general service on a preaching day, though not usually a Sunday, since that precluded feasting after the ceremony.[139] These were also the preferences of many English Puritans. From very early in Elizabeth's reign the bishops issued injunctions against the practice of baptizing in basins, rather than in the traditional font. Questions about the use of baptismal equipment figured in many visitations. On the timing of baptism the bishops were, as so often, cautious: infants should be baptized on the Sunday or next holy day after their birth, though the ceremony could be performed on other days in case of need, and private baptism was not absolutely excluded if there was 'peril of death'. While no very substantial ideological difference was evident in these choices, the practices came sharply to differentiate groups. The godly were particularly troubled by the issue of private baptism, which they feared opened the way for the continuation of such 'popish remnants' as baptism by midwives, and which risked representing the sacrament as essential to salvation.[140]

Church court evidence suggests that ordinary parishioners often erred towards the views stigmatized by the godly. When Mr Udall, the minister of Kingston-on-Thames, preached in 1586 that it did not matter if a child died before baptism, he was delated to the ecclesiastical authorities.[141] There are numerous complaints against clergy who refused to baptize except on Sundays, even though the child might be in danger of death.[142] Baptism by midwives seems to have been uncommon in the Elizabethan church, but individuals were prepared to defend it as a necessity, as in the case of George Bourne, the son of William, who was christened by the midwife of the parish of Bobbingworth, Essex, in 1569 'by mother Wright the midwife of the parish, and in the presence of nine other honest

---

[138] J.D.C. Fisher, *Christian Initiation: The Reformation Period* (1970), 80–4.

[139] Cowan, *Scottish Reformation*, 150–2. Knox, ii. 252. Cameron, *First Book of Discipline*, 91, 182.

[140] D. Cressy, *Birth, Marriage and Death: Ritual, Religion and the Life-Cycle in Tudor and Stuart England* (Oxford, 1997), 97–123, 140–8.

[141] A. Peel (ed.), *The Second Part of a Register*, 2 vols. (1915), ii. 45.

[142] Cressy, *Birth, Marriage and Death*, 114–22.

women of the parish'.[143] Even profound religious differences did not
necessarily modify popular beliefs about the urgency of baptism: in seventeenth-century Ireland, for example, Catholics and Presbyterians were
equally keen to baptize within a few days of birth.[144] It was to allay these
fears that Richard Barnes, bishop of Durham, instructed his clergy to
assure parishioners that a child dying without baptism was 'not to be
condemned or adjudged as a damned soul'. It could be buried in the
churchyard, secure in consecrated ground, though there could be no
service if it had not been received into the church.[145] By the end of the
century there is some evidence that the Church of England's emphasis on
the priority of public baptism was beginning to take effect. Berry and
Schofield, studying St Peter's, Cornhill, in London, showed that the average period between birth and baptism gradually lengthened, and that by
1596–8 82 per cent of baptisms took place on a Sunday.[146] It has also been
suggested that the changing use of the term 'chrisom child' in the parish
registers of the early seventeenth century, to denote a growing number of
unbaptized children, is indication of popular acceptance that the ceremony was not essential for salvation.[147]

The Scottish Kirk took a predictably severe view of private baptism and
insisted on a more rapid transformation of the nature of the baptismal rite
than occurred in England. It also sought to assail the strong traditional social
commitment to godparentage. In the early years of the Scottish Reformation the Kirk conceded the continuation of godfathers (though not apparently godmothers) but their function was changed from that of sponsor,
speaking for the child, to that of witness, only the father actually being
permitted to speak for his offspring. Because he acted as sponsor the father
was required to show understanding of the Lord's Prayer and the Creed
before the ceremony.[148] The English church continued to accept the idea of
the artificial kinship constructed by sponsors at baptism, but it also insisted
that knowledge of the faith was now an essential part of their duties, and
they were in theory interrogated on the basic points of the catechism.[149]

[143] Ibid., 120. Maltby, *Prayer Book and People*, 52–6.
[144] Gillespie, *Devoted People*, 76–7.
[145] *Injunctions of Bishop Barnes*, 18.
[146] B.M. Berry and R.S. Schofield, 'Age at baptism in pre-industrial England', *Population Studies* 25 (1971), 462–3.
[147] W. Coster, 'Tokens of innocence: infant baptism, death and burial in early modern Eng-
land', in Gordon and Marshall, *Place of the Dead*, 283–6.
[148] Cowan, *Scottish Reformation*, 151–2. Bardgett, *Scotland Reformed*, 103–4. The concerns of
the Kirk, and of the godly in England, were two-fold: there was no scriptural legitimation
for godparentage, and no individual could stand warrant for another in the face of God.
[149] Cressy, *Birth, Marriage and Death*, 151–6. D. Meads (ed.), *The Diary of Lady Margaret Hoby
1599–1605* (1930), 107, 118, 192, 195, 222.

Similar negotiations between public doctrine and customary behaviour marked the other rites of passage. Marriage, no longer a sacrament, nevertheless retained strong sacramental elements for the Protestant Church in England. The solemnization of marriage underlined the fact that it was a religious contract in which the church ceremony was the focal activity. In contrast to the late medieval church the ceremony was conducted entirely in the body of the church, not at the church door, to reinforce the church's commitment to the 'honourable estate' of matrimony.[150] Scottish marriages were also emphatically kirk-based, public events: from 1571 onwards a General Assembly statute insisted that all had to be celebrated 'in the face of the congregation' and as part of a preaching service.[151] This created the same difficulties as for baptisms: the threat of festivity on the sabbath.[152] Apart from the firm insistence upon the relationship between the Church and marriage it is most striking to note how much of earlier custom survived even in the official attitudes of Protestant reformers. Both churches retained a table of prohibited degrees; banns continued to be read in both England and Scotland; both followed the practice of the medieval Church in regarding public consent to marriage as binding, though only the Scots drew the conclusion that the Church should not pronounce couples man and wife; the English retained forbidden days, effectively closing off nearly 40 per cent of the calendar year.[153] Marriage, although far more firmly under the control of the ecclesiastical authorities than in the medieval past, continued to exhibit some of the social and cultural flexibility that must have helped it to retain continuity of meaning in the eyes of many parishioners.

The rites of burial provide perhaps the most potent evidence of the impact of religious change on congregations and the individuals who composed them. A rich vein of surviving evidence indicates the significance of these last things for sixteenth-century parishioners: indeed so rich is the material that it has in the last few years spawned a historical industry in its own right.[154] It was through the processes of interment and memorialization that men expressed their understanding about the relationship between the living and the dead, an understanding that the Reformation

---

[150] E.J. Carlson, *Marriage and the English Reformation* (Oxford, 1994), 105–42. Cressy, *Birth, Marriage and Death*, 285–339.

[151] *BUK* i. 192.   [152] Cowan, *Scottish Reformation*, 152–5.

[153] Though on the last point Carlson indicates that there is scarcely any evidence of church court prosecution for marriage at an inappropriate season: *Marriage*, 132–3.

[154] The first stimulus to new work on death was provided by P. Aries, *The Hour of our Death*, tr. H. Weaver (1981). For England there are three particularly important works: C. Gittings, *Death, Burial and the Individual in Early Modern England* (1984); Cressy, *Birth, Marriage and Death*; R. Houlbrooke, *Death, Religion and the Family in England 1480–1750* (Oxford, 1998). There are several essays pertinent to England in this period in R. Houlbrooke (ed.), *Death, Ritual and*

had in theory changed out of all recognition. Since the doctrine of purgatory was anathematized, the living could no longer aid the dead with their prayers, and the community that bound them was shattered. Burial now served primarily to offer closure upon a life past and to comfort the living with the assurance that, to quote a contemporary funeral sermon, the dead may 'sleep quietly till they be awakened by the sound of the last Trumpet'.[155] As Duffy has compellingly argued, there was a traumatic moment of liturgical and doctrinal transition when the Book of Common Prayer instructed the priest to address the survivors, not the corpse being sent on its last journey.[156] Commemoration recorded reputation, fame, and virtuous achievements: exemplars to survivors also intended to warn of the transitoriness of mortal things.

The Scottish Kirk appeared to achieve the most dramatic break with its Catholic heritage and to constrain traditional parochial behaviour most fiercely. The funeral service was reduced to a minimalist form in the Book of Common Order. There was to be no singing or reading, simply a committal within the churchyard, though there was a concession that the minister might exhort the people on the nature of death and expound the Kirk's teaching on resurrection. Dignity in the practice of burial was to be combined with a total rejection of the efficacy of any form of prayer for the dead.[157] The Kirk's assault upon burial within the walls of the church gathered momentum from the 1580s onwards: it reflected a fear that if men kneeled on the graves of their ancestors, or even saw their tombs, it might stimulate them to pray for the latters' repose.[158] That this fear was not wholly irrational is suggested by the 1593 case in which two parishioners of Logic admitted to entering the kirk and removing the pew of the local laird, David Balfour, because it stood 'on our forebears' bones'.[159] In the disputes about place of burial it is possible to observe both the determination of the reformed Kirk, and some of the limitations on its capacity to change attitudes to death and the family.[160] While

Bereavement (1989). Distinctive themes on doctrine and popular beliefs are introduced in the volume edited by Gordon and Marshall, *The Place of the Dead*. For Scotland see A. Spicer, '"Rest of their bones": fear of death and reformed burial practices', in W.G. Naphy and P. Roberts (eds.), *Fear in Early Modern Society* (Manchester, 1997), 167–83. There is, as so often, no equivalent work on Ireland, though note J. Bossy, 'The Counter-Reformation and the people of Catholic Ireland, 1596–1641', in T.D. Williams (ed.), *Historical Studies 8* (1971) and R. Gillespie, 'The image of death 1500–1700', *Archaeology Ireland 6/1* (1992), 8–10.

[155] R. Pricke, *A Verie Godlie and Learned Sermon treating of Mans mortalitie* (1608), sig. D3.
[156] E. Duffy, *The Stripping of the Altars: Traditional Religion in England, c.1400–1580* (Yale, 1992), 475.
[157] J. Cumming (ed.), *Liturgy of the Church of Scotland* (1840), 105. Cowan, *Scottish Reformation*, 155.
[158] *BUK* i. 6.   [159] Graham, *Uses of Reform*, 179.
[160] Spicer, 'Burial and burial aisles', 153–9.

funerals were, it seems, conducted according to the new norms wherever the Kirk became strongly established, burials continued, in one form or another, to be linked to kin identity and to a strong sense of familial continuity. Both lairds and ordinary laymen often defied the demands of the General Assembly and insisted on kirk burial: and ultimately the sessions conceded to this view of the world by accepting such burials in return for fines.[161] Moreover, leading laymen sometimes took the unusual step of continuing to seek burial in monasteries or collegiate churches founded by their ancestors and now redundant, as did the Frazers of Lovat at Beauly, Invernesshire, or the Kennedys at Maybole, Ayrshire. The Kirk could not object, since such sites were no longer consecrated, but the choice of these families seems to indicate a more intimate linkage between the living and the dead than it would have wished to accept.[162] The choices of the elite *mutatis mutandis* are unlikely to have been very different from those of the ordinary population, and the sense of dramatic break in understanding of mortality much less than the change in the funeral service would indicate.

The Elizabethan Prayer Book made greater concessions to formal rite at burial than its Scottish counterpart. Prayer and reading were acceptable parts of a service that never precluded committal in church rather than churchyard, making the location of burial a matter of discretion for the minister. 'Sure and certain hope of resurrection' was proclaimed, to the disquiet of some Puritans.[163] But the Book of Common Prayer, no less than its Scottish counterpart, sought to break belief in service to the dead, and the idea that burial was merely part of an elaborate process of supporting them into an afterlife through obits, month-minds, and cycles of prayer. In the first two decades of the reign the bishops remained unconvinced that the traditional view was subverted. Parker, visiting Canterbury diocese in 1569, continued to use the language of the Elizabethan Injunctions, reminding the parishes that 'obits, dirges, trentals, or any such like use' were outlawed.[164] A decade later Richard Barnes of Durham was still having to insist in his northern territory that there should be 'no communions or commemorations' for the dead or associated rituals.[165] In the 1560s wills often continued either to request prayers for the dead, or to provide forms of benevolence that suggest a continuing belief in the

---

[161] Margo Todd has shown convincingly that Spicer exaggerates the success of the Kirk on burial. Initially kirk sessions demanded penance for offences, even from the elite, but by the turn of the century they had often abandoned the struggle to exclude the laity from burial, and turned the arrangement to financial advantage by taking fines. *Culture of Protestantism*, 333–8.

[162] Spicer, 'Burial and burial aisles', 156–8.

[163] Cressy, *Birth, Marriage and Death*, 396–8.

[164] *VAI* iii. 215.   [165] *Injunctions of Bishop Barnes*, 16.

efficacy of such prayer.[166] By the 1570s explicit requests for prayer had virtually disappeared, and so it seems had most resistance to Prayer Book committal outside determinedly Catholic areas.[167]

This process of acculturation must surely have been aided by the reluctance of the churches to intervene in the rest of funeral custom. In some ways it positively endorsed continuity with the past. The tolling of bells was maintained (to the dismay of the godly), the ritual of funeral processions was not challenged, neither were offerings to the poor.[168] In Ireland keening continued, and was reluctantly tolerated.[169] The most that the bishops sought to do was to regulate excess or overtly 'superstitious' behaviour. Bells, for example, were to be tolled only briefly, not rung endlessly, and no crosses were to be used in the church or churchyard or on the graves of the dead. Regulation of these types of popular tradition proved difficult, especially in the North. In the late 1570s several sextons in Chester diocese were still ringing 'more peals at funerals than is decent'.[170] Celebration of a godly life, endorsed even by many Puritans through the preaching of the funeral sermon, maintained its hold in the wider culture through almsgiving and feasting.[171] The Elizabethan church legitimated the expression of loyalty to the dead, or as Hooker put it, 'that love toward the party deceased which nature requireth'.[172] The process of remembering, reinforced as it was by legacies, church monuments, and other cultural forms, still nurtured the idea of bonds between the dead and the living.[173] The weaning of the population from a belief in purgatory did not, perhaps, create quite such a traumatic divide between the present and hereafter as Duffy's argument suggests.

The Practice of Discipline

The Scots Confession of 1560 had followed the French reformed church in making ecclesiastical discipline the third mark of the 'true Kirk of

---

[166] C. Litzenberger, *The English Reformation and the Laity: Gloucestershire 1540–1580* (Cambridge, 1997), 118–24, 152–60. F.G. Emmison (ed.), *Wills of the County of Essex*, 12 vols. (Washington, D.C., 1982–), i. 365–6; ii. 142, 194–5.

[167] For an example of continuing resistance see H. Aveling, *Northern Catholics: The Catholic Recusants of the North Riding of Yorkshire 1558–1790* (1966), 21.

[168] Cressy, *Birth, Marriage and Death*, 398–403. Houlbrooke, *Death and the Family*, 264–71. For Scotland see D.B. Thoms, *The Kirk of Brechin* (Perth, 1972), 21, 45.

[169] S.A. Meigs, *The Reformations in Ireland* (Basingstoke, 1997), 136–8.

[170] *VAI* iii. 256, 289, 309, 383. Purvis, *Tudor Parish Documents*, 73, 160.

[171] Maltby, *Prayer Book and People*, 56–63.

[172] Hooker, *Laws of Ecclesiastical Polity*, v. 75. 2.

[173] J.S.W. Helt, 'Women, memory and will-making in Elizabethan England', in Gordon and Marshall, *Place of the Dead*, 188–205.

Christ'.[174] Upon that statement of belief was erected a system of congregational discipline that in theory, and increasingly in practice, sought to construct a society regulated according to the principles of the reformed faith.[175] Kirk sessions, presided over by a consort of ministers and elders, disciplined erring laymen, ordered penance, and, as an ultimate threat, excommunicated offenders. From the 1580s onwards the presbyteries provided powerful regional support for the efforts of individual communities. Meanwhile, the Kirk had managed to free itself from much of the business of the old church courts: from 1564 onwards disputes about teinds, testaments, and defamation were heard by a separate commissary system established by the Privy Council.[176] The ministers were enabled to concentrate on the true business of bringing godly discipline to an unregenerate society. It was small wonder that English Puritans looked northwards with envious eyes. Instead of this steady movement towards true order, the English church was saddled, in the words of the *Admonition to the Parliament*, with a local court system that was 'but a petty little stinking ditch' which 'punisheth whoredoms and adulteries with toyish censures, remitteth without satisfying the congregation...and committeth a thousand such like abominations'.[177] Rather than making discipline a defining mark of the Church, the English hierarchy was, in this view, content to compromise with the secular world by continuing the old business of the Catholic courts; to employ a law almost entirely papal in its content; and to use such powers as it possessed against virtuous ministers, not against sinners. Few aspects of the Reformation seemed so clearly to divide England and Scotland as the practice of discipline.[178]

The bitterness of English Puritan invective had some justification. Formal rights to self-discipline within the congregation were officially closed by the nature of the Elizabethan settlement, and even the most sympathetic prelate could not surrender jurisdictional rights to any nascent presbytery. The promised reform of the ecclesiastical law was stillborn, and the courts

---

[174] G.D. Henderson (ed.), *The Scots Confession, 1560 and the Negative Confession, 1581* (Edinburgh, 1937), 75–7. For a valuable analysis of the origins of the emphasis on discipline see J.K. Cameron, 'Godly nurture and admonition in the Lord: ecclesiastical discipline in the reformed tradition' in L. Grane and K. Horby (eds.), *Die Danische Reformation vor ihrem internationalem Hintergrund* (Gottingen, 1990), 264–76.

[175] Parker, 'St Andrews', 159–92. Graham, *Uses of Reform*, 4 ff.

[176] G. Donaldson, 'The church courts', in *An Introduction to Scottish Legal History* (Stair Society, Edinburgh, 1958), 363–73.

[177] W.H. Frere and C.E. Douglas (eds.), *Puritan Manifestoes* (1954), 33–4.

[178] M. Ingram, 'Puritans and the church courts, 1560–1640', in Durston and Eales, *Culture of English Puritanism*, 58–91. It should be noted that the Channel Islands also aspired to the true discipline of the Calvinist church, and established a standard of godly control that made Guernsey an attractive place of exile for Thomas Cartwright in the 1590s: D.M. Ogier, *Reformation and Society in Guernsey* (Woodbridge, 1996), 89, 104–8.

were staffed with lawyers, often laymen, who were trained in the civil law and who, at least in the early part of the reign, were routinely conservative in religious sympathy.[179] Accusations of corruption and inertia can sometimes be substantiated. Meanwhile, the General Assembly of the Kirk threw itself enthusiastically into the task of establishing discipline. Some flavour of its sentiments can be gained from the 1569 *Ordoure of Excommunicatioun and of Public Repentance*, which established a tariff of punishments. Murderers, witches, and open blasphemers were all deserving of death by scriptural law, and must therefore be excommunicate; fornicators, drunks, and those who displayed open contempt for the Kirk were to do public penance; lesser offenders, including absentees from church, were normally to be offered private reproof by the session.[180] The Kirk also achieved some notable disciplinary triumphs that seemed to affirm godly rule: the abolition of Yuletide celebration being merely the most spectacular example.

Yet, when viewed from the perspective of the parish, the sharp differences between the two systems become blurred. This is partly because the broad objectives of episcopal and presbyterian discipline were often identical. Both churches aspired to impose regular patterns of Sunday worship, and of communion reception; both sought to punish sin, especially sexual sin, and to regulate the aspects of social behaviour that might lead to delinquency; both were acutely aware of the threat of Catholicism. In practice, both systems addressed much of their energy to issues of sexuality and marriage: they represented approximately a third of cases in mid-Elizabethan Wiltshire; as much as two-thirds in Aberdeen in the 1570s.[181] There are also parallels in the problems that the English courts and Scottish sessions encountered in forcing appearance and imposing punishment. In the 1560s the kirk session for Canongate, Edinburgh, and St Andrews had modest 'no show' rates, but two decades later Anstruther Wester failed to persuade a third of those complained against to attend. As soon as cases moved from the local court to the presbytery no-show rates tended to climb, so that at the end of the 1580s Stirling presbytery could not compel the attendance of well over a third of those summoned.[182] Even the last figure looks very impressive when compared with Marchant's calculation that barely 30 per cent of defenders in disciplinary cases in the Diocese of Chester in 1595 appeared and were obedient to the court's orders.[183] But in England, as in Scotland, it seems that the more local the

---

[179] R.A. Marchant, *The Church under the Law: Justice, Administration and Discipline in the Diocese of York, 1560–1600* (Cambridge, 1969), 236–45.

[180] Knox, vi. 447–70.

[181] Ingram, *Church Courts*, 66–9. Graham, *Uses of Reform*, 120–1.

[182] Graham, *Uses of Reform*, 86–7, 100, 167, 225.

[183] Marchant, *Church under the Law*, 204–35.

court, the more likely to secure some response: figures for the Wiltshire archdeaconries, for Chichester, and for Leicester show appearance rates that average about 75 per cent.[184]

In both systems certain social groups were routinely resistant to discipline. The mobile poor, though particularly prone to be accused of illicit sexual behaviour, were notoriously difficult to control, and rarely seem to have been pursued with tenacity by the ecclesiastical authorities. At the other end of the social spectrum the elites were more than likely to escape the disciplinary net, particularly in sexual cases. Even the Scots, says Graham, did not peer 'into the bedrooms of the notables' with the same zeal as those of lesser mortals.[185] A small category of persons were also self-consciously contumacious, particularly some of those accused of major sexual offences. William Flower of Northallerton, Yorkshire, for example, was said in 1575 to live in an adulterous relationship, to be 'full of contempt' for his local minister, and to care 'for no law'.[186] Such individuals were small in number, but represent a substratum of 'irreligion' against which the court system had little effect, and communal norms probably also failed. More predictably, both the English and the Scottish courts found it particularly difficult to handle determined religious dissent: the ecclesiastical commission, and ultimately the apparatus of the secular state, had to be invoked against Catholicism: in Scotland the General Assembly took up the struggle, only intermittently supported by the crown.[187]

The success or failure of discipline, when viewed from the perspective of the parishioners who were its prime targets, lay above all in its compatibility with communal values. Sexual offences made up much of the business of the courts largely because wardens and elders wished to police these aspects of lay behaviour, particularly since the outcome of sin was so often bastardy. The mantra often repeated by churchwardens at visitation, that so and so was suspected of unchastity 'to the offence of the parishioners', seems to reflect the sentiments of at least the substantial householders.[188] Even less glaring sins, like carting on a Sunday, began to be described as offensive to

---

[184] The calculations for appearance are complex, since adjustments have to be made to the crude figures to arrive at any realistic conclusions: they are discussed systematically in Ingram. Some diocesan evidence runs counter to the assumption that the archidiaconal courts could exercise the most effective discipline. Most notably, attendance levels for disciplinary proceedings in the Diocese of Ely after the 1590–1 visitation reached 93 per cent on Ingram's adjusted figures: *Church Courts*, 340–54.

[185] Graham, *Uses of Reform*, 259–79. B.P. Lenman, 'The limits of godly discipline in the early modern period, with particular reference to England and Scotland', in von Greyerz, *Religion and Society*, 124–45. Ingram, *Church Courts*, 353–8.

[186] Sheils, *Grindal's Visitation*, 64–5.

[187] M. Lynch, *Edinburgh and the Reformation* (Edinburgh, 1981), 214–22.

[188] For the language of complaint from the wardens see Sheils, *Grindal's Visitation*, passim, and Hussey, 'Visitations of Canterbury', 33 ff.

'well-disposed people' as the reformation of manners had impact in some parishes towards the end of the century. Miscreants who failed to perform penance did not give 'satisfaction' to the parish: the language of the wardens here often implying that the courts had been deficient as well for their failure to enforce penalties. But the social role of the courts went beyond the control of sexual misdemeanour: they represented the outlet for those disputes that could not be settled by local arbitration and peacemaking. When, towards the end of Elizabeth's reign, the volume of business being conducted in the English ecclesiastical courts began to grow significantly it may be that this reflects the failures of local processes of dispute-resolution rather than an increasing interventionism from above.[189] There is no particular evidence that ecclesiastical judges in England sought to abrogate to themselves more sexual and social business. Here, however, there is some contrast with the Scottish sessions. The intense localism of Scottish congregational discipline encouraged the Kirk to assume a more explicitly mediatory role, resolving the conflicts of the community.[190] For example, the Canongate kirk session held meetings in the 1560s that were a prelude to communion celebration, reconciling neighbours, and, if necessary, imposing penance on those who failed in Christian charity.[191] This was precisely the sort of activity, backed by enforceable penalties, that was the envy of the English Puritan movement, and it may well be that it would have been quite widely acceptable to ordinary parishioners concerned about order and discipline in their communities. One can imagine the wardens of Mildenhall, Suffolk, so closely studied by Craig, warming to a system that gave greater powers of enforcement to the parish.[192]

The disciplinary systems of the two churches were not, however, driven only by social and sexual concerns. Both aspired to enforce conformity, and, towards the end of the century, to link this with regularity of worship and good order on the sabbath. Both were pressed from above by bishops and by the leaders of the presbytery. Whitgift's regime at Canterbury produced a notable tightening of control and ecclesiastical initiative.[193] In Scotland the development of the network of Presbyterian

---

[189] Carlson, *Marriage*, 156–80, stresses very strongly that the role of the ecclesiastical courts in communal affairs was that of a safety net. Large numbers of disputes and cases emerging from a particular parish is, he suggests, indicative of the failure of internal mechanisms of management and control, and often as well as showing a weakness in clerical leadership. There is a danger that this line of analysis excludes too completely the initiatives of the ordinaries, but it is better attuned to an understanding of how the courts were seen than studies that work purely from the evidence provided by the courts themselves.

[190] Parker, 'St Andrews', 174–7.

[191] Graham, *Uses of Reform*, 102–3.   [192] Craig, 'Co-operation and initiatives', 370–80.

[193] J. Strype, *The Life of John Whitgift DD* (1718), 209–10. Brinkworth, *Archdeacon's Court*, vol. ii, pp. v–vi.

synods from the 1580s, although interrupted by political conflict, established a fuller grid of discipline upon the very variable endeavour of the local sessions. Before this period there is genuine uncertainty about how many congregations could be said to live under discipline: by the 1590s the question remains relevant only for the Highland zone. Drives for conformity, energetic attacks on sabbath-breaking in the case of the Scots, and a steadier insistence on regular Sunday worship characterize the last years of the century. Yet, even then, the courts often reflect particular, local concerns and conflicts, rather than a systematic disciplinary agenda from above. A godly, but contentious, cleric in an English parish could fundamentally change the court record. Thus Simon Hacksuppe, rector of Weston Colville, Cambridgeshire, from 1583 to 1605, who called himself a 'teacher of God's Word', had his parish in deep conflict about his refusal to wear the surplice and attacked individuals in his sermons. A flow of presentments came to the courts from Weston Colville about non-attendance and sabbath failures. Few cases involved community disputes and both before and after Hacksuppe's ministry the parish appears to have been quiet.[194] The Scottish system could produce similar abrupt transitions: notably in small kirk sessions like that of Monifieth, where a key minister, Andrew Clayhills, pushed a disciplinary agenda with great vigour at the turn of the century. Within three years the initiative was spent, and the session went back to performing its routine task of assailing sexual delinquency.[195]

Perhaps the ultimate contrast between the two disciplinary systems established by the English and Scots lies in the visible contrast in 'performing repentance' in church and kirk.[196] English parishioners were intermittently exposed to a traditional penitent standing in white sheet before the congregation on a Sunday confessing to sins as ordered by the church courts and asking forgiveness. The performances were sporadic, repeated at most only three times and apparently undertaken with great reluctance: commutation to a fine or simple evasion of punishment were the preferred English modes of behaviour. The Scottish congregation, by contrast, seems to have accepted communal discipline with unconcealed enthusiasm. The ritual of discipline, with its processions of penitents, its sermons urging repentance, and its unique use of the stool, or bench,

---

[194] Carlson, *Marriage*, 173–4.   [195] Graham, *Uses of Reform*, 239–45.

[196] I owe the discussion of 'performing repentance' to Margo Todd, who gave a stimulating paper on this theme to the Religion in the British Isles seminar in Oxford in Trinity Term 2001. This was a preview of her important book on Protestantism in Scotland. Cameron also emphasizes the drama of repentance: 'Godly nurture and admonition', in Grame (ed.), *Die danische reformation*, 272–5. The significance of repentance is indicated in the unique survival in Scotland of stools and benches designated for the sinner: Hay, *Scottish Churches*, 196.

placed in front of the preacher, all spoke to the central significance of the experience. Kirk session records indicate that there was a regular expectation of several members of the congregation performing repentance at any one time, and serious offences involved many weeks of sitting upon the stool. While some individuals inevitably resisted the pressure to confess sin publicly, the importance of reincorporation into communities that had accepted discipline so enthusiastically led others to seek forgiveness with apparent alacrity. This public expiation of sin had by the end of the century indeed become the third defining mark of the 'true' Kirk in Scotland.[197]

Inclusion and Exclusion

When Richard Gough wished to anatomize his community of Myddle, Shropshire, a hundred years after the death of Queen Elizabeth, he described the parish at prayer, seated in its pews.[198] The period between the Elizabethan settlement and the civil war had been of great significance for the articulation of local hierarchy and order through the fixing of church seating. The primary purpose of such pewing—the provision of more comfortable conditions in which sermons and public prayer could be heard—did not conflict with the secondary benefit, that of assuring and stabilizing social structures which might otherwise have remained fluid and uncertain.[199] There were various methods by which the churchwardens, who were normally in charge of the process, could act. Pews could in certain circumstances be erected by individuals, and maintained by them, a route particularly favoured by the elite. But more generally the wardens proceeded to erect and allocate pews, usually in return for rent, often by the end of the sixteenth century designating the whole church for pewing at the same time. Pew plans were drawn up 'for the parish to have good order', and by the early seventeenth century there was an expectation that they would be revised from time to time.[200] Certain general conventions governed allocation, but much was driven by custom, above all the choice of whether space should be allocated by householders (the most favoured method) or by holdings or tenements (the method adopted at Myddle).

---

[197] Parker, 'St Andrews', 180–2.

[198] D. Hey (ed.), *Richard Gough: The History of Myddle* (1981).

[199] K. Dillow, 'The Social and Ecclesiastical Significance of Church Seating Arrangements and Pew Disputes, 1500–1740', University of Oxford D.Phil. (1990). Marsh, '"Common Prayer"', 66–83.

[200] Marsh, '"Common Prayer"', 81–2.

The erection of seating in English, Welsh, and Scottish churches gave rise to a rich vein of disputes about allocation, bearing on such key sensitivities as the reputation of individuals and the failure of charity.[201] In Scotland, where general pewing post-dates our period, the ambition of individual families and groups such as guilds drove the process in earlier years. By the end of the century kirk sessions were regularly hearing disputes about the placing of seats by prominent individuals 'for keeping of peace and quietness and good order both in kirk and country'.[202] In England and Wales, where pewing was quite general before 1600, it is possible at times to use the evidence available to gain insight into the choices made about who was defined as belonging fully to the community. The most common pattern appears to be that pews were assigned on the basis of rank, so that the wardens had to consider 'the dignity and degree of the party' and their 'antiquities and callings'.[203] Landed families would occupy the front rows of the nave, or sometimes even penetrate into the chancel if the church had not been separated to provide a communion room. Lesser mortals had to rely on their good standing with the wardens, and the subtle variations of status inevitably led to conflict. These could be so difficult to adjudicate that by the early seventeenth century some urban parishes, such as St John's, Chester, actually appointed commissioners for 'Placing and Displacing'.[204] To possess a pew came to indicate identity in the community and to express the precise nature of that identity. There are no absolute rules, since matters were clearly governed as much by local custom as by broad social convention. However, a common pattern was for all married householders who could afford any rent to hold a pew, sometimes with their whole family, sometimes with the women and children separated in another seat.[205] Children might be seated on stools at the pew ends, as at Great Haddenham in Essex, or assigned benches at the back of the church, as at Hornchurch. This may have been a practical matter of space, but is likely also to have been indicative of their marginal status in the order of the church. Unmarried men and maidens were usually, following the ancient practice of the church, allocated distinct seats. Thus far the arrangements within the

---

[201] Dillow, 'Church Seating', 120 ff. Marsh, '"Common Prayer"', 86–90.

[202] Todd, *Culture of Protestantism*, 318–24; the quotation is at p. 321. Hay, *Scottish Churches*, 195–9. The importance of guild pews, a logical development from the guild altars of the pre-Reformation church, seems to be unique to Scotland within the British Isles.

[203] McIntosh, *Community Transformed*, 199–201. Dillow, 'Church Seating', 142–5.

[204] Alldridge, 'Loyalty and Identity', 95.

[205] On gender separation in England see M. Aston, 'Segregation in church', in W.J. Sheils and D. Wood (eds.), *Women in the Church*, SCH 27 (Oxford, 1990), 237–94. For Scotland, McMillan, *Worship*, 155. D. Hey, *An English Rural Community: Myddle under the Tudors and Stuarts* (Leicester, 1974), 219–20.

church were designed to reflect those of the wider community.[206] The difficult question is what happened to the poor: those unable to pay church rate, or pew rents, or those who were strangers. The general maxim adopted by the wardens seems to have been 'no church rate, no seat'. Most plans indicate the existence of 'common' or free seats at the back of the church where the poor in theory sat. At St Michael's, Chester, in 1578, for example, they were probably occupied by the twelve cellar-dwellers who could pay nothing for their own space.[207]

Free benches were of their nature undifferentiated and inferior, symbolic of the weak attachment of the poor and outsiders to community. There has been debate about how far these marginalized groups ever attended church.[208] To begin with mechanisms of enforcement: it seems clear that neither church made sustained efforts to control non-attendance in the first decades after the settlements. In Scotland it was only in the 1580s, and more consistently from the 1590s, that a number of the kirk sessions began to pursue absenteeism and sabbath-breaking with the diligence initially reserved for the assault on sexual misconduct.[209] In the case of England it was the growing fear of recusancy that prompted sustained action. Although the 1559 Act of Uniformity had imposed a 12d. fine for absence from church, the state acted vigorously only in the 1580s with the imposition of crippling monthly fines on the resolutely non-conformist. Though weekly attendance at church was the key issue, a willingness to receive annual communion became a major way of identifying those who were essentially conformist.[210] Local studies for participation at Easter communion, like that for Havering in 1562, suggest that between 71 and 85 per cent of the population received.[211] The situation in Scotland was complicated by the relative powerlessness of the Kirk to enforce its will outside certain favoured centres in the first decades of the Reformation and by its dependence on the support of the local elites. It has been calculated that in godly St Andrews perhaps a half to two-thirds of the population were communicant members of the congregation in the 1570s.[212] Thereafter in both countries percentages were

[206] Dillow, 'Church Seating', 143.

[207] D. Underdown, *Revel, Riot and Rebellion: Popular Politics and Culture in England 1603–1660* (Oxford, 1985), 31. Alldridge, 'Loyalty and identity', 94–8.

[208] See, for example, K.V. Thomas, *Religion and the Decline of Magic* (1971), 189–90. M. Ingram, 'From reformation to toleration: popular religious cultures in England, 1540–1690', in T. Harris (ed.), *Popular Culture in England, c. 1500–1850* (Basingstoke, 1995), 115–17.

[209] Graham, *Uses of Reform*, 204 ff.

[210] Walsham, *Church Papists*, 10–11. M.C. Questier, *Conversion, Politics and Religion in England, 1580–1625* (Cambridge, 1996), 98–115.

[211] McIntosh, *Community Transformed*, 197–8.

[212] K. Wrightson and D. Levine, *Poverty and Piety in an English Parish: Terling 1525–1700* (New York, 1979), 156.

increased by disciplinary campaigns of the kind identified by Wrightson and Levine for Terling in Essex from 1583 to 1597. At their most impressive the results can be seen in the carefully orchestrated Easter communions held in Southwark in the 1590s where over 90 per cent of the population considered eligible seem to have received.[213]

Regular attendance at Sunday worship was another matter. In the 1570s Archbishop Grindal acknowledged in his visitation that those who were not householders did not necessarily attend church.[214] A generation later a Wiltshire householder declared that men had 'as good send their horses' to prayer as their servants.[215] The godly ministers of Dedham, Essex, discussing discipline in the 1580s, saw householders as the key to attendance on the sabbath, though they aspired to an inclusive church.[216] Alldridge's figures for Chester, based on pew rents, show high percentages of assumed regular attendance in the middle decades of Elizabeth's reign: 83 per cent in St Michael's parish, and much lower 61 per cent in St Oswald's.[217] The difficulty is that these figures do not include the poor who did not pay their rents. Ingram, looking at a longer time span for the area of Wiltshire, is cautiously optimistic about the growing habit of attendance at Sunday worship, as a steady drive for attendance by the diocesan officials after the 1570s, and again particularly from the 1590s, made its mark.[218] In Essex it was not until after the end of the century that a number of parishes began to take simple absenteeism from church seriously.[219] Much the same story could probably be told in Scotland: in the rural parish of Monifieth, for example, attendance at annual communion involved most of the population, but until the 1580s weekly attendance seems to have been only about 10 per cent of the communion figure.[220] The Scots, however, strove to establish a clear discipline of

---

[213] Boulton, 'Limits of formal religion', 142–3.   [214] *VAI* iii. 266, 288.

[215] Ingram, 'Reformation to toleration', 116.   [216] Collinson, *Religion of Protestants*, 218.

[217] Alldridge, 'Loyalty and identity', 94–8.   [218] Ingram, *Church Courts*, 107–8.

[219] Wrightson and Levine, *Terling*, 156–7. Attempts at calculating what percentage of the English population was included within the church community have produced wildly varying conclusions. The figures are inherently unreliable, and have to be worked on the basis of evidence that is not necessarily commensurate: change over time is particularly difficult to gauge. The conclusions of Peter Clark, that church absenteeism was rising as fast as the population rate in Elizabethan England, is not sustained by any adequate quantitative data: P. Clark, *English Provincial Society from the Reformation to the Revolution* (Hassocks, 1977), 156–7. Among the groups poorly represented at Sunday worship were children: in some instances young children were specifically excluded, as in Guernsey, where children under four were banned from sermons: Ogier, *Guernsey*, 141. The Canons of 1604 required that everyone above fourteen years should be present. For England see P. Griffiths, *Youth and Authority: Formative Experiences in England, 1560–1640* (Oxford, 1996), 181–3, who emphasizes the ambiguity of the evidence, but the assumption that youth should be present.

[220] Bardgett, *Scotland Reformed*, 158–60.

church attendance. Unlike their Dutch Calvinist counterparts, whose control was restricted to the minority of full church members, Scottish divines were free to try to comprehend the regenerate and unregenerate within the confines of the kirk.[221] It must have been with some complacency that the St Andrews Session recorded in 1600 that 'the people convene so frequently to the preaching that the kirk may not conveniently contain them'.[222]

Although the late sixteenth-century parish was capacious, and the ecclesiastical authorities sought to make it inclusive, it was in practice marked by a series of involuntary and voluntary exclusions. Least remarked by historians are those who were excluded from the parish community and from the discipline of churchgoing by the continuing weakness of the parochial structure. The pre-Reformation pattern of large and scattered parishes with chapelries in the uplands of the British Isles, and particularly in the Gaelic territories, was not altered in any fundamental way at the Reformation. At its most extreme this could still isolate communities from religious support for prolonged periods: when the minister of Kintail, Wester Ross, visited the Isle of Lewis in 1610 he claimed that he had to marry people who had been co-habiting for years and to baptize mature men and women.[223] This pattern of distribution does not explain the strength of Catholicism in Lancashire, or the resistance to change in Elizabethan Ireland, but it facilitated those developments. In Lancashire it was some (though by no means all) of the large upland parishes that proved most difficult for clergy and churchwardens to supervise.[224] In the case of Gaelic Ireland the population proved willing to continue its pre-Reformation habits of accepting a variety of environments as holy: parish churches and other sites where Mass had been said, but also former monastic sites and holy wells. The pervasiveness of the idea of the holy in Catholic Ireland ensured that there was only a weak connection to the idea of fixed community that was so valued in England and Lowland Scotland.[225] It is an interesting paradox that it was the Scottish Calvinists, in many ways so hostile to the idea of a building possessing any peculiar sanctity, who, at the very end of the sixteenth

---

[221] Lenman, 'Limits of godly discipline', 135. Graham, *Uses of Reform*, 204 ff.

[222] Hay Fleming, *Register of St Andrews*, ii. 925.

[223] T.P. McCaughey, 'Protestantism and Scottish Highland culture', in J. Mackey (ed.), *An Introduction to Celtic Christianity* (Edinburgh, 1989), 188.

[224] C. Haigh, *Reformation and Resistance in Tudor Lancashire* (Cambridge, 1975), 316–20.

[225] Gillespie, *Devoted People*, 87–92. Peter Clark is one of the few historians who notes the likely connection between scattered parishes and absenteeism, calculating that in Kent extra-parochial areas like Blean Forest, and areas poorly served by parish churches like Romney Marsh, could have accounted for 2 per cent of the local population: Clark, *English Provincial Society*, 437 n. 26.

century, slowly began the most effective exercise in fixing the location of congregations in Gaelic territory.[226]

Another form of physical separation was that provided by the great household. Household worship was a deeply ingrained habit for the nobility and greater gentry in the generations before the Reformation, and there was little incentive thereafter to adapt to new practices. The impulse to associate this automatically with dissent or alienation from the established faith must be resisted: the earls of Bedford worshipped in their own chapel, precisely as did the earls of Arundel. When the 1559 Act of Uniformity exempted the private worship of the nobility from its disciplinary provisions, it was a reflection both of the specific need to secure noble support and the more general belief that it was inappropriate to challenge the patriarchal authority of these men.[227] Whitgift was understandably uncomfortable with the idea of private worship, but in the Admonition controversy he argued that it was acceptable to have ministry, preaching, and sacraments apart from the parish if, for example, a nobleman's house was far from a church.[228] Although the Scottish Kirk felt no such inhibition, the state in the person of James VI proved equally tolerant of the private devotions of the great nobility: it would indeed have been difficult to be otherwise given that as many as a third of the nobility and gentry remained Catholic in sympathy.[229] The Irish nobility managed to achieve a virtual separation from the church through the use of their own chaplains, who, as a hostile commentator observed of the earl of Clanricard's priests, favoured papistry and had a 'sacrificing function'.[230] Below the level of the greatest magnates there was a more general expectation that members of the elite would be present in church from time to time and, in the case of the English and Welsh, would take communion publicly. From at least the 1570s private chapels that were licensed by the English bishops were subject to the proviso that communion must be taken once a year in the parish church. Yet there was an understandable fear that this would not suffice, and that the great household would be a breeding ground for 'conventicles', or would nurture a 'nest of papists'. At the end of the century Bancroft noted with

---

[226] Dawson, 'Calvinism and the Gaidhealtachd', 243–6.

[227] L. Stone, *The Crisis of the Aristocracy* (Oxford, 1965), 730–1. F. Heal and C. Holmes, *The Gentry in England and Wales, 1500–1700* (Basingstoke, 1994), 368–9. W. Gibson, *A Social History of the Domestic Chaplain, 1530–1840* (1997), 16–28.

[228] Ayre, *Works of Whitgift*, i. 207–12.

[229] J. Wormald, *Court, Kirk and Community, Scotland 1470–1625* (1981), 133–4, though James equally did nothing to stop the Kirk sending godly ministers into Catholic households to 'reason' with the nobility.

[230] B. Cunningham (ed.), 'A view of religious affiliation and practice in Thomond, 1591', *Archivium Hibernicum* 48 (1994), 16.

deep disapproval the French Calvinist *Discipline* that allowed princes and nobles to have 'particular consistories in their private homes'.[231]

Mobility, in its various forms, was a third manner in which contemporaries might be separated from their parish churches. Sailors and merchants, drovers and carriers, all had respectable reasons for non-attendance, while at the end of the century the growing mobility of the English and Welsh elites, and the development of a London season, rendered aspirations to parochial control more difficult. Above all the mobile poor were a self-excluded category, and one that the wardens only intermittently regarded as ripe for discipline.[232] In contrast, the local poor and disaffected, those who preferred the alehouse to the pew, were the subject of growing complaints about sabbath-breaking. Such individuals were subject to community pressures in that they were present and visible to the authorities, but resistant, in that many cared little for the sanctions that the courts and locality could impose. William Scrowton, accused of absenteeism by the wardens of Thirsk, Yorkshire, in 1575, 'did give opprobrious words and answers for executing their office, calling them knaves'.[233] A St Andrews man came before the kirk sessions in 1593 for 'playing on the sabbath, extraordinary drinking, dinging of his wife, and passing forth of the kirk before the blessing be given'.[234] From individuals such as these emanated a whole range of compromise behaviour: appearing in church only for the second half of the service, or escaping before the sermon; regarding the churchyard as a proxy for the building itself; putting in an appearance once a month. Trading or playing sports were usually regarded as more than satisfactory alternatives to listening to a sermon. Even when the disciplinary noose was tightening in Scotland in the 1590s the fishermen of Dunblane still preferred their Sunday market to attendance at the kirk.[235]

Beyond those who were not fully assimilated by the parish by virtue of physical or social circumstances, or indifference to religious sanctions, are the minorities who self-consciously rejected the Protestant settlements. Not all refused a measure of protective integration into the community. For many of those who are labelled as church papists in particular, the political

---

[231] R. Bancroft, *A Survey of the Pretended Holy Discipline* (1593), 98. The canons of 1604 allowed for the consecration of chapels, but with the proviso that communion should rarely be ministered on Sundays, and that the family should attend the parish church : G. Bray (ed.), *The Anglican Canons, 1529–1947* (Woodbridge, 1998), 362–3.

[232] Ingram, *Church Courts*, 99–100, 106. Ingram shows that in the case of Keevil, Wiltshire, which he subjected to in-depth study, most of those who were excommunicated and remained contumacious were transients or servants: Ingram, 'Religion, communities and moral discipline in the late sixteenth and early seventeenth centuries: case studies', in K. von Greyerz (ed.), *Religion and Society in Early Modern Europe, 1500–1800* (1984), 189.

[233] Sheils, *Grindal's Visitation*, 47.

[234] Hay Fleming, *Register of St Andrews*, ii. 771. McMillan, *Worship*, 158–9.

[235] Graham, *Uses of Reform*, 178.

and social advantages of minimal conformity outweighed their distaste for the Protestant settlements. But the church papist was often placed so reluctantly in the pew, that he or she would not make the necessary gestures of outward obedience.[236] Lancashire Puritans complained of those who with 'scoffing and laughing countenances' withdrew themselves to the farthest corners of the churches, or scuffled and chattered during the sermon. Thomas Blenerhasset, a Norfolk gentleman, so troubled the local vicar with his 'loud talking, laughing and reading' that the latter was on one occasion forced to vacate the church.[237] In Ireland, as ever, resistance was prone to be particularly dramatized: wine was poured from communion cups and consecrated bread flung about, the minister was sometimes forced to stop the service 'until the hostile auditors were expelled from the parish church'.[238] Public gestures of this sort articulate a claim to separation, while following the basic legal obligation to be present in church. Most church papists probably opted for quieter forms of withdrawal, especially the evasion of communion. It is notoriously difficult to quantify and differentiate recusants and church papists, but Lancashire figures for the beginning of the seventeenth century suggest more than half the known Catholics were thought to come into the latter group.[239]

Non-conformists at the other end of the ideological spectrum also practised outward obedience. Most notably the adherents of the Family of Love, a Netherlandish sect which gained a foothold in parts of East Anglia in the 1550s and 1560s and consciously encouraged its adherents to be nicodemist and to blend into their own parishes.[240] However, it was critical for those who sought to challenge the prevailing ideology of the established churches that they developed networks separated from the community, sustaining spiritual identity through kin groups, households, and the role of itinerant leaders. The network of gentry households that sustained the Catholic mission under Elizabeth is so well known as to need no detailed discussion here.[241] In Scotland such arrangements were

---

[236] Walsham, *Church Papists*, 89–91.

[237] J.F. Williams (ed.), *Bishop Redman's Visitation of 1597*, Norfolk Record Society 18 (1946), 47.

[238] P.F. Moran, *A History of the Catholic Archbishops of Dublin since the Reformation* (Dublin, 1864), 72.

[239] For example, a survey of Prescot, Lancashire, one of the 'affected' parishes in the country, enumerated 204 recusants and 244 non-communicants: C. Talbot (ed.), *Recusant Records*, Catholic Record Society 53 (1961), 146. Purvis, *Tudor Parish Documents*, 77. On the methodological problems of identifying forms of conformity see Questier, *Conversion*, 98–102.

[240] On the Family of Love see C. Marsh, *The Family of Love in English Society, 1550–1630* (Cambridge, 1994).

[241] On Catholic recusancy the fullest study remains J. Bossy, *The English Catholic Community 1570–1850* (1975). See also A. Dures, *English Catholicism 1558–1642* (Harlow, 1983). The vivid narrative of John Gerard provides the best insight into these networks from a contemporary perspective: P. Caraman (ed.), *John Gerard: The Autobiography of an Elizabethan* (1951).

slower to develop, partly because the control the Kirk could exercise was imperfect. The most striking case, as ever, is that of Ireland, where even within the Pale the networks sustaining Catholic recusancy possessed the qualities of an alternative church by the 1580s. Dublin patricians and Waterford merchants did nurture militant Catholicism through household chaplaincies and kin loyalties, but there was also a distinctive sense of a full challenge to the Protestant Church in operation. When the president of Munster happened to arrive in Waterford early one Sunday morning in 1576 he was amazed to see the inhabitants 'resort out of the [Catholic] churches by heaps'.[242]

When an English Protestant found that the bounds of parish religious routine proved too constraining, a range of alternatives presented themselves. The most orthodox of these fell within that Collinsonian category of 'voluntary religion'.[243] Sermon-gadding was the favoured pastime of the godly, who, like John Winthrop the future governor of Massachusetts, 'could not miss a good sermon, though many miles off'.[244] Urban lecturerships broke the parochial habit with their emphasis on shared spiritual fellowship and the edifying of the soul provided by great preachers. The next development from the pattern of individual sermon-gadding was attendance at a fast, like that orchestrated at Southill in Bedfordshire in 1603, when four ministers presided over a day of preaching, prayer, and psalm-singing. By then such behaviour was well established: the first famous example being the Stamford fast of 1580 proclaimed in the aftermath of the earthquake of that year. The parallels with past Catholic activities sometimes struck observers. In 1586 the town clerk of Barnstaple, Devon, recorded that 'an exercise or holy fast' was held at Pilton in Devon, previously a major Marian pilgrimage centre, and that 'there some offered [money] as they did when they went on pilgrimage'.[245] Ecclesiastical authorities were not opposed to the principle of public fast and repentance, but as ever they were deeply suspicious of occasions not deliberately sanctioned by authority, and particularly of the way in which parochial boundaries were transcended.[246] The English godly could once again only look with longing at their Scottish counterparts, who fasted

---

[242] H.H.W. Robinson-Hammerstein, 'Aspects of the Continental education of Irish Students in the reign of Elizabeth I', *Historical Studies* 8 (1971), 146.

[243] Collinson, *Religion of Protestants*, 242–83.

[244] *Winthrop Papers*, vol. i: *1498–1628* (Massachussetts Historical Society, Cambridge, Mass., 1929), 155.

[245] Collinson, 'Elizabethan and Jacobean Puritanism', in Durston and Eales, *Culture of English Puritanism*, 51–4.

[246] The 1604 canons were explicit on the need for fasts to be sanctioned by authority: Bray, *Anglican Canons*, 363–5.

with remarkable regularity, making whole weeks periods of abstinence, to 'avert the Lord's wrath'.[247]

The development of such fellowship in the Lord was also likely to generate inward-looking bonds: those of the spiritualized household, and of the gathered community. Meetings to repeat sermons and discuss them became part of the 'accepted economy of religious practice' among English Protestants.[248] The problem was that such meetings quickly became tarred with the brush of non-conformity, especially after Whitgift had uncovered the 'classis' movement. So the archbishop who had earlier defended the possibility of private household worship became morbidly sensitive to any display of privatized piety. In 1583 'preaching, reading, catechism and other such exercise' undertaken in private and involving more than one family was prohibited. The canons of 1604 repeated the prohibition, and episcopal instinct continued to associate the most constrained of Calvinist devotional meetings with unorthodox behaviour.[249] The fears of authority were not wholly irrational, however. Coming together to repeat sermons and to pray, perhaps to enjoy the hospitality of a like-minded family, left open the possibility of overturning the established religious order. There could be active ideological dissent, or simply too great a lay initiative in interpretation. Women might speak on the basis of a knowledge that they should not and could not display in the public sphere.[250] Groups sometimes went further, and covenanted among themselves to 'turn unto the Lord with all our hearts in sincerity' and avoid 'outward hindrances'.[251] Thus in the late Elizabethan years some groups of the godly arrived either at 'quasi-separatism', defining themselves as distinct among the unregenerate but not wholly detached from the parish, or at the full separatism of a few. Among the last are the congregations at London and Amsterdam, under the leadership of Henry Barrow, clearly intent on not 'staying for the magistrate' in the establishment of a godly church. But they were a small minority among those who sought spiritual solace beyond the defining bounds of parochial Protestantism.[252]

---

[247] I.P. Hazlett, 'Playing God's card: Knox and fasting, 1565–6', in R.A. Mason (ed.), *John Knox and the British Reformations* (Aldershot, 1998), 176–200. For national fasts see *APS* 3:40, 353, 453; 4:70. For local fasts see Todd, *Culture of Protestantism*, 344–8.

[248] Collinson, *Religion of Protestants*, 264–76.

[249] Wilkins, *Concilia*, iv. 307. Bray, *Anglican Canons*, 365.

[250] P. Crawford, *Women and Religion in England, 1500–1720* (1993), 119–24.

[251] R. Rogers, *Seven Treatises, containing such direction as is gathered out of the holie scriptures* (1603), 487, 489

[252] B.R. White, *The English Separatist Tradition* (Oxford, 1971). S. Brachlow, *The Communion of Saints: Radical Puritan and Separatist Ecclesiology, 1570–1625* (Oxford, 1988). M.R. Watts, *The Dissenters*, i: *From the Reformation to the French Revolution* (Oxford, 1978), 14–40.

The concerns that drove minorities into semi-separation or a full detachment from the church 'by law established' were diverse. The London congregation located in Holy Trinity in the Minories that so mortified Grindal in the 1560s was strongly Calvinist in tendency, baptizing by 'the Geneva book' and showing an alarming unwillingness to behave reverently before the magistrate.[253] The chronicler John Stow swiftly labelled them as 'Anabaptists who are called puritans'.[254] Grindal was particularly disconcerted by the truculence of the women who invaded his palace and hooted him in the pulpit calling 'ware horns'.[255] The few radical recusants uncovered in Gloucester diocese in the 1570s seem to have been of the same type. They refused to have children baptized in the parish church or to participate in its ceremonies since 'malefactors and papists [be not] excluded out of the church'.[256] It is likely that these and other early recusants had some connection with mid-Tudor opposition to Catholicism, to which the Londoners at least looked back as a time of heroic resistance when there was no hierarchy but 'a congregation of us in this city in Queen Mary's days and a congregation at Geneva'.[257] More remarkable is the evidence of the tenacity of a hard-core of separatists in the face of persecution by the bishops: several of those arrested by Grindal refused conformity and remained permanently imprisoned; several of those in trouble in Gloucestershire in the early 1570s were still imprisoned or under renewed investigation in the 1580s.[258]

The more organized Calvinist dissenting congregations of the last decades of Elizabeth's reign took as their point of departure a refusal to compromise upon ceremony and a determination not to integrate with the ungodly. The Brownists and others found assurance in Revelation 3. 16: 'because thou art lukewarm and neither cold nor hot, it will come to pass I will spew thee out of my mouth'.[259] And vitriol against the established

---

[253] P. Collinson, *Archbishop Grindal, 1519–1583* (1979), 176–83. H.G. Owen, 'The Liberty of the Minories: a study in Elizabethan religious radicalism', *East London Papers* 8 (1965), 81–97.

[254] J. Stow, *Three Fifteenth-Century Chronicles*, ed. J. Gardiner, CS NS 28 (1880), 143.

[255] W. Nicholson (ed.), *The Remains of Edmund Grindal* (PS, Cambridge, 1843), 288–9.

[256] C. Litzenberger, 'Defining the Church of England: religious change in the 1570s', in S. Wabuda and C. Litzenberger (eds.), *Belief and Practice in Reformation England* (Cambridge, 2000), 146–9.

[257] On the networks of godly Protestantism in London from Mary's reign to the 1570s see B. Usher, 'Backing Protestantism: the London godly, the Exchequer and the Foxe circle', in D. Loades (ed.), *John Foxe: An Historical Perspective* (Aldershot, 1999), 105–25.

[258] Litzenberger, 'Defining the Church of England', 147.

[259] There were continuities from earlier non-conformity to outright separation in East Anglia, where leaders of the Brownist movement in the 1580s, such as Henry Copping, had an earlier history of trouble with the authorities: D. MacCulloch, *Suffolk and the Tudors* (Oxford, 1986), 204–7. It was Copping who made particular play of the quotation from St Paul. M.E. Moody, 'Trials and troubles of a non-conformist layman: the spiritual odyssey of Stephen Offwood, 1564–c.1635', *Church History* 51 (1982), 159.

church, unconstrained by the formalities of much mainstream Calvinist discourse, became a defining feature of the separatists. This sometimes issued in millenarian 'incidents' like that provoked by William Hackett, the Northamptonshire man who claimed to speak with the spirit of John the Baptist, and who prophesied imminent doom for the Church of England unless it adopted a full Calvinist programme of regeneration.[260] Or there was the vitriol of John Penry, whose agonies over the tragedy of his own Welsh church did much to propel him from non-conformity to the more radical solution of separatism.[261] The circumstances of the early 1590s, with a number of the leaders of separatism imprisoned and then tried for sedition, pushed others such as Francis Johnson across the boundary from non-conformity to full separation, and Johnson's flight to Amsterdam provides a defining moment in the development of later sectarianism.[262]

Although the label of anabaptism was freely dispensed by the opponents of radicalism, it is difficult to detect in Elizabethan England much identity with Continental Anabaptist thought.[263] Only the Family of Love, with its emphasis on a spiritualized mysticism and inner illumination, stands out as a distinctive movement opposed to the fundamental Calvinist principles of Elizabethan Protestantism. The teachings of the movement's founder, Hendrik Niclaes, had taken the form of a combination of Catholic mystical and of Anabaptist radical ideas and melded them into a belief system based upon the idea that the true disciple could be 'godded with God', set apart for spiritual perfection in this world. This produced a group who were both antipathetic to the unregenerate and were themselves not easily integrated into a sect-type movement. Their radical individualism and willingness to conceal belief behind a façade of conformity made them both elusive and, perhaps, attractive to those who found the prevailing ideology spiritually barren. The recent historian of the movement may have been unduly ambitious in discovering familist tendencies not only in the Elizabethan court but also in the person of the queen. He is surely correct, however, to suggest that the mysticism of Niclaes had a potential appeal for those who sought a personal spirituality beyond that of the congregation.[264]

---

[260] W.J. Sheils, *The Puritans in the Diocese of Peterborough, 1558–1610* (Northampton, 1979), 136–9. A. Walsham, ' "Frantick Hacket": prophecy, sorcery, insanity and the Elizabethan Puritan movement', *HJ* 41 (1998), 27–66.

[261] J. Penry, *Three Treatises concerning Wales*, ed. D. Williams (Cardiff, 1960).

[262] White, *English Separatist Tradition*, 82–115.

[263] I.B. Horst, *The Radical Brethren: Anabaptism and the English Reformation to 1558* (Nieuwkoop, 1972), 54, 76, 152–4.

[264] Marsh, *Family of Love*, 162 ff.

Rejection of the established Church of England by those seeking further reform is an interestingly circumscribed phenomenon: limited both by numbers and by geography. Neither in northern England, nor Wales, if we discount the lone voice of John Penry in the latter, is there evidence of full separatism or sectarianism.[265] It may be that in both these cases pressure on Protestants to adopt a fully conformist position was less intense than in southern England, and the incentive to exclude oneself from an imperfect church correspondingly less. There is silence also from Ireland, where recusancy was simply and automatically identified with Catholicism. Scotland also shows no evidence of any move to reject the Kirk from any more radical position: again those who chose exclusion were almost by definition Catholic. In these two last cases the stark contrasts between the churches seem to have left little space for any third way. The binary divisions of confessionalization demanded allegiance that tended to preclude such longings as those of the English familist who explained that he belonged neither to the Church of England, nor to the Romanist Church 'but hoped yet there was a third Church, which should stand where both these shall fail'.[266]

Assimilating the Reformation?

Looking back from the vantage point of the early years of the united reign of James VI and I, British Protestants had many reasons to offer thanks to the Lord for 'restoring the purity of religion'.[267] England was now reformed, at least to the extent that its people had all been exposed to three generations of official Protestant settlement, to a stable liturgy, and to an increasing range of preaching across the realm. The Scottish Kirk had emerged bloody but unbowed from the battles of the previous decades, and was providing settled witness of the truth of the gospel. Ireland was another matter, but its papists showed through their unassailable obstinacy that Satan and his minions still walked the earth and that there must be perpetual vigilance and perpetual preaching by the defenders of God's truth. It was, however, unduly optimistic of the preacher Thomas Baughe to claim even in 1614 that there was 'no nook, nor angle of this Isle, where the language of the gospel is not heard'.[268] There were, in fact, great swathes of territory where the effort of primary evangelism

---

[265] On the absence of separatism in the north see R.C. Richardson, *Puritanism in North-West England* (Manchester, 1972), 86, though there were some household conventicles. On Wales, Williams, *Wales and the Reformation*, offers nothing on radicalism.

[266] Quoted in C. Marsh, 'The gravestone of Thomas Lawrence revisited', in M. Spufford (ed.), *The World of Rural Dissenters* (Cambridge, 1995), 228.

[267] R. Tynley, *Two Learned Sermons* (1609), 66–8.

[268] T. Baughe, *A Summons to Judgement* (1614), 33. A. Walsham, *Providence in Early Modern England* (Oxford, 1999), 287–95.

by Protestant ministers had scarcely begun. Even in the heartlands, there had been insufficient preaching and catechizing: in the Celtic territories the dissemination of Protestantism was still in its infancy. Only in Wales, where the work of biblical translation was beginning to take effect, did the decades around the turn of the century see a sustained commitment to the conversion of the people in their own tongue. William Morgan's revised Welsh version of the Book of Common Prayer, published in 1599, and the Homilies, translated by Edward James in 1606, were the most visible fruit: equally intriguing were the struggles to translate the Psalms into Welsh verse, finally resolved by Edmwnd Prys in 1620.[269] But even in Wales some sense of the continuing difficulties of evangelization through print is revealed in one distinctive vignette. In the Breconshire parish of Talachddu there was a collection of twenty-five parish books: only three were in Welsh, though the population must have been largely monoglot.[270] 'God only knows how pathetic is the situation of the poor commonalty' remained an appropriate lament for divines who depended upon the power of the Word.[271]

Elsewhere the picture was even less promising. The Irish New Testament was finally published in 1603 with the support of Dublin Protestants, and the translated Book of Common Prayer was printed in 1608.[272] But the newly formed Trinity College failed to live up to the expectation that it would begin to produce an Irish-speaking ministry. Only one of the founding fellows, William Daniel, encouraged the study of Irish: the rest followed Archbishop Loftus's policy of anglicization. Despite cautious interest from both Elizabeth and later James in the construction of a mission to the Irish orchestrated through Trinity, little was achieved. The failure was one both of institutional capacity and of recruits: to quote Ford, 'in order to convert the native Irish, [the Church] needed native ministers; but the supply of native ministers was meagre because the Irish were unconverted'.[273] Moreover, a striking feature even of those like William Daniel who were firmly committed to evangelization was that they

---

[269] Williams, *Wales and the Reformation*, 382–6, 393–4; *The Welsh and their Religion* (Cardiff, 1991), 158–61.

[270] W.P. Griffith, *Learning, Law and Religion, c.1540–1642* (Cardiff, 1996), 305.

[271] This is from the Welsh tract on witchcraft *Tudor and Gronow* by Robert Holland, cited in S. Clark and P.T.J. Morgan, 'Religion and magic in Elizabethan Wales: Robert Holland's dialogue on witchcraft', *JEH* 27 (1976), 40.

[272] Ford, *Protestant Reformation*, 107–10. H.R. McAdoo, 'The Irish translations of the Book of Common Prayer', *Eigse* 2 (1940), 250–7. C. O'Hainle, 'The *Pater Noster* in Irish Reformation texts to c.1650', *Celtica* 22 (1991), 145–6. As the author points out it is odd that when Sir William Herbert later arranged for the translation of the essentials of the catechism into Irish for his tenants, he appeared unaware of the Kearney translation.

[273] Ford, *Protestant Reformation*, 98.

discussed conversion in a severely confessionalized language. The indigenous Irish were despised for following the 'filthy frogs of the synagogue of Antichrist', even while there was an attempt to wrestle for their souls. The process of wrestling came, of course, too late to stem the other evangelical initiative emanating from the Continent, as the Louvain Franciscans provided the tools for conversion in Gaelic.[274]

The situation in the Scottish Highlands was again different, since there was a slow process of conversion as the General Assembly established its network of kirks, many with Gaelic-speaking pastors. But a tension remained between the desire to disseminate Protestantism in an appropriate medium and the cultural contempt in which much Gaelic culture was held. The 1609 Statutes of Iona, through which James VI and I assailed the clans and their language, were not of the making of the Kirk. However, they reinforced the message that Protestantism was identified with the interests of the Lowland Scots. The 1616 reinforcement of the Statutes insisted that the 'vulgar English tongue be universally planted, and the Irish language, which is one of the chief and principal causes of the continuance of barbarity...be abolished and removed'.[275] Lack of enforcement helped to soften the impact of the Statutes.[276] Yet some of that hopeful evangelical environment which John Carswell had earlier nurtured was soured in these new circumstances. Finally we might note that much the same was true of the Isle of Man, where John Phillips, the bishop of Sodor and Man, in the first decade of the seventeenth century produced a 'Mannish book of Common Prayer', but received no backing for its publication. In the Restoration period his successor Bishop Barrow was apparently totally ignorant of the existence of such a text.[277]

These Celtic worlds were alien to London, Edinburgh, and even Dublin. In much of Britain and Ireland the Reformation had been tamed and become either a defining part of the culture, or apprehended and consciously rejected. In Ireland and Scotland the choices presented to the population appeared stark: a rigorous Calvinism driven by a determined body of clerics, or Catholicism increasingly sustained by counter-Reformation mission. In the Irish case, in John Hooker's apocalyptic language, military

---

[274] P. Jenkins, 'The Anglican Church and the unity of Britain: the Welsh experience, 1560–1714', in S.G. Ellis and S. Barber (eds.), *Conquest and Union: Fashioning a British State, 1485–1725* (1995), 121–4. Meigs, *Reformations in Ireland*, 81–9, 101–2. From Louvain emanated a crucial metrical catechism by Ó hEodhusa, as well as much devotional literature: J. Brady, 'The catechism in Irish', *Irish Ecclesiastical Record* 83 (1955), 167–76.

[275] *Register of the Privy Council of Scotland*, i. ser. x. 671–2. McCaughey, 'Scottish Highland culture', 177–83. J. Bannerman, 'Literacy in the Highlands', in I.B. Cowan and D. Shaw (eds.), *The Renaissance and Reformation in Scotland* (Edinburgh, 1983), 225–6.

[276] J. Goodare, 'The Statutes of Iona in context', *SHR* 77 (1998), 31–57.

[277] Moore, *Common Prayer in Manx*, vol. i, pp. ix–xii.

defeat was the 'just judgement of God upon such a Pharisical and stiff-necked people', who would not 'serve God in true religion'.[278] However, in early modern society nothing was quite as stark as this rhetoric suggests. Even the most aggressively self-righteous Scottish clerical leadership had to negotiate localist lay interests, and the complex politics of Jacobean Scotland constantly disrupted the ambitions of the Kirk.[279] In Ireland at the turn of the century occasional conformity still remained an option for sections of the Anglo-Irish elite as a means of preserving office and political connection. But in neither realm was there any longer much cultural space between ideological alternatives. John Penry identified the stark demands of Scottish clericalism very clearly when he debated with his hosts and protectors what liberty individual members of kirk assemblies should have.[280] The Kirk had established its control through an apparently draconian disciplinary policy. Yet the remarkable feature of the system was that it attracted levels of popular support of which the English church could only dream. Control was not the defining aspect of either the Protestant or the Catholic Church in Ireland, and forms of popular devotion and belief flourished often in a symbiotic relationship with the views of elites. But political circumstance and the growing influence of the clergy sharpened the ideological divide and led to the representation of Irish religion in clear binary terms.[281]

Even in these confessionalized realms, however, ideological labels and disciplinary structures may not be the best ways of understanding the assimilation of religious change.[282] The taming of the Reformation involved constant negotiation between clergy and laity, elites and ordinary men and women: negotiations that modified the religious landscape in ways not necessarily anticipated in official formulae. The effect was certainly to modify 'the economy of the sacred', compelling individuals and groups to redefine their relationship with the Church, and with the Deity: it was not necessarily to ensure full communities of informed and com-

---

[278] Hooker's comment reflects his own observations of the sufferings of Munster in the early 1580s: R. Holinshed, *Chronicles of England, Ireland and Scotland*, 6 vols. (1808), vi. 460.

[279] Parker, 'St Andrews', 190–1.

[280] D.G. Mullan, *Scottish Puritanism, 1590–1638* (Oxford, 2000), 267–8. Calderwood, v. 696–8.

[281] Both Alan Ford and Brendan Bradshaw point out that Irish Protestants had by this time adopted the language of the true and false churches as a way of articulating the conflict with indigenous Catholicism: A. Ford, 'The Protestant Reformation in Ireland', in C. Brady and R. Gillespie (eds.), *Natives and Newcomers* (Dublin, 1986), 67–8; B. Bradshaw, 'The Reformation in the cities: Cork, Limerick and Galway, 1534–1603', in J. Bradley (ed.), *Settlement and Society in Medieval Ireland* (Kilkenny, 1988), 465–6.

[282] The case for not being obsessional about the confessional divide in Ireland at the expense of studying religious culture is made most powerfully in Gillespie, *Devoted People*, esp. 10–14.

mitted Catholics or Protestants.[283] It has become fashionable to label the world that emerged from these exchanges as post-Reformation, rather than specifically confessional. Parochial identities in this post-Reformation world have been the main burden of this chapter. But the experience of religion did not confine itself to church or community: it also found outlets in the processes of reading and listening, of debate and rumour, of festivity and of seeking to explain misfortune.[284]

Tessa Watt has argued that the best access into post-Reformation mentalities is through the medium of cheap print, the ballads, broadsides, and predecessors of the 'penny dreadfuls' that found a ready market and wide circulation in late Elizabethan England. Alexandra Walsham's work on providentialism uses similar material, reinforced by more elaborate printed texts and by the evidence of sermons. Both reveal a culture in which the sacred jostles with the profane, residual Catholic narratives are sometimes dressed in Protestant weeds, and godly preachers seem almost as willing as balladeers to accept the miraculous and occult. God's providences unveiled through prodigies, wonders, and miracles, ghostly armies clashing in the clouds, or fire falling out of heaven on a Lincolnshire town, seem far removed from the sober insistence on divine judgement found in the official formulae of the established church.[285] Yet the former were the routine offerings of the press, and could inculcate a crude but powerful understanding of God's purposes for his people. Biblical and moralizing stories could be rendered appealing by the addition of the miraculous, as in the ballad version of Tobias, when the protagonist chases an evil spirit away with smoke from the heart of a fish.[286] Conversely, secular tales of

[283] R.W. Scribner, 'Cosmic order and daily life: sacred and secular in pre-industrial German society', in K. von Greyerz (ed.), *Religion and Society in Early Modern Europe, 1500–1800* (1984), 17–32. The idea of a 'sacred economy' has been developed in some outstanding Continental and American case studies, notably D. Gentilcore, *From Bishop to Witch: The System of the Sacred in Early Modern Terra d'Otranto* (Manchester, 1992); Sabean, *Power and the Blood*; and D.D. Hall, *Worlds of Wonder, Days of Judgement: Popular Religious Belief in Early Modern New England* (Cambridge, Mass., 1990).

[284] There are now a series of important studies on this 'post-Reformation' world-view for England: D. Cressy, *Bonfire and Bells: National Memory and the Protestant Calendar in Elizabethan and Stuart England* (1989); Hutton, *Merry England*; T. Watt, *Cheap Print and Popular Piety, 1550–1640* (Cambridge, 1991); Walsham, *Providence*.

[285] Walsham, *Providence*, 65–115. Peter Lake has argued that we should discard the idea that much Protestant thought was hostile to the assumptions of traditional religion: P. Lake, 'Deeds against nature: cheap print, Protestantism and murder in early modern England', in K. Sharpe and P. Lake (eds.), *Culture and Politics in Early Stuart England* (1994), 313–34. Most of the current research on this topic emphasizes that these 'popular' providentialist views were as much the possession of the elites as of ordinary men. When Sir Henry Sidney reported armies having been seen in the sky over County Louth, he added to his commentary, 'doubtless there was such a thing seen': quoted in Gillespie, *Devoted People*, 108–9. For providentialism and the London mercantile elite see D. Hickman, 'Religious belief and pious practice among London's Elizabethan elite', *HJ* 42 (1999), 943–4.

[286] Watt, *Cheap Print*, 118–19.

wickedness undone, like that of the cruel landlord who, having evicted a poor widow, was driven to suicide, are strongly rhetoricized as examples of divine judgement. And the preachers readily took up these themes, formalizing their message, while rarely losing the narrative impact of the exempla. Most of this had little contact with Calvinist soteriology and in its assumptions was not inimical to Catholic views of providence: indeed in Ireland tales of this kind were being used a century and more later with equal force on both sides of the confessional divide.[287]

Were the godly writers and preachers who used the worlds of miracles and wonders simply pandering to the sensationalist instincts of their audiences? The desire to instil proper fear as a route to repentance could no doubt involve the manipulation of narrative: Richard Bernard, in his book on clerical behaviour, recommended that the preacher should keep a stock of 'home observed' providences to focus the attention of his congregation.[288] It is more appropriate, however, to see these ways of understanding the world as shared between preacher and audience. The preachers were, to quote Walsham, rehearsing 'visible sermons'.[289] When John Rogers described the case of a clerical supporter of the Familists who dropped dead after recanting at Paul's Cross, he surely internalized the assertion that it was a 'terrible example' of the punishment God meted out to heretics.[290] Indeed preachers whose own world-view was intensely informed by the immanence of the divine, and the importance of special providence, were likely to be empathetic to popular views of disasters and wonders. It was the *ministers* who constantly repeated to the people of Scotland that they must fast to atone for their abounding 'sin and impiety' which led to plague, harvest disaster, fire, and flood, all witness to God's wrath.[291] The 1580 earthquake that shook much of southern England also moved several preachers to denounce the apostasy of God's people, while also offering ideal opportunities for the sensationalism of the pamphleteers.[292] The jeremiad sermons preached at Paul's Cross in the early seventeenth century traded in an economy of the sacred that must have resonated with most of their auditors.[293]

---

[287] Gillespie, *Devoted People*, 40–63.

[288] Bernard, *Faithfull Shepheard*, 68. George Herbert makes much the same suggestion in 'The Country Parson': F.E. Hutchinson (ed.), *The Works of George Herbert* (Oxford, 1941), 233.

[289] Walsham, *Providence*, 116 ff. where the language is drawn from a Joseph Mede newsletter of 1627 on violent storms near Boston, Lincolnshire.

[290] Marsh, *Family of Love*, 94–5.

[291] J. Maidment (ed.), *Chronicle of Perth* (Edinburgh, 1831), 3–34. Todd, *Culture of Protestantism*, 349 ff.

[292] A. Golding, *A Discourse upon the earthquake* (1580). A. Munday, *A View of Sundry Examples* (1580).

[293] On jeremiads see Walsham, *Providence*, 281–325, and M. McGiffert, 'God's controversy with Jacobean England', *AHR* 88 (1983), 1151–74.

The obvious difficulty, both for the preachers and for the historian, is to understand how far audiences were detaching themselves from traditional providential narratives. Were they responding in a 'post-Reformation' manner to tales and ballads? A part of the answer to this must lie in the nature of the texts: a part of the output of the English presses Watt labels 'Godly tables for good householders', simple instructional texts that might be nailed to walls or doors conveying explicitly Protestant messages.[294] More generally, it is the shifting content of popular works over the late sixteenth century that is important. The sins and sufferings of individuals might have a universal quality; the changes in the experience of church and nation were another matter. Here Foxe's *Book of Martyrs* is the obvious point of departure. Even though the text of Foxe was beyond the reach of most ordinary Englishmen, his contemporary narratives were of paradigmatic importance in fixing the providentialist understanding of the world upon Protestantism. His tales of the abominable deaths of Catholic persecutors carry little conviction across the centuries, but were consistent with a desire to explain the world in a way congruent with his understanding of God's purposes.[295] The whole form of the martyrology was an adaptation of a Catholic genre for Protestant ends. Foxe, while denying that England was *the* elect nation, offered some hostages to fortune in his insistence that God had placed 'us Englishmen here in one commonwealth, also in one Church, as in one ship together'.[296]

From Foxe it appears but a short step to the anti-Catholic providentialism of the post-Armada period. In 1588 even those godly preachers whose usual impulse was to denounce the unregenerate masses were prepared to urge thanksgiving because the Lord had been on 'our' side against the Goliath of Spain.[297] The bonfires and bells that had initially greeted Elizabeth's accession day in the late 1560s, often under local official sponsorship, had become by the 1580s a national celebration, not so much because it was generally ordained as because it had been adopted by a myriad of individual communities across the land.[298] By the early years of James's

---

[294] Watt, *Cheap Print*, 217 ff.

[295] P. Collinson, 'Truth, lies and fiction in sixteenth-century historiography', in D.R. Kelley and D.H. Sacks (eds.), *The Historical Imagination in Early Modern Britain: History, Rhetoric and Fiction, 1600–1800* (Cambridge, 1997), 49–62. T. Freeman, 'Fate, faction and fiction in Foxe's *Book of Martyrs*', *HJ* 43 (2000), 601–23.

[296] Foxe, i. 520. P. Collinson, 'Biblical rhetoric: the English nation and national sentiment in the prophetic mode', in C. McEeachern and D. Shuger (eds.), *Religion and Culture in Renaissance England* (Cambridge, 1997), 34–5.

[297] C.Z. Wiener, 'The beleaguered isle: a study of Elizabethan and early Jacobean anti-Catholicism', *PP* 51 (1971), 27–62.

[298] R.C. Strong, 'The popular celebration of the accession day of Queen Elizabeth I', *Journal of the Warburg and Courtauld Institutes* 21 (1958), 86–103. Cressy, *Bonfire and Bells*, 50–7. Hutton, *Merry England*, 146–51, 186–7.

reign the specific celebration of monarchical events had merged with the far more intense memorialization of the 'great miracle[s] of our latter age', in which deliverance from the Gunpowder Plot, from Jesuit conspiracy and from the power of Spain were woven into an 'intoxicating mixture of jingoism'.[299] God had intervened decisively on behalf of 'his Englishmen': all the subtleties of general rather than special providence were thrown aside. The popular view here parted company with that of the prophetic preachers, who still saw the people as corroded by sin, and imminent ruin as facing the nation unless they repented and atoned for their sins.[300]

Scotland was not immune from the desire to establish a providential association between the victory of Protestantism and the integrity of the realm. Thanksgiving came even less naturally to the leaders of the Kirk than to their southern colleagues, though public events such as James's deliverance from the Gowrie Plot, or later from Gunpowder, were made solemn moments of celebration.[301] But it was in the purity of the Reformation, the liberty with which the gospel was preached and discipline properly ministered, that the Scots found their greatest assurance of divine favour. 'God dwelt never in no nation of the earth . . . so long with such sincerity and purity . . . as he hath done with us.'[302] The people of Scotland were covenanted, as Israel had been, to fulfil divine imperatives: a view of the world whose consequences proved even more revolutionary than England's jingoistic confidence in the Deity's support.[303] The Irish also emphasized their exceptional relationship with the Deity, though it was far more difficult for the Protestant minority to associate this with any affirmation of collective political identity. Instead, it was the righteousness or sinfulness of individuals and groups on one side or other of the confessional divide that was believed to invoke divine wrath or blessing. Ireland had its language of providentialism in the early modern period, but it was employed, says Gillespie, to provide confessional groups with 'a divine justification for their distinctiveness'.[304]

To suggest that the majority of early seventeenth-century Britons derived a strong sense of cultural and political identity from their Protestantism is not to argue that they had collectively become experiential

---

[299] E. Bourcier (ed.), *The Diary of Sir Simonds D'Ewes, 1622–4* (Paris, 1975), 164.

[300] Walsham, *Providence*, 246–7.

[301] *APS* iv. 213–14.

[302] W. Cunningham (ed.), *Sermons by the Reverend Robert Bruce* (Edinburgh, 1843), 288.

[303] Mullan, *Scottish Puritanism*, 267–73. Mullan points out that Scottish ministers were, however, even less likely than their English counterparts to think exclusively of Scotland as *the elect* nation, given the continuing commitment to the 'Calvinist international'. Moreover, after 1603 their rhetoric is more likely to embrace England as well as Scotland.

[304] Gillespie, *Devoted People*, 57.

Calvinists, still less proto-rationalists.[305] Their soteriology no doubt often corresponded to the characterization of Antilegon in Arthur Dent's *Plaine-Man's Pathway*: 'if a man . . . say no body harm nor do any body no harm and do as he would be done to; have a good faith God-ward and be a man of God's belief, no doubt he shall be saved'.[306] Moreover, even a sacred landscape peopled by men and women with access to God's word, alerted to his Protestant purposes for the individual, community, and nation, was also occupied by witches, fairies, and cunning men. For most it seems unlikely that the world was either 'disenchanted' or 'demystified' by the coming of a logocentric religion.[307] Men were, it seems, capable of inhabiting multiple, even contradictory, mental worlds simultaneously. But there were also processes of adaptation, as the old surrendered to the new. For example, the changed liturgy steadily redefined the sacred year, with fewer days of festival (or scarcely any in the case of Scotland). We may infer that this was successful partly because of the pressures usually labelled 'social control', partly because even in Scotland there remained a means of marking out God's time from the mundane through holy days and fast. Or, to take another critical example, the idea of the Mass as re-enactment of Christ's sacrifice was destroyed by the reformed churches, yet the centrality of that sacrifice was reaffirmed in the solemnity of the Protestant communion.

The precise impact of these changes must have depended on accommodation and adjustment. Negotiation was undertaken in the parish between the most austere forms of clericalism and communal interests, or at least the interests of those who exercised local power. The critical importance of this process of negotiation is most clearly suggested by its failure in Ireland. In the Pale and other Anglo-Irish territories there was by the 1590s a resolute refusal by both the gentry and ordinary parishioners to engage with the established church. In Bishop Lyon's vivid report on Cork, the Prayer Book services were being denounced as the devil's service, and ministers as spreading diabolical contagion.[308] Elsewhere in the British Isles forty years of Protestantism, of the majority sitting in the

---

[305] There is extensive debate on what sort of Protestants the English became after the Elizabethan settlement. Many of the main issues are well summarized in P. Collinson, 'The Elizabethan church and the new religion' and C. Haigh, 'The Church of England, the Catholics and the people', in C. Haigh (ed.), *The Reign of Elizabeth I* (Basingstoke, 1984).

[306] A. Dent, *The Plaine-Man's Pathway to Heaven* (1601), 27. For similar sentiments see G. Gifford, *A Briefe Discourse of Certaine Points of the Religion which is among the Common Sort of Christians, which may bee Termed the Countrie Divinitie* (1581).

[307] R.W. Scribner, 'Reformation and desacralisation: from sacramental world to moralized universe', in R. Po-Hsia and R.W. Scribner (eds.), *Problems in the Historical Anthropology of Early Modern Europe* (Wiesbaden, 1997), 90–1.

[308] Bradshaw, 'Cork, Limerick and Galway', 464.

pew, or on the stool, assimilating the reformed liturgy and preaching, had produced the opposite effect. Conformity to national settlements was the norm. Acceptance of godly preaching and the denunciation of sin was common in Scotland, and perhaps even in England, though in the latter case there was highly varied tolerance of Puritan zeal and manipulation of the Prayer Book. Despite the aspiration of the reformers to make worship common, local arrangements continued to modify the Protestantism of the settlements in a variety of directions. In the process a distinctively post-Reformation religion was grounded in community and in daily experience.[309]

[309] One of the most useful discussions on these problems is the conclusion of Haigh, *English Reformations*, 289–95. For a recent restatement, with some modifications, of this position by Haigh, see 'The taming of Reformation: preachers, pastors and parishioners in Elizabethan and early Stuart England', *History* 85 (2000), 572–88. In both cases the argument that parishioners tamed the ambitions of the reformers, rather than vice versa, underestimates the transactional element emphasized above.

BIBLIOGRAPHY

Primary

ADAMSON, P. *A declaratioun of the kings maiesties intentioun and meaning toward the lait actis of parliament* (Edinburgh, 1585) [*RSTC* 21948]

AIKMAN, J. (ed. and trans.) *George Buchanan's History of Scotland*, 4 vols. (Glasgow, 1827)

ALCOCK, J. *Gallicantus in Sinodo apud Bernwell* (1498) [*RSTC* 277]

ALESIUS, A. *Of the auctorite of the word of God agaynst the bisshop of London* (?Strasbourg, 1544) [*RSTC* 292]

ALLEN, P.S. and H.M. (eds.) *The Letters of Richard Fox* (1929)

ARBER, E. (ed.) *Thomas Lever: Sermons* (1870)

The Arte or Crafte to Lyve Well and to Dye Well (1505) [*RSTC* 792]

AVELING, H. and PANTIN, W.A. (eds.) *The Letter Book of Robert Joseph*, Oxford Historical Society NS 19 (1967)

AYLMER, J. *A harborowe for faithfull and trewe subjects agaynst the late blowne blaste concerninge the government of wemen* (Strasbourg, 1559) [*RSTC* 1005]

AYRE, J. (ed.) *The Sermons of Edwyn Sandys* (PS, Cambridge, 1842)

——— *Thomas Becon: Prayers and Other Pieces* (PS, Cambridge, 1845)

——— *The Works of John Jewel*, 4 vols. (PS, Cambridge, 1845–9)

——— *The Works of John Whitgift*, 3 vols. (PS, Cambridge, 1851)

BALE, J. *Expostulation or complaynte agaynste the blasphemyes of a frantike papyst of Hamshyre* (? 1552) [*RSTC* 1294]

BALNAVES, H. *The Confession of Faith* (Edinburgh, 1584) [*RSTC* 1340]

BANCROFT, R. *A sermon preached at Paule's Cross the 9 of Februarie . . . Anno 1588* (1589) [*RSTC* 1346]

——— *Dangerous Positions and Proceedings, published and practised within this Island of Brytaine under pretence of Reformation and for the Presbiteriall Discipline* (1593) [*RSTC* 1344]

——— *A Survay of the pretended Holy Discipline* (1593) [*RSTC* 1352]

BARNES, R. *A supplicatyon made by Robert Barnes doctoure in divinite unto the most excellent and redoubted prince henrye the eyght* (Antwerp, 1538) [*RSTC* 1470]

BARNUM, P.H. (ed.) *Dives and Pauper*, 2 vols., EETS OS 280 (1976–80)

BARRATT, D.M. (ed.) *Ecclesiastical Terriers of Warwickshire Parishes*, Dugdale Society 22 (1955)

BATEMAN, S. *A christall glasse of christian reformation* (1569) [*RSTC* 1581]

BATESON, M. (ed.) 'A collection of original letters from the bishops to the Privy Council, 1564', *Camden Society Miscellany* 9, CS NS 53 (1895)

BAUGHE, T. *A Summons to Judgment* (1614) [*RSTC* 1594]

BAYNE, R. (ed.) *The Life of Bishop Fisher*, EETS extra ser. 27 (1921)

BECON, T. *David's harpe, ful of moost delectable armony* (1542) [*RSTC* 1717]

BEER, B.L. (ed.) 'A letter of William Lord Paget of Beaudesert', *Huntingdon Library Quarterly* 34 (1971), 277–83

BEER, B.L. and JACK, S.M. (eds.) 'The letters of William, Lord Paget of Beaudesert', *Camden Society Miscellany* 25, CS 4th ser. 13 (1974)

BERNARD, R. *The faithfull shepherd . . . to further young divines in the studie of divinitie. With shepherds practise in preaching* (1621) [*RSTC* 1941]

BEZA, T. *Epistolae*, 2nd edn. (Geneva, 1575)

BINNEY, J.E. (ed.) *The Accounts of the Wardens of the Parish of Morebath, Devon, 1520–1573* (Exeter, 1904)

BISSE, J. *Two Sermons, preached at Paules Crosse and Christes Church* (1581) [*RSTC* 3099]

BONNER, E. *A Profitable and Necessarye Doctryne* (1555) [*RSTC* 3281.5]

Book of Common Order, in J. Knox, *Works*, 6 vols., ed. D. Laing (Wodrow Society, Edinburgh, 1846), vol. vi

BOOTY, J.E. (ed.) *Jewel's: An Apology for the Church of England* (Ithaca, N.Y., 1983)

BOURCIER, E. (ed.) *The Diary of Sir Simonds D'Ewes, 1622–4* (Paris, 1975)

BRADSHAW, W. *A plaine and pithy exposition of the second epistle to the Thessalonians* (1620) [*RSTC* 3523]

BRAY, G. (ed.) *Documents of the English Reformation* (Cambridge, 1994)

—— *The Anglican Canons, 1529–1947*, Church of England Record Society (Woodbridge, 1998)

—— *Tudor Church Reform: The Henrician Canons of 1535 and the Reformatio Legum Ecclesiasticum*, Church of England Record Society 8 (Woodbridge, 2000)

BREWER, J.S. *et al.* (eds.) *Letters and Papers, Foreign and Domestic, of the Reign of Henry VIII*, 23 vols. (1862–1932)

BRIGDEN, S. 'The letters of Richard Scudamore to Sir Philip Hoby, September 1549–March 1555', *Camden Society Miscellany* 30, CS 4th ser. 39 (1990)

BRIGHT, T. *An Abridgement of the Booke of Acts and Monuments* (1589) [*RSTC* 11229]

BRIGHTMAN, T. *Workes* (1644)

BRINKWORTH, E.R.C. (ed.) *The Archdeacon's Court: Liber Actorum, 1584*, 2 vols., Oxfordshire Record Society 23–4 (1942–6)

BRUCE, J. (ed.) *The Works of Roger Hutchinson* (PS, Cambridge, 1842)

BRYNE, M. St. C. (ed.) *The Letters of King Henry VIII* (1936)

—— *The Lisle Letters*, 6 vols. (1980)

BUCER, M. *De Regno Christi*, ed. F. Wendel, Opera Latina 15 (1955)

BULLINGER, H. *A hundred Sermons upon the Apocalips of Jesu Christe . . .* (1561) [*RSTC* 4061]

CALDERWOOD, A.B. (ed.) *The Buik of the Kirk of the Canagait, 1564–1567*, SRS OS 90 (Edinburgh, 1961)

Calendar of the Patent Rolls

Calendar of the Patent and Close Rolls of Ireland

Calendar of State Papers Domestic

Calendar of State Papers Foreign

Calendar of State Papers Ireland

Calendar of State Papers Scotland

Calendar of State Papers Spanish

Calendar of State Papers Venetian

Calendars of Entries from the Papal Registers, ed. J.A. Twemlow, M. Haren, A.P. Fuller (Dublin, 1978–86)

CAMERON, J.K. (ed.) *The First Book of Discipline* (Edinburgh, 1972)

CANNY, N.P. (ed.) 'The dysorders of the Irishry, 1571', *Studia Hibernica* 14 (1979)

CARAMAN, P. (ed.) *John Gerard: The Autobiography of an Elizabethan* (1951)

—— *William Weston: The Autobiography of an Elizabethan* (1955)

CARLETON, G. *The Life and Death of Bernard Gilpin* (1727 edn.)

CARR, S. (ed.) *The Early Writings of Bishop Hooper* (PS, Cambridge, 1843)

CARTWRIGHT, T. *The Second Replie of Thomas Cartwright against Master Doctor Whitgifts second Answere touching Churche Discipline* (Heidelberg, 1575) [RTSC 4714]

CHADERTON, L. *A Fruitfull Sermon upon the 3, 4, 5, 6, 7, & 8 verses of the 12 Chapiter of the Epistle of St Paule to the Romanes* (1584) [RSTC 4926]

CHRISTMAS, H. (ed.) *The Works of Nicholas Ridley* (PS, Cambridge, 1843)

—— *Select Works of Bishop Bale* (PS, Cambridge, 1849)

CLAY, W.K. (ed.) *Liturgies and Occasional Forms of Prayer set forth in the Reign of Queen Elizabeth* (PS, Cambridge, 1847)

CLIFFORD, A. (ed.) *The State Papers and Letters of Sir Ralph Sadler*, 3 vols. (Edinburgh, 1809)

COLEMAN, J. (ed.) 'A medieval Irish library catalogue', *Bibliographical Society of Ireland* 2 (1921–5), 111–20

CORRIE, G.E. (ed.) *The Sermons and Remains of Hugh Latimer*, 2 vols. (PS, Cambridge, 1844–5)

COSIN, R. *An Apologie: of and for Sundrie Proceedings by Jurisdiction Ecclesiasticall* (1591) [RSTC 5820]

COX, J.E. (ed.) *Miscellaneous Writings and Letters of Thomas Cranmer* (PS, Cambridge, 1846)

—— *The Works of Thomas Cranmer, Archbishop of Canterbury, Martyr, 1556*, 2 vols. (PS, Cambridge, 1844–6)

CRAIGIE, J. (ed.) *The Basilikon Doron of King James VI*, 2 vols., STS 3rd ser. 16, 18 (1942–4)

CRANSTOUN, J. (ed.) *Satirical Poems of the Time of the Reformation*, 2 vols., STS, 20, 28 (Edinburgh, 1891–3)

CRASHAW, W. *Preface to William Perkins' Of the Calling of the Ministrie* (Cambridge, 1608) [RSTC 19649]

CUMING, J. (ed.) *The Liturgy of the Church of Scotland or John Knox's Book of Common Order* (1840)

CUNNINGHAM, B. (ed.) 'A view of religious affiliation and practice in Thomond, 1591', *Archivium Hibernicum* 48 (1994), 13–23

CUNNINGHAM, W. (ed.) *Sermons of Revd Robert Bruce* (Wodrow Society, Edinburgh, 1843)

DASENT, J.R. (ed.) *Acts of the Privy Council*, 32 vols. (1890–1907)

DAVIDSON, J. *Bancroft's rashnes in Rayling against the Church of Scotland* (Edinburgh, 1590) [*RSTC* 6322]

DAVIES, J.H. (ed.) *Yny Lhyvyr Hwnn . . .* (Bangor, 1902)

DAVIS, N. (ed.) *Paston Letters and Papers of the Fifteenth Century*, 2 vols. (Oxford, 1971)

DENT, A. *The Plaine Mans Pathway to Heaven* (1601) [*RSTC* 6626]

DERING, E. *A briefe and necessarie Catechisme or instruction, very needful to be known to all Housholders*, in *Workes* (1614)

——*A Sermon preached before the Queenes Maiestie*, in *Workes* (1614) [*RSTC* 6676]

DEWAR, M. (ed.) *Sir Thomas Smith's De Republica Anglorum* (Cambridge, 1982)

DICKENS, A.G. (ed.) *The Chronicle of Butley Priory* (Winchester, 1951)

——'Robert Parkyn's narrative', in *Reformation Studies* (1982), 287–312

DICKINSON, W.C., DONALDSON, G., and MILNE, I.A. (eds.) *A Source Book of Scottish History*, 3 vols. (Edinburgh, 1952–4)

DOWLING, M. (ed.) 'William Latymer's Chronickille of Anne Bulleyn', *Camden Society Miscellany* 30, CS 4th ser. 39 (1990)

DOWLING, M. and SHAKESPEARE, J. (eds.) 'The recollections of Rose Hickman', *BIHR* 55 (1982), 97–102

DUNLOP, A.I. *Acta Facultatis Artium Universitatis Sanctandree, 1413–1588*, 2 vols., SHS 3rd ser. 54–5 (1964–5)

DUNLOP, A.I. and COWAN, I. *Calendar of Scottish Supplications to Rome 1428–32*, SHS 4th ser. 7 (1970)

DUNLOP, A.I. and MACLAUCHLAN, D. (eds.) *Scottish Supplications to Rome 1433–47*, SHS 4th ser. 7 (1982)

DYBOSKI, R. (ed.) *Songs, Carols and other Miscellaneous Poems*, EETS extra ser. 101 (1907)

DYKE, J. *A Worthy Communicant: or a treatise Shewing the Due order of Receiving the Lord's Supper* (1636) [*RSTC* 6626]

EARLE, J. *Microcosmographie*, facs. edn. (1966)

EASTING, R. (ed.) *St. Patrick's Purgatory*, EETS OS 298 (1991)

EDELEN, G. (ed.) *William Harrison: The Description of England* (Ithaca, N.Y., 1968)

ELDER, J. 'A proposal for uniting Scotland with England', *Bannatyne Miscellany* 1 (Bannatyne Club, Edinburgh, 1827), 1–18

ELLIS, H. *Original Letters Illustrative of English History*, 3 vols. (1827)

ELRINGTON, C.R. (ed.) J. Ussher, *A discourse of the religion anciently professed by the Irish and British*, in *The Whole Works of James Ussher*, 17 vols. (Dublin, 1864), vol. iv.

EMMISON, F.G. (ed.) *Wills of the County of Essex*, 12 vols. (Washington D.C., 1982–)

ERASMUS, D. *An Exhortation to the Diligent Study of the Scripture* (Antwerp, 1529), trans. W. Roye [*RSTC* 10493]

ERBE, T. (ed.) *Mirk's Festial: A Collection of Homilies by Johannes Mirkus*, EETS extra ser. 96 (1905)

FISHER, J. (ed.) *William Salesbury: Kynniver Llith a Ban* (Cardiff, 1931)

FITZGERALD, W. (ed.) *William Whitaker: A Disputation of the Holy Scriptures* (PS, Cambridge, 1848)

FOXE, E. *The True Dyfferens between the regall power and the ecclesiastical power*, trans. Henry, Lord Stafford (1548) [*RSTC* 11220]

FRERE, W.H. and DOUGLAS, C.E. (eds.) *Puritan Manifestoes: A Story of the Origin of the Puritan Revolt* (1954)

FRERE, W.H. and KENNEDY, W.M. (eds.) *Visitation Articles and Injunctions of the Period of the Reformation*, 3 vols. (1910)

GALLOWAY, D. (ed.) *Norwich 1540–1642*, Records of Early English Drama (Toronto, 1984)

GARDINER, J. (ed.) *John Stow: Three Fifteenth-Century Chronicles*, CS NS 28 (1880)

GIBBINGS, R. (ed.) *John Calfhill's Answer to John Martiall's Treatise of the Cross* (PS, Cambridge, 1846)

GIFFORD, G. *A Briefe Discourse of Certaine Points of the Religion which is among the Common Sort of Christians, which may bee Termed the Countrie Divinitie* (1581) [*RSTC* 11845]

—— *Sermons upon the Whole Book of the Revelation* (1596) [*RSTC* 11866]

GILBY, A. *An answere to the devillish detection of Stephane Gardiner* (1547) [*RSTC* 11884]

—— *A commentarye upon the Prophet Mycha* (1551) [*RSTC* 11886]

—— *A commentarye upon the Prophet Malaky* (1553) [*RSTC* 11885.5]

GOLDING, A. *A Discourse upon the Earthquake that hapned the sixt of Aprill* (1580) [*RSTC* 11987]

GORHAM, G.C. (ed.) *Gleanings of a Few Scattered Ears during the Period of the Reformation in England*, 2 vols. (1857)

GREET, W.C. (ed.) *Reginald Pecock: The Reule of Crysten Religioun*, EETS OS 171 (1927)

GREG, W.W. (ed.) *Respublica*, EETS OS 226 (1952)

GRIFFITHS, J. (ed.) *The Two Books of Homilies appointed to be Read in Churches* (Oxford, 1859)

HALL, E. *Chronicle: The Life of King Henry VIII*, ed. C. Whibley (1904)

HALL, F. (ed.) *William Lauder: Ane Compendious and Breve Tractate concerning the Office and Dewtie of Kyngis, Spirituall Pastoris and Temporall Iugis*, EETS OS 4 (1864)

HAMILTON, W.D. (ed.) *Charles Wriothesley: A Chronicle of England during the Reigns of the Tudors from AD 1485 to 1559*, 2 vols., CS NS 18, 20 (1875–7)

HANNAY, R.K. and MACKIE, R.L. (eds.) *Letters of James the Fourth, 1505–1513*, SHS 3rd ser. 45 (1953)

HANNAY, R.K. and HAY, D. (eds.) *Letters of James V* (Edinburgh, 1954)

HAPPÉ, P. and KING, J.N. (eds.) *The Vocacyon of Johan Bale*, Medieval and Renaissance Texts and Studies 70 (Binghamton, N.Y., 1990)

HARDING, T. *An Answere to Maister Juelles Chalenge* (Antwerp, 1565); English Recusant Literature facs. 229 (1975)

HARRISON, W. *The difference of hearers. On an exposition of the parable of the sower* (1614) [*RSTC* 12870]

HARTLEY, T.E. (ed.) *Proceedings in the Parliaments of Elizabeth I: 1584–89* (1995)

HARTSHORNE, C.H. (ed.) *William Fulke: A Defence of the Sincere and True Translation of the Holy Scriptures into the English Tongue* (PS, Cambridge, 1843)

HAY FLEMING, D. (ed.) *The Register of the Minister, Elders and Deacons of the Christian Congregation of St Andrews, 1559–1600*, 2 vols., SHS, 4, 7 (1889–90)

HAYNES, S. (ed.) *A Collection of State Papers relating to affairs in the Reigns of King Henry VIII, King Edward VI, Queen Mary and Queen Elizabeth*, 2 vols. (1740)

HEATH, P. (ed.) *Bishop Geoffrey Blythe's Visitations, ca. 1515–75*, Staffordshire Record Society 4th ser. 7 (1973)

HENDERSON, G.D. (ed.) *The Scots Confession, 1560 and the Negative Confession, 1581* (Edinburgh, 1937)

HENNESSY, W. (ed.) *Annals of Loch Cé*, 2 vols. (1871)

HENRY VIII *Assertio Septem Sacramentorum adversus M. Lutherum* (1521); trans. *An Assertion of the Seven Sacraments against Martin Luther* (1687)

HEROLT, J. *Sermones Discipuli* (Rothomagi, 1511)

HERRTAGE, S.J. (ed.) *Thomas Starkey's Life and Letters*, EETS extra ser. 32 (1878)

HEY, D. (ed.) *Richard Gough: The History of Myddle* (1981)

HIMELICK, R. (ed.) *The Enchiridion of Erasmus* (Bloomington, Ind., 1963)

HITCHCOCK, E.V. (ed.) *William Roper: The Life of Sir Thomas More, Knight* (1935)

HITCHCOCK, E.V. and CHAMBERS, E.K. (eds.) *John Harpsfield: The Life and Death of Sir Thomas Moore, Knight*, EETS os 226 (1932)

HOGARDE, M. *The displaying of the Protestantes* (1556) [*RSTC* 13557]

HOGG, J. (ed.) *Richard Whytford: A Werke for Housholders*, Salzburg Studies in English Literature 89 (1979), vol. v.

HOLINSHED, R. *Chronicles of England, Ireland and Scotland*, 6 vols. (1808)

HOOKER, J. alias VOWELL *Description and Account of the City of Exeter* (Exeter, 1765)

HORNE, R. *Whether Christian faith maye be kepte secret in the heart without confession therof openly to the worlde* (? 1553) [*RSTC* 5160.3]

HOSKINS, E. (ed.) *Horae Beatae Mariae Virginis* (1901)

How the Plowman lerned his pater noster (1510) [*RSTC* 20034]

HUGHES, P.L. and LARKIN, J.F. (eds.) *Tudor Royal Proclamations*, 2 vols. (New Haven, Conn., 1964, 1969)

HUSSEY, A. (ed.) 'Visitations of the archdeacon of Canterbury', *Archaeologia Cantiana* 25 (1902)

HUTCHINSON, F.E. (ed.) *The Works of George Herbert* (Oxford, 1941)

Injunctions and other Ecclesiastical Proceedings of Richard Barnes, Bishop of Durham from 1575 to 1587, Surtees Society 22 (Durham, 1850)

JANELLE, P. (ed.) *Stephen Gardiner: Obedience in Church and State* (Cambridge, 1930)

JENKYNS, H. (ed.) *The Works of Thomas Cranmer*, 4 vols. (Oxford, 1833)

JESSOP, A. (ed.) *Visitations of Norwich, 1492–1532*, CS 2nd ser. 43 (1888)

JONES, E. (ed.) *The New Oxford Book of Sixteenth-Century Verse* (Oxford, 1991)

JORDAN, W.K. (ed.) *The Chronicle and Political Papers of King Edward VI* (Ithaca, 1966)

KEATINGE, W. (ed.) *Liturgies and Occasional Forms of Prayer set forth in the Reign of Queen Elizabeth* (PS, Cambridge, 1847)

KEAVENEY, A. and MADDEN, J.A. (eds.) *Sir William Herbert: Croftus sive de Hibernia Liber* (1992)

KEBLE, J. (ed.) *The Works of . . . Richard Hooker*, 3 vols. (Oxford, 1841)

KEITH, R. *History of the Affairs of Church and State in Scotland from the beginning of the Reformation to the year 1568*, ed. J.P. Lawson, 3 vols. (Spottiswoode Society, Edinburgh, 1844–50)

KETLEY, J. (ed.) *The Two Liturgies, AD 1549 and AD 1552, with Other Documents set forth by authority in the Reign of Edward VI* (PS, Cambridge, 1844)

KIRK, J. (ed.) *The Second Book of Discipline* (Edinburgh, 1980)

—— *Stirling Presbytery Records, 1586–1589*, SHS 4th ser. 17 (1981)

—— *The Visitation of the Diocese of Dunblane and Other Churches, 1586–1589*, SRS 11 (Edinburgh, 1984)

—— *The Books of Assumption of the Thirds of Benefices: Scottish Ecclesiastical Rentals at the Reformation*, British Academy Records of Social and Economic History NS 21 (1995)

KITCHIN, G.W. (ed.) *The Records of the Northern Convocation*, Surtees Society 113 (Durham, 1907)

KLEIN, E.J. (ed.) *The Imitation of Christ from the First Edition of an English Translation made c. 1530 by Richard Whitford* (New York, 1941)

KNIGHTON, C.S. (ed.) *Acts of the Dean and Chapter of Westminster, 1543–1609* Westminster Abbey Record, 5th ser. 1 (1997)

KNOX, T.F. (ed.) *The First and Second Diaries of the English College, Douay* (1887)

LAING, D. (ed.) *John Row: History of the Kirk of Scotland from the Year 1558 to August 1637* (Wodrow Society, Edinburgh, 1842)

—— *John Knox: Works*, 6 vols. (Wodrow Society, Edinburgh, 1846)

LASKI, J. *Brevis ac dilucida de sacramentis ecclesiae Christi tractatio* (1552) [*RSTC* 15259]

LAW, T.G. (ed.) *The Catechism of John Hamilton, Archbishop of St Andrews 1552* (Oxford, 1884)

—— *The New Testament in Scots*, 3 vols., STS 44, 49, 52 (1901–5)

LEIGHTON, W.A. 'The register of Sir Thomas Butler, vicar of Much Wenlock', *Transactions of the Shropshire Archaeological and Natural History Society* 6 (1883), 93–132

LESLIE, J. *The History of Scotland*, ed. T. Thomson (Bannatyne Club, Edinburgh, 1830)

LLOYD, C. (ed.) *Formularies of Faith put forth by Authority during the Reign of Henry VIII* (Oxford, 1825)

LOADES, D.M. (ed.) *The Papers of George Wyatt, Esquire*, CS 4th ser. 5 (1968)

LOUIS, C. (ed.) *The Commonplace Book of Robert Reynes of Acle* (New York, 1980)

LUTHER, M. *Works*, ed. J. Pelikan and H. Lehman (St Louis, Mo., 1955–) vol. ix.

LYALL, R. (ed.) *Sir David Lindsay of the Mount: Ane Satyre of the Thrie Estatis* (Edinburgh, 1989)

MACCARTHY, B. (ed.) *Annals of Ulster*, 4 vols. (Dublin, 1895)

MACDONALD, A. (ed.) *The Register of Ministers, Exhorters and Readers and of their Stipends after the Period of the Reformation* (Edinburgh, 1830)

MACKAY, A.J.G. (ed.) *History of Greater Britain, compiled by John Major*, SHS 10 (1892)

MASON, J.A. (ed.) *John Knox: On Rebellion* (Cambridge, 1994)

MAXEY, A. *The Golden Chaine of Mans Salvation* (1610) [*RSTC* 17687]

MAYER, T.F. (ed.) *Thomas Starkey: A Dialogue between Pole and Lupset*, CS 4th ser. 37 (1989)

MEADS, D. (ed.) *The Diary of Lady Margaret Hoby 1599–1605* (1930)

MEECH, S.B. and ALLEN, H.E. (eds.) *The Book of Margery Kempe*, EETS os 212 (1940)

MITCHELL, A.F. (ed.) *Compendious Book of Godly and Spiritual Songs known as the 'Gude and Godlie Ballatis' (1567)*, STS 1st ser. 39 (Edinburgh, 1897)

MOORE, A.W. (ed.) *The Book of Common Prayer in Manx Gaelic* (Manx Society, 1895)

MORE, T. *Complete Works*, 10 vols. (New Haven, Conn., 1963–90)

MULLER, J.A. (ed.) *The Letters of Stephen Gardiner* (Cambridge, 1933)

MUNDAY, A. *A View of Sundry Examples Reporting many straunge murthers* (1580) [*RSTC* 18281]

MURRAY, J.A.H. (ed.) *The Complaynt of Scotlande*, EETS extra ser. 17 (1872)

MUSCULUS, W. *Common places of Christian Religion* (1563) [*RSTC* 18308]

NEVINSON, C. (ed.) *The Later Writings of Bishop Hooper* (PS, Cambridge, 1852)

NICHOLS, J.G. (ed.) *The Diary of Henry Machyn, Citizen of London*, CS os 42 (1848)

—— *The Chronicle of Queen Jane and Queen Mary*, CS os 48 (1850)

—— *Chronicle of the Grey Friars of London*, CS 1st ser. 53 (1852)

—— *Literary Remains of King Edward VI*, 2 vols. (Roxburghe Club, 1857)

—— *Narratives of the Days of the Reformation*, CS os 57 (1859)

NICHOLSON, W. (ed.) *The Remains of Edmund Grindal* (PS, Cambridge, 1843)

OCHINO, B. *Certayne Sermons of the ryghte famous and excellente Clerke Master Bernardine Ochine* (1550) [*RSTC* 18766]

O'KEARNEY, J. *Aibidil Gaoidheilge & Caiticiosma* (Dublin, 1571) [*RSTC* 18793]

OLDE, J. *A confession of the most auncient and true christen catholike olde beliefe* (Emden, 1556) [*RSTC* 18798]

PAFFORD, J.H. (ed.) *King Johan by John Bale* (Malone Society, Oxford, 1931)

PANTIN, W.A. (ed.) *Chapters of the English Black Monks*, CS 3rd ser. 47, 54 (1933, 1937)

—— 'Instructions for a devout and literate layman', in J.G. Alexander and M.T. Gibson (eds.), *Medieval Learning and Literature* (Oxford, 1976), 389–422

PARKER, M. *De Antiquitate Britanniae Ecclesiae et privilegiis Cantuariensis* (1572) [*RSTC* 19292]

PARKHURST, J. *Ludicra sive Epigrammata Juvenilia* (1573) [*RSTC* 19299]

PATRICK, D. (ed.) *Statutes of the Scottish Church, 1225–1559*, SHS 54 (1907)

PATTEN, W. 'The expedition into Scotland', in A.J. Pollard, (ed.), *Tudor Tracts, 1532–1588* (1903), 53–156

PECK, F. (ed.) *The History and Antiquities of the Isle of Man*, in *Desiderata Curiosa* (1779)

PEEL, A. (ed.) *The Seconde Parte of a Register: Being a Calendar of Manuscripts . . . intended for publication by the puritans about 1593*, 2 vols. (1915)

—— *The Notebook of John Penry*, CS 3rd ser. 67 (1944)

PERKINS, W. *A Reformed Catholicke: Or a Declaration shewing how neer we may come to the present Church of Rome in sundrie points of Religion* (Cambridge, 1598) [*RSTC* 19736]

—— *Works*, 3 vols. (Cambridge, 1631) [*RSTC* 19653]

PEROWNE, T. (ed.) *The Correspondence of Matthew Parker* (PS, Cambridge, 1853)

PETHERAM, J. (ed.) *A brief discours off the troubles begonne at Franckfort* (1846)

PITCAIRN, R. (ed.) *Ancient Criminal Trials of Scotland*, 3 vols. (Bannatyne Club, Edinburgh, 1829–33)

—— (ed.) *The Autobiography and Diary of Mr James Melvill* (Wodrow Society, Edinburgh, 1843)

PLUCKNETT, T.F.T. and BARTON, J.L (eds.) *St German's Doctor and Student*, Selden Society 91 (1974)

PRICE, F.D. (ed.) *The Commission for Ecclesiastical Causes in the Dioceses of Bristol and Gloucester*, Bristol and Gloucester Archaeological Society record section 10 (Gateshead, 1972)

Pregethau a osodwyd allan trwy awdurdod (1606) [*RSTC* 13678]

PRICKE, R. *A Verie Godlie and Learned Sermon treating of Mans mortalitie* (1608) [*RSTC* 20338]

PRYDE, G.S. (ed.) *Ayr Burgh Accounts, 1534–1624*, SHS 3rd ser. 28 (1937)

PURVIS, J.S. (ed.) *Tudor Parish Documents of the Diocese of York* (Cambridge, 1948)

—— *Select Sixteenth Century Causes in Tithe from the York Diocesan Registry*, York Archaeological Society 94 (1949)

QUENTIN, J. *The Maner to Lyve Well* [included in E. Hoskins (ed.) *Horae Beatae Marie Virginis* (1901)]

RAIT, R.S. (ed.) *The Warrender Papers*, 2 vols., SHS 3rd ser. 18 (Edinburgh, 1931)

REBHOLZ, R.A. (ed.) *The Complete Poems of Thomas Wyatt* (1978)

RINGLER, W.A. and FLACHMANN, M. (eds.) *Beware the Cat by William Baldwin: The First English Novel* (San Marino, Calif., 1988)

ROBINSON, H. (ed.) *The Zurich Letters*, 2 vols. (PS, Cambridge, 1842)

—— *Original Letters Relative to the English Reformation*, 2 vols. (PS, Cambridge, 1846–7)

ROGERS, E.F. (ed.) *The Correspondence of Thomas More* (Princeton, N.J., 1947)

ROGERS, R. *Seven Treatises, containing such direction as is gathered out of the holie scriptures* (1603) [*RSTC* 21215]

ROLLOCK, R. *Certain sermons upon severall places of the epistles of Paul* (Edinburgh, 1599) [*RSTC* 21271]

ROWLANDS, R. *A declaration of the True Causes of the Great Troubles presupposed to be intended against the Realm of England* (Cologne, 1592) [*RSTC* 10005]

RUSSELL, T. (ed.) *The Works of the English Reformers William Tyndale and John Frith*, 3 vols. (1831)

SALTER, H.E. (ed.) *Chapters of the Augustinian Canons*, Oxford Historical Society 74 (1920)

SAMUEL, W. *The abridgement of Goddes statutes in myter* (1551) [*RSTC* 21690.2]

SARAVIA, H. *Of the diverse degrees of the ministers of the gospel* (1591) [*RSTC* 21749]

SCHAFF, P. *The Creeds of the Evangelical Protestant Churches* (1877)

SCOLEFIELD, J. (ed.) *The Works of Bishop Pilkington* (PS, Cambridge, 1842)

SHEILS, W.J. (ed.) *Archbishop Grindal's Visitation, 1575*, Borthwick Texts and Calendars 4 (York, 1977)

SHIRLEY, E.P. (ed.) *Original Letters and Papers in Illustration of the Church in Ireland during the Reigns of Edward VI, Mary and Elizabeth* (1851)

SHUTTE, C. *A compendious forme and summe of Christian doctrine* (1584) [*RSTC* 22693]

SIMMONS, T.F. (ed.) *The Lay Folks' Mass Book* (Oxford, 1879)

SMITH, J. (ed.) *The Hammermen of Edinburgh and their Altar in St Giles, Edinburgh* (Edinburgh, 1906)

SNEYD, C.A. (ed.) *A Relation of the Island of England about the Year 1500*, CS os 37 (1847)

STANDISH, J. *A discourse wherin is debated whether it be expedient that the Scripture should be in English for al men to reade that wyll* (1555) [*RSTC* 23208]

STOCKWOOD, J. *A Sermon Preached at Paules Crosse on Barthelmew day* (1578) [*RSTC* 23284]

STUBBES, P. *The Anatomie of Abuses* (1583) [*RSTC* 23376]

SURTZ, E. and MURPHY, V. (eds.) *The Divorce Tracts of Henry VIII* (Angers, 1988)

SUTCLIFFE, M. *A Treatise of Ecclesiastical Discipline* (1590) [*RSTC* 23471]

SWINBURN, L.M. (ed.) *The Lanterne of Light*, EETS os 151 (1917)

TALBOT, C. (ed.) *Recusant Records*, Catholic Record Society 53 (1961)

TALBOT, C.H. (ed.) *Letters from the English Abbots to the Chapter at Cîteaux, 1442–1521*, CS 4th ser. 4 (1967)

TANNER, N. (ed.) *Norwich Heresy Trials, 1428–31*, CS 4th ser. 20 (1977)

TAVERNER, R. *The Epistles and Gospelles with a brief Postill upon the same from after Easter tyll Advent* (? 1545)

This Prayer of Salisbury Use etc., printed by F. Regnault (Paris, 1531)

THOMAS, H. (ed.) *Wever, R. Lusty Juventus* (New York, 1982)

THOMPSON, A.H. (ed.) *Visitations in the Diocese of Lincoln, 1517–1531*, LRS 33, 35 (1940–4)

THOMSON, R.L. (ed.) *John Carswell's 'Foirm na n-Urrnuidheadh'*, Scottish Gaelic Text Society 11 (Edinburgh, 1970)

THOMSON, T. (ed.) *A Diurnal of Remarkable Occurrents* (Edinburgh, 1833)

—— *Acts and Proceedings of the General Assemblies of the Kirk of Scotland from the year MDLX*, 3 vols. (Bannatyne and Maitland Clubs, 1839–45)

—— *The True History of the Church of Scotland by Mr David Calderwood*, 8 vols. (Wodrow Society, Edinburgh, 1842–9)

TORRANCE, T.F. (ed.) *Robert Bruce: Sermons on the Sacrament preached at Edinburgh, 1589* (1958)

TOULMIN-SMITH, L. (ed.) *The Itineraries of J. Leland*, 5 vols. (1906–8)

TOWNSEND, A. (ed.) *The Writings of John Bradford*, 2 vols. (PS, Cambridge, 1848, 1853)

TOWNSHEND, G. and CATTLEY, S.R. (eds.) *John Foxe's Acts and Monuments*, 8 vols. (1837–41)

TRAHERON, B. *An Exposition of the 4. Chapter of St John's Revelation* (1573) [*RSTC* 24171]

TURNER, W. *The Huntyng and Fyndyng out of the Romishe Foxe* (Bonn, 1543) [*RSTC* 24353]

TYNLEY, R. *Two Learned Sermons* (1609) [*RSTC* 24472]

TYTLER, P.F. (ed.) *England under the Reigns of Edward VI and Mary*, 2 vols. (1839)

UDALL, J. *A demonstration of the trueth of that Discipline which Christe hath prescribed for the governement of his Church* (1588) [*RSTC* 24499]

UDALL, N. (ed.) *The First Tome or Volume of the Paraphrases of Erasmus upon the Newe Testamente* (1548) [*RSTC* 2854]

Valor Beneficiorum Ecclesiasticorum in Hibernia (Dublin, 1741)

Valor Ecclesiasticus, 6 vols. (Record Comm., 1825–34)

VERSTEGAN, R. *A declaration of the True Causes of the Great troubles presupposed to be intended against the realm of England* (Antwerp, 1592) [*RSTC* 10005]

VOSSER, A.F. (ed.) *Edmund Campion: Two Bokes of the Histories of Ireland* (1963)

WALTER, H. (ed.) *William Tyndale's Doctrinal Treatises and Other Works*, 4 vols. (PS, Cambridge, 1848–9)

WESTFALING, H. *A treatise of Reformation in Religion preached in Oxeford* (1582) [*RSTC* 21215]

WHITE, J. *A Defence of the Way of the True Church* (1614) [*RSTC* 25390]

WHITE KENNETT, F. *The Case of Impropriations Truly Stated* (1704)

WILKINS, D. *Concilia Magnae Britanniae et Hiberniae*, 4 vols. (1737)

WILLIAMS, D. (ed.) *John Penry: Three Treatises concerning Wales* (Cardiff, 1960)

WILLIAMS, J. (ed.) *Bishop Redman's Visitation of 1597*, Norfolk Record Society 18 (1946)

WILLIAMSON, T. *The Sword of the Spirit to smite in pieces that anti-Christian Goliath* (1613) [*RSTC* 25740]

WILSON, J. (ed.) *Sermons very fruitfull, godly and learned: Roger Edgeworth Preaching in the Reformation, c.1535–c.1553* (Woodbridge, 1993)

WILSON, T. *The Arte of Rhetorique*, ed. G.H. Mair (Oxford, 1909)

Winthrop Papers, 6 vols. (Massachusetts Historical Society, Boston, 1929–)

WOLF, A. (ed.) *William Roye's Dialogue between a Christian Father and his Stubborn Son* (Vienna, 1874)

WOOD, H. (ed.) *Sir James Perott: The Chronicle of Ireland, 1584–1608* (Dublin, 1933)

WOOD-LEGH, K.L. (ed.) *Kentish Visitations of Archbishop William Warham and his Deputies, 1511–1512*, Kent Records 24 (1984)

WOOTTON, D. (ed.) *Thomas More: Utopia; Desiderius Erasmus: The Sileni of Alcibiades* (Indianapolis, Ind., 1999)

The Workes of that Famous and Worthy minister of Christ . . . Mr William Perkins, 2 vols. (Cambridge, 1608–9)

WRIGHT, D.P. (ed.) *The Register of Thomas Langton, Bishop of Salisbury, 1485–93,* Canterbury and York Society 74 (1985)

WRIGHT, T. (ed.) *Three Chapters of Letters Relating to the Suppression of the Monasteries,* CS OS 26 (1843)

WYNN, SIR JOHN *History of the Gwydir Family* (Ruthin, 1827)

WYNTER, P. (ed.) *The Works of Joseph Hall,* 10 vols. (Oxford, 1843)

Secondary

ADAMS, J.H. 'The medieval chapels of Cornwall', *Journal of the Royal Institution of Cornwall* NS 3 (1957), 48–65

ADDLESHAW, G.W.O. and ETCHELLS, E. *The Architectural Setting of Anglican Worship* (1948)

ALEXANDER, G. 'Bonner and the Marian persecutions', in C. Haigh (ed.), *The English Reformation Revised* (Cambridge, 1987), 157–75

ALFORD, S. *The Early Elizabethan Polity: William Cecil and the British Succession Crisis, 1558–1569* (Cambridge, 1998)

ALLDRIDGE, N. 'Loyalty and identity in Chester parishes, 1540–1640', in S.J. Wright (ed.), *Parish, Church and People: Local Studies in Lay Religion* (1988), 85–124

ANDERSON, M. 'Rhetoric and reality: Peter Martyr and the English Reformation', *C16J* 19 (1988), 451–61

ARIES, P. *The Hour of our Death* (1981)

ARNAULT, S.L. '"Spiritual and sacred publique actions". The Book of Common Prayer and the understanding of worship in the Elizabethan and Jacobean Church of England', in E.J. Carlson (ed.), *Religion and the English People, 1500–1640,* Sixteenth-century Essays and Studies 45 (Kirksville, Mo., 1998), 25–47

ASTON, M. *England's Iconoclasts, vol. i: Laws against Images* (Oxford, 1988)

—— 'Segregation in church', in W.J. Sheils and D. Wood (eds.), *Women in the Church,* SCH 27 (Oxford, 1990), 237–94

—— *Faith and Fire: Popular and Unpopular Religion, 1350–1600* (1993)

—— *The King's Bedpost: Reformation and Iconography in a Tudor Group Portrait* (Cambridge, 1994)

—— 'Puritans and iconoclasm, 1560–1660', in C. Durston and J. Eales (eds.), *The Culture of English Puritanism, 1560–1700* (Basingstoke, 1996), 92–121

AVELING, H. *Northern Catholics: The Catholic Recusants of the North Riding of Yorkshire 1558–1790* (1996)

AVIS, P.D.C. *The Church in the Theology of the Reformations* (1981)

AYRIS, P. 'Continuity and change in diocese and province: the role of a Tudor bishop', *HJ* 39 (1996), 291–313

AYRIS, P. and SELWYN, D. (eds.) *Thomas Cranmer, Churchman and Scholar* (Woodbridge, 1993)

BAILEY, D.S. *Thomas Becon and the Reformation of the Church of England* (Edinburgh, 1952)

BAINBRIDGE, V.R. *Gilds in the Medieval Countryside: Social and Religious Change in Cambridgeshire, c.1350–1558* (Woodbridge, 1996)

BANNERMAN, J. 'The Lordship of the Isles', in J. Brown (ed.), *Scottish Society in the Fifteenth Century* (1977), 209–40

—— 'Literacy in the Highlands', in I.B. Cowan and D. Shaw (eds.), *The Renaissance and Reformation in Scotland* (Edinburgh, 1983), 221–8

BARDGETT, F. *Scotland Reformed: The Reformation in Angus and the Mearns* (Edinburgh, 1989)

—— 'The Monifieth kirk register', *RSCHS* 23 (1987–9), 175–95

BARNES, G.L. 'Laity formation: the role of the early English printed primers', *JRH* 18 (1994), 139–58

BARRON, C.M. 'The parish fraternities of medieval London', in C.M. Barron and C. Harper-Bill (eds.), *The Church in Pre-Reformation Society: Essays in Honour of F.R.H. Du Boulay* (Woodbridge, 1985), 13–37

BASKERVILLE, E.J. *A Chronological Bibliography of Propaganda and Polemic published in English between 1553 and 1558* (American Philosophical Society, 1979)

BAUCKHAM, R. *Tudor Apocalypse* (Appleford, Oxon., 1976)

—— 'Hooker, Travers and the Church of Rome in the 1580s', *JEH* 29 (1978), 37–50

BAYNE, C.G. 'The coronation of Queen Elizabeth', *EHR* 22 (1907), 650–73

BECKETT, W. 'Sheen Charterhouse', University of Oxford D.Phil. (1993)

BECKWITH, M. 'The Bridgettine Monastery of Syon, with special reference to its Monastic Usages', University of Oxford D.Phil. (1975)

BEER, B. 'London parish clergy and the Protestant reformation, 1547–1559', *Albion* 18 (1986), 375–93

—— 'Episcopacy and reform in mid-Tudor England', *Albion* 23 (1991), 231–52

BERNARD, G.W. *War, Taxation and Rebellion in early Tudor England* (Brighton, 1986)

—— 'The making of religious policy, 1533–46: Henry VIII and the search for a middle way', *HJ* 41 (1998), 321–49

BERRY, B.M. and SCHOFIELD, R.S. 'Age at baptism in pre-industrial England', *Population Studies* 25 (1971), 453–64

BETTERIDGE, T. *Tudor Histories of the English Reformation: 1530–83* (Aldershot, 1999)

BICKNELL, E.J. *A Theological Introduction to the Thirty-Nine Articles* (1955)

BLENCH, J.W. *Preaching in England in the Late Fifteenth and Sixteenth Centuries* (Oxford, 1964)

BLOCK, J. *Factional Politics and the English Reformation, 1520–1540* (Woodbridge, 1993)

BOOTY, J.E. 'Preparation for the Lord's Supper in Elizabethan England', *Anglican Theological Review* 49 (1967), 131–48

BOSSY, J. 'The Counter-Reformation and the people of Catholic Europe', *PP* 47 (1970), 51–70

—— 'The Counter-Reformation and the people of Catholic Ireland, 1596–1641', *Historical Studies* 8 (1971), 155–70

—— *The English Catholic Community 1570–1850* (1975)

—— 'The social history of Confession in the age of the Reformation', *TRHS* 25 (1975), 21–38

BOSSY, J. 'The Mass as a social institution', *PP* 100 (1983), 29–61

—— *Christianity in the West, 1400–1700* (Oxford, 1985)

—— 'Privacy, Christianity and the State, 1400–1650', in J.-Ph. Genet and B. Vincent (eds.), *Etat et Eglise dans la Genèse de l'Etat Moderne* (Madrid, 1986), 103–11

BOTTIGHEIMER, K.S. 'The failure of the Reformation in Ireland: une question bien posée', *JEH* 36 (1985), 196–207

BOTTIGHEIMER, K.S. and BRADSHAW, B. 'Revisionism in the Irish Reformation: a debate', *JEH* 51 (2000), 581–92

BOTTIGHEIMER, K.S. and LOTZ-HEUMANN, U. 'The Irish Reformation in European perspective', *ARG* 89 (1998), 268–309

BOULTON, J.P. 'The limits of formal religion: the administration of holy communion in late Elizabethan and early Stuart England', *London Journal* 10 (1984), 135–54

BOWERS, R. 'The chapel royal, the first Edwardian Prayer Book and Elizabeth's settlement of religion, 1559', *HJ* 43 (2000), 317–44

BOWKER, M. *The Secular Clergy in the Diocese of Lincoln, 1495–1520* (Cambridge, 1968)

—— 'Lincolnshire 1536: heresy, schism or religious discontent', in D. Baker (ed.), *Heresy, Schism and Religious Protest*, SCH 9 (1972), 227–43

—— 'The Supremacy and the episcopate, the struggle for control, 1534–1540', *HJ* 18 (1975), 227–43

—— *The Henrician Reformation: The Diocese of Lincoln under John Longland* (Cambridge, 1981)

—— 'The Henrician Reformation and the parish clergy', in C. Haigh (ed.), *The English Reformation Revised* (Cambridge, 1987), 75–93

BOZEMAN, T. 'Federal theology and the "National Covenant": an Elizabethan Presbyterian case-study', *Church History* 61 (1992), 394–407

BRACHLOW, S. *The Communion of Saints: Radical Puritan and Separatist Ecclesiology, 1570–1625* (Oxford, 1988)

BRADSHAW, B. 'The opposition to the ecclesiastical legislation in the Irish Reformation parliament', *IHS* 16 (1968–9), 285–303

—— 'George Browne, first Reformation archbishop of Dublin, 1536–54', *JEH* 21 (1970), 301–26

—— *The Dissolution of the Religious Orders in Ireland under Henry VIII* (Cambridge, 1974)

—— 'The Edwardian Reformation in Ireland, 1547–53', *Archivium Hibernicum* 34 (1976), 83–99

—— 'Sword, Word and strategy in the Reformation in Ireland', *HJ* 21 (1978), 475–502

—— *The Irish Constitutional Revolution of the Sixteenth Century* (Cambridge, 1979)

—— 'The Reformation in the cities: Cork, Limerick and Galway, 1534–1603', in J. Bradley (ed.), *Settlement and Society in Medieval Ireland* (Kilkenny, 1988), 455–76

BRADSHAW, B. and DUFFY. E. (eds.) *Humanism, Reform and Reformation: The Career of Bishop John Fisher* (Cambridge, 1989)

BRADSHAW, B. and MORRILL, J. (eds.) *The British Problem, c. 1534–1707: State Formation in the Atlantic Archipelago* (Basingstoke, 1996)

BRADSHAW, B. and ROBERTS, P. (eds.) *British Consciousness and Identity: The Making of Britain 1533–1707* (Cambridge, 1998)

BRADSHAW, C. 'David or Josiah? Old Testament kings as exemplars in Edwardian religious polemic', in B. Gordon (ed.), *Protestant History and Identity in Sixteenth-Century Europe*, 2 vols. (St Andrews, 1996), i. 77–90

BRADY, C. 'Conservative subversives: the community of the Pale and the Dublin administration, 1556–1586', in P.J. Corish (ed.), *Radicals, Rebels and Establishments*, Historical Studies 15 (1985), 11–32

—— *The Chief Governors: The Rise and Fall of Reform Government in Tudor Ireland, 1536–1588* (Cambridge, 1994)

—— 'Comparable histories? Tudor reform in Wales and Ireland', in S. Ellis and S. Barber (eds.), *Conquest and Union: Fashioning a British State, 1485–1725* (Harlow, 1995), 67–86

BRADY, J. 'The catechism in Ireland: a survey', *Irish Ecclesiastical Record* 5th ser. 83 (1955), 167–76

BRENNAN, G. 'Patriotism, language and power: English translations of the Bible, 1520–1580', *History Workshop* 27 (1989), 18–36

BRIGDEN, S. 'Tithe controversy in Reformation London', *JEH* 32 (1981), 285–301

—— 'Youth and the Reformation', *PP* 95 (1982), 37–67

—— 'Thomas Cromwell and the "brethren"', in C. Cross, D. Loades, and J.J. Scarisbrick (eds.), *Law and Government under the Tudors* (Cambridge, 1988), 31–49

—— *London and the Reformation* (Oxford, 1989)

—— 'Henry Howard, earl of Surrey and the "conjured league"', *HJ* 37 (1994), 507–37

BRIGHTMAN, F.E. *The English Rite*, 2 vols. (1915)

BROOK, V.V.K. *A Life of Archbishop Parker* (Oxford, 1962)

BROOKE, C.N.L. 'The missionary at home: the Church and the towns, 1000–1250', in G.J. Cuming (ed.), *The Mission of the Church and the Propagation of the Faith*, SCH 6 (Cambridge, 1970), 59–83

BROOKS, P.N. *Thomas Cranmer's Doctrine of the Eucharist* (1965)

BROWN, A.D. *Popular Piety in Late Medieval England: The Diocese of Salisbury 1250–1550* (Oxford, 1995)

BROWN, A.J. *Robert Ferrar: Yorkshire Monk, Reformation Bishop and Martyr in Wales (c.1500–1555)* (1997)

BROWN, K.D. 'The Franciscan Observants, 1482–1559', University of Oxford D.Phil. (1986)

—— 'Wolsey and ecclesiastical order: the case of the Franciscan Observants', in S.J. Gunn and P.G. Lindley (eds.), *Cardinal Wolsey: Church, State and Art* (Cambridge, 1991), 219–38

BROWN, K.M. 'In search of the godly magistrate in Reformation Scotland', *JEH* 40 (1989), 553–81

BUCKINGHAM, C. 'The movement of clergy in the Diocese of Canterbury, 1552–1562', *Recusant History* 14 (1978), 219–41

BURGESS, C. '"For the increase of divine service": chantries in the parish in late medieval Bristol', *JEH* 36 (1985), 46–65

BURGESS, C. and KÜMIN, B. 'Penitential bequests and parish regimes in late medieval England', *JEH* 44 (1993), 610–30

BURNET, G. *History of the Reformation of the Church of England*, 3 vols. in 6 (1820)

BURNS, J.H. *Scottish Churchmen and the Council of Basel* (1962)

—— 'The conciliarist tradition in Scotland', *SHR* 42 (1963), 89–104

—— *The True Law of Kingship: Concepts of Monarchy in Early Modern Scotland* (Oxford, 1996)

BURRELL, S.A. 'The covenanting idea as a revolutionary symbol: Scotland 1596–1637', *Church History* 27 (1958), 338–50

BURROWS, M.A.J. 'Fifteenth-century Irish provincial legislation and pastoral care', in W.J. Sheils and D. Wood (eds.), *The Churches, Ireland and the Irish*, SCH 25 (Oxford, 1989), 55–67

BUSH, M.L. *The Government Policy of Protector Somerset* (1975)

—— *The Pilgrimage of Grace* (Manchester, 1996)

BUSSBY, F. (ed.) *Winchester Cathedral, 1079–1979* (Southampton, 1979)

BUTTERWORTH, C.C. *The English Primers: 1529–45* (Philadelphia, 1953)

BUTTERWORTH, C.C. and CHESTER, A.G. *George Joye: 1495–1553* (Philadelphia, 1962)

BYFORD, M. 'The Price of Protestantism: Assessing the Impact of Religious Change on Elizabethan Essex: The Cases of Heydon and Colchester, 1558–94', University of Oxford D.Phil. (1989)

—— 'The birth of a Protestant town: the process of reformation in Tudor Colchester, 1530–1580', in P. Collinson and J. Craig (eds.), *The Reformation in English Towns, 1500–1640* (Basingstoke, 1998), 23–47

BYMAN, S. 'Ritualistic acts and compulsive behaviour: the pattern of Tudor martyrdom', *AHR* 83 (1978), 625–43

CAMERON, A.I. *The Apostolic Camera and Scottish Benefices, 1418–1488* (1934)

CAMERON, E. *The European Reformation* (Oxford, 1991)

—— 'Philipp Melanchthon: image and substance', *JEH* 48 (1997), 705–22

CAMERON, J. *James V: The Personal Rule, 1528–42* (Edinburgh, 1998)

CAMERON, J.K. 'The Renaissance tradition in the Reformed Church of Scotland', in D. Baker (ed.), *Renaissance and Renewal in Church History*, SCH 14 (1977), 251–70

—— '"Catholic Reform" in Germany and in the pre-1560 Church in Scotland', *RSCHS* 20 (1979), 105–17

—— 'Godly nurture and admonition in the Lord: ecclesiastical discipline in the Reformed tradition', in L. Grame and K. Horby (eds.), *Die Danische Reformations vor ihren Internationalem Hintergrund* (Gottingen, 1990), 264–76

CANNY, N.P. *The Elizabethan Conquest of Ireland: A Pattern Established 1565–76* (Hassocks, 1976)

—— 'Why the Reformation failed in Ireland: une question mal posée', *JEH* 30 (1979), 423–50

—— *From Reformation to Restoration: Ireland 1534–1660* (Dublin, 1987)

—— 'Identity formation in Ireland: the emergence of the Anglo-Irish', in N.P. Canny and A. Pagden (eds.), *Colonial Identity in the Atlantic World, 1500–1800* (Princeton, 1987), 159–212

—— *Kingdom and Colony: Ireland in the Atlantic World* (Baltimore, 1988)

CARGILL THOMPSON, W.D. 'A reconsideration of Richard Bancroft's Paul's Cross sermon', *JEH* 20 (1969), 233–66

—— 'Who wrote "The Supper of the Lord"', in his *Studies in the Reformation: Luther to Hooker* (1980), 83–93

CARLETON, K.W.T. *Bishops and Reform in the English Church, 1520–1559* (Woodbridge, 2001)

CARLSON, E.J. 'The marriage of William Turner', *HR* 65 (1992), 336–9

—— *Marriage and the English Reformation* (Oxford, 1994)

—— 'The origins, function and status of the office of churchwarden, with particular reference to the diocese of Ely', in M. Spufford (ed.), *The World of Rural Dissenters, 1520–1725* (Cambridge, 1995), 191–200

—— (ed.) *Religion and the English People, 1500–1640*, Sixteenth-Century Essays and Studies 45 (Kirksville, Mo., 1998)

CARLSON, L.H. *Martin Marprelate, Gentleman: Master Job Throckmorton Laid Open in his Colors* (San Marino, Calif., 1981)

CARPENTER, C. 'The religion of the gentry in fifteenth century England', in D. Williams (ed.), *England in the Fifteenth Century* (Woodbridge, 1987), 53–74

—— *Locality and Polity: A Study of Warwickshire Society, 1401–1499* (Cambridge, 1992)

—— 'Gentry and community in medieval England', *JBS* 33 (1994), 340–80

CARTER, P. 'Mary Tudor, Parliament and the renunciation of First Fruits', *HR* 69 (1996), 340–6

—— 'Economic problems of provincial urban clergy during the Reformation', in P. Collinson and J. Craig (eds.), *English Towns* (1998), 147–58

—— '"Certain, continual and seldom abated": royal taxation of the Elizabethan Church', in S. Wabuda and C. Litzenberger (eds.), *Belief and Practice in Reformation England* (Aldershot, 1998), 94–112

CATTO, J.I. and EVANS, T.A.R. (eds.) *The History of the University of Oxford: Late Medieval Oxford* (Oxford, 1992)

CHADWICK, O. 'Richard Bancroft's submission', *JEH* 3 (1952), 58–73

CHAMBERS, D.S. *Cardinal Bainbridge and the Court of Rome* (Oxford, 1965)

CHARLES-EDWARDS, T. *Saint Winefride and her Well* (1964)

CHESTER, A.G. 'Robert Barnes and the burning of the books', *Huntington Library Quarterly* 14 (1951), 216–19

CHIBI, A.A. *Henry VIII's Conservative Scholar: Bishop John Stokesley and the Divorce, Royal Supremacy and Doctrinal Reform* (Berne, 1998)

CHRISTIE, G. *The Influence of Letters on the Scottish Reformation* (Edinburgh, 1908)

CLARK, J.G. 'Reformation and reaction at St Alban's Abbey, 1530–1558', *EHR* 115 (2000), 297–328

CLARK, P. 'The prophesying movement in Kentish towns in the 1570s', *Archaeologia Cantiana* 93 (1978 for 1977)

—— *English Provincial Society from the Reformation to the Revolution* (Hassocks, 1977)

—— 'Reform and radicalism in Kentish towns, *c.*1500–1553', in W.J. Mommsen (ed.), *Stadtbürgertum und Adel in der Reformation* (Stuttgart, 1979), 107–27

CLARK, S. and MORGAN, P.T.J. 'Religion and magic in Elizabethan Wales: Robert Holland's dialogue on witchcraft', *JEH* 27 (1976), 31–46

CLARKE, A. 'Varieties of uniformity: the first century of the Church of Ireland', in W.J. Sheils and D. Wood (eds.), *The Churches, Ireland and the Irish*, SCH 25 (Oxford, 1989), 105–22

CLARKE, M. 'Northern light? Parochial life in a "dark corner" of Tudor England', in K.C. White, C.G. Gibbs, and B. Kümin (eds.), *The Parish in English Life, 1400–1600* (Manchester, 1997), 56–73

CLEBSCH, W.A. *England's Earliest Protestants, 1520–1535* (New Haven, Conn., 1964)

CLEMENT, C.J. *Religious Radicalism in England, 1535–1565* (1997)

COLLINSON, P. 'The authorship of "A Brieff discours off the troubles begonne at Franckford"', *JEH* 9 (1958), 188–208

—— *The Elizabethan Puritan Movement* (1967)

—— *Archbishop Grindal 1519–83: The Struggle for a Reformed Church* (1979)

—— 'Cranbrook and the Fletchers: popular and unpopular religion in the Kentish Weald', in P.N. Brooks (ed.), *Reformation Principle and Practice* (1980), 171–202

—— *The Religion of Protestants: The Church in English Society 1559–1625* (Oxford, 1982)

—— *Godly People: Essays on English Protestantism and Puritanism* (1983)

—— 'The Elizabethan church and the new religion', in C. Haigh (ed.), *The Reign of Elizabeth I* (Basingstoke, 1984), 169–94

—— 'Truth and legend: the veracity of John Foxe's Book of Martyrs', in A.C. Duke and C.A. Tamse (eds.), *Clio's Mirror: Historiography in Britain and the Netherlands* (Zutphen, 1985), 31–54

—— 'The English conventicle', in W.J. Sheils and D. Wood (eds.), *Voluntary Religion*, SCH 23 (Oxford, 1986), 223–59

—— 'Shepherds, sheepdogs and hirelings: the pastoral ministry in post-Reformation England', in W.J. Sheils and D. Wood (eds.), *The Ministry: Clerical and Lay*, SCH 24 (Oxford, 1988), 185–220

—— *The Birthpangs of Protestant England* (Basingstoke, 1988)

—— *Elizabethan Essays* (1994)

—— 'The coherence of the text: how it hangeth together: the Bible in Reformation England', in W.P. Stephens (ed.), *The Bible, the Reformation and the Church*, Journal for the Study of the New Testament, Supplement Series 105 (Sheffield, 1994), 84–108

—— 'Ecclesiastical vitriol: religious satire in the 1590s and the invention of puritanism', in J. Guy (ed.), *The Reign of Elizabeth I* (Cambridge, 1995), 150–70

—— 'William Tyndale and the course of the English Reformation', *Reformation* 1 (1996), 72–97

—— 'The religion of Elizabethan England and of its Queen', in M. Ciliberto and N. Mann (eds.), *Giordano Bruno 1583–1585: The English Experience* (Florence, 1997), 3–22

—— 'Biblical rhetoric: the English nation and national sentiment in the prophetic mode', in C. McEarchern and D. Shuger (eds.), *Religion and Culture in Renaissance England* (Cambridge, 1997), 15–45

COLLINSON, P. and CRAIG, J. (eds.) *The Reformation in English Towns 1500–1640* (Basingstoke, 1998)

COLMICILLI, C. 'Decline and attempted reform of the Irish Cistercians, 1445–1531', *Collectanea Ordinis Cisterciensium Reformatorum* 18 (1956), 290–305; 19 (1957), 142–62, 371–83

CONLAN, P. *Franciscan Ireland* (Dublin, 1988)

COOLIDGE, P. *The Pauline Renaissance in England: Puritanism and the Bible* (Oxford, 1970)

COOPER, R. *Abbeys and Priories of Wales* (Swansea, 1992)

COOPER, W.R. 'Richard Hunne', *Reformation* 1 (1996), 221–51

CORISH, P.J. *The Irish Catholic Experience: A Historical Survey* (Dublin, 1985)

CORNWALL, J. *Wealth and Society in Early Sixteenth-Century England* (1988)

COSTER, W. 'Tokens of innocence: infant baptism, death and burial in early modern England', in B. Gordon and P. Marshall (eds.), *The Place of the Dead* (Cambridge, 2000), 266–87

COURATIN, A.H. 'The service of Holy Communion, 1552–1662', *Church Quarterly Review* 163 (1962), 431–42

COWAN, I.B. *The Parishes of Medieval Scotland* (SRS, 1967)

—— 'Some aspects of appropriation', *RSCHS* 13 (1971), 203–22

—— 'The Medieval Church in the diocese of Aberdeen', *Northern Scotland* 1 (1972), 19–48

—— 'Vicarages and the cure of souls in medieval Scotland', *RSCHS* 16 (1974), 111–27

—— 'Church and society', in J. Brown (ed.), *Scottish Society in the Fifteenth Century* (1977), 112–35

—— 'The Medieval Church in Argyll and the Isles', *RSCHS* 20 (1978), 15–29

—— *The Scottish Reformation* (1982)

COWAN, I.B. and EASSON, D.F. *Medieval Religious Houses: Scotland*, 2nd edn. (1976)

COWAN, W. 'The Scottish Reformation psalmody', *RSCHS* 1 (1926), 29–47

CRAIG, J. 'Co-operation and initiatives: Elizabethan churchwardens and parish accounts of Mildenhall', *Social History* 18 (1993), 357–80

—— 'Reformers, conflict and revisionism: the Reformation in sixteenth-century Hadleigh', *HJ* 42 (1999), 1–23

CRANKSHAW, D. 'Preparations for the Canterbury Provincial Convocation of 1562–3: a question of attribution', in S. Wabuda and C. Litzenberger (eds.), *Belief and Practice in Reformation England* (Aldershot, 1998), 60–93

CRAWFORD, P. *Women and Religion in England 1500–1700* (1993)

CRESSY, D. *Bonfire and Bells: National Memory and the Protestant Calendar in Elizabethan and Stuart England* (1989)

—— *Birth, Marriage and Death: Ritual, Religion and the Life Cycle in Tudor and Early Stuart England* (Oxford, 1997)

CROSS, C. *The Royal Supremacy in the Elizabethan Church* (1969)

—— 'Dens of loitering lubbers: Protestant protest against cathedral foundations, 1540–1640', in D. Baker (ed.), *Schism, Heresy and Religious Protest*, SCH 10 (1972), 231–8

—— 'Parochial structures and the dissemination of Protestantism in sixteenth-century England: a tale of two cities', in D. Baker (ed.), *The Church in Town and Countryside*, SCH, 16 (Oxford, 1979), 269–78

—— 'Priests into ministers: the establishment of Protestant practice in the city of York', in P.M. Brooks (ed.), *Reformation Principle and Practice* (1980), 203–26

—— 'Lay literacy and clerical misconduct in a York parish during the reign of Mary Tudor', *York Historian* (1980), 10–15

—— 'Protestant attitudes towards episcopacy in the early Elizabethan Church', *Miscellanea Historiae Ecclesiasticae* 8 (Louvain, 1987), 221–8

—— 'Monasticism and society in the diocese of York, 1520–1540', *TRHS* 5th ser. 38 (1988), 131–45

—— 'Communal piety in sixteenth-century Boston', *Lincolnshire History and Archaeology* 25 (1990), 33–8

CROSS, C. (ed.) *Patronage and Recruitment in the Tudor and Early Stuart Church*, Borthwick Studies in History (York, 1996)

D'ALTON, C.W. 'The Suppression of Heresy in Early Henrician England', University of Melbourne Ph.D. (1999)

D'ARCY, J. 'Late Medieval Catholicism and the Impact of the Reformation in the Archdeaconry of Derby, *ca.*1520–*ca.*1570', University of Nottingham Ph.D. (1996)

DANIELL, D. *William Tyndale: A Biography* (New Haven, Conn., 1994)

DANNER, D.G. 'The contribution of the Geneva Bible of 1560 to the English Protestant tradition', *C16J* 12 (1981), 5–18

DAVIDSON, D. 'The influence of the English printers on the Scottish Reformation', *RSCHS* 1 (1926), 75–87

DAVIES, C.S.L. 'International politics and the establishment of presbyterianism in the Channel Islands: the Coutances connection', *JEH* 50 (1999), 498–522

DAVIES, H. *Worship and Theology in England from Cranmer to Baxter and Fox* (Princeton, N.J., 1970)

DAVIES, J.G. *The Architectural Setting of Baptism* (1962)

DAVIES, R.G. 'Lollardy and locality', *TRHS* 6th ser. 1 (1991), 191–212

DAVIES, R.R. *The Matter of Britain and the Matter of England* (Oxford, 1996)

DAVIS, J.F. *Heresy and Reformation in the South East of England, 1520–1559* (1983)

DAVIS, N. 'From "popular culture" to religious cultures', in S.E. Ozment (ed.), *Reformation Europe: A Guide to Research* (St Louis, Miss., 1982), 321–41

DAWSON, J. 'Two kingdoms or three? Ireland in Anglo-Scottish relations in the middle of the sixteenth century', in R.A. Mason (ed.), *Scotland and England, 1286–1815* (Edinburgh, 1987), 113–38

——'William Cecil and the British dimension of early Elizabethan foreign policy', *History* 74 (1989), 196–216

——'The two John Knoxes: England, Scotland and the 1558 tracts', *JEH* 43 (1991), 555–76

——'"The face of the perfyt Reformed Kyrk": St Andrews and the early Scottish Reformation', SCH Subsidia 8 (Oxford, 1991), 413–35

——'The Scottish Reformation and the theatre of martyrdom', in D. Wood (ed.), *Martyrs and Martyrology*, SCH 30 (Oxford, 1993), 259–70

——'Calvinism and the Gaidhealtachd in Scotland', in A. Duke, G. Lewis and A. Pettegree (eds.), *Calvinism in Europe* (Cambridge, 1994), 231–53

——'Anglo-Scottish Protestant culture and the integration of sixteenth-century Britain', in S. Ellis and S. Barber (eds.), *Conquest and Union* (1995), 87–114

——'Trumpeting resistance: Christopher Goodman and John Knox', in R.A. Mason (ed.), *John Knox and the British Reformations* (Aldershot, 1998), 131–53

——'Clan, kin and kirk: the Campbells and the Scottish Reformation', in N. Scott Amos, A. Pettegree and H. Van Nierop (eds.), *The Education of a Christian Society* (Aldershot, 1999), 211–41

DEAN, D.M. and JONES, N.L. (eds.) *The Parliaments of Elizabethan England* (Oxford, 1990)

DELUMEAU, J. *Catholicism from Luther to Voltaire* (1977)

DENT, C.M. *Protestant Reformers in Elizabethan Oxford* (Oxford, 1983)

DEVEREUX, J.C. 'Protestant propaganda in the reign of Edward VI: a study of Luke Shepherd's "Doctour Doubble Ale"', in E.J. Carlson (ed.), *Religion and the English People, 1500–1640* (Kirksville, Mo., 1998), 121–46

DICKENS, A.G. *Lollards and Protestants in the Diocese of York, 1509–1558* (Oxford, 1959)

——*Reformation Studies* (1982)

——*The English Reformation*, 2nd edn. (1989)

——*Late Monasticism and the Reformation* (1994)

DICKINS, B. 'The Irish broadside of 1571 and Queen Elizabeth's Types', *Transactions of the Cambridge Bibliographical Society* 1/1 (1949/53), 48–60

DICKINSON, J.R. *The Lordship of Man under the Stanleys: Government and Economy in the Isle of Man, 1580–1704* (Chetham Society, 3rd ser. 41, 1996)

DILLOW, K. 'The Social and Ecclesiastical Significance of Church Seating Arrangements and Pew Disputes 1500–1740', University of Oxford D.Phil. (1990)

DILWORTH, M. *Scottish Monasteries: Monastic Life in the Sixteenth Century* (Edinburgh, 1994)

——'Franco-Scottish efforts at monastic reform', *RSCHS* 25 (1994), 204–21

DINN, R. ' "Monuments answerable to men's worth": burial patterns, social status and gender in late medieval Bury St Edmund's', *JEH* 46 (1995), 237–55

DOBSON, R.B. 'Mendicant ideal and practice in late medieval York', in P.V. Addyman and V.E. Black (eds.), *Archaeological Papers from York presented to M.W. Barley* (York, 1984), 109–22

—— 'The bishops of late medieval England as intermediaries between Church and State', in J.-P. Genet (ed.), *Etat et Eglise dans la Genèse de l'Etat Moderne* (Madrid, 1986), 227–38

—— 'Citizens and chantries in late medieval York', in D. Abulafia *et al.* (eds.), *Church and City 1000–1500* (Cambridge, 1992), 311–32

—— 'The religious orders, 1370–1540', in J.I. Catto and T.A.R. Evans (eds.), *The History of the University of Oxford: Late Medieval Oxford* (Oxford, 1992)

DONALDSON, G. 'The Church Courts', in *An Introduction to Scottish Legal History* (Stair Society, Edinburgh, 1958), 363–73

—— *The Scottish Reformation* (Cambridge, 1960)

—— *Scotland: James V–James VII* (Edinburgh, 1971)

—— *All the Queen's Men: Power and Politics in Mary Stewart's Scotland* (1983)

—— *Scottish Church History* (Edinburgh, 1985)

—— *Reformed by Bishops: Galloway, Orkney and Caithness* (Edinburgh, 1987)

—— *The Faith of the Scots* (1990)

—— 'The Reformation to the Covenant', in D. Forrester and D. Murray (eds.), *Studies in the History of Worship in Scotland*, 2nd edn. (Glasgow, 1996), 41–7

DORAN, S. 'Elizabeth I's religion: the evidence of her letters', *JEH* 51 (2000), 699–720

DOWLING, M. 'The Gospel and the Court: reformation under Henry VIII', in P. Lake and M. Dowling (eds.), *Protestantism and the National Church* (1987), 36–77

—— 'John Fisher and the preaching ministry', *ARG* 82 (1991), 287–309

—— 'Anne Boleyn as patron', in D. Starkey (ed.), *Henry VIII: A European Court in England* (1991), 107–11

—— *John Fisher* (Basingstoke, 1999)

DU BOULAY, F.R.H. 'The quarrel between the Carmelite friars and the secular clergy of London, 1464–1468', *JEH* 6 (1955), 156–74

DUFFY, E. *The Stripping of the Altars: Traditional Religion In England 1400–1580* (New Haven, Conn., 1992)

—— 'The long Reformation: Catholicism, Protestantism and the multitude', in N. Tyacke (ed.), *England's Long Reformation 1500–1800* (1998), 33–70

—— *Voices of Morebath: Reformation and Rebellion in an English Village* (New Haven, Conn., 2001)

DUGGAN, L.G. 'Fear and confession on the eve of the Reformation', *ARG* 75 (1984), 153–75

DUGMORE, C.W. *The Mass and the English Reformers* (1958)

DUNBAR, L.J. 'Synods and superintendence: John Winram and Fife, 1561–72', *RSCHS* 27 (1997), 97–125

DUNNING, R. 'The last days of Cleeve Abbey', in C.M. Barron and C. Harper-Bill (eds.), *The Church in Pre-Reformation Society* (Woodbridge, 1985), 95–107

DUNNING, R. and ROSS, A. 'Early Scottish libraries', *Innes Review* 9 (1958), 5–172

DURES, A. *English Catholicism 1558–1642* (Harlow, 1983)

DURKAN, J. 'The cultural background in sixteenth-century Scotland', in D. McRoberts (ed.), *Essays on the Scottish Reformation* (Glasgow, 1962), 274–331

—— 'Chaplains in late medieval Scotland', *RSCHS* 20 (1980), 91–103

—— 'Scottish "evangelicals" in the patronage of Thomas Cromwell', *RSCHS* 21 (1982), 127–56

—— 'The Observant Franciscan Province in Scotland', *Innes Review* 35 (1984), 51–7

—— 'Heresy in Scotland: the second phase, 1546–8', *RSCHS* 24 (1992), 320–65

—— 'Scottish Reformers: the less than golden legend', *Innes Review* 45 (1994), 1–28

DURKAN, J. and KIRK, J. *The University of Glasgow, 1451–1577* (Glasgow, 1977)

DURSTON, C. and EALES, J. (eds.) *The Culture of English Puritanism 1560–1700* (Basingstoke, 1996)

DYKEMA, P.A. and OBERMAN, H.A. (eds.) *Anticlericalism in Late Medieval and Early Modern Europe*, Studies in Medieval and Reformation Thought 51 (Leiden, 1993)

EAGLESTON, A.J. *The Channel Islands under Tudor Government, 1485–1642* (Cambridge, 1949)

EASTERLING, R. 'The friars in Wales', *Archaeologia Cambrensis* (1914), 323–56

EDINGTON, C. *Court and Culture in Renaissance Scotland: Sir David Lindsay of the Mount, 1486–1555* (East Linton, 1995)

EDWARDS, R.D. *Church and State in Tudor Ireland* (1935)

—— 'Ireland, Elizabeth I and the Counter-Reformation', in S.T. Bindoff, J. Hurstfield and C.H. Williams (eds.), *Elizabethan Government and Society* (1961), 315–39

—— 'The Irish Reformation Parliament of Henry VIII, 1536–7', *Historical Studies* 6 (Dublin, 1968), 59–84

EGAN, P.K. 'Diocesan organisation: Clonfert', *Proceedings of the Irish Catholic Historical Commission* (1956), 4–8

EIRE, C.M.N. *War Against the Idols: The Reformation of Worship from Erasmus to Calvin* (Cambridge, 1986)

ELLIS, P.B. *The Cornish Language and its Literature* (1974)

ELLIS, S.G. 'The Kildare rebellion and the early Henrician reformation', *HJ* 19 (1976), 807–30

—— 'Thomas Cromwell and Ireland, 1532–40', *HJ* 23 (1980), 497–519

—— 'John Bale, bishop of Ossory, 1552–3', *Journal of the Butler Society* 2 (1984), 283–93

—— *Tudor Ireland: Crown Community and the Conflict of Cultures, 1470–1603* (1985)

—— 'Economic problems of the Church: why the Reformation failed in Ireland', *JEH* 41 (1990), 239–74

—— *Tudor Frontiers and Noble Power: The Making of the British State* (Oxford, 1995)

ELTON, G.R. 'The evolution of a Reformation statute', *EHR* 64 (1949), 174–97
—— *Policy and Police: The Enforcement of the Reformation in the Age of Thomas Cromwell* (Cambridge, 1972)
—— *Reform and Reformation* (1977)
—— *The Parliament of England, 1559–1581* (Cambridge, 1986)
EMMISON, F.G. 'Tithes, perambulations and Sabbath-breach in Elizabethan Essex', in F.G. Emmison and R. Stephens (eds.), *Tribute to an Antiquary: Essays presented to Marc Fitch* (1976), 199–206
ENSSLE, N.R. 'Patterns of godly life: the ideal parish minister in sixteenth- and seventeenth-century English thought', *C16J* 28 (1997), 3–28
EVANS, N. 'The descent of dissenters in the Chiltern Hundreds', in M. Spufford (ed.), *The World of Rural Dissenters* (Cambridge, 1995), 288–308
FACEY, J. 'John Foxe and the defence of the English church', in P. Lake and M. Dowling (eds.), *Protestantism and the National Church in Sixteenth-Century England* (1987), 169–92
FAIRFIELD, L.P. *John Bale: Mythmaker for the English Reformation* (W. Lafayette, Ind., 1976)
FAWCETT, R. *Scottish Medieval Churches: An Introduction to the Ecclesiastical Architecture of the Twelfth to Sixteenth Centuries* (Edinburgh, 1985)
—— *Scottish Architecture from the Accession of the Stewarts to the Reformation, 1371–1560* (Edinburgh, 1994)
FINCHAM, K. *Prelate as Pastor: The Episcopate of James I* (Oxford, 1990)
—— 'Clerical conformity from Whitgift to Laud', in P. Lake and M. Questier (eds.), *Conformity and Orthodoxy in the English Church, c.1560–1660* (Woodbridge, 2000), 125–58
FINES, J. 'Heresy trials in the Diocese of Coventry and Lichfield, 1511–12', *JEH* 14 (1963), 160–74
—— *A Biographical Register of Early English Protestants*, section A–C (Sutton Courtenay, 1983); remainder in Bodleian typescript
FINUCANE, R.C. *Miracles and Pilgrimages: Popular Beliefs in Medieval England* (1977)
FIRTH, K.R. *The Apocalyptic Tradition in Reformation Britain, 1530–1645* (Oxford, 1979)
FISHER, J.D.C. *Christian Initiation: The Reformation Period* (1970)
FITCH, A.-B. 'The Search for Salvation: Lay Faith in Scotland, 1480–1560', University of Glasgow Ph.D. (1994)
FLEMING, P.W. 'Charity, faith and the gentry of Kent, 1422–1525', in A.J. Pollard (ed.), *Property and Politics: Essays in Late Medieval English History* (Gloucester, 1984), 36–58
FLETCHER, A.J. 'The civic pageantry of Corpus Christi in fifteenth- and sixteenth-century Dublin', *Irish Economic and Social History* 23 (1996), 73–96
FLETCHER, A. and MacCULLOCH, D. *Tudor Rebellions*, 4th edn. (1997)
FLOWER, R. 'William Salesbury, Richard Davies and Archbishop Parker', *National Library of Wales Journal* 2 (1941/2), 7–14
FLYNN, T.S. *The Irish Dominicans: 1536–1641* (Dublin, 1993)

FORD, A. 'The Protestant Reformation in Ireland', in C. Brady and R. Gillespie (eds.), *Natives and Newcomers: The Making of Irish Colonial Society, 1534–1641* (Dublin, 1986), 50–74

—— 'The Church of Ireland, 1558–1634: a Puritan church?', in A. Ford, J. McGuire, and K. Milne (eds.), *As by Law Established: The Church of Ireland since the Reformation* (Dublin, 1995), 52–68

—— ' "Standing one's own ground": religion, polemic and Irish history since the Reformation', in A. Ford *et al.* (eds.), *As by Law Established: The Church of Ireland since the Reformation* (Dublin, 1995), 1–14

—— 'Dependent or independent: the Church of Ireland and its colonial context, 1536–1647', *The Seventeenth Century* 10 (1995), 163–87

—— *The Protestant Reformation in Ireland, 1590–1641* (Dublin, 1997)

FORRESTER, D.B. and MURRAY, D.M. (eds.) *Studies of the History of Worship in Scotland* (Edinburgh, 1984)

FOSTER, A. 'Churchwardens' accounts of early modern England and Wales', in K. French, C.C. Gibbs, and B. Kümin (eds.), *The Parish in English Life 1400–1600* (Manchester, 1997), 74–93

FOSTER, W.R. *The Church before the Covenants: The Church of Scotland 1596–1638* (Edinburgh, 1975)

FOX, A. *Thomas More: History and Providence* (Oxford, 1982)

FOX, A. and GUY, J. *Reassessing the Henrician Age: Humanism, Politics and Reform, 1500–1550* (Oxford, 1986)

FREEMAN, T. 'Fate, fact and fiction in Foxe's *Book of Martyrs*', *HJ* 43 (2000), 601–23

FRENCH, K.L., GIBBS, C.C., and KÜMIN, B. (eds.) *The Parish in English Life, 1400–1600* (Manchester, 1997)

FRITZE, R. ' "A rare example of godlyness amongst gentlemen": the role of the Kingsmill and Gifford families in promoting the Reformation in Hampshire', in P. Lake and M. Dowling (eds.), *Protestantism and the National Church* (1987), 144–61

FUGGLES, J.F. 'The parish clergy in the archdeaconry of Leicester, 1520–1540', *Transactions of the Leicestershire Archaeological and Historical Society* 46 (1970–1), 25–44

FULLER, T. *The Church History of Britain*, ed. J.S. Brewer, 6 vols. (Oxford, 1845)

GABEL, G. *Benefit of Clergy in England in the Later Middle Ages* (New York, 1969)

GALPERN, A. 'The legacy of late medieval religion in sixteenth-century Champagne', in C. Trinkhaus and H. Oberman (eds.), *The Pursuit of Holiness* (1974), 141–76

GARRETT, C. *The Marian Exiles* (Cambridge, 1938)

GASQUET, A. and BISHOP, E. *Edward VI and the Book of Common Prayer* (1928)

GEE, H. *The Elizabethan Clergy and the Settlement of Religion, 1558–1564* (Oxford, 1898)

—— *The Elizabethan Prayer Book and its Ornaments* (1902)

GENTILCORE, D. *From Bishop to Witch: Belief and Religion in Early Modern Terra d'Otranto* (Manchester, 1992)

GERRISH, B.A. *Grace and Gratitude: The Eucharistic Theology of John Calvin* (Minneapolis, Minn., 1993)

GIBSON, E.C.S. *The Thirty-Nine Articles of the Church of England*, 2 vols. (1910)

GIBSON, W. *A Social History of the Domestic Chaplain, 1530–1840* (1997)

GILLESPIE, R. *Devoted People: Belief and Religion in Early Modern Ireland* (Manchester, 1997)

—— 'Differing devotions: patterns of religious practice in the British Isles, 1500–1700', in S.J. Connolly (ed.), *Kingdoms United? Great Britain and Ireland since 1500* (Dublin, 1999), 67–77

GITTINGS, C. *Death, Burial and the Individual in Early Modern England* (1984)

GOODARE, J. 'Scotland', in R. Scribner *et al.* (eds.), *The Reformation in National Context* (Cambridge, 1994), 95–110

—— 'The Statutes of Iona in context', *SHR* 77 (1998), 31–57

—— *State and Society in Early Modern Scotland* (Oxford, 1999)

GOODMAN, A. 'Henry VII and Christian renewal', in K. Robbins (ed.), *Religion and Humanism*, SCH 17 (Oxford, 1981), 115–25

GORDON, B. and MARSHALL, P. (eds.) *The Place of the Dead: Death and Remembrance in Late Medieval and Early Modern Europe* (Cambridge, 2000)

GRAHAM, M.F. 'Equality before the Kirk? Church discipline and the elite in Reformation-era Scotland', *ARG* 84 (1993), 289–309

—— *The Uses of Reform: 'Godly Discipline' and Popular Behaviour in Scotland and Beyond, 1560–1610* (Leiden, 1996)

—— 'Knox on discipline: conversionary zeal or rose-tinted nostalgia', in R.A. Mason (ed.), *John Knox and the British Reformations* (Aldershot, 1998), 268–86

GRAVES, C.P. 'Social space in the English medieval parish church', *Economy and Society* 18 (1989), 297–319

GRAVES, M.A.R. *The House of Lords in the Parliaments of Edward VI and Mary* (Cambridge, 1981)

GREAVES, R. 'The Knoxian paradox: ecumenism and nationalism in the Scottish Reformation', *RSCHS* 18 (1972), 85–98

—— *Society and Religion in Elizabethan England* (Minneapolis, Minn., 1981)

GREEN, I. '"The necessary knowledge of the principles of religion": catechisms and catechizing in Ireland, *c.*1560–1800', in A. Ford, J. McGuire, and K. Milne (eds.), *As By Law Established: The Church of Ireland since the Reformation* (Dublin, 1995), 69–88

—— *The Christian's ABC: Catechisms and Catechizing in England, c.1530–1740* (Oxford, 1996)

—— *Print and Protestantism in Early Modern England* (Oxford, 2001)

GREENSLADE, S.L. (ed.) *Cambridge History of the Bible*, vol. iii: *The West from the Reformation to the Present Day* (Cambridge, 1965)

GRIFFITH, P. *Youth and Authority: Formative Experiences in England, 1560–1640* (Oxford, 1996)

GRIFFITH, W.P. *Learning, Law and Religion in Wales, c.1540–1642* (Cardiff, 1996)

GRIFFITHS, N.D. 'Early translations of the Book of Common Prayer', *The Library* 6th ser. 3 (1981), 1–16

GRIFFITHS, R.A. *Sir Rhys ap Thomas and his Family* (Cardiff, 1993)

GUREVICH, A. *Medieval Popular Culture: Problems of Belief and Perception* (Cambridge, 1988)

GUY, J. *The Political Career of Sir Thomas More* (Brighton, 1980)

—— 'Henry VIII and the *praemunire* manoeuvres of 1530–31', *EHR* 97 (1982), 481–503

—— 'The Elizabethan establishment and the ecclesiastical polity', in J. Guy, (ed.), *The Reign of Elizabeth I: Court and Culture in the Last Decade* (Cambridge, 1995), 126–49

GWYN, P. *The King's Cardinal: The Rise and Fall of Thomas Wolsey* (1990)

GWYNN, A.O. *The Medieval Province of Armagh, 1470–1543* (Dundalk, 1946)

—— *Anglo-Irish Church Life in the Fourteenth and Fifteenth Centuries* (Dublin, 1968)

GWYNN, A.O. and HADCOCK, R.N. *Medieval Religious Houses: Ireland* (1970)

HAAS, S.W. 'Henry VIII's *Glasse of Truthe*', *History* 64 (1979), 353–62

HACKETT, H. *Virgin Mother, Maiden Queen* (Basingstoke, 1995)

HADFIELD, A. 'Translating the Reformation: John Bale's Irish *Vocacyon*', in B.I. Bradshaw, A. Hadfield, and W. Maley (eds.), *Representing Ireland: Literature and the Origins of the Conflict, 1534–1660* (Cambridge, 1993), 43–59

HAIGH, C.A. *Reformation and Resistance in Tudor Lancashire* (Cambridge, 1975)

—— 'Puritan evangelism in the reign of Elizabeth I', *EHR* 92 (1977), 30–58

—— (ed.) *The Reign of Elizabeth I* (1984)

—— 'Anticlericalism and the English Reformation', in C. Haigh (ed.), *The English Reformation Revised* (Cambridge, 1987), 19–33

—— *English Reformations: Religion, Politics and Society under the Tudors* (Oxford, 1993)

—— 'Communion and community: exclusion from communion in post-Reformation England', *JEH* 51 (2000), 721–40

—— 'The taming of the Reformation: preachers, pastors and parishioners in Elizabethan and early Stuart England', *History* 85 (2000), 572–88

HAINES, R.M. *Ecclesia Anglicana: Studies in the English Church of the Later Middle Ages* (Toronto, 1989)

HALL, B. *The Genevan Version of the English Bible* (1957)

—— 'Cranmer, the Eucharist and the foreign divines in the reign of Edward VI', in P. Ayris and D. Selwyn (eds.), *Thomas Cranmer, Churchman and Scholar* (Woodbridge, 1993), 217–58

—— 'Martin Bucer in England', in D.F. Wright (ed.), *Martin Bucer: Reforming Church and Community* (Cambridge, 1994), 144–60

—— 'The Genevan version of the English Bible: its aims and achievements', in W.P. Stephens (ed.), *The Bible, the Reformation and the Church: Essays in Honour of James Atkinson*, Journal of the Study of the New Testament, Supplement 105 (1995), 124–49

HALL, D.D. *Worlds of Wonder, Days of Judgement: Popular Religious Belief in Early Modern New England* (Cambridge, Mass., 1990)

HALLAM, E. 'Henry VIII's monastic refoundations of 1536–7 and the course of the dissolution', *BIHR* 51 (1978), 124–31

HAMILTON, A. *The Family of Love* (Stony Point, S.C., 1981)

HAMILTON-THOMPSON, A. *The English Clergy and their Organisation in the Later Middle Ages* (Oxford, 1947)

HAMMOND, G. *The Making of the English Bible* (New York, 1983)

HANNEY, R.K. 'On the church lands at the Reformation', *SHR* 16 (1918), 52–72

HAPPÉ, P. *John Bale* (1996)

HARDING, V. '"And one more may be laid there": the location of burials in early modern London', *London Journal* 14 (1989), 112–29

—— 'Burial choice and burial location in late medieval London', in S. Bassett (ed.), *Death in Towns* (Leicester, 1992), 119–35

HARDWICK, C. *A History of the Articles of Religion*, 3rd edn. (1895)

HAREN, M.J. 'A description of Clogher cathedral in the early sixteenth century', *Clogher Record* 12/1 (1985), 48–54

HAREN, M.J. and PONTFAREY, Y. de *The Medieval Pilgrimage to St Patrick's Purgatory: Lough Derg and the European Tradition* (Clogher Historical Society, Enniskillen, 1988)

HARPER-BILL, C. 'A late medieval visitation: the Diocese of Norwich in 1499', *Proceedings of the Suffolk Institute of Archaeology and History* 34 (1977), 35–47

—— 'Archbishop John Morton and the province of Canterbury, 1486–1500', *JEH* 29 (1978), 1–21

—— 'Dean Colet's Convocation Sermon and the pre-Reformation Church in England', *History* 73 (1988), 191–210

—— *The Pre-Reformation Church in England, 1400–1530* (1989)

HARRIS, B. 'A new look at the Reformation: aristocratic women and nunneries, 1450–1540', *JBS* 32 (1993), 89–113

HARVEY, B. *Living and Dying in Medieval England 1100–1540: The Monastic Experience* (Oxford, 1995)

HARVEY, M. *England, Rome and the Papacy, 1417–1464* (Manchester, 1993)

HAUGAARD, W. *Elizabeth and the English Reformation: The Struggle for a Stable Settlement of Religion* (Cambridge, 1968)

HAWS, C.W. 'Continuity and change: the clergy of the diocese of Moray, 1560–74', *Northern Scotland* 5 (1983), 91–8

HAY, G. *The Architecture of Scottish Post-Reformation Churches, 1560–1843* (Oxford, 1957)

HAYS, R.W. 'Welsh students at Oxford and Cambridge in the Middle Ages', *Welsh History Review* 4 (1968–9), 325–61

HAZLETT, W.I.P. 'The Scots Confession 1560: context, complexion and critique', *ARG* 78 (1987), 287–320

—— 'Playing God's card: Knox and fasting, 1565–66', in R.A. Mason (ed.), *John Knox and the British Reformations* (Aldershot, 1998), 176–200

HEAD, D. 'Henry VIII's Scottish policy: a reassessment', *SHR* 61 (1982), 1–24

HEAL, F. 'The Bishops of Ely and their Diocese, 1515–ca.1600', University of Cambridge Ph.D. (1972)

—— 'The bishops and the Act of Exchange of 1559', *HJ* 17 (1974), 227–46

—— 'Clerical tax collection under the Tudors: the influence of the Reformation', in R. O'Day and F. Heal (eds.), *Continuity and Change* (Leicester,1976), 97–122

—— 'Economic problems of the clergy', in F. Heal and R. O'Day (eds.), *Church and Society in England, Henry VIII to James I* (Basingstoke, 1977), 99–118

—— 'Parish clergy and the Reformation in the Diocese of Ely', *Cambridge Antiquarian Society* 66 (1977), 141–63

—— *Of Prelates and Princes: A Study of the Economic and Social Position of the Tudor Episcopate* (Cambridge, 1980)

HEAL, F. and HOLMES, C. *The Gentry in England and Wales, 1500–1700* (Basingstoke, 1994)

HEALY, R.M. 'The preaching ministry in Scotland's First Book of Discipline', *Church History* 58 (1989), 339–53

HEATH, P. *English Parish Clergy on the Eve of the Reformation* (1969)

—— 'Urban piety in the later Middle Ages: the evidence of Hull wills', in R.B. Dobson (ed.), *The Church, Politics and Patronage in the fifteenth century* (Gloucester, 1984), 209–34

HELMHOLZ, R. *Roman Canon Law in Reformation England* (Cambridge, 1990)

HELMHOLZ, R. (ed.) *Canon Law in Protestant Lands* (Berlin, 1992)

HELT, J.S.W. 'Women, memory and will-making in Elizabethan England', in B. Gordon and P. Marshall (eds.), *The Place of the Dead* (Cambridge, 2000), 188–205

HERBERT, A.S. *A Historical Catalogue of Printed Editions of English Bibles* (1968)

HERR, A.F. *The Elizabethan Sermon: A Survey and Bibliography* (Philadelphia, 1940)

HEWITT, G.R. *Scotland under Morton* (Edinburgh, 1982)

HEY, D. *An English Rural Community: Myddle under the Tudors and Stuarts* (Leicester, 1974)

HICKMAN, D. 'Religious belief and pious practice among the London elite', *HJ* 42 (1999), 941–60

HICKS, M.A. 'The Piety of Margaret, Lady Hungerford', *JEH* 38 (1987), 19–38

HIGGS, L.M. *Godliness and Governance in Tudor Colchester* (Ann Arbor, Mich., 1998)

HIGMAN, F. 'Calvin's works in translation', in A. Pettegree, A. Duke, and G. Lewis (eds.), *Calvinism in Europe* (Cambridge, 1994), 82–99

HILL, J.E.C. *Economic Problems of the Church from Archbishop Whitgift to the Long Parliament* (Oxford, 1956)

—— *The English Bible and the Seventeenth-Century Revolution* (Penguin edn., 1994)

HINNEBUSCH, W.A. *The Early English Friars Preachers* (Rome, 1951)

HOAK, D.E. *The King's Council in the Reign of Edward VI* (Cambridge, 1976)

HOPE, A. 'Lollardy: the stone the builders rejected?' in P. Lake and M. Dowling (eds.), *Protestantism and the National Church in Sixteenth-Century England* (1987), 1–35

HOPF, C. *Martin Bucer and the English Reformation* (Oxford, 1946)

HORIE, H. 'The Lutheran influence on the Elizabethan Settlement, 1558–1563', *HJ* 34 (1991), 519–38

HORST, I.B. *The Radical Brethren: Anabaptism and the English Reformation to 1558* (Nieuwkoop, 1972)

HOTLE, C.P. *Thorns and Thistles: Diplomacy between Henry VIII and James V, 1528–42* (1996)

HOULBROOKE, R. 'Persecution of heresy and Protestantism in the Diocese of Norwich under Henry VIII', *Norfolk Archaeology* 25 (1972), 308–26

—— 'The decline of ecclesiastical jurisdiction under the Tudors', in R. O'Day and F. Heal (eds.), *Continuity and Change* (Leicester, 1976), 239–57

—— 'The Protestant episcopate, 1547–1603: the pastoral contribution', in F. Heal and R. O'Day (eds.), *Church and Society in England, Henry VIII to James I* (Basingstoke, 1977), 78–98

—— *Church Courts and People during the English Reformation, 1520–70* (Oxford, 1979)

—— *Death, Religion and the Family in England 1480–1750* (Oxford, 1998)

HOUSE, S.B. 'Literature, drama and politics', in D. MacCulloch (ed.), *The Reign of Henry VIII* (Basingstoke, 1995), 181–201

HOWARD, D. *The Architectural History of Scotland: Scottish Architecture from the Reformation to the Restoration, 1560–1660* (Edinburgh, 1995)

HOYLE, R.W. 'The origins of the dissolution of the monasteries', *HJ* 38 (1995), 275–305

—— *The Pilgrimage of Grace and the Politics of the 1530s* (Oxford, 2001)

HUBERT, J. 'Sacred beliefs and beliefs of sacredness', in J. Carmichael and J. Hubert (eds.), *Sacred Sites, Sacred Places* (1994), 9–17

HUDSON, A. *The Premature Reformation: Wycliffite Texts and Lollard History* (Oxford, 1988)

HUDSON, W.S. *The Cambridge Connection and the Elizabethan Settlement of 1559* (Durham, N.C., 1980)

HUGHES, J. *Pastors and Visionaries: Religion and Secular Life in Late Medieval Yorkshire* (Woodbridge, 1988)

HUGHES, S.F. 'The problem of "Calvinism": English theologies of predestination *c.*1580–*c.*1630', in S. Wabuda and C. Litzenberger (eds.), *Belief and Practice in Reformation England* (Aldershot, 1998), 229–49

HUME BROWN, P. *Early Travellers in Scotland* (Edinburgh, 1891)

HUNT, A. 'The Lord's Supper in early modern England', *PP* 161 (1998), 39–83

HUTTON, R. 'The local impact of the Tudor Reformations', in C. Haigh (ed.), *English Reformation Revised* (Cambridge, 1987), 114–38

—— *The Rise and Fall of Merry England: The Ritual Year, 1400–1700* (Oxford, 1994)

IDIGORAS, J.I. TELLECHEA *Fray Bartolomé Carranza y el Cardinal Pole* (Pamplona, 1977)

INGRAM, M. *Church Courts, Sex and Marriage in England, 1570–1640* (Cambridge, 1987)

—— 'From reformation to toleration: popular religious cultures in England, 1540–1690', in T. Harris (ed.), *Popular Culture in England, c.1500–1850* (Basingstoke, 1995), 95–123

——'Puritans and the church courts 1560–1640', in C. Durston and J. Eales (eds.), *Culture of English Puritanism* (Basingstoke, 1996), 58–91

IVES, E.W. *Anne Boleyn* (Oxford, 1986)

——'Anne Boleyn and the early Reformation in England: the contemporary evidence', *HJ* 37 (1994), 389–400

JACK, R.I. 'Religious life in a Welsh Marcher Lordship: the lordship of Dyffryn Clwyd in the later Middle Ages', in C. Barron and C. Harper-Bill (eds.), *The Church in Pre-Reformation Society* (Woodbridge, 1985), 143–57

JACK, S. 'Dissolution dates for the monasteries dissolved under the act of 1536', *BIHR* 43 (1970), 161–81

——'English bishops as tax-collectors in the sixteenth century', in S.M. Jack and B.A. Masters (eds.), *Protestants, Property, Puritans: Godly People Revisited*, Parergon NS 14 (1996), 129–64

JAGGER, M. 'Bonner's episcopal visitation of London, 1554', *BIHR* 45 (1972), 306–11

JAMES, M. 'Ritual, drama and the social body in the late medieval English town', *PP* 98 (1983), 3–29

JANSEN, S. *Dangerous Talk and Strange Behavior: Women and Popular Resistance to the Reforms of Henry VIII* (Basingstoke, 1996)

JARDINE, L. 'The place of dialectic teaching in sixteenth-century Cambridge', *Studies in the Renaissance* 21 (1974), 31–62

JEFFERIES, H.A. 'The Irish Parliament of 1560: the Anglican reforms authorised', *IHS* 26 (1988), 128–41

——'The Church Courts of Armagh on the eve of the Tudor Reformations', *Seanchas Ard Mhacha* 16 (1995), 120–32

——*Priests and Prelates of Armagh, 1518–1558* (Dublin, 1997)

——'The Diocese of Dromore on the eve of the Tudor Reformations', in L. Proudfoot (ed.), *Down: History and Society* (Dublin, 1997)

——'The laity in the parishes of Armagh inter Anglicos on the eve of the Tudor Reformations', *Archivium Hibernicum* (1998), 73–84

——'The early Tudor Reformation in the Irish Pale', *JEH* 52 (2001), 34–62

JENKINS, P. 'The Anglican Church and the unity of Britain: the Welsh experience, 1560–1714', in S.G. Ellis and S. Barber (eds.), *Conquest and Union* (Harlow, 1985), 115–38

JONES, M.K. and UNDERWOOD, M.G. *The King's Mother: Lady Margaret Beaufort, Countess of Richmond and Derby* (Cambridge, 1992)

JONES, N. *Faith by Statute: Parliament and the Settlement of Religion, 1559* (1982)

——*The Birth of the Elizabethan Age: England in the 1560s* (Oxford, 1993)

——*The English Reformation: Religion and Cultural Adaptation* (Oxford, 2002)

JONES, R.F. *The Triumph of the English Language: A survey of Opinions concerning the Vernacular from the Introduction of Printing to the Restoration* (Oxford, 1953)

JORDAN, W.K. *Edward VI: The Young King* (1968)

——*Edward VI: The Threshold of Power* (1970)

KAUFMAN, P.I. 'John Colet's *Opus de sacramentis* and clerical anticlericalism: the limitations of "Ordinary Wayes"', *JBS* 22 (1982), 1–22

KEELING, S.M. 'The Reformation in the Anglo-Scottish Border counties', *Northern History* 15 (1979), 24–42

KEISER, G.R. 'The progress of Purgatory: visions of the afterlife in late medieval English literature', *Analecta Cartusiana* 107 (1987), 72–100

KELLAR, C. '"To Enrich with Gospel Truth the Neighbour Kingdom": Religion and Reformation in England and Scotland, 1534–1561', University of Oxford D.Phil. (1999)

KELLY, H.A. *The Matrimonial Trials of Henry VIII* (Stanford, 1976)

KELLY, M.J. 'Canterbury Jurisdiction and Influence during the Episcopate of William Warham, 1503–1532', University of Cambridge Ph.D. (1963)

—— 'The submission of the clergy', *TRHS* 5th ser. 15 (1965), 97–120

KENDALL, R.T. *Calvin and English Calvinism to 1649* (Oxford, 1979)

KENNEDY, W.M. *Elizabethan Episcopal Administration*, 3 vols. (1924)

KENNETH, BROTHER 'The popular literature of the Scottish Reformation', in D. McRoberts (ed.), *Essays of the Scottish Reformation*, (Glasgow, 1962), 169–84

KING, J.N. *English Reformation Literature: The Tudor Origins of the Protestant Tradition* (Princeton, N.J., 1982)

—— *Tudor Royal Iconography* (Princeton, N.J., 1989)

—— 'Henry VIII as David: the King's image and Reformation politics', in P.C. Herman (ed.), *Rethinking the Henrician Era* (Urbana, Ill., 1994), 78–92

KIRK, J. *Patterns of Reform: Continuity and Change in the Reformation Kirk* (Edinburgh, 1989)

—— (ed.) *Humanism and Reform: The Church in Europe, England and Scotland, 1400–1643*, SCH Subsidia 9 (1991)

—— 'The religion of early Scottish Protestants' in Kirk (ed.), *Humanism and Reform: The Church in Europe, England and Scotland, 1400–1643*, SCH Subsidia 9 (1991), 361–411

—— 'Iconoclasm and Reformation', *RSCHS* 24 (1992), 366–83

KITCHING, C. 'Church and chapelry in sixteenth-century England', in D. Baker (ed.), *The Church in Town and Countryside*, SCH 16 (Oxford, 1979), 279–90

KNOWLES, D. *The Religious Orders in England*, 3 vols. (Cambridge, 1948–61)

KNOWLES, D. and HADCOCK, R.H. *Medieval Religious Houses: England and Wales*, 2nd edn. (1971)

KNOX, R. BUICK *James Ussher, Archbishop of Armagh* (Cardiff, 1967)

KOEBNER, R. 'The imperial crown of this realm', *BIHR* 26 (1953), 29–52

KREIDER, A. *English Chantries: The Road to Dissolution* (Cambridge, Mass., 1979)

KÜMIN, B. *The Shaping of a Community: The Rise and Reformation of the English Parish, c.1400–1650* (Aldershot, 1996)

KÜMIN, B. (ed.) *Reformations Old and New: Essays on the Socio-Economic Impact of Religious Change, c.1470–1630* (Aldershot, 1996)

KYLE, R. 'The nature of the Church in the thought of John Knox', *Scottish Review of Theology* 37 (1984), 485–501

LAKE, P. 'Matthew Hutton: a puritan bishop?' *History* 64 (1979), 182–204

—— 'The significance of the Elizabethan identification of the pope as Antichrist', *JEH* 31 (1980), 161–78

—— *Moderate Puritans and the Elizabethan Church* (Cambridge, 1982)

—— 'Presbyterianism, the idea of a national church and the argument from divine right', in P. Lake and M. Dowling (eds.), *Protestantism and the National Church in Sixteenth-Century England* (1987), 193–224

—— 'Calvinism and the English church, 1570–1635', *PP* 114 (1987), 38–59

—— 'Conformist clericalism? Richard Bancroft's analysis of the socio-economic roots of presbyterianism', in W. Sheils and D. Wood (eds.), *The Church and Wealth*, SCH 24 (Oxford, 1987), 219–29

—— *Anglicans and Puritans? Presbyterian and English Conformist Thought from Whitgift to Hooker* (1988)

—— 'Deeds against nature: cheap print, Protestantism and murder in early modern England', in K. Sharpe and P. Lake (eds.), *Culture and Politics in Early Modern England* (1994), 313–34

—— 'Predestinarian propositions', *JEH* 46 (1995), 110–23

LAKE, P. and QUESTIER, M. (eds.) *Conformity and Orthodoxy in the English Church, c.1560–1660* (Woodbridge, 2000)

LAMBURN, D.J. 'Petty Babylons, godly prophets, petty pastors and little churches: the work of healing Babel', in W. Sheils and D. Wood (eds.), *The Ministry, Clerical and Lay*, SCH 26 (Oxford, 1989), 237–48

LANDER, S. 'The Diocese of Chichester: Episcopal Reform under Robert Sherburne and its Aftermath', University of Cambridge Ph.D. (1974)

—— 'The church courts and the Reformation in the Diocese of Chichester', in R. O'Day and F. Heal (eds.), *Continuity and Change* (Leicester, 1976), 215–38

LAWRENCE, C.H. (ed.) *The English Church and the Papacy in the Middle Ages* (1965)

LEAVER, R. *Goostly Psalmes and Spirituall Songs: English and Dutch Metrical Psalms from Coverdale to Utenhove, 1535–66* (Oxford, 1991)

LEE, M. 'James VI and the revival of episcopacy in Scotland: 1596–1600', *Church History* 43 (1974), 49–64

LEHMBERG, S.E. 'Supremacy and vicegerency: a re-examination', *EHR* 81 (1966), 225–35

—— *The Reformation Parliament, 1529–1536* (Cambridge, 1970)

—— *The Later Parliaments of Henry VIII, 1536–1547* (Cambridge, 1977)

—— *The Reformation of Cathedrals: Cathedrals in English Society, 1485–1603* (Princeton, N.J., 1988)

LENMAN, B. 'The limits of godly discipline in the early modern period with particular reference to England and Scotland', in K. von Greyerz (ed.), *Religion and Society in Early Modern Europe* (1984), 124–45

LENNON, C. 'The Counter-Reformation in Ireland 1542–1641', in C.F. Brady and R. Gillespie (eds.), *Natives and Newcomers: Essays on the Making of Irish Colonial Society* (Dublin, 1986), 75–86

—— *The Lords of Dublin in the Age of Reformation* (Dublin, 1989)

—— *Sixteenth-Century Ireland: The Incomplete Conquest* (Dublin, 1994)

LIPKIN, J.A. 'Pluralism in Pre-Reformation England: A Quantitative Analysis, c.1490–1539', Catholic University of America, Washington D.C., Ph.D. (1979)

LITTLE, A.G. 'Introduction of the Observant Friars into England', *Proceedings of the British Academy* 10 (1921–3), 455–71

LITZENBERGER, C. 'Richard Cheyney, bishop of Gloucester: an infidel in religion', *C16J* 25 (1994), 567–84

—— *The English Reformation and the Laity: Gloucestershire, 1540–1580* (Cambridge, 1997)

—— 'St. Michael's Gloucester, 1540–1580: the cost of conformity in sixteenth-century England', in K.L. French, G.C. Gibbs and B.A. Kümin (eds.), *The Parish in English Life 1400–1600* (Manchester, 1997), 230–49

—— 'Defining the Church of England: religious change in the 1570s', in S. Wabuda and C. Litzenberger (eds.), *Belief and Practice in Reformation England* (Aldershot, 1998), 137–53

LLEWELYN, N. *Funeral Monuments in Post-Reformation England* (Cambridge, 2000)

LOACH, J. 'Conservatism and consent in parliament, 1547–59', in J. Loach and R. Tittler (eds.), *The Mid-Tudor Polity, 1540–1560* (Basingstoke, 1980), 9–28

—— 'The Marian establishment and the printing press', *EHR* 101 (1986), 135–48

—— *Parliament and the Crown in the Reign of Mary Tudor* (Oxford, 1986)

LOADES, D.M. *The Oxford Martyrs* (1970)

—— *The Reign of Mary Tudor* (1979)

—— *Mary Tudor: A Life* (Oxford, 1989)

LOCKWOOD, S. 'Marsilius of Padua and the case for the royal ecclesiastical supremacy', *TRHS* 6th ser. 1 (1990), 89–119

LOGAN, F. 'Thomas Cromwell and the vicegerency in spirituals: a revisitation', *EHR* 103 (1988), 658–67

LORIMER, J.P. *John Knox and the Church of England* (1875)

LUCAS, M.D. 'Popular Religious Attitudes in Urban Lincolnshire during the Reformation Period, 1520–1600', University of Nottingham Ph.D. (1998)

LUNT, W. *Financial Relations with the Papacy 1327–1534* (Cambridge, Mass., 1962)

LUSARDI, J.P. 'The career of Robert Barnes', in L.A. Schuster (ed.), *The Complete Works of St Thomas More* (New Haven, Conn., 1973)

LYDDON, J.F. *Ireland in the Later Middle Ages* (Dublin, 1973)

LYNAM, E.W. 'The Irish character in print, 1571–1923', *The Library* 4th ser. 4 (1924), 288–92

LYNCH, A. 'Religion in late medieval Ireland', *Archivium Hibernicum* 36 (1981), 3–15

LYNCH, M. *Edinburgh and the Reformation* (Edinburgh, 1981)

—— 'From privy kirk to burgh church: an alternative view of the process of Protestantisation', in N. MacDougall (ed.), *Church, Politics and Society: Scotland 1408–1929* (Edinburgh, 1983), 85–96

—— 'Religious life in medieval Scotland', in S. Gilley and W.J. Sheils (eds.), *A History of Religion in Britain* (Oxford, 1994), 99–124

—— 'Preaching to the converted? Perspectives on the Scottish Reformation', in A.A. MacDonald, M. Lynch and I.B. Cowan (eds.), *The Renaissance in Scotland* (Leiden, 1994), 301–43

——— 'A nation born again? Scottish identity in the sixteenth and seventeenth centuries', in D. Brown, R.J. Finlay, and M. Lynch (eds.), *Image and Identity: The Making and Remaking of Scotland through the Ages* (Edinburgh, 1998), 82–104

LYONS, M.A. 'Sidelights on the Kildare ascendancy: a survey of Geraldine involvement in the Church, c.1470–c.1520', *Archivum Hibernicum* 48 (1994), 73–87

——— *Church and Society in County Kildare, c.1470–1547* (Dublin, 2000)

LYTLE, G.F. *Reform and Authority in the Medieval and Reformation Church* (Washington D.C., 1981)

McADOO, H.R. 'The Irish translations of the Book of Common Prayer', *Eigse* 2 (1940), 250–7

MacCAFFREY, W. *Exeter, 1540–1640* (Cambridge, Mass., 1958)

McCAUGHEY, T.P. 'Protestantism and Scottish Highland culture', in J.P. Mackey (ed.), *An Introduction to Celtic Christianity* (Edinburgh, 1989), 177–83

McCLELLAND, J.C. 'The Reformed doctrine of predestination according to Peter Martyr', *Scottish Journal of Theology* 8 (1955), 255–71

——— *The Visible Words of God: An Exposition of the Sacramental Theology of Peter Martyr Vermigli: AD 1500–1562* (Edinburgh, 1957)

McCLENDON, M. *The Quiet Reformation: Magistrates and the Emergence of Protestantism in Tudor Norwich* (Basingstoke, 1999)

McCONICA, J. *English Humanists and Reformation Politics under Henry VIII and Edward VI* (Oxford, 1968)

McCONICA, J. (ed.) *The History of the University of Oxford*, vol. iii: *The Collegiate University* (Oxford, 1986)

McCOOG, T. *The Society of Jesus in Ireland, Scotland and England, 1541–88* (Leiden, 1996)

MacCRAITH, M. 'The Gaelic reaction to the Reformation', in S.J. Ellis and S. Barber (eds.), *Conquest and Union* (Harlow, 1995), 139–61

McCRIE, T. *The Life of Andrew Melville*, 2 vols. (Edinburgh, 1819)

MacCULLOCH, D. *Suffolk under the Tudors* (Oxford, 1988)

——— *The Later Reformation in England, 1547–1603* (Basingstoke, 1990)

——— 'The myth of the English Reformation', *JBS* 20 (1991), 1–19

——— *Thomas Cranmer* (1996)

——— (ed.) *The Reign of Henry VIII: Politics, Policy and Piety* (Basingstoke, 1998)

——— 'Worcester: a cathedral city in the Reformation', in P. Collinson and J. Craig (eds.), *English Towns* (Basingstoke, 1998), 94–112

——— *Tudor Church Militant: Edward VI and the Protestant Reformation* (1999)

——— 'The importance of Jan Laski in the English Reformation', in C. Strom (ed.), *Johannes a Lasco, 1499–1560* (Emden, 2000), 315–45

McCULLOCH, D. and BLATCHLY, J. 'Pastoral provision in the parishes of Tudor Ipswich', *C16J* 22 (1991), 457–74

McCULLOUGH, P. *Sermons at Court: Politics and Religion in Elizabethan and Jacobean Preaching* (Cambridge, 1998)

MacDONALD, A.M., LYNCH, M., and COWAN, I.B. (eds.) *The Renaissance in Scotland: Essays in Honour of J. Durkan* (Leiden, 1994)

MacDonald, A.R. *The Jacobean Kirk, 1567–1625: Sovereignty, Polity and Liturgy* (Aldershot, 1998)

MacDougall, N. (ed.) *Church, Politics and Society: Scotland 1408–1929* (Edinburgh, 1993)

McEntegart, R. 'England and the League of Schmalkalden, 1531–1547: Faction, Foreign Policy and the English Reformation', London School of Economics Ph.D. (1992)

McFarlane, I.D. *Buchanan* (1981)

Macfarlane, L. 'The primacy of the Scottish church, 1472–1521', *Innes Review* 20 (1969), 111–29

—— 'Was the Scottish church reformable by 1513?' in N. MacDougall (ed.), *Church, Politics and Society: Scotland 1408–1929* (Edinburgh, 1983), 23–43

—— *William Elphinstone and the Kingdom of Scotland, 1431–1514* (Aberdeen, 1995)

McGiffert, M. 'William Tyndale's concept of covenant', *JEH* 32 (1981), 167–84

—— 'Grace and works: the rise of the covenant divinity in Elizabethan Puritanism', *Harvard Theological Review* 75 (1982), 496–502

—— 'God's controversy with Jacobean England', *AHR* 88 (1983), 1151–74

—— 'From Moses to Adam: the making of the covenant of works', *C16J* 19 (1988), 131–55

McGoldrick, J.E. *Luther's Scottish Connection* (Rutherford, N.J., 1989)

McGrade, A.S. *Richard Hooker and the Construction of Christian Community*, Medieval and Renaissance Texts and Studies 165 (1997)

McGrath, A. *Iustitia Dei: A History of the Christian Doctrine of Justification*, 2 vols. (Cambridge, 1986)

McHardy, A.K. 'Careers and disappointments in the late medieval Church: some English evidence', in W. Sheils and D. Woods (eds.), *The Ministry, Clerical and Lay*, SCH 26 (1989), 111–30

McIntosh, M. *A Community Transformed: The Manor and Liberty of Havering, 1500–1620* (Cambridge, 1991)

McKay, D. 'Parish life in Scotland, 1500–1560', in D. McRoberts (ed.), *Essays on the Scottish Reformation* (Glasgow, 1962), 85–115

Mackay, W.N. 'Sheen Charterhouse from its Foundation to its Dissolution', University of Oxford D.Phil. (1992)

McKerrow, R.B. and Ferguson, F.S. (eds.) *Title-Page Borders Used in England and Scotland, 1485–1640* (1932)

Mackie, P. 'Chaplains in the Diocese of York, 1480–1530: the testamentary evidence', *YAJ* 58 (1986), 123–33

McLennan, B. 'The Reformation and the burgh of Aberdeen', *Northern Scotland* 2 (1974–7), 119–44

MacLure, M. *The Paul's Cross Sermons, 1534–1642* (Toronto, 1958)

—— *Register of Sermons Preached at Paul's Cross, 1534–1642*, revised by P. Pauls and J.C. Boswell (Ottawa, 1989)

McMillan, W. *The Worship of the Scottish Reformed Church, 1550–1638* (1950)

McNair, P. 'Peter Martyr in England', in J.C. McLelland (ed.), *Peter Martyr Vermigli and the Italian Reformation* (Waterloo, Ont., 1980), 85–105

McNeill, J.T. 'Alexander Alesius, Scottish Lutheran', *ARG* 55 (1964), 161–91

—— *The History and Character of Calvinism* (New York, 1967)

McRoberts, D. 'Material destruction caused by the Scottish Reformation', in D. McRoberts (ed.), *Essays on the Scottish Reformation* (Glasgow, 1962), 415–62

—— (ed.) *Essays on the Scottish Reformation* (Glasgow, 1962)

—— 'Scottish Sacrament Houses', *Transactions of the Scottish Ecclesiological Society* 15 (1965), 30–56

—— 'The Rosary in Scotland', *Innes Review* 23 (1972), 81–101

Mahoney, M. 'The Scottish hierarchy, 1513–65', in D. McRoberts (ed.), *Essays on the Scottish Reformation* (Glasgow, 1962), 39–84

Maltby, J. '"By this book": parishioners, the Prayer Book and the established church', in K. Fincham (ed.), *The Early Stuart Church, 1603–1642* (Basingstoke, 1993), 115–37

—— *Prayer Book and People in Elizabethan and Early Stuart England* (Cambridge, 1998)

Manning, R.B. *Religion and Society in Elizabethan Sussex* (Leicester, 1969)

—— 'The crisis of episcopal authority during the reign of Elizabeth I', *JBS* 11 (1971), 1–25

—— 'Elizabethan recusancy commissions', *HJ* 15 (1972), 23–35

Manson, T.M.Y. 'Shetland in the sixteenth century', in I.B. Cowan and D. Shaw (eds.), *The Renaissance and Reformation in Scotland* (Edinburgh, 1983), 200–13

Marchant, R.A. *The Church under the Law: Justice, Administration and Discipline in the Diocese of York, 1560–1640* (Cambridge, 1969)

Marcombe, D. 'The Durham dean and chapter: old abbey writ large?' in R. O'Day and F. Heal (eds.), *Continuity and Change* (Leicester, 1976), 125–44

—— 'Bernard Gilpin: anatomy of an Elizabethan legend', *Northern History* 16 (1980), 20–39

—— *English Small Town Life: Retford 1520–1642* (Nottingham, 1993)

Marcombe, D. and Knighton, C.S. (eds.) *Close Encounters: English Cathedrals and Society since 1540* (Nottingham, 1991)

Marsh, C. *The Family of Love in English Society, 1550–1630* (Cambridge, 1994)

—— 'In the name of God? Will-making and faith in early modern England', in G.H. Martin and P. Spufford (eds.), *The Records of the Nation* (Woodbridge, 1996), 215–49

—— *Popular Religion in Sixteenth-Century England* (Basingstoke, 1998)

—— 'Common Prayer in England 1560–1640: the view from the pew', *PP* 171 (2001), 66–94

Marshall, P. *The Catholic Priesthood and the English Reformation* (Oxford, 1994)

—— 'The rood of Boxley, the Blood of Hailes, and the defence of the Henrician church', *JEH* 46 (1995), 689–96

—— *The Face of the Pastoral Ministry in the East Riding, 1525–95*, Borthwick Papers 88 (1995)

MARSHALL, P. 'Discord and stability in an Elizabethan parish: John Otes and Carnaby, 1563–1600', *YAJ* 71 (1999), 185–99

—— '"The map of God's word": geographies of the afterlife in Tudor and early Stuart England', in B. Gordon and P. Marshall (eds.), *The Place of the Dead: Death and Remembrance in Late Medieval and Early Modern Europe* (Cambridge, 2000), 110–30

MARTIN, F.X. 'The Irish friars and the observant movement in Ireland', *Proceedings of the Irish Catholic Historical Commission* (1960), 10–16

—— 'The Irish Augustinian reform movement in the fifteenth century', in J. Watt *et al.* (eds.), *Medieval Studies* (Dublin, 1961), 230–64

MARTIN, J. 'Leadership and priorities in Reading during the Reformation', in P. Collinson, and J. Craig (eds.), *The Reformation in English Towns* (Basingstoke, 1998), 113–29

MARTIN, J.W. *Religious Radicals in Tudor England* (1989)

MASON, R.A. 'Covenant and commonweal: the language of politics in Reformation Scotland', in N. MacDougall (ed.), *Church, Politics and Society: Scotland 1408–1929* (Edinburgh, 1993), 97–126

—— 'George Buchanan, James VI and the presbyterians', in R.A. Mason (ed.), *Scots and Britons: Scottish Political Thought and the Union of 1603* (Cambridge, 1994), 112–37

—— *Kingship and Commonweal: Political Thought in Renaissance and Reformation Scotland* (East Linton, East Lothian, 1998)

—— (ed.) *John Knox and the British Reformations* (Aldershot, 1999)

MATTINGLEY, J. 'The medieval parish gilds of Cornwall', *Journal of the Royal Institution of Cornwall* NS 10 (1989), 290–329

MAYER, T.F. *Reginald Pole: Prince and Prophet* (Cambridge, 2000)

MAYHEW, G. *Tudor Rye* (Brighton, 1987)

MEIGS, S.A. *The Reformations in Ireland: Tradition and Confessionalism, 1400–1690* (Basingstoke, 1997)

MERRIMAN, M.H. 'The assured Scots: Scottish collaborators with England during the Rough Wooing', *SHR* 48 (1968), 10–34

—— 'James Henrisoun and "Great Britain": British union and the Scottish Commonweal', in R.A. Mason (ed.), *Scotland and England, 1286 to 1815* (Edinburgh, 1987), 85–112

MERRIMAN, R.B. *The Life and Letters of Thomas Cromwell*, 2 vols. (Oxford, 1902)

MERTES, R.G.K.A. 'The household as a religious community', in J. Rosenthal and C. Richmond (eds.), *People, Politics and Community in the Later Middle Ages* (Gloucester, 1987), 123–39

MILTON, A. *Catholic and Reformed: The Roman and Protestant Churches in English Protestant Thought, 1600–1640* (Cambridge, 1995)

MOLLER, J. 'The beginnings of Puritan covenant theology', *JEH* 14 (1963), 46–67

MOODY, M.E. 'Trials and troubles of a non-conforming layman: the spiritual odyssey of Stephen Offwood, 1564–*ca.*1635', *Church History* 51 (1982), 157–71

MOODY, T.W., MARTIN, F.X., and BRYNE, F.J. (eds.) *A New History of Ireland*, vol. iii: *Early Modern Ireland* (Oxford, 1976)

MOONEY, C. *Devotional Writings of the Irish Franciscans, 1224–1950* (Killiney, 1952)
—— *The Church in Gaelic Ireland* (1969)
MOORE, A.W. *A History of the Isle of Man* (1900)
MORAN, J.A.H. 'Clerical recruitment in the Diocese of York, 1340–1530', *JEH* 34 (1983), 19–54
MORRILL, J.S. 'A British patriarchy? Ecclesiastical imperialism under the early Stuarts', in A. Fletcher and P. Roberts (eds.), *Religion, Culture and Society in Early Modern Britain* (Cambridge, 1994), 209–37
MOZLEY, J.E. *Coverdale and his Bibles* (1953)
MULLAN, D.G. *Episcopacy in Scotland: The History of an Idea, 1560–1638* (Edinburgh, 1986)
—— *Scottish Puritanism, 1590–1638* (Oxford, 2000)
MULLER, J.A. *Stephen Gardiner and the Tudor Reaction* (1926)
MULLER, R.A. 'Perkins' *A goldene Chaine*: predestination system or schematized *ordo salutis?*' *C16J* 9 (1978), 70–7
—— *Christ and the Decree. Christology and Predestination in Reformed Theology from Calvin to Perkins* (Durham, N.C., 1986)
MURPHY, J. 'The illusion of decline: the Privy Chamber 1547–1558', in D. Starkey (ed.), *The English Court from the Wars of the Roses to the Civil War* (1987), 119–46
MURPHY, V. 'The literature and propaganda of Henry VIII's first divorce', in D. MacCulloch, *The Reign of Henry VIII* (Basingstoke, 1995), 135–58
MURRAY, J. 'Archbishop Alen, Tudor reform and the Kildare Rebellion', *Proceedings of the Royal Irish Academy* sect. C 89 (1989), 1–16
—— 'Ecclesiastical justice and the enforcement of the Reformation: the case of Archbishop Browne and the clergy of Dublin', in A. Ford, J. McGuire, and K. Milne (eds.), *As by Law Established* (Dublin, 1995), 33–51
—— 'The Tudor Diocese of Dublin: Episcopal Government, Ecclesiastical Politics and the Enforcement of the Reformation, 1534–90', Trinity College Dublin Ph.D. (1997)
MURRAY, L. 'A calendar of the register of Primate George Dowdall', *Journal of the County Louth Archaeological Society* 6 (1927), 148–52
—— 'The ancient chantries of County Louth', *Journal of the County Louth Archaeological Society* 9 (1939), 181–208
NEALE, J.E. 'The Elizabethan Acts of Supremacy and Uniformity', *EHR* 64 (1950), 304–32
—— *Elizabeth I and Her Parliaments*, 2 vols. (1957)
NICHOLLS, D. 'The theatre of martyrdom in the French Reformation', *PP* 121 (1988), 49–73
NICHOLLS, J. *The Progresses of Queen Elizabeth*, 3 vols. (1810)
NICHOLLS, K.W. 'Rectory, vicarage and parish in the Western Irish dioceses', *Royal Society of Antiquaries of Ireland Journal* 101 (1971), 53–83
—— *Gaelic and Gaelicised Ireland in the Middle Ages* (Dublin, 1972)
NICHOLS, A.E. 'The etiquette of pre-Reformation confession in East Anglia' *C16J* 17 (1986), 145–63

NICHOLS, A.E. *Seeable Signs: The Iconography of the Seven Sacraments, 1350–1544* (1994)

NICHOLSON, G. 'The Nature and Function of Historical Argument in the Henrician Reformation', University of Cambridge Ph.D. (1977)

—— 'The Act of Appeals and the English Reformation', in C. Cross, D. Loades, and J.J. Scarisbrick (eds.), *Law and Government under the Tudors* (Cambridge, 1988), 19–30

NICHOLSON, R. *Scotland: The Later Middle Ages* (1978)

NIMMO, D. *Reform and Division in the Medieval Franciscan Order* (Rome, 1987)

NUSSBAUM, D. 'Whitgift's "Book of Martyrs": Archbishop Whitgift, Timothy Bright and the Elizabethan struggle over John Foxe's legacy', in D. Loades (ed.), *John Foxe* (Aldershot, 1999), 135–53

OAKLEY, F. 'Almain and Major: conciliar theory on the eve of the Reformation', *AHR* 70 : 2 (1965), 671–90

O'CONNELL, M. 'The idolatrous eye: iconoclasm, anti-theatricalism and the image of the Elizabethan theatre', *Journal of English Literary History* 52 (1985), 279–310

O'DAY, R. *The English Clergy: The Emergence and Consolidation of a Profession* (Leicester, 1979)

—— 'Hugh Latimer: prophet of the kingdom', *HR* 65 (1992), 258–76

O'DONOHOE, J.A. *Tridentine Seminary Legislation: Its Sources and Formation* (Louvain, 1957)

O'DONOVAN, O. *On the Thirty-Nine Articles* (Exeter, 1986)

O'DWYER, P. 'The Carmelite Order in pre-Reformation Ireland', *Proceedings of the Irish Catholic Historical Commission* (1968), 49–62

OGIER, D.M. *Reformation and Society in Guernsey* (Woodbridge, 1996)

OGLE, A. *The Tragedy of the Lollards' Tower* (1949)

O'GRADY, P. *Henry VIII and the Conforming Catholics* (Collegeville, Minn., 1990)

O'HAINLE, C. 'The *Pater Noster* in Irish', *Celtica* 22 (1991), 145–67

ONG, W. *The Presence of the Word* (New Haven, Conn., 1967)

—— *Orality and Literacy: The Technologizing of the Word* (1982)

ORME, N. 'The medieval parishes of Devon', *Devon Historian* 33 (1986), 3–9

—— (ed.) *Unity and Variety: A History of the Church in Devon and Cornwall* (Exeter, 1991)

OSBOROUGH, N. 'Ecclesiastical law and the Reformation in Ireland', in R.H. Helmholz (ed.), *Canon Law in Protestant Lands* (Berlin, 1992), 223–52

O'SIOCHRU, M. 'Foreign involvement in the revolt of Silken Thomas, 1534–5', *Proceedings of the Royal Irish Academy* sect. C 96 (1996), 49–66

OTTO, R. *The Idea of the Holy* (Oxford, 1923)

OVERELL, M.A. 'Peter Martyr in England, 1547–1553: an alternative view', *C16J* 15 (1984), 87–104

OWEN, H.G. 'Parochial curates in Elizabethan London', *JEH* 10 (1959), 66–73

—— 'The episcopal visitation: its limits and limitations in Elizabethan London', *JEH* 11 (1960), 179–85

—— 'Tradition and reform: ecclesiastical controversy in an Elizabethan London parish', *Guildhall Miscellany* 11 (1961), 63–70

—— 'The Liberty of the Minories: a study in Elizabethan religious radicalism', *East London Papers* 8 (1965), 81–97

OXLEY, J.E. *The Reformation in Essex* (Manchester, 1965)

PALLISER, D. *Tudor York* (Oxford, 1979)

PALMER, W.M. 'Village gilds of Cambridgeshire', *Transactions of the Cambridgeshire and Huntingdonshire Archaeological Society* 1 (1902), 330–402

PANTIN, W.A. 'Abbot Kidderminster and monastic studies', *Downside Review* 47 (1929), 198–211

PARISH, H. *Clerical Marriage and the English Reformation* (Aldershot, 2000)

PARKER, G. 'Success and failure during the first century of the Reformation', *PP* 136 (1992), 43–82

—— 'The "Kirk by Law Established" and the origins of the "Taming of Scotland": St Andrews 1559–1600', in R. Mentzer (ed.), *Sin and Calvinists: Moral Control and the Consistory in the Reformed Tradition* (Kirksville, Mo., 1994), 158–97

PARKER, K. and CARLSON, E.J. *'Practical Divinity'. The Works and Life of the Revd Richard Greenham* (Aldershot, 1998)

PARKER, W. *The History of Long Melford* (1873)

PARRY, G.J.R. *A Protestant Vision: William Harrison and the Reformation of Elizabethan England* (Cambridge, 1987)

PASTOR, L. *The History of the Popes from the Close of the Middle Ages*, 40 vols. (1890–1953)

PEARSE, M.T. *Between Known Men and Visible Saints: A Study of Sixteenth Century English Dissent* (1994)

PENNY, D.A. *Freewill or Predestination: The Battle over Saving Grace in Mid-Tudor England*, Royal Historical Society Studies in History 61 (1990)

PETERS, C. 'Women and the Reformation: Social Relations and Attitudes in Rural England, *ca.*1470–1570', University of Oxford D.Phil. (1994)

PETTEGREE, A. *Foreign Protestant Communities in Sixteenth-Century London* (Oxford, 1986)

—— 'Rewriting the English Reformation', *Nederlands Archief voor Kerkgeschiedenis* 72 (1992), 37–58

—— *Marian Protestantism: Six Studies* (Aldershot, 1996)

—— 'The reception of Calvinism in Britain', in W.H. Neusner and B.G. Armstrong (eds.), *Calvinus sincerioris religionis vindex*, Sixteenth-Century Essays and Studies 36 (1997), 267–89

—— (ed.) *The Reformation of the Parishes: The Ministry and the Reformation in Town and Country* (Manchester, 1993)

PFAFF, R.W. *New Liturgical Feasts in Late Medieval England* (Oxford, 1970)

—— 'The English devotion of St Gregory's Trental', *Speculum* 49 (1974), 75–90

PHILIP, G. 'Queen Mary Tudor's benefaction to the university', *Bodleian Library Record* 5 (1954), 27–37

PHILLIPS, J. *The Reformation of Images: Destruction of Art in England 1535–1660* (Berkeley, 1973)

PHILLIPS, P. *English Sacred Music, 1549–1649* (Oxford, 1991)

PHYTHIAN-ADAMS, C. 'Ceremony and the citizen: the communal year at Coventry, 1450–1550', in P. Clark and P. Slack (eds.), *Crisis and Order in English Towns 1500–1700* (1972), 57–85

—— *Desolation of a City: Coventry and the Urban Crisis of the Late Middle Ages* (Cambridge, 1979)

PINEAS, R. *Thomas More and Tudor Polemics* (Bloomington, Ind., 1968)

PLUMB, D. 'The social and economic spread of rural Lollardy: a reappraisal', in W.J. Sheils and D. Wood (eds.), *Voluntary Religion*, SCH 23 (Oxford, 1986), 111–29

—— 'A gathered church? Lollards and their society', in M. Spufford (ed.), *The World of Rural Dissenters, 1520–1725* (Cambridge, 1995), 132–63

POCOCK, J.G.A. 'British history: a plea for a new subject', *Journal of Modern History* 47 (1975), 601–28

POGSON, R. 'Revival and reform in Mary Tudor's Church: a question of money', *JEH* 25 (1974), 249–65

—— 'Reginald Pole and the priorities of government in Mary Tudor's Church', *HJ* 18 (1975), 3–20

—— 'The legacy of schism: confusion and change in the Marian clergy', in J. Loach and R. Tittler (eds.), *The Mid-Tudor Polity: c.1540–1560* (1980), 116–36

—— 'God's law and man's: Stephen Gardiner and the problem of loyalty', in C. Cross, D. Loades, and J.J. Scarisbrick (eds.), *Law and Government under the Tudors* (Cambridge, 1988), 67–90

POLLARD, M. *Dublin's Trade in Books, 1550–1800* (Oxford, 1989)

PORTER, H. *Reformation and Reaction in Tudor Cambridge* (Cambridge, 1958)

—— 'The nose of wax: Scripture and the Spirit from Erasmus to Milton', *TRHS* 5th ser. 14 (1964), 155–74

POUND, J. 'Clerical poverty in early sixteenth-century England: some East Anglian evidence', *JEH* 37 (1986), 389–96

POUNDS, N.J.G. *A History of the English Parish* (Cambridge, 2000)

POWELL, K.G. *The Marian Martyrs and the Reformation in Bristol* (Bristol, 1972)

PRICE, F.D. 'Gloucester diocese under Bishop Hooper', *Transactions of the Bristol and Gloucestershire Archaeological Society* 60 (1938), 51–151

—— 'An Elizabethan church official: Thomas Powell, chancellor of Gloucester diocese', *Church Quarterly Review* 128 (1939), 94–112

PUCCI, M.S. 'Reforming Roman emperors: John Foxe's characterization of Constantine in the *Acts and Monuments*', in D. Loades (ed.), *John Foxe: An Historical Perspective* (Aldershot, 1999), 29–51

QUESTIER, M.C. *Conversion, Politics and Religion in England, 1580–1625* (Cambridge, 1996)

RATCLIFF, E.C. 'Liturgical work of Archbishop Cranmer', *JEH* 7 (1956), 189–203

REBOLZ, R. A. (ed.), *The Complete Poems of Thomas Wyatt* (1978), 195–216

REDWORTH, G. 'A study of the formulation of policy: the genesis and evolution of the Act of Six Articles', *JEH* 37 (1986), 42–67

—— 'Whatever happened to the English Reformation?' *History Today* 37 (1987), 29–35

—— *In Defence of the Church Catholic: The Life of Stephen Gardiner* (Oxford, 1990)

REID, W.S. 'Clerical taxation: the Scottish alternative to the dissolution of the monasteries, 1530–1560', *Catholic Historical Review* 35 (1948), 129–53

REX, R. 'The English campaign against Luther in the 1520s', *TRHS* 5th ser. 39 (1989), 85–106

—— *The Theology of John Fisher* (Cambridge, 1991)

—— *Henry VIII and the English Reformation* (1993)

—— 'The crisis of obedience: God's Word and Henry's Reformation', *HJ* 39 (1996), 863–94

RICHARDSON, R.C. *Puritanism in North-West England* (Manchester, 1972)

RICHARDSON, W.B. 'The Religious Policy of the Cecils, 1588–98', University of Oxford D.Phil. (1994)

RICHMOND, C. 'Religion and the fifteenth-century English gentleman', in R.B. Dobson (ed.), *Church, Politics and Patronage in the Fifteenth Century* (Gloucester, 1984), 193–208

—— 'The English gentry and religion c.1500', in C. Harper-Bill (ed.), *Religious Belief and Ecclesiastical Careers in Late Medieval England* (Woodbridge, 1991), 121–50

ROBERTS, P. 'Wales and England after the Tudor "union": 1543–1624', in C. Cross, D. Loades, and J.J. Scarisbrick (eds.), *Law and Government under the Tudors* (Cambridge, 1988), 111–38

—— 'The Welsh language, English law and Tudor legislation', *Transactions of the Honourable Society of Cymmrodorion* (1989), 19–76

—— 'Tudor Wales, national identity and the British inheritance', in B. Bradshaw and P. Roberts (eds.), *British Consciousness and Identity* (Cambridge, 1998), 8–42

ROBERTSON, D.H. *The Reformation in Scotland* (Edinburgh, 1909)

ROBERTSON, J.J. 'Scottish legal research in the Vatican Archives: a preliminary report', *Renaissance Studies* 2 (1988), 339–46

ROBINSON-HAMMERSTEIN, H.H.W. 'Aspects of the Continental education of Irish students in the reign of Elizabeth I', *Historical Studies* 8 (1971), 137–54

ROBINSON, M. 'Language choice in the Reformation: the Scots Confession of 1560', in J.D. McClure (ed.), *Scotland and the Lowland Tongue* (Aberdeen, 1983), 59–78

RONAN, M.V. 'Religious customs of Dublin medieval gilds', *Irish Ecclesiastical Record* 5th ser. 26 (1925), 225 41, 364–85

—— *The Reformation in Dublin, 1536–1558* (Dublin, 1926)

ROSENTHAL, J. *The Purchase of Paradise: Gift Giving and the Aristocracy 1307–1485* (1972)

ROSMAN, D.M. *From Catholic to Protestant: Religion and the People in Tudor England* (1996)

ROSSER, G. 'Communities of parish and guild in the late Middle Ages', in S. Wright (ed.), *Parish, Church and People: Local Studies in Lay Religion, 1350–1700* (1988), 29–55

—— 'Parochial conformity and voluntary religion in late medieval England', *TRHS* 6th ser. 1 (1991), 173–89

ROSSER, G. 'Going to the fraternity feast: commensality and social relations in late medieval England', *JBS* 33 (1994), 430–45

ROTH, F. *The English Austin Friars, 1249–1538*, 2 vols. (New York, 1961–6)

ROWSE, A.L. *Tudor Cornwall*, 2nd edn. (1969)

RUBIN, M. *Corpus Christi: The Eucharist in Late Medieval Culture* (Cambridge, 1991)

—— 'Religious culture in town and country: reflections on a great divide', in D. Abulafia, M. Franklin, and M. Rubin (eds.), *Church and City 1000–1500: Essays in Honour of Christopher Brooke* (Cambridge, 1992), 3–22

RUIZ, T.F. 'Unsacred monarchy: the kings of Castile in the late Middle Ages', in S. Wilentz (ed.), *Rites of Power: Symbolism, Ritual and Politics since the Middle Ages* (Philadelphia, 1985), 109–44

RUPP, G. *Studies in the Making of the English Protestant Tradition* (Cambridge, 1947)

RUSSELL, G.H. 'Vernacular instruction of the laity in the late Middle Ages in England', *JRH* 2 (1962), 98–119

RYRIE, A. 'English Evangelical Reformers in the Last Years of Henry VIII', University of Oxford D.Phil. (2000)

SABEAN, D. *Power and the Blood: Popular Culture and Village Discourse in Early Modern Germany* (Cambridge, 1984)

SANDERSON, M.H.B. 'Some aspects of the Church in Scottish Society in the era of the Reformation' *RSCHS* 17 (1970), 81–98

—— *Cardinal of Scotland: David Beaton, c.1494–1546* (Edinburgh, 1986)

—— *Ayrshire and the Reformation* (East Linton, East Lothian, 1997)

SCARISBRICK, J.J. 'The Conservative Episcopate in England, 1529–1535', University of Cambridge Ph.D. (1955)

—— 'Clerical taxation in England, 1485–1547', *JEH* 11 (1960), 41–54

—— *Henry VIII* (1968)

—— 'Cardinal Wolsey and the commonweal', in E.W. Ives, R.J. Knecht, and J.J. Scarisbrick (eds.), *Wealth and Power in Tudor England: Essays Presented to S.T. Bindoff* (1978), 45–69

—— *The Reformation and the English People* (Oxford, 1984)

SCHMIDT, L.E. *Holy Fairs: Scottish Communions and American Revivals in the Early Modern Period* (Princeton, N.J., 1989)

SCHMUTZ, R.A. 'Medieval papal representatives, legates, nuncios, etc.', *Studia Gratiana* (1972), 443–63

SCHOECK, R.J. 'Canon law in England on the eve of the Reformation', *Medieval Studies* 25 (1963), 125–43

SCOFIELD, A.N.E.D. 'The first English delegation to the Council of Basel', *JEH* 12 (1961), 167–96

SCRIBNER, R. *Popular Culture and Popular Movements in Reformation Germany* (1987)

—— 'Reformation and desacralisation: from sacramental world to moralised universe', in R. Po-Hsia and R.W. Scribner (eds.), *Problems in the Historical Anthropology of Early Modern Europe* (Wiesbaden, 1997), 75–92

—— (ed.), with Porter, R. and Teich, M. *The Reformation in National Context* (Cambridge, 1994)

SEAVER, P. *The Puritan Lecturerships: The Politics of Religious Dissent 1560–1662* (Stanford, Calif., 1970)

SHAGAN, E. 'Protector Somerset and the 1549 rebellions: new sources and new perspectives', *EHR* 144 (1999), 34–63

SHAW, D. *The General Assemblies of the Church of Scotland 1560–1600* (Edinburgh, 1964)

SHEILS, W.J. *The Puritans in the Diocese of Peterborough, 1558–1610*, Northants Record Society 30 (1979)

—— 'Profit, patronage and pastoral care: the rectory estates of the archbishopric of York, 1540–1640', in R. O'Day and F. Heal (eds.), *Princes and Paupers in the English Church, 1500–1800* (Leicester, 1981), 91–109

—— ' "The right of the church": the clergy, tithe and the courts of York, 1540–1640', in W.J. Sheils and D. Wood (eds.), *The Church and Wealth*, SCH 24 (Oxford, 1987), 231–55

—— *The English Reformation, 1530–1570* (Harlow, 1989)

SHEILS, W.J. and SHEILS, S. 'Textiles and reform: Halifax and its hinterland', in P. Collinson and J. Craig. (eds.), *The Reformation in English Towns* (Basingstoke, 1998), 130–46

SHEPARD, A. and WITHINGTON, P. (eds.) *Communities in Early Modern England: Network, Place, Rhetoric* (Manchester, 2000)

SHEPPARD, E.H. 'The Reformation and the citizens of Norwich', *Norfolk Archaeology* 38 (1981–3), 44–58

SHERLOCK, P. 'Funeral Monuments: Piety, Honour and Memory in Early Modern England', University of Oxford D.Phil. (2000)

SHORT, B. *The English Rural Community: Image and Analysis* (Cambridge, 1992)

SIMMS, K. 'Frontiers in the Irish church—regional and cultural', in T. Barry, R. Frame, and K. Simms (eds.), *Colony and Frontier in Medieval Ireland* (1995), 177–200

SKEETERS, M.C. *Community and Clergy: Bristol and the Reformation, c.1530–c.1570* (Oxford, 1993)

SLAVIN, A.J. 'Cromwell, Cranmer and Lord Lisle, a study in the politics of reform', *Albion* 9 (1977), 316–36

—— 'The Rochepot Affair', *C16J* 10/1 (1979), 3–19

SMITH, L.B. *Tudor Prelates and Politics, 1536–1558* (Princeton, N.J., 1953)

—— *Henry VIII: The Mask of Royalty* (1971)

SMITH, R.B. *Land and Politics in the England of Henry VIII: The West Riding of Yorkshire* (Oxford, 1970)

SOMMERVILLE, C.J. 'On the distribution of religious and occult literature in seventeenth-century England', *The Library* 5th ser. 29 (1974), 221–5

SOUTHGATE, W.M. *John Jewel and the Problem of Doctrinal Authority* (Cambridge, Mass., 1962)

SPENCER, H.L. *English Vernacular Preaching in the Late Middle Ages* (Oxford, 1993)

SPICER, A. ' "Rest of their bones": fear of death and reformed burial practices', in W.P. Naphy and P. Roberts (eds.), *Fear in Early Modern Society* (Manchester, 1997), 167–83

SPICER, A. ' "Defyle not Christ's kirk with your carrion": burial and the development of burial aisles in post-Reformation Scotland', in B. Gordon and P. Marshall (eds.), *The Place of the Dead* (Cambridge, 2000), 149–69

SPIELMANN, R.M. 'The beginnings of clerical marriage in the English Reformation: the reigns of Edward and Mary', *Anglican and Episcopal History* 56 (1987), 251–63

SPUFFORD, M. 'Can we count the "godly" and the "conformable" in the seventeenth century?' *JEH* 36 (1985), 428–38

—— (ed.) *The World of Rural Dissenters, 1520–1725* (Cambridge, 1995)

STACHNIEWSKI, J. *The Persecutory Imagination: English Puritanism and the Literature of Religious Despair* (Oxford, 1991)

STARKEY, D. *The Reign of Henry VIII: Personalities and Politics* (1985)

STEPHENS, W.P. *The Holy Spirit in the Theology of Martin Bucer* (Cambridge, 1970)

—— 'The Church in Bucer's commentaries on the Epistle to the Ephesians', in D. Wright (ed.), *Martin Bucer: Reforming Church and Community* (Cambridge, 1994), 45–60

STEVENS BENHAM, L.M. 'The Durham clergy, 1494–1540, a study of continuity and mediocrity among the unbeneficed', in D. Marcombe (ed.), *The Last Principality: Politics, Religion and Society in the Bishopric of Durham, 1494–1660* (Nottingham, 1987), 6–32

STEVENSON, D. *King's College, Aberdeen, 1560–1641* (Aberdeen, 1990)

STONE, L. *The Crisis of the Aristocracy* (Oxford, 1965)

—— 'The size and composition of the Oxford student body, 1580–1910', in Stone, L. (ed.), *The Universities in Society*, 2 vols. (Princeton, N.J., 1975), i. 3–110

STRONG, R.C. 'The popular celebration of the accession day of Queen Elizabeth I', *Journal of the Warburg and Courtauld Institutes* 21 (1958), 86–103

STRYPE, J. *The Life of John Whitgift DD* (1718)

—— *Life of the Learned Sir John Cheke, Knight* (Oxford, 1821)

—— *The Life of Aylmer* (Oxford, 1821)

—— *Ecclesiastical Memorials of the Reformation of Religion under . . . Henry VIII . . . Edward VI . . . and Mary*, 6 vols. (Oxford, 1822)

—— *Annals of the Reformation . . . during Queen Elizabeth's Happy Reign*, 7 vols. (Oxford, 1824)

—— *Memorials of . . . Thomas Cranmer*, 2 vols. (Oxford, 1840)

SUTHERLAND, N. 'The Marian exiles and the establishment of the Elizabethan regime', *ARG* 78 (1987), 253–86

SWANSON, R.N. 'Learning and livings: university study and clerical careers in late medieval England', *History of Universities* 6 (1986–7), 81–103

—— *Church and Society in Late Medieval England* (Oxford, 1989)

—— 'Problems of the priesthood in pre-Reformation England', *EHR* 105 (1990), 845–69

—— 'Standards of living: parochial revenues in pre-Reformation England', in C. Harper-Bill (ed.), *Religious Belief and Ecclesiastical Careers in Late Medieval England* (Woodbridge, 1991), 151–96

SWENSEN, P. 'Patronage from the Privy Chamber: Sir Anthony Denny and religious reform', *JBS* 27 (1988), 25–44

SWENSEN, P.C. 'Noble Hunters of the Romish Fox: Religious Reform at the Tudor Court, 1543–1564', University of California, Berkeley, Ph.D. (1981)

TAIT, W.B. 'The Brigettine Monastery of Sheen', University of Oxford D. Phil. (1975)

TANNER, N.P. *The Church in Late Medieval Norwich, 1370–1532* (Toronto, 1984)

TARGOFF, R. *Common Prayer: The Language of Public Devotion in Early Modern England* (Chicago, 2001)

TEMPERLEY, N. *The Music of the English Parish Church* (Cambridge, 1979)

THOMAS, K.V. *Religion and the Decline of Magic* (Penguin, 1973)

THOMSON, J.A.F. 'Tithe disputes in later medieval London', *EHR* 53 (1963), 1–17

—— *The Later Lollards 1414–1520* (Oxford, 1965)

—— 'Innocent VIII and the Scottish church', *Innes Review* 19 (1968), 23–31

—— '"The well of grace": Englishmen and Rome in the fifteenth century', in R.B. Dobson (ed.), *The Church, Politics and Patronage in the Fifteenth Century* (Gloucester, 1984), 99–114

—— *The Early Tudor Church and Society, 1485–1529* (1993)

THOMPSON, S. 'The Pastoral Work of the English and Welsh Bishops, 1500–1558', University of Oxford D.Phil. (1984)

THORP, M.R. 'Religion and the Wyatt Rebellion of 1554', *Church History* 47 (1978), 363–80

TITTLER, R. *The Reformation and Towns in England* (Oxford, 1998)

TJERNAGEL, N.S. *Henry VIII and the Lutherans: A Study in Anglo-Lutheran Relations from 1521 to 1547* (St Louis, Mo., 1965)

TODD, J.R. 'Pre-Reformation cure of souls in Dunblane diocese', *Innes Review* 26 (1975), 28–34

TORRANCE, J. 'The covenant concept in Scottish theology and politics and its legacy', *Scottish Journal of Theology* 34 (1981), 225–43

TRUEMAN, C. *Luther's Legacy: Salvation and the English Reformers, 1525–47* (Oxford, 1994)

TUDOR-CRAIG, P. 'Religious instruction for children and adolescents in the early English Reformation', *JEH* 35 (1984), 391–413

—— 'Henry VIII and King David', in D. Williams (ed.), *Early Tudor England* (Woodbridge, 1989), 183–206

—— 'Protestant books in London in Mary Tudor's reign', *London Journal* 15 (1990), 19–28

TUPLING, G. 'The pre-Reformation parishes and chapelries of Lancashire', *Transactions of the Lancashire and Cheshire Antiquarian Society* 67 (1957), 1–16

TURNER, V. and Turner, E. *Image and Pilgrimage in Christian Culture: Anthropological Perspectives* (New York, 1978)

TYACKE, N. *Anti-Calvinists: The Rise of English Arminianism, c.1590–1640* (Oxford, 1987)

—— (ed.) *England's Long Reformation, 1500–1800* (1998)

TYLER, P. 'The significance of the ecclesiastical commission at York', *Northern History* 2 (1967), 27–44

ULLMANN, W. 'Julius II and the schismatic cardinals', in D. Baker (ed.), *Schism, Heresy and Religious Protest*, SCH 9 (1972), 177–94

—— ' "This realm of England is an Empire" ', *JEH* 30 (1979), 175–203

UNDERDOWN, D. *Revel, Riot and Rebellion: Popular Politics and Culture in England 1603–1660* (Oxford, 1985)

USHER, B. 'Expedient and experiment: the Elizabethan lay reader', in R.N. Swanson (ed.), *Continuity and Changes in Christian Worship*, SCH 35 (Woodbridge, 1999), 185–98

—— 'Backing Protestantism: the London godly, the Exchequer and the Foxe circle', in D. Loades (ed.), *John Foxe: An Historical Perspective* (Aldershot, 1999), 105–34

USHER, R.G. *The Reconstruction of the English Church*, 2 vols. (New York, 1910)

—— *The Rise and Fall of the High Commission*, ed. P. Tyler (1969)

VERSCHAUR, M.B. 'The Perth Craftmen's Book', *RSCHS* 23 (1988), 157–74

VISSER, D. 'The covenant in Zacharius Ursinus', *C16J* 18 (1987), 531–44

VON ROHR, J. *The Covenant of Grace in Puritan Thought* (Atlanta, 1986)

WABUDA, S. 'The Provision of Preaching during the English Reformation, with special reference to Itineration, c.1530 to 1547', University of Cambridge Ph.D. (1991)

—— 'Equivocation and recantation during the English Reformation: the "subtle shadows" of Dr Edward Crome', *JEH* 44 (1993), 224–42

—— 'The bishops and the provision of homilies, 1520–1547', *C16J* 25 (1994), 551–66

WALKER, G. *Plays of Persuasion: Drama and Politics at the Court of Henry VIII* (Cambridge, 1991)

—— *Persuasive Fictions: Faith, Faction and Political Culture in the Reign of Henry VIII* (Aldershot, 1996)

WALL, J.N. 'Godly and fruitful lessons: the English Bible, Erasmus's Paraphrases and the Book of Homilies', in J.E. Booty (ed.), *The Godly Kingdom of Tudor England* (Wilton, Conn., 1981), 47–138

WALL, T. 'The Catechism in Irish', *Irish Ecclesiastical Record* 5th ser. 59 (1942), 36–48

WALLACE, D.D. 'Puritan and Anglican: the interpretation of Christ's descent into hell in Elizabethan theology', *ARG* 69 (1978), 248–87

—— *Puritans and Predestination: Grace in English Protestant Theology 1525–1695* (Chapel Hill, N.C., 1982)

WALSH, K. 'Cranmer and the fathers, especially in the *Defence*', *JRH* 11 (1980), 227–47

—— 'Clerical Estate', in J. Bradley (ed.), *Settlement and Society in Medieval Ireland* (Kilkenny, 1988), 361–78

WALSHAM, A. *Church Papists: Catholicism, Conformity and Confessional Polemic in Early Modern England*, Royal Historical Society Studies in History 68 (1993)

—— ' "Frantick Hacket": prophecy, sorcery, insanity and the Elizabethan Puritan movement', *HJ* 41 (1998), 27–66

—— '"A Glose of Godlines": Philip Stubbes, Elizabethan Grub Street and the invention of Puritanism', in S. Wabuda and C. Litzenberger (eds.), *Belief and Practice in Reformation England* (Aldershot, 1999), 177–206

—— *Providence in Early Modern England* (Oxford, 1999)

WALSHE, H.C. 'Responses to the Protestant Reformation in sixteenth-century Meath', *Riocht na Midhe* 7 (1987), 97–109

—— 'Enforcing the Elizabethan Settlement: the vicissitudes of Hugh Brady, bishop of Meath', *IHS* 26 (1989), 352–74

—— 'The rebellion of William Nugent, 1581', in R.V. Comerford *et al.* (eds.), *Religion, Conflict and Co-existence in Ireland* (Dublin, 1990), 26–52

WARD, J.P. 'Religious diversity and guild unity in early modern London', in E.J. Carlson (ed.), *Religion and the English People, 1500–1640* (Kirksville, Mo., 1998), 77–97

WARD, P. 'The politics of religion: Thomas Cromwell and the Reformation at Calais', *JRH* 17 (1992), 152–71

WARDHAUGH, R. *Languages in Competition* (Oxford, 1987)

WATT, J.A. *The Church in Medieval Ireland* (Dublin, 1972)

—— 'The Church and the two nations in late medieval Armagh', in W.J. Sheils and D. Wood (eds.), *The Churches, Ireland and the Irish*, SCH 25 (Oxford, 1989), 37–54

WATT, T. *Cheap Print and Popular Piety, 1550–1640* (Cambridge, 1991)

WATTS, M. *The Dissenters from the Reformation to the French Revolution* (Oxford, 1978)

WEBB, J. 'Peter Moone of Ipswich (d.1601): a Tudor tailor, poet and gospeller and his circle', *Proceedings of the Suffolk Institute of Archaeology and History* 38 (1993), 35–55

WEIDERMANN, G. 'Alexander Alesius, Scottish Lutheran (1500–1565)', *ARG* 55 (1964), 161–91

—— 'Martin Luther versus John Fisher: some ideas concerning the debate on Lutheran theology at the University of St Andrews, 1525–30', *RSCHS* 22 (1984), 13–34

—— 'Alexander Alesius's lectures on the Psalms at Cambridge, 1536', *JEH* 37 (1986), 15–41

WESKE, D.B. *Convocation of the Clergy* (1937)

WESTFALL, S. *Patrons and Performance: Early Tudor Household Revels* (Oxford, 1990)

WESTLAKE, A. *The Parish Gilds of Medieval England* (1919)

WHITAKER, T. *A History of the Original Parish of Whalley* (Manchester, 1872)

WHITE, A. 'The impact of the Reformation on a burgh community: the case of Aberdeen', in M. Lynch (ed.), *The Early Modern Town in Scotland* (1987), 81–101

—— 'The Regent Morton's mission: the Reformation of Aberdeen, 1574', in A. MacDonald *et al.* (eds.), *The Renaissance in Scotland* (Leiden, 1994), 246–63

WHITE, B.R. *The English Separatist Tradition* (Oxford, 1971)

WHITE, P. *Predestination, Policy and Polemic: Conflict and Consensus in the English Church from the Reformation to the Civil War* (Cambridge, 1992)

WHITE, P.W. *Theatre and Reformation: Protestantism, Patronage and Playing in Tudor England* (Cambridge, 1993)

WHITING, R. *The Blind Devotion of the People: Popular Religion and the English Reformation* (Cambridge, 1989)

—— *Local Reactions to the English Reformation* (1997)

WIENER, C.Z. 'The beleaguered Isle: a study of Elizabethan and early Jacobean anti-Catholicism', *PP* 51 (1971), 27–62

WILKIE, W.E. *The Cardinal Protectors of England: Rome and the Tudors before the Reformation* (Cambridge, 1974)

WILLIAMS, G. *The Welsh Church from Conquest to Reformation* (Cardiff, 1962)

—— *Welsh Reformation Essays* (Cardiff, 1967)

—— *Reformation Views of Church History* (Richmond, Va., 1970)

—— *Recovery, Reorientation and Reform: Wales 1415–1642* (Oxford, 1987)

—— 'The Edwardian Reformation in Wales', *Journal of Welsh Religious History* 2 (1994), 14–30

—— *Wales and the Reformation* (Cardiff, 1997)

WILLIAMSON, A.H. *Scottish National Consciousness in the Age of James VI* (Edinburgh, 1979)

WILSON, J.M. 'The sermons of Roger Edgeworth: Reformation preaching in Bristol', in D. Williams (ed.), *Early Tudor England* (Woodbridge, 1989), 223–40

WINNING, T. 'Church councils in sixteenth-century Scotland', in D. McRoberts (ed.), *Essays on the Scottish Reformation* (Glasgow, 1962), 332–58

WOODCOCK, B.L. *Medieval Ecclesiastical Courts in the Diocese of Canterbury* (1952)

WOODGER, A. 'Post-Reformation mixed Gothic in Huntingdonshire: church towers and the campanological associations', *Archaeological Journal* 141 (1984), 269–308

WOODING, L. *Rethinking Catholicism in Reformation England* (Oxford, 2000)

WOODWARD, G.W.O. *The Dissolution of the Monasteries* (1968)

WORMALD, J. *Court, Kirk and Community: Scotland 1470–1625* (1981)

—— '"Princes" and the regions in the Scottish Reformation', in N. MacDougall (ed.), *Church, Politics and Society* (Edinburgh, 1983), 65–84

—— 'No bishop, no king: the Scottish Jacobean episcopate 1600–1625', in B. Vogler (ed.), *Bibliothèque de la Revue d'Histoire Ecclésiastique: Miscellania Historiae Ecclesiasticae VIII* (Louvain, 1987), 259–67

—— *Mary Queen of Scots: A Study in Failure* (1988)

—— 'Ecclesiastical vitriol: the kirk, the Puritans and the future king of England', in J. Guy, (ed.), *The Reign of Elizabeth I* (1995), 171–91

WRIGHT, D.F. (ed.) *The Bible in Scottish Life and Literature* (Edinburgh, 1988)

—— *Martin Bucer: Reforming Church and Community* (Cambridge, 1994)

WRIGHT, S.J. (ed.) *Parish, Church and People: Local Studies in Lay Religion, 1350–1700* (1988)

WRIGHTSON, K. and LEVINE, D. *Poverty and Piety in an English Parish: Terling 1525–1700* (New York, 1979)

YATES, N. *Buildings, Faith and Worship: The Liturgical Arrangement of Anglican Churches, 1600–1900* (Oxford, 1991)

YELLOWLEES, M.I. 'The ecclesiastical establishment in the Diocese of Dunkeld at the Reformation', *Innes Review* 36 (1985), 74–85

YODER, D. 'Toward a definition of folk religion', *Western Folklore* 33 (1974), 2–14

YOST, J.K. 'German Protestant humanism and the early English Reformation: Richard Taverner and official translations', *Bibliothèque d'Humanisme et Renaissance* 32 (1970), 613–25

YOUINGS, J. *The Dissolution of the Monasteries* (1969)

YULE, G. 'James VI and I: furnishing the churches in his two kingdoms', in A. Fletcher and P. Roberts (eds.), *Religion, Culture and Society in Early Modern Britain: Essays in Honour of Patrick Collinson* (Cambridge, 1994), 182–208

ZELL, M. 'The personnel of the clergy of Kent in the Reformation period', *EHR* 89 (1974), 513–33

—— 'Economic problems of the parochial clergy in the sixteenth century', in R. O'Day and F. Heal (eds.), *Princes and Paupers in the English Church, 1500–1800* (Leicester, 1981), 19–43

ZIM, R. *English Metrical Psalms: Poetry as Praise and Prayer, 1535–1601* (Cambridge, 1987)

INDEX

LENSEN

The d'Anethan Dispatches

OTHER BOOKS BY GEORGE ALEXANDER LENSEN

Report from Hokkaido:
The Remains of Russian Culture in Northern Japan

Russia's Japan Expedition of 1852 to 1855

The Meaning of Yalta:
Big Three Diplomacy and the New Balance of Power
WITH JOHN L. SNELL (ED.), CHARLES F. DELZELL,
AND FORREST C. POGUE

The Russian Push Toward Japan;
Russo-Japanese Relations, 1697–1875

The World Beyond Europe:
An Introduction to the History of Africa, India,
Southeast Asia, and the Far East

Russia's Eastward Expansion (edited)

Revelations of a Russian Diplomat: the Memoirs of
Dmitrii I. Abrikossow (edited)

Korea and Manchuria Between Russia and Japan 1895–1904:
The Observations of Sir Ernest Satow, British Minister
to Japan (1895–1900) and China (1900–1906) (edited)

The Soviet Union: An Introduction

The Russo-Chinese War

BARON D'ANETHAN AT WORK *(from a photo by Professor Conder)*

THE D'ANETHAN
DISPATCHES
FROM JAPAN, 1894–1910

The observations of Baron Albert d'Anethan
Belgian Minister Plenipotentiary and
Dean of the Diplomatic Corps

SELECTED, TRANSLATED, AND EDITED, WITH
A HISTORICAL INTRODUCTION BY
GEORGE ALEXANDER LENSEN

SOPHIA UNIVERSITY · TOKYO
IN COOPERATION WITH
THE DIPLOMATIC PRESS
TALLAHASSEE · FLORIDA

PUBLISHED BY

SOPHIA UNIVERSITY

7, KIOI-CHŌ, CHIYODA-KU

TOKYO

IN COOPERATION WITH

THE DIPLOMATIC PRESS

2305 AMELIA CIRCLE

TALLAHASSEE, FLORIDA

Library of Congress Catalog Card No. 67–26670

PRINTED AND BOUND IN JAPAN

PETER BROGREN, THE VOYAGERS' PRESS, TOKYO

To 'Lotta'

Contents

Introduction

KOREA and Manchuria have been a "cradle of conflict" for China, Japan, Russia and the United States for many years. Chinese and Japanese involvement in Korea dates back to prehistoric times. The first armed conflict between Chinese and Japanese forces occurred in the seventh century A.D. over Korea. In the 13th century Chinese and Koreans participated in the Mongol invasions of Japan, launched from Korea, and in the 16th century Japanese armies overran the Korean peninsula and invaded Manchuria.

Russian interest in Manchuria goes back to the 17th century, when Russian adventurers crossed into it. Manchuria formed part of the Russo-Chinese frontier, delineated by the Treaty of Nerchinsk (1689). With the annexation of the northern bank of the Amur River in 1858, Russian contact with Manchuria was extended. The cession by Manchu China of the region east of the Ussuri River in 1860, gave Russia not only a portion of Manchuria but also a common border with Korea.

American interest in Korea and Manchuria developed in the nineteenth century. It was essentially commercial, with the preservation of the "Open Door" for American business as the chief objective.

In 1876, Japan, which but two decades before had herself been opened to the West by American, Russian and English pressure, concluded a treaty with Korea in Perry-like fashion. Korea at the time was a tributary of the Chinese Empire. The conclusion of an agreement directly with Korea was a challenge to Chinese suzerainty. The American treaty with Korea (1882), though it was negotiated through a Chinese official, also implied the independence of the peninsular kingdom. When the Chinese in the 1880's belatedly tried to reassert their authority, a number of clashes between Chinese and

A

Japanese troops resulted. In 1894 the Sino-Japanese rivalry over Korea culminated in full-scale war.

The tragedy of Korea lay in the weakness, corruption, and division of her government. Unable to keep her house in order, Korea invited foreign intervention, for her strategic location made her not only a tempting prize, but also a potential threat, should she fall into the hands of another Power. Victorious over China, Japan secured the independence of the Korean kingdom and sought to dominate it indirectly. Her heavy hand and Chinese and Russian intrigues were to hinder her plans until another war, with Russia in 1904–05, permitted her to gain direct control over Korea and eventually to annex it (1910).

Rivalry over Korea was complicated by rivalry over Manchuria. The Treaty of Shimonoseki, which concluded the Sino-Japanese War in 1895, provided for the cession of the Liaotung Peninsula in South Manchuria to Japan, along with Formosa and the Pescadores Islands. But Russia, Germany and France intervened and "advised" Japan to retrocede the Liaotung Peninsula in exchange for an increased war indemnity. Unable to take on the three Powers singlehandedly, Japan backed down sullenly, the more irate when Russia in 1898 obtained a lease on Port Arthur and Dalny, the very places which she had denied her.

In 1900 the Boxer Uprising swept China. Foreigners and Christian converts were massacred, and an international expeditionary force had to be dispatched to lift the siege of the foreign legations in Peking. In Manchuria, through which the Russians had received permission to build their trans-continental railroad following their intervention "on behalf" of China, sizable Russian armies defeated the Boxers and regular Manchu troops. While the Russians were justified in the rescue of their nationals, they aroused Japanese, English and American hostility when they delayed withdrawing, once Manchuria had been pacified.

At first Japan seemed willing to renounce all interests in Manchuria, if Russia in turn renounced all interests in Korea. But as Russia refused to negotiate with Japan seriously, the position of the latter hardened. Convinced that Russian domination of Manchuria would eventually lead to Russian domination of Korea and ultimately to Russian domination of Japan, the Japanese in 1904 struck Russia, while the military advantage was still on their side.

This time Japan had made diplomatic preparations, the Anglo-Japanese Alliance of 1902 isolating Russia from French or other support. No one interfered when Japan established a protectorate over Korea, and as long as she professed to be fighting for the Open Door in China, Great Britain and the United States cheered her on from the sidelines. But while the Japanese victory over Russia was of global significance, making Japan a World Power, exploding the myth of white supremacy, and shaking the Russian monarchy to its very foundations, it did not restore Manchuria to China or guarantee its Open Door to Western enterprise. Victorious, Japan stepped into Russian footsteps and, effecting a reconciliation with her recent enemy, joined hands with Russia in the exploitation of Manchuria. American attempts to neutralize Manchuria only strengthened Russo-Japanese collaboration, for neither Russia nor Japan could have competed with American enterprise in a free market.

Chinese impotence endangered more than the fringes of the Manchu Empire. The partition of China proper by the Powers became a distinct possibility. The Revolution of 1911, which toppled the Manchu Dynasty, compounded Chinese disunity, and in 1915 Japan tried to make China into a Japanese satellite. In this she was blocked by the Western Powers and though she succeeded in the 1930's in carving out the puppet state of Manchukuo, her attempted conquest of China was foiled by the United States and her allies, including the Soviet Union, in World War II. The total defeat of Japan and the resurgence of a strong, belligerent China dramatically changed the balance of power in the Far East. Manchuria passed back into Russian and ultimately Chinese hands, and Korea, temporarily liberated and united, became the battleground for a new "East-West" conflict. The division of the peninsula into North and South Korea takes one back to ancient times, when the Chinese ruled the north, except that now American troops have displaced the Japanese as allies of the southern government.

While the present world conflict is often viewed in ideological terms, it is deeply rooted in the past. Korean, Manchurian, Chinese, Russian, American and Japanese attitudes have been molded particularly by the events of the 1890's and early 1900's. There are a number of studies on the Sino-Japanese War and the Russo-Japanese War and their consequences. They are based to a large extent on English and American sources and to a lesser extent on Russian, Japanese, and Chinese materials. Many of these sources are biased in favor of one side or another. While it is possible to a certain degree to "balance out" the opposing views, it is important to refer to more or less neutral sources for information and appraisal. One such source, completely unexplored by historians until now, is the collection of unpublished diplomatic dispatches of Baron Albert d'Anethan, the Belgian Minister to Japan.

D'Anethan came from a distinguished family. His uncle, Baron Jules d'Anethan, had been successively Minister of Justice, Minister of State, Minister of Foreign Affairs and President of the Senate. D'Anethan thus had the proper background for a diplomatic career. His wife, an English lady by the name of E. Mary Haggard, broadened his horizon. An author in her own right, she was the sister of the novelist Sir Henry Rider Haggard, author of *King Solomon's Mines*, as well as the sister of a diplomat, Sir William Haggard, and of two Army officers, Andrew and Arthur Haggard.

D'Anethan's contact with Japan dates back to 1871, when

the Iwakura Mission visited Europe and America. A young
official of the Foreign Office at that time, d'Anethan was
assigned to the Iwakura Mission during its visit to Belgium
and accompanied its members to various places. In 1873–75
d'Anethan served as Secretary of the Belgian Legation in
Tokyo, becoming well acquainted with his English counterpart, Sir Ernest Satow, with whom he was to share the stage
again in later years. In 1893, after service in London, Rio de
Janeiro, Washington, Constantinople, and Vienna, d'Anethan
returned to Japan as Minister Resident of the King of the
Belgians. The following year he was promoted to Envoy
Extraordinary and Minister Plenipotentiary, a position he
held from 1894 until his death on July 25, 1910, at the age of
61. His length of service in Japan and his serious study of
Japanese history made d'Anethan a discerning observer. His
old friendship with notable Japanese and European personages
won him many insights. His mounting status—he became
Dean of the Diplomatic Corps—gained him influence in counsels and "inside" information, while his Belgian nationality
provided him with a neutral and relatively objective point of
view.

D'Anethan was struck by the many changes that had
occurred in the manners and customs of the country and especially of the Imperial Court during the two decades of his
absence.

*The Princes who live in palaces, built and furnished in the
European style, all hold rank in the Army or in the Navy and
exercise actual command.*

*The majority have travelled in Europe, and upon return to
Japan have made a point of following our customs and have
succeeded so well, that it is difficult to imagine that one is in the
presence of the same Princes who only yesterday had been brought
up in the seclusion and exclusivism, customary in the countries of
the Orient.*

Today everything has been borrowed from Europe for the cere-

monial, the organization of the civil and military households, the service of the Chamberlains and the Ladies-in-waiting.

We meet them frequently now when they honor us with their presence at dinners and soirées, given by the Ministers to the Diplomatic Corps, and they are particularly gracious to foreigners.

In view of the fact that anti-foreignism now prevails in certain classes . . . , I believe it to be of interest to add that these hostile feelings have not penetrated into the high sphere. . . .[1]

On New Year's Day, 1894, the Diplomatic Corps paid its respects to Emperor Meiji and the Empress. D'Anethan described the ceremonial and the boycotting of the reception by some of his colleagues.

Upon arrival at the Palace we gathered in a room next to the Throne Room until the Grand Master of Ceremonies invited us to go before their Majesties who received, surrounded by the Princes and Princesses and by their civil and military households. All we did was to salute the Imperial Family, and were led into another room where we found the Minister of Foreign Affairs and were served refreshments.

After several minutes the Grand Chamberlain guided us into a third room where we met the Emperor and the Empress. Legation by legation we filed past their Majesties who conversed with the heads of Missions and the ladies. . . .

The Ministers of France [Sienkiewicz] and Italy [Renato de Martini] were not present at the reception, believing that the ceremonial followed compromised the dignity of the foreign Representatives. They considered that the first défilé [filing] before the Emperor is a mistake and that we should have been led directly into the room where the meeting was held. Perhaps it would have been better this way, but it is carrying sensitivity too far to see in it an intention to offend. . . .

This account, I fear, belongs to the category of diplomatic rivalry, which holds little interest for Your Excellency [d'Anethan remarked to the Foreign Minister]. If I mention it, it is because

*events at Court have become important. Since its organization
along European lines, the Japanese have been very touchy and
easily offended. They show themselves friendly toward us, but in
return expect the foreign diplomats not to behave in a free and
easy manner that would not be tolerated at any Occidental Court....*

*It is discouraging to the Japanese to see so little obligingness on
the part of certain foreign agents. The lack of respect for the Court
is especially regrettable at a time when the High Spheres seek to
counteract the anti-European feeling, prevalent in certain lower
classes.*

*It is fortunate that except for the Ministers of France and Italy,
who willingly give rise to irritating incidents, the heads of Missions are well disposed toward the Japanese, and recognize that
at Court and in the official world we are welcomed with great
amiability. The grievances voiced against the ceremonial and etiquette can be attributed more often to the foreigners than to the
Japanese.*[2]

Emperor Meiji, or Mutsuhito as d'Anethan still called
him, was an extraordinary personality. What he had accomplished "seemed to belong more to the realm of fiction than
fact, so rapid and radical had been the changes." D'Anethan
reviewed the transformation of Japan during the past quarter
of a century:

*What was Japan like when he succeeded to the throne? A country
less known and less important than Siam and Korea in our own day.
And now he sees about him the Representatives of all the Sovereigns
of Europe, the most powerful of whom will soon vie for his alliance.*

*The few junks which hugged the coast as they sailed to fish, have
now been replaced by hundreds of steamers that are engaged in
large-scale trade in the Inland Sea and with China and Korea.
Japanese lines transport native products as far as Bombay and are
getting ready to compete with European companies in the ports
of America and England.*

The railway allows the Sovereign to scour all parts of his

Empire in thirty-six hours. . . . In the palace, from where he can communicate by telephone, electricity has been installed.

Material progress is matched by moral advances of even greater significance. Public spirit has developed. Instruction at all levels has spread everywhere. In the remotest villages children find schools, and in Tokyo superb buildings of universities and colleges of higher education rise proudly. . . .

The nation is prosperous and satisfied, the taxes are moderate, the foreign debt is insignificant, the budget shows a surplus. The most absolute order reigns in all the provinces. . . .

If the most complete peace reigns in the interior, Japan possesses also the means of making herself respected by the foreign countries. Her Army, constantly drilled and commanded by trained officers, can match European troops. . . .

In his determined pursuit of Western progress and civilization, the Emperor has bestowed on his people a liberal Constitution, and Japan alone in Asia has respect for individual rights, religious tolerance for all creeds, equal justice for all, and the abolition of torture.

The few difficulties which the institution of a parliamentary regime has created for the Government are no greater than in countries long accustomed to liberty. They do not diminish in any way the grandeur of the conception [of the Constitution] of 1889, which more than any of the reforms of the past quarter of a century has contributed to placing Japan on a footing of equality with the civilized nations.[3]

As can be seen from the dispatches just quoted, d'Anethan was sympathetic toward Japan. Baron Kato Takaaki, Japanese Minister to Great Britain (1895–1900), attributed d'Anethan's sympathy to the fact that d'Anethan, entering into the life and sentiment of the Japanese people, "understood the Japanese to a degree very rare among foreigners residing in Japan, however long their residence in that country may be."[4] For seven out of the sixteen and a half years of his service as

Minister in Tokyo, d'Anethan was Dean of the Diplomatic Corps. Praising the "singular tact and ability" with which d'Anethan discharged the duties of this position to the satisfaction of his colleagues as well as of the Japanese Government, Kato reflected:

The credit was all the greater because, although the Japanese have made considerable progress in the ways of Western civilization, their intercourse with the outside world has been of comparatively short duration, and their manners, modes of expressions, nay, even sentiments were in several respects somewhat different from those of other nations. Thus unpleasantness might unwittingly have resulted in the relations between the Japanese Government and foreign Representatives unless things were very adroitly handled; but in Baron d'Anethan's skilful hands no untoward incident was allowed to happen, and the relations between the two were always of a most smooth and pleasant description.

The friendly sentiments which Baron d'Anethan entertained towards Japan and its people were cordially appreciated and reciprocated by the Emperor and such of his subjects as had the privilege of coming into contact with him officially or otherwise. In consequence, they held him in respect and affection while he lived, and they sincerely lamented his death. The Belgian Government is to be indeed envied in having so long had a Representative in Tokyo who, while always endeavouring to promote the interests of his country, knew so well how to gain the respect and sympathy of the nation to which he was accredited.[5]

The dispatches of Baron d'Anethan are of a very different nature from the memoirs of his wife, published under the title *Fourteen Years of Diplomatic Life in Japan*. They deal with affairs of state rather than with personal and social experiences. When the same subject is covered, the description is more elaborate, if not different. Thus in her diary the Baroness merely states that the Ministers of Italy and France and their wives did not attend the Imperial reception of January 1,

1894 because they were "indisposed," as they were officially. In the Baron's dispatches, on the other hand, we find, as seen above, that the indisposition was purely diplomatic, that the ministers were boycotting the reception in protest against some of the ceremonial.

In depicting the monumental changes that were transforming Meiji Japan into a Great Power, d'Anethan described the chauvinism and militarism that gripped the nation and swept along its leaders. But throughout he remained a friend of Japan, his monarchist leanings welcoming a halt in democratization, which in his view was bound to lead to corruption and disunity. Surveying the international scene, d'Anethan reported in 1894, that China opposed Russian intrigues in Korea as much as she could, but at the same time refused to act in concert with Japan. He himself was suspicious of Russian designs and assurances in Korea. As he asked tongue-in-cheek: "Does Russia ever have an objective other than 'the good of her neighbors'?!" He wrote that Japan in 1894 was very much afraid of Russia "and does not let herself be lulled into sleep by the sweet words of the Representative of the Tsar in Tokyo." But he appreciated the reasons for Russian involvement in the peninsula. "An independent Korea, making progress after the example of Japan, would no longer be the easy prey that Russia covets for possessing ports on the Pacific, ports which she needs from a political as well as a commercial standpoint."

D'Anethan understood the wider implications of the struggle over Korea, for the intervention of Russia in the traditional Sino-Japanese rivalry would awaken the feelings of England. "And who knows what complications would come from conflicts between the European nations concerning this country?" he asked in June, 1894. In another dispatch that month d'Anethan warned that the Korean question involved the peace of Europe. D'Anethan described the intensity of national feeling in Japan. "Japanese chauvinism is awake and pushes the Government to act," he reported in June of 1894. "The enthusiasm for war is general in all classes, from the highest to the lowest," he wrote in July.

D'Anethan foresaw that Japan would not be able to settle her differences with China over Korea without provoking European intervention. He thought that the Japanese government showed "little perspicacity" in failing to recognize this, and becried that Japanese illusions of an easy victory and rich rewards were "threatened by a rude awakening, should Russia throw the weight of her influence to the side of China." He reported how Japan refused English and other European advice to halt hostilities and how she was determined not to negotiate until after the Chinese had been driven from Korea.

The smashing victories of Japan over China made it obvious to d'Anethan that "in the future the influence of Japan will be felt beyond her frontiers." He found popular anger in Japan so great, when Russia, Germany and France intervened to block Japanese acquisition of a foothold on the Asian continent and the Japanese government backed down, that neither the lives of the Representatives of the three Powers nor of the leading Japanese statesmen were safe. The Tripartite Intervention demonstrated that Russia had taken up the gauntlet dropped by China. D'Anethan noted that the Japanese Government, therefore, was taking "all measures" to become a "formidable military power" on land and on sea. "There is the danger—and it is very serious—that it may be pushed to act too precipitatedly and may not be strong enough to control and restrain the military spirit and belligerent excitement of the nation. . . ."

While d'Anethan was very sympathetic toward the Japanese, he was disturbed by their conduct in Formosa and Korea. He expressed the fear, in August 1896, "that the Japanese have not the desired qualities, or have not yet attained a degree of civilization advanced enough, to exercise a salutary influence beyond their own territory." Just the same, d'Anethan repeated in December of 1897, that he was convinced that Japan someday would exercise "a preponderant influence in Far Eastern politics."

D'Anethan described how agitated the Japanese were in 1898, when the Russians, who had blocked their acquisition of Port Arthur and Talien-wan, obtained a lease in the very region themselves, and how deeply the Japanese were concerned about continued Russian inroads in Korea. "For Japan the annexation of Korea by Russia would be the greatest of dangers and the Government would not hesitate before any sacrifice to oppose this," he reported in March, 1898. Describing the mounting rivalry of Japan and Russia, d'Anethan wrote in July of the same year: "The memory of the retrocession of Liaotung and of the intervention of the three Great Powers is still vivid in Japan and she only looks for a favorable opportunity to take revenge." A Russian proposal for world disarmament met with skepticism in Japan. As d'Anethan reported, the difficulty in coming to a disarmament agreement with Russia lay, according to Viscount Aoki, in one's inability to control the military forces of Russia. "In that vast empire . . . closed to foreigners in the Asiatic regions, where there is no parliament, [no] freedom of the press, [no] budget with exact and convenient figures for verifying the state of the army, how will one be able to make sure that the Tsar abides scrupulously by the rules which he proposes to other nations?"

Following the outbreak of the Boxer Uprising, d'Anethan wrote that Japan feared "lest Russia benefit by the Chinese complications to pursue her ambitious designs in China as well as Korea." "The future relations between Japan and Russia are one of the very black spots on the already very dark Far Eastern horizon," he reflected in July of 1900. "If Russia declares war on China and takes possession of Manchuria, Japan will then seize the opportunity to install herself in Korea," d'Anethan predicted. When the Russians concluded a secret agreement with China, providing for Chinese acceptance and consultation of a Russian Political Resident at Mukden and Chinese assistance in the construction of the Russian railroad in Manchuria in return for Russian evacuation, the Japanese were greatly aroused. "This Russo-Chinese entente, which would put all of North China under Russian domination, seems to jeopardize the maintenance of peace in the Far East," d'Anethan noted in January, 1901. In March he reported: "In the military world the idea is now expressed loudly and publicly that the present time would be most favorable for making war, and that one must not wait until Russia has built the formidable fleet which she will have in a few years." In May d'Anethan wrote that the Japanese people were "firmly in favor of an aggressive policy against Russia."

The conclusion of the Anglo-Japanese Alliance in 1902 seemed to increase rather than to decrease the likelihood of war between Russia and Japan. Georges de Man, who replaced d'Anethan while he was on leave in Europe, noted that while the Japanese public received news of the alliance with "exuberant joy," English residents in Japan felt "a bit humiliated by the alliance of their country with a people of the yellow race." Upon his return to Tokyo in November of 1902, d'Anethan found Japan preparing for any eventuality and determined, as he reported in January of 1903, "to establish her complete and exclusive influence in Korea." In January, 1904, d'Anethan observed that the Japanese Government, while still negotiating, feverishly continued military preparations. Japan was waiting only, he believed, for two warships, recently purchased by her, to clear the Suez canal and for some of her merchant ships to return to Japanese ports.

Following the rupture of diplomatic relations between Japan and Russia, in February of 1904, d'Anethan reviewed the situation. "During the long negotiations conducted between Japan and Russia," he recalled, "we never thought of a peaceful solution, knowing that the concessions demanded of Russia could hardly be given by her and that, on the other hand, we had too much proof of the stubborn resolution of Japan."

During the Russo-Japanese War d'Anethan related the confidence with which the Japanese carried the struggle to victory. Following the conclusion of peace, he described in some detail the indignation and wave of riots that swept through the country when the public felt that the aims for which Japan had fought had been abandoned. He described the unheroic return of Baron Komura, the Japanese negotiator, from the United States. Yet by 1907, d'Anethan reported that both St. Petersburg and Tokyo seemed "animated by conciliatory feelings, and the desire to re-establish not only normal but friendly relations between the two countries is evident." American efforts to neutralize the railroads of Manchuria drove Japan and Russia closer together, and in 1910 d'Anethan attested to "the perfect understanding which exists... between the Cabinet of Tokyo and of St. Petersburg concerning the railroads in which they are interested in Manchuria." Mounting unrest in China favored a Russo-Japanese *rapprochement*, as the two Powers sought to exploit the weakness of China by working with each other rather than at cross-purposes. When Russia and Japan in 1910 concluded an agreement maintaining the *status quo* in Manchuria, the demarcation of Russian and Japanese interests and their protection against aggression by a third power, d'Anethan hailed the event as "of all the diplomatic victories won by Japan..., the most striking and lasting in effect."

Well informed, d'Anethan was often trenchant and usually right. Obvious as some of his observations may appear in retrospect, they were perspicacious at the time. His expectation of war between Russia and Japan, for example, contrasts sharply with the view held by his German colleague, who believed until the very last moment that Japan was merely rattling her saber and would eventually back down. D'Anethan's major misappraisal was his failure to foresee the continuity, indeed the mounting momentum, of Japanese military ambitions. Making light of the heritage of hatred which others ascribed to racial discrimination in California, d'Anethan believed that "war between Japan and the United States would be a crime against civilization" and "would be such folly, that. . . it will never enter the mind of any Japanese statesman." His short range observations were borne out, however. As he predicted, Russia shifted her major attention from the Far East to the Near East following her defeat in the Russo-Japanese War, and resumed friendly relations with Japan.

Publication of all of d'Anethan's dispatches in full was not feasible. Reproduction of the excerpts in the original French was tempting, but would have limited the circle of American readers. The present format was chosen to make d'Anethan's observations most readily available to students of Far Eastern international relations. The chapter headings have been given to underline the theme which runs through many of the dispatches. "Extraneous" material of interest, such as Japanese reaction to American annexation of the Philippines and revolutionary unrest in China, has been retained, so that the coverage of the book is broader than the divisions suggest. The idea of segregating such entries in a "miscellaneous" chapter proved impractical, as their significance and impact lay in a chronological context.

Cumbersome as my translation may appear at times, it is, if anything, more lucid than the original. I have disentangled long and involved "trailer" passages and have broken them up into more coherent sentences, making every effort, of course, to leave the meaning intact. By extracting the key sections of the dispatches and joining them together with transitional paragraphs that put the material into historical context, I have tried to give to d'Anethan's observations continuity, if not narrative force. In translating the dispatches I have rendered Russian names in accordance with the Library of Congress system of transliteration, Japanese and Chinese names in accordance with the style of Kenkyūsha and Wade-Giles respectively. Place names are given as in the *Columbia-Lippincott Gazeteer of the World*.

Since the dispatches of d'Anethan form the bulk of the book, it would have looked awkward to indent them. At the same time, their rendition in small type would have made the work difficult to read. After some experimentation, it was decided to differentiate between d'Anethan's words and mine by printing the former in italics, the latter in roman style. Italics seemed appropriate not only because they underlined the thoughts of d'Anethan, but because they preserved most nearly the "feel" of the handwritten dispatches.

The original dispatches are kept in the Belgian Ministry of Foreign Affairs under "Correspondance Politique. Legations. Japon," a file that covers the period from 1866 to 1913. I am most grateful to the Belgian Ministry of Foreign Affairs and External Commerce for making the documents available to me for publication and to the Florida State University Research Council for making possible their photoduplication and translation. I am indebted to Mr. P.-H. Desneux, Archivist of the Belgian Ministry of Foreign Affairs, for supplying me with biographical information about Baron d'Anethan and some of his colleagues. Last but not least I wish to acknowledge the assistance of my friend, the Countess Ellen de Sercey, with whom I discussed the entire translation, and of Tony, my Girl Friday, who typed the final manuscript, helped read the galleys, and compiled the index. Needless to say any errors are solely my own responsibility.

GEORGE ALEXANDER LENSEN
Tokyo, July, 1967

CHAPTER ONE

The Sino-Japanese War

IN THE early days of May, 1894, Kim Ok-kiun, a Korean politician who collaborated with the Japanese, was murdered by Korean patriots in Shanghai. His body was returned to Korea, where it was publicly dismembered and exposed. The slayers too were returned to Korea and were rewarded rather than punished for the killing. A great outcry went up in Japan. Describing the ugly course of events, Baron Albert d'Anethan wrote to Count de Mérode Westerloo, the Belgian Minister of Foreign Affairs:

This murder has greatly aroused public opinion in Japan not only because Kim had attracted much sympathy, however badly misplaced, but because it is felt that the Chinese authorities by honoring the assassin had purposely manifested...their disapproval of the asylum given to the revolutionary by the Imperial Government during the past ten years. The Government has denied supporting Kim and his partisans in Korea and favoring any intrigue against the King [of Korea]. Nevertheless his presence in Japan, the arrival during the last years of many refugees, and the frequent plots against the ministers in Korea were cleverly exploited by the Minister of China in Seoul. The influence of Japan has suffered in consequence to the great advantage of that of China which had never, anyway, stopped regarding Korea as a tributary state.

Certain organs of the press have insinuated also that the Russian Legation was involved in the departure of Kim by financing his voyage. I do not believe that one should attach importance to this rumor. Yet the moment Korea is mentioned, one thinks of Russia in Japan and asks immediately what the intentions and views of the powerful neighbor of Korea may be.

Alert to the dangers which menace Korea from that direction, the Imperial Government would like to come to an understanding with China to take common action in Seoul and protect that country. Until now, however, all negotiations begun to this effect have faltered, and with every incident the rivalry is accentuated. China opposes the Russian intrigues as much as she can, but at the same time she refuses to act in concert with Japan.

Lately the Russian Government has sought to gain the consent of the King of Korea to establish a colony of one hundred Russians in the province of Kankyo-do. According to the Russian proposal, the colony would be limited to a period of five or seven years. The colonists would live in tents on the conceded land, which would be returned to the Korean Government after having been exploited and cultivated for those seven years! So unselfish on the part of Russia—does Russia ever have an objective other than "the good of her neighbors"?—this offer was made solely to bring prosperity to the province of Korea (not far from the sea!). Nevertheless it was rejected thanks to wise counsels from Peking.

The solicitude of Russia towards Korea remains undaunted. Japan is very much afraid of her and does not let herself be lulled into sleep by the sweet words of the Representative of the Tsar in Tokyo.

The dispatch of Chinese troops to Korea in the summer of 1894, following the outbreak of the Tonghak rebellion with which the Korean Government could not cope, triggered also Japanese "assistance." As large forces from China and Japan poured into the peninsula, the most serious consequences were apparent. Looking at the total picture, d'Anethan wrote to the Belgian Minister of Foreign Affairs:

If the question can remain limited to the ancient rivalry between China and Japan, we need not be worried about Korea. But the intervention of Russia would awaken the feelings of England, and who knows what complications would result from conflicts between the European nations concerning this country, which is so admirably situated for arousing the covetousness of the maritime powers and of the [country] which aspires to become one.

Your Excellency will remember that in April 1885, the British Government "in view of the uncertainty with Russia" temporarily occupied the island of Port Hamilton, to the south of Korea. The British flag was lowered in February 1887, when the cabinet of St. Petersburg gave the assurance "that Russia would not occupy any point of Korea."[6]

As Japanese forces pushed into Korea, the Japanese Government announced that they were sent merely to protect Japanese subjects and that Japan had no designs upon Korea. It promised that as soon as order was restored, Chinese and Japanese troops would be withdrawn in accordance with the Tientsin Convention of 1885. But while Japan wished to collaborate with China in rejuvenating Korea, the Chinese continued to regard Korea as their tributary and hence as their sole responsibility. In the words of d'Anethan:

By the Tientsin Convention of 1885, the Governments of China and Japan agreed not to send troops to Korea without forewarning each other. The Cabinet of Peking observed this clause of the Convention when it informed the Cabinet of Tokyo that it had ordered some troops to cross the frontier, but in so doing it added the words: "Korea being a dependency of China." The Imperial Government was very vexed by this statement and responded to it by dispatching an Army Corps.[7]

The speed and extent of Japanese mobilization were admirable. Yet they reflected on the sincerity of Japanese assurances that troops would be withdrawn upon the restoration of order. D'Anethan voiced mounting concern:

This large deployment of troops, which is not consistent with the avowed official objective [merely] to quell the Korean insurrection and to protect the interests of [Japanese] nationals, can entail the most serious consequences for the relations between Japan and China.

Public opinion in Japan is extremely excited. It is passionate on the subject of Korea. It sympathizes with the rebels and hates the Royal Government, which it considers to be in feudal subjection to China. Backed by popular feeling, the Imperial Government would claim most emphatically [that its objective is] to preserve the independence of Korea and to liberate her from Chinese suzerainty. It has been doing so since 1876, when it concluded a treaty with Korea.

The statesmen in power are too wise and prudent to plunge into such a serious adventure as war with China without first exhausting the diplomatic means for an agreement. But they will not shrink from resorting to arms, if negotiations fail.

The speed with which 5,000 men were assembled in Korea, and the entry into the capital in force give a primary advantage to Japan. If complications ensue, another 20,000 men can be sent in less than a week. The occupation corps will not leave Korea as long as one Chinese soldier will be there.

The situation hence is critical, and if it continues, may bring other interventions. For this reason the Korean question unfortunately involves also the peace of Europe.[8]

When the Chinese claimed that the rebellion had been suppressed and the presence of foreign troops in the peninsula was no longer necessary, the Japanese refused to withdraw their troops, in fact continued to augment their forces. "In the opinion of the Japanese, Korea cannot continue to live under the corrupt and degenerate Government which rules today, since administrative and military reforms will not be effective so long as this country will remain under Chinese domination and will be a cause of constant conflicts between the two countries [China and Japan]," d'Anethan observed. Reporting that the Japanese had no intention of withdrawing until some of their reform demands were met, d'Anethan commented:

The Japanese Government has gone so far that it is difficult for it to pull back. Public feeling is too overheated and overexcited for it to be able to confine itself to a simple demonstration in

Korea. If it will not get satisfaction from China, it will resort to force. Japanese chauvinism is awake and pushes the Government to act.

I fear that one does not fully realize here what a war with China would cost. The harm that Japan can do unto her strong neighbor is insignificant compared to that which can be inflicted upon her. . . .

Should China, which is now negotiating, seek merely to gain time, I believe that Japan will precipitate events in order to impede the arrival of Chinese troops in Korea and not to lose the superiority which she has today, being master of the capital, of Chemulpo and Fusan.

As before, the situation was complicated by the danger of foreign intervention, particularly of Russia, which shared a common frontier with Korea. D'Anethan continued:

Russia has offered to Japan the good offices of the Tsar to facilitate an amicable arrangement between China and Japan. Mr. Hitrovo,[a] the Russian Minister in Tokyo, yesterday made the offer, adding that the Emperor acted at the request of the Chinese Government, which had asked Russia to support . . . its demand that the Japanese Government withdraw its troops from Korea.

"I replied to the Minister of Russia," the Foreign Minister told me, "that we were very grateful to the Emperor for this proof of his friendship toward Japan and that we shall always welcome the proposals of His Majesty with the greatest deference; that we were animated by the greatest desire to settle our differences with China by peaceful means and that consequently we would always be disposed to show ourselves conciliatory. As for withdrawing Japanese troops, we could not do it until after having received assurances that a new intervention would not be necessary soon. China proposes that we negotiate after the withdrawal of troops; we wish to negotiate first. If the negotiations succeed, the army of occupation will return immediately to Japan."

[a] Mikhail Aleksandrovich Khitrovo.

The intervention of Russia—an intervention entirely peaceful and well-meaning—was not at all to the liking of the Imperial Government, as it fears the friendly advances of the strong neighbor of Korea and hoped—showing little perspicacity in this—to settle the Sino-Korean questions directly with China without the help of a European Power.

It is very regrettable that at this moment the British Legation is virtually without a head. Since the death of Mr. Fraser, it has been run by a very young 3rd Secretary who has no authority or experience. The French Legation is in the hands of the Consul General of Shanghai, Monsieur Dubail, who has been sent to carry on until the arrival of the new Minister, Monsieur J. Harmand, who is expected next month.[9]

The position of Japan remained firm. She refused to heed Chinese demands to withdraw her armed forces from Korea. The British Government through Viscount Aoki Shuzo, the Japanese Minister in London, tried to induce Japan to pull back her troops "in the interest of peace," but to no avail. In the words of d'Anethan:

The Cabinet of Tokyo continues to show itself very firm on this point. . .and will not give in to any influence, either that of Russia or of England. . . . .At Seoul the Representatives of several Powers have intervened to try to bring about an amicable arrangement, but without success so far.

The European intervention to be effective should be joint. But in view of the relations which exist between the Powers that are most interested in Korea and in Far Eastern politics, an entente seems rather difficult, and under the circumstances the counsels of prudence given to Japan by England as well as by Russia lose much of their value.[10]

The Japanese Government rejected a Chinese demand to ease the situation by keeping Chinese and Japanese warships out of each other's waters. Frustrated in her attempts to attain military and administrative reforms in Korea through diplomatic pressure by Chinese counterpressure, Japan was ready to impose her will by force, and demanded the withdrawal of Chinese troops from Korea in a note that was a veritable ultimatum. Transmitting an article from the Japanese newspaper *Nichi Nichi Shimbun* on the theme that "Japan does not like war, but is compelled to fight," d'Anethan pointed out that the article accurately reflected the views not only of the Japanese Government, but of the public at large.

The enthusiasm for war is general in all classes, from the highest to the lowest. The confidence in the strength of the Army and Navy is absolute, and it is with the "lightest heart" that one prepares for war. The circulation of newspapers has increased considerably; crowds besiege all the offices where news from Korea is posted. The enthusiasm and struggle for newspapers extends to the smallest villages.[11]

On July 28, d'Anethan reported that although there had not been a declaration of war, hostilities had begun. Asserting that one of their warships had been attacked by a Chinese vessel, the Japanese had leaped into action. The Chinese Minister in Tokyo expressed no hope for an amicable settlement. "The Japanese Government has decided on war, and rejects all Chinese proposals," he told d'Anethan. He said that China had kept her forces in Korea small to avoid giving the Japanese a pretext for war. Now, as a result, she was unprepared for the struggle. But the Minister voiced confidence in the ultimate outcome: "China is strong and rich enough to continue the war for twenty years, if necessary." He added:

Korea is a tributary state of China, but according to the system of my Government, we leave to her, as to other tributaries, complete independence in internal affairs. Japan, which proclaims so highly the independence of Korea, on the other hand, wants to impose reforms by force; more than that, she occupies the country with troops. All the people's sympathies have turned towards China; the idea of a Japanese yoke is odious to Korea.

To the words of the Chinese Minister, d'Anethan appended some observations of his own on the nature of the conflict and the reaction of the Powers:

The Japanese ravenously hasten their arming. More than 20,000 men are now in Korea and every day new transports are sent out. They occupy all the strategic positions of the country and have connected them with military telegraph lines. The Reserve has been called and the men rally to the colors with extraordinary spirit and enthusiasm. One dark spot in this picture—from the Japanese point of view—are the daily visits of the Minister of Russia to the Minister of Foreign Affairs. He insists that the Government make an arrangement with China and avoid war. His intervention has had little success so far. Very favourable and well-disposed as he had been toward Japan, he has become hostile and almost menacing. If the attitude of Mr. Hitrovo accurately reflects the feeling of the Cabinet of St. Petersburg, it is evident that at this moment Russian sympathies are on the side of China.

Should one be surprised? An independent Korea, making progress after the example of Japan, would no longer be the easy prey that Russia covets for possessing ports on the Pacific, ports which she needs from a political as well as a commercial standpoint.

In spite of the pressure which the Representative of the Tsar seeks to exert, the enthusiasm for war is manifested every day by new demonstrations. The officials give up part of their pay, and presents in kind and in money pour in for the Army. The Government has established a special office to receive and distribute the gifts which amount already to several thousand dollars. The confidence in victory surpasses all bounds. The Japanese see themselves already as the protectors of Korea and the masters of the island of Formosa, [regard] the occupation of Peking as a simple military march, and calculate already the use to which they will put the billions in gold which China will pay. Complacently chauvinism indulges in these bright dreams, and not one voice is raised to show how much these illusions are in danger of a cruel awakening, should Russia throw the weight of her influence to the side of China.

Without question the superiority of the Japanese Army in numbers as well as quality is striking, but on sea the forces are about equal, in numbers at least. Without drawing a parallel between the two invasions of Korea by Japan in the 16th century and the expedition projected today, it is interesting, in rereading the history of the campaigns of Taiko-sama [Toyotomi Hideyoshi]. . . that it was the inferiority of the Navy that lost the fruit of the victories then constantly gained on land. As regards courage, ardor and love of war, the Japanese [of today] still resembles the Japanese of 1592, and now as before the statesmen and the nation are passionate on the subject of Korea, which they continue to regard as the road to supremacy in the Orient.

Since the Minister of England will not arrive until the end of next month, English action is taken through the Japanese Minister in London. We are thus not well informed here about the nature of the advice given by Lord [John Wodehouse] Kimberley [the British Foreign Secretary]. The Japanese Government counts on the sympathy of England as long as Russia stresses her preference for China. It forgets perhaps too much, however, that Europe—first of all England—has commercial interests of such great importance in the Far East, that it is not likely to observe neutrality toward the belligerents. The maritime Powers will not fail to take measures necessary to protect their commerce, and Japan will find herself blocked, if she tries to carry onto Chinese soil the successes which in all probability she will gain in Korea.

D'Anethan added in a postscript:

The English Chargé d'Affaires has just told me that he received a telegram from Lord Kimberley this morning ordering him to urge the Imperial Government not to make war and to resume negotiations with China. England offers her good offices and proposes that Japan halt troop movements, confining her positions to the south of Korea, so as not to trouble China in the North. The same day the Ministers of France, Germany, Russia and Italy received instructions to support the démarche *of England. They immediately went to the Ministry but the collective intervention had no result whatsoever. Mr. Mutsu [Munemitsu, the Japanese Foreign Minister] replied to them that the hostilities having been begun by China, Japan would not consent to negotiate until after the expulsion of the Chinese troops from Korea.*[12]

A fortnight after the eruption of war, d'Anethan summarized an official Japanese account of the fateful clash between Chinese and Japanese warships, and described Japanese successes since that time.

On July 25, three Japanese warships, the Yoshino Kan, *the* Naniwa Kan *and the* Hiyei Kan, *left Jinsen or Chemulpo (the port of Seoul is named one way or the other according to whether one uses the Chinese or Japanese word). They were going to meet the* Yayeyama Kan *which was bringing dispatches. Their course took them to the south of the island of Kanghwa near Asan, where the Chinese troops were stationed. The same day two Chinese vessels, the* Tsi-yuen *and the* Kwangyi, *came out from Asan in order to meet the transport* Kowshing *and the warship* Tsao-chiang *which escorted the latter. Perceiving the Japanese vessels in the strait which separates the island of Kanghwa from the mainland, they set out in pursuit, running out their guns.*

The Japanese turned about and also prepared for action. At that moment the Chinese vessels hoisted a white flag above a Japanese flag. This signal prompted the Japanese to approach peacefully. But when the distance which separated them was not more than about 300 meters [less than 1,000 feet], one of the Chinese vessels launched a torpedo and opened fire. An engagement followed, the Yoshino Kan *and the* Hiyei Kan *fighting against the* Tsi-yuen *and the* Kwangyi, *while the* Naniwa *directed its attention to the transport vessel* Kowshing *and the vessel which escorted her. These two vessels flew the English flag but the* Naniwa, *recognizing that one belonged to the Chinese Navy and that the other one had Chinese troops on board, shot a cannonball across the bow of the* Tsao-chiang *and signalled it as well as the transport to lie to. The transport obeyed and cast anchor. The* Naniwa *sent a boat with an officer, to whom the captain of the transport, an Englishman, declared that 1,500 Chinese soldiers were aboard and that these would prevent him from obeying the Japanese orders. When the boat returned, the* Naniwa *signalled to the transport to weigh anchor and to place itself behind the warship. Captain Galsworthy was disposed to comply, but, as he had foreseen, the Chinese opposed it, threatening him and the officers with death.*

The Naniwa *thereupon fired a 28 pound missile from an Armstrong cannon, and sank the ship. The English on board jumped into the sea and were saved by the boats of the* Naniwa. *Only 83 Chinese were picked up. The fire against the* Tsi-yuen *and the* Kwangyi *was maintained for a couple of hours, and the two vessels were put to flight. The* Tsao-chiang *surrendered, and was led to Sasebo. The Japanese vessels were very superior to their adversaries in tonnage and speed, but the Chinese had sufficient armament to make the victory less easy, had they shot more accurately.*

Since war had not yet been declared, the Japanese commander exceeded his authority in firing on an English vessel which could legitimately transport troops. The affair will not entail any complications, however. I believe the Imperial Government will give all satisfaction and indemnities that the Government of the Queen could claim. What will simplify things anyway is that the Company to which the Kowshing *belongs will not lodge a complaint, because it had collected from the Chinese Government an advance of 40,000 pound sterling as insurance for the vessel.*

On land the Japanese have likewise attained the first successes. On the 29th, they gained a victory over the Chinese at Songhwan and took Asan. Chinese losses amounted to 500 men. Several flags, five cannons, ammunition and all the field equipment were taken. Seventy Japanese, including seven officers, were killed or wounded. The Chinese numbered about 3,000; the Japanese troops were very superior in number. . . .

On the basis of very reliable information, I think that unless China will submit completely to all Japanese demands or unless there will be reverses on the sea, we shall soon see the Imperial Army invade Chinese territory and march on Peking.

D'Anethan enclosed the English text of the Chinese declaration of war, which presented the Chinese side of the story:

Corea has been our tributary for the past two hundred odd years. She has given us tribute all this time, which is a matter known to the world. For the past dozen or so years Corea has been troubled by repeated insurrections, and we in sympathy with our small tributary have as repeatedly sent succour to her aid, eventually placing a Resident in her capital to protect Corea's interests. In the 4th moon (May) of this year another rebellion was begun in Corea, and the King repeatedly asked again for aid from us to put down the rebellion. We then ordered Li Hung-chang to send troops to Corea, and they having barely reached Yashan the rebels immediately scattered. But the Wojen *(an ancient name for Japanese, expressive of contempt), without any cause whatever, sent their troops to Corea, and entered Seoul, the capital of Corea, reinforcing them constantly until they have exceeded ten thousand men. In the meantime the Japanese forced the Corean King to change his system of government, showing a disposition every way of bullying the Coreans. It was found a difficult matter to reason with the* Wojen. *Although we have been in the habit of assisting our tributaries we have never interfered with their internal government. Japan's treaty with Corea was as one country with another; there is no law for sending large armies to bully a country in this way, and compel it to change its system of government. The various Powers are united in condemning the conduct of the Japanese, and can give no reasonable name to the army she now has in Corea. Nor has Japan been amenable to reason, nor would she listen to the exhortation to withdraw her troops and confer amicably upon what should be done in Corea. On the contrary, Japan has shown herself bellicose without regard to appearances, and has been increas-*

ing her forces there. Her conduct alarmed the people of Corea as well as our merchants there, and so we sent more troops over to protect them. Judge of our surprise then when half-way to Corea, a number of the Wojen ships suddenly appeared and taking advantage of our unpreparedness opened fire upon our transports at a spot on the seacoast near Yashan, and damaged them, thus causing us to suffer from the treacherous conduct which could not be foretold by us.

As Japan has violated the treaties and not observed inter-national laws, and is now running rampant with her false and treacherous actions, commencing hostilities herself and laying herself open to condemnation by the various Powers at large, we therefore desire to make it known to the world that we have always followed the paths of philanthropy and perfect justice throughout the whole complications, while the Wojen on the other hand have broken all the laws of nations and treaties which it passes our patience to bear with. Hence we command Li Hung-chang to give strict orders to our various armies to hasten with all speed to root the Wojen out of their lairs. He is to send successive armies of valiant men to Corea in order to save the Coreans from the dust of bondage. We also command the Manchu Generals, Viceroys and Governors of the Maritime Provinces, as well as the Commanders-in-Chief of the various armies, to prepare for war and to make every effort to fire on the Wojen ships if they come into our ports, and utterly destroy them. We exhort our Generals to refrain from the least laxity in obeying our commands in order to avoid severe punishment at our hands. Let all know this Edict as if addressed to themselves individually. Respect this![13]

In September d'Anethan reported that a great battle was in the offing in Korea. Describing the magnitude of Japanese preparations, he observed that it was evident that Japan had decided not to confine her operations to Korea, but to push into China. Transmitting the text of a treaty which Japan had concluded with Korea on August 26, he commented:

The treaty, imposed on Korea by force, is a clever maneuver of Japanese diplomacy. It is, indeed, of great interest for Japan to show by the said convention that the Korean Government, by virtue of its right as [the government of] an independent state, has entrusted Japan with the expulsion of the Chinese. Korea thus indicates once more that she wants to break her bonds of vassalage to China.

As Your Excellency already knows, the offers of mediation and good offices of the Great Powers have been rejected by Japan. England and Russia know that for the moment any new attempt at intervention is useless. The Representatives of these Powers are instructed, however, to seek the first opportunity to make Japan listen to counsels of moderation. Such opportunity will not arise until after conspicuous successes [have been achieved by Japan]. Before then the Imperial Government will not listen to any proposal.[14]

The great battle which d'Anethan had reported imminent took place on September 16, and resulted in a brilliant victory for Japan. D'Anethan analyzed the situation.

This victory is of enormous importance, because it makes Japan master of Korea. The road to the border is free and the Japanese army can march on Mukden in Manchuria.

But Mukden is about 260 miles from Pyongyang. The roads are terrible. There are rivers to cross, several fortresses to subdue. The army . . . could not besiege Mukden until the first days of November. By that time the cold would be an enemy far more dangerous than the Chinese. We believe that Japan will concentrate her efforts on an attack against Port Arthur and will confine herself to preventing [Chinese] reinforcements from coming to Korea.

If they succeed in capturing this invaluable strategic position and thereby make their power felt on the soil of China proper, the Japanese will be disposed to stop. As long as they have success in Korea only, China will not waver, and the war will drag on to the great detriment of the Japanese, without any serious harm to China.

I know that the Imperial Government believes that the day that its armies will have conquered a piece of Chinese territory, China will show herself disposed to negotiate peace. On its part, the Government would like very much to be able to end the war before winter. . . . The Government realizes the enormous difficulties that threaten its armies if the hostilities continue in the winter as well as the danger to Japan of prolonging a struggle which effects the interest of other powers to such a high degree.

Financially and commercially the disastrous effects of the war are felt already in Japan. Her trade with China, amounting to 25,000,000 dollars, has stopped and the reserve funds, accumulated over a number of years from revenue surplus, have been used up. The Government has just floated an internal loan of 30,000,000 dollars. Though it has been oversubscribed twice, this cannot be repeated frequently.

There are very serious reasons, therefore, militating in favor of peace. Once the Chinese have been expelled from Korea, Japan can honorably make peace, and I would be very much surprised if the Government would not eagerly take the first opportunity that presented itself to suspend hostilities honorably.[15]

The land battle of September 16, was followed the next day by a major naval engagement. Again the Japanese were triumphant. "This naval victory shows most strikingly the superiority of Japan on sea as well as on land," d'Anethan reported. Prior to the war China had appeared to be the dominant Far Eastern nation. The changing power relationship that Japanese successes presaged required a re-examination of policy in many capitals. D'Anethan observed a change in Russian attitude:

At the beginning of the war the Minister of Russia seemed hostile toward the Japanese. His attitude has changed completely, especially since the arrival of the Russian military agent Colonel

*Wogack[b] who is also accredited to China. Colonel Wogack recently
gave a big dinner for the Ministers of War and Navy. The French
Military Attaché was present. The toasts to "victories gained and
to future success" were very ardent. These two officers will shortly
go to the Headquarters of the Emperor at Hiroshima.*

*Is there some arrangement between Japan, Russia and France?
Are we witnessing a diplomatic maneuver of Japan to give pause
to England, whom the Government suspects of being sympathetic
toward China? The situation will become clearer after some time,
when the Japanese armies will find themselves on Chinese territory.*

*The press during the past few days made several allusions to the
possibility of a new triple alliance of Japan, France and Russia.[16]*

After reading European newspapers, d' Anethan felt compelled to warn his government against the dispatches from
Shanghai, which claimed Chinese victories and Japanese reverses. He reflected on the international implications of
various Japanese steps and on the danger of European intervention.

*The Japanese are actually masters of all of Korea, where there
is not a Chinese soldier left. . . . In view of the extraordinary
disorganization of the Chinese Army, the Japanese have little to
fear, and can establish their winter quarters in towns, where
they will be sheltered from the cold.*

*The inferiority of the Chinese Navy assures them free com-
munication by sea. If no foreign Power intervenes, Japan will
without doubt emerge victorious from this war.*

*Reports from the Legation in Peking should show Your Excel-
lency the disarray in which the whole political administration is,
and how much the power of the Dynasty has been shaken. In taking
Mukden, where the ancestral tombs of the reigning Dynasty are,
and Peking, the Japanese will be able, if they so desire, to inflict
mortal blows on the Dynasty and thus usher in an era of terrible
revolutions in China.*

  [b] Konstantin Ippolitovich Vogak.

In Korea, the Imperial Government has undertaken the reorganization of the country. To this end Count Inouye [Kaoru], one of the most remarkable men of Japan, who for more than twenty years has held the highest positions, has been appointed Envoy Extraordinary. The choice of a Minister of such high rank clearly indicates that the protectorate which Japan henceforth will exercise in the peninsula is not an empty word. Nominally the independence of Korea will remain intact, and one will leave her the attributes of sovereignty. . . . This is a clever policy, because it avoids the intervention of England and Russia, both of whom have declared that they would oppose the annexation of Korea by Japan.

Once again d'Anethan dwelled on Japanese enthusiasm for the war, but also on Japanese adherence to the Geneva Convention pertaining to the humane treatment of the wounded, prisoners of war, and civilians:

I have repeatedly had occasion to point out to Your Excellency how general the enthusiasm for the war is. . . . Hundreds, millions of dollars pour in to further the well-being of the soldiers; and—uniquely, I think, in a war between Asians—the sick and the wounded are not forgotten. The Red Cross, under the high patronage of the Empress, has carried out its admirable work with perfect correctness, that is to say, it extends its solicitude to the wounded enemies as well as to the [wounded] nationals. This circumstance seems quite natural for European nations, but is without precedent in Asia. The manner in which Japan treats the Chinese prisoners and takes care of the wounded would suffice to rank her with the civilized nations.[17]

On November 6, d'Anethan reported that China had been invaded from two directions. Three Japanese Army Corps were pushing overland, across the Yalu into Manchuria, and from the sea, into the Liaotung Peninsula. They met little or no resistance. The second Corps, for example, landed without loss of a single soldier. Writing that the Japanese "made war like a civilized nation," assuming the administration of the

c

conquered territory, and looking after the welfare of the people, d'Anethan mused:

The rapidity and sureness of Japanese movements and their skillful strategic plans no longer allow any doubt about the outcome of the war. China is at their mercy.

Where are the millions of soldiers that the colossus could put in the field? Until now China has assembled only some 40,000 men, who are but bands of undisciplined bandits. The extent of the terrible corruption of the whole Chinese system that is laid bare is incredible. Among the large booty taken by the Japanese army, there are many excellent cannons and rifles of all makes and calibers. The unfortunate Chinese had not been able to use them for lack of the right ammunition. Certain regiments are still armed with bows and arrows. Amid the trophies brought from the battlefield, I saw yesterday enormous, formidable-looking sabers, whose blades were made of tin. Veritable harlequin's bats! There were also cannon balls of painted mortar!

The origin of these new-type cannon balls is amusing and well illustrates the character of the Chinese administration. Several months ago a great Mandarin was to inspect a Tientsin depot, containing on paper I do not know how many thousands of cannon balls. But the depot was empty. What to do? Time was short; the inspection was scheduled for the following week. The Mandarin in charge of that department was not embarrassed by such a trifle. He had the brilliant idea of making the required number of cannon balls out of mortar, and had them covered with a good layer of black paint. On the appointed day the inspector would have to marvel at the admirable order which reigned in the depot!

There is no commissariat to supply the armies in the field, which live by pillage and marauding. Doctors are likewise unknown in the Chinese army. How great is thus the astonishment of those poor devils who fall into the hands of the Japanese and find themselves treated with kindness and nursed in hospitals, where they enjoy a well-being of which they have never dreamed.

During the battle of Pyongyang several wounded Japanese were

surprised by the Chinese. Their corpses were found atrociously mu-
tilated. Two young Japanese, arrested in Shanghai, and accused of
espionage, were put to death after terrible torture. What a contrast
here. Chinese who have remained in Japan attend to their affairs
in complete safety. No one molests or insults them, and the author-
ities guarantee them absolute protection of property and person.

I often call attention to the humanitarian principles which re-
gulate the conduct of the Japanese. This proves that moral progress
has kept abreast with political and material changes.[18]

Chinese efforts to end the war through European mediation
were thwarted by Japan, which insisted on direct negotiation.
Foreign Minister Viscount Mutsu assured d'Anethan, however, that Japanese demands would be reasonable. The excessive weakening of China or the toppling of its regime were
not in the interest of Japan. As Mutsu confided to d'Anethan:

The Imperial Government will be conciliatory and moderate. It
does not want to reduce the strength of China to the point of making
her immense territories too easy a prey for Franco-English-Russian
covetousness. The power of the monarchy has been greatly shaken.
There is danger of insurrections as terrible as those of the Taipings.
In the event of unpredictable revolutionary turmoil, Japan would
have to prolong the occupation of the territory and would no longer
have [legally] constituted authorities with whom to negotiate.

Conveying Mutsu's assurances d'Anethan commented:

I think one can trust the declarations of Viscount Mutsu, when
he assures us that Japan will not seek to take excessive advantage of
her victories and that she fears a change in dynasty and the dis-
memberment of China. The statesmen in power today are as prudent
as they are able, and are afraid of too great an increase in the in-
fluence and power of the European nations, which are ready to
profit from the break-up of China. But to what extent will Japan
be able to control events? Will she be able to move skillfully enough
not to become involved with one of the three rival Powers whose
possessions touch China?

Meanwhile England, France and Russia are reinforcing their squadrons enormously. The garrison of Hong Kong has been augmented by 10,000 Indian troops; the Russians are massing forces on the borders of Manchuria. These three Powers make claims on China and demand satisfaction—Russia for the incursions of Chinese bandits into Russian territory, France for the murder of a missionary in Korea and the abduction of "des Dames du Chaillet" [ladies of easy virtue], and England for the arbitrary removal of Japanese from a warship flying the British flag.[19]

In November, the Japanese took Port Arthur. D'Anethan described the magnitude of the achievement:

This fortress is fortified according to all the rules of modern military science and with any enemy other than the Chinese would have been impregnable for many months, and a very long siege would have been necessary. But the Japanese took it in two days. Their losses do not exceed, it appears, 300 dead and wounded. The Chinese have lost more than 3,000 men and 6,000 prisoners. The latter have been freed as there is little to fear from them.[20]

In December, the Japanese Government refused to deal with a German, in the service of China, who had been sent with a letter from Li Hung-chang to Count Ito Hirobumi, the Japanese Premier, on the grounds that he was not properly accredited. Nor did Japan prove more receptive to American offers of mediation than she had been to those of the European Powers.

Meanwhile the exemplary restraint of the Japanese forces, recently lauded by d'Anethan, snapped in the Port Arthur campaign. D'Anethan reported:

The occupation of Port Arthur by the Japanese army was made conspicuous by the extremely regrettable excesses committed by the coolies (bearers and helpers) against the peaceful inhabitants and even, it is asserted, against women and children.

Without excusing a cruelty so brutal and useless and contrary to the spirit of discipline and humanity which heretofore had charac-

terized the army of invasion, one must attribute it to exasperation aroused by Chinese atrocities. . . .[21]

Later d'Anethan amended the atrocity report, finding it greatly exaggerated. As he wrote toward the end of the month:

The massacres, alleged to have been committed by the Japanese army at Port Arthur, had been exaggerated very much by the newspaper correspondents, especially by the one of the New York World. I saw Viscount de Labry, the French Military Attaché, who had been present. He assured me that the men who had been killed were soldiers who had thrown away their uniforms, and that it was not true that women and children had been put to death. Several days before the taking of Port Arthur nearly all the inhabitants had fled and there remained in town only soldiers and arsenal employees. . . .

The Japanese soldiers, provoked beyond measure by the sight of the mutilated bodies of their comrades, exercised too full a vengeance and shed too much blood, when they could have limited themselves to taking their enemies prisoner. But there is a great difference between such reprehensible yet understandable reprisals and the atrocious massacres about which Your Excellency will read in the newspapers.

I bring this to your attention, because it would be unjust to draw sweeping, unfavorable conclusions concerning Japan on the basis of some excesses, committed under exceptional circumstances.[22]

Chinese efforts to learn through the American Ministers in Peking and Tokyo under what conditions Japan would make peace were fruitless. Japan replied that, if China seriously desired to negotiate, she must accredit an Ambassador of high rank to Japan. If he proved acceptable to Japan, he would be received. Until then the Japanese Government would not divulge its conditions for peace.

Not all Japanese were bent on pursuing the war as long as possible. D'Anethan analyzed the conflicting forces within Japan:

The President of the Council and the members of the Cabinet desire to conclude peace as soon as possible. The military party, on the other hand, wants to go all the way and dictate peace in Peking. It is to be hoped in the interest of Japan that the wise and prudent men who are in power will have enough influence to impose their point of view. They fear the intervention of the great European Powers and understand that if the war is prolonged, England and Russia will appear on the scene. The cordiality which seems to exist today between the cabinets of London and St. Petersburg seriously preoccupies the Government of the Emperor. Until now it counted very much on the rivalry of the great Powers, but it has begun to understand that China is big enough to satisfy many appetites.[23]

The unpredictable consequences of prolonged warfare in the Far East prompted the European powers to renew their diplomatic pressure on Peking and Tokyo to conclude peace. D'Anethan wrote to Count de Mérode Westerloo:

As Your Excellency knows, England and Russia have advised China to make overtures to Japan, and at present the Representatives of the two great Western Powers are actively pressing the Imperial Government not to prolong the war by excessive demands.

Joint action by the Powers will not fail to influence the decisions of the Imperial Government greatly. It counted much on the rivalry of the European Powers, but confronted with the entente which seems to exist today between England and Russia, Count Ito and Viscount Mutsu, the most important members of the Cabinet, understand that in spite of the victories [already] won and yet to be won [by Japan], Europe does not intend to allow Japan alone to decide the fate of China.[24]

In February, 1895, d'Anethan reported that Chinese plenipotentiaries (Chang Ying-huan and Shao Yu-lien) had arrived in Hiroshima and had met with Count Ito and Viscount Mutsu, but had been turned back for lack of satisfactory credentials. In the words of d'Anethan:

The [credentials] of the Chinese Ministers did not indicate the object of their mission. They did not give them the right to conclude any agreement; indeed, they strictly ordered them to act only as intermediaries between the Imperial Government and the Tsungli Yamen (Foreign Office).

Under the circumstances, the Government did not consent to open negotiations. Its refusal was announced the following day in a very short conference. But the Count told the Chinese Plenipotentiaries, that the Imperial Government would be willing to receive duly accredited envoys.

D'Anethan added:

Will the [Japanese] successes at Weihaiwei finally open the eyes of the Cabinet of Peking? The failure of this new mission must show them that it is futile to rely on procrastination or on apparent negotiations. The Japanese are too clever and know too well the bad faith of their enemies to be fooled.[25]

The rebuff of Chang and Shao forced the Chinese Government to appoint a key official. As d'Anethan wrote to Count de Mérode Westerloo:

Your Excellency is no doubt aware that Li Hung-chang has just been named Ambassador. It seems, therefore, that the Chinese Government at last understands that to obtain peace it must choose a negotiator who by his rank and his high position can inspire confidence and whose role will not be confined to acting merely as an intermediary between the Tsungli Yamen and the Cabinet of Tokyo.

The date of departure of the Chinese Ambassador has not yet been set, nor has it been decided where the negotiations will be opened. Thanks to the procrastination of Chinese diplomacy, it would not be surprising if the negotiations would not begin seriously until after the entrance of the Japanese army into Peking.

The Chinese fleet no longer exists. The vessels which were not sunk by the Japanese or destroyed by the Chinese themselves are in the hands of the Japanese. Admiral Ting [Ju-ch'ang], who sur-

rendered them at Weihaiwei, subsequently committed suicide.

Japanese troops are en route to the island of Formosa, which they will take in several days.

At the beginning of March, with the thaw, the advance on Peking can start. In view of the demoralization of the Chinese soldiers, it does not seem that the Japanese need to fear serious resistance. Only when victory has been concluded, and this should occur soon, will the victorious army halt its advance.

Wondering whether Chinese procrastination was due to the hope that Japanese demands would soften with time or due to the expectation of foreign intervention, d'Anethan reverted to the international aspects of the situation:

England, since the outbreak of the war, has shown more sympathy for China than Japan. The English Minister in Tokyo [P. le Poer Trench] is definitely hostile toward Japan. He has . . . doubted too much the real strength of Japan. He believed that her financial resources would be insufficient for the prolongation of the war. Misled by dispatches from Peking, he counted on more effective Chinese resistance. Until now all his predictions have been proven wrong by events. He resents it, and his feelings of personal grudge, acerbated by ill health, reveal themselves not only in his dispatches and reports but also in his talks with the Minister of Foreign Affairs.

The English Admiral, commanding the squadron, on his part shows himself not very friendly toward the Japanese fleet. Repeatedly he has hindered its action. For example, at the beginning of the war he saluted the Japanese flag in the open sea just when several [Japanese] ships were pursuing Chinese vessels; forewarned by the noise of the cannons, the latter were able to take refuge at Weihaiwei.

On another occasion Sir A. Fremantle likewise delayed the action of the Japanese fleet at Port Arthur by placing himself between it and the line of forts and demanding an interview with Admiral Ito. He threatened—but in this he was repudiated by his Govern-

ment—to oppose by force [Japanese] search of English ships suspected of transporting contraband of war.

These actions did not have any unfortunate consequences for the Japanese, but they show a not very friendly attitude on the part of England. If it worsens, it will cause a rapprochement between Japan and Russia, a rapprochement which Japan fears on account of Russian designs on Korea.

The reorganization of the Korean Government proceeds not without difficulty. According to all the reports that we receive, the Japanese are hated in Korea, all sympathy going to China. The Minister of Japan in Seoul nonetheless works with ardor to improve the Government, to build an army, and change the system of taxation; a railway is to be built between Seoul and Gensan. But there is no money in Korea to make reforms. The Japanese Government, therefore, presented a bill to the Chamber of Deputies, authorizing a loan of three million dollars to the Korean Government. The Chamber adopted the project unanimously.

Count Ito and Viscount Mutsu always proclaim very loudly that they do not want to annex Korea, that they desire, on the contrary, to maintain her independence and to make her able to defend herself. It is nonetheless obvious from all their policy toward Korea, that Japan wants to establish herself as protector in imitation of the example of England in Egypt, France in Tunisia and Madagascar and Austria in Bosnia and Herzegovina!

Russia, which does not seem to have embarrassed Japan until now, has assembled a powerful fleet in the Far Eastern seas, the largest that she has ever had in one spot without being at war. The Pacific squadron will soon be reinforced by a part of the Mediterranean one. This deployment of forces must have been made with possible complications regarding Korea in mind, because Japan would not object to Russian rectification of her border with China in Manchuria.

Japan will soon enter the difficult phase of the war, as far as her relations with England and Russia are concerned. As the Government has realized from the beginning, the moment that negotia-

tions with China start, it will have to gain diplomatic victories, not only over China but also over the Western Powers. Understanding fully well that England and Russia will not fail to protect their political and commercial interests in China, the Government nurses the hope, I fear, that it will be able to forestall all intervention, if the peace which it imposes on China will not injure the commercial interests of Europe.

Against China alone, Japan could certainly continue the war for a long time . . . Japan is . . . stronger after seven months of war. The losses in men have been very small. The fleet is larger, and they have captured an enormous amount of war material at Port Arthur and Weihaiwei. The illusions which the Japanese statesmen cherish are thus understandable, but they are dangerous if England and Russia will appear on the scene and force Japan to negotiate peace in a congress, at which the Western Powers will be represented along with the belligerent nations. The idea of a congress greatly preoccupies the Cabinet of Tokyo.[26]

On March 18, d'Anethan reported that Li Hung-chang was expected at Shimonoseki the following day and that, if his credentials gave him the required full powers, negotiations would be opened at Hiroshima. But d'Anethan did not expect quick results:

It is to be feared that negotiations will not proceed quickly. The desire to sign peace only after the taking of Peking has so gripped the spirit of the nation and of the Army that, I fear, the hand of the Government will be forced. It thus makes large preparations with a view to continuing the war.[27]

Li Hung-chang duly arrived with a large retinue and the appropriate credentials. He demanded the conclusion of an armistice. The Japanese countered that China must first agree to the cession of the Kwantung Peninsula and a piece of territory in Southern Manchuria. D'Anethan commented:

Enormous as the concessions exacted from China are, no territory of China proper (that is to say the 18 provinces) is encroached upon. That is the point, I am assured on very good authority, that Li Hung-chang was most concerned about and on which his instructions were uncompromising. . . .

The military party in Japan, as I had the honor to write your Excellency recently, shouts loudly that honor demands the taking of Peking. This is a source of difficulty for the Government. Let us hope in the interest of Japan that the Government, if it obtains all that it demands without inflicting this last humiliation on China, will know how to prevail.[28]

Later d'Anethan learned that Japanese conditions had been still more severe, and that Li had given up the idea of an armistice prior to discussing the peace terms.[29] But that day, as Li was leaving the conference, an incident occured that d'Anethan in spite of his misgivings, had not foreseen. He reported:

Coming out from this conference (on the 24th) Li Hung-chang fell victim to the most criminal attempt on his life. A man by the name of Koyama Rokunosuke fired a pistol at him almost point-blank. The bullet made a deep wound under the eye. Koyama was arrested before he had time to fire a second shot.

It has not yet been possible to extract the bullet. In the opinion of the Japanese doctors and of those in the Ambassador's retinue the wound will close without an extraction being necessary. To-morrow morning, however, the Surgeon [Julius] Scriba, a German professor of great talent, will arrive in Shimonoseki and decide if an operation will be of use. The condition of the patient has been satisfactory up to now.

The indignation caused by this outrage is as profound as it is general. In a proclamation, countersigned by the Ministers, the Emperor has publicly expressed his regrets. The Parliament, the press, and the associations of all Parties have sent thousands of telegrams to convey their condolences. The police force had been strongly reinforced in Shimonoseki, but the precautionary measures had been insufficient. The Government had made the great mistake of not forbidding all traffic on the streets which the Ambassador was to take. Vigilance must have been aroused the more, because on the morning of the assassination attempt six men of suspicious charac- ter, armed with sword-sticks, had been arrested.

The assassin is a fanatic, but not insane. He had premeditated the crime since March 12, the date when he bought a revolver in Yokohama.

It is hoped that recovery will be relatively quick if there will be no complications—a danger always to be feared, especially with an old man of 73. The Viceroy has assured the Japanese Plenipoten- tiaries that he will continue the negotiations as soon as he will recover.[30]

The dastardly deed proved a blessing in disguise for China. Japan agreed to an armistice without the conditions which it had posed earlier. D'Anethan observed:

The Government of the Emperor acted in this case with a cour- tesy which was bound to be appreciated by the European Cabinets. It could not have chosen a better way of alleviating as much as possible the unfortunate impression made by the shameful attempt on the life of the Ambassador of China.[31]

On April 5, d'Anethan reported the Japanese conditions of peace and a fortnight later their acceptance with minor mo- difications. China was to recognize the independence of Korea, pay an indemnity of 200,000,000 taels (nearly 150 million gold dollars) open new ports to foreign trade and cede For- mosa, the adjacent Pescadores islands, and the Kwantung (southern tip of the Liaotung) Peninsula, including Port Arthur, to Japan. D'Anethan commented:

The Imperial Government had to fight against the military party which pressed for the taking of Peking. The outbreak of cholera in the occupied provinces occured just in time to cool the enthusiasm for the continuation of the war, and the wise counsels of Count Ito have prevailed.

It is fully in Japan's interest, anyway, to cease hostilities, and she could never have concluded a more advantageous peace.

One can criticize, and perhaps with reason, that in annexing a part of Chinese territory, Japan loses the advantages of her insular position. As a result of this conquest, we shall see Japan obliged to strengthen her means of defense considerably more and to keep part of her Army on a war footing for a long time. On the other hand, she assures thereby the independence [of Korea] or rather her "protectorate" over Korea, making a land attack against the peninsula extremely difficult. With the network of railroads, which will soon cover the peninsula, she will be able to concentrate troops at any point with a speed that will prevent all aggression.

The telegrams [of the Reuter news agency] announce that the Cabinet of St. Petersburg wants to oppose any annexation of Chinese territory. The Russian Minister—at least so the Vice Minister of Foreign Affairs assures me—has made no declaration in this regard to the Imperial Government and has not protested.

Japan, at any rate, would be able to resist Russia. One must not lose sight of the fact, that the war did not weaken Japan and that her fleet instead of sustaining [losses] has been increased by the ships taken from China and by those bought since the beginning of hostilities. . . .

The news of peace was received with very little enthusiasm in Tokyo. There seems to be a general feeling of great disappointment that Japanese victories were not crowned with a triumphant entry into Peking. The Government was forced to suppress most capital newspapers, nearly all of which contained articles condemning "the weakness of the negotiators." When successes had been announced, the entire city had displayed flags, and joy and animation had lit up all faces. Since yesterday there is not a banner in the streets; all flags were removed at once. [There are] no festivities; no rejoicing! Instead of cheerfulness which would seem natural, [there is] a despondency which assumes the proportions of national mourning.

The victory of Japan necessitated policy reappraisals in many capitals. D'Anethan noted to Count de Mérode Westerloo:

In March of 1894, I had the honor of writing to Your Excellency "that it would not be long before the Great Powers would seek the alliance of Japan and that henceforth one had to count with that country." I did not anticipate at that time, any more than anyone else, the China War and the smashing successes of Japan. But seeing the progress [that Japan had] made in twenty years and the management of [her] finances, considering the valor and the admirable organization of [her] army of more than 300,000 men, and listening to what competent experts told me about the quality of [her] fleet, the skill of [her] commanders, and the perfection of her war preparations, I felt that one had to be blind not to understand that a great Power was coming to the fore in the world.

Events have proven [right] those who believed, on the basis of the ever progressive general policy of the Imperial Government, that the future held a new era in store for Japan. I do not think that I am mistaken if I say, without the ridiculous pretension of being a prophet, that in the future the influence of Japan will be felt beyond her frontiers. Excellent administrators, and methodical, precise, honest, and respectful of authority, the Japanese will bring to China the institutions and statutes of law, police, and finance, which function admirably in their own country. They will spread education to inculcate modern ideas in the young generation.

Your Excellency is in a better position to judge what the attitude of the Great Powers will be in regards to the position acquired by Japan and to know to what extent there exists an entente between the European Cabinets interested in Asian questions. What I have been able to ascertain in Japan is that the Representatives of the Great Powers do not get along well at all and that their actions have no weight whatsoever on the decisions of the Japanese Government.

The Ministers of England, France and Russia have not seen Count Ito or the Minister of Foreign Affairs for the past three weeks. Not one of them has gone to Hiroshima or Shimonoseki.

All the offers of mediation or of good offices of England or of Russia have been politely declined.

The Cabinet of St. James has never, since the beginning of the war, been well informed. Mr. Fraser died in the month of June; his successor [P. le Poer Trench] arrived only in August, having already the germs of the disease which softened [his] brain. The Legation is now run by a Chargé d'Affaires who has not had time to acquaint himself with the situation.

The Minister of France, former doctor and administrator in Tonkin and for some time consul in Calcutta (from where he was recalled after a brief stay at the request of the English Government), is known as a diplomat only for the singular failure of his mission to President ... [José Manuel] Balmaceda in Chili, and does not seem to be held in great respect by the Japanese Government.

As for Mr. Hitrovo, it is difficult to express an opinion about him. His past in Bulgaria and Rumania lead one to believe that he thrives above all on intrigue and political agitation. I do not see that he has found fertile ground for talents of this kind in Japan.

Japanese statesmen are not easily fooled. Although most of my colleagues feel that Russia will obtain from Japan the cession of Gensan (Port Lazareff) in Korea, it is hard for me to believe that the Imperial Government, which fears the proximity of Russia, will consent. It would not have to do so, unless England— and she is not likely to adopt a policy so contrary to her interests— would take a decidedly hostile attitude toward Japan.

Germany does not seek to exercise political influence in Japan. She has only commercial interests there.

The Minister of Italy, Mr. de Martino, who left six weeks ago for service in Brazil, was a restless agent who loved to be in the limelight and wished to involve his Government. But the latter would not be dragged in, and in answer to the numerous dispatches of its Representative merely replied that the state of Italian finances did not allow the very expensive luxury of telegraphic dispatches.

I got these details from Mr. de Martino's successor, the Chargé d'Affaires Count Ercole Orfini, a sensible man who understands that Italy does not have to play the role of a Great Power in Japan, where her commercial interests are minimal.[32]

The Japanese public was not satisfied with the terms of the Treaty of Shimonoseki. Yet even these were to be whittled down by Western intervention. Successful in the field of battle, Japan had not made the necessary diplomatic preparations for securing the fruits of victory. D'Anethan described the impact of the Tripartite Intervention on the already aroused Japanese populace:

The peace treaty concluded at Shimonoseki between Japan and China did not satisfy public opinion. The Army and the Navy, elated by their victories, did not want to stop the triumphal march of the troops until [they had reached] the walls of Peking. The political parties of the opposition were unanimous in most violently attacking the negotiators, Count Ito and Viscount Mutsu. The Prime Minister in particular was the object of reproaches as fiery as they were unjust. The conditions imposed on China gave Japan far more than anyone had a right to expect at the beginning of the hostilities.

Masters of Port Arthur, the Liaotung Peninsula and South Manchuria, the Japanese were in firm control of Korea and posed a constant threat to Peking. In spite of the enormous advantages gained by Japan, the Powers most concerned with Far Eastern politics, did not raise any objections. It would seem, therefore, that the entire nation would have recognized the ability of the negotiators. This was not the case, however. The Emperor had to issue a rescript to calm his people somewhat and to silence the opposition which had manifested itself in the Army.

If the Peace of Shimonoseki had been greeted with so little enthusiasm, Your Excellency can imagine the effect made on Japan by the intervention of Russia, Germany and France and the need to retrocede to China her possessions on the mainland.

The action of Germany took the Government completely by surprise. Her intervention was particularly unexpected as the Cabinet of Berlin had always been lavish with marks of sympathy and the German Minister in Tokyo [Baron von Gutschmid] had telegraphed to Viscount Mutsu his congratulations on the occasion of the glorious peace concluded by Japan! Your Excellency will have been informed by Berlin and the unofficial organs of the press that the Imperial Government [of Germany] had informed the Japanese Government as early as March, that it would oppose the cession of Chinese territory on the mainland. The Representative of the [German] Empire had not been this explicit. He had confined himself to mentioning during a general conversation with the Vice Minister of Foreign Affairs on March 26, that his Government, out of its feelings of friendship for Japan, advised her to be moderate in her demands, because if the Imperial Government [of Japan] sought to annex permanently too much Chinese territory certain Powers would intervene. Baron von Gutschmid said nothing to imply that his Government would be on the side, indeed in the forefront, of these "certain Powers."

The illusion harbored by the [Japanese] Government, that Russia would watch such an enormous increase in the power of Japan without protest appears the more difficult to explain in view of the impressive deployment of Russian naval forces. To understand it, one must not lose sight of the fact, that Japanese statesmen, counting on the rivalry of England and Russia in the Orient, believe that Japan is capable of waging war against Russia alone.

As for France, the Japanese were well informed about the cordial relations which existed between the Republic and Russia, but they did not think that the entente—in the event of complication between the latter Power and Japan—would extend to military cooperation.

Be that as it may, the combined action of the Representatives of the new and unexpected Triple Alliance and the strong tone used by them, especially by the Representative of Germany, have deeply

D

impressed the [Japanese] Government, which realized that resistance would have been foolhardy.

The foreign intervention created the more difficulties for the Government by coming only after the signing of the peace [treaty], when the Emperor had already proclaimed it and in letters, made public, had expressed his satisfaction to his Ministers. Under the circumstances it was twice as hard for the Sovereign to state in a new rescript "His intention to accept the friendly *counsels of the Powers."*

The conditions of peace, presented to Li Hung-chang, had been telegraphed by him to Peking and from there to the Great Powers. It would have been possible to counsel moderation at that time without wounding the national pride [of Japan] so deeply. Furthermore, the Japanese negotiators—who, as I know from a very good source, were under pressure from the military—would have been in a much stronger position to impose their far more moderate views, namely occupy Port Arthur only until the payment of the war indemnity.

Japan has not yet restored the Liaotung Peninsula. She wants to do so after an arrangement [has been made] directly between the Imperial Government and the Chinese Government following the payment of an indemnity by the latter. The arrangement must be negotiated in China by the Minister of Japan. The Representatives of the three Powers recently asked the Minister of Foreign Affairs again to fix the date of evacuation. The Minister replied that the Government would be disposed to do so under the condition which I have mentioned. The amount demanded will be, I believe, 50,000,000 dollars. This answer has been telegraphed to Berlin, Paris, and St. Petersburg, and my colleagues are waiting for their instructions. The Imperial Government does not expect difficulties with France and Germany regarding the conditions for the "retrocession" of Liaotung.[33]

The three Western powers continued their pressure on Japan. D'Anethan wrote:

The Ministers of Russia, France and Germany have once again approached the Japanese Government concerning the evacuation of the Liaotung Peninsula. Article VI of the Treaty of Shimonoseki stipulates that China will conclude a treaty of commerce with Japan. Negotiations concerning this will begin in Peking. The Imperial Government intended to arrive at an agreement about the return of the territories mentioned in Article II, Section 1 at the same time. It is the object of the latest démarche *of the three Powers to compel the Japanese Government to separate the two negotiations and not to make fulfillment of the promise given to the Powers depend on the conclusion of the treaty of commerce.*

The Japanese Minister in Peking [Otori Keisuke] has been ordered accordingly to open negotiations without delay to determine the conditions of the retrocession [of the Liaotung Peninsula].

The question of the indemnity to be paid by China—and the Far Eastern Triplice does not contest Japan's right to demand financial compensation—will give rise to great difficulties, because the Chinese Government, counting on foreign support, seeks to avoid direct negotiation with Japan. It is the European Powers and not China that have asked the abrogation of Article II section 1 of the Treaty. Japan has yielded to the pressure of these Powers. It is they, therefore, who must intervene to have the commitment, made by the Imperial Government, carried out. China would rather lose the provinces than suffer new financial sacrifices.

Such is the position of the Chinese Government according to information received by the Minister of Foreign Affairs from Peking. If it persists in it, the Powers will have to exert all their influence to compel China to indemnify Japan.

The negotiations threaten to drag out, and the Cabinet of Tokyo seems to me little disposed to hasten them greatly, since it understands that once it will have given up the pawn which it still holds today, it will be in a less strong position to obtain the commercial concessions to which it is entitled by virtue of Article VI of the Peace Treaty.[34]

Public resentment at the surrender of the Japanese Government to Western demands was translated into action. D'Anethan related :

A few days ago the police arrested an individual by the name of Watanabe on the eve of the day when he planned to assassinate Marquis Ito, the Prime Minister. A number of accomplices in the projected outrage are also behind bars. The authorities are very guarded in the information which they give out, and it is not yet possible to know whether it is a matter of a plot, organized merely by some fanatics, or of a conspiracy, concocted by political enemies of the eminent statesman.

As I had the honor to write Your Excellency, the forced retrocession of the territories conquered from China has provoked serious agitation in the country, and the lives of Government leaders, especially of Marquis Ito and of Count Mutsu, are evidently in danger. The precautions taken by the police are evidence of the anxiety which exists in this regard. The Ministers of Russia, Germany, and France also are escorted still constantly by a number of gendarmes.[35]

In November, 1895, China paid Japan an additional 30,000,000 taels (over 20 million gold dollars) in lieu of the Kwantung Peninsula. "This question seems to be settled for the moment," d'Anethan observed. He continued :

The troops of the Imperial Guard, sent to Formosa, have been recalled and will be replaced by a division of 30,000 men, counting soldiers, officers, coolies, and laborers. This impressive force indicates that Japan expects further conflicts before the final subjugation of the island.

Another division of the same size will occupy Weihaiwei until the final payment of the war indemnity. The evacuation of Liaotung begins. It must be carried out in three months. The point which remains very black at the moment is Korea. . . .[36]

CHAPTER TWO

Korea between Russia and Japan

THE cession of Formosa by the Treaty of Shimonoseki did not of itself guarantee Japanese control. The island had yet to be conquered effectively and the semi-savage Hakkas, adept at guerilla warfare, subdued. But Korea, rivalry over which had triggered the Sino-Japanese War, remained Japan's major concern. In the words of d'Anethan:

The difficulties and complications possible, indeed very likely, in Korea demand the full attention and vigilance of the Imperial Government. The policy of reforms, order and civilization, which Japan wants to impose on Korea, finds hardly any supporters in this country, where sympathies remain tied to China. It is fought also by Russia, which flatters and supports the Court and government officials hostile to Japan.

There are between six and seven thousand Japanese troops in Korea. Will Russia not insist soon on the withdrawal of these troops? Hitrovo has not yet made known the views of his Government on this subject, but the Imperial Government expects a step in this direction. According to the Ministers of Germany and France. . .the entente between the three Powers does not provide for possible intervention in the affairs of Korea; Russia alone will have to settle that question with Japan.

The Tripartite Intervention had made it crystal clear that the defeat of China would not leave Japanese ambitions unchecked. The gauntlet dropped by China was taken up by Russia. Japan for whom the war literally had paid, stepped up her military preparations. D'Anethan observed:

The Imperial Government is taking all measures to make Japan a formidable military power on land and on sea, a policy for which it will have full and unanimous support. There is the danger—and it is very serious—that it may be pushed to act too precipitatedly and may not be strong enough to control and restrain the military spirit and bellicose excitement of the nation....

Following the intervention of the Powers to deprive Japan of some of the fruits of her victory, the Government was preoccupied with anti-foreignism. It deemed it wise to protect the foreign Representatives against possible attack or insult by fanatics. Until recently all of us were accompanied by gendarmes wherever we went. During my stay in the University Hospital in June, two agents guarded the door of my room night and day. Now only the Ministers of Russia, France and Germany are escorted in this way.[37]

Unable as yet to challenge Russia, not to mention the triplice, directly, Japan spawned sinister "internal" intrigues in Korea to insure the peninsula's independence from everyone but herself. On October 10, 1895 d'Anethan reported:

Grave news comes to us from Korea. The Queen who, it has been said with reason, is the only "statesman" of Korea, is [reported] to have been assassinated yesterday. She was the leading spirit of the opposition to Japan, finding support in the Representative of Russia.[38c]

A week later d'Anethan was able to elaborate:

On the 8th, at the instigation of the Tai-wön-kun, the old Regent and avowed enemy of the Sovereign, the palace had been invaded and the Queen and her two Ladies-in-Waiting massacred. Among the murderers there were persons wearing Japanese clothes. One seeks to pretend here, that they were Koreans thus disguised "to frighten the palace guards." But according to news received by different Legations, it is evident that a number of Japanese took part in the crime. General Miura [Goro], the [Japanese] Minister Plenipotentiary in Seoul, arrived at the palace a few minutes after the outrage.

The King, who is a complete idiot, on the 11th issued an edict

    c Aleksei Nikolaevich Shpeier.

*which stripped the Queen of her rank and degraded her to the
position of a woman of the lowest class. A second decree stated
that out of consideration for the feelings expressed by the Crown
Prince, the King agreed to leave her the title of Concubine. At the
same time he announced that he would assume henceforth the title
of Emperor instead of King. The ludicrousness of these decrees to
a corpse (the Queen had been dead for three days) shows the utter
abjectness of this barbaric court.*

D'Anethan reflected on the situation:

*These events are very deplorable for Japan and render her
position very difficult, even critical. Without effective occupation
[of Korea] and [without] absolute control of affairs, she cannot make the reforms, which she had loudly advocated. Having
solemnly pledged herself to respect the independence of Korea, the
Imperial Government understands—and should it forget, Russia
is quite ready to remind it—that it alone cannot fulfill the task
which it has undertaken. It wants to attempt an entente with the
Great Powers to guarantee the integrity and neutrality of Korea.*

*If Japan had not been deprived of her conquests in China by the
foreign intervention, she would have become virtual master of
Korea. The situation has changed, and if she does not want to
become embroiled in a conflict with Russia, she must negotiate.
The troubles which one expects in Korea—still greater disorganization than before the beginning of the war (if that is possible). . . ,
hostility and hatred toward Japan, and the threat of a demonstration by the Russian fleet—constitute a constant source of complications, which could very rapidly become most serious.*

*England, no doubt, fears an occupation of Korea by Russia, and
the Government in Tokyo continues to count on the advantages
which it can derive from the rivalry of the two great Asio-European
Powers. But until now Japanese diplomacy has not been fortunate;
it has failed to legalize the military victories. Badly informed
about the intentions of the Powers at the time of the peace negotiations, I fear it still does not appreciate fully the political situation*

*in Europe, and believes too readily that England would be willing
to intervene actively, if Russia set foot in Korea.*

*The prestige of the Government has greatly diminished of late,
and we can expect difficulties in internal politics. If the Government does not find an honorable solution to the Korean question, it
will have trouble remaining in power. There is also the danger
that should the national pride be wounded again by the abandonment of work undertaken in Korea, members of the Cabinet will be
subject to attack by a number of fanatics. In every period of crisis
le crime politique [assassination] has been all too frequent in this
country and, judging by the precautions taken to protect the
Ministers, the authorities are very apprehensive. Fortunately the
police is run admirably, and watches most actively.*[39]

Toward the end of October, d'Anethan supplemented his
previous account of the Japanese involvement in the murder of
the Korean Queen, and dwelled on world reaction:

*We have since learned that General Miura, the Minister of
Japan, knew about the conspiracy against the Palace, and if it
has not yet been proven that he had premeditated the murder of the
Queen, it is admitted that by the presence of his soldiers he had
provoked and aided the attack against the Palace guard. He has
not only been recalled, but relieved of his duties. He will soon be
tried in court.*

*Russia refuses to recognize the new Administration of Korea,
which is virtually in the hands of the Tai-wön-kun, and demands
that actual power be restored to the King. The Russian Representative in Seoul has offered the King a guard to replace the Japanese
guard. The offer has been declined.*

*Count Inouye has left for Seoul again in great haste in order to
give the most formal assurances that the Imperial Government is
sincere in its intentions to respect the independence of Korea and to
explain that General Miura has acted not only in violation of all
his instructions, but also completely contrary to the views of the
Government.*

It is a critical moment for Japan. The Cabinet has decided to abandon Korea and to withdraw its troops. Marquis Ito, the Prime Minister, announced this to the English Minister, who repeated it to me. The Cabinet only waits for assurance that the other Powers will not seek to substitute their control for its own. It must make haste, for however painful the renunciation is to national pride, it is imperative for the preservation of internal peace in Japan that no foreign intervention occur again. Russia is on the point of demanding the withdrawal of the troops.

The Ministers of France and Germany say that they have not been instructed to intervene in the affairs of Korea. But I feel that their utterances must not be taken as more than personal opinions, for I know that their respective Governments do not consult them on the policies to be followed. The Cabinets of Berlin and Paris negotiate with the Cabinet of St. Petersburg, and my two colleagues are not informed of the intentions of their Governments until the moment when they must act with the Russian Minister, who directs them. . . .

A large part of the Russian fleet has left Vladivostok. It is not yet known where it is headed, but presumably for a point not far from the Korean ports.[40]

The Korean outrage had important repercussions within Japan. D'Anethan related:

Information from Korea indicates that the revolution of October 8 in Seoul had been directed by the Minister of Japan. Recalled, as I wrote in my last report, he has been arrested and imprisoned in Hiroshima.

The inquiry continues. Nothing has as yet leaked out about his interrogation. The Legation personnel as well as some forty Japanese, expelled from Korea, are also in prison. The Imperial Government is determined to deal most severely with the instigators of the shameful assassination of the Queen, hoping to prove thereby that it has had no part in the crime.

The position of Marquis Ito is very shaky in the wake of these events. With some reason he is held responsible for the acts which have shamed Japan before the foreigner. I hasten to add, that no one accuses him of having instigated the assassination of the Queen, but one reproaches him for not having foreseen it and for not having taken the necessary measures to make such a scandal impossible. His resignation is demanded quite generally; his prestige has been impaired by the blow dealt to national honor. We can expect his retirement soon.[41]

Within Korea the situation was critical and fraught with danger for all concerned. In the words of d'Anethan:

The King is all but prisoner of the party which, with the aid of the Japanese, took power after the assassination of the Queen. The foreign Representatives in Seoul refuse to recognize this Government and have asked the Japanese Minister to expel the Korean guard from the palace and to replace it with a Japanese guard. The Russian Chargé d'Affaires is most active in pushing this scheme!!

The Imperial Government refuses to take this course until it knows whether the foreign Representatives at Seoul have acted according to their own views or according to instructions from their Governments. As I had the honor to write to Your Excellency, the Cabinet of Tokyo has informed the Great Powers that Korea would be evacuated at the same time as the Chinese territories. In view of this declaration, it is understandable, that it hesitates to take the responsibility for events which may happen in Korea.

To entrust the Palace Guard to the Japanese is to give them virtually control of this unfortunate kingdom. Supported above all by the Russian agent, the proposal arouses, of course, the suspicion of the Imperial Government. It would accept the mandate to maintain order in Korea, if it were conferred upon it by the interested Powers after an agreement between them and itself. But before the return of Count Inouye, who was sent to Seoul as Ambassador, two days hence, no final solution will be reached.

Although we are not directly interested in the Korean question, I take the liberty of writing about it to Your Excellency, because it is the sort of question that can most seriously disturb world peace and, therefore, deserves to be called to the attention of the Government of the King.

English diplomacy has lost considerable prestige in China as a result of the master stroke of Russia, which with French gold presented herself as the friend of the Celestial Empire [which needed money to pay the war indemnity, increased with the retrocession of Liaotung]. She too—judging at least by the attitude of her Minister—seeks to avoid an intervention by Russia in Korea.[42]

The situation in Korea went from bad to worse. D'Anethan related:

The situation in Korea becomes ever more complicated. A new émeute broke out on the 28th. The guard which had been expelled from the palace at the time of the assassination of the Queen in turn tried to drive out the guard which was loyal to the Tai-wön-kun. Among the ringleaders, there was a missionary by the name of Underwood. His wife is a doctor and frequently attended the late Queen. The presence of this individual has no political significance whatsoever. What is more serious, is that several Koreans— Li Han Yo, former Minister of Education, Li In Yo, former Chief of Police, Li Karu Kin and Gen Ko Taku, Commanders of the old Royal Guard of the Queen, and Li Sai Eu, former Minister to the United States—who had taken refuge at the Russian Legation since October 8, headed the conspiracy. This time the Japanese were not involved at all. The palace guard repulsed the assailants.

In Korea the tragic is always mixed with the incredibly grotesque. A royal decree has just restored the Queen to her rights of spouse and her rank of Sovereign! At the same time, her death has been announced only now, and deep, public mourning for one year has been ordered. In view of the idiocy of the King, of the intrigues of the Tai-wön-kun on one hand and of the supporters of the Min

family to which the Queen belonged on the other, of general cor-
ruption, in a word, of the absence of all government, it is obvious
that a foreign intervention must be regarded as imminent.

As I had the honor of writing to Your Excellency in my last
report, Japan draws back and hesitates to take the initiative in
this matter until an understanding with the European Govern-
ments interested [has been reached]. A joint occupation with
Russia does not appeal to her, and the Government fears such a
solution. Nevertheless, the rapid succession of events in Korea,
the constant danger to the King's life and the threat to foreign
interests force the Imperial Government to make a decision soon.
Reluctant as it is to negotiate with Russia only, it will do so if
England will not support it.[43]

D'Anethan had expressed the belief that the situation in
Korea could lead to complications between Russia and Japan.
In February of 1896, he wrote:

A new revolution which has just occured in Korea bears out these
forecasts. The King and the Crown Prince have been refugees in
the Russian Legation since the 11th of this month. On the 10th,
two hundred Russian marines arrived from Chemulpo, and at
dawn the following day the King proceeded to the said Legation.
From there he at once issued the following proclamation:

"Our country is constantly torn by civil wars, incited by crimi-
nals and traitors. We have, therefore, gone in person to the Russian
Legation to put ourselves under the protection of the Ministers of
several Powers. Our beloved subjects, be without fear and attend
to your usual business. We order that U Tons-son, Yi Tu-ho, Yi
Tom-nai, Yichin-ho, Chowi-yon and Kwom Yong-chin be beheaded,
and that their heads be presented to us."

Three of these former Ministers were immediately assassinated.

What will the attitude of Japan be now that the King and the
Korean Government are virtually prisoners of the Russians? Her
position is very critical. [On one hand,] after proclaiming first
that the object of the war was to assure the independence of Korea,

then that she would maintain it and at no cost would tolerate the intervention of another Power, [Japan finds it] very humiliating to have to watch the ruin of these hopes without protesting. On the other hand, the Russian naval forces in the waters of the Far East are so superior to the ones of Japan, that the Imperial Government will hardly dare to resort to arms. It is likely, therefore, that for the moment Japan will have to bow before accomplished fact and for a while leave to Russia the influence which it had vainly sought to exercise in Korea.

The assassination of the Queen in October, organized and executed by the Japanese Minister in Seoul, was not only an atrocious crime but also a colossal mistake from a political point of view, because it alienated from Japan the most influential party which alone possessed some sort of authority.

The trial of General Miura and the officers who took part in the October conspiracy has taken place. Unfortunately for the honor of Japan, all defendants have been acquitted. The judgment is the more iniquitous and scandalous, because it is clearly evident from the grounds which precede the sentence ... that Miura has repeatedly and to a large number of persons given the order to kill the Queen. The acquittal was justified on the grounds that it had not been established sufficiently that it was one of the Japanese defendants who had actually inflicted the death blow.

The King of Korea is a wretched puppet without will, dominated by fear. It is understandable, therefore—particularly since the conduct of the Japanese authorities has justified the most well-founded fears—that Russia was easily able to terrify the King and to show him the danger of relying on the Japanese, who do not shrink from assassinating those who oppose them.

Marquis Ito, President of the Council of Ministers, was getting ready to leave for Russia with Prince Fushimi ... to attend the coronation of the Tsar. But the [real] object of his mission had been the negotiation of an agreement concerning the affairs of Korea directly with the Cabinet of St. Petersburg. The events of the past days took him completely by surprise, and it is not known whether he will

*be able to leave now. The chauvinists are very much overexcited
and everyone feels the humiliation which the new Russian diplomatic victory has inflicted on Japan.*

The moment news of the Russian coup d'état *reached Tokyo, the
opposition delegates laid the question before Parliament. The discussion was brief, as the Emperor immediately suspended the Diet
for ten days.*[44]

In March, d'Anethan reported that Prince Fushimi-no-miya
would represent the Japanese Emperor at the coronation of
Nicholas II, and that Marshal Yamagata Aritomo would go to
Moscow as Ambassdor. He observed:

*Aside from his mission of courtesy, the Ambassador is charged
with negotiating with the Cabinet of St. Petersburg an agreement
that, while guaranteeing the independence of Korea, provides for
joint action by Japan and Russia to assure order in that miserable
kingdom.*

*For the moment the Imperial Government is firmly resolved not
to provoke any conflict with Russia. In view of the indifference
which England seems to show, at least for the present, toward the
Korean question, Japan must be very prudent. She feels still suspended over her head the triple sword that had forced her to evacuate
Liaotung! Russia, meanwhile, lavishes the most pacific assurances
on the Imperial Government, and denies any intention of annexing
Korea.*

*The King is still at the Russian Legation in Seoul. The guard
provided by the warships has increased. A number of Japanese have
been massacred and the telegraph line between Chemulpo and Fusan, which belongs to the Japanese, is constantly cut. At several
points new insurrections have occurred. Russian influence, therefore, is as unable as Japanese influence to restore a semblance of order or of government.*[45]

In June, d'Anethan communicated that Count Mutsu Munemitsu had resigned for reasons of health, and that Marquis

Saionji Kimmochi, then Minister of Education, had succeeded him as Foreign Minister. He reflected:

The retirement of the Count is very regrettable, because he and Marquis Ito were the only members of the Cabinet with some experience in foreign affairs. The full weight of this now falls on the Prime Minister. Absorbed as he is in internal politics, he will find the task very heavy.

Count Mutsu has the honor of having achieved the revision of the treaties with most of the Great Powers. In this he rendered a signal service to his country and has laid the groundwork for a more intimate and friendly understanding with the nations of the West in the future. He was not so successful in his negotiations after the war, and relations between Japan and Russia remain delicate to this day on the subject of Korea.

As Your Excellency is aware, the King of Korea still resides at the Russian Legation in Seoul. His Majesty returned to his palace only once for one hour to receive the Japanese Minister who, promoted to Envoy Extraordinary, had to present new credentials. Russian soldiers, moreover, escorted the King and guarded the palace during the audience.

The Russian Government has loaned 5,000 rifles to the Korean Government. Russian officers will train a guard European-style for the protection of the royal family. These Korean troops will wear Russian uniforms. Coal and supply depots are being set up by Russia at the entrance of the port of Chemulpo.

A few hundred Japanese soldiers are still there for the security of the concessions in the open ports and to defend the telegraph line which connects Seoul and Fusan and which the Koreans continually try to destroy. But for the moment Japanese influence has been lost completely, and Russia is master of the situation. This is understood in Tokyo and bitterly though it is resented, one yields to necessity, wanting to avoid all cause of conflict. For the past two months the efforts of Japanese diplomacy have been confined to seeking to obtain from Russia assurance that she does not intend to annex Korea and at the same time to coming to an understanding about the number of soldiers that the two Powers are to keep in the peninsula. I have been told by the Foreign Office in Tokyo that a provisional accord on these points has been concluded in Seoul between the Chargé d'Affaires of Russia [Karl Ivanovich Waeber] and the Minister of Japan [Komura Jutaro]. We cannot attach much importance to arrangements negotiated in Seoul, however. It is in St. Petersburg that the questions will be really dealt with by Marquis Yamagata, who attended the coronation festivities as Ambassador.

Though serious complications are not to be expected in the near future, one must not lose sight of the fact that large military preparations are being made on both sides. The Japanese Army, which will be reinforced by two divisions, remains on a war footing. Several ships have been ordered in England, France and the United States. Coastal defenses are pushed actively and a number of strategic railroads are being studied. On her part, Russia keeps a squadron of fifteen ships in her waters, among them five of the most powerful of the Russian Navy, [including] the Emperor Nicholas, Pamiat' Azova, Admiral Nakhimov *and* Dimitrii Donskoi. *For the past several months the line from Odessa to Vladivostok transports an enormous number of men and munitions. The garrisons of Vladivostok and of the Amur have been reinforced by more than 70,000 men.*[46]

Meanwhile Japan was plagued with insurrections on Formosa. Her manner of dealing with the natives raised some far-reaching questions. D'Anethan wrote:

Several Japanese posts were surprised and a rather large number of soldiers and officers massacred. The Japanese troops retained the upper hand, however, and the repression was terribly bloody. Whole villages were set on fire and the inhabitants put to death. It is difficult to determine the exact number of victims, since the Government tries to conceal as much as possible the atrocities committed by the army of occupation. But according to information provided in trustworthy private letters, it must be not less than six

or seven thousand. And this figure includes unfortunately many wo-
men and children.

What are the causes of these constant insurrections and of the
opposition that the Japanese encounter in pacifying the island? Ac-
cording to the Government it is merely a struggle with brigands,
half-savages who live in the mountains and whom China had not
been able to subdue. Information drawn from very reliable sources
shows the situation in a very different light. The Japanese are said
to have overcome these brigands easily and in this campaign even to
have received the help of the Chinese population. Instead of gaining
the favor of the population by an intelligent and benevolent admin-
istration, they have done everything to exasperate it. Japan has
been determined, without regard for the manners, customs, pre-
judices, and needs of race and climate, right away, without any
transition, to apply to her new possession the laws and rules which
govern the other parts of the empire. The Japanese, sent to Formosa,
show themselves arbitrary, arrogant and cruel. They have made
themselves so hated, that the entire population revolts, and no sooner
is an insurrection put down in one place than it breaks out in
another.

It is natural that taking possession of the Island of Formosa was
not accomplished without difficulty and that it was necessary to
resort to force to impose order and submission. Have not the Euro-
pean nations encountered the same obstacles and have they not also
had to use arms to secure their conquests in Asia and Africa? Had
Japan thus limited herself to repression that I could call legitimate,
there would be no ground for blame. But unfortunately instead of
seeking to conciliate and appease first and striking only if kind meth-
ods did not succeed, she has from the beginning, without sufficient
provocation, used the greatest severity in her governing of Formosa,
and has instituted a veritable reign of terror.

It is much to be feared from what we already saw in Korea that
the Japanese do not have the desired qualities, or have not yet attain-
ed a high enough degree of civilization to exercise a salutary in-
fluence beyond their own territory.[47]

E

On September 7, d'Anethan reported the resignation of Prime Minister Ito. He explained:

The position of Marquis Ito has been severely shaken for several months. The total defeat of the Government in Korea and the bad administration on Formosa have aroused against him animosity that is as violent as it is desperate. The opposition parties have formed a coalition and have united to a point that his excellency realizes that he will have to retire from power for some time.

His retirement—which will probably be only temporary—is very regrettable under the present circumstances, for it is to be feared that the next cabinet will not show the same prudence. The Marquis, who was not able to impose his moderate views at the time of the conclusion of peace with China, had at least the wisdom, when the European Powers intervened, to recognize that the interest of his country demanded that he yield and that Japan, in spite of her victories, lie low and avoid all cause for conflict with Russia as long as the entente between the Cabinets of St. Petersburg, Berlin, and Paris concerning the questions of the Far East exists.

The self-respect, or more accurately, the national pride continues to be very much hurt by the way Russian influence has supplanted that of Japan in Korea, and it took great moral courage on the part of Marquis Ito to resist a chauvinistic course that could have involved the Empire in the greatest dangers. What is happening in Korea is not of a nature to sooth feelings because, as I have said above, the defeat of Japan is complete and the situation is worse than before the war.

Some months ago the Korean Government granted to Japan the concession of the railroad from Seoul to Fusan; it has just withdrawn it. The telegraph line which Japan laid between those two points and which she owns, is now being contested. All the Koreans suspected of the slightest sympathy toward Japan are thrown in prison, if not put to death. Commercial transactions are hampered as much as possible. The Chinese are returning in great numbers to Korea and commercially have regained their ancient preponderance there.

All these humiliations and vexations are deeply felt here, and it will take much ability, prudence and firmness to prevent a provocative and aggressive policy. To explain the fall of Marquis Ito, one must consider also the difficulties which result, on one hand, from a spirit of reaction that now animates certain influential political groups, and, on the other hand, from an exaggerated confidence in the power of Japan.[48]

Count Matsukata Masayoshi succeeded to the premiership, with Count Okuma Shigenobu assuming the role of Foreign Minister. Okuma had not been in office very long, when he was confronted with an embarrassing incident. D'Anethan confided to de Favereau:

I feel I must inform Your Excellency of an unfortunate and ridiculous incident which just happened in Tokyo and of which Baron von Gutschmid, the Minister of Germany and Dean of the Diplomatic Corps, is the sad hero.

On December 30, two Japanese students, Maeda Masakishi and Arikado Shuji, while walking quietly, were menaced by the Minister with whip lashes from the top of his phaeton, which he was driving himself. One was out of reach, but the other allegedly was severely lashed. Baron von Gutschmid denies that he hit them. He insists he merely touched them lightly with the cracker of the whip for fun. Is it not a singular pastime for a man of the age and position of our colleague thus to tickle the noses of passers-by?

Whatever the frolicsome intentions of Baron von Gutschmid may have been, the students took the pleasantry in very bad part and went immediately to the German Legation to complain. Not admitted, they presented a complaint to the Minister of Foreign Affairs, who likewise held them off. They then addressed themselves to the Police Bureau, which refused to do anything. Determined to receive redress, they wrote to the Prefect of Police and at the same time apprised the press of the affair and interested several members of Parliament in their cause.

For the past ten days the Japanese newspapers have been full of violent and malicious articles against the Representative of Germany, asking that the Government demand his recall. The opposition has gotten hold of this incident and has grossly exaggerated it in order to disparage the Cabinet and especially the Minister of Foreign Affairs. The affair thus has become altogether political and consequently is of interest to us.

A demand for an interpellation, signed by twelve members, has been laid on the table of the House of Representatives. It is worded as follows:

"It seems beyond doubt that on December 30, the Minister of Germany, who was in a carriage, menaced Maeda with his whip, but not reaching him, lashed Arikado. If this is what happened, the Minister was guilty of a criminal act. Since a Foreign Representative cannot be prosecuted in a Japanese court, it is proper that the affair be treated in accordance with international law. What measures has the Government taken?"

The sessions of the Diet having been suspended because of the death of the Empress Dowager, the Government has not yet replied. It would have liked to hush the matter up, but the opposition will not lay down arms soon and will be supported by public opinion.

I shall keep Your Excellency informed of this incident, whose consequences threaten, I fear, to be as unpleasant for the Minister of Germany as for Count Okuma. The Diplomatic Corps can only deplore the ridiculous situation in which its Dean has placed himself.[49]

The matter ended with an apology on the part of the German Minister. Okuma, for all his tact, was determined to uphold the dignity of Japan. As d'Anethan observed on another occasion:

"Asia for the Asiatics," Count Okuma said in times past. If now, that he is in office, he moderates his language, he remains no less eager to increase the prestige and power of his country.

To take the place of a Great Power, Japan does not shrink

from any sacrifice. The enormous sums devoted to the increase of the Army and Navy are the most striking proof of this. At the same time that Japan wants to be a first class military nation, she seeks to develop commercial relations throughout the whole world. The flag of the Rising Sun now waves on all oceans.[50]

In March of 1897, the d'Anethans went on leave.[51] Monsieur E. de Cartier de Marchienne, one of the Belgian Secretaries, remained behind as Chargé d'Affaires. In Europe d'Anethan was offered the post of Lisbon. "He preferred, however, to remain in the absorbing centre of the Far East, so we returned to Japan in December 1897, a few days before Christmas, after nine months very pleasant leave, during which time, after a dangerous operation, d'A.s health was restored," Baroness d'Anethan recorded in her diary.[52]

Prior to his departure from Japan, d'Anethan had transmitted to his Government the text of the two agreements concerning Korea, concluded between Russia and Japan the previous year: the Komura–Waeber accord of May 14, 1896 and the Yamagata–Lobanov convention of June 9.[53] Though the agreements ameliorated some of the issues between the two Powers, the basic conflict remained. Only a few days after d'Anethan had forwarded the documents, E. de Cartier de Marchienne, acting as Chargé d'Affaires, reported home an incident, caused by a group of drunken Japanese soldiers who assaulted the carriage in which the small daughter of the Russian Chargé d'Affaires was riding with her governess, after one of them had been slightly hit by the horses. Tact, restraint and the desire of Russian and Japanese officials not to make an issue of the incident, led to a "prompt and happy solution of the affair," however.[54]

In May 1897, a more serious question affected Russo–Japanese relations: the employment of Russian military instructors in Korea. Reporting the controversy and attempts, once again, to smooth over relations between Russia and Japan, de Cartier noted: "One must remember that the recent Sino-Japanese War was caused by the Korean question. Today it is Russia which occupies the preponderant position that the Celestial Empire enjoyed in Seoul not long ago."[55]

In August, 1897, de Cartier reported that three officers and six noncommissioned officers of the Russian Army had arrived in Seoul "ostensibly as tourists, but actually to serve as military instructors of the guard regiment of the King of Korea." He added:

By a strange coincidence the new Minister of Russia to Tokyo, Baron [Roman Romanovich] de Rosen, who is charged with settling with the Japanese Government the question whether the engagement of Russian officers is contrary to the Lobanov-Yamataga protocol, signed at St. Petersburg in 1896, arrived in Japan several days after the entry of his compatriots in Seoul.

The Japanese press shows itself on the whole rather reserved, and limits itself to deploring what it calls the lack of good faith of Moscovite diplomacy.[56]

It was during d'Anethan's absence also that the annexation of Hawaii was projected by the United States. De Cartier reported in June, that when President William McKinley submitted the annexation treaty to the Senate for ratification, Japan protested against it. She felt that the *status quo* was necessary to maintain the balance of power in the Pacific and that the annexation of the Sandwich Islands (Hawaii) could imperil the interests of Japanese residents.[57]

D'Anethan's dispatches, after his return to Japan in December of 1897, reveal the allaying of Japanese fears and the eventual settlement of the Hawaiian question. In the summer of 1898, the American Congress passed a joint resolution of annexation; it was approved by the President on July 7. On July 27, d'Anethan commented on Japanese reaction:

The annexation of Hawaii by the United States has not aroused any protest from Japan. The Government is satisfied with the assurances of the American Government regarding the safe-keeping of the interests of Japanese subjects and emigrants on the island. The press is unanimous in urging the Government to work in unison with the United States. It is believed in Japan that an agreement with the powerful Republic concerning Far Eastern affairs would greatly assist the protection of Japanese interests in China and would be an effective counterweight to the influence of the European Powers. Japan is particularly concerned with the encroachment of Germany. There is grave apprehension here concerning German plans in the Philippines. If one does not go so far as to fear that Germany will attempt to establish herself in Manila, one is apprehensive lest she obtain naval bases in the islands, which belong to Spain. All the efforts of the Government will be directed toward preventing it, and to succeed in this, it wishes to come to an understanding with England and the United States.

Japan still remembers vividly the retrocession of Liaotung and the Tripartite Intervention, and only looks for a favorable opportunity to take revenge. As the fate in store for the Philippines is as yet very uncertain and America, in spite of her naval victory and numerical superiority . . . experiences great difficulties, the Cabinet of Tokyo has not departed so far from the neutrality which it has pledged. Should a foreign intervention in favor of Spain and against the Americans materialize, however, Japan would immediately extend her support to the United States.[58]

In September of 1898, d'Anethan was to describe the settlement of the Hawaiian question:

On the eve of the annexation of the islands by the United States, the Government of Hawaii paid the sum of 75,000 dollars in gold to the Imperial Government. [The money had been] claimed by the latter as reparations for injuries suffered by Japanese during the past year, when the Hawaiian Authorities had refused to let 1,200 emigrants land. The settlement grew out of an exchange of notes between the Minister of the United

States and the Hawaiian Government [to the effect] that it was the express demand of President McKinley that the affair be settled to the satisfaction of Japan. . . .

The Japanese Government has been criticized rather sharply by the press for the way in which the negotiations were conducted. It is considered humiliating for Japan to have obtained satisfaction only with the help of the United States and that payment thus made is not compensation for an insult, but a "sweet" bestowed from charity. The dignity of Japan has been impaired by this gift of a few dollars. It was a matter of principle; not merely a question of money. One points out also that the Government's policy toward Hawaii was weak and vacillating. When the annexation was seriously discussed, Count Okuma first protested to Washington, that the balance of power would be upset in the Pacific and the peace of the Far East threatened. When, contrary to the treaties, Japanese emigrants were not permitted to land and were forced to return to their country, the Imperial Government sent a warship, thereby giving the impression that it would back up its demands. To what did these protestations and demonstrations lead? To a miserable handful of dollars, paid to facilitate an annexation which was detrimental to Japan. The Government ignores this campaign of the press, and considers the affair ended.

Japanese interests in Hawaii will be safeguarded, and in accordance with an agreement concluded in Washington—the text of which has not yet been published in Japan, however—Japanese immigration will continue to be authorized in conformity with the laws relative to the immigration of Europeans.[59]

The Russian military advisers in Korea had by their mere presence undermined the position of the Matsukata-Okuma cabinet in Japan. As de Cartier de Marchienne had related during d'Anethan's absence:

Public opinion reproaches Count Okuma not without reason for not having kept the brilliant promises which he had made but lately, when becoming Minister of Foreign Affairs. Since he came to power, Japan has seen her influence at the Court of Seoul gradually disappear, while Russia in contrast gained all the ground that she had lost. For the past six weeks Russian officers have been giving instruction to Korean soldiers; yet six months ago the entire Japanese press had declared that if this were to happen, Japan would be justified in regarding it a casus belli *[cause of war]! And now, to crown the disgrace, it is announced that Mr. [Kir Alekseevich] Alekseev is about to be appointed Russian adviser to the Government in Seoul in place of Mr. McLeavy Brown, the present adviser to the Government, who has always shown himself favorable toward the Japanese and who has succeeded in putting Korean finances a little in order. Besides, the probable annexation of the Sandwich Islands by the United States has greatly shaken the popularity of Count Okuma and of the entire Cabinet.*[60]

As expected, the Cabinet fell. After reiterating the factors that had discredited Okuma, de Cartier evaluated the significance of his replacement by Baron Nishi Tokujiro:

The replacement of Count Okuma by Baron Nishi does not necessarily entail a new orientation in Japanese foreign policy. Baron Nishi spent several years in France and Russia, performing his diplomatic duties to everyone's satisfaction. The new Minister is fluent in Russian, and speaks a little French. He has made a good impression on all who have approached him. The Emperor has bestowed the title of Minister of State without portfolio on Count Okuma, and has called on Marquis Hachisuka [Mochiaki] to sit in the Privy Council! In sum, there has been no change in the principles of government, only a change in persons.[61]

De Cartier de Marchienne soon had occasion to observe the reaction of the new Foreign Minister to another slap-in-the-face to Japanese ambitions on the part of Germany. He wrote:

News of the capture of Kiaochow by the German fleet caused the greatest surprise in Japan—surprise that soon gave way to indignation, when it was learned that the occupation might well last longer than had been expected at first. The newspapers observed with bitterness, that it was one of the very Powers whose concerted action had necessitated the retrocession of the Liaotung Peninsula to China, that now seemed to have profited from Japan's political idea of establishing bases on Chinese territory. The press and public opinion generally seem convinced that the action of Germany is the consummation of a long premeditated and cleverly prepared plan. One almost believes in political circles and elsewhere, that before landing her troops Germany had first assured herself of the disposition of the other Great Powers, and that the capture of Kiaochow was but the prelude to the division of the Celestial Empire between Russia, France, Germany and Great Britain! It is with great uneasiness, if not anxiety, that Japan follows the development of the different phases of this question. In spite of the most violent attacks of the opposition press, the Government does not yet seem to have agreed on the attitude to be taken. Ministerial councils are held one after another, almost daily, without visible results. It is very difficult to obtain exact information on this question at the Ministry of Foreign Affairs, because Baron Nishi, under the pretext of illness, receives no one, and his subordinates know nothing or do not want to say anything. The spread of all kinds of alarmist rumors, which in all likelihood have no basis in truth whatsoever, are probably due to this strangely reserved attitude of the Ministry of Foreign Affairs.[62]

The retirement of Count Okuma had entailed the defection of his political supporters, so that Premier Matsukata and his Cabinet had faced a chamber of deputies, almost unanimously hostile. D'Anethan related upon his return from leave:

Public opinion too is against him. He inspires no confidence whatever either in foreign affairs or in domestic affairs. Under the circumstances, there is no doubt that the Emperor will very soon call on other councillors. . . .

The Matsukata Cabinet so far has done nothing; it has taken no decision. Surprised by . . . the action of Germany at Kiaochow and the presence of Russian warships at Port Arthur, it has not been able to decide on the line of policy to adopt.

Internal division and lack of determination had been reflected in a weak foreign policy. But this, d'Anethan felt, was merely a temporary situation. In his words:

The inability of the present Cabinet has no doubt contributed strongly to keeping Japan thus in the background. Under a capable and experienced Government, such as one led by Marquis Ito, there will be less self-effacement of the Empire. If the moment has come when the dismemberment of China must begin, little serious and lasting work will be accomplished if one continues to ignore Japan.

One must not lose sight of the fact that, in spite of financial difficulties, which are temporary and will be surmounted without much trouble by a good Administration, Japan has great resources. Her insular position and the strength of her Army make her territory safe from attack; her fleet, though not yet fully developed, is already very respectable. Since the arrival of the Fuji *and the* Yashima, *the most powerful battleships of the world along with English vessels of the same class (the* Magnificent *and the* Majestic), *the [Japanese] fleet is 104,000 tons strong. In comparison, the foreign squadrons in the Far Eastern seas [total]: England, 67,000 tons; Russia, 47,000 tons; Germany, 34,000 tons; and France, 12,000 tons.*

Japan still occupies Weihaiwei. To be sure, according to the treaty with China, she must withdraw her troops after the payment of the war indemnity, but meanwhile she has sent reinforcements.

Marquis Ito favors a rapprochement between China and Japan. Should this happen, how rapidly will the relations between China and the Powers that want to annex or protect territories or provinces change?

In taking the liberty of making these observations to Your Excellency, I realize that they may not be of immediate importance and that I am little qualified to discuss such complicated problems. If I dare to express an opinion, it is that I am convinced that Japan, in spite of her self-effacement, which is more apparent than real, will yet exercise a preponderant influence in Far Eastern politics.[63]

Decrying the do-nothing policy of the Matsukata Cabinet, d'Anethan looked forward to Marquis Ito's return to office. "Under the present circumstances, so grave for Japan, no statesman can be of greater service than he."[64]

In mid-January, 1898, d'Anethan conveyed a conversation he had had with Ito:

Marquis Ito told me, that he was taking office under difficult conditions at home and abroad. He did not hide that the steadily growing influence of Parliament, the unruliness of the Parties, the freedom or rather excess of freedom of the press, and opposition to levying new taxes would cause him great difficulties. But for the moment, the dominant question is that of foreign policy.

"We do not want to disturb the peace in the Far East, but we shall not let our interests be attacked. The Government is firmly resolved to exercise the legitimate influence to which it is entitled in China."

He added that, according to information from Peking, the Chinese Government had not given to the German Government its consent to the occupation of Kiaochow for a period of ninety-nine years. The arrangement had been concluded in Berlin, but the authorities in Peking had not ratified it. Marquis Ito asserted that Russia had not taken possession of Port Arthur. The Chinese Government has authorized only the temporary presence of a few Russian ships. Japan will oppose with all her might the "exclusive and permanent" establishment of Russia in Korea.

The relations between China and Japan, the Prime Minister tells me, are now very cordial, and all his efforts will be directed toward improving them further. The Chinese Government asked him already several months ago for advice on the most urgent reforms that it would be fitting to introduce in China. He replied:

grant railroad concessions; allow the establishment of banks by foreigners, because the people in China would not have confidence in banknotes issued by a Chinese bank; establish a military academy at Peking; and curtail the unlimited power of present-day Viceroys. There would be many other things to do in China, of course, but Marquis Ito felt, these were the four principal points which must underlie all reorganization of this vast Empire, so shaken today.

The Marquis of Salisbury told him when he passed through London, that he did not believe in the imminent dismemberment of China and that, if other Powers would seek to annex territory, England would oppose it.

D'Anethan reflected on the international situation:

Under the present circumstances, it is natural to hear many rumors about alliances. As Your Excellency will have noticed in Japanese and European newspapers, there is much discussion about an entente between England and Japan.

I do not think that any agreement has yet been made between the Cabinets of St. James and Tokyo. But the relations between them are very intimate, and Her British Majesty's Minister in Tokyo [Sir Ernest Satow] shows himself very favorable toward Japan.

The Imperial Government, as Marquis Ito told me, is eager to do nothing that might disturb the peace. But it prepares itself for any eventuality. The Army is ready to be mobilized; the whole fleet is armed, and an imposing squadron will shortly leave for an unknown destination. The garrison at Weihaiwei has been reinforced, and unless a general coalition against Japan is formed, the Government is fully determined not to abandon this strategic position.[65]

In February, d'Anethan reported that China, which still owed Japan 83,500,000 taels, had requested a delay in payment. He described the reaction of the Japanese Government:

The Imperial Government has refused to grant a delay and

insists on the execution of the Treaty of Shimonoseki. China will probably be able to meet her obligations; if not, new complications may be feared, because the Imperial Government seems to me fully determined not to permit China to elude her obligations.

So far, the Japanese Government acts with restraint, and the Cabinet members keep absolutely secret their attitude toward events in the China theater.[66]

In March of 1898, Russo-Japanese contradictions, dormant for a while, came to the fore again. D'Anethan related:

At the time when Russia had obtained Chinese permission to station warships at Port Arthur, the Minister of Russia had informed the Japanese Government of the Chinese concession, adding that the occupation would be only temporary. The [Japanese] Government at that time replied simply that it took note of the Russian declaration.

Today we learn from Peking, that Russia asks for the cession of Port Arthur and of Talien-wan, as well as for a part of Manchuria, for a period of ninety-nine years. She wants, furthermore, the preferential right to build a railroad which would lead to Port Arthur. The Russian demand is very pressing and even threatening; if our information from Peking is correct, she is giving China only until the 26th of this month to make a decision.

This news has aroused great excitement in Japan. The Government seems inclined to shed the restraint which it had imposed on itself until now. It [does] not [want] to remain a stranger to the negotiations under way in St. Petersburg concerning the occupation of the territories which it had conquered by arms and which it had been forced to restore in order not to disturb the peace of the Far East.

In Korea the Japanese have succeeded lately in creating difficulties for Russia. After the repeated failure of Japanese diplomacy at Seoul, the Russian Minister had the game in hand, and it appeared that his influence was absolutely dominant. Even the Russian Representative, Mr. [Alexis] de Speyer (recently

*named Minister to Peking), admits [however] that Korea is
recalcitrant. On the 7th of this month, he presented a strange note
[to the Korean Government]:*

*"At the request of the Emperor of Korea Russia has sent army
instructors, a financial adviser and other officials to help and reform the administration of the country. Recently, however, the
Court has shown little inclination to rely on Russia. Does the
Korean Court really believe that it will no longer be necessary to
ask help from Russia? The Minister of Russia demands a categorical reply within twenty-four hours."*

*The following day the Korean Government asked for a delay of
three days for its answer. At a Council of Ministers meeting on the
9th, everyone but Foreign Minister Min Chun Mak agreed to reply by sending back the Russian employees. The Foreign Minister, who is a creature of Russia, has submitted his resignation. The
opinion of his colleagues has prevailed, and a note to this effect has
been addressed to the Russian Minister.*

*While the Ministers deliberated, public meetings were held at
different points in town regarding the position to be taken toward
Russia. The United States Minister in Seoul, Dr. [Horace N.]
Allen, has played an important role in the instigation of these
anti-Russian manifestations. The Consul General of England
has been raised to the rank of Minister Resident.*

*Japan thus is not the only Power interested in the affairs of
Korea. England, furthermore, clearly warned some time ago, that
she intended to maintain her rights in the peninsula. Mr. McLeavy
Brown has been employed for a number of years by the Korean
Government to control the finances. At the instigation of the Russian Minister, the Emperor of Korea wanted to annul the contract
of this Englishman. When this became known, the English Admiral appeared at Chemulpo with six warships ... and Mr. Brown
was kept in his position.*

*For Japan the annexation of Korea by Russia would be the
greatest of dangers, and the Government would not hesitate before any sacrifice to oppose this.*[67]

Two and a half weeks later d'Anethan was able to report that Russia had recalled the officers and employees, whom she had put at the disposal of Korea. Reciting the course of events, he pondered about their implications:

To the dispatch of Mr. de Speyer, which I mentioned in my report, the Government replied ... that thanks to the good counsels of Russia, Korea was now in a position to govern herself and asked that the Russians in her service be relieved of their functions. It added that the Emperor had the intention of sending an Ambassador to St. Petersburg to thank the Tsar.

The Russian Chargé d'Affaires in Seoul answered:

"I acknowledge receipt of the note by which you inform me that Your Sovereign has the intention of sending an Ambassador to St. Petersburg. I have just been ordered by my August Sovereign to let you know that the presence of an Envoy is not at all necessary, and the Russian Government does not desire to receive any thanks. Russia only wishes to offer her friendship, but she never seeks [?]to impose herself on anyone. When your Government asked me to send military instructors and a financial adviser, we acceded to its desire. Now your Government considers the presence of Russians no longer necessary, and you declare that Korea can settle her affairs without the aid of Russia. Russia can only congratulate Korea on having made such great progress in such a short space of time, that she is capable of maintaining her independence without the help of foreigners. I have already given the necessary instructions for our officers and advisers to cease their functions in your service.

(Signed) Speyer."

In Japan this new [Russian] attitude towards Korea is welcomed, and removes at least for the present a dangerous cause of conflict. The Imperial Government has been notified officially of the principal clauses of the Sino-Russian agreement concerning the occupation of Port Arthur and of Talien-wan. The text has never reached it, however, and I gather from the Foreign Office that it will not let its views be known until it is in possession of the document.

For the moment, the Japanese Government shows the greatest prudence. Disconcerted by the rapidity with which Germany and Russia have made China accept their arbitrary demands, misled by the tolerance of England, preoccupied with the difficulties which can still arise next month when the war indemnity payment is [scheduled] to be made, Marquis Ito—the soul of the present Government—has successfully recommended a wait-and-see policy. As far as we can determine here, under the present circumstances Japan will not undertake anything likely to disturb the peace. While ardently continuing to augment her Army and Navy, she will not rush into a foolhardy policy. Excluded from the negotiations that took place in Europe concerning the acquisition or occupation of Chinese territory, she senses her isolation and inability [?] to resist a combination of the European Powers. When Germany acquired Kiaochow Bay, the garrison of Weihaiwei was reinforced, but no new troops are being sent and today Japan keeps only about 4,000 men there. Will Japan be able to conclude an agreement with China, similar to those of Germany and Russia to continue occupation of this post? According to a reliable source, the Government intends to open negotiations with China on this subject.

Will it not be too late and has it not been forestalled by another power? Rather persistent and not unfounded rumors indicate that England will establish herself at Weihaiwei after the payment of the war indemnity to Japan in order to counterbalance to some extent the taking of Port Arthur by Russia.[68]

In May, 1898, d'Anethan sent back the text of a protocol concerning Korea, signed by Foreign Minister Nishi and Baron Rosen in Tokyo on April 25. He commented:

The first article recognizes the sovereignty and independence of Korea. The value of this declaration is not very great, if we judge it by the way in which the Russians and the Japanese have so far acted in Korea.

F

The second article is important. Russia and Japan commit themselves in the future, if Korea wants to receive military instructors and financial advisers, not to take any measures whatever without first coming to a mutual agreement. Russia had not interpreted the convention signed by Prince Lobanov and Marquis Yamagata in this way, when she had eagerly furnished the Emperor of Korea with officers without notifying the Japanese Government and had ignored the latter's protests.

The commercial interests of Japan in Korea are considerable, and a great number of Japanese are established there. It is significant that this should be stated in a diplomatic document, and that Russia pledges not to hinder the development of commercial and industrial enterprises of Japan. Under the present circumstances, when relations between the Powers are strained everywhere, it is a pleasure to find that in regard to Korea the difficulties between Japan and Russia seem to have been removed at least for the moment.

Russo-Japanese relations were not exclusively bilateral. England lurked in the shadows. As d'Anethan noted:

The war indemnity having been paid, the [Japanese] Government is recalling the troops from Weihaiwei. By the end of the month the garrison will have left, and will cede the place to the English. The occupation of this port by England has Japanese approval. It is now known that the Cabinet of St. James had come to an understanding with that of Tokyo beforehand, and the great importance of not leaving Russia sole mistress of the Gulf of Pechili is appreciated. The relations between the two countries are most cordial. No treaty of alliance has been signed nor any definite commitment made by either side—at least, so I believe; the Japanese Ministers are so reserved always, that it is dangerous to make an assertion. But there is the general feeling that Japan and England have so many common interests, that if one or the other is attacked, they will act in concert. The two Governments also seem agreed to work against the dismemberment of China. For this rea-

son Japan has so far not asked to lease a Chinese port. She has confined herself to obtaining merely [the assurance] that China would not cede the province of Fukien to any Power.[69]

In spring of 1898, the molesting of English, American and German subjects by the common people in Kobe prompted over 300 foreign residents to petition d'Anethan to "take such steps with regard to the same as shall seem advisable with a view to having the evils remedied." The residents complained of an "exceedingly hostile" attitude of "the lower classes of the Japanese, especially of the coolie class" and of "unprovoked assaults" and "gross insults." D'Anethan referred the petition, which had been transmitted to him through the Dean of the Consular Corps, to the Ministers of the various countries, as he had not been empowered by them to act on their behalf in this matter.[70] Eventually the Consular Corps in Kobe addressed the local Governor directly. D'Anethan relayed their protest and an English translation of the Governor's reply. Promising to make every effort to prevent future incidents, the Governor wrote:

Recently, as a consequence of the sudden and rapid development of every description of industrial enterprise in this country, ignorant persons of the country have thronged in large numbers to this district, and it is a matter of great regret to me that these persons have been apt to conduct themselves in a rude, insulting and violent way towards foreigners giving rise to frequent trouble whereby a feeling of irritation has been excited. At the same time such conduct on their part is not to be regarded as being necessarily prompted by a spirit of ill will directed solely and exclusively against foreigners; on the contrary instances of the exactly same behaviour by them towards their fellow countrymen are of frequent occurrence.[71]

Within Japan foreign policy was a major issue. During the first session of the Chamber of Deputies the spokesman for the Liberal Party posed five questions to the Government:

1. *What diplomatic action has the Government taken concerning*

the leasing of Kiaochow by Germany and of Port Arthur and of Talien-wan by Russia, and has the Government opened negotiations on this subject with these Powers or other Powers?

2. Is there an exchange of correspondence with England or does there exist an agreement with this Power concerning the cession of Weihaiwei?

3. What measures does the Government intend to take and what will be its attitude toward China to maintain the peace and balance of power in the Far East?

4. What measures will the Government take regarding the outrages committed at Shasi?

5. How does the question of Hawaii stand?

D'Anethan relayed the queries put by the spokesman of the Liberal Party, and continued:

He declared that in posing these questions he did not intend to make a political issue out of the diplomatic question. It was his aim to establish complete harmony between the Government and Parliament regarding the policy to be followed, in view of the very important events now unfolding in the Far East. He stated that the leasing of Kiaochow to Germany was contrary to all international practice, and that Germany had succeeded only because of China's weakness. It was evident from the fact that more than a month had passed between the murder of the German missionaries and the acquiescence of China to the demands of the German Government, that China must have tried everything to reject the claims of Germany. The speaker added that he was inclined to believe that an agreement existed between Germany and Russia concerning the Chinese question as a result of the meeting of Emperor William and Emperor Nicholas last summer.

In England the Government and the nation both were opposed to the occupation of Kiaochow. In view of the opposition manifested in England against the action of Germany in China and the efforts made by China to evade the German demands, Japan should have taken the necessary measures for safeguarding the peace and the balance of power. Had the Government taken such measures? Had it received from Germany notification about the occupation of this port and its opening to foreign trade?

The speaker thought there must have been an agreement between Russia and China concerning the cession of Port Arthur and Ta-lien-wan. What action had the Government taken, when public opinion in England had been so opposed to these cessions? Did the Government dare to remind Russia what she, together with France and Germany, had told Japan in advising her to return the Liao-tung Peninsula to China? The speaker hoped that the Government would not confine itself to responding that it had no knowledge of diplomatic negotiations between Russia and China and that it did not have the opportunity to intervene.

The speaker admitted, that from an economic and financial standpoint the occupation of Weihaiwei was not advantageous; but looked at from a strategic point of view, the question became most important. He wished to know, therefore, whether or not a definite agreement on this subject existed between England and Japan. He concluded by asking, if the Government was determined to preserve the territorial integrity of China. Would it seek to spread civilization in China to this end or did it regard its opposition to the dismemberment of China an impossible task?

To these demands for an explanation by the Government, Mr. Ogaki in the name of the Progressive Party, added four others:

1. When Japan retroceded Liaotung in accordance with the advice of Russia, France and Germany, did she receive from them any assurance that none of them would in the future demand the cession of this territory? If such had been the case, he wanted an explanation.

2. Russia had obtained not only the cession of Port Arthur and of Talien-wan, but other privileges, such as the construction of rail-roads and mining concessions. What did the Government know of these transactions?

3. Germany, France and England also had acquired, or were on the point of acquiring, preferential rights in China. Had the

Government received any information on the nature of these prefer-
ential rights?

4. *In view of the state of current relations between China and the*
European Powers, what measures would the Government take to
maintain the status quo *in the Far East and defend the rights and*
interests of Japan?

As is the custom, the Foreign Minister replied to these questions
in writing. His message . . . is most guarded, and sheds no light on
the policy which the Cabinet intends to follow. He refused to say
one word about the occupation of Kiaochow by Germany. As for
Port Arthur and Talien-wan, the Government states that the
Russian Government notified it of the lease of these two ports and
that Talien-wan would be open to foreign trade. It desired to do
what it could to help China maintain her independence and her
[territorial] integrity. The Minister said that the English Govern-
ment had inquired of him whether the Japanese Government would
oppose the leasing of Weihaiwei [by the British] after the Jap-
anese troops withdrew. Japan had replied, that she had no objec-
tions. . . .

The brevity of Baron Nishi's reply to Parliament indicates
continued caution. The reason for this extreme prudence and the
refusal to publish the text of the note by which the Cabinet of Tokyo
has informed the Cabinet of St. James of its views is difficult to
understand, if it is merely a matter of adhering purely and simply
to the plans of England. There has probably been an exchange of
views to establish that the occupation of Weihaiwei by England
would not hurt Japanese interests and would not hinder, in
certain eventualities, the action of her fleet.

D'Anethan appended to his dispatch the answer of the
Japanese Government. To the five questions raised by the
Liberals, the Government replied:

1. *The Government does not believe that the moment has*
come for giving a fuller response to this question.

2. *The English Government inquired of the Japanese Govern-*

ment whether the latter saw any objection to [Great Britain] leasing Weihaiwei after the evacuation of the Japanese troops, and Japan answered that she did not see any objection to it.

    3. The Government intends to make every effort to preserve the peace and territorial integrity of China.

    4. The Government is presently negotiating with China on the subject.

    5. The Governments of Hawaii and Japan have resolved to submit the question to arbitration by a friendly nation, and the points on which arbitration will bear are now being considered.

To the four questions of Mr. Ogaki, the Government responded:

    1. No assurance was given by the Powers, because circumstances did not permit it at the time.

    2. The Russian Government informed the [Japanese] Government of the cession of Port Arthur and Talien and the opening of Talien to foreign trade. Russia, furthermore, told Japan of her preferential right to construct a branch-line of her Transasiatic Railway to a suitable point on the Liaotung Peninsula.

    3. The information of the Government does not differ appreciably from what has been published in the newspapers. Nevertheless, certain facts have not yet been confirmed.

    4. The Government cannot disclose at present the policy that it deems best to follow in regard to the internal and external affairs and interests of the Empire.[72]

In June, the Government dissolved Parliament over an internal issue. The issue itself was secondary to the basic division between Government and Parliament. D'Anethan reflected:

The perpetual antagonism which exists between Government and Parliament and which is becoming more acute with every session will not cease until the Ministry abandons the present system, that is the Government of the clans. It is not yet prepared

*to do so, and the deplorable conflicts that we witness will be re-
peated every session.*

*The Imperial Diet met for the first time on November 29, 1890.
Since then, there have been six dissolutions. It was only during
the period of the war against China that the sessions took place in
a satisfactory manner, the highly developed patriotism in Japan
silencing all dissent.*[73]

Quoting Marquis Ito's letter of resignation, d'Anethan
reflected on his tenure in office:

*The political conduct of Marquis Ito in the management of the
internal affairs of Japan during his Administration is difficult
to understand. He did not seek to conciliate Parliament, which
at the beginning of the session at least had not shown itself hostile;
instead he offended and threatened it. He reiterated loudly that
the Cabinet was responsible to the Emperor and that it would be
futile for the Chamber to try to impose its views. On the other
hand, as soon as Parliament was dissolved, he sought to form a
Government Party and showed his intention of entering the
scene of political battles.*

*In presenting his resignation to the Emperor, he asked to be
relieved of his titles and ranks. This unusual step seems to indicate
that he wants to abandon the independent position which he has
held towards Parliament up to now. Impressed by the unanimity
with which the press and the political Parties after the dissolution assailed the statesmen in whose hands power has rested al-
ternately for the past 30 years, the Marquis feels that the time
has come when a change is necessary, and that instead of leaving
the direction of Japan's destinies during this period of evolution
to inexperienced men, it is up to him to take leadership of the
movement. . . .*

*The liberal ideas which appear in the press and in the political
world are vigorously fought by the chiefs of the military party.
These, in contrast, relegate parliamentary institutions more and
more to the background, and a number of them even go so far as*

to suggest the suspension of the constitution. In a recent council meeting with the Emperor, attended by several marshals and field officers besides the members of Cabinet, this question was raised.[74]

The Cabinet of Marquis Ito was followed by that of Count Okuma Shigenobu, with Okuma as both Premier and Foreign Minister and Count Itagaki Taisuke as Minister of the Interior. D'Anethan commented:

The accession of this Ministry is a landmark in the political life of Japan. If it maintains itself, it will alter the system of government, followed until today. The change of regime has occured with remarkable suddenness and under conditions which it is difficult to understand. It is Marquis Ito who has advised the Emperor to form a parliamentary ministry and to call Count Okuma to power. The attitude of this illustrious statesman is incomprehensible, when one remembers the way he treated the last Parliament. One could understand his conduct, had he bowed to the wishes of the majority of the Chamber and had he tendered his resignation the day after the vote against the financial projects of the Government he had headed. Instead, he had dissolved Parliament, declaring that he was determined to take drastic measures as often and as long as the deputies offered opposition.

Your Excellency will easily understand also how astonished one is to see him suddenly put himself at the head of a movement, which he has consistently fought. As I have written Your Excellency, he has gone so far as to beseech the Emperor to relieve him of his titles and ranks. His Majesty has refused, however, and he remains Marquis, Grand Order of the Chrysanthemum, and retains the first rank after the Imperial Princes and before the Prime Minister himself.

A few days ago, the Emperor convened a grand council, composed of the principal statesmen and the chiefs of the Army, at the Palace. At this meeting Count Inouye, Marquis Yamagata, Count Matsukata and a number of prominent Japanese expressed the opinion that the Constitution should be suspended for several years. The proposal to touch the Constitution, of which he is the principal author, greatly excited Marquis Ito, and he brusquely broke away from the men with whom he had guided so long the destinies of Japan.

The alliance of Count Okuma and Count Itagaki, heads of the Progressive and Liberal Parties, is as extraordinary as it is unexpected. In view of the relentlessness with which they fought each other for years, it is hard to believe in a long duration of their entente.

Preoccupied with domestic issues, Japan was less active abroad. In the words of d'Anethan:

Public attention is completely absorbed by the internal politics of Japan, so complicated these days, and rather little attention seems to be paid to foreign questions. Count Okuma, who during his previous service in the Ministry stressed the need for an active policy on the part of Japan, today seems much more moderate and understands that it is in the interest of the country to continue the wise and prudent line of his predecessor toward the foreign Powers.[75]

On July 7, 1898, Grand Duke Cyril [Kirill Vladimirovich] of Russia, a junior officer on one of the Russian warships in the Far East, arrived in Tokyo to stay for four days in a palace, put at his disposal by Emperor Meiji. D'Anethan observed:

The visit is not without political significance and the more important because the Emperor has not invited Prince Henry. The Government has on the contrary indicated to the German Minister that it would prefer, that the brother of the Emperor of Germany did not come to Japan. The Grand Master of Ceremonies of the Court, Baron Sannomiya, went to Count de Leyden several days ago to ask him, if His Imperial Highness intended to visit Japan. The Minister had answered that he had no news in this regard. Continuing the conversation, Baron Sannomiya said that in consequence of Germany's intervention after the China War a certain section of the press had published very violent articles against Germany and that at the time of the incident, two [1½] years ago, over the lashing of two students by the German Minister, there had been more agitation. It was to be feared, therefore, that some young people, influenced by these press campaigns, or some rash person would be disrespectful to the Prince. The German Minister, from whom I have these details, told me, that he had strongly advised that Prince Henry did not come to Japan.

The Grand Duke of Russia, on the other hand, will be received with the highest honors. The Russo-Japanese agreement about Korea, concluded under the Ito Ministry has eased relations between the two Governments. As long as Russia does not try to thwart Japanese influence in Korea, the Government will do everything to avoid a conflict until the fleet has been fully armed.

English newspapers have published telegrams from St. Petersburg to the effect that Russia sought to lure Japan into a joint protest against the occupation of the Philippines by the United States. We do not know of any request in this sense by the Russian Minister in Tokyo. Baron Nishi told me the day before he left the Ministry, that he had received no communication on that subject.

After the China War, there had been a movement for Japanese expansion to the Philippines. Count Okuma himself had said one day in a public speech, "that Asia should belong to the Asians and that if Spanish domination ceased in Manila, it would be the duty of Japan to prevent the annexation [of the Philippines] by a European Power." He was not Minister then, and has been more moderate since. I do not think that the Government has the slightest thought of extending the borders of the Empire. When the time will come for changing the map of the Far East, Japan will establish her sphere of influence in Korea and in Fukien Province in China, which she needs to defend the Island of Formosa. The Japanese Government would view without fear the

annexation of the Philippines by the United States; it would
fear annexation by one of the European Great Powers.

Japan has observed absolute neutrality so far, but she is sym-
pathetic towards America. This is shown in the difference with
which the idea of the annexation of Hawaii by the United States
is welcomed today.

There are only two Japanese warships in Manila, whereas the
greater part of the German squadron is assembled there. This
deployment of German forces has aroused concern in Japan; it
seems quite considerable, if it is intended merely to protect German
interests and residents.[76]

In a subsequent dispatch d'Anethan reviewed the Grand
Duke's stay in Japan:

The visit of Grand Duke Cyril to the Emperor passed without
incident and was simply one of courtesy. Although no political
question was raised. . . , the presence of a Russian Prince in Tokyo
was not without interest under the present circumstances, if only
as a manifestation of normal relations between Russia and
Japan.

His Imperial Highness received the Japanese Ministers and
the Heads of Missions. We were introduced to him separately by
the Russian Minister in order of precedence. The following day
the Prince left his card with the Diplomatic Corps. He acted the
same way toward the Prime Minister.

The Government was very anxious during the Grand Duke's
sojourn, and increased precautions to assure his safety. All the
police of Tokyo and numerous corps of gendarmes protected the
road which the Prince followed. Apprehension was the more
acute, as strange rumors circulated among the public about the
possibility of an attempt on his life. There was even a rumor that
opponents of the Government wanted to incite a hostile demon-
stration to embarrass the Cabinet. Fortunately the measures
taken were effective, and no disagreeable incident occurred. After
the official visit in Tokyo, the Prince went aboard his vessel at

Yokohama and remained there for several days. He then left for Kobe and visited Kyoto.[77]

Toward the end of July, d'Anethan wrote to the Belgian Foreign Minister about Marquis Ito's concentration on foreign affairs and about political changes within Japan:

Marquis Ito is going to Korea and China. For the moment, as a result of his strange attitude in leaving office, he must stay away from the controversies of domestic politics, but he can render great service to his country abroad. He wants to familiarize himself with the situation in Peking and. . .strengthen the bonds of friendship between the two countries. As I had the honor of writing you in January, he believes it to be in the interest of Japan to draw closer to China and to support her; he also sees the need for reforms in that vast empire, which is falling to pieces. He will try to shake the Chinese out of their apathy and torpor. During his short Administration he succeeded in establishing excellent relations between Peking and Tokyo, which his successor is fully determined to preserve. The mission entrusted to Marquis Ito is the best proof thereof.

While the present government is prudent and wise in its foreign policy, the same cannot be said of its conduct of internal affairs. In an effort to secure the cooperation of supporters in the Diet, it throws the whole Administration into confusion, and gives employment and positions to political friends. Except occasionally in the case of Prefects and Vice-Ministers, officials did not change with different administrations; today the Government is introducing the system followed in the United States. The result will be disastrous, because it will inevitably entail corruption. No longer assured of an independent position, but exposed to all the risks of political combinations, Japanese officials will have to draw the greatest profit from the positions which they will hold only for a certain time.

I believe, there soon will be a reaction against this movement of democratic tendencies. The Army chiefs are very apprehensive

*about the new form of government, which will be responsible to
Parliament. They do not yet show their opposition, because . . . the
Ministers of War and Navy consider themselves independent of the
Cabinet. This anomalous situation cannot last, and conflicts will
arise at the slightest pretext.*

*Among the police, and this is very serious, a hostile tendency
toward the new order of things is apparent. The chief of police,
Baron Sonoda, a very esteemed and very influencial man, was
dismissed recently. He deserved it, for he had made a very violent
speech against the members of the Cabinet to the inspectors under
his command, going so far as to incite them to insubordination.*[78]

In the summer of 1898, Tsar Nicholas II invited the Powers,
including Japan, to participate in a conference to limit armaments. D'Anethan conveyed the reaction of the Japanese
Foreign Minister:

*Count Okuma told me that the Government has not yet replied,
and that it was making inquiries about the reception which the
Russian proposal had received in Europe. It is the impression of
the Foreign Minister, that the projected conference has little
chance of obtaining any practical result. On the basis of information
from Japanese diplomatic agents, Count Okuma is inclined to
believe, that Russia had come to an agreement only with Germany
before sending out invitations to the conference.*

*The negotiations that will take place in Paris to settle the fate
of the Philippines disturb the Imperial Government greatly. It
tries to obtain the [promise], that should the United States not
keep possession of these islands, they would be put under the protection of Japan, England and the United States. It has approached
London and Washington about this.*[79]

Three weeks later, d'Anethan reported the official response
of the Imperial Government to the Tsar's invitation. He
wrote:

*In reply to the disarmament proposal, made by the Emperor
of Russia, the Japanese Government declared that, "the Govern-*

ment of His Majesty was in sympathy with the Tsar's proposal, which was designed to preserve peace and to secure the happiness of humanity. It admired the benevolent and generous intentions of the Tsar."

If a conference will be held to discuss the question raised by the Russian Emperor, the Japanese Government will not fail to be represented, happy to seize the occasion to sit in a meeting of European Powers. Government circles and the press are rather skeptical about the practical results which the projects of the Russian Emperor can bring. Japan will not support any measure that would oblige her to reduce or limit her land and sea forces.

In spite of the rather difficult present financial situation, the military and naval budgets have not been cut. On the contrary, the Government does all it can to hasten the construction of ships in England, and has placed large orders for cannons in Germany and France.[80]

In March of 1899, d'Anethan assured his Government that Japan would participate in the arms-limitation conference:

The Imperial Government will not fail to be represented at the conference. Viscount Aoki told me that he will send at least two delegates, one of whom will be one of the Representatives accredited in Europe. Mr. Motono [Ichiro], the Minister at our Court, will probably be the diplomat selected. On the basis of reports from Europe, Viscount Aoki does not believe that the Conference will have practical results. He finds it difficult to understand, in view of the activity of all the Great Powers, including Russia, to increase their land and sea forces, how one will succeed in limiting armaments.

According to Viscount Aoki, a principal obstacle to the Powers' commitment in this regard lies in their inability to control the military forces of Russia. In that vast empire, closed to foreigners in the Asiatic regions, where there is no parliament, [no] freedom of the press, [and no] budget with exact and convenient figures for verifying the state of the Army, Viscount Aoki adds, how will one be able to make sure that the Tsar abides scrupulously by the rules which he proposes to the other nations?

The Japanese Army is so inferior in numbers compared to the armies of the Powers whose size and population do not exceed those of Japan, that there will be no question of limiting her or of making her subscribe to any agreement that would weaken her action. Nonetheless, the Imperial Government will voice its adherence to humanitarian measures for ameliorating the horrors of war. The respect shown by Japan during the war against China for the stipulations of the Geneva Convention and the establishment of the admirably organized Red Cross Society, are sufficient proof of Japan's desire to rank with the most civilized nations. . . .

I shall take great care to continue keeping Your Excellency informed of the appraisals that I shall hear of the Tsar's proposal. The press hardly deals with the question now. When it does make allusions to it occasionally, it is very much with doubt and skepticism.[81]

From June 11 to September 16, 1898, China was in the throes of "the Hundred Days' Reform." The attempts of Emperor Kuang-hsü and his young advisers, notably K'ang Yu-wei, to transform China into a modern state were cut short, however, by a *coup d'état.* In a lengthy dispatch d'Anethan reviewed Japanese policy and developments within China:

On several occasions I have had the opportunity to point out to Your Excellency, that Japan's policy sought to establish friendly relations with China and to help her maintain her independence by encouraging indispensable reforms in the system of Government, the Army and education. Marquis Ito inaugurated this policy, and his successor adhered to it. The recent mission of the eminent statesman [Ito] to China takes on particular interest because of the grave events which have just occurred in Peking.

The Foreign Minister told me that the Marquis was received by the Emperor and the Government with great honors. At the audience which the Emperor granted him on the 18th, he told of his desire to continue in the path of the reforms which he had just inaugurated, spoke in very flattering terms of Japan, and asked the Marquis to reply in writing to the questions which he would pose to him.

The radical measures which the Emperor decreed encountered the most vigorous opposition of the Manchu Ministers. With the aid of Li Hung-chang, [who was] incensed at having been pensioned off, they made the coup d'état *which has put the Empress in power. . . .*

Count Okuma does not think that the taking of power by the Empress will be the signal for extreme reaction in China, nor that the friendly relations with Japan will suffer from it. Wanting to go fast, the advisers of the Emperor had attempted too radical a change without sufficient preparation. While encouraging progress, the Japanese Representative at Peking had always counselled prudence too. The Japanese Government has urged the Chinese Government to begin with a system of education more suitable to modern ideas, and this suggestion has been adopted. A thousand Chinese students are to come to Japan to study. One hundred young men, chosen by Chang Chih-tung, the Viceroy of Hupeh, and fifty from the Province of Hunan will arrive soon. For the time being, Japan will not send officers or military advisers, but professors and engineers.

His Excellency does not believe that the coup d'état was provoked by any European Power. Chang Yin-yuen [Yin-huan], who was arrested and condemned to death, has been pardoned at the insistence of Japan and the Minister of Great Britain [Sir Claude MacDonald]. K'ang Yu-wei, the apostle of the reforms in China, who has escaped from Peking, is on board the English warship Esk, *which gave him asylum by order of Sir C. MacDonald. One thinks highly in Japan of the talents of K'ang Yu-wei and of the influence that he is yet to exercise in China. He has established a school in Yokohama. It is directed by one of his followers and is frequented by a rather large number of Chinese.*

Marquis Ito expects to leave Peking shortly. Before returning

G

to Japan he will go up the Yangtze again and will visit Chang Chih-tung at Hankow. A Mr. Okuzo [?], a member of Parliament, will accompany Marquis Ito on his trip. In a communication to a Tokyo newspaper, he asserts that Li Hung-chang said to the Japanese Minister: "Our Emperor is seriously engaged in administrative reforms and spares no effort in improving the condition of the country. He willingly consults those whose opinion may be useful to him. One talks here of asking you to become our Prime Minister and of entrusting you with the task of transforming our national policy." Mr. Okuzo is well known and one believes what he reports. At the same time, however, the remarks attributed to Li are regarded as an irony on his part or as exaggerated flattery!

The reception, accorded to Marquis Ito in Peking by the influential men of all parties, seems to justify the confidence of Count Okuma in the preservation of good relations between the two countries and the desire of China to lean on Japan.

Japan evidently seeks to preserve the independence of China as long as possible and to halt the partition of the empire between the European Powers. In this, her interests seem to merge with those of England. There has not yet been an understanding between the two Governments, however, on the means to be employed, if necessary, to back the policy of consolidating the Chinese Empire.

If it seeks to propagate progressive ideas in China by peaceful means, the Japanese Government does not conceal, however, that the task is bristling with difficulties and may even be impossible. The rivalries of the Western Powers threaten to precipitate a crisis. Japan will then have to make her voice heard. She does not want to give rise to complications. She has conducted herself with prudent restraint since the war, but will be ready, if her interests are ignored, to claim energetically the share that she considers should revert to her in the settlement of the Chinese question.[82]

A month later d'Anethan wrote another long dispatch in which he examined developments in China and Japan:

The opinion which Count Okuma expressed, and which I conveyed to Your Excellency in my report of September 29, "that the taking of power by the Empress will not be the signal for extreme reaction in China" has not been confirmed by events. The Japanese Government, which wants to use all its influence to encourage and support the reform party in China, is aroused by the violent and bloody measures taken by the Empress against the men, ready to set out on the road to progress.

As Japanese have been insulted and mistreated, the Government has followed the example of the European Powers and sent 30 marines to Peking. Absent for the past several months, the Japanese Minister is returning to his post with orders to demand an immediate audience with the Emperor and to assure him of the sympathies of Japan. Will he arrive in time? According to news from Peking, the Emperor is already on the verge of being dethroned.

The Cabinet is strongly attacked in the press on the grounds that its foreign policy is hesitant and timid. It is urged to come to an agreement with England and to assert more energetically its intention to prevent the dismemberment of the Chinese Empire. These attacks are unjust, for the Government is prudent not to precipitate a crisis, liable to bring results contrary to the interests of Japan. . . .

The opposition that the Government encounters because of its domestic policy is better founded. The Cabinet is weak and entirely absorbed in petty questions of local interests and individuals. It seeks to gain supporters by giving politicians seats and positions to the detriment of the good administration of the country. Thus its position is shaky, and I expect imminent and important Cabinet changes.

The politicians who represent the clans, that is to say those who have ruled for the past thirty years, do not want to submit to the new and excessively democratic liberal regime, inaugurated

*by Count Okuma and Count Itagaki. The army supports them,
and they always gain the sympathy of the Emperor. The House
of Peers is getting ready to lead a very active campaign against
the Cabinet in the next session.*

*In spite of Marquis Ito's resignation and his energetic declara-
tions that he was renouncing office and honors for ever, it is probable that we shall soon see him take up the reins of government
again. A serious crisis can thus be avoided in Japan. But the
Marquis should not delay in making his influence felt anew and
in replacing the present Administration. Only he will be able to
suspend the Constitution without resorting to violent means.*

*A very dangerous feature of the newspaper polemic against the
Cabinet—and this has never happened before—is that the person
of the Emperor is frequently discussed. So far there has been no
attack against His Majesty. One speaks of him only with the most
profound respect. But one accuses the Cabinet of seeking to diminish
the prestige of the Crown, and one depicts it as not having the
confidence of the Sovereign. It is out of a feeling of loyalty that
one thus alludes to the Throne. It is nonetheless very dangerous
to spread the idea that a Cabinet is imposed on the Emperor. When
the present Cabinet was formed, I had the honor of reporting to
Your Excellency how serious all encroachment on the rights and
prerogative of the Emperor would be for this country. This feeling
is shared by all the ruling classes and by the Army, which will
oppose, if necessary by force, the excessively democratic liberalism
of the Government.*

*A speech by the Minister of Education [Ozaki Yukio] on the
need of introducing certain reforms in the system of youth education has produced a great sensation. The Minister uttered the
phrase: "If a thousand years from now, a republic may perhaps
be established in Japan." These words have aroused general
indignation and, although the speech as a whole was not republican,
have greatly harmed the Cabinet. To admit even for so distant a
future the mere possibility of a change in regime is considered as a
crime of lese majesty.*[83]

As d'Anethan had predicted, the Okuma-Itagaki cabinet did not last long. Reporting its fall, he wrote to de Favereau on November 2:

The Okuma–Itagaki Cabinet lasted for four months, and during this period its work was absolutely fruitless. The members of the Cabinet could not agree on any of the important questions which merited the full attention of the Government, such as balancing the budget and a definite and determined foreign policy.

As I wrote you in my last report, personal questions were the only concern of the Cabinet. There was a mad scramble for administrative and governmental posts and as it was not possible to satisfy equally the two Parties represented in the Government, the crisis exploded even before the meeting of the Parliament. It was precipitated by the resignation of the Minister of Education who, as I wrote you recently, had uttered a phrase, regarded as revolutionary, concerning the possible eventuality a thousand years hence of the advent of a republic in Japan.

Count Itagaki wanted the immediate dismissal of this Minister. Count Okuma, on the other hand, supported him. The Emperor cut short the dispute by exacting the resignation of the Minister of Education. Count Okuma was obliged to yield, but at the same time, without the knowledge of his colleagues of the Itagaki Party, submitted the nomination of Mr. Ozaki's successor for the Emperor's signature. Resenting the irregularity of this procedure, Count Itagaki and his liberal colleagues offered their resignation. . . . The Emperor at first invited the Count to withdraw his resignation. Understanding that he no longer had the confidence of His Majesty, Count Okuma then also asked to be relieved of his duties.[84]

Marshal Yamagata succeeded Okuma as Premier. Party government was pushed aside. D'Anethan reflected:

Of the nine Ministries which form the Cabinet, five are entrusted to Generals and Admirals, all of whom did not hide during the past few months their opposition to the liberal regime that the last Cabinet had wanted to inaugurate. Viscount Aoki and Count Matsukata also believe that the time has not yet come for Japan to adopt a parliamentary regime, which would make the life of the Cabinet depend on the vote of the Houses. The present Cabinet does not want to be the servant of any Party. It is responsible only to the Emperor and not concerned with the Houses.

Parliament has assembled and is electing committees. It will be opened by the Emperor in a few days. There is every reason to believe that the Representatives, with an immense majority, will pass a noconfidence vote as early as the first meeting. Immediately thereafter the House will be dissolved.

What will the Cabinet do then? It can make a new appeal to the country and for the last time try to form a House, which would not be concerned solely with the overthrow of the Government. Experience shows that there is little chance of realizing this hope. Your Excellency remembers how ephemeral the Cabinets have been during the past ten years, and how Marquis Ito as well as Count Matsukata and Count Okuma failed miserably to establish some sort of harmony between the parliamentary and executive branches. It seems, therefore, that the present Cabinet, if it acts in accordance with the principles which everyone of its members constantly proclaims, will suspend the Constitution. If it will not do so, the prestige of the Emperor will emerge diminished from this last crisis.

The Emperor has actually demonstrated a great deal of decision, and has openly shown his sympathy for the Party which wants to preserve the government of the clans backed by the Army. . . . The policy of the new Cabinet must be formed without delay, because it is dangerous to allow much longer the agitation, incited in the meetings and gatherings and spread by the press. . . . The press in general receives the Yamagata Cabinet with great disfavor. . . .

In the interest of the Empire, it is desirable that the Marshal [Yamagata] will have enough vigor to suspend the Constitution. He will do so not without danger, because the ousted politicians and journalists will seek revenge, and it is to be feared that they will not shy away from acts of violence and assassination attempts.[85]

Internal division distracted attention from foreign affairs and undermined Japanese strength. Yet when it came to problems of foreign policy, there was far greater unanimity than on domestic issues. In the words of d'Anethan:

The constant disagreements between Parliament and the different Cabinets that have succeeded each other to power during the past decade paralyze the Government in the attainment of progress and internal development as well as in matters of foreign policy.

In view of the daily more serious complications in China, Japan must protect her interests by continuing, indeed by hastening, her defenses, completing her armaments and the construction of warships, ordered in Europe and America. On these points there is no difference of opinion whatsoever between the Parties. All of them are unanimous in wanting Japan powerful and prepared to exercise due influence in the Far East. No voice is ever raised against military expenses. Yet at the same time Parliament after Parliament refuses [to vote] the means that would increase the budgets of the Army and the Navy without harming other works of public interest, both in Japan proper as well as on the Island of Formosa and of Yezo [Hokkaido].

The new Cabinet follows the prudent course of Marquis Ito and of Count Okuma in its relations with the Great Powers of the West. "I state with joy and you can rejoice with me," Marquis Yamagata yesterday told the House, "that the relations of the Empire with the Foreign Powers become more intimate every year and, though the situation in the Far East may be more and more complicated, our relations with these Powers are very peaceful and friendly."

Korea continues to be the scene of grave disorders and the Emperor has requested the help of Japan, Viscount Aoki told me.

His Excellency added, that the Government refused to intervene, as it does not want to raise delicate questions with Russia.

Japan views the annexation of the Philippines by the United States with satisfaction, but fears the acquisition of the Carolines by Germany. She does not deem herself in a position to protest, however. With Viscount Aoki at the [helm of] Foreign Affairs, the domestic policies of Japan will be as conciliatory as possible. His enemies accuse him even of excessive timidity and of a tendency to show himself too submissive to the Foreign Powers.[86]

The resurgence of the anti-reform elements in China and the weakness of this strife-torn country directed attention from Korea to China. D'Anethan forwarded the text of a speech by Marquis Ito. Stating that neither the Army nor the Administration of China were capable of maintaining peace within the Empire, Ito had declared:

Would it be possible under the circumstances for China to preserve her integrity and independence vis-à-vis the Powers, one of which is more aggressive than the other? Given the present state of affairs, I do not hesitate to declare this impossible.

One is justified, therefore, in calling the Far Eastern situation extremely critical. The causes for this situation have not necessarily originated in this hemisphere. Complications in the rest of the world aggravate matters. Look how the repercussions of the Fashoda question are felt in the Far East. Has it not caused the gathering of the English squadron at Weihaiwei? It is conceivable that a new development in the Peking situation might have occurred in consequence of this other complication at a remote point of the globe. China is not even able to control her internal affairs. How can a country, incapable of governing herself, be able to cope with international complications? One must remember meanwhile, that when a country shows herself powerless to introduce reforms at home, other nations may intervene to this end.

Fortunately the disorders in the interior of China at present still are only isolated and not too important. But what would result, if incidents, such as the massacres of missionaries or the destruction of churches, began to prevail in the whole country? When things get that far, the consequences can be most serious.

Moreover, the Powers regard each other with mistrust and each watches the attitude of the other toward China. Let us assume for a moment, that one of the Powers would seize some territory belonging to this vast empire. What would be the consequences? One can say almost with certainty, that in order to maintain the balance of power and also because of mutual jealousy, a general conflagration would probably result. Japan, due to her close relations with China, will be the first to feel the effects of any great change in that empire.

It is absolutely impossible to predict the measures that we would have to take in this case. They will have to meet the needs of the moment. I cannot boast then of being a supporter, at any cost, of the celebrated energetic foreign policy. But one thing is certain. Japan must be ready to protect her rights and interests in case of crisis. To achieve this end, it is evident that every sincere patriot must strive to maintain the national interests in ordinary times.

Not only China, but Korea also finds herself in an extremely difficult situation. It is obvious that if Korea continues her state of permanent revolts, she will end up by losing her independence. Her situation, consequently, is very dangerous. To recapitulate, Gentlemen, let me assure you that the situation of China and the Far East in general is much more critical than the majority of our compatriots think. Other nations regard the situation as very grave. It seems to me that the nations which are far away and are fighting only for personal interests in China devote much more attention to Chinese affairs than the neighboring nations![87]

In January of 1899, Lord Charles Beresford arrived in Japan. Delegated though he was by the English Chamber of Commerce to study commercial and political conditions in China, he aroused in Japan animated discussion regarding the desirability of Anglo-Japanese collaboration. D'Anethan reported

on the visit of Lord Charles Beresford and the speculations
which it stimulated:

*He has received the most enthusiastic welcome, and his presence
under the present circumstances is not without political significance. The honors which have been shown to him are evidence of
[Japanese] sympathy for England and the desire to safeguard
the interests of Japan through an understanding with this Power.*

*Lord Charles has not come on an official mission of the Govern-
ment . . . , but represents, as he told us in a speech . . . , the greatest
power in England, the Association of the Chambers of Commerce.
In China and in Hong Kong he began a campaign for a commercial alliance between England, Germany, the United States
and Japan. He continues it actively in Tokyo, and in a few weeks,
after a brief stay in America, intends to propagate the idea of this
alliance in England, [asserting that it is] necessary for the maintenance of peace in the Far East. Similar declarations made by Mr.
Chamberlain in Birmingham, Manchester and recently in Wakefield, lead one to assume that Lord Charles Beresford is not un-
acquainted with the views or projects of his Government.*

*Yesterday, at a meeting of 500 persons, presided over by Prince
Konoye, the President of the House of Peers, and the President of
the Tokyo Chamber of Commerce, and composed of the most influential members of the governmental, political, and industrial
world, he pointed to the identity of English and Japanese interests and the need for concluding a commercial alliance or—going
already further—an entente to defend the "open door" policy in
China. In view of the need for outlets for her industry in China
and Korea, Japan must watch "with the greatest care what the
other nations are doing, and if these take a preponderant position
and hurt commerce and industry, it is her absolute duty, as is that
of England, to take measures which her interests dictate."*

*Lord Charles Beresford insisted also, that "if the door must re-
main open, the interior of the house must also be kept in order."
Diplomatic declarations, treaties or protocols will not be sufficient
to obtain this result, when other Powers will have formidable*

armies to realize their projects. One must help China to build an Army and a Police, without which there can be no security. He added: "The Japanese understand the Chinese better than does any nation in the world. Japanese officers have told me that the Chinese will make good soldiers. Why don't Japanese officers undertake to organize the Chinese Army on condition that China leaves the door open?"

Lord Charles had long interviews with Viscount Aoki, Marquis Ito and the major statesmen. As he did not speak in the name of the English Government, he conveyed only his personal views, and the Japanese Ministers . . . were rather reserved in what they said. The [Japanese] Government wants to be very prudent and not become involved in an alliance before having very clear-cut and formal assurances of effective support from England.

The idea of an entente with Germany does not inspire confidence. The Government remembers the support given by the Emperor to Russian projects in China after the war, the taking of Kiaochow, and German projects in Shantung Province, which it regards as incompatible with the integrity of China! It fears an agreement between Berlin and St. Petersburg, which would be detrimental to Japan.

The Okuma Cabinet had favored an entente between Japan, England and the United States. Viscount Aoki is less enthusiastic about the growth of American might. He does not believe that the United States which so far has shown herself most protectionist, will extend a liberal regime to her new territories. The question of Hawaii also concerns Japan. The Japanese Minister in Washington is to claim for Japanese subjects living in those islands the [same] rights [as those] accorded to nationals of other countries, rights of which they are deprived, if the laws in force in the United States concerning the yellow race are applied.

Viscount Aoki told me very recently: "It is evident that England and Japan have common interests in the Far East. We can thus act in concord, and it is natural that the question of an alliance between the two countries be often in the press. It is easy to talk of an alliance; it is another thing to conclude one. There is actually no alliance between England and Japan, but the relations which exist between the two countries are such as to render common action not only possible, but necessary under certain circumstances. We both want to preserve in China a market open to commerce and, consequently, to prevent as long as possible the partition [of the country]. We proved after the war, that we were not seeking exclusive benefits, and the new ports, opened by the Treaty of Shimonoseki, are open to all nations."

He does not conceal, however, that the situation of China is most critical, and that he does not believe serious reforms possible. "We must be prepared, therefore, for any eventuality. But before committing ourselves, we must specify exactly under what conditions we will make common cause with a foreign Power." His Excellency added that he [?] did not expect an imminent crisis which would disturb the peace.

Advocates of an alliance with England are enthusiastic about the appeal of Mr. Chamberlain for the cooperation of Japan with Germany and the United States in defense of the "open door" policy. The Japanese Government does not forget that in an earlier statement (the speech at Wakefield), Mr. Chamberlain advocated an understanding between England and Russia concerning the affairs of China. Russia is, of course, the Power that Japan fears. She will not expose herself to a conflict with this Power until she is certain that the negotiations between London and St. Petersburg concerning the Chinese question have failed.

The Japanese Government has just asserted itself in Korea by advancing the sum of 1,800,000 yen to a Japanese syndicate for the repurchase of the railroad from Chemulpo to Seoul from an American.

Lord Charles Beresford no doubt thought to flatter Japanese vanity, when he spoke of entrusting Japan with the mission of reforming the Chinese Army. Judging from the language of the principal newspapers, he was not mistaken. The Government will probably not be opposed to embarking on this road, if it can do so with-

out coming into conflict with the foreign Powers. Several months ago, it made an offer of military instructors to the Chinese Government and invited Chinese to come and study in Japan. Forty young Chinese, among them a grandson of Viceroy Chang Chih-tung, have just arrived with this intention from Wuchang and Nanking. It is said that they have come to study for three years.

Since no general reform is possible in China at the moment, there could actually be a question only of forming several regiments at certain specified points. England has already decided to enlist one thousand men at Weihaiwei, and for this purpose has appointed a commission of English officers and noncommissioned officers. Germany will probably follow this example at Kiaochow.

Japan is in a completely different position, having neither taken nor received lease territory in China. Lord Charles Beresford who, bearing no responsibility, is not afraid to voice the boldest ideas, has tried to persuade Viscount Aoki to take possession of a point in Fukien Province, opposite Formosa.

I think it unlikely that the Government will let itself be drawn into an action which would be so contrary to its former declarations and thus would precipitate a crisis, which her diplomacy tries to avert or at least to defer as much as possible.[88]

Insurrection in the Philippines against American rule had its repercussions in Japan. Rebel agents solicited Japanese support. But Japan turned her back on them,[89] and reciprocated American neutrality during the Sino-Japanese War. Nevertheless, Japan was concerned and not quite sure what to do if the United States annexed the Philippines permanently. D'Anethan observed:

I do not think that the Government has yet decided on a line of conduct. It is difficult for it to do so, because in view of opposition in America itself to the permanent occupation of the Philippines, it does not know what policy the President of the United States will choose to follow.[90]

Overshadowed as the Korean question was at times by

events in China, it kept reasserting itself. In June of 1899, d'Anethan wrote:

The state of anarchy which has prevailed in Korea since the Sino-Japanese War is becoming more critical with every day. Seoul has just been the scene of very serious troubles. A number of dynamite bombs have been thrown near the palace of the Emperor and the homes of the Ministers. These anarchistic outrages have made the more of an impression in Tokyo, because the bombs were made in a house belonging to a Korean refugee in Japan and presently occupied by Japanese. There is a large number of Korean refugees in Japan, and one believes that they are the instigators of the plots against the Emperor and the Government.

An Imperial edict has recently reinstituted the barbaric law of extending to the entire family the punishment inflicted on one of its members. There is much excitement as a result among the political refugees, who have left their parents in Korea.

It is very regrettable that Japanese are involved in these criminal acts. The Government, therefore, wants to take energetic measures to purify the Japanese colony in Seoul. To this end, it has just forbidden Japanese emigration to Korea and has ordered its Minister in Seoul to send back to Japan all individuals, implicated in subversive activities. Humiliating as these measures are to Japanese pride, they are necessary to preserve the influence of Japan in Korea.

One has not forgotten the assassination of the Queen. If it is with bombs that Japan must implant civilization in the peninsula, the Emperor, who lives in constant terror of suffering the fate of the unfortunate Queen, will understandably prefer to seek the support of Russia.[91]

In June of 1899, Prince Henry of Prussia arrived in Tokyo. He had wanted to come the year before, but Japan had deemed it inadvisable then. D'Anethan commented:

The Government did not desire it at that time, fearing that the memory of the German intervention following the Sino-Japanese

War and of the then recent taking of Kiaochow might provoke troublesome incidents. We must believe, therefore, that the relations between Germany and Japan are once again more friendly. . . .

As Germany by her position in Kiaochow and the acquisition of the Carolines is a neighbor of Japan, it is in the interest of both countries to live in harmony. The remarks made by Baron [Bernhard] von Bülow [the German Secretary of State for Foreign Affairs] when he announced the treaty ceding the Carolines have made a good impression in Japan.[92]

In August 1899, the new treaties went into effect. For many years Japan had striven to revise the unequal provisions of the old. Now she joined the world community on a footing of equality. D'Anethan conveyed Japanese feeling on the occasion of the new treaties going into force:

Glorious for Japan, the event was celebrated splendidly in Tokyo and in Yokohama with banquets and reunions, at which foreigners and natives met and mingled with the greatest cordiality.

Your Excellency will read with interest the speeches made by the Ministers and the notables. They reflect the profound joy which the Government and the nation feel at the thought of being treated henceforth on an equal footing by the European Powers. They testify at the same time to the value that the Government attaches to complete harmony between its subjects and the foreigners.[93]

The arrival of a Chinese trade mission aroused much speculation, but d'Anethan did not foresee a basic change in Japanese policy. In his words:

Viscount Aoki does not want to change the political line adopted by Japan toward China. He seeks to preserve the best relations with China, but will not plunge into adventures that would involve Japan in difficulties with the Western Powers.

Contrary to what is believed in certain diplomatic circles in Peking, there neither was nor now is any question of an alliance, by which Japan would commit herself to defend China.[94]

In fall of 1899, Russo-Japanese friction over Korea came to the fore again. D'Anethan related:

Several months ago, a Russian wanted to buy land at Masampo in Korea. The transaction could not be concluded, and a Japanese became the buyer of the land, coveted by the Russian. The diplomatic Representative of Russia at Seoul protested against the acquisition and asked the Government to forbid the sale of land to Japanese. The Korean Government replied that it was a transaction between private persons, that the land sold did not belong to the Government, and that it could not intervene.

The Japanese Government is seriously concerned about this affair. It wants to avoid a conflict with Russia, but is determined to defend the interests of its nationals in Korea and not to permit Russia to install herself at any point of the peninsula. The firmness shown by the Korean Government in this question shows that it feels itself supported by Japan. One fears in Government circles, that Russia exaggerates the importance of her claims regarding Masampo in order to justify a demand for the cession of another point on the coast. It is feared that Russia covets Deer Island near Fusan. But Japan will not back down in her opposition to Russian encroachment in Korea, and hopes to be supported by England. One does not forget, that in 1885, when the latter restored Port Hamilton, Russia bound herself not to occupy a port in Korea.

The possession of Deer Island would make Russia mistress of Fusan. This would constitute a permanent menace to Japan. This possibility could not be realized without the most serious consequences. In view of the very calm but at the same time firm attitude of the Japanese Government, it is probable that Russia, at least for the moment, will not carry out projects which would disturb the peace.[95]

A *Times* telegram declared that the intensification of Russo-Japanese friction over Korea had brought Japan to the verge of taking extreme measures. D'Anethan disagreed:

Japan has no intention of shedding her restraint and, barring hostile action on the part of Russia in Korea, she will not let herself be drawn into a belligerent policy. The struggle for influence in the Korean Peninsula can, it is true, become acute later and provoke serious difficulties, but so far it is confined to diplomacy. The question of ceding land at Masampo, which had aroused Russian objections, has been more or less settled for the moment. It is not apt to lead to hostilities unless Rusia has aggressive plans.

There seem to be many rumors in Europe (echoed by the Diplomatic Corps in Peking) of a Sino-Japanese alliance. I am convinced, that . . . Japan has made no commitment to defend Chinese territory against foreign aggression. The present Japanese Government is composed of men who are too intelligent and too well informed about the weakness of China to plunge into complications of this sort.

I feel that one must take the alarming reports that are and probably will be spread again by the press concerning the belligerent intentions of Japan with the greatest reservation. The country needs peace to develop itself, and the Government will not make war, if its interests in Korea and in the provinces of China, next to Formosa, are not threatened.[96]

A fortnight later d'Anethan reverted to the question of Japanese military action in China and Korea. Taking no stock in persisting rumors of war, d'Anethan wrote:

Japan will use all her influence to prevent the dismemberment of China, and seeks to support the Chinese Government. But the Imperial Government did not and will not commit itself to defend the territory of China against the aggression of her neighbors. As Viscount Aoki told me only today, the Government will not risk the life of a single Japanese soldier in the interest of China. The idea that Japan would restore to China part of the fleet, captured during the war, makes one smile, for one asks oneself with reason in which Chinese ports these ships would be safe!

Japan views with envy, resentment and jealousy the advantages gained by the European Powers, and hopes to have her share in the

H

*industrial and commercial exploitation of China. Exploratory missions have been sent into the Provinces of Chekiang and Fukien. There are plans for the establishment of a bank founded by Chinese and Japanese capital. These enterprises, as well as mining and railroad concessions, cannot succeed unless peace is maintained. Nonetheless, belligerent plans are persistently attributed to Japan. I read in American and English newspapers of the beginning of this month, that one believes war has been set for spring (*New York Herald *and *Daily Mail, November 7). According to the [Japanese] Foreign Minister, these news reports are spread by Russia in order to arouse the mistrust of the other Powers toward Japan. The disseminators [of these stories] may also be invloved in stock market speculation. The Chinese press, particularly the *North China Daily News, *specializes in sensational hoaxes. What faith can one have in a newspaper which announced on November 13, that "the Mandarins of Shanghai have received from Peking the following *official *telegram: "The Russians having decided to acquire the port of Masampo (Korea) in the face of energetic Japanese opposition, diplomatic relations have been severed between the two countries." As many inaccuracies as there are words.*

The Russian Minister, Baron Rosen, has just been recalled. He succeeds Mr. [Aleksandr Petrovich] Izvolskii in Munich, Izvolskii taking his place in Tokyo. Baron Rosen, who is very much liked in Japan, where he was twice, in 1875 and 1885, as Secretary of the Legation, has been Minister for only a little more than two years. He is a conciliatory man and too well informed about Japan not to understand the danger of a policy of intrigues and provocations. Is he considered in St. Petersburg as too prudent and moderate towards Japan? His change of post will no doubt be interpreted this way, especially as his successor has the reputation of being shrewd, active and turbulent.

The delicate issues which divide the Russians and the Japanese in Korea obviously can become more or less critical, depending on whether they will be handled with or without consideration for the legitimate susceptibilities of the two nations concerned. How-

ever, as long as the independence of Korea will not be threatened to any extent, Japan will not want to provoke war. She will be the more prudent now that England and the United States, on whose support she had hoped to be able to count if she were threatened, are engaged in difficult wars, the quick end of which cannot be foreseen.

Since the war of 1894, Japan has shown moderation and wisdom. She did not shed her restraint over the occupation of Port Arthur and Kiaochow by Russia and Germany, even though she felt deeply humiliated. When the war indemnity was paid, she abandoned Weihaiwei in agreement with England, in order to avoid complications. What does France do today at Kwangchow? Japan neither intervenes nor protests. She has not opposed the claims of Italy to Sanmen Bay and is not responsible for the defeat of the Italians. Viscount Aoki, Marquis Ito, Marquis Yamagata and the military advisers of the Emperor are determined not to depart from this line of conduct.[97]

In the closing days of 1899, the *Times* once again depicted Russo-Japanese friction over Korea as "very critical." D'Anethan persisted in his disagreement and quoted Japanese sources:

Japanese newspapers, influenced by the Government, notably the paper which ordinarily reflects the views of Marquis Ito faithfully, formally deny the alarming rumors. "There is no question in Korea now, important enough to lead to conflict," says the Jiji Shimbun. *"The question of land at Masampo was a private matter, and has not led to an exchange of correspondence between Tokyo and St. Petersburg. The conventions, concluded between the two Governments, assure Japan that the independence of Korea will be maintained and that no obstacle will be raised in the development of her commercial and industrial interests. Japan does not ask for more, and so far Russia has faithfully observed the conventions. She has neither opposed nor hindered Japan in regard to the Seoul-Ninsen and Seoul-Fusan railway concessions or the mining demands. One seems persuaded in Europe that Japan wants to go to war with Russia to take revenge for the retrocession of Liaotung. Let us have confidence in our statesmen, who have always shown themselves able to carry out a prudent policy and not let themselves be carried away by a spirit of inopportune chauvinism. Japan does not want to be aggressive; her military preparations are purely defensive."*

All the Ministers talk in the same vein as the article. Far from wanting to provoke Russia, the Government will try as much as possible to avoid a break. While it does not fear complications now, it has some misgivings about the future designs of Russia. It does not ignore that Russia covets a port in Korea to assure her communications between Vladivostok and Port Arthur. Remembering the joint action of France, Germany and Russia in 1895, it fears a new entente between these Powers. Very poorly informed by her diplomatic service in Europe and ignorant whether the accord in question still exists, the Government does not want to expose itself again to the humiliation which she suffered after the war.

Germany too has interests in Korea today and has obtained mining concessions. Prince Henry stopped rather long in Korea. The Japanese Government is somewhat uneasy. It remembers Emperor William's picture "The Yellow Peril," and knows that it cannot count on great sympathy in Berlin.

The sudden recall of Baron Rosen and his replacement by Mr. Izvolskii have aroused some apprehension. The Government is suspicious, perhaps not without reason, of Russian diplomats who have occupied a number of posts in the Balkans. Nor is the return of Mr. [Aleksandr Ivanovich] Pavlov to Korea apt to calm Japan, in spite of the very friendly assurances which he gave in Washington at the time of his departure.

Baron Rosen's successor will have under him a whole new staff. The First Secretary, the Naval Attaché, the Military Attaché and the Consul of Yokohama are leaving in a few days. The complete transformation of the Legation at the time that the Minister is changed is rather unusual. It will be interesting to know the composition of Mr. Izvolskii's mission.[98]

The year 1900 opened with d'Anethan's attention still focussed on Korea and Russo-Japanese relations there:

The Russian Chargé d'Affaires in Korea stopped several days in Japan on his way back to his post. He saw the Foreign Minister, who was very satisfied with the way Mr. Pavlov answered questions about Masampo and does not believe that Russia intends to poison the discussions. The Japanese Minister in Korea has spent two weeks in Tokyo; he leaves for Seoul tomorrow. The Shanghai newspapers attach great importance to this very simple and natural fact and dwell in this connection on the allegedly very acute relations between Russia and Japan. Mr. Hayashi (the Minister in Korea) told me, on the other hand, that he did not foresee the danger of a break with Russia. "The Russians will buy land at Masampo and will establish coal depots there; the Japanese will do likewise and thus counterbalance Russian preponderance. Japanese emigration to Korea is very considerable. There are now more than 25,000 Japanese in the peninsula. The Government owes them aid and protection. But so far the Government did not have to intervene, as the Russians created no difficulties for them."

As long as Russia does not seek to occupy or fortify a port in Korea, the accord between the two Governments will be preserved. It will be broken, of course, the day that Russia ceases to conform to the protocol, signed in Tokyo in April 1898 by the Minister of Foreign Affairs [Nishi] and the Representative of Russia [Rosen], concerning the Korean question. According to this agreement, "the Imperial Governments definitely recognize the sovereignty and full independence of Korea" (articles I and III) and "in view of the large growth of Japanese commercial enterprises in Korea as well as the considerable number of Japanese subjects residing in that country, the Imperial Government of Russia will not hinder the development of commercial and industrial relations between Japan and Korea."[99]

By the end of the month, d'Anethan acknowledged a deterioration in Russo-Japanese relations. He wrote:

The latest news from Korea is not reassuring. It appears that Russia is sending troops from Port Arthur to the northern frontier and warships to the mouth of the Yalu. The Russian Chargé d'Affaires at Seoul asserts that Russia is merely forming a sanitary cordon to protect her territories from the plague. Since not a single case of plague has been found on the Russian-Korean frontier according to reports in Tokyo, the Government views these troop movements with some apprehension. We learn also that difficulties have arisen between England and Russia at Seoul concerning the concession of the In-san gold mine to an English subject, Mr. Pritchard Morgan. Russia claims to have received two years ago the Emperor's assurance that no mines belonging to the Imperial Household Ministry would be granted to foreigners other than Russians. Since the mine, granted to Morgan, seems to fall in this category, the Russian Chargé d'Affaires has protested. Paying no heed to Russian opposition and allegedly backed by the English Representative, Morgan is said to have installed himself already at the mine with fifty Japanese workers. Russia, on her part, has allegedly asked for the concession of gold mines, belonging to the Crown. So far the Korean Government has not acceded to the demand. Russia thus begins to show much activity in Korea. If she backs her claims with troops, Japan, in spite of her desire to avoid a conflict, will find herself driven also to take measures of precaution to protect her interests.[100]

The absence of a Russian Minister in Tokyo was noted by d'Anethan. He commented:

The new Minister of Russia will arrive in Tokyo only in June. The Japanese Government, which had been affected by the brusque recall of Baron Rosen, feels that the lack of eagerness which his successor shows in proceeding to his post indicates that the Russian Government does not intend to modify its policy toward Japan.[101]

In spring d'Anethan described the mounting uneasiness of Japan:

The Japanese Government views with apprehension the constant increase of Russian forces in the Far East. Viscount Aoki told me that the declarations of the Emperor and of his Government are friendly and pacific, but that the Russian Representatives in China and Korea are very hostile toward Japan. In Seoul especially, the Russian Chargé d'Affaires has been very active in recent months. He has pushed the Emperor to oppose mining concessions to Englishmen; he has pressed for the acceptance of a loan of several million dollars; he urges the Government to procure permission for the Russians to acquire much land outside the foreign concession at Masampo as well as two islands in the vicinity of this port. The Governor of Port Arthur came to back up this demand. He appeared at the Imperial Palace with a number of officers and while Russian vessels took up position in the port.

In spite of the display of force, the Government did not yield. The English work the mine; the Russian gold has been declined; and the transactions of land do not go beyond the limits of the concession. Japanese influence, strengthened under the circumstances by that of England, has thus not been seriously injured yet.   But we cannot conceal from ourselves [the fact] that this continued friction is apt to lead to complications. As long as Russia will not stop opposing Japan in Korea, the relations between the two countries will remain dangerous notwithstanding the peaceful assurances of the Cabinets.

Russia now has more than 100,000 men in Manchuria, Port Arthur and Vladivostok. Every ship of the Volunteer Fleet on its frequent trips reinforces them and the big stocks of arms and ammunitions. The new Danish Navigation Company, which is subsidized by Russia, will inaugurate a service to the Far East. Since Denmark has no important trade with China or Japan, this fleet will serve as auxiliary troop transport to the Volunteer Fleet. It is noted also that Russia plans to increase her Far Eastern squadron considerably.

The Government believes that this great display of force is directed against Japan. The latter on her part consequently does everything to prepare her defenses. When I visited the state arse-

nals recently, I ascertained how busy they were. One works day and night to forge cannons, make cartridges, cast bullets and bombs, build and equip torpedo boats, etc. On all sides of the Inland Sea new forts are being built and batteries established. Much ammunition and many cannons also come from Europe. Large quantities of coal have recently been purchased from Cardiff and stored in the arsenals of Kun and Sasebo. Japan shrinks from no expenditure and spares no effort to prepare for any eventuality.

The great naval maneuvers, decided upon a year ago, have just begun. More than forty warships, not counting torpedo boats, are taking part. The plan of the maneuvers is kept secret; not one foreign Naval Attaché has been invited. There is no doubt, however, that the exercises are being held in the south, not very far from the Korean coast.[102]

On March 30, d'Anethan telegraphed home: "In spite of repeated friendly assurances by the Russian Government, the Minister of Foreign Affairs looks with anxiety at Russian action in Korea. But the press exaggerates the seriousness of the situation."[103] The following day d'Anethan elaborated:

I deemed it necessary to telegraph yesterday to bring to Your Excellency's attention that the doings of Russia in Korea have caused anxiety to the Government, but also to put you on guard against the exaggerations of the press concerning the gravity of the situation.

In view of the repeated friendly declarations of Baron Rosen in Tokyo and of the Minister of Foreign Affairs in St. Petersburg, Viscount Aoki does not want to believe in aggressive plans [on the part of Russia]; on the other hand, he cannot understand what Russia seeks to attain by constantly raising irritable questions.

As I have repeatedly stated to Your Excellency, the Japanese Government is determined not to tolerate an attack against the independence of Korea, and will oppose any real or disguised occupation of one of the ports by Russia. Viscount Aoki and his colleagues do not conceal their firm intentions in this regard.

They will show themselves resolute, though they will avoid doing anything that might provoke a conflict. But if Russia persists in demanding the concession of territory at Masampo or elsewhere outside of the concessions or in seeking to evade the protocols of June 9, 1896, and of April 25, 1898 by interfering in the internal affairs of the country, as Mr. Pavlov did recently in offering a loan of several million dollars, the Government will call St. Petersburg to account. In that case the situation can become critical, especially since the naval maneuvers, in which all the biggest and most powerful vessels of Japan are engaged, will readily prompt an impressive demonstration.

My English, German and Italian colleagues do not believe in immediate complications, as they have asked and obtained leave, which they plan to take in May. The French Minister has told me, that he does not expect war, since neither of the two Governments desires it. Nor does he think that Emperor Nicholas will let subordinate agents in the Orient involve him [in war]. He added that such was his hope, "since France, though she has no interest whatever in Korea, would find herself obliged, by virtue of the alliance, to support Russia."[104]

CHAPTER THREE

Manchuria

In autumn of 1900 the Yamagata Cabinet fell. Marquis Ito Hirobumi resumed the premiership. By this time he had created his own political party, the Rikken Seiyukai. Whether Japan had progressed from the days of the Okuma-Itagaki Cabinet to responsible party government was another matter, however. D'Anethan observed:

We have seen no indication in the political ways of Japan during the past two years, that would justify the expectation that a parliamentary ministry would have greater chances for permanence today than before. No political party—no more that constituted by Marquis Ito than the Progressive, Liberal, Radical, Socialist or Reform Party—has a clearly defined program based on principles. I have not succeeded in finding out, and no one can explain to me, the difference between the various political groups, which have borrowed the names of European political parties. Under the circumstances, it is to be feared that in spite of the undisputed prestige of Marquis Ito in Japan, the moment has not yet come to broaden the prerogatives of Parliament. Many years will yet pass before a parliamentary regime will function regularly in Japan. Furthermore, the question seems to me merely theoretical for the time being. It is more important and urgent to know whether the vassals of the Satsuma and Choshu Clans will resign themselves to being deprived of the influence that they have exercised in the counsels of the Crown since the Restoration. Until today, Ministries in which this element was not represented, have been short-lived.[105]

In 1900 the anti-Christian, anti-foreign Boxer Uprising brought China to a state of war with the Powers. Following the example of the Western States, Japan sent marines to protect her nationals. D'Anethan related:

The powerlessness or rather the unwillingness of the Empress to quell the attacks against the foreigners will soon necessitate the intervention of the Powers to maintain order and to assure the security of foreigners.

Marquis Ito and Viscount Aoki told me very recently that the Empress is becoming increasingly reactionary and that the insurgents not only are not acted against, but are even encouraged by the Mandarins of her entourage. As long as the Empress will be at the helm of power, there will be disorder, corruption and anarchy. According to the Japanese statesmen the moment approaches when the Powers interested in China will have to take the law in their hands and act with energy.

Japan does not want to be alone in restoring and then maintaining order and peace; she will seek to come to an understanding with the other Powers concerning the means to be used. The Government is prepared to act in concert with the Powers, and will not hesitate to send a contingent of troops if the uprising spreads.[106]

Two weeks later d'Anethan elaborated on developments in China and on Japanese reaction:

All the news reports that we receive from China indicate that the Boxer Uprising grows with every day. The Boxers, according to particulars sent by Baron Nishi, number between eighty and one hundred thousand, and are reinforced by deserters from the Army, charged with putting them down. One dreads in Tokyo lest the movement, fomented against the Christians and the foreigners, spread to other parts of China. Uprisings are feared in the Provinces of Shensi and Kansu. The French Consuls have urged the foreigners to quit Yunnan. At Canton too, attacks against foreigners are feared. The situation would be the more serious in the South, as the insurrection would have at its disposal a large quantity of arms and ammunition. The Governor of Hong Kong, who is passing through Japan, has told me that in his opinion a revolution at Canton was certain, and that it would break out soon. One has been preparing it for two years.

It seems increasingly evident, that the Government of Peking encourages the Boxers and that the foreign Powers can rely only on their own forces to defend their interests and their nationals. Japan at present has four warships at Tientsin and Taku; one squadron is gathered at Sasebo; she will be able to send considerable forces to China very rapidly. As Russia has already lined up several thousand men, Japan also will have to take measures to guard her commercial and political interests.

The [Japanese] Government does not want to act, however, without a previous understanding with the Powers. If differences in view arise between the European Powers, it will seek to proceed in concert with England and the United States. It does not want to contribute to the dismemberment of China; on the contrary, it dreads this eventuality as fraught with dangers for Japan. To avoid it, it deems. . .a radical change in the highest governmental circles in Peking necessary. . .and would be inclined to dethrone the Empress. One almost believes in Japan that if the influence of the present councillors would persist in spite of the unseating of the Empress, a change in dynasty would be needed.

Russian policy arouses Japanese fears. Apprehensions are the more acute, now that the Korean Government, supported evidently by the Russian Chargé d'Affaires, has taken an attitude of independence, incompatible with its weakness.[107]

Several days later, d'Anethan reported on the extent of Japanese involvement in the Boxer crisis:

Japan now has 9 warships in the China Seas, and is sending a corps of 3,000 troops—infantry, artillery and cavalry. She joined the other Powers in the first measures taken to rescue the Legations in Peking and to protect the foreigners in Tientsin. Her vessels participated in the bombardment of the Taku forts. As I wrote you in one of my last reports, she does not take an independent course of action and does not want to embark on an expedition against China without a mandate from the Powers or an accord with them. Alone, among the Powers, with the possible exception of Russia, Japan is in a position to send to China very quickly an army sufficient for restoring order. She will shun this extreme measure, however, if she does not have formal assurances that the services which she would thus render for the common cause would not lead her into dangerous complications.

Public opinion was aroused, of course, by the murder of Mr. Sugiyama, Chancellor of the Peking Legation, and presses the Government to send imposing forces to China. But the Government does not shed its prudent caution. It believes that we are now only at the beginning of great upheavals which the present revolutionary movements are preparing.

If it were merely a question of repressing the insurrection of several thousand brigands and fanatics, the cooperation of the foreign Powers would be sufficient, and order would soon be restored. But in the opinion of the Japanese Government the revolution that is taking place in China will lead to a complete change in government. Japanese statesmen understand that in view of this eventuality, the consequences of which would vitally affect the interests not only of the nations bordering unto China but of the whole world, they must act in concert with the Powers which want to maintain the [territorial] integrity of the Empire and adhere to the "open door" policy, whatever regime will govern China. The Minister of Foreign Affairs, through his Representatives in Europe and America, has already initiated an exchange of views to learn the attitudes and intentions of the Cabinets of the Great Powers and of Washington.

According to my information, only the American Government has answered so far, [stating] that the Government of the United States "true to its principles of not interfering in the internal affairs of a foreign Government will only take those measures necessary for safeguarding the lives and interests of its nationals." It is with the German and English Governments that the Imperial Government especially desires to make an understanding, fearing lest Russia take advantage of the Chinese complications to ursue herp ambitious designs in China as well as in Korea.[108]

By the end of the month, Japanese involvement had grown.
D'Anethan observed:

*The Government has ordered the mobilization of a division;
an Imperial ordinance has appropriated the sum of 50,000,000
yen to meet the expenses. The mobilization order is dated the 26th;
the transports are ready, and the troops can be delivered to China
very quickly. . . .*

*On the 23rd, upon receipt of alarming reports from the Japa-
nese Admirals who insisted, following the capture of the Taku
forts, that reinforcements be sent, Viscount Aoki had assembled
the Representatives of the Powers which had warships in China.
He read to them the dispatches from the Admirals, explained
to them the gravity of the situation, called their attention to the
urgent need of taking measures to protect the foreigners in China,
and asked them to telegraph to their respective Governments to
ascertain their intentions. . . .*

*Immediately after the meeting Viscount Aoki kindly gave me
an account of what had happened. "We want to act in concert
with the Powers," he repeated again and again, "but are determined not to pull the chestnuts out of the fire for others. We seek
no exclusive advantage. Since the beginning of the troubles in
China our attitude has been frank and faithful. We sent a detachment to protect the Legations in Peking at the same time as the
others. Our forces participated with the Russians, Germans,
French and English in the capture of the Taku forts. Although
we are in a position to dispatch considerable forces into China very
quickly, we have confined ourselves to sending 3,000 men in order
not to arouse the suspicions or susceptibilities of the Powers."*

*When he informed me of the mobilization of a division [on
the 26th], the Viscount told me: "We are not yet ordering the
embarkation of this imposing number of troops, because we do not
want to plunge alone into an adventure without first having a
joint plan with the other Powers. Our hesitation is not due to lack
of preparations or transports, for we could, if necessary, send one
or two divisions more without difficulty."*

The language of the Foreign Minister is as firm as it is prudent. He did not let himself be swayed either by those who from the beginning demanded energetic action or by those who counselled too passive an attitude.

It is regrettable that the dispatch of a sufficient force for protecting the lives and property of the foreigners has been delayed so long. One must not blame the Japanese Government, which would have gone ahead, had it been encouraged by the Powers. But the latter have been most reserved toward it, and have not acquainted it with the views that they have no doubt exchanged.

The common and daily more acute danger makes necessary the sending of a coalition of forces to China. Having just been assured by the principal Powers that they would favor the dispatch of Japanese troops to China, the Japanese Government will not delay sending them. Measures have already been taken to mobilize two more divisions. A division is composed of about 12,000 men plus 1,000 to 2,000 porters and coolies. More than 40 vessels have been chartered and orders have been given to all navigation companies to have their equipment at the disposal of the Government.

The Japanese fleet, mobilized for the April maneuvers, is ready for action. Gathered at Sasebo and Kure, it can radiate to the coasts of China and Korea. Besides the ships at Taku, there are cruisers at Shanghai, Amoy, and Chefoo. A squadron will soon be sent also to South China. . . . In view of the lack of information about events in Peking since June 14, the Government cannot make final plans and confines itself to preparing for all eventualities. The Japanese Government pays close attention to the attitude of the Viceroys of the southern provinces, who seem to want to separate from the Peking Government. Without perhaps having encouraged them as yet, it wants to obtain powerful auxiliaries for the restoration of order and the maintenance of the [territorial] integrity of the Chinese Empire.

A change of dynasty is imperative. Japanese statesmen think that in order for the Government to be replaced by one which would

have power and a certain chance of permanence, the transforma-
tion must be effected by the Chinese themselves and that it will
be the duty and interest of the Powers to support any Govern-
ment capable of preventing the dismemberment of the Empire.
This task the Japanese Government cannot and will not attempt
with her forces alone, but will proceed in agreement with those
powers which will not take advantage of the circumstances to seize
Chinese provinces. Should the regeneration of China be impossible,
however, Japan will look after her interests, and will secure them
commercially and politically.

The question of Korea preoccupies Japan perhaps even more
than that of China. In that which concerns China, Japan can
find many points of possible agreement with the Great Powers,
including Russia. Any attack against the independence of Korea
by the latter will very much complicate the situation, and I am
convinced that the firmness of Japan will not weaken. She will
not stop at war to prevent Russia from establishing herself on any
point of the peninsula.[109]

In July the Japanese Government proposed an entente of
the Powers regarding the military expeditions that were being
prepared. Conveying the gist of the telegram sent by Viscount Aoki to the Japanese Representatives abroad, d'Anethan
wrote:

The situation in North China is increasingly serious and the
insurrection is taking on such proportions, that it will require
large forces to subdue it. He [Viscount Aoki] repeats that Japan
is prepared to send troops and to act in concert with the Powers,
but that it is urgent to decide on a common plan of action.

The Japanese Government believes like the German Emperor. . .
that the Powers must march on Peking. It merely asks to join with
the European nations, but first wants assurances that Japan will
participate on an equal footing with the Powers in the settlement
of the numerous questions which an expedition against China will
raise.

I

As Your Excellency already knows, the English are sending 12,000 men and the French and Germans an almost equal number. The Russians will have more, and the Japanese can send several divisions.[110]

With foreign approval Japanese efforts gained momentum. D'Anethan observed:

Having received satisfactory assurances from all the Powers and encouragement from a number of them concerning the sending of large forces to China, the Japanese Government now will resolutely go ahead. In number of men already used or about to be used, Japan holds first place among the Powers that have decided to intervene in China. If necessary, she can add after a brief delay several other divisions to the twenty-five thousand men who are en route to Taku, where a great number have arrived already. Her military preponderance will only become more pronounced, and simultaneously her political influence will be strengthened.

The task undertaken by Japan is most difficult, and will be accomplished only at the cost of enormous sacrifices in men and money. She does not shrink from her share of responsibility, however, and will work to the end in concert with the Powers who, in restoring order in China, want to establish a Government, strong enough to maintain the integrity of the Chinese Empire and restore peace. The Imperial Government does not dream of new conquests in China. It does not favor the acquisition of spheres of influence which, it feels, would entail endless complications and would close the vast territories to general commerce.

Japanese statesmen believe that serious and effective reforms can be introduced in China only with the cooperation of the Chinese themselves. They favor, therefore, using men who are animated by ideas of progress and presenting themselves to China as liberators and not as conquerors.

A number of Viceroys and chiefs of provincial armies presently oppose Peking. They refuse to send subsidies and no longer obey the last edicts, which they regard as coming from a rebel. The

Viceroys friendly toward foreigners are insufficiently prepared for maintaining order and at the same time inaugurating a new Government. Members of the Government feel that sympathetic Governors will have to be supported. It is the only way of preventing the insurrection of the North from spreading to the whole Empire. News of Boxer massacres of missionaries and attacks on foreigners reach us from all points. If the provincial armies join the Boxers as they have done in the north, the already dreadful situation will take on such proportions, that armies numbering in the hundreds of thousands of men will be needed.

The first effort of the Allied forces is to be directed against Peking. The campaign, according to the Japanese, will be very rough and difficult, and will require at least 50 to 60,000 men. The 15,000 foreign troops find it very hard to maintain themselves in Tientsin. At this time of the year the plain between Tientsin and Peking is under water. The army will have to take everything along as the whole region is devastated; everything will be lacking, even drinking water. It is doubtful that the advance on Peking will be possible before the beginning of September.

So far we have not learned of serious disagreements between the chiefs of the combined troops. How long will this harmony last as the foreign contingents increase? The Japanese with their numerical superiority will have high pretensions. Recent news that Russia was sending 30,000 men by way of Manchuria and that she had forces on the frontier of Korea concerns the Japanese Government. It is feared that Russia will not concert her movements with those of the other Powers, and that she plans a campaign of conquest.

Russia has raised no objections to the sending of Japanese troops, and the relations between Tokyo and St. Petersburg are always very correct, Viscount Aoki tells me. One has nevertheless great apprehensions concerning Russian future designs. Preparations are made, therefore, firmly though without provocation, to oppose them should they threaten the vital interests of the country. The future relations between Japan and Russia are one of the very black spots on the already very dark Far Eastern horizon. The tendency of an accord between England and Japan, with the sympathetic support of the United States, becomes increasingly marked. The views and plans of Germany are less clearly indicated, and there is constant fear of the Triple Alliance of 1895. The situation has since changed greatly for Japan; new sacrifices would not be so easily imposed on her.

The present expedition against China does not arouse the popular enthusiasm that the earlier campaign had awakened; there is no hate in Japan today against China as a nation. The feeling which prevails is more one of pity for a great people whose rights have been ignored and who is the victim of a cruel and corrupt Government. The general feeling is that Japan now has the mission of helping up the colossus whom she had knocked down, but who had been supported momentarily, to the detriment of Japan, by the other Powers in order to rob him the more surely a few years later. The cruel and humiliating recollection of the taking of Port Arthur [by Russia] and of Kiaochow [by Germany] is still very vivid, and Japan will take all possible measures not to lose the fruit of victory again.

The Imperial Government will keep its commitments toward the Powers, but while cooperating strenuously with them for the repression of crimes and abuses, it will seek to remain the friend of China. When Marquis Ito was in Peking two years ago, he gave assurances that Japan would like to aid China carry out reforms in the system of Government at Peking and in the Provinces; Count Okuma and the influential men of Japan have always spoken in the same sense. It is remembered, that for a long time Japanese policy toward China was friendly to the point that last year the rumor of an alliance between the two countries was credited in Europe. The reports were false, but the intentions of the Government thus are well known; it wishes to realize them in concert with the Powers that will not attempt new conquests.[111]

The Chinese sought to separate Japan from the Western

Powers. The Chinese Minister in Tokyo handed Viscount
Aoki a telegram from the Emperor of China to the Emperor
of Japan. D'Anethan summarized its content and the Japanese
reply:

*The Emperor of China expresses his regrets at the assassination of the Chancellor of the Legation and says that he has had the
culprits arrested and punished.*

*He asks the aid of the [Japanese] Emperor in defending
China against the insurgents and the foreigners on account of the
common interests of the two countries. He speaks of the danger
which will threaten Japan, if China is destroyed.*

*The Emperor of Japan in his response makes no allusion to the
request for an alliance, and says that the Chinese Government
must first rescue the Foreign Representatives; no negotiations will
be possible until they are free.*[112]

A week and a half later d'Anethan elaborated on Japanese
reaction to the telegram of the Emperor of China:

*Not much importance has been attached to the message of the
Emperor of China, as one ignores here under whose inspiration it
was drafted. The Government has deemed it necessary, however,
to reply to make it clear that it does not want to pursue toward
China a line of conduct different from that of the other Powers.*

*The Emperor disdainfully ignores the proposal that Japan
"make common cause" with China.*

Reporting that Boxer unrest had spread to Korea and that
the Russians had even been attacked along the frontier,
d'Anethan continued:

*The Korean Government is said to have asked the Japanese
Government to send troops to Korea to maintain order. For the
moment Japan will be careful not to embark on this course; but
large Russian troop movements, said to be taking place in Manchuria, may precipitate events.*

If Russia declares war on China and takes possession of Manchuria, Japan will seize the opportunity to install herself in

Korea. Japan has been disposed to act in concert with the European nations to reestablish peace in China. But the moment that Russia threatens the whole of North China, Japan will defend her interests in the Peninsula.[113]

In August 1900, d'Anethan reported that the relief forces were heading toward the Chinese capital. He wrote:

They have captured Pehtsang, eight miles from Tientsin. They are Japanese troops, entrusted with the most important part of the expedition. They would have been able to respond to the desperate appeals of the Ministers sooner, had the other contingents been ready with provisions and transportation. . . . The strategic obstacles seem to be serious. Have they not been increased by political considerations? It is with difficulty, that the different commanders have come to an agreement, and the absence of a commander-in-chief is felt acutely. Will the appointment of Count von Waldersee remove the obstacles to common action in the future?

The German Emperor proposed to the Japanese Emperor, at the suggestion of Russia, that the supreme command of operations in North China be entrusted to this famous general. The Emperor approved. Emperor William's proposal would be of very great importance, if Count von Waldersee were already in China and could take effective command of the campaign. By the time he will get to China, however, it is more than probable that Peking will already be in Allied hands. The Imperial Government's objective in sending 25,000 men to China will largely be attained; whether it will continue an aggressive policy against China will depend on many circumstances, impossible to predict now. The words of the German Emperor, proclaiming a war to the bitter end and without mercy against China, have not met a favorable response in Japan.

The [Japanese] Government has decided to free the foreigners in Peking and to restore order in China without violating the independence and integrity of the Empire; it is in accord so far with most of the Great Powers of Europe and the United States. The understanding will be endangered the day that one Power will want to secure exclusive advantages or a separate sphere of influence. From that moment Japan will be governed by her interests.

The Government seriously dreads, lest the revoltion which has broken out in the north, spread to the whole Empire. Hope to halt the insurrection lies in maintaining order in the Yangtze valley and in the provinces of the south. The Viceroys at Wuchang [Chang Chih-tung] and Nanking [Liu Kun-yi] are showing themselves favorable to foreigners and openly oppose the revoluntionary Government in Peking. The Imperial Government feels that one must support and encourage the Viceroys and not make naval or military demonstrations in these provinces. One is convinced in Tokyo, that if some or all of the Powers do not confine themselves to allied action against Peking and the restoration of peace with the aid of enlightened Chinese, but wage war against China, the whole country will rise up and make common cause against the foreigners.

The Japanese who know China best do not believe it possible to impose on China a stable Government by force alone, without the cooperation of the Chinese themselves. I do not think that the Government considers sending more troops to China if the number sent for the liberation of Peking is sufficient. It will keep its forces intact to defend its interests in Korea.

The advance of a Russian army in Manchuria forces Japan to take steps to thwart Russian plans in the peninsula. Furthermore, England is preparing to defend the Yangtze valley and Shanghai, with naval and military forces, and she must retain troops to preserve her influence in the Provinces of Fukien and Kiangsi. It is with some apprehension that Japan sees England act independently at Shanghai and the Yangtze, diverting troops which in Japanese opinion were supposed to participate in the liberation of Peking....

It is Japan's desire, as her attitude from the beginning of the troubles in China proves, to gain the sympathy of the European Powers and to convince them that she does not seek exclusive advantages but works with them to find a solution to the very serious problems, raised by the Chinese question. She envisages and would even be willing to bring about an international conference to lay the basis for common action. She wants to appear at such a congress, if it convenes, free from any commitment, yet ready to claim the legitimate share of influence due her in China as well as in Korea.[114]

The question of supreme command was as complex as it was unstable, and operations did not proceed without differences among the allies. D'Anethan commented:

Lieutenant General Baron Yamaguchi was to preside over the Council of the Chiefs of the different contingents, called together to decide the march on Peking. The last minute arrival of a Russian Lieutenant General, senior in rank, modified the situation, and the presidency fell to the latter.

The Germans and Russians, it appears, were in favor of postponing the advance until more troops were landed. The English, Americans and Japanese refused to delay any longer to bring help to their Ministers.[115]

In the southeast, in Amoy, Chinese hostility was directed primarily against the Japanese, who had annexed Formosa in 1895. Here the Japanese were prepared to act on their own. D'Anethan observed:

The Japanese Government is very anxious about the disorders which have allegedly broken out at Amoy. The movement is said to be directed principally against the Japanese, one of whose Buddhist temples has been set afire. Since the acquisition of Formosa, Amoy has been the center of conspiracies against the new order of things. It is there too that the enemies of the Japanese take refuge. The latter believe that there now is a vast conspiracy at Amoy to incite a general uprising on the island.

In view of this very dangerous situation, the Government has landed 250 marines and has dispatched two warships. Between fifteen and twenty thousand men, garrisoned on Formosa and on the Pescadores, are ready to land at Amoy and Fuchow if the insurrection grows. The English, German, and American Consuls feel that the security of the foreigners is not threatened and disapprove of the landing of Japanese forces.

According to the telegrams received yesterday, Europeans are aroused by the independent action of Japan in that part of China. As I have not ceased to write to Your Excellency, if the Western Powers take steps in China to guarantee the fulfillment of obligations which she will assume later, Japan wants to be prepared to affirm her rights equally. With the exception of the 250 marines, she has not occupied any point of Fukien Province; but it is quite certain that she is in the position to do so very quickly.

We have not had reliable news from Peking since the entry of the allied troops. The telegraph seems to be reserved almost exclusively for the communications of the military commanders. The Marquise Salvago-Raggi, wife of the Italian Minister, is to arrive today in Nagasaki from Peking on a warship. Her departure was telegraphed to the Legation here by the Admiral and not by the Minister. No one has had a reply to the numerous telegrams, sent since the 18th.

It seems established that the Court with the principal councillors has taken refuge at Shansi; on the other hand, there are rumors about the return of the Empress to negotiate. The [Japanese] Government does not comment on the nature of the negotiations that it wants to open with China, nor with whom it will be possible to begin them.

Russia has announced her intention of recalling her Minister and her troops from Peking. The [Japanese] Cabinet at this moment deliberates on the answer to make to the Russian Government. It is very eager not to disrupt the unison of the Powers which had collaborated in the liberation of Peking, and wants to continue acting in concert with them. But it would not favor abandoning Peking before a Government of some strength has been established there. Because of the numerical superiority of its troops and their brilliant action in the occupation [of the city], it plays a preponderant role in Peking today and will not let itself be overshadowed by the European Powers.

We must keep in mind that the Japanese have some apprehension about the future attitude of Europe toward them. They are very sensitive about the articles of an influencial part of the English and Continental press, which considers that because they belong to the yellow race, they are not worthy of being treated on an equal footing. They realize that most of the Governments have accepted their assistance only with a certain repugnance and mistrust. They feel also how delicate and dangerous their task is.

Russia inundates Manchuria with troops without arousing any objections; Germany sends an army; England has landed 4,000 men at Shanghai and concentrated her fleet at the Yangtze. The moment Japan shows the slightest inclination to take precautionary measures for the protection of her possession of Formosa, protests are raised at once.[116]

In fall, China once again tried to secure Japan's good offices. D'Anethan commented:

The Emperor of China has once again telegraphed to the Emperor [of Japan] to request Japanese intervention on behalf of the restoration of peace. His Majesty has replied that he could not act before the instigators and leaders of the insurrection had been punished and the Government was composed of men worthy of inspiring confidence. His Majesty also recommended the return of the Emperor to Peking. This advice does not seem to have been heeded; in fact, we learn that the Imperial Court is going to Sian, moving even farther away from the capital. The Japanese Government still wants to act in concert with the European Powers and accepts in principle the proposals recently made by Germany and France. It does not believe, however, that it would be advisable to forbid the entry of arms into China, as this would make it impossible for the Chinese Government to maintain order and protect the foreigners. It deems also that the occupation of Peking by international troops would present great inconveniences. It would prefer to see each Legation protected by its own nationals.[117]

Japanese policy was impeded by the illness of Marquis Ito,

who had succeeded to the premiership in October. The responsibility of negotiating with China rested squarely on the shoulders of the Foreign Minister, Kato Takaaki. D'Anethan remarked:

*Until now Mr. Kato follows the political line, traced with so
much prudence and competence by Viscount Aoki.... Mr. Kato
does not have very much confidence in the possibility of maintaining
the apparent harmony which seems to exist between the allies up to
a certain point. He foresees, on the contrary, that the differences
will become accentuated, when negotiations are begun with the
Chinese plenipotentiaries. Not wishing to leave the negotiations in
the hands of a diplomat who has gone through the horrors of the
siege of Peking, the Government is recalling Baron Nishi. Mr.
Komura Jutaro, presently Minister to Russia, has been named to
replace him.*

Speaking of Russia, d'Anethan was reminded of Russian
activity in Korea. He continued:

*Russian activity in Korea seems to have abated of late, but the
calm is only apparent. It manifests itself anew in the support
given by Mr. Pavlov to a French Company which seeks to obtain
the concession of a railroad from Seoul to Wiju. This line would
be of great strategic importance for Russia, as it would be connected to the railroad of Manchuria. For this reason Japan will
make every effort to prevent the granting of the concession.*[118]

In a subsequent dispatch, d'Anethan elaborated on Japanese policy:

*As long as the appearance of accord between the Powers is main-
tained in Peking, the Japanese Government ... tries not to do anything to break the harmony. When it will become impossible to preserve it, the Government will arrange itself with the Powers whose
demands are most moderate.*

*As for the conditions which one wants to impose on China before
negotiating, it has ordered its Representative in Peking to join in
[making] them, even though it is critical of some of them. Mean-*

while it has called the attention of the Powers to two points: the punishment of the principal culprits and inciters of the disorders and the question of the indemnity. Like the Government of the United States, it thinks that a delay in the opening of the negotiations may entail the most serious complications. It is disposed to demand the exemplary punishment of the principal culprits, but does not deem it advisable to present an ultimatum *demanding the execution of a whole list of high personages. All negotiations would be rendered impossible thereby, because the Chinese plenipotentiaries will not be able to subscribe to this condition. Besides, if they accepted it, their commitment would be without value, for they would be disavowed at once. As to the question of the indemnity, the Japanese Government, again like that of the United States, judges that the lump sum to be demanded must not be excessive nor exceed what the resources of China permit. Once the amount is fixed, it should be divided equitably between all the interested Powers.*

One is convinced here, that the negotiations will be illusory, as long as the Court does not return to Peking; that one should therefore facilitate this return by suspending the measures of war and threats.

Before deciding on a definite political line, however, the Government awaits further developments. With Russia and the United States increasingly manifesting the intention of negotiating separately with China, Japan will be free to pursue a more independent policy.

The consequences of the anarchy which reigns in China weigh heavily upon Japan. The very considerable trade between the two countries has stopped almost completely; the stagnation of business has resulted in a very serious economic crisis which can lead to real financial disaster.

The prolonged closing of the big market of China will be ruinous not only for Japan, but here the effects are felt sooner. This consideration alone would suffice to explain the interest that the Government attaches to seeing the negotiations at Peking offer a program, moderate enough to be accepted by China.[119]

Two weeks later d'Anethan dwelled on the nature of the Japanese demands presented to China:

It was only just and natural that in the first note addressed to the Chinese since the horrible events of the summer, the crime committed against the member of the Imperial Legation should be recalled and that the Powers should demand suitable reparations on the part of China for the death of Chancellor Sugiyama. But Japan appreciates the unanimity with which the mention was added to the preamble. The Government continues to insist that it is impractical to stipulate capital punishment for Chinese Princes and to determine in advance who the guilty persons are. The prudence of its counsels has been recognized. The clause demanding the prohibition of all articles used in the manufacture of arms has also been modified in accordance with the views of the Japanese Government. In limiting the prohibition to the importation of products which are used exclusively in the manufacture of arms or ammunitions, the original purpose will hardly be obtained—what product would not have multiple uses? The Japanese Government has always been against prohibiting the introduction of arms to China, it has agreed to the proposal only out of the desire to show itself as conciliatory as possible. When one wanted to go further and make it impossible for China to manufacture instruments of war herself, Japan objected. She feels that if China is to remain an independent state, she must not be deprived of the means of maintaining order and of meeting the obligations that the treaties impose on her.

As I have often written to Your Excellency, there is no hatred for China in Japan. One desires, on the contrary, to help her raise herself up and, as long as there is any chance that she can do so, to give her support and protection. While having exerted a restraint which the chauvinistic party in Japan has found excessive, and acting very loyally towards the Western Powers, the Government cannot hide its sympathy for China, when it refuses to demand the execution of the high personages who instigated the massacres of foreigners and opposes measures which would reduce the Chinese Government to complete impotence.

Very great importance seems to be attached here to the Imperial decree ordering Tung [Fu-hsiang] to disband the major portion of his army and to resume his command in Kansu. The news that the Viceroys of Nanking and of Wuchan each are sending a corps of 2,500 men to Sian to protect the Court is received with favor. It is hoped that with the removal of Tung and Tuan [Tsai-i] and the protection of the Viceroys of the Yangtze the Emperor will be able to return to Peking. Mr. Kato thinks, as his predecessor foresaw from the beginning, that as long as the Court, and thus the Government, is in flight, hundreds of leagues in the interior, the negotiations will be faced by almost insurmountable obstacles.

The Foreign Minister does not rise above generalities when he comments on questions regarding the indemnity that China will have to pay and the revision of the treaties of commerce. He declares that the demands of Japan will be moderate. If one requires too heavy sacrifices on the part of China, one will not be able to indemnify oneself except by claiming pieces of territory. Japan, which has such a high interest in the preservation of the [territorial] integrity of the Empire and in keeping open the doors of the big commercial market in the entire country, would view with repugnance the settlement of the indemnity question in ways that would involve the dismemberment of China. But she will have to take into account the attitude of the other Powers. If these will be led, in the protection of their interests, to extend the zone of their possessions in China, Japan will be forced likewise to seek compensations.[120]

Japanese reaction to an American proposal to remove negotiations with China to the West was prompt. D'Anethan noted:

The proposal made by the United States that the seat of the negotiations with China concerning the treaties of commerce and the indemnities questions be transferred either to Washington or a European capital has not been received with favor by the Imperial Government. The Government believes that the American proposal far from accelerating or facilitating the negotiations, would tend to hinder them seriously. It feels that the rank of the Chinese pleni-

potentiaries must be as high as possible, much higher in any case than that held by any of the Ministers of China accredited abroad. It would be difficult to choose among the Princes, who could represent China in Washington or in Europe.

The Government deems also that the abnormal, even unique, conditions in which China finds herself, require [the sort of] knowledge and experience that can be acquired only in China herself by men familiar with the customs and resources of that country. This point of view . . . is shared by most of the Powers.

Japan has declined the American proposal without consulting the other Governments.[121]

In the international relief force, which had hastened to the rescue of the beleaguered foreign Legations in Peking, Russians and Japanese had fought side by side. But in Manchuria the foreign armies were strictly Russian, and as the Boxer threat died down, their continued presence was viewed with alarm by the other Powers. In the closing months of 1900 Russia made a secret agreement with China, turning civil administration back into Chinese hands in return for Chinese assistance in the construction of the Russian railway and Chinese acceptance and consultation of a Russian Political Resident at Mukden. Before long, news of the secret agreement leaked out. In January, 1901, the text was published, and d'Anethan sent a copy to his Government. He commented:

The publication of the so-called secret treaty between Russia and China concerning Manchuria. . . has aroused great excitement among the public and the press of Japan. The Russo-Chinese entente, which would place all of North China under Russian domination, seems to jeopardize the maintenance of peace in the Far East. The press, almost unanimously and without distinction as to political views, sees in it a serious future threat to Japanese supremacy in Korea.

Prince Konoye, President of the House of Peers and leader of an influential political group in Parliament, has frankly and freely commented on current events in an interview. He feels that obtaining Manchuria is a vital question for Russia at this time. The acquisition of this province will provide her with an outlet for the greatly increasing population of Siberia. But Manchuria is too near a neighbor of Korea to delude oneself for one instant about the future plans of the Cabinet of St. Petersburg. Once established in the north of China, the Russians will not delay coming to Seoul. "If the advance of the Russians toward Korea is to be stopped, it must be done now," the Prince concluded. "The moment has come."

Your Excellency is aware that Prince Konoye belongs if not to the opposition, so at least to a political group whose views regarding the China question do not agree entirely with those of Marquis Ito and the Government now in power. His ideas accurately reflect the aspirations of the military party, which would like to see the Government take a more determined and, in view of the latest events in China, less passive attitude. All deem that the moment has come for Japan to shed her restraint and usual prudence and loudly assert her displeasure—to say the least—at Russian violation of the Anglo-German convention concerning the maintenance of the [territorial] integrity of China, a violation which seriously threatens Japanese prospects in Korea.

Japan is particularly interested in preventing Moscovite domination of Manchuria. The advocates of an energetic policy go so far as to think that once the Cabinets of London and Berlin have been consulted on this question, Japan—as a party to the Anglo-German convention—would have the right to oppose the annexation of Manchuria even singlehandedly.

Japanese pride has been noticeably wounded by these events. She is reminded of her own occupation of Manchurian territory five years ago . . . [and of]the coalition of 1895 [which] had forced her to restore it on the ground that a prolonged occupation would endanger the peace of the Far East. Today when another Power wants to occupy the same territory without being at war with China, no protest is raised to prevent her. Even the most restrained

voices advise the Imperial Government "to seize this opportunity—
the annexation of Manchuria by Russia seeming to be an accom-
plished fact—to come to an agreement [with Russia] which
would leave Japan full freedom of action in Korea."

It is rather difficult to predict the attitude of the Government
in the face of such a formidable outburst of national feeling. After
taking office last October, Marquis Ito retired to the country under
the pretext of illness, and has only now actively resumed the
presidency of the Council. Moreover, the state of domestic politics,
the proceedings instituted against several members of the Municipal
Council of Tokyo for corruption, and the sudden resignation of
Mr. Hoshi Toru, hinder the freedom of action of the Cabinet at
the present time.

The financial condition of the country is far from satisfactory.
The costs of the China expedition and the ever growing needs of the
Army and Navy will require the levying of new taxes. It does not
seem very likely, therefore, that the Government will find at this
time the sums necessary for large military operations. It will
probably endeavor again to meet the present crisis with peaceful
means, satisfying national feeling in so far as possible by obtaining
compensation on the part of Korea.[122]

A fortnight later d'Anethan elaborated on the position
of the Japanese Government:

Public opinion in Japan is becoming increasingly aroused about
Russian policy in Manchuria. But the Government remains pru-
dently restrained. It understands too well the folly of the chauvinis-
tic party, which seeks to pose as the champion of China and the
defender, at any cost, of the [territorial] integrity of the Em-
pire. If England and Germany do not protest against the occu-
pation, annexation, protectorate or whatever the form under which
Russia will establish her domination in Manchuria, the present
Government will not go beyond diplomatic discussion.

Marquis Ito told me recently:

"We do not have positive information about the agreement

which has allegedly been concluded at Mukden between two gener-als. At any rate, the Governments have not ratified it, and it is too soon for Japan to be able to define absolutely the policy she will have to follow.

"Russia has considerable interests in Manchuria, and it is legitimate for her to protect them. During last year's troubles, she was the only one to send troops and maintain order in this part of China. She thereby helped the other Powers, limiting the area where their troops had to intervene. If she continues to maintain order in North China without hindering the commercial develop-ment of the other nations, Japan will be able to safeguard her interests, in spite of the presence of military forces.

"Our already considerable economic interests in Manchuria tend to increase with every day, and it is absolutely essential for us, that the port of Newchwang remain open and free to our mer-chant marine. The situation will become critical, if obstacles and hindrances are put in the way of our commercial transactions. We shall not be the only ones hurt then, and our interests will merge with those of the other European Powers and of America."

The Marquis, in the course of conversation, reiterated that he was concerned above all with the commercial and industrial interests of Japan in China. "In Europe one is too inclined to believe that we strive primarily for a political influence that would be detrimental to the Western nations. One says that the Japanese and the Chinese are of another race and that the yellow race will always have the tendency to draw together and unite against the white race. Nothing is farther from the truth or more absurd. We know too well—better than the Occidentals—the faults, the ignorance, the prejudices and the backward ideas of the Chinese to consider for an instant uniting with them. We deem it necessary to help them establish a progressive government, capable of main-taining the integrity of China, but we want to attempt this difficult task in cooperation with the European nations.

"Without foreign support China will never succeed in making the financial, moral and political reforms in her Government,

without which she is bound to perish. The Governments of Europe, Japan and America, therefore, must agree on a general plan of reforms for China. Our Government, which knows China well, could propose a program of reforms. We hesitate to take the initiative, because of the still very deep-rooted prejudice against us and the mistrust of advice by statesmen of the yellow race.

"If haste is not made to collaborate in the restoration of order and stability in China, however, the situation will get worse. For several months there has been fruitless discussion of the reparations that should be exacted from China. I see no indication of a change for the better in the future.

"So far the uprisings and disorders have broken out in a limited region. The Viceroys and Governors of the richest and most populous provinces have maintained peace. One must take advantage of the good disposition which now exists, and not let the anarchy that reigns in the north spread to all of China. New and bloodier disturbances will be avoided only by lending benevolent support to the Viceroys who have resisted the orders given by the leaders of the revolution at Peking. We shall join any common action designed to give new life to the Government of China.

"I cannot say and repeat enough that Japan does not seek any exclusive or particular advantage. Our interests in China are identical with those of the industrial powers of both worlds. All our efforts are directed toward the development of our trade and our industry, and the big market which is at our door must be open wide to us as much and even more than to others and offer full security. Since this goal can be attained only through the collaboration and agreement of all Powers, Japan would commit national suicide were she to refuse to cooperate faithfully [in working] toward a better administration of the Chinese Empire."

The views expressed by Marquis Ito are shared by the leading statesmen of Japan. They will prevail, if the European Cabinets do not ignore the legitimate role due Japan in the settlement, or the attempts at settlement, of the China question. If, on the other hand, mistrust should dominate and Japan be side-stepped or

*placed in an inferior position in the negotiations to come, the
military party will force the hand of the Government.*

*We cannot conceal from ourselves, that there exists in the
country an influential party which is sympathetic toward China
and advocates the union of the yellow race. This party is fought by
the Government and will not gain power and stability, unless
the wise and moderate policy of the present Cabinet . . . fails to
safeguard the primary interests of Japan and China in Korea.*[123]

By late March, Japanese excitement had reached a fever
pitch, and war with Russia had become a distinct possibility.
D'Anethan observed:

*Very great excitement has been aroused in Japan by Russian
policy in North China. The Army and the Navy seek to persuade
the Government to take a firmer attitude toward Russia. Belligerent ideas are encouraged by an influential group in the House
of Peers, and in the House of Representatives the Ministers are
constantly queried how they will protect the interests of the country.
The press is almost unanimous in echoing the attacks against the
weakness and incapacity of the Government, and keeps all classes
of society in a state of excitement, the seriousness of which we
cannot conceal from ourselves. Marquis Ito, whose prestige was
unquestioned for years, now is attacked more seriously. The House
of Peers, where he had only supporters and friends a short time ago,
set the example of revolt against the eminent statesman. It recently
refused to vote the new taxes decreed by the Government and voted
by the House of Representatives. In vain the Marquis adduced
evidence in several speeches that the funds requested were indispensable . . . for the maintenance of the Japanese forces in China—
the Peers did not want to listen to reason. The session was, therefore, suspended for five days to permit reaching an agreement
between the Ministry and the Upper House. Marquis Yamagata,
Count Matsukata, Count Okuma, Marquis Saigo, Count Inouye—
all of them former prime ministers—vainly used their influence
to [try to] bring the Peers around to a more reasonable view.*

The Emperor thus had to intercede, and called on Prince Konoye, the President of the House [of Peers], to convey to the Peers his will, that the projects of the Government be voted in view of the gravity of the situation. The Peers bowed to the authority of the Sovereign, and the law was adopted.

The immediate efficacy of the direct intervention of His Majesty shows how profound the feeling of respect and love for the dynasty still are. At the same time, however, it is a great proof of weakness for the Ministry to have been constrained to expose the person of the Emperor.

In the House of Representatives the Ministry's action was the subject of a very animated discussion, and a motion of censure against it was defeated by only a small majority. The members of the Cabinet also disagree on foreign policy. The Ministers of War and of the Navy push for energetic action, and are controlled with difficulty by Marquis Ito and Mr. Kato. The danger of the situation is evident, and it is to be feared that the military element will gain the upper hand.

The Foreign Minister declared to the House that Russia informed the Government, that she did not want to annex Manchuria, that she had forces there solely to maintain order and protect her railways. One is not satisfied with these pacific assurances in Japan, and urges the Government to take immediately appropriate measures to assure the independence of Korea, which would be threatened directly by the annexation of Manchuria.

I do not say that war is imminent, but it is far from improbable. In the present state of mind in Japan, it would be popular and undertaken with confidence. It is believed here that the fleet is superior to that which Russia can send now, and in a very short time at least two hundred thousand men could attack the Russians in Manchuria or in Korea. In the military world the idea is now expressed loudly and publicly, that the present time would be most favorable for making war, and that one must not wait until Russia has built the formidable fleet which she will have in a few years.

The President of the Council has much more peaceful views and would like to obtain certain compensations by diplomatic means. But his authority is so shaken, that he will have great difficulty to resist the pressures which are exerted on him from all sides to induce him to be less timid in his protests against Russian infringements.[124]

In April, 1901, Russia backed down, but talk of war continued. In the words of d'Anethan:

The Russian Minister has notified the Japanese Government, that Russia has given up concluding a treaty with China concerning Manchuria. For the moment the cause of the crisis, which rendered relations between Tokyo and St. Petersburg so tense, has thus been averted.

Japan has obtained a diplomatic success. By her encouragement of China and by the firmness of her remonstrances in St. Petersburg, she has prevented the signing of a convention which would have sanctioned the dismemberment of China.

We cannot conceal from ourselves, however, that the situation is still full of danger, and the slightest incident can put fire to the powder. The prudent and moderate element of the Government, represented by Marquis Ito and Mr. Kato, will continue to seek to safeguard the interests of Japan by peaceful means before resorting to extreme measures. The Ministers of War and of the Navy, on the other hand, push for an aggressive policy. The country agrees with them. The idea that war with Russia must break out one day has so taken hold of the public mind, that the Government will have much trouble to calm those who want to precipitate it.

Count Okuma, former Prime Minister, who may regain the position shortly, has publicly stated: "I condemn any foreign policy which merely adapts itself timidly to the attitude of other Powers. There is only one alternative: to deal a decisive blow to Russia in Manchuria or to lose all prestige in China. Here is a magnificent opportunity for your patriotism. The war will be a just war, because it will be made against an enemy of justice, of commerce, of peace and of civilization."[125]

On April 20, the Baroness d'Anethan left for Europe. D'Anethan himself deferred taking leave, because of the worsening international situation. As the Baroness had recorded in her diary on April 2: "The political atmosphere gets more and more gloomy, and it certainly seems as if Japan is on the eve of a war with Russia."[126] On April 8, Foreign Minister Kato had told her that the Russians had decided that morning not to insist on the Convention regarding Manchuria. She jotted down: "This is, of course, a great diplomatic victory for Japan; but though the present crisis is passed, it is doubtful whether matters are improved between the two Powers for any length of time. The situation is now exactly where it was before there was any talk of a Convention and A. [Albert d'Anethan] is, I see, perfectly convinced that the danger of war is merely averted for a period of a year or two."[127]

In May, d'Anethan forwarded the translation of an article written for a Japanese journal by Prince Konoye Atsumaro, President of the House of Peers, on the subject of Manchuria. In it Konoye continued the campaign against Russia and, d'Anethan remarked, the number of advocates of a strong policy was increasing steadily.

There are disagreements in the bosom of the Cabinet concerning the financial conduct, and the Ministry is much criticized. We expect a change in Ministry shortly. Marquis Ito loses his authority more and more, and I am afraid that he will soon be replaced by the party which represents more the current aspirations of the Japanese people, who are firmly in favor of an aggressive policy against Russia.[128]

In June the Ito Cabinet fell and General Katsura Taro became Premier. D'Anethan telegraphed to his Government: "The anti-parliamentary Ministry is ready for an energetic policy, should the interests of Japan be menaced by Russia."[129]

That month Hoshi Toru, Minister of Communications in the former Cabinet, was assassinated. D'Anethan related the incident and reflected on its causes and the nature of the current government.

Mr. Hoshi Toru, former Minister in the last Cabinet of Marquis Ito, was assassinated yesterday by a Mr. Iba Sotaro in one of the drawing-rooms of the municipal hotel. He had attended a meeting of the town council and was talking in a neighboring room with several of his friends, when a person wearing the Japanese dress of the rich classes suddenly entered. He approached Hoshi Toru, spoke a few words, and with the speed of lightning seized a short sword and plunged it twice into the chest and side of his victim, who died almost instantly. Arrested and disarmed without offering resistance, the murderer declared with much calm and composure, that he had committed the crime for the good of his country. He is a well-off man in his fifties, who had occupied important positions in a provincial bank and was president of a committee established by the Government to study questions concerning the progress of instruction in Yotsuya.

Mr. Hoshi Toru, whose dominant role in the Party formed by Marquis Ito had ruined not only the influence of that Party but also had been the principal cause of the Cabinet's forced resignation, had as enemies all honest people. Intelligent and very able, he lacked any feeling of honor and honesty. Making him a lieutenant, Marquis Ito ruined for long. . .the great and exceptional position that he had occupied with such brilliance in the counsels of the Crown.

The present Ministry is composed of men who do not belong to any political Party. It will not be preoccupied with the opposition that it may encounter in the House of Representatives. Supported by the House of Peers, it will not hesitate to dissolve the Diet and at the least indication of trouble will suspend the Constitution. In foreign policy too, it will show much firmness. The accession of the Cabinet was warmly welcomed by the military world and the political group led by Prince Konoye, who recently launched an active newspaper campaign against Russia.[130]

Field Marshal Count von Waldersee, Commander-in-Chief of the allied forces during the Boxer Uprising, visited Tokyo at this time, and was greeted with great honors and festivity. D'Anethan reflected:

The original announcement of the Marshal's visit was received with little enthusiasm. The semi-official press did not fail to recall the part played by Germany after the war against China; it also had reservations about the conduct of the Marshal in China and the expeditions which he had deemed necessary and which were regarded as useless slaughter. The tone has changed, since the result of the visit can only be favorable for Japanese-German relations. An article inspired by Jiji states: "We only ask to forget the past and to remember the debt Japan owes Germany both in the military and intellectual realms, and hope that the visit of the Marshal will strengthen the cordial relations existing between the two peoples, relations which are still far from what they should be."

Japan, of course, attaches the greatest importance to knowing what the attitude of Germany would be in case of a conflict with Russia. She believes she can count on the benevolent neutrality, if not on the support, of England and the United States, and does not believe that France would declare war on Japan to help Russia in Manchuria or in Korea. The great enigma which always worries them is Germany.

The situation seems calm enough at the moment, but the preparations for war do not cease. General Yamaguchi, who has just returned from China, considers that the supposed strength of the Russian armies is very much exaggerated and that the time has come for Japan to seize Korea. In the opinion of Japanese officers, the favorable season for beginning hostilities would be autumn, when ice closes the port of Vladivostok. It would be easy then to immobilize the greater part of the Russian squadron. All that I see and hear seems not very reassuring for the maintenance of peace. The defenders of a prudent policy, such as Marquis Ito, Count Inouye and Count Matsukata are set aside. The head of the

Cabinet, who is one of the most brilliant officers of Japan—it was he who in '94 directed the campaign in Manchuria—would not have kept his present Ministers of War and of the Navy, if he were animated by peaceful feelings.[131]

In July d'Anethan transmitted an article from a Japanese newspaper, which took issue with the belligerent attitude of those who spoke "as if Russia were not one of the Powers with which Japan had peaceful diplomatic relations." D'Anethan remarked: "The question of Manchuria has temporarily lost the acute character that had threatened to disturb the peace at the time when Russia wanted to impose an agreement on China. It is no longer in the forefront of Japanese policy."[132]

By November Russo-Japanese relations had improved further. D'Anethan observed:

For some time relations between Russia and Japan seem to have been such as to diminish the apprehensions which had been aroused last spring by Russia's plan to impose a treaty on China concerning Manchuria. In Korea, we do not hear of Russian intrigues to counterbalance the action and interests of Japan.

Japan has obtained satisfaction by the repeal of the decree forbidding the exportation of rice. Construction of the Seoul-Fusan railway has been started. France does not seem to insist on the building of a railway from Seoul to Wiju, which Japan would oppose, since the line could only be of strategic interest for Russia. As long as Russia will not threaten Korea, a conflict can be avoided, and if the commercial interests of Japan are not impeded by the occupation of Manchuria, an entente between Russia and Japan is not impossible. The French Chargé d'Affaires, Monsieur Dubail, has been instructed to do all he can to induce Japan to establish friendly relations with Russia. . . .

Our Russian colleague, Mr. Izvolskii, who from the beginning of his mission had shown himself rather arrogant and little concerned with sparing even the most justified susceptibilities of Japan, now is much more conciliatory and amiable. According to Monsieur Dubail, he has been ordered very explicitly by St. Petersburg not to cause any difficulties with Japan. My French colleague added, that we owe the change in the Russian Minister's attitude to his reports, which the Cabinet of Paris communicated to that of St. Petersburg.[133]

In January, 1902, d'Anethan joined his wife in Europe.

Russo-Japanese relations had been like a pendulum, swinging from amity to hostility, back and forth. Interested in Korea, Manchuria and China proper, Russian and Japanese statesmen were confronted repeatedly with the choice of working with each other or against each other. Marquis Ito leaned toward Russo-Japanese collaboration but Russian reluctance to come to terms with him played into the hands of those who favored an alliance with Great Britain, Russia's major rival. In February of 1902, in d'Anethan's absence, Georges de Man reported the conclusion of the Anglo-Japanese Alliance and transmitted the text of the treaty. In doing so he commented:

News of the conclusion of this treaty has been received in the Diplomatic Corps and in Japanese circles with some surprise, if not with a great deal of astonishment. So scrupulously had the secret of these negotiations been observed, that not even the Russian Legation in Tokyo had gotten wind of the bomb which burst so suddenly, as the English Minister put it. Only the American Legation had been informed recently of the clauses of the new treaty which had received, it is said, the full approval of the American Government. Its eagerness to congratulate Japan tends to prove this.

No one doubts that the Anglo-Japanese treaty of alliance, though affecting the appearance of an instrument of peace, is a weapon aimed against Russia and her ally France, even against Germany. I believe we shall soon see whether Russia, whose political interests are so powerful in the Far East, will tolerate this new state of affairs, which she can regard only as a provocation. According to a conversation which I just had with one of the most influential members of the Russian Legation in Tokyo, Russia cannot remain indifferent to this humiliation, and must without delay deal a striking blow before the eyes of the Japanese to nullify the psychological effect of the new treaty. When I asked him if he thought that Russia could eventually make this demonstration in Manchuria, he replied with a smile: "But Manchuria is ours. We shall complete its conquest in a slow and sure way and neither the Japanese Army allied to the remains of the English Army of the Transvaal nor any other Power will ever dislodge us from there. No, no," my colleague added, "the blow that we shall strike will be loud and brilliant and will only tend to abate the arrogance of the Japanese towards us and prove to them the absurdity of the treaty of alliance that they have just concluded."

As I persisted, intrigued, to get more detailed information, my colleague remained stubbornly silent, except to tell me: "Whatever it may be, this treaty will sooner or later be the pretext for the inevitable war between Russia and Japan, not because it injures us directly of itself, but because it constitutes for Japan a dangerous weapon which will allow her to provoke us without let-up. . .and finally, at the end of our patience, exasperated, we shall accept the challenge."

The predictions of my colleague appear to me quite pessimistic, if not somewhat exaggerated. Would one not be inclined rather to believe that the answer of Russia, like the conquest of Manchuria, will be slow and sure?

After this somewhat bitter note, it is fitting to acknowledge that the new treaty has received the warmest welcome on the part of the Japanese public and especially the political and commercial circles. Demonstrations are being organized on all sides, political clubs of every shade, the Chambers of Commerce, and the most diverse associations express their exuberant joy with banquets adorned with flamboyant speeches. The Japanese press exults in dithyrambic articles. Yesterday a torch parade, organized by 1,500 students

marched past the British Legation, intoning a chorus, improvised
for the occasion, to the glory of England the new friend.

The local English press congratulates itself on the agreement
concluded between its country and Japan in view of the interests
of England in China, but its enthusiasm is rather cool. I am told
that a number of English residents who have lived in Japan for
many years and are used to regarding the Japanese as a generally
inferior nation are a bit humiliated by the alliance of their country
with a people of the yellow race, and they must think, I imagine, as
does the majority of the members of the Diplomatic Corps in
Tokyo, that England is much lowered for having come to that.

As regards the treaty of alliance itself. . . , it is limited to the
affairs of the Far East and appears to seek only the maintenance of
the status quo and universal peace, having as its goal respect for
the independence and territorial integrity of the Chinese Empire
and of Korea. The different organs of the press specifically note,
that the preamble of the treaty explicitly states "the Empire" of
China, to let it be known that Manchuria has not been excluded.

What is particularly serious about the alliance consecrated by this
treaty, is that it is offensive as well as defensive, which one day will
allow England to launch Japan on very dangerous adventures—
without running any risk of her own.[134]

In November of 1902, de Man provided the Belgian
Government with a lengthy report on the organization and
strength of the Japanese Army. He was not very impressed:

The level of studies, except at the War College, is generally
very low. The instruction given in the different schools is equivalent
to that acquired by the noncommissioned officers in Europe, and is
confined to about ten months of study.

Japanese officers generally have only a very vague idea about
European military science, and the strategy of the Old World is,
so to speak, unknown to them. They are most meticulous in insignifi-
cant details, but have no idea of the whole, and in unforeseen cases
very quickly lose their heads. They have the great fault of not spar-

ing their men enough and of sacrificing their lives uselessly. It has been authenticated that during the Sino-Japanese war one third of the soldiers remained lying on the road, felled by fatigue and starvation, and another third was sent uselessly to death. . . .

The Japanese soldier is brave and scorns death. He is docile, but little disciplined. He has no endurance on marches and does not stand cold. His nourishment is bad and insubstantial. He is rather sober and very cruel. . . .

The cavalry is the weakest branch of the Japanese Army because of the absolutely inferior quality of the horses, which have defective rumps, narrow chests, and bad hoofs. . . . The number of men who could leave the country in case of war with a foreign power on the Asian Continent is estimated as, at the very maximum, 150,000.[135]

But Japan was making every effort to strengthen her armed forces and ready herself for any eventuality. D'Anethan, who had returned to Tokyo with his wife on November 6, after a long leave, wrote at the end of January, 1903:

In spite of the pacific assurances of St. Petersburg, the action of the Russian agents in Port Arthur, Peking and Seoul has not, in the opinion of the Japanese Government, ceased to be provocative. Only today news has been received, that Mr. Pavlov seeks to obtain concessions at Masampo and at Chin-lin-wan (?) to establish coal depots there.

According to newspapers reports and. . .well-informed travelers coming from Port Arthur and Manchuria, Russian officers openly express their contempt for the Japanese Army and their conviction that Japan will not dare to attack Russia. They see in Japan's moderation, proof of her weakness. . . .

It is true, that Japan simply asked that the categorical refusal given to the Japanese proposals concerning Manchuria be reconsidered. But at the same time, we see that she has been preparing Imperial Ordinances, purchasing ships, and completing her arrangements for war.

Whether Russia at the last moment will again find a way to post-pone the denouement and prolong the negotiations, we cannot know in Tokyo. The information which it is our duty to furnish deals only with the intentions and decisions of the Japanese Government. These are now clearly indicated: to establish its complete and exclusive influence in Korea; to impose it, if threatened or attacked.[136]

In February d'Anethan commented on the relations of Korea with Russia and Japan:

Finance Minister Li Yong-ik, who formerly seemed inclined to submit to Japanese influence, today seems entirely devoted to Russia. Since he took refuge in the Russian Legation last year and on a Russian warship fled from Korea to Port Arthur, whence he was brought back again on a vessel of the same Power, he has. . . adopted a hostile attitude toward Japan. He wants to prohibit the circulation of Japanese banknotes, take back the ginseng monopoly from a Japanese company, and contract a loan abroad.

The intrigues of the Ministers and officials of the Korean Court concern the Japanese Government only from the standpoint of its relations with Russia; the Korean Government has neither the strength nor the resources to cause it serious trouble.

In the protocols of June 9, 1896 and June 25, 1898, signed in St. Petersburg and Tokyo, the Japanese and Russian Governments stipulated, that no obstacle be raised to the development of Japanese commerce and industry in Korea and that, if Korea had to resort to foreign loans, the two Governments jointly lend her support. The Japanese Government watches that these advantages not be compromised, and will not allow Korea to violate them either directly or indirectly.[137]

Manchuria remained in the limelight. D'Anethan related:

The Russian occupation of Manchuria is much discussed by the Japanese press, and we see the same emotion that was manifested about two years ago, when it was imputed that Russia intended to occupy this part of the Chinese Empire permanently. Without letting ourselves be carried away by the alarming and exaggerated

*considerations of the press, we cannot conceal from ourselves that
the present situation is not sufficiently reassuring.*

*I feel one must not believe the rumors, which part of the Euro-
pean press will probably echo, to the effect that a break between the
two countries is imminent. So far, the Foreign Minister recently
told me, the interests of Japan have not suffered from the presence
of Russian troops in Manchuria. On the contrary, he added, the
Russian occupation has been profitable first to the Chinese and then
to the Japanese, who today number two thousand in this province
and are increasing constantly. We have, the Minister says further,
considerable trade with Manchuria; much navigation with Newchwang. We must insist, therefore, that our commercial relations
not be impeded, that no restriction be put on the residence and
free movement of our nationals. The port of Newchwang must
remain absolutely open to foreign dealings, like all the other ports
of China. The Foreign Minister's words seem to indicate, that
the Government now is concerned with this side of the question:
it desires assurances and guarantees that Russia will not injure
business transactions in Manchuria.*

*One is convinced in Japan that England and the United States
want to keep the vast and rich market of North China open for their
commerce and industry. The similarity of views and identity of
interests from the commercial standpoint of the three nations which
have most business with Manchuria allay Japan's present fears
to some extent.*[138]

Japan was determined not to forfeit Manchuria. In the
words of d'Anethan:

*The Japanese Government is very firm in the pressure which it
exerts in Peking to prevent the conclusion of arrangements that
would make Russia mistress of Manchuria. At St. Petersburg too,
it protests against the continuation of the Russian occupation. . . .*

*The Foreign Minister told me today, he considered the situation
would become very grave, if Russia persisted in occupying Manchuria with her. . . .large forces. For the past two years, Russia has*

*made extensive military preparations; she has in particular seri-
ously augmented her squadrons, and has her best and most powerful
ships in the China seas. But Japan will not be intimidated by this
show of force, and will not flinch.*

*Fortunately the present Minister is as prudent as he is firm. He
does not let himself be pushed by the military parties, which want
drastic measures now. He will consent to any negotiations that
promise a peaceful solution. If these fail, we shall see Japan resort
once again to arms with as much ardor and enthusiasm as in
1894. She was ready to do so two years ago.*

*In the keen game between Russia and Japan today, the latter
puts her cards on the table and—to use the expression of an American game that has become part of the diplomatic vocabulary—does
not bluff.*[139]

Japan stood united in girding her strength. As d'Anethan
reported in June of 1903 :

*The Japanese Parliament has voted the projects, presented by
the Government, to increase the Navy considerably. The expenses
over a period of ten years will amount to 115,000,000 yen or
nearly 300 million francs. On the other hand, there will be no
reduction in the budget of the Ministry of War [i.e. the Army].*[140]

D'Anethan reported that once Japan had made clear to St.
Petersburg how much importance she attached to the question of Russian troops in Manchuria, which Russia was
negotiating with China, she conducted herself on the whole
with prudent reserve. But d'Anethan warned:

*One should not conclude from the calm shown by Japan under
the present circumstances, however, that she no longer demands the
carrying out of the arrangements by which Russia has consented,
under certain conditions, to return to China the government of the
part of her territory. . . . Russia now administers.*

*The Russian Minister of War is expected very soon with a large
retinue, and will be received with great respect by the Emperor and
his Government. Yet I believe that unless General [Aleksei*

L

Nikolaevich] Kuropatkin brings proposals that would absolutely permit the realization of Japanese aspirations in Korea—which would hardly be in the tradition of Russian diplomacy—the mission of the Count will not result in the establishment of a more reassuring situation in the Far East. . . .

Japan will never consent to the neutrality of Korea, the guaranteeing of her independence, the division of spheres of influence, or a joint occupation. As a Japanese diplomat, who is well known and appreciated in Brussels and formerly was Minister of Foreign Affairs, told me only recently, Korea does not have the necessary strength to allow the very possibility of such diplomatic combinations. . . . "You know our country too well" he told me, "not to know that we all have but one and the same foreign policy. We do not have cause for satisfaction about the future of Korea; the question will have to be decided on the battlefield."

It is in Korea that a fire threatens to break out which, once lit, will spread far in Asia. Under the circumstances, the foreigners whose advice the Korean Government will seek will have an almost insurmountably difficult task, because the counsels that they will give in all sincerity and absolute neutrality for the good of the country alone will be interpreted according to the situation of the moment, favorably or unfavorably, depending on whether Russia or Japan will have an interest in approving or disapproving them.[141]

In the second half of June General Kuropatkin visited Japan. The Russians always treated Japanese guests with the greatest hospitality at Court; Kuropatkin in turn was received with high honors by the Japanese, receiving the Paulownia Cross, which was most rarely bestowed on foreigners. The visit that was to have lasted only three days was prolonged to over a week, giving rise to stories of a Russo-Japanese agreement. Passing on the text of the alleged agreement, denied by the Authorities, providing for a limited withdrawal of Russian forces from Manchuria and recognition of Japanese privileges in Korea, d'Anethan commented:

Without believing in the authenticity of this memorandum, one seems inclined to accept that General Kuropatkin actually seeks to calm the apprehensions of Japan concerning Manchuria by offering her concessions in Korea.

The publication of this document has given rise to a series of articles in all shades of the press, showing how unfavorably public opinion would receive any agreement that would sacrifice the interests of Japan in China for some problematical advantages in Korea.

Should telegram reports that Mr. [Pavel Mikhailovich] Lessar [the Russian Minister in Peking] has signed a secret convention with Prince Ch'ing be confirmed, we can expect to see Japan protest more energetically than she has done until now.

Feeling about the occupation of Manchuria has become the more acute, as Russia displays great activity on the banks of the Yalu, where she has stationed some troops under the pretext of protecting the exploitation of forests.[142]

Queried by his Government about the prospects of war and peace, d'Anethan responded:

In the excerpt of the reports from St. Petersburg of April 28, which Your Excellency has kindly sent me. . . , I read: "According to well-informed persons, Japan would at present still be able to drive the Russians out of Manchuria by herself, but one doubts that the situation will remain the same as time passes." These words correspond exactly to Japanese thinking. They want to settle their differences with Russia, because they believe that they are stronger today and fear that in a very few years they will have lost the superiority in number of troops and vessels. So deeply is this feeling embedded in all classes of society, civilian and military, that with every day that passes without bringing changes in the already very tense situation, we see the danger of a break increase.

The moderate language of Russia in Europe and the assurances which she gives in London and in Washington regarding her guarantees to foreign interests make no impression in Tokyo. Im-

portance is attached only to the negotiations begun in Peking. Their nature does not allow one to have much faith in declarations made by Russia elsewhere.

For the moment the efforts of Japanese diplomacy are concentrated on preventing the Chinese Government from giving in to the demands of Russia. It is generally believed, that the energetic language used just recently by the Minister of Japan to Prince Ch'ing has stopped the latter from signing an accord with Mr. Lessar.

This situation cannot continue, however. If China, unable to reject the Russian demands by herself, shows the vigor that one recommends, Japan will lend her effective assistance. It is to St. Petersburg that Japan will then have to carry her protests and to formulate the conditions under which she will preserve her peaceful attitude. There is reason to fear that if things reach that stage, the negotiations will be short-lived!

The Ministry now in power avoids precipitating events, but it will not content itself with vain promises. Even if it wanted to do so, it would be swept away by national feeling.

The attitude of the Japanese Government has been correct and prudent up to now. Neither in the Diet nor in private interviews can one find one word of hostility or provocation toward Russia on the part of the members of the Cabinet. Yet the Government does not prevent the press from expressing itself very freely, and has accepted without protest the memorial that seven distinguished professors of the Imperial University of Tokyo have addressed to the Minister of Foreign Affairs [maintaining that Japan should demand the withdrawal of all Russian troops from Manchuria].

The influence of the elder statesmen Marquis Ito, Count Inouye, and Marshal Yamagata has been exerted lately to temper Japanese chauvinism, but only in the sense that no provocative policy should be pursued. If the day comes, when there can be no longer any doubt about Russian intentions to ignore Japanese interests in China and Korea, they will be the first to support and encourage the warlike sentiments of the nation.

Had Russia not pledged herself to evacuate Manchuria, thereby forcing Japan to content herself with a diplomatic victory, two years ago, we would have seen arise at that time the danger that is the more threatening today. Without doubt Japan has confidence in the alliance with England and believes she can count on the sympathy of the United States. She does not expect armed intervention, but is not afraid, should the occasion arise, to attack her powerful neighbor alone.[143]

Rumors of a Russo-Japanese understanding, prevalent during Kuropatkin's visit, did not linger beyond his departure. D'Anethan related:

Leaving Japan, General Kuropatkin went to Port Arthur, where he met with the Russian Minister to Peking, the Russian Representative to Korea, Admiral [Evgenii Ivanovich] Alexeev, and General [Konstantin Ippolitovich] Vogak, the former Military Attaché in Japan.

Following these conferences a large Russian troop movement was noticed on the Yalu border. The Russians have tried to set up telegraph lines partly on Korean territory. One is convinced in Tokyo, furthermore, that Mr. Pavlov has demanded a railway concession (considered here as purely strategic) from Seoul to Wiju. In the wake of these conferences too, the Cabinet of St. Petersburg addressed a memorandum to London, Berlin, Washington and Tokyo to the effect that Russia would not oppose the opening of new ports in Manchuria; she would oppose the establishment of foreign concessions and would not admit foreigners to the towns of the interior, including Harbin.

These conditions are not apt to calm Japanese susceptibilities, and the recrudescence of Russian activity in Korea only increases the apprehensions, which I often expressed in my correspondence, that Japan will take a very determined attitude.[144]

In September of 1903, d'Anethan reviewed the state of negotiations between Russia and Japan:

The negotiations, begun in St. Petersburg to reach an agreement between Russia and Japan concerning Manchuria and Korea, do not seem to have progressed favorably, and I learn, though the fact is still being kept secret, that they have been transferred to Tokyo and will be conducted by Baron Rosen, the Russian Minister.

Japanese demands at St. Petersburg seemed moderate enough as they implied the recognition of Russia's special position in Manchuria. The Japanese Minister had believed at first that he could count on a conciliatory attitude on the part of Count [Vladimir Nikolaevich] Lamsdorf [the Foreign Minister] and find a basis for agreement.

The nomination of Admiral Alexeev, with the widest powers, to the position of Viceroy and the new demands made by Russia on China have not only rekindled but also poked the fire which had been smouldering for over two years and which threatens increasingly to bring about a terrible conflagration.

The continuation of the negotiations in Tokyo virtually puts the direction of Russian policy in the Far East in the hands of Admiral Alexeev. Japan feared this eventuality, because in her eyes it is the Governor of Port Arthur who is responsible for the provocative action of the Russian Representative in Korea. One believes also that he is most hostile toward Japan.

The preservation of peace depends on Russia. Japan demands assurances that her political and economic policy will not be impeded by Russia in any way. She wants to reserve for herself the construction of a railway from Seoul to Wiju, and will not tolerate the occupation, exploitation or leasing of a point of Korean territory by Russia, in whatever form the Power may seek to obtain it. If Russia accedes to these claims, the conflict between the two Powers can be delayed. If not, Japan will forge ahead. The Government does not want to precipitate events, but is prepared to face them.

A society, called Patriots Watching Russia, holds frequent discussions during which the most hostile feelings are expressed. At numerous banquets, celebrating the anniversary of the naval battle of the Yalu and Japanese victories in China, Army and Navy officers made the most bellicose speeches. Unable to attend a banquet, a Lieu-

tenant General, who in case of war would be called to a position of high command, telegraphed: "In celebrating the victory of Pyong-yang, let us pray that we see another one like it soon." The victory is the one Marshal Yamagata won, when he crossed the Yalu and invaded China.

The high officers of the Crown, who are close to the Emperor and usually are prudent and reserved, do not conceal that the situation has reached a point where, unless Russia suddenly changes her atti-tude completely, Japan will no longer let her rights be violated. The negotiations which have been begun or are about to be begun between Baron Komura and Baron Rosen will entail the most serious con-sequences.

Offended by new Russian demands to Peking while it was nego-tiating at St. Petersburg and made the more mistrustful by the no-mination of Admiral Alexeev, the Government will show itself less conciliatory than it had been inclined to show itself toward Count Lamsdorf.[145]

On October 9, Baroness d'Anethan confided to her diary:

Japan and Russia are on the eve of a war. It is difficult to see how it can be averted. It does not look as though Russia, in spite of her promises, seems inclined to give up the occupation of Manchuria. Baron Rosen has been to Port Arthur to confer with Viceroy Alex-ev, and is back again. All negotiations are being carried on here. The Japanese are most bellicose and equally indignant. Russia thinks the latter are playing a game of bluff, but there they are mis-taken, and there is not the slightest doubt but that the Japanese are in deadly earnest.[146]

A month later d'Anethan wrote further about the negotia-tions between Baron Rosen and Foreign Minister Komura:

Baron Komura told me, that since the two Governments were eager to arrive at a peaceful solution, he was quite hopeful that this end would be attained. The interests at stake are so important and vital for both countries, that one cannot expect a speedy conclusion of the negotiations. The questions concerning the occupation of

Manchuria and the relations with Korea are most complex and must be discussed in all their aspects and be resolved only after due deliberation.

Sincerely animated by peaceful intentions, the Imperial Government does not let itself be carried away by press incitements and popular excitement which, according to the Minister, is not so deep and general as the journalists and enemies of the Cabinet represent. The views of the Imperial Government have been stated very frankly to Russia, and it will not abandon the calm and moderation which it has persistently shown toward Russia. Baron Komura told me also, that he was persuaded that the Russian Minister was working to reconcile the interests of the two Powers.

Your Excellency will know already from the declarations made by the Japanese Representatives in London, Paris and Berlin, "that the relations between Russia and Japan are good, and that the Imperial Government refuses to admit that there is ground to fear an imminent break." The optimistic views of the Government are not shared in Japan, because one finds it hard to believe that Russia will make serious enough concessions to Japan to render the maintenance of peace possible.

If Russia accedes to all of Japan's claims, war evidently will be postponed or perhaps even avoided. Not knowing the exact nature of the Japanese demands, we cannot comment on the importance of the sacrifices asked of Russia. But it is absolutely certain that the Government, even if it so desired, would not be powerful enough to make the Army and Navy accept a diplomatic arrangement that did not clearly safeguard the interests of Japan in China and Korea.

It would be difficult for the Foreign Minister to speak otherwise while negotiations are in progress. It is astonishing, however, that not a single newspaper regards the situation in so favorable a light. I do not speak of the newspapers of the opposition, but of those which are in favor of his ideas and in many instances are semi-official mouthpieces. All without exception . . . predict war if Russia does not accept the Japanese proposals.

Notwithstanding the freedom accorded to the press, the Govern-

ment knows how to restrain and direct the latter, when it desires. Recently sensational bulletins were issued daily in Tokyo about the break in relations, the movements of troops and of the fleet. The newspaper editors received a warning from the Minister of the Interior, and since then no such bulletins have been published. No brake has been applied, however, to their political appraisals.

At the beginning of the negotiations a Japanese squadron, composed of 21 ships and 30 torpedo boats, was at Masampo. Almost the entire fleet cruises in the south, armed and ready for battle. If the negotiations drag out, the Government is expected to send a division to Korea to "protect" the few miles of railway, constructed between Seoul and Fusan.[147]

Assertions in the European press, that Japanese hatred of foreigners was increasing year by year, that xenophobia was more rampant in Japan than in China, and that in the event of a Russo-Japanese war the foreign community in Japan might be massacred, elicited from d'Anethan strong dissent:

If it were merely a question of the lucubrations of a newspaper man seeking to create sensational news, I would not waste Your Excellency's time in writing about this subject. I believe I must do so, however, because in Japan itself, especially among the residents in Yokohama and I regret to state among certain members of the Diplomatic Corps, one contemplates with some apprehension what the fate of the foreigners would be in case of a defeat.

Hate or hostility toward the foreigner does not exist in Japan. Were it true that we are tolerated and that every Japanese hates us at the bottom of his heart, by what acts, by what crimes is this hostility expressed? In what most remote place of Japan can the foreigner not move around and live alone, without arms or guards, day or night in perfect safety? Hundreds of American ladies, traveling alone or accompanied by a maid who is usually Japanese, annually traverse Japan in all directions. Let someone cite me one example, one only, where they have been molested or embarrassed in any way whatsoever!

*Look at the missionaries, Catholic, Protestant and Russian!
Have they been the object of insults or persecution of any sort?
They establish themselves wherever they wish, erect schools, chapels,
cathedrals. They preach and teach in all freedom.*

*Yes, one replies to me, until now the Japanese have not translated
their hate into action, but wait till the day when national feeling
will be hurt or overexcited, and they will give free rein to their
passions. I was in Japan when Japanese pride received the wound
from which it has not yet recovered. I remember the extent to which
Japanese partiotism suffered, when the intervention of the three
Great Powers, Russia, Germany and France, deprived it of the
fruit of victory. One could fear the outburst of a great anti-
European movement at that time. Did it materialize? As a precautionary measure the Government had the Legations guarded,
and the foreign Ministers were escorted by two policemen; at the
demand of the diplomats themselves this police surveillance was
soon discontinued. Has a single foreigner, in any village, been
provoked or even insulted?*

*Instead of harboring absurd and unjustified fears, I like to
place my confidence in the way in which the Japanese have always
in the past conducted themselves toward foreigners. There is no
trace of popular uprisings and plots against foreigners in the
history of Japan since the opening of the country. There have been
a number of assassinations—few indeed, if one considers that for
centuries [during the seclusion period] the Japanese had been
taught to hate foreigners. Is it not absurd, therefore, to speak of
massacres?*

*A visionary, a fanatic can in Japan, as in our most civilized
countries, make an attempt on the life of a foreigner; several such
crimes have been committed in recent years. Who have been the
victims? Japanese statesmen. The criminal in all cases acted alone,
without an accomplice, believing that he was rendering a service
to his country. The assassins of Count Kido [Koin]*[d] *and Marquis*

---

[d] Kido narrowly escaped being killed, thanks to the help of a geisha, whom he later married.

Okubo [Toshimichi], the perpetrator of the dynamite attack on
Count Okuma, and the murderer, two years ago, of Minister [of
Communications] Hoshi Toru, sacrificed their lives beforehand,
and voluntarily surrendered themselves to the police.

The attempt on the life of the Emperor of Russia [Nicholas II,
while still Crown Prince] was carried out by a madman who was
part of the escort ᵉ of the Sovereign. Li Hung-chang at the time of
the negotiations at Shimonoseki was the victim of a deluded person
who came on foot from the far end of Japan, without having re-
vealed his sinister project to anyone.

I do not deny, that isolated cases can unfortunately occur again,
and they threaten to be more frequent, of course, at moments of
popular excitement. But I repeat, apprehension concerning the
security of foreigners in the event of war, be it successful or unsuc-
cessful, is needless. They will not be exposed to more dangers than
they had been during the Sino-Japanese war, the period of peace
negotiations, and the days of mourning when victorious Japan gave
in to the pressure of Russia, France and Germany.[148]

At the opening of the nineteenth session of the Diet foreign
policy tripped the Government. The Emperor had made the
opening statement, urging support for the negotiations that
were under way "to preserve the peace of the Far East,"
when unprecedented opposition was voiced. D'Anethan related:

It is customary that the Presidents of the House of Peers and of
the House of Representatives present to the Emperor an address,
voted by the respective Houses, to thank him for having honored
Parliament with the August presence of His Majesty. The House
of Peers conformed to the fixed precedent. The President of the
House of Representatives, on the other hand, wanted to seize this
occasion to attack the Ministers and express the Assembly's lack
of confidence in them: "It is an incessant cause of fear and anxiety

---

ᵉ He was a policeman, guarding the route of Nicholas's tour through
Otsu.

*for the humble subjects of Your Majesty to see that in the unique
period of prosperity and power in which Japan now finds herself,
the Ministers of State are powerless to cope with the situation.
Following an opportunist policy at home, they do not take advantage
of circumstances to assert their foreign policy." The address,
written by the President, was unanimously approved by the House
and taken to the Palace. His Majesty refused to receive it, and
yesterday an Imperial decree dissolved the House. . . .*

*The conduct of the House has been condemned generally, because
it has hurt the feelings of profound respect or, better, veneration
which still exists in the Japanese soul toward the Sovereign.
A direct appeal to the Emperor is considered a crime of* lèse-
majesté, *a crime so inconceivable to the Japanese, that they have
no expression for it in their language. The severe measure taken
against Parliament thus is justified and will not give rise to any
serious opposition.*

*While the lack of respect for the Sovereign is justly condemned,
one must not conclude that the attacks against the Ministry do not
correspond to the apprehensions aroused in all classes of society
by its apparent inertia. . . . On the contrary, the censure motion
proposed by the president of the House and, I repeat, voted unanimously, strikingly reflects the state of Japanese feeling.*

*The secrecy of the negotiations opened between Russia and Japan
has been guarded so scrupulously, that no one in Japan knows the
nature of the assurances demanded by the Imperial Government.
It is kept in mind, however, that the negotiations first begun in
St. Petersburg fell through; that they were transferred to Tokyo,
and that until now they do not seem to have given any satisfaction
to Japan. It is noticed also that in Manchuria as in Korea Russian
activity becomes more threatening every day. The Russian fleet,
a few months ago much inferior to that of Japan, is today in number
of ships and tonnage almost equal. The occupation troops in Manchuria and the frontier garrisons have been reinforced. In the
negotiations with China, the Russian diplomatic agents do not
conceal how little attention they pay to the protests of Japan. In*

Korea, Mr. Pavlov opposes the opening of Yongmanpho and presses for strategic railroad concessions.

These facts are recognized, published and discussed every day by the organs of the press. They are the constant object of deliberation of all political associations formed, not only in Tokyo, but throughout the whole of Japan.

The political agitation will not subside unless the Government will soon be in a position to declare formally that the Russian concessions are serious and effective and apt to avert, not merely delay till she has completed her armaments, a conflict that Japan may not desire, but for which she believes herself sufficiently prepared.

Until now Count Katsura and his colleagues, backed by the wise and level-headed influence of Marquis Ito and the statesmen who have founded [Meiji] Japan [the Genro], do not let themselves be carried away by the popular voice which unanimously demands a more energetic attitude. They want to exhaust all diplomatic means with calm and dignity before taking extreme decisions. They heed the opinion of the European Powers and by their policy of conciliation seek to prove to the world, that if war breaks out the responsibility must be borne by Russia. On their part, they will have done everything to avoid it.[149]

D'Anethan added toward the end of the dispatch that the day before, on December 11, Baron Rosen had presented a note from his Government to the Japanese Minister of Foreign Affairs. On December 25, 1903, he wrote that the delivery of the Russian note "far from calming tempers and ameliorating the situation redoubles anxiety and makes negotiations ever more difficult."

It appears that Russia refuses to discuss with Japan the questions relating to her position in Manchuria and offers unacceptable conditions concerning the rights that Japan wants to reserve for herself in Korea.

Although deeply offended and wounded by the unconciliatory attitude of Russia, the Imperial Government still tries not to sever negotiations. It has addressed a moderate note to the Russian Government in which it asks it kindly to reconsider its reply. It is not a question, as rumored persistently, of an ultimatum or of a note apt to make a peaceful solution impossible. The Government hopes, nevertheless, that the answer of the Imperial Government will not be delayed as long as the one presented on the 11th.

We cannot understand in Tokyo the confidence which seems to exist in Europe that peace will definitely be maintained between Russia and Japan. My English, French, American and Spanish colleagues believe that the [Japanese] Government is determined on war, if Japan does not receive serious concessions. My Russian colleague says, that the Government does let itself be influenced by the press and national opinion, which unanimously clamor for war.[150]

Ten days later, d'Anethan reported the floating of a large loan to provide the Government with emergency funds:

As fears of war have become ever more serious, the Government has decided to make a domestic loan of 100 million yen at 5%, redeemable in five years. The bonds will be issued at 95. The Government also will increase taxes to 50 million yen. It is not known yet, whether this will be decreed by Imperial Ordinance or whether the Diet, which is to convene in May, will be asked to act on the matter.

One does not doubt that the loan will be subscribed to immediately; indeed, one is surprised that the amount of the loan is not higher. The opinion, once held so widely, that lack of money would force the Government to follow a peaceful policy, proves in no way justified.

The country will have to bear heavy sacrifices. A commercial crisis is inevitable. Public works in progress will be suspended. But funds in Japan will suffice to cover the expenses of a war with Russia[151]

On January 22, 1904, d'Anethan weighed the delicate balance of war and peace. He wrote:

We are informed by news telegrams, that Russia continues to give peaceful assurances and that Berlin and Paris believe that war can be avoided. It is true that the negotiations between Russia and Japan have not been severed. The Government replied to the last note, which, according to Russia, gave Japan certain concessions regarding Korea that were not satisfactory, and asked that the Russian Government reconsider them once more. The Foreign Minister insisted, as he informed us of this new Japanese demand, that the Japanese note did not have the character of an ultimatum; the Imperial Government was not departing from the conciliatory spirit which it had shown throughout these long and difficult negotiations.

As I had the honor to write in my last report, the Government, while still negotiating, feverishly continues military preparations and all measures are taken to occupy Korea. It is not possible to give full details concerning troop and fleet movements, the newspapers having received orders not to publish any military news. We know, however, that a number of divisions are ready for embarkation in the south; that the first reserve has just been called to arms; and that more than sixty vessels are equipped as transports. The navigation lines have suspended their service to Europe, Australia and America, and the ships which left in December have received orders to return to Japan as soon as possible. Japan is in a position to begin hostilities without a moment of delay.

If negotiations were not halted on receipt of the Russian note, it was not because it was hoped that Russia would change her attitude to the point of reassuring Japan completely of the sincerity of her intentions, but because of Japan's desire to see the two recently purchased Argentine warships pass through the Suez Canal. Large loads of coal from Cardiff also are on the way and are due to arrive any day. Furthermore, it was in the interest of Japan to give the merchant marine ships time to return to Japanese ports.

For months Russia has very skillfully used the period of negotia-

tions to bring most of her fleet to the Far East and to strengthen her military defenses; Japan on her part wants merely a few days to face any eventuality under the best conditions. The time has passed when Japan can content herself with any last minute Russian promises unless the promises be backed by the withdrawal of the enormous fleet that Russia has assembled at Port Arthur. . . .

During the long period of suspense and anxiety, when Japanese patriotism was awakened and overexcited to a point that cannot be appreciated from afar and that is well understood only by the foreigner who has studied the history and character of this essentially military people, the Government defied unanimous public opinion to maintain peace. The pressure has become too strong and unless Russia capitulates, there will be war.

We know that in the history of great countries agitation and popular emotion sometimes swept the Government into an imprudent and reckless policy in spite of itself. When this happened, however, cool-headed men always thought to calm the spirits by their counsels and influence and to show the dangers of thoughtless action. For the past two years Japan has been passing through one of these fatal crises. But vainly do I look for wise and moderate counsels outside of the Cabinet.

It would be natural to think that ideas of peace would prevail in the world of business and finance. It is unusual for bankers and capitalists to express warlike sentiments. Yet in Japan there is this surprising phenomenon.

D'Anethan noted that he had appended the text of a discourse by Mr. Sonoda, director of one of the principal banks of Tokyo (Sonoda Kokichi, President of the Yokohama Specie Bank and subsequently of the Fifteenth Bank). He observed:

The excess of jingoism would not be important, if it expressed merely an individual opinion. Unfortunately this is not the case. Mr. Sonoda has spoken in the name of all the bankers of Tokyo, the directors of the big railroad and maritime companies and the principal merchants of the capital. All these capitalists joined in a ban-

*quet for the military correspondents of the English and American
newspapers and the military and naval attachés of the two great
nations [Great Britain and the United States], one of which is
the ally and the other the friend of Japan.*

*At all Japanese festivities the main attraction consists of musi-
cians and dancers. Here, in brief, is the scenario [of the perform-
ance] which preceded the toast . . . . A female dancer, dressed like
an ancient samurai, is sitting, leaning on her sword; another female dancer arrives carrying the head of the Britannic Lion;
she is followed by a third female dancer, dressed like . . . John
[Bull]. The Britannic Lion gives the samurai a warship and
John a bag of flour. The samurai gets up and brandishes his sword.
. . . When the dance ends, the curtain rises, and a troop of female
dancers advance carrying the English, American and Japanese
flags. They begin to sing this war song: "Lion, Lion, the king of
beasts, is the famous emblem of Great Britain. What do we have
to fear? The bear who wants to choke us can dance and howl, showing us his fearful claws. His grimaces do not deceive us. Let us march,
let us march, now is the time to crush him. Let us unite our warships, our armies—we are tired of waiting. Our ally approves of
us, and America sympathizes with us in the war for civilization.
Let us be courageous and without fear. Now is the happy time
for the Japanese people. We shall show the world what we can
accomplish.". . .*

*The newspapers have given an account of this banquet and the
accuracy of the details was confirmed to me by the military and
naval attachés who had been present. The latter excuse their presence on the ground that they did not expect such an outburst of war
cries and such violent and direct attacks against Russia. We must
admit, that it constituted a singular infraction of diplomatic custom and of the reserve that their official position demands. Besides,
their presence was not needed to bolster the confidence that the English alliance inspires in Japan. Nor does one doubt that Japan has
gained American sympathy and in case of war can count on the benevolent neutrality of her great Pacific neighbor.*[152]

M

CHAPTER FOUR

The Russo-Japanese War

O N FEBRUARY 6, 1904, d'Anethan telegraphed his Government first about the rupture of diplomatic relations between Russia and Japan, then about a declaration of the Foreign Minister on the state of war between them. Two days later[f] he reviewed the situation:

During the long negotiations conducted between Japan and Russia we never thought of a peaceful solution, knowing that the concessions demanded of Russia could hardly be given by her and that, on the other hand, we had too much proof of the stubborn resolution of Japan.

The note addressed by the Cabinet on January 13, 1904, had been the last attempt to prolong the negotiations. Although the Government had not given to this note the form of an ultimatum, it had wanted to wait but a few days for the Russian answer. On the 23rd, Mr. Kurino was instructed to press the Imperial [Russian] Government, which had given him only an evasive statement, when the note would be delivered. The Japanese Minister learned at the same time, that it would not be satisfactory. Deeming that under the circumstances the prolongation of negotiations would only be detrimental to the interests of Japan and profitable solely to Russia, which had profited so well from delays and dilatory procedures to increase her means of war, the Imperial Government resolved not to wait for the Russian note, and resumed her freedom of action.

---

[f] The dispatch is dated January 8, but deals with events through February 7. It must have been written on February 8. Strangely it was marked as received in Bruxelles on February 12, delivery normally taking about a month. In view of the importance of the dispatch it may have been telegraphed. The document is bound in the files of the Belgian Ministry of Foreign Affairs in the January position. The original document number places it just before a dispatch of February 9, however.

*On the 5th [of February], it telegraphed its Representative in St.
Petersburg to leave Russia; on the 6th, it notified Baron Rosen in
Tokyo of the break in diplomatic relations, and informed him that
it was forced to return his passports to him.*

*The Russian note arrived in Tokyo on the morning of the 7th,
but the time for presenting it had passed. Had it been transmitted
earlier, the situation would not have been altered.*

*The two warships recently purchased in Italy have now left Sin-
gapore and can reach Japan without danger; this had been the Government's only consideration in postponing the breaking of relations a few days. Mobilization orders had been published and the
second reserves called to arms. Besides, for a long time already, all
measures had been taken for an immediate entry into battle.*

*It is rather surprising that the Government has not yet made a
declaration of war, though, as the Foreign Minister told me today,
it will be promulgated in a few days. But as of now, the Government
considers itself in a state of war with Russia. Hostilities thus are
imminent and we shall probably have the declaration after the first
act or engagement of war. At the time of the war with China, the
Emperor did not proclaim the declaration until after the attack on
the Chinese transport* Kowshing.

*According to the military and naval attachés, Japan is in a posi-
tion to win the fighting on sea and on land. Competent officers state
that her fleet, continually drilled and on the move for months, is
superior to that of its adversaries. Should a naval victory assure her
freedom of the sea, Japan with her admirably organized system of
transports would be able very rapidly to concentrate considerable
forces either in Korea or in Manchuria.*

*Korea, as Your Excellency is aware, has proclaimed that she
would remain neutral in case of conflict between Russia and Japan!
The Japanese Government, which received this notification of neutrality through the French Consul at Chefoo, regarded it as a simple
joke, and did not take it into consideration. Everyone realizes that
one will deal with Korea, in her own country, without her opinion.*

The Japanese Government has urged the Chinese Government

to observe strict neutrality. It considers that in view of uprisings which one must always fear in China, it would be dangerous to employ the several thousand soldiers commanded by the Viceroy of Pechili.[153]

On February 9, d'Anethan transmitted without comment the official communiqué of the Japanese Government announcing the rupture of diplomatic relations. "Animated by a sincere desire for peace, the Japanese Government exercised the utmost patience, but now is reluctantly compelled by the action of Russia to give up all hopes of reconciliation and to break off negotiations," the communiqué concluded after a review of the differences between Russia and Japan.[154]

The dispatches preserved in the Legation file of the Belgian Ministry of Foreign Affairs are strangely silent about the actual outbreak of the war. The only reference is a dispatch in which d'Anethan describes the annual celebration of the founding of the dynasty by Emperor Jimmu on February 11, and conveys the text of the Imperial address, regretting that Japan "had to sever peaceful relations with a neighboring Power." D'Anethan commented: "The day commemorating the first Emperor, who according to historic legend reigned in the year 660 B.C., is religiously observed in Japan. The Emperor could not have found a more solemn occasion for announcing the war against Russia to his people himself."[155]

On February 12, Baron Rosen, his family, and the staff of the Russian Legation embarked at Yokohama. D'Anethan described Rosen's departure from Tokyo:

He had left Tokyo the preceding evening. The entire diplomatic corps was at the station to salute him. A large number of Japanese were also present: the Minister of the Imperial Household and Viscountess Tanaka, the Vice-Minister of Foreign Affairs, ladies in waiting of the Empress, chamberlains and several friends. The Empress sent valuable presents to Baroness Rosen and through a lady of the palace conveyed the nicest message and her regrets.

This excess of civilities is somewhat astonishing under the present circumstances, particularly since the Emperor on the same day forbade the wearing of Russian decorations and asked the foreign diplomats not to put them on at Court functions.

Baron Rosen, who on different occasions had carried out diplomatic missions to Japan,[g] personally was persona grata *at Court and had many friends in all classes of society. The Press was unanimous in praising his goodwill and sympathy for Japan and one is convinced that he is in no way responsible for the break in relations.*

Great precautions and police measures were taken to insure his safety on the way from the Legation to the station. I had the honor and the painful duty to lead Baron Rosen from the waitingroom to the railroad car which had been reserved. Escorted and surrounded by gendarmes and policemen, we had to walk the length of the platform along the crowded train. Some jeers by third class travellers were quickly quelled by the policemen. A squad of gendarmes occupied the carriage ahead of that of the Legation.

In Yokohama too police measures were very thorough, and no untoward incident occurred.[156]

Fully supported by its own subjects, the Japanese Government had also the sympathy and support of many foreigners. D'Anethan related:

Japan received numerous and striking signs of English and American sympathy in the form of offers of military enlistments, the sending of doctors, hospital attendants and nurses, donations of money, etc. . . . The Red Cross Societies of Italy, Spain, France and Germany show themselves equally disposed to lend their charitable and devoted help to Japan.

The Emperor of Germany has telegraphed directly to the Empress to inform Her Majesty that he has put the German hospitals of Yokohama and Kiaochow at the disposal of the Government. The gracious act of the Emperor is greatly appreciated and

---

[g] Baron Rosen had been Chargé d'Affaires and Secretary of the Legation (1877-83) and Minister (1897-99 and again 1903-05).

one sees in it proof of Germany's friendly disposition toward Japan. Since German intervention to compel the abandonment [by Japan] of the conquests of the [Sino-Japanese] war and the occupation of Kiaochow, Japanese feelings toward Germany have been very hostile. One was uncertain lately about the intentions of the Emperor in case of conflict with Russia. The promptness with which the German Government has declared that it would remain absolutely neutral during the war has calmed uneasiness about this for the time being.

France too, in spite of her alliance, has resolved to remain neutral. The explanations given by the French Government to Mr. Motono [Ichiro, the Japanese Minister in France] regarding the presence of Russian warships at Djibouti seemed satisfactory. Little importance is attached here consequently to the attacks of the French press against the so-called violation of the rights of men, committed by Japan, in opening hostilities before making a declaration of war.[157]

In March, 1904, Marquis Ito proceeded to Seoul with a large retinue to convey to the Emperor of Korea Emperor Meiji's "feelings of friendliness and sympathy." D'Anethan commented:

The selection of the noted statesman for this extraordinary embassy has great significance. It indicates that the Government has decided to institute without delay the necessary reforms in Korea. Marquis Ito's mission is not to be of long duration. He will explain to the Emperor the means by which Japan will help the ruling House maintain the independence and integrity of Korea. No one is in a better position than Marquis Ito to convey most conciliatingly what Japan demands in return for the services that she is so anxious to render to her feeble and impotent neighbor.[158]

The success with which Japan marshaled her resources was remarkable. D'Anethan observed:

The confidence in the resources of the country to meet the expenses of the war has been strikingly justified. The subscriptions opened

*on March 1 for a war-loan of 100,000,000 yen have been closed,
with 452,225,775 yen or one billion one hundred and eight million
francs collected. Of these 452 million, 418,000,000 were subscribed at the issue price of 96 yen; 34,000,000 above that price.
Redeemable in 5 years, the loan carries an interest of only 5%,
which is considered low for investments in Japan.*

*The highly admirable patriotism of the entire nation shows itself
ready for any sacrifice, and will not shrink from any privation to
pursue the war to the end. The ardent desire of all classes, even the
less well-to-do, to contribute to the war funds is seen in the fact that
nearly 50,000,000 represented payments of not more than 200
yen. The subscription of 33,000,000 [sic] at above the price of
issue is another manifestation of unselfishness.*

*The Government estimates that the proceeds of the loans, to
which it will resort only as the war requires, will be sufficient for
continuing operations for more than three years. These resources
will be supplemented by 60 to 70,000,000 in new taxes which
Parliament will soon be asked to vote. If we add also some fifty
million in economies made in various budgets with the suspension
of public works . . . , we see that the Government is far from being
in the financial difficulties, that the enemies of Japan had predicted
and desired.*[159]

With the opening of Parliament the Representatives of
the people were informed of the war which was in progress.
The Emperor regretted the "lack of sincerity" on the part
of Russia, which had forced Japan's hand, but pledged, now
that recourse had been taken to arms, to pursue the war till
the objective was attained. Foreign Minister Komura thereupon reviewed the course of negotiations, and D'Anethan
transmitted the text of his discourse. The tenor, as before,
was that the Japanese attack had been defensive, that Japan
was waging a preventative war. Komura asserted:

*. . . Russia, while professing peaceful intentions, made great
naval and military preparations, dispatching all her most powerful*

warships to the Far East and sending military reinforcements, tens of thousands strong, to Manchuria and the neighboring regions. She showed unusually great activity in purchasing and transporting arms, ammunition, stores and coal to the same region, so that it became [clear] beyond the shadow of doubt that Russia had no sincere desire for conciliation and only wanted to force us to yield to her designs. The warlike activities of Russia accelerated to such an extent by the end of January that Japan would certainly have been placed in serious danger, had she allowed further procrastination. The Imperial Government most sincerely desired peace, but under the circumstances, after a full and careful survey of the situation, could not but decide to break off negotiations with Russia and take all necessary measures for self-defense.[160]

A large number of military observers came to Japan from Europe and the United States. As yet the Japanese refused to let any of them accompany the armies in the field. Censorship was very severe. But d'Anethan could convey some general impressions:

The foreign officers are very impressed by the perfect system of mobilization, the order and method down to the smallest detail in the commissariat, and the number and quality of the artillery as well as of arms and ammunitions. The general opinion of the military experts is favorable to the Japanese.

We cannot comment on these technical questions. But knowing the national character well, we can affirm that in courage, spirit, discipline, bravery to the extent of foolhardiness, contempt for death, and the will to die rather than retreat, the Japanese soldier deserves to rank first class.[161]

Convoked in an emergency session to provide the funds necessary for war, the Diet supported the Government proposals and stated unanimously: "The time is still remote when peace can be restored; the Chamber will never hestitate to vote all the necessary funds to continue the war." D'Anethan remarked: "The House, in its patriotic manifestations, is the echo of the entire nation, which is prepared for all sacrifices to maintain the glory and honor of Japan.''[162]

In May d'Anethan summarized the international situation to de Favereau:

In all the reports, I have always written Your Excellency, that Japan was determined on war, if she did not obtain all the concessions which she demanded from Russia. I emphasized that the slowness of the negotiations, which greatly hurt national pride, should not be attributed to faintheartedness or fear. On the contrary, I have incessantly given the impression, indeed the assurance, that Japan had an unshaken faith in her means of action and that she relied solely on her own forces to back by arms the demands that she deemed vital for the defense of her interests and the security of her territory. So far, events have justified Japanese confidence and prove that she had not exaggerated the power of her armies and fleets.

With the exception of five ships, immobilized at Vladivostok, the Russian squadron has been destroyed or blockaded at Port Arthur. One Japanese army, repeating the exploits of 1894, has crossed the Yalu and after taking 28 out of 40 cannons and a large number of prisoners has put to flight twenty to thirty thousand Russians, charged with defending the river. A second army has landed on the Liaotung peninsula. According to the most authoritative forecasts, a third army corps will capture Newchwang. Advancing by three different roads toward Liaoyang, about 200,000 Japanese (not counting bearers, the commissariat, Red Cross, etc.) prepare to engage the Russian Army before continuing against Mukden.

Without wanting to prejudge the fate reserved for the belligerents by the God of Battles, we can for a moment examine the relative importance of a defeat or an indecisive battle. The Japanese Army, supported by her fleet, which is mistress of the sea, is in constant and direct communication with its base of operations, and can without hindrance receive reinforcements, supplies, munitions, and war material. . . . The Japanese armies will operate in terrain which was traversed in the past . . . and of which they have studied and know the smallest nooks and corners. They fight in populated regions whose sympathies they have gained and that will furnish them with provisions, with which the Oriental can content himself better than the European.

Russia, on the other hand, has only one way for receiving all that she needs—from her base, thousands of miles away, with the last thousand in enemy country. Thus for Japan a defeat at Liao-yang or at Mukden would be a simple reverse, a delay, a pause; for Russia, it would be a disaster that would begin the campaign of 1812 in reverse. . . .

The voice of the cannon is the only one that will resound for some time to come. Will that of diplomacy be very long in making itself heard, if not listened? Your Excellency will know of it before us, since it is probable that the friendly or neutral Powers will seize the first occasion to offer their good offices.

As far as Japan is concerned, I am convinced—and if Your Excellency will be so good as to reread my correspondence, you will see that I get my information from reliable sources—that the Imperial Government will not demand after the war or at a moment favorable for peaceful intervention from Europe or from Washington *more complete assurances than those formulated for Russia during the negotiations. It wants neither "one stone of the fortresses of Port Arthur nor one inch of Chinese territory." It will not demand any concessions or any privilege that would not be accorded to all the nations interested in China, and will even recognize the economic interests acquired by Russia through the construction of railroads.*

Japan . . . does not want to attempt the revival of China single-handedly. She wants to work with the European nations and America. It has been her ambition—consistent with her interests—to join the Concert of the Great Powers. She has succeeded partly by her attitude at the time of the siege of Peking and by her alliance with England. Today she wants that no difference be made in the orchestra between her and the musicians of the white race.

In . . . 1901 . . . Marquis Ito told me, that "Japan would commit national suicide if she refused to cooperate loyally [with the Powers] toward a better administration of the Chinese Empire" and also that, "in Europe one is inclined too much to believe that we strive primarily for a political influence which would be detrimental to the Western Nations. One says the Japanese and Chinese are of another race and the yellow race will always have the tendency to draw together and unite against the white race. Nothing is farther from the truth or more absurd."

Desirous to work harmoniously with the European Powers, a victorious Japan will forego many demands ordinarily made of the defeated. In one of my reports I wrote that "the question of war depends on Russia"; today I do not hesitate to say: "Japan will surprise the world as much by the moderation of her demands after the war, as she has surprised it by the crushing blows inflicted on her enemy on land and on sea."[163]

Finding little support at home and abroad for her war against Japan, Russia tried to sway public opinion by resorting to the Yellow Peril bugaboo. Japan, of course, took every opportunity to reassure the other Powers that her conflict with Russia was not racial. Transmitting some comments of Premier Katsura on this subject, d'Anethan wrote:

What does the yellow race still demand today of Japan in regard to the no less yellow race of Manchuria? Not a voluntary or forced union between them, but on the contrary, that they remain independent one from another. Manchuria alone cannot force Russia to keep her promise to evacuate; Japan comes to her help. Her work accomplished, she will retire, and the rich and populous province, put back under the legitimate dominance of China, will definitely be opened to the trade and exploitation of the world.

"No war of race, no war of religion," says Count Katsura, and he speaks not only as a private individual, but as Prime Minister in the name of the Emperor. His view is shared by all policy-makers. Japan's history during the past fifty years shows that not a single day has the policy of progress inaugurated in 1868 taken one step

backwards. All the progressive tendencies of Japan have been di-
rected toward the West. She has taken from the West not only her
arms, her war materials, her cruisers, mines and torpedoes, but
also, above all, her system of education, the spirit of freedom and
tolerance, and the principles of right and justice, written in her
codes.

A dispatch from our Legation in Washington, kindly sent to
me by Your Excellency, says that there are misgivings in certain
circles that Japan one day will want to head a movement of "Asia
for the Asians," a slogan coined a few years ago by Count Okuma.
Considering the policy followed by Japan for the past half a century
and trusting the words of the statesmen who under the direction
of the Emperor have presided over the extraordinary destinies of
this country, which has astonished the world with her progress as
much as she has now made it shudder with the exploits of her armies
and fleets, we do not hesitate to say that these fears are absolutely
fanciful. Strong in her insular position and secured by her pro-
tectorate over Korea, Japan will only ask to develop her resources,
expand her industries, and share with the other commercial Powers
the great market of China. If her rights are respected, Japan will
not threaten either England or the United States, or France, or
even Russia, which (except for China where they have occupied
only certain points) have divided the richest part of the Asian
continent among themselves.

As for our country, which has only economic interests, it will be
to our advantage to work in concert with Japan . . . in the develop-
ment of our commerce and the expansion of our industrial enter-
prises.

I am aware that there is a fairly general feeling in Europe that
Russia will emerge from the war victorious, that Japan, in view of
the numerical force of the Russians, will soon be drained of men
and money. One thought the same in Europe when Japan attacked
China. The delusions under which one labors today regarding the
relative strength of the Powers facing each other are due to the fact,
that one ignores in Europe the enormous preparations made in

Japan for years to fight and sustain the war until the desired objective has been attained.

If it were a question of a war to conquer Russian territory and if the Japanese armies had to pursue the enemy into the plains of Siberia, thought of a Russian triumph would be justified. The circumstances are completely different: Japan merely wants to drive Russia out of Manchuria. The field of operations thus being limited, Japan, mistress of the sea, can concentrate forces superior to those of the Russians. The brilliant victories already achieved by the Japanese, the crossing of the Yalu, the taking of Kinchow and Nanshan and shortly of Port Arthur and Dalny will allow her to concentrate all her forces for the advance on Mukden and, if necessary, on Harbin.[164]

Japanese refusal to let foreign correspondents and observers accompany the troops made it difficult to obtain objective news. The observations of Miss McCaul of the British Red Cross, for whom the Japanese made an exception, were therefore of particular interest. Conveying some of her impressions, d'Anethan wrote:

The solicitude of the Japanese for the Russian wounded and prisoners is. . .admirable. Miss McCaul has seen a number of them in Manchuria; they were unanimous in their praise of the treatment that they were receiving. At Matsuyama, in Japan, where one thousand Russian prisoners whom she also visited are interned, she did not hear any complaint. The French Minister gave me the same information about the treatment of the latter. The myth of Japanese hatred for the foreigner will vanish like many other myths unfavorable to Japan by the very testimony of her enemies, who will bear witness to the humanitarian feelings of their conquerors.[165]

The advance of a Russian squadron of four vessels from Vladivostok to Tokyo Bay caused little concern in Japan. D'Anethan commented:

The calm, I would say indifference, with which the Government and the population have learned that the Russian squadron threatened the coasts of Japan is truly extraordinary. So absolute is the confidence concerning the outcome of the war, the taking of Port Arthur and the defeat of Kuropatkin, that some material damage is regarded as insignificant. The victories achieved up to now, moreover, justify this confidence.[166]

The Vladivostok squadron sank a Japanese transport, and it went down without survivors. D'Anethan wrote:

An impressive funeral service was just celebrated in Tokyo in memory of the 635 officers and soldiers of the Imperial Guard who perished in this catastrophe. An immense crowd, estimated at more than two hundred thousand people, followed calm and collected behind the cortege which proceeded to the cemetery where a stone monument had been erected in remembrance of these heroes.

Almost the same day there arrived in Japan the 601 prisoners whom the Japanese had saved when the Rurik *sank in the naval battle of August 12. Two of the prisoners had succumbed to their wounds, and they were buried with military honors according to the rites of the Orthodox Church. The officiating priest was the chaplain of the* Rurik *whom the Japanese had promptly freed in conformance with the Geneva Convention.*

I take the liberty of directing Your Excellency's attention to these two funeral ceremonies, because they are a striking example of the attitude of the Japanese toward their enemies.

The Vladivostok squadron has sunk not only the Hitachi Maru; *several other transports have gone down also. But did the Japanese take reprisals? Did they depart from the humanitarian rules prohibiting the striking of a combatant who could no longer defend himself? Did they sacrifice to the spirits of their departed the 600 Russians whom victory had delivered to them and whose fate depended on their generosity? On the contrary, the Russian sailors are treated and nursed with as much kindness as Japanese soldiers.*

I read in some French newspaper that the Japanese have committed atrocities against the Russian wounded; on the other hand, official reports make public several cases where Japanese are said to have been mutilated. In all wars belligerents accuse each other of such deeds. As it is impossible to verify them, it is useless to draw general conclusions from isolated acts perpetrated in the heat of Battle. It is different when we can ascertain—and we have the testimony of the prisoners themselves—the solicitude with which the Japanese Red Cross has organized its aid to the wounded enemies.

As for religious tolerance, it remains as complete as before the war. The Russians themselves are obliged to recognize it, because the Metropolitan of the Orthodox Church, Bishop Nicholas, has remained in Tokyo and has declared in a letter addressed to the authorities of the Church in Moscow and published in Novoe Vremia *that "the Cathedral is protected by the police and the services continue without incident or interruption." What more striking example does one want, that Japan under all circumstances intends to respect the article of the Constitution of 1889, granting freedom of worship. It is particularly remarkable to see the correct attitude of the population in Tokyo toward the Russian Cathedral, this vast edifice, one of the most imposing of the capital, situated on a hill from which it dominates the town, for it offends pride and popular feeling, its construction having been demanded by Russia after the attempt of a lunatic on the life of the present Emperor [Nicholas] during his trip in 1891.*

I have written to Your Excellency many a time about the perfect safety enjoyed by foreigners in Japan. If I revert to this subject, it is because in spite of facts so obvious that one must be blind or systematically ill-disposed to ignore or hide them, there are influential. . .people in Tokyo who continue to refuse to admit that Japan has attained a degree of civilization equal to that of the Western nations.[167]

Meanwhile Japanese efforts to "rejuvenate" Korea aroused native opposition. D'Anethan observed:

A rather large meeting was held in Seoul and feelings of

animosity toward the Japanese were expressed in violent terms. Yet in Tokyo one does not attach much importance to these whims of Korean independence. One does not doubt that Japan will obtain all the concessions that she will want. Twenty-four hours after having declined to see the Minister of Japan under the pretext that it was too hot, the Emperor received him and lavished on him the most friendly assurances regarding Japan and her Sovereign.

An anti-Japanese meeting was broken up by the Japanese police and the leaders were arrested. A squad of police, furthermore, has just been sent from Tokyo and will maintain order in Seoul. It would thus be erroneous to believe, that the hostility which no doubt exists in some spheres of the Korean Court is serious or strong enough to stop Japanese action in the task of regeneration that she wants to accomplish.

The intrigues that occur in the palace among the Emperor's entourage have long been one of the principal causes of the deplorable state into which this unfortunate country has fallen. Under a timid and ignorant prince, who thought only of his pleasures and of ways to procure money to satisfy them, the courtesans continued intriguing. This did not fail to encourage Japanese and Russian diplomacy. Now that the situation is changing, and Japan alone will exercise a preponderant influence, she will apply herself to put an end to the abuses caused by the corruption and the embezzlements of the counsellors of the Emperor. I believe that if the latter delays in submitting to Japanese demands, we shall soon see a change of Sovereign.[168]

The war was progressing in Japan's favor, but slower and with more sacrifices than the Japanese had anticipated. In October of 1904 d'Anethan observed: "The resistance of Port Arthur has lasted longer than expected here. The Russians fight with the heroism of despair, and the Japanese who had hoped to take the place by storm were forced to change tactics and to send reinforcements."[169] Yet the Japanese economy was in strong shape, and Japan was determined

N

to continue the war to the bitter end. D'Anethan communicated to de Favereau on October 22:

The Foreign Minister told me today that no serious offer of mediation or of good offices to bring about peace negotiations had been addressed to Japan. According to reports that His Excellency receives from Europe, Russian policy continues to be controlled by the party which brought on the war and still holds the confidence of the Emperor. Under the circumstances Japan can only redouble her efforts and not shrink from any sacrifice to prolong the struggle. She can do so the more easily because so far the economic situation of the country has hardly suffered from the war.[170]

The third of November, Emperor Meiji's birthday, was a great national holiday in Japan. D'Anethan observed:

This year it was celebrated with so much more enthusiasm and love, since the whole nation sees in the Sovereign the living symbol of its strength and grandeur. It attributes the triumphs of the armies and fleets to the almost divine character of the Emperor. Sustained by their unswerving faith in the power of the Emperor, the Japanese, from the humblest coolie to the princes, fear no enemy and march to new battles with absolute confidence.[171]

The foreign colony in Peking was full of "strange illusions" about Japan, and as these were conveyed to Europe and thence referred to d'Anethan for comment, he repeatedly took strong issue with them.[172] Convinced that Japan's cause was at once just and limited, d'Anethan ridiculed the idea that the growing imperialistic tendencies in Japan and the United States would sooner or later lead to a conflict between the two countries. He wrote:

Perhaps certain spheres which foresee the eventuality of war between the two great Pacific Powers have such reliable sources of information that the future holds no mystery for them? They would serve humanity, in the interest of world peace, if they indicated them to us. We who do not have this occult power of reading the secrets of the future in the stars will have to limit ourselves to ascertaining events that are happening under our eyes and to speaking only of facts that are apt to influence the relations between the nations. . . .

According to Peking opinion all Powers except England with possessions in Asia must fear the triumph of Japan. It is predicted that Japan wants to declare war on the whole world. There is not a single statesman in Japan who contemplates such folly. It is Japan's ambition to take an important place in the concert of the civilized Powers; she knows at the same time that she will succeed only by respecting the interests of these Powers. The present war is not a war of conquest as far as China is concerned. The protection of Japanese interests in Korea and the security of the Empire itself demand that Manchuria does not become a Russian province. As soon as this goal will have been attained, that Manchuria will have been restored to China, we shall see Japan, like the other Powers, work to develop her economic interests there.

After the war Japan will concentrate all her efforts to recoup her weakened forces, to stimulate her industries, to organize Korea, and to exploit her resources. No Power will have more interest in peace than Japan and I know that the Emperor, his Government and all Japanese statesmen perfectly realize that peace, to be durable, must neither threaten nor compromise the acquired possessions and existing interests of other Powers.[173]

The twenty-fifth session of the Diet, which opened on November 30, 1904, was held in an atmosphere of loyalty and seriousness. In the words of d'Anethan:

Parliament will show itself this year equal to the situation, the seriousness of which is felt by the whole world.

The Government does not conceal from the country that Japan must yet make gigantic efforts and painful sacrifices to emerge victorious from the war with Russia.[174]

The fall of Port Arthur, which ushered in the new year, was of great significance. As d'Anethan wrote: "Japan has obtained a triumph which no one contests any more."[175] The flow of prisoners into Japan was increasing. D'Anethan observed:

There now are close to 40,000 Russian prisoners, including 400 officers, in Japan. General [Anatolii Mikhailovich] Stoessel and about 400 officers, having signed a pledge not to participate any further in the war, are en route to Russia. They had been treated with great respect at Nagasaki both by the authorities and the population.

The Japanese, so terrible and heroic during combat, become gentle, well-meaning and polite as soon as the fight is over. What must be the astonishment of those thousands of prisoners at thus being treated by people, who were represented to them as savage heathens and barbarians?[176]

Japanese successes raised fear of Japanese expansion in the post-war era. To d'Anethan there seemed no cause for alarm. He wrote:

It appears that French opinion has been aroused by an article said to have been written by General Kodama [Gentaro] on the subject of the conquest of Indo-China. Baron Kodama, Marshal Oyama [Iwao]'s Chief-of-staff, former Minister of War and Governor of Formosa, is not only one of the most brilliant and most learned officers of the Japanese army, but also one of the best informed statesmen. He has consequently never written the absurd opinions ascribed to him. Japan does not have and never has had the intention to create difficulties for France either in Cochin China or in Tonkin. There was never any question of aggressive action against France.

Japan prepared for war against Russia and against Russia alone. She threatens no other Power and, I do not cease repeating, she will respect the interests and possessions of all Powers in Asia. She has made the present war to stop the Power which alone was in a position to endanger her vital interests in China and whose policy was a danger to her security. Once this aim has been achieved, we shall see Japan strive to live in harmony with all the nations, including Russia.[177]

The spread of peace rumors in February of 1905 prompted d'Anethan to reassure his Government again concerning the moderation of Japanese demands and ambitions. He stated:

All my information confirms the assurances which I have already given Your Excellency concerning Japanese postwar demands. They will hardly differ from the demands made to Russia during the diplomatic negotiations in 1903. Japan will continue the war until the Russian armies have evacuated Manchuria, but does not intend to replace them by a general or partial Japanese occupation.

The Government knows too well that any annexation of Chinese territory far from strengthening Japan, would be a cause of weakness and of danger. It would entail enormous sacrifices in men and money and, more important, would awaken the mistrust of even those Powers with whom Japan was on most intimate terms. On February 17, Baron Komura wrote to the Chinese Minister: "Japan has gone to war not for the sake of conquest, but only in defense of her rights and her interests. The Imperial Government, therefore, has no intention of acquiring territory at the expense of China."

Very well informed of Russia's internal political situation, the Japanese know that Russia could continue playing an important role in part of the world only with the help of other Powers. Consequently, they will avoid giving umbrage to any of the Powers who have interests in North China or possessions or concessions in other parts of the Chinese Empire.[178]

Internal unrest in Russia and Japanese victory at Mukden added to speculations about Russian ability to continue the war and about the prospects of peace. D'Anethan commented:

At the beginning of the month, when the terrible battles that the bulletins of General Kuropatkin transformed into victories or wise withdrawals took place, the European press discussed the conditions under which Russia would consent to make peace. . . . The trial balloons regarding peace have hardly been taken seriously in Japan, because one considers it up to the victorious nation to impose her demands and to formulate the preliminaries that would allow the opening of negotiations.

The prospect of seeing Russia prolong the fight does not move anyone. The Japanese know that once they will be in possession of Harbin and Vladivostok, which will fall into their hands if the war continues, making them masters of the sole two points by which the Russians can send reinforcements, considerable troop movements will be impossible. Besides, as a Japanese newspaper says, if Russia had not been able to provide Kuropatkin with more than 500,000 men (at the very most) during one year, how could she in view of internal events completely dismantle her strongholds on the borders of Poland, Finland and the Caucasus? The myth of Russia's inexhaustible might in men and money and of her Cossacks who were to sweep everything before them does not frighten Japan.

The more peace is delayed, the harder conditions will be; demands will increase in proportion to the sacrifices that Japan must bear. . . .[179]

On March 25, and again the following month, d'Anethan reiterated that in her peace demands Japan neither could nor would encroach upon the interests of the other Powers. He remarked:

There is no foundation for the apprehension manifested in certain political circles in the United States concerning the attitude of Japan regarding the Philippines.

The task of organizing and administering the Government of Korea, which will devolve upon Japan, is too arduous and complicated for her to provoke conflicts with any Power. In view of the constant growth of her population, Japan has sought to expand, but Korea is a vast and rich enough field for her not to have to acquire new territories. With what Power does Japan have a more vital interest to live in harmony than with the United States? And it is this nation which she would arouse against herself in provoking difficulties in the Philippines![180]

In April 1905, d'Anethan reported that the fleet of Admiral Zinovii Petrovich Rozhestvenskii was en route to the Far East and that a large naval engagement could be expected sooner or later. He commented:

After the taking of Port Arthur the Japanese believed that the Baltic fleet would not continue its advance. Nonetheless they took all measures for new action. No one knows where Admiral Togo [Heihachiro] is. The secrecy which has been kept so completely regarding the military operations is even tighter for the movement of squadrons. Except for the presence several days ago for half a day of several cruisers in Singapore, the arrival of warships has not been reported anywhere. The only thing we know is that the Japanese fleet is not in Japan. The ships which for almost one year cruised before Port Arthur came to repair their damages, but went out to sea again at once.

The Japanese seem as confident of the issue of the coming battles on the sea, as they had been on the eve of the battle of Mukden.

They believe that they are superior to the Russian forces in homogeneity in type of ships, higher average speed, more modern armament and cannons with a longer range. They have, it is true, two battleships less than the Russians, but their cruisers are more numerous and their fleet of torpedo boats, so important already at the beginning of the war, has been considerably increased during the past year, new ones being built in the dockyards and arsenals of the state day and night. Disposing over all the transport vessels which it might need, the Government never has any trouble supplying its squadrons and sending reinforcements and ammunition. Very fast vessels plough the seas and keep the Admiralty informed of the movements of the enemy, while the latter does not know where he will meet Admiral Togo.

If the Japanese were not convinced that they were strong enough to inflict new defeats on the Russians, they would have sought to open peace negotiations after the Mukden disaster. Instead we find that they are more determined than ever to push their success until the object of the war has been attained.[181]

Two months later d'Anethan reported:

On May 27, Admiral Togo telephoned to the Minister of the Navy: "The Russian fleet has been sighted. I am going to attack it and annihilate it." The confidence of the illustrious Admiral was shared by all the officers, and explains the vigor of the attack and the heroism shown in this naval battle which erases Russia from the list of naval nations for a long time. . . .

Will Russia decide at last to ask for peace and submit to the demands of the victor? Japan is determined to continue the war; she will not make the first advances.[182]

Though d'Anethan had concluded the above dispatch with the assertion that Japan wished to negotiate the terms of peace directly with Russia, without foreign intervention, he reported a fortnight later that the Japanese Government had accepted President Theodore Roosevelt's offer to help arrange peace negotiations between the two belligerents (and Roosevelt, it might be added, had acted at Japanese prompting). D'Anethan wrote to de Favereau:

The Imperial Government has accepted the invitation. . . .addressed to it by the President of the United States on June 9 to bring together the Japanese and Russian Plenipotentiaries to come to an understanding for the restoration of peace.

The Foreign Minister replied the following. . .day that the Imperial Government "desiring, in the interest of the world as of Japan, the reestablishment of peace with Russia on the terms and conditions which will fully guarantee its permanence, will, in accordance with the wishes of the President, appoint Plenipotentiaries to meet with those of Russia at the time and place which will be mutually convenient for the purpose of negotiating and con-cluding the conditions of peace directly and exclusively between the belligerents."

Russia proposed that the meeting take place in Paris; Japan wanted a spot closer-by, Chefoo. Washington has been chosen.

As for peace at this time, one must be aware that the negotiations threaten to drag out and that the hopes of friends and promoters of a prompt end to hostilities are likely to be disappointed. . . . The very cordial and friendly relations that exist between Japan and the United States demanded that the approach made by the latter be welcomed with the deference and readiness due to the intervention of a friend, whose straightforwardness and loyalty are beyond suspicion. The Imperial Government also did not hesitate to agree with the views of President Roosevelt. It has agreed to discuss or negotiate, but at the same time, it "wants to conclude" peace.

Japan will not be a party to dilatory negotiations, resulting only in a "suspension of hostilities," "a truce," "an armistice" or a hasty [?] agreement, which would leave the situation in a status quo *bad for Japan and would be favorable for her adversary.*

Japan regrets that the peace overtures were made before the military successes, which she hopes to gain soon against the Russians in Manchuria, were an accomplished fact. Strong as her position is—she considers it unassailable—she has, though reluctantly, not only listened but acceded to the proposal of the Washington Cabinet.

She knows, furthermore, that American diplomacy is very straight, sincere, "outspoken" as one says in English. Japan follows the same school as we have seen in the negotiations preceding the war. She had never wanted to discuss the question of Korea, and until the break had shown great conciliation vis-à-vis the Russians in regards to Manchuria. A little skill on the part of Russian diplomacy would certainly have delayed the war.

The Japanese statesmen, as I have written in several reports, do not let themselves be influenced by the victories which have surprised the world, but which have not astonished them. Carried away, forced into the war, they have undertaken a gigantic task, knowing the objective they wanted to attain. They have reached this objective today and I know that though their triumphs have exceeded their hopes, they do not dream of increasing their demands or of imposing a harsher peace than that which they had proposed to obtain at the time when they had decided on the supreme effort of attacking the giant who made Europe tremble.

Your Excellency will certainly have read in the press telegrams from Tokyo the conditions that Japan would impose: the right shore of the Amur and Sakhalin to be ceded to Japan; the railroads and the territory belonging to Russia in Manchuria to be trans-ferred to Japan; withdrawal of all Russian forces from Man-churia and annulment of all rights acquired; an indemnity of 3,000,000,000 yen; the delivery to Japan of all Russian vessels that have taken refuge in neutral ports; assurance of Japanese rights of navigation and fishing on the Amur; Blagoveshchensk and Stretensk [?] to be opened to foreign trade; occupation of Vladivostok, etc. etc. The chauvinistic [?] parties from which these Draconian conditions emanate, demand the humiliation of Russia besides the demands that victorious Japan has a legitimate right to claim.

Neither the Emperor nor the Government share these extreme views. His Majesty knows, as do his Ministers and Councillors, that if Japan by her victories had gained the admiration and sympathy of her ally England and her friend America, she has also aroused many disappointments and apprehensions among the other nations interested in Asia. He is aware that Japan, separated from Europe by race, religion, customs and way of life, can enter the concert of nations on a footing of equality only by respecting the rights of other nations, helping them to maintain them, and not demanding for herself any exclusive advantage.

A Japanese statesman recently told me: "We are strong enough to be moderate in our demands. Had we been only half-victorious, this moderation would have been considered a sign of weakness. Now one will have proof that we were sincere when we declared at the beginning of the war, that we were waging it in the interest of progress and civilization and in the interest of all nations. If we want to keep the sympathy of our friends and win that of those who understand us less well, . . . we can make no diplomatic faux pas.[183]

Two weeks later d'Anethan commented on Japanese reaction to the Russian choice of negotiators:

The appointment of Mr. Muravev as principal Russian Pleni-potentiary has been received. He was, one believes, formerly hostile to Japan and an advocate of an aggressive policy. The sudden change which must have occured in his views seems to augur well.

Baron Rosen is persona grata *in Japan. At the time of his departure . . . he had been showered with Imperial kindness and . . . high functionaries had accompanied him to the station.*

The addition of the Russian Minister at Peking [Dmitrii Dmitrievich Pokotilov], former director of the Russo-Chinese Bank, to the Russian Mission charged with opening the peace negotiations, is regarded with some mistrust.[184]

In July Baron Komura, the Foreign Minister of Japan, set out for the United States. D'Anethan observed:

On the 8th, Baron Komura embarked for Seattle, cheered by an immense crowd. The enthusiastic greeting extended to the Foreign Minister, sent on a mission of peace, is not an indication of the nation's desire to see the war end, but of the confidence one has in him and of the conviction that he will not sign a treaty which will not give complete satisfaction to Japan. In spite of all the bloodshed, the various sacrifices, and the increase in charges and taxes, the bellicose and patriotic ardor remains as strong as at the beginning of hostilities. There do not exist in Japan advocates of peace at any price!

Peace, to be lasting, requires sacrifices on the part of Russia. But she will gain nothing by dragging out the negotiations. The military operations will not be halted by the negotiations and by the time that they can be started at Portsmouth [which had been substituted for Washington], Japan will have gained new victories and will have pawns not only in China, but on Russian territory.

Your Excellency will know already, that Sakhalin Island has been occupied without resistance. National pride had always chafed at the cession [of the island] to Russia in 1875. This land, which since time immemorial belonged to Japan, will henceforth remain a part of the Empire.

The financial situation of Japan is favorable for continuing the war. The last loan of £30,000,000, floated the day of Baron Komura's departure, shows clearly that if peace will not be concluded, there will be no lack of resources for the prolongation of the struggle. . . .

The indemnity that Russia will have to pay, will play a large part in the calculations of the Government. Your Excellency is in a better position to know to what extent Russia will give in to Japanese demands in this respect. What we do know here and can affirm is that Japan will not put down her arms until she is reimbursed for her war expenses.[185]

As Komura headed for the United States, word reached d'Anethan that China wished to be included in the impending negotiations between Russia and Japan. D'Anethan commented:

It appears that a certain party at the Court in Peking would like China to be represented at the peace conferences. Overtures are said to have been made to the American Government. The Chinese step has provoked Japanese derision.

Japan will not admit any [third] Power to the conference. She will deal with Russia alone. After Manchuria has been put back under the dominance of China, Japan will deal with her concerning arrangements to be made in the general interest of the Powers to bolster the regime that will guarantee her security.

It seems that this Chinese step was inspired by the new Russian Minister, Mr. Pokotilov. The latter is [said] to have assured China, that Russia intends to leave Manchuria and to renounce her Liaotung lease! Mr. Pokotilov allegedly maintains that the railways do not constitute an enterprise of the Russian Government, having been constructed with funds of the Russo-Chinese Company, and that China consequently must oppose their cession to Japan. He is said to have added, that if the occupied lines were not returned, Russia would demand an indemnity from China.

I do not think that Japan will accept this point of view. The occupation and the exploitation of the lines can give rise to arrangements connected with the indemnity, but Japan does not consider it a question of private enterprise but of Russian Government property.

According to a rumor emanating from Shanghai, the Company is said to contemplate ceding its network to a foreign syndicate, made up of French and Belgian capitalists. As the Japanese Government deems that it is not in effect a private company but the Russian Government itself which wants to dispose of one of its properties, due Japan by right of conquest, it will not recognize the validity of a transaction of this kind.

The addition of Mr. Pokotilov to the Russian Plenipotentiaries is viewed unfavorably. The very active and predominant role played by him as director of the Bank at Peking in the policy of absorption, projected by Russia in China, inspires mistrust in the Japanese.

The defeat of Russia has dealt a terrible blow to the [Russo-Chinese] Bank. Manchuria will be closed to it for a long time and China will have the support of Japan, if the bank seeks to obtain new concessions in other parts of the Empire. The foreign companies interested in the Russo-Chinese [Bank] or having worked with it in China will, I fear, encounter very serious opposition by Japan, if they continue to confound their interests with hers.[186]

That month William Howard Taft, then Secretary of War of the United States, stopped over in Japan with a Commission of over eighty distinguished Americans, including Miss Alice Roosevelt, the President's daughter, en route to the Philippines. D'Anethan commented:

They were treated like royal guests and were accorded the ceremonial observed at the time of the visits of foreign Princes. His Majesty put the Imperial Palace of Shiba-Rikyu at the disposal of Mr. Taft. High dignitaries of his household were attached to them. At the Court banquet Miss Roosevelt took precedence over

Mrs. Griscom (at the demand of the American Minister).

At a garden-party given at the American Legation, the daughter of the President was paid homage next to and on the same level as the Princesses Fushimi and Hashimi. She presided over one of the tables of honor at which H.I.H. Prince Fushimi, Princess Higashi-Fushimi, Marquis Oyama, Count Inouye and Your servant [d'Anethan] were seated. If I mention the exceptional privileges accorded to Miss Roosevelt by the Japanese Court, which ordinarily is so punctilious and very well informed about protocol, it is to make it clear how much importance one attaches to the friendship of the President of the United States. . . .

The Honorable Mr. Taft did not come on a mission to Japan and consequently had no official status. The welcome extended to him is thus the more significant. One has seized this occasion, coinciding with the meeting between the Emperors of Germany and Russia, to proclaim the solidarity between Japan and America. The enthusiasm was the more extraordinary as it was rumored, falsely or correctly, that Mr. Cassini[h] had protested a month ago against the visit of Mr. Taft to Tokyo. In view of such evident marks of understanding and sympathy between the Cabinets of Tokyo and Washington, one should not attach great importance to the opposition of the legislatures of several western states to the immigration of Japanese. Fears of the Yellow Peril will not influence relations as long as President Roosevelt will remain in power. Instead of fearing contact with Japanese, Americans generally soon will share Mr. Taft's outlook.[187]

The Treaty of Portsmouth, which ended the Russo-Japanese war, was a terrible disappointment to the Japanese public. D'Anethan related:

The news of the peace which is to be signed in several days has been received in Japan with a feeling of profound and universal sorrow. The intense patriotism which animated and animates the

---

[h] Artur Pavlovich Kassini, the Russian Ambassador in Washington.

country feels stricken and humiliated. The few flags that are hoisted are veiled with crape!

At the time of Baron Komura's departure, on July 11, I had written to you that the cheers which saluted him showed not the desire to see the end of the war but the confidence that a glorious peace would be concluded. In telling you furthermore, that Japan would not give in on the question of an indemnity, I relied on the highest and most responsible authorities. Till the last day, Japanese public opinion never doubted that the Government would stick to its claims in this regard.

It is to be feared that the Ministry of Count Katsura will be faced with the most serious difficulties, because popular excitement exceeds all bounds.

The text of the agreements is not yet known here. The Government does not let anything be published officially. One sees only, that there will be no indemnity and that Japan will keep merely part of Sakhalin.

The silence observed by the Government during the negotiations has been fatal because public opinion was not prepared in any way to give up the hopes that had been aroused in it. With the exception of the government newspaper Kokumin, *the press is unanimous in condemning the Government's weakness. Unfortunately it contributes by this imprudent and unreasonable attitude to provoking great disorders in the near future.*

Sensible people and real statesmen will soon understand that the peace is a great blessing for the country, because all in all it will bring her considerable advantages and the realization of the end of the war.

The psychological effect is also immense. No longer will one contest Japan's status as a Great Power, preponderant in the Pacific and in the entire Far East.[188]

Popular disappointment with the peace terms exploded in riots. Three telegrams, sent by d'Anethan on September 7 and 8, highlighted the course of events. The first read:

"Grave disorders aroused by popular movement hostile to the peace. The foreigners are not threatened so far. Government protects the Legations."[189] Later in the day d'Anethan wired further: "Martial law proclaimed. Government takes necessary measures to protect churches and missions."[190] The next day he reported: "All measures taken by the Government to maintain order. Consequently calm reigns in capital."[191]

On September 10, d'Anethan elaborated on his telegrams:

The disorders which have broken out in Tokyo have been occasioned by the general feeling, that the peace, instead of bringing glory to Japan, humiliated her undeservedly after her great feats on sea and land. This feeling, inspired by patriotism that was perhaps exaggerated but of the sort that had animated the nation since the beginning of the war, found expression at a popular meeting in Hibiya Park, situated in the center of the section of the city, where the Palace, the Ministries and Legations are located.

The meeting had been announced for several days and its promoters, a number of lawyers, professors and deputies, do not belong to parties of anarchy or disorder. It was merely a question of protesting against the peace terms and against the weakness of the Ministry. The press was unanimous in approving of this demonstration. Neither the Government, nor the municipal authorities, nor the chief of police had forbidden the planned meeting. The thousands of demonstrators, therefore, neither believed in nor wanted to commit any act against the law.

Unfortunately, without previous notice, one hour before the meeting, the six gates of the park had been closed and barriers erected to prohibit entrance. The crowd, indignant at this arbitrary procedure, flung itself against the barriers. The police were powerless to resist the shock, and the park was invaded. Mr. Kono, former President of the House and Chief of the Kowa Doshikai (Association Against the Peace) made a speech demanding that the peace not be ratified. Several orators made remarks that were lost in the noise. At this moment all the gates were opened, and the crowd dispersed. If the chief of police had not, on his own authority, given the unfortunate order to forbid the meeting arbitrarily, no disorder would have occurred. The failure of the police, which did not have the strength to implement its orders, had serious consequences in making possible the very regrettable incidents that followed.

The indignation of the mob, which heretofore had been inspired by a perhaps insufficiently thought-through but noble and patriotic feeling, changed in character and turned against the police and the Minister of Home Affairs under whom it was. Several times the mansion of Viscount Yoshikawa [Akimasa], the Minister of Home Affairs, was attacked, and fire was set to several wooden outbuildings. The mansion itself was not damaged.

A hundred police posts were destroyed in different quarters of the town. These offices or rather "Aubettes" [little huts] consist of a roof and four walls of boards; they can hold only five to six or seven persons. A pickax and a box of matches suffice to destroy them completely in five minutes. From a material point of view the damage thus is insignificant. During the evening and the night some thirty streetcars were burned in the streets; also three Christian chapels, among them a Catholic one.

As the police lost all control, the Government called out a division of the Imperial Guard, and with it protects the Ministries, the Legations, the churches and missions. Martial law was proclaimed by Imperial ordinance. The troops were welcomed everywhere enthusiastically, and order thus was restored immediately.

During the day the Russian Cathedral was invaded, but no damage was done; a platoon arrived in time to clear the church. At no time did the movement have an anti-foreign character. The Legations were guarded as an extra precaution. . . .

As there were some apprehensions concerning a possible attack by some rogues against the churches and convents, the Government took all steps necessary to assure their safety. The sisters of St. Paul of Charity, who have a convent in Tokyo, took refuge for one night in the French Legation. Their convent was not molested or threatened any more than the other missions.

o

The burning of the three chapels justified the anxieties to a certain extent and gave the appearance of truth to the opinion that an attack was being prepared against the foreign religious establishments. The unjustified crimes were the work of a number of bandits who took advantage of the unrest and the absence of police, to execute their plan, with pillage and theft as their objective. The number of thefts in Japanese houses was considerable and committed by evildoers of the same sort. It would hardly be correct, therefore, to consider these excesses as the result of a preconceived plan or of one concocted out of hostility toward the European nuns or missionaries.

In other large cities, in Kyoto, Osaka, Kobe, Nagoya and in many less important localities, there have been demonstrations against the conclusion of the peace. But the disorders do not seem to have been serious, and calm has been restored without the help of troops.

The tumultuous scenes which have recently occurred in Tokyo are the more surprising because no such events have ever happened before. There had always existed under all circumstances the greatest respect for the police and no one, least of all the Government, could conceive of an occasion when it would be powerless to perform its duty. It is improbable that similar acts will recur in the future, because the Government will hasten to reinforce the police and to assure it of the help of the army, on which it can always count fully. There is no reason, therefore, to be alarmed about the fate of foreigners in Japan, nor to be afraid that they will be in danger in consequence of some disturbances caused by popular excitement. There is some apprehension concerning the moment when the exchange of ratifications of the peace will take place. Excesses and crimes could occur. But should this sad eventuality materialize, they would be directed against the Japanese Ministers. *They would be committed by some determined or hot-headed fanatics who sacrifice their lives beforehand. There will be neither a conspiracy, nor an organized attack, nor any hostile demonstration against foreigners. When there are disorders in the Orient, one is inclined in Europe to exaggerate their importance and to jump to the conclusion that they are necessarily directed against the Europeans. At present Japan is passing through an internal political crisis that is not apt to endanger or compromise the interests of foreigners of any nationality.*[192]

Toward the end of the month the conclusion of a new treaty of alliance with Great Britain was made public in Japan. The announcement was received with general and unanimous satisfaction. In the words of d'Anethan:

No hostile criticism has been expressed either in the press or among statesmen, even those ordinarily most opposed to the Ministry. One had been aware that an agreement replacing the treaty of 1902 had been signed in London, but its terms and duration had been kept strictly secret. Had it been known earlier, there would not have been the commotion provoked by the peace treaty with Russia. With the feeling of security that the alliance with England inspires, the country will soon understand that her true interests require the end of the war, considering that Russia has accepted the Japanese protectorate in Korea, is abandoning Port Arthur and evacuating Manchuria.[193]

On October 19, d'Anethan described the unheroic return of Baron Komura from the United States:

The Diplomatic Corps was at the station to meet him to express their sympathy and congratulate him on the occasion of the conclusion of the peace. Only the foreign Ministers and the officials were admitted inside the station. A large number of troops and police guarded the approaches to the station and the route to the Imperial Palace, where His Excellency went directly in a Court carriage, preceded and followed by a squadron of cavalry.

No hostile demonstration occurred, but the immense crowd, massed in the vicinity of the station, kept the most profound silence. Not one hurrah, not one banzai! This mournful attitude of the populace, so strangely in contrast with the cheers that had accompanied Baron Komura when he had departed in July, unfortunately shows that popular indignation against the peace treaty has not abated.

*The press continues to show itself very hostile to the peace and at-
tacks the Ministry ever more violently. The proclamation of the
Emperor . . . has unfortunately not calmed the spirits. The agitation will continue, I fear, until the Emperor chooses other councillors. It is believed, that he will do so before or immediately after the
convocation of the Diet.*

*It is against the Ministry alone that the general dissatisfaction
is directed. The press does not attack the President of the United
States and no one doubts the loftiness of his views and the disin-
terestedness of his policy. The welcome given recently to Secretary
of War Taft on his return from the Philippines and the ovations
which greeted Mr. [William Jennings] Bryan show well that
the cordial relations between the two countries have not changed in
any way.*

*An imposing English squadron under the command of Admiral
Noel came to celebrate the alliance which is unanimously approved.
During the visit of the English Admiral and of thousands of sailors
the town had regained its usual festive and gay air. It was the more
painful, therefore, to see the almost mournful welcome extended to
the statesman who had contributed so effectively to bringing about
this alliance.*[194]

A different reception awaited Admiral Togo. D'Anethan
related:

*Admiral Togo made a triumphal entrance into Tokyo, cheered
by millions of spectators who had come from all parts of the Empire.
The most perfect order was maintained throughout by this huge
throng, which had only one thought: homage to a hero who had
brought such high renown to the fleets put under his command. One
forgot during the festivities the deception felt at the conclusion of the
peace, and took patriotic joy in the pride felt in recalling the victories of the illustrious admiral.*

*The same enthusiasm was aroused at the naval revue held by His
Majesty in Tokyo Bay. All the combined fleets assembled between
Yokohama and Tokyo. One hundred and sixty-six vessels! The*

captured Russian vessels could be recognized by the different color of the chimneys. I believe we witnessed a unique spectacle in history, the victorious fleet comprising after a naval war the same number of vessels as at the beginning of hostilities.

Several refloated Russian ships still bear the marks of destruction but the captured ships are little damaged, especially those surrendered by Admiral [Nikolai Ivanovich] Nebogatov. The Bedovyi, *on which Admiral Rozhestvenskii was taken prisoner, and the* Chinyen, *a ship captured during the war with China and on board which Admiral Ting had committed suicide, likewise fired triumphal salvos as the Emperor passed aboard the* Asama.

The English squadron, sent on the occasion of the alliance, was present as was the American cruiser Wisconsin.

In spite of the alliance with England and the sacrifices of the war, the build-up of the navy does not stop. At the dockyards of Kure and Yokosuka three cruisers and one battleship are now under construction and two others will soon be begun. In England the ships ordered before the war are being finished. The conclusion of peace thus will not lead to any reduction in naval expenditures and Japan will continue to take all necessary measures to retain command of the Pacific and of the seas which bathe her territories.[195]

Upon hearing of the signing of the peace treaty, d'Anethan, as Dean of the Diplomatic Corps, had requested an audience with the Emperor to permit him and his colleagues to present their felicitations. On October 31, the reception took place. D'Anethan remarked on its unusually intimate atmosphere:

The Emperor today received the heads of Missions, and was so kind as to keep us for lunch. Their Imperial Highnesses Prince Fushimi and Prince Higashi-Fushimi as well as the President of the Council and Baron Komura were at the banquet. . . .

We were seated at the table of His Majesty and the meal was served European style. It is very rare, except when foreign Princes visit, that the Emperor invites to his table. Exceptions to this rule were made at the time of the celebration of the silver wedding anniversary of Their Majesties in 1894, at the time of the coming into force of the new treaties in 1899, and at a luncheon given to me by the Emperor on the eve of my departure on leave in 1902.

The Dean did not have to make a speech because the gathering had an intimate character and each of the foreign Representatives was allowed to offer his congratulations to His Majesty.

D'Anethan added:

On November 3, we shall lunch again at the Palace and the Emperor will refer to the conclusion of the peace, and I shall reply in the name of my colleagues. This will be the last time that I shall have the honor to exercise my functions as Dean of the Diplomatic Corps, since the promotion of the English Legation to the rank of Embassy has been settled in principle.[196]

This year the birthday of Emperor Meiji was celebrated with particular rejoicing. As d'Anethan observed:

The birthday of the Emperor was celebrated with even greater enthusiasm than usual. The opposition to the terms of the Portsmouth peace has abated, and the population cheers the troops which return from the battle fields. It is to the Emperor and to his virtues that the triumphs which have been won are attributed, and the feeling of veneration for the Sovereign is as sincere as it is general.[197]

The arrival of an American bishop to convey the thanks of the Pope for the treatment accorded to the Catholic missions in Korea and Manchuria during the war, led d'Anethan to comment:

The choice of an American prelate for this confidential mission has impressed the Japanese who have followed with interest the anti-clerical policy of the French Republic in regard to the future protection of the Catholic missions in China.

In Japan the Christian missionaries, whatever their nationality or the doctrines they profess and teach, enjoy the most complete religious freedom. The baptized natives are not the object of any hatred and are neither molested nor persecuted.

The policy of religious tolerance, which Japan has followed for more than thirty years, will continue in this country and will extend to those, where she exerts and will exert influence. We see it on the Island of Formosa in regards to the Catholic Mission of the Dominicans and the English Mission of the Presbyterians and we shall see it in Korea when—before long—the administration of this unfortunate country will pass into the hands of Japan.

The missionaries in Japan have never occupied themselves with politics, have not sought to obtain privileges or advantages superior to those given to other foreigners. They have scrupulously followed the rule of not interfering in the relations of the native converts with the Authorities. In conformance with Article XXVIII of the Constitution and those of the treaties, the missionaries, in complying with the laws, have thus been able to devote themselves to their worship and exercise their ministry without any opposition or difficulty. They reside not only in big centers but in more than 50 towns and villages. They number eleven or twelve hundred, more than 600 being women. The number is considerable when we note that the foreign population in Japan (not counting the Chinese) amounts to barely more than 6,000.

I do not think it useless to recall these facts and the attitude of Japan toward Christians, because one of the questions that will have to be solved in Korea is the position of the missionaries and of religious congregations. It will be settled according to the spirit of tolerance which animates the Japanese, but also in accordance with the strict observance of regulations that will be decreed. The Christian religion, be it Catholic or Protestant, which a rather large number of Koreans have adopted, henceforth will not shield them from laws, and the support or jurisdiction that the missionaries exerted in their favor will no longer be tolerated.[198]

On November 7, d'Anethan reported that Baron Komura had departed for Peking as Ambassador to negotiate Chinese consent to the terms of the Treaty of Portsmouth. He commented:

One attaches the highest importance to this mission and the selection of the Foreign Minister is universally approved.

The following points are to be settled: cancellation and reversion to Japan of the lease of Liaotung; the transfer to Japan of the railway south of Changchun; connection of the Manchurian railroads with those of Korea; concessions to exploit the mines in Manchuria; the opening of Antung, Mukden, Harbin and Kirin to foreign commerce; measures to be taken to assure the security of the foreigners; the question of the railway guards; and the date and the conditions of the evacuation of the Japanese armies.

According to news from Peking the Chinese commissioners will allegedly seek to drag out the negotiations. They supposedly intend to withdraw all the concessions that they have accorded to foreigners in Manchuria, and attach great importance to obtaining a cut in the period of occupation, the discontinuing of foreign railway guards, and the restitution of the buildings occupied by Japanese and Russian troops.

Agreement on these points would not be difficult with Japan, but as the consent of Russia too is necessary, one suspects that Chinese diplomacy wants to raise them from the beginning of the negotiations to gain time and create new difficulties between Russia and Japan. China has always shown herself skillful in the game of sowing discord between the Powers, but now the game has less chance of succeeding. The Japanese negotiator has a well-defined program, and Chinese dilatory cunning will be powerless to modify it.

Besides, the intentions of Japan toward China are most benevolent. Not only does she want to come to an agreement with her on points raised by the treaty of peace, but also to place the relations between the two Empires on solid and amicable foundations and thereby definitely assure peace in the Far East. Faithful to her promises, Japan wants to restore Manchuria to China, but with the guarantees necessary to establish order and tranquility there and avoid in the future the dangers of foreign intervention.

The question of the return of the railways and the construction of new lines will be one of the hardest to solve. I am inclined to believe that an English-Japanese-Chinese Syndicate is in the making to acquire and exploit the present network as well as that which is planned.[199]

That day d'Anethan wrote also that Marquis Ito was going to Korea as Ambassador Extraordinary to lay the groundwork for the new organization and administration of that country. He observed:

There has been no improvement in the Government so far, and the Emperor is incapable of taking any decision. Japan thus will set to work seriously and create a protectorate that will leave the Emperor merely the appearance of Power.

Korea will no longer accredit Ministers and will have no more foreign diplomatic Representatives at Seoul. The conduct of foreign affairs thus will be in the hands of Japanese advisers. Order will be maintained by Japanese troops and police. The finances and customs will be reorganized and managed in accordance with Japanese procedures.

The foreigners will not suffer from this new state of affairs, because their rights will be respected and the country will remain open to their commercial activity.[200]

Toward the end of the month d'Anethan relayed the text of the Korean agreement, concluded in the wake of the negotiations conducted by Marquis Ito in Seoul. D'Anethan remarked:

As you will note, the convention is explicit only in that which concerns the control and conduct of the foreign relations of Korea. The prerogatives of the Japanese Resident General and those of the Residents who will be installed at different points of the territory are not defined beyond the sphere of diplomatic affairs. The silence regarding the powers that will devolve to the Resident General in the matter of internal administration does not indicate, however, that his role will be limited to conducting Korea's foreign policy. On the contrary, it means that the influence of this high functionary will be fully exerted in all branches of Government. The need for total financial, military, economic, administrative, and judicial reforms in Korea and the maintenance of the appearance of sovereignty of the Emperor made it impossible to formulate in a treaty the regime that henceforth will be applied to the Government of the nation, placed under the protectorate of Japan.

Before inaugurating the system of reforms and making her protectorate effective, Japan had to remove the difficulties which could arise from the diplomatic relations existing between Korea and the foreign Powers. She had to affirm her right of intervention in the foreign affairs of Korea, a right which she acquired by the Treaty of Portsmouth (Article II). The Treaty of Alliance with England (Article III) also recognized Japan's right to take measures of control and protection, necessary for the safeguarding of her interests.

The friendly relations existing between the United States and Japan do not let one believe that any difficulty will be raised by the former. It has even been announced that the American Minister to Seoul has been recalled. No doubt the other Powers soon will follow this example.

Foreign Consuls will undoubtedly be able to remain in Korea to take care of the interests of their nationals. The question of consular jurisdiction will have to be settled.[201]

In January of 1906, d'Anethan reported that the negotiations in Peking regarding the provisions of the Treaty of Portsmouth had ended to the complete satisfaction of the Japanese. He commented:

China has recognized the advantages and concessions acquired by Japan by the Treaty of Portsmouth and has agreed to the opening of new centers to foreign commerce and to the question of the railways and their connection with those of Korea.

Baron Komura went to Peking not as the representative of a conquering nation wanting to impose humiliating conditions. Instead he came animated by feelings of conciliation, and with due decorum spared the susceptibilities of China. As a result he has

*obtained for his country all the advantages to which, he considered,
the Japanese victories entitled her.*

*At Portsmouth as at Peking Baron Komura showed a great
spirit of conciliation, and avoided hurting or humiliating the
Russian and Chinese plenipotentiaries. Public opinion in Japan
reproached him for his moderation. He was accused of weakness
and of diplomatic unfitness. He did not let himself be influenced by
these attacks, and today one does him justice.*

*Baron Komura, like the Government, realized that the peace
with Russia, to be durable, had to be honorable and such as not to
render impossible a future rapprochement between the two Powers.
It seems, according to the newspapers, that relations between
England and Russia are taking a more friendly turn. The Japanese
Government too desires to see her friendly relations with Russia
revived as soon as possible.*[202]

In a lengthy dispatch of the same date, d'Anethan reviewed
the whole Far Eastern situation:

*The objective of the war, which Japan undertook to chase the
Russians out of Manchuria and establish her protectorate in Korea,
has been attained. Will the results of her victories be durable and
is the maintenance of peace in the Far East assured for a long
time?*

*In Korea, it does not seem that the difficulties which the creation
of the new order may encounter will be apt to lead to foreign complications. Under the wise and prudent direction of Marquis Ito,
order will be established, and it will be possible to develop the
resources of the country, offering a large field of exploitation both
to Japanese and foreigners, who will work harmoniously.*

*It is in regard to China that there are apprehensions about the
possibility of maintaining calm and peace. Very well informed
about happenings in China, the Japanese Government is aware
that hostility against foreigners now is very strong and that the
secret societies are restless in all parts of the Empire. China is at
last coming out of her long lethargy and wants to affirm her rights*

of sovereignty and to escape the bondage with which the European Powers had burdened her so long. The anti-American movement, extending as far as the Chinese residents in Singapore and Hongkong, is considered very serious.

In Japan, there are now more than ten thousand Chinese students of all ages and all positions. The young men are put in schools under the supervision and direction of the Chinese Minister and the Japanese Government, and quietly pursue their studies. Under the guise of students there have come also Chinese of a certain age who do take courses, but whose object is to propagate from here revolutionary ideas in China. The Japanese Government, far from encouraging this movement, has tied them to all the regulations other students must follow. More than a thousand have just left Japan. . . .

All Japanese statesmen are agreed on the policy to be followed toward China. This policy can be summed up as follows: strict observance of the treaties and respect of persons and property; encouragement of reforms in the administrative and judicial system; and reorganization of the armed forces and the police. The goodwill and protection of Japan are and will remain extended to China. But if the latter does not understand the urgent need for reforms through governmental and regular channels and does not herself suppress. . .the revolutionary movements threatening the foreigners, Japan will not separate her cause from that of the West and of America. Japan will work toward the maintenance of the integrity of China only as long as the Authorities of the Celestial Empire will not violate the treaties and will know how to make them respected.

It is a great mistake to believe—and the view is still too prevalent in Europe—that because Japan belongs to the yellow race, she would prefer, by virtue of her tastes, customs or sympathies, to make common cause with Orientals of the same color. Starting out from this false idea, one sees Japan already as the ally of China stirring up Asia against the white race! One is not far from believing, that she will seek to incite troubles and disorders to attain her ends and that she will instigate redoubled hostility against the for-eigners.

It cannot be repeated enough: nothing is further from the mind of any thinking Japanese. The interest of Japan forbids such a policy, for she knows better than anyone, that in a China given over to anarchy, no difference would be made between Japanese subjects and other nationals and that they would be the object of the same hatred and the same outrages. For the development of her commerce and her industries, Japan has as much and perhaps more interest than Europe in seeing China calm and prosperous. If an insurrection of Boxers or others would break out again, Japan would be forced [to send] a new expedition and to [make] new sacrifices of men and money.

Japan wants to avoid the partition of China, since territorial expansion would be a cause of weakness for her and would involve her in very serious rivalries with the nations already occupying positions in China. In short, Japan aspires to be the principal factor in the maintenance of the status quo in China, if the blindness, corruption and ignorance of the Court and of the Mandarins do not pose insurmountable obstacles.

Yüan Shih-k'ai is considered today as the statesman most likely to lead China on the road to progress. It is him, consequently, that Japan encourages and supports.

Will Japan succeed in furthering. . .improvements in Chinese administration and the avoidance of new, bloody conflicts? This is the big problem that the Imperial Government poses itself, and it wants to resolve it in harmony with the European Powers and the United States. [203]

In April, Japan announced the opening of several ports in Manchuria. D'Anethan observed:

A dispatch from Peking states that China protests the opening of territory in Manchuria, maintaining that it is up to her and not up to Japan to take measures of this kind. According to the pledge made by Japan, her military occupation of South Manchuria must end in 18 months, unless the evacuation of the part occupied by Russia occurs sooner. China, which has not yet reconstituted a regular government in these regions, is not disposed to assure the protection of foreigners.[204]

CHAPTER FIVE

Shifting Sands

In March of 1906, the Baroness d'Anethan left for Europe and in the summer her husband joined her. The Baroness's diary, *Fourteen Years of Diplomatic Life in Japan*, ends at this point. But by the end of the year both she and her husband were back in Japan.[i] During d'Anethan's absence, Maurice Rooman d'Ertbuer kept the Belgian Government informed of the international situation. In October he reported that Russian removal of restrictions on the Japanese in North Manchuria had accelerated the Russo-Japanese negotiations which were taking place in St. Petersburg, while the exclusion of Japanese children from the public schools in San Francisco had aroused the Japanese public and damaged Japanese-American relations. In December he wrote about the arrival of a Korean mission in Tokyo, as well as about the return of Prince Ito from Seoul. Toward the end of the month he reported a snag in Russo-Japanese negotiations to settle the remaining issues and conclude a new treaty of amity and commerce regarding the opening of the Amur and its tributaries and the fisheries in the territorial waters of Russia in the Pacific. He confirmed the steady worsening of relations between Japan and the United States.

Back in Japan, d'Anethan reported:

The negotiations with Russia will soon be concluded. Both in St. Petersburg and in Tokyo one shows oneself animated by con-

---

[i] The diplomatic dispatches are impersonal and do not indicate whether or not the Baroness accompanied him. I am indebted for the information to Mr. P.-H. Desneux, Archivist of the Belgian Ministry of Foreign Affairs. The Baroness returned with Baron d'Anethan on December 22, 1909 and left Japan for the last time on November 9, 1910 after the death of her husband.

ciliatory feelings, and the desire to reestablish not only normal but friendly relations between the two countries is evident.

The diplomatic position of Japan is superb and for a long time we shall hear no more talk of her belligerent and encroaching inclinations. We do not have to fear any complications between Japan and the United States and Europe. It is not the same as far as her relations with China are concerned.

On every occasion the Chinese Government shows its hostility against Japan. The reactionary movement in Peking is directed above all against statesmen suspected of having Japanese sympathies. It is realized in Tokyo that when anti-foreignism will break out again in China, it will be directed primarily against the Japanese. The Imperial Government, therefore, will seek to act in accord with the Powers interested like itself in the maintenance of order.[205]

On June 18, d'Anethan commented on the signing of a Franco-Japanese agreement. He observed:

The entente concluded between France and Japan, published yesterday, was favorably received by the press and [public] opinion. The agreement in effect reconfirms Japan as a Great Power and considerably increases her strength and her diplomatic influence in the Far East.

Viscount Hayashi, in an interview granted to one of the editors of the liberal press, showed that the convention had no aggressive character and was not directed against any other Power. The territorial clauses concern the maintenance of Chinese integrity and the guarantee of the possessions and spheres of influence of the two contracting parties in the Far East. The Foreign Ministry in its statements to the press has likewise insisted on the pacific side of the entente.

It is to be noticed, however, that the convention, while guaranteeing the independence and sovereignty of China, constitutes a powerful weapon for Japanese diplomacy in the latter country. As you know.... "divide et impera" [divide and conquer] has always been the political doctrine of the Chinese leaders. Most recently China tried to apply this doctrine in her campaign to recover her territorial rights and her real independence. . . . From now on she will find herself facing three Great Powers, acting in harmony and agreeing beforehand on all the questions that concern them.

This new political orientation will probably be completed by a Russo-Japanese entente that the press foresees as a logical consequence of the accord which has just been concluded. There is room for doubt, however. Russia would have to renounce the role which she has always played in the Far East, that of confidante of China and of broker between her and the other Powers. One can even presume that Russia will try to profit from the excitement that the Franco-Japanese entente has caused in Peking to recapture her former influence.[206]

In July d'Anethan evaluated the extent to which racial discrimination in California had affected the course of Japanese-American relations:

The incidents which have recently occurred in San Francisco against Japanese workers and merchants naturally affect Japanese pride and national feeling. But one must not exaggerate the importance of the hostility of a few thousand troublemakers in California in regard to political relations between the Imperial Government and that of the United States. They have not ceased to be most cordial. The difficulties in carrying out the treaties which assure the rights and privileges of the Japanese in the United States will be settled through diplomatic channels.

It is absurd to speak of war between the two countries and we must put ourselves on guard against the false news, spread by certain newspapers of the American and European press. The Japanese press which in this case faithfully reflects public opinion is very wise and very moderate; it is unanimous in rejecting all thought of possible conflict with the great nation which has always been the sincere friend of Japan. . . .

From whatever point of view we judge the state of relations

P

between Japan and the United States, it is evident that the Imperial Government is firmly determined to keep them friendly and peaceful. If they will lose this character one day, the provocation will not come from Japan. As it is unlikely, that the United States on her part intends to plunge into so senseless an adventure, we can await with confidence the result of the negotiations in progress to settle the differences aroused by the municipality of San Francisco.[207]

D'Anethan sent his government the text of the new convention, concluded between Japan and Korea on July 5th. He commented:

The Resident General becomes in fact the chief of state, as he has authority to make appointments to all the posts that may be occupied by Koreans or Japanese. In leaving an Emperor on the throne, the Japanese Government keeps to the letter of the treaties which guarantee the independence of Korea.

There are some disorders in Seoul, but they will be repressed promptly. The international relations are unchanged, and the treaties concluded by Korea and the Foreign Powers are still in force.[208]

In October, Secretary Taft once again stopped in Japan en route to Manila. D'Anethan observed:

This is the third time that Mr. Taft visits Japan. The welcome which he received on two occasions was most enthusiastic and the Government and the population eagerly seized the opportunities to manifest their feelings of affection toward the great republic, which had always shown herself the friend of Japan. If today we see less popular demonstrations, the official reception is no less correct and cordial. . . . No one in Japan desires war. Everybody, on the contrary, understands that it is of the greatest interest to retain the most intimate relations with America. . . .

For what reason would Japan make war on the United States? Why attack a Power whose territory she could not seriously invade? This would be such folly, that, I cannot repeat enough, it will never enter the mind of any Japanese statesman.[209]

Dwelling on the subject of war between the two countries, Taft declared in a speech, summarized by d'Anethan: "War. . .between Japan and the United States would be a crime against civilization. The two peoples do not desire it and the two Governments will make every effort to avoid such a catastrophe."[210]

The recall of the Japanese Ambassador from Washington gave birth to all kinds of rumors. To counteract them, d'Anethan telegraphed that Aoki had been removed for incompetence, and that his recall was of no political importance, a replacement to be sent shortly.[211] In a longer dispatch of the same day, d'Anethan elaborated:

Viscount Aoki has exceeded and badly interpreted his instructions. Instead of conforming to the views of the Foreign Minister, he had . . . followed too personal a line of conduct. He has failed in his efforts both in Washington and in Tokyo, and has aroused public opinion against himself in Japan. He is said to have promised to President Roosevelt to induce his Government to consent to the revision of Article 2 of the Japanese-American treaty and to join the Russian-American fisheries treaty.

As these declarations of Viscount Aoki were not ratified by the Japanese Government, the President was placed in a delicate position. In his message of last year he had in effect announced the adhesion of Japan to the said Russo-American treaty. In his efforts to settle the difficulties aroused by the expulsion of Japanese children from the schools, the President, relying on the opinion expressed by the Viscount, had made certain commitments to the authorities and the congressmen of California.

The confidence of the President being thus shaken, Aoki could not carry on with any chance of success the delicate negotiations now in progress. His replacement in the near future will be the best denial of the importance that the press has sought to give to his recall. Insofar as Japan is concerned, the situation has not changed. The Ministry will not let itself be influenced by the incitements of the native or foreign Press.[212]

At this time Ivan Shipov, former Finance Minister of Russia, visited Japan. D'Anethan commented:

He conversed primarily with businessmen and bankers and at a number of public meetings expressed his admiration for the progress made by Japan and deplored that more important dealings did not exist between the two countries. He says that the object of his trip is to work to increase the common interests.

Are the excellent relations which exist today between Russia and Japan and the very prompt reconciliation which has occurred between them, very real and will they last? The Japanese Government believes in the sincerity of the Russian assurances. It does not fear new aggression on the part of the adversary, which cost it so much blood and money. I do not know on what agreements the confidence of the Imperial Government is based, but I have it from the most reliable source that such confidence exists.

Is the mission of Mr. Taft to St. Petersburg apt to shake it? I am not inclined to think so, when I consider with what calm one envisages in Tokyo the trip of the Secretary of War to Russia. The reason is perhaps that one is well informed about the policy that the Russian Foreign Minister wants to follow in a less distant Orient.

I remember perfectly that Mr. Izvolskii, when he was my colleague in Tokyo, told me: "Our policy in Manchuria is fifty years ahead of time. We must, before getting involved in the Far East, realize our historic program in the Balkans and in Turkey."[213]

Word of the impending retirement of the Empress Dowager, refocussed attention on China. D'Anethan related:

The most contradictory rumors circulate about the palace intrigues and the rivalries between the viceroys and governors. It is unanimously held in Japan, however, that the state of things in China will not last without serious modifications.

The statesmen who know China best do not believe in a united movement or a sudden [?] change, which under another sovereign or a dictatorship would continue the present system with some ameliorations. The numerous reform decrees and the new organization of the Neiwupuh [Ministry of Internal Affairs] will not find sufficient groundwork done to have a lasting effect. There is the tendency, however, to upset and destroy everything without having conceived a fixed plan of reconstruction.

All the Powers which have interests in China are threatened by the disturbances that one fears. . . . In this respect the Japanese are no more privileged than the other Powers. On the contrary, having different and more complicated relations with the Chinese, they run into more numerous difficulties. Immediately after the war Chinese feelings seemed favorable to Japan. The situation has radically changed today. I do not presume to comment on the value or merit of Japanese claims or of the opposition of China. I limit myself to state the facts as exactly as possible. I must bring them to Your attention, however, because there are some which, if they are not settled amicably, will create conflicts and lead to an armed intervention on the part of Japan. . . .

Your Excellency knows from the reports of our Minister in Peking what excitement was aroused by the agreements concluded between Japan, Russia and France. Will China seize this pretext to seek a rapprochement with Germany and the United States? One is not entirely reassured in Japan about the intentions of Germany. The relations between Berlin and Tokyo are very correct. The particularly friendly welcome accorded to Admiral Ijuin by Emperor William was appreciated. Yet there is no confidence, and the famous drawing [of the Emperor], the "Yellow Peril", is not forgotten.[214]

China and Japan were at odds over railways. D'Anethan explained:

China wants to extend her railroad from Hsinmintun to Tsitsihar via Fakumen. The Japanese Government has protested against this project on the basis of the protocol of the treaty of 1905, by which China committed herself not to construct lines parallel to or in the vicinity of the Japanese line or any other which would compete with the latter. The Waiwupu maintains its right [to do so], alleging that the line will not be parallel or prejudicial to the Japanese railroad.

The question is complicated by the intervention of foreign capitalists, to whom China is said to have turned to obtain the funds necessary for the construction of the line in question. In stipulating guarantees against possible competition with the railroads of South Manchuria, the Japanese followed the example set by Russia, which before constructing the Manchurian railroad had received from China assurances identical with those claimed by Japan in the above-mentioned protocol.

Russia had prevented the line from Mukden to Hsinmintun. During the war she had united the two towns with a temporary line for strategic reasons. When the line fell into the possession of the Japanese, the latter rebuilt it in a permanent way and ceded it to China. Japan is very determined to maintain the rights which she has acquired by her treaty with China, and will not tolerate the line from Hsinmintun to Tsitsihar.[215]

In the summer of 1908, rebellion in Yunnan Province and the penetration of some of the insurgents into neighboring Indo-China, brought on a crisis in Franco-Chinese relations. D'Anethan described the attitude of Japan:

It is expected in Tokyo that China will refuse to bow to French demands. If she is not strong enough to resist, the national party will see its influence considerably increased and the relations of the other Powers with China will be rendered the more delicate and difficult.

Japan has too much interest in deferring the time of new and more serious complications with China to be in a position to support the claims of France. Her entente with this power, brought about by her alliance with England, is limited, as far as I can learn, to assuring France concerning the Empire of Indo-China. The Imperial Government is consequently not committed to intervene, and I have reason to believe that she will remain an impartial spectator.[216]

In 1908, the Russian Legation was raised to the rank of Embassy, and Nikolai Nikolaevich Malevskii-Malevich, who arrived in July as the new Russian Representative, thus came as the first Russian Ambassador. D'Anethan observed:

The first Ambassador of Russia, Mr. Malevich, has just arrived. He has been welcomed with sympathy in Japan, because it is felt that the appointment of a Representative who has not occupied an important post abroad and whose functions in the Ministry dealt with consular affairs indicates that the Russian Government does not intend to create political difficulties [but wants] to maintain the most cordial relations with Japan.

Mr. [Iurii Petrovich] Bakhmetev, who had renewed diplomatic relations [between Russia and Japan] and who had succeeded in gaining the confidence of the Imperial Government, was surprised that he was not promoted to Ambassador in Tokyo. But he assured me in taking leave of me, that very soon after his return to Europe he will be named Ambassador either to Vienna or to Rome. He added: "We now agree perfectly with Japan on all points. For quite a long time there will be only commercial questions to regulate; it is of great mutual interest for us to work together in this regard. It is to Turkey and the Balkans that Russia will direct her efforts. Austria and Italy are too interested in the question of the Orient for the [Russian] Emperor not to send an Ambassador there who knows it well. I have made almost my whole career in the Orient and was involved in important events; if one had listened to me more, the influence of Russia would have remained intact."

I deem it interesting, Monsieur le Ministre, *to inform you very confidentially of this conversation, for* if it is correct *that Mr. Bakhmetev is slated for one of the two big posts in question, we can expect to see Russia strengthen her posture in Constantinople.*

Mr. Bakhmetev's career in the Orient has shown him enter-

prising, intriguing and not always very scrupulous in the means employed. With him in Rome or Vienna, it can only be a question of a policy of action to prepare or provoke an intervention in the restless and disorderly Turkish provinces.[217]

In October d'Anethan reported that Japan had decided to reduce drastically the number of troops which she had kept in China following the Boxer Rebellion, and was recalling over half the infantry and all the cavalry. She felt that the political situation no longer required the presence of such large forces, and would be disposed to evacuate Peking, Tientsin and Shanhaikwan completely. D'Anethan commented:

If she does not do so now, it is because she is bound by pledges made with the Powers who likewise have troops in China and must come to an agreement with them beforehand. The Chinese Government, as one might expect, bitterly resents the humiliation inflicted on her by the foreign Powers and can only welcome the proof of friendship that Japan has given her.

One of the objectives of the mission of Mr. Tung, who is going to America and to Europe, is to obtain the withdrawal of all foreign garrisons. Japan's attitude facilitates his task. The United States, which seeks every opportunity to show her sympathy for China, will no doubt take the initiative of proposing the repeal of the Peking Protocol (September 1901), by which the Powers bound themselves to maintain garrisons as proof of continued common action. At present one does not fear disturbances against the foreigners in Peking. If contrary to expectations protective measures would be necessary, the Japanese would very rapidly send troops, stationed in Manchuria.

In view of the progress made by the military authorities and the excellent organization of the part of the Chinese Army, drilled in the European way, the foreign contingents, which amount to less than 600 men, would not be of any effective help. Under the circumstances Japan deems it time to relieve China of the humiliating treatment, similar to that which so hurt Japanese national pride when French and English detachments occupied (until 1875) the foreign concession in Yokohama.

It cannot be concealed that Peking is not animated by sympathetic feelings toward Japan. Hostility is manifested also and perhaps to a greater extent in Canton and on the Yangtze. We have seen it during that already rather long boycott . . . of Japanese goods. The tense situation is improving, but absolutely cordial relations have not yet been restored.

The meddling and influence of the foreign [commercial] houses established in China have contributed not a little to sustaining hostility against Japan. In acting thus, the foreign merchants imprudently play with a two-edged sword. The momentary advantage that they were able to obtain from the reduction of transactions between China and Japan will be of little import the day when they in turn will also be boycotted. Japan had well understood the danger of the situation, when Chinese merchants two years ago refused American goods. She had, therefore, at the time lent her support to ending the boycott.

With the awakening of patriotic feeling in China, we shall see the Chinese, whenever difficulties arise between the Chinese Government and any other Power, put more serious obstacles to the trade of those Powers, which injure their rights or dignity.[218]

In October of 1908, d'Anethan wrote that relations between the United States and Japan were very good:

The campaign waged by the New York Herald *and several "yellow" newspapers will not succeed in influencing a single sensible person in the United States any more than it will cause the slightest excitement in Japan. The idea of a war with the United States makes every thinking man shrug his shoulders. The relations between the two countries have never been more intimate, more confident, more sincerely friendly. . . .*

The United States has great interests in China. Moreover the questionable success . . . of its colonization in the Philippines depends also on its future relations with China. It is rational, there-

fore, that an accord must be established between Peking and Washington.

The Japanese Government understands the situation well and will not work against the American interests in Peking. On the other hand, it will not tolerate any entente or alliance apt to compromise its own interests. The Cabinets of Tokyo and Washington are in agreement on this subject, and . . . there is no foreseeable danger that peace between the two Pacific Powers will be endangered.

The United States has given up the portion of the indemnity, which was imposed on China in excess [of damages]. The High Commissioner Na-t'ung will go to America to convey the thanks of the Chinese Government. I have reason to believe that it is being considered in Washington to raise the American Legation to an Embassy. . . . The sending of an Ambassador would be of great importance for China.

The Chinese Government likes to think that it can count on American sympathy. It is justified in this view, but would be mistaken in believing that it could establish more intimate relations with the United States at the expense of or counter to the interests of Japan.

Japan does not claim any exclusive advantage in China; she has acted and will act in harmony with Europe and America in her policy toward China. She would not change her political course, if the impossible should happen and the theories of the New York Herald concerning an anti-Japanese alliance between China and the United States came to be realized.[219]

The arrival of an American squadron cemented Japanese-American amity. D'Anethan observed:

The American squadron, which had departed from Hampton Roads on December 16, arrived at Yokohama yesterday, after visiting Trinidad, Brazil, Chili, San Francisco, Honolulu, New-Zealand, Australia and the Philippines. This enormous fleet of sixteen first-class cruisers, which have just completed the long voy-

age of two thousand eight hundred miles, is anchored for eight days near an equal number of Japanese vessels.

The reception, accorded to the American fleet not only by the Emperor and His Government but by the entire nation, has great political significance. It will strengthen more intimately than ever the relations of amity and confidence between the two countries. Far from giving umbrage or inspiring any fear in Japan, this deployment of forces is . . . regarded as a guarantee of peace.

In my report of July 9, 1907 . . . I had the honor to write: "If the American squadron had time to visit Japan and receive the sympathetic welcome that it certainly would be accorded, the welcome would be no less cordial than that given to the squadron of Admiral Ijuin at Jamestown. This visit would strongly contribute to consolidating the good mutual understanding." At the time it was merely a question of reinforcing the Pacific squadron. When the Government of the United States later decided to send the fleet around the world, the Imperial Government officially invited it to come to Japan. The invitation was accepted most amiably. Today we witness this splendid scene.

On the eve of the arrival of the fleet, the Emperor addressed a proclamation to his people, expressing his desires concerning the political lines which he wants to follow and recommends. They can be summed up as follows: peace with all nations, cooperation in concert with the Powers, appeal to the most noble instincts of the race to work for the prosperity of the Empire. . . .

The Emperor's infallibility is a dogma that every Japanese accepts without reservation and before which he bows with the deepest and sincerest respect. . . . In the great duel with Russia He had appealed to the martial spirit of his nation to assure victory. More than three hundred thousand men died in response to their Emperor's confidence! Upon the conclusion of peace, a peace which did not satisfy national pride, the Emperor expressed his approval of the obtained results. As if by magic, the murmurs, complaints, and objections ceased completely. Today the Emperor declares: My Empire must live in peace with the world and dedicate itself to developing her resources to keep its rank in the world. His voice will be heard and heeded by his people with the same confidence, with which it acquired the high position that it occupies by sacrificing the best of its forces, riches, and blood.

Telegraphic dispatches from London state: "The proclamation of the Emperor has made a good impression—proof of peace." Those from New York: "Proclamation coinciding with the arrival of the fleet indicates desire of more intimate union with the United States." The London version is more accurate. Japan—and this, I repeat, is the important point—wants peace, but the proclamation was not influenced by the arrival of the fleet. As I wrote you, Monsieur le Ministre, *on December 17, 1904, Japan—once the war with Russia will have ended after a moderate peace— will only desire to follow a policy of peace with all nations of the world.*

Attacks, we can even say, wars of the press and of financiers have been and are being directed against the Japanese. The Japanese Government does not get aroused, does not deviate from the path which it has laid out for itself. It says and proclaims today through the voice of its beloved Emperor, that it wants peace with the same conviction and the same resolution that it went to war with China and Russia.

When information from the Legation of the King [i.e. from d'Anethan himself] stated that Japan would not retreat before her powerful enemy, I do not think that it was taken very seriously. Yet today I am no less positive in the pacific sense than I was at the time, when I announced that war would be inevitable, unless Russia would make concessions.[220]

While Japanese-American relations seemed to be improving, Japanese-German relations deteriorated again. D'Anethan related:

The declarations of the Emperor of Germany concerning the role that the German Navy would be called upon to play in the waters of the Pacific and the allusions to the Yellow Peril have caused in Japan not so much excitement as astonishment. But they revive the feeling of defiance of German aims in the Far East.

Since the war the Emperor of Germany seemed to seek opportunities to show his sympathy for Japan. The call for a possible union of European fleets in the Pacific erases the good impression that the kindnesses of the Emperor toward Prince Arisugawa and recently toward Prince Kuni had produced. The press has been very sober in its comments and has exercised great restraint. The German Ambassador was instructed to give the most amiable explanations of the meaning of the words of the Emperor. They are received nonetheless with a certain skepticism.

The alliance with England, the entente with France and Russia, and the most friendly assurances of the United States guarantee Japan against the eventuality of complications that Germany under the present circumstances, however powerful she may be in Europe, could not arouse or create in the Far East. The intervention of the Emperor and his famous picture of the Yellow Peril had not been forgotten, but one preferred not to speak about it further! The remarks attributed to the Emperor have awakened the painful memory.[221]

Later in the month d'Anethan communicated:

Baron Mumm, the German Ambassador in Tokyo, has formally and publicly declared that the words attributed to the Emperor and reproduced by The American *and* The World *are apocryphal. He added, that he had been informed officially that these remarks had been contradicted in the* Reichsanzeiger. *His Excellency also said that according to information from the highest authority, the news that the German Government had paid fifty thousand dollars to stop the publication in the* Century *of the account of the conversations of His Majesty with Dr. Hale, was utterly false and mendacious.*

The assurances given by the German Government spontaneously in Berlin and Tokyo . . . do not suffice to establish confidence. It matters little to the Japanese whether the conversations of the

Emperor were reproduced more or less verbatim. They figure that they express the intimate views of the Emperor and that consequently the intentions of His Majesty are not benevolent toward Japan. One is convinced that the Emperor resents seeing Japan take a place among the Great Powers and conclude an alliance with England. One fears equally lest the Emperor's diplomatic efforts seek to provoke difficulties between the United States and Japan. The feeling of defiance of German policy in the Far East has been reawakened, and a few friendly exchanges and banal assurances will not suffice to calm them.[222]

Upon the conclusion of the Root-Takahira Agreement, Baron Mumm gave an interview to the Japanese press, in which he publicly stated that the Japanese-American understanding "was a matter of great satisfaction" to Germany. D'Anethan commented:

The publicity given by the Ambassador himself to his instructions will make a good impression. Not wanting to remain isolated in Far Eastern policy, Germany desires, it appears, also to come to an agreement with Japan with a view to declaring that she does not seek to modify the status quo *in China. The line of conduct of Japan is so plain and clearly defined, that the Cabinet of Tokyo will undoubtedly have no objection to accepting an exchange of views with that of Berlin.*

German commerce, which has developed so rapidly in the Far East, is passing through a serious crisis at this moment. The bankruptcy of very important houses in China is expected. Baron Mumm says German policy is guided solely by commercial interests. Under the circumstances, it is evident that the German Government must be anxious to avoid as much as possible all cause of enmity or even of friction with Japan.

The memorandums exchanged between the United States and Japan have opened the eyes of the most shortsighted, and the rumors of war between the two great Pacific Powers have been relegated to the category of sensational news, of which the yellow

American organs are fond and which, as regards Japan, the German press has frequently spread with little discernment.[223]

On November 14, Emperor Kuang-hsü of China died; on November 15, the Empress Dowager passed away also. The demise of both left the throne in the hands of a minor. D'Anethan wrote:

It is difficult as yet to predict the impact that the death of the Emperor and of the Empress Dowager of China will have on the destinies of China. As long as power rested in the hands of this Princess, who was clever, cunning and unscrupulous but energetic and possessed a will-power that always overcame all opposition, the Government of Peking exercised its authority in all of China. The Court intrigues fomented against her were frustrated and the rivalries between the different branches of the Imperial family were made ineffectual. The foreign Powers thus had an interest in seeing her authority maintained. With her gone, will the dynasty continue? Will we not witness a general upheaval in China?

The Japanese Government has some apprehensions, and is rather inclined to consider the internal situation of China as perilous for foreign interests. If the lives or properties of foreigners are threatened, the commerce impeded, or the treaties violated, the Powers will intervene. The preponderant position that Japan exercises in the Far East today will give her the major role.

It is interesting, therefore, to be sure of her intentions and of the policy that she plans to follow in regard to China. The last service rendered by the Empress Dowager was to regulate the succession to the throne and to nominate a Regent. The Japanese Government will use its influence to maintain the present dynasty, aware that rebellions against it will accentuate the hatred of the Chinese against the Manchus. The danger would be the more serious as half the army is composed of Chinese.

One of the basic principles of Japanese policy is to maintain the integrity of China. With respect to this she has given the most formal assurances not only to Europe but to the United States, and has committed herself by her treaty with England and her ententes with France and Russia to work to this end in concert with the Powers. Fears of Japan taking advantage of China's difficulties to inaugurate an aggressive policy are thus unfounded. As long as possible she will use the greatest consideration toward China and continue her efforts to prevent all complications.

It would be foolish to believe that Japan seeks to foment insurrection and civil war in China. Should these break out, as I said above, foreign intervention would be needed to protect the Legations in Peking and the concessions in the open ports. Because of her proximity to China and the great forces that she could send promptly, Japan would have to bear the heaviest burden of the enterprise.

Japan does not desire to intervene in China, and should she be forced to do so, she will do it only after consulting with the European Powers and the United States and act in concert with them. Please rest assured, Monsieur le Ministre, *that Japan will not follow in China a line of conduct different from that of the other nations interested in maintaining order, security and peace.*

Foreign Minister Count Komura speaks clearly and categorically in the sense that I have just indicated. His predecessor, Count Hayashi, also often made similar statements. Mr. Kato, the former Foreign Minister, who is going to London as Ambassador, does not conceal that he has instructions to maintain harmony between his country and Europe in regards to the affairs of China.

It seems that the American Government desires an accord with Japan . . . concerning the policy to be followed in China. I think there are talks between the Cabinets of Tokyo and Washington about this. It is not believed that the exchange of views will entail a written agreement. The two Governments will probably confine themselves to a declaration (confirming only what exists), to the effect that the two Governments, respecting the independence and territorial integrity of China and the principle of freedom of commerce of all nations, commit themselves to maintain the state of affairs now existing without receiving exclusive advantages.

Unity between Japan and the Occident is imperative to safe-

*guard the interests of the capital invested in China, amounting to
billions, not to mention the trade, railroads, etc., etc. If harmony
ceased, the losses that Europe would suffer would be incalculable.*

*Japan, whose commercial prosperity will depend above all on the
vast market that she will find in China, is too interested in preventing the dismemberment of China to abandon the straightforward,
correct, and sincere policy that she followed at the time of the Boxer
disturbances and of subsequent treaties. She made common cause
with Europe in the most dangerous crisis through which the foreigners passed in China. Her help will be of use today, when the grave
Chinese problem poses itself in particularly alarming circumstances.*[224]

A week and a half later d'Anethan reported:

*The Foreign Minister told me that according to news that he is
receiving from all parts of China, the situation is calm and he does
not apprehend disturbances or difficulties for the moment. There is
unity among the members of the Imperial family and no opposition
against the powers of the Regent. All rumors about the suicide of
the Empress, the poisoning of Prince Ch'ing, the disfavor of Yüan
Shih-k'ai, and the palace intrigues were but pure fabrications propa-
gated around Shanghai.*

*Count Komura is of the opinion that Prince Chun is a capable and
intelligent man, imbued with ideas of progress, and that he will
have sufficient energy to put them into effect. He believes that he
will hasten the proclamation of a Constitution and will accomplish
reforms in the administration of the finances.*

*The only attempted disturbance took place at Anking in the Pro-
vince of Anhwei. Several soldiers revolted, but the affair had no
consequences and was promptly quelled. The boycott against Japanese goods in Canton will soon be suppressed. It was instigated by
a society of revolutionaries in Canton. The latter has just been dissolved and the leaders arrested. The resumption of normal business
is therefore expected soon.*[225]

On November 30, Secretary of State Elihu Root signed an

Q

agreement with Takahira Kogoro, the Japanese Ambassador in Washington. D'Anethan commented:

The sincerity of the welcome given to the American fleet by the Japanese nation in October cemented the traditional friendship of the two countries, and presented a favorable occasion for making their concordant political views public. The Imperial Government seized the occasion to make a proposal to that of the United States, which happened to share the opinion regarding a public declaration. Consequently an exchange of notes took place on November 30, and the agreement was published officially two days later.

The declaration states the resolution of the two Governments to maintain the status quo *in the Pacific, respecting their mutual territorial possessions; to encourage the peaceful development of commerce; to defend the common interests of all Powers in China, protecting by all means the independence and integrity of this Empire as well as the principle of commercial and industrial equality for all nations; and finally, should the occasion arise, to act in concert to stop by whatever measures necessary any occurrence that would threaten the* status quo *or the above-mentioned principles.*

The form of the entente dispenses with subsequent ratification either by the American Senate or the Japanese Privy Council, which a regular treaty would have necessitated. Nonetheless, as the Tokyo press and a number of influential statesmen agree in remarking, it completes the series of ententes concluded by the Empire with two of the great continental Powers of Europe and her treaty of alliance with England. It is hoped the accord will be effective in preventing in the future every cause of possible misunderstanding, misunderstanding which furthermore is rendered improbable by the traditionally frank and sincere diplomacy of the two countries and the historical friendship that unites them.[226]

Tsai-feng, who assumed the role of Regent for the new child Emperor Hsüan-t'ung, did dismiss Yüan Shih-k'ai, the influential confidant of the late Empress Dowager. D'Anethan commented:

The disfavor of Yüan Shih-k'ai does not arouse in Japan the excitement that it has provoked in Europe. The Government does not apprehend that the withdrawal of this statesman will be likely to produce serious disorders or to orient Chinese policy in a reactionary, anti-foreign sense. Nor does one believe in an imminent struggle between the Manchus and the Chinese. The attitude of Yüan Shih-k'ai toward the deceased Emperor rendered his position close to the Prince Regent untenable; one deems that his retirement will facilitate harmony between the members of the Government.

It is felt in Japan that the influence attributed to Yüan Shih-k'ai has been exaggerated. One recognizes his great qualities as administrator, but realizes that he has many enemies among the Chinese. His supporters are not powerful enough to be able to attempt a rebellion against the Dynasty. It is thought that the army which he formed and organized on a rather solid basis would not give him its support, now that he has lost the prestige of power. He has returned to his province of Honan and according to declarations made by the Regent, no other severe measures will be taken against him.

A number of questions must yet be settled between China and Japan, and the Cabinet of Tokyo, wanting to deal with them in an amicable and conciliatory spirit, does not think that the negotiations will be hindered or compromised by the retirement of Yüan. Consequently, it does not want to interfere in the internal politics of China. The interests of Japan require that order not be disturbed in China; she believes that the best way to maintain it is to abstain from any step that might create difficulties for the Government of Peking. She would consider it imprudent on the part of the foreign Powers, therefore, to lend their support to Yüan Shih-k'ai or his partisans.

Is the optimism, shown by the Japanese Government concerning the maintenance of tranquility in China, justified? It is not shared, I know, by most residents in China. I can only report the views of the Government, taking the liberty of adding, that it is ordinarily very accurately informed about events not only in Peking but in other parts of the Empire.[227]

A week later d'Anethan added:

The resignation of Yüan Shih-k'ai, as you are aware, has surprised the Representatives of the foreign Powers in Peking. They wanted to approach the Chinese Government without delay to express their sympathies and regard for the statesman who had been dismissed. The Ministers of America and England agreed to call their colleagues together and try to bring them to make a collective protest.

The correspondent of the Times *in Peking has telegraphed that the Japanese Government had pressed for the disfavor of Yüan Shih-k'ai. I think it not useless to establish the truth of the matter and to relate to you the action of the Japanese Government.*

One realized in Tokyo that the position of Yüan Shih-k'ai was difficult, but was surprised at the rapidity with which the stern measures against him were taken. As soon as the news reached Tokyo, Viscount Komura ordered the Japanese Minister in Peking to call the attention of the Chinese Government to the serious inconveniences that could result from measures of a general character taken by the partisans or friends of the statesman, expelled from the Government. As for the protest, contemplated by the foreign Ministers, the Cabinet of Tokyo told its Representative: "We do not oppose your joining in an action, implying that all the Powers agree to express the desire that no change be brought in the Government of China, which would be apt to lead to internal complications, but you must abstain from discussing personal questions or attacking any member of the Government." Faithful to the line of conduct that it has followed for years, the Japanese Government does not want to separate itself from the Great European Powers and from America in her policy toward China.

According to reports that we have received here, the nervousness of the perhaps somewhat overzealous Representatives in Peking has been calmed by instructions from their Governments. The rather hostile bent of **Dr.** *[George Ernest] Morrison, correspondent of the* Times, *formerly a very just and perspicacious observer of Japanese action in China, has changed perceptibly since a very powerful financial group in England has become interested in the construction of the Fakumen railroad.*[228]

In June of 1908, d'Anethan had reported the opposition of the Japanese Government to Chinese extension of the South Manchurian Railway with English financial help.

The proposed prolongation of the railway from Hsinmintun to Tsitsihar via Fakumen with the help of English capital is opposed by the Japanese Government by virtue of the protocol of the treaty of 1905, by which China committed herself not to construct lines parallel or neighboring to the Japanese line. Since last August, it had reminded the Chinese Government on three different occasions that the construction of the line in question would be a violation of this previous agreement. In spite of these warnings, a contract for the extension of the line was signed last November with a British firm, Pauling and Co. When in January of this year the Cabinet of Tokyo learned of the conclusion of the contract, it could only file a formal protest with the Chinese government against carrying out the works.

As early as the beginning of 1906, the aforementioned stipulation of the protocol of Peking had been communicated to the British Government, which, it appears, did not question the validity of Japanese objections. But the Chamber of Commerce of Newchwang, composed mainly of merchants of English origin, deemed it proper in March 1908 to adopt a resolution of energetic protest against the obstacles put by Japan to the extension of the North Chinese railways from Hsinmintun to Fakumen and beyond.[229]

In February of 1909, the London *Times* reacted to a speech of Count Komura on this subject by attacking the views of the Japanese Government as being "absolutely irreconcilable with the policy of the Open Door." D'Anethan commented:

The reasoning of the Japanese Government is the following:

The operation of railways is by nature a monopolistic enterprise and the existence of exclusive rights is indispensable for them. If then a Government grants a railway concession, it is understood that this railway will have the power to exercise certain privileges necessary for its existence. Now everyone has acknowledged the transfer of the South Manchurian railway by Russia to Japan as a legitimate consequence of the events, and its existence is indispensable. No one has dreamed of saying that the South Manchurian railways controlled by Japan constitute an impediment to the policy of the Open Door. It is the right and duty of Japan to protect this railway and to maintain its privileges. Now, considering the special situation of the country which it traverses, it is essential for this railway to be protected in certain zones against competition, and it is thus that China by the protocol signed at Peking in 1905 renounced the construction of any line parallel or neighboring to the South Manchurian railway. Nothing in this is opposed to the policy of the Open Door either. But the line now proposed by China threatens the exempted zone, and it is only natural for Japan to oppose its construction, or the article of the protocol of Peking has no reason for being.

In any case, Japan fights for the very existence of her South Manchurian railway. . . . The pretensions of the English syndicate of which the Times *has made itself the spokesman are incompatible with the undertakings made in 1905. Consequently the Imperial Government, which is in the process of negotiating about this with the Chinese Government, is firmly resolved not to make any concession which would injure the interests of the Manchurian railways.*[230]

In the summer of 1909, while d'Anethan was absent, Baron Henri de Woelmont dealt with another railway dispute. He wrote:

Among the difficulties now existing between Japan and China, none has reached a more acute state than that aroused by the projected rebuilding of the railway from Antung to Mukden by the

Japanese South Manchurian Company, which has twenty million yen at its disposal for this work.

The existing railway is only a military line completely unsuitable for the transportation of passengers and goods. The time seems to have come for Japan there to make improvements of great importance for the junction of the main line from Korea with the South Manchurian, improvements which would result in "opening" Korea to the world and in shortening the distance between Japan and Europe.

The proposals made to Viceroy Hsi Liang, who has been entrusted by the Chinese Government with the negotiations on this subject, have received an answer that the Japanese press and public opinion agree in calling insolent. Not only does the Viceroy of Manchuria oppose Japanese control of the police and military guards in the railway zone, where he would like a purely Chinese police force, but he also maintains that widening the existing light narrow gauge railway to the standard gauge is not reconstruction, but the construction of an entirely new line. Consequently the Chinese Commissioner opposes the reconstruction of the railway, except with the present gauge.

Such a claim is manifestly untenable, if one refers to the terms of Article VI of the Treaty of Peking of December 22, 1905, an article inserted for the sole purpose of giving Japan the right to change the existing strategic railway into a railway geared to commerce, or to build a new commercial line. The exact term of the treaty is "transformation." Article VIII of the Supplementary Agreement of 1908 gives Japan even more explicitly the right to rebuild the line from Antung to Mukden.

Faithful to the temporizing tactics dear to tortuous diplomacy, Viceroy Hsi moreover intends to leave on a tour of inspection in North Manchuria, so as to drag out the question until it will be too late to reach a solution in 1909, the region's climate allowing work during only a short period of the year.

It is believed in Tokyo that China tries once more to get out of the obligations which she assumed by treaty. The negotiations continue, and an official note has informed the public that the Japanese Government has every reason to believe that the question will be solved to its full satisfaction.[231]

In August Woelmont related:

After six weeks of fruitless negotiation, the Japanese Government, convinced of its inablility to overcome Chinese diplomacy, has, it is said, decided to put an end to the question. The need for a more vigorous attitude, which the "military party" had not ceased to advocate, was recognized in a conference of the principal statesmen of all Parties. Following the meeting, Count Komura is said to have cabled to Mr. Ijuin to ask the Chinese Government for a final answer in eight days and to notify him that Japan would take whatever measures the situation required. Whatever the response of China will be, the reconstruction of the railway will be begun on the 15th of this month in every one of the fourteen sections into which it has been decided to divide the line from Antung to Mukden for this purpose. Materials have been prepared and it is said that the Japanese Government is ready for any eventuality, such as the general boycott of Japanese goods in China, which could lead to the reconstruction of the railway line by force.[232]

A few days later Woelmont dwelled on the decision of the Japanese Government to proceed immediately and without the cooperation of China to the rebuilding of the Antung-Mukden railway:

This decision was communicated to the Waiwupu on the afternoon of the 6th by the Japanese Minister in Peking, and on the evening of the same day, on orders received from Tokyo, the reconstruction of the line was started at the tunnel of Fuktsen-ling. On the 7th the Gaimusho (the Japanese Foreign Ministry) issued a statement to the press. . . .

General Viscount Oshima, Commander-in-Chief of the Japanese forces in Manchuria, has received orders to avoid any military demonstration, the incident not to be regarded in any way as a break in the friendly relations between the two Empires. "Far from it," General Terauchi [Masatake] Minister of War adds. "Please inform the troops collectively and individually that their conduct has to be most circumspect and in harmony with the best traditions of the Japanese army."[233]

On September 4, China and Japan signed a convention settling their differences in Manchuria and along the Sino-Korean frontier. Transmitting the text of the agreement Woelmont commented:

This courteous compromise, based on skillful mutual concessions, which "saves the face" of the Chinese Government in attributing to it almost invariably the initiative of every arrangement, is generally regarded here as a very great success for Japanese diplomacy and for Mr. Ijuin in particular. The sovereign rights of China are recognized in the rich, disputed territory of Chientao and Kando (!), but the 90,000 Koreans who live in this region, whose size is nearly equal to that of the Island of Kyushu, will continue to enjoy the suzerain protection of the Japanese Government.

One point stipulated by the new Convention of Peking, which must be mentioned, is the construction at common expense of a railway, extending the line from Changchun to Kirin as far as the southern border of Yenchi [Yenki], to join a Korean railway at Hoiryong. A railway thus laid out is bound to assume real importance, both from a strategic point of view and an economic point of view.[234]

When the American Government sought to neutralize the Manchurian railway, Japanese reaction was prompt. In the words of d'Anethan, who was back in Tokyo:

The proposal of the Cabinet in Washington to neutralize the railways of Manchuria has not failed to awaken serious excitement in Japan. But the comments of the press have not generally departed from the calm and moderate tone which serves the solution of international problems better than the exaggerations of violent and chauvinistic articles. The press does not refrain from pointing out, however, how difficult it would be to put in practice the perhaps somewhat fanciful plan of Mr. [Philander C.] Knox [the American Secretary of State], and what little chances it had of being acceptable to the interested parties. The plan of the American project, so simple in appearance, does not seem to take into account the realities of the present situation in Manchuria.

The United States Ambassador in Tokyo [Thomas J. O'Brien], interviewd by an editor of the Jiji Shimpo and asked to make a statement, answered him in substance "that the Government of the United States had suggested that all the railroads of Manchuria be returned to China; that a line be built between Chinchun and Aigun, via Tsitsihar; and that no doubt the nationals of various Powers could furnish the necessary funds for the cost, both of the lines already constructed and the above mentioned lines and of others which in the future it might seem in China's interest to build. He added that the countries most immediately concerned were, of course, Japan, Russia and China, and that it appeared to his Government that these Powers would naturally be desirous of resolving all conflict and all difficulty in the manner proposed and of helping the Chinese Government to develop her own domain in peace."

The Ambassador remarked that a few years ago the United States had presented to the Powers a plan, according to which every one of them would pledge itself to reject all temptation of obtaining special privileges in China, so that the territories of China would remain free for the commercial benefit of all. The Powers accepted the suggestion, and that which is proposed today is only a logical step in the same direction. The Government of the United States thinks that a plan that has these principles as an objective would result in lasting benefits for all the parties concerned.

The Japanese Cabinet is now preparing a reply to the American note. I have no doubt that it will be negative. I am the more certain, because I can attest to the perfect understanding which exists at present between the Cabinet of Tokyo and of St. Petersburg concerning the railways in which they are interested in Manchuria.

As a postscript d'Anethan directed the attention of his Government to an article on Russo-Japanese relations by Monsieur de Caix [de St. Aymour] in the *Journal des Débats* of December 27th, and added: "Perhaps the correspondence of the Legation before, during and after the Russo-Japanese war could be reread on this occasion."[235]

In January of 1910, Count Komura addressed the Diet regarding the foreign relations of Japan. Transmitting a copy of the speech, d'Anethan observed:

The Foreign Minister stated that the relations were eminently satisfactory and energetically repudiated the completely unfounded rumors which had been spread on different occasions concerning Russo-Japanese relations. These relations of friendship and of good neighborliness are constantly being strengthened and continue to become more cordial, Count Komura said.

As to the negative response of the Imperial Government to the American proposal of neutralizing the railway of Manchuria, the Foreign Minister explained its reason: the possession by Japan of the South-Manchurian railway is in no way contrary to the principle of the Open Door that the Imperial Government is determined to respect scrupulously in the future as in the past. Furthermore, the surrender of this railway would entail radical changes in the state of affairs established in Manchuria by the Treaties of Portsmouth and of Peking, and thus would have serious consequences. Affirming its policy of remaining faithful to the principle of the Open Door, Count Komura added, the Imperial Government has decided to open Port Arthur, so as to contribute to the development of Manchuria and to facilitate the commerce of all nations.[236]

In spring a serious rebellion broke out in the city of Changsha in Hunan Province as the result of the famine and misery that had followed a recent flood. D'Anethan commented on the unrest of China:

Changsha has always been one of the very antiforeign centers of the province, and it has been only a few years that foreigners could reside there. The Japanese, numbering 120, and the other foreigners were threatened by the insurgents and were forced to abandon their houses. Taking refuge in the palace of the Governor, they did not find there enough protection, and sought safety on vessels to go to Hunan. The Japanese consulate has been destroyed. The buildings of the American Wesleyan Mission and the Christian churches have been set afire. English and Japanese gunboats have been sent to protect the residents and their belongings.

Recently there have also been grave disturbances in Hangchow, incited especially against the Japanese, a number of whom have been wounded and their stores plundered. The Japanese Government has addressed very firm protests to the Waiwupu and expects to obtain prompt satisfaction of its just claims.

One must not exaggerate the importance or the extent of these uprisings. But they embarrass the Japanese Government, whose present policy is to avoid as much as possible all difficulties with China.[237]

In April, during maneuvers near Hiroshima, a Japanese submarine sank. When it was salvaged and the corpses of its fifteen-men crew were removed, a last letter from its commander, Lieutenant Sakuma, was found. D'Anethan transmitted a translation of this unique document. It read:

Words of excuse fail me for having lost Your Majesty's submarine No. 6. My subordinates are perishing by my fault. But it is with pride that I inform you that the crew fulfilled its duties, without exception, with the greatest coolness till the last moment, as befits sailors.

We now are sacrificing our lives for our country, but I fear lest this disaster affect the future development of submarines. That is why I hope that nothing will stop your determination to study the submarine until it has become a perfect machine, absolutely trustworthy. If this be the case, we can die without regret.

In submerging with the gasoline engine the ship sank deeper than desired, and in our efforts to close the water-tight door the chain broke. We tried to stop the entrance of water with our hands, but too late. The water came in at the stern and the ship sank at an angle of 25 degrees.

When it touched bottom, it was at an angle of 13 degrees. The stream of water flooded the electric generator, extinguishing the light, and the electric wires burned.

In a few minutes there developed bad gas which made our breathing difficult. It was 10 A.M., *the 15th of this month, when the ship sank. Surrounded by poisonous gas, the crew tried to pump water. As soon as the ship had sunk, one started pumping out the water from the main tank. The electric light was out, and the leak invisible, but it seems that the water from the main tank was pumped out completely.*

The electric current has now become useless, one can not produce gas and the hand-pump is our only hope. The ship is in the dark, and I write these notes by the light which comes from the turret at 11:45 A.M.

The crew is now wet and it is extremely cold. It is my opinion that men who embark on submarines must have the qualities of coolness and nerve and be tireless; it takes courage and daring to handle the ship. One can make fun of this opinion, seeing my failure, but it is the truth.

We have worked hard to pump the water, but the ship is still in the same position. It is now noon. *The depth of the water here is about ten fathoms.*

The crew of a submarine must be chosen from the bravest and those who have the most presence of mind, otherwise they would be useless at a moment of crisis, like the one in which we are. My brave men do their best.

I always expect death when I am away. Consequently my last will is prepared; it will be found in my chest, but these are my private affairs. I hope that Mr. Taguchi will be so good as to send it to my father.

A word to His Majesty the Emperor. It is my fervent hope that

Your Majesty will furnish the means of existence to the poor families of the crew. This is my only wish, and I am very anxious to see it realized.

My respects and best remembrances to the following persons: to Admiral Saito, Minister of the Navy, to Vice Admiral Shimamura and Fujii, to Rear Admirals Nawa, Yamashita and Narita
—The air pressure is so light that it seems to me that my ear drums will burst—*to Captains Oguri and Ide, to Commander Matsumura, to Lieutenant Commander Matsumura (the latter is my elder brother), to Captain Funakoshi, to Mr. Narita and Mr. Ikuta*—It is now 12:30—my breathing is so difficult and painful. I thought I could turn off the gasoline but it poisons me—*to Captain Nakano*—It is now 12.40.

Here ended the report. D'Anethan commented:

Ignorant persons in Europe think to explain the calm of the Japanese soldier before death by his indifference to life and by I do not know what Oriental fatalism. This touching testament, left by Commander Sakuma, proves that it is from the feeling of duty accomplished, the respect for and obedience to his Sovereign, his love for his fatherland, and the honor of the name that he must leave to his family intact, that the Japanese draws the courage, of which he has given so many examples in combat. Nothing can surpass in noble heroism the last act of Commander Sakuma, cooly and soberly writing a report, and dropping the pen only at the time of death—a time which he recorded himself![238]

In June of 1910, d'Anethan reviewed the international situation in the Far East:

The English Government continues to give assurances of its will to maintain the alliance with Japan in full force. We observe that while in government circles there is not the least hesitation about the usefulness of the alliance, in certain spheres—urban businessmen, principally in financial centers interested in the affairs of China—the alliance is no longer considered with the same favor. It does not seem, however, that this position will influence the policy of the Cabinet of St. James, nor of the political group which eventually may replace it. I see a very clear indication of this in the confirmation for another two years of the appointment of the present Ambassador of England in Tokyo. The term of his appointment expired this year, and has just been prolonged until 1912. Sir Claude MacDonald has lately been very much attacked in the financial circles, of which I have just spoken, where he is reproached for not defending English interests with enough energy. Sir Edward Grey [Secretary of State for Foreign Affairs] has strongly denied these accusations, and has paid tribute to the very enlightened policy pursued by the Ambassador.

The Ambassador of Germany has been recalled rather brusquely to Berlin. His relations with the Emperor and the Government have been very good; thus there is no sense of his disfavor in this measure. It is announced that he will occupy himself with the question of treaty revision and negotiations which will soon begin. Already last year, in Germany, certain organs of the press put his name forward to replace Baron [Wilhelm] von Schoen. This appointment, while not at all impossible, does not seem very likely. Baron Mumm, I fear, would find serious difficulties when it came to Parliamentary debates. It is always with a certain emotion that he is compelled to speak in public, and his speeches must be carefully prepared beforehand. To be sure, too much facility of speech is not always an advantage for a Foreign Minister and he can carry out his functions very properly without having the gift of eloquence.

Baron Mumm is a Representative of agreeable relations, very fond of questions of protocol, of decorations, and of precedence. In flattering this rather innocent mania, one easily puts oneself on intimate terms with him. He belongs to the German diplomatic school which is firmly hostile to English diplomacy and would always be happy to join any unfriendly scheme against his British colleague. He was, as you are aware, the German plenipotentiary who negotiated the peace with China after the Boxer rebellion. Toward Orientals he understands only a policy of force, and will never bring himself to treat them on an equal footing. Forced by circumstances to show himself amiable and hospitable towards the Japanese, he has not succeeded, after three years, in inspiring confidence in them. If he becomes Foreign Minister one day, the relations with Japan will perhaps remain correct since he is not excessively aggressive by nature, but they will certainly not become more confident or more cordial.

Mr. A. Gerard [the French Ambassador] had decided to go on leave last month; he has postponed his departure till late autumn. It does not seem that this alteration of his plans is due to anything other than his personal convenience. No thorny question has existed between France and Japan for three years. The very important interests which are now being discussed between Russia and Japan have the full cooperation of the French Government and do not compromise those of the Republic. Mr. Gerard thus has not had the opportunity to give play to his natural inclination for intrigues, which in his previous posts had made him suspect to the Governments to which he was accredited.[239]

In July 1910, d'Anethan described the mounting anti-dynastic agitation in China, which was to explode in revolution the following year and ultimately change the face of Far Eastern history, and the continuing rapprochement between Japan and Russia which sought to exploit the weakness of China by working with each other rather than at cross-purposes. The Russo-Japanese agreement concluded at St. Petersburg on July 4, 1910 provided for the maintenance of the *status quo* in Manchuria, the demarcation of Russian and Japanese interests and their protection against aggression by a third power. D'Anethan reported:

The movement of dissatisfaction in China seems general. The movement is chiefly anti-dynastic. The power of the monarchy seems to lose prestige daily. Everything is a pretext for attacking the Manchus. The few more or less organized military forces have no cohesion and, furthermore, the Authorities cannot trust them. The secret societies, be they organized to agitate for the recovery of the railways by the Chinese or for the establishment of national assemblies, newspaper articles which are widely disseminated throughout China, and the students who return from Europe and America and especially from Japan seem unanimous in their animosity to the established regime. We must add to this anti-dynastic propaganda a most unfavorable economic situation. Crop prospects are generally bad.Disastrous floods have already undermined the hopes of prosperity in the Yangtze valley.

The revolutionary movement does not seem to be inspired by hatred for the foreigner. Nonetheless the foreigners will, of course, suffer from the state of affairs in China, though protective measures could be taken. The gravity of the movement comes above all from the universal hatred of the Government of Peking. As the Foreign Minister and my English Colleague, the two best informed authorities, recently told me, one sees this highly dangerous state of affairs, but cannot get a clear idea of the form, place and extent of the movement, and when it will break out. The revolutionary elements are so diverse in nature, and infiltrate all the machinery of provincial administration. Nor are the interests identical from province to province. The general movement can thus be set back, but a series of troubles and insurrections in all branches are to be feared. In Peking no member of the Imperial family any longer enjoys the least prestige, and unfortunately one does not see any upcoming man of energy or intelligence among the younger Princes and the councillors of the Crown.

In diplomacy the same infantile and pusillanimous spirit which for years has characterized the relations of the Waiwupu with the Diplomatic Corps is noticeable. For several months the attempts of the American Government, supported by the German Legation, to play the part of friend and protector of China gave Peking hope that they would lead to differences between the Powers to the benefit of Chinese policy. The illusions of the unfortunate Government were brief. The agreements and treaties which have just been concluded between Japan and Russia had the assent of France and England,

R

and have quickly opened the eyes of the blindest Chinese statesmen.

In Manchuria, for the moment, there is no reason to fear troubles and difficulties. Nor does there seem to be danger in Peking. The speed with which troops would be transported removes all cause of apprehension. It is in the interior of China, in almost all the provinces, that revolution threatens. On the coasts, in the ports, order will easily be reestablished. But when it will be a matter of penetrating into the interior, the foreign Powers will have to send troops, and in spite of the absence of an army in China, the obstacles will be gigantic. Japan and Russia are aware what a long and costly adventure they will have to undertake. They will do all they can, therefore, to avoid conflicts and will seek, as long as there will be a ray of hope, to maintain a semblance of Government at Peking.

As I have had the honor to write to the Department for years, the policy of Japan has not changed in this regard and the Government of the Emperor understands that . . . it is only with the help of Russia that it could delay the time of a general upheaval in China. Of all the diplomatic victories won by Japan and personally by Count Komura, the most striking and most lasting in effect is that which has just been sealed in St. Petersburg.[240]

Notes on the Text

¹ D'Anethan to Count de Mérode Westerloo, Minister of Foreign Affairs, No. 330/94, dated Tokyo (hereafter deleted), 7 December 1893.

² D'Anethan to de Mérode, Confidential, No. 1/1, 2 January 1894.

³ D'Anethan to de Mérode, No. 54/16, 12 March 1894.

⁴ Baroness Albert d'Anethan, *Fourteen Years of Diplomatic Life in Japan. Leaves from the Diary of Baroness Albert d'Anethan* (London: Stanley Paul and Co., 1912; second edition), p. 15.

⁵ *Ibid.*, p. 16.

⁶ D'Anethan to de Mérode, No. 116/43, 8 June 1894.

⁷ D'Anethan to de Mérode, No. 120/47, 12 June 1894.

⁸ D'Anethan to de Mérode, No. 124/49, 20 June 1894.

⁹ D'Anethan to de Mérode, Confidential, No. 129/51, 29 June 1894.

¹⁰ D'Anethan to de Mérode, No. 139/55, 13 July 1894.

¹¹ D'Anethan to de Mérode, No. 146/59, 20 July 1894.

¹² D'Anethan to de Mérode, No. 152/62, 28 July 1894.

¹⁰ D'Anethan to de Mérode, No. 161/65, 9 August 1894.

¹⁴ D'Anethan to de Mérode No. [?], 11 September 1894.

¹⁵ D'Anethan to de Mérode, No. 189/75, 19 September 1894.

¹⁶ D'Anethan to de Mérode, No. 195/77, 29 September 1894.

¹⁷ D'Anethan to de Mérode, No. 217/84, 17 October 1894.

¹⁸ D'Anethan to de Mérode, No. 230/87, 6 November 1894.

¹⁹ D'Anethan to de Mérode, Confidential, No. 235/90, 16 November 1894.

²⁰ D'Anethan to de Mérode, No. 244/91, 30 November 1894.

²¹ D'Anethan to de Mérode, No. 245/92, 7 [?] December 1894.

²² D'Anethan to de Mérode, No. 259/99, 28 December 1894.

²³ D'Anethan to de Mérode, No. 252/96, 20 December 1894.

²⁴ D'Anethan to de Mérode, No. 259/99, 28 December 1894.

²⁵ D'Anethan to de Mérode, No. 24/10, 4 February 1895.

²⁶ D'Anethan to de Mérode, Confidential, No. 30/12, 25 February 1895.

²⁷ D'Anethan to de Mérode, No. 38/16, 18 March 1895.

²⁸ D'Anethan to de Mérode, No. 49/19, 29 March 1895.

²⁹ D'Anethan to de Mérode, No. 52/21, 1 April 1895.

³⁰ D'Anethan to de Mérode, No. 47/18, 28 March 1895.

³¹ D'Anethan to de Mérode, No. 52/21, 1 April 1895.

³² D'Anethan to de Mérode, No. 83/30, 18 April 1895.

³³ D'Anethan to Mr. de Burlet, Belgian Foreign Minister, No. 110/35, 13 August 1895.

³⁴ D'Anethan to de Burlet, No. 125/42, 17 September 1895.

35 D'Anethan to de Burlet, No. 139/47, 10 October 1895.

36 D'Anethan to de Burlet, No. 162/55, 25 November 1895.

37 D'Anethan to de Burlet, No. 110/35, 13 August 1895.

38 D'Anethan to de Burlet, No. 139/47, 10 October 1895.

39 D'Anethan to de Burlet, No. 140/48, 17 October 1895.

40 D'Anethan to de Burlet, Confidential, No. 142/49, 26 October 1895.

41 D'Anethan to de Burlet, No. 147/52, 6 November 1895.

42 D'Anethan to de Burlet, No. 162/55, 25 November 1895.

43 D'Anethan to de Burlet, No. 166/57, 1 December 1895.

44 D'Anethan to de Burlet, No. 11/6, 17 February 1896.

45 D'Anethan to the Minister of Foreign Affairs, No. 15/8, 3 March 1896.

46 D'Anethan to Monsieur de Favereau, Belgian Minister of Foreign Affairs, No. 60/18, 4 June 1896.

47 D'Anethan to de Favereau, No. 112/37, 27 August 1896.

48 D'Anethan to de Favereau, No. 115/38, 7 September 1896.

49 D'Anethan to de Favereau, Confidential, No. 10/4 [?] 18 January 1897.

50 D'Anethan to de Favereau, No. 35/12, 27 February 1897.

51 Baroness d'Anethan, *Fourteen Years of Diplomatic Life in Japan*, p. 179.

52 *Ibid.*, p. 185.

53 D'Anethan to de Favereau, No. 46/17, 2 March 1897.

54 E. de Cartier de Marchienne to de Favereau, No. 53/20, 7 May 1897.

55 De Cartier de Marchienne to de Favereau No. 93/32, 19 May 1897.

56 De Cartier de Marchienne to de Favereau, No. 164/62, 20 August 1897.

57 De Cartier de Marchienne to de Favereau, No. 122/45, 24 June 1897.

58 D'Anethan to de Favereau, No. 150/61, 27 July 1898.

59 D'Anethan to de Favereau, No. 158/64, 1 September 1898.

60 De Cartier de Marchienne to de Faverau, No. 219/92, 31 October 1897.

61 De Cartier de Marchienne to de Favereau, No. 226/94, 9 November 1897.

62 De Cartier de Marchienne to de Favereau, No. 235/97, 30 November 1897.

63 D'Anethan to de Favereau, No. 249/104, 23 December 1897.

64 D'Anethan to de Favereau, No. 249/104, 23 December 1897.

65 D'Anethan to de Favereau, No. 11/8, 15 January 1898.

66 D'Anethan to de Favereau, No. 26/13 or 25/13 (looks like a "5" converted into a "6" but not clear), 23 February 1898.

67 D'Anethan to de Favereau, No. 46/20, 13 March 1898.

68 D'Anethan to de Favereau, No. 61/23, 1 April 1898.

69 D'Anethan to de Favereau, No. 90/35, 20 May 1898.

70 D'Anethan to de Favereau, No. 45/19, 12 March 1898.

71 D'Anethan to de Favereau, No. 115/43, 15 June 1898.

72 D'Anethan to de Favereau, No. 96/39, 26 May 1898.

73 D'Anethan to de Favereau, No. 114/42, 23 June 1898.

74 D'Anethan to de Favereau, No. 120/49, 27 June 1898.

[75] D'Anethan to de Favereau, No. 129/51, 6 July 1898.
[76] D'Anethan to de Favereau, Confidential, No. 132/54, 7 July 1898.
[77] D'Anethan to de Favereau, No. 148/59, 25 July 1898.
[78] D'Anethan to de Favereau, No. 149/60, 27 July 1898.
[79] D'Anethan to de Favereau, No. 164/67, 8 September 1898.
[80] D'Anethan to de Favereau, No. 182/77, 29 September 1898.
[81] D'Anethan to de Favereau, No. 38/15, 6 March 1899.
[82] D'Anethan to de Favereau, No. 183/78, 29 September 1898.
[83] D'Anethan to de Favereau, No. 187/83, 25 October 1898.
[84] D'Anethan to de Favereau, No. 201/86, 2 November 1898.
[85] D'Anethan to de Favereau, No. 207/88, 11 November 1898.
[86] D'Ancthan to de Favereau, No. 227/92, 9 December 1898.
[87] D'Anethan to de Favereau, No. 233/95, 30 December 1898.
[88] D'Anethan to de Favereau, No. 14/8, 22 January 1899.
[89] D'Anethan to de Favereau, 21/11, 31 January 1899.
[90] D'Anethan to de Favereau, Very Confidential, No. 41/18, 6 May 1899.
[91] D'Anethan to de Favereau, No. 85/43, 20 June 1899.
[92] D'Anethan to de Favereau, No. 99/51, 6 July 1899.
[93] D'Anethan to de Favereau, No. 126/31, 9 August 1899.
[94] D'Anethan to de Favereau, No. 127/62, 15 August 1899.
[95] D'Ancthan to de Favereau, No. 147/76, 20 October 1899.
[96] D'Anethan to de Favereau, No. 165/89, 14 November 1899.
[97] D'Anethan to de Favereau, No. 172/91, 29 November 1899.
[98] D'Anethan to de Favereau, No. 178/95, 28 December 1899.
[99] D'Anethan to de Favereau, No. 12/9, 11 January 1900.
[100] D'Anethan to de Favereau, No. 28/11, 24 January 1900.
[101] D'Anethan to de Favereau, No. 30/12, 5 February, 1900.
[102] D'Anethan to de Favereau, No. 46/22, 26 March 1900.
[103] D'Anethan, ciphered telegram, No. 1, 30 March 1900.
[104] D'Anethan to de Favereau, No. 50/23, 31 March 1900.
[105] D'Anethan to de Favereau, No. 151/76, 21 October 1900.
[106] D'Anethan to de Favereau, No. 71/38, 1 June 1900.
[107] D'Anethan to de Favereau, No. 83/46, 14 June 1900.
[108] D'Anethan to de Favereau, No. 85/48, 19 June 1900.
[109] D'Anethan to de Favereau, No. 93/51, 3 July 1900.
[110] D'Anethan to de Favereau, No. 95/53, 5 July 1900.
[111] D'Anethan to de Favereau, No. 98/55, 15 July 1900.
[112] D'Anethan to de Favereau, No. 101/57, 16 July 1900.
[113] D'Anethan to de Favereau, No. 107/60, 26 July 1900.
[114] D'Anethan to de Favereau, No. 113/62, 10 August 1900.
[115] D'Anethan to de Favereau, No. 115/64, 15 August 1900.
[116] D'Anethan to de Favereau, No. 122/67, 3 September 1900.
[117] D'Anethan to de Favereau, No. 147/74, 15 October 1900.

[118] D'Anethan to de Favereau, No. 164/80, 9 November 1900.
[119] D'Anethan to de Favereau, No. 178/86, 29 November 1900.
[120] D'Anethan to de Favereau, No. 185/87, 13 December 1900.
[121] D'Anethan to de Favereau, No. 6/6, 15 January 1901.
[122] D'Anethan to de Favereau, No. 8/8, 24 January 1901.
[123] D'Anethan to de Favereau, No. 14/11, 8 February 1901.
[124] D'Anethan to de Favereau, No. 41/20, 20 March 1901.
[125] D'Anethan to de Favereau, No. 70/26, 10 April 1901.
[126] Baroness d'Anethan, *Fourteen Years of Diplomatic Life in Japan*, p. 292.
[127] *Ibid.*
[128] D'Anethan to de Favereau, Confidential, No. 83/31, 2 May 1901.
[129] D'Anethan, ciphered telegram, No. 7, 4 June 1901.
[130] D'Anethan to Baron de Favereau, No. 101/42, 22 June 1901.
[131] D'Anethan to de Favereau, No. 102/43, 22 June 1901.
[132] D'Anethan to de Favereau, No. 107/45, 4 July 1901.
[133] D'Anethan to de Favereau, No. 178/62, 28 November 1901.
[134] Georges de Man to de Favereau, No. 13/3 ,15 February 1902.
[135] De Man to de Favereau, No. 224/37, 5 November, 1902.
[136] D'Anethan to de Favereau, No. 1/1 [?], 30 January 1903.
[137] D'Anethan to de Favereau, No. 23/12, 10 February 1903.
[138] D'Anethan to de Favereau, No. 51/21, 13 April 1903.
[139] D'Anethan to de Favereau, No. 66/28, 30 April 1903.
[140] D'Anethan to de Favereau, No. 83/37, 5 June 1903.
[141] D'Anethan to de Favereau, Confidential, No. 93/45, 10 June 1903.
[142] D'Anethan to de Favereau, No. 98/49, 24 June 1903.
[143] D'Anethan to de Favereau, No. 108/55, 1 July 1903.
[144] D'Anethan to de Favereau, No. 116/59, 23 July 1903.
[145] D'Anethan to de Favereau, No. 136/47, 19 September 1903.
[146] Baroness d'Anethan, p. 341.
[147] D'Anethan to de Favereau, No. 156/80, 18 October 1903.
[148] D'Anethan to de Favereau, No. 159/82, 20 October 1903.
[149] D'Anethan to de Favereau, No. 217/88, 12 December 1903.
[150] D'Anethan to de Favereau, No. 234/89, 25 December 1903.
[151] D'Anethan to de Favereau, No. 21/14, 4 January 1904.
[152] D'Anethan to de Favereau, No. 17/12, 22 Januray 1904.
[153] D'Anethan to de Favereau, No. 24/15, 8 January [February?], 1904.
[154] D'Anethan to de Favereau, No. 25/16, 9 February 1904.
[155] D'Anethan to de Favereau, No. 37/21, 13 February 1904.
[156] D'Anethan to de Favereau, No. 38/22, 15 February 1904.
[157] D'Anethan to de Favereau, No. 43/25, 23 February 1904.
[158] D'Anethan to de Favereau, No. 51/32, 15 March 1904.
[159] D'Anethan to de Favereau, No. 52/33, 15 March 1904.
[160] D'Anethan to de Favereau, No. 63/38, 29 March 1904.

[161] D'Anethan to de Favereau, No. 70/44, 7 April 1904.

[162] D'Anethan to de Favereau, No. 71/45, 7 April 1904.

[163] D'Anethan to de Favereau, No. 85/52, 7 May 1904.

[164] D'Anethan to de Favereau, No. 101/58, 28 May 1904.

[165] D'Anethan to de Favereau, No. 123/68, 29 June 1904.

[166] D'Ancthan to de Favereau, No. 150/84, 5 August 1904.

[167] D'Anethan to de Favereau, No. 172/99, 29 August 1904.

[168] D'Anethan to de Favereau, No. 147/82, 3 August 1904.

[169] D'Anethan to de Favereau, No. 192/108, 5 October 1904.

[170] D'Anethan to de Favereau, No. 206/117, 22 October 1904.

[171] D'Anethan to de Favereau, No. 221/121, 10 November 1904.

[172] D'Anethan to de Favereau, No. 235/129, November [date left blank], 1904.

[173] D'Anethan to de Favereau, No. 254/133, 17 December 1904.

[174] D'Anethan to de Favereau, No. 245/131, 5 December 1904.

[175] D'Anethan to de Favereau, No. 19/12, 15 January 1905.

[176] D'Anethan to de Favereau, No. 21/13, 19 January 1905.

[177] D'Anethan to dc Favereau, No. 22/14, 19 January 1905.

[178] D'Anethan to de Favereau, No. 38/22,15 February 1905.

[179] D'Anethan to de Favereau, No. 54/28, 15 March 1905.

[180] D'Anethan to de Favereau, No. 62/32, 25 March 1905.

[181] D'Anethan to de Favereau, No. 76/40, 10 April 1905.

[182] D'Anethan to de Favereau, No. 127/66, 8 June 1905.

[183] D'Anethan to de Favereau, No. 134/68, 22 June 1905.

[184] D'Anethan to de Favereau, No. 149/74, 7 July 1905.

[185] D'Anethan to de Favereau, No. 152/77, 11 July 1905.

[186] D'Anethan to de Favereau, No. 153/78, 11 July 1905.

[187] D'Anethan to de Favereau, No. 159/82, 29 July 1905.

[188] D'Anethan to de Favereau, No. 170/88 [?], 31 August 1905.

[189] D'Anethan, telegram No. 13, 7 September 1905.

[190] D'Anethan, telegram No. 14, 7 September 1905.

[191] D'Anethan, telegram No. 15, 8 September 1905.

[192] D'Anethan to de Favereau, No. 171/89, 19 September 1905.

[193] D'Anethan to de Favereau, No. 181/95, 28 September 1905.

[194] D'Anethan to de Favereau, No. 190/98, 19 October 1905.

[195] D'Anethan to de Favercau, No. 193/100, 26 October 1905.

[196] D'Anethan to de Favereau, No. 195/101, 31 October 1905.

[197] D'Anethan to de Favereau, No. 199/103, 7 November 1905.

[198] D'Anethan to de Favereau, No. 200/104, 7 November 1905.

[199] D'Anethan to de Favereau, No. 201/105, 7 November 1905.

[200] D'Anethan to de Favereau, No. 202/106, 7 November 1905.

[201] D'Anethan to de Favereau, No. 223/110, 28 November 1905.

[202] D'Anethan to de Favereau, No. 7/4, 8 January 1906.

[203] D'Anethan to de Favereau, No. 10/7, 8 January 1906.

[204] D'Anethan to de Favereau, No. 73/26, 26 April 1906.

[205] D'Anethan to de Favereau, No. 175/42, 15 May 1907.

[206] D'Anethan to Foreign Minister Monsieur Davignon, No. 200/52, 18 June 1907.

[207] D'Anethan to Davignon, No. 207/56, 9 July 1907.

[208] D'Anethan to Davignon, No. 221/64, 26 July 1907.

[209] D'Anethan to Davignon, No. 257/85, 1 October 1907.

[210] D'Anethan to Davignon, No. 258/86, 2 October 1907.

[211] Ciphered telegram No. 11, 7 December 1907.

[212] D'Anethan to Davignon, No 293/103, 7 December 1907.

[213] D'Anethan to Davignon, No. 294/104, 7 December 1907.

[214] D'Anethan to Davignon, No. 296/106, 7 December 1907.

[215] D'Anethan to Davignon, No. 301/111, 31 December 1907.

[216] D'Anethan to Davignon, No. 156/71, 25 June 1908.

[217] D'Anethan to Davignon, Very Confidential, No. 169/177, 13 July 1908.

[218] D'Anethan to Davignon, No. 269/110, 7 October 1908.

[219] D'Anethan to Davignon, No. 270/111, 9 October 1908.

[220] D'Anethan to Davignon, No. 279/119, 19 October 1908.

[221] D'Anethan to Davignon, Confidential, No. 306/128, 10 November 1908.

[222] D'Anethan to Davignon, No. 337/142, 28 November 1908.

[223] D'Anethan to Davignon, No. 349/149, 6 December 1908.

[224] D'Anethan to Davignon, No. 323/135, 17 November 1908.

[225] D'Anethan to Davignon, No. 336/141, 28 November 1908.

[226] D'Anethan to Davignon, No. 346/148, 3 December 1908.

[227] D'Anethan to Davignon, No. 10/7, 9 January 1909.

[228] D'Anethan to Davignon, No. 15/10, 15 January 1909.

[229] D'Anethan to Davignon, No. 147/67, 12 June 1908.

[230] D'Anethan to Davignon, No. 38/23, 16 February 1909.

[231] Woelmont to Davignon, No. 231/91, 7 July 1909.

[232] Woelmont to Davignon, No. 263/107, 6 August 1909.

[233] Woelmont to Davignon, No. 269/110, 11 August 1909.

[234] Woelmont to Davignon, No. 310/128, 9 September 1909.

[235] D'Anethan to Davignon, No. 16/8, 14 January 1910.

[236] D'Anethan to Davignon, No. 41/49, 31 January 1910.

[237] D'Anethan to Davignon, No. 154/58, 18 April 1910.

[238] D'Anethan to Davignon, No. 165/61, 22 April 1910.

[239] D'Anethan to Davignon, *Very Confidential*, No. 317/111, 23 June 1910.

[240] D'Anethan to Davignon, No. 335/115, 8 July 1910.

Index